P9-DFR-662

ANTIQUES Handbook & Price Guide

Miller's Antiques Handbook & Price Guide
By Judith Miller

First published in Great Britain in 2013 by Miller's, a division of Mitchell Beazley,
imprints of Octopus Publishing Group Ltd., Endeavour House,
189 Shaftesbury Avenue, London, WC2H 8JY.
www.hachette.co.uk

Distributed in the US by Hachette Book Group USA,
237 Park Avenue, New York NY 10017, USA.
Distributed in Canada by Canadian Manda Group,
165 Dufferin Street, Toronto, Ontario, Canada M6K 3H6.

Miller's is a registered trademark of Octopus Publishing Group Ltd.
www.millersguides.com

ISBN: 9781845337919

A CIP record for this book is available from the Library of Congress

Set in Frutiger

Printed and bound in China

Publisher Alison Starling
Head of Editorial Tracey Smith
Editorial Co-ordinator Katy Armstrong
Editorial John Wainwright
Advertising Sales Christine Havers
Indexer Hilary Bird

Art Director Jonathan Christie
Design and Prepress Ali Scrivens, TJ Graphics

Senior Production Manager Peter Hunt

Photograph of Judith Miller by Chris Terry

Page 1: One of two early 20thC Egyptian Revival chairs. $10,000-15,000 pair DN
Page 3: A Goldscheider figure of 'Tricorne'. $2,500-3,500 DOR
Page 4 from left to right: A Meissen 'Goldchinesen' teapot and cover. $15,000-20,00 TEN;
A Northern Italian carved walnut armchair. $5,000-7,000 FRE;
A Biedermeier commode clock. $2,500-3,500 DOR;
A Scottish silver castle top card case. $5,500-7,500 L&T
Page 5 from left to right: A Bohemian lidded goblet. $5,500-6,500 FIS;
A Fischer tinplate clockwork limousine. $4,000-6,000 SAS;
'Dancing Polar Bear', in stone, by Davie Atchealak. $8,000-12,000 WAD;
A Cowan 'Jazz' bowl, designed by Viktor Schreckengost. $100,000-150,000 DRA

ANTIQUES Handbook & Price Guide

Judith Miller

MILLER'S

Contents

LIST OF CONSULTANTS

At Miller's we are extremely lucky to be able to call on a large number of specialists for advice. My colleagues and friends on the BBC Antiques Roadshow have a wealth of knowledge and their advice on the state of the market is invaluable. It is also important to keep in touch with dealers as they are really at the coalface dealing directly with collectors. Certain parts of the market have been extremely volatile over the past year, so up-to-date information is critical.

CERAMICS

John Axford
Woolley & Wallis
51-61 Castle Street
Salisbury SP1 3SU, UK

Fergus Gambon
Bonhams
101 New Bond Street
London W1S 1SR, UK

Steven Moore
Anderson & Garland
Anderson House, Crispin Court,
Newbiggin Lane
Westerhope,
Newcastle upon Tyne
NE5 1BF, UK

John Howard
Heritage
6 Market Place, Woodstock
OX20 1TA, UK

DECORATIVE ARTS

Michael Jeffrey
Woolley & Wallis
51-61 Castle Street
Salisbury, SP1 3SU, UK

John Mackie
Lyon & Turnbull
33 Broughton Place
Edinburgh EH1 3RR, UK

Will Farmer
Fieldings
Mill Race Lane
Stourbridge DY8 1JN, UK

Mike Moir
www.manddmoir.co.uk

FURNITURE

Lennox Cato
1 The Square, Edenbridge
Kent TN8 5BD, UK

Lee Young
Lyon & Turnbull
33 Broughton Place
Edinburgh EH1 3RR, UK

ORIENTAL

John Axford
Woolley & Wallis
51-61 Castle Street
Salisbury SP1 3SU, UK

Lee Young
Lyon & Turnbull
33 Broughton Place
Edinburgh EH1 3RR, UK

GLASS

Jeanette Hayhurst
www.antiqueglasslondon.com

SILVER

Alistair Dickenson
90 Jermyn Street
London SW1 6JD, UK

JEWELRY

Trevor Kyle
Lyon & Turnbull
33 Broughton Place
Edinburgh EH1 3RR, UK

Steven Miners
Cristobal
26 Church Street
London NW8 8EP, UK

CLOCKS & BAROMETERS

Paul Archard
Derek Roberts
25 Shipbourne Road
Tonbridge TN10 3DN, UK

MODERN DESIGN

Mark Hill
www.markhillpublishing.com

John Mackie
Lyon & Turnbull
33 Broughton Place
Edinburgh EH1 3RR, UK

HOW TO USE THIS BOOK

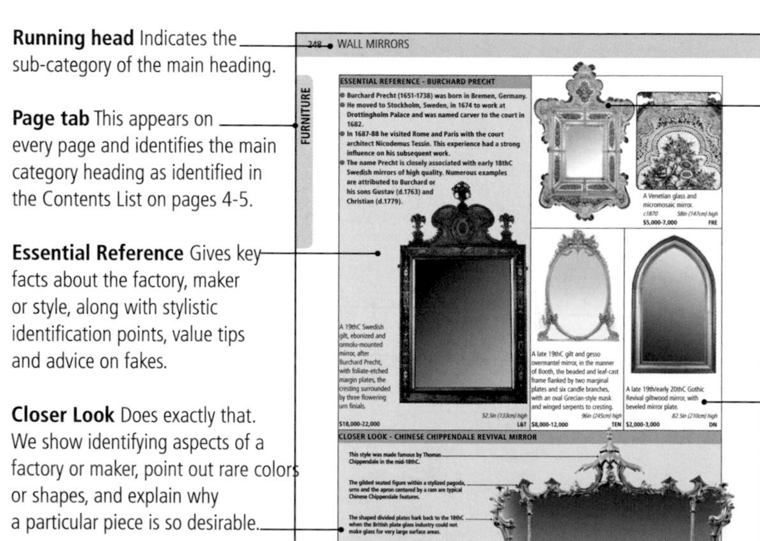

Running head Indicates the sub-category of the main heading.

Page tab This appears on every page and identifies the main category heading as identified in the Contents List on pages 4-5.

Essential Reference Gives key facts about the factory, maker or style, along with stylistic identification points, value tips and advice on fakes.

Closer Look Does exactly that. We show identifying aspects of a factory or maker, point out rare colors or shapes, and explain why a particular piece is so desirable.

The object The antiques are shown in full color. This is a vital aid to identification and valuation. With many objects, a slight color variation can signify a large price differential.

Caption The description of the item illustrated, including when relevant, the period, the maker or factory, medium, the year it was made, dimensions and condition. Many captions have **footnotes**, which explain terminology or give identification or valuation information.

The price guide These price ranges give a ball park figure of what you should pay for a similar item. The great joy of antiques is that there is not a recommended retail price. The price ranges in this book are based on actual prices, either what a dealer will take or the full auction price.

Judith Picks

When I first began collecting, I fell in love with 18thC Worcester. There was something about these pots that struck a chord. Much as I admire the superior quality of Meissen and Sèvres, there is something special about the early soft-paste porcelain produced in Worcester. I love this octagonal shape with the slightly misshapen lid, and the attempt to compete with the Chinese porcelain that was flooding the market, much as now, with the enameled Chinese famille verte-style decoration. I believe Worcester porcelain to be undervalued and certainly some of the more common patterns are cheaper than when I bought them 20-30 years ago. Unfortunately, antiques are not always a good investment, although some of my rarer patterns have seen a substantial increase in value.

A First Period Worcester 'famille verte' teapot and cover, painted with Buddhistic auspicious objects, two tall ladies and arrangements of vases and tables in garden settings.

An undated price card for the factory's London warehouse, probably produced not long after it opened in 1756, lists 'tea pots fluted panelled and octagon' at 30 shillings a dozen wholesale price.

A First Period Worcester cream boat, molded with scroll rocaille-edged panels.
c1750-58 4.25in (11cm) long
$1,200-1,800 TEN

A First Period Worcester bottle vase, painted with the 'Waiting Chinaman' pattern, with some restoration and missing part.
c1753 4.5in (11.5cm) high
$1,500-2,000 A&G

A First Period transfer-printed ... the 'Red Bull'
c1757
$550-750

Judith Picks Items chosen specially by Judith, either because they are important or interesting, or because they're good investments.

A late 19thC gilt and gesso overmantel mirror, in the manner of Booth, the beaded and leaf-cast frame flanked by two marginal plates and six candle branches, with an oval Grecian-style mask and winged serpents to cresting.
96in (245cm) high
$8,000-12,000 TEN

Source code Every item has been specially photographed at an auction house, a dealer, an antiques market or a private collection. These are credited by code at the end of the caption, and can be checked against the Key to Illustrations on pages 632-633.

INTRODUCTION

Welcome to the new edition of the 'Antiques Handbook & Price Guide'. As always, the book is packed full of thousands of images all of which are completely new to this edition. We've also included even more special feature boxes, which should help explain why some pieces are more sought after than others and help you spot that hidden treasure!

As you are undoubtedly aware, the antiques market has gone through a very difficult period recently. We are experiencing one of the worst global recessions in memory and as a consequence many antiques shops have closed and prices for many antiques have fallen. Even the Oriental market is showing signs of softening.

However, the situation is not as bleak as it might appear. More and more people are becoming convinced that 'Antiques are Green' and are choosing antique furniture over disposable MDF pieces. Campaigns such as the 'Young Guns' campaign of 2013 are encouraging younger dealers, who will hopefully become key figures in the trade in the years to come. Many areas of the market, such as Arts & Crafts and Art Deco, continue to perform well. Dealers and auctioneers have also reported strong sales for top end pieces in more traditional areas of the antiques market, such as 18thC furniture. In fact, high quality items in good condition and with good provenance are breaking records all around the world. One of the most interesting things we've noticed while compiling this book is that, due to the power of the internet, smaller or less well-known auction houses are getting incredible results for rare pieces.

Additionally, while mid-range and low-end pieces are generally seeing falling or stagnant sales, this should not be seen as a disaster. It is a very good time to buy, which gives new collectors a chance to enter the market. Items that are not currently fashionable may prove to be good investments later as tastes change and prices rise.

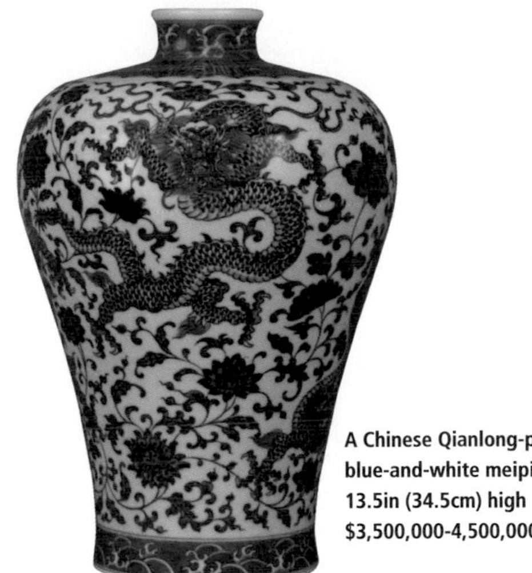

A Chinese Qianlong-period blue-and-white meiping vase. 13.5in (34.5cm) high $3,500,000-4,500,000 RTC

As well as the new edition of the 'Antiques Handbook & Price Guide', 2013 will also see an updated edition of our best-selling 'Antiques Encyclopedia' and a brand new book of 'Antiques Marks'. These three books complement each other perfectly and together they will help any budding antiques expert. We do try and give you as many little 'Essential References' throughout the 'Antiques Handbook & Price Guide' as possible, but if you're looking for in-depth information on the history of antiques, you'll need the 'Encyclopedia'. Meanwhile, the much requested 'Antiques Marks' book features more than 6,000 marks (most in full color) - far more than we have space to include in either of the other books. 'Antiques Marks' is also pocket sized (unlike this book or the Encyclopedia!), which means you can carry it with you wherever you go to help identify and date silver, ceramics, glass, costume jewelry and more.

As for 2014 2015... I have a feeling that things are improving. All the indicators point to a slight reinvigoration of all markets. I wouldn't be at all surprised if unfashionable areas like Victoriana and 'brown furniture' begin to see an upturn soon. Until then, I hope you continue to enjoy your collection and buy what you love.

Judith Miller.

A pair of 19thC ormolu-mounted Blue John urns. 15.25in (38.5cm) high $250,000-300,000 TEN

THE PORCELAIN MARKET

As with all the antiques covered in this book, with the possible exception of Chinese and Russian pieces, there has been considerable nervousness in the porcelain market, fueled by porcelain collectors' concerns about the economy. However, there are many indicators that collectors are prepared to buy when rare and high-quality items are on offer.

In most respects the last few years have seen relatively little change. The leaders – Sèvres and Meissen – have remained in demand, particularly early 18thC examples. Even damaged pieces can fetch high prices if they are rare, such as the pair of Meissen swans sold at Tennants in 2012 (see p.29).

Later 18thC pieces have tended to struggle, unless the piece has some rare features. Dresden and Limoges pieces have to be particularly impressive to sell well at the moment. The Paris factories have also struggled, and buyers are suspicious of many so-called 'Samson' pieces that do not have the quality of the true Samson copies of original pieces.

Another area that is still in the doldrums is British blue-and-white porcelain from the 18thC and 19thC. What buyers really want are pieces in exceptional condition, decorated with rare, early patterns. Worcester has been in demand, but only the First Period Dr Wall pieces with rare hand-painted patterns. Later transfer-printed pieces have struggled to find pre-recession prices and many auctioneers are combining pieces in job lots. In some cases I paid more in the early 1970s for 18thC transfer-printed Worcester than I would now. Of course, there are exceptions. In early 2013, I was excited to find a late 18thC transfer-printed 'fence' pattern saucer with the very rare 'man in the moon' mark. I paid the appropriate price, which was ten times as much as the piece would have been worth with a more standard mark! Lowestoft has also continued to buck the trend. In 2011 Lowestoft Porcelain Auctions sold an exceptionally rare guglet and basin for over $60,000 (see p.25).

Royal Worcester ewers and vases painted by artists such as the Stintons, Charles Baldwin and Harry Davis still have their collectors and prices have remained steady. In fact, prices have risen for Baldwin swans.

It is always good to buy from a reputable dealer or auction house, as there are many fakes on the market. Publicity about fakes always causes nervousness in the marketplace. Marks alone will not guarantee authenticity. The Meissen crossed-swords mark, for example, has been applied to many Dresden pieces, and can appear on 18thC soft-paste English porcelain and other European hard-paste examples. It is important to study the quality of good Meissen examples.

If you are considering beginning a collection of 18thC and 19thC porcelain, this is a pretty good time to start.

Top Left: A First Period Worcester tea cup and saucer. See p.44.

Left: A 19thC Meissen vase and cover. See p.31.

A KPM Berlin plaque, painted with a portrait of a girl, with impressed 'KPM' and scepter mark.

c1860 *6.75in (17cm) wide*

$1,200-1,800 TEN

A KPM Berlin plaque, painted with a young boy, with impressed 'KPM' and scepter mark, incised '9-6', in a giltwood frame.

c1870 *9in (23.5cm) high*

$12,000-18,000 TEN

A late 19thC KPM Berlin plaque, painted with a girl reading a letter, after the original by Jean Étienne Liotard, with impressed 'KPM' and scepter mark.

10in (25.5cm) high

$1,000-1,500 H&L

A late 19thC KPM Berlin plaque, after the original by Pieter Cornelisz van Slingelandt, in a giltwood frame.

$5,000-7,000 FRE

CLOSER LOOK - KPM BERLIN PLAQUE

The Berlin porcelain factory made its name with the creation of sumptuous portraits of beauties, particularly after 1870.

Scantily-clad beauties are particularly collectible.

This image is exquisitely painted with natural skin tone and shading, painstakingly detailed face and hair and barely concealed breasts.

The quality of the giltwood frame enhances the plaque and adds to its desirability.

A late 19thC KPM Berlin plaque, painted with 'Odalisque', after the original by Angelo Asti, signed 'Wagner', with impressed marks and 'Enbluch nou'h Asti', in a giltwood frame.

13in (33cm) high

$15,000-20,000 FRE

A late 19thC KPM Berlin plaque, painted with a dark-haired beauty, in a giltwood frame.

9in (23cm) high

$4,000-6,000 FRE

A late 19thC KPM Berlin plaque, painted with a reclining woman, with impressed 'KPM', 'H' and scepter mark, with incised '15-12', in a Florentine giltwood frame.

15in (38cm) high

$10,000-15,000 FRE

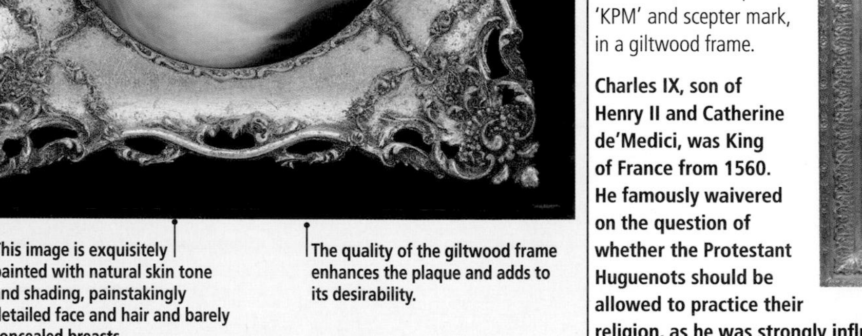

A KPM Berlin plaque, painted with Charles IX, signed lower right 'J. B. Schwerin', with impressed 'KPM' and scepter mark, in a giltwood frame.

Charles IX, son of Henry II and Catherine de'Medici, was King of France from 1560. He famously waivered on the question of whether the Protestant Huguenots should be allowed to practice their religion, as he was strongly influenced by both his Catholic mother and Admiral Gaspard de Coligny, the military and political leader of the Huguenots. In 1572 Charles IX conclusively sided with his mother. This resulted in the murder of Coligny and many other prominent Huguenots in the St Bartholomew's Day Massacre.

1905 *13in (32.5cm) high*

$8,000-12,000 DOR

A KPM Berlin plate, painted with a bouquet of flowers, with 'KPM' and scepter marks.

c1860 *9in (23cm) diam*

$1,200-1,800 **DOR**

A pair of early 20thC KPM Berlin dishes, painted with floral sprays, with 'KPM' and scepter marks.

11in (28cm) wide

$500-700 **GORL**

A KPM Berlin pâte-sur-pâte charger, depicting Venus writing in a book held by Cupid, signed 'E. Dietrich', with blue scepter and red orb marks.

c1860 *13.5in (34.5cm) diam*

$12,000-18,000 **SK**

A pair of late 19thC KPM Berlin cache pots, painted with exotic birds and butterflies, with impressed 'KPM' and scepter marks.

9.5in (24cm) diam

$500-700 **FRE**

A KPM Berlin cup and saucer, with the coat-of-arms of the von Reichel family of East Prussia, with blue scepter and penny mark.

1849-70 *3.25in (8.5cm) high*

$1,000-1,500 **DOR**

A pair of late 19thC KPM Berlin cups and saucers, painted with birds, with blue scepter mark.

$500-700 **SWO**

A late 19thC KPM Berlin candlestick, painted with panels of figures in boats, with blue scepter mark, with chip to footrim.

6in (14cm) high

$200-300 **WW**

A KPM Berlin figure of 'Danae', with blue scepter mark.

7.5in (19cm) high

$700-900 **DMC**

BERLIN MARKS

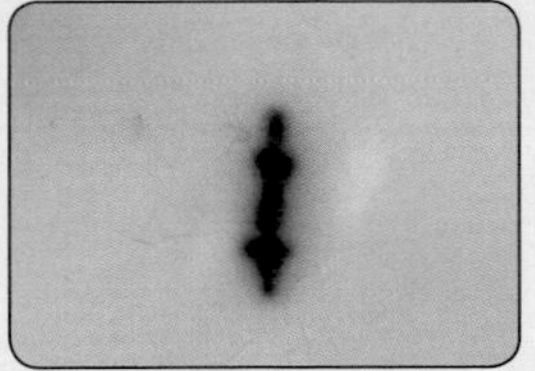

Scepter mark (variations)
1820-37

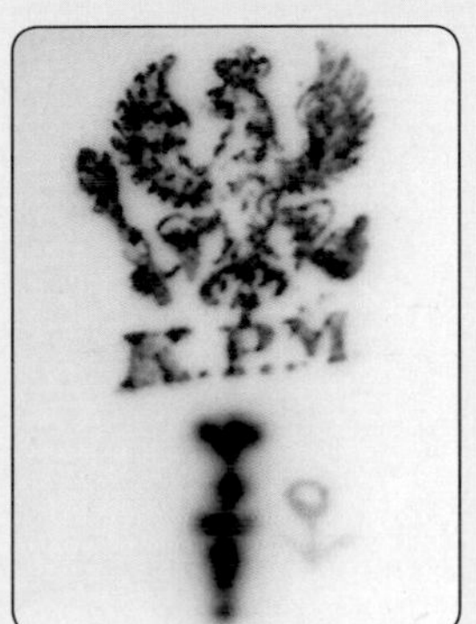

Crowned eagle
1820-32

Orb, KPM and scepter mark

1832-present

Scepter and KPM
1837-44

Eagle penny mark
1847-49

An early Bow white-glazed sauce boat, deeply molded with garlands of flowers beneath a scrolling rim, with crack to handle.

c1750 *8in (20.5cm) long*

$4,000-6,000 **WW**

A rare Bow blue-and-white sweetmeat or pickle dish, formed as three shells around a central dolphin, the tip of the fishtail replaced with metal.

c1750 *7.25in (18.5cm) high*

$800-1,200 **WW**

A Bow blue-and-white bowl, painted with the 'Cross-Legged Chinaman' pattern, with painted blue '8'.

c1752-6 *6in (15cm) diam*

$500-700 **DN**

A Bow blue-and-white plate, painted with the 'Golfer and Caddy Boy' pattern, with blue painted mark.

c1760 *8.75in (22cm) wide*

$1,000-1,500 **L&T**

A Bow frill vase and cover, modeled with flowers and masks, the cover surmounted with an eagle, restored.

c1765 *13in (33cm) high*

$500-700 **DN**

A Bow mug, painted with flower sprays beneath an iron-red scroll and loop pattern border, with restored chip.

c1770 *5in (12cm) high*

$1,000-1,500 **DN**

A rare late 18thC Bow basket, of large size, painted with apples.

12in (30cm) wide

$13,000-15,000 **GORL**

An 18thC Bow figure of a street cook, with restoration.

6in (15cm) high

$1,500-2,000 **GORL**

A near pair of 18thC Bow bocage figures of lady and gentleman musicians, on Rococo bases.

7.25in (18cm) high

$1,000-1,500 **GORL**

A Caughley blue-and-white leaf-molded mask jug.

c1785 *7.5in (19cm) high*

$400-600 **DN**

A Caughley blue-and-white baluster coffee pot, printed with the 'Stalked Apple' pattern with supplementary flowers, with printed 'S' mark, with dry base.

6.5in (16.5cm) high

$1,500-2,500 **BRI**

Miniatures

A Caughley blue-and-white miniature water guglet and wash bowl, painted with the 'Island' pattern.

$7,000-9,000 **BRI**

A Caughley blue-and-white miniature cider jug, painted with the 'Island' pattern, with 'S' mark.

On one occasion, the Chamberlain's factory at Worcester complained to Thomas Turner at Caughley that the toy teawares they had been sent to decorate and sell were 'too small'. Clearly these very tiny pieces proved unpopular with Chamberlain's customers at the time, which may account for their great rarity today. Much of the miniature Caughley on the market today is painted with the 'Island' pattern or printed with the 'Fisherman and Cormorant' pattern.

2.5in (6.5cm) high

$2,500-3,500 **BRI**

A Caughley blue-and-white star-shaped salt, painted with the 'French Sprigs' pattern.

2.25in (6cm) high

$1,000-1,500 **BRI**

A Caughley pounce pot, printed with the 'Stalked Apple' pattern.

This piece still has a label from the 1999 Caughley Bicentenary Exhibition. Many of the other pieces on this page were also shown at this exhibition.

3.5in (9cm) high

$6,500-8,500 **BRI**

A Caughley blue-and-white baluster vase, printed with the 'Apple and Floral' pattern, with cellular friezes, with 'C' mark, with some small chips.

5.5in (14cm) high

$1,200-1,800 **BRI**

A Caughley blue-and-white egg cup, painted with 'Chantilly Sprigs', with painted 'S' mark.

1.5in (4cm) high

$2,000-3,000 **BRI**

A Caughley blue-and-white dessert tureen, cover and stand, painted with the 'Scrolled Landscape' pattern.

9.25in (23.5cm) high

$1,200-1,800 **BRI**

A Chamberlain's Worcester jug, inscribed with loyal support for William Gordon's 1807 victory by a 'Glorious Majority of 352', with gilt 'Chamberlain's Worcester' mark.

William Gordon (1772-1823) obtained the seat at Worcester in 1807 in a contested by-election, having previously been defeated in the General Election of 1806. He succeeded Henry Bromley, whose lavish bribes were so blatant that he resigned rather than let Gordon's petition against his election proceed to a vote in the House of Commons. Gordon represented the 'independent' faction in a constituency that was notoriously expensive to contest due to the high number of non-resident voters and the ingrained corruption. He stood down in 1818 as the expense of election had ruined his business. As his clerk wrote, 'no business could stand £25,000 for contested elections, £20,000 for house and furniture in Portland Place, and £19,000 for jewels to Lady Gordon...'. Two examples of this jug are to be found in the Worcester Porcelain Museum.

7in (18cm) high
$1,200-1,800 **H&C**

An early 19thC Chamberlain's Worcester dish, possibly from the Abergavenny service, painted with a coat-of-arms, with red mark.

10in (25.5cm) wide
$15,000-20,000 **SK**

A Chamberlain's Worcester ink well, decorated with named view 'Moxhull Hall - Warwickshire'.

c1820 *5in (12cm) high*
$800-1,200 **ROS**

A Chamberlain's Worcester 'Lord Nevill service'-type campana vase, probably painted by Humphrey Chamberlain with a scene from Shakespeare's 'Othello'.

c1815 *6in (15cm) high*
$2,500-3,500 **DN**

An early 19thC Chamberlain's Worcester watch stand.

6.5in (17cm) high
$500-700 **GORL**

An early 19thC Chamberlain's Worcester vase and cover, painted with the 'Dragons in Compartments' pattern, with some restoration.

13in (32.5cm) high
$650-850 **WW**

An early 19thC Chamberlain's Worcester pen tray, painted with a view of the Pittville Pump Room in Cheltenham, with printed mark.

6.25in (16cm) long
$400-600 **WW**

A pair of early 19thC Chamberlain's Worcester dishes, with painted puce marks, with impressed marks.

10in (25cm) wide
$1,000-1,500 **AH**

A Chelsea silver-shaped dish, painted with flowers, insects and a butterfly, with applied anchor mark to the base, restored.

c1748 *10in (24.5cm) wide*

$1,000-1,500 **WW**

A Chelsea 'Kakiemon' plate, painted with the 'Flying Fox and Rooting Squirrel' pattern, with scattered flowerheads disguising small firing flaws, with chip to footrim.

c1755 *9in (22.5cm) diam*

$1,500-2,500 **WW**

A pair of Chelsea plates, painted with flowers within molded scrolled borders, with brown anchor mark, with slight wear.

c1760 *8in (21.5cm) diam*

$1,500-2,500 **SWO**

ESSENTIAL REFERENCE - CHELSEA

Founded in c1744 by Nicholas Sprimont, the Chelsea factory was the first porcelain factory in England.

- **Pieces from the Raised Anchor Period (c1749-52) are typically decorated with copies of Japanese Kakiemon wares or Meissen-style European landscapes.**
- **During the Red Anchor period (c1752-56) Chelsea was known for innovative decoration, which included painted fruit and botanical motifs.**
- **Porcelain produced during the Gold Anchor Period (c1756-69) was strongly influenced by Sèvres.**
- **The Chelsea factory was sold in 1770 to William Duesbury of Derby, who ran it until 1784. Pieces from this period are known as Chelsea-Derby.**

This mark 1752-56

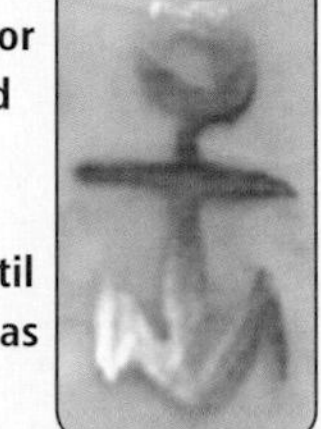

This mark c1756-69

A Chelsea molded peony dish, the handle formed as a stalk terminating in a bud, with red anchor mark, with some small chips.

c1755 *9in (23cm) diam*

$3,500-4,500 **WW**

An 18thC Chelsea strawberry-leaf molded sauceboat, painted with floral sprays, with red anchor mark.

8in (20cm) long

$3,000-4,000 **GORL**

A Chelsea scroll-molded and pierced basket and stand, painted with flowers, the basket with red anchor mark, with cracks to basket.

c1756 *Stand 9in (22cm) diam*

$3,000-4,000 **DN**

A large Chelsea basket, the interior painted with long-tailed birds amid foliage, the pierced sides applied with blue flowerheads, with brown anchor mark, with minor restoration.

c1763 *11in (28cm) long*

$550-750 **WW**

A Chelsea fluted tea bowl, with two panels of water mills, the interior with a ruin in landscape, with some restoration.

c1753 *2in (5cm) high*

$1,200-1,800 A&G

An 18thC Chelsea fluted tea bowl and saucer, with panels of harbour scenes and insects.

Saucer 6.5in (16.5cm) diam

$8,000-12,000 GORL

A Chelsea tureen and cover, painted with flower bouquets and insects, with red anchor mark and stilt mark beneath, with restoration to cover.

1752-56 *9.5in (24cm) diam*

$3,500-4,500 GORL

An 18thC Chelsea tureen and cover, the body decorated with flowers and exotic birds, with floral handle.

11in (28cm) wide

$7,000-9,000 ECGW

A Chelsea figure of the 'Vauxhall Singer', modeled in theatrical costume, with gold anchor mark.

c1760 *11.5in (29cm) high*

$5,000-7,000 DN

A pair of Chelsea musician bocage groups, on Rococo bases, with gold anchor marks.

c1765

10.5in (27cm) high

$1,500-2,500 POOK

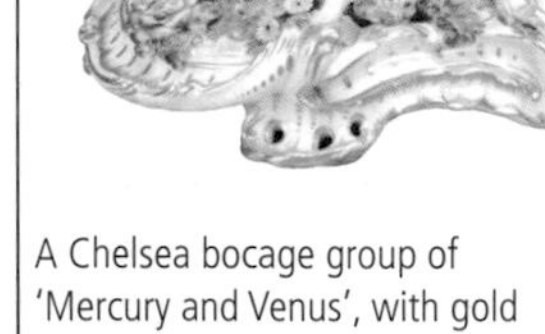

A Chelsea bocage group of 'Mercury and Venus', with gold anchor mark.

c1765 *9in (24cm) high*

$4,000-6,000 DN

A Chelsea figure of 'Winter', personified as a man in a fur cloak, seated beside a brazier of hot coals and smoking a pipe, with gold anchor mark, with some damage and restoration.

c1765 *5.25in (13.5cm) high*

$1,200-1,800 WW

A Coalport botanical part dessert service, comprising five dishes, a pair of sauce tureens, covers and stands, a bowl and twelve plates, painted with different botanical specimens.

c1815

$3,500-4,500 DN

Four Coalport botanical plates, painted with different botanical specimens within molded borders, each titled to the reverse.

c1820 *9.25in (23.5cm) diam*

$2,500-3,500 WW

A Coalport cabinet plate, painted with fruit by Frederick Chivers, signed, with blue printed crown mark and gilder's number '5351/R', with impressed '18A23'.

Frederick Chivers (1881-1965) was a fruit and flower painter. He originally worked for Royal Worcester, but by 1906 he had moved to Coalport where he specialized in fruit studies. He achieved the stippled-effect background of his paintings by working the ceramic color with a matchstick.

c1920-30 *11in (27cm) diam*

$350-450 TEN

A 20thC Coalport part tea service, comprising six cups and saucers and five plates, painted in the 'Strawberry' pattern, with printed marks.

$80-120 set CAPE

An early 20thC Coalport vase and cover, painted with flowers by F Howard, with printed marks.

16in (41cm) high

$1,200-1,800 GORL

A pair of Coalport Sèvres-style vases and covers, painted with panels of fallen fruit by Frederick Chivers, with green printed marks, one cracked.

c1900 *13in (34cm) high*

$3,500-4,500 DN

A Coalport ornithological vase and cover, painted with three panels of birds of prey by John Randall, with gilt ampersand mark to cover, with damage.

John Randall (1810-90) was one of Coalport's best-known artists. He was apprenticed to his uncle Thomas Martin Randall and painted at the Rockingham factory before joining Coalport in 1835. His earlier work typically featured exotic birds, but in the 1860s he began to paint more local birds of prey and other naturalistic studies. In addition to his ceramic painting, he was a botanist, geologist, published local historian and journalist, all of which helped make him a local celebrity.

$3,500-4,500 MAB

A pair of mid-19thC Coalport ice pails, painted with colorful birds including a bullfinch and golden oriole, with painted 'CBD' monograms.

9in (24cm) high

$1,200-1,800 WW

CLOSER LOOK

The scene of Chinese gentlemen standing beside a table with a basket of flowers is extremely unusual for Western porcelain of this period, as it implies interaction between the figures. There is the impression of a story going on that the viewer is not entirely privy to.

Although it depicts Chinese subjects and uses the traditional blue-and-white palette, the style of the image isn't in the Chinese taste.

Given the unusual subject matter, it is likely that this dish was specially commissioned.

This is a good early piece of rare hand-painted Derby.

A Derby blue-and-white saucer dish, with a scroll and half flower border, incised 'A5'.
c1760 *6.25in (16cm) diam*
$1,500-2,500 **M&K**

A rare Derby blue-and-white coffee cup, painted with plantain and tendrils.

Derby coffee cups of this shape are rare in polychrome and very rare in blue-and-white. A pair of cups in this pattern is held in the Derby Museum & Art Gallery and is illustrated in H G Bradley's 'Ceramics of Derbyshire 1750-1975'.
c1760 *2.25in (5.5cm) high*
$1,200-1,800 **M&K**

A Derby blue-and-white sauceboat, painted with trailing flower sprays under a 'Fitzhugh' border.
c1775-80 *7in (18cm) long*
$350-450 **SWO**

A Derby three-tier shell centerpiece, the interior of the shells painted with flowers and insects, with extensive damage.
c1765 *12in (31cm) high*
$1,500-2,500 **DN**

A very large Derby 'famille verte' dish, with painted red mark.
c1800 *16.5in (42cm) wide*
$2,000-3,000 **M&K**

A Derby 'Kakiemon' plate, after a Meissen original, painted with flowers tied with ribbon, a cricket and moth, with painted blue crossed swords mark and small red Derby mark to footrim.

Provenance: Collection of John Haslem (1808-84). In his 1879 catalog Haslem observes that this plate (no.111 in his collection), is 'an amusing instance' of the factory applying another's mark 'at the desire of certain London dealers ...who doubtless passed them off as genuine.'.
c1805 *9.75in (25cm) diam*
$2,000-3,000 **M&K**

Two Derby trout-head stirrup cups, both inscribed 'The Fisher's Delight'.
c1810
Largest 4.75in (12cm) long
$4,000-6,000 **L&T**

A Derby hare-head stirrup cup, with red crowned-'D' mark.
c1820 *6.75in (17cm) long*
$3,500-4,500 **L&T**

A pair of rare Derby white-glazed figures of a seated gentleman and female companion, with labels to base.
c1760 *Taller 7in (18cm) high*
$8,000-12,000 **HAN**

A Derby white-glazed dry-edge figure of 'Feeling' from 'The Five Senses', modeled as a lady in contemporary European dress with a parrot pecking her thumb.

To try and stop the glaze running under the base during the firing process, early Derby figures were held upside down in a liquid glaze and then either wiped clean after dipping or only partially dipped. This left a 'dry' or unglazed edge.

c1750-55 *6.5in (16.5cm) high,*
$3,000-4,000 **M&K**

A Derby figure of 'Britannia', modeled standing before a bocage of oak leaves and acorns, with small chips and missing spear
c1765 *10.5in (26.5cm) high*
$550-750 **DN**

A pair of Derby figures of a rustic and his companion.
c1765 *8.25in (21cm) high*
$550-750 **DN**

A pair of 18thC Derby figural blackamoor sweetmeat dishes, each modeled holding a shell, on Rococo bases.
7.75in (20cm) high
$2,500-3,500 **GORL**

A pair of Derby figures of 'Bacchus' and 'Aria', incised 'N. 193'.
c1800 *8.75in (22cm) high*
$700-900 **DN**

A pair of Bloor Derby figures of 'William Shakespeare' and 'John Milton', with red marks.
c1830 *Taller 10.25in (26cm) high*
$1,000-1,500 **DN**

A Derby model of a leopard, painted with well-defined markings, on thin sprigged base.
c1760 *2.5in (6.5cm) high*
$1,500-2,500 **M&K**

A Derby model of a pug, with incised '3' mark.
c1820 *2.5in (6cm) high*
$400-600 **DN**

A Crown Derby plate, from the 'Gladstone Service', designed by Richard Lunn, painted by James Rouse Snr from sketches by Count Holtzendorf, with a central panel of figures on a Derbyshire moor, with inscription 'DESIGNED AND MANUFACTURED BY THE DERBY CROWN PORCELAIN CO LIMITED FOR PRESENTATION TO THE RT HONLE W E GLADSTONE MP BY THE LIBERAL WORKING MEN OF DERBY 1883', with red 'PODR' mark for 5 December 1883, further inscribed 'Rouse Flowers' and 'J Rouse Snr/ Derwent Edge Peak/Duplicate'.

Count Holtzendorf made several sketches of the Derbyshire countryside exclusively for use on the Gladstone Service. The finished service of 26 pieces was presented to Gladstone in the Library of Hawarden Castle on Saturday, 22nd December 1883. This piece is one of a very small number of duplicate plates that were made in addition to the 26.

1883 *9.5in (24cm) diam*
$2,500-3,500 **M&K**

A Royal Crown Derby vase and cover, painted by Desiré Leroy with exotic birds after a Sèvres original, signed and with date code, the cover repaired.

1898 *8in (20cm) high*
$3,000-4,000 **SWO**

A Royal Crown Derby vase and cover, painted by W Mosley, with iron-red printed mark and pattern number '7054/1409'.

c1900 *10in (25cm) high*
$1,500-2,500 **GORL**

A Royal Crown Derby vase, painted with a flower spray, with lizard handles and paw feet, with red mark.

1902 *15in (41cm) high*
$4,000-6,000 **TEN**

A Royal Crown Derby vase and cover, decorated with sprays of roses, with iron-red marks and date code.

1909 *8.25in (21cm) high*
$350-450 **DN**

A Royal Crown Derby 'Imari' 80-piece dinner service, comprising a soup tureen, cover and stand, three vegetable tureens and covers, two soup tureens, covers and stand, two sauceboats and stands, seven meat dishes, 18 dinner plates, 18 soup plates and 18 dessert plates, with printed marks.

c1910
$4,000-6,000 **TEN**

A pair of Royal Crown Derby vases and covers, painted by George Darlington with exotic birds, signed, with red marks.

1918 *10in (23.5cm) high*
$2,000-3,000 **TEN**

A Royal Crown Derby plate, from the Judge Gary service, painted by Albert Gregory, signed, with gilded signature of George Darlington, with gilt marks and date code.

1911 *10in (24.5cm) diam*
$2,500-3,500 **WW**

A late 19thC Stevenson & Hancock Derby bramble and flower-encrusted four-strand basket, on raised branch feet, with pad mark.

9in (23cm) diam
$150-250 **DN**

ESSENTIAL REFERENCE - GRAINGER'S WORCESTER

Thomas Grainger (1783-1839), a former apprentice at Robert Chamberlain's Worcester factory, established his porcelain company in Worcester in 1801.

- **Grainger's factory initially specialized in rich patterns, such as Japanese-style Imari. During the 1830s and '40s, wares were Rococo in style.**
- **In 1889 the factory was sold to Royal Worcester. Production in the Royal Worcester-style continued until 1902 when the Grainger's factory was closed. Many Grainger's employees transferred to Royal Worcester, including the famous Stinton family of painters.**

A Grainger's Worcester model of a red squirrel, with impressed 'Grainger, Lee & Co Worcester', restored.

c1830-40 *2.5in (6cm) high*

$350-450 **TEN**

A mid-19thC Grainger's Worcester dessert service, comprising twelve dessert plates and four tazzas, painted in the style of Birket Foster, retailed by Sandbach & Co., Manchester.

1845 *Plate 10in (25cm) high*

$800-1,200 **AH**

A Grainger's Worcester cider mug, painted with scenes of Worcester.

5.75in (15cm) high

$250-350 **GORL**

A Grainger's Worcester cabinet plate, painted with pattern no.2513 of a spray of flowering heather, with impressed marks.

9.25in (23cm) diam

$120-180 **GORL**

A Grainger's Worcester pâte-sur-pâte moon flask, with restoration.

c1880 *6.75in (17cm) high*

$150-250 **DN**

An early 19thC Grainger's Worcester campana ice pail and cover, painted with a large panel of English flowers, the cover repaired.

14in (34.5cm) high

$800-1,200 **WW**

A pair of Grainger's Worcester wall pockets, each modeled as a bud, with printed marks.

9.5in (24cm) high

$200-300 **GORL**

A Grainger's Worcester pot pourri vase and cover, painted with blue tits on a blush ground, with printed mark and date code.

1897 *8in (20cm) high*

$400-600 **WW**

A Grainger's Worcester Japanese-style vase and cover, painted with an exotic bird on gilt tree, with printed mark and date code.

1899 *11.75in (30cm) high*

$500-700 **CAPE**

A late 19thC Grainger's Worcester vase and cover, decorated with birds.

8in (21cm) high

$350-450 **CHT**

A late 19thC Grainger's Worcester reticulated bud vase.

6in (15cm) high

$100-150 **AH**

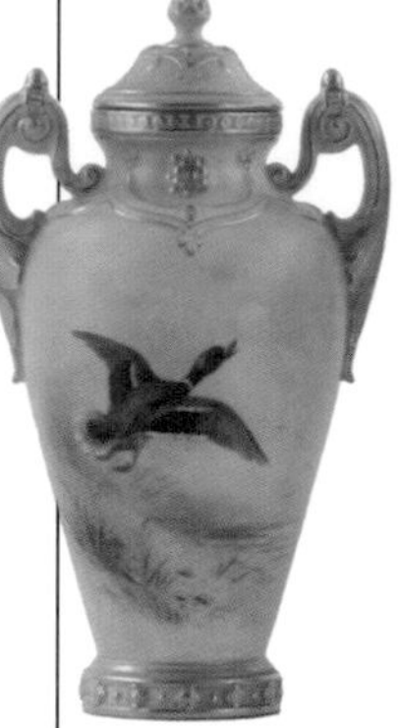

A pair of Grainger's Worcester vases and covers, painted with ducks on a blush ground, with printed marks and date codes.

1901 *8in (21cm) high*

$1,000-1,500 **WW**

A pair of Grainger's Worcester vases, painted by John Stinton with cattle in a meadow, depicting sunrise and sunset, shape no.1001, signed, with printed marks and date codes.

1902 *10in (24cm) high*

$3,500-4,500 **WW**

A Grainger's Worcester ewer, painted by John Stinton with cattle standing in a meadow, shape no.965, with printed mark and date code.

1902 *6in (16.5cm) high*

$700-900 **WW**

ESSENTIAL REFERENCE - HADLEY'S WORCESTER

James Hadley (1837-1903) was an apprentice modeller at Kerr & Binns of Worcester in the 1850s.

- **By 1870 he had become the principal modeller at Royal Worcester.**
- **In 1875 he set up his own modeling studio where he produced ornamental vases and figures. Until 1895 he sold almost all his output to Royal Worcester, often inscribing his name on the base of his master models.**
- **In 1897 Hadley began to build a new factory with the support of his business partner Frank Littledale. This factory became known for softly painted roses, now known as 'Hadley Roses', and figures.**
- **In 1905 Royal Worcester purchased the Hadley factory, which continued to produce wares until 1906. All the workforce, molds and designs were then moved to the Royal Worcester factory where production of some of Hadley's designs continued. The letter 'H' was added to the shape design number of such pieces.**

A James Hadley's Worcester figural hat pin holder, modeled by James Hadley as a young girl, with printed mark and date code.

1882 *7.5in (18cm) high*

$250-350 FLD

A James Hadley's Worcester figure of a 'Yankee', modeled by James Hadley, from the 'Countries of the World' series, with date code.

1893 *7in (17.5cm) high*

$500-700 A&G

A James Hadley's Worcester figure of a Cairo water seller, modeled by James Hadley, with printed mark and date code.

1896 *9in (22.5cm) high*

$400-600 WW

A pair of James Hadley's Worcester figures of children, in typical Hadley colors, with printed marks.

8in (20cm) high

$250-350 GORL

A James Hadley's Worcester blush figure of a dancing girl, modeled by James Hadley, with a spill vase tree stump behind, shape no.1129, with molded Hadley signature, with puce mark.

1898 *10in (24.5cm) high*

$350-450 WHP

A James Hadley's Worcester blush figural candlestick, modeled as a young boy resting on a tree stump, by James Hadley, shape no.1175, with puce mark.

1898 *7.5in (22cm) high*

$350-450 WHP

A pair of James Hadley's Worcester dessert baskets, shape no.1364, with puce mark and year mark, impressed mark and '011', with some restoration.

1890 *8in (21cm) high*

$800-1,200 TEN

A James Hadley's Worcester blush fern centerpiece, modeled and incised by James Hadley, in the style of Kate Greenaway, shape no.1233, with puce marks and date code, with rivetted crack to base.

1895 *19in (49cm) wide*

$350-450 DN

A James Hadley's Worcester faience vase, painted with pink orchid sprays within typical Hadley borders, with printed marks.

7.75in (20cm) high

$150-250 **GORL**

A James Hadley's Worcester jardinière, with printed and painted marks.

c1900 *7.5in (16.5cm) high*

$500-700 **TOV**

A James Hadley's Worcester vase and cover, painted by A C Lewis, signed, with green printed marks and red painted marks 'F106/36.67', with minor hairline crack.

c1901

11in (29cm) high

$1,000-1,500 **TOV**

A James Hadley's Worcester vase, painted with daffodils and other spring flowers, with green printed mark.

1902-05 *10in (25.5cm) high*

$300-500 **ROS**

A James Hadley's Worcester vase, painted by Charles White with peacocks in a naturalistic setting, signed, with date code.

1903 *10.25in (26cm) high*

$350-450 **TRI**

A James Hadley's Worcester ewer, painted by William Powell with a stork by a river, signed, with date code.

1904 *8.75in (22cm) high*

$1,200-1,800 **A&G**

A James Hadley's Worcester vase, painted by A Shuck with pheasants and a hare in a landscape.

c1905 *10in (26cm) high*

$550-750 **SWO**

A pair of James Hadley's Worcester vases, painted by C V White, signed, with green printed and red painted marks.

c1905 *8in (20cm) high*

$800-1,200 **TOV**

An early 20thC James Hadley's Worcester pot pourri with pierced cover, with printed and painted marks.

5in (11cm) high

$350-450 **TOV**

A James Hadley's Worcester pot pourri, with mark and date code.

1928 *5in (13cm) high*

$120-180 **TRI**

A probably Isleworth blue-and-white coffee cup, painted with a mountainous Chinese landscape, with minor chips and firing faults.

c1760-70 *3in (8cm) high*

$1,000-1,500 **WW**

An Isleworth blue-and-white teabowl, transfer-printed with figures on a boat, a hut beside rocks and a pine tree.

c1765-75 *3in (7.5cm) diam*

$550-750 **WW**

An Isleworth flower-molded sauceboat, painted with flower sprays.

This shape is one of around six known sauceboat shapes used by Isleworth.

c1768-75 *7.5in (19cm) wide*

$1,500-2,500 **SWO**

A rare Isleworth feeding cup, transfer-printed with scattered flowers and a moth.

c1775-80 *3.75in (9.5cm) high*

$6,500-8,500 **M&K**

A Lowestoft blue and-white scallop shell dish.

The distinctive blue glaze has pooled attractively in the molding.

$1,200-1,800 **LOW**

A rare Lowestoft powder-blue-and-white saucer dish.

7in (18cm) diam

$5,000-7,000 **LOW**

A Lowestoft jug, with inscription 'Thos Davy, Fressingfield 1782', with scroll handle.

7in (18cm) high

$15,000-20,000 **LOW**

A Lowestoft guglet and basin, painted with views of the High Light, two windmills and St Margaret's Church, flanked by views of the Low Light, the Battery and ships in the Roadstead, with painter's mark '5'.

c1764 *Bottle 9in (23cm) high*

$60,000-70,000 **LOW**

A Lowestoft coffee pot and cover, painted with a Chinese river scene with pagodas on islands.

c1770-75 *9.75in (25cm) high*

$2,500-3,500 **GORL**

A rare Lowestoft blue-and-white coffee can, in the 'Cottage and Fence' pattern.

$1,500-2,500 LOW

A Lowestoft blue-and-white transfer-printed bowl, in the 'Argument' pattern.

The Lowestoft factory was active c1757-99.

9in (23cm) diam

$700-900 LOW

A Lowestoft polychrome sparrowbeak jug, painted by the 'Tulip painter'.

$1,000-1,500 LOW

A Lowestoft teapot and cover, transfer-printed with the 'Garden Party' pattern, clobbered with iron-red flowers and gilding.

$1,200-1,800 LOW

An early Lowestoft blue-and-white jug, painted with a three-tier pagoda, with decorator's mark '3'.

Workmen's marks painted in underglaze blue often appear on early Lowestoft c1760-75, particularly on the edge of the footrim. The numbers '3' and '5' are fairly common.

5in (12.5cm) high

$3,500-4,500 LOW

A rare Lowestoft blue-and-white plate, in the 'Oriental Boy on a Bridge' pattern, with decorator's mark '3'.

c1760-75 *8.5in (21.5cm) diam*

$3,500-4,500 LOW

A rare early Lowestoft blue-and-white coffee cup, with compressed handle, with decorator's mark '6'.

$700-900 LOW

An early Lowestoft blue-and-white teabowl and saucer, with berry border, the saucer with decorator's mark '6'.

$1,000-1,500 LOW

A Lowestoft blue-and-white transfer-printed mug, decorated with flowers and butterflies.

4.25in (11cm) high

$1,500-2,500 LOW

Judith Picks: Meissen

The 'golden era' of Meissen - the Rolls-Royce of porcelain - lasted from the 1720s to the 1750s, during which time many pieces were modeled by Johann Joachim Kändler and enameled with the brilliant colors introduced by Johann Gregorius Höroldt. Such is the desirability of these early figures, that many collectors will overlook issues of condition. This particular figure group lacks the tree the courting couple were leaning against and was restored probably in the late 19thC. It is now showing serious discoloration. I am constantly repeating how important condition is (and of course in perfect condition this could be worth $35,000) but the over-riding value factor here is desirability.

A Meissen group of a 'Shepherd and Shepherdess', modeled by J J Kändler, with dog and sheep.

c1740 *6in (16cm) high*

$8,000-12,000 **TEN**

A Meissen figure of 'Gianqurqolo', modeled by Peter Reinicke and J J Kändler, from the 'Duke of Weissenfels' series, with indistinct marks to base, with some restoration.

c1745 *6in (14cm) high*

$20,000-30,000 **TOV**

A Meissen figure of 'Barbara Uttman', modeled by J F Eberlein, with faded crossed swords mark, with restoration.

Barbara Uttman (1514-75) established the lacemaking industry in her home town of Annaberg, Germany. Her tombstone credits her with the invention of bobbin lace in 1561.

c1745 *5in (12cm) high*

$3,500-4,500 **WW**

A pair of Meissen figures of a fisherman and fisherwoman, models no.2 and 3, with blue crossed swords mark, with some restoration to fisherman.

c1745 *6.25in (16cm) high*

$35,000-45,000 **DOR**

A Meissen group of 'The Betrothal', modeled by J J Kändler, with a putto in a tree behind, a further putto holding a torch.

c1750 *7in (18cm) high*

$12,000-18,000 **TEN**

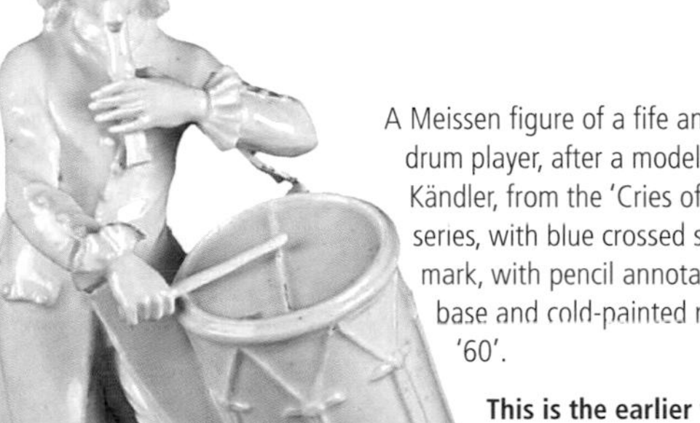

A Meissen figure of a fife and drum player, after a model by J J Kändler, from the 'Cries of Paris' series, with blue crossed swords mark, with pencil annotations to base and cold-painted number '60'.

This is the earlier version of this figure, modeled by Kändler who based the design on the drawings of Edmé Bouchardon.

c1750 *8in (21cm) high*

$3,500-4,500 **A&G**

A Meissen figure of a 'Vinegar Seller', modeled by Peter Reinicke after a design by Christophe Huet, from the 'Cris de Paris' series, with blue crossed swords mark.

c1757 *5.25in (13.5cm) high*

$15,000-20,000 **TEN**

A Meissen figure of a Russian fish seller, modeled by Peter Reinicke, with blue crossed swords mark, with some restoration.

c1760 *6in (16.5cm) high*

$7,000-9,000 **DN**

An early 19thC Meissen figure of 'Aphrodite and Cupid' in her shell carriage, model no.2260, after the model (no.94) by J J Kändler, with blue crossed swords mark, with minor restoration.

6.75in (17cm) high

$4,000-6,000 **DOR**

An early 19thC Meissen figural group of a bagpipe-playing cavalier and a listening lady, model no.B17, modeller no.122, painter no.56, with blue crossed swords mark, with minor restoration.

10in (25cm) high

$3,500-4,500 **DOR**

A 19thC Meissen group of three ladies and putti, with blue crossed swords mark.

19.5in (50cm) wide

$20,000-30,000 **LHA**

A late 19thC Meissen group of 'Venus and Attendants' emblematic of 'Water', modeled after the original by J C Schönheit, from a series of the 'Elements', with blue crossed swords mark, with incised 'D81', with extensive restoration.

9in (23cm) high

$2,500-3,500 **DN**

A pair of Meissen figures of 'Day' and 'Night', modeled by Heinrich Schwabe, model no. L134 and L135, with blue crossed swords marks, with minor chips and 'Night' restored.

c1877-80 *Taller 15in (36.5cm) high*

$3,500-4,500 **KAU**

A late 19thC Meissen figure of a lady on a chair, her hand kissed by a kneeling cavalier, her head turned toward a Moor in the background, after the model by J J Kändler, with blue crossed swords, with minor restoration.

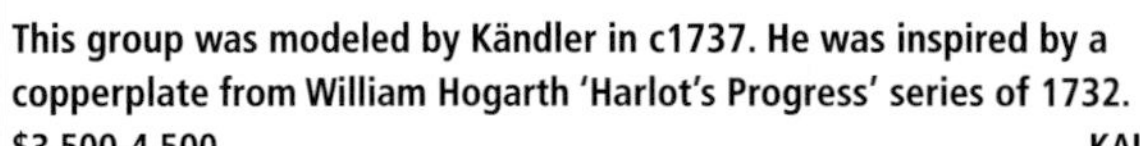

This group was modeled by Kändler in c1737. He was inspired by a copperplate from William Hogarth 'Harlot's Progress' series of 1732.

$3,500-4,500 **KAU**

A 19thC Meissen figure of 'Cupid', after a model by Rudolphe Hoelbe, a lyre hangs to the side with a banner inscribed 'Philomell', with blue crossed swords mark, with impressed 'N195 & 196'.

16.5in (42cm) high

$4,000-5,000 **FRE**

A late 19thC Meissen group of 'The Parcae', after a model by J J Kändler, modeled as Chronos assisting the three Fates, with blue crossed swords marks, incised 'N33', impressed '137' and '57'.

15in (38cm) high

$10,000-15,000 **FRE**

A 19thC Meissen figure group of 'Castor and Pollux', after Christian Gottfried Jüchtzer, with blue crossed swords and incised marks.

14in (36cm) high

$5,000-6,000 **FRE**

A late 19thC Meissen nodding figure, with articulated hands.

6.5in (16.5cm) high

$3,500-4,500 **LC**

A Meissen figure of 'Harlequin Alarmed', after a model by J J Kändler, incised '259', with blue crossed swords mark, with small chips.

c1900 *6.25in (16cm) high*

$1,500-2,500 **DN**

A Meissen figure of a girl drinking from a blue onion cup, designed by Konrad Hentschel in 1905, with blue crossed swords mark, with restoration.

c1920 *6.5in (16.5cm) high*

$2,500-3,500 **DOR**

A pair of Meissen models of swans, modeled by J J Kändler, with blue crossed swords marks, with one wing restored.

c1750 *5.25in (13.5cm) high*

$20,000-30,000 **TEN**

A large 19thC Meissen model of a parakeet, model no.A436, with blue crossed swords mark and incised model number.

16in (40.5cm) high

$5,500-6,500 **GORL**

A late 19thC Meissen model of a pug and puppy, with blue crossed swords mark, with incised '1169'.

9in (22cm) high

$2,000-3,000 **DN**

A Meissen coffee pot, painted with figures and boats in a merchant harbour, with blue crossed swords mark, missing cover.

c1730 *6in (16.5cm) high*

$1,500-2,500 **WW**

A Meissen tea caddy with lid, painted with Indian flowers, birds, a lion and fabulous animals, with Johanneum Palace number 'N=308 w', with blue crossed swords mark.

This piece was owned by Augustus the Strong, King of Poland and Elector of Saxony. Augustus owned the Meissen factory during the late 1720s and early 1730s. He also owned a palace (Johanneum) dedicated entirely to porcelain, which he aimed to fill with Asian ceramics and specially commissioned pieces from the Meissen factory.

c1730 *4in (10cm) high*

$8,000-12,000 **DOR**

MEISSEN MARKS

Mark for Augustus Rex, Elector of Saxony
1723-40

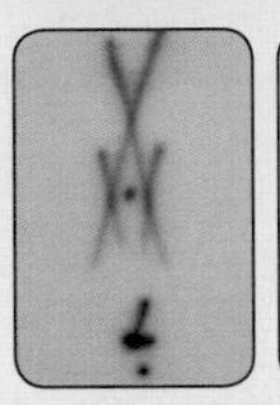

Crossed swords (dot mark)
1763-74

Crossed swords with star
Marcolini period: c1774-1814

Crossed swords
19thC -c1925

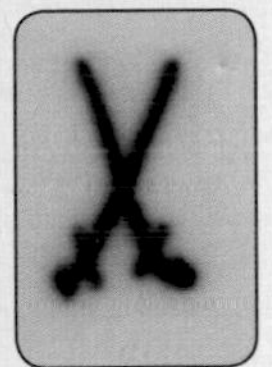

Crossed swords with dot above
Pfeiffer period: 1924-34

Blindstamp crossed swords
Biscuit only: 1814+

Blindstamp crossed swords with 'Weiss'
Only for white porcelain: 20thC-

A Meissen 'Goldchinesen' teapot and cover, decorated in the Augsburg workshop of Abraham Seuter, with chinoiserie scenes of figures in hammocks, with indistinct luster '13' marks.

c1725 *4.5in (11.5cm) high*

$15,000-20,000 **TEN**

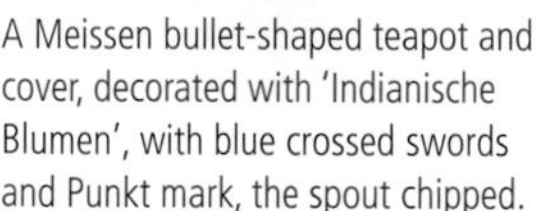

A Meissen bullet-shaped teapot and cover, decorated with 'Indianische Blumen', with blue crossed swords and Punkt mark, the spout chipped.

Carl Christopher Punkt was a sculptor and modeller at Meissen 1761-65.

c1760 s

$1,200-1,800 **DN**

A late 19thC Meissen coffee pot with lid, decorated with miners, with gilt 'AR' for Augustus Rex, with blue crossed swords.

9in (22cm) high

$3,500-4,500 **DOR**

A Meissen cup and saucer, painted with quails, prunus tree and Kikyo plant, with the Johanneum Palace number 'N=345 w', with blue crossed swords mark, with some restoration.

This set was owned by Augustus the Strong.

c1732 *3in (7.5cm) diam*

$7,500-8,500 **DOR**

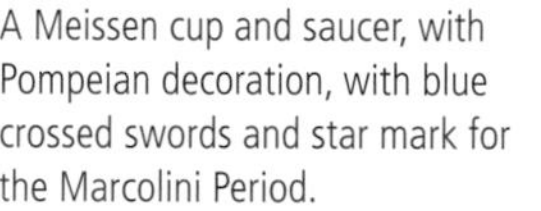

A Meissen cup and saucer, with Pompeian decoration, with blue crossed swords and star mark for the Marcolini Period.

c1780 *5in (13cm) diam*

$2,500-3,500 **DOR**

A Meissen cup and saucer, painted with Bavarian mountain landscape, with blue crossed swords mark.

c1814 *Cup 3.5in (9cm) high*

$2,500-3,500 **DOR**

A Meissen jug, encrusted with flowers, the handle and feet with gilt leafy-branches, with blue crossed swords mark, with minor restoration.

c1740 *6.75in (17cm) high*

$1,000-1,500 **DOR**

A Meissen bowl, painted with Höroldt-style chinoiserie figures, the interior with a man holding a parrot and a child with a fly-swat, with blue crossed sword mark.

c1735 *6.75in (17.3cm) diam*

$2,000-3,000 **L&T**

A large late 19thC Meissen flower-encrusted mirror, with applied birds and putti, with some damage.

72in (183cm) high

$15,000-20,000 **DN**

A late 19thC Meissen ormolu-mounted box, painted with mythological and battle scenes, with gilt enhancements, with blue crossed swords mark.

11.5in (29cm) wide

$10,000-15,000 **FRE**

One of a pair of Meissen ormolu-mounted vases, decorated with forget-me-nots, painted with figural panels, with blue crossed swords marks, with restoration.

c1745 *9in (23cm) high*

$12,000-18,000 pair KAU

CLOSER LOOK

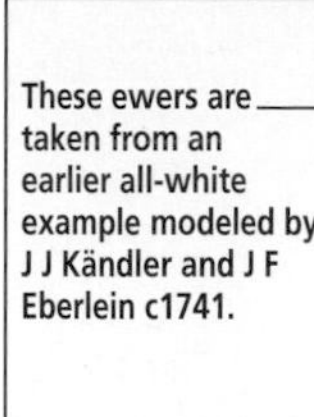

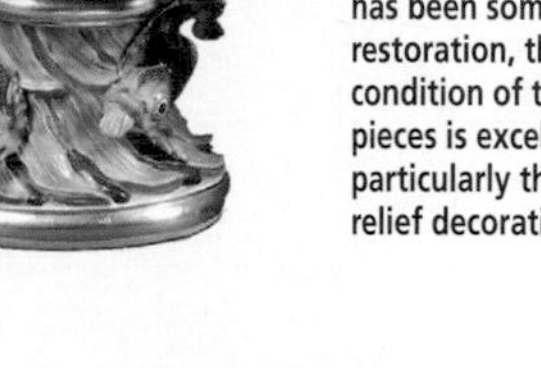

These ewers are taken from an earlier all-white example modeled by J J Kändler and J F Eberlein c1741.

The attention to detail is typical of the Meissen factory. These ewers are certainly statement pieces.

Even though there has been some restoration, the condition of these pieces is excellent, particularly the high-relief decoration.

Two Meissen ewers emblematic of 'Fire' and 'Water', after the 18thC models by J J Kändler, with blue crossed swords marks, 'Fire' incised '310', 'Water' incised '320', with some restoration.

c1880 *27in (68.5cm) high*

$50,000-70,000 SK

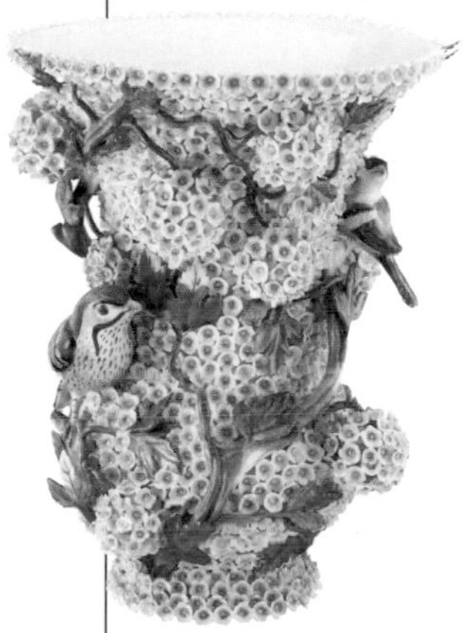

A pair of Meissen snowball vases, modeled by J J Kändler, encrusted with flowers and with applied birds, with blue crossed swords, with minor restoration.

c1745 *9.75in (25cm) high*

$35,000-45,000 KAU

An early 19thC Meissen vase, decorated with flowers and hunting scenes, with blue crossed swords mark.

19in (48cm) high

$5,500-6,500 DOR

A Meissen 'Limoges enamel' vase and cover, in the style of Ernst August Leuteritz, with cobalt-blue ground, with blue crossed swords mark, with incised 'L191' and impressed '8', with minor faults.

c1860 *13in (34cm) high*

$15,000-20,000 TOV

A 19thC Meissen vase and cover, with molded scrolls, encrusted with flowers, with an applied cherub and woman with basket of flowers, with painted figural panels, with blue crossed sword mark.

26in (65cm) high

$6,500-7,500 L&T

A late 19thC Meissen vase, painted with Classical figures, with blue crossed sword marks.

19in (48cm) high

$10,000-15,000 L&T

A late 19thC Meissen urn, with cobalt-blue ground and gilt decoration, with blue crossed swords mark.

24.25in (62cm) high

$2,000-3,000 LHA

A pair of late 19thC Meissen snowball vases, with blue crossed swords marks, with damage.

10in (22.5cm) high

$2,500-3,500 KAU

A Meissen ormolu and porcelain figural centerpiece, painted in polychrome and gold.

c1750 *11.5in (29cm) high*

$20,000-30,000 **KAU**

A Meissen double salt, painted with flower posies and scattered 'Deutsche Blumen'.

c1750 *7in (18cm) wide*

$2,000-3,000 **WW**

A Minton parian group of 'Una and the Lion', from the model by John Bell, with pad mark 'JOHN BELL' and registration mark for 19th August, with small chip.

1847 *4in (36cm) long*

$500-700 **DN**

A set of eleven Minton cabinet plates, painted with aquatic scenes by William Mussill, retailed by Davis, Collamore & Co., New York, with printed crowned globe mark, signed, with date mark.

1880 *9.5in (24cm) diam*

$6,500-7,500 **FRE**

A pair of Meissen ormolu and porcelain figural candelabra, featuring amoretti with bagpipes and drums, with some restoration, the mounts later.

c1750 *5.25in (13.5cm) high*

$7,000-9,000 **DOR**

A late 19thC Meissen clock case, modeled with Cupid and a pair of doves, with blue crossed swords mark, with incised 'F56', with old damage and repair.

12in (31cm) high

$3,500-4,500 **DN**

A Minton parian group of 'The Three Mary's', with indistinct mark.

c1852 *13.75in (35cm) high*

$300-500 **DN**

An unusual Minton brown transfer-printed porcelain footbath, in the 'Genevese' pattern, with vignettes of Swiss mountain scenes, with brown-printed scroll, floret mark and 'M'.

c1850 *19in (49.5cm) wide*

$2,500-3,500 **TEN**

A Mintons pâte-sur-pâte cabinet plate, decorated by Louis Solon, retailed by Phillips of Oxford Street, London, signed, with gilt globe mark, with initials 'SMS'.

c1880 *9.5in (24cm) diam*

$3,500-4,500 **DN**

A Minton pâte-sur-pâte vase and cover, decorated by Albion Birks, the body carved with a recumbent Diana and Cupid, signed 'ABirks', with gilt globe mark, with firing cracks to base.

c1905 *7in (17.5cm) high*

$1,000-1,500 **DN**

A Nantgarw dish, painted with flowers including poppy and convolvulus, with impressed 'NANTGARW CW' mark.

c1815-20 *9.5in (24cm) wide*

$3,500-4,500 **WW**

A Nantgarw soup bowl, possibly from the 'Brace' service, probably decorated in London, perhaps in the Bradley workshop, decorated with fruit, flower and bird vignettes around a central floral spray.

c1820 *8in (20.5cm) diam*

$2,000-3,000 **TEN**

A pair of Nantgarw ice pails, covers and liners, from the 'Cardiff Castle' service, probably decorated by Thomas Pardoe, one with damage.

Provenance: Acquired directly from the Marquis of Bute, from Cardiff Castle in 1943.

c1820 *8in (21.5cm) high*

$100,000-150,000 **DN**

A Nantgarw plate, painted by William Billingsley, with impressed mark.

c1820 *10in (24cm) diam*

$2,000-3,000 **TEN**

A pair of Paris vases, by Darte, decorated with figures including a Native American.

c1820 *16.5in (42cm) high*

$6,500 7,500 **POOK**

ESSENTIAL REFERENCE - PARIS

Following the relaxation of laws protecting the Sèvres monopoly, a large number of porcelain factories were established in Paris in the late 18thC.

- **Paris porcelain was decorative, especially late 18thC tablewares, but rarely innovative.**
- **François-Maurice Honoré founded a factory in the petite rue Saint-Gilles in 1785. By 1807 it had become the leading Paris porcelain factory. It closed in 1867.**
- **Jean-Baptiste Locré de Roissy's La Courtille factory (1771-c1840) was the most productive of the Paris factories.**

A pair of late 19thC Paris tea caddies and covers, probably by Paul Bocquillon, in the Worcester style.

8in (21cm) high

$500-700 **SWO**

A mid-19thC Paris Sèvres-style part dessert service, probably by Feuillet, comprising a pair of baskets, a pair of sauce tureens, covers and stands, an ice pail, 12 plates and a pair of tazzas.

$4,500-5,500 **DN**

A pair of late 19thC Paris cupid figural groups, by Balthasar Augustin Le Hujeur, with blue faux Sèvres mark.

Taller 13in (34cm) high

$2,500-3,500 **DOR**

A late 19thC Paris ormolu-mounted lidded vase, signed 'G. Poitevin', with blue faux Sèvres mark.

Georges-Émile Poitevin was a Parisian porcelain painter who worked with his father. He was a participant in various Paris salons.

1876-79 *21in (53cm) high*

$8,000-12,000 DOR

A Paris lattice basket, by André-Marie Leboeuf, marked 'Manufacture de la Reine', with red crown mark.

c1790 *9in (24cm) long*

$1,800-2,200 DOR

A Paris cabinet cup and saucer, with a portrait by or after Sophia Hawes, titled in the interior 'Marc Isambart [sic] Brunel né à Hacqueville Normandie 1769', with 'Honoré' Paris red printed mark.

1769 *Saucer 5in (15cm) diam*

$4,000-6,000 TOV

Four mid-19thC Paris Sèvres-style 'jeweled' plates, painted with portraits of Madame de Pompadour, Madame du Barry, Madame Elizabeth and Elizabeth D'Autriche, with blue faux Sèvres marks.

9.75in (25cm) diam

$5,500-6,500 DN

A pair of mid-19thC Paris Sèvres-style seaux with stands, with green-ground.

7.75in (19.5cm) high

$800-1,200 DN

A Paris bisque figure of Venus, with incised 'AR' and black script 'Medaille d'Or Exposition Universelle de Paris 1878', with green printed anchor mark, cracked.

c1878

$1,200-1,800 TEN

A 19thC French model of Francis I on horseback, after the 1540 painting by François Clouet, with blue faux Sèvres mark, with some damage and restoration.

15in (38.5cm) high

$4,000-6,000 WW

An early 20thC Paris group of three young people with a swing, with minor chips and restoration.

15in (38.5cm) high

$800-1,200 KAU

A late 19thC Samson vase, decorated in the Worcester style with exotic birds within a scale-blue ground, with faux Worcester marks.

8.5in (22cm) high

$150-250 **GORL**

A late 19thC Samson vase and cover, with inventory label 'St.E. 5241', with Samson mark.

27.5in (73cm) high

$2,500-3,500 **KAU**

A large late 19thC Samson Meissen-style pagoda figure, with nodding head, protruding tongue and articulated upturned palms, with faux Meissen mark, with minor damage.

11in (28cm) high

$1,500-2,500 **WW**

A late 19thC Samson Meissen-style group of 'Minerva for War, Science and Music', with faux Meissen mark, with some damage.

17in (42cm) high

$650-850 **DN**

A Samson bonbonnière in the form of a cat's head, with gilt-metal mount.

c1900 *2.75in (7cm) high*

$250-350 **SWO**

A pair of Samson models of Dogs of Fo, unmarked.

10.5in (27cm) high

$1,000-1,500 **AH**

A late 19thC Samson Yongzheng-style charger, painted with two pheasants among flowering peony.

22in (56cm) diam

$3,500-4,500 **SWO**

A set of late 19thC Samson armorial plates, comprising ten dinner plates and ten luncheon plates, each with a different heraldic crest and motto.

Dinner plate 9.75in (25cm) diam

$1,500-2,500 **FRE**

ESSENTIAL REFERENCE - VINCENNES

The Vincennes factory was established in c1740. In 1745 it was granted a 20-year monopoly for the production of decorative porcelain. In 1753 Louis XV became the principal shareholder and the factory became known as the 'Manufacture Royale de Porcelaine'.

- **All pieces were of soft-paste porcelain.**
- **The factory's 'great period' began in 1751 with the appointment of Jean-Jacques Bachelier as art director.**
- **The crossed 'L's of the Royal cypher were adopted as the Vincennes (and later Sèvres) mark in 1753.**
- **The factory moved to Sèvres in 1756.**

A small rare Vincennes bottle/glass cooler, painted in the manner of Meissen in puce camaïeu with Classical shrine to one side and with figures in boats to the other, within gilt cartouches, with blue interlaced 'L's mark and dot mark.

c1750-52 *5.25in(11cm) high*

$20,000-30,000 **WW**

A Vincennes jug, painted with a gilt-edged cartouche of birds in flight, with blue interlaced 'L's mark, with traces of painter's mark.

While the painter's mark is barely legible, the most likely candidate is Jean-François Grison, who worked at Vincennes 1749-51.

c1750 *4.5in (11.5cm) high*

$4,000-6,000 **SWO**

A Vincennes sugar bowl and cover, decorated in gilt with panels of exotic birds, with blue interlaced 'L's mark.

c1753 *3.5in (9cm) high*

$6,500-7,500 **DN**

A Sèvres coffee cup and saucer, probably later decorated with scenes of exotic birds in landscapes, with interlaced 'L's marks, with painter's marks in blue enamel.

c1760

$2,000-3,000 **MAB**

A Sèvres cup and saucer, decorated with marine scenes in the manner of Morin, with interlaced 'L's marks, with date letter 'P'.

1768

$1,500-2,500 **DN**

A Sèvres milk jug, painted with two panels of flowers in a green ground, cracked.

c1780 *4in (10.5cm) high*

$800-1,200 **DN**

One of a pair of Sèvres sauce tureens and cover, painted by Nicolas Bulidon, the design incorporating large gilt 'D's, with blue printed interlaced 'L's mark, with date letter 'S'.

From the service 'Petit Vases et Guirlandes' de Madame du Barry.

1771 *9in (24cm) long*

$10,000-15,000 pair **TEN**

A late 18thC Sèvres ecuille and underplate, decorated in gilt with panels of storks among foliage, with blue interlaced 'L's mark.

Ecuille 8.75in (22cm) wide

$1,500-2,500 **L&T**

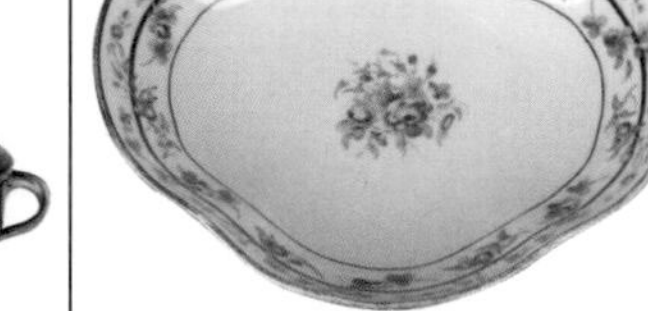

A Sèvres scallop-shaped dish, with painted 'RF' mark for the First Republic.

c1795 *9in (22.5cm) wide*

$350-450 **DN**

Judith Picks: Sèvres

To add to the delight of the exquisitely painted pieces of Sevres porcelain, we collectors always like a good story or provenance. These ice cream pails and sucriers were probably part of the 95-piece service presented to Sir Thomas Lawrence (1769-1830) by Charles X in recognition of the portraits he painted of the King and his son the Dauphin in Paris in 1825.

The service is reputed to have cost 8,100 livres in 1825, but one wonders: did the King have to pay? Sir Thomas Lawrence (1769-1830) was a leading portrait painter and president of the Royal Academy. Lawrence's love affairs were not happy (his tortuous relationships with Sally and Maria Siddons became the subject of several books). It is said about him, he was 'Always in love and always in debt'.

A pair of Sèvres ice cream pails, probably from the Sir Thomas Lawrence service, with botanic decoration bordered with gilt and platinum-decorated blue bands, with internal liners and covers, with green painted '29 AV 24 GU', 'Ex' and 'M'.

11.5in (29.5cm) wide

$10,000-15,000 CLV

A pair of Sèvres two-handled sucriers, covers and stands, probably from the Sir Thomas Lawrence service, with botanic decoration and gilt and platinum-decorated blue borders, with pineapple finials, with blue interlaced 'L's marks, with green painted '29 AV 24 GU Ex' and brown 'DT', with incised 'JB'.

10in (25.25cm) wide

$6,500-7,500 CLV

A Sèvres bisque profile plaque of the Duke of Wellington, signed 'Brachard Fe', in original frame, with 'Colnaghi & Co.' label.

Three members of the Brachard family worked as modellers at the Sèvres factory. Around 1817, both Jean Charles Nicholas and his younger brother Alexandre worked there.

c1817 *7.5in (19.5cm) high*

$1,800-2,200 H&C

A 19thC Sèvres silver-plate-mounted chocolatière, painted with chinoiserie panels on a brown ground, incised 'FR', with minor damage.

4.75in (12cm) high

$2,500-3,500 GORB

A pair of 19thC Sèvres ormolu-mounted center bowls, painted with Classical figures in a landscape.

24in (61cm) wide

$12,000-18,000 LHA

A 19thC Sevres ormolu-mounted vase and cover, painted with a Napoleonic scene.

17.5in (44.5cm) high

$2,000-3,000 GORL

One of a pair of early 19thC Sèvres ormolu-mounted vases, with blue interlaced 'L's marks, with restoration.

Taller 22.5in (60cm) high

$8,000-12,000 pair KAU

A Sèvres coffee and tea service, comprising a coffee pot, a tea pot, a sugar bowl, twelve coffee cups, twelve saucers, eleven tea cups, eleven saucers and twelve dessert plates, decorated with couples in landscapes, with chromium green mark with line.

1871-76 *Coffee pot 8in (20cm) high*

$5,500-6,500 set DOR

A Swansea cabinet cup and saucer, the cup with initials 'EN', with three gilt lion's paw feet, with gilt script marks.

c1815

$2,500-3,500 **DN**

A Swansea dessert plate, painted with flowers including daffodil, rose and auricula, unmarked.

c1815-7 *8.5in (21.5cm) diam*

$2,500-3,500 **WW**

A Swansea dessert plate, painted with strawberries and flowers, with stenciled iron-red mark.

c1815-17 *8.5in (21.5cm) diam*

$2,500-3,500 **WW**

A Swansea footed dessert dish, painted in the style of Henry Morris, with minor wear to gilding.

c1820 *12.5in (32cm) wide*

$2,500-3,500 **WW**

A 19thC Swansea cabinet cup and saucer, with painted iron-red 'Swansea'.

6in (15.2cm) high

$3,500-4,500 **WW**

A Vauxhall tea canister, decorated with flowers and a large butterfly, missing cover.

c1752-54 *4in (10cm) high*

$3,500-4,500 **WW**

A Vauxhall teabowl and saucer, painted with a pine tree issuing from rocks.

c1755-60

$3,500-4,500 **DN**

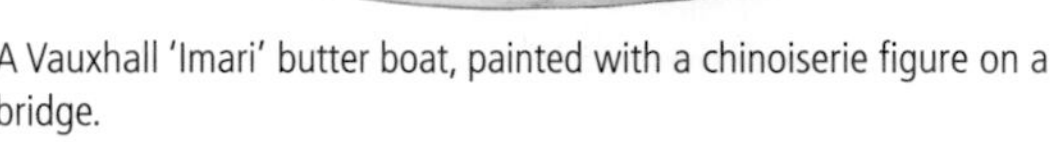

A Vauxhall 'Imari' butter boat, painted with a chinoiserie figure on a bridge.

c1760 *5in (10cm) long*

$1,500-2,500 **TEN**

ESSENTIAL REFERENCE - VIENNA

The first porcelain factory in Vienna was founded in 1718 by Claudius Du Paquier with the assistance of former Meissen employees C C Hunger and Samuel Stölzel.

- **Vienna was the second European factory to make hard-paste porcelain after Meissen.**
- **Early wares were similar in form to those of Meissen, but have denser decoration.**
- **Du Paquier sold the factory to the state in 1744. Around this time, the Rococo style was introduced and chief modeller Johann Josef Niedermayer began producing a wide variety of figures.**
- **In 1784 Konrad Sörgel von Sorgenthal was made director. The Rococo style was abandoned during this era in favor of the Neo-classical style.**
- **The factory declined in the 1820s and closed in 1864.**

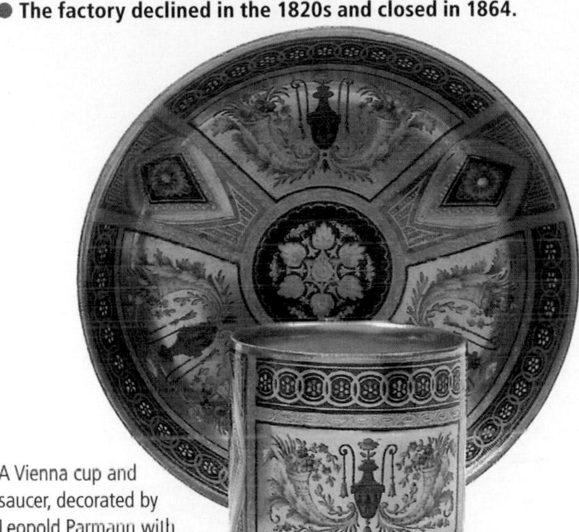

A Vienna cup and saucer, decorated by Leopold Parmann with Etruscan vases, with blue shield mark, dated. 1789, *1796* *5in (13cm) diam*
$12,000-18,000 DOR

A Vienna cup and saucer, painted én grisaille by Johann Schiffauer with acanthus leaves, vases and rosettes within purple reserves, with blue shield mark, dated, with minor restoration.
1790, 1817 *5in (13cm) diam*
$2,000-3,000 DOR

A Vienna teacup and saucer, painted by Paul Schwaiger, with copper-luster ground, with blue shield mark, dated.
1796, 1798 *5in (13.5cm) diam*
$15,000-20,000 DOR

A Vienna plate, decorated with 'Cupid wird von Nymphen gefesselt' (Cupid bound by Nymphs) after Angelica Kauffmann, with blue shield mark, dated, with small scratches.
1805 *10in (24.5cm) diam*
$4,000-6,000 DOR

A Vienna cup and saucer, decorated with circus entertainers, with blue shield mark, dated, with hairline crack.
1811 *5in (13.5cm) diam*
$14,000-16,000 DOR

A Vienna Egyptian-style cup and saucer, decorated with hieroglyphs, with blue shield mark, dated.
1815, 1821 *3.5in (9cm) high*
$10,000-15,000 DOR

A Vienna Veduti cup and saucer, painted with 'Le Chiosk dans le parc à Baden', with blue shield mark, dated.
1817, 1818 *7.5in (15cm) diam*
$4,500-5,500 DOR

A Vienna Veduti cup, painted with 'The Metropolitan church of St Stefan in Vienna', with impressed shield mark, dated.
1846 *4in (10cm) high*
$4,000-6,000 DOR

A Vienna Oriental-style plate, with blue shield mark, turner no.19, painter no.14.

c1750 *9in (24cm) diam*

$1,200-1,800 **DOR**

A Vienna plate, painted with a hunting scene, with blue shield mark, dated.

From 1780 to 1815 the Vienna factory enjoyed a golden age under the management of Conrad Sörgel von Sorgenthal. This period of Classicism (known as the Sorgenthal Period) celebrated the return to artistic styles from Antiquity. Porcelain produced during this period often features relief gold decoration, palmettes and horns of plenty.

1799 *10in (24.5cm) diam*

$3,500-4,500 **DOR**

A Vienna plate, painted with 'Hercules at the Crossroads', with blue shield mark, with year mark.

The plate is marked with turner number '15' for Georg Schwindel, who worked at Vienna 1803-27, and with gilt-painter number '93' for Franz Schulz, who worked at Vienna 1802-47.

1823 *9in (24cm) diam*

$5,000-6,000 **DOR**

A 19thC Vienna charger, painted with 'Opferung der Iphigenie'.

16.25in (41cm) diam

$3,500-4,500 **GORL**

A large 19thC Vienna plaque, painted with the 'Consecration of Decius Mus' after Reubens, signed 'O Her'.

24.25in (62cm) diam

$6,500-7,500 **GORL**

A late 19thC Vienna charger, painted with a scene of bathing beauties after Angelica Kaufmann, with blue shield mark.

19.25in (49cm) diam

$8,000-12,000 **L&T**

A set of early 20thC Vienna cabinet plates, painted with portraits of European Royal ladies, including Elizabeth I, Maria de Medici, Marguerite de Provence, Anne Boleyn, Anna von Osterreich, Louise of Mecklenburg-Strelitz, Katherine Howard, Henrietta Maria, Mary Stuart, Maria Therese and Josephine Bonaparte, with blue shield mark.

9.5in (24cm) diam

$20,000-30,000 **FRE**

A pair of Vienna urns and covers, painted with Classical subjects, with blue shield marks.
c1900 *15in (38cm) high*
$4,000-6,000 **DN**

A 19thC Vienna campana vase, painted with a garland of spring flowers.
13.5in (34cm) high
$3,500-4,500 **GORL**

A pair of Vienna epergnes with lids, with blue shield mark, dated, with minor scuffing to gilding.
1822 *14in (35.5cm) high*
$4,000-6,000 **DOR**

A Vienna Oriental-style bottle cooler, with blue shield mark, dated, with some restoration.
1798 *5.25in (13cm) high*
$1,200-1,800 **DOR**

A Vienna pedestal dish, painted with Cupid and Psyche, with impressed marks, with blue shield mark, dated.
1817 *5.75in (14.5cm) diam*
$1,200-1,800 **DN**

An early 19thC Vienna plaque, painted with 'Juno visits Jupiter', in the style of Annibale Carraci, Bologna School, signed 'A. Kothgasser' and probably by a contemporary of Anton Kothgasser.

Juno was the Roman goddess of marriage, birth and motherhood. Her counterpart in the Greek pantheon was Hera. Juno/Hera was the Royal spouse of Jupiter (Greek counterpart: Zeus), god of the sky and weather. Together with Minerva (Greek counterpart: Athena), Juno and Jupiter were worshipped as a triad on Rome's Capitoline Hill.
$12,000-18,000 **DOR**

A Vienna bisque allegorical figure group, with some restoration, unmarked.
c1780 *9in (22.5cm) high*
$2,000-3,000 **DOR**

A Vienna group of the birth of Crown Prince Rudolf, featuring his parents Archduke Franz Karl and Archduchess Sophie, with impressed mark and year stamp, with hairline crack and some small losses.
1858 *10in (26cm) high*
$5,000-6,000 **DOR**

A Vienna Rococo clock, modeled by H Paul Painstingel, with blue shield mark, with some restoration.
c1765 *9in (23cm) high*
$4,000-6,000 **DOR**

ESSENTIAL REFERENCE - PRUNUS ROOT PATTERN

- **The 'Prunus Root' pattern was introduced at Worcester in c1753, making it one of the factory's earliest blue-and-white patterns. It was also one of the most popular.**
- **It was probably copied from a Chinese export original, although no record of this has been found.**
- **The pattern occurs on plain and fluted teawares, mustard pots and mugs, as well as toy and miniature Worcester porcelain objects.**

A very rare First Period Worcester blue-and-white miniature tea kettle, painted with the 'Prunus Root' pattern, with blue crescent mark.
c1753 *4in (10cm) high*
$5,500-6,500 **LC**

One of a pair of First Period Worcester blue-and-white butter boats, molded as acanthus leaves.
c1755 *3in (8cm) long*
$1,000-1,500 pair **SWO**

A First Period Worcester blue-and-white coffee cup, painted with the 'Fisherman & Willow Pavilion' pattern, with workman's mark.
c1755-7 *2in (5cm) high*
$650-850 **AH**

A First Period Worcester blue-and-white coffee cup, painted with the 'Warbler' pattern, with painter's mark.
c1758 *2.5in (6cm) high*
$800-1,200 **TEN**

A First Period Worcester blue-and-white cream jug, painted with the 'Prunus Root' pattern, with workman's mark.
c1757 *3.5in (9cm) high*
$700-900 **AH**

A First Period Worcester blue-and-white silver-shaped sauce boat, with chinoiserie landscapes, with workman's marks.
c1760 *7in (19cm) long*
$1,000-1,500 **SWO**

A First Period Worcester blue-and-white leaf-shaped pickle dish, painted with the 'Rock Warbler' pattern, with arrow painter's mark.
c1760 *4in (10.5cm) long*
$1,200-1,800 **TEN**

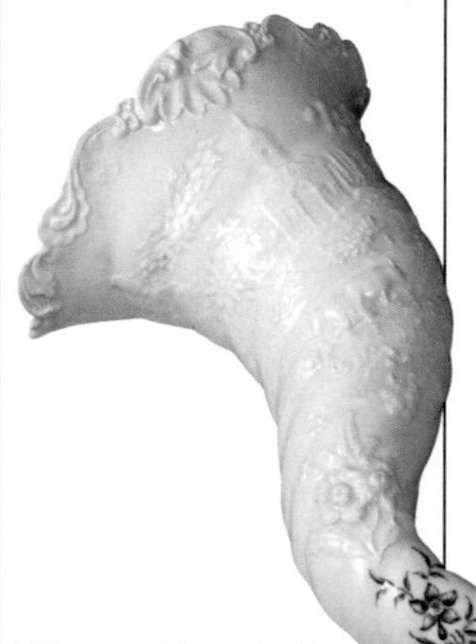

A Worcester blue-and-white cornucopia wall pocket, molded with cattle and gazebo in a garden, painted with a flower to foot.
c1765 *8in (21cm) long*
$3,500-4,500 **SWO**

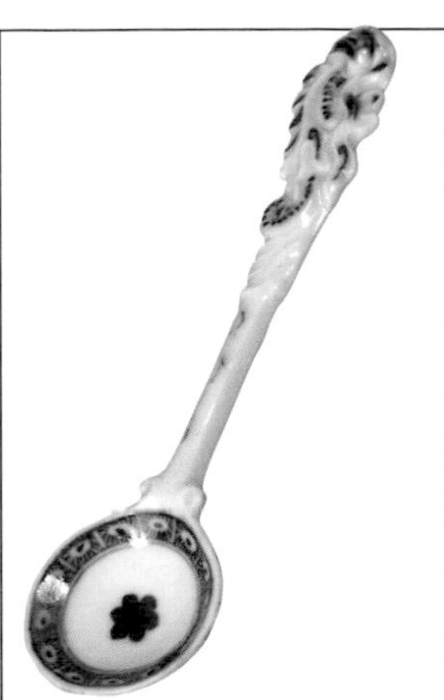

A rare First Period Worcester blue-and-white salt spoon.
c1765 *4in (10cm) long*
$1,200-1,800 **SWO**

A First Period Worcester blue-and-white cabbage-leaf mask jug, transfer-printed with a floral pattern.
8in (20cm) high
$350-450 **TRI**

An 18thC First Period Worcester blue-and-white lidded mustard pot and spoon, transfer-printed with floral sprays and a moth.
Pot 4in (10.2cm) high
$1,000-1,500 **GORL**

A First Period Worcester blue-and-white mug, transfer-printed with the 'Pecking Parrot' pattern, with script 'W' mark.
c1775 *3.25in (8.5cm) high*
$650-850 **SWO**

A First Period Worcester blue-and-white rice spoon, with 'Maltese Cross' decoration, with open crescent mark.
c1775 *6in (14cm) long*
$700-1,000 **SWO**

A First Period Worcester blue-and-white sauceboat, painted with a chinoiserie pattern of a stylized garden with bamboo.

This pattern is possibly un-recorded.
c1775 *7in (18.5cm) diam*
$650-850 **DN**

A First Period Worcester blue and white tea caddy, transfer-printed with the 'Fence' pattern, with hatched crescent mark.
5in (13cm) high
$700-1,000 **GORL**

A First Period Worcester tea canister and lid, transfer-printed with the 'Cormorant' pattern.
c1770 *5in (12cm) high*
$350-550 **SWO**

A First Period Worcester blue-and-white mug, transfer-printed with the 'Man Holding a Gun' pattern, with crescent mark.
c1780 *4.5in (11.5cm) high*
$650-850 **AH**

WORCESTER MARKS

First Period Worcester
c1755-92 (painted/or printed).

First Period Worcester
c1755-75 (painted)

Flight period
c1788-92 (painted)

Barr, Flight & Barr period
c1807-13 (impressed)

Flight, Barr & Barr period
c1813-40 (printed)

Royal Worcester
1891-1943 (printed)

PORCELAIN

Judith Picks

When I first began collecting, I fell in love with 18thC Worcester. There was something about these pots that struck a chord. Much as I admire the superior quality of Meissen and Sèvres, there is something special about the early soft-paste porcelain produced in Worcester. I love this octagonal shape with the slightly misshapen lid, and the attempt to compete with the Chinese porcelain that was flooding the market, much as now, with the enameled Chinese famille verte-style decoration. I believe Worcester porcelain to be undervalued and certainly some of the more common patterns are cheaper than when I bought them 20-30 years ago. Unfortunately, antiques are not always a good investment, although some of my rarer patterns have seen a substantial increase in value.

A First Period Worcester 'famille verte' teapot and cover, painted with Buddhistic auspicious objects, two tall ladies and arrangements of vases and tables in garden settings.

An undated price card for the factory's London warehouse, probably produced not long after it opened in 1756, lists 'tea pots fluted panelled and octagon' at 30 shillings a dozen wholesale price.

c1752-55 *5in (11.5cm) high*
$3,500-4,500 TEN

A First Period Worcester cream boat, molded with scroll rocaille-edged panels.
c1750-58 *4.25in (11cm) long*
$1,200-1,800 TEN

A First Period Worcester bottle vase, painted with the 'Waiting Chinaman' pattern, with some restoration and missing part.
c1753 *4.5in (11.5cm) high*
$1,500-2,000 A&G

A First Period Worcester bowl, transfer-printed and painted with the 'Red Bull' pattern.
c1757 *4in (10.5cm) diam*
$550-750 TEN

A First Period Worcester scale-blue mug, painted with exotic birds, with seal mark.
3.5in (9cm) high
$1,000-1,500 GORL

A rare First Period Worcester inkwell, painted with a large flower spray and two insects, with small chip.
c1760 *2.5in (6cm) high*
$10,000-15,000 WW

A First Period Worcester cabbage-leaf molded sauce boat.
c1765 *4in (10.5cm) wide*
$650-850 SWO

A First Period Worcester Japanese-style coffee cup and saucer, with blue fret mark.
c1765
$1,000-1,500 SWO

A First Period Worcester tea cup and saucer, painted with the 'Jabberwocky' pattern, with blue fret mark.
c1770
$400-600 SWO

A First Period Worcester sauce tureen, cover and stand, painted with the 'Dragons in Compartments' pattern.
c1770 *Tureen 7in (18cm) wide*
$3,000-4,000 L&T

A First Period Worcester plate, painted with the 'Blind Earl' pattern, with molded and enameled leaves.

This pattern was first used at the Chelsea porcelain factory and was produced at Worcester from the 1750s. It became known as the 'Blind Earl' pattern in the 19thC after the Earl of Coventry (who had lost his sight in a riding accident) ordered a service in this pattern so he could feel the raised decoration.

c1770 *7.75in (19.5cm) diam*
$2,500-3,500 WW

CLOSER LOOK - FLIGHT & BARR VASE

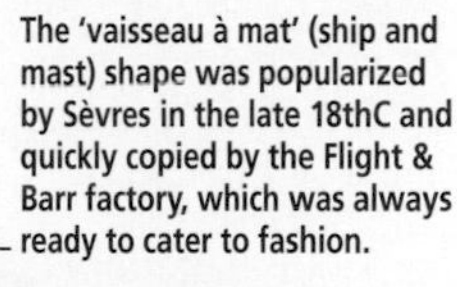

This vase is well-known amongst Worcester collectors. It was given a full-plate illustration in Henry Sandon's 'Flight & Barr Worcester Porcelain, 1783-1840', Antique Collector's Club Ltd, 1978.

The 'vaisseau à mat' (ship and mast) shape was popularized by Sèvres in the late 18thC and quickly copied by the Flight & Barr factory, which was always ready to cater to fashion.

This vase's rarity was attested to in 1875 by connoisseur collector Charles Schreiber, who negotiated its purchase for the Arkwright family, who were then living in the castellated country house depicted on the vase.

A very rare Flight & Barr Worcester vase and cover, painted with a view of Hampton Court country house, Herefordshire.

c1795 *14.5in (37cm) high*

$25,000-35,000 BRI

A Flight & Barr Worcester inkwell, painted in the manner of Baxter with a ship, with incised 'B' mark.

3in (7.5cm) high

$1,200-1,800 GORL

One of a pair of Flight & Barr Worcester ice pails, covers and liners, painted with the 'Royal Lily' pattern, with incised 'B' marks, both feet with silver-mounted repairs.

c1800 *11.75in (30cm) high*

$1,500-2,000 pair DN

A Barr, Flight & Barr Worcester egg cup, with impressed 'BFB' mark.

c1810 *19.75in (5cm) high*

$250-350 TRI

A Flight, Barr & Barr Worcester tea cup and saucer, stamped 'FBB'.

c1813-40 *Saucer 6in (15cm) diam*

$250-350 ECGW

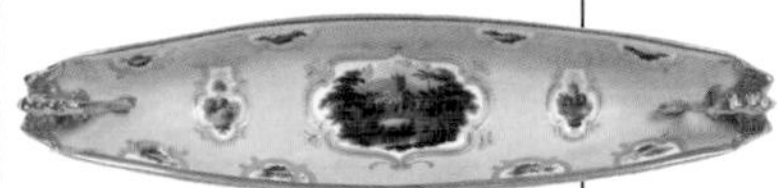

A Flight, Barr & Barr Worcester pen dish, painted with Malvern church, with impressed crown and 'FBB' mark, with red script 'Flight Barr & Barr Royal Porcelain Works Worcester London House 1. Coventry St'.

c1820 *12in (31.5cm) long*

$1,500-2,500 TEN

A Flight, Barr & Barr Worcester teacup and saucer, in the 'Princess Charlotte Breakfast Service' pattern, with gilt factory marks.

This decorative pattern was used in 1816 on a breakfast service for HRH Princess Charlotte on her marriage to Prince Leopold of Saxe-Coberg-Saalfeld. This piece is clearly a teacup and not a breakfast cup so it is unclear whether it was made for the Princess or is simply in the same pattern. Factory records do not survive from this period.

$400-600 DN

A Flight, Barr & Barr Worcester inkwell, painted with a view of Windsor Castle from the river, unmarked.

c1820 *3.5in (9cm) high*

$1,200-1,800 TEN

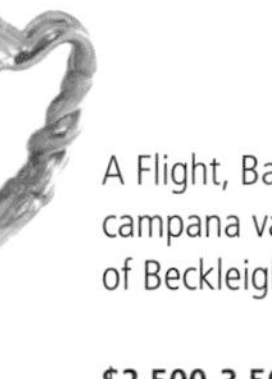

A Flight, Barr & Barr Worcester campana vase, painted with a view of Beckleigh Vale.

6.75in (17cm) high

$2,500-3,500 GORL

A rare Kerr & Binns Worcester 'Medici' vase, gilt and painted with Renaissance portraits, with red printed shield mark, date and faux Registration of Design mark.

1862 *7.5in (21.5cm) high*

$1,500-2,000 SWO

A Royal Worcester twin-handled vase and cover, painted by C Baldwin with swans in flight against a powder-blue ground, with twin mask handles and pedestal base, with date code.
1895 *10.5in (27cm) high*
$8,000-12,000 **GORL**

A late 19thC Royal Worcester hors d'oeuvres dish, transfer-printed in the 'Willow' pattern.
1884 *10.5in (27cm) diam*
$150-250 **DA&H**

A Royal Worcester vase, painted by R Seabright with Michelmas daisies within pink and gilded borders, dated.
1904 *9in (23cm) high*
$400-600 **GORL**

A pair of Royal Worcester plaques, painted by John Stinton with cattle watering in landscapes, titled 'On the Thames' and 'On The Avon', signed, with puce marks, in glazed gilt frames.
1914 *4in (10.5cm) diam*
$5,000-6,000 **TEN**

A Royal Worcester vase and cover, shape no.2032, painted by Harry Davis with sheep to a mountainous landscape within gilded borders, signed, with printed marks, dated.
1914 *12.5in (29cm) high*
$10,000-15,000 **FLD**

A small Royal Worcester pot pourri vase and cover, shape no.278H, painted by Harry Stinton with cattle near a thatched bothy in a Highland landscape, signed, with printed crown and wheel mark, dated.
1924 *5in (13cm) high*
$2,500-3,500 **TEN**

A pair of early 20thC Royal Worcester vases, painted by James Stinton with pheasants in woody clearings, with puce printed marks, dated, with damage.
1928, 1929 *10in (25.4cm) high*
$3,000-4,000 **CAPE**

A Royal Worcester teapot and cover, painted by Edward Townsend with fruit and brambles, with solid gilded spout and ribbed C-handle, with printed crown and wheel mark, dated.
1939 *5in (13cm) high*
$1,200-1,800 **TEN**

A 1970s Royal Worcester vase, shape no.1286, painted by Brian Leaman with peaches, grapes, apples and raspberries above a gilt basket-molded lower section, signed, with black printed crown and wheel mark.
8in (21cm) high
$1,200-1,800 **TEN**

A Royal Worcester cream jug, painted by Horace H Price with fruit, signed, with puce printed crown and wheel mark, dated.
1930 *3.75in (9.5cm) high*
$550-650 **TEN**

A Royal Worcester shot-enameled figure of a Chinese man holding an opium pipe.

7in (18cm) high

$1,000-1,500 **GORL**

A Royal Worcester figure of 'The Bather Surprised', model no.486, with puce mark, impressed 'T Brock. St., London', dated.

1913 *25in (63.5cm) high*

$1,500-2,000 **AH**

CLOSER LOOK - 'LADY MOTORIST'

Due to the introduction of electricity, there was a dramatic drop in demand for candlesnuffers.

This is a particularly rare example. Only four 'Lady Motorists' were recorded as having been made in 1909 and, of those, only two were colored.

She is very much 'the radical chic woman', dressed in Suffragette colors and ready to get behind the wheel.

A Royal Worcester 'Lady Motorist' candle snuffer, shape no.2489, with puce mark, dated.

1909 *5in (12.5cm) high*

$20,000-30,000 **FLD**

A pair of Royal Worcester colored bisque piano babies.

8in (20cm) high

$400-600 **DA&H**

A pair of Royal Worcester figures of water carriers, with printed puce marks, dated.

1923, 1924

Taller 18in (46cm) high

$1,500-2,500 **TEN**

A Royal Worcester figure of the 'Sea Urchin', shape no.2917, modeled by Margaret Cane, with puce mark, dated.

1936

6.25in (16cm) high

$300-400 **AH**

A Royal Worcester figure of 'Wellington' on horseback, modeled by Bernard Winskill, from a limited edition of 750, from the 'Famous Military Commanders' series, with certificate and box.

17.5in (43cm) high

$1,500-2,500 **FLD**

One of a pair of Royal Worcester Dorothy Doughty birds, 'Blue-Gray Gnatcatcher', on dogwood branches.

c1955 *11.5in (29cm) high*

$1,200-1,800 **LHA**

A Royal Worcester limited edition 'Brahman Bull', 'J.D.H. De Ellary Manso', modeled by Doris Lindner.

1967 *8in (21cm) high*

$550-750 **CHT**

Amstel

The Weesp porcelain factory was founded near Amsterdam, Holland, in 1757. It produced gold quality hard-paste porcelain wares, predominantly tableware and some figures. After briefly closing in 1768, it moved to Oude Loosdrecht in 1771, Amstel in 1784 and Nieuwer Amstel in 1809. It closed in 1814.

A selection of Amstel coffee wares, painted with rustic vignettes, comprising two coffee cans and saucers, a coffee pot and a bowl, with blue script marks.

c1800 *Pot 5in (12.5cm) high*

$3,500-4,500 **DN**

An Ansbach figure of a lady, on a mound base, with impressed shield mark.

c1765 *5in (12.5cm) high*

$6,500-7,500 **TEN**

A Copeland parian bust of 'Love', after Raffaelo Monti, made for the Crystal Palace Art Union, her dress with gilt-lined detail, incised 'R Monti Sept 1871', with impressed marks.

c1870 *13in (34cm) high*

$1,200-1,800 **TEN**

A Royal Copenhagen vase, decorated with horseman and boar hunt, with blue mark.

c1900 *25in (61.5cm) high*

$3,500-4,500 **DOR**

A pair of Copenhagen silver-mounted fish etui, with restoration.

c1775 *5.5in (14cm) long*

$1,200-1,800 **MAB**

An H & R Daniel punch bowl, painted with panels of sportsmen in landscapes.

The Henry and Richard Daniel Factory was based at London Road, Stoke, Staffordshire, 1822-46.

12.25in (31cm) diam

$2,500-3,500 **GORL**

BELLEEK MARKS

A First Period Belleek oval basket and cover, decorated with roses, thistles and shamrocks.

12in (30.5cm) long

$2,000-3,000 **GORL**

The First Period Belleek black mark was used 1863-c1890.

The Third Period Belleek black mark was used 1926-46.

The Second Period Belleek black mark (with the inclusion of 'Co. Fermanagh' and 'Ireland' was used c1891-1926.

The Fourth Period Belleek green mark was used 1946-55.

ESSENTIAL REFERENCE - DAVENPORT

In c1793 John Davenport founded a pottery factory in Longport, Staffordshire. A porcelain factory was added in c1820.

- **Davenport was one of the most productive of all the Staffordshire factories.**
- **Wares were decorated in the style of Derby, partly because several of the Davenport painters also worked at Derby. One of the most notable was Thomas Steel (1772-1850), who was best known for painting fruit.**
- **Tea and dessert services were staple products of the factory.**
- **It developed a type of luster glaze in the early 19thC.**
- **The factory closed in 1887.**

A Davenport plate, from the service used at the banquet on 9th November 1837 at the Guildhall to celebrate the accession of Queen Victoria, centered by 'VR' monogram and painted with crown, floral sprays and arms of the City of London, the reverse with gilt printed marks.

The accession banquet was a lavish affair, commencing at 3.30pm and lasting until 8.30pm. The Queen rode from Buckingham Palace in a procession of 58 carriages carrying foreign ambassadors and others. She was received at Temple Bar before proceeding to the Guildhall. This plate is reputedly one of 24 commissioned for the event.

1837 *9in (23cm) diam*
$4,000-6,000 **H&C**

A Fischer & Reichenbach Veduta cup and saucer, painted with 'Cortis Coffee house upon the Bastey', with impressed mark.

1810-46 *4in (10.5cm) high*
$3,000-4,000 **DOR**

A Fulda cup and saucer, the cup molded with a portrait of a lady, with gilt flowers to base and gilt edging, with blue mark, with hairline crack.

c1765-88 *5in (13.5cm) diam*
$1,500-2,500 **DOR**

An Aimeé Jovin plaque, signed, with gilt relief wooden frame (not shown), dated.

Jeanne Marie Aimeé Cheron née Jovin (1778-1847) was a Parisian portrait miniature painter. She was pupil of François Meuret and exhibited at the Salon in Paris in 1848 and 1852-70.

1841 *Plaque 11in (29cm) high*
$15,000-20,000 **DOR**

A Limehouse blue-and white Oriental-style pickle dish, in the form of a scallop shell, painted with scroll and trailing leaves.

c1746-48 *3.25in (8.5cm) wide*
$3,500-4,500 **GORL**

One of a pair of very rare Limehouse blue-and-white silver-shaped sauce boats, painted with houses to one side and a landscape to the other, unmarked.

The Limehouse factory was one of the pioners of English porcelain. Positive identification of Limehouse pieces has only been possible from 1989 when fragments were unearthed at the factory site.

c1750 *8.7in (22cm) long*
$60,000-80,000 pair **FLD**

A Samuel Gilbody coffee cup, painted with peony and chrysanthemum.

c1755-60 *3in (8cm) high*
$3,000-4,000 **WW**

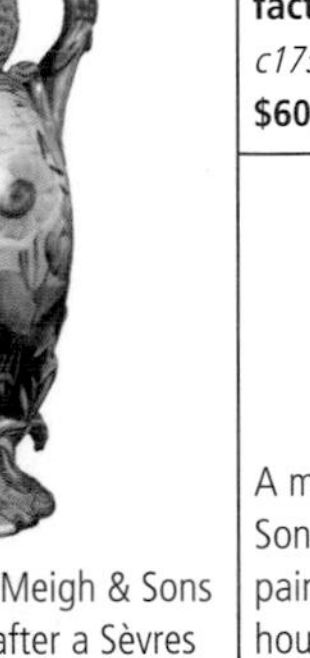

A mid-19thC Charles Meigh & Sons swan ewer, modeled after a Sèvres original.

9.5in (24cm) high
$250-350 **DN**

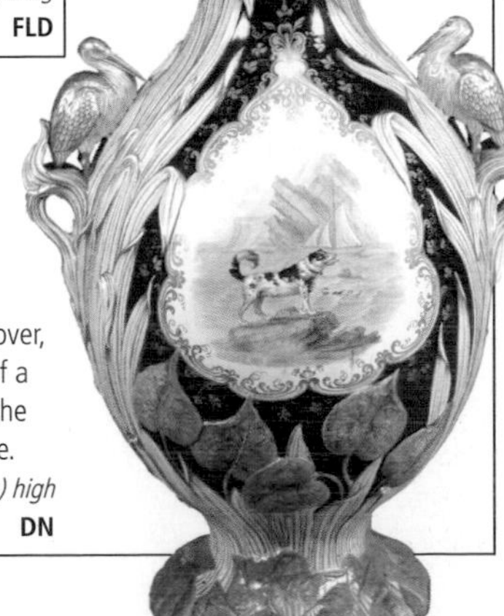

A mid-19thC Charles Meigh & Sons floor-standing vase and cover, painted with two panels, one of a hound in a coastal landscape, the other with sheep in a landscape.

41.25in (105cm) high
$1,000-1,500 **DN**

ESSENTIAL REFERENCE - NEW HALL

New Hall was established in 1781 in Staffordshire.

- **Early wares were heavily decorated in the style of Chinese Export porcelain, often with groups of mandarins in landscapes.**
- **From 1791 simpler patterns were used under the direction of key decorator Fidelle Duvivier. Sprigs of flowers in famille rose colors are typical.**
- **In c1781 New Hall was the first porcelain factory to use pattern numbers. A printed factory mark was used from c1812.**
- **Figures and vases are rare, as New Hall's wares were intended as mass-market pieces, rather than luxury wares.**
- **The factory closed in 1835.**

A New Hall saucer dish, painted in the manner of Fidelle Duvivier with birds in landscape.

Fidelle Duvivier was born and learned his craft in Tournai, Belgium, in 1740, and is known for decorating English porcelain. Besides working in London and at Worcester, he was employed by William Duesbury for four years from 1769. A letter to Duesbury from Duvivier proves that Duvivier also worked at New Hall and was about to leave that factory in 1790. Various New Hall wares have been attributed to Duvivier because they share style qualities with five items that are signed by Duvivier - one of these is a Worcester teapot currently in the Ashmoleon Museum, Oxford.

c1790 *8in (20cm) diam*

$700-1,000 **TEN**

A Pinxton slop bowl, decorated with figures fishing beside a river, beneath an overhanging tree.

c1800 *6.25in (16cm) diam*

$1,200-1,800 **WW**

A Pinxton dish, painted with two figures in a rowing boat with trees, with star and crescent mark.

c1800 *12in (30.5cm) wide*

$1,500-2,500 **WW**

A Pinxton mug, painted with a large spray of flowers.

c1800 *4.25in (11cm) high*

$1,500-2,000 **WW**

A Pinxton topographical coffee cup, painted with a river valley view (perhaps Dovedale), with indented C-shape handle, unmarked.

c1800 *2.75in (7cm) high*

$4,000-6,000 **TEN**

A Spode matched part dinner service, comprising 28 plates, twelve bowls, three tureens and covers and five platters, decorated in the 'Imari' pattern.

c1815-30

$6,500-8,500 **L&T**

A Spode part dessert service, comprising a sauce tureen, cover and stand, four dishes and twelve plates (one a Copeland replacement), painted in pattern no.4011 with flowers, most with printed marks for Spode Felspar.

c1820

$1,500-2,500 set **WW**

A Spode pedestal urn, with iron-red script mark.

c1820 *9in (23cm) high*

$2,000-3,000 **DN**

One of two Tucker jugs, with decorated grisaille landscapes.
c1825 *9.5in (24cm) high*
$1,000-1,500 two **POOK**

A Tucker basket, with gilt highlights.
c1825 *9.5in (24cm) high*
$3,500-4,500 **POOK**

A late 19thC 'American Belleek' jug, by Willets Manufacturing Company of Trenton New Jersey, with printed mark.
14in (35.5cm) high
$350-450 **DN**

An English parian figure of 'Morning' or 'Spring', modeled as a nude young woman in floating pose.

For a similar figure see 'The Parian Phenomenon, A Survey of Victorian Parian Porcelain Statuary & Busts', edited by Paul Atterbury, published by Richard Dennis, p.251. This figure is similar in style to Worcester figures such as 'Morning Dew' and 'Evening Dew'.

c1860 *14in (35.6cm) high*
$1,000-1,500 **TEN**

A 19thC English plaque, possibly Worcester, painted with figures before Windsor Castle, in giltwood frame, with damage to frame.
9in (23cm) wide
$800-1,200 **WW**

A rare English jug, painted with a cavalryman on horseback, inscribed in gilt 'Success to the Manchester Cavalry', also inscribed 'To Protect our Families & Property' and on the reverse 'In Defence of our King & Country'.

Following the riots in the spring of 1817, magistrates in Manchester decided to form the Manchester and Salford Yeomanry Cavalry. The 120 volunteers came from a broad spectrum of occupations but tended to hold Tory political views and to have a hatred of radicals. On 16th August 1819 the same Yeomanry was called out to initially arrest the speakers and subsequently disband the meeting on St Peter's Field, Manchester, resulting in the death of fifteen people. This event became known as the 'Peterloo Massacre'. The regiment was disbanded in 1824.
c1817 *8.5in (21.5cm) high*
$4,000-6,000 **H&C**

A pair of English portrait busts of William IV and Queen Adelaide.
c1831 *7in (17.5cm) high*
$4,000-6,000 **H&C**

A white bisque figure of Queen Victoria, with a band inscribed 'Honni Soit' (sic) on her left arm, with wood stand and glass dome (not shown).
8.25in (21cm) high
$1,000-1,500 **H&C**

A late 19thC Continental Worcester-style inkstand, painted with exotic birds, butterflies and insects.
6in (16cm) wide
$120-180 **WW**

THE POTTERY MARKET

As with most areas of the antiques market, pottery collectors have been affected by the economic climate. Having said that, when good, rare, early pieces come fresh to the market, top prices are paid. In contrast to this, mid-priced and low-end pieces have struggled.

The interesting thing about the pottery market is that the American market for British pottery is stronger than the British market at the moment. Business is mainly conducted on the internet, because there are fewer American buyers traveling to Britain than in the past.

Victorian pottery and Staffordshire figures either have to be exceptionally rare - such as those sold at Holloway's in 2012 - or very cheap, to attract any interest. This is reflected in the pieces in this chapter - five years ago, many of the figures shown would have been worth twice as much (or more) as they are today. Prices may improve, but it's worth noting that antiques are not always an immediate investment. So always buy what you love because, as an old dealer used to say to me, 'you may have to live with it for a long time!'

There is also the problem of fake 'Staffordshire' figures, which are being manufactured in China. These are made from porcelain rather than pottery and are really quite easy to spot. If in any doubt you should buy from a reputable dealer or auction house. I recently spotted at a car boot sale a stall of 'Staffordshire' figures all selling for $30-60. Even in this depressed market, these are very unlikely to be genuine.

Delftware, again, has to be early and a rare shape to achieve strong prices. For the more modest collector interested in delft and slipware, this is an excellent time to buy. At many sales there is strong competition for the top-end pieces, but the market is generally sluggish for the more common pieces and damaged examples.

There have, however, been some dramatic prices paid for some early pottery, particularly the Italian maiolica plates and dishes created in the 16thC. One of the most striking examples is the Urbino maiolica charger decorated with 'The Feast of Herod', sold at Charterhouse in early 2013. It fetched over $900,000 (see p.62), including the buyer's premium, and the Guide price of up to $1,200,000 is certainly justified, especially as this example had a re-stuck chip – damage, given the piece was early and rare enough, collectors were willing to overlook.

American stoneware continues to have a strong collectors' market, particularly for rare shapes and makers. Redware, however, has undergone a sluggish period, during which only the most unusual pieces have been fetching high prices.

The good news is, again, that this is an excellent time to start a collection.

Right: A Castelli majolica chemist's jar. See p.63.

Top Left: An early 19thC Spode Dutch-shape jug. See p.69

A William III probably Bristol delft blue-dash charger, painted with stylized tulips, with small rim chip.

c1700 *13.5in (34cm) diam*

$5,000-6,000 **DN**

An unusual Bristol delft plate, painted in iron-red with a vase of flowers, with small chips.

c1740 *10in (25.5cm) diam*

$500-700 **SWO**

A pair of Bristol delft plates, each painted with a 'Long Eliza' figure with fan under a tree, with flaking to rims.

c1750 *9in (23cm) diam*

$650-850 **H&L**

A mid-18thC Bristol delft chinoiserie plate, painted with rocks and flowers, with faux Chinese mark in manganese, with slight rim chips.

9in (22cm) diam

$400-600 **SWO**

Election Plates

A Bristol delft Taunton by-election commemorative plate, inscribed 'SIR In. Pole, For Ever, 1754', with restoration.

Following the death of the 'Dissenter' John Halliday, who had been elected as MP for Taunton in the General Election of 1754, there followed 'one of the severest contests that ever disturbed a town'. The six-month campaign proved to be so costly that the previous Taunton MP Robert Webb was frightened off. Eventually Robert Maxwell was induced to stand on the promise of financial support. Maxwell's eventual victory was so unpopular that the town rioted, leading to many injuries and two deaths. This plate is the earliest recorded for a by-election.

1754 *9in (22.5cm) diam*

$2,500-3,500 **H&C**

A very rare Bristol delft General Election commemorative plate, inscribed 'Martin & Calvert, For Ever 1754, Sold by Webb', with restoration.

The April 1754 General Election was noteworthy in the otherwise placid constituency of Tewkesbury in that a number of the electorate agreed 'to choose no members but such as will give £1,500 each towards mending the roads.' As the two incumbents initially refused to stand on such conditions, John Martin (who had unsuccessfully contested the seat in 1734 before successfully holding it 1741-47) and Nicholson Calvert, both Whigs, came forward and subsequently won by a good margin. Banners proclaiming 'Calvert & Martin' and 'Good Roads' were displayed in the town. The arrangement 'Martin & Clavert' has only ever been recorded on this, thought to be uniquely surviving, plate, which may have been from a batch commissioned by Martin himself.

1754 *9in (22.5cm) diam*

$3,000-4,000 **H&C**

CLOSER LOOK - ENGLISH DELFT

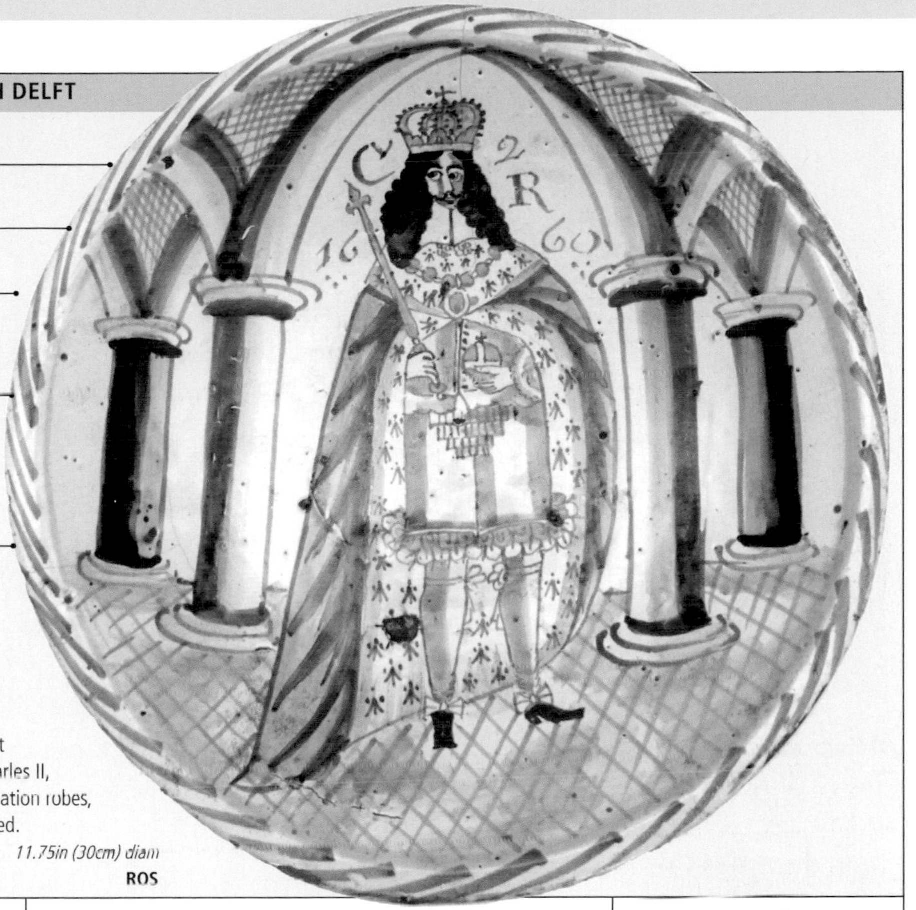

This is an important delft plate in excellent condition.

The decoration is extremely sophisticated.

This charger was previously unrecorded.

Chargers with dates are more desirable than similar undated chargers.

The fact that this charger features the date '1660' (the year of the Restoration) makes it particularly rare and desirable. Other, later examples survive but very few from the Restoration itself.

A London blue-dash Royal portrait Restoration charger depicting Charles II, painted with the king in his coronation robes, flanked by the initials 'C R 2', dated.

1660 *11.75in (30cm) diam*

$200,000-300,000 **ROS**

A Bristol delft chinoiserie plate, painted with a lady seated on a branch of a tree, holding a flat fan, with small rim chip.

c1760 *9in (22.5cm) diam*

$200-300 **WW**

A Bristol or Liverpool delft chinoiserie charger, painted with a bird in a stylized landscape.

c1760 *13in (33.5cm) diam*

$2,000-3,000 **DN**

A mid-18thC Lambeth delft chinoiserie dish, painted with a figure in a garden, the rim with white florets and sgraffito foliage, with chips.

12in (30.5cm) diam

$550-750 **SWO**

A probably Liverpool delft shallow dish, painted with two cockerels in a landscape.

A similar dish is illustrated in F H Garner's article on Liverpool delftware.

c1745 *14in (36.5cm) diam*

$1,000-1,500 **TEN**

A possibly Liverpool delft plate, painted with an unusual scene of a tower billowing smoke, with rubbing to the rim.

8in (21.5cm) diam

$500-700 **SWO**

A late 17thC London delft chinoiserie plate, painted with seated figure among rocks.

c1680 *7in (19cm) wide*

$1,200-1,800 **L&T**

A London delft chinoiserie plate, painted with fishermen.

c1745 *9in (22.5cm) diam*

$500-700 **SWO**

A mid-18thC probably London delft chinoiserie plate, painted with a man seated in a landscape, with small chips.

9in (22.5cm) diam

$400-600 **WW**

A pair of probably London delft chinoiserie plates, painted with flowers.

c1765 *9.25in (23cm) diam*

$650-850 **POOK**

A 17thC delft dish, painted with a swirling center and primitive brush strokes, on circular foot.

c1670 *12.5in (32cm) diam*

$800-1,200 **DA&H**

A rare delft plate, initialed 'HTE', dated.

This plate belongs to one of a small number of services made for Chester County (America) Quakers.

1738 *8.75in (22cm) diam*

$12,000-18,000 **POOK**

One of a pair of mid-18thC delft plates, painted with a parakeet seated on rockwork above peony, with some chipping to the glaze.

12in (29.5cm)

$550-750 pair **WW**

A delft charger, painted with a flower spray within a border of five flower sprays.
c1760 *13in (34cm) diam*
$550-750 **TEN**

A pair of delft chinoiserie plates, painted after Chinese originals with a figure and a dog on a punt.
c1760 *9in (23cm) diam*
$350-450 **SWO**

An 18thC delft charger, painted with a fisherman before a boat on a lake.
13.75in (35cm) diam
$350-450 **GORL**

An 18thC delftware chinoiserie charger, painted with a squirrel and flowers.
11.75in (30cm) diam
$800-1,200 **AH**

An 18thC delft chinoiserie charger, decorated with flowers.
12in (30cm) diam
$400-600 **GORL**

An 18thC delft chinoiserie dish, painted with flowers.
8.75in (22cm) diam
$250-350 **GORL**

A late 18thC delft plate, decorated with an urn of flowers within a floral border and yellow rim.
9in (22.5cm) diam
$250-350 **L&T**

A mid-18thC delft punch bowl, painted with flowering foliage and insects, with chips and cracks.

10in (26cm) diam

$1,000-1,500 **SWO**

A mid-18thC delft bowl.

11.5in (29cm) diam

$700-1,000 **POOK**

A mid-18thC delft polychrome bowl.

8.75in (22cm) diam

$1,000-1,500 **POOK**

A mid-18thC delft bowl.

10.75in (27cm) diam

$1,000-1,500 **POOK**

A London delft posset pot, painted with birds and flowers.

c1710 *9.5in (24cm) high*

$5,000-7,000 **DN**

An English delft sack bottle, dated.

Sack, a sweet wine fortified with brandy (known today as sherry), was very popular with the Elizabethans and early American colonials. It was cheap enough that all classes could drink it. The most famous use of sack was in the making of sack-posset, the traditional drink of weddings and christenings.

1650 *5.75in (15cm) high*

$10,000-15,000 **POOK**

An unusually large late 17thC London delft dry-drug jar, painted with angels holding flower stems above a cartouche with the inscription 'THER:EDENSIS', with chips.

'THER:EDENSIS' is an abbreviation for Theriaca Edinensis, a formula from Greek times, which included the flesh of vipers and was a general cure-all. By the 19thC it was little more than treacle.

12in (30cm) high

$5,000-7,000 **SWO**

A delft posset pot and cover, painted with four panels of geometric floral designs, with a scrolling border, with damage and restoration.

c1780 *9in (23cm) high*

$650-850 **WW**

A late 18thC delft ointment jar, painted with 'O. LILIORUM' within a cartouche of peacocks and winged masks.

Lily ointment or Oil of Lily was traditionally used to relieve a sore or swelling.

11in (27.5cm) high

$250-350 **WW**

A late 18thC delft dry-drug jar, painted with angels holding flower stems above a cartouche with the inscription 'U: ALB: CAMPH'.

***Unguentum album camphorum* was camphorated white ointment. An 18thC account reports that 'this unguent [was] often used to the frettings of the skin in young children'.**

7in (19cm) high

$1,500-2,500 **WW**

A pair of 18thC delft tiles, each depicting a soldier, with chips.

5in (12.5cm) wide

$150-250 SWO

A pair of delft tile-panels, each painted with a large parrot sitting on a hanging perch.

15in (38cm) high

$1,000-1,500 WW

A probably London delft coffee cup, with rockwork, flowers and a bird on a branch, with ocher rim.

c1760 *2.25in (5.5cm) high*

$5,000-7,000 SWO

A mid-18thC delft flower brick, painted with coastal scenes.

6.25in (16cm) wide

$500-700 POOK

A delft heart-shaped inkwell, with matching lid, lacking well.

c1760 *4.5in (11.5cm) wide*

$400-600 SWO

A late 17thC probably Brislington delft chinoiserie bulb-pot, painted with birds and stylized foliage, with restoration.

7in (18cm) diam

$2,000-3,000 WW

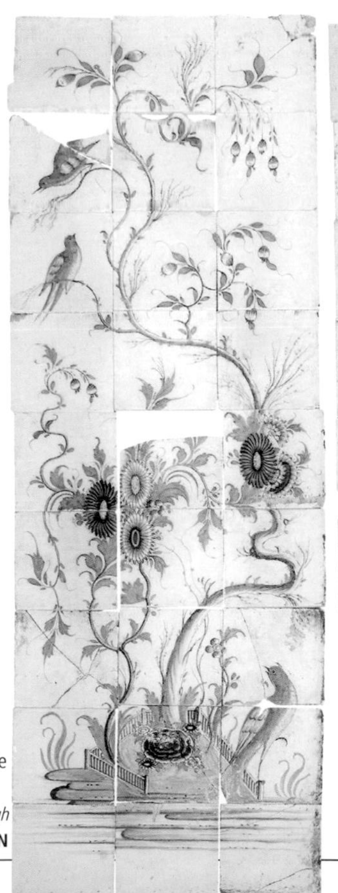

A pair of Bristol or Liverpool delft polychrome chinoiserie tile panels, painted with birds perched in trees.

c1760 *44.5in (113cm) high*

$15,000-20,000 DN

ESSENTIAL REFERENCE - DUTCH DELFT

Dutch potters were making tin-glazed earthenware from the late 15thC. By the late 17thC Delft was the most important center of manufacture.

- **The industry expanded rapidly from c1650 as the importing of Chinese porcelain had briefly ceased and Dutch pottery filled the gap in the market. As a consequence, early Dutch Delft pieces are often based on Chinese patterns and include motifs such as Dogs of Fo.**
- **By the late 17thC a wide range of colors, such as purple, red, green and black, had been produced. Biblical scenes became common motifs.**
- **Dutch Delft has a gritty texture and thick glaze, as opposed to British 'delftware', which has a smoother glaze.**
- **By the mid-18thC many Dutch Delft factories had gone out of business.**

A pair of Dutch Delft vases and covers, painted with figures in a boat before a bridge, with restoration.
c1760 *15in (39cm) high*
$400-600 WW

A late 18thC Dutch Delft garniture, painted with a dense floral and foliate design, with restoration.
13in (34cm) high
$2,000-3,000 WW

A late 19thC Dutch Delft vase, painted with a scene of a lady seated with a musician in a landscape.
8.75in (22cm) high
$150-250 GORL

A Dutch Delft charger, painted with a bowl of flowers and typical precious objects and flowers, with some restoration.
c1670 *15in (38.5cm) diam*
$350-450 SWO

A Dutch Delft earthquake commemorative plate, with inscription 'den 18 Septembe wasser een aertbeving' within a double line border, dated.

The inscription translates as 'The 18th September was an earthquake everywhere'. It refers to the 1692 earthquake centered on the Belgian Ardennes, which caused widespread damage from Kent to the Rhinelands and Champagne. This earthquake is believed to have been between 6 and 6.25 in magnitude. This plate is sold with a letter from the Rijksmuseum, Amsterdam, suggesting that there is only one other known example of the plate shown.
1692 *9in (22cm) diam*
$2,500-3,500 TEN

A mid-18thC Dutch Delft dish, painted with a parrot perched on a basket of fruit.
13.5in (34.5cm) diam
$550-750 CHEF

A Dutch Delft Battle of Dogger Bank commemorative plate, painted with a Dutch man o'war and Dutch inscription, within a husk border.

The plate commemorates the Battle of Dogger Bank, which took place on the 15th August 1781 during the Fourth Anglo-Dutch War, as part of the American War of Independence. Thirteen British ships under the command of Admiral Hyde Parker fought a similar number of Dutch ships under Admiral Zoutman. The British claimed 104 men killed and 339 wounded, while the Dutch claimed 142 killed and 403 wounded, however, private reports suggest the Dutch casualties were actually much higher, possibly reaching 1,100. This battle was celebrated as a victory by the Dutch, but is generally believed to have been a strategic win for the British.
c1781 *9in (23.5cm) diam*
$2,500-3,500 TEN

An 18thC Dutch Delft plate, painted with a figure holding a flag, inscribed 'Vivat Orange'.
9in (23cm) diam
$550-750 L&T

A Dutch Delft six-tile panel, inscribed 'FREDERICA LOUISA WILHELMINA PRINCESS VAN ORANGE - NASSAUW, GEBN. VAN PRUYSSA & R', with substantial damage, with paper label, framed.

Frederica (b. 1770) was the daughter of William V, Prince of Orange. She married Karl, Hereditary Prince of Braunschweig, in 1790 and this panel presumably commemorates that event.

c1790 *15in (39cm) high*

$650-850 **SWO**

An 18thC Dutch Delft model of a parrot, sponge-painted in green, with blue beak and feet, with some cracks and restoration.

7in (19cm) high

$550-750 **WW**

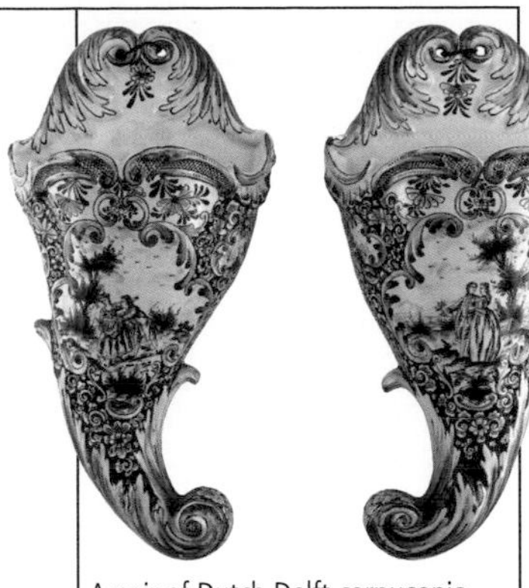

A pair of Dutch Delft cornucopia wall pockets, painted with scenes of young lovers in rural landscapes, with 'AK' marks, with minor chipping.

c1850 *13in (33.5cm) high*

$300-500 **WW**

A German Frankfurt/Hanau faience chinoiserie jar, painted with panels.

c1700 *12in (31cm) high*

$3,000-4,000 **DN**

A German Zittau faience plate, with date below a flower in the center, with minor edge chip.

1705 *10in (26.5cm) diam*

$2,500-3,500 **DOR**

A late 18thC French Nevers faience jardinière, painted with buildings in a wooded landscape, with restored cracks.

13.75in (35cm) wide

$2,500-3,500 **WW**

A Slovakian faience jug, painted with lions holding an animal skin, with the monogram 'M.F.M', dated.

1783 *10in (24.5cm) high*

$3,500-4,500 **DOR**

A late 18thC Austrian faience jug, painted with a couple, with pewter lid and base ring, with restoration.

10in (25cm) high

$3,000-4,000 **DOR**

A mid-late 18thC German Nuremberg or Schrezheim faience tankard, with pewter lid.

9in (23cm) high

$3,500-4,500 **KAU**

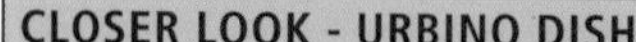

CLOSER LOOK - URBINO DISH

This is a magnificent example of Renaissance pottery.

Professor Timothy Wilson of the Ashmolean Museum aided in the identification of the charger, dating it to Urbino c1540. The scene was identified as 'The Feast of Herod' by Dr Mercedes Ceron.

The source for the ambitious decoration is an engraving by the German printmaker Sebald Beham (1500-50).

The only significant imperfection on this piece was a 1.5in (3.5cm) re-stuck chip. Condition is, of course, vitally important when assessing the value of an antique, but when something of such an early date and as rare as this example appears on the market, its desirability renders the damage almost insignificant.

An Urbino maiolica charger, decorated with 'The Feast of Herod', with re-struck chip.
c1540 *16.5in (42cm) diam*
$900,000-1,200,000 **CHT**

A Deruta maiolica dish, painted with an 'istoriato' scene of 'the Procession of Silenus', with a border of scrolling foliage, the footrim pierced with two holes.

Donkey motifs are seen on some Deruta dishes of this period. They usually illustrated local proverbs or had satirical meaning. The source image for this dish may have been an engraved print by Agostino Veneziano, after a drawing by Raphael or Giulio Romano. The image shown has an additional figure pouring wine over Silenus, perhaps intended as a satirical commentary on drunkenness.
c1520-60 *16in (40.5cm) diam*
$120,000-180,000 **L&T**

A Venice maiolica jar, probably from the workshop of Domenego Da Venezia, painted with a continuous landscape and a figure on a promontory, with inscription 'PESTAEN' (Pestem), with incised mark on the base probably reading 'AS'.
c1560-70 *10.5in (27cm) diam*
$45,000-55,000 **L&T**

An Urbino maiolica 'Bella Donna' dish, with inscription 'ANGELLA BELLA' scratched through the blue ground.

This dish is strongly related to an example in the Victoria & Albert Museum, London, which has 'Amaro chi me amara' scratched through the background in much the same way, except the letters are picked out in fired luster.
c1535 *8.75in (22cm) diam*
$15,000-20,000 **L&T**

A large Cantagalli Urbino-style maiolica pedestal bowl, the center with a portrait bust of a lady, with inscription 'VIVA VIVAED VCHAD VRBINO', with cockerel mark, with loss and chips.

On her shoulder, the girl wears the Arms of Guidoboldo I di Montefecro, Duke of Urbino (1482-1508). The Medici arms are top left.

16in (40.5cm) diam

$5,000-6,000 SWO

A 17thC possibly Deruta maiolica wall-plaque, moulded in relief with the Virgin and Christ Child in the Heavens above St Agnes, cracked in half.

20.5in (52cm) high

$2,500-3,500 DN

A 16th/17thC Deruta maiolica relief-moulded plaque of the Virgin and Christ Child, in giltwood frame, cracked.

The image is possibly taken from a terracotta relief attributed to the 'Maitre des Enfants Animes'.

18in (44.5cm) high

$3,500-4,500 TEN

A probably Savona maiolica tazza, painted with three birds, the footrim badly chipped.

c1740 12in (30.5cm) diam

$1,200-1,800 WW

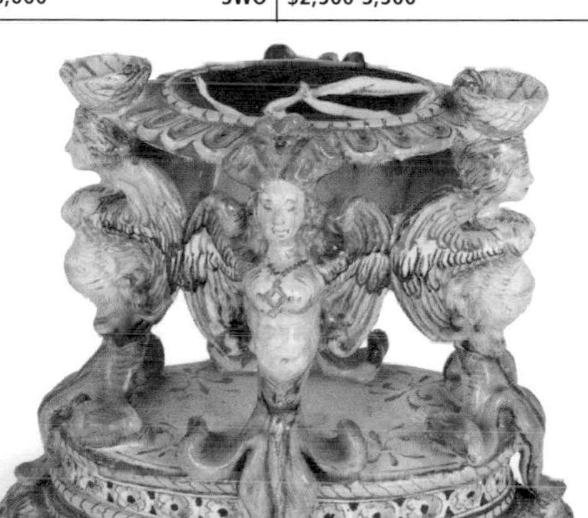

A late 16thC Urbino maiolica salt, supported by four winged caryatids, the depression painted with a female nude, with restoration.

5.75in (14.5cm) high

$2,500-3,500 MAB

A Castelli majolica chemist's 'Sy De SUCO CN' jar, decorated in Orsini Collonna style, decorated with two bust portraits, with dragon spout, with restoration and loss of glaze.

10.75in (27.5cm) high

$30,000-40,000 A&G

A 17thC maiolica wet-drug jar, with inscription 'S.D. CICORIA. COMP', with a sun medallion with 'IHS' monogram, unmarked, with minor typical fritting.

7.5in (18.5cm) high

$2,000-3,000 TOV

A maiolica Persian-style charger, by Torquato Castellani, with black painted mark '18 TC 79 ROMA', dated.

1879 19in (47.5cm) diam

$2,500-3,500 DN

A late 19thC maiolica figure of a monkey, with 'AP' mark.

14.5in (37cm) high

$800-1,200 GORL

A rare mid-18thC Whieldon-type creamware model of a billy goat, decorated in a running treacle glaze, the eyes enameled red, with some good restoration.

5in (13cm) wide

$4,000-6,000 **WW**

A rare green-glazed 'landskip' creamware teapot, probably Whieldon or Wedgwood, moulded with a Georgian house behind sheep and cattle, with swans swimming around the base, with repair to handle.

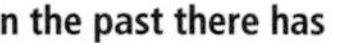

In the past there has been some tentative attribution of the mould for these teapots to William Greatbatch, based on an invoice discussed by David Barker in his book on the Staffordshire potter. However, there is no definite evidence supporting this theory and block moulds have been discovered at several factory sites including Wedgwood, making a definite attribution difficult.

c1765 *8in (20.5cm) high*

$4,000-6,000 **WW**

A rare Cockpit Hill General Election commemorative creamware mug, painted with profile portrait above the ribboned inscription 'Clarke For Ever Huzza', with crack.

The 1768 General Election in Derbyshire was, unusually, a contested affair. The Cavendish family, being one of the consistent incumbents of the seats, was represented by Lord George Cavendish. The sitting MP, Sir Henry Harpur, was contested by Godfrey Baghnall Clarke. Cavendish secured 2,767 votes, Clarke 1,768 and Harpur 1,314 votes. Cavendish and Clarke went on to represent the county until Clarke's death at the age of 32.

c1768 *5in (13cm) high*

$9,000-11,000 **H&C**

A Newcastle-under-Lyme General Election commemorative creamware tankard, inscribed 'CHEWTON AND HAY For Ever'.

The General Election of 1774 saw Earl Gower's interest, George Waldegrave, Viscount Chewton and the incumbent, George Hay, elected to the seat of Newcastle-under-Lyme. Chewton was aide-de-camp to Cornwallis, Commander of the British troops during the American Wars of Independence. Hay was a judge and former MP for Stockbridge, Calne and Sandwich. He later fell ill and was found to be a lunatic. He was committed to an asylum, but in 1778 he escaped and drowned himself.

1774 *5.25in (13.5cm) high*

$2,500-3,500 **H&C**

A creamware mask jug, painted with three agricultural vignettes and with inscription 'THOMAS SUTTON 1775'.

1775 *7.5in (19.5cm) high*

$3,000-4,000 **TEN**

A Wedgwood & Co. creamware teapot and cover, printed with 'ELISEE COHU, GUERNSEY, 1789', with impressed mark, with chips.

1789 *7.5in (16cm) high*

$2,500-3,500 **SWO**

A Wedgwood & Co. creamware mug, printed with 'CHARITY' above three girls, a boy and a rhyme, with impressed marks, with basal star crack.

c1800 *5in (15cm) high*

$650-850 **SWO**

A 'Smith For Ever' political commemorative creamware mug, with restoration.

Several Smiths contested parliamentary elections during the latter quarter of the 18thC, some successfully, some not. The sentiment 'For Ever' is generally associated with political support.

c1790 *5in (12.5cm) high*

$800-1,200 **H&C**

A 18th/19thC creamware tankard, printed with 'A South East VIEW of the stupendous bridge over the Wear near Sunderland built under the patronage of R Burdon Esq MP engineer TW', marked 'J Dawson & Co Low Ford', with chips and minor crack.

John Dawson & Co. produced printed and luster wares at South Hylton and Ford Potteries Sunderland, Durham, c1799-1864.

c1800 *4.5in (11.5cm) high*

$1,200-1,800 **A&G**

A pair of rare Wedgwood & Co. creamware bough pots, painted by Fidelle Duvivier (attr.) with maroon landscapes, with impressed marks, with restoration to both.

For more information about Duvivier see p.50.

c1800 *5in (15.5cm) wide*

$3,500-4,500 **SWO**

An early 19thC political commemorative creamware tankard, printed with 'Liberty' and a shield-shaped vignette inscribed 'John Vause Esq, Mayor Elected 4th Oct 1800'.

1800 *4.75in (12cm) high*

$1,500-2,500 **H&C**

A commemorative creamware jug for The Treaty of Amiens, printed with Britannia, Peace and France attended by 'H.M. The King, Gen. Cornwallis, Ireland, Buonaparte (sic), Gen. Lauriston and Citizen Otto', with some chips.

c1802 *4.5in (11.5cm) high*

$1,500-2,500 **WW**

A Dutch-decorated English creamware plate, painted with a soldier waving the Dutch Flag and inscribed with Dutch script.

This plate commemorates the popular revolts against Napoleon by Dutch nobles which saw the return of William I. The Dutch translates as 'I do not wave for France or Spain, but for the Prince of Orange'.

c1813 *10in (25.5cm) wide*

$3,500-4,500 **A&G**

A Queen Caroline commemorative lusterware plaque, with integral frame.

1820 *5.25in (13.5cm) high*

$550-650 **H&C**

A commemorative creamware tankard, inscribed 'Lambton the terror of the black coats and defender of our rights', with restoration.

Born in 1792 John George Lambton (later 1st Earl of Durham) represented Durham from 1813 until his elevation to the peerage in 1828. He headed the radical wing of the Whigs, becoming known as 'Radical Jack' after he refused to evict his tenants in order to allow open-cast coal mining on his estates. The reference to 'the terror of the black coats' on this tankard presumably refers to this incident.

c1822 *6in (15cm) high*

$3,500-4,500 **H&C**

A Scottish pink lusterware soup bowl, painted with the inscription 'Maule & Freedom'.

William Ramsay Maule represented Forfarshire briefly during 1796 and later 1805-31. He was by all accounts a debauched violent rake as a youth, maturing to become a Foxite. Raised to the peerage in 1831, he was a poor attendee of both houses. Lord Cockburn said of him 'A spoiled beast from his infancy… he was insanely brutal… with everyone who [dared] to resist the capricious and intolerant despotism of his will.'

c1826 *10in (25.5cm) diam*

$1,500-2,500 **H&C**

ESSENTIAL REFERENCE - NELSON MEMORABILIA

Horatio Nelson (1758-1805) was a British naval officer, famous for his service during the Napoleonic Wars and for his love affair with Lady Emma Hamilton. He was killed during his most notable victory at the Battle of Trafalgar.

- **Nelson was an extremely popular figure in his time and remains so to this day. Numerous monuments, most notably Nelson's Column in Trafalgar Square, London, have been created in his memory.**
- **Items owned by Nelson command a premium, though proven provenance is very important. In 2002 a large collection of letters and other items were discovered in the possession of the descendants of Alexander Davison, Nelson's banker and close friend.**
- **Nelson's hair is also highly collectible. In January 2011 Salisbury auction house Woolley & Wallis sold a small locket of hair for a record price of around $80,000.**

A rare Nelson in Memoriam pearlware jug, printed with a panel depicting Nelson attended by three figures, the reverse with figures grieving at an obelisk monument.

1805 *9.5in (24.5cm) high*

$8,000-12,000 **H&C**

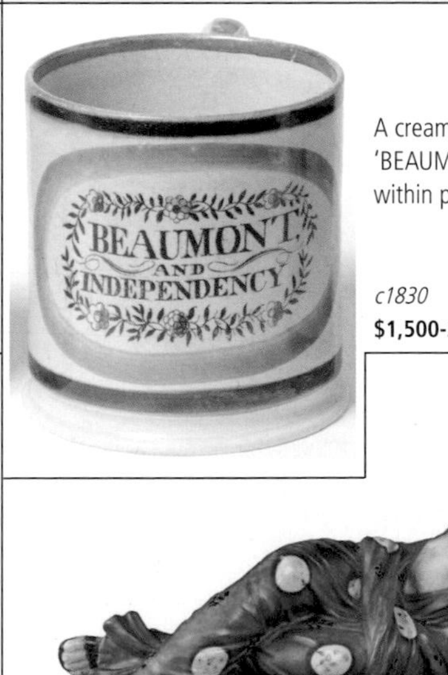

A creamware mug, printed with 'BEAUMONT AND INDEPENDENCY' within pink luster cartouche.

c1830 *5in (12.5cm) high*

$1,500-2,500 **TEN**

A Staffordshire pearlware bull-baiting group, with impressed '33'.

c1790 *7in (17.5cm) long*

$3,000-4,000 **DN**

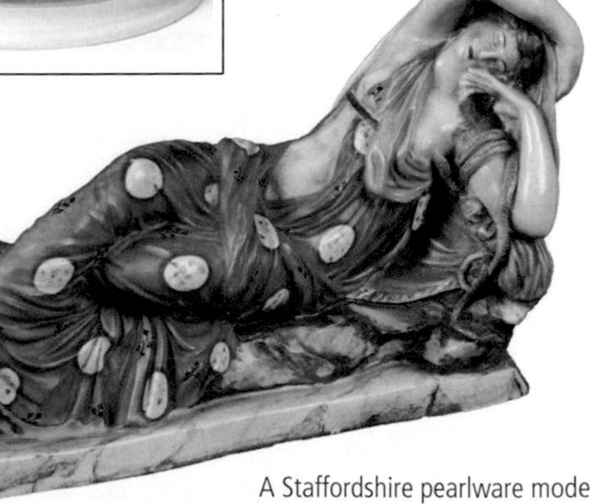

A Staffordshire pearlware model of Cleopatra, being bitten by an asp.

c1800 *12in (31cm) long*

$350-450 **DN**

A Borrowstounness pearlware bowl, printed with blue borders and decorated in a typical Pratt palette, with the inscription 'John & Helen Fisher, 'Borrowstoness (sic) 1811', with cracks and staining chips.

1811 *10in (28.5cm) diam*

$1,500-2,500 **SWO**

A rare yellow pearlware luster jug, of pugilist interest, commemorating the fight between Tom Molyneux and Tom Cribb at Thistleton Gap in Rutland, printed with the boxers in fighting stance, the other side with a verse about boxing in Britain.

The 1811 match between former slave Molyneux and Bristolian Cribb ended in the 11th round when Cribb broke his opponent's jaw. Their first meeting in 1810 saw them so closely matched that the fight went to 35 rounds, with Cribb again the victor.

c1811 *5.75in (14.5cm) high*

$3,500-4,500 **WW**

A pair of Ralph Salt pearlware models of sheep, each standing before bocage on mound bases with a lamb, with indistinct scroll mark.

c1830 *6in(15.5cm) high*

$1,000-1,500 **TEN**

An early 19thC pearlware arbour group of 'Perswaition' (sic), modeled as a couple with a potted plant, a dog and parasol.

8in (20.5cm) high

$2,500-3,500 **HT**

An early 19thC pearlware bust of the poet Matthew Prior, wearing his characteristic turban.

Matthew Prior (1664-1721) of Wimborne was one of 'Lord Dorset's Boys' and a sometime member of the notorious Kit-Cat Club.

7in (17cm) high

$650-850 **WW**

ESSENTIAL REFERENCE - PEARLWARE

Pearlware was introduced by Josiah Wedgwood in c1779 as an improvement on creamware. Pearlware includes more white clay and flint in the body than creamware and thus has a whiter body.

- **The glaze on pearlware does, however, have a bluish tinge due to the addition of cobalt oxide.**
- **Pearlware is often decorated in underglaze blue by painting or transfer-printing. One of the most famous printed patterns is the chinoiserie 'Willow' pattern.**
- **Much pearlware is useful ware, such as dishes, plates, teapots, and jugs.**
- **Many figure groups were also made.**

An early 19thC pearlware group, modeled as a hurdy-gurdy man with a female companion, a dancing bear and a monkey riding a dog.

5.75in (14.5cm) high

$3,500-4,500 **HT**

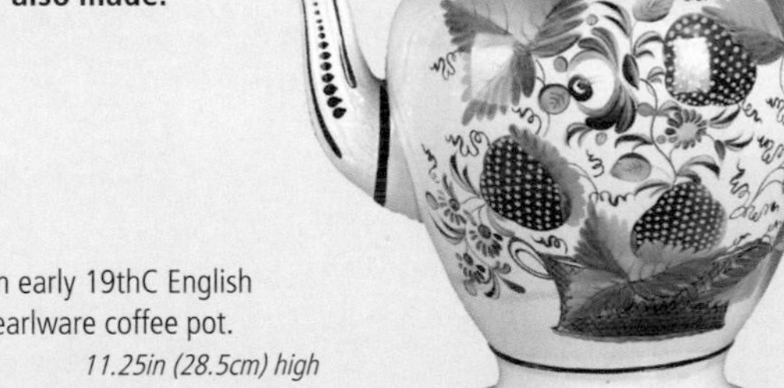

An early 19thC English pearlware coffee pot.

11.25in (28.5cm) high

$2,000-3,000 **POOK**

POTTERY

A pair of commemorative pearlware tankards, inscribed with loyal tributes to John George Lambton (later 1st Earl of Durham) from the Humin families, dated.

For more information about Lambton see p.66.

1822 *5.75in (14.5cm) high*

$2,500-3,500 **H&C**

A rare Duke of York in Memoriam pearlware mug.

This mug was previously unrecorded.

1827 *4.5in (11.5cm) high*

$1,200-1,800 **H&C**

A rare commemorative pearlware jug, decorated with named portrait of Daniel O'Connell, with restoration.

O'Connel was one of the most important figures in the campaign for Catholic emancipation, establishing the Catholic Association in 1823. He was elected to the seat of County Clare, Ireland, in the by-election of 1828 but was barred from taking his seat until the passing of the Catholic Relief Act of 1829. O'Connell was re-elected, unopposed, in July 1829 and took his seat in Westminster in February 1830.

c1828 *6.5in (16.5cm) high*

$1,800-2,200 **H&C**

A Staffordshire commemorative pearlware mug, printed with a bust portrait and with inscription 'TRIED MARCH 31st 1829 BEFORE MR BARON HULLOCK AND SENTENCED TO CONFINEMENT DURING HIS MAJESTY'S PLEASURE', the reverse with a titled scene 'YORK MINISTER ON FIRE FEBRUARY 2nd 1829'.

1829 *2.5in (9.5cm) high*

$1,800-2,200 **TEN**

A rare Princess Victoria pearlware child's plate, the borders moulded with a monkey, dogs, a cat and cupids in a horse-drawn chariot, with inscription 'PRINCESS VICTORIA'.

c1831 *7in (17.5cm) diam*

$4,500-5,500 **TEN**

A pearlware jug, moulded with Isaac van Amburgh dressed as a gladiator among his big cat menagerie, with restoration to spout.

By far the most famous of the early wild animal keepers, Van Amburgh debuted at the June, Titus and Angevine menagerie in 1833-34 in New York. He traveled with the company until July 1838 when he left for a seven-year stay in Europe that further enhanced his fame.

6.75in (17cm) high

$650-850 **WW**

A large political commemorative pearlware tankard, printed with a portrait and 'Saml J. Prescod elected Member of the Barbados house of assembly, 6th June 1843', the reverse with inscription 'Great fire in Bridge Town Barbados 3rd Feb 1845. 200 house destroyed and a great many families rendered destitute', with restoration.

Born in 1806 of a free black mother and wealthy white father Samuel Prescod began to actively participate in politics in 1829 and worked as a journalist from 1836. In 1843 he was one of the two people elected for the new constituency of Bridgetown - a place plagued with fires. The 1845 fire started in Tudor Street and destroyed property on about ten acres of land.

8in (20cm) high

$1,200-1,800 **H&C**

A Spode pearlware marbled drainer, printed in blue with the 'Cracked Ice and Prunus' pattern, with printed and impressed marks.

c1810 *13in (33cm) wide*

$200-300 **DN**

A Staffordshire soup tureen, cover and stand, printed in blue with the 'Beemaster' pattern, sometimes attributed to William Adams, with crack.

c1815 *Stand 15in (38cm) wide*

$1,500-2,500 **DN**

A Spode pearlware drainer, printed in blue with the 'Antique Fragments at Limisso' pattern, from the 'Caramanian' series, with impressed marks.

c1815 *13in (33.5cm) wide*

$550-650 **DN**

A Spode pearlware serving dish, printed in blue with the 'Driving a Bear Out of Sugar Canes' pattern, from the 'Indian Sporting Series', with impressed and printed marks.

c1815 *16.5in (42cm) wide*

$700-1,000 **DN**

An early 19thC Staffordshire pearlware part supper-set and tin tray, printed in blue with a pagoda pattern, with damage.

28.25in (72cm) wide

$350-450 **DN**

A Staffordshire pearlware Freemasonry serving dish, printed in blue with a town house within a Masonic border.

c1820 *19in (48.5cm) wide*

$1,000-1,500 **DN**

An early 19thC Spode Dutch-shape jug, printed in blue with the 'Chinese of Rank' pattern.

This is a rare pattern and an excellent quality transfer.

6.75in (17cm) high

$1,500-2,000 **DN**

A commemorative mug, by E. & C. Challinor, printed in green with a portrait entitled 'WELCOME' flanked by inscriptions 'TO COMMEMORATE THE VISIT OF OUR ESTEEMED SAILOR PRINCE' and 'ALFRED Second Son of OUR BELOVED QUEEN VICTORIA, GOD BLESS HER', with printed mark.

The Prince, a keen sailor, undertook two cruises on his yacht 'Galatea', the first of which ran 1866-68. During the second cruises (1868-71) he commenced a three-month tour of India, starting from the end of 1869. While the portrait and title shown on this example are not dissimilar to those that appear on a mug produced for the Prince's return from the West Indies in 1861, the ship, foliage, flags and inscription all differ. The firm of Challinor used the initials 'E. & C.' in their mark 1862-91.

4.75in (12cm) high

$1,000-1,500 **H&C**

A Staffordshire commemorative jug for the 1832 Reform Act, printed in black with portraits of notable Whigs.

c1832 *6.5in (16.5cm) high*

$350-450 **DN**

A mid-18thC Staffordshire agateware model of a cat, with black marbling, with blue marks to front and ears.

4in (10cm) high

$2,500-3,500 **HT**

A late 18thC Whieldon-type model of a cat, decorated with spots of brown and ocher.

3in (8cm) high

$2,500-3,500 **WW**

ESSENTIAL REFERENCE - STAFFORDSHIRE POTTERIES

The Staffordshire ceramics trade emerged in the mid-17thC around the five towns of Stoke, Burslem, Hanley, Longton and Tunstall. By the 19thC Staffordshire was home to more than 1,000 pottery and porcelain factories.

- **The first Staffordshire figures were made in c1740 as an affordable alternative to porcelain figures by factories such as Meissen.**
- **In the early 18thC, the factories of John Astbury and Thomas Whieldon produced some of the best wares, with Robert Wood producing some attractive rustic figures in the mid-18thC.**

A pair of 19thC Staffordshire treacle-glazed models of lions, with unusually large teeth.

9in (23cm) long

$2,500-3,500 **GORL**

A pair of 19thC Staffordshire groups of a cat and kittens.

6.75in (17cm) high

$1,200-1,800 **AH**

An early 19thC Staffordshire model of a lion, glazed in brick-red, with a judge's wig-mane and manic grin, with restoration.

5.5in (14cm) long

$1,200-1,800 **SWO**

A Staffordshire model of a lion, with a paw raised on a silver luster globe.

c1820 *12.5in (31cm) long*

$1,500-2,500 **TEN**

A near pair of Staffordshire models of lions, standing in front of spill vases.

7.25in (18.5cm) high

$2,500-3,500 **RGA**

A pair of mid-19thC Staffordshire groups of lion and lambs.

There has been speculation that this group was inspired by the American lion-tamer Isaac van Amburgh, who had mixed cages of lions, leopards and a lamb in his act at Drury Lane Theatre. For more information about Van Amburgh see p.68.

10.25in (26cm) high

$5,000-7,000 **DN**

A very rare Staffordshire figure of a seated monkey, wearing a square hat, playing a trumpet, possibly part of a band set.

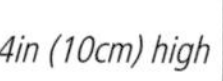

4in (10cm) high

$1,200-1,800 **RGA**

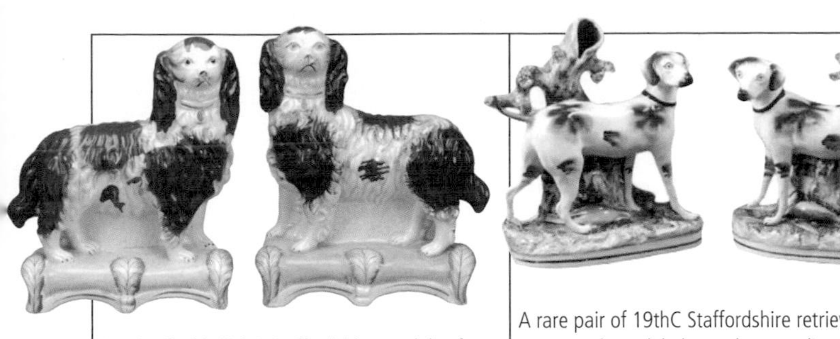

A pair of mid-19thC Staffordshire models of spaniels, standing on pink-painted cushion bases, one with old restoration.

8in (21cm) long

$2,500-3,500 **DN**

A rare pair of 19thC Staffordshire retriever spill vases, each modeled as a dog standing above a pheasant, with restoration to tail tips and muzzles.

c1860 *9in (23cm) wide*

$2,500-3,500 **SWO**

A pair of Staffordshire modles of spaniels, painted in red and white, with black and white pups on blue bases.

6.25in (16cm) high

$1,200-1,800 **RGA**

A rare pair of Staffordshire models of Irish setters, on superior bases.

11.75in (30cm) high

$4,500-5,500 **RGA**

A pair of Staffordshire models of spaniels, sitting on cushions.

4.75in (12cm) high

$3,000-4,000 **RGA**

A late 18thC Whieldon-type manganese-glazed model of a parrot, on a domed and moulded base.

9in (23cm) high

$4,000-6,000 **HW**

A Staffordshire model of a bird, painted in bright colors.

12.75in (32.5cm) high

$650-850 **RGA**

A pair of Staffordshire models of zebras, with restoration to tails and ears.

c1860 *7in (17.5cm) wide*

$800-1,200 **SWO**

A pair of Victorian Staffordshire models of rabbits, on moulded mossy bases.

4.75in (12cm) wide

$3,500-4,500 **HW**

A pair of Staffordshire salt-glazed stoneware figures, of a lady and gentleman, on hollow and domed bases.

c1760s *Taller 4in (10cm) high*

$1,500-2,500 **HW**

A late 18thC Staffordshire figure of 'Apollo', by Ralph Wood, glazed in earth tones.

8.25in (22cm) high

$2,000-3,000 **HW**

A rare Staffordshire figure of a lion, with two cherubs on its back, in front of a bower.

10in (25.5cm) high

$1,200-1,800 **RGA**

A pair of early 19thC Wood-type figures of 'Simon' and 'Iphigenia', glazed in blue, green and ocher, on square bases.

$1,200-1,800 **HW**

A pair of Victorian Staffordshire figures of the American Evangelists Ira David Sankey and Dwight Lyman Moody.

c1880 *9.75in (24.5cm) high*

$120-180 **HW**

A 19thC Staffordshire figure of the Rev. Christmas Evans.

13in (33.5cm) high

$800-1,200 **TEN**

A Staffordshire bust of John Wesley, with simulated marble base.

John Wesley is often credited as one of the founders of the Methodist movement.

c1840 *11.5in (29cm) high*

$800-1,200 **DN**

A 19thC Staffordshire figure of George Washington.

This figure was modeled as Benjamin Franklin, but it was often titled and released as Washington. It is believed that only one model with a true likeness of Washington was ever made.

16in (39.5cm) high

$650-850 **WW**

A pair of Victorian Staffordshire figures, of Queen Victoria and Prince Albert.

Taller 11.5in (29cm) high

$120-180 **HW**

A large Victorian Staffordshire figure, of Victoria 'Queen of England'.

17.25in (44cm) high

$350-450 **HW**

A matched pair of Victorian Staffordshire groups, of the Royal children with sheep.

$200-300 **HW**

A Victorian Staffordshire figure, of 'The Martyrdom of Ridley and Latimer'.

9.5in (24cm) high

$1,000-1,500 **HW**

A Victorian Staffordshire group, of Saul presenting his daughter to King David.

9.5in (24cm) high

$120-180 **HW**

A Victorian Staffordshire group probably of Boaz and Ruth/ Rebecca.

8.75in (22cm) high

$150-250 **HW**

A matched pair of Victorian Staffordshire figures, of a fisherman and a fishwife.

Taller 13in (32cm) high

$150-250 **HW**

Palmer's House

A Victorian Staffordshire model of 'Palmers House', inscribed to the base.

7.25in (18cm) high

$200-300 **HW**

POTTERY

A late 18thC English earthenware Toby jug, with brown tricorn hat, blue hair and jacket.

10in (25cm) high

$3,000-4,000 **AH**

A late 18thC Ralph Wood-type Toby jug.

10in (25cm) high

$1,500-2,000 **FLD**

A Staffordshire pearlware Collier-type Toby jug.

c1790 *10.5in (26.5cm) high*

$2,500-3,500 **DN**

A rare late 18thC Ralph Wood-type 'Admiral Lord Howe' toby jug, modeled seated on a barrel with a dog at his feet.

10in (25cm) high

$2,500-3,500 **GORL**

A Staffordshire creamware Toby jug.

c1800 *9.5in (24.5cm) high*

$3,500-4,500 **DN**

A rare Yorkshire 'Crown Mark' Toby jug, with sponging to hat and base, holding a miniature toby jug, a small dog at his feet, with impressed large crown mark to base, with restoration.

10in (25.25cm) high

$1,000-1,500 **A&G**

A Staffordshire pearlware 'Hearty Goodfellow' Toby jug.

c1820 *11.5in (29cm) high*

$250-350 **DN**

A set of nine Royal Staffordshire (Wilkinson Ltd.) World War I leaders Toby Jugs, after F Carruthers Gould, with bright enamel and gilding.

Tallest 12.5in (30cm) high

$5,500-6,500 **TEN**

A rare limited edition Winston Churchill Toby jug, modeled by Leonard Jarvis, painted in Ralph Wood-style colors, with incised marks, with restoration to fingers.

c1947 *7in (17.5cm) high*

$1,500-2,500 **DN**

ESSENTIAL REFERENCE - WEDGWOOD BLACK BASALT

Other Staffordshire potteries had produced 'Egyptian Black' wares before Josiah Wedgwood introduced 'Black Basaltes' (now called black basalt) in 1768, but the color of the earlier wares was not as rich.

- **The new black body was used to make Neo-classical vases, plaques, portrait medallions, library busts and candlesticks.**
- **It was made of a reddish-brown clay that burned black with firing. The richer color was a result of the addition of manganese.**
- **Wedgwood patented two new forms of decoration for black basalt: bronzing and 'encaustic' painting in the style of ancient Greek and Roman vases. Rather than the simple reds and black of the Classical originals, Wedgwood's encaustic painting included blue, green, pink, orange and white.**
- **Josiah Wedgwood said of black basalt, 'Black is Sterling and will last forever'.**
- **Black basalt wares are still made by Wedgwood today.**

A Wedgwood Egyptian Revival black basalt candlestick, with impressed mark.
c1805-10 *7in (18cm) high*
$3,500-4,500 DN

A pair of Wedgwood black basalt figures of Greek sphinxes, both impressed 'WEDGWOOD', one impressed 'W', the other 'E'.

Sphinxes of this form were in production from c1770, sometimes with 'lotus' nozzles or candle holders. By 1773 at least eight models of Grecian and Egyptian sphinxes were in production.
c1800 *9in (22.5cm) high*
$3,500-4,500 TEN

An early 19thC Wedgwood Egyptian Revival 'Rosso Antico' vase and cover, with chocolate-brown ground, with crocodile finial, with impressed mark.
8in (20.5cm) high
$12,000-18,000 SK

An early 19thC Wedgwood encaustic-decorated black basalt vase, with impressed mark, with professional restoration.
15in (38cm) high
$7,500-8,500 SK

A pair of 19thC Wedgwood black basalt wine and water ewers, depicting Bacchus and Neptune, with impressed 'WEDGWOOD', with damage to one base.
17in (43cm) high
$1,500-2,500 WW

A mid-19thC Wedgwood Egyptian Revival 'Pearl'-bodied black basalt Canopic inkstand, or 'Gondola Ecritoire', with impressed marks.
11.25in (28.5cm) long
$4,500-5,500 DN

A Wedgwood black basalt bicentenary vase and cover, with impressed and printed 'WEDGWOOD' marks and 'Only Fifty of these vases were made of this is number 4, 1930', with restoration to finial.
1930 *10.25in (26cm) high*
$2,000-3,000 SWO

ESSENTIAL REFERENCE - THE PORTLAND VASE

The original 'Portland Vase' is a Roman cameo-glass vessel decorated with mythological scenes. It was probably made around 5-25 AD. Although it is not known exactly where and when it was discovered, it was part of the Cardinal del Montes collection in Italy in 1601.

- **In 1786 it belonged to the third Duke of Portland, who lent it to Josiah Wedgwood.**
- **Wedgwood made the vase famous by replicating it in jasper ware, a task that took four years of trials to perfect. He put the first edition on private show in 1790.**
- **The original 'Portland Vase' was deposited in the British Museum by the fourth Duke of Portland in 1810 and officially purchased by the Museum in 1945.**

A 19thC Wedgwood black jasper dip Portland vase, stamped 'WEDGWOOD'.

10in (25cm) high

$4,000-6,000 DRA

A pair of Wedgwood sage-green jasper dip vases, sprigged with lion head pilasters suspending rose swags and lilac medallions, with impressed marks and date letter.

1877 7in (18cm) high

$1,000-1,500 DN

A pair of late 19thC Wedgwood sage-green jasper dip pedestal urns and covers, sprigged with a band of Classical figures, with impressed marks.

7.5in (19cm) high

$1,000-1,500 DN

A pair of 19thC Wedgwood pale-green jasper dip vases and covers, with impressed marks, with minor restoration to one finial.

12in (30cm) high

$2,500-3,500 TOV

An early 20thC Wedgwood green jasper dip vase and cover, with impressed mark.

15.5in (39cm) high

$1,500-2,500 SK

An early 19thC Wedgwood caneware bamboo spill vase, with impressed mark.

9.5in (24.5cm) high

$3,000-4,000 SK

An early 19thC Wedgwood three-color jasper dip vase and cover, with impressed mark.

7.75in (20cm) high

$5,500-6,500 SK

A Wedgwood earthenware charger, painted by G Siever, with impressed 'WEDGWOOD' and printed 'G L Siever & Co, Worcester', with date code.

1882 19in (47.5cm) diam

$250-350 SWO

A Rhenish stoneware 'Cardinal Bellarmine' ewer, moulded in relief with an elaborate coat-of-arms beneath a Bellarmine mask, dated.

1607 *13.75in (35cm) high*

$12,000-18,000 **DN**

An Annaberg stoneware jug, moulded with a mother and child, with pewter lid, with chip and dented cover.

c1690 *10in (25.5cm) high*

$1,200-1,800 **WW**

An 18thC probably Lambeth salt-glazed stoneware tankard, decorated with trees, with silver-plated rim.

8.5in (21.5cm) high

$4,500-5,500 **GORL**

A late 18thC German salt-glazed stoneware puzzle jug, with pewter tappit lid, with minor faults.

7.5in (19cm) high

$500-700 **TOV**

A Nottingham brown salt-glazed stoneware commemorative jug, inscribed 'Thomas Riley 1843 and Nottingham, Independent Order of odd Fellows', and sprigged in relief with the Arms of the Odd Fellows and the heads of Washington and Franklin, dated.

1843 *6in (15cm) high*

$350-450 **DN**

A mid-18thC Staffordshire salt-glazed stoneware teapot and cover, painted with a couple and a gentleman playing a flute with a building beyond, with crabstick handle and spout.

3.5in (9cm) high

$1,000-1,500 **HT**

A Staffordshire Queen Caroline in Memoriam white stoneware jug.

Caroline of Brunswick-Wolfenbuttel (1768-1821) was Queen consort to King George IV 1820-21 and mother to Princess Charlotte of Wales. The latter died in childbirth in 1817 and Charlotte herself died in 1821 shortly after failing to gain entrance to her husband's coronation (they were by this time estranged). Caroline evoked much public sympathy, which is presumably why many commemorative pieces were fashioned.

c1821 *7in (18cm) high*

$400-600 **DN**

A mid-18thC Staffordshire salt-glazed stoneware mansion teapot and cover, with rampant lion above the door.

5.25in (13.5cm) high

$2,500-3,500 **SK**

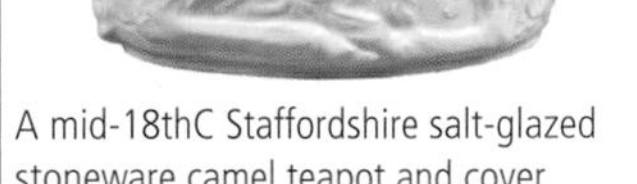

A mid-18thC Staffordshire salt-glazed stoneware camel teapot and cover.

6.5in (16.5cm) high

$3,500-4,500 **SK**

An incised patriotic stoneware jug, by Absalom Stedman, New Haven, Connecticut, incised and painted in cobalt-blue with an American eagle with Masonic shield breast, holding an American flag and arrows, with incised 'Made by A. Stedman'.

c1825-30 *19.25in (49cm) high*

$500,000-600,000 **POOK**

Judith Picks: Jug

I'm always fascinated by the extraordinary – even if the object is not immediately attractive! This jug was retrieved from the interior of a vessel inscribed 'Monkey Jug - made at Bath S.C. 1862 by negro slaves/Aiken S.C.'.

Early southern American face vessels, such as the example shown, were made by enslaved African-American potters and were probably influenced by anthropomorphic clay vessels made in West Africa (the chief source of the Atlantic slave trade). The larger face jugs were used as water vessels called 'monkey' jugs, after 'monkeyed', a southern term for the dehydrating effect of the summer heat. Small jugs such as this one have aroused curiosity as to their use, as they are so small that they would not hold enough liquid to quench a thirsty individual! It may well be that the small jugs were used by the slaves in possible religious or ritual practices.

A late 19thC alkaline-glazed stoneware face jug, attributed to the Bath, Aiken County, South Carolina area, with applied white kaolin eyes and teeth.

4.5in (11.5cm) high

$60,000-80,000 **SK**

A rare 19thC Cowden & Wilcox four-gallon stoneware jug, painted in cobalt-blue with a dog holding a basket.

15.25in (38.5cm) high

$65,000-75,000 **POOK**

A 19thC two-gallon stoneware crock, painted in cobalt-blue with a bird, with impressed 'Fulper Bros., Flemington NJ'.

9.25in (23cm) high

$400-600 **POOK**

A 19thC stoneware pitcher, Baltimore, Maryland, painted in cobalt-blue, with impressed 'P. Herrmann'.

10.5in (27cm) high

$550-650 **POOK**

A stoneware cooler, with cobalt-blue inscription 'Robt. Benson 1855/Geddes/Onondaga Co. N.Y.', with impressed maker's mark 'W.H. Farar/Geddes, N.Y.'.

1855 *21.5in (55cm) high*

$5,000-6,000 **SK**

A 19thC five-gallon stoneware butter churn, painted in cobalt-blue with flowers, with impressed 'Evan R. Jones Pittston PA'.

18in (46cm) high

$400-600 **POOK**

A late 19thC Haxstun, Ottman & Co. stoneware five-gallon crock, Fort Edward, New York, with Albany slip-glazed interior, with impressed maker's marks, with minor chips and stains.

12in (30cm) high

$15,000-20,000 **SK**

An 18thC Prattware figure of 'Autumn', modeled as a boy.

4.5in (11.5cm) high

$350-450 **GORL**

A Prattware Duke of York and Prince Coburg commemorative jug. **From 1793 to 1795 Frederick Augustus, Duke of York and Albany (1763-1827), second son of George III, commanded the British in Flanders. His contingent of 10,000 men was part of the army of Prince Josias of Saxe-Coburg. These jugs were probably made to celebrate the victorious campaigns of 1793.**

c1794 7in (18.5cm) high

$650-850 **TEN**

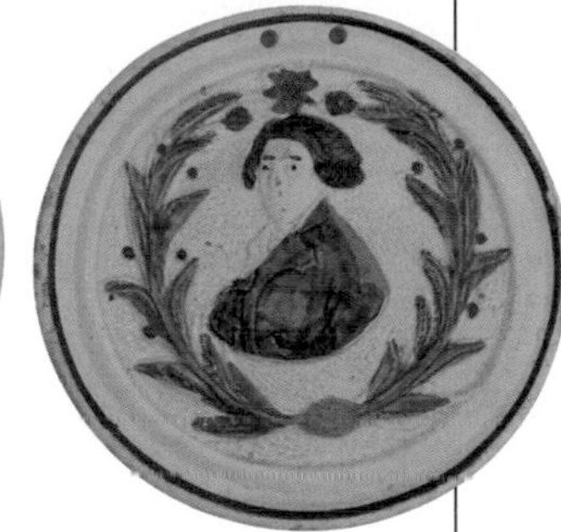

A rare pair of Prattware plaques, each moulded with a head and shoulders portrait, one of Charles James Fox, the other of Earl Howe.

c1795 5in (13cm) diam

$2,500-3,500 **H&C**

A Prattware model of a ewe and lamb.

c1800 5in (10.5cm) wide

$1,200-1,800 **TEN**

An early 19thC Prattware shepherd group, the young shepherd leaning on a spade beside a large ram, his dog at his feet.

6in (15cm) high

$2,000-3,000 **HT**

A unique Prattware tricorn vase, with three pictures, 'I See You My Boy' (311), 'The Poutry Woman' (349) and 'The Fishbarrow' (58).

For more information see K V Mortimer's 'Pot-Lids and Other Colored Printed Staffordshire Wares', Antique Collectors' Club, 2003.

$5,000-6,000 **H&C**

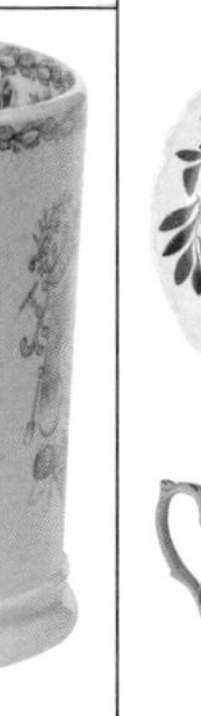

A Staffordshire anti-slavery mug, printed in black with a slave released from chains, inscribed 'WILBERFORCE' and 'Isaiah Chap 58.6', the reverse with 'Farmers' Creed' and 'God Speed the Plough', the base with a further verse.

Lincoln Hallinan suggests in 'British Commemoratives' (published by the Antique Collectors' Club) that no ceramics bearing Wilberforce's name seem to exist. This makes it likely that this mug is rare.

c1830 4.5in (11cm) high

$3,000-4,000 **TEN**

A 19thC Staffordshire 'Adams Rose' dinner set, consisting of 28 bowls, 99 plates, 24 cups and saucers, four creamers, two pitchers, three platters, three waste bowls, a mug and three trays.

Largest plates 10in (25cm) diam

$10,000-15,000 set **POOK**

POTTERY

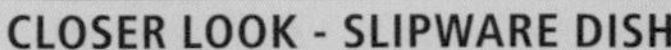

A North Devon slipware harvest jug, with sgraffito decoration of a songbird perched on a leafy branch, with small chips and losses, dated.

1876 *12.25in (31cm) high*

$3,500-4,500 **WW**

CLOSER LOOK - SLIPWARE DISH

The demand for early slipware exceeds supply.

Few slipware bowls of this age survive without any damage.

The stylized designs often used on slipware pottery means such pieces fit into modern interiors, making them desirable.

This example is in extremely good condition for its age.

A large English slipware press-moulded dish, the dark treacle glaze decorated with cream colored slip-trailed cascading swirls, with pie-crust rim.

c1880 *14.5in (36.5cm) diam*

$5,500-6,500 **HALL**

An English slip-decorated redware shallow bowl.

c1800 *8in (20.3cm) diam*

$5,500-6,500 **POOK**

A rare Rye lead-glazed pottery flask, inscribed 'MOSES*ROOTS. RYE. SEP.1846., STEAL NOT THIS BOTTLE DISHONEST FRIEND, FOR FEAR THE GALLOWS SHOULD BE YOUR END, BUT IF YOU DO MAY CONSCIENCE SAY, TAKE BACK THE BOTTLE YOU STOLE AWAY.', with incised mark beneath 'Rye Pottery', dated.

1846 *10.5in (26cm) high*

$1,800-2,200 **GORL**

A rare early 19thC Alamance Co. earthenware sugar bowl and cover, North Carolina, with splash decoration.

7.75in (19.7cm) high

$40,000-50,000 **POOK**

A 19thC red and yellow rainbow Spatterware sugar, with drape pattern and a blue cornflower.

4.25in (11cm) high

$5,500-6,500 **POOK**

A late 18thC green-glazed redware lidded-pitcher, Bristol County, Massachusetts, with reeded bands around the cover rim and shoulder of vessel, with minor chips and glaze-loss.

11in (28cm) high

$10,000-15,000 **SK**

An English commemorative harvest jug, printed with the 'Farmer's Arms' pattern and with 'J.R. PALETHORPE WILMER GRANGE HARLAXTON GRANTHAM'.

c1835 *7.25in (18.5cm) high*

$350-450 **DN**

A Staffordshire agateware urn, with clear lead glaze on brown, tan and white marbled clay, with lion mask and scroll handles.

c1850 *22.5in (57.5cm) high*

$6,500-7,500 **SK**

ESSENTIAL REFERENCE - MASON'S PATENT IRONSTONE

Charles James Mason (1791-1856) patented his Ironstone China wares in 1813 in Staffordshire. The white stoneware body of Ironstone was more durable than porcelain.

- **Mason's Patent Ironstone was used for simple objects, such as plates and jugs decorated with blue-and-white transfer-printed patterns, but also large and elaborate objects, such as vases, which were usually decorated in rich, bright colors. The strength of Ironstone allowed for the production of very large pieces.**
- **Designs were typically inspired by Chinese and Japanese patterns.**
- **Mason's firm, which traded as G M & C J Mason and C J Mason & Co., closed in 1848.**
- **From the 1820s to 1840s, other Staffordshire manufacturers also produced similar wares with names such as 'Granite China' and Stone China'.**

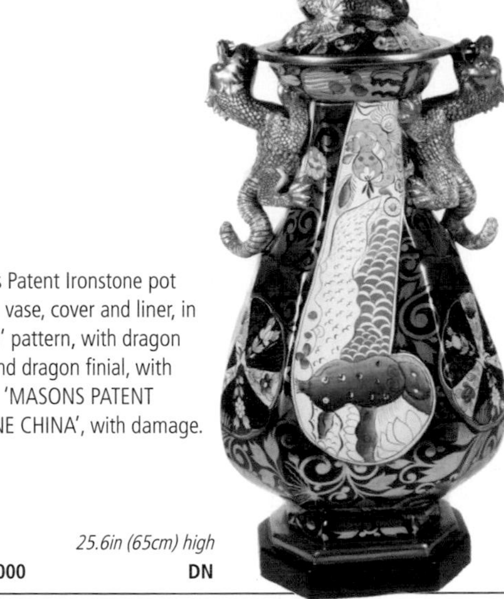

A Mason's Patent Ironstone pot pourri hall vase, cover and liner, in the 'Japan' pattern, with dragon handles and dragon finial, with impressed 'MASONS PATENT IRONSTONE CHINA', with damage.

c1820 *25.6in (65cm) high*

$5,000-6,000 **DN**

This mark c1820

This mark c1813-25

An early 19thC Mason's Patent Ironstone ewer.

25.25in (64cm) high

$2,000-3,000 **CHEF**

Six mid-19thC Damm pottery models of children, after Höchst porcelain originals modeled by J P Melchior, with blue wheel and incised marks.

6.75in (17cm) high

$2,500-3,500 **DN**

A pair of late 19thC Rozenburg figures of a fisherman and fishwife, with inscribed marks.

Taller 8in (20cm) high

$4,000-6,000 **L&T**

A late 19thC terracotta luster-glaze Classical vase, with relief laurel wreath swags.

68.5in (174cm) high

$2,000-3,000 **L&T**

Fern Chair

A very rare late 19thC Drury Pottery fern chair, with tree trunk-shape base and fern support-back.

This is a one-off piece. It came from the estate of Kereone Station, Matamata. The owner of the station was a director of the Drury Pottery.

34in (86cm) high

$8,000-12,000 **DS**

THE ORIENTAL MARKET

Over the past few years, it has seemed as though not a week passed without some record for Oriental jade or ceramics being broken. However, there are rumours that the 'gold-rush' frenzy may well be coming to an end.

Nevertheless, having attended various fairs and auctions in the last few months, I have seen that there is still a real buzz when anything Chinese of importance comes to the market. This is particularly true if a piece is new to the market and has Imperial connections, by which I mean that it was specifically made for the Chinese Emperor and the Imperial household. The first specifically Imperial kiln was set up in Jingdezhen during the Yuan dynasty (1279-1368). During the Ming and Qing dynasties, Imperial porcelain was made at the Imperial kiln at Zhushan (Pearl Hill).

It is also true that, although many are still primarily interested in Imperial ware, Chinese collectors are slowly becoming more interested in good quality export and armorial porcelain. This is an entirely new development. Previously, shipwreck cargoes have been of very little interest to Chinese buyers, but they are now starting to buy the 'Hatcher Junk' cargo. The ship sank in c1643. And there are still the odd flutters, for example when a rare and important Northern Song Dynasty 'Ding' bowl bought at a US garage sale for $3 sold in March 2013 in Sotheby's New York for $2.2 million.

However, the era of the £17 million Song Dynasty bowl may be coming to an end. In 2012 a Portugal-based marine-archaeology company, Arqueonautas Worldwide, discovered 700,000 pieces of shipwrecked Ming (1368-1644) porcelain off the coast of Indonesia. The collection was estimated by Bloomberg at £30 million. But how much will it be worth a year from now, when that amount of porcelain comes onto a market that appears to be slowing down?

The latest Christie's Hong Kong auctions show that demand for traditional Chinese porcelain may be softening. During the 'Chinese Ceramics and Works of Art' auction of early 2013, over a third of the lots failed to reach their reserve price (the lowest price sellers were willing to accept).

It could be that Chinese buyers have had second thoughts because of a weakening economy. It has also been suggested that sellers are becoming too greedy and reserves were too high. Also the choice of goods available may be less attractive as collectors are less willing to part with their pieces.

By way of comparison, Christie's managed a 'white-glove' wine auction in the same week ('white glove' means all lots were sold). Perhaps, in times of stress and economic uncertainty, alcohol is more sought after than antiques!

Left A Chinese Qianlong period blue-and-white ewer and cover. See p.97.
Far Left: An 18thC Chinese celadon jade cup. See p.130.

CHINESE REIGN PERIODS AND MARKS

Imperial reign marks were adopted during the Ming dynasty, and some of the most common are illustrated here. Certain emperors forbade the use of their own reign mark, lest they should suffer the disrespect of a broken vessel bearing their name being thrown away. This is where the convention of using earlier reign marks comes from – a custom that was enthusiastically adopted by potters as a way of showing their respect for their predecessors.

It is worth remembering that a great deal of Imperial porcelain is marked misleadingly, and pieces bearing the reign mark for the period in which they were made are, therefore, especially sought after.

EARLY PERIODS AND DATES

Xia Dynasty	*c2000 - 1500BC*	Three Kingdoms	*221 - 280*	The Five Dynasties	*907 - 960*
Shang Dynasty	*1500 - 1028BC*	Jin Dynasty	*265 - 420*	Song Dynasty	*960 - 1279*
Zhou Dynasty	*1028 - 221BC*	Northern & Southern Dynasties	*420 - 581*	Jin Dynasty	*1115 - 1234*
Qin Dynasty	*221 - 206BC*	Sui Dynasty	*581 - 618*	Yuan Dynasty	*1260 - 1368*
Han Dynasty	*206BC - AD220*	Tang Dynasty	*618 - 906*		

EARLY MING DYNASTY REIGNS

Hongwu	*1368 - 1398*	Jingtai	*1450 - 1457*
Jianwen	*1399 - 1402*	Tianshun	*1457 - 1464*
Yongle	*1403 - 1424*	Chenghua	*1465 - 1487*
Hongxi	*1425 - 1425*		
Xuande	*1426 - 1435*		
Zhengtong	*1436 - 1449*		

MING DYNASTY MARKS

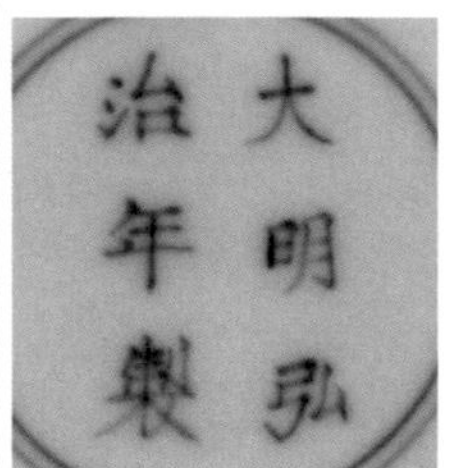

Hongzhi
1488–1505

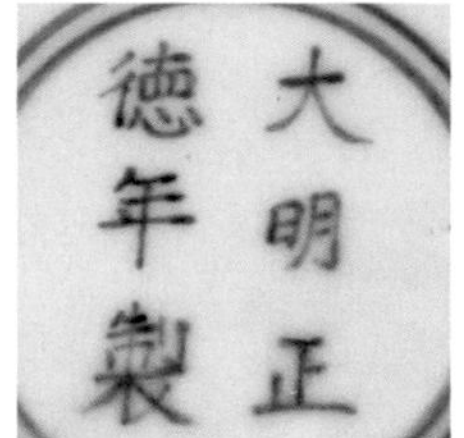

Zhengde
1506–21

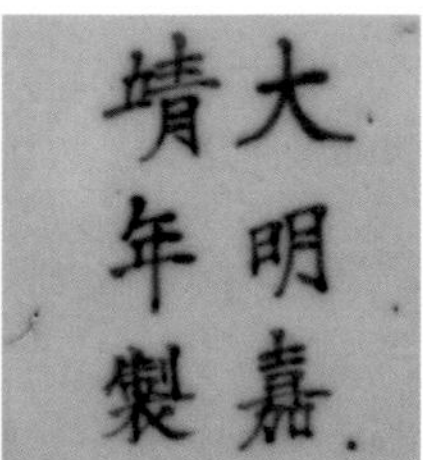

Jiajing
1522–66

Wanli
1573–1619

Chongzhen
1628–44

QING DYNASTY MARKS

Kangxi
1662–1722

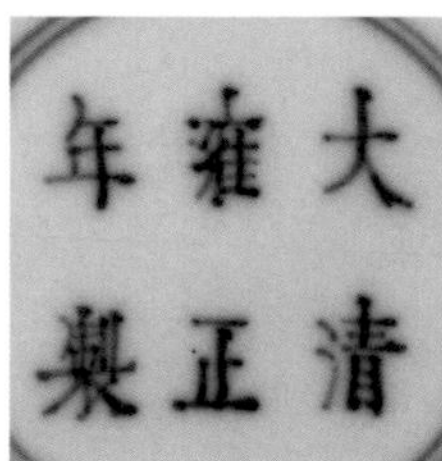

Yongzheng
1723–35

Qianlong
1736–95

Jiaqing
1796–1820

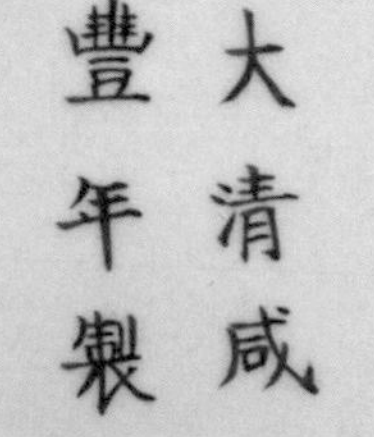

Xianfeng
1851–61

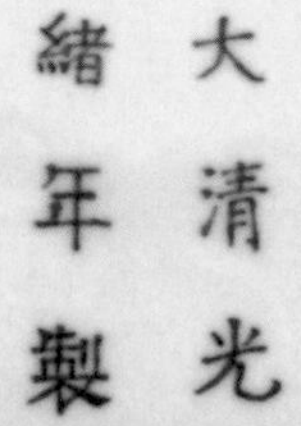

Tongzhi
1862–74

Guangxu
1875–1908

Xuantong
1909–11

Hongxian
1915–16

A rare 3rd/2ndC BC Chinese painted pottery bottle, with minor chips.

10in (28cm) high

$2,500-3,500 KAU

A Chinese Neolithic pottery vessel, with geometric decoration.

17.25in (44cm) high

$3,500-4,500 SWO

A Chinese probably late Zhou period dou-type sacrificial vessel.

This period is called the 'Warring States' period.

5th-3rdC BC 7.75in (19.5cm) high

$2,000-3,000 KAU

A rare Chinese Tang dynasty black-ware ewer, the mirror-black glaze splashed with phosphatic brown.

This ewer was made at a pottery in Duandian, Lushan county, Henan province. The nearest comparable ewer is in the Asian Art Museum of San Francisco, USA. This class of ware led to junyao and, in turn, to ruyao.

7.25in (18.5cm) high

$6,500-7,500 SWO

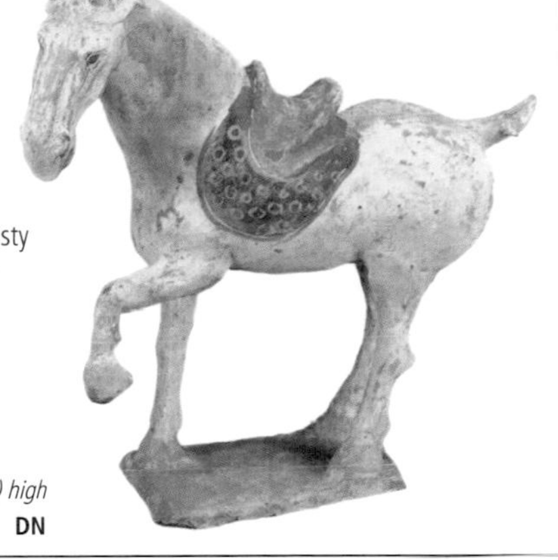

A Chinese Tang dynasty cold-painted pottery model of a prancing horse, with TL test.

12.5in (32.5cm) high

$4,500-5,500 DN

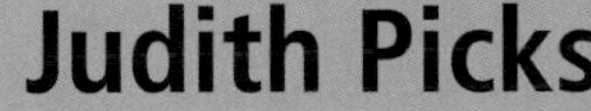

Judith Picks

These horses were produced in what is arguably China's golden age of literature and art. This horse is in a typical prancing position and the court lady retains much of her original clothing and color. Horses imported from the Near East were precious. In Tang China, the horse was the emblem of wealth and power. They are meant to embody rank and speed. These statues were often included in burials to ensure that the dead enjoyed the pleasures of life on earth. Due to the number of Chinese modern fake 'Tang' horses on the market, it is essential that the horse should have a TL (thermoluminescence) certificate, as this one has.

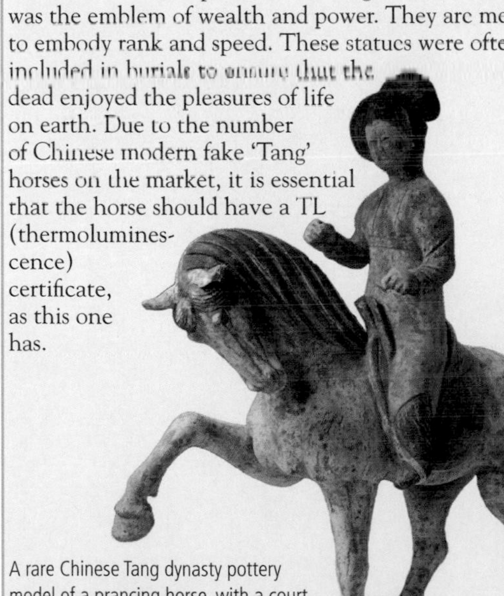

A rare Chinese Tang dynasty pottery model of a prancing horse, with a court lady sitting in a saddle on its back.

17in (43cm) high

$12,000-18,000 RGA

A Chinese Tang dynasty pottery model of a polo player, painted in polychrome colors, with TL test.

13.5in (34.5cm) high

$7,000-8,000 KAU

A Chinese Tang dynasty pottery model of a horse, with restoration, with TL test.

24.5in (62.5cm) high

$3,500-4,500 SWO

A Chinese Tang dynasty pottery model of a horse.

9.75in (25cm) high

$1,500-2,500 DN

A 17thC Chinese 'blanc de Chine' figure of Guanyin, with seal marks.

7.5in (20.5cm) high

$4,500-5,500 **DN**

A 17thC Chinese 'blanc de Chine' group of a dignitary and attendant immortals, with detachable figure of a devil.

7.5in (21cm) high

$5,000-6,000 **DN**

A late 17thC Chinese 'blanc de Chine' figure of Guanyin, sitting on a lotus leaf supported by a tall column of water, with extensive damage.

12.5in (31.5cm) high

$5,000-6,000 **WW**

A Chinese Qing dynasty Dehua 'blanc de Chine' figure of Guanyin.

c1700 *7.5in (19cm) high*

$15,000-20,000 **CAN**

A pair of 18thC Chinese 'blanc de Chine' seals, each surmounted by a Buddhist lion dog and a puppy, with minor damage.

5.25in (13.5cm) high

$20,000-30,000 **WW**

A Chinese 'blanc de Chine' figure of Guandi, seated with feet thrust forward in an aggressive attitude, with four-character inscription 'Chen-ho-chin Ch'i', probably the name of a workshop.

c1700 *8.25in (21cm) high*

$20,000-30,000 **WW**

An 18thC Chinese 'blanc de Chine' figure of Buddhai Ho Shang, on a wood stand, with damage.

6.75in (17cm) high

$3,000-4,000 **WW**

A 19thC Chinese 'blanc de Chine' figure of a monk, standing on scrolling waves, with impressed factory marks, with wood stand.

13.5in (34.5cm) high

$12,000-18,000 **WW**

A Chinese 'blanc de Chine' ewer and cover, with dragons forming the handle, spout and knop, with chips.

c1680 *4.75in (12cm) high*

$8,000-12,000 **SWO**

ESSENTIAL REFERENCE - CELADON

Celadon glaze is usually semi-translucent and greenish, deriving its color from iron. The glaze was first used while the Song court was situated in northern China (960–1127).

- **Yaozhou in the Shaanxi Province was one of the first important centers of celadon production. Early celadons typically have incised or molded decoration and are covered in an olive-green glaze.**
- **After the court moved south in 1127, Longquan became one of the most important areas of production. It gave its name to the second period of celadon production.**
- **Longquan celadon typically has a pale-gray body with a thick, opaque, bluish-green glaze. Decoration is typically sparse, with some pieces carved or stamped with decoration under the glaze.**

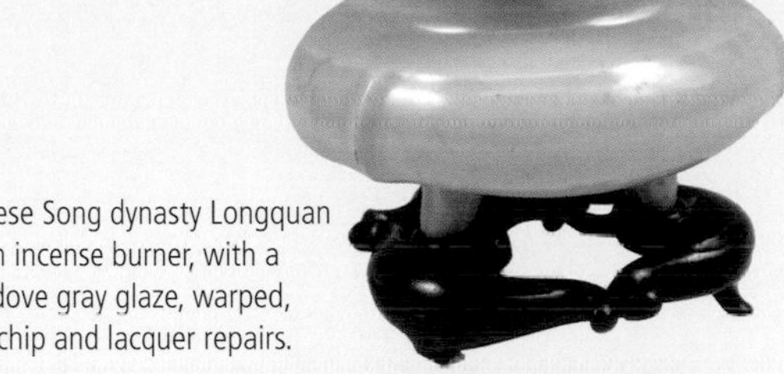

A Chinese Song dynasty Longquan celadon incense burner, with a green-dove gray glaze, warped, with a chip and lacquer repairs.

This koro sagged in the kiln and was a 'kiln waster' that wasn't wasted. It may have gone straight to Japan where the tea masters would have found it more appealing than a perfect example. The stand is probably 18thC Chinese.

4in (10.5cm) diam

$10,000-15,000 SWO

A Chinese Yuan dynasty Longquan celadon dish.

9.5in (24cm) diam

$2,000-3,000 DN

A Chinese Yuan dynasty Longquan celadon vase, with crackled sea-green glaze, incised with scrolling peony, the foot with a lappet border.

22in (56cm) high

$12,000-18,000 DOY

A rare 14thC Chinese celadon dish, inscribed with the four characters 'jing yu man tang' (hall of abundant gold and jade), with wear to glaze.

13in (33cm) diam

$2,500-3,500 WW

A 14thC Chinese Yuan dynasty 'purple splash' junyao bowl, with a pale lavender glaze with purple splash.

6.75in (17.5cm) diam

$2,000-3,000 DN

A 15thC Chinese carved celadon bowl.

12.5in (31.5cm) diam

$15,000-20,000 DN

An early 15thC Chinese Longquan celadon dish, carved with a five-clawed dragon amid cloud scrolls, with crack, with a hardwood stand.

15in (38.5cm) diam

$45,000-55,000 WW

A 15thC Chinese Longquan celadon tazza.

6.5in (16.5cm) diam

$2,500-3,500 DN

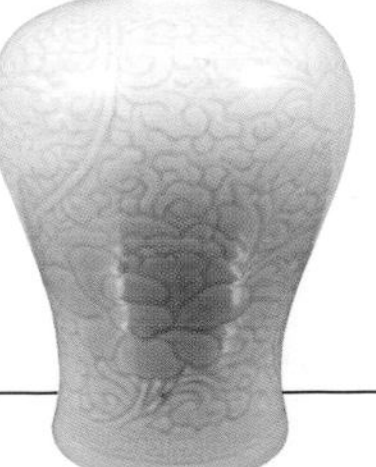

An 18thC Chinese pale celadon vase.

5in (15.5cm) high

$8,000-12,000 SWO

A Chinese Qianlong period 'sang de boeuf' water pot.

3.75in (9.5cm) diam

$120,000-180,000 **CAN**

A Chinese Daoguang period pink bottle vase, with seal mark.

7.5in (18cm) high

$55,000-75,000 **TEN**

A 19thC Chinese 'sang de boeuf' inkwell, mounted with European silver-plate rim and lid, with Chinese white jade finial carved as a boy and cat.

5in (12.5cm) high

$15,000-20,000 **DOY**

A Chinese Guangxu period 'sang de boeuf' hu-form vase, the neck with arrow handles, incised 'ta Qing Guangxu nian zhi', with wood stand.

12.5in (31cm) high

$20,000-30,000 **SWO**

A large 19thC Chinese 'sang de boeuf' baluster vase.

22.5in (57cm) high

$1,500-2,000 **DN**

A Chinese Qianlong period 'liver-red' dish, with underglaze blue 'Ta Qing Qianlong nizn zei' mark, with chips.

7in (18cm) diam

$3,500-4,500 **SWO**

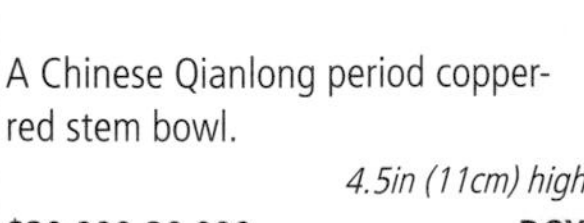

A Chinese Qianlong period copper-red stem bowl.

4.5in (11cm) high

$20,000-30,000 **DOY**

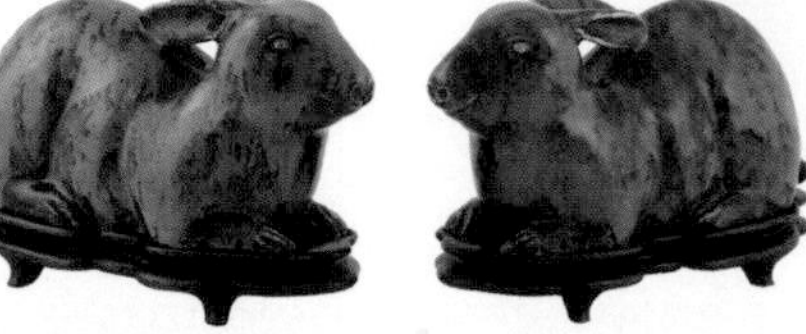

A pair of Chinese flambé-glazed rabbits, with streaked red and lavender glazes, with hardwood stands.

c1800 *7.75in (19.5cm) long*

$5,000-6,000 **WW**

A Chinese Qianlong period Imperial yellow ceremonial vessel, relief-decprated with archaistic motifs beneath a band of key fret, with kui dragon handles, the cover with wing-shaped fins around a dragon and clouds, with Qianlong seal mark.

11in (28cm) high overall

$70,000-90,000 **M&K**

A Chinese Hongzhi-period Imperial yellow bowl, with Hongzhi mark.

Hongzhi yellow-glazed bowls of this size are rare.

8in (20.5cm) diam

$150,000-200,000 **DUK**

A Chinese Xianfeng period Imperial yellow ceremonial vessel, relief-decorated with archaistic patterns, with double-rope-twist loop handle, with Xianfeng seal mark.

9.75in (25cm) high

$80,000-120,000 **M&K**

A large Chinese Zhengde period yellow saucer dish, with six-character Zhengde mark, with faint cracks and wear.

8.5in (21.5cm) diam

$20,000-30,000 **WW**

A Chinese Yongzheng period yellow tea bowl, with blue six-character Yongzheng mark.

2.5in (8cm) diam

$10,000-15,000 **TEN**

A Chinese Yongzheng period Imperial yellow saucer dish, the base carved with the eight Buddhist emblems, with six-character Yongzheng mark.

7.75in (19cm) diam

$6,500-7,500 **SWO**

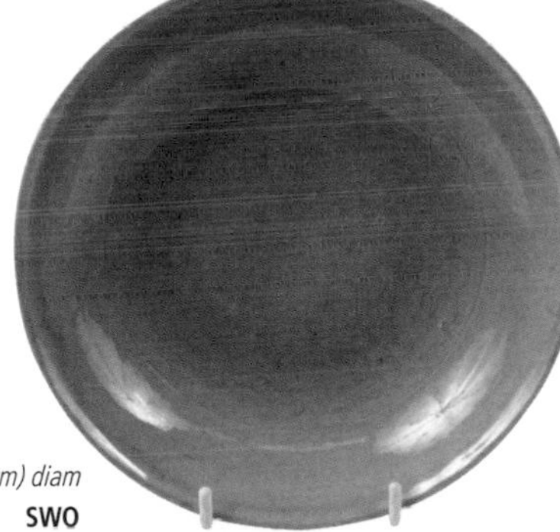

A Chinese Daoguang period Imperial yellow saucer dish, incised with a five-clawed dragon chasing a flaming pearl, with Daoguang seal mark.

6.75in (17cm) diam

$10,000-15,000 **SWO**

A pair of Chinese Daoguang period yellow bowls, incised with stylized flowerheads and clouds above a lappet band.

4.75in (12cm) diam

$15,000-20,000 **DOY**

A 19thC Chinese yellow saucer dish, incised with a dragon among clouds with a flaming pearl, the exterior with dragons, with apocryphal Qianlong seal mark.

6.75in (17cm) diam

$4,000-6,000 **DN**

A 13thC Chinese Yuan dynasty Guan-type ewer, with pale grayish-olive crackle glaze.

3in (7.5cm) high

$5,000-6,000 SK

A Chinese Kangxi period white 'Dragon' vase, incised with a four-clawed dragon chasing flaming pearls, with a light blue wash, with apocryphal six-character Chenghua mark, with chip.

15.75in (40cm) high

$35,000-45,000 CAN

A Chinese Kangxi period peach-bloom Guanyin or 'willow leaf' vase.

6.75in (17cm) high

$3,500-4,500 DN

An 18thC Chinese white stem cup, the interior molded with a 'Phoenix' design, with apocryphal Yongle mark.

3.25in (8.5cm) high

$10,000-15,000 CAN

A Chinese Kangxi period green crackle-glaze beehive water pot, with six-character Kangxi mark.

3.7in (9.5cm) high

$6,500-7,500 L&T

A Chinese Kangxi period green teapot and cover, modeled with bamboo.

4.5in (11.5cm) high

$6,500-7,500 L&T

A Chinese Tongzhi period Imperial blue bowl, with six-character Tongzhi mark.

6in (15cm) diam

$3,500-4,500 WW

A Chinese Guangxu period Imperial pale duck-egg blue fanghu-form vase, with six-character Guangxu mark.

12.25in (31cm) high

$35,000-45,000 WW

A Chinese Guangxu period lavender-blue censer, with six-character Guangxu mark.

5in (12cm) diam

$1,000-1,500 DN

A small late 17th/early 18thC Chinese Yixing hexagonal teapot and cover, applied with sprigs of prunus, pine and bamboo, with gilt-metal mounts, with square seal mark.

4.5in (12cm) high

$18,000-22,000 **WW**

A Chinese Yixing teapot and cover, decorated with triangles interlocking into hexagons, the cover with a lion dog finial, with chips.

c1700-25 7in (18cm) high

$15,000-20,000 **WW**

A Chinese Yixing teapot and cover, with four roundels containing the 'Three Friends of Winter' above swastika-type motifs, the cover with a mythical beast, with minor restoration.

c1700-25 5.5in (14cm) high

$55,000-75,000 **WW**

ESSENTIAL REFERENCE - YIXING

Unglazed red-brown stoneware has been produced by the Yixing potteries in the Jiangsu Province from the late Ming dynasty. This pottery was exported to Europe from the mid-17thC until the end of the 18thC.

- **Yixing is best known for teapots, which were widely exported. These were either left plain or decorated in relief with garden scenes or sprigged decoration, such as prunus branches. Most forms were simple, but extremely elaborate forms are also known.**
- **In the 1670s, Dutch Delft potters began producing redware in imitation of Yixing pottery. Staffordshire potteries produced a similar ware in the late 17thC.**
- **Yixing wares are still produced today.**

A small Chinese Yixing teapot and cover, the body sprigged with prunus, with restoration.

c1675-1700 5.25in (13.5cm) high

$8,000-12,000 **WW**

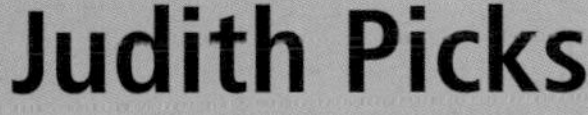

Judith Picks

These teapots are made from clay produced near Yixing (pronounced yeeshing) in the Eastern province of Jiangsu. From the early 16thC Yixing teapots were popular with the scholarly class and their fame spread.

It is said that if you use a Yixing teapot for many years, you can brew tea by just pouring boiling water into the empty pot. The very simplicity and early date of this teapot add to its desirability.

A 17thC Chinese Yixing deep-brown teapot and cover, on a slightly flared lipped foot, with script mark.

7in (17.5cm) high

$200,000-300,000 **WW**

A rare Yixing teapot and cover, decorated with a raised design of tribal-type figures among leaves and chrysanthemum flowers, the cover with a lion dog finial.

c1700 6in (15cm) high

$55,000-75,000 **WW**

A Chinese Yixing phoenix teapot and cover, the cover with a flaming pearl finial.

c1700-25 6.5in (16.5cm) high

$25,000-35,000 **WW**

A small 18thC Chinese Yixing teapot and cover, modeled with bamboo stems, the cover with two leaf motifs, decorated with splashes of orange pigment.

6in (15cm) high

$70,000-90,000 **WW**

An 18thC Chinese Yixing lobed chrysanthemum-form teapot and cover, with gilt-metal mounts, the cover with later stag finial mount.

6.25in (16cm) high

$100,000-150,000 **WW**

A rare Chinese Yixing robin's-egg blue teapot and cover, with seal mark.

c1780 *7in (17.5cm) high*

$200,000-300,000 **WW**

A rare late 18thC Yixing teapot and cover, with warming stand, enameled in two shades of blue with butterflies.

10.5in (27cm) high

$50,000-70,000 **WW**

An early 19thC Chinese Yixing duanni prunus teapot and cover, probably by Shao Daheng, applied with darker blossoms, with impressed marks.

Shao Daheng was the Senior Master during the reign of the Daoguang Emperor (1821-50).

8.5in (22cm) high

$20,000-30,000 **WW**

A 19thC Chinese Yixing teapot and cover, modeled as bamboo, with mark probably for Menghou, with some restoration.

5.75in (14.5cm) high

$120,000-180,000 **WW**

A 19thC Chinese Yixing brush pot, modeled as bamboo, marked 'Qing Xi Leng Ba Jia Ni Feng Nian Xing Duan Dao Guang Nian Yang Ji'.

5.5in (14cm) high

$15,000-20,000 **SK**

ESSENTIAL REFERENCE - EARLY BLUE-AND-WHITE

Chinese potters first used underglaze blue decoration around c1330. The cobalt was imported from Persia until the late Chenghua period (1465-87) when local ores were used. The quality of blue was later improved during the Jiajing period (1522-66).

- **The finest blue-and-white wares were produced during the Chenghua period with quality declining from the Hongzhi period (1488-1505) onward.**
- **Glazes were viscous in the Yuan dynasty. During the early Ming dynasty, the glaze often featured a pitted 'orange peel' effect. Pieces produced for export often have a high gloss glaze, tending to thin on the base.**

A Chinese Ming dynasty blue-and-white dish, painted with a scrolling lotus pattern, with fitted box.

15in (38cm) diam

$120,000-180,000 DRA

An early Chinese Xuande period blue-and-white grape jar, painted with fruiting vines, the rim with shaped panels of flowers.

5.25in (13.5in) high

$70,000-100,000 JN

A Chinese Jiajing period blue-and-white brush pot, painted with figures in landscapes, with six-character mark.

6.5in (16.5cm) high

$20,000-30,000 GORL

A Chinese blue-and-white provincial dish, painted with a mythical beast within a floral and foliate scroll border.

c1550 13.5in (34cm) diam

$1,500-2,500 L&T

A rare Chinese blue-and-white stem bowl, painted with figures in a garden beneath bamboo, the interior with a seated sage, with apocryphal six character Xuande mark, with small faults.

c1570 4.25in (11cm) high

$20,000-30,000 WW

A Chinese Wanli period blue-and-white molded lotus-shaped dish, painted with Sanskrit characters, with hairline crack and minor restoration.

The Sanskrit character on the front relates to the Chinese character 'fo' and can represent the word 'Buddha'.

8.25in (21cm) diam

$12,000-18,000 CAN

A rare Chinese Wanli period blue-and-white burner, painted with a band of eight five-clawed dragons chasing flaming pearls above waves.

6in (15.5cm) wide

$50,000-70,000 WW

A Chinese Wanli period blue-and-white 'Lotus' bowl, the rim ground down, with small hairline crack.

6in (15cm) diam

$35,000-45,000 CAN

A rare Chinese Wanli period blue-and-white incense burner, painted with pairs of five-clawed dragons contesting flaming pearls above waves, with fish handles, with some restoration.

8.75in (22cm) wide

$35,000-45,000 **WW**

Kraak

A rare Chinese Kraak blue-and-white dish, painted with pheasants, with panels of flowers, lotus and insects, with egret mark.

The egret mark is rare and appears mainly on Kraak wares, and only on pieces of good quality. It is commonly accepted that pieces bearing this mark were produced in one particular kiln. Maura Rinaldi lists only 45 known examples in 'Kraak Porcelain' (1989).

c1620 *8.25in (20.5cm) diam*

$18,000-22,000 **WW**

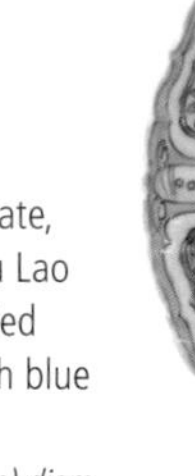

A Chinese Kraak blue-and-white plate, painted with Shou Lao fishing, with molded lappet panels, with blue egret mark,

8.25in (21cm) diam

$20,000-30,000 **LC**

A Chinese Chongzhen period blue-and-white bidong (brush pot), painted with a woman dancing with a sword while an artist and attendants work in a garden, with chips and wear.

c1640 *7.5in (19cm) high*

$7,000-8,000 **SWO**

A mid-17thC Chinese Transitional blue-and-white vase and cover, painted with a warrior on horseback, others approaching past a rock and clouds, the cover associated.

14.5in (37cm) high

$7,000-8,000 **SWO**

A mid-17thC Chinese Transitional blue-and-white vase and cover, painted with a mother and boys in a garden, with some restoration.

15in (38cm) high

$3,500-4,500 **SWO**

A pair of Chinese Shunzhi period Transitional blue-and-white vases, painted with Immortals and boys in a landscape.

5.5in (14cm) high

$14,000-16,000 **SWO**

A Chinese Kangxi period 'Master of the Rock' blue-and-white dish, painted with figures and huts beneath trees in a mountainous landscape.

c1670 *10.75in (27.5cm) diam*

$8,000-12,000 **WW**

A rare Chinese Kangxi period blue-and-white vase, painted with a wide band of stylized taotie and with smaller bands to the shoulder and foot.

5.25in (13cm) high

$250,000-350,000 **WW**

A Chinese early Kangxi period blue-and-white brush holder, painted with a supplicant on his knees to a scholar and boy attendant with a large fan on a terrace, with apocryphal six-character Chenghua mark.

c1670 *5.5in (13.5cm) high*

$10,000-15,000 **SWO**

A late 17thC Chinese Kangxi period lotus-petal molded blue-and-white dish, painted with butterflies and flowers, with apocryphal six-character Chengua mark.

10.2in (26cm) diam

$2,500-3,500 **SWO**

A late 17thC Chinese Transitional blue-and-white mallet-shaped vase, painted with fish in a stormy ocean, converted to a lamp.

With fitting 18in (46cm) high

$8,000-12,000 **L&T**

Kangxi Bowls

A pair of Chinese Kangxi period blue-and-white bowls, painted with figures in gardens, with small rim chips.

Kangxi blue-and-white porcelain is usually very economically potted and neatly trimmed around the base. The glaze is very thin and glassy with the blue varying from a silver to a purple-blue tone.

6.5in (16.5cm) diam

$7,000-8,000 **WW**

A 17thC Chinese blue-and-white vase and cover, painted with flowering shrubs and rocks between strapwork and diaper, with crack.

19in (48cm) high

$10,000-15,000 **SWO**

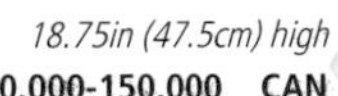

A Chinese Kangxi period blue-and-white yen-yen vase, painted with panels of sages, with label.

17.75in (45cm) high

$40,000-60,000 **GORL**

A near pair of Chinese Kangxi period blue-and-white vases, painted with scholars on a terrace, with apocryphal Chenghua marks, one cracked and restored.

18.75in (47.5cm) high

$100,000-150,000 **CAN**

A Chinese Kangxi period blue-and-white vase, painted with an audience scene.

12.75in (32.5cm) high

$14,000-16,000 SWO

A Chinese Kangxi period blue-and-white bowl, painted with panels of figures, fish, flowers and landscape scenes, with chips.

12.25in (30cm) diam

$12,000-18,000 WW

A Chinese Kangxi period blue-and-white gu beaker vase, painted with figures in landscapes, the central section with two pomegranate-shaped panels of seal marks, with restoration.

18in (46cm) high

$20,000-30,000 WW

A Chinese Kangxi period blue-and-white bowl and cover, painted with figures in interiors and with a Buddhist shrine, the cover with eight boys playing in a garden, missing one metal handle.

c1700 8in (20.5cm) wide

$20,000-30,000 WW

A Chinese Kangxi period blue-and-white brush pot, painted with sages in a rocky river landscape.

6.25in (16cm) high

$20,000-30,000 DN

A Chinese Kangxi period blue-and-white brush pot, painted with antiques and precious objects, with a panel of sages in a landscape.

6in (15.5cm) high

$20,000-30,000 DN

One of a pair of Chinese Kangxi period blue-and-white saucers, painted with figures eating on riverboats, with six-character Kangxi marks.

6in (15.5cm) diam

$15,000-20,000 pair L&T

A Chinese Kangxi period blue-and-white plaque, painted with warriors and pagoda in a mountainous landscape, in a hardwood frame.

Plaque 8in (20cm) diam

$8,000-12,000 L&T

A Chinese Kangxi period blue-and-white jar and cover, painted with maidens and jardinières in a fenced garden, with Yu mark, the cover associated.

7in (18cm) high

$2,000-3,000 L&T

CLOSER LOOK

This high quality porcelain meiping has a slender tapering neck with high shoulders rising to the short slightly waisted neck.

Meipings were inspired by the shape of a young female body.

Such vases were meant to hold a single branch of plum tree blossoms.

The realistically painted decoration of fruits and flowers leaves most of the exquisite white porcelain on show.

Even though the vase has extensive damage such is its quality that it commands a strong price.

The high quality of the painting can be seen in the stiff leaves toward the foot.

A rare Chinese Qianlong period blue-and-white meiping vase, painted with fruits and flowers beneath a band of lappets, the foot with stiff leaves, with extensive damage.

12.75in (32.5cm) high

$90,000-120,000 WW

A Chinese Kangxi period monteith, painted with panels of flowering plants.

12.25in (32cm) diam

$8,000-12,000 LC

A pair of Chinese Kangxi period blue-and white molded dishes, painted with hunting scenes, with apocryphal six-character Chenghua mark.

8in (20cm) diam

$2,500-3,500 WW

A mid-18thC Chinese blue-and-white yen-yen vase, painted with stylized chrysanthemums, with minor damage.

18in (45.5cm) high

$12,000-18,000 SWO

A rare pair of Chinese Qianlong blue-and-white vases, painted with two dragons chasing flaming pearls amid clouds, the shoulders with the eight Buddhist Emblems, one with faint hairline crack.

7.75in (19.5cm) high

$120,000-180,000 WW

A Chinese Qianlong period blue-and-white stem bowl, painted with the eight Buddhist emblems above flowering lotus, with six-character Qianlong mark, with minor restoration.

4.5in (12cm) high

$4,000-6,000 SWO

A Chinese Qianlong period blue-and-white ewer and cover, painted with flowers and scrolling lotus vines, with Qianlong mark, with a fitted box.

8.25in (21cm) high

$70,000-100,000 LHA

A large Chinese Qianlong period blue-and-white 'lotus' bowl.

15.5in (39cm) diam

$3,500-4,500 **DN**

One of a pair of 18thC Chinese Ming-style blue-and-white bowls, painted with scrolling prunus, with apocryphal six-character Chenghua marks, with hardwood stands.

4in (10cm) diam

$15,000-20,000 pair **L&T**

Judith Picks

This is a particularly fine Qianlong meiping with classic Ming-style 'heaping and piling' decoration. It has been suggested that the iconography of this vase, which includes three five-clawed dragons and one three-clawed dragon, indicates that this vase was made in the third year of the reign of the emperor Qianlong (1735-96) out of reverence for his father. According to Chinese Imperial tradition, three years was the time in which Chinese emperors kept the ruling traditions of their predecessors alive.

The Qianlong emperor's reign has been termed one of China's golden ages, during which the economy expanded, and China was the wealthiest and most populous country in the world. Qianlong is known for his scholarship and patronage of the arts.

A Chinese Qianlong-period blue-and-white meiping vase, with three five-clawed dragons and one three-clawed dragon, with Qianlong mark.

13.5in (34.5cm) high

$3,500,000-4,500,000 **RTC**

A pair of 18thC Chinese Ming-style blue-and-white bowls, painted with scrolling prunus, with apocryphal six-character Chenghua marks, with hardwood stands.

4in (10cm) diam

$15,000-20,000 **L&T**

A 19thC Chinese blue-and-white meiping vase, painted with stylized lotus leaves and flowerheads, the foot with chrysanthemums.

12.75in (32.5cm) high

$15,000-20,000 **WW**

A Chinese Qianlong period blue-and-white moon flask, painted with a continuous lotus scroll above a band of lappets, the neck with stiff leaves beneath breaking waves.

12.75in (32.5cm) high

$40,000-60,000 **WW**

A 19thC Chinese blue-and-white fish bowl, painted with figures in a landscape.

14.5in (37cm) high

$2,500-3,500 **SWO**

A 19thC Chinese blue-and-white bowl, painted with a willow tree and a pavilion in a landscape.

10.5in (26.5cm) diam

$1,200-1,800 **L&T**

A 19thC Chinese Ming-style hu-form vase, painted with bands of scrolling foliage and lotus blossoms, with apocryphal Qianlong seal mark.

17in (43cm) high

$10,000-15,000 **L&T**

A Chinese late Qing/early Republic period blue-and-white figure of Guanyin, her robes decorated with blossoming foliage, with two impressed seal marks.

30in (76cm) high

$70,000-100,000 **DUK**

A pair of Chinese blue-and-white double-gourd vases, painted with prunus between rui heads, the foot with false gadroons.

c1870 *23.5in (60cm) high*

$14,000-16,000 **SWO**

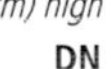

A 19thC Chinese blue-and-white jar and cover, painted with a riverside landscape, with metal collar and clasp.

23.25in (59cm) high

$6,500-7,500 **DN**

A 19thC Chinese blue-and-white vase, painted with a battle scene, with apocryphal six-character Qianlong seal mark.

15.4in (39cm) high

$5,000-7,000 **SWO**

A late 19thC Chinese Tongzhi period blue-and-white jar, painted with four ladies watching boys playing, with apocryphal Kangxi mark.

9in (23cm) high

$1,000-1,500 **DN**

A Chinese Guangxu period blue-and-white yuhuchunping (bottle vase), painted with bamboo and plantain amid rockwork, the neck with leaf-shaped lappets, with a hardwood stand.

11.5in (29cm) high

$50,000-70,000 **WW**

A pair of late 19thC Chinese vases, painted with panels of figures in a geometric ground, drilled.

18in (46cm) high

$6,500-7,500 **L&T**

A Chinese Kangxi period famille verte rouleau vase, painted with a battle scene.

17in (43cm) high

$20,000-30,000 **DN**

A Chinese early Kangxi period famille verte dish, painted with ladies in a terrace in front of a pavilion.

c1670 *13in (33.5cm) diam*

$3,500-4,500 **DN**

Two late 17thC Chinese famille verte fluted dishes, painted with panels of mythical and real beasts, with minor chips and wear.

Largest 9.5in (24.5cm) diam

$10,000-15,000 **SWO**

A pair of Chinese Kangxi period famille verte chargers, each painted with a phoenix above a kylin, with small chips.

A kylin is a mythical beast that resembles a dear with horns and scales. It is one of the 'Four Divine Creatures' and is an auspicious symbol.

15in (38.5cm) diam

$40,000-50,000 **WW**

A Chinese Kangxi period famille verte tankard, painted with flowering prunus beneath stylized peonies.

6.75in (17cm) high

$2,500-3,500 **LC**

A Chinese Kangxi period famille verte artemesia-form tile, painted with two maidens, in a damaged wood stand.

12.5in (32cm) wide

$6,500-7,500 **WW**

A pair of Chinese Kangxi period famille verte tea canisters, painted with figures in a walled garden with auspicious items.

11.5in (29cm) high

$6,500-7,500 **L&T**

A pair of Chinese famille verte dishes, painted with a large cicada and peony blooms.

c1710 *13in (33cm) wide*

$3,000-4,000 **WW**

A Chinese Kangxi period famille verte dish, painted with two ladies and a gentleman in a garden terrace.

15in (38cm) diam

$5,000-6,000 **DN**

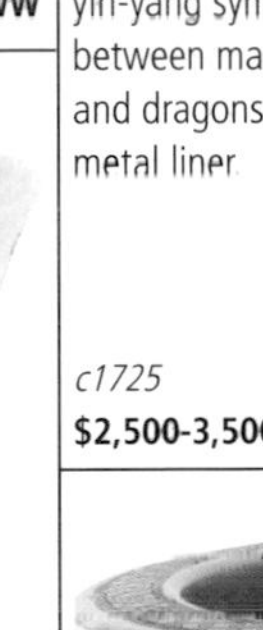

An unusual Chinese famille verte stand, painted with shou characters and yin-yang symbols between maidens and dragons, with a metal liner.

c1725 *7.75in (19.5cm) high*

$2,500-3,500 **WW**

A Chinese Jiaqing period famille verte wine cup, painted with magnolia and tree peony.

1.75in (4cm) high

$1,200-1,800 **WW**

A 19thC Chinese famille verte dish, painted with dignitaries and bannermen beneath a tree.

13.5in (34cm) diam

$1,200-1,800 **DN**

A Chinese yellow famille verte fish tank, painted with a battle scene, the interior with carp.

19in (48cm) diam

$12,000-18,000 **L&T**

A large 19thC Chinese famille verte rouleau vase, painted with a battle, some warriors riding mythical beasts.

23in (58.5cm) high

$1,500-2,500 **DN**

A 20thC Chinese famille verte vase, painted with a peacock, the reverse with deities and a bear below trees.

24in (61cm) high

$4,000-6,000 **MEA**

A Chinese famille rose vase and cover, painted with birds, insects, pheasants and flowers, with cracks and restoration.

c1730 *24in (61cm) high*

$8,000-12,000 **WW**

A Chinese Yongzheng period famille rose saucer dish, painted with a river scene with figures on boats and pagodas.

21.25in (54cm) diam

$4,500-5,500 **L&T**

A Chinese famille rose teapot and stand, painted with flower sprays.

c1730 *4.25in (11cm) high*

$2,500-3,500 **L&T**

A Chinese famille rose baluster vase and cover, painted with fruit and flowers in a fenced garden, with some restoration.

c1750 *21.75in (55cm) high*

$9,000-11,000 **WW**

A Chinese Qianlong period famille rose-verte brushpot, with three men in a pleasure boat traveling down a river.

7.25in (18.5cm) diam

$50,000-70,000 **LHA**

A Chinese famille rose snuff box, painted with birds, flowers and insects, the lid interior with pheasants, with gilt-metal mounts.

c1760 *2.75in (7cm) wide*

$4,000-6,000 **SWO**

ESSENTIAL REFERENCE - FAMILLE ROSE

The famille rose palette was developed during the Yongzheng period (1723-35) and virtually replaced the earlier famille verte palette.

- **Famille rose is comprised of predominantly rose-pink and purple shades, combined with green and yellow. The pink hue was developed from gold chloride, which had been introduced to China by Jesuit missionaries.**
- **The new colors were significantly more opaque than famille verte colors. This allowed the depiction of more complex images. Typical famille rose decoration includes panels of figures, landscapes and interior scenes, as well as motifs such as rockwork, branches, flowers and birds.**
- **Large quantities of famille rose ceramics were exported to the West in the 18thC and 19thC.**

A Chinese Qianlong period famille rose figural candlestick in the form of a female attendant, with a peacock to one side.

9.5in (24cm) high

$6,500-7,500 **FRE**

A pair of Chinese famille rose candlesticks in the form of ladies, with some restoration.

c1790 *11.5in (29.5cm) high*

$4,000-6,000 **WW**

A large rare Chinese Jiaqing period famille rose Baxian (Immortals) vase, painted with the eight Daoist Immortals, scholars and meiren in a landscape, with a river and bridge, across which Li Tieguai walks with his crutch, carrying his double gourd vase on his back, with restoration.

27.5in (69.5cm) high

$350,000-450,000 **WW**

A Chinese export Qianlong period famille rose lantern-form box and cover, painted with panels of geese in lotus groves and village scenes.

12in (30.5cm) high

$4,000-6,000 **FRE**

A Chinese Jiaqing period Imperial famille rose tripod incense burner, with the eight Buddhist emblems among lotus flower and scrolling foliage, with restoration.

10.5in (27cm) high

$40,000-60,000 **SWO**

A rare Chinese Daoguang period Imperial famille rose bottle vase, painted to simulate cloisonné with stylized flower heads, bats, shou characters and swastika motifs, with chips.

11.5in (29cm) high

$120,000-180,000 **WW**

A large Chinese Daoguang period famille rose 'phoenix' garlic-neck vase.

25in (63.5cm) high

$3,500-4,500 **DN**

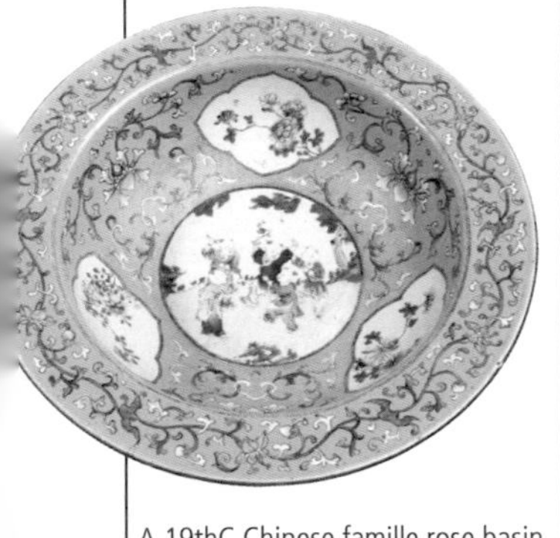

A 19thC Chinese famille rose basin, painted with five playing boys, cracked.

15.5in (39cm) diam

$12,000-18,000 **SWO**

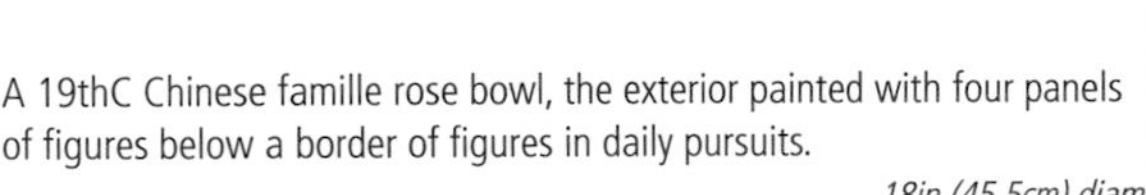

A 19thC Chinese famille rose bowl, the exterior painted with four panels of figures below a border of figures in daily pursuits.

18in (45.5cm) diam

$35,000-45,000 **WW**

A 19thC Chinese famille rose vase and cover, painted with grumpy pigeons on a rock between peony and bamboo, with minor frits.

29in (74cm) high

$15,000-20,000 **SWO**

A large pair of 19thC Chinese Canton famille rose vases, painted with dignitaries and warriors, with damage.

24.5in (62.5cm) high

$12,000-18,000 **WW**

A pair of late 19thC famille rose garden seats, painted with bands of butterflies, lotus, birds, fruit and precious objects.

18.25in (46.5cm) high

$10,000-15,000 **SWO**

A late 19thC famille rose goldfish bowl, painted with pendants hung from butterfly and lotus, the interior with red shibumkin, with wood stand.

With stand 31in (79cm) high

$10,000-15,000 **SWO**

A late 19thC Chinese Guangxu period famille rose bottle vase, painted with bats and clouds and a five-clawed dragon.

16in (41cm) high

$12,000-18,000 **L&T**

A Chinese famille rose vase, with scattered flowerheads on a cloud turquoise ground, with crack.

c1900 *15.5in (39cm) high*

$9,000-11,000 **SWO**

A 20thC Chinese famille rose vase and cover, painted with pink peonies with underglaze blue tendrils, with apocryphal Qianlong mark.

10.25in (26cm) high

$4,500-5,500 **SWO**

A Chinese famille rose vase, painted with flowers in vases and baskets, with stylized dragon handles.

c1930 *13.5in (34cm) high*

$4,000-6,000 **SWO**

A Chinese Kangxi period famille jaune dish, painted with a radiating design of stylized flowerheads, with small chips.

14.5in (36.5cm) diam

$4,500-5,500 **WW**

A late 19thC Chinese famille noire vase, painted with birds among prunus branches, rockwork, bamboo and flowers, with apocryphal Kangxi mark.

20in (53.5cm) high

$3,000-4,000 **DN**

A Chinese armorial plate, painted with the arms of Grant.

c1730 *8.75in (22.5cm) diam*

$4,500-5,500 **WW**

A Chinese Yongzheng period armorial dish, painted with the arms of Peers of Chislehampton Lodge, Oxfordshire, the border with the family griffin crest, with chip.

15.4in (39cm) diam

$4,000-6,000 **SWO**

A Chinese Yongzheng export armorial charger, painted with the arms of Hamilton quartering Douglas, Duke of Hamilton, above the motto 'Nemo Me Impune Lacessit', with crack.

c1733 *12.5in (32cm) wide*

$5,500-6,500 **SWO**

A mid-18thC Chinese armorial plate, painted with the arms of Yonge, vases and other auspicious objects in red and gilt.

c1740 *9in (23cm) diam*

$3,500-4,500 **WW**

Judith Picks

Provenance is all and a dash of Royalty helps too! The Lyon family are one of the oldest and most distinguished families in Scotland. The family name became Bowes-Lyon after the 9th Earl married wealthy heiress Mary Bowes in 1767. Elizabeth Bowes-Lyon was the wife of George VI and mother of Queen Elizabeth II. This service was gifted to the Royal couple at their wedding in 1923, but returned to Glamis Castle in 1952 at the death of George VI. The service at Glamis contains three sauceboats and it is possible that this is the only piece of that service not at Glamis Castle.

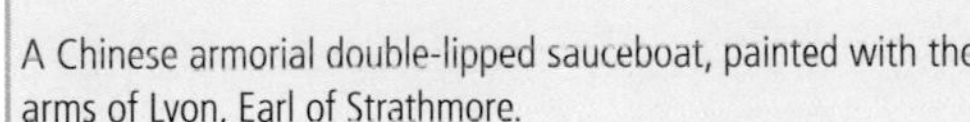

A Chinese armorial double-lipped sauceboat, painted with the arms of Lyon, Earl of Strathmore.

c1740 *7.5in (19.5cm) wide*

$3,500-4,500 **WW**

A Chinese armorial tankard, painted with the arms of Nassau quartering the Earl of Rochford impaling Young.

This mug was made for the 4th Earl of Rochford, Secretary to George II and Ambassador at the Courts of Madrid and Versailles.

c1745 *5.75in (14.5cm) high*

$4,000-6,000 **WW**

A Chinese armorial teapot and cover, painted with the arms of Hare.

The family of Hare descend from Sir Nicholas Hare, Speaker of the House of Commons during the reign of Queen Elizabeth I.

c1755 *8.25in (21cm) wide*

$2,500-3,500 **WW**

A Chinese armorial tea canister and cover, painted with the arms of Poley impaling Coffin, and with parrots perched on foliate scrolls.

c1755 *4.5in (12cm) high*

$5,000-7,000 **WW**

An extremely rare Chinese armorial plate, painted with the arms of Fitzroy, Duke of Grafton, above a scene of large exotic birds and a figure fishing from a small boat.

The 11th Duke of Grafton was unaware of the existence of this service and has found no record of it at Euston Hall, the family seat in Suffolk. No other pieces from this service are known.

c1755 *9in (22.5cm) diam*
$18,000-22,000 **WW**

A Chinese armorial plate, painted with the arms of Stones impaling Machell.

c1760 *8.5in (21.5cm) diam*
$650-850 **SWO**

A Chinese armorial coffee cup and saucer, painted with the arms of Lennox, Duke of Richmond and Lennox, with restoration.

c1760 *Saucer 4.5in (11.5cm) diam*
$3,000-4,000 **WW**

A Chinese armorial plate, painted with the arms of Stepney with Lloyd in pretence.

c1760 *9in (23cm) diam*
$2,500-3,500 **WW**

A Chinese armorial mug, painted with the arms of Phipps quartering Baron Mulgrave.

c1767 *5.25in (13.5cm) high*
$5,500-6,500 **WW**

A Chinese armorial quatrefoil dish, painted with the arms of Duff, Earl of Fife, the border with fruiting vine and small squirrels.

c1775 *5in (12.5cm) wide*
$1,500-2,500 **WW**

A Chinese armorial sauce tureen on stand, with crest and rampant lions.

c1780 *Tureen 6.5in (30.5cm) wide*
$5,000-7,000 **DRA**

A Chinese famille rose armorial ashet, painted with the arms of Johnstone impaling Stewart quartering Lorne (Appin Stewart), with crest and motto 'Nunquam Non Paratus'.

c1780 *11.5in (29cm) wide*
$1,500-2,500 **L&T**

A Chinese Shunzhi period Transitional doucai 'rolwagen' vase, painted with an unusual scene of two mothers and children playing among rocks.

10in (25.5cm) high

$10,000-15,000 **SWO**

A rare Chinese Kangxi period doucai longevity dish, painted with a crane inside a peach over a shou character, surrounded by scrolling ruyi-head emblems, with hairline cracks.

8.5in (21cm) diam

$25,000-35,000 **WW**

A rare Chinese Yongzheng period Imperial doucai stem bowl, painted with the eight Buddhist emblems, with Yongzheng mark, with chip and hairline crack.

It is rare to find a stem bowl painted in the doucai color scheme.

c1730 *6.25in (16cm) diam*

$300,000-400,000 **CAN**

A Chinese Wanli period wucai vase, painted in red, green and black with a stylized design of flowers growing from rockwork.

9in (23cm) high

$50,000-70,000 **WW**

ESSENTIAL REFERENCE - 'CHICKEN' CUP

- **The 'Chicken' cup design is a classic associated with Imperial porcelain.**
- **It was originally conceived during the Ming Dynasty, during the reign of the Chenghua Emperor (1465-1487).**
- **The design's popularity was revived during the early Qing Dynasty, as the Yongzheng and Qianlong Emperors revered the Chenghua prototypes.**
- **The combination of the chicken (gongji) and cockscomb plant (jigusanhua) is a pun for 'May you continuously rise in rank' (guanshang jiaguan). The second character (guwan) in the name of the flower is a pun for 'official'.**
- **The cockerel also bears a cockscomb, yet another pun for 'official'.**

A rare Chinese Yongzheng period doucai 'Chicken' cup, painted with a cockerel, hen and five chicks and plants to one side, the reverse with rocky outcrop, with apocryphal six-character Chenghua mark.

3.5in (9cm) diam

$350,000-450,000 **CAN**

A mid-19thC Chinese doucai vase, painted with peaches, flowers, bats and precious objects.

14.75in (37.5cm) high

$3,000-4,000 **SWO**

A Chinese Wanli period wucai box and cover, painted with dragons among cloud scrolls.

5.25in (13.5cm) long

$2,500-3,500 **L&T**

A Chinese Shunzhi period wucai jar, painted with two panels of dignitaries and attendants.

11.75in (29.5cm) high

$12,000-18,000 **SWO**

Kangxi Bowl

A rare Chinese Kangxi period Imperial wucai 'Pheasant' bowl, painted with a pair of pheasants among flowers and foliage issuing from rockwork.

It is rare to find a Kangxi bowl of this design incorporating underglaze blue and copper-red within the wucai palette. A very similar bowl of Kangxi mark and period from the Qing court collection is in the Palace Museum, Beijing.

6in (15.5cm) diam

$400,000-600,000 **CAN**

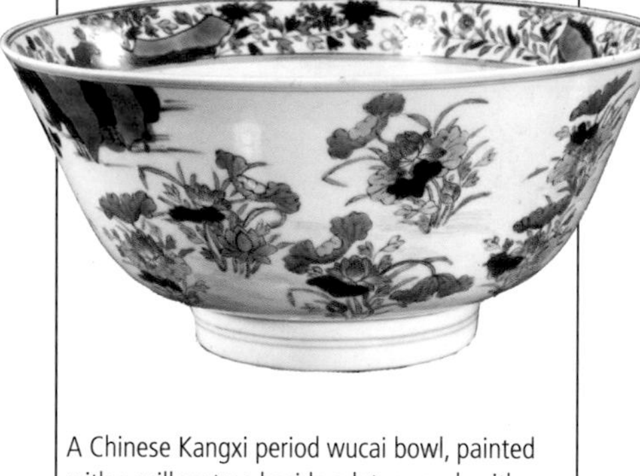

A Chinese Kangxi period wucai bowl, painted with a willow tree beside a lotus pond, with apocryphal Xuande mark, with small chip.

8.25in (20.5cm) diam

$8,000-12,000 **WW**

A 19thC Chinese wucai vase and cover.

24.75in (63cm) high

$2,000-3,000 **SWO**

A Chinese Koi-Imari plate.

c1700 *12.25in (31cm) diam*

$1,000-1,500 **KAU**

A pair of early 18thC Chinese Imari tea caddies and covers, with unmarked English silver covers.

5in (13.5cm) high

$1,000-1,500 **DN**

A mid-18thC Chinese Imari bowl, with mid-19thC ormolu mount.

Bowl c1740 *10in (26.5cm) diam*

$1,200-1,800 **SWO**

A pair of 19thC Chinese Imari vases, painted with panels of Geisha.

38.5in (98cm) high

$1,000-1,500 **A&G**

A pair of Chinese Qianlong period Imperial coral-ground bowls, painted with bamboo stems and leaves.

4.5in (11.5cm) diam

$150,000-200,000 **WW**

A pair of Chinese Qianlong period Imperial blue and yellow 'Dragon' bowls, painted with two five-clawed dragons chasing flaming pearls, the interiors with central dragon medallions.

4in (10.5cm) diam

$120,000-180,000 **CAN**

A Chinese Daoguang period Ming-style Imperial 'Dragon' dish, painted with a five-clawed dragon amid crashing waves.

7in (17.5cm) diam

$35,000-45,000 **CAN**

A 16thC Chinese Jiajing period 'Heavenly Horse' jar, with double-ring six-character Jiajing mark, with wood cover and stand.

Jar 8.5in (21.5cm) high

$40,000-60,000 **SK**

ESSENTIAL REFERENCE - DRAGON CHASING PEARL

Dragons are a popular motif in Chinese art as they are viewed as blessed and benevolent animals. They can symbolize cosmic energy, high rank, power and good fortune. A five-clawed dragon represents the emperor.

- **The pearl is symbolic of wisdom, rebirth and qi, the creator of all energy and life.**
- **A dragon shown chasing a flaming pearl is thus usually symbolic of the quest for perfection and enlightenment, particularly if the dragon represents the emperor. The pearl can also represent the moon, with the dragon disgorging or devouring it as the moon waxes and wanes.**

A pair of Chinese export models of cows.

c1750 *8in (20.5cm) wide*

$12,000-18,000 **DRA**

A Chinese Kangxi period dish, painted with two five-clawed dragons chasing a flaming pearl, the exterior with four further dragons.

15in (38cm) diam

$40,000-60,000 **DRA**

An 18thC Chinese Qianlong period flask, painted with a leaping dragon encircling a flaming pearl, with stylized crested waves, with restoration.

16in (40.5cm) high

$250,000-350,000 **SK**

A 19thC Chinese Daoguang period vase, painted with five dragons among clouds.

15.5in (39.5cm) high

$12,000-18,000 **SK**

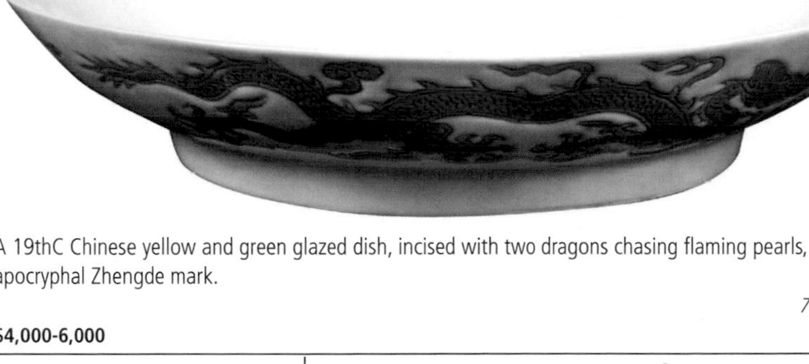

A 19thC Chinese yellow and green glazed dish, incised with two dragons chasing flaming pearls, with apocryphal Zhengde mark.

7.5in (19cm) diam

$4,000-6,000 **DN**

A pair of 19thC Chinese vases, painted with a jardiniere of flowers on a rock, precious objects and peony, with apocryphal Xuande mark.

17.25in (44cm) high

$12,000-18,000 **SWO**

A 19thC Chinese pair of cockerels, with restoration.

15.5in (39.5cm) high

$4,500-5,500 **SWO**

A 19thC Chinese archaic-style vase, with low-relief decoration of bands of linghzi and rising leaves, the handles made to resemble bronze and 'hung' with auspicious symbols, with apocryphal Qianlong seal mark.

12.25in (31cm) high

$12,000-18,000 **L&T**

A late 19thC Chinese vase, painted with panels of ladies in a garden, deer, a crane, precious objects and landscapes, with apocryphal Qianlong mark, drilled.

24in (61cm) high

$4,500-5,500 **SWO**

A pair of late 19thC Chinese millefleurs vases, with apocryphal Qianlong mark.

10.25in (26cm) high

$8,000-12,000 **L&T**

Republic Period

A Chinese Republic period eggshell vase, painted with a soldier on horseback returning from the spring hunt, with apocryphal Qianlong mark.

The period between the Xinhai Revolution (which saw the end of the Qing dynasty) and the War Lord Era is known as the Chinese Republic period (1914-16). Good quality wares from this relatively recent period continue to rise in value, with many pieces proving more valuable than lesser-quality late 19thC pieces.

7.25in (18.5cm) high

$15,000-20,000 **L&T**

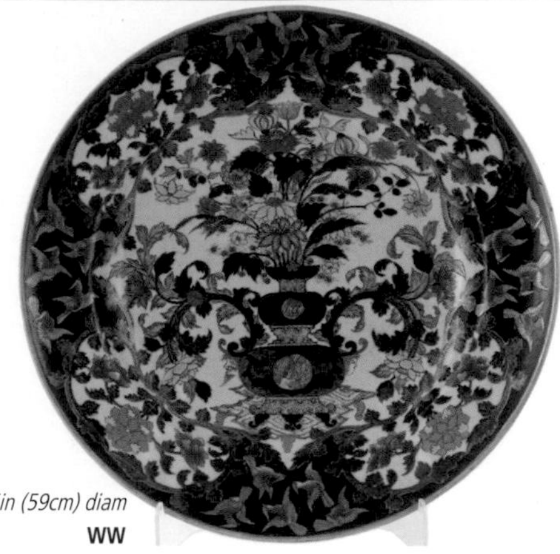

A large Japanese Imari dish, painted with a central vase, flowers and foliage, the border with panels of birds in flight.

c1700 *23.25in (59cm) diam*

$6,500-7,500 **WW**

A large 18thC Japanese Imari dish, painted with a vase issuing flowers, the reverse with further flowers and a six-character mark.

The characters on the back of Japanese Imari were often copies of Chinese marks. This practice was possibly adopted to make such pieces more saleable in Europe during the period when Chinese porcelain exports ceased as a result of the fall of the Ming dynasty in 1644.

$5,500-6,500 **RGA**

A large 18thC Japanese Imari vase and cover, painted with landscape and figural reserves, with some damage.

21.5in (54.5cm) high

$2,000-3,000 **GORL**

A pair of 19thC Japanese Imari bottle vases, with gilt decoration of dragons.

24in (61cm) high

$3,500-4,500 **LHA**

A pair of large Japanese Meiji period Imari vases, painted with phoenix and dragon mon and with fan-shaped reserves, with four-character marks.

22.5in (57cm) high

$2,000-3,000 **GORL**

A 19thC Japanese Imari vase and cover.

15.75in (40cm) high

$1,000-1,500 **KAU**

A 19thC Japanese Imari barber's bowl.

11in (28cm) diam

$350-450 **WW**

A near pair of 19thC Japanese Imari vases and covers.

13.5in (34.5cm) high

$650-850 **KAU**

A pair of Japanese Meiji period Imari vases, by the Fukugawa family, with iron-red four character mark, one damaged.

The Fukugawa family produced porcelain in the Arita region from the 17thC. Following the collapse of the feudal system and the subsequent economic recession, the family decided to concentrate on export porcelain that combined traditional Japanese designs with Western stylistic elements.

14.5in (36.5cm) high

$550-750 **GORL**

A Japanese Imari dish, painted with hydra, within a brocade-pattern paneled border, with apocryphal Ming mark.

c1900 *15in (36cm) diam*

$500-700 **DN**

A miniature Japanese Satsuma vase, by Shizan, painted and gilt with a band of children at play, one with a flag bearing the artist's signature.

c1880 *2in (5cm) high*

$1,500-2,000 **SWO**

A Japanese Satsuma vase, painted with figures in a garden, the shoulders with complex diaper, with gilt Shimazu mon and Suizan mark.

c1880 *4.5in (11.5cm) high*

$650-850 **SWO**

A pair of miniature Japanese Satsuma vases, painted with figures, fish and a hare, both signed 'Mizan' in gilt.

c1880 *3in (7.5cm) high*

$4,500-5,500 **WW**

A Japanese Meiji period Satsuma bowl, painted with figures and pavilions, with a 'thousand flower' border, the exterior decorated with a river landscape and trailing wisteria.

11.75in (30cm) diam

$4,500-5,500 **GORL**

A Japanese Meiji period Satsuma koro and cover, painted with overlapping fan-shaped reserves of figures practicing the various arts and traditions of Japan, with damage.

4.75in (12cm) high

$10,000-15,000 **GORL**

A Japanese Satsuma vase, by Kinkozan, painted and gilt with a flying eagle and kingfisher above a river, the reverse with geese, with impressed and gilt 'Kinkozan zo'.

c1890 *8.25in (21cm) high*

$3,000-4,000 **SWO**

A Japanese Satsuma koro and cover, painted with figures and plants, signed 'Tomoyama' and with seal mark.

c1890 *4in (10cm) high*

$3,000-4,000 **SWO**

A late 19thC Japanese Satsuma tea jar and cover, by Kinkozan, painted with women and children to obverse, the reverse with a lake scene, signed by the artist 'Konen'.

3.75in (9.5cm) high

$5,500-6,500 **RGA**

A Japanese Satsuma bowl, painted with a female figure surrounded by groups of figures, signed 'Seikozan'.

2.5in (6cm) high

$8,000-12,000 **RGA**

A Japanese Satsuma vase, painted with figures, flowers and a magical gourd with fruits, with gilt signature for 'Ryozan', with restoration.

c1900 *9.5in (24cm) high*

$1,200-1,800 **WW**

A Japanese Satsuma vase, by Shoko Takebe for Thomas B. Blow, painted with a parade of figures, with small crack.

c1900 *5in (12.5cm) high*

$2,500-3,500 **SWO**

A large Japanese Satsuma koro and cover, with a lion-dog knop, with some restoration.

A koro is a Japanese censer often used in tea ceremonies.

c1900 *19.25in (49cm) high*

$650-850 **WW**

A Japanese Satsuma vase, by Kinkozan, painted with flowers overflowing from a gilded basket, with impressed mark, with some rim wear.

c1900 *7in (18cm) high*

$2,500-3,500 **WW**

A pair of Japanese Satsuma vases, by Kinkozan, painted with panels of figures, signed 'Sozan', 'Okahashi' and 'Fuzan (?)'.

c1900 *14in (36cm) high*

$8,000-12,000 **WW**

CLOSER LOOK - SATSUMA DISH

Satsuma ware can vary tremendously in quality.

This large plate has high quality painting of many different scenes and figures.

It features many children's pastimes, including playing cards, a miniature theatre, modeling clay, dressing up and as 'sleeping lions'.

A known and respected artist and studio is likely to increase value. Kinkozan Sobei VI (1824-84) is credited with being the first to export Satsuma wares, which he did from 1872.

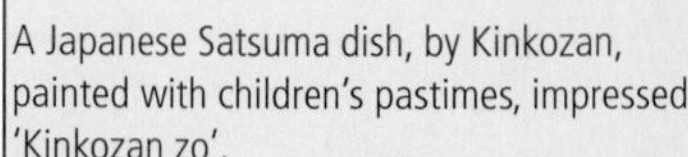

A Japanese Satsuma dish, by Kinkozan, painted with children's pastimes, impressed 'Kinkozan zo'.

c1900 *15in (37cm) diam*

$6,500-7,500 **SWO**

A 17thC Japanese Arita charger, painted in cobalt-blue under a thick glassy glaze with a central vase of three peony sprays on a platform.

22in (56cm) diam

$15,000-20,000 **RGA**

ESSENTIAL REFERENCE - NABESHIMA

Nabeshima ware was made at Okawachi near Arita in Kyūshū under the authority of the Nabeshima clan. It is arguably the most refined kind of pre-19thC Japanese porcelain.

- **Breaking from the tradition of Chinese-inspired ceramics, Nabeshima ware was decorated with striking Japanese motifs against empty space. The resulting designs were often reminiscent of late 17th/18thC textiles.**
- **Popular themes include seasonal flowers or wintry trees.**
- **The most common ceramic shapes were food dishes, usually produced in sets of five.**
- **The foot rims of Nabeshima ceramics are usually decorated in underglaze blue with a comb-tooth pattern (kusitakade).**
- **Very few examples were exported.**

A late 18thC Japanese Nabeshima dish, painted with fruiting branches, on a comb-tooth foot.

7.25in (18cm) diam

$4,000-6,000 **WW**

A Japanese Arita coffee pot, painted with five of the Seven Gods of Good Fortune, the neck with hares, with restoration and crack.

c1700 *17.5in (44.5cm) high*

$2,500-3,500 **SWO**

A Japanese Arita dish, painted with dragons enclosing a cockerel and ho-oh, with fuku mark, with restoration, with 19thC gilt-metal mounts.

c1720 *5in (15cm) wide*

$1,200-1,800 **SWO**

A small 18thC Japanese Arita vase, modeled as a leaping carp.

4.5in (11cm) high

$1,200-1,800 **WW**

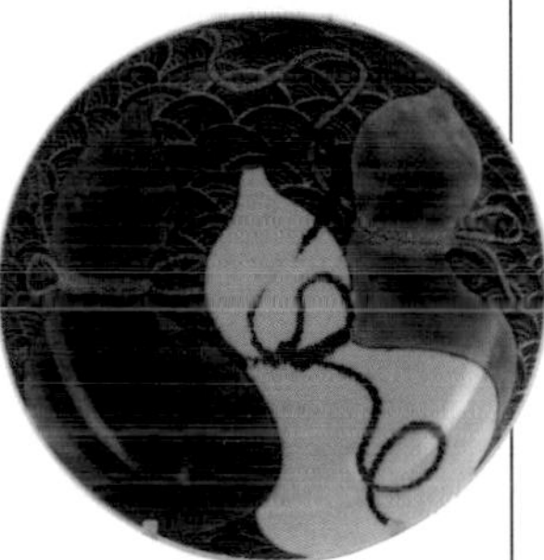

A 19thC Japanese Nabeshima dish, painted with tied bottle gourds on a ground of waves, on a high comb-tooth foot.

7in (17.5cm) diam

$1,000-1,500 **WW**

A 19thC Japanese Nabeshima dish, painted in blue on a celadon ground with three peaches, with a comb-tooth foot.

8in (20cm) diam

$2,000-3,000 **DN**

A 19thC Japanese Nabeshima dish, painted with irises against a mi-parti ground of stylized waves.

8in (20cm) diam

$2,000-3,000 **DN**

A pair of Japanese Kutani vases and covers, by Zoshuntei Sanpo, signed in red 'Zoshuntei Sampo (sic) sei', with restoration, with wood stands.

c1880 15in (35cm) high

$800-1,200 SWO

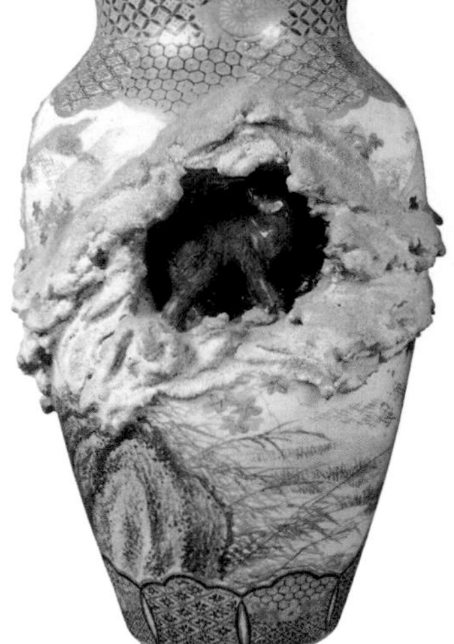

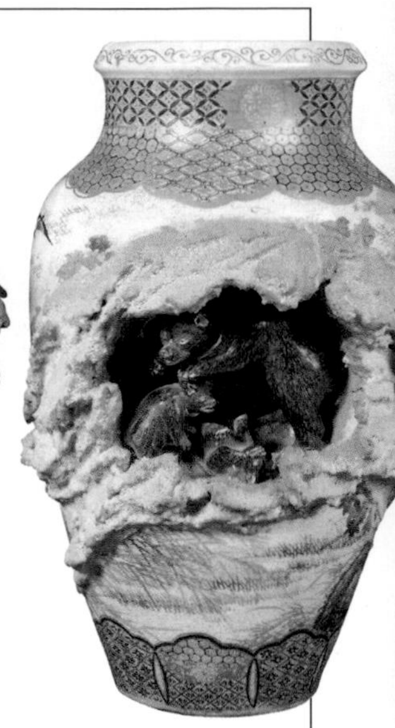

A pair of Japanese earthenware vases, modeled with inverted cave scenes of bears with cubs.

c1900 12.5in (32cm) high

$15,000-20,000 DN

A Japanese Kakiemon saucer dish.

c1700 5.75in (14.5cm) diam

$650-850 WW

A Japanese Kakiemon vase, painted with peony and prunus issuing from rockwork, with restored crack.

c1700 10.5in (26.5cm) high

$3,500-4,500 WW

A Japanese Nanban Vase, depicting seven Dutch gentlemen.

c1800 12in (30.5cm) high

$4,000-6,000 SK

A Japanese gourd dish, painted with aubergine, fish roe and buildings on a promontory, with ken mark.

10.5in (27cm) wide

$300-500 SWO

ESSENTIAL REFERENCE - HIRADO

Some of the earliest Japanese blue-and-white porcelain was produced on the island of Hirado, near Arita, from the early 17thC. The most characteristic pieces were made at the Mikawachi kilns from c1760.

- **Hirado porcelain was made from a very pure, white clay found on the island of Amakusa. The purity of the clay allowed for intricate modeling. The glaze had a soft, bluish hue.**
- **Popular decorative themes include children at play or mountainous landscapes. Birds and plants were also used.**

A Japanese Hirado jar and cover, painted with Immortals beside rocks under a pine tree, signed 'Dai Nihon Mikawachi sei'.

c1890 7.75in (19.5cm) high

$800-1,200 SWO

A 17thC Japanese dish, painted with two dragons chasing a flaming pearl among clouds and waves, with apocryphal Ming marks.

14in (35.5cm) diam

$2,500-3,500 SK

A late 19thC Japanese Seto celadon umbrella stand, painted with a shrike grabbing a frog, with six-character mark possibly for Denkichi.

23.5in (60cm) high

$650-850 SWO

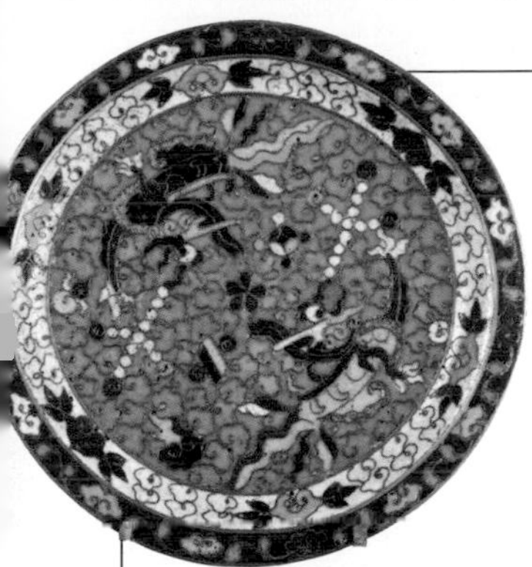

A 16th/17thC Chinese Ming dynasty cloisonné dish, decorated with two dragons, fruits and flowers.

5in (13cm) diam

$6,500-7,500 **DN**

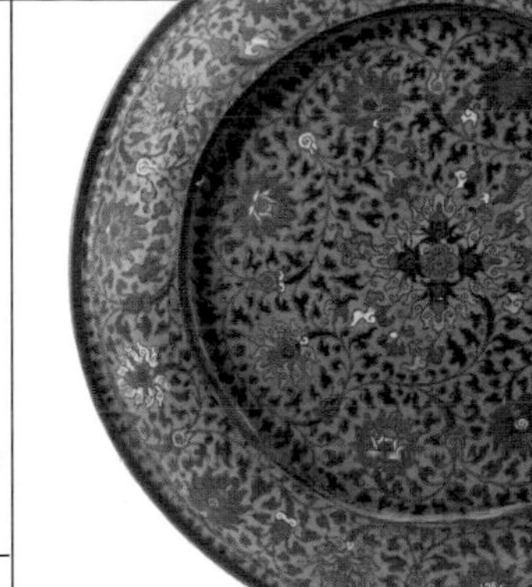

A 17thC Chinese cloisonné dish, decorated with a large dragon and phoenix contesting a flaming pearl among cloud scrolls, with a tall flared foot.

The dragon and the phoenix together represent happy omens and are considered to be the most auspicious of the mythical animals. They represent good fortune and blessings for the emperor and empress. This message is emphasized by the clouds, which symbolize the granting of all wishes.

21in (53cm) diam

$70,000-90,000 **WW**

A Chinese Qianlong period cloisonné tripod censer and cover, decorated with scrolling foliage beneath a band of ruyi heads, with some wear.

4.25in (11cm) high

$70,000-90,000 **WW**

A Chinese Qianlong period cloisonné vase, decorated with six lotus flower heads among scrolling foliage, with some wear.

5.75in (15cm) high

$15,000-20,000 **WW**

An 18thC Chinese cloisonné tripod censer and cover, decorated with stylized lotus, with gilt dragon handles, with some restoration.

11.25in (28.5cm) high

$20,000-30,000 **WW**

An 18thC Chinese ormolu and cloisonné box and cover, decorated with a cricket and two quail.

2.25in (5.5cm) high

$20,000-30,000 **WW**

A pair of Chinese Qing dynasty cloisonné gu-form vases.

13in (33cm) high

$25,000-35,000 **L&T**

A large 18thC Chinese cloisonné dragon censer and cover, decorated with dragons divided by shou characters.

21.3in (54cm) high

$20,000-30,000 **WW**

Judith Picks

Elephants have special significance to the Imperial court. Elephants carrying vases on their backs were part of a procession to celebrate the Qianlong Emperor's birthday. The Qing rulers commissioned elephants to be made in jade and cloisonné and pairs of these models flanked the Imperial thrones (see p.149 for more on throne room groups). This particularly large example of a cloisonné elephant is of exceptional quality and rarity. The decoration is extremely detailed. It is overall decorated with flower scrolls and the ormolu saddle has panels of scaly dragons contesting flaming pearls.

A rare Chinese Qianlong period cloisonné model of a caparisoned elephant, the saddle surmounted by a covered vase and decorated with dragons contesting flaming pearls.

14.5in (37cm) high

$120,000-180,000 **WW**

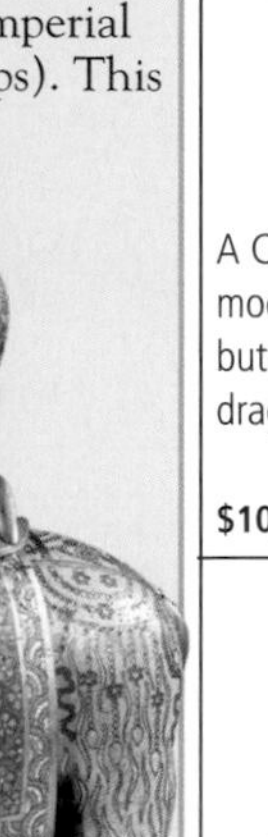

A Chinese Jiaqing period cloisonné moon flask, decorated with butterflies and flowers, with ormolu dragon handles.

11.75in (30cm) high

$10,000-15,000 **DN**

One of a pair of 19thC Chinese cloisonné censors, the covers decorated with lotuses and a band of chilong dragons, the finials with double-lotus bases and pierced with a dragon among clouds, the interiors with removable bowls.

25.25in (64cm) high

$20,000-30,000 pair **SK**

A 19thC Chinese cloisonné fish vase, the face decorated with scrolling lotus flowers and jewels, with 'Da Qing Qianlong Nian Zhi' mark.

9in (23cm) high

$18,000-22,000 **SK**

A 19thC Chinese cloisonné tripod censer and cover.

6.75in (17cm) high

$30,000-40,000 **WW**

A large 19thC Chinese cloisonné panel.

28in (71cm) high

$50,000-70,000 **WW**

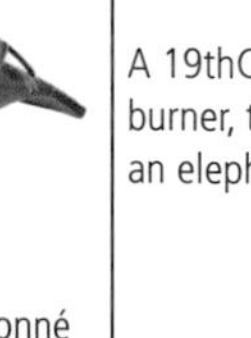

A pair of 19thC Chinese cloisonné birds.

6in (15cm) high

$2,500-3,500 **L&T**

A 19thC cloisonné incense burner, the cover surmounted by an elephant and cloud knop.

9.5in (24cm) high

$4,000-6,000 **SWO**

A 19thC Chinese cloisonné crane.

As cranes have a comparatively long life span for a bird, they are associated with longevity, immortality and wisdom in China.

28in (72cm) high

$8,000-12,000 **DN**

A Chinese export silver bowl, Tuck Chang, Shanghai.

c1870 *4.75in (12cm) diam 5.4oz*

$1,500-2,500 **L&T**

A Chinese export silver card case, Wang Hing, Hong Kong, decorated with repousse foliage, marked 'WH' and '90'.

c1880 *3in (8cm) high 1.83oz*

$1,000-1,500 **L&T**

A Chinese export silver mug, Kwan Wo, Canton, engraved with dragons, marked 'KW'.

c1890 *2.5in (6.5cm) high 2.1oz*

$350-450 **L&T**

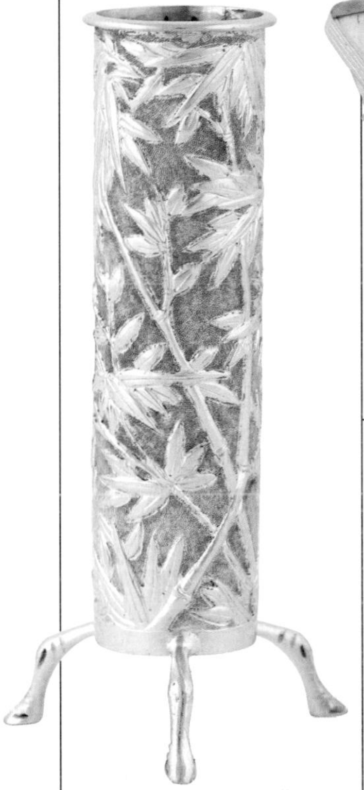

A Chinese export silver rickshaw condiment set, Wang Hing, Hong Kong.

c1895 *8in (20cm) long 7.5oz*

$800-1,200 **L&T**

A Chinese export silver tea canister, Kan Mao Hsing, Jiujang, chased with foliage and dragons.

c1895 *4.25in (11cm) high 5oz*

$3,500-4,500 **L&T**

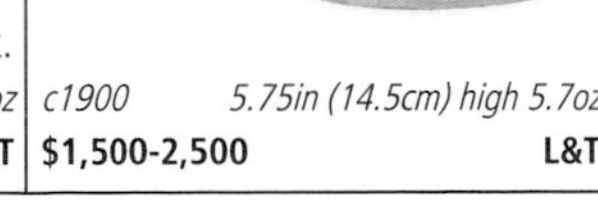

A Chinese export silver spill vase, Wang Hing, Hong Kong, marked 'WH', '90' and with character mark.

c1890 *4.25in (11cm) high 1.5oz*

$500-700 **L&T**

A Chinese export silver table bell, Wang Hing, Hong Kong, the handle decorated with prunus blossom, marked 'WH' and '90'.

c1900 *5.75in (14.5cm) high 5.7oz*

$1,500-2,500 **L&T**

A large silver presentation bowl, Wang Hing, Hong Kong, inscribed 'presented to the Hon Mr Edward Osborne by Mr Wong Kam Fuk and the Chinese staff of the Hong Kong and Kowloon Wharf and Godown Coy Ld on his retirement 1913'.

c1900 *12.5in (31.5cm) diam*

$35,000-45,000 **SWO**

A Chinese export silver three-piece tea set, Gan Mao Xing, with chased panels of foliage, dragons and figures.

c1900 *Teapot 6.75in (17cm) high 31oz*

$4,500-5,500 **L&T**

A late 19thC Japanese patinated-bronze and ivory group of two tigers attacking an elephant, with ivory tusks.

28in (71cm) high

$3,000-4,000 **FRE**

A Japanese Meiji period bronze group of two tigers attacking an elephant, Genryusai Seiya, one tusk broken.

17in (43.5cm) high

$2,500-3,500 **SWO**

An early 20thC Japanese bronze elephant lamp base.

15.5in (39.5cm) long

$2,000-3,000 **DN**

A Japanese Meiji period bronze model of a lion, the eyes inlaid in glass, signed 'Koku Saku'.

17in (43cm) long

$2,500-3,500 **DN**

A Japanese Meiji period bronze group of an eagle pinning a crane to the ground.

1868-1912

30in (76cm) wide

$4,000-6,000 **WW**

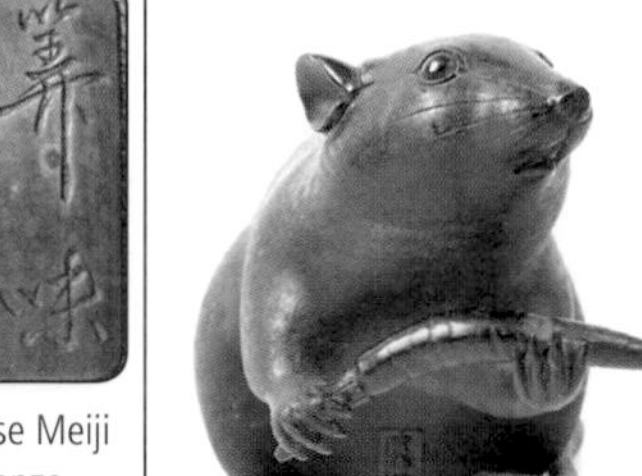

A Japanese bronze model of a rat, holding a pepper in its paws, marked 'Saneyoshi chu'.

c1890 *4.25in (11cm) high*

$1,200-1,800 **SWO**

A late 19thC Japanese bronze figure of Hotei.

8.25in (21cm) high

$1,500-2,500 **SWO**

A Japanese Meiji period bronze figure of a warrior, possibly Tokugawa Ieyasu, signed 'Miyao' with seal, with original stand.

14.5in (37cm) high

$25,000-35,000 **DN**

A mid-19thC gold-splashed bronze incense burner, in the form of a peach, with small crack.

9.5in (24cm) wide

$3,500-4,500 **SWO**

A 19thC Japanese bronze, gold and shakudo urn, decorated with two phoenix and scrolling lotus in a roundel, above a taotie mask with inlaid gold eyes, the dragon handles inlaid with gold.

Shakudo is an alloy of copper, invented by the Japanese, which is very dark blue, almost black, in color.

29.75in (75.5cm) high

$50,000-70,000 **SK**

A Japanese bronze vase, inlaid in silver and shakudo with an iris on the coppery ground, chased 'Ichiyosai Atsuhiro Koku'.

c1900 *4.5in (11.5cm) high*

$2,500-3,500 **SWO**

A late 19thC bronze vase, inlaid in copper, gold, silver and shakudo with swallows flying through sycamore, the neck chased with dragons.

7in (18cm) high

$5,500-6,500 **SWO**

A Komai miniature chest of drawers, decorated in gold and silver with ho-ho, butterflies and cranes, the sides decorated with Fujiyama and buildings, marked in gilt 'Nihon kuni Tokyo ju Komai sei'.

c1880 *4.25in (11cm) high*

$5,500-6,500 **SWO**

A Komai iron koro and cover, inlaid in gold and silver with panels of country scenes, with unusual mark in grass-script-like seal characters 'Kyoto Komai sei tsukuru', with minor wear.

c1880 *6.5in (16.5cm) high*

$6,500-7,500 **SWO**

ESSENTIAL REFERENCE - KOMAI WARE

In the mid-19thC the Komai family invented a form of damascening that is now named after them. Damascening is a technique in which silver, gold or copper wire is inlaid into a pattern of fine grooves and hammered flush with the surface. Komai ware typically had a base of iron or steel.

- **The Komai technique was originally designed to ornament swords. The family held the office of sword-mounters to the Japanese court for over seven years.**
- **Following the Meiji restoration in 1868, samurai were no longer allowed to openly wear swords, so the Komai family began to decorate other luxury objects, such as cigarette cases, pins and bracelets.**

A late 19thC Japanese copper box, inlaid in gold, silver and copper, signed and stamped 'Koma'.

4.75in (12cm) high

$1,000-1,500 **SWO**

A Japanese Meiji period Komai koro, decorated with a bird on a blossoming tree, signed in gold.

4.25in (11cm) high

$5,000-7,000 **L&T**

A Japanese silver and shibayama jar and cover, the ivory body set with doves amongst wisteria, with enameled silver mounts, signed 'Masakazu'.

c1880 *6.75in (17cm) high*

$3,500-4,500 **SWO**

A Japanese Meiji period silver and enamel koro, decorated with roundels depicting flowers and butterflies, with two character mark.

4.75in (12cm) high

$4,500-5,500 **L&T**

A 1930s Japanese silver cigarette case, inlaid in copper and niello with a yori-i lighthouses, buildings and boats, stamped 'Pagoda' and 'sterling', in fitted case.

6.25in (16cm) high

$350-450 **SWO**

A Japanese Meiji period cloisonné vase, with mark of Gonda Hirosuke Studio.

12in (30.5cm) high

$4,000-6,000 **L&T**

A silver and cloisonné box, Namikawa Yasuyuki (1845-1927).

5.5in (14cm) wide

$14,000-16,000 **L&T**

A Japanese cloisonné vase and cover, decorated with birds among wisteria, with some damage.

c1890 *4in (10cm) high*

$2,000-3,000 **SWO**

A Japanese cloisonné tray, attributed to Namikawa Sosuke (1847-1910).

11.5in (29cm) diam

$5,500-6,500 **LHA**

A Japanese Meiji period silver and cloisonné tea set, decorated with blossoming branches, signed.

Teapot 6.75in (17cm) high

$9,000-11,000 **L&T**

Totai Jippo

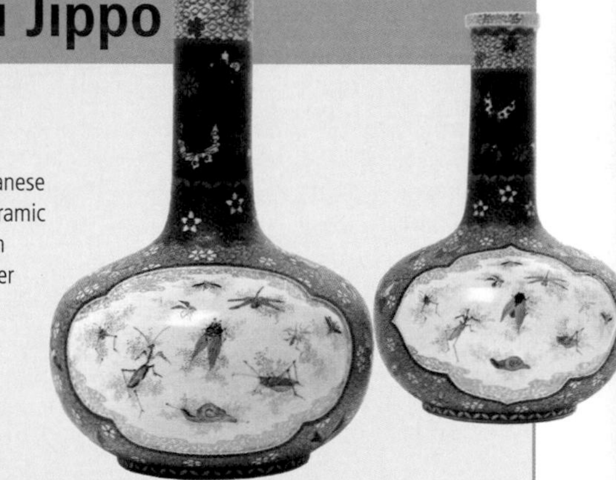

A pair of Japanese totai jippo ceramic vases, with an eight-character mark.

Tsukamoto Kaisuke introduced the technique of jiki shippo (literally porcelain-enamel) more commonly known as totai jippo (which includes all ceramics). This is a type of Japanese cloisonné whereby wires are applied to a ceramic body, rather than a metal one. The cloisonné cells are then filled with powdered enamel and fired.

$3,500-4,500 **LHA**

A pair of Japanese ginbari vases, decorated with pine and bamboo on a nanako ground, inscribed 'Nagoya Hayashi saku'.

Ginbari designs look like cloisonné, but the outside of the cells are not wire, they are the raised edges of embossed foil.

5in (12.5cm) high

$1,500-2,500 **DN**

A Japanese Meiji period Hayashi Tangaro enameled vase, stamped on base.

18in (45.5cm) high

$4,000-6,000 **DOY**

An 18thC armorer's oxidized-iron inro, in the form of a bag embroidered with a dragon, the cover in the form of an oni face, the ojime as a Buddhist pearl gripped by the oni's hand.

3.5in (9cm) high

$1,000-1,500 **SWO**

An 18thC Tibetan ormolu figure of White Tara, with painted detail, with monastery mark to base.

10in (26cm) high

$250,000-350,000 **KAU**

A 17thC Tibetan bronze figure of a seated monk, his hands in vitarka and bhumisparsa mudra, his eyes inlaid with silver.

6.75in (17cm) high

$35,000-45,000 **WW**

An 18thC Sino-Tibetan bronze figure of White Tara, seated in dhayanasana on a double-lotus throne.

7in (18cm) high

$25,000-35,000 **DN**

A 19thC Tibetan ormolu and emerald figure of Yuganaddha Hayagriva, Lhasa , on a lotus throne, with painted detail, set with 36 emeralds.

23in (58cm) high

$12,000-18,000 **KAU**

An early 20thC Tibetan ormolu eight-armed bodhisattva, on a lotus throne, with painted detail.

16in (41cm) high

$5,500-6,500 **KAU**

A 17thC Ottoman Tombac censer, with tulip decorated base.

12.75in (32.5cm) high

$6,000-8,000 **GORL**

An 18thC Turkish Tombac censer, on an engraved floral tray.

5.75in (14.5cm) high

$10,000-15,000 **GORL**

A Persian silver damascened steel ewer.

13in (33cm) high

$12,000-18,000 **L&T**

An early 17thC Persian Safavid tinned-copper bowl, decorated with foliate and animal motifs, with three owners' marks.

15in (38cm) diam

$5,500-6,500 **GORL**

An early 17thC Chinese ivory carving of a young girl, playing the shen.

4in (10cm) high

$6,500-8,500 **SWO**

A mid-18thC ivory appliqué in the form of the He He Erxian, with traces of color.

3.5in (8.5cm) high

$10,000-15,000 **SWO**

A late 19thC ivory figure of Guanyin, holding a basket of lotus, with a feng at her feet, her hair enclosing a figure of Buddha, with apocryphal Qianlong mark.

25.5in (65cm) high

$15,000-20,000 **SWO**

A late 19thC ivory head of Guanyin, set with 18ct gold, four rubies and twelve sapphires, with mahogany torso.

6.75in (17 cm) high

$8,000-12,000 **KAU**

A Chinese ivory carving of a fishing boat, with nine figures steering and lifting a large fishing net, on wooden stand.

15.25in (39cm) long

$4,000-6,000 **SWO**

ESSENTIAL REFERENCE - COURT TABLETS

- **Ivory court tablets were carried by officials while in the Imperial presence.**
- **They were used at least as early as the Tang dynasty.**
- **In the Ming dynasty they were plain except for a single character denoting the category of the official concerned.**
- **They helped direct the eyes down the length of the hu and discreetly away from the face of the emperor.**
- **All court tablets were preserved by court door-keepers and collected only upon entering the palace. It was an offence to retain a tablet after an audience, as it gave access to restricted areas.**

An 18thC Chinese ivory hu (court tablet), carved with Guanyin and an attendant on a mountain ledge, the reverse with figures in a mountain landscape.

10.5in (26.5cm) high

$10,000-15,000 **WW**

A rare mid-20thC Chinese polychrome-painted ivory figure of a mandarin, on silver-inlaid wooden stand.

5in (15.5cm)

$70,000-100,000 **SWO**

A late 19thC Chinese ivory ruyi scepter, carved as a branch sprouting with lingzhi fungus and two cicadas in embrace.

14in (35.5cm) high

$30,000-40,000 **DN**

A pair of early 20thC Chinese ivory wrist-rests, carved with ladies in mountainous landscapes, with wooden stands and fitted box.

7in (17.5cm) high

$12,000-18,000 **DN**

A 19thC Chinese Canton ivory jewelry casket, carved with figures in pavilions, the feet carved with bats.

10in (25.5cm) wide

$10,000-15,000 GORB

A 19thC Chinese Canton ivory workbox, carved with figures among pavilions, the interior with lift-out tray containing turned and carved accessories.

10in (25cm) wide

$10,000-15,000 DN

A 19thC Chinese ivory bidong, carved with pheasants on rocks among lingzhi and peony, the base broken and detached.

4.75in (12cm) high

$15,000-20,000 SWO

A 19thC Chinese Canton ivory card case.

4.25in (11cm) high

$2,500-3,500 DN

A 19thC Chinese Canton ivory casket, carved with figures, buildings and foliage.

7.5in (20.5cm) wide

$25,000-35,000 SWO

A 19thC Chinese Canton ivory jewelry casket, carved with figures in pavilions, royal processions and flowers, within decorated borders.

7.5in (19cm) wide

$35,000-45,000 GORB

A 19thC Chinese Canton ivory letter rack, carved with a hunting scene, mounted on a later velvet backboard

13.75in (35cm) high

$25,000-35,000 L&T

A 19thC Chinese ivory vase and cover, carved with figures in mountain landscapes and with Immortals standing on clouds.

16in (41cm) high

$70,000-100,000 WW

Mother-of-Pearl

An early 19thC Chinese export mother-of-pearl tea chest, the handles decorated with silver-colored metal leaf, with stamped marks, the plush-lined interior fitted with three canisters.

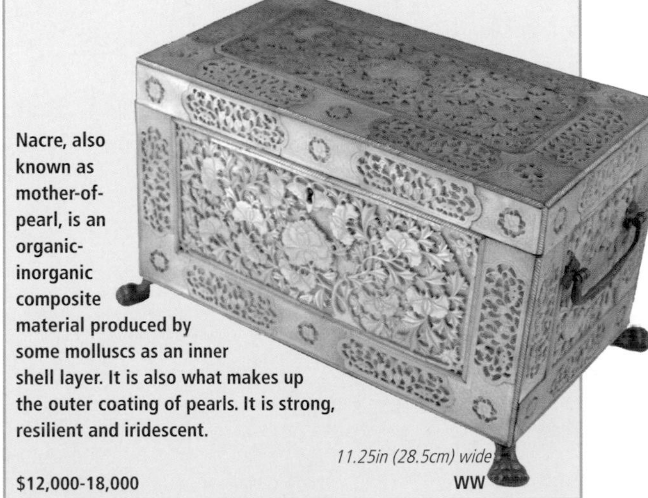

Nacre, also known as mother-of-pearl, is an organic-inorganic composite material produced by some molluscs as an inner shell layer. It is also what makes up the outer coating of pearls. It is strong, resilient and iridescent.

11.25in (28.5cm) wide

$12,000-18,000 WW

A Japanese Tokyo-school ivory okimono of a man holding a child, attributed to Goshi, with his daughter by his side and a dog tangled within vines.

c1880
13.25in (33.5cm) high
$50,000-70,000 JN

A Japanese amusing figure of an ivory fisherman, struggling to stop two eels escaping from his creel.

c1880 *2.5in (6cm) high*
$1,500-2,500 SWO

A Japanese ivory group of a farmer and his son, with a yoked basket and drawers with a shell on his left, signed 'Myoe'.

c1880 *5in (12.5cm) wide*
$5,000-7,000 SWO

A Japanese Tokyo-school cormorant fisherman, signed 'Shizuoka'.

c1890 *12.25in (31cm) high*
$3,000-4,000 SWO

A Japanese ivory Bijin figure, the girl in embroidered kimono and elaborate obi, signed 'Michiaki'.

The term 'Bijin' refers to beautiful women in Japanese art.

c1900 *8.5in (21.5cm) high*
$3,000-4,000 SWO

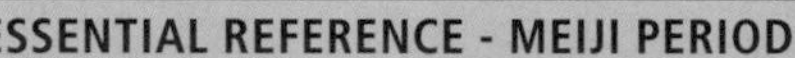

ESSENTIAL REFERENCE - MEIJI PERIOD

From 1633 Japan was isolated under the 'sakoku' policy, which dictated that no foreigner could enter and no Japanese citizen could leave the country on penalty of death.

- **Japanese ports were eventually re-opened in 1853 after an American naval squadron arrived in the Bay of Edo demanding Japan open to trade with the West.**
- **The combination of external pressure and internal unrest eventually led to the restoration of the Meiji Emperor in 1868. The new government realized Japan would have to transform itself along western lines if the country was to compete with the military and industrial might of the West.**
- **The 'opening' of Japan aroused enormous interest in the West and led to a craze for all things Japanese.**
- **This was known as Japonism.**

A Japanese Meiji period ivory okimono of a basket seller, with a red lacquer reserve signature.

2.5in (6.5cm) high
$7,000-10,000 L&T

A Japanese Meiji period ivory okimono of a farmer holding a basket of chicks, signed.

9.5in (24cm) high
$3,500-4,500 L&T

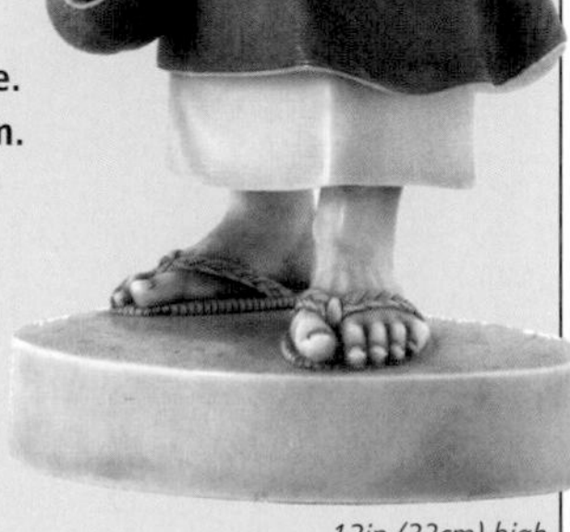

A Japanese Meiji period ivory figure of a man, wearing long flowing robes.

13in (33cm) high
$3,500-4,500 WW

An 18thC Japanese ivory netsuke, in the form of a child with an axe above two monkeys.

1.5in (4cm) high

$700-1,000 **SWO**

A 19thC Japanese ivory netsuke, in the form of a recumbent puppy.

1.25in (3cm) wide

$650-850 **DN**

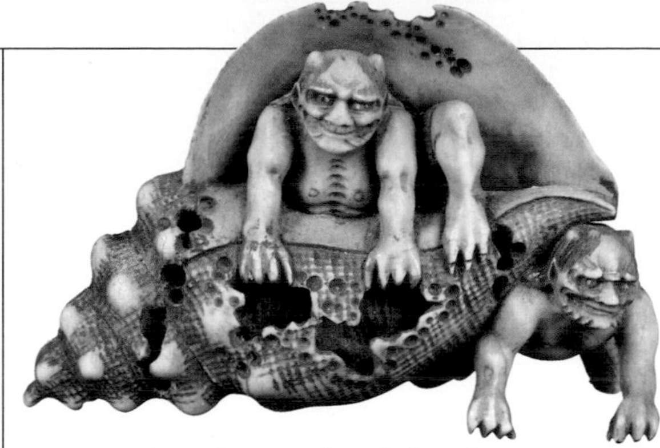

A Japanese Meiji period ivory netsuke, in the form of two oni on a conch shell, signed on a red seal.

Oni are Japanese mythological creatures, roughly analogous to demons or trolls.

2.5in (6cm) wide

$2,500-3,500 **DN**

A Japanese Meiji period ivory netsuke, in the form of a gamma sennin with an oni on his shoulder.

4in (10cm) high

$4,000-6,000 **L&T**

A Japanese Meiji period ivory netsuke, in the form of a standing Shishimai dancer, signed 'Hideaki'.

$800-1,200 **DN**

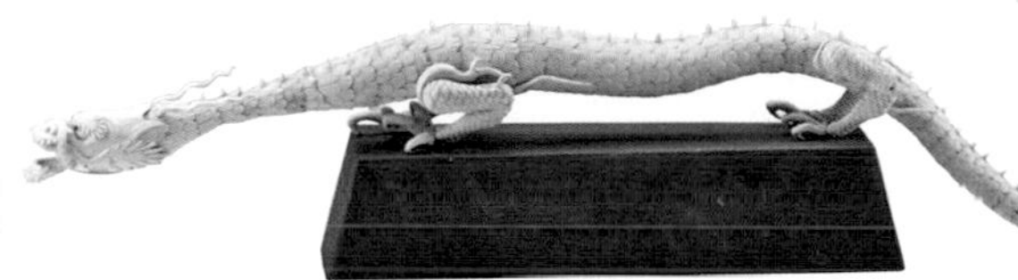

A Japanese Meiji period articulated ivory model of a dragon.

29in (73.5cm) long

$7,000-10,000 **DRA**

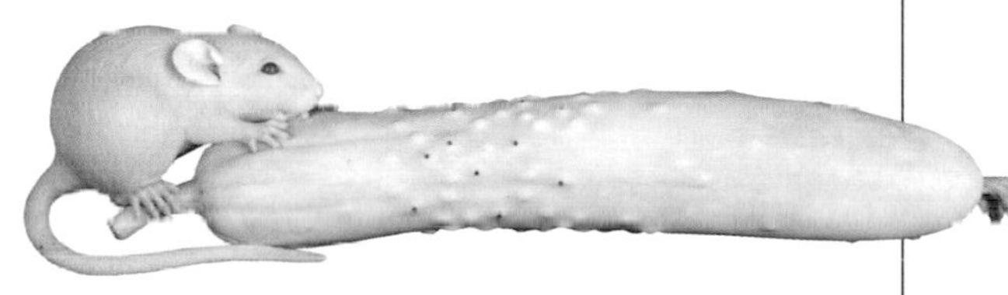

A Japanese Meiji period ivory okimono of a field mouse, gnawing on a large gherkin, the eyes inlaid in coral, signed 'Raku(?)zan saku'.

8.5in (21.5cm) long

$8,000-12,000 **DN**

A Japanese ivory group of the 'Three Wise Monkeys'.

c1860 *1in (2.5cm) high*

$500-700 **SWO**

An ivory okimono of a monkey in engraved coat, signed 'Tomomasa'.

c1870 *1.5in (3.5cm) high*

$1,000-1,500 **SWO**

A Japanese ivory okimono of a squirrel, signed in red 'Rakushin'?, with restoration to foot.

c1900 *4in (10cm) high*

$1,000-1,500 **SWO**

An early 20thC Japanese stained ivory model of a mallard duck, with two-character mark.

5.5in (14cm) long

$2,500-3,500 **L&T**

A Japanese Meiji period Shibayama kodansu, decorated with pheasants on prunus trees, the doors opening to six drawers with crane decoration, signed.

8in (20.5cm) high

$9,000-11,000 **GORB**

A Japanese carved and decorated ivory tusk, carved and detailed in black with two crocodiles and eight tigers, with ivory plug and silver mount, signed 'Orizawa'.

c1890 *29.5in (75cm) long*

$2,000-3,000 **SWO**

A Japanese ivory and shibayama inro, ojime and manju, the inro decorated with a flower-filled urn on a chariot, signed.

$4,500-5,500 **LC**

A Japanese Shibayama tusk vase, decorated with flowers and birds, missing base plate.

c1900 *6.25in (16cm) high*

$2,000-3,000 **WW**

A rare 16thC Chinese archaistic rhinoceros horn libation cup, carved with a band of stylized scrolls and chilong dragons.

6.25in (16cm) long

$300,000-400,000 **WW**

ESSENTIAL REFERENCE - ZHONG KUI

Zhong Kui is a Chinese mythological figure, who is known as the vanquisher of ghosts and evil beings. Highly intelligent but physically disfigured, he is said to be able to command 80,000 demons.

- **His story became popular after the Tang emperor Xuanzong dreamt of him while ill. Once the emperor recovered, he commissioned a painting of Zhong Kui based on his dream. This image strongly influenced later representations.**
- **Zhong Kui's image is often painted on household gates or in businesses to act as a guardian spirit.**

A 19thC Chinese stag-antler figure of Zhong Kui the demon queller.

5.75in (14.5cm) high

$2,500-3,500 **SK**

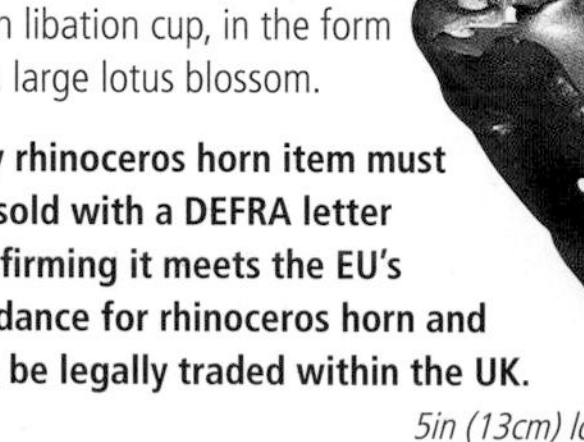

A 17thC Chinese rhinoceros horn libation cup, carved with flowering prunus and magnolia branches, the base with stalk terminal.

2.75in (7cm) high

$150,000-200,000 **DN**

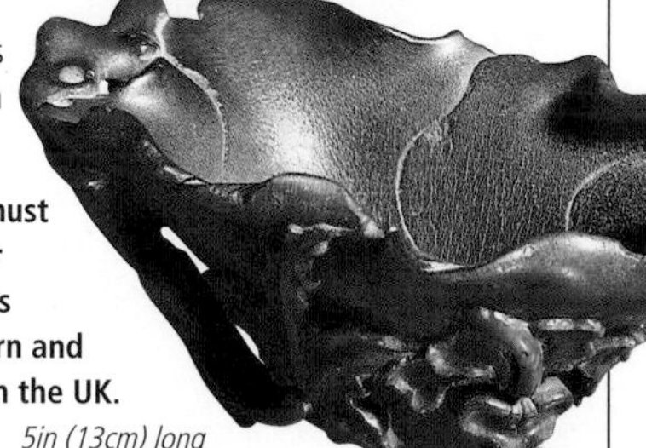

An 18thC Chinese rhinoceros horn libation cup, in the form of a large lotus blossom.

Any rhinoceros horn item must be sold with a DEFRA letter confirming it meets the EU's guidance for rhinoceros horn and can be legally traded within the UK.

5in (13cm) long

$70,000-100,000 **L&T**

A Chinese Northern Song dynasty celadon jade box and cover, carved with a peony bloom.

960-1127 *3in (8cm) diam*

$10,000-15,000 **WW**

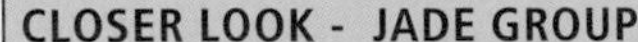

CLOSER LOOK - JADE GROUP

Carvings of animals with their young were a popular theme during the Ming and Qing dynasties.

A large lion together with a small lion represents the wish for the recipient and their descendants to achieve high rank.

The carving on this piece is particularly fine and crisp.

The high quality is noticeable in the lion's finely incised tail and mane, and the body issuing flame-like motifs and lingzhi.

A Chinese Qianlong period pale celadon jade group of mythical animals, the large beast with its head turned facing its pup.

5.5in (14cm) wide

$180,000-200,000 **WW**

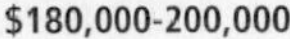

A 17thC Chinese jade model of a mythical beast.

1.5in (4cm) high

$9,000-11,000 **L&T**

A pair of 17thC Chinese celadon jade cups.

3in (7.5cm) wide

$8,000-12,000 **DN**

A Chinese Qianlong period white jade conjoined vase and cover, formed from a single stone as two sections with vertical ribs to the body, the cover with a coiled dragon holding a lingzhi in its jaws, on a hardwood stand.

7.5in (19cm) high

$2,500,000-3,500,000 **WW**

A Chinese Qianlong period jade bamboo-shaped spill vase, carved with a phoenix and a peony, of pale green tone with a brown inclusion.

4in (10cm) high

$20,000-30,000 **CAN**

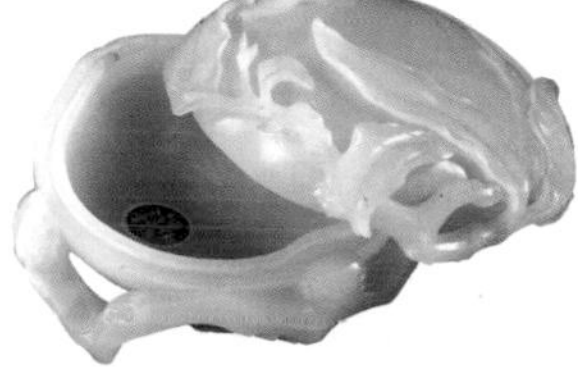

A Chinese Qianlong period white jade peach box and cover, carved with a small bat creeping upon the surface.

Bats and peaches are auspicious symbols in China and often depicted together. The bat (fu) symbolizes blessings, the peach (shoutao) for longevity. The combination of the two results in the proverb fushou shangquan: 'May you possess both blessings and longevity'.

4in (10cm) diam

$120,000-140,000 **WW**

A Chinese Qianlong period white jade model of a phoenix, holding a lingzhi spray in its beak.

The phoenix is the emperor of all birds and also symbolizes the empress. A phoenix reputedly appeared when Conficius was born. Consequently it is believed that the phoenix's appearance in China augers the arrival of a great man.

4.25in (11cm) high

$40,000-60,000 **WW**

An 18thC Chinese pale celadon jade carving of a qilin, seated with a raised head and open mouth, the base later inscribed with calligraphy.

3.25in (8.5cm) high

$150,000-250,000 **WW**

A rare Chinese Qianlong period Imperial white jade teapot and cover, unmarked, with two paper exhibition labels.

It is probable that this piece was made toward the end of the Qianlong period when large jade boulders of this quality became available.

4.75in (12cm) high

$3,500,000-4,500,000 **WW**

An 18thC Chinese celadon jade cup, with two dragon handles.

4.7in (12cm) diam

$8,000-12,000 **WW**

An 18thC Chinese jade figure, of two sleeping cats.

1.6in (4cm) wide

$25,000-35,000 **L&T**

ESSENTIAL REFERENCE - RUYI SCEPTERS

- **The ruyi scepter is a wish-granting wand and amongst the most auspicious of Chinese symbols.**
- **The head is usually shaped as a lingzhi fungus, an important symbol of longevity and the scepters are often decorated with further auspicious Buddhist symbols such as bats and peaches.**
- **Ruyi were customarily given to the emperor and empress on occasions such as birthdays and also used as gifts among other members if the Qing court.**

An 18thC Chinese Imperial celadon jade ruyi scepter, carved with a poem by the Qianlong Emperor.

14.5in (36.8cm) long

$500,000-700,000 **WW**

A rare Chinese white jade gourd-shaped 'bats and clouds' vase. Qianlong Period

The Chinese word for bottle gourd, hulu, is a pun for both 'blessings and wealth'. Used together with bats, fu, it can mean 'may you have blessings and wealth for ten thousand generations'. This is re-emphasized by the clouds which represent fortune or luck.

6in (15.5cm) high

$120,000-140,000 **WW**

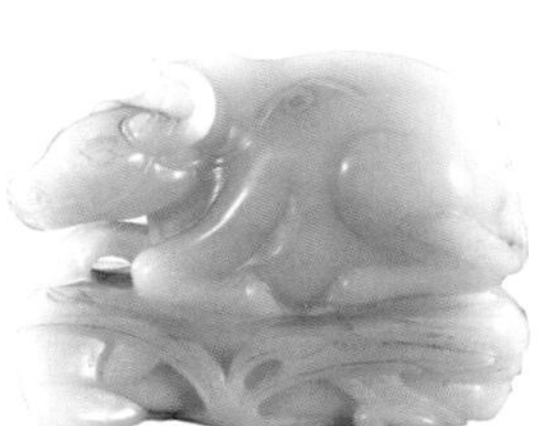

An 18thC Chinese pale celadon jade carving of a water buffalo, the face delicately detailed with a beatific expression.

The water buffalo is the traditional symbol of Spring, strength and tranquillity. As the reputed mount of the philosopher Laozi, the buffalo has strong Daoist connotations and is an important animal in all rice cultivation societies. Buffaloes are also depicted in art dating back thousands of years.

5in (12.5cm) wide

$100,000-150,000 **WW**

An 18th/19thC Chinese light green jade model of a monkey with a peach.

4.25in (11cm) high

$30,000-40,000 **L&T**

An 18th/19thC Chinese jadeite covered-vase.

5.5in (14cm) high

$35,000-45,000 **L&T**

A 19thC Chinese celadon jade qing (musical chime), carved with a ruyi scepter, a vase, bats, clouds and other auspicious symbols, with wooden frame.

With frame 19.75in (50cm) high

$18,000-22,000 **WW**

A 19thC Chinese archaistic jade ewer, carved in relief with a chilong dragon, the handle in the form of a phoenix.

6.5 in (16.5cm) high

$25,000-35,000 **SK**

A 19thC Chinese celadon jade model of a recumbent horse.

The horse (ma) is a symbol of speed and persistence.

6in (15.5cm) wide

$9,000-11,000 **WW**

A 19thC Chinese light green jade model of a qilin.

4in (10cm) long

$8,000-12,000 **L&T**

A 19thC Chinese yellow jade model of a qilin.

The qilin is a mythical and auspicious Chinese creature with ox's hooves, a dragon's head, antlers and a scaly body. It is first recorded in Chinese literature in the Western Zhou period (1028-221BC) and became a popular subject of jade carvings during the Qing dynasty.

3.75in (10cm) long

$100,000-150,000 **WW**

A pair of 19thC Chinese celadon jade models of Buddhist lion dogs, inlaid with lapis lazuli, jadeite, agate and other hardstones, decorated with auspicious emblems.

7.25in (18.5cm) high

$8,000-12,000 **WW**

A late 19thC Chinese celadon jade model of a chilong dragon.

1.75in (4.5cm) high

$2,500-3,500 **WW**

A Chinese coral figure of a robed woman, with floral headdress and flowing scarves, holding a footed dish containing five peaches, on an ivory base.

9.5in (24cm) high

$35,000-45,000 **LHA**

A late 19thC Chinese coral carving, inlaid with silver, on a wooden base.

7in (17.5cm) wide

$5,500-6,500 **KAU**

An Oriental coral figure of a woman in front of a flowering shrub, on a wooden base.

6.75in (17cm) high

$4,000-6,000 **CAPE**

A Chinese coral figure of a lady, her robes carved with a floral design, on a wooden base.

c1900

9.5in (24cm) high

$12,000-18,000 LHA

A Chinese coral carving, in the form of various immortals and figures, with a parade of figures hoisting a dragon into the air, Shoulao holding a peach, on a wooden base.

8.75in (22cm) wide

$10,000-15,000 **LHA**

A Chinese coral figure of Kuan Yin holding a child, on a lotus base, on a wooden stand.

6in (15cm) high

$2,500-3,500 **SK**

A 20thC Chinese lapis lazuli model of a horse.

12.5in (32cm) high

$1,000-1,500 **SWO**

A 20thC Chinese lapis lazuli figure of Buddha, seated in padmasana on a lotus throne.

10.5in (26.5cm) high

$4,000-6,000 **SK**

A 20thC Chinese Mughal-style lapis lazuli jar with cover, with elephant-head handles suspending loose rings.

14in (35.5cm) high

$5,000-7,000 **SK**

An 18thC Chinese soapstone figure of a lohan, with remnants of painted decoration.

The Chinese call the eighteen disciples of Gautama Buddhla the 'lohan'. Lohans are well-known for their great wisdom, courage and supernatural power. Due to their abilities to ward off evil, lohans have become the guardians of Buddhist temples.

12.5in (34.5cm) high

$10,000-15,000 **DN**

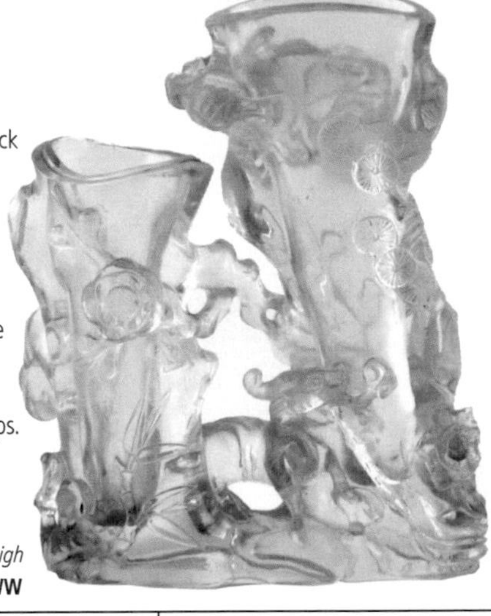

A 19thC Chinese rock crystal vase, in the form of the 'Three Friends of Winter' carved as two trunks, one of pine with two cranes, the other of prunus, with lingzhi and a deer, with small chips.

6in (15.5cm) high

$20,000-30,000 WW

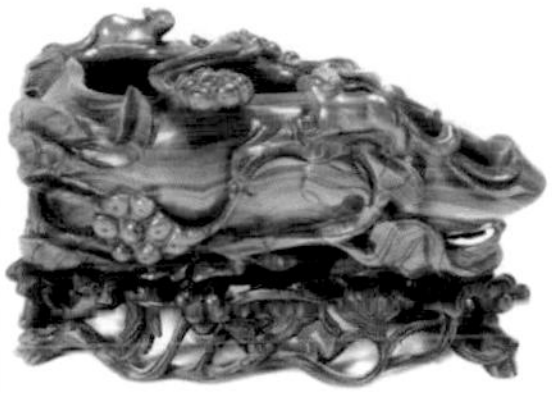

A Chinese malachite brushwasher, carved with squirrels and vines, on a wood stand.

10.5in (27cm) wide

$8,000-12,000 **DN**

A 19thC chalcedony brush washer, carved with rui against a rock.

5in (11.5cm) wide

$4,000-6,000 **SWO**

A Chinese Qing dynasty soapstone figure of a lohan, sitting on the back of a recumbent mythical beast, on a hardwood stand carved as a rocky outcrop.

5in (12.5cm) high

$15,000-20,000 **TEN**

A 15thC Chinese wood figure of a Bhodisatva, with traces of pigment, the hands possibly replaced.

25in (63cm) high

$3,500-4,500 **SWO**

A rare mid-18thC Chinese export amboyna and ebony table bureau, the interior with pigeonholes and drawers, with two keys.

Provenance: by repute from the Austrian Royal Family Collections. The monogram is Queen Adelaide's.

18in (46cm) wide

$5,500-6,500 **L&T**

Tea Box

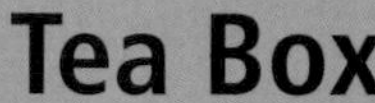

A Chinese rosewood tea box, the sides inset with yellow and brown jade tablets inscribed with a poem and framed in white jade, the top inlaid with mother-of-pearl images of the 'Hundred Antiques', the base with two seals and 'Ch'ien Lung 'nien chih" mark in tortoiseshell-colored jade.

c1770 *8.5in (22cm) high*

$30,000-40,000 **SK**

A set of three late 18thC Chinese wooden wine cups, carved with literati or Immortals.

The literati, although by natural inclination solitary, did meet to play 'go', discuss scrolls and recite poetry. The form of these wine cups is influenced by rhinoceros horn cups.

Largest 2.25in (5.5cm) high

$12,000-18,000 **SWO**

A Chinese huanghuali table cabinet, the removable five-sided cover inlaid in hardstone with flowers around a swastika and central shou character with five bats, the cabinet with two reverse-painted mirrored sides, the third side with similarly painted doors and drawers, the fourth side with pigeonholes.

c1800 *11in (29cm) wide*

$30,000-40,000 **DN**

A 19thC Chinese boxwood Guqin, inlaid with bone and inscribed on the surface.

The guqin is the modern name for a seven-string Chinese musical instrument of the zither family. It has been played since ancient times and has traditionally been favored by scholars and literati as an instrument of great subtlety and refinement.

11.25in (28.5cm) long

$8,000-12,000 **DOY**

A 19thC Chinese boxwood figure of a woman with a monkey.

14in (35.5cm) high

$5,500-6,500 **LHA**

A 19thC Chinese huanghuali brushpot or scroll holder, formed from a single trunk.

9in (23cm) high

$18,000-22,000 **LHA**

A 19thC Chinese agarwood ruyi scepter, carved with scholars and attendants among the 'Three Friends of Winter'.

21in (53.5cm) long

$25,000-35,000 SK

A late 19thC Japanese wood and ivory figure of a Samurai.

16in (40.5cm) high

$5,000-7,000 DRA

A late 19thC Japanese wood and ivory group of a Samurai and a boy, inlaid with carved mother-of-pearl and abalone, the samurai with elephant-head mon to his robes.

15in (41cm) high

$6,000-8,000 DN

A 19thC Japanese wooden okimono, in the form of a toad seated on a discarded waraji, signed 'Masanao'.

$1,800-2,200 DN

A 19thC Chinese bamboo brush pot, carved with a mountainous landscape with scholars and attendants in a boat, with a calligraphic inscription.

5.75in (14.5cm) high

$5,000-7,000 SK

ESSENTIAL REFERENCE - BAMBOO

Bamboo represents integrity and a source of artistic inspiration in Chinese artwork.

- **In the 16thC bamboo was adopted by scholars as a medium for carving figures, landscapes and objects for their writing desks.**
- **From the early 19thC bamboo stem was used for cylindrical objects, such as brushpots.**
- **The great centers of bamboo carving were Nanjing and Jiading, both in south-eastern China.**

A 19thC Chinese bamboo libation cup, carved with fruiting pomegranate.

3.25in (8cm) high

$6,500-8,500 DN

A 19thC Chinese bamboo figure of a seated sage.

4.5in (11.5cm) high

$6,500-7,500 WW

A pair of 19thC Chinese bamboo libation cups, in the form of lion dogs, inverting to reveal hollowed and lacquered interiors.

4.75in (12cm) high

$35,000-45,000 WW

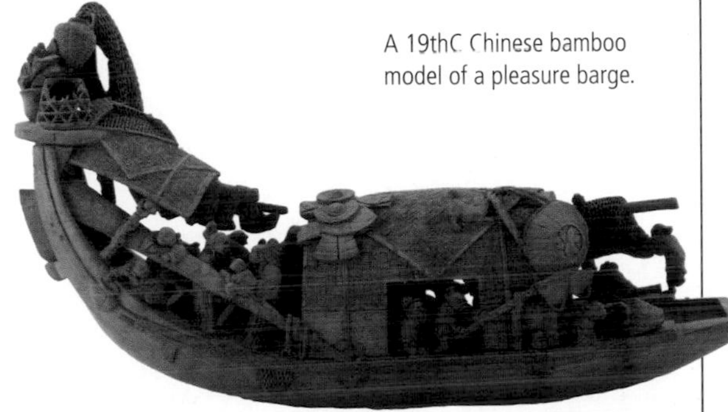

A 19thC Chinese bamboo model of a pleasure barge.

14.5in (37cm) long

$15,000-20,000 WW

A Chinese Yongle period cinnabar lacquer bottle vase, the body deeply chased with four flowering peonies.

5in (13cm) high

$100,000-150,000 **PBE**

A 17thC Chinese guri lacquer tray, carved through red and black lacquer with rui, with some damage.

15in (37cm) wide

$10,000-15,000 **SWO**

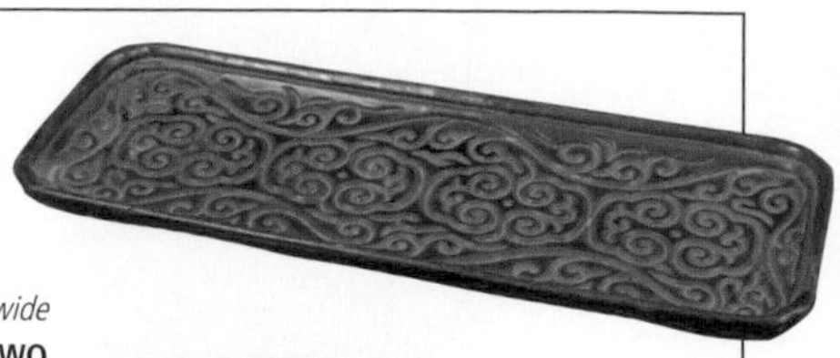

A rare Chinese Qianlong period red lacquer box and stand, the plum-blossom-form cover carved with scholars and attendants, opening to a fitted polychrome lacquer box, the interior top lifting to a tray, the base tier with six fitted boxes.

6.5in (16.5cm) wide

$120,000-180,000 **DOY**

A Chinese Kangxi period xipi lacquer brush pot, the base lacquered black.

The term 'xipi' literally means rhinoceros skin. It describes a type of lacquer where the pattern was made by applying successive layers of different colors on a base of raised molded lacquer. The enamel was then polished flat to reveal the nodular pattern.

5.25in (13.5cm) high

$60,000-80,000 **WW**

A 19thC Chinese cinnabar lacquer and porcelain supper box, the interior with six famille rose porcelain compartments.

15.75in (40cm) wide

$70,000-100,000 **L&T**

A large Japanese lacquer Kodansu, decorated in gold lacquer nashiji, with engraved silver mounts.

c1880 *18in (44.5cm) wide*

$10,000-15,000 **SWO**

One of a pair of 19thC Chinese black lacquer brushpots, with apocryphal Yongzheng marks.

7in (18cm) high

$3,500-4,500 pair **DN**

A Japanese Meiji period lacquer box, decorated in takimaki-e and hiramaki-e.

16.5in (42cm) wide

$2,500-3,500 **L&T**

A late 19thC Japanese gold lacquer box and cover, decorated in gold and silver hiramaki-e, the interior decorated in nashiji.

6.5in (17cm) wide

$3,500-4,500 **WW**

A Chinese Qianlong period enameled glass vase, painted with flowers, bamboo and rockwork, a butterfly and other insects.

4.5in (11cm) high

$6,500-7,500 **WW**

An early 19thC Chinese Peking yellow glass vase, carved with birds among lotus flowers and leaves.

7.5in (19cm) high

$1,200-1,800 **SK**

An early 19thC Chinese Peking glass vase, carved with a phoenix among clouds and a dragon chasing a flaming pearl, with apocryphal Qianlong mark.

8.25in (21cm) high

$1,200-1,800 **SK**

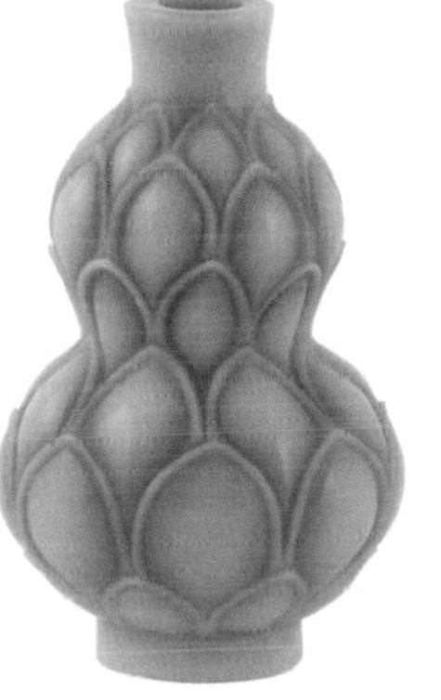

A 19thC Chinese Peking pink glass gourd-shaped vase, with apocryphal Qianlong mark.

4.75in (12cm) high

$3,500-4,500 **WW**

A Chinese Qianlong period famille rose porcelain snuff bottle.

2.25in (5.5cm) high

$6,500-8,500 **WW**

A Chinese famille rose porcelain snuff bottle, painted with flowers in the 'Compagnie des Indes' style.

c1780 *3.5in (9cm) high*

$1,500-2,500 **WW**

A 19thC Chinese Peking glass bottle vase, with red overlay over white ground.

10in (26cm) high

$4,000-6,000 **L&T**

An 18thC Chinese agate snuff bottle, carved with a silhouette of a swimming goose.

2.75in (7cm) high

$5,000-7,000 **WW**

An 18thC Chinese '100 Boys' porcelain snuff bottle.

2in (5cm) high

$10,000-15,000 **L&T**

A late 18th/early 19thC chalcedony snuff bottle, carved to reveal two ducks and lotus.

$8,000-12,000 **SWO**

ESSENTIAL REFERENCE - SNUFF BOTTLES

Snuff-taking was introduced to China from the West, probably in the late 17thC. By the 18thC dedicated snuff bottles were being made in large numbers.

- **Many snuff bottles date from the Daoguang period (1821-50).**
- **Most were made from glass or, particularly in the late 18thC, hardstone. Porcelain, lacquer, amber, coral and ivory were also used.**
- **Snuff bottles are still produced in China today, mostly for the tourist industry.**

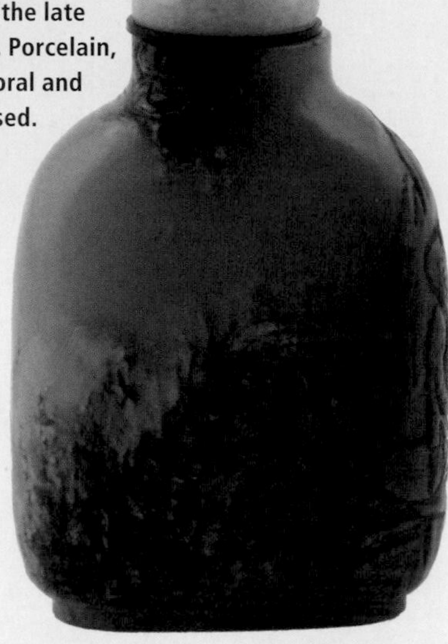

A late 18thC Chinese pebble jade snuff bottle, carved with Shoulao holding a staff.
3in (7.5cm) high
$6,500-8,500 WW

An 18thC Chinese white jade 'boys' snuff bottle, each figure holding a Buddhist symbol.
2.5in (6.5cm) high
$50,000-70,000 DN

A late 18th/early 19thC Chinese pale celadon jade snuff bottle, decorated with gilt.
3in (8cm) high
$15,000-20,000 DN

A Chinese amber snuff bottle.
2.75in (7cm) high
$10,000-15,000 WW

A late 18th/early 19thC Chinese rock crystal snuff bottle.
2.75in (7cm) high
$2,500-3,500 WW

A late 18th/early 19thC Chinese Baltic amber snuff bottle.
2in (5.5cm) high
$2,000-3,000 WW

A late 18th/early 19th Chinese moss-agate snuff bottle.
3in (7.5cm) high
$3,500-4,500 WW

A Chinese Daoguang period porcelain snuff bottle, painted with a figure on a riverbank waving to a fisherman, the reverse with a poem.
3.5in (9cm) high
$4,000-6,000 WW

A Chinese famille rose porcelain 'Eighteen Lohan' snuff bottle.
c1840 3in (7.5cm) high
$650-850 DN

A Chinese famille rose porcelain snuff bottle, painted with figures fighting a dragon.
c1840 2.75in (7cm) high
$2,000-3,000 WW

A 19thC Chinese white jade snuff bottle, carved with a viewing pavilion on a mountainside and a bat.
3.25in (8cm) high
$10,000-15,000 WW

A late 18th/early 19thC Chinese jade snuff bottle, with later soapstone, tortoiseshell, mother-of-pearl, lacquer, silver and pearl embellishment by the Isuda Family, depicting a courtesan with attendant.

The Isuda Family were active in Kyoto, Japan 1900-40.

2.5in (6.5cm) high

$25,000-35,000 DOY

A 19thC Chinese brown stoneware snuff bottle, with seal mark.

2.75in (7cm) high

$5,500-7,500 L&T

A Chinese famille rose porcelain snuff bottle, painted with a fisherman.

c1870 *2.75in (7cm) high*

$1,500-2,500 WW

A 19thC Chinese celadon jade snuff bottle, with inscriptions.

2in (5.5cm) high

$2,500-3,500 DN

A 19thC Chinese Peking glass snuff bottle.

3in (7.5cm) high

$800-1,200 WW

A 19thC Chinese agate snuff bottle, with seaweed-form inclusions.

3.25in (8cm) high

$3,000-4,000 WW

A late 19thC Chinese internally decorated glass snuff bottle.

2.75in (7cm) high

$1,500-2,500 L&T

An early 20thC Chinese internally decorated glass snuff bottle, painted with landscapes and calligraphy.

3.5in (9cm) high

$1,000-1,500 L&T

A Chinese internally painted glass snuff bottle, painted with figures and a donkey, signed 'Yeh chung san' and dated.

1922 *3.5in (9cm) high*

$5,000-7,000 WW

A Chinese internally painted glass snuff bottle, painted with two oxen, the reverse with poem, signed 'Wang Xiao Cheng' and dated.

1962

$1,500-2,500 DN

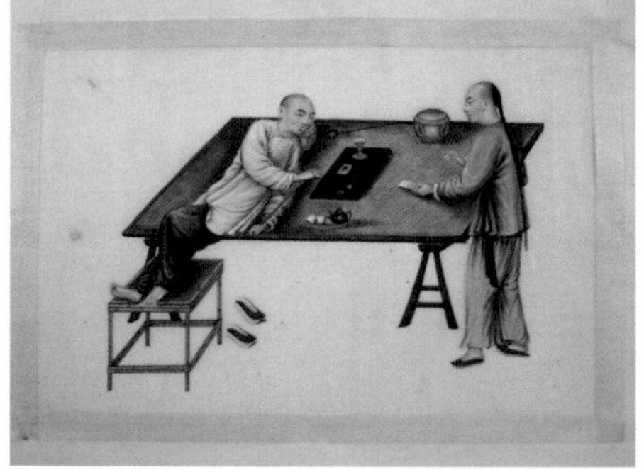

An early 19thC Chinese album of six pith paper paintings, 'The Rake's Progress' by Youqua, showing a gentleman smoking opium and slowly ending in a hovel, with cloth binding.

11in (28cm) wide

$6,500-8,500 **SWO**

Judith Picks: Chinese Painting

From the late 1700s, an increasing number of international merchant vessels began returning home with cargos of exotic objects from China. An insatiable interest in things Oriental resulted in a range of objects created by Chinese artisans specifically for the European market.

Among the items that filled the holds of the ships were ceramics, furniture, silk embroideries and a fascinating variety of paintings. These 'China Trade' paintings offered first-hand documentation of the ships that plied the Far East Trade and the exotic ports they visited. Early paintings, such as this example, are considered to be some of the finest harbour views and ship portraits ever produced. To me they are so evocative of the period with the colonial buildings that were allowed to be constructed at the harbour – even the Christian church!

A Chinese-school oil on canvas view of the Shamien Island Settlement, depicting small ships and a paddle steamer.

c1870-75 *56.5in (143.5cm) wide*

$250,000-350,000 **WW**

An early/mid-19thC Chinese Imperial red-ground silk robe, decorated with three-clawed dragons.

59in (150cm) long

$40,000-60,000 JN

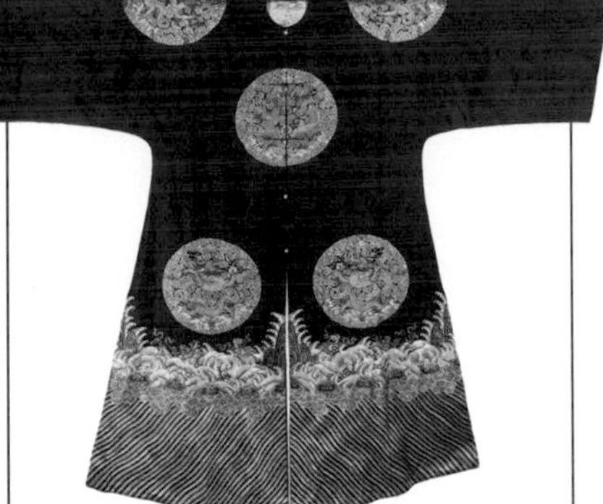

A 19thC Chinese silk robe, decorated with eight gold dragons above waves and among swirling clouds.

58in (147.5cm) long

$40,000-60,000 DOY

A 19thC Chinese green silk semi-formal robe, embroidered with five-clawed dragons chasing flaming pearls among clouds, bats and stylized symbols.

52.75in (134cm) long

$12,000-18,000 L&T

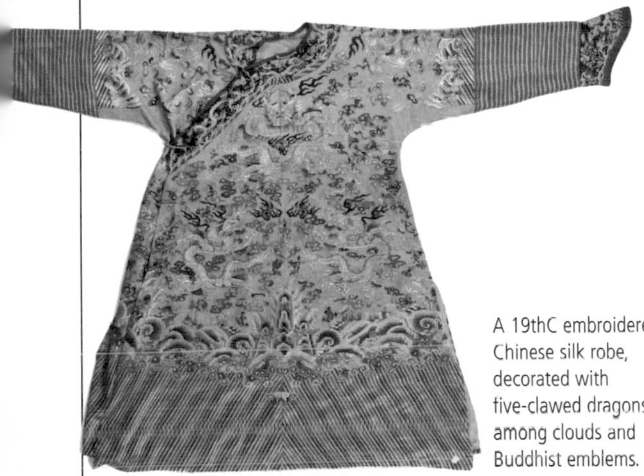

A 19thC embroidered Chinese silk robe, decorated with five-clawed dragons among clouds and Buddhist emblems.

50.5in (128cm) long

$15,000-25,000 LHA

An early 20thC Chinese silk three-quarter-length lady's informal robe, embroidered with birds and 'Pekin knot' peonies.

$2,000-3,000 CAN

One of a pair of 19thC Chinese silk panels, embroidered with a writhing, five-clawed dragon.

59.5in (151cm) long

$20,000-30,000 pair LHA

A 19thC Chinese embroidered textile, depicting a lion among clouds and flames, the lion with silk and metallic thread tapestry.

13.75in (35cm) wide

$8,000-12,000 SK

A Chinese embroidered silk panel, depicting the guardian Guan Yu in dragon robes.

80in (203cm) long

$8,000-12,000 LHA

A 20thC Chinese yellow silk brocade panel, woven with nine pairs of dragons chasing a flaming pearl among clouds.

79in (200.5cm) long

$2,000-3,000 SK

A late 18thC Chinese ivory fan, the guards carved with Immortals and the finely-pierced leaf with figures playing 'go' and musical instruments, with minor damage.

13in (33.5cm) wide

$5,000-7,000 **SWO**

A Chinese Canton ivory brisé fan, carved and pierced with pagodas and figures, the guards with feng and dragons.

c1820 *7in (18cm) high*

$2,000-3,000 **SWO**

A mid-19thC Chinese Canton fan, the splines in ivory, stained ivory, tortoiseshell, sandalwood and mother-of-pearl, the leaf painted with figures with applied ivory faces, with carved ivory guards, with original box.

10in (25.5cm) wide

$1,200-1,800 **SWO**

A mid-19thC Chinese Canton fan, the splines in mother-of-pearl, lacquer, sandalwood, ivory and stained-ivory, the paper leaf painted with figures with applied ivory faces, framed and glazed.

Frame 22in (56cm) wide

$3,500-4,500 **SWO**

A Chinese ivory brisé fan, carved with figures in pursuits, with a monogram in a shield.

c1850 *13in (33cm) wide*

$4,000-6,000 **WW**

A 19thC Chinese ivory and lacquer fan, decorated with figures, with a fitted box.

15in (38cm) wide

$3,500-4,500 **WW**

A 19thC Chinese black and gold lacquer fan, decorated with figures, flowers and foliage, the ribbon perished.

17.5in (45cm) wide

$3,500-4,500 **WW**

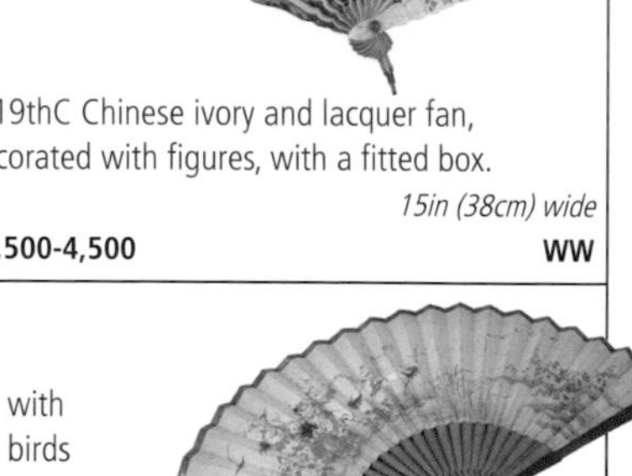

An early 20thC Chinese fan, with bamboo sticks, painted with birds among flowers.

39.5in (100cm) wide

$350-450 **WW**

A 20thC Chinese fan, attributed to Zhang Daqian, painted with a landscape and inscription on one side and calligraphy on the other, with one seal.

17in (43cm) wide

$45,000-55,000 **SK**

An early 19thC Indian lapis lazuli model of an elephant, painted in polychrome and gold.

9in (23cm) high

$25,000-35,000 **KAU**

An early 19thC Indian miniature model of an elephant, painted in polychrome and gold.

1.5in (4cm) high

$5,500-6,500 **KAU**

A rare 19thC Indian ivory 'phallic' symbol, carved with two figures possibly depicting chastity.

10.5in (26.5cm) long

$8,000-12,000 **JN**

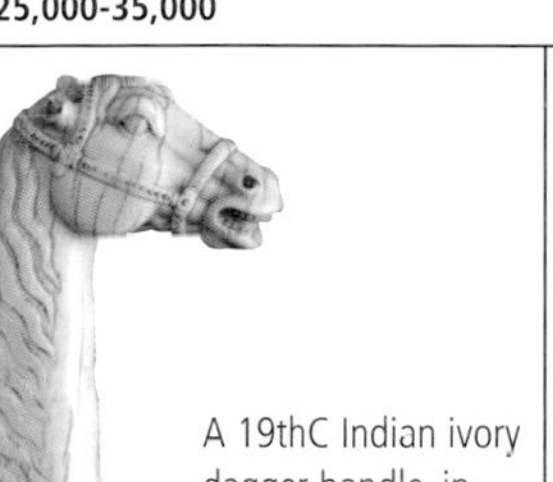

A 19thC Indian ivory dagger handle, in the form of a horse's head, with chip to ear.

5.75in (14.5cm) high

$3,500-4,500 **SWO**

A 19thC Indian bronze figure of Durga, with flaming hair and eight arms holding various attributes including a trident.

17.75in (45cm) high

$1,500-2,500 **DN**

A large 19thC Indian white-metal turban box, decorated with exotic birds and flowers.

20in (51cm) high

$5,000-7,000 **GORL**

Ivory Figures

A group of 19thC Indian Rajastani ivory figures of female musicians, gilt and partially painted in colors.

Tallest 8in (20.5cm) high

$5,500-7,500 **KAU**

An 18thC Chinese 'Southern official's hat' huanghuali armchair, with white-brass-mounted feet.

$50,000-70,000 **SK**

CLOSER LOOK - LACQUER THRONE

The throne has many motifs with significance to the Chinese, such as shou characters amidst cloud scrolls to the interior and bat roundels to the reverse.

It has excellent provenance, having been owned by Sackville, 5th Earl of Yarborough. It has the remains of a Sackville paper label on the base.

Even though it has elements from many periods, is severely distressed and will require expensive restoration, the significance of this throne demands a high value.

A rare Chinese red lacquer throne, the back with five panels, three inset with mother-of-pearl motifs, the panels decorated with shou characters, cloud scrolls and bat roundels, the five panels Ming dynasty, the remainder later, extensively distressed.

50in (126.5cm) wide

$20,000-30,000 **WW**

A pair of 19thC Chinese hardwood lowback armchairs, the backs inset with burrwood panels.

$6,500-7,500 **DN**

A pair of 19thC Chinese hongmu chairs.

$1,500-2,500 **L&T**

An early 20thC Chinese hardwood and burrwood armchair.

$2,500-3,500 **L&T**

An early 20thC Chinese hardwood and burrwood armchair.

$2,500-3,500 **L&T**

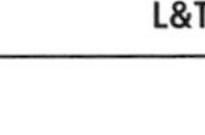

One of pair of Chinese huali moongaze chairs, with sliding foot rest.

c1900

$10,000-15,000 pair **SWO**

A pair of 19thC Chinese huanghuali barrel-form stools.

18in (46cm) high

$3,500-4,500 **L&T**

An 18thC Chinese huanghuali painting table.

64in (163cm) wide

$20,000-30,000 **POOK**

A 19thC Chinese huanghuali recessed trestle-leg table, the apron carved with dragons, bats, ruyi and shou longevity symbols, the legs enclosing a panel of wu-fu (five bats) encircling a stylized shou character.

110.25in (280cm) wide

$5,500-6,500 **RTC**

A Chinese nanmu altar table, Shanxi Province, the frieze carved with dragons and lingzhi, both ends carved with a crane holding a fungus in its beak.

c1880 *81in (207cm) wide*

$8,000-12,000 **WW**

A 19thC Chinese huanghuali side table, with a pierced and scroll-carved frieze, the straight column legs with stylized scroll feet.

48in (122cm) wide

$20,000-30,000 **L&T**

A late 19thC Chinese huanghuali Kang low table.

47.5in (119cm) long

$15,000-20,000 **DN**

A 19thC Chinese huanghuali altar table, the underside with Chinese script.

$7,000-10,000 **L&T**

An early 19thC Chinese huali table, carved with scrolling lotus, the top inset with black marble.

41.25in (105cm) wide

$10,000-15,000 **SWO**

A Chinese export amboyna-, ebony- and ivory-inlaid library table, the drawers with turned horn handles and a Chinese character mark.

c1830 *47in (119cm) wide*

$12,000-18,000 **L&T**

A mid-19thC Chinese rosewood and marble-inset center table.

46in (117cm) diam

$40,000-60,000 **L&T**

A mid-19thC Chinese hardwood partners' desk, carved with dragons among swirling clouds, on paw feet.

74in (187.5cm) wide

$10,000-15,000 **SWO**

A Chinese export black lacquer and gilt work-table, opening to an arrangement of divisions and accessories, missing some lids from the interior.

c1880 *25.5in (64.5cm) wide*

$650-850 **DN**

A 19thC Chinese hardwood side table, the marble inset top with a gadrooned edge.

36.5in (93cm) wide

$2,000-3,000 **L&T**

A late 19thC Chinese hongmu games table, on dragon-carved cabriole legs with stylized raised claw feet.

22.5in (57cm) wide

$4,000-6,000 **L&T**

An early 20thC Chinese hardwood and burrwood pedestal desk.

$8,000-12,000 **L&T**

A 19thC Chinese hardwood pedestal desk, the pierced apron carved with bats, songbirds and pomegranates, on carved cabriole legs.

41in (104cm) wide

$10,000-15,000 **L&T**

A 15thC Japanese Buddhist lacquered-negoro altar table, with perforated kosama apron and border, on 'heron-shaped' legs, with metal fittings.

22.25in (56.5cm) wide

$10,000-15,000 **SK**

A 19thC Chinese black lacquer and gilt cabinet-on-stand, decorated with mountainous landscapes, opening to galleried tiers, painted panels, drawers and pigeonholes.

$12,000-18,000 **L&T**

A Chinese hardwood display cabinet, heavily-carved with foliage scrolling dragons.

c1900 *90in (231cm) high*

$15,000-20,000 **TEN**

ESSENTIAL REFERENCE - CHINESE WOOD NAMES

Many of the hardwoods used in antique Chinese furniture were not native to China, but were introduced to China through trade.

- **Huali (rosewood) has a lighter hue than other rosewoods. It is one of the least valuable.**
- **Huanghuali (yellow rosewood) was popular for Ming scholar's furniture.**
- **Hongmu (mahogany) was often used for Qing dynasty furniture.**
- **Jichimu (native Chinese wood, known as 'chicken-wing wood') is an expensive, highly patterned wood, sometimes used for Ming and Qing palace furniture.**
- **Nanmu (southern elm) was popular in the Ming dynasty as it was resistant to decay.**
- **Zitan (red-purple sandal wood) is the most prized and expensive wood used in Ming and Qing furniture.**

A late 19th/early 20thC Chinese hongmu display cabinet.

32.25in (82cm) wide

$8,000-12,000 **L&T**

An early 20thC Chinese blackwood display cabinet, carved with dragons and clouds.

59in (150cm) wide

$25,000-30,000 **CAN**

A Chinese hardwood and burrwood cabinet.

64.5in (166cm) high

$6,500-8,500 **DN**

A Japanese hardwood display cabinet, carved with birds among prunus, chrysanthemum and flag-iris, all beneath a feng.

c1880 *88in (223cm) high*

$9,000-11,000 **SWO**

A Japanese carved and patinated wood cabinet-on-stand, inset with bone, mother-of-pearl, bronze and lacquer.

c1890 *80in (201cm) high*

$12,000-18,000 **KAU**

A Japanese wood and shibayama cabinet, the pierced cornice carved with phoenix.

46.5in (118cm) wide

$5,000-7,000 **L&T**

A late 17thC ivory table screen and stand.

10.5in (27cm) high

$6,500-8,500 **SWO**

A late 19thC Chinese hardstone-mounted 'marriage' table screen, pierced with prunus and set with ten jade precious objects around a double shou, with cracks.

13in (33.5cm) high

$6,500-8,500 **SWO**

A late 19thC Chinese ivory battle scene panel, on silver inlaid hardwood stand.

12in (30.5cm) wide

$20,000-30,000 **CAN**

A pair of 19thC Chinese ivory table screens, carved and stained with scholars, the reverse with calligraphy.

10.75in (27cm) high

$20,000-30,000 **CAN**

An early 20thC Chinese rosewood and marble 'dreamstone' table screen, the frame and stand probably hongmu.

17.25in (44cm) wide

$2,000-3,000 **DN**

An early 20thC Chinese rosewood and needlework screen, with exotic birds.

40.5in (103cm) high

$6,500-8,500 **L&T**

A Chinese lacquer and hardstone six-leaf screen.

72in (183cm) high

$15,000-20,000 **LHA**

A Japanese lacquer tsuitate, inlaid with ivory, mother-of-pearl, stag horn and bone, signed.

c1900 *67.75in (172cm) high*

$6,500-8,500 **DN**

A Japanese Meiji period ivory and lacquer two-leaf screen, decorated with a landscape with pagoda and figures.

26.75in (68cm) wide

$10,000-15,000 **L&T**

A 19thC Chinese hardwood and parcel-gilt marriage bed, the cornice panels carved and gilt with prunus, the back with small drawers, compartments and gilt panels carved with phoenix.

An added piece of provenance always helps! This bed appeared in the TV program 'Monarch of the Glen'.

99.5in (253cm) long

$6,500-7,500 **L&T**

An 18thC Chinese huanghuali bed.

90.5in (230cm) long

$150,000-200,000 **WW**

A 19th/20thC Chinese hardwood bed, with detachable rigid sides, the headboard carved with scrolling dragons.

80.25in (204cm) long

$3,500-4,500 **WW**

ESSENTIAL REFERENCE - QIANLONG 'THRONE-ROOM GROUPS'

In 'Splendours of China's Forbidden City, the Glorious Reign of the Emperor Qianlong', Hu Desheng describes the Qianlong Emperor's throne rooms as containing: 'a throne in the center, a screen at the back; and on either side of the throne, an elephant statue with a vase on its back (symbolizing peace), a standing fan, a luduan unicorn statue, and a vertical censer. This assemblage is commonly referred to as the 'throne-room group'.

- **The word for elephant in Chinese is 'xiang,' which can also mean 'sign' and which additionally sounds like a word meaning happiness. Elephants also provide other messages when combined, for example, with precious vases. The word for vase in Chinese is 'ping', which sounds the same as the word for 'peace'. The combination of an elephant with a vase on its back thus suggests the phrase 'taiping youxiang,' 'when there is peace there are signs'.**
- **The luduan was a mythical animal with a single horn and scaly body, which was believed to be capable of distinguishing between good and evil. Censers of this form thus protected the emperor and ensured that he was both virtuous and wise.**

A rare 18thC Chinese zitan and other hardwood fan stand, from a throne room, carved as a recumbent caparisoned elephant with a vase upon his back, the base carved with stylized mythical beasts and bands of ruyi heads, with damage to the vase.

23.25in (57cm) high

$150,000-200,000 **WW**

THE FURNITURE MARKET

Very little has changed since I wrote about the state of the antique furniture market two years ago. If anything the market has polarized. In the mid-to-low end, some sources are actually claiming a 20 to 30 percent drop in prices. Brown furniture has nose-dived in value, whereas 20thC furniture, especially Mid-Century Modern, has continued its renaissance. The work of firms such as Knoll International and Herman Miller is selling particularly well, with buyers on the look out for classic pieces by the likes of Charles and Ray Eames.

High-end, exceptional quality period furniture also continues to do well, particularly pieces that are new to the market, which regularly fetch record prices. The old adage 'buy the best you can afford' certainly applies. Attractive decorator's pieces, such as fine lacquer cabinets, can also make good money.

The reason for the decline in value of 'average', mid-range furniture is complex, but may be at least partially attributed to fashion and a lack of really good quality examples on the market. Additionally, many vendors are naturally reluctant to enter good antique furniture to auction while prices are depressed.

However, I think it would be fair to say that there are hints of resurgence, with dealers reporting more customers and interest. And there is no doubt that 18thC Chippendale and Federal pieces sell better than their heavy late 19thC counterparts.

Oak dressers, unless of exceptional quality, are also unfashionable. Where have all the buyers gone who liked to display their collections of blue-and-white transfer-printed ware? Many other pieces are too bulky for modern houses, with only the best examples fetching high prices. Additionally, pieces such as the bureau have no real function in today's interiors.

So has the low- to mid-range furniture market reached its nadir? Some of the prices achieved at auction are ridiculously low for pieces fashioned from solid wood by craftsmen and not merely machine-cut and assembled from laminated MDF (medium-density fiberboard). Many auction houses are being forced to turn away such furniture!

I believe that prices may well improve in the near future. People are being persuaded that 'antiques are green' and that recycling old furniture is more responsible than cutting down more of the Amazon jungle or Scandinavian pine trees.

Also, with some prices so low, younger buyers are looking at auctions when furnishing their first apartment or house. Sturdy, good-quality, highly functional pieces are excellent value for money: a solid mahogany, 19thC chest-of-drawers can be found at around $350. These pieces could well provide good investment potential, as prices must surely increase with a strengthening economy – whenever that happens.

Above: A mid-18thC George II mahogany-framed library armchair. See p.166.

Left: A George III gilt and japanned chinoiserie chest. See p.210.

A mid-17thC ash and oak turned or 'thrown' armchair, with baluster-turned arm finials and legs, with stretchers.

$15,000-20,000 **DN**

A Philadelphia comb-back Windsor armchair, previously owned by John Bartram, possibly from the workshop of Thomas Gilpin, the peaked toprail decorated with a painted image of St Peter, patron saint of fishermen.

John Bartram is widely considered to be the father of American Botany. This chair is a copy of one used by the president of the State in Schuylkill (the first angling club in the America). It was given to Bartram by the club as a token of friendship because he allowed members free access to his shore line.

c1750

$20,000-30,000 **POOK**

A mid-18thC Thames Valley ash, elm and beech high-back Windsor armchair.

$2,500-3,500 **DN**

A George II and later yew, oak and elm high-back Windsor armchair.

c1750

$3,000-4,000 **DN**

Two of a set of four 18thC country dining chairs, with pierced splat backs and paneled seats.

$80-120 set **ECGW**

One of a pair of mid-late 18thC elm Windsor armchairs, with turned legs and back rails.

$2,500-3,500 pair **DOR**

A Delaware Valley painted Windsor bench, on baluster-turned legs with bulbous stretchers, with original dark-green painted surface.

c1770

83in (210cm) wide

$20,000-30,000 **POOK**

Judith Picks

This is the Rolls-Royce of Windsor chairs. This type of chair is commonly attributed to the Thames Valley region. It is often referred to as being of the 'Strawberry Hill' design after the house at Twickenham that was remodeled in the Gothic style by Horace Walpole. (He delightfully said 'It is a plaything-house… and it is the prettiest bauble you ever saw.')

A chair of this quality was not destined for life in a rural cottage. As an example of the best of all Windsor type chairs, it demonstrates that in the 18thC Windsor chairs could be situated in the most esteemed interiors. Henry Williams supplied the Prince of Wales with several mahogany Windsor armchairs for St James's Palace in 1729. The rich patina and Gothic detailing add to the appeal.

A George III Gothic-style yew and elm Windsor armchair.

c1770

$12,000-18,000 **DN**

A New England painted ladderback chair, possibly Matteson School, South Shaftsbury, Vermont, with rush seat, with original salmon-pink and black-painted surface.

c1800

$1,500-2,500 **POOK**

An early 19thC painted elm comb back Windsor armchair, with green painted finish.

$6,500-7,500 **SWO**

A Regency yew Windsor child's highchair.

c1820 *38in (97cm) high*

$1,500-2,500 **DN**

An early 19thC cherrywood and elm Windsor armchair, on four cabriole legs with pad feet.

$12,000-18,000 **SWO**

A 19thC yew, cherry and ash Windsor child's armchair, with low double-bow back, on turned legs with a crinoline stretcher.

$1,500-2,500 **TEN**

A harlequin set of six 19thC yew Windsor armchairs, of high double-hoop form, on ring-turned legs with ball feet and crinoline stretchers.

$4,500-5,500 **AH**

A harlequin set of thirteen 17thC and later oak joined chairs, Derbyshire/South Yorkshire, each with double crescent toprails carved with scrolls, masks and stylized foliage.

$9,000-11,000 set **SWO**

A rare set of six William and Mary walnut dining chairs, the toprails flanked by a carved boy's heads, with later upholstered seats.

c1690

$8,000-12,000 set **SWO**

A pair of George I red-walnut dining chairs, the backs with carved scroll motifs, the drop-in seats with original needlework covers, on cabriole legs with carved scallop shell knees and claw-and-ball feet, with some faults.

$5,000-7,000 **TOV**

An 18thC Italian carved oak dining chair, with floral-painted leather upholstery, with X-frame stretcher and turned feet.

$550-650 **GORL**

A Delaware Valley Queen Anne walnut dining chair, the cupid's-bow toprail above a solid splat, on cabriole legs with pad feet.

c1760

$1,500-2,500 **POOK**

A pair of Philadelphia, Pennsylvania Chippendale walnut chairs, the serpentine toprails with shell centers and scrolled ears, the vasiform splat backs with beaded edges, on shell-carved cabriole legs with claw-and-ball feet.

c1760

$3,000-4,000 **FRE**

A set of eight George III Chippendale dining chairs, including two armchairs, the pierced and interlocking splats with carved anthemion, the overstuffed seats upholstered with floral tapestry, with H-stretchers.

$25,000-35,000 set **TEN**

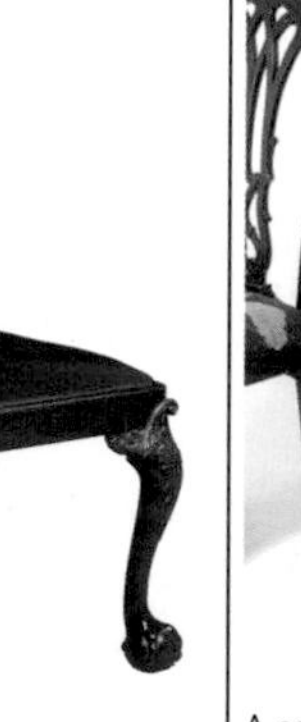

An Irish George III mahogany dining chair, with pierced vase splat, upholstered in red velvet, on acanthus-carved cabriole legs with claw-and-ball feet.

c1770

$800-1,200 **DN**

A set of three George III Chippendale dining chairs, with pierced interlacing splats, the overstuffed seat upholstered in floral needlework fabric, on square chamfered legs, with restoration.

$2,500-3,500 **TEN**

A set of eight Irish George III mahogany dining chairs, including two armchairs, the shaped toprails centered by a raised oval above pierced tapered splats between reeded uprights, mid-rails and sabre legs, with green overstuffed seats.

$10,000-15,000 **L&T**

Two of a set of eight George III mahogany dining chairs, including armchairs, with reeded uprights, on ring-turned tapered forelegs.

$3,000-4,000 set **TEN**

One of a set of six Southern American mahogany dining chairs, probably Virginia, each with a scalloped toprail and pierced splat, with juniper rear seat rail and cedrela corner blocks.

c1775

$4,000-6,000 set **POOK**

Two of a set of twelve George III mahogany dining chairs, including two armchairs, with reeded pierced vasiform splats above drop-in seats, on square tapered legs.

c1790

$10,000-15,000 set **L&T**

A set of eight George III mahogany dining chairs, with X-shaped back supports, with turned upright arm supports, on square tapered legs with stretchers.

c1800

$5,000-7,000 **DN**

A set of ten George III mahogany dining chairs, including two armchairs, the splats and front legs reeded, the seats upholstered in striped silk.

c1810

$9,000-11,000 **DN**

CLOSER LOOK - FEDERAL DINING CHAIRS

The elegant backs with a central arched crest, and the splat with a central stylized Prince of Wales feather and pierced vasiform upright with drapery swags, are all products of top-level craftsmanship.

The high quality tapered legs and spade feet add to the elegant appeal of the set.

A set of twelve New York Federal carved mahogany dining chairs, including two armchairs, three chairs later.

c1800

$15,000-20,000 **POOK**

Sets of twelve chairs are always at a premium. The rule is that compared to the value of a single chair: a pair – 3 times, set of four – 6-7 times, a set of six – 10-12 times, a set of eight – 15 plus times, a set of 10 or 12 – 20 times.

A set of ten George III mahogany and marquetry dining chairs, including two armchairs, the backs with scroll finials, the central bars with satinwood inset panels and acanthus carving, with drop-in seats, on sabre legs.

c1810

$5,000-7,000 **DN**

A set of six late George III Chippendale dining chairs, with scrolling pierced splats, four upholstered in worn red leather, two in silk damask, on square chamfered forelegs with H-stretchers.

$3,500-4,500 **TEN**

A set of seven Regency mahogany and brass-strung dining chairs, including one armchair, with reeded and scrolling uprights, on ring-turned and spiral forelegs.

$4,000-6,000 **TEN**

One of a set of twelve Irish Regency simulated-rosewood dining chairs, with palmetted carved bar-backs, on sabre legs.

$4,000-6,000 set **L&T**

A set of twelve Regency brass-inlaid dining chairs, including two armchairs, the horizontal splats carved with rosettes and lotus, with caned seats, on sabre legs, with original horsehair tufted pads.

$40,000-60,000 **L&T**

A set of ten Regency mahogany dining chairs, including two armchairs, with overstuffed green velvet seats, on reeded tapered legs.

$5,500-6,500 **GORL**

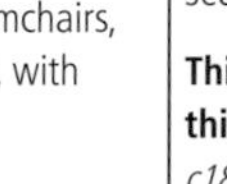

A set of eight Regency japanned dining chairs, including two armchairs, the backs with caned panels and chinoiserie decorated reserves, with caned seats, on round tapered ring-turned legs.

c1810

$3,500-4,500 **FRE**

Five of a set of ten Regency carved rosewood dining chairs, probably by Gillows, including two armchairs, with green velvet upholstered drop-in seats, one stamped 'K' to the seat rail.

This design was in use by 1813 as it appears in two room settings of this date drawn for customers by Gillows of Oxford Street, London.

c1815

$40,000-50,000 set **DN**

A set of seven Regency mahogany dining chairs, including two armchairs, with X-frame backs, on turned and tapered legs.

$4,000-6,000 GORL

A set of thirteen Regency mahogany dining chairs, including two armchairs, the back with upright supports, with bowfront upholstered seats, on square tapered legs.

c1815

$6,500-7,500 set DN

A set of eight George IV mahogany dining chairs, with leather overstuffed seats.

c1820

$9,000-11,000 SWO

A set of twenty two William IV ebonized dining chairs, carved with paterae, with padded backs and seats, on tapered and fluted forelegs.

c1835

$9,000-11,000 set DN

ESSENTIAL REFERENCE - BIEDERMEIER

Biedermeier is a simplified version of the French Empire style (see p.224). It features simple, clean lines and geometric shapes in light-colored woods. Decoration is generally limited to pilasters, columns and palmettes in ebony, which provides a contrast to the light base wood.

- **The style was was popular in Germany, Austria and Scandinavia, mainly between c1805 and 1850. By the mid-19thC it had begun to seem dowdy and was given the derogative name 'Biedermeier, derived from a satirical term meaning 'the decent, if slightly dull common man'.**
- **The best Biedermeier furniture was made by Josef Danhauser of Vienna, Austria.**
- **Biedermeier was primarily a middle-class style, but was also used in the private areas of some noble houses.**

A set of six German Biedermeier cherrywood-veneered chairs, Munich area, the splats printed and inked with Classical figures, the upholstery later, with some heavy wear.

c1820

$10,000-15,000 DOR

A set of six George IV mahogany dining chairs, the reeded frames with cable-molded toprails, with drop-in bow seats, on reeded and tapered legs.

c1820

$2,500-3,500 DN

A set of six William IV mahogany dining chairs, with scrolling leaf carved splats, with drop-in seats, on ring-turned reeded legs.

$2,500-3,500 set TEN

A set of twelve William IV mahogany dining chairs, including two armchairs, the bar backs with carved acanthus-scroll corners above reeded center rails, with drop-in seats upholstered in patterned red damask, on turned and reeded tapered legs.

$12,000-18,000 TOV

A set of fifteen William IV mahogany dining chairs, including one armchair, with reeded uprights, with upholstered seats, on turned and tapered legs.

c1835

$15,000-20,000 L&T

A set of six Pennsylvania painted plank-seat dining chairs, with original salmon-pink painted surface and fruit and floral stenciled decoration.

c1840

$2,000-3,000 POOK

A set of six French balloon-back dining chairs, partly walnut-veneered.

c1860

$1,500-2,500 KAU

A set of twelve late 19th/early 20thC green-painted and floral-decorated dining chairs, with pierced vasiform splats and padded seats, on tapered legs.

$7,000-9,000 set DN

A set of six late 19thC mahogany Chippendale Revival dining chairs, with acanthus-carved and pierced splats, on cabriole legs with claw-and-ball feet.

$5,500-6,500 set DN

A set of ten 19thC George III-style mahogany dining chairs, including two armchairs, with serpentine toprails and wavy horizontal splats, with overstuffed seats, on straight chamfered legs with H-stretchers.

$7,000-10,000 set L&T

A set of fifteen late 19thC 17thC-Flemish-style carved oak dining chairs, carved with acanthus and paterae, with embossed leather seats, on turned legs with X-shaped stretchers, with applied label 'James Shoolbred, Tottenham'.

$15,000-20,000 set DN

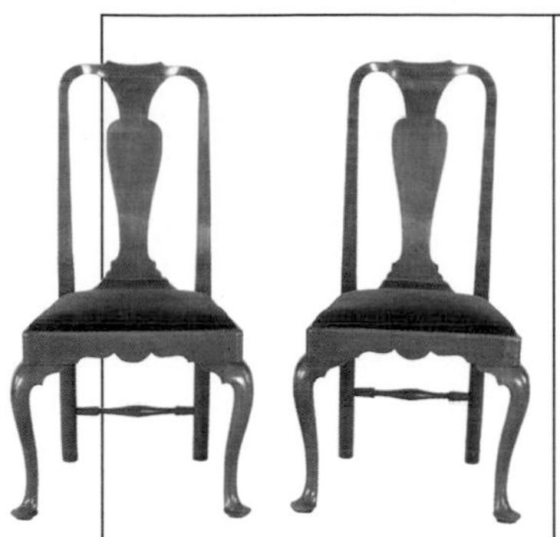

A pair of Connecticut Queen Anne carved walnut side chairs, with baluster splats and shaped apron, on cabriole legs with pad feet.

$2,500-3,500 POOK

A pair of American Queen Anne beech side chairs, with a carved crests and vasiform splats, with scalloped apron, on cabriole legs with crooked feet, retaining an old black surface.

c1740

$5,500-6,500 POOK

A pair of 18thC Pennsylvania Transitional walnut side chairs, with yoked toprail and solid vasiform splat, on cabriole legs with trifid feet.

$2,500-3,500 FRE

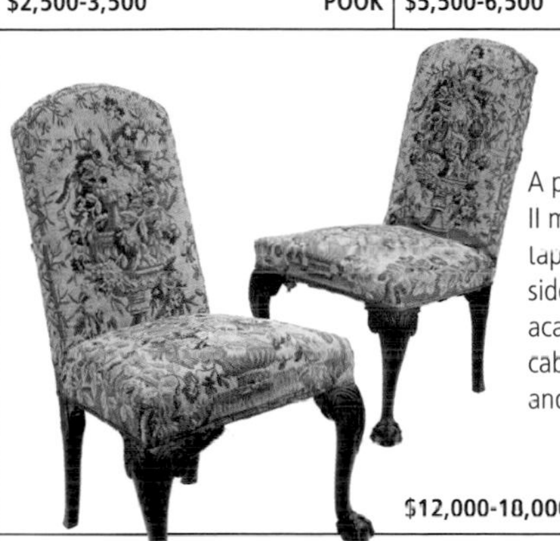

A pair of George II mahogany and tapestry-upholstered side chairs, on acanthus-carved cabriole legs with claw-and-ball feet.

$12,000-18,000 L&T

A George II carved walnut side chair, with solid splat carved at the crest with a shell, on shell-carved cabriole legs with claw-and-ball feet.

$2,000-3,000 POOK

A 18thC satinwood Burgomaster chair, with caned back panels and seat.

It is likely that the 'Burgomaster' chair derives from the circular or hexagonal seats used by dignitaries in southern India and Sri Lanka. From the mid-17thC these seats were adapted by Singhalese or Tamil furniture makers for officers of the European East India companies, particularly the Dutch Vereenigde Oostindische Compagnie (VOC). Some early example were made of ebony inlaid with ivory, while others are typically of satinwood. The form was copied throughout the Dutch East Indies – many of these later examples are made of teak. The term 'Burgomaster' chair was introduced in the 19thC (the contemporary name was 'round chair'), presumably inspired by the notion that they were made for prosperous, middle-ranking administrators in the VOC.

$4,000-6,000 SWO

A six-piece Louis XV beechwood salon suite, Francois Reuze, including two fauteuils and four side chairs, each stamped 'FRC*REVZE', on carved cabriole legs.

$8,000-12,000 RTC

A set of six George III mahogany side chairs, upholstered in 20thC gros point floral woolwork, on chamfered Gothic blind-fret forelegs and splayed back legs with stretchers.

$7,000-10,000 AH

A pair of George III mahogany side chairs, the serpentine toprail carved with a ribbon-tied garland, the pierced splat carved with anthemion, on square straight legs with stretchers, stamped with crowned 'WR'.

$2,000-3,000 FRE

A pair of George III Chippendale Gothic mahogany side chairs.

c1780

$1,000-1,500 DN

A late 18thC Philadelphia Chippendale carved mahogany side chair, with pierced Gothic splat, on cabriole legs with claw-and-ball feet.

$3,000-4,000 POOK

A set of four late George III painted side chairs, the wheel-backs painted with Greek keys and on eagle leg supports, the apron painted with palmettes, with caned seats, on simulated-reeded turned legs.

c1800

$5,000-7,000 L&T

A pair of Regency black lacquer and brass -mounted side chairs, with caned seats, on tapered octagonal forelegs and sabre back legs.

c1815

$2,500-3,500 FRE

A pair of small mid-19thC Danish walnut side chairs, attributed to M G Bindesboll, the overstuffed seats upholstered in the original red Genoa velvet, on ring-turned splayed legs with spindle stretchers.

$2,500-3,500 L&T

A pair of Renaissance Revival carved side chairs, the toprail carved with foliage and with urn finials, with needlepoint-upholstered back and seats.

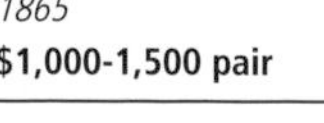

$2,500-3,500 LHA

One of a pair of Victorian mahogany and upholstered side chairs, attributed to Gillows, with foliate-carved scroll backs, upholstered in buttoned red faux-leather, on reeded turned tapered legs, one chair signed 'J. Barlow' and dated.

1865

$1,000-1,500 pair L&T

A George II mahogany corner chair, with vasiform splats, on cabriole legs with pad feet.

$1,500-2,500 FRE

A George II walnut corner chair, the toprail with chair-back pediment, with re-upholstered seat, on a carved cabriole foreleg with pad foot and straight turned back legs.

$2,500-3,500 TRI

A late 18thC possibly Massachusetts Chippendale tiger-maple, sycamore and birch roundabout chair, with pierced splats, with probably original rush seat, on beaded legs with cross-stretchers.

Provenance: Old Taft Tavern, North Uxbridge, Massachusetts, where Washington stayed in late 1789.

$6,500-8,500 SK

Miller's Compares: Hall Chairs

Hall chairs were introduced in Britain in the late 17thC. They may have been inspired by 'sgabelli', which were popular in Italian palaces in the 16thC. Hall chairs were designed to be placed in the entrance hall or passageway where they would be used mainly by tradesmen or tenants waiting to be called into one of the main rooms. Consequently they were not upholstered and lacked arms. Recently hall chairs have fallen out of fashion, as few of us have hallways or visiting tradespeople lingering in them! However, good quality examples will always find a buyer.

These chairs may have been made by society cabinetmakers Mayhew & Ince.

The fluted frieze with turned roundels adds elegance, as do the tapered and fluted legs.

These chairs have an excellent color and patination.

A pair of George III mahogany hall chairs, in the manner of Mayhew & Ince, with radiating backs and dished seats, the fluted friezes with turned roundels, on square tapered legs.

c1780

$15,000-20,000 DN

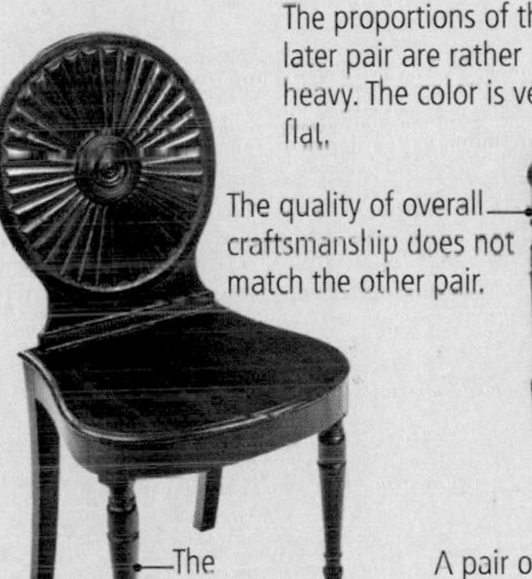

The proportions of this later pair are rather heavy. The color is very flat.

The quality of overall craftsmanship does not match the other pair.

The baluster turned legs are rather pedestrian.

A pair of George III mahogany hall chairs, with radiating backs, on baluster-turned legs and feet.

$2,000-3,000 L&T

A matched pair of hall chairs, including a George III mahogany chair (left) and a late 19th/early 20thC oak chair (right).

$4,000-6,000 DN

A pair of Regency mahogany hall chairs, with brass-inlaid cresting rails above oval splats, on ring-turned splayed legs.

$1,200-1,800 GORL

A New Zealand rimu hall chair, with naively carved decoration.

While English hall chairs were used for servants or callers of lower social status, hall chairs in New Zealand colonial houses were typically no more than a decorative element adding an air of elegance to the entrance way.

c1885

$400-600 DS

A probably late 16th/early 17thC provincial walnut stool.

$2,500-3,500 **DOR**

A late 17thC oak joint stool, on turned gun-barrel legs with block feet and stretchers.

22in (57cm) high

$2,000-3,000 **TEN**

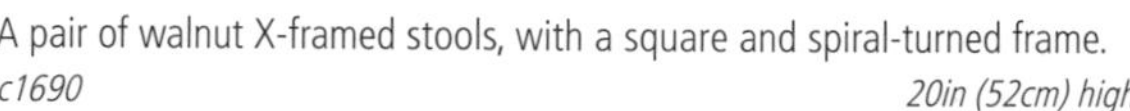

A pair of walnut X-framed stools, with a square and spiral-turned frame.

c1690 *20in (52cm) high*

$4,000-6,000 **DN**

A mahogany stool, with a scalloped apron, on carved cabriole legs with pad feet.

c1740 *20.25in (51cm) long*

$4,000-6,000 **POOK**

A George III mahogany stool, the shaped apron carved with flowers and C-scrolls, upholstered in floral machine-tapestry, on acanthus leaf-capped legs with claw-and-ball feet.

c1760 *23.5in (59.5cm) long*

$1,500-2,500 **WES**

A George III carved giltwood stool, upholstered in silk brocade, on cabriole legs headed by pataera and with scroll feet.

c1780

$2,000-3,000 **DN**

A pair of Regency rosewood foot stools, the upholstered seats within carved gadrooned borders, on X-shaped legs with turned stretchers.

$5,500-6,500 **SWO**

A Regency rosewood and leather-upholstered stool.

c1815 *37in (94cm) long*

$3,500-4,500 **DN**

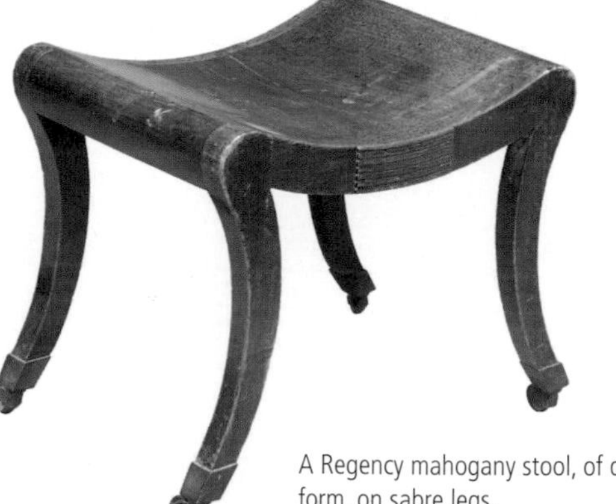

A Regency mahogany stool, of dished form, on sabre legs.

c1815 *22in (56cm) long*

$2,000-3,000 **DN**

A joined oak armchair, the back carved with Gothic tracery, with recessed linen-fold panels to base and sides.

$15,000-20,000 **TEN**

A Charles I joined oak panel-back armchair, the applied molded back with parquetry borders, on turned and block legs with stretchers, stamped 'G:CATCHP?L'.

$5,000-7,000 **WW**

An early 17thC and later oak panel-back armchair, on square-section legs with stretchers.

$12,000-18,000 **DN**

A joined oak panel-back armchair, the back flanked by carved scrolls and stylized foliage and carved with a lozenge issuing scrolls, on baluster-turned legs with stretchers, dated.

1642

$8,000-12,000 **DN**

A Charles I oak panel-back armchair, with foliate carved toprail and coat-of-arms to back panel, on turned legs with square-section feet and stretchers.

Provenance: These arms are believed to be those of Sir Richard Wilbraham of Woodhey, Co, Chester (1579-1643) impaling those of his wife Grace, daughter of Sir John Savage of Rocksavage, Bart. The arms contain four quaterterings of the Wilbraham Coat and twelve for Savage. The Wilbraham-Savage marriage took place in or before 1601. Sir Richard Wilbraham was born in 1579 was knighted 4th September 1603 and was created a Baronet on 5th May 1621. He died in 1643, making it likely this chair was made between 1621 and 1643.

c1640

$8,000-12,000 **DN**

ESSENTIAL REFERENCE - SETTLES

The box-settle (so called because of the box or well beneath the seat) was known in northern Europe by the 15thC.

- **The earliest examples typically have planked seats and a pierced trellis or linen-fold paneled backs. They are often richly carved.**
- **Box-settles are usually of oak, although elm, chestnut and fruitwood were increasingly used in the 18thC.**
- **The 'monk's table' settle (which had a hinged back that could be converted into a table) was extremely popular in Britain and the Low Countries in the 16thC.**
- **Provincial settles continued to be made into the 19thC. Many of the most elaborately carved settles were either made or embellished during the 19thC.**

A Charles II and later oak panel-back armchair, possibly Lancashire, with a carved and scrolling toprail, the panel carved with stylized tulips and roses, on turned legs.

$4,000-6,000 **DUK**

A mid-17thC joined oak panel-back armchair, probably South Yorkshire, the back carved with stylized flowerheads and lunettes, on baluster-turned legs with stretchers.

$12,000-18,000 **DN**

A 17thC and later joined oak panel-back settle, the back with three foliate and scrolling relief panels surrounded by an egg-and-dart border over five fielded panels, initialed 'IL' and dated, the hinged box-base with paneled frieze, dated.

1686 *64in (163cm) wide*

$2,500-3,500 **TEN**

A 17thC and later Continental walnut and marquetry caqueteuse armchair, the arched top with relief lunette decoration above a dolphin carved frieze, the paneled back with marquetry of an urn issuing flowers, on turned legs with bun feet and stretchers.

$2,500-3,500 DN

A mid-17thC joined oak panel-back armchair, possibly West Midlands, the back with shaped scrolling foliate motifs centered by a palmette, initialed 'I M' and 'T K', on block and square-section baluster legs with stretchers.

Square-section legs and arm-supports of this kind are extremely rare on English armchairs, which normally have turned supports.

$30,000-40,000 DN

A joined oak panel-back armchair, West Country, the crest carved with hounds, with a foliate carved panel and lunette carved frieze, on turned and block legs with stretchers, the reverse with initials 'D' over 'RS'.

$8,000-12,000 WW

A mid-late 17thC Connecticut joined oak panel-back armchair, the panel top carved with tulips, with late 19thC upholstery, with plaque reading 'Presented to Fraternity Lodge by James Kimball Nov. 18th 1880', with losses and restoration, refinished.

$3,500-4,500 SK

An early 18thC American Northern Colonies red-oak panel-back armchair, on block- and baluster-turned legs.

c1710

$15,000-20,000 POOK

A late 17thC and later probably Spanish stained walnut-framed armchair, the molded scroll arms on tapered column supports, on conforming legs with molded X-stretcher.

$1,200-1,800 L&T

A probably Chester County, Pennsylvania William and Mary walnut banister-back armchair, with ring- and baluster-turned arm-supports, on ring- and block-turned legs with turned frontal stretcher and box stretchers to sides, with domed ball feet.

c1730

$5,000-7,000 POOK

A Southeastern Pennsylvania William & Mary banister-back armchair, the back with punched star decoration, retaining an old black-painted surface.

c1735

$30,000-40,000 POOK

A Delaware Valley Queen Anne walnut armchair, the cupid's bow toprail above a solid splat, the slip seat concealing the original close stool frame, on shell-carved cabriole legs with trifid feet.

A pair of related chairs featuring a virtually identical splat, made by Solomon Fussell for Benjamin Franklin, are currently held in the Henry Ford Museum.

c1755

$9,000-11,000 POOK

A mid-18thC mahogany armchair, the toprail carved with foliage and a rocaille crest, with a carved and pierced vasiform splat, with a drop-in seat, on acanthus-carved cabriole legs with claw-and-ball feet.

$800-1,200 WW

CLOSER LOOK - GEORGE II ARMCHAIR

This chair displays the influence of French design on mid-18thC English cabinetmakers who sought to offer furniture in the French style to their clientele.

The shell and leaf carving is crisp and original.

London cabinetmaker Thomas Chippendale and his contemporaries Mayhew & Ince, both included designs for French-style furniture in their respective pattern books.

The chair has wonderful proportions.

A mid-18thC George II mahogany-framed library armchair, the armrests with shell- and leaf-carved handrests, the seat rails carved with C-scrolls and centered by a shell on a diaper ground, on leaf-carved cabriole legs with scroll feet, formerly with casters.

c1755

$50,000-70,000 FRE

A pair of Louis XV provincial walnut-framed armchairs, the toprails and seat rails carved with scrolls, flowers and leaves, on cabriole legs.

$5,000-7,000 DN

A pair George III mahogany-framed Gainsborough chairs, upholstered in foliate tapestry, on square chamfered legs with H-stretchers.

c1760

$14,000-16,000 L&T

A George III mahogany elbow chair, the arched back carved with flowerheads, leaves and husks, the pierced waisted splat carved as an anthemion and scrolls.

c1760

$5,000-7,000 SWO

A New England Queen Anne yoke-back armchair, retaining an old black painted surface.

c1760

$3,500-4,500 POOK

A pair of George III mahogany-framed Gainsborough chairs, made for Hackwood Park, upholstered in foliate-pattern silk fabric, with reeded outscrolling arms, on carved cabriole legs with scroll feet and castors.

c1765

$100,000-150,000 L&T

Two of a set of six George III mahogany salon chairs, the oval backs with molded channel carving, the swept arm-supports carved with tapering vitruvian scrolls, with channel-carved serpentine seat rails, on turned tapered and fluted legs.

$15,000-20,000 set SWO

An unusual George III mahogany-framed wing armchair, with upholstered wings and arms.

It's likely this chair was made for life on board a ship.

$700-1,000 SWO

A George III mahogany- and beech-framed upholstered armchair, with outswept scroll arms, on blind-fret carved square-section legs with stretchers.

c1780

$5,000-7,000 DN

A pair of George III mahogany-framed armchairs.

c1780

$3,500-4,500 DN

A pair of George III satinwood shield-back armchairs, in the manner of George Hepplewhite, the frames carved with guilloche, the backs with five reeded and foliate-clasped splats each terminating in fan medallions, on turned tapered reeded legs headed by rectangular panels with flowerheads, with pinched feet.

c1780

$10,000-15,000 DN

A pair of 18th/19thC Italian-Baroque-style walnut-framed armchairs, upholstered in leather, on baluster legs with stretchers.

$9,000-11,000 FRE

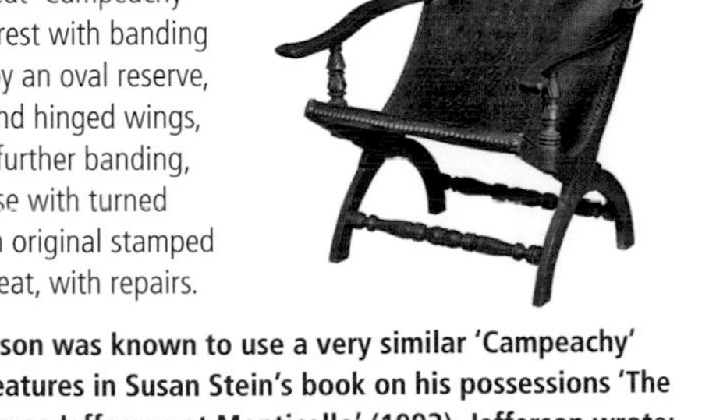

A Mid-Atlantic States Federal inlaid and carved mahogany-framed sling-seat 'Campeachy' armchair, the crest with banding and centered by an oval reserve, with padded and hinged wings, the arms with further banding, on a curule base with turned stretchers, with original stamped black leather seat, with repairs.

Thomas Jefferson was known to use a very similar 'Campeachy' chair, which features in Susan Stein's book on his possessions 'The Worlds of Thomas Jefferson at Monticello' (1993). Jefferson wrote: 'While too weak to sit up the whole day and afraid to increase the weakness by lying down, I long for a Siesta chair, which would have admitted the medium position. I must therefore pray you to send by Henry the one made by Johnny Hemmings...'

1810-25

$8,000-12,000 SK

A New England Federal inlaid mahogany-framed lolling armchair, the arm supports with central flowerhead and line inlays, on line-inlaid square tapered legs with banded cuffs.

c1800

$10,000-15,000 POOK

A pair of French Empire swan's neck chairs.

c1810

$4,000-6,000 SWO

A Regency painted and gilded armchair, the back with lattice design, on square tapered forelegs with spade feet.
c1810
$1,000-1,500 DN

A Gillows rosewood-framed armchair, upholstered in close-nailed green leather, with scrolling anthemion-carved toprail, the arms with reeded hand-rests and acanthus-carved arm-supports, on turned and tapered reeded forelegs, stamped 'Gillow'.
c1825
$8,000-12,000 TEN

Three of a set of six rare German Biedermeier cherrywood armchairs, with upholstered seats and backrests, with later covers.
c1830
$4,000-6,000 set DOR

A Northern Italian carved walnut armchair, Florence, attributed to Giuseppe Colzi, with foliate-carved toprail, dolphin- and wing-carved scrolling part-upholstered arms and fluted carved seat rail, on acanthus-carved tapered legs.
c1830
$5,000-7,000 FRE

A pair of William IV simulated-rosewood armchairs, in the manner of Gillows, with gadrooned and scroll serpentine carved back rails, with caned seats with cushions, on reeded tapered legs.
c1835
$2,000-3,000 DN

A Victorian low armchair, with turned mahogany arm-supports, upholstered in burgundy leather, with ceramic castors.
$800-1,200 WW

One of a pair of 19thC Baltic States or Scandinavian gold-painted hardwood-framed armchairs, the backrests painted with flowers and a medallion, the armrests carved as snakes on C-scroll supports, on reeded legs, with restored upholstery.

$10,000-15,000 pair DOR

A 19thC Venetian carved walnut-framed armchair, after Andrea Brustolon, the scrolled arms carved with putti and supported by carved male figures.
$5,000-7,000 FRE

A 19thC walnut-framed armchair, upholstered in floral verdure tapestry, on S-scroll legs with H-stretcher.
$2,000-3,000 TOV

A Victorian mahogany-framed revolving tub armchair, on cabriole legs with ball feet and casters, with label for 'Globe Wernicke Co. Limited, London, Paris and Buenos Aires'.
c1890
$1,000-1,500 DN

A Victorian George III-style carved mahogany and marquetry-framed armchair, the back with carved drapery and sphinx supports, on turned legs.

This chair is after a design by Robert Adam for an armchair in Osterley Park.

c1900

$1,200-1,800 DN

An early 20thC Sheraton Revival satinwood and polychrome-decorated armchair, painted with feather plumes, drapes, husks, paterae and foliage, with cane seat.

$2,500-3,500 WW

ESSENTIAL REFERENCE - LATER REPRODUCTIONS

As most reproduction furniture made from the mid-19thC onward was produced by machines, rather than by hand, such pieces are usually of a lower quality and are less valuable than originals.

- **It is often possible to tell a reproduction piece by ensuring the wood that it is made from is right for the period. Indigenous woods, such as oak, were used in the 16thC and early 17thC. Walnut became predominant in the mid-late 17thC and was largely superseded by mahogany from the mid-18thC.**
- **Machine-made furniture is likely to have circular saw marks, whereas a handmade piece will have more irregular marks. Similarly, irregularities of embellishment are likely to indicate that the decoration was carried out by hand.**
- **Early pieces typically have cabinet-maker's joins, whereas machine-made pieces are likely to be joined together with screws or glue.**

An Edwardian mahogany dressing-room armchair, with boxwood line inlays, the pierced back with floral-inlaid panel, upholstered in gold-colored floral fabric, on cabriole forelegs with H-stretcher, with additional stretcher across back legs.

$250-350 CAPE

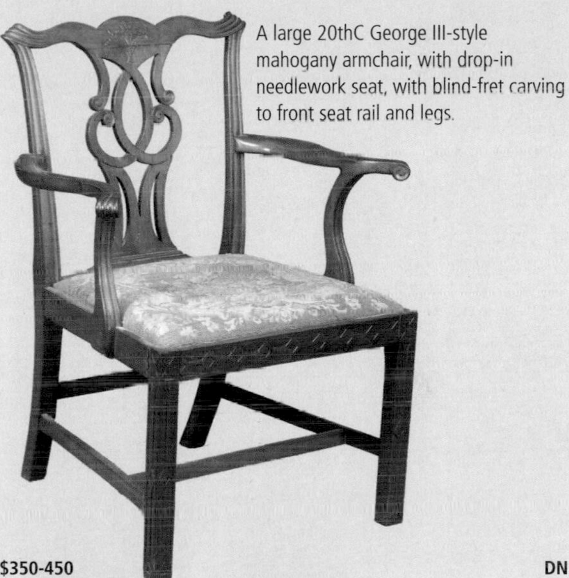

A large 20thC George III-style mahogany armchair, with drop-in needlework seat, with blind-fret carving to front seat rail and legs.

$350-450 DN

A Regency mahogany library bergère armchair, with brass-mounted book rest.

c1800

$5,500-6,500 CHEF

A Regency mahogany library bergère armchair, the reeded back and arms with split cane upholstery and loose squab cushions, the reading slope on ratchet support for use either side, with sliding foot-rest, on lotus-turned tapered legs with brass castors.

$4,000-6,000 L&T

A George IV mahogany library bergère armchair, with upholstered arms and loose squab cushions.

c1825

$4,000-6,000 DN

ESSENTIAL REFERENCE - WING ARMCHAIRS

The 'wings' at the back of armchairs were designed to keep out drafts. The first recorded examples were made in France from the early 1670s.

- Wing armchairs were made in the UK from the late 17thC. They were popular until the mid-18thC and are still produced today.
- Early wing armchairs were made of walnut or stained beech, with mahogany being used from the 18thC in Britain. Walnut and maple were used in North America during the same period.
- 17thC wing armchairs generally have highly carved legs and stretchers. Queen Anne and George I wing armchairs have pad feet and are often carved with husks and shells on the top of the knees. The most refined examples were upholstered in needlework.

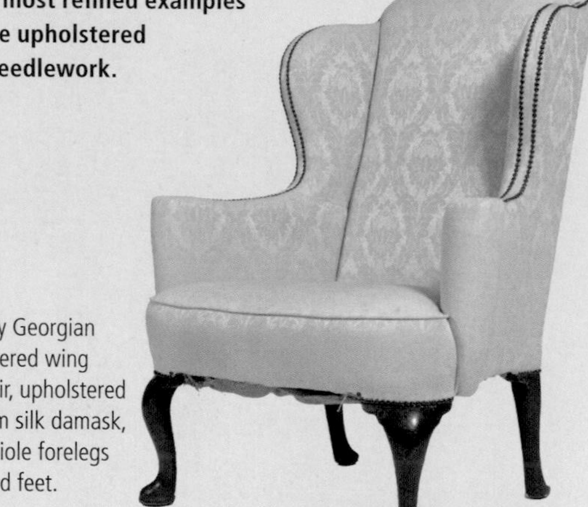

An early Georgian upholstered wing armchair, upholstered in cream silk damask, on cabriole forelegs with pad feet.

$6,500-7,500 TEN

A Queen Anne-style walnut-framed upholstered wing armchair, on possibly associated cabriole legs with pad feet, re-railed.

$1,000-1,500 L&T

A George II carved and upholstered wing armchair, the back and seat upholstered with needlework, on acanthus-carved cabriole forelegs and outswept back legs with turned stretchers.

c1740

$5,000-7,000 DN

A New England Queen Anne mahogany-framed upholstered wing armchair, upholstered in 18thC-style needlework, on cabriole legs with pad feet and block-and-ring turned stretchers.

c1750-70

$5,000-7,000 POOK

A mid-18thC Massachusetts Queen Anne walnut-framed upholstered wing armchair, with loose cushion, on cabriole legs with pad feet and block-and-ring stretchers.

$5,000-7,000 POOK

A Philadelphia Chippendale mahogany-framed upholstered wing armchair, with loose cushion, on square legs with Marlborough feet and stretchers.

1760-80

$10,000-15,000 POOK

A Georgian upholstered wing armchair, with button-tufted back and sides and overstuffed seat, on forelegs with claw-and-ball feet and plain back legs.

$3,000-4,000 FRE

A large George III-style mahogany-framed upholstered armchair, on chamfered straight legs with H-stretcher.

$500-700 TRI

A late 18th/early 19thC Federal barrel-back upholstered armchair, on square tapered legs with brass casters.

$2,000-3,000 **FRE**

A Regency mahogany-framed leather-upholstered library armchair, the back and seat surrounded by brass nail-heads, with scroll handrests, on carved tapered forelegs and outswept back legs with brass casters.

$3,000-4,000 **FRE**

A late George IV mahogany-framed upholstered library armchair, with acanthus-carved arms, on reeded tapered legs.

$2,500-3,500 **GORL**

A George IV rosewood-framed upholstered bergère armchair, upholstered in blue striped velvet, on shaped profile supports with bun feet, both mounted with brass.

$3,500-4,500 **L&T**

A pair of Regency ebonized-framed upholstered library armchairs, with gilt-metal mounts, upholstered in tassled-rope pattern ivory fabric, on turned tapered legs with brass caps and castors.

c1820

$5,000-7,000 **L&T**

A George IV rosewood- and mahogany-framed upholstered bergère armchair, the molded toprail with scroll-carved terminals, the arm supports with acanthus carving, on quatrefoil headed reeded tapered legs with lion's paw feet.

c1825

$10,000-15,000 **DN**

A William IV patent mahogany-framed upholstered library armchair, with carved acanthus leaf sides, with reclining action and pull-out foot rest, on turned lobed forelegs and outswept back supports.

Although in poor condition, this chair's flamboyant design indicates a prominent maker. Surprisingly this example does not appear to be stamped or labeled.

$15,000-20,000 **SWO**

A near pair of William IV mahogany-framed leather-upholstered armchairs, attributed to Gillows, with lotus-carved turned arm-supports, on lotus-carved tapered legs headed by stylized flowerheads with brass castors.

c1835

$7,000-10,000 **DN**

A late Victorian upholstered armchair, Howard & Sons, on turned walnut legs with brass castors, stamped 'HOWARD AND SON'S LTD LONDON'.

$3,500-4,500 **WW**

A Victorian ebonized-framed upholstered wing armchair, upholstered with a carpet fragment and green velvet.

c1880

$1,000-1,500 **DN**

A pair of late 19thC/early 20thC George II-style walnut-framed and upholstered wing armchairs, with loose cushions, on shell-carved cabriole legs with stylized pad feet.

$12,000-18,000 **DN**

Library Armchairs

A pair of early Victorian oak-framed leather-upholstered library armchairs, with scrolled armrests, on lappet-carved legs with brass caps and castors, one with adjustable bookrest and with plaque inscribed 'HMS Brittania/the wooden home of/Will. F. Blair/for 7 years/1842', the other with plaque inscribed 'The Royal George/Sunk at Spithead Aug 19th 1782/1100 souls perished/Recovered 1840'.

c1842

$5,000-7,000 **L&T**

An early 20thC probably Colonial ebonized-rosewood-framed upholstered armchair, on carved cabriole forelegs with claw-and-ball feet.

$1,200-1,800 **DN**

A late 19thC Chippendale carved mahogany-framed upholstered wing armchair, the frame carved with acanthus leaves, flowerheads and shells, upholstered in floral needlework tapestry, on square legs with block feet and pierced H-stretcher.

$5,000-7,000 **TEN**

One of a pair of 20thC George IV-style mahogany-framed leather-upholstered library armchairs, on square tapered legs.

$4,000-6,000 pair **DN**

A late Victorian mahogany- and ebony-framed tub armchair, with later green leather upholstery, on fluted tapered forelegs with ceramic castors.

$1,000-1,500 **WW**

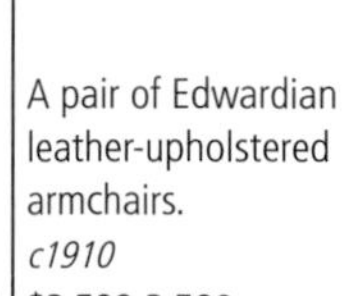

A pair of William IV-style mahogany-framed upholstered armchairs, with scroll terminals centered by paterae, on tapered legs with carved lion's paw feet.

c1900

$3,000-4,000 **DN**

A pair of Edwardian leather-upholstered armchairs.

c1910

$2,500-3,500 **DN**

CLOSER LOOK - GEORGE II SETTEE

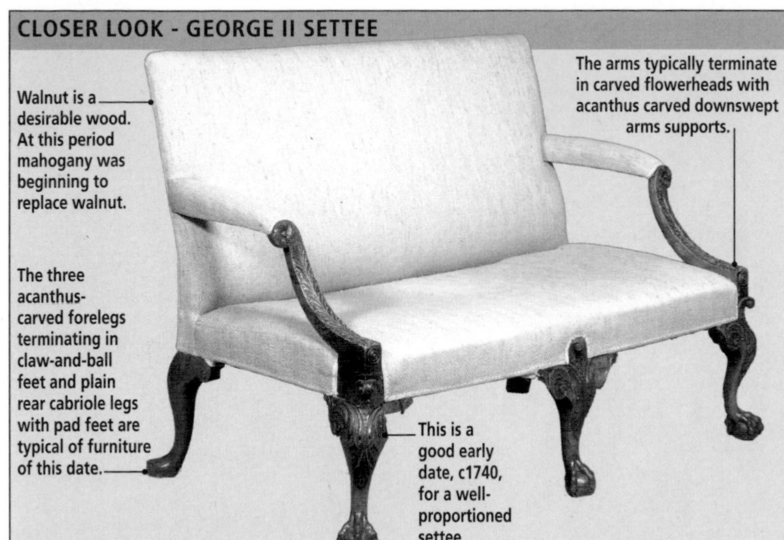

A George II walnut-framed upholstered settee, the upholstered arms terminating in carved flowerheads with acanthus-carved arm-supports, on three acanthus-carved forelegs with claw-and-ball feet and three cabriole back legs with pad feet.

c1740 *55in (140cm) wide*

$35,000-45,000 **DN**

A George II walnut-framed upholstered settee, on cabriole legs headed by scroll terminals with pad feet and leather castors.

55in (140cm) wide

$6,500-7,500 **H&L**

A George II walnut-framed upholstered 'shepherds crook' settee, upholstered with 17thC needlework, on shell-carved cabriole forelegs with paw feet and splayed back legs.

c1750 *77in (195cm) wide*

$15,000-20,000 **DN**

An 18thC Italian Baroque-style painted wooden bench, painted with putti and the coat-of-arms of the Giustiniani family.

84in (214cm) wide

$25,000-35,000 **DOR**

A George III and later mahogany-framed upholstered settee, upholstered in foliate-patterned gold-colored fabric, on square chamfered legs with stretchers.

46in (118cm) wide

$1,200-1,800 **L&T**

A George III mahogany quadruple chairback settee, the shield-shaped backrests with carved toprails above Prince of Wales feathers and swags, with padded seat, on square tapered legs with spade feet.

c1780 *72in (183cm) wide*

$7,000-10,000 **FRE**

A late 18thC satinwood and caned settee, the toprail painted with landscapes, the frame with flowers and ribbons.

69in (174cm) wide

$2,500-3,500 **SWO**

A Regency mahogany-framed upholstered settee, upholstered in cream floral damask, with turned and reeded arm-supports and ebony-strung spandrels, on turned and reeded tapered legs with castors.

72in (183cm) wide

$4,000-6,000 **TEN**

A late George III mahogany-framed upholstered campaign sofa, with a removable back and arms and a loose cushion, on reeded legs with stretchers.

90.5in (230cm) wide

$6,500-7,500 **L&T**

A Regency mahogany-framed upholstered settee, with fluted scroll back. on sabre legs with hairy-paw caps and castors.

c1820 *87in (222cm) wide*

$1,500-2,500 **L&T**

A George IV carved giltwood-framed upholstered scroll-end sofa, in the manner of Gillows, with some later paintwork.

c1825 *79in (200cm) wide*

$3,500-4,500 **DN**

A William IV rosewood-framed upholstered settee, with acanthus-carved scroll arms, upholstered in gray and plum-colored foliate patterned fabric, on lappet-carved turned tapered legs with brass caps and castors.

c1830 *87in (220cm) wide*

$2,500-3,500 **L&T**

A New York Rococo Revival rosewood-framed upholstered 'Stanton Hall' settee, J. & J.W. Meeks, with scrolled and pierced cresting centered by roses and molded apron, on molded cabriole legs with casters.

65.5in (166cm) wide

$2,500-3,500 **FRE**

A Victorian walnut-framed upholstered conversation settee, the central support with leaf-carved and scrolling arm-support above a sprung base, upholstered in peach button-back dralon, on stout cabriole legs with brass castors.

$1,500-2,500 **TEN**

A pair of 19thC Biedermeier upholstered settees, with pinwheel and ebonized half-column decoration.

71in (180cm) wide

$5,500-6,500 **DRA**

A 19thC Dutch mahogany- and floral marquetry-framed upholstered sofa, with chequer-banding, upholstered in black and gold cut-velvet, on carved dolphin feet.

88in (223.5cm) wide

$6,500-7,500 **HT**

A late 19thC George III-style mahogany-framed triple chairback settee, with green silk damask upholstered seat.

$3,500-4,500 **WES**

A late 19thC New York Renaissance Revival carved rosewood-framed upholstered three-piece parlor suite, attributed to John Jelliff (1813-1893), comprising a kidney-shaped sofa with lion's mask arms and two side chairs.

Settee 69in (175cm) wide

$3,500-4,500 **FRE**

A German antler-mounted upholstered settee, the back panel embossed with an image of a pig hunt within a frame of fallow and red deer antlers, the seat and arms upholstered in later brown hide, on outswept antler legs.

c1880 *69in (175cm) wide*

$3,500-4,500 **TEN**

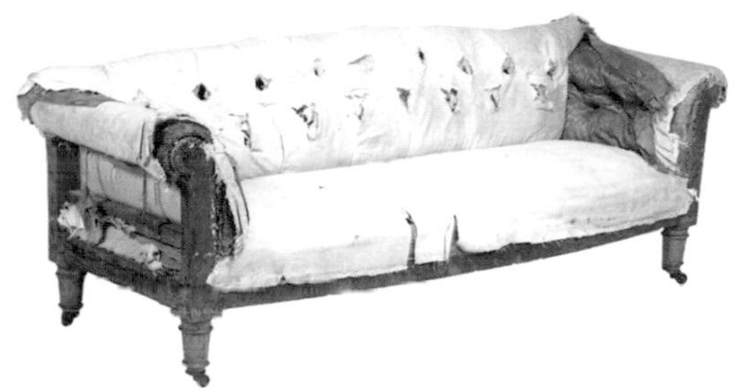

A Victorian satin-birch-framed upholstered settee, stamped 'Gillows', on turned tapered legs with brass castors.

c1880 *77in (195cm) wide*

$5,000-7,000 **DN**

One of a pair of late 19th/early 20thC William and Mary-style carved oak-framed upholstered settees, on short cabriole legs with carved shaped stretchers.

63in (159cm) wide

$3,500-4,500 pair **DN**

A Louis XV-style giltwood-framed Aubusson tapestry salon suite, comprising a settee and four armchairs and four side chairs, on cabriole legs with castors.

c1900 *Settee 75in (190cm) wide*

$9,000-11,000 set **TEN**

An Edwardian Neo-classical Revival walnut-framed upholstered settee, the arched toprail carved with berried laurel leaves, the arm supports carved with bellflowers and the frieze carved with floral swags, upholstered in foliate patterned green damask, on fluted tapered legs with brass castors.

87in (220cm) wide

$3,000-4,000 **TOV**

One of a pair of 17thC-style settees, with cartouche-shaped back, upholstered in red and cream moquette, on turned baluster legs with scrolling paw feet on sledge bases.

By repute from the Dorchester Hotel, London.

c1920 *65in (165cm) wide*

$4,000-6,000 pair **TEN**

FURNITURE

A Regency mahogany cockfighting chair, the back fitted with a pivoting and adjustable baize-lined reading slope above vertical splats, with brown leather-upholstered seat, on turned tapered legs with brass caps and castors.

32in (82cm) high

$8,000-12,000 **L&T**

A rare miniature Pennsylvania painted wooden chair, Joseph Lehn (1798-1892), with decoupage floral decoration on a salmon-pink painted ground with red pinstriping and gilt.

13.5in (34cm) high

$5,000-7,000 **POOK**

An early Victorian mahogany and caned folding Robinson & Sons campaign chair, on baluster turned legs with brass caps and ceramic castors.

c1840

$500-700 **DN**

A walnut and beech children's twin-seat rocking chair, the central pierced uprights supporting two tiers and surmounted by Prince of Wales feathers, with two tub-shaped armchairs carved with scrolls and foliage.

c1860 *67in (170cm) long*

$1,200-1,800 **DN**

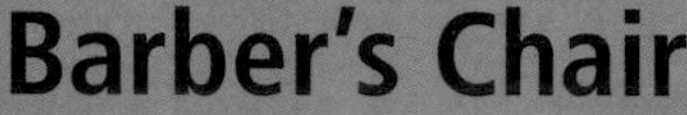

Barber's Chair

An American child's barber chair, attributed to the workshop of Marcus Charles Illions, the white enamel and cast-iron base supporting a fully-carved leopard with glass eyes and original painted surface.

Marcus Charles Illions was a Lithuanian-born Jewish carver, who opened his own carving company in Brooklyn, New York in 1909 and began to develop the 'Coney Island style' of carousel horse carving. His animals are notable for their animation and elaborate decoration.

$25,000-35,000 **POOK**

A New Zealand serpentine box seat, with original carpet top and mottled kauri front, on bun feet, missing interior.

The existence of the original carpet insert is rare.

c1880 *23in (59cm) long*

$400-600 **DS**

An Edwardian pine folding pushchair, on spoked wheels.

$120-180 **WHP**

A 17thC oak refectory table, with a single plank top, on six legs with stretchers, with alterations and replacements.

103in (262cm) long

$10,000-15,000 **SWO**

A 17thC Spanish walnut and wrought-iron trestle table, with three carved frieze drawers, on turned legs with bulbous feet with iron brackets.

70.25in (178cm) long

$12,000-18,000 **FRE**

A mid-17thC oak refectory table, the one-plank top above a molded frieze with zig-zag and stamped cross decoration, on six turned and block legs with stretchers.

134.25in (341cm) long

$30,000-40,000 **WW**

A mid-late 17thC French Baroque walnut refectory table, with three paneled frieze drawers, on baluster-turned legs with stretchers.

111.4in (283cm) long

$7,000-10,000 **SK**

A possibly Spanish walnut, elm and pine refectory table, with molded frieze, on bobbin-turned legs with stretchers.

c1700 *73in (186cm) long*

$3,000-4,000 **DN**

An early 18thC and later stained-oak refectory table, the carved arcaded front-frieze with leaf scroll brackets, on six block and turned tapered legs with stretchers.

101in (256.5cm) long

$4,000-6,000 **WW**

An 18thC and later oak refrectory table.

144in (367cm) long

$10,000-15,000 **DN**

An early 19thC French cherrywood refectory table, with one drawer and an opposing retractable cutting board.

79in (200cm) long

$5,000-7,000 **DN**

A rare Cromwellian oak gate-leg table, on paneled trestle-end legs and central vertical support, with molded feet and stretcher.

c1650 *Extended 51.5in (131cm) wide*

$8,000-12,000 **WW**

A Charles II oak gate-leg table.

c1680 43in (110cm) wide

$150-250 **DN**

A George I oak gate-leg table, with one drawer, on barley-twist turned legs with stretchers.

29.25in (74cm) long

$5,000-7,000 **POOK**

A New England William and Mary maple drop-leaf dining table, with one drawer, on baluster and ring-turned legs.

c1740 *40.75in (104cm) long*

$5,000-7,000 **POOK**

A George II mahogany triangular drop-leaf table, with three drop-flaps supported by pull-out slides (two missing), on club legs with pad feet, with depository label for George Milton & Sons, with old damage and restoration.

35.75in (91cm) long

$7,000-9,000 **WW**

A George II mahogany drop-leaf dining table, on cabriole legs with hoof feet.

c1750 *29in (74cm) high*

$3,500-4,500 **DN**

A mid-18thC New England Queen Anne red-painted maple drop-leaf dining table.

Extended 47.5in (120.5cm) long

$10,000-15,000 **SK**

A probably Irish George II mahogany drop-leaf dining table, with molded edge, on tapered legs with pad feet.

c1750 *29in (73cm) high*

$2,000-3,000 **DN**

A New York Sheraton drop-leaf dining table, on six legs.

c1840 *49in (124cm) long*

$600-800 **POOK**

ESSENTIAL REFERENCE - PEDESTAL TABLES

Pedestal dining tables were introduced during the reign of George II and were popular into the 19thC. Most are made of mahogany and have D-shaped ends.

- **Early pedestals were simple, much like the legs of contemporary tripod tables. During the 1760s, pedestals became increasingly rich in form and carving before becoming simpler to coincide with the popularity of Neo-classicalism in the 1780s and '90s. Ring-turned column pedestals were popular around the turn of the century.**
- **Table tops were usually covered by cloths and were thus typically plain as they would not be seen.**

A George III mahogany quadruple-pedestal D-end dining table, after a Gillows design, on turned column supports with cabriole legs with raised pad feet, with three additional leaves.

The same pattern was made for Bellamour, Staffordshire in 1798 by cabinet-maker George Atkinson, who executed a number of similar dining tables for Gillows between 1790 and 1802.

c1800 *Extended 182.5in (464cm) long*

$20,000-30,000 L&T

A George III mahogany triple-pedestal dining table, on downswept legs with brass caps and casters, with four additional leaves.

This table was previously owned by Sir Alexander Glen, former MI5 operative and friend of Ian Fleming, who reputedly based James Bond on Glen.

c1800 *Extended 135.75in (345cm) long*

$12,000-18,000 DN

A late Georgian mahogany dual-pedestal dining table, with reeded edge, on carved baluster supports with acanthus-carved and reeded downswept legs with brass caps and casters, with one additional leaf.

116in (295cm) long

$8,000-12,000 FRE

A New York Federal carved mahogany triple-pedestal dining table, attributed to the workshop of Duncan Phyfe, with reeded edge, each pedestal with four column uprights centered by a carved pineapple, on acanthus-carved and reeded legs with reeded brass cuffs.

c1805 *126.5in (321cm) long*

$12,000-18,000 POOK

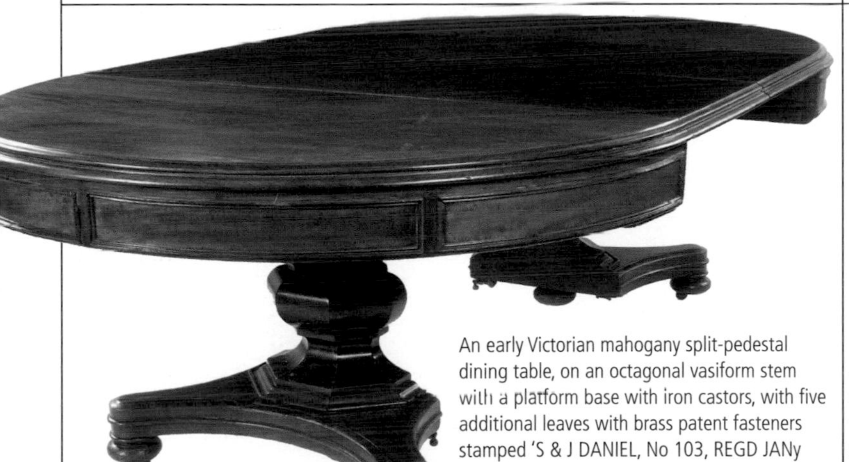

An early Victorian mahogany split-pedestal dining table, on an octagonal vasiform stem with a platform base with iron castors, with five additional leaves with brass patent fasteners stamped 'S & J DANIEL, No 103, REGD JANy 1844'.

Extended 151in (383.5cm) long

$8,000-12,000 WW

A 19thC-style Irish mahogany dual-pedestal dining table, with acanthus-carved and baluster-turned pedestals with downswept legs with scroll feet and recessed castors, adapts to a pair of side tables, with three additional leaves.

110in (279cm) long

$12,000-18,000 DN

A George III mahogany D-end extending dining table, on square tapered legs, with two hinged leaves.

Extended 120in (306cm) long

$5,000-7,000 **TEN**

A George III mahogany extending dining table, on turned tapered legs with brass caps and casters, with two additional leaves.

c1810 *Extended 78.75in (200cm) long*

$2,500-3,500 **DN**

A New England Sheraton mahogany extending dining table, with banded edges, on reeded legs with brass casters.

c1820 *48in (122cm) long*

$5,000-7,000 **POOK**

A George IV mahogany extending dining table, with three additional leaves.

c1825 *Closed 51in (129cm) long*

$15,000-20,000 **DN**

A Regency mahogany extending dining table, in the manner of Gillows, with reeded edge and brass handles to the shortest friezes, on baluster-turned tapered and reeded legs with brass caps and casters, with three additional leaves.

c1815 *Extended 137in (348cm) long*

$8,000-12,000 **DN**

Jupe-type Table

A Jupe-type mahogany expanding dining table, on a quadriform cluster column and plinth with paw feet, expanding with segment sections.

Robert Jupe patented the design for this table in 1835 stating that the table was 'an improved expanding table so constructed that the sections composing its surface may be caused to diverge from a common center and that the spaces caused thereby may be filled by inserting leaves or filling pieces'. Tables of this design were produced by Jupe in association with the cabinetmaker John Johnstone of New Bond Street, London.

Expanded 95in (241cm) diam

$20,000-30,000 **LC**

A 19thC mahogany extending dining table, with acanthus-carved split octagonal column support, with brass claw caps and castors, with four additional leaves.

60in (152cm) diam

$10,000-15,000 **GORL**

A Victorian burr-walnut extending dining table, in the manner of Johnstone & Jeanes, the quarter-veneered top on carved baluster supports with quadriform undertier, with bun feet, with four full additional leaves, two three-quarter leaves and five half leaves.

Extended 171in (434cm) long

$15,000-20,000 **L&T**

A Victorian mahogany extending dining table, on four bulbous gadrooned fluted tapered legs, with four additional leaves.

c1860 *Extended 142.5in (362cm) long*

$6,500-8,500 **TEN**

An Edwardian mahogany and satinwood-banded D-end extending dining table, with two square additional drop-leaves and additional D-ends, on square tapered legs with spade feet, stamped JOHN TAYLOR & SONS MANUFACTURERS EDINBURGH LTD.

c1900 *97.5in (245cm) long*

$2,500-3,500 **TEN**

A Scottish Regency mahogany dining table, the tilt top with lipped edge, on an octagonal acanthus-carved pedestal and gadrooned collar, the triform base with reeded bun feet and castors.

71in (181cm) diam

$12,000-18,000 **L&T**

A Regency mahogany and brass-inlaid octagonal dining table, the crossbanded tilt-top with a foliate brass-inlaid and bead-molded frieze, on brass-inlaid triform base with acanthus-carved scroll feet.

c1820 *54in (137cm) wide*

$20,000-30,000 **L&T**

A 19thC French cherrywood dining table, with frieze drawer, on square tapered legs.

138in (351cm) long

$7,000-10,000 **DUK**

A probably Charleston, South Carolina Federal mahogany inlaid drop-leaf breakfast table, the top chequer-banded, on foliate-inlaid and strung tapered legs with brass caps and casters, refinished.

c1800 *Closed 20.5in (52cm) long*

$20,000-30,000 **SK**

A Scottish Regency mahogany breakfast table, in the manner of William Trotter, the top with gadrooned edge, the concave quadriform base with paw feet with volute scrolls and wooden castors, with some losses.

53in (134cm) diam

$5,500-7,500 **SHAP**

A Regency rosewood breakfast table, the top with a satinwood border inlaid with scrolls and foliage, on downswept legs with brass caps and castors.

c1815 *57in (146cm) long*

$5,000-7,000 **L&T**

A George IV parquetry, specimen wood and mahogany breakfast table, the tilt top on a turned column support with paw feet.

c1825 *49in (124cm) diam*

$7,000-10,000 **L&T**

An early Victorian Gonçalo alves-veneered breakfast table, in the manner of Gillows, the tilt top with inlaid hexagonal motif and ebony stringing, the column support with leaf-carved collar and gadrooned base, with carved bun feet and later castors.

53.5in (136cm) diam

$2,000-3,000 **A&G**

A Victorian specimen-wood-inlaid breakfast table, the tilt top with a chequer-inlaid star in a satinwood ground within an ebonized border with entwined bandwork enclosed by an outer zig-zag border, on geometric-inlaid base with hairy paw feet.

45in (115cm) diam

$7,000-10,000 **L&T**

ESSENTIAL REFERENCE - JACKSON & GRAHAM

- **Jackson & Graham was established in 1836 by Thomas Jackson and Peter Graham at 37 Oxford Street, London.**
- **The company produced very high-quality furniture. It was notable for fine marquetry work, the use of Wedgwood plaques, ivory inlay, rare woods and fine casting of bronze mounts.**
- **Many leading designers of the period were employed by Jackson & Graham, including Owen Jones, Bruce Talbert, Alfred Lorimer and Eugene Prignot.**
- **The company represented Britain at many international exhibitions.**
- **Clients included Queen Victoria, Napoleon III, the Grand Khedive at Cairo and the royal palace in Siam.**
- **Jackson & Graham's workforce and assets were bought by Collinson & Lock in 1885.**

A Victorian coromandel, macassar ebony, amboyna, bone and satinwood marquetry breakfast table, probably Jackson & Graham, stamped '2/ 2065'.

c1870 *47in (120cm) diam*

$8,000-12,000 **DN**

CLOSER LOOK - VIENNESE CENTER TABLE

This table is inspired by French designs for tables by Lepautre, c1685.

The later marble top does not seriously affect the value.

The aprons (three later) are carved with acanthus and scrolls centered by a Diana mask. These replacements do have an impact on the value.

The elaborately carved square tapered legs with carved stretchers are typically centered by an urn.

This is a dramatic statement piece, with all the hallmarks of good Venetian craftsmanship.

A mid-18thC Viennese painted and parcel-gilt center table, with later pink-marble top, with restoration.

63in (160cm) long

$18,000-22,000 **MFA**

An early 18thC and later Italian scagliola and carved walnut side or center table, the top with a central armorial cartouche with lion rampant, with carved frieze, on straight tapered legs with recessed guilloche motifs.

c1700 *56in (142cm) long*

$7,000-10,000 **DN**

ESSENTIAL REFERENCE - MOREL & HUGHES

- **The London firm Morel & Hughes was established in 1805 by Nicholas Morel and Robert Hughes.**
- **Morel was strongly associated with the architect Henry Holland. Under Holland's direction, he worked on the decoration of Carlton House, the official London residence of the Prince of Wales (later George IV).**
- **As well as George IV, who was a frequent client, Morel & Hughes supplied furniture for nobles including the Dukes of Buccleuch, Northumberland, Bedford and the Earl of Mansfield.**
- **Morel and Hughes had ended their partnership by 1827. Morel subsequently went into partnership with George Seddon.**

An early 18thC Spanish painted and gilt center table, with later black-marble top, on a foliate-carved support with later ebonized base.

35in (89cm) wide

$5,000-7,000 **L&T**

A Neo-classical mahogany center table, with gray marble top, the frieze with ormolu foliate decoration, on three columnar legs with triform stretcher.

38.5in (98cm) diam

$5,500-7,500 **LHA**

A Regency tulipwood, ebonized and parcel-gilt center table, in the manner of Morel and Hughes, the top with an ebony-inlaid laurel border, on an anthemion-molded and gadrooned column with triform base with paw feet.

c1815 *51in (130cm) diam*

$30,000-40,000 **DN**

A Regency parcel-gilt and specimen-marble inlaid rosewood center table, on gilt scroll legs and a turned central column with triform base with scroll and paw feet, the top later.

31in (78.5cm) diam

$10,000-15,000 **WES**

An early 19thC Austrian Biedermeier mahogany-veneered and marquetry table, Vienna.

c1815-20 *37in (95cm) diam*

$6,500-7,500 **DOR**

A George IV rosewood, ebony and burl-walnut center table, the tilt top with an inlaid band of bellflowers, the column support carved at the base with rising leaves, with triform base with lobed bun feet.

c1825 *48in (122cm) diam*

$8,000-12,000 **FRE**

A George IV pollard-oak center table, on an octagonal column with turned collar, with bun feet.

c1825 *54in (137cm) diam*

$5,000-7,000 **DN**

A Charles X mahogany and specimen-marble inset center table, the top with radiating bands of specimen and sample hardstones, on hexagonal column with three voluted supports with paw feet, the top later.

c1830 *38in (97cm) diam*

$3,500-4,500 **DN**

CLOSER LOOK - MICROMOSAIC CENTER TABLE

This table was created in the workshop of Michelangelo Barberi (Italian,1787-1867) – highly distinctive high-quality Roman cabinetmakers.

The micromosaic's show monuments of Rome: St. Peter's Basilica/St. Peter's square, The Colosseum, Roman Forum, Baths of Caracalla, Castel Sant Angelo (Hadrian's Tomb), Pantheon, Temple of Vesta.

The giltwood bacchanalian base with putti exudes quality.

This table has tremendous pedigree – similar examples are in The Hermitage, St Petersburg and the Victoria and Albert Museum, London.

An Italian micromosaic and scagliola center table, the micromosaics depicting monuments of Rome, on giltwood base with putti, signed 'Cav. Barberi' and dated.

1855 *32in (81cm) diam*

$50,000-70,000 **DRA**

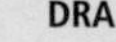

A large Victorian oak center table, the parquetry top with gadrooned edge and carved frieze, the carved Renaissance-style base comprised of four balusters around a central wrythen, on X-form base with castors.

89in (225cm) long

$3,000-4,000 **TEN**

A mid-Victorian burr-walnut center table, the quarter-veneered top with a molded edge above a shaped apron, on foliate-strapwork supports with acanthus-scroll feet.

49in (125cm) long

$1,500-2,500 **TOV**

A Louis XIV-style boulle center table, the top with a chariot enclosed by foliate arabesques and strapwork, with two frieze drawers centered by a cupid mount, on cabriole legs with satyr mask-mounts and hairy-paw feet.

c1860 *48.5in (123cm) long*

$12,000-18,000 **L&T**

A Victorian walnut center table, the top with carved molded border, the carved base with four scrolling legs centered by a squat finial and acanthus, with scroll feet.

c1880 *63in (160cm) long*

$20,000-30,000 **DN**

A late 19thC/early 20thC Louis XV-style carved giltwood and walnut-veneered center table, on a triform base with toupie feet.

36in (91cm) diam

$2,000-3,000 **L&T**

A carved center table, from the collection of the Empress Elisabeth of Austria, on turned feet with X-stretcher centered by an urn and dolphins, stamped 'Privatfond I K. K. Majestät' and with the Imperial double-eagle, with extendable flaps, the table-top associated.

c1890 *53in (135cm) long*

$12,000-18,000 **DOR**

An early-19thC-style mahogany center table, with white-marble top, with plain crossbanded frieze, on a reeded column and beaded ring-turned base with lappet-carved paw feet.

50in (124.5cm) diam

$10,000-15,000 **DN**

A Continental Renaissance-style gilt and malachite-veneered center table, the top with leaf-cast edge and foliate frieze, on three winged-serpent supports with pierced scrolling brackets and circular base.

42.5in (110cm) diam

$12,000-18,000 **TEN**

ESSENTIAL REFERENCE - JAMES MOORE

- **James Moore (c1670-1726) is best-known for for his rich, gilt gesso furniture. Such pieces were actually only a small part of his output, which also included fine walnut and mahogany furniture.**
- **Moore was the cabinetmaker to George I.**
- **He was in partnership with John Gumley from 1714.**
- **He completed the furnishing of Blenheim Palace after Sarah Churchill, Duchess of Marlborough, quarreled with her architect, John Vanbrugh. By 1714 the Duchess referred to Moore as 'my oracle, Mr. Moore' who 'certainly has very good sense and I think him very honest and understanding in many trades besides his own'.**
- **Benjamin Goodison, who became the next Royal cabinetmaker, trained in Moore's workshop.**

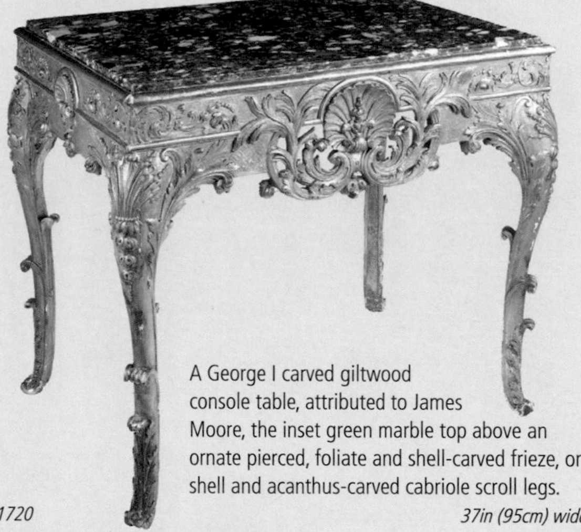

A George I carved giltwood console table, attributed to James Moore, the inset green marble top above an ornate pierced, foliate and shell-carved frieze, on shell and acanthus-carved cabriole scroll legs.

c1720 *37in (95cm) wide*

$10,000-15,000 L&T

A George I giltwood and gesso console table, in the manner of James Moore, with later red-marble top, on leaf-carved scrolling corner brackets and square tapered legs with leaf-carved block feet, with alterations.

39in (98cm) wide

$5,000-7,000 TEN

An 18thC and later Italian Baroque gold-painted console table, with damaged red-velvet top, on legs with rocaille ornament, with some restoration.

67in (170cm) wide

$6,500-7,500 DOR

A mid-18thC and later giltwood console table, with white marble top, the pierced foliate frieze over eagle support.

60in (152cm) wide

$7,000-9,000 DN

A small 18thC Italian carved and painted console table, with marble top.

32in (81cm) high

$8,000-12,000 DOR

A late 18thC Italian giltwood and painted console table, the marble top above a frieze carved with scrolling foliage and centered with a mask, on leaf-carved and fluted tapered legs, with some restoration.

46.75in (118.5cm) wide

$10,000-15,000 WW

A Regency painted pine, gilt and marble console table, the top with leaf-carved gilt molding, on tapered pillars with leaf-carved capitols, the back panel painted with a gilt mask of Apollo, on a plinth.

63in (160cm) wide

$5,000-7,000 TEN

A pair of Regency cream-painted and parcel-gilt console tables, on spiral wrythen legs.

47.5in (120.5cm) wide

$12,000-18,000 LC

A pair of Regency rosewood and marble console tables, on acanthus-carved scroll supports, with green silk-lined back panels, on shaped plinth bases.

31in (79cm) wide

$12,000-18,000 **L&T**

One of a pair of Regency carved giltwood, ebonized and black-marble console tables.

c1815 *30in (76cm) high*

$12,000-18,000 pair **DN**

A George IV rosewood and Carrara marble console table, on scroll-carved supports with paw feet, with damage.

44in (112.1cm) wide

$2,000-3,000 **WW**

A pair of George IV mahogany and marble console tables, with plain and bead-molded friezes, on gilt metal mounted legs with bead-molded bases.

c1825 *42in (107cm) wide*

$12,000-18,000 **DN**

A Regency amboyna and parcel-gilt mirrored console table, with marble top on twin lappet-carved fluted turned supports.

c1820 *44in (111cm) wide*

$12,000-18,000 **L&T**

One of a pair of New York Neo-classical rosewood-veneered mirrored pier tables, with black Egyptian marble tops, the frieze with gilt decoration of a lion's mask within a wreath, on ormolu-mounted supports with acanthus-carved wood and gesso feet with simulated vert antique surfaces.

c1820-30 *41.75in (106cm) wide*

$60,000-80,000 pair **SK**

A mid-19thC carved beech and marble console table, with arched mirror frame, the table with molded and acanthus-carved edge, on lion monopodia legs, missing upper mirror plate.

Provenance: Crookham House, Crookham, Newbury, Berkshire. In 1830 Crookham House was involved in the so-called 'Captain Swing' riots when agricultural workers roamed the countryside breaking machinery, which they believed was keeping wages down. On the evening of 17 November 1830 a group of men arrived at Crookham House intending to smash machines owned by the lord of the manor, Richard Tull. They were met by Tull himself, his own laborers and special constables. Tull and his men seized the ringleaders and a dozen or so of them were taken to Reading gaol.

89.5in (228cm) wide

$30,000-50,000 **DN**

A 19thC Continental carved giltwood console table, the green marble top above a flower-enclosed Greek key frieze with crowned mask, on acanthus-carved cabriole legs with claw-and-ball feet.

46in (117cm) wide

$5,000-7,000 **FRE**

A 19thC Italian Neo-classical giltwood console table, the later rouge and white marble top above a frieze carved with foliate scrolls and an urn, on foliate-carved and fluted tapered legs.

52in (132cm) wide

$5,000-7,000 **FRE**

One of a pair of Victorian Louis XVI-style giltwood pier tables, the marble tops above pierced foliate friezes, on tapered fluted legs.

c1870 *22.5in (54cm) wide*

$4,000-6,000 pair **DN**

A George II-style carved wood and painted console table, the faux-marble top above a leaf-carved cornice and floret-carved frieze with a central shell and fruiting swags, on griffin-headed scroll legs with hairy-paw feet.

This table is a copy of an example at Ditchley Park, Oxfordshire.

55in (139.5cm) wide

$7,000-10,000 **WW**

A George II-style carved giltwood and faux-porphyry console table, with ogee-molded frieze and acanthus-carved pierced apron centered by a shell, on acanthus-carved cabriole legs with paw feet.

84in (213cm) wide

$5,500-7,500 **L&T**

ESSENTIAL REFERENCE - THOMAS SHERATON

Thomas Sheraton (1751-1806) gave his name to the elegant and sophisticated Neo-classical furniture produced in the late 18thC and early 19thC. Sheraton favored simple shapes with flat (painted or inlaid) decoration, sometimes with stringing and contrasting veneers.

- **He settled in London in c1790 but left in 1800 having been ordained as a Baptist minister.**
- **It is unlikely that Sheraton himself had a workshop or ever made any furniture. His fame rests on his books of designs, especially 'The Cabinet-Maker and Upholsterer's Drawing-Book' (1791-94). This highly influential book was a practical guide that aimed to acquaint cabinet-makers with the most up-to-date designs.**
- **The Sheraton style was revived in the late 19thC.**

A late 19thC/early 20thC Sheraton Revival satinwood, parcel-gilt and painted console table, the frieze painted with a Neo-classical scene of cherubs, on square tapered legs headed by ram's masks with spade feet.

54in (137cm) wide

$4,000-6,000 **DN**

A pair of late 19th/early 20thC George II-style carved pine and marble console tables, with patera- and roundel-carved friezes, each supported by an eagle, on simulated-marble plinths.

44.5in (113cm) wide

$9,000-11,000 **DN**

A pair of Regency-style simulated-burrwood and parcel-gilt mirrored console tables, with shell- and acanthus-carved friezes, on carved cabriole legs with paw feet, on plinth bases.

48in (122cm) wide

$4,000-6,000 **L&T**

A pair of George I carved giltwood and gesso side tables, the later breccia-marble tops with a ribbon-and-rosette edge, the frieze with a flowerhead-filled chain centered by a plumed mask, the apron edged with acanthus-scrolls and carved with swags, on cabriole legs centered by grotesque masks with dolphin feet, with restoration.

c1720 41.5in (105cms) wide

$70,000-90,000 MEA

A George II red walnut side table, with later top, with three drawers, on hipped tapered legs, with pad feet.

47.5in (120cm) wide

$3,500-4,500 H&L

A pair of burr-elm and elm demi-lune side tables.

c1740 and later 45in (114cm) wide

$12,000-18,000 DN

A Irish George II marble-topped side table, with ogee-molded frieze and shaped apron centered by a shell, on cabriole legs with hoof feet.

41in (104cm) wide

$5,500-7,500 L&T

A George II giltwood side table, the top and frieze carved with scrolling foliage, on cabriole legs with carved pad feet, re-gilded.

38in (97cm) wide

$12,000-18,000 L&T

A mid-18thC and later mahogany side table, with later verde-antico top, the egg-and-dart molded frieze with coat-of-arms between foliate scrolls, on cabochon-, harebell- and acanthus-carved cabriole legs with hairy-paw feet, with restoration.

The arms are probably those of Craycroft of Lincoln.

64.25in (163cm) wide

$30,000-40,000 MEA

A mid-18thC Neapolitan giltwood side table, with quarter-veneered Siena marble top, the pierced frieze centered by stylized foliage on a pounced ground, on molded scrolled cabriole legs headed by scrolling foliage and harebells.

56.5in (144cm) wide

$30,000-40,000 MEA

A late 18th/early 19thC Italian Neo-classical onyx, marble and painted side table, the frieze carved with garlands and wreaths, on tapered stop-fluted legs with laurel-leaf carved ball feet.

77in (196cm) wide

$3,500-4,500 FRE

CLOSER LOOK - GEORGE II SIDE TABLE

An Irish George II mahogany side table, the molded top above an ornate high-relief shell- and foliate-scroll-carved frieze with mask, on acanthus-carved cabriole legs with trefoil feet.
c1750 *47in (120cm) wide*
$400,000-500,000 **L&T**

A late George III mahogany and crossbanded side table, with frieze drawer above deep two-as-one drawer, on ring-turned legs with brass caps and castors.
19in (48cm) wide
$2,000-3,000 **TEN**

A possibly Irish George III mahogany side table, with egg-and-dart molded frieze, on cabriole legs headed by lion's masks and with hairy-paw feet.
49.5in (119cm) wide
$15,000-20,000 **L&T**

A late George III rosewood and ormolu-mounted side table, the shaped supports carved with Byzantine masks.
51in (130cm) wide
$3,500-4,500 **FRE**

A late George III Gillows burrwood side table, the top with reeded edge, the turned column supports with turned stretcher, on sabre legs with foliate caps and castors.
33.5in (85cm) wide
$5,500-6,500 **L&T**

A late 19thC Sheraton Revival mahogany side table, with quarter-veneered and crossbanded top, with frieze drawer, on tapered legs with stretchers.
28in (70cm) high
$2,500-3,500 **TEN**

A French kingwood, rosewood, tulipwood and gilt-metal-mounted side table, in the manner of François Linke, the top with quarter-veneered lozenge within four quarter-veneered panels and crossbanding, with drawers, on gilt-metal-mounted cabriole legs with gilt-metal sabots.
32.25in (82cm) wide
$6,500-7,500 **DN**

A pair of Regency mahogany occasional tables, on possibly associated octagonal rosewood columns, the shaped platform bases with paw feet.

28.5in (72cm) high

$4,000-6,000 **ECGW**

A Sèvres-style porcelain and gilt-metal mounted guéridon table, the top with central plaque of Louis XVI, signed 'Wen Tenn', surrounded by seventeen oval plaques of aristocratic French women.

31in (79cm) diam

$20,000-30,000 **LHA**

A Continental pietra dura and giltwood occasional table, the black slate and onyx top with inset hardstones depicting a magnolia blossom, with carved frieze, on C-scroll- and foliate-carved column with triform base carved with grotesque masks and scrolled feet.

26.5in (67cm) high

$3,500-4,500 **FRE**

A Louis XVI-style marquetry and ormolu-mounted tulipwood table en chiffonier, attributed to Stéphane Boudin, decorated with marquetry floral sprays with scrolling borders, with small drawer and candle slide, on cabriole legs with sabots with undertier.

28in (71cm) high

$20,000-30,000 **LHA**

A near pair of late 19thC French inlaid walnut bijouterie tables, with beveled glass sides, on cabriole legs.

34in (86cm) wide

$2,000-3,000 **GORL**

'Caricature'

A William IV mahogany and specimen-wood inlaid 'caricature' occasional table, the tilt top depicting caricatures of figures such as the Duke of Wellington around a Punch and Judy show and inscribed 'Punch for Ever', on triform platform base with scrolling feet and castors.

c1835 *30in (75cm) high*

$12,000-18,000 **DN**

A George III mahogany drum library table, the top with red leather inset above four drawers and four dummy drawers, the baluster column on three reeded downswept legs with brass paw caps and castors.
c1790 *53in (134cm) diam*
$12,000-18,000 **DN**

An early 19thC mahogany library table, attributed to Gillows, the top with a green leather inset above two drawers and two opposing dummy drawers, on leaf- and shell-carved claw-and-ball feet with turned stretcher.
60in (152cm) long
$12,000-18,000 **TEN**

A Regency mahogany octagonal drum library table, the top with leather inset, above four drawers, one with adjustable writing surface, and four dummy drawers, on downswept legs with brass caps and castors.
c1810 *45in (114cm) wide*
$6,500-7,500 **DN**

ESSENTIAL REFERENCE - DRUM TABLES

Drum tables (also known as library or writing tables) were popular from c1790 to 1820. They had round tops and were predominantly used for writing. Most have leather-covered surfaces and a slight lip above the frieze, rather than a large overhanging edge. Some examples have a revolving top.

- **Some drum tables had wedge-shaped drawers, others had a combination of real and dummy drawers. 'Rent' tables had drawers labeled with the days of the week, thus providing an elegant storage system for landlords. The grandest drum tables also incorporated bookshelves.**
- **The central pillars were usually turned or faceted. Inward-curving reeded legs were popular in c1800. Early 19thC drum tables often had platform bases and carved feet.**
- **Late 18thC drum tables were typically made of mahogany, with rosewood becoming popular in the early 19thC.**

A Regency mahogany library or 'rent' table, in the manner of Marsh & Tatham, the top with radiating banded panels and central compartment with lid, above four drawers with lettered plaques and with anthemion ormolu mounts, with four ormolu-mounted scroll legs with castors.
c1810 *45in (115cm) diam*
$40,000-60,000 **DN**

A Regency mahogany drum library table, the top with leather inset, above four drawers and four dummy drawers, on four reeded downswept legs with brass caps and castors.
c1815 *31in (80cm) diam*
$8,000-12,000 **L&T**

A Regency rosewood and marquetry library table, in the manner of George Bullock, with oak parquetry inset top, with one drawer, on tapered trestle supports with paw feet and concealed casters.
c1815 *33.5in (86cm) long*
$2,000-3,000 **DN**

A William IV mahogany library table, attributed to Gillows, the top with tooled leather inset and gadrooned edge, above two frieze drawers, on reeded and lobed turned supports with platform bases and bun feet with concealed castors.
c1830 *54in (138cm) long*
$8,000-12,000 **L&T**

A William IV Gillows mahogany library table, with two frieze drawers, on turned tapered and reeded legs with plinth base and turned feet, stamped 'GILLOWS'.

c1835 *42in (106.5cm) long*

$2,500-3,500 **DN**

A William IV rosewood library table, the crossbanded top above two frieze drawers, on acanthus-carved trestle supports with downswept legs and with stretchers, brass paw feet and castors.

c1835 *71in (181cm) long*

$20,000-30,000 **DN**

A 19thC Gillows mahogany partners' library table, the top with leather inset, above four paneled drawers one stamped 'Gillow', on square tapered legs headed with lions' masks and scroll terminals, the brass castors stamped 'Strong'.

54in (137cm) long

$7,000-10,000 **SWO**

A George IV mahogany library table, the top with green leather inset, on curved downswept legs with brass paw caps and casters.

44in (112cm) diam

$3,000-5,000 **FRE**

A 19thC Italian Renaissance Revival carved walnut library table, the foliate- and scroll-carved frieze with two drawers, on acanthus-carved supports headed by lions' masks and with galleried stretcher, scroll feet and brass casters.

54in (137cm) long

$2,500-3,500 **FRE**

A Victorian giltwood and composition library table, the top with leather inset above anthemion-carved frieze, the baluster supports decorated with scrolls and cherub masks, on downswept legs headed by winged female terms with acanthus-decorated stretcher and scroll feet.

c1880 *52.5in (133cm) long*

$4,000-6,000 **DN**

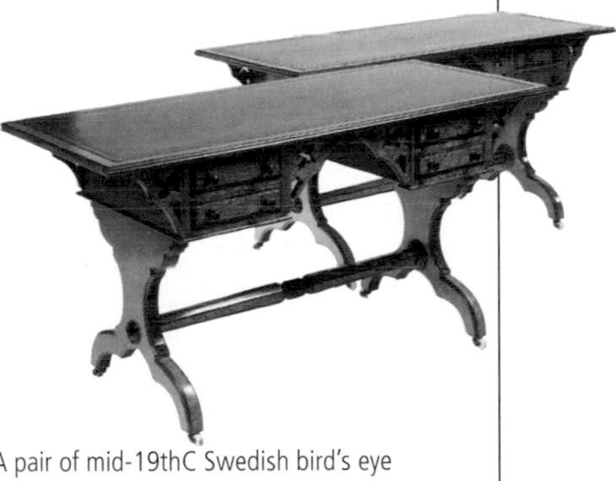

A pair of mid-19thC Swedish bird's eye maple library tables, the top with gilt-tooled leather inset, with quadriform pierced aprons and spandrels, with four drawers each, on downswept legs and tapered faceted stretchers and with ceramic castors.

57in (146cm) long

$10,000-15,000 **L&T**

A late 18thC George III satinwood writing table, with pierced brass gallery and adjustable leather-lined writing slope, with two frieze drawers, on square tapered legs with brass casters.

41.5in (105cm) wide

$5,000-6,000 **FRE**

A Regency rosewood writing table, in the manner of Gillows, the top with tooled leather inset, on gilt-metal mounted downswept supports with three spindles, with cast acanthus caps and brass casters.

The pedestal pattern, including the palm-wrapped castor-sockets, features in the Gillows 1818 'Estimate Sketch Book' (nos.2079 and 2084).

c1815 *31in (78cm) wide*

$5,000-7,000 **DN**

A William IV mahogany writing table, on gadroon-molded legs with castors.

c1840 *53.5in (137cm) wide*

$5,000-7,000 **CHEF**

An early Victorian giltwood lady's writing table, C. Hindley & Sons, London, the raised spindle back with a brass gallery, the husk- and floret-decorated frieze with drawer stamped by the maker, on petal-carved and fluted supports with an undertier, on turned legs with brass castors, the leather insets replaced.

Charles Hindley & Sons, originally carpet, rug and floor-cloth manufacturers, acquired the business of Miles & Edwards in 1844, and subsequently stamped their furniture with their address as 134 Oxford Street, London.

42in (107cm) wide

$2,000-3,000 **WW**

A William IV rosewood bureau plat, the inverted breakfront top with leather inset and crossbanded in padouk, with three drawers and three opposing dummy drawers, on cabriole legs headed by keeled angle clasps and with foliate sabots.

c1830 *53in (135.cm) wide*

$15,000-20,000 **MEA**

A late 19thC French Louis XV-style kingwood and gilt-metal bureau plat, with gilt-tooled red leather inset above a frieze drawer and two deep drawers, on cabriole legs with leaf-cast mounts and sabots with scrolling toes.

47.5in (118cm) wide

$10,000-15,000 **TEN**

CLOSER LOOK - LOUIS XV BUREAU PLAT

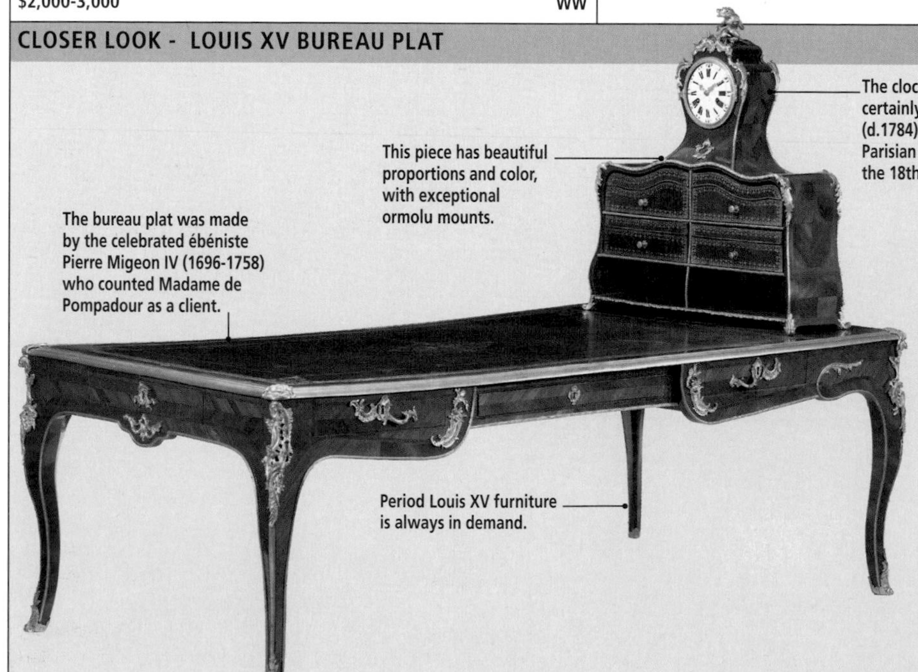

The clock movement was almost certainly made by Denis Masson (d.1784), who was one of the great Parisian clock makers working in the 18thC.

This piece has beautiful proportions and color, with exceptional ormolu mounts.

The bureau plat was made by the celebrated ébéniste Pierre Migeon IV (1696-1758) who counted Madame de Pompadour as a client.

Period Louis XV furniture is always in demand.

A mid-18thC Louis XV ormolu-mounted kingwood bureau plat and cartonnier, the bureau plat stamped 'Migeon', the top with gilt-tooled red leather inset above five drawers, on cabriole legs with sabots, the cartonnier dial signed 'Masson, Paris', the underside stamped 'LVE', with six pigeon holes and surmounted by an ormolu monkey.

88in (223.5cm) wide

$20,000-30,000 **FRE**

A George III flame-mahogany sofa table, with two drawers, on four downswept legs with paw feet and castors.

c1790-1820 *51in (130cm) wide*

$10,000-15,000 **DS**

A Regency rosewood sofa table, the top crossbanded and inlaid with flowering foliage, with a floral-inlaid drawer to each side, on twin turned and reeded cup-and-cover supports with outscrolled legs with turned tapered feet and stretcher.

54in (136.5cm) wide

$15,000-20,000 **SWO**

A Regency rosewood, satinwood and brass-inlaid sofa table, in the manner of John Mclean, the crossbanded top above two frieze drawers flanked by reeded brass panels, on trestle side-supports with downswept brass-inlaid legs with brass caps and casters.

c1815 *Closed 37.25in (95cm) wide*

$8,000-12,000 **FRE**

Judith Picks

This Pembroke table came from Dumfries House. The furniture collection is exceptional, and ranks as the most important collection of works from Thomas Chippendale's Director period and the most comprehensive range of pieces produced by Edinburgh furniture makers Alexander Peter, William Mathie and Francis Brodie. Whilst it has proven a challenge to firmly attribute this table to a particular cabinetmaker, the overall design and quality of the piece strongly suggests one the finest cabinetmakers of the period. Whilst attribution of the making or design of this table is possible to a number of firms, research and evidence at this time has pointed positively toward an attribution to the firm of Mayhew & Ince.

A George III burr-yew and sycamore crossbanded Pembroke table, with one drawer, on square tapered legs with castors.

c1780 *35in (89cm) wide*

$20,000-30,000 **DN**

A George III mahogany 'harlequin' Pembroke table, with sycamore-banded top, the rising structure with five burr-yew-veneered drawers enclosed by a leather-lined writing surface/door, on square tapered legs with brass caps and castors, the flaps slightly bowed.

A 'harlequin' Pembroke table has a small concealed box-like structure, which springs open to reveal drawers and compartments.

32in (81cm) wide

$7,000-10,000 **WW**

A Baltimore Hepplewhite mahogany Pembroke table, the frieze ends with diamond-shaped maple panels, on square tapered legs with bellflower-chain and banded cuffs.

c1800 *34.5in (88cm) wide*

$8,000-12,000 **POOK**

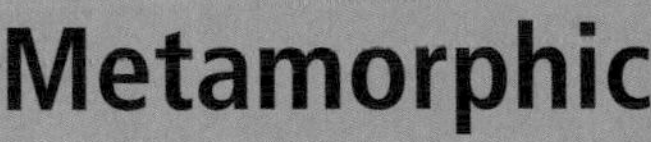

A Sheraton Revival satinwood foliate-marquetry and crossbanded Pembroke table, on square tapered legs.

30in (76cm) wide

$10,000-15,000 **GORL**

Metamorphic

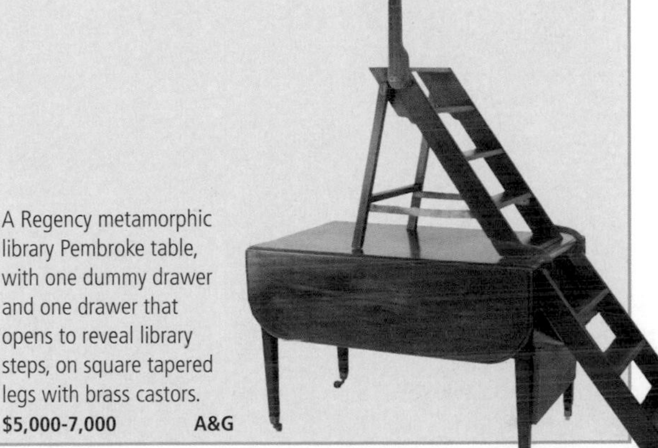

A Regency metamorphic library Pembroke table, with one dummy drawer and one drawer that opens to reveal library steps, on square tapered legs with brass castors.

$5,000-7,000 **A&G**

CLOSER LOOK - CHIPPENDALE CARD TABLE

This card table has never been published or exhibited before, which is always desirable to collectors.

The ornamentation of this card table has been attributed to the as-yet-unidentified master Philadelphia craftsman known as the 'Garvan Carver'. His work is distinguished by graceful, fluid naturalistic forms, such as sinuous leaves, shells, vines and flowerheads.

The carving is especially distinctive at the leaf ends, which twist and turn back on themselves. Depth is created by groupings of fine parallel cuts. The apron of this table exhibits such leaves.

The sinuous lines of the cabriole legs are accentuated with scrolls and elongated acanthus leaves ending in powerfully carved claw-and-ball feet.

A Philadelphia, Pennsylvania Chippendale carved mahogany card table, the carving attributed to the 'Garvan Carver', the hinged top revealing playing surface with candlestick and counter recesses, the apron carved with acanthus leaves, with hidden drawer in swing rail, on acanthus leaf-carved cabriole legs with claw-and-ball feet.

This table was probably made for merchant Tench Francis, Jr. (1730-1800) and Anne Willing (1733-1812), daughter of Philadelphia mayor Charles Willing and Anne Shippen, at the time of their marriage at Christ Church in 1762. Tench Francis, Jr., a successful businessman and patriot contributed to the Revolutionary cause from his personal wealth. As a result of his actions, Francis was appointed First Cashier of the Bank of North America and Purveyor of Public Supplies.

c1760 *32in (81cm) wide*

$250,000-350,000 **FRE**

A George II mahogany games and tea table, the triple-hinged top with one plain surface and one baize-lined playing surface with candlestands and counter wells, on leaf- and husk-carved cabriole legs with scroll feet.

33in (83.5cm) wide

$12,000-18,000 **WW**

A mid-18thC Irish mahogany card table, the folding top re-lined in green baize, the frieze carved with acanthus scrolls on a punched ground and centered by a lion's mask, on acanthus-carved cabriole legs and paw feet.

33in (84cm) wide

$50,000-70,000 **AH**

A Philadelphia Chippendale carved mahogany card table, the hinged top above a frieze drawer, the apron carved with a recessed shell, on acanthus-carved cabriole legs with claw-and-ball feet.

c1755 *30in (76cm) wide*

$10,000-15,000 **POOK**

An Irish George III combination card and tea table, with double hinged top, one side with baize inset and wells, on carved cabriole legs and a central leg with shell- and bellflower-carving to the knee.

c1760 *35in (90cm) wide*

$6,500-7,500 **DN**

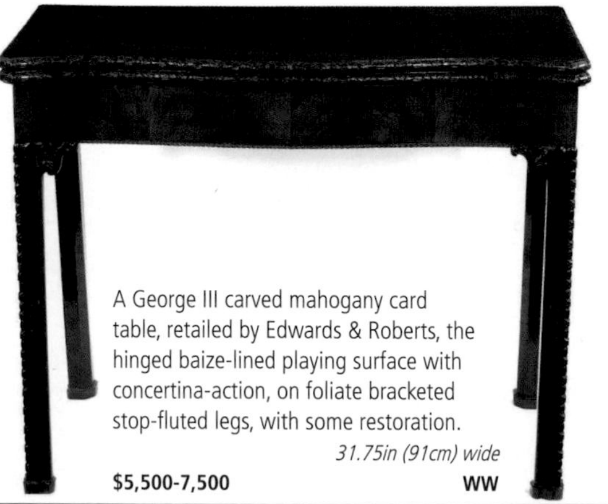

A George III carved mahogany card table, retailed by Edwards & Roberts, the hinged baize-lined playing surface with concertina-action, on foliate bracketed stop-fluted legs, with some restoration.

31.75in (91cm) wide

$5,500-7,500 **WW**

A George III mahogany tilt-top games table, the top inlaid with a sycamore and mahogany backgammon board, on a turned baluster column with tripod base.

25in (64cm) wide

$2,500-3,500 **L&T**

A pair of George III satinwood and marquetry card tables, decorated with foliage and floral motifs.

c1780 *36in (91cm) wide*

$20,000-30,000 **DN**

A George III satinwood and kingwood crossbanded card table, with baize-inset playing surface, on square tapered legs with spade feet.

c1790 *35in (89cm) wide*

$1,500-2,500 **DN**

A pair of George III rosewood and yew crossbanded card tables, each with line inlay, with baize playing surfaces, on collared square legs.

c1800 *36in (91cm) wide*

$20,000-30,000 **L&T**

A pair of Regency mahogany and ebony-strung card tables, with green baize lined interiors, the friezes with recessed rectangular tablets, on square tapered legs headed by brass lion's mask drop-handles and with spade feet.

35in (90cm) wide

$4,000 6,000 **TEN**

A Regency padouk and brass-marquetry card table, the swivel top with baize-lined playing surface, on twin baluster-turned stems on quadriform base with foliate-carved downswept legs with paw feet and brass castors.

36.5in (92.5cm) wide

$7,000-10,000 **WW**

A pair of Regency mahogany and rosewood crossbanded card tables, with baize-lined interiors, on baluster and ring-turned column supports and quadriform bases with castors.

35.5in (90cm) wide

$7,000-10,000 **GORL**

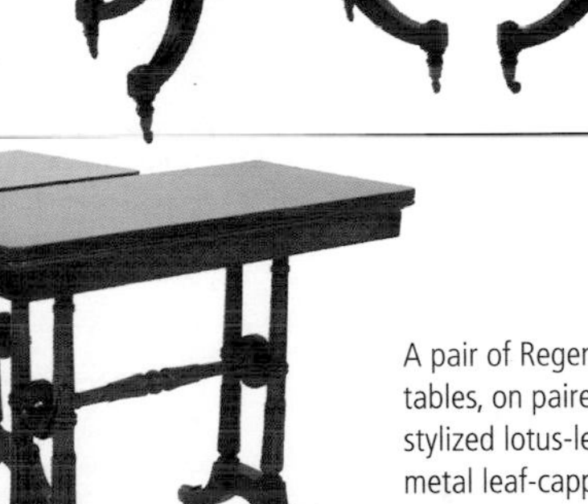

A pair of Regency pollard-oak card tables, on paired end supports with stylized lotus-leaf moldings, with gilt-metal leaf-capped anthemion sabots.

35in (92cm) wide

$10,000-15,000 **WHP**

A Gillows rosewood games table, with green baize playing surface, on foliate-carved trestle supports with paw feet.

c1835 *33.75in (86cm) wide*

$7,000-10,000 **L&T**

A pair of mid-19thC satinbirch and walnut-crossbanded serpentine card tables, with swivel tops, on cabriole legs.

36in (91cm) wide

$8,000-12,000 **GORL**

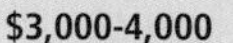

A mid-19thC Irish Killarney yew and marquetry games table, the swivel top with a marquetry image of 'Muckross Abbey' flanked by ferns within decorative borders, the playing surface with marquetry chess, backgammon and cribbage boards within reserves of Glena Cottage and a ruin, with paw feet.

31in (79.5cm) wide

$6,500-7,500 **TOV**

A pair of Sheraton mahogany, satinwood and rosewood crossbanded card tables, with baize-lined interiors above strung friezes, on square tapered legs.

36in (92cm) wide

$12,000-18,000 **TEN**

ESSENTIAL REFERENCE - BOULLE

Boullework is an intricate form of marquetry in which brass is inlaid into a dark background of either tortoiseshell or ebony. The technique was invented in Italy in the 16thC and perfected by French cabinetmaker André-Charles Boulle (1642-1732), who gave his name to the technique.

- **The process of cutting out the materials for one set of designs produced an opposing set, known as contre-partie. This could either be used to decorate a pair of items (one in the première-partie, the other in the contre-partie) or the insides of doors.**
- **Boullework was fashionable during the 18thC and 19thC.**

A Napoleon III ormolu-mounted, boulle and ebonized games table, the top with brass and pewter foliate inlay centered by an ormolu mask, on cabriole legs headed by female terms and with sabots.

35.5in (90cm) wide

$3,000-4,000 **FRE**

A Gillows amboyna, ebonized and parcel-gilt games table, the swivel top with tooled green leather inset and inlaid border enclosing a baize inset, on twin turned and fluted supports with splay legs and stretcher, on brass castors.

c1890 *37in (94cm) wide*

$6,500-7,500 **L&T**

A pair of 20thC George II-style carved hardwood card tables, the plain interiors with counter wells, on shell-carved cabriole legs with claw-and-ball feet.

33in (84cm) wide

$15,000-20,000 **DN**

A George II mahogany tripod table, the tilt top revolving on a birdcage, on a ring-turned inverted baluster column.

31.25in (79.5cm) diam

$1,000-1,500 **WW**

An Irish George III mahogany tray-top table, the tilt top with a fret pierced gallery, on a fluted column with acanthus-carved tripod base with claw-and-ball feet.

c1760 *28in (72cm) high*

$10,000-15,000 **L&T**

A George III mahogany tilt-top table, the top with a reeded edge, on a turned and spiral-fluted column with shell-carved cabriole legs with pad feet and brass castors.

26in (66cm) diam

$10,000-15,000 **GORB**

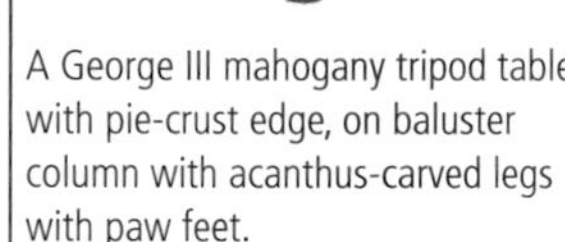

A George III mahogany tripod table, with pie-crust edge, on baluster column with acanthus-carved legs with paw feet.

c1770 *29.25in (74cm) high*

$8,000-12,000 **DN**

A George III mahogany tripod table, on turned column with fluted base with pad feet.

c1790 *27.5in (71cm) high*

$1,200-1,800 **DN**

A Victorian carved walnut tripod table, the top inset with agates and hardstone specimens into a scagliola ground, the edge carved with acorn and oak leaves, on a spiral-twist column with acanthus-carved cabriole legs with scroll feet, with old damage and restoration.

29.25in (74cm) high

$3,500-4,500 **WW**

A Victorian mahogany apprentice tripod table, the turned column on shell-carved cabriole legs with pad feet.

18in (46cm) high

$400-600 **GORL**

A Massachusetts Queen Anne mahogany drop-leaf tea table, on cabriole legs with pad feet, refinished.

c1740-60 *32in (81cm) diam*

$12,000-18,000 **SK**

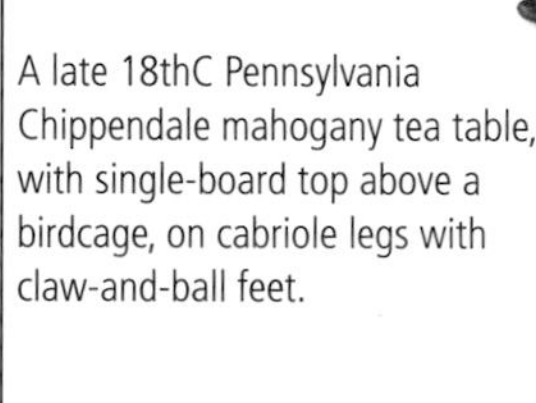

A late 18thC Pennsylvania Chippendale mahogany tea table, with single-board top above a birdcage, on cabriole legs with claw-and-ball feet.

$10,000-15,000 **FRE**

A George III-style malachite-inset mahogany tea table, with gadrooned edge, on a reeded and acanthus-carved column with claw-and-ball feet.

28.5in (72cm) high

$3,500-4,500 **FRE**

A rare 18thC mahogany and satinwood-banded work table, with drawers over slide, on tapered and strung legs with brass castors and with stretchers.

28in (71cm) high

$8,000-12,000 DS

A Gillows satinwood work table, the leather-inset top with ratchet slope, over two drawers and a basket flanked by two narrow drawers and drop-leaf sides, on turned supports and swept legs with castors, stamped 'Gillow' and dated.

The table was made by Mr W Johnston (pencil signed to bottom of top drawer) for a Mr Young, via Maple & Co. £5 2s 0d was paid to Mr Johnson and the total cost to make was £10 3s 9d.

1869

$4,000-6,000 SWO

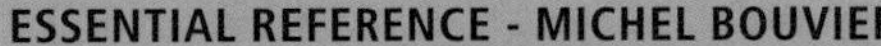

ESSENTIAL REFERENCE - MICHEL BOUVIER

Michel Bouvier (1792-1874) was apprenticed to his father in Pont-Saint-Esprit, France.

- **Bouvier left France after the defeat of Napoleon in 1815 and immigrated to Philadelphia, USA where he opened a cabinetmaking shop. His customers included Joseph Bonaparte (elder brother of Napoleon) and Stephen Girard.**
- **Bouvier's furniture was French in style, although the gilding and other ornament was influenced by English furniture.**
- **Bouvier marked his furniture with a maker's stencil from c1830 onward.**
- **He was also successful in the real estate business.**
- **Michel Bouvier was the great-great-grandfather of Jackie Kennedy Onassis.**

A Philadelphia, Pennsylvania Neo-classical mahogany, bird's eye maple and ivory-inset work table, attributed to Michel Bouvier, with fitted drawer over second drawer and slide, on a lyre pedestal with sabre legs with brass paw feet and casters, with brass plaque engraved 'Presented to/Trent Chapter/D.A.R./by/Mary Scudder Jamieson/Regent 1894'.

The Trent Chapter of the Daughters of the American Revolution was founded January 29th 1895 in Trenton, New Jersey

c1810-20 *28.75in (73cm) high*

$20,000-30,000 FRE

A Maryland Hepplewhite mahogany and line-inlaid work table, with lift-lid, on square tapered legs with banded cuffs.

c1795 *30.25in (77cm) high*

$5,000-7,000 POOK

A Regency rosewood work table, with fitted drawer over second drawer and silk-lined work box, on lyre supports with downswept legs with brass caps and casters and with stretcher.

c1815 *20.5in (52cm) wide*

$700-1,000 DN

A George IV rosewood work table, attributed to Gillows, with end frieze drawers and a pull-out bag, on turned and petal-carved supports with scroll legs with leaf feet and brass castors and with turned stretcher.

29in (73.5cm) high

$5,000-7,000 WW

A William IV oak work table, the top opening to a lined interior, on reeded turned column with carved triform base with scroll feet.

The top bears a brass inset plaque 'The Oak of which this table is made was under the foundations of Old London Bridge, upwards of six hundred & fifty six years and taken up from thence in 1833 by, Sir Edward Banks and William John Jolliffe Esq, the contractors & builders of, New London Bridge'.

c1835 *30in (75cm) high*

$4,000-6,000 L&T

A Victorian satinwood and painted work table.

c1860 *28in (72cm) high*

$3,000-4,000 DN

An early 17thC Salisbury joined oak folding table, possibly from the Beckham workshop, the folding top with double-knuckle hinges over a molded frieze with drawer, the apron with spilt moldings, on block and turned legs with solid undertier.

36.25in (92cm) wide

$12,000-18,000 DN

A 17thC and later oak folding table, the frieze carved with mythological beasts, with acorn finials, with supports carved as stylized figures, with rear gate-leg action.

35.5in (90cm) wide

$15,000-20,000 DN

A Charles II oak credence table, with frieze drawer, on bobbin and ring-turned supports with stretchers.

c1680 *42in (106cm) wide*

$12,000-18,000 SWO

An unusual 18thC oak ship's table, with drawers to each end, on reeded block supports and decorative brackets, with two undertiers, with iron mounts.

53in (135cm) long

$7,000-10,000 SWO

Miniature

A miniature 19thC Jupe-type mahogany extending dining table, on part-fluted and fluted tapered legs, with three additional leaves, in a fitted case with ivory label 'Stenhouse & Savage/Makers/London'.

Table 8.5in (22cm) diam

$8,000-12,000 FRE

A George II mahogany architect's table, with ratchet-operated hinged table top, candle slides and drawers to each side, on turned legs headed by lappets and with pointed pad feet with barrel castors.

34in (87cm) high

$5,000-7,000 L&T

A mid-Georgian mahogany architect's table, with ratchet-operated hinged table top, candle slides, pull-out and fitted leather-inset writing surface, on column and chamfered carved legs, with original brass fittings.

36in (91cm) wide

$3,000-5,000 TRI

A George II Chinese Chippendale mahogany silver table, with overall pierced fretwork.

c1755 *34in (86cm) wide*

$40,000-60,000 FRE

A late 19thC French-style mahogany serving table, with bronze mounts and C-scroll supports, on fluted legs.

35in (90cm) high

$6,500-7,500 DOR

A mid-17thC carved oak low dresser, the two-plank top above three paneled drawers, on turned and block forelegs.

66in (168cm) wide

$5,000-7,000 **GORL**

A William & Mary oak low dresser, with geometric paneled fronts, on stile feet.

71in (180cm) wide

$3,500-4,500 **GORL**

A William & Mary oak low dresser, with three drawers, on square and baluster-turned forelegs with turned feet.

c1690 *87.5in (222cm) wide*

$12,000-18,000 **DN**

An early 18thC oak low dresser, with three paneled drawers, on baluster-turned and block forelegs, with restoration and replacements.

75in (190.5cm) wide

$2,000-3,000 **WW**

A George II oak low dresser, with three cockbeaded drawers, on cabriole forelegs with carved pad feet.

65in (165cm) wide

$5,000-7,000 **FRE**

A George II oak low dresser, with three frieze drawers over three fielded cupboard doors, on bracket feet.

71in (180cm) wide

$6,500-7,500 **TEN**

A George III oak and mahogany crossbanded low dresser, with three drawers above scrolling apron, on cabriole forelegs and square tapered back legs.

c1780 *85in (216cm) wide*

$7,000-10,000 **DN**

An mid-18thC oak high dresser, with three drawers, with pine back boards.

74in (189cm) high

$4,000-6,000 **SWO**

A George II oak high dresser, the two fixed shelves with iron cup-hooks, with three drawers above a field panel and two cupboards, on bracket feet.

77.5in (198cm) high

$8,000-12,000 **TEN**

A mid-18thC Welsh oak pewter cupboard, the base with three drawers.

75.5in (192cm) high

$5,500-6,500 **POOK**

A George III oak, mahogany and inlaid high dresser, the two cupboards with paterae marquetry and crossbanding, the base with three crossbanded and inlaid drawers, on square tapered legs.

c1770 *78in (197cm) high*

$5,500-6,500 **DN**

A George III oak high dresser, the associated delft rack shelves flanked by four small shelves, the base with mahogany banding, with three frieze drawers over eight drawers and a cupboard, with brass drop handles, on ogee bracket feet.

85in (216cm) high

$5,000-7,000 **AH**

A George III oak high dresser, with three open shelves, the base with two drawers, on square legs, with a solid pot board.

c1780

74in (188cm) high

$2,500-3,500 **DN**

An 18thC and later oak high dresser, with three drawers above three cupboards, on block legs, with restoration.

75in (191cm) wide

$8,000-12,000 **TOV**

A 16thC oak dole cupboard, with two doors between paneling, on later turned feet.

67in (170cm) high

$20,000-30,000 **SWO**

A 17thC carved oak hunt cupboard, of peg construction, with triple-paneled sides, the box base with hinged cover, on stile legs.

67in (170cm) high

$6,500-7,500 **TRI**

A mid-17thC carved oak livery cupboard, with scroll-carved frieze over leaf-carved central door flanked by panels, with one frieze drawer, on baluster-turned supports, with solid undertier.

51.5in (131cm) wide

$12,000-18,000 **DN**

A Charles II carved oak court cupboard, with two cupboards flanked by cup-and-cover supports above two cupboards.

c1680 *74in (188.5cm) wide*

$3,000-4,000 **DN**

A late 17thC oak court cupboard, with a carved frieze.

67in (171cm) high

$4,000-6,000 **SWO**

A 17thC and later oak side cupboard, with three drawers above two cupboards.

55in (140cm) wide

$1,500-2,500 **DN**

An early 18thC German Baroque veneered elm cupboard, with original key.

90in (231cm) high

$10,000-15,000 **KAU**

A 18thC Hudson Valley three-part gumwood kas, with two raised panel doors, the base one drawer, on bun feet, retaining old dry surface.

76in (193cm) high

$7,000-10,000 **POOK**

One of a pair of George III coromandel and lacquer press cupboards, formed from earlier Chinese lacquer screen panels, decorated with figures among pavilions, the interior with shelves and two drawers, on bracket feet.

c1760 *72.5in (185cm) high*

$60,000-80,000 pair **DN**

A mid-18thC Austrian Baroque walnut-veneer and marquetry hall cupboard, with original lock and key, with damage.

94in (238cm) high

$15,000-20,000 **DOR**

A George III oak livery cupboard, with single paneled door flanked by two panels, the open interior with pegs, the base three panels above two drawers, on bracket feet.

58in (147cm) wide

$5,000-7,000 **DUK**

A Lancaster County, Pennsylvania Chippendale walnut shrank, the raised panel doors flanked by fluted columns, the base with three drawers, on ogee bracket feet.

c1775 *89in (226cm) high*

$30,000-40,000 **POOK**

A small late 18thC New England painted cupboard, the interior with shelves, with old olive-green surface over earlier red.

71.5in (181cm) high

$25,000-35,000 **SK**

An early 19thC Pennsylvania Federal cherrywood corner cupboard, with glazed door, the base with two recessed panel doors, on flared bracket feet.

91.75in (233cm) high

$3,000-4,000 **POOK**

An early 19thC oak cupboard, with three drawers above two paneled doors opening to later hanging rail, with later brass handles.

66.75in (169.5cm) high

$4,000-6,000 **WW**

An early 19thC mahogany cupboard, with doors with applied dummy boards painted with a lady and gentleman above two paneled doors opening to four drawers.

85in (217cm) high

$3,000-4,000 **SWO**

A Dresden Biedermeier mahogany-veneered corner cupboard, with original key.

c1825 *85in (217cm) high*

$3,000-4,000 **KAU**

A 19thC carved chestnut cupboard, the arched spindled frieze over two sliding doors and two hinged doors carved with vases issuing flowers and birds, the base with three drawers.

76in (193cm) high

$5,000-7,000 **LHA**

A 19thC Salzburg carved cherrywood and softwood Knochenbarock hall cupboard, with removable cornice, with one drawer.

85in (215cm) high

$5,000-7,000 **DOR**

A late 19thC French provincial painted cupboard, with two paneled doors above two cupboards, on cabriole legs with scroll feet.

92in (233cm) high

$4,000-6,000 **DN**

A rare 17thC German Baroque oak, birch and fruitwood wardrobe, with original key, with restoration.

92.5in (235cm) high

$5,000-7,000 **KAU**

ESSENTIAL REFERENCE - PHILIP BELL

- **Bell's family business was founded in 1736 by Philip's father Henry. Philip and his mother Elizabeth took over the firm following Henry's death in 1740. (For more information about Elizabeth Bell see p.212). By 1758 Philip was operating independently. He was succeeded by Henry Kettle in 1774.**
- **Like Giles Grendey, Philip Bell favored complex re-entrant panels and the use of high-quality, well-figured timbers.**
- **Bell commissioned Matthias Darly, the engraver who worked on Chippendale's 'Director', to design a new Rococo-style pictorial label.**
- **Bell exported furniture to America and there is evidence to suggest that in 1761 George Washington ordered a mahogany bottle case from Bell for which he was charged £17.7.0.**

A George II mahogany linen press, by Philip Bell, London, the Greek key-carved cornice above two fielded panel doors opening to slides, the base with four cockbeaded drawers with brass handles, on bracket feet, with maker's label.

c1750 *74.75in (190cm) high*

$15,000-20,000 **L&T**

A late George III Gillows mahogany crossbanded linen press, with two cupboard doors opening to sliding trays, the base with four drawers, on splayed feet, stamped 'Gillows, Lancaster'.

75.25in (196cm) high

$12,000-18,000 **L&T**

A late 18thC Dutch mahogany and marquetry linen press, with foliate cresting above two cupboard doors with bird and flowering urn inlay opening to shelves and drawers, the base with three drawers, on bracket feet.

87in (221cm) high

$10,000-15,000 **L&T**

A rare New Brunswick, New Jersey Chippendale walnut linen press, by Matthew Egerton Junior, the crotch-veneer frieze above scalloped panel cupboard doors, the base with three drawers, on bracket feet, with maker's label.

c1790 *78in (198cm) high*

$50,000-70,000 **POOK**

An Austrian carved, mahogany-veneer and later painted wardrobe, attributed to F O Schmidt, Vienna, carved with putti, rams' heads, festoons and floral garlands, with three doors above three drawers.

This wardrobe has screw construction to enable dismantling.

c1900-20 *86.5in (220cm) high*

$6,500-7,500 **DOR**

A large 16thC oak chest, with four carved Gothic tracery panels to the front, the sides with two parchment carved panels.

53in (134cm) long

$10,000-15,000 **SWO**

A 16thC Italian Renaissance walnut and poplar cassone, Tuscany, with simple panels and carved applied ornament, on paw feet, with some damage.

69in (176cm) long

$12,000-18,000 **DOR**

A 17thC and later oak and inlaid nonesuch chest, the top with zig-zag- and plain-banding, the front decorated with buildings, the interior with lidded till and two drawers, on shaped stile feet.

42in (108cm) long

$5,500-6,500 **WW**

A small 17thC oak coffer, the top and front with three panels each, carved '16 Francis Buluck 97'.

44in (112cm) long

$2,500-3,500 **SWO**

A late 17thC paneled oak coffer.

50in (128cm) long

$350-450 **DN**

A 16thC French Gothic carved oak coffer, the interior with candle box, the front with Gothic tracery panels divided by spire pilasters, the sides with linen-fold panels.

61in (155cm) long

$20,000-30,000 **L&T**

An early 18thC Italian carved walnut cassone, the paneled front with grotesques and bands of leaves, on paw forefeet, with damage.

70.5in (179cm) long

$4,000-6,000 **WW**

An 18thC walnut-veneer and engraved-brass mounted coffer, the quarter-veneered top and front with cross- and featherbanded borders, the sides crossbanded, with later removable trays, on later bun feet.

51in (130cm) long

$4,000-6,000 **H&L**

A mid-18thC Tyrolean Sockeltruhe-type painted pine coffer, with relief-carved imbrications, monogrammed and dated 'TF 1746', the interior with one drawer, with some damage.
1746 *55in (140cm) long*
$5,000-7,000 DOR

An 18thC Colonial mahogany and brass marquetry coffer, the interior with candle box, the front with brass marquetry depicting an urn issuing flowers, the sides and back with arrowhead carving, on bracket feet.
52.25in (132.5cm) long
$1,200-1,800 DN

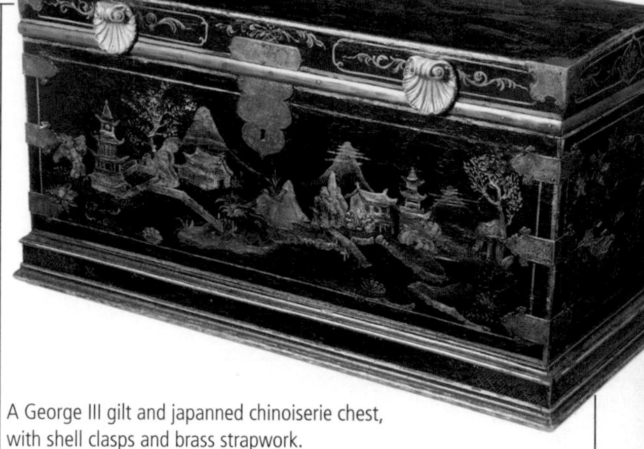

A George III gilt and japanned chinoiserie chest, with shell clasps and brass strapwork.
50.4in (128cm) long
$10,000-15,000 L&T

A possibly Chester County, Pennsylvania inlaid walnut blanket chest, the interior with till, above two lip-molded drawers with molded base, the case inlaid with tulips, heart and the initials 'AB' surrounded by the date '1784'.

Provenance: The blanket chest was made for Anna Brownback (b.1730), daughter of Gerhard Brumbach later Garrett Brownback (1662-1757), a native of Würtemberg, Germany. Garret sailed from Amsterdam in 1683 and settled in Germantown, Pennsylvania, before moving to Chester County. There he founded the first tavern on the north side of the Lancaster pike as well as Brownback's German Reformed church. Anna Brownback married Paul Benner (1726-1783) in c1752.
1784 *48.5in (123cm) long*
$5,000-7,000 FRE

A George III mahogany architect's chest, the long drawer with a sliding baize inset above a divided interior, with three further drawers to each side, on square feet.
c1760 *41in (105cm) long*
$5,000-7,000 DN

A late 18thC Continental mahogany and iron-mounted chest.
60in (152.5cm) long
$1,500-2,500 DN

A Batavian satinwood and ebony-banded chest, on boldly-turned stands.
c1800 *66in (168cm) long*
$4,000-6,000 SWO

A set of three early 19thC Colonial Indian painted and metal-mounted chests, with hinged lids, painted with floral motifs.
Largest 34.25in (87cm) long
$5,000-7,000 DN

A 19thC-Tyrolese-style rustic pine coffer, the front with arched panels painted with stenciling and scattered floral panels.
65in (168cm) long
$2,500-3,500 DOR

A William III walnut and crossbanded chest-of-drawers, with three long drawers, on bracket feet.

c1700 *33in (85cm) high*

$5,000-7,000 **DN**

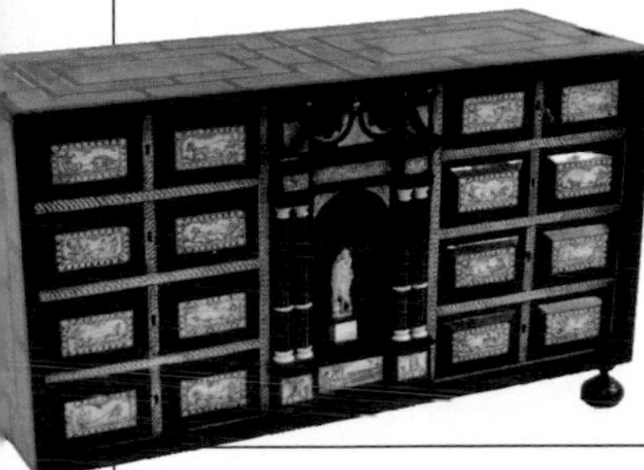

A late 17thC Spanish bone-inlaid walnut vargueno, with an arrangement of drawers around a 19thC Dieppe ivory figure of Winter, the drawers with later bone and ebony veneers and decorated with figures and chariots, on bun feet.

37in (94cm) wide

$6,000-8,000 **GORL**

An early 18thC burr-walnut chest-of-drawers, the top cross- and featherbanded, with two short and three long drawers, on bracket feet, with original brass handles and escutcheons, one missing.

39.5in (100.5cm) wide

$6,000-8,000 **A&G**

A Queen Anne oyster-walnut, stained bone and floral marquetry chest-of-drawers, with two short and three long drawers, on bun feet.

c1705 *37.5in (97cm) wide*

$15,000-20,000 **DN**

A George I walnut chest-of-drawers, the top featherbanded and molded, with brushing slide and four drawers, on compressed shell-carved cabriole legs with claw-and-ball feet.

c1720 *36.25in (92cm) wide*

$15,000-20,000 **DN**

A George II walnut crossbanded and inlaid chest-of-drawers, with two short and three long drawers, on bracket feet.

c1730 *36.5in (93cm) high*

$3,000-4,000 **FRE**

A George II walnut chest-of-drawers, the top quarter-veneered, crossbanded and featherbanded, with brushing slide and three short and three long drawers, on bracket feet.

c1740 *32in (82cm) high*

$12,000-18,000 **DN**

A French Louis XV rosewood-veneer, marquetry and bronze-mounted salon chest-of-drawers, Adrien Fleury, Paris, with original marble top, with restoration.

50in (127cm) wide

$25,000-35,000 **DOR**

ESSENTIAL REFERENCE - ELIZABETH BELL

- **Elizabeth Bell never served an apprenticeship. However, she was permitted by Guild regulations to carry on the business established in 1736 by her late husband Henry (d.1740).**
- **She was based at the White Swan, St Pauls Churchyard, London.**
- **Elizabeth's trade label was identical to that of her husband, with the word 'Elizabeth' substituted for 'Henry'. Some later labels also had '& SON'. For more information about Elizabeth's son Philip see p.208.**
- **Elizabeth Bell retired, or died, in c1758.**
- **In his 1996 book 'Pictorial Dictionary of Marked London Furniture 1700-1840', Christopher Gilbert noted that Elizabeth Bell's label had only been found on quality walnut and mahogany cabinet furniture.**

A George III mahogany serpentine chest-of-drawers, with reeded-chamfered corners and carved outer edge, one drawer with label of 'Elizabeth Bell, London'.
c1780 *37in (95cm) wide*
$8,000-12,000 DN

A Massachusetts Chippendale carved mahogany block-front chest-of-drawers, with four drawers, on bracket feet.
c1760-80
32.25in (82cm) high
$50,000-70,000 POOK

An Italian burr-veneer serpentine chest-of-drawers.
c1760
55in (140cm) wide
$12,000-18,000 POOK

A probably South German late Baroque oak and spruce painted chest-of-drawers, with two drawers, with restoration.
c1760-70 *36in (92cm) wide*
$12,000-18,000 DOR

A 19thC New England red-stained blanket chest, with a lift lid and two drawers, on cutout feet.
41.5in (105cm) high
$1,000-1,500 POOK

A New York Chippendale mahogany chest-of-drawers, with four long drawers above rope-carved apron, on claw-and-ball feet.

The top drawer has interior 'slide' slots.
c1770 33.5in (85cm) wide
$12,000-18,000 FRE

A George III mahogany serpentine chest-of-drawers, with three long drawers, the upper with writing slide and compartmented interior, on bracket feet.
42in (107cm) wide
$12,000-18,000 GORL

A George III mahogany and satinwood-banded serpentine chest-of-drawers, with four long drawers, on bracket feet.
36in (91cm) wide
$6,500-7,500 GORL

Miller's Compares: George III Chests

When valuing a late 18th/early 19thC chest-of-drawers, a great deal of importance is placed on originality, color, proportion and detail. While both these serpentine-fronted chests are good quality, the example on the left has many indications of a higher status piece, such as the distinctive 'flame' mahogany, the arrangement of two small drawers with fitted dressing drawer and fluted segmental columns. The brass hardware is also original to the piece, unlike the brass on the right. The chest on the left looks like a London piece, rather than a provincial one, and quite simply made to a higher spec.

This piece is made from beautiful 'flame' mahogany.

A George III mahogany serpentine chest-of-drawers, with slide and fitted dressing drawer flanked by narrow drawers, over three further long drawers, on bracket feet.

39in (100cm) wide

$40,000-60,000 **TEN**

This chest has a slightly dull patina and has been re-finished.

The handles are good quality replacements, rather than originals.

A George III mahogany serpentine chest-of-drawers, with pull-out slide over four cockbeaded drawers, on bracket feet.

38.75in (98cm) wide

$7,000-10,000 **POOK**

A Russian Empire mahogany and brass chest-of-drawers, with three drawers.

36in (91cm) wide

$6,500-7,500 **FRE**

A George III mahogany chest-of-drawers, with two banks of four drawers.

c1800 *41in (105cm) wide*

$2,000-3,000 **DN**

A Connecticut Valley Federal cherrywood inlaid chest-of-drawers, with four cockbeaded and strung drawers inlaid with fans, on string-inlaid ogee bracket feet, with replaced brasses.

c1800 *45.5in (116cm) wide*

$12,000-18,000 **SK**

A Pennsylvania painted pine chest-of-drawers, attributed to Jacob Knagy, Somerset County, the drawers with stenciled urns, flowers and pinwheels on a red ground, inscribed 'Benjamin Mast' and dated.

1855 *44in (111.5cm) high*

$15,000-20,000 **POOK**

A Victorian campaign chest-of-drawers, by Ross, Dublin, in two sections with five drawers in total, on bun feet, with maker's label, named for Major J.W.H Houghton R.A.M.C.

E. Ross was listed in the 1855 Dublin Street Directory as 'army cabinet furniture, portmanteau, and camp equipage manufactory' at 9, 10 and 11 Ellis's Quay.

c1880 *41in (103cm) high*

$3,000-4,000 **DN**

A late 19thC/early 20thC Louis XV-style rosewood, kingwood, parquetry and ormolu-mounted cartonnier, with six gilt leather-faced drawers above four drawers, on scrolling leaf cast feet.

45in (117cm) wide

$4,000-6,000 **TEN**

A Chester County, Pennsylvania Queen Anne walnut Octorara tall chest, with five short and four long drawers, on tall pierced ogee feet.
c1770 *61in (155cm) high*
$8,000-12,000 **POOK**

A Regency mahogany double Wellington chest, with two columns of ten drawers, with locking columns to either side.
63in (159cm) high
$5,000-7,000 **L&T**

An early 19thC Austrian Biedermeier mahogany-veneered semainier, Vienna, with ebonized contouring, with seven drawers, with replaced lock.
c1820 *53in (135cm) high*
$10,000-15,000 **DOR**

An early Victorian rosewood Wellington chest, with seven drawers, with locking bars.
50in (127cm) high
$4,000-6,000 **GORL**

A mahogany Wellington chest, with eight green leather document files.
c1880 *64in (163cm) high*
$2,000-3,000 **DN**

A Victorian satin-birch Wellington chest, with six graduated drawers between locking bars.
c1880 *47.5in (121cm) high*
$5,000-7,000 **L&T**

A late 19thC French floral marquetry tall chest-of-drawers, with seven drawers, with gilt-metal banding and applied scrolling motifs, with marble top.
50in (127cm) high
$1,000-1,500 **A&G**

A stained pine collector's chest, the twenty-two drawers with removable frame sections, with paper label for 'W CRANE, Naturalist, Taxidermist and Furrier 31a Hope Street'.
c1900 *57in (146cm) high*
$700-1,000 **DN**

A rare 17thC Spanish yew commode, the five long drawers with carved brickwork decoration, on a later ebonized plinth base.

67in (170cm) wide

$10,000-15,000 **L&T**

A 17th/18thC Italian Baroque walnut commode, with three long drawers with carved head handles, with term columns, on grotesque mask feet.

57.5in (146cm) wide

$8,000-12,000 **FRE**

An 18thC Régence japanned and parcel-gilt commode, with two drawers, on short cabriole legs.

40.5in (103cm) wide

$20,000-30,000 **FRE**

A small 18thC Italian Rococo walnut and gilt-metal mounted commode, the inlaid and crossbanded top above three long drawers, on short cabriole legs.

33in (84cm) high

$3,000-4,000 **FRE**

A Louis XV kingwood, parquetry and gilt metal mounted commode, by François Mondon, with a later white and gray marble top, with three drawers, on splayed feet, stamped 'Mondon'.

François Mondon (1693-1775) was made Master Craftsman in c1730.

57in (146cm) wide

$15,000-20,000 **TEN**

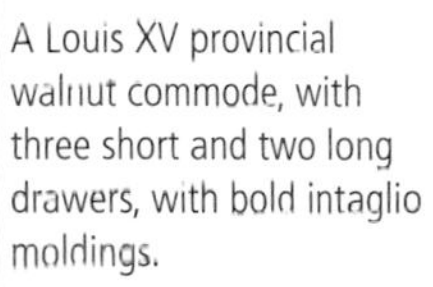

A Louis XV provincial walnut commode, with three short and two long drawers, with bold intaglio moldings.

50.5in (128cm) wide

$6,500-7,500 **LC**

An 18thC South German Baroque walnut, ebony and mahogany-veneered commode, with original key.

47.5in (118cm) wide

$7,000-10,000 **KAU**

A mid-18thC Italian late Baroque rosewood-marquetry commode, Naples, with two drawers and marble top.

59in (150cm) wide

$40,000-60,000 **DOR**

A 18thC Swedish walnut, tulipwood, ebonized and parquetry commode, by Mathias Engström, with three drawers, with ebonized outswept corners and gilt-metal mounts.

Mathias Engström (1725-1804) was taught by Erik Bergström, and was a master cabinetmaker 1758-97.

49.25 (125cm) wide

$8,000-12,000 **DN**

ESSENTIAL REFERENCE - JOHN COBB

- **John Cobb (1715-1778) completed his apprenticeship in 1736 and went into partnership with William Vile in 1751. The firm was awarded the Royal warrant 1761-64.**
- **In 1755 Cobb married cabinetmaker Giles Grendey's daughter, Sukey.**
- **Vile retired in 1764 and Cobb took over the firm, with the assistance of his foreman Samuel Reynolds. Cobb began producing more Neo-classical pieces from the mid-1760s.**
- **He was well known for high quality marquetry.**
- **He was described as a 'singularly haugty (sic) character... one of the proudest men in England... he always appeared in full dress of the most superb and costly kind, in which state he would strut through his workshops giving orders to his men'.**
- **On Cobb's death, Reynolds went into partnership with John Graham.**

A George III mahogany, crossbanded and ormolu-mounted commode, attributed to John Cobb, with brushing slide above three drawers, on splayed bracket feet with sabots.

c1760 *50in (126cm) wide*

$80,000-120,000 **L&T**

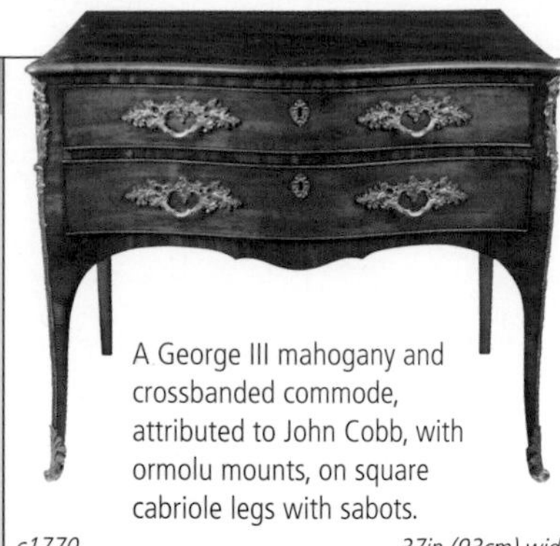

A George III mahogany and crossbanded commode, attributed to John Cobb, with ormolu mounts, on square cabriole legs with sabots.

c1770 *37in (93cm) wide*

$50,000-70,000 **L&T**

A late 18thC and later Dutch walnut and floral-marquetry bombe commode, with gilt-brass mounts, with four graduated drawers.

36.25in (91.5cm) wide

$4,000-6,000 **WW**

A pair of late 18thC Italian Neo-classical olivewood and walnut parquetry commodes, Lombardy, the kingwood-banded and quarter-veneered tops above two drawers, on square tapered legs.

47in (120cm) wide

$30,000-40,000 **L&T**

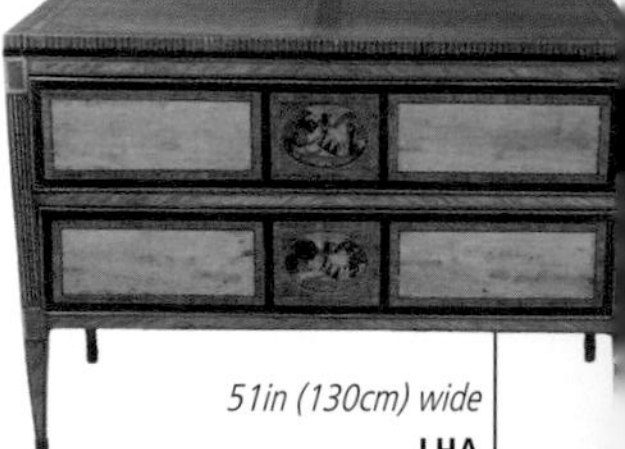

A Continental Neo-classical commode, the two drawers with inlaid trophies to center, on tapered legs.

51in (130cm) wide

$8,000-12,000 **LHA**

A late 18thC Continental possibly Maltese walnut serpentine commode, with figured walnut panels within crossbanded and line-inlaid borders, with three drawers, the fall concealing drawers and pigeonholes, on short cabriole legs.

54in (137cm) wide

$50,000-70,000 **DN**

An 18thC North-Italian-style serpentine commode, painted with acanthus-scrolls, flowers and foliage, with marble top above two drawers, on molded cabriole legs.

52.5in (131cm) wide

$20,000-30,000 **DN**

A possibly Salem, Massachusetts Queen Anne walnut and maple chest-on-stand, with swan's neck pediment and three flame-carved finials.

c1740-60 *40in (101.5cm) wide*

$60,000-80,000 **SK**

A Charles II oyster olivewood and floral-marquetry chest-on-stand, with two short and three long drawers, the stand with a drawer, on turned legs with turned feet and shaped stretchers.

c1680-85 *48in (122cm) high*

$40,000-60,000 **DN**

A William & Mary oyster-veneer and inlaid chest-on-stand, with two short and three long drawers with line inlay, the stand on baluster legs with bun feet and shaped stretchers.

c1690 *37.5in (95cm) wide*

$7,000-9,000 **L&T**

A Queen Anne oak chest-on-stand, the three drawers with molded fronts and brass drop-handles, the later stand on spiral-turned legs with bun feet and stretchers.

40in (102cm) wide

$6,500-7,500 **DUK**

A George II walnut chest-on-stand, the cornice with cushion drawer above two short and three long drawers, the stand with three drawers, on cabriole legs with hoof feet.

c1750 *63in (161cm) high*

$10,000-15,000 **DN**

A George III mahogany chest-on-stand, the top drawer with brushing slide, the stand with carved foliate decoration, on acanthus- and cabochon-carved legs with scroll feet.

c1760 *40in (103cm) wide*

$20,000-30,000 **DN**

A late 18thC New Hampshire Queen Anne black-painted carved maple chest-on-stand, attributed to Peter Bartlett, Salisbury, with five drawers, the stand with long and three short drawers, on cabriole legs with pad feet, with old replaced brasses and old black paint over earlier red.

Provenance: Once the property of John Page, who was Governor of New Hampshire 1839-41.

38.25in (97cm) wide

$50,000-70,000 **SK**

A Charles II joined oak and snakewood chest-on-chest, inlaid with ivory and mother-of-pearl, with thin drawer over deep drawer, the base with two cupboard doors opening to three oak drawers, on flattened bun feet.

c1665 *47.5in (123cm) wide*

$6,500-7,500 **TEN**

An early 18thC Queen Anne walnut and feather-banded chest-on-chest, with three short and three long drawers, the base with three long drawers, on ogee bracket feet.

63in (161cm) high

$3,000-4,000 **ROS**

A George I walnut chest-on-chest, with a brushing slide.

67in (170cm) wide

$20,000-30,000 **SWO**

A George III mahogany chest-on-chest, with three short and three long drawers flanked by gadrooned columns, the base five drawers, on bracket feet.

78in (198cm) high

$3,000-4,000 **FRE**

A George III oak chest-on-chest, with elm sides, with later pierced brass handles and escutcheons, with old restoration.

69.75in (177cm) high

$1,000-1,500 **WW**

ESSENTIAL REFERENCE - CHIPPENDALE STYLE

Thomas Chippendale (1718-79) was an English cabinetmaker and furniture designer. He began working in London in c1747 and published his influential design book 'The Gentleman and Cabinet-Maker's Director' in 1754.

- **The term 'Chippendale' is generally taken to mean 'in the Chippendale-style', rather than a piece that was made by Chippendale himself.**
- **By the mid-1760s Chippendale-style had spread to the USA. The American Chippendale furniture tends to be similar to its European counterpart, but is less ornate. Veneers are uncommon, with most pieces being made in solid walnut, mahogany or maple.**
- **The Chippendale style was revived in the mid- and late 19thC.**

A probably New Hampshire Chippendale maple chest-on-chest, attributed to the workshop of Moses Hazen, Weare, the broken scroll pediment with turned finial, with three-panel drawer over three drawers, the base with four drawers, on short ogee legs with claw-and-ball feet, with original red stained surface.

c1800 *83in (210cm) high*

$40,000-60,000 **POOK**

A Queen Anne walnut and featherbanded secrétaire chest, the interior with drawers, pigeonholes and cupboards, the base with two short and two long drawers, on bun feet.
c1700
$5,000-7,000 **DN**

A George II figured walnut and boxwood-strung secrétaire chest, the interior with drawers and pigeonholes.
c1740 *71in (181cm) high*
$6,500-7,500 **DN**

A George III mahogany, marquetry and bronze-mounted secrétaire, in the manner of Thomas Hope, with marble top, with Egyptian masks and feet to columns, the interior with drawers and pigeonholes, the base with cupboard doors, the locks stamped 'G.R'.
c1810 *54in (137cm) high*
$2,500-3,500 **DN**

An Empire ormolu mounted mahogany secrétaire à abattant, the black marble top above a drawer flanked by caryatids, the interior with drawers, the base with two cupboard doors concealing a shelf, on gilt leaf-carved paw feet.
c1810 *56in (142cm) high*
$4,000-6,000 **FRE**

A Regency parcel-ebonized wood and mahogany secrétaire-chiffonier, attributed to Morel & Hughes, with shelves on serpent supports, the interior with drawers and pigeonholes, the base with paneled doors, on paw feet.
c1815 *57.25in (145.5cm) high*
$3,000-4,000 **WES**

A 19thC Continental Biedermeier ash secrétaire à abattant, with drawer over fall-front, the interior with drawers, pigeonholes and secret compartments, the base with three drawers, on block feet.
62.25in (157.5cm) high
$8,000-12,000 **WW**

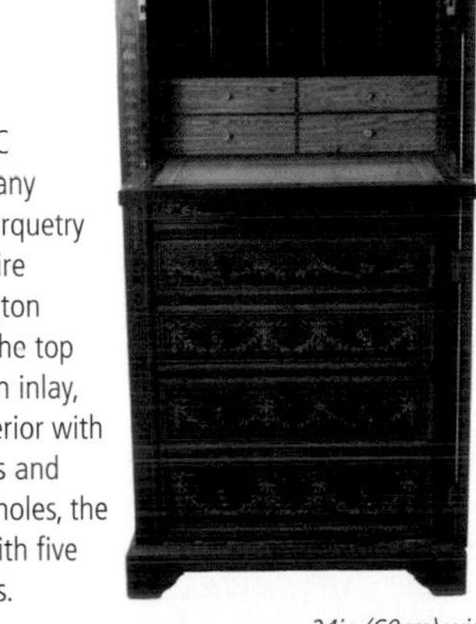

A 19thC mahogany and marquetry secrétaire Wellington chest, the top with fan inlay, the interior with drawers and pigeonholes, the base with five drawers.
24in (60cm) wide
$6,500-7,500 **BELL**

A 19thC French rosewood serpentine secrétaire à abattant, the bird's eye maple interior with a green leather gilt-tooled inset over drawers, on turned legs.
54.25in (138cm) high
$400-600 **GHOU**

An Auckland rimu and kauri secrétaire chest, with fitted interior.
c1885 *56in (142cm) high*
$10,000-15,000 **DS**

An Irish George III mahogany kneehole secrétaire bookcase, the two cupboard doors above two drawers, the fitted interior above an apron drawer and kneehole drawers flanked by six drawers, on bracket feet, lacking eagle finial and one flowerhead roundel.

c1760 *93in (235cm) high*

$30,000-40,000 **DN**

A Massachusetts Federal-style inlaid mahogany secrétaire breakfront bookcase, with a serpentine crest above glazed and mullioned doors, the crossbanded base with fitted interior above two drawers, flanked by drawers and cupboards, on tapered legs.

c1880 *79in (201cm) high*

$8,000-12,000 **POOK**

A Regency rosewood secrétaire bookcase.

c1815 *88in (223cm) high*

$3,000-4,000 **DN**

ESSENTIAL REFERENCE - MARSH & TATHAM

- **In 1790 William Marsh (active 1775-1810) went into partnership with George Elward. Thomas Tatham (1763-1818) joined the partnership in 1795 and the firm became known as Elward, Marsh & Tatham. From 1803 the firm was called Marsh & Tatham and it was in this period that it was the most successful and influential.**
- **The firm attracted many Royal and aristocratic patrons, such as the Prince of Wales who commissioned several pieces for Carlton House, including a cabinet with a similar use of ebony marquetry to the secrétaire bookcase shown.**
- **In 1794 Tatham's brother, Charles Heathcote Tatham was sent to Rome by the architect Henry Holland in order to collect Classical fragments. C H Tatham later published drawings of these objects as 'Etchings of Ancient Ornamental Architecture'. This publication provided Marsh & Tatham, as well as other designers, with the inspiration for much of their furniture.**

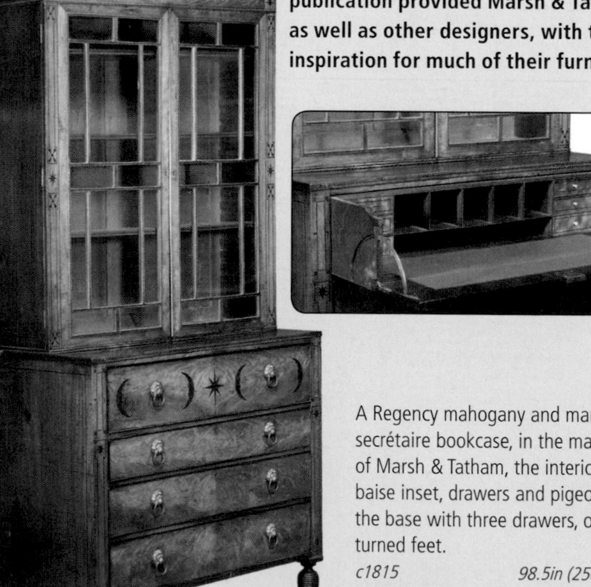

A Regency mahogany and marquetry secrétaire bookcase, in the manner of Marsh & Tatham, the interior with baise inset, drawers and pigeonholes, the base with three drawers, on turned feet.

c1815 *98.5in (250cm) high*

$6,500-7,500 **DN**

A 19thC and later mahogany secrétaire bookcase, with four carved astragal-glazed doors, the associated base with fall-front over later leather inset and burr-walnut-veneered drawers and pigeonholes, flanked by two drawers over cupboards, stamped 'T & A BLAIN'.

104in (264cm) high

$10,000-15,000 **WW**

An Edwardian mahogany and satinwood-banded secrétaire bookcase, with astragal-glazed doors, the base with fitted interior of small drawers, pigeonholes and gilt-tooled leather inset, above cupboard doors.

c1900 *92.5in (238cm) high*

$3,000-4,000 **TEN**

An Edwardian and later Sheraton Revival mahogany, satinwood-banded and marquetry secrétaire bookcase, the base Edwards & Roberts, the interior with pigeonholes, drawers and gilt-tooled leather inset, above cupboard doors, on bracket feet, the later bookcase with swan-neck pediment and four astragal-glazed doors.

110in (280cm) wide

$10,000-15,000 **TEN**

CLOSER LOOK - BUREAU BOOKCASE

John Coxed worked at the White Swan in St Paul's Churchyard c1711-18. Coxed's business was continued until 1735 by his widow Grace Coxed and brother-in-law Thomas Woster.

The White Swan workshop is best-known for stained burr-maple veneered furniture.

Many features of this bookcase are typical of Coxed and his successors, for example the mirrors are held by a narrow half-round molding rather than the more usual ovolo.

The top of the base is veneered, indicating it was initially made as a bureau.

The base has two small drawers flanking the interior well. This construction is not typical of Coxed's successors and suggests that John Coxed is the maker.

A stained burr-maple, rosewood-crossbanded and white-metal strung bureau bookcase, attributed to John Coxed, with mirrored doors above three drawers and candle slides, the base with fitted interior and drawers, on bun feet.

c1715 *81in (205cm) high*

$30,000-40,000 SWO

A George I burr-walnut bureau bookcase, with two mirrored doors opening to fitted interior, the base with fall-front opening to pigeonholes and drawers, with concealed frieze drawer above short and long drawers, on bracket feet, with alterations and restoration.

97in (247.5cm) high

$50,000-70,000 TOV

An 18thC Dutch walnut and marquetry bombe bureau bookcase, the shell cresting above two paneled cupboard doors, the base with stepped, fitted interior above two short and three long drawers, on later bun feet.

92in (234cm) high

$12,000-18,000 L&T

A George II red-lacquered and parcel-gilt chinoiserie bureau bookcase, with gilt and pierced carved crest above two mirrored doors, the base with fitted interior above drawers, on bracket feet.

93in (236cm) high

$200,000-300,000 LHA

A late George III mahogany bureau bookcase, the frieze inlaid with oval patera above astragal-glazed doors, the base with fitted interior over drawers, on ogee bracket feet.

92in (233cm) high

$3,000-4,000 TEN

An 18thC-style Dutch walnut marquetry bureau bookcase, the shell-carved pediment over two doors opening to fitted interior, the bombé base with further fitted interior over three drawers, with carved shaped apron, on paw feet.

$7,000-8,000 A&G

A Queen Anne-style walnut double-domed bureau bookcase, with two glazed doors opening to drawers, with fitted interior above two short and two long drawers, on bracket feet.

77in (196cm) high

$4,000-6,000 GORB

A George II mahogany breakfront bookcase, with three sash-bar glazed doors opening to shelves, the base with a panel door opening to drawers, flanked by cupboards.

63in (160cm) wide

$5,000-7,000 **DUK**

A late George III mahogany breakfront bookcase, with four astragal-glazed doors opening to adjustable shelves, the base with cupboards, on splayed bracket feet.

95in (241cm) wide

$15,000-20,000 **TEN**

A George III Irish mahogany breakfront bookcase, the arched pediment above astragal-glazed doors opening to shelves, the base with cupboard with stylized leaf decoration.

c1790 94in (240cm) wide

$7,000-10,000 **DN**

A Regency and later rosewood and brass-inlaid breakfront bookcase, with three glazed doors flanked by open shelves, the base with cupboard doors opening to shelves.

148in (375.5cm) wide

$15,000-20,000 **WW**

A late Regency plum-pudding mahogany breakfront bookcase, the crossbanded base with a pair of central cupboard doors opening to drawers, flanked by banks of drawers, flanked by cupboard doors opening to drawers.

152in (385.5cm) wide

$10,000-15,000 **WW**

An early 19thC possibly Baltic mahogany breakfront bookcase, with six astragal-glazed doors, the base with two flame-veneered mahogany cupboard doors, flanked by banks of drawers and cupboard doors.

114in (290cm) high

$8,000-12,000 **FRE**

A Victorian mahogany breakfront bookcase, the five glazed doors with bracketed arches and divided by applied scrolls, the base with drawers around a central panel with an applied reserve engraved 'JD'.

122in (309cm) wide

$6,500-7,500 **TEN**

A Victorian mahogany breakfront bookcase, the open bookcase with adjustable shelves flanked by carved corbels, the base with paneled cupboard doors.

113.25in (287.5cm) wide

$6,500-7,500 **WW**

A 19thC mahogany breakfront bookcase, with four glazed and mullioned doors, the base with four short drawers above four cupboard doors, on a foliate-carved base with carved bracket feet.

105.5in (268cm) high

$7,000-10,000 **FRE**

A Victorian carved rosewood and glazed breakfront bookcase.

c1870 *106in (270cm) high*

$3,000-4,000 **DN**

A mid-19thC Philadelphia Renaissance Revival walnut breakfront bookcase, the leaf- and scroll-carved cresting above mirrored cupboard door on two-drawer base, flanked by bookcases with glazed doors.

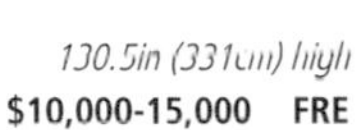

130.5in (331cm) high

$10,000-15,000 **FRE**

A late 19thC oak ecclesiastical breakfront bookcase, the quatrefoil guilloche frieze above arched glazed doors, the base with cupboard doors.

105in (267cm) wide

$15,000-20,000 **TEN**

An early 20thC 'Chippendale' mahogany breakfront bookcase, by Whytock & Reid, the pierced foliate cresting above astragal-glazed doors carved with wheat sheaves divided by uprights carved with roses, the base with foliate-scroll carved doors, on foliate-carved scrolled feet.

85in (216cm) wide

$20,000-30,000 **L&T**

A mid-18thC Palladian-style mahogany bookcase, with glazed doors, the base with six cockbeaded drawers.

117in (298cm) high

$20,000-30,000 **SWO**

A George II mahogany library bookcase, the pierced and carved swan-neck pediment above a dentil molded frieze and glazed doors, the base with dummy-drawer cupboard doors over two drawers, on shaped bracket feet.

c1750 *97.5in (248cm) high*

$10,000-15,000 **L&T**

A Victorian mahogany library bookcase, by Edwards & Roberts, the cavetto-molded cornice above three glazed panel doors, the base with three arched panel doors.

95in (242cm) high

$5,000-7,000 **L&T**

ESSENTIAL REFERENCE - EMPIRE STYLE

The Empire style is a form of the Neo-classical style, named after the period during which Napoleon Bonaparte ruled France (1804-14). The style was specially created to idealize Napoleon's leadership and the French state.

- **Classical forms and ornaments were combined with motifs associated with Napoleon, such as bees, 'N's, laurel wreaths, eagles and Egyptian motifs.**
- **Furniture was typically made of a single wood, generally mahogany, with ormolu decoration.**
- **Drapery was very popular in the Empire style.**
- **The style spread across Europe with Napoleon's armies and remained popular after his defeat. It was revived in the late 19thC.**

A pair of Empire-style mahogany open bookcases, the friezes with central ormolu double-anthemion mounts and outer rosettes, flanked by tapered ribbed terminals headed by Egyptian masks, on plinth bases.

c1900 *38in (97cm) high*

$6,500-7,500 **L&T**

A Victorian walnut, marquetry and gilt-metal-mounted bookcase, with two glazed doors, the base with two cupboard doors concealing shelves.

c1860 *82in (209cm) high*

$10,000-15,000 **DN**

A large Victorian limed-oak library bookcase, the foliate-carved frieze above three glazed panel doors opening to adjustable shelves, the base with three relief-carved panel doors.

c1880 *120in (305cm) high*

$8,000-12,000 **L&T**

A 19thC-style oak open library bookcase, surmounted by four turrets with painted shield to center.

172.5in (436cm) wide

$12,000-18,000 **DN**

A Regency rosewood breakfront dwarf bookcase, Gillows, the three fielded cupboard doors inset with brass grills, on reeded bun feet.

36in (91cm) wide

$15,000-20,000 GORL

A George IV mahogany double-waterfall bookcase, with openwork spindle-shaped and reeded end-supports, on lobed bun feet.

c1815 *39in (98cm) high*

$7,000-10,000 L&T

A small Regency rosewood open bookcase, with frieze drawers, on square column supports carved with pilasters headed by anthemion, the base with two drawers and dummy drawers.

c1820 *29.25in (74cm) high*

$5,500-6,500 L&T

A George IV rosewood library bookcase, attributed to Gillows, the top with leather inset, the sides with leather-bound book-spine panels, on lobed feet.

c1825 *32.5in (83cm) high*

$15,000-20,000 L&T

A George IV satinwood dwarf bookcase, with white marble top above stylized Doric pilasters.

c1830 *48in (122cm) wide*

$5,000-7,000 L&T

A Victorian mahogany, satinwood and marquetry revolving bookcase, the top with central mahogany panel within satinwood marquetry border.

c1890 *32.5in (85cm) high*

$2,500-3,500 DN

A George II hexagonal oak book table, the dish top with turned upright supports and undertier, on a tripod base with castors.

c1750 *32in (82cm) high*

$4,000-6,000 L&T

A Victorian walnut revolving library table, the burr-walnut veneer top with candle stand, on a turned baluster stem with revolving bookcase, on a tripod base.

30.75in (78cm) high

$800-1,200 A&G

An Edwardian satinwood and marquetry revolving bookcase, surmounted by a tazza top, on quadiform base with hairy-paw feet.

c1910 *52in (132cm) high*

$5,500-6,500 L&T

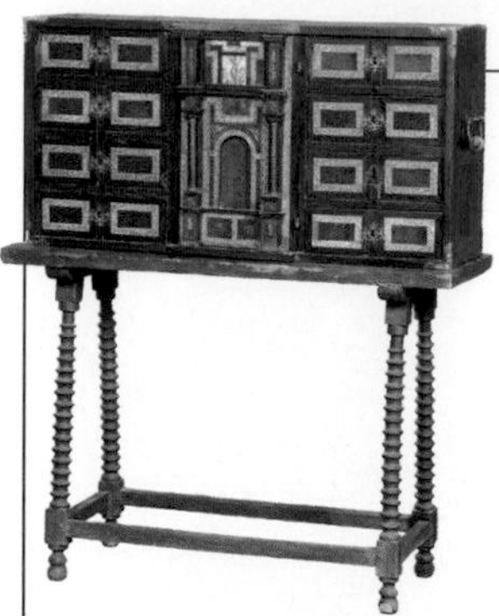

A Spanish Baroque ivory and tortoiseshell-mounted cabinet-on-stand, composed of antique elements, the cabinet with nine drawers and a central cupboard door opening to drawers, mounted with foliate-engraved ivory plaques and brass mounts, the stand with bobbin-turned legs and with stretchers.

55in (140cm) high

$7,000-10,000 **SK**

A late 17thC Flemish ebonized cabinet-on-stand, the cabinet with hinged top above drawers, later painted with allegorical scenes, on associated stand with cabriole legs and pad feet.

57in (145cm) high

$4,000-6,000 **GORL**

A late 17thC and later William & Mary oyster-veneered, walnut and floral marquetry cabinet-on-stand, with cushion frieze drawer above cupboard doors opening to drawers and a further cupboard door, the stand reduced in height, on later bracket feet.

42.5in (108cm) wide

$15,000-20,000 **L&T**

A Queen Anne japanned chinoiserie cabinet-on-stand, the cabinet doors opening to drawers, the later giltwood stand carved with scrolls, flowers and foliage, with old damage and restoration.

65.25in (165.5cm) high

$12,000-18,000 **WW**

An early 18thC German walnut, burr-walnut, mahogany and plumwood cabinet-on-stand.

75in (193cm) high

$10,000-15,000 **KAU**

A George III satinwood, marquetry and brass-banded cabinet-on-stand, the two cupboard doors opening to two shelves, on square tapered legs.

c1780 *57.5in (144cm) high*

$12,000-18,000 **DN**

A 18thC red-lacquered chinoiserie cabinet-on-stand, with two cupboard doors opening to ten drawers, the stand possibly later.

61in (155cm) high

$35,000-45,000 **DS**

A near pair of late 19thC Neo-classical Revival ebonized and part burlwood-veneered salon cabinets, with porcelain portrait and flower medallions, the friezes with three drawers, the central drawer with writing surface.

59in (150cm) wide

$30,000-40,000 **DOR**

A Queen Anne walnut cabinet-on-chest, with two feather-banded cupboard doors opening to drawers, the base with two short and two long drawers, with gilt-brass ring handles, on replaced turned bun feet.

67.25in (171cm) high

$12,000-18,000 WW

A William & Mary walnut cabinet, with cushioned frieze drawer above two quarter-veneered and feather-banded cupboard doors, opening to drawers and a cupboard, the base with drawers, on bun feet.

68in (172cm) high

$8,000-12,000 SWO

A late 17thC and later iron-bound oak cabinet-on-chest, with two cupboard doors opening to drawers and a cupboard, the base with two short and two long drawers, on bracket feet.

59in (151cm) high

$1,200-1,800 SHAP

A George III mahogany cabinet-on-chest, with four paneled doors opening to adjustable shelves, the base with thirteen drawers.

72in (183cm) high

$8,000-12,000 SWO

A rare German Baroque walnut, burl-walnut, mahogany, pearwood and satinwood cabinet-on-chest, with replacements and some damage to veneer.

82.5in (212cm) high

$12,000-18,000 KAU

An early George III mahogany cabinet-on-chest, the pierced foliate-carved cornice above two paneled doors opening to drawers, the base with three long drawers, with replaced brass handles, on paneled bracket feet with rosettes.

78in (198.5cm) high

$5,000-7,000 WW

A 19thC Dutch Baroque-style red-japanned chinoiserie cabinet-on-chest, with two cupboard doors opening to shelves, the base with two short and two long drawers, on block feet.

98.5in (250cm) high

$3,000-4,000 SK

A Queen Anne walnut bureau cabinet, with two cupboard doors opening to fitted interior, the base with further fitted interior, on possibly replaced bun feet.

76in (193.5cm) high

$25,000-35,000 **DS**

An early 18thC walnut and crossbanded bureau cabinet, with two panel doors opening to shelves, the base with covered well, pigeonholes and drawers, above three long drawers, on bracket feet.

77in (196cm) high

$8,000-12,000 **L&T**

A George I walnut bureau cabinet, the mirrored door opening to a cupboard, shelves and pigeonholes, the base with fitted interior of drawers and pigeonholes, above two short and three long drawers, on bracket feet.

c1720 *83in (211cm) high*

$12,000-18,000 **DN**

A George II walnut and feather-banded bureau cabinet, the two paneled doors opening to pigeonholes and two candle slides, the base with fitted interior above three short and two long drawers, on bracket feet, with later inlay.

75in (191cm) high

$1,500-2,500 **GORB**

A George III mahogany bureau cabinet, the swan-neck cornice over a mirrored door opening to pigeonholes, a shelf, drawers and a cupboard, the base with fitted interior with pigeonholes, drawers and a cupboard, above two short and three long drawers, on ogee bracket feet.

87in (222cm) high

$30,000-40,000 **SWO**

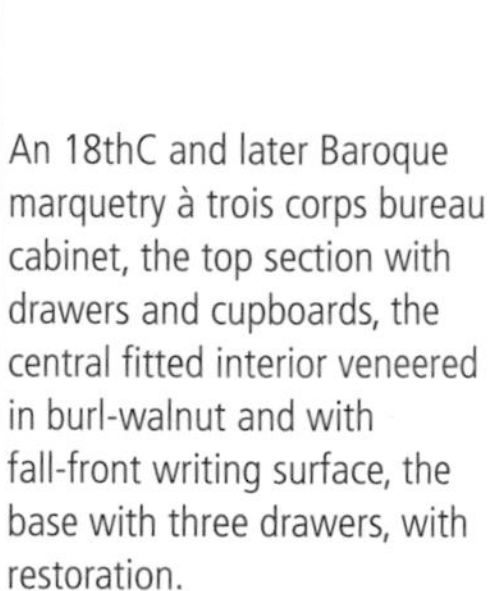

A George III mahogany writing cabinet, the dentil cut molded cornice above a fluted frieze, with two flame-veneered cupboard doors opening to shelves, drawers and removable recess, the base with writing slide over two cupboard doors, on banded bracket feet with spandrels.

78in (198cm) high

$30,000-40,000 **L&T**

An Austrian/German Neo-Classical walnut à trois corps bureau cabinet, with two cupboard doors above fitted interior, the base with two cupboard doors.

c1780 *83in (210cm) high*

$12,000-18,000 **DOR**

An 18thC and later Baroque marquetry à trois corps bureau cabinet, the top section with drawers and cupboards, the central fitted interior veneered in burl-walnut and with fall-front writing surface, the base with three drawers, with restoration.

84in (213cm) high

$40,000-60,000 **DOR**

A French ormolu-mounted display cabinet, by Jean Baptiste Fromageau, Paris, with marble top, signed 'I B Fromageau' and with Paris guild stamp 'AV'.

c1755 *55in (139cm) high*

$15,000-20,000 **KAU**

A George III mahogany and glazed display cabinet.

The overall form of this cabinet and its astragal glazing relate closely to a design by Gillows.

c1780 *98in (249cm) high*

$12,000-18,000 **DN**

An early 19thC Dutch walnut and floral-marquetry display cabinet, retailed by Edwards & Roberts, with glazed door above four long drawers, on claw-and-ball feet.

71in (180cm) high

$5,500-6,500 **GORL**

CLOSER LOOK - VICTORIAN DISPLAY CABINETS

A pair of cabinets of this complexity of design and materials commands a premium.

For the provenance appeal – the rear of each section bears paper inventory label for 'Shelburne', a former nobleman owner.

Each pagoda top has high quality stiff-acanthus-leaf mounts at the corner and is centered by a double scroll mask and unusual dragon mount.

The cabinets are on exceptional tapered banded cabriole legs with ornate mounts to the knees and feet.

If the mounts were not actually made by the Sèvres porcelain factory, they are of an equal quality.

These cabinets exude quality and sophistication.

A pair of Victorian kingwood, ormolu- and porcelain-mounted display cabinets, the interiors now mirror glazed, on tapered banded cabriole legs.

59in (149cm) high

$40,000-60,000 **L&T**

A Victorian mahogany, satinwood and floral marquetry display cabinet, the base with two doors decorated with flowers and leaves, flanked by shelves.

85in (215cm) high

$6,500-7,500 **TEN**

A late 19thC Sheraton Revival satinwood display cabinet, with marquetry swag inlays to the pediment and drawer front.

c1870 *76in (195cm) high*

$5,000-7,000 **CHEF**

A late 19thC French painted and gilt vitrine, the glazed door and panels with gilt reeded pilasters, the apron applied with giltwood and gesso flower baskets and festoons, on cabriole legs with hairy-hoof feet and undertier.

This cabinet was previously used in Arundel Castle to display Mary Queen of Scots' Rosary.

71in (180cm) high

$6,000-8,000 **TOV**

A New Zealand specimen cabinet, constructed and carved by H B Dobbie, Whangarei, including 19thC fern specimens.

Provenance: Herbert Dobbie (1852-1940) was an British-born engineer, traveller, writer, botanist and expert wood carver. He traveled extensively on his penny farthing bicycle and on foot, collecting ferns to collate the first book on New Zealand ferns in 1880.

c1880 *65in (166cm) wide*

$30,000-40,000 DS

A pair of late 19thC satinwood, rosewood and crossbanded ormolu-mounted side cabinets, painted with Grecian motifs, the reeded and turned pilasters with carved flowerheads, on toupie feet.

41in (104cm) wide

$30,000-40,000 TEN

A late 19thC Louis XV-style kingwood and ormolu-mounted vitrine, the marble top above three glazed doors, on square cabriole legs with sabots.

78.75in (200cm) high

$10,000-15,000 L&T

A Victorian mahogany and gilt-metal-mounted display cabinet, the frieze with pierced decoration, on square tapered legs with paw-cast sabots.

c1890 *74.5in (184cm) high*

$6,500-7,500 DN

An Edwardian satinwood and marquetry secrétaire display cabinet, attributed to Edwards & Roberts, inlaid with flowering urns, baskets and foliate scrolls, the base with two cupboard doors and a fall-front drawer with fitted interior, on square tapered splayed legs with undertier.

c1905 *50.5in (128cm) high*

$6,500-7,500 L&T

An Edwardian inlaid satinwood breakfront display cabinet, with three glazed doors above two drawers and cupboards, on splayed feet.

73in (186cm) high

$4,000-6,000 SWO

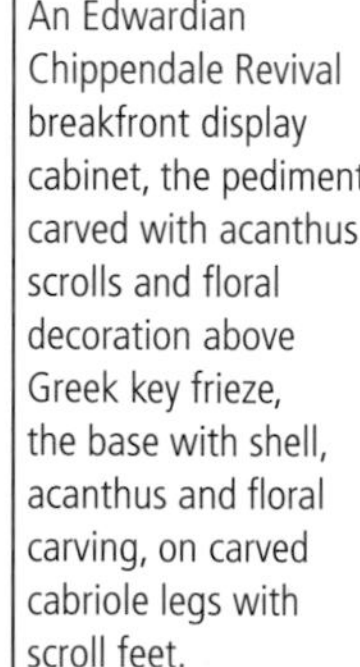

An Edwardian Chippendale Revival breakfront display cabinet, the pediment carved with acanthus scrolls and floral decoration above Greek key frieze, the base with shell, acanthus and floral carving, on carved cabriole legs with scroll feet.

77.75in (185cm) wide

$12,000-18,000 A&G

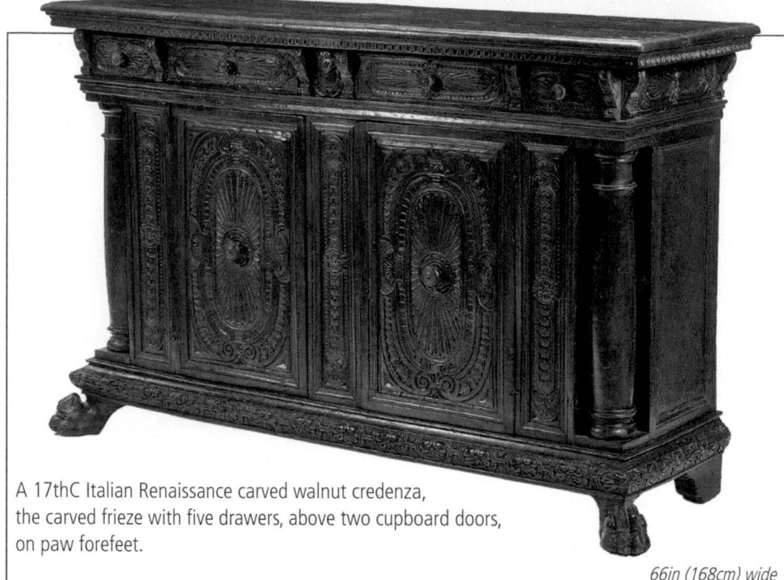

A 17thC Italian Renaissance carved walnut credenza, the carved frieze with five drawers, above two cupboard doors, on paw forefeet.

66in (168cm) wide

$20,000-30,000 **FRE**

A 17thC and later Italian walnut credenza, with short frieze drawers and foliate-carved brackets, above two cupboard doors, on paw feet.

48.5in (123cm) wide

$3,000-4,000 **FRE**

A Victorian walnut and gilt-metal-mounted credenza, the marquetry frieze above an ebonized central cupboard with floral marquetry, flanked by gilt metal caryatids and two glazed cupboards.

75in (191cm) wide

$5,500-6,500 **ROS**

A late Victorian ebonized and gilt-metal-mounted breakfront credenza, with two cupboard doors with inset Jasperware plaques, flanked by glazed doors, divided by Ionic capitals, on turned feet.

75in (189cm) wide

$3,000-4,000 **TOV**

A pair of George III and later satinwood, harewood and line-inlaid chiffoniers, each with one drawer above two silk-backed doors, on bracket feet.

c1880 50in (126cm) high

$10,000-15,000 **DN**

A Regency rosewood chiffonier, with mirrored superstructure above marble top, above two frieze drawers and two brass-grille cupboard doors flanked by columns with marble capitals, on turned feet.

49in (125cm) high

$4,000-6,000 **TEN**

A Regency painted pine chiffonier, with two shelves, with frieze drawer above a two grille doors, on turned tapering legs.

61.5in (156cm) high

$5,000-7,000 **WW**

A pair of Regency rosewood chiffoniers, each with one shelf and two gilt-metal grill doors.

30in (76cm) wide

$15,000-20,000 **TOV**

A 16th/17thC and later oak buffet, the marquetry frieze with stylized masks and one drawer, with griffin supports, above another frieze drawer and shell- and acanthus-carved cup-and-cover supports.

50in (128cm) wide

$10,000-15,000 **DN**

ESSENTIAL REFERENCE - GEORGE HEPPLEWHITE

George Hepplewhite (c1727-86) was not a particularly well-known or successful cabinetmaker during his lifetime. He became known after his book of designs 'The Cabinet-maker and Upholsterer's Guide' was published in 1788, two years after his death. His designs epitomized Neo-classicalism.

- **Hepplewhite's 'Guide' was widely used as a trade catalog, especially by provincial makers. Much 'Hepplewhite' furniture was probably made after the style had gone out of fashion in London.**
- **Bow- and serpentine-fronted chests-of-drawers and shield-back chairs are typical of the style.**

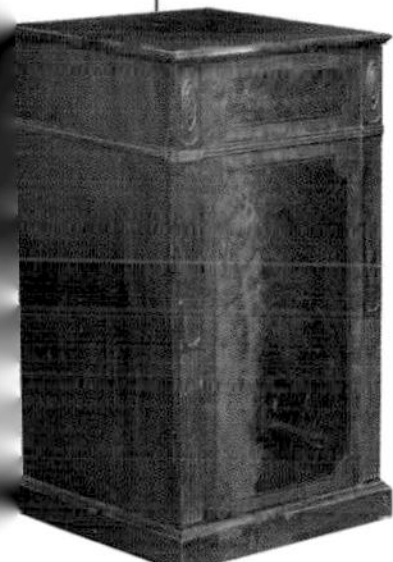

A pair of mahogany and tulipwood crossbanded dining room pedestals, one with a frieze drawer and cupboard opening to cupboard and drawer, the other with a cupboard door opening to later shelves.

c1770 *37in (95cm) high*

$4,000-6,000 **DN**

A New York Hepplewhite mahogany sideboard, with fan-inlaid drawers flanked by inlaid columns, on square tapered legs with bellflower inlays.

c1790 *71.5in (182cm) wide*

$10,000-15,000 **POOK**

A George III mahogany and inlaid serving table, the frieze inlaid with fan motifs with trailing bellflower swags and with one drawer, on reeded tapered legs headed by paterae.

90in (229cm) wide

$20,000-30,000 **L&T**

A George III mahogany and satinwood-banded demi-lune sideboard, with two drawers flanked by cellaret drawers and cupboards, on later tapered square legs.

c1780 *72in (184cm) wide*

$4,000-6,000 **DN**

A George III mahogany, tulip and chevron banded sideboard, with bow-shaped rear-edge, one side with revolving lead-lined cellaret drawer, the other with revolving drawer and a cupboard, on square tapered legs with spade feet.

c1800 *72in (183cm) wide*

$2,500-3,500 **DN**

An early 19thC Salem, Massachusetts Federal mahogany sideboard, with five drawers and two cupboard doors, on reeded and ring-turned legs.

55.5in (141cm) wide

$6,500-7,500 **FRE**

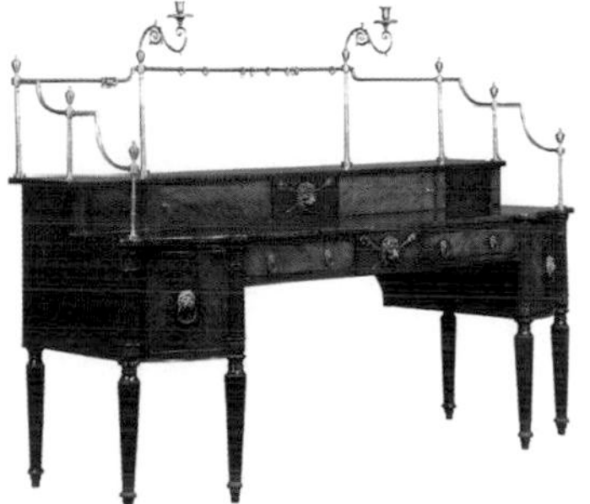

A Scottish George III mahogany stageback sideboard, the frieze with drawers and central Classical tablet, on turned legs.

c1810 *87in (220cm) wide*

$7,000-10,000 **DN**

ESSENTIAL REFERENCE - GEORGE SMITH

Along with Thomas Hope, George Smith (1756–1826) brought the taste for the Neo-Egyptian and Neo-classical to English furniture design.

- **Egyptian motifs were first incorperated into the Regency style in 1807 in Thomas Hope's influential work 'Household Furniture and Interior Decoration'. George Smith's 'Collection of Designs for Household Furniture and Interior Decoration' (1808) included sphinxes and other strange Egyptian iconography.**
- **Smith was inspired by French and Classical sources, as well as the designs of Thomas Hope and Thomas Sheraton (see p.188 for more on Sheraton).**

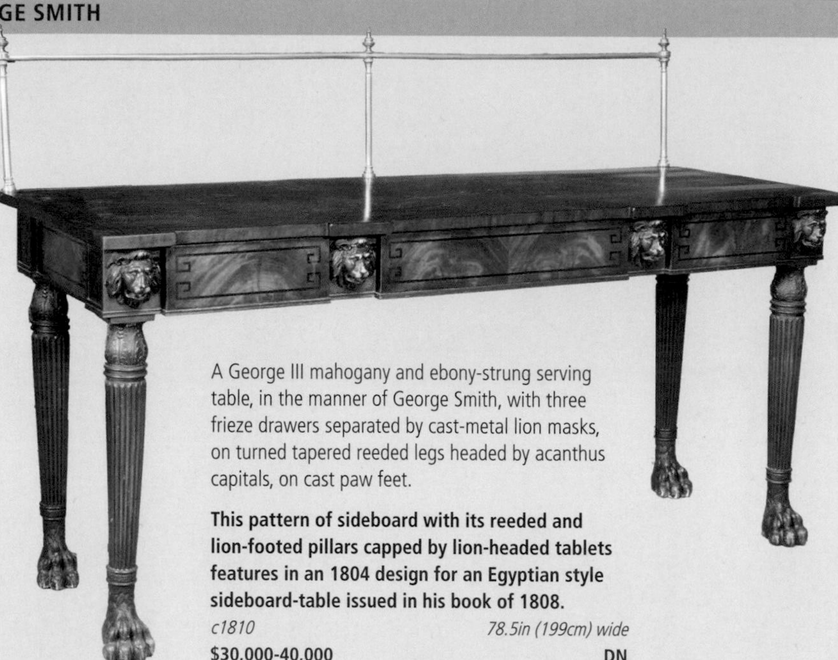

A George III mahogany and ebony-strung serving table, in the manner of George Smith, with three frieze drawers separated by cast-metal lion masks, on turned tapered reeded legs headed by acanthus capitals, on cast paw feet.

This pattern of sideboard with its reeded and lion-footed pillars capped by lion-headed tablets features in an 1804 design for an Egyptian style sideboard-table issued in his book of 1808.

c1810 *78.5in (199cm) wide*

$30,000-40,000 **DN**

An early 19thC provincial sideboard, with beech top, with two cupboard doors.

65in (166cm) wide

$4,000-6,000 **DOR**

A George IV mahogany breakfront sideboard, in the manner of Gillows, with a pierced gallery, with frieze and apron drawers and two revolving cellaret drawers, on turned and fluted legs with brass caps and castors.

c1825 *85in (215cm) wide*

$20,000-30,000 **DN**

A George IV Gillows mahogany inverted-breakfront sideboard, with three frieze drawers above cupboard doors, on turned and gadrooned feet, stamped 'GILLOW'.

c1825 *71.5in (181.5cm) wide*

$2,000-3,000 **DN**

A George III mahogany and ebony-inlaid serving table, in the manner of Thomas Hope, with two small drawers and concave center section.

c1810 *90in (228.5cm) wide*

$6,500-7,500 **DN**

A Scottish George IV mahogany serving table, the brass gallery with thistle finials, with two columnar-carved drawers, on turned and reeded legs.

c1825 *79in (200cm) wide*

$10,000-15,000 **L&T**

A William IV metamorphic pollard-oak serving table, attributed to Gillows, with carved scroll and panel back, on fluted baluster floral legs.

66in (168cm) wide

$4,000-6,000 **GORL**

A William IV mahogany breakfront serving table, in the manner of George Smith, with three drawers, one carved with the head of Apollo, with carved lion masks, on lappet carved, turned and reeded tapered legs and turned feet.

c1835 *94in (240cm) wide*

$6,500-8,500 **DN**

A William IV mahogany bowfront serving table, attributed to Gillows, with frieze drawer, on lappet-carved and reeded tapered legs with reeded bun feet.

c1835 *94.5in (240cm) wide*

$12,000-18,000 **DN**

A Victorian pollard-oak mirror-back sideboard, carved with foliage and birds, the mirror flanked by caryatid pilasters, the base with one frieze drawer and two cupboard doors.

c1880 *85.5in (217cm) wide*

$7,000-10,000 **L&T**

A William IV mahogany sideboard, with carved scrolling crest above two small drawers, the central frieze drawer above a carved and recessed drawer flanked by a cellaret drawer and cupboard, on ring-turned and carved legs.

78in (199cm) wide

$3,500-4,500 **TEN**

A late 18thC Boston, Massachusetts Federal mahogany inlaid sideboard, attributed to John and Thomas Seymour, the central drawer with fitted interior, flanked by drawers and cupboards, with 'General Washington' brass handles.

68.25in (173cm) wide

$20,000-30,000 **SK**

A mid-20thC Adam-style satinwood and painted sideboard, with fruitwood marquetry inlaid doors.

77.25in (196cm) wide

$5,000-7,000 **RTC**

An early George III crossbanded mahogany bedside cabinet, with two cupboard doors above a drawer, on square tapered legs.

c1760 *31.5in (80cm) high*

$4,000-6,000 **L&T**

One of a matched pair of George III mahogany bowfront bedside cabinets, later adapted.

c1770 *Tallest 29.25in (74cm) high*

$2,000-3,000 pair **DN**

A pair of George III mahogany tray-top bedside cabinets, enclosed by tambour shutters, on square legs, one with pull-out base.

c1780 *30in (77cm) high*

$8,000-12,000 **DN**

A pair of early 19thC mahogany, boxwood-strung and crossbanded bedside cabinets, with frieze drawers above cupboards, both with pull-out close stools, on strung spade feet.

21.5in (54cm) high

$20,000-30,000 **A&G**

A pair of George IV Gillows mahogany bedside cabinets, with cupboard doors, on turned and reeded tapered legs.

c1825 *31in (79cm) high*

$12,000-18,000 **DN**

A pair of 19thC Regency-style mahogany bedside cabinets, with cupboards, on turned tapered legs.

29.5in (75cm) high

$3,000-4,000 **L&T**

A pair of French kingwood and ormolu-mounted encoignure, the marble tops above cupboards, on bracket feet.

35.5in (90cm) high

$4,000-6,000 **DN**

A late 19thC French mahogany bedside cabinet, the marble top above four drawers and two dummy drawers concealing a cupboard, with pot castors.

36in (91.5cm) high

$800-1,200 **CAPE**

An early 18thC walnut feather- and crossbanded kneehole desk, the quarter-veneer top above a slide, with two frieze drawers above seven drawers and door, on bracket feet.

33in (84cm) high

$10,000-15,000 **GORB**

A George II red walnut secrétaire kneehole desk, the frieze drawer with hinged fall enclosing a fitted interior with pigeonholes and drawers, above six drawers, a shaped apron drawer and a central recessed cupboard, on bracket feet.

32.75in (83cm) wide

$2,000-3,000 **H&L**

A George III mahogany kneehole desk, on ogee bracket feet.

37in (93cm) wide

$6,500-7,500 **SWO**

A George III mahogany partners' desk, with a green leather writing surface, above three long frieze drawers on each side, the twin pedestals each with three drawers and two cupboard doors, one with adjustable dividers, the other with pigeonholes.

This desk has several features that are similar to those used by Thomas Chippendale, such as the pigeonholes and dividers.

73in (185cm) wide

$25,000-35,000 **TEN**

A George III mahogany bureau pedestal writing table, attributed to Gillows, the ratcheted and hinged slope above a two-as-one secrétaire drawer, the sliding tray inset with a gilt leather skiver, above a well and lidded compartments, with six drawers and opposing dummy drawer.

c1790 *48in (122cm) wide*

$7,000-10,000 **TEN**

A French Empire rosewood and ormolu-mounted desk, with four drawers above a paneled top with pull-out drawer on a wheel mechanism, with a hinged fall and gilt tooled leather inset above drawers, one with lift-out tray and lockable slide, the well with two cupboard doors, signed 'LESAGE & GRANDVOINNET, Rue de la Chaussee-d'Antin, No:11, Paris'.

66in (167cm) wide

$18,000-22,000 **WW**

A Regency and later rosewood, parcel-gilt and gilt-metal mounted pedestal desk, in the manner of Marsh & Tatham, the gilt-tooled leather-inset top above six drawers and three dummy frieze drawers with patterae and wreath mounts.

60in (153cm) wide

$15,000-20,000 **DN**

A Regency mahogany writing desk, attributed to Gillows, with two short and one long drawer, on reeded tapering legs with brass caps and castors.

The earliest sketch of this model occurs in the Gillows Estimate Book, 1803-1815, dated 12 March 1806.

c1815 *41in (105cm) wide*

$5,500-6,500 **DN**

A 19thC mahogany pedestal writing desk, the leather-inset top above three frieze drawers, with three short drawers in each pedestal and cupboard at side, stamped 'C.J Freemans Furniture Manufactory, 37 London Street, Norwich'.

82.5in (212cm) wide

$15,000-20,000 **SWO**

A Victorian Sheraton Revival satinwood, banded and painted Carlton House desk, with hinged stationery compartments and a pull-out inset leather writing surface, with three drawers one stamped 'JAS SHOOLBRED & CO', on square tapered legs with brass castors.

45.25in (114.5cm) wide

$10,000-15,000 **WW**

A Neo-classical Revival painted kneehole desk, with frieze drawer and two cupboards.

c1860 and later *60in (153cm) wide*

$2,500-3,500 **DN**

ESSENTIAL REFERENCE - GILLOWS

Gillows of Lancaster was founded in c1727 by joiner Robert Gillow (1703-72). The company became the UK's leading factory manufacturer outside of London, known for well-made Georgian, Regency and Victorian furniture.

- **In the 1760s Gillows was the first English company to stamp its furniture.**
- **Gillows established a London saleroom in 1776.**
- **By the late 18thC Gillows had introduced several new types of furniture, including the Davenport desk.**
- **Gillows absorbed Collinson & Lock in 1897 and merged with S J Waring & Sons in 1900 to become Waring & Gillow.**
- **In 1980 the company joined with Maple & Co, becoming Maple, Waring & Gillow.**

A Victorian Holland & Sons satinwood partners' pedestal desk, with three frieze drawers and three drawers in each pedestal, the opposing side with dummy drawers and two cupboards, stamped.

c1860 *62.5in (157.5cm) wide*

$18,000-22,000 **DN**

A Victorian Gillows coromandel and mahogany-crossbanded kidney-shaped desk, with graduated drawers.

c1870 *51in (130cm) wide*

$30,000-40,000 **DN**

CLOSER LOOK - LOUIS XV-STYLE BUREAU

Henry Dasson is one of the most important French furniture makers of the second half of 19thC. He was known as the finest makers of ormolu-mounted furniture as shown with this bureau.

He is very famous for the high quality of his ormolu mounts with extraordinary mercurial gilding.

He specialized in the production of furniture and works of art inspired by Louis XIV, Louis XV and Louis XVI styles.

He was very successful at the 1878 Paris Universal Exhibition, which adds to the cachet of this piece.

One mount bears his makers stamp and the date of 1878.

A Louis XV-style tulipwood, kingwood and ormolu-mounted bureau Rognon, by Henri Dasson, with three leather-faced drawers and leaf-cast candle holders, with three frieze drawers, on cabriole legs with acanthus leaf scrolling mounts and paw feet, stamped.

1878 *55in (139cm) wide*

$20,000-30,000 **TEN**

A Wright & Mansfield olivewood and ebonized desk, with a pierced brass gallery on fluted columns, with frieze drawers and pull-out slides, on tapered legs with stop-fluted corner blocks, stamped.

c1880 *55in (140cm) wide*

$15,000-20,000 **L&T**

A 19thC mahogany and calamander-crossbanded pedestal desk, by Thomas Willson, London, with three frieze drawers and three drawers in each pedestal, the opposing side with dummy drawers, with recessed castors, stamped.

Thomas Willson (1799-1854) is recorded as furniture broker, auctioneer and appraiser. Some speculation exists as to whether Willson's were furniture makers or brokers.

58in (148cm) wide

$3,000-4,000 **L&T**

A late 19thC Chinese Chippendale carved mahogany desk, the frieze drawer carved with scrolling leaves and flowerheads, with four drawers to each pedestal, on acanthus leaf-carved scrolling feet with castors.

59in (151cm) wide

$7,000-10,000 **TEN**

A late 19th/early 20thC 18thC-style Italian rosewood and bone-marquetry desk.

57.5in (146cm) wide

$5,000-7,000 **DN**

An Edwardian satinwood and marquetry Carlton House desk, retailed by S & H Jewell, the cylinder superstructure with fitted interior over drawers and flanked by cupboards and drawers, with five drawers around the central arch, on tapered square legs.

39in (100cm) wide

$5,000-7,000 **BELL**

A pair of Victorian Louis XVI-style kingwood, porcelain-inset and gilt-metal-mounted bonheur du jours, each with two cupboards above four drawers, on cabriole legs.

c1870 *45in (115cm) high*

$10,000-15,000 **DN**

A Victorian walnut and marquetry bonheur du jour, with mirror above a drawer with silver presentation plaque, flanked by two cupboards, above a fall front with fitted interior, on cabriole legs.

c1880 *56in (142cm) high*

$2,000-3,000 **DN**

A late Victorian amboyna, ebonized and porcelain-mounted bonheur du jour, with central mirrored recess flanked by cupboards mounted with porcelain plaques, the corners with gilt-metal figures of Shakespeare and Milton, above frieze drawers, one with writing slope, on fluted and gilt-metal-mounted legs with shelf and undertier, on toupie feet.

59in (150cm) high

$6,500-7,500 **L&T**

A George III mahogany and strung cylinder bureau, the fall front opening to fitted interior and sliding writing surface, with two frieze drawers, on square tapered legs with brass caps and castors.

41in (105cm) wide

$3,000-4,000 **TEN**

A George III rosewood and satinwood-banded cylinder writing desk, the alternating-veneered tambour opening to hinged writing surface and fitted interior, with two drawers, on square tapered legs with brass caps and castors.

39.25in (99.5cm) high

$15,000-20,000 **WW**

CLOSER LOOK - LOUIS XVI BUREAU

The complexity and sophistication of the overall design of the piece is stunning, with exotic woods, including tulipwood and amaranth, and marquetry and parquetry decoration.

It achieves a three-dimensional scene with a large number of elements, including animals, people and Classical ruins.

The marble top could have been more sympathetically replaced.

The interior is well appointed.

The provenance speaks for the quality of the piece – it was part of the Battersea Collection owned by Constance de Rothschild, Lady Battersea (d.1931).

A Louis XVI amaranth, tulipwood, marquetry and parquetry and ormolu-mounted cylinder bureau, the later marble top above three frieze drawers, the cylinder with marquetry decoration of Classical ruins opening to inlaid fitted interiors, the well with oak drawer flanked by inlaid drawers, on inlaid tapered legs, with restoration.

c1780

$40,000-60,000 **MEA**

A late 18thC French kingwood and rosewood-banded cylinder bureau, the marble top above three parquetry drawers, the gilt-brass-mounted cylinder opening to fitted interior and leather-inset writing surface, with three frieze drawers with bellflower and ram's head mounts, on strung tapered legs with brass feet.

43in (109cm) high

$15,000-20,000 **L&T**

A William & Mary walnut and featherbanded bureau, the fall front opening to a fitted interior, above two short and two long drawers.

37.75in (96cm) wide

$8,000-12,000 **LC**

A George I burr-walnut, walnut and featherbanded bureau, the fall front opening to a serpentine fitted interior, above six drawers and a dummy drawer.

c1720 *41in (104cm) high*

$10,000-15,000 **DN**

An early 18thC walnut and crossbanded bureau, with fitted interior above two short and three long drawers, on bracket feet.

36in (92cm) wide

$3,000-4,000 **WHP**

A George I cross- and featherbanded walnut bureau, the fall front opening to fitted interior of drawers, pigeonholes and a cupb oard, above two short and two long drawers, on replaced bracket feet, with restoration.

c1720 *38in (96.5cm) wide*

$7,000-10,000 **L&T**

A Louis XV walnut bureau, by Louis Cresson, Paris, the fall front opening to a fitted interior with drawers and shelves, above three short drawers and two long drawers, on cabriole legs, stamped.

c1745 *40.5in (103cm) high*

$4,000-6,000 **FRE**

A German Baroque burr-walnut, walnut and mahogany bureau, with restoration.

c1740–50 *47.5in (122cm) wide*

$6,500-7,500 **KAU**

A probably Maltese olivewood and walnut serpentine bureau, with restoration.

c1750 *51in (130cm) wide*

$15,000-20,000 **DN**

A George III mahogany bureau, the fall front opening to fitted interior with pigeonholes, drawers, a cupboard and two faux-book-spine compartments, above four drawers, on bracket feet.

41.5in (105cm) high

$4,000-6,000 **WW**

A George III mahogany bureau, the fall front opening to drawers and a cupboard, above four drawers, on ogee bracket feet.

c1760 *42.5in (107cm) high*

$1,000-1,500 **DN**

A late 18thC Provincial Neo-Classical walnut desk, the fall front with intarsia panels, above three long drawers, with cracks.

49.25in (125cm) wide

$5,000-7,000 **DOR**

A late Georgian mahogany bureau, the fall front opening to fitted interior, above two short and two long drawers, on bracket feet.

41in (103cm) high

$500-700 **ROS**

A tiger-maple bureau, the fall front opening to valanced and fitted interior, above four drawers, on bracket feet.

c1800

$4,000-6,000 **FRE**

ESSENTIAL REFERENCE - WOOTON DESKS

- **The Wooton desk was patented by William S Wooton in 1870. Wooton established a company to produce his design in the same year. Production continued until 1884.**
- **The Wooton desk is a variation of the fall-front bureau that boasts a large number of drawers, pigeonholes and compartments. The complicated nature of the desk was its biggest selling point, as wealthy Americans purchased these elaborate and clearly expensive items of furniture to display their economic power.**
- **As a practical item of furniture, the Wooton desk was arguably obsolete. By the time it was patented, office work had changed drastically to include far greater amounts of paperwork than before. It was no longer efficient to have to fold and title each document before placing in a pigeonhole. Filing cabinets, that could be filled with unfolded paper in folders, became popular around this time for this reason.**

An Eastlake burl-walnut and parcel-gilt Wooton desk, incised with geometric and foliate devices, the spindle-inset cresting above fall front opening to drawers and pigeonholes, above paneled doors opening to fitted interior with forty drawers, a letter box and pigeonholes.

c1874 *69in (175cm) high*

$12,000-18,000 **SK**

A large early 19thC Dutch walnut and floral-marquetry bureau, the fall front opening to fitted interior with drawers and pigeonholes, above three drawers, on splayed bracket feet with gilt-metal sabots.

50in (127cm) high

$5,500-7,500 **ROS**

A 19thC Georgian-style lacquered chinoiserie bureau, the fall front opening to fitted interior, above four drawers, on bracket feet.

43in (109cm) high

$2,500-3,500 **LHA**

A Regency mahogany Davenport, the sliding top with inset side slides, the base with four side drawers, on gilt-metal paw feet.
c1815 *31in (78cm) high*
$2,500-3,500 DN

A William IV burr-walnut Davenport, the sliding top with a later leather-inset slope, one side with a pull-out hinged writing drawer above drawers the other with a slide and dummy drawers, on turned ribbed feet with brass castors, stamped 'T. Willson, 68 Great Queen Street, London'.
34in (86.5cm) high
$4,000-6,000 WW

ESSENTIAL REFERENCE - DAVENPORTS

The first Davenport desk was created by Gillows of Lancaster in the 1790s. The basic form, which comprised a chest-of-drawers with a desk compartment on top, changed very little over the next century.

- **Although the Davenport was generally used by women, the first person to order one was a man, Captain Davenport.**
- **Most Davenports have four drawers to the base with dummy drawers on the opposing side. Some have cupboards to both sides.**
- **Early Davenports had a sliding desk section. From c1840, the desk section of most Davenports was fixed in place and supported by scrolled or turned supports. This change in design allowed more legroom.**
- **Most Davenports were made of mahogany, although some of the best examples were made from rosewood and burr-walnut.**
- **Some of the finest mid-19thC examples had brass galleries and ormolu candle sconces.**

A George IV rosewood Davenport, attributed to Gillows, the writing surface opening to two drawers and two dummy drawers, the side with an inkwell drawer, a slide and three drawers, on lobed bun feet with castors.
29in (74cm) high
$3,000-4,000 WW

An early Victorian oak pedestal Davenport, Holland & Sons, with sliding top, the side with a pen drawer above four drawers, with two slides.
c1840 *31in (80cm) high*
$700-1,000 DN

A Victorian burr-walnut piano-top Davenport, with pop-up stationery box, with four side drawers, on turned feet.
22in (56cm) wide
$4,000-6,000 GORL

A 19thC Irish walnut and marquetry Davenport, the hinged writing slope opening to fitted interior, with lyre supports and platform base, on compressed bun feet.
22.5in (57cm) wide
$1,000-1,500 TRI

A Victorian walnut, crossbanded, boxwood and ebony-stung Davenport, with fitted stationery compartment above writing surface opening to drawers and a maple-veneered desk, with four drawers and four dummy drawers.
32in (81.5cm) high
$600-800 A&G

A Victorian burr-walnut and marquetry Davenport, the raised top with fitted interior, the base with a side cupboard door enclosing four drawers, with old restoration.
44in (111.5cm) high
$1,200-1,800 WW

A mid-Victorian burr-walnut and floral-marquetry piano-top Davenport, with pop-up compartment, writing slide and drawers, with cabriole supports, the side with four drawers, on bun feet, with alterations and restoration.
$5,000-7,000 TOV

A Regency mahogany Canterbury, in the manner of Gillows, with turned spindle supports, the base with drawer, on reeded tapered legs with brass caps and castors.

c1815 *28in (72cm) high*

$5,000-7,000 DN

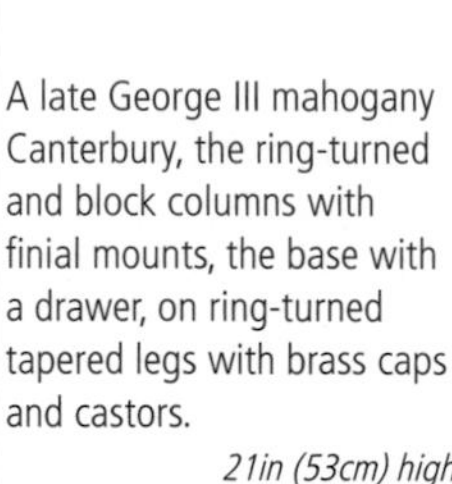

A late George III mahogany Canterbury, the ring-turned and block columns with finial mounts, the base with a drawer, on ring-turned tapered legs with brass caps and castors.

21in (53cm) high

$1,200-1,800 TEN

A 19thC rosewood Canterbury, the front carved with a laurel wreath and ribbon swag, the base with one drawer, on turned legs with castors.

$1,500-2,500 TOV

A Victorian black lacquer and parcel-gilt Canterbury.

c1840 *22in (55cm) high*

$700-1,000 DN

An unusual Victorian fretwork Canterbury, the fret carved with 'VR' and surmounted by a coronet, the base with one drawer, on baluster-turned legs with brass caps and castors.

c1860 *20in (51cm) wide*

$1,200-1,800 L&T

A Victorian walnut and inlaid Canterbury, with gadrooned finials and petal-carved and gadrooned supports, the base with one drawer, on gadrooned legs with castors.

23in (58cm) wide

$400-600 DA&H

A Victorian walnut oval Canterbury, with turned and pierced supports, the base with one drawer, on baluster-turned legs.

c1870 *25in (63.5cm) wide*

$1,000-1,500 DN

An unusual laburnum Canterbury, with one drawer, on block feet with brass castors.

20in (50cm) wide

$1,000-1,500 TEN

A late Victorian brass Canterbury, on tripod stand with paw feet.

16in (41cm) wide

$400-600 GORL

A Victorian walnut Canterbury whatnot.

24in (61cm) high

$600-800 GORL

A late 17thC probably Baltic oak mirror, the frame carved with cherubs supporting cartouches, exotic fruit, trees, animals and beauty products, with traces of original paint.

55in (140cm) high

$15,000-20,000 **SWO**

A French Régence gilt and verre églomisé mirror, the original mercury plates within a gilt composition leaf frame and marginal plates, with scrolling shell apron and pierced scrolling cartouche plume.

47in (120cm) high

$8,000-12,000 **TEN**

A large early 18thC Italian giltwood mirror, Rome, with a rocaille-shaped carved frame and later mirror plate.

80in (203cm) high

$45,000-55,000 **DOR**

Judith Picks

This mirror was originally cataloged as an 18thC Italian mirror and, as such was, estimated at $200-300. It is also in need of extensive, sensitive and expensive restoration. However in the antiques world we always like to find a 'sleeper' - something that has gone unnoticed, and due to the interest generated by this mirror, everyone looked more closely. Word went out that it was possibly an early work by William Kent (1685-1748), one of Britain's greatest designers. He was a painter, architect, garden designer, interior and furniture designer. Such is his desirability that the mirror is now valued at $40,000-60,000.

A George I giltwood mirror, possibly an early work by William Kent.

$40,000-60,000 **AS&S**

A Queen Anne walnut mirror, with beveled and engraved mirror plates.

c1710 *40in (102cm) high*

$5,500-6,500 **L&T**

An early 18thC oyster-veneered mirror, the rectangular beveled plate in a cushion-molded frame.

26.5in (67cm) high

$1,000-1,500 **L&T**

An unusual Queen Anne walnut, giltwood and needlework mirror, the inner frame embroidered with figures, flower-filled urns and animals, the cushion-molded outer frame surmounted by a carved hippocamp and C-scrolls.

71.5in (182cm) high

$35,000-45,000 **FRE**

A George I carved giltwood mirror, surmounted by an angel mask, the frame carved with foliate scrolls and shells, the plate later.

c1720 *41in (104cm) high*

$3,000-4,000 **L&T**

A pair of George II giltwood and verre églomisé mirrors, each surmounted by an eagle and surrounded by C-scrolls and foliage, the mirror plates with later decoration of Chinese figures.

34in (86cm) high

$5,500-6,500 **FRE**

A George II walnut and giltwood mirror, surmounted with Prince of Wales feathers, with a shaped apron.

c1740 *48.5in (123cm) high*

$8,000-12,000 **DN**

A large Rococo silver-gilt, wood and velvet mirror, the silver stamped 'FP', Prague, assembled from various pieces.

1760 *57in (145cm) high*

$12,000-18,000 **DOR**

An 18thC giltwood salon mirror, carved with flowers and birds, with later mirror plate, with some restoration.

The execution of the mirror and the form of the birds are reminiscent of the designs of Thomas Chippendale.

62in (158cm) high

$30,000-40,000 **DOR**

An Irish George III giltwood mirror, carved with vine leaves, grapes and acanthus scrolls, surmounted with ho ho birds, C-scrolls and a pierced shell, with later mirror plate, re-gilded.

58in (147.5cm) high

$30,000-40,000 **MEA**

An Irish George III giltwood mirror, attributed to Francis & John Booker, Dublin, the openwork frame carved with Rococo scrolls, castle turrets and trailing oak leaves, the plate later.

c1765 *39.5in (100cm) high*

$15,000-20,000 **L&T**

A George III giltwood girandole mirror, surmounted by an eagle and leaf cresting, with two candle arms, with carved laurel wreath swags below.

37.5in (95cm) high

$6,500-7,500 **FRE**

A late 18thC giltwood and gesso mirror, the sunburst crest above foliate carved mirror, with molded fish to base.

57in (145cm) high

$6,500-7,500 **ROS**

An Irish George III oval mirror, framed by blue and milk glass enriched with gilt.

c1800 *28in (70cm) high*

$8,000-12,000 L&T

A Regency parcel-ebonized and giltwood overmantel mirror, the cornice with applied frieze of a double-headed eagle holding a laurel festoon, the plate flanked by lions' heads and reeded pilasters, with restoration.

58.5in (148.5cm) wide

$10,000-15,000 WES

A Regency giltwood and ebonized girandole mirror, with twin-branch candle arms.

c1815 *57in (145cm) high*

$25,000-35,000 DN

A Regency giltwood and gesso overmantel mirror, surmounted by an openwork scroll carving, flanked by applied anthemions and acanthus.

c1815 *65in (164cm) wide*

$3,000-4,000 L&T

A verre églomisé, giltwood and composition pier mirror, the reverse-painted maritime panel depicting a naval duel, beneath a beaded architrave.

The scene is an almost exact copy of an oil by Thomas Whitcombe and engraving by T. Sutherland of the 1812 conflict between HMS 'Pelican' and USS 'Argus'. After a fifteen minute action, the 'Argus', which had been harassing British merchantmen off Ireland, surrendered. The first commander of the 'Argus' was Stephan Decatur, who notably defeated HMS 'Macedonian' later in the war.

c1815 *30in (76cm) high*

$1,200-1,800 DN

A Regency giltwood girondole mirror, with rockwork cresting surmounted by a hippocamp, the candlearms terminating in female-Egyptian bust candle nozzles, above a drop finial with foliage and acorns.

c1815 *36.5in (118cm) high*

$5,500-6,500 L&T

An 18thC Italian-style carved, painted and parcel-gilt mirror, carved with palm branches, leaves and scrolls, the crest centered by bulrushes draped with giltwood garlands.

82.5in (208cm) high

$15,000-20,000 DN

A large 19thC George III-style giltwood mirror, the plate divided by borders of rocaille, within a carved frame surmounted by a C-scroll.

111in (282cm) high

$30,000-40,000 DN

ESSENTIAL REFERENCE - BURCHARD PRECHT

- Burchard Precht (1651-1738) was born in Bremen, Germany.
- He moved to Stockholm, Sweden, in 1674 to work at Drottingholm Palace and was named carver to the court in 1682.
- In 1687-88 he visited Rome and Paris with the court architect Nicodemus Tessin. This experience had a strong influence on his subsequent work.
- The name Precht is closely associated with early 18thC Swedish mirrors of high quality. Numerous examples are attributed to Burchard or his sons Gustav (d.1763) and Christian (d.1779).

A 19thC Swedish gilt, ebonized and ormolu-mounted mirror, after Burchard Precht, with foliate-etched margin plates, the cresting surrounded by three flowering urn finials.

52.5in (133cm) high

$18,000-22,000 **L&T**

A Venetian glass and micromosaic mirror.

c1870 *58in (147cm) high*

$5,000-7,000 **FRE**

A late 19thC gilt and gesso overmantel mirror, in the manner of Booth, the beaded and leaf-cast frame flanked by two marginal plates and six candle branches, with an oval Grecian-style mask and winged serpents to cresting.

96in (245cm) high

$8,000-12,000 **TEN**

A late 19th/early 20thC Gothic Revival giltwood mirror, with beveled mirror plate.

82.5in (210cm) high

$2,000-3,000 **DN**

CLOSER LOOK - CHINESE CHIPPENDALE REVIVAL MIRROR

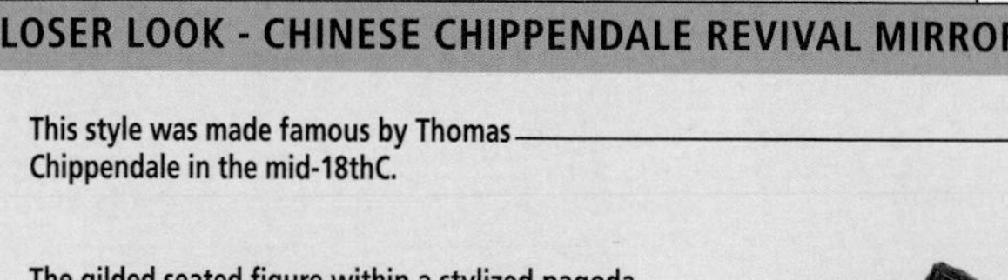

This style was made famous by Thomas Chippendale in the mid-18thC.

The gilded seated figure within a stylized pagoda, urns and the apron centered by a ram are typical Chinese Chippendale features.

The shaped divided plates hark back to the 18thC when the British plate glass industry could not make glass for very large surface areas.

The ornate Rococo scroll-carved frame is delicate and graceful.

Original mid-18thC pieces are extremely rare and very expensive. If you like the style, a late 19thC copy may be the answer.

A large late 19thC Chinese Chippendale Revival giltwood mirror.

67in (170cm) wide

$15,000-20,000 **L&T**

An Empire mahogany and ormolu-mounted cheval mirror, the free-standing columns with urn finials, the apron cast with rinceaux, the flat supports cast with acanthus scrolls.

A rinceau is a decorative strip of stylized vines and leaves, often with fruit or flowers. Classical rinceaux typically feature a pair of vines growing from a vase.

68.5in (174cm) high

$6,500-7,500 **FRE**

A George IV mahogany cheval mirror, with cushion-molded frame on two section supports, each with two acanthus-carved outswept legs on brass caps and castors.

c1825 *49in (125cm) high*

$800-1,200 **DN**

An Edwardian Sheraton Revival mahogany and satinwood-banded cheval mirror, the tapering S-shaped scrolling uprights with brass finials, on splayed legs with brass caps and castors.

59in (151cm) high

$2,000-3,000 **TEN**

An early 18thC walnut dressing table mirror, the base with molded and featherbanded top over six curved drawers with brass handles, on bracket supports.

31in (80cm) high

$2,500-3,500 **ROS**

A George III mahogany and crossbanded dressing table mirror, the serpentine-fronted base with three drawers.

c1790 *22in (55cm) high*

$700-1,000 **DN**

A George III mahogany and marquetry dressing table mirror, the frame with chequer-banding, the top with marquetry of a fan and trailing leaves.

c1800 *24in (60cm) high*

$1,500-2,000 **DN**

A William IV mahogany dressing table mirror, with carved dolphin supports, the base with two short drawers, on carved scroll feet, stamped 'A Blaine Liverpool'.

c1835 *34.25in (87cm) high*

$2,000-3,000 **L&T**

One of a pair of Neo-classical patinated metal étagères, with a Greek key borders, the columnar supports with paw feet.

36in (91cm) high

$6,500-7,500 pair FRE

An early 19thC ebonized and gilt étagère, with damage.

34in (86.5cm) high

$1,000-1,500 WW

One of a pair of Regency palmwood étagères, the top tier with pierced gallery and turned corner finials, on turned legs with brass casters.

c1820 39.75in (101cm) high

$5,000-7,000 pair FRE

A Continental foliate-marquetry corner étagère, the two lower tiers with drawers, on cabriole legs.

40in (102cm) high

$1,200-1,800 LHA

One of a pair of late 19thC French kingwood and parquetry étagères, with rouge marble tops, on tapered legs.

14in (36cm) wide

$3,000-4,000 pair GORL

An early 20thC French mahogany and ormolu-mounted étagère, the marble top on dolphin supports, the central tier with radiating veneers and floral garland frieze, the X-stretcher centered by a basket with an onyx base, the scroll legs with paw sabots.

35.5in (90cm) high

$6,500-7,500 WW

A late 19thC French kingwood, walnut and gilt-metal-mounted étagère, with one drawer, on cabriole legs.

36in (91cm) high

$2,500-3,500 GORL

A Victorian amboyna and ebonized étagère, the tapered turned legs with ceramic castors.

43in (110cm) high

$300-500 L&T

An Edwardian mahogany and strung étagère, with detachable tray top.

$700-1,000 WHP

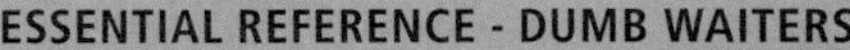

An Irish George III mahogany two-tier dumb waiter, the lower tier with plate and bottle coasters, on turned stem with three reeded splay-legs with brass caps and castors, with damage.

38in (96.5cm) high

$6,500-7,500 WW

ESSENTIAL REFERENCE - DUMB WAITERS

The dumb waiter was conceived in Britain in c1725. The form comprises a tripod stand with trays (often revolving) that increase in size from top to bottom.

- **Sheraton described it as 'a useful piece of furniture, to serve in some respects the place of a waiter, whence it is so named.'.**
- **By the end of the 18thC dumb waiters were also known in France and Germany. In Britain the dumb waiter was becoming increasingly decorative.**
- **In 1803 Sheraton designed two new models. One had a layer of marble on the top level and knife trays, shelves for plates and holes for bottles and decanters on a lower level. The other had two levels, rather than three and drawers for cutlery underneath.**

A George III mahogany three-tier dumb waiter, on baluster-turned supports, the tripod base with pointed pad feet.

c1780 47in (120cm) high

$1,000-1,500 DN

A George III mahogany two-tier dumb waiter, the folding tiers with reeded edges, on baluster-turned stem with reeded outswept supports with brass caps and castors.

36.75in (93.5cm) high

$1,500-2,000 WW

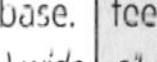

A Regency mahogany two-tier dumb waiter, with turned and reeded supports, on a molded base.

27.5in (73cm) wide

$1,200-1,800 WHP

One of a pair of large George IV mahogany three-tier dumb waiters, the revolving tiers on turned and petal-carved supports with scroll legs with brass castors.

48in (122cm) high

$12,000-18,000 pair WW

A late 19thC George III-style mahogany and gilt-metal-mounted revolving dumb waiter.

39in (98cm) high

$800-1,200 DN

An Edwardian satinwood and marquetry revolving dumb waiter.

c1910 38in (97cm) high

$700-1,000 DN

A 19thC and later two-tier dumb waiter, the galleried white marble tiers on fluted column support with tripod base with slipper feet.

37in (94cm) high

$800-1,200 GORB

A George III mahogany wine cooler, after Adam, with two brass faun-head drop handles, on molded tapered square legs with brass castors.

31in (79cm) wide

$7,000-10,000 GORB

A mahogany and brass-banded wine cooler, with brass handles and hinged lid, on three legs with casters, missing liner.

27in (68cm) high

$4,000-6,000 DOR

A George III mahogany and brass-banded wine cooler, on stand with square-section tapering legs, with lead liner.

c1780 27in (68cm) wide

$3,000-4,000 DN

A George III mahogany wine cooler, with loop and lion mask handles, on square legs cornered by pierced spandrels, with hinged lid.

c1780 28in (71cm) high

$3,000-4,000 DN

A late George III mahogany and brass-banded wine cooler, with swing handles, with later zinc liner.

26in (65cm) wide

$2,000-3,000 DN

A George III mahogany wine cooler.

27in (68cm) high

$2,000-3,000 A&G

ESSENTIAL REFERENCE - WINE COOLERS

Although marble and metal wine coolers were made in Britain from the late 17thC, the lead-lined mahogany wine cooler did not appear until the mid-18thC.

- **Georgian wine coolers were often hexagonal or oval in form, made from mahogany and held together with two or three brass bands. Some have stands.**
- **Sarcophagus-form wine coolers were first made in the 1780s and '90s, but became common in the Regency period.**
- **Victorian wine coolers are often squat and heavy.**

An early 19thC mahogany wine cooler, with ormolu wreath handles, on plinth base with later square tapered legs with brass roller castors, with lead lining, with restoration.

28.5in (72.5cm) wide

$5,500-6,500 WW

A George III mahogany wine cooler, with original bottle divisions.

14in (36cm) high

$1,200-1,800 SWO

A George III yew and brass-bound wine cooler, with lion's-head handles, on a fruitwood stand.

c1780 *34in (87cm) high*

$3,500-4,500 **L&T**

An early 19thC mahogany sarcophagus-form wine cooler, in the manner of Mack, Williams & Gibton, the hinged lid with a leaf-carved border and scroll pilasters, on paw feet with castors.

John Mack founded his cabinet-making business in Abbey Street, Dublin in the late 18thC and was joined by William Gibton in c1801. In 1806, they were appointed 'Upholsterers and Cabinet Makers to his Majesty, His Excellency the Lord Lieutentant and His Majesty's Board of Works'. Robert Gibton died in 1812 and was succeeded by his son William Gibton (1789-1842). Zachariah Williams also joined the management in c1812, thus creating Mack, Williams & Gibton. The firm became highly sucessful. It ceased trading in 1852.

40in (103cm) wide

$6,500-7,500 **DN**

An early 19thC mahogany and brass-bound twin bottle wine cooler, with two hinged lids, one with brass antique dealer's label to underside, with brass handle, on ball feet.

15in (38cm) wide

$10,000-15,000 **H&L**

A late Regency mahogany sarcophagus-form wine cooler, with hinged lid, the interior fitted for bottles, on scroll feet.

c1825 *12.25in (31cm) long*

$2,500-3,500 **FRE**

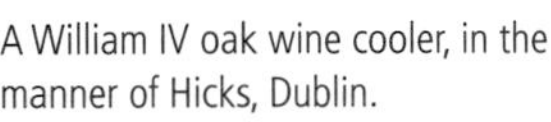

A William IV oak wine cooler, in the manner of Hicks, Dublin.

c1835 *34in (86cm) wide*

$2,500-3,500 **DN**

An early 19thC-style mahogany wine cooler, with an outswept top and acanthus carved frieze, with carrying handles, on stepped flame-veneered plinth, lined.

35in (87.5cm) wide

$7,000-10,000 **DN**

Wine Cooler

A Regency mahogany sarcophagus-form combined cellaret and teapoy, with metal-lined cellaret section and a pair of mahogany tea canisters, the stand with drawer, on baluster-turned legs with brass caps and casters.

c1815 *20.5in (52cm) wide*

$2,500-3,500 **DN**

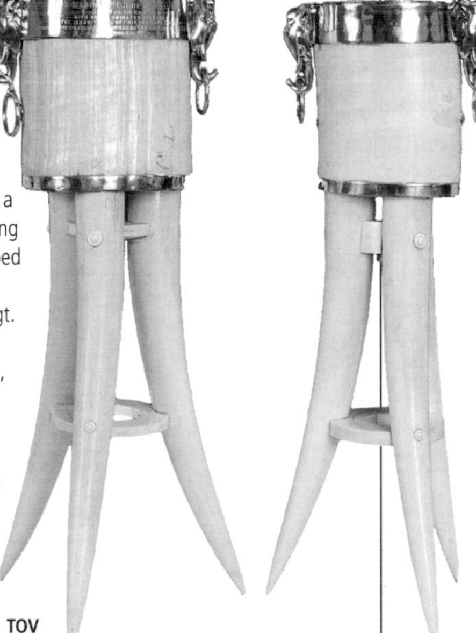

A pair of early 20thC metal-mounted elephant tusk wine coolers, each with a pair of elephant mask and ring handles, one with rim inscribed 'Presented to Major WM. Forrest, D.S.O. 3rd Welsh Regt. with an illuminated address by the inhabitants of Prieska, Cape Colony in appreciation of his valuable services as Commandant of the District, Sept. 1900 - Nov. 1901', the tusks incised 'T.J', metal mounts marked with two stars.

23in (59.5cm) high

$10,000-15,000 **TOV**

A George III mahogany jardinière, with brass handles, on cabriole legs with pad feet and leather castors, lead-lined.

13.5in (34.5cm) wide

$7,000-10,000 L&T

An Empire mahogany jardinière, set with a brass bowl.

34in (86cm) high

$1,000-1,500 LHA

A Regency rosewood planter, the ogee-molded, acanthus-carved top on acanthus-carved cabriole legs with scroll feet, with inset brass liners.

c1820 *37in (95cm) high*

$10,000-15,000 L&T

ESSENTIAL REFERENCE - LOUIS XV REVIVAL

During the 19thC numerous earlier styles were revived across Europe. In France, designs from the reigns of Louis XV and Louis XVI were resurrected. Napoleon III, who ruled France 1852-70, hoped to use the style to help remind the country of a golden age.

- **Sèvres porcelain plaques were much used on 18thC French furniture and this trend was copied during the 19thC. Many 19thC plaques were not made by Sèvres, but by other Paris factories.**
- **19thC furniture was often made of dark woods, such as mahogany, with pale inlays of mother-of-pearl or ivory and ormolu mounts.**

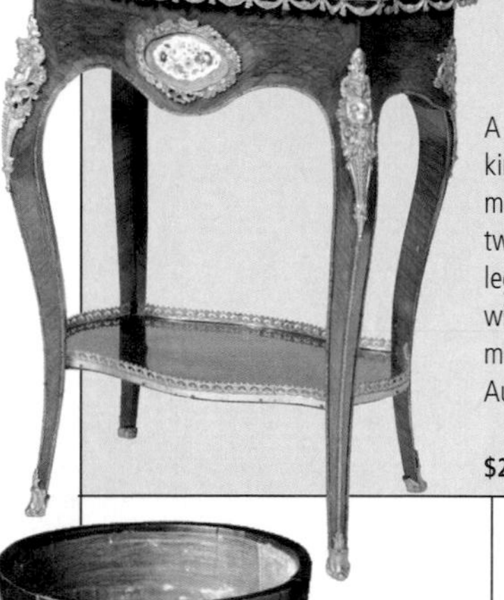

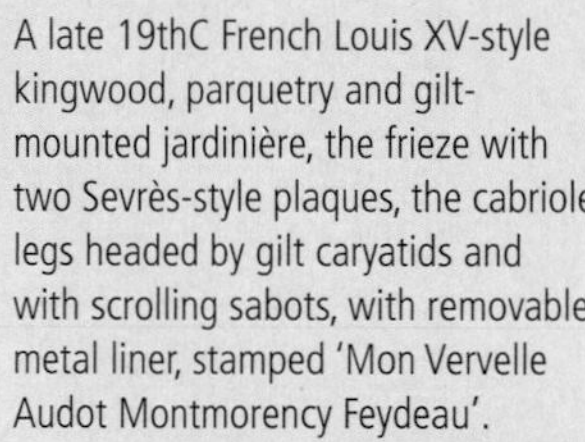

A late 19thC French Louis XV-style kingwood, parquetry and gilt-mounted jardinière, the frieze with two Sevrès-style plaques, the cabriole legs headed by gilt caryatids and with scrolling sabots, with removable metal liner, stamped 'Mon Vervelle Audot Montmorency Feydeau'.

27.5in (73cm) high

$2,500-3,500 TEN

A George IV gonçalo alves jardinière table, attributed to Gillows, the top with gadrooned edge, the baluster-turned, lappet-carved and fluted column on paw feet with casters, with metal liner.

Gonçalo alves is a stripy hardwood, often referred to as zebrawood or tigerwood.

c1825 *29in (74cm) high*

$3,000-4,000 DN

A 19thC mahogany and brass-bound jardinière.

31in (78cm) high

$1,000-1,500 SWO

A late 19thC French boulle, walnut and ebonized jardinière, with zinc liner.

$700-1,000 GORB

A William IV bird's-eye maple jardinère table, the lappet-carved baluster column with stylized flowerhead feet and castors, with removable liner.

c1835 *28.75in (73cm) high*

$2,500-3,500 DN

An Edwardian satinwood jardinière, the square tapered splayed legs with brass spade feet, with brass liner.

$1,000-1,500 GORL

A pair of William & Mary floral-marquetry torchères, the octagonal tops inlaid with a flower-filled urn within crossbanded borders.

34in (86.5cm) high

$2,500-3,500 **LC**

A pair of 19thC Continental ebonized and parcel-gilt torchères, the pierced Greek key friezes with brass lions' heads, with fluted tapering columns and lattice supports centered by rosettes, on paw feet.

33in (84cm) high

$6,500-7,500 **WW**

A Regency painted plaster torchère, by Robert Shout, Holborn, modeled as a Classical maiden holding a brass lamp, signed, on a later oak plinth.

Figure 45in (114.5cm) high

$7,000-10,000 **WW**

A Regency-style ebonized, painted and specimen-marble torchère, the decorated frieze with ring terminals, on outswept legs with hoof feet.

43.5in (110cm) high

$2,500-3,500 **DN**

A pair of carved giltwood and painted torchères, the stylized Corinthian quadriform capitals with leaf and berry decoration, held aloft by putti.

63in (159cm) high

$5,000-7,000 **L&T**

A pair of late 19thC Continental carved giltwood torchères, the columns carved with S-scrolls and trailing cornflowers, on scrolling foliate carved tripod feet.

62in (157cm) high

$3,000-4,000 **FRE**

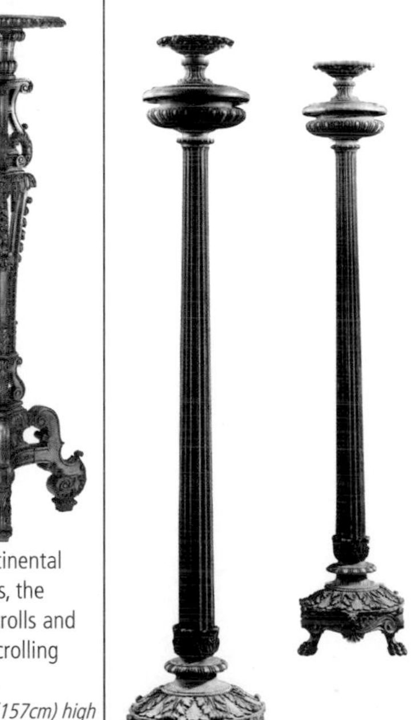

A pair of 19thC-style green-patinated bronze torchères, with leaf cast collars supporting compressed, gadrooned and leaf-cast holders, the bases with acanthus, on paw feet.

80in (203cm) high

$10,000-15,000 **DN**

A pair of early 20thC Irish carved and turned mahogany torchères, the tops with reeded edges.

59.75in (151.5cm) high

$1,200-1,800 **WW**

A George III mahogany tray, with pierced rim.

c1770 *18.5in (47cm) wide*

$1,200-1,800 **POOK**

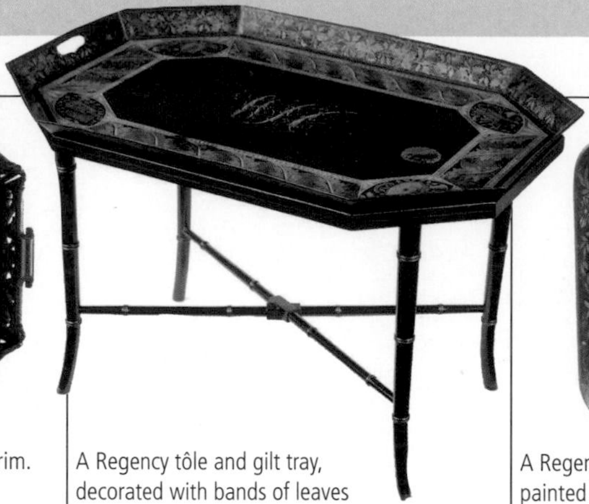

A Regency tôle and gilt tray, decorated with bands of leaves and musical instruments, on later stand.

30in (76.5cm) wide

$1,200-1,800 **WW**

A Regency painted and gilt papier-mâché tray, painted with flowers and foliage, impressed 'Clay, King St. Cov't. Garden'.

30in (77cm) wide

$1,200-1,800 **SWO**

A Victorian black lacquered papier-mâché tray, painted with flowers, inlaid with mother-of-pearl and decorated with gilt.

30in (76cm) wide

$500-700 **TRI**

A 19thC tôleware tray, gilt with butterflies, flowers and foliage.

24in (61cm) wide

$250-350 **MOR**

A 19thC mahogany and inlaid tray.

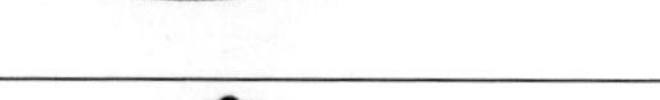

28in (72cm) wide

$350-450 **SWO**

A large mid-19thC American tin tray, decorated with fruit and vegetables.

28in (70cm) wide

$5,500-6,500 **POOK**

A Regency burr-elm teapoy, opening to four mahogany caddies and a recess for a sugar bowl, on square tapered legs headed by cusped brackets and with brass socket-castors.

29in (73cm) high

$2,500-3,500 **TEN**

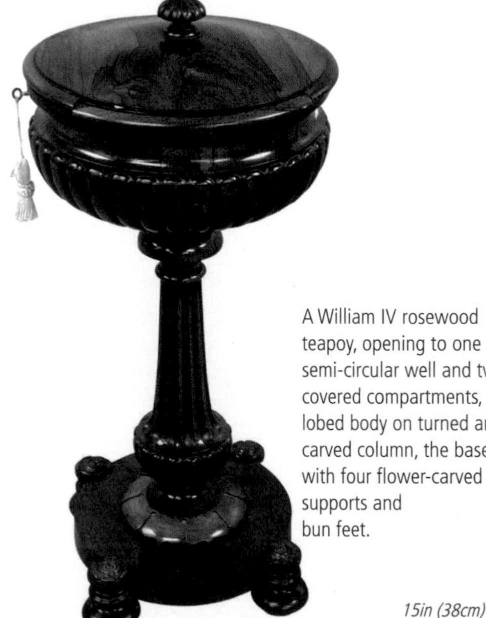

A William IV rosewood teapoy, opening to one semi-circular well and two covered compartments, the lobed body on turned and carved column, the base with four flower-carved supports and bun feet.

15in (38cm) diam

$2,500-3,500 **ECGW**

An early 19thC mahogany four-tier whatnot, the hinged and ratchetted top with bookrest, with central drawer, on brass castors.

51.5in (131cm) high

$2,000-3,000 **WW**

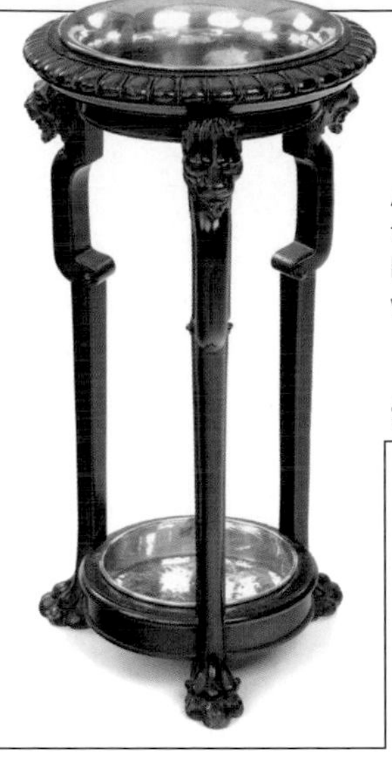

A Victorian mahogany stick stand, the gadrooned top on three lion's head-carved Chinese-scroll legs with paw feet, with brass liners

28in (71cm) high

$2,000-3,000 **L&T**

A mid-19thC rosewood folio stand, with trellis-shaped framed wings and turned stretcher, on ring turned feet with recessed brass castors.

46in (116cm) high

$3,000-4,000 **TEN**

An early 19thC French mahogany easel, with geometric intarsia and carved swan and dolphin heads.

92.5in (235cm) high

$12,000-18,000 **DOR**

A late 18thC Chester County, Pennsylvania cherrywood candlestand, the tilt top on a circular birdcage, on cabriole legs with slipper feet.

28.5in (72cm) high

$12,000-18,000 **POOK**

A Regency mahogany reading stand, the tilt top on a spiral-fluted support, on three splayed legs.

c1805 *17in (43cm) wide*

$5,000-7,000 **DN**

Judith Picks

When I talk about valuing any antique, I usually talk about condition, age, rarity and desirability, with a good dash of provenance thrown in. But there are more subtle reasons that people are drawn to objects. For example, many people are attracted to objects because they are great conversation pieces and, of course, there is also sentimentality – if you love dogs you are going to love this stick stand. Just look at the facial expression and the adorable pleading eyes. And I'm not alone in thinking this way! On a perfectly reasonable estimate of $150-250, this little fellow soared to the price shown below.

A tôle stick stand, with a painted cut-out of a poodle.

25in (64cm) high

$8,000-12,000 **LC**

A late 19thC carved and painted figural towel holder.

28.5in (72cm) high

$2,500-3,500 **DOR**

Judith Picks

This is a fine American walnut fire screen from the highly desirable Queen Anne period and made in one of the centers of excellence in furniture making, Philadelphia. But collectors are also interested in the history of a piece – its provenance. This stand was originally owned by Philadelphian abolitionist, Anthony Benezet (1713-84). The image of this great man sitting in front of the fire writing with this screen protecting him gives it a great deal of added value.

A rare Philadelphia Queen Anne walnut fire screen, the oblong screen with fixed demi-lune candle shelf, the baluster support on cabriole legs with pad feet.
c1760 *47in (119.5cm) high*
$60,000-80,000 **POOK**

A mid-Victorian black and gilt papier-mâché firescreen, attributed to Jennens & Bettridge, painted with a view of Salisbury Cathedral within an pierced shell border, the baluster stem with scrolling legs.
c1860 *51in (130cm) high*
$3,000-4,000 **L&T**

An early George III mahogany and needlework pole screen, the panel embroidered with a courting couple in a landscape, with Chippendale-triform base.
65in (164cm) high
$1,000-1,500 **SWO**

A large George III polychrome-painted dummy board, in the form of a Royal Scots Fusilier, 21st Foot Regiment.
c1760 *84in (213cm) high*
$10,000-15,000 **L&T**

A pair of Victorian oak and needlework pole screens, each mounted with part of a saddle cloth of the 16th Lancers, the tripod base with scrolled feet.

The saddlecloth belonged to Colonel Frederick Gordon Blair, 26th Laird, who was commissioned in the 16th Lancers in 1874.
58.5in (149cm) high
$1,500-2,500 **L&T**

A Victorian polychrome-painted dummy board, in the form of a lady with a whippet on her lap, on simulated marble base.
38in (97cm) high
$2,500-3,500 **L&T**

A Victorian giltwood, composition and Aubusson-style needlework firescreen, the frame decorated with foliage.
c1860 *49in (125cm) high*
$1,500-2,500 **DN**

An 18thC painted four-leaf screen, decorated with courtly and gallant scenes, with damage.

90.5in (230cm) high

$10,000-15,000 **DOR**

A large 19thC French carved oak and giltwood four-leaf screen, each leaf with a scroll and oak leaf carved pediment above two inset gold-brocade panels.

112in (284cm) high

$2,500-3,500 **FRE**

A 19thC polychrome and painted leather four-leaf screen, painted with exotic birds.

77.5in (198cm) high

$2,500-3,500 **TEN**

A Victorian Moorish-style ebony and painted leather four-leaf screen, the leaves with three painted and parcel-gilt panels on each side, in an ebony-veneered frame.

82.5in (210cm) high

$10,000-15,000 **L&T**

A 19thC four-leaf needlework and petit-point floor screen, the shaped panels depicting mythological scenes within a scrolling border.

69.75in (177cm) high

$3,000-4,000 **LHA**

An Edwardian mahogany four-leaf screen, each leaf with a carved top and large painted panel depicting either a knight or a maiden.

$2,000-3,000 **SWO**

ESSENTIAL REFERENCE - EARLY BEDS

The earliest European beds were basic structures and the hangings that decorated them were of greater value. When noblemen moved around the country, they took their bedding and curtains, but left the bed!

- **By the early 16thC most European beds were made of oak and featured highly carved paneled headboards. Carved posts and testers (canopies) were added around the middle of the century.**
- **Mattresses were supported by ropes, which needed to be pulled tight to provide a well-sprung bed. This is most likely the origin of the phrase 'sleep tight'.**
- **During the 17thC beds were typically made of beech. The back was generally covered in the same fabric as the curtains.**
- **Most ordinary beds were hung with cloth, linen and moreen (a sturdy ribbed fabric of wool, cotton, or wool and cotton).**

A 17thC and later oak tester bed frame, with paneled canopy and head, the baluster-turned uprights with cup-and-cover terminals.

79.5in (202cm) long

$5,000-7,000 **DN**

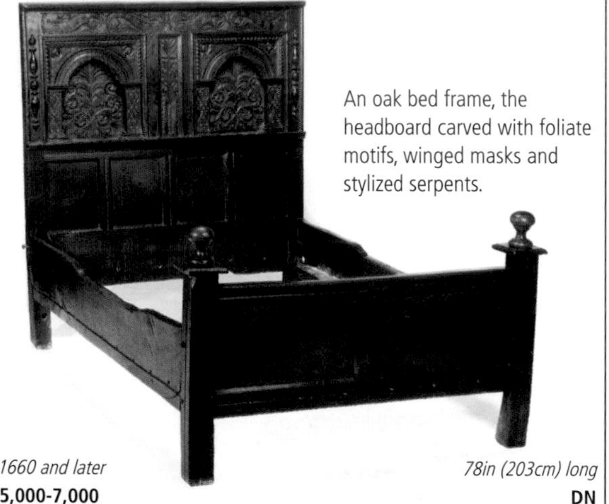

An oak bed frame, the headboard carved with foliate motifs, winged masks and stylized serpents.

c1660 and later *78in (203cm) long*

$5,000-7,000 **DN**

A Regency mahogany bed, the dentil-molded cornice above fluted and foliate carved posts, with deep-red and cream silk hangings and bedskirt.

79.5in (202cm) long

$12,000-18,000 **L&T**

A pair of early 19thC Biedermeier walnut, mahogany and stained-beech children's beds, each with a pedimented cornice on baluster-turned supports, the arched footboards centered by gilt-metal mounts, with chintz hangings.

188cm (74in) long

$10,000-15,000 **L&T**

An early 19thC mahogany bed, with cluster columns and canopy top.

100in (254cm) high

$1,500-2,500 **SWO**

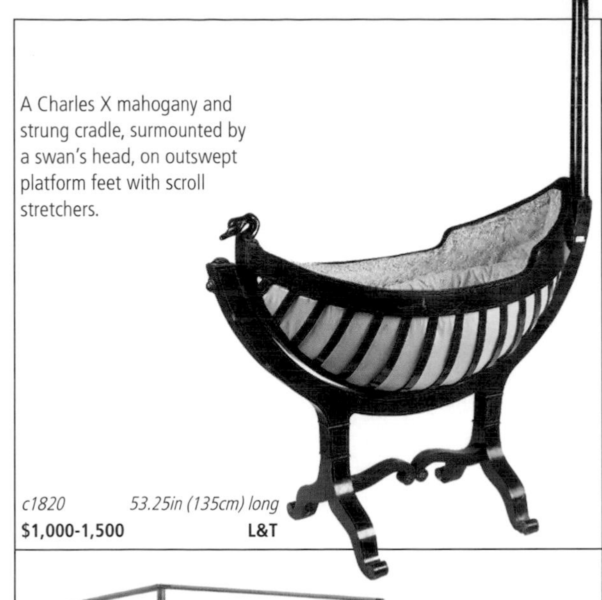

A Charles X mahogany and strung cradle, surmounted by a swan's head, on outswept platform feet with scroll stretchers.

c1820 *53.25in (135cm) long*

$1,000-1,500 **L&T**

A Federal maple canopy bed.

c1825

$1,000-1,500 **POOK**

A 19thC Pennsylvania painted tester bed, with later black and salmon painted surface.

85.5in (217cm) high

$3,000-4,000 **POOK**

A Baroque Revival walnut bed, the headboard and footboard carved with maidens, festoons and putti.

Headboard 79.5in (202cm) high

$8,000-12,000 **LHA**

A pair of Baroque Revival walnut and walnut-veneer beds, partly composed of 18thC elements, with marquetry panels.

74.75in (190cm) long

$5,000-7,000 **DOR**

A 19thC and later mahogany and painted composite bed, the arched cornice and urn-shaped finials painted with foliate scrolls, with leaf-carved and reeded supports, on fielded panel square section block feet, with blue and yellow silk tasseled drapes.

83.75in (213cm) long

$20,000-30,000 **L&T**

A Victorian walnut bed, with spindle and carved crest, with clover and acanthus decoration.

79.5in (202cm) high

$700-1,000 **LHA**

An Austrian mahogany-veneer and painted bed, attributed to F O Schmidt, Vienna, the headboard and footboard carved with putti, a coat-of-arms, festoons and floral garlands.

c1900-20 *84.5in (215cm) long*

$7,000-10,000 **DOR**

A French oak and beech bed, Breton, the arched and pierced frame with spindles and foliate carving, the headboard with spindles and carved scenes of farmers and men playing boules, with turned corner posts.

c1900 *82in (208cm) long*

$7,000-10,000 **L&T**

Bedroom Suite

An American Victorian bedroom suite, comprising a bed, side cabinet and chest with mirror (not shown), the cabinet and chest with shaped marble tops.

$6,500-8,500 set **LHA**

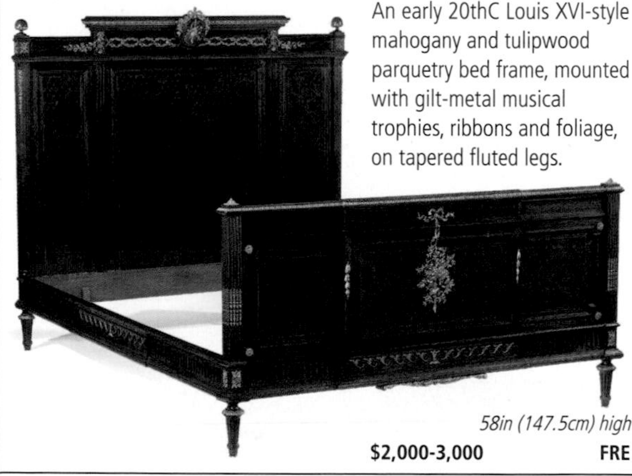

An early 20thC Louis XVI-style mahogany and tulipwood parquetry bed frame, mounted with gilt-metal musical trophies, ribbons and foliage, on tapered fluted legs.

58in (147.5cm) high

$2,000-3,000 **FRE**

An Austrian painted pine bed frame, Losensteinleithen area, with floral rocaille decoration on painted faux veneer, with some wear.

c1820 *Mattress 70in (175cm) long*

$5,500-6,500 **DOR**

ESSENTIAL REFERENCE - PLATE BUCKETS

Plate buckets were designed to help servants ferry warm plates from the kitchen to the dining room. They were usually made in pairs and each one had a vertical slot in the side to enable the easy removal of plates.

- **As they were designed to be used during elaborate meals, early plate buckets were frequently embellished. Carving and marquetry are common.**
- **In the late 18thC plate buckets of this form were made redundant by the warmers enclosed within dining-room pedestals. Later examples were consequently plain, as all plates were carried to the dining room before guests arrived.**

A pair of Irish late George III mahogany and brass-bound slatted plate buckets, with swing handles.

Provenance: Dromoland Castle, Co. Clare, Ireland.

14.5in (37cm) high

$10,000-15,000 WW

A pair of George III mahogany plate buckets.

c 1770 *15in (38cm) diam*

$6,500-7,500 DN

An early 19thC mahogany and brass-bound peat bucket, with brass liner.

13in (33cm) high

$2,000-3,000 GORL

A 19thC American painted miniature bucket, with inscription 'Good Boy' and decorated with American flags, horses and stars on a yellow ground.

3.25in (8.5cm) high

$1,500-2,500 POOK

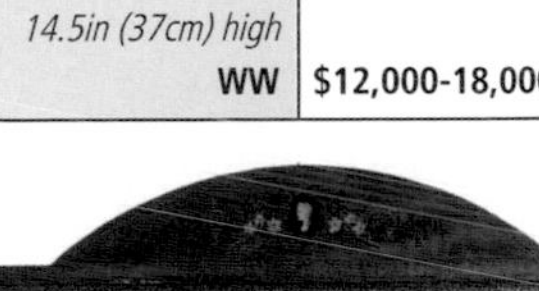

A Pennsylvania painted bucket, Joseph Lehn (1798-1892), with salmon grain surface decoration and bands of leafy vines, with swing handle.

7in (18cm) high

$12,000-18,000 POOK

A Regency-style red-japanned and giltwood hanging corner shelf, carved with bamboo.

36.5in (93cm) high

$2,000-3,000 FRE

An Edwardian painted satinwood and parcel-gilt hanging wall shelf, the pediment with portrait medallion, with tapering apron.

c1910 *43in (109cm) high*

$3,500-4,500 L&T

An 18thC painted child's carriage, painted with flowers, cherubs, a crowned figure, a bull and coats-of-arms, the scrolling ends with eagle's head terminals, dated.

1750 *39.5in (100cm) long*

$1,200-1,800 DN

Judith Picks: Tea Caddy

Tea was a precious commodity, worth more than its weight in gold during the 18thC and early 19thC, and only the wealthiest could afford a fresh cuppa. Tea caddies in the shape of fruit became extremely popular. The most common were in the shape of apples and pears. Many were made from fruitwood and were colored with sponge paint effects, which would have worn away quite quickly. You would be unlikely to find one for less than $5,000 and some of the extremely rare ones, particularly pumpkins and squashes, have been known to fetch between $25,000 and $35,000.

A late 18thC George III fruitwood tea caddy in the form of a melon, the body with six divisions, one of the sections plumwood, another with the remnants of a green-stained finish.

$5,000-7,000 **DN**

A late 18thC George III fruitwood tea caddy in the form of a pear, with traces of metal lining, the stalk broken but still attached.

6in (15cm) high

$3,000-4,000 **DN**

A late 18thC George III green-stained fruitwood tea caddy in the form of an apple, with traces of metal lining, staining worn off, with replaced hinge.

4.75in (12cm) high

$5,000-7,000 **DN**

A George III satinwood twin-division tea caddy, inlaid with scrolls, fleur-de-lys, a Classical urn and swags, with ivory escutcheon.

7in (19cm) wide

$1,500-2,500 **ROS**

A George III satinwood barrel-front tea caddy, with tulipwood crossbanding and stringing, the cover with a foliate marquetry spray, with cast-brass handle, the lid warped and sides bowed.

11.25in (28.5cm) wide

$1,200-1,800 **WW**

A George III papier-mâché tea caddy, painted with figures in rural scenes, with a hinged lid.

5in (11cm) high

$4,000-6,000 **SWO**

A silver-mounted tortoiseshell tea caddy, the sides with applied silver cartouches engraved with monograms and crests, with original key.

Opening the hinged cover reveals apertures for cutlery (now missing), a pair of caddies for green and black tea and a central box for mixing. All are engraved with monograms and armorials, including the cockerel crest of John Lyall who immigrated to Barbados in c1800. The case seems to date from around this period, but the unmarked suite is stylistically a generation or more earlier, perhaps c1755.

c1755, c1800 *10in (23cm) wide*

$30,000-40,000 **BELL**

An early 19thC tôle peinte tea caddy, painted with a mourning sailor besides a monument to Lord Nelson, inscribed '1805, Conquer'd & Died, Nelson', with divided interior, with loop handle, with key.

This value of this tôle tea caddy is relatively high due to the Admiral Lord Nelson interest.

4.5in (11cm) high

$1,500-2,500 **WW**

An early 19thC ribbed ivory tea caddy, with tortoiseshell stringing and applied white-metal shield.

5in (13cm) high

$5,000-7,000 **SWO**

A George III tortoiseshell tea caddy, with ivory stringing, with silver loop handle and escutcheon.

5.25in (13cm) wide

$4,000-6,000 **GORL**

A George III rolled paper hexadecagon tea caddy, with kingwood feather-banding and stringing, with plated ring handle and key, with crack to top panel, locked and missing key.

8in (20cm) wide

$1,000-1,500 **WW**

An early 19thC tortoiseshell and mother-of-pearl inlaid tea caddy, the top with ivory stringing, on white-metal ball feet, with faulty lock.

7in (17cm) wide

$2,500-3,500 **H&L**

An early 19thC green-tortoiseshell tea caddy, with ivory and pewter stringing, the cover with an applied plaque marked 'S W C', the divided interior with two lids, each with turned ivory handles.

7.25in (18.5cm) wide

$8,000-12,000 **WW**

A small Regency tortoiseshell tea caddy, with silvered ball finial and feet.

c1820 *4in (11cm) high*

$1,500-2,500 **L&T**

A tortoiseshell-veneered tea caddy, the lid with applied metal cartouche and wire stringing, the interior with two compartments, each with turned bone mushroom handles, on 'vegetable ivory' bun feet.

c1830 *7in (17.5cm) wide*

$1,200-1,800 **TEN**

An Indian Vizagapatam antler-mounted tea chest, the sandalwood-lined interior with two ivory-veneered caddies and a sugar bowl aperture, on antler coronet feet, missing bowl.

15in (37.5cm) wide

TEN

A Victorian tortoiseshell-veneered tea caddy, with pewter stringing, on coquilla nut feet, the interior with two subsidiary tortoiseshell-veneered covers, with missing keyhole escutcheon and old restoration.

c1860 *8in (20cm) wide*

$1,000-1,500 **DN**

A George V silver-mounted tortoiseshell tea caddy, with maker's mark 'BS', Sheffield, of miniature 'knife box' form.

1910 *5in (11.5cm)*

$1,500-2,500

A George III stained-sycamore and marquetry workbox, with fitted interior, with period and later accessories including a needle case, a pin cushion and a straw-work snow flake.
c1790 *9in (22cm) wide*
$1,200-1,800 **TEN**

A Regency red leather sewing box, by Gaimes, St Paul's Church Yard, London, the inside lid with printed harvest scene including Demeter, with lion mask and ring handles.
10.5in (27cm) wide
$650-850 **A&G**

A 19thC Anglo-Indian sandalwood, ivory and tortoiseshell workbox, the interior with removable tray fitted with purple plush-lined compartments.
9.5in (24.5cm) diam
$2,500-3,500 **L&T**

A late 19thC ebonized and brass-inlaid scent/sewing box, with ormolu mounts, with sewing accessories.
16.5in (42cm) wide
$1,500-2,500 **DRA**

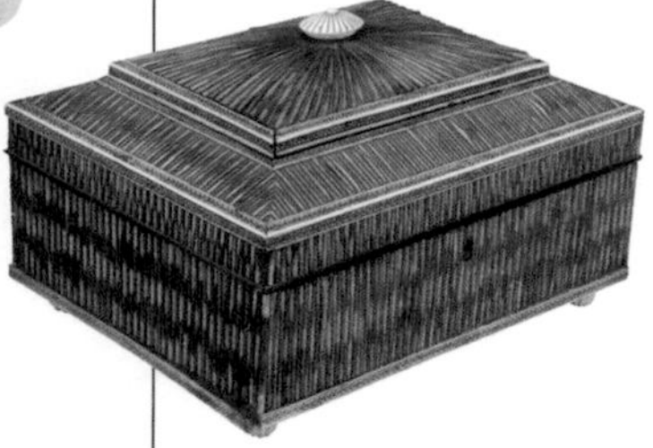

An Anglo-Ceylonese straw-work and penwork ivory-mounted sandalwood workbox, probably Galle (Sri Lanka), the fully-fitted interior with lift-out tray, with some losses.
c1830 *12.5in (31cm) wide*
$4,000-6,000 **DN**

A mid-19thC Pennsylvania birdseye-maple sewing box, with pin cushion.
6.5in (17cm) high
$800-1,200 **POOK**

A late 19thC Louis XIV-style boulle and ormolu work box, inlaid with mother-of-pearl portrait busts and mythical beasts.
13.75in (35cm) wide
$3,000-4,000 **L&T**

Palais-Royal

A 19thC French Palais-Royal ormolu-mounted tortoiseshell scent/sewing casket, the interior with two enamel and ormolu-mounted glass scent bottles and eleven sewing implements.

In 1784, Duke Louis Philippe II opened a public shopping arcade in the gardens of the Palais-Royal, once the home of Cardinal Richelieu. Not long after the arcade was opened, a group of Parisian master craftsmen began specializing in elaborate sewing tools made from gold, silver, enamel, precious stones, mother-of-pearl and tortoiseshell. Their distinctive and high quality work was only sold in a few select shops and boutiques in the Palais-Royal and thus it became known by that name. Palais-Royal craftsmen marked their work with small enameled diamonds or shields or, most notably, a small gold oval with an enameled pansy.

8in (20cm) wide
$[illegible]00-6,000 **GORL**

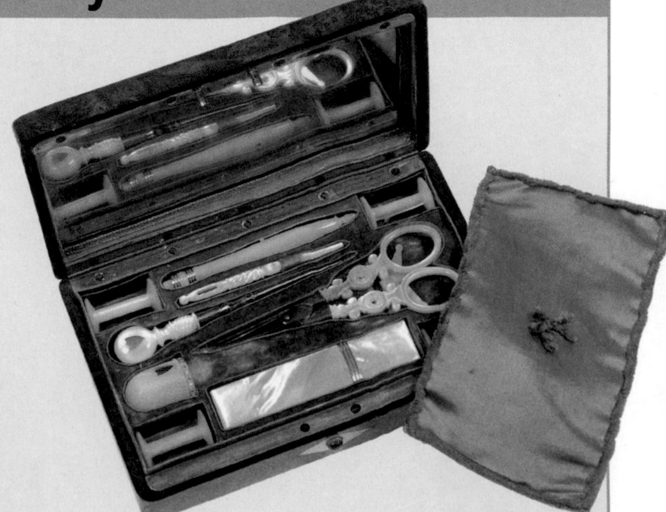

A French probably Palais-Royal sewing nécessaire, the richly figured wood case with vacant lid cartouche, the inner lid with mirror, with mother-of-pearl accessories.
c1820 *6in (14cm)*
$1,500-2,500

A 17thC Flemish engraved ivory and ebonized table cabinet, the central door enclosing a mirror and drawer, surrounded by nine short drawers.

25in (62cm) wide

$3,500-4,500 **SWO**

A 17thC Indo-Persian table cabinet.

15.25in (38.5cm) wide

$3,000-4,000 **DRA**

A late 17thC Dutch walnut table cabinet, with ripple moldings, the top with hidden compartment, the interior with ten drawers, the drawers and dividers removing to reveal ten further concealed compartments.

19in (48cm) wide

$2,000-3,000 **DN**

An early 18thC Anglo-Portuguese tortoiseshell and ivory table cabinet, the fitted interior with eight small drawers.

13in (32cm) wide

$15,000-20,000 **L&T**

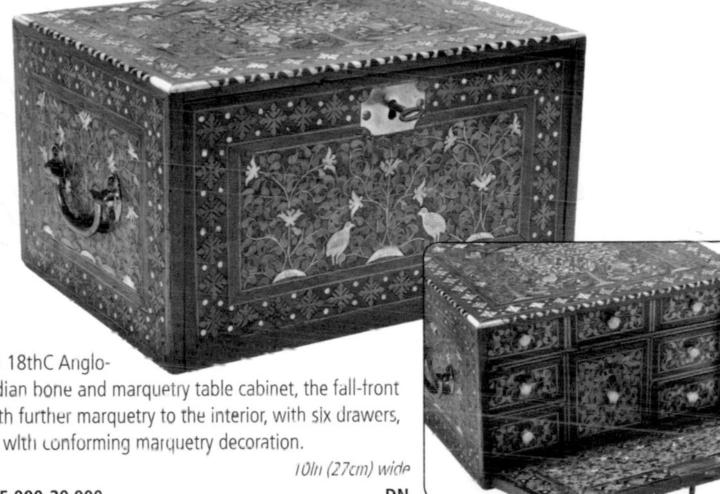

An 18thC Anglo-Indian bone and marquetry table cabinet, the fall-front with further marquetry to the interior, with six drawers, all with conforming marquetry decoration.

10in (27cm) wide

$15,000-20,000 **DN**

A 19thC gilt-metal-mounted ivory table cabinet, inset with 25 Viennese enamel plaques painted with Classical figures.

15in (37cm) high

$25,000-35,000 **TOV**

A late 18thC partly burlwood-veneered table cabinet, missing one section of molding.

20in (50cm) wide

$4,000-6,000 **DOR**

A 17thC-style tortoiseshell-veneered, ivory-mounted and ebonized table cabinet.

c1900-20 13in (32cm) wide

$1,200-1,800 **DN**

An early 15thC French iron and leather-mounted document box, the lid with openwork Gothic-window pierced panels and tooled leather strips depicting figures, animals and stylized wording.

12in (30cm) wide

$5,500-6,500 **TEN**

An Italian Baroque tortoiseshell, ivory, mother-of-pearl and pewter-inlaid writing box, with geometric parquetry and floral inlay, with silvered-wrought iron hardware.

c1700 *15.75in (40cm) wide*

$10,000-15,000 **WAD**

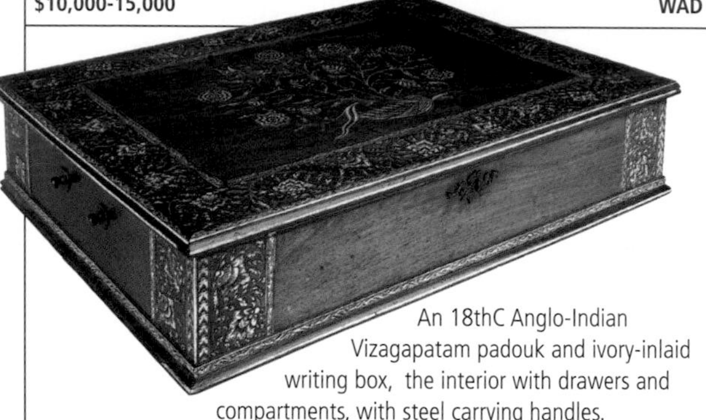

An 18thC Anglo-Indian Vizagapatam padouk and ivory-inlaid writing box, the interior with drawers and compartments, with steel carrying handles.

Provenance: The box was reputedly owned by Apphia, Baroness Lyttelton (1743-1840), who traveled to Bengal with her first husband Colonel Joseph Peach (1731-1770), an officer in the 1st Bengal European Regiment. Apphia married her second husband Thomas, 2nd Baron Lyttelton (1744-1779) of Hagley Hall in Worcestershire in 1772.

21in (53cm) wide

$5,000-7,000 **L&T**

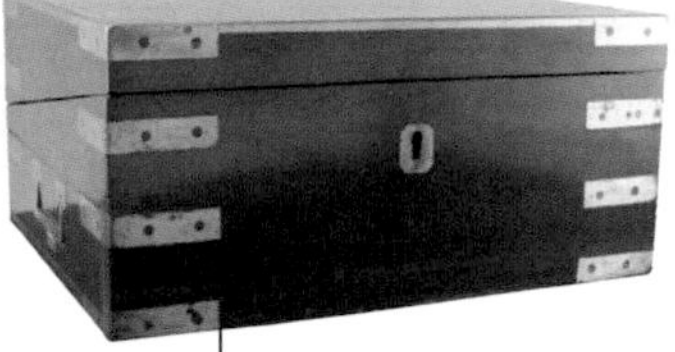

A Regency brass-bound mahogany gentleman's portable desk, by William Gaimes, London, the drawer with brass mechanism engraved 'Gaimes Fecit, 54 St Paul's Church Yd & 56 Cornhill, London'.

c1810 *15in (38cm) wide*

$1,000-1,500 **GORL**

An early 19thC brass-bound mahogany writing slope, with a hinged velvet-lined slope, the later brass lock stamped 'J.BRAMAH PATENT', the front with a plaque inscribed 'Sir Theophilus Lee, G.C.H. G.C.C., The Elms, Bedhampton'.

Sir Theophilus Lee was the second cousin of the Duke of Wellington.

20.75in (52.8cm) wide

$3,500-4,500 **WW**

ESSENTIAL REFERENCE - AMBOYNA

- **Amboyna is the burr form of padouk (*Pterocarpus indicus*). It takes its name from the Dutch trading station on the island of Ambon, where the best wood was exported from.**
- **Amboyna has an attractive grain and can therefore be used as a highly decorative veneer. It is also used for the keys on a marimba (a type of xylophone with resonators).**
- **Numerous amboyna boxes, similar to the example shown, survive today. Some are mounted with silver that is hallmarked for Batavia, the chief Dutch settlement in the Moluccas, Indonesia.**
- **These amboyna boxes had diverse uses, but the smaller, silver-mounted boxes were known as sirih boxes. These contained the ingredients to make a quid of sirih, which comprised a folded sirih (betel) leaf spread with lime, shavings of areca nut and a piece of gambir (dried sap of the Jasmine bush). The chewing of sirih, which turned teeth black and saliva blood red, was a widespread Asian custom adopted by both male and female Dutch settlers.**

An 18thC Dutch Colonial amboyna (padouk) document box, with ornately cast and stamped corners, hinges, back plates, handles and escutcheons.

13in (32cm) wide

$1,500-2,500 **SWO**

A George IV brass-bound mahogany stationery box, by Bayley & Blew, London, the red leather-lined interior with secret document folder and later compartmented removable tray, with compartmented apron drawer, with brass maker's label.

c1825 *17.25in (44cm) wide*

$2,000-3,000 **L&T**

An early Victorian Tunbridgeware writing slope, the double-hinged lid with a geometric panel within a border of mosaic flowers, with fitted interior.

15in (38cm) wide

$1,000-1,500 **TOV**

Traveling Box

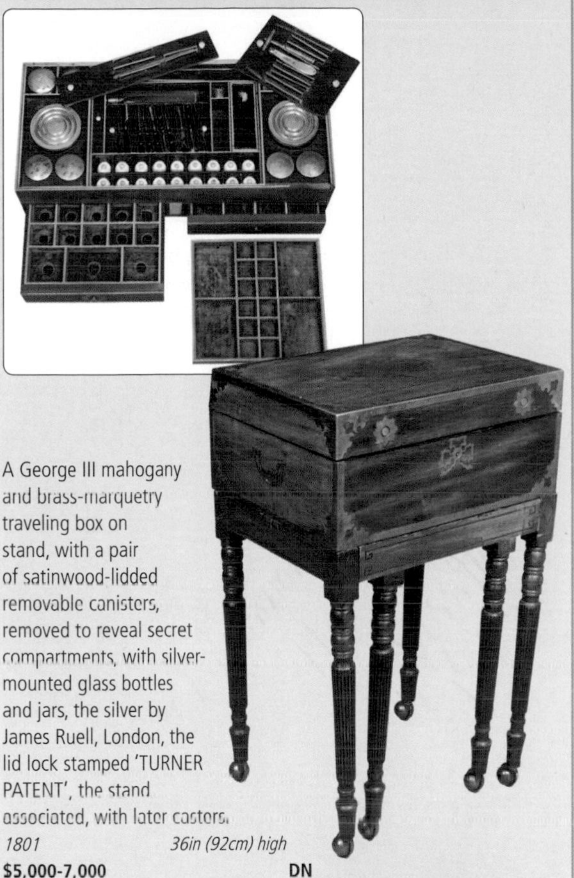

A George III mahogany and brass-marquetry traveling box on stand, with a pair of satinwood-lidded removable canisters, removed to reveal secret compartments, with silver-mounted glass bottles and jars, the silver by James Ruell, London, the lid lock stamped 'TURNER PATENT', the stand associated, with later casters.
1801 *36in (92cm) high*
$5,000-7,000 **DN**

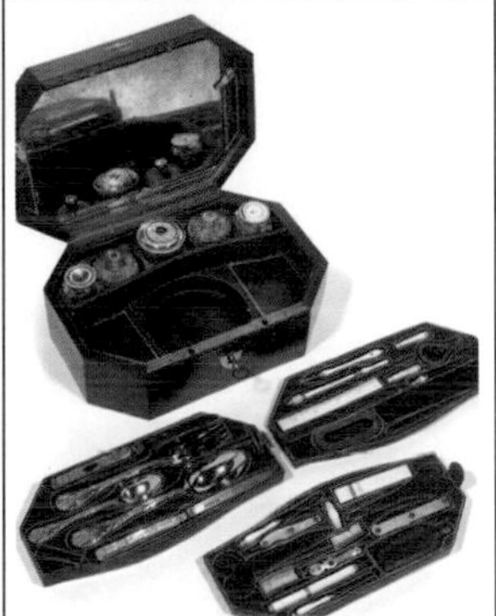

A Napoleon I writing/dressing box, by J C B Dallemagne, Paris, including writing set, manicure set and travel cutlery, some in silver-gilt.
Case 11in (28.5cm) wide
$5,500-6,500 **DOR**

A George IV coromandel dressing box, by Archibald Douglas, London, the interior with twelve silver-mounted jars and a manicure set.
1828 *14in (35.5cm) wide*
$1,000-1,500 **TEN**

An early Victorian brass-bound rosewood dressing box, the drawer with ivory glove-stretchers, three hairbrushes and a penknife, the interior with silver-gilt-lidded bottles, jars and boxes, the silver by 'F.D', London.
1837 *13.25in (33.5cm) wide*
$1,500-2,500 **WW**

A Victorian brass-bound burr-walnut dressing box, the fitted interior with thirteen silver-topped, hobnail-cut glass bottles and a manicure set, the silver by Halstaff & Hannaford, London, with two later bottles by Wright & Davies, London, the lock engraved 'S Mordan's Patent'.
c1851 *15in (38cm) wide*
$1,200-1,800 **TEN**

A Victorian walnut and brass-inlaid dressing box, with eleven silver-topped glass bottles, the silver by 'J.H.'.
1853 *13in (32cm) wide*
$3,500-4,500 **LC**

A 19thC brass-bound mahogany campaign writing/dressing box.
12.75in (32.5cm) wide
$1,200-1,800 **WW**

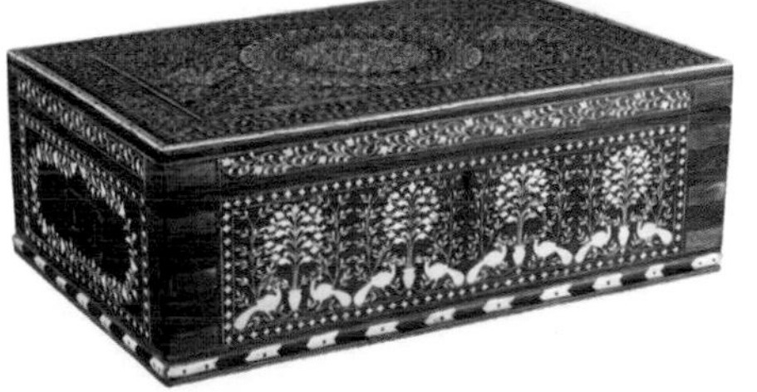

A 19thC Anglo-Indian ebony- and ivory-inlaid dressing box, with floral motifs, peacocks and banding, with fitted interior and mirror.
18in (46cm) wide
$1,200-1,800 **A&G**

An Art Deco green-leather dressing box, the silver by Walker & Hall, Birmingham/Sheffield.
1930 *14.25in (36cm) wide*
$1,000-1,500 **LC**

A George II shagreen knife box, with twelve silver-handled knives and forks by John Wood.

12.5in (31.5cm) high

$2,000-3,000 **WW**

A George III mahogany, crossbanded and white-metal-mounted knife box, the refitted interior with three associated glass decanters with stoppers and six associated drinking glasses.

c1780 *15in (38cm) high*

$400-600 **DN**

A pair of George III mahogany and kingwood-banded knife boxes, with fitted interior.

14.5in (37cm) high

$3,500-4,500 **WW**

A pair of 18thC Russian brass-inlaid mahogany knife boxes, with lockable swivel fronts enclosing fitted interiors.

19in (48cm) high

$5,000-7,000 **GORL**

A pair of George III satinwood, rosewood and chequer-banded knife boxes, with fitted interiors.

c1790 15in (38cm) high

$4,000-6,000 **DN**

A pair of George III satinwood, rosewood and chequer-banded knife boxes, with fitted interiors.

c1790 *15in (38cm) high*

$4,000-6,000 **DN**

ESSENTIAL REFERENCE - FOLK DECORATION

American folk art is extremely desirable, with exceptional and rare pieces commanding very high sums. The most sought-after painted items feature a striking use of color and strong, graphic decoration.

- **Popular motifs include the tulip (a symbol of contented home life), the peacock (associated with the resurrection of Christ) and the red rose (a symbol of God's love).**
- **All pieces should have the original paint applied to the piece by its maker or first decorator.**
- **Pieces inscribed with a name, date and/or place are particularly desirable.**

A pair of George III mahogany and line-inlaid knife boxes, with fitted interiors.

c1800 *14.5in (37cm) high*

$2,000-3,000 **FRE**

A pair of late 19thC George III-style mahogany, boxwood- and ebony-inlaid cutlery urns, with fitted copper inserts.

24in (61cm) high

$2,500-3,500 **FRE**

A 19thC American tôle-decorated cutlery box, with leaf and fruit decoration, with heart cut-out handle.

12.4in (31cm) wide

$8,000-12,000 **POOK**

A 16thC parcel-gilt pastiglia casket, with pastiglia decoration throughout, on later bun feet.

Pastiglia (an Italian term meaning 'pastework') is a form of low-relief decoration that was popular during the Italian Renaissance. Normally modeled in gesso or white lead, the decoration was applied to a surface and could then be gilded, painted or left plain. Today, the term 'pastiglia' is mostly used to describe gilded work on small wooden caskets.

8in (20cm) wide

$8,000-12,000 **L&T**

A mid-17thC boarded oak box, the front carved with anthemions, arcading and scrolls.

28in (71cm) wide

$1,000-1,500 **SWO**

A late 17thC japanned and decoupaged strongbox, decorated with landscapes and hunting scenes, with wavy brass mounts, the interior veneered in rosewood and with secret compartments.

15in (38cm) wide

$1,500-2,500 **SWO**

A 17thC French Medieval-style iron-bound wood table strong box, with double-hinged locks, decorated with panels of pierced Gothic tracery.

9.5in (24cm) wide

$3,000-4,000 **GORL**

ESSENTIAL REFERENCE - THE TOWN OF SPA

The small town of Spa, Ardennes, Belgium, was a popular 18thC summer retreat for kings, princes and nobles. It was christened 'Le Café de l'Europe' by the Holy Roman Emperor Joseph II after a visit in 1781.

- **Spa became so popular that its name has now become a common noun, meaning any place with medicinal or mineral springs.**
- **The town's main spring (Le Pouhon Pierre-le-Grand) is named after Peter the Great, who visited in 1721.**
- **The first casino in Europe opened in Spa in 1761.**
- **With so many rich patrons, a trade in luxury goods and souvenirs flourished. Spa's souvenir speciality was the 'Bois de Spa' (or sometimes 'Boites de Spa'): a lacquered box often painted with views of the town and surroundings.**

A mid-18thC Belgian grisaille-painted 'Bois de Spa' (box), painted by Antoine Le Loup with a hunting party in an Italian landscape, the interior later lined with patterned cream silk, the lid signed.

Antoine Le Loup (1730-1802), a native of Spa, was known for his finely detailed monochrome views, many of which were mounted on boxes such as the one pictured.

12in (30.5cm) wide

$10,000-15,000 **MAB**

A Queen Anne olivewood Bible box, the cover inlaid with interlaced strapwork.

19.5in (50cm) wide

$1,500-2,500 **POOK**

An 18thC American tiger-maple pipe box, with a dovetail constructed drawer.

18.25in (46cm) high

$10,000-15,000 **SK**

A late George III mahogany and marquetry wall-mounting candle box, with marquetry conch shell motif, with damage.

21in (53cm) high

$800-1,200 **DN**

A late George III mahogany and marquetry decanter box, with six parcel-gilt-topped glass decanters with gilt-metal wine labels, two glass phials and a glass tray, missing two liqueur glasses.

12.5in (32cm) wide

$1,000-1,500 **DN**

A Berks County, Pennsylvania trinket box, possibly painted by Heinrich Bucher with the initials 'C.P.' for Christian Prenzer above a basket of flowers, the sides with typical tulip decoration.

c1800 *10.25in (26cm) wide*

$5,500-6,500 **POOK**

A Regency rosewood ballot box.

c1815 *25in (63cm) wide*

$1,200-1,800 **DN**

A Regency Scottish penwork box, by Charles Stiven, Laurencekirk, the lid depicting Drumtochty Castle, the removable tray with lidded compartments, with stamped mark.

Charles Stiven (1753-1820) was a renowned box maker who commonly used the 'invisible hinge' thought to have been invented by John Sandy of nearby Alyth. Stiven's boxes were made of sycamore, decorated with penwork and paint, and were heavily varnished. The town of Laurencekirk became so well known for this sort of box that they became known as 'Laurencekirk boxes'. After 1821, the focus for production of this type moved to Mauchline.

12in (30cm) wide

$10,000-15,000 **L&T**

An early 19thC mahogany apothecary cabinet, with a fitted interior and five drawers with 21 glass jars and various accessories.

13.5in (34.3cm) wide

$2,000-3,000 **GORL**

A mid-19thC Pennsylvania wallpaper-covered bentwood hat box, painted in salmon-pink with floral decoration on a blue ground.

19.5in (50cm) wide

$1,000-1,500 **POOK**

A 19thC Indian hardwood and ivory-inlaid box.

11.5in (29cm) wide

$3,500-4,500 **GORL**

A Napoleon III coromandel, boulle marquetry and ormolu-mounted table casket, the cedar-lined interior with three drawers, the ormolu lock plate inscribed 'Giroux a Paris'.

c1870 *25in (63.5cm) wide*

$1,500-2,500 **DN**

A late 19thC Napoleon III boulle marquetry perfume casket, with three gilt-accented scent bottles.

6.25in (16cm) wide

$1,000-1,500 **FRE**

A 19thC Indian parquetry box, the frieze drawer with ivory handles, with a secret drawer.

17in (43cm) wide

$3,000-4,000 **A&G**

A Victorian brass-bound burr-walnut humidor, the interior with three compartmented drawers, the doors with Bramah locks.

19.75in (50cm) wide

$1,500-2,500 **L&T**

A Victorian gilt-brass-mounted coromandel decanter box, by Mappin & Webb, the satin-birch-lined interior with a pair of cut glass decanters with glass stoppers and six glasses.

c1880 *19in (48cm) wide*

$2,000-3,000 **DN**

A 19thC French brass-inlaid and tortoiseshell-mounted rosewood box.

12in (30cm) wide

$2,000-3,000 **GORL**

A Victorian silver-mounted tortoiseshell dressing table bowl, by William Comyns, London, with silver strapwork borders and a silver-filled foot.

1888 *5in (11.5cm) high*

$1,000-1,500 **H&L**

A late 19thC brass-bound walnut box, by Charles Asprey, London, the later lined interior with a lift-out jewelry tray, with maker's plaque, missing clasps and with minor damage.

8.5in (21.5cm) wide

$400-600 **WW**

A late 19thC teak plantation accounting box, with account books and a Jamaican almanac, the lock stamped 'W H Castrell, 165 Sussex Place, London SW'.

25in (63cm) wide

$1,500-2,500 **SWO**

A late 19thC Brazilian ormolu-mounted presentation casket, mounted with 20 specimen hardwood shields, with white-metal presentation plaques, one dated.

c1889 *16in (40.5cm) wide*

$6,500-7,500 **GORL**

An Anglo-Ceylonese coromandel and lac-heightened ivory box, Galle (Sri Lanka), the lift-out tray with nineteen compartments, with another lift-out tray below.

c1900 *16in (40cm) wide*

$2,500-3,500 **DN**

An oak cigar box in the form of a railway carriage, one side with inscription 'FRED CROWTHER, COAL MERCHANT. No.1, Dewsbury.'.

c1900 *12.5in (33cm) wide*

$1,500-2,000 **SWO**

CLOSER LOOK

This tankard appears to form a 'missing link' between the earliest of Scottish drinking vessels (the mazers) and the standard tankard/mugs of the late 17thC onward.

The wooden body mounted with simple bands of decorated silver is very reminiscent of the engraved rims of mazers. The decoration to the cover is obviously of a later style, although contemporary with the piece.

A rare mid-17thC silver-mounted laburnum tankard, by Thomas Cleghorn, Edinburgh, the silver heavily engraved with flowers, foliage and masks, the handle with angel figure, the cover centered by a later engraved armorial, engraved 'OMNE SOLUM FORTI PATRIA 1610'.

c1640 *6in (15cm) high*

$40,000-60,000 L&T

The motto engraved to the foot rim appears to be for Balfour.

The armorial is for the Prince Regent (later George IV). This later engraving may have connections with the Royal visit of King George IV to Scotland, when many Scottish people became interested in their history and restored relics for use, display, etc.

Although it is unlikely, this cup may form one of the pair given to King George by Walter Scott for use at the ceremonial closing dinner for his state visit. It noted that 'the goblets which the King would drink were antique, two centuries old'.

A late 17thC Norwegian burr-birch peg tankard, carved with scrolling flower tendrils, with S-scroll handle ending in a square terminal carved with a praying man, on three ribbed ball feet.

7.75in (19.5cm) high

$12,000-18,000 WW

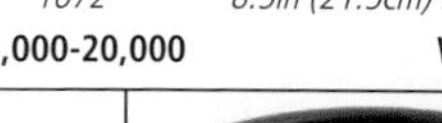

A late 17thC Norwegian burr-birch tankard, the lid carved with a sleeping figure within serpents, fruits and leaves, the S-scroll handle with later lion and ball finial, the body carved with figures including Apollo and Mercury, the outer border inscribed 'ONSILIV... INNOCTE', on later lion and ball feet, the base with initials 'R S', dated.

1672 *8.5in (21.5cm) high*

$15,000-20,000 WW

A Charles II *lignum vitae* wassail bowl and cover, the cover with three finials around an integral spice chalice.

Provenance: A typed paper label stuck to the interior of the bowl states it was formerly the property of Lord Richard Cavendish.

21.7in (55cm) high

$10,000-15,000 DN

A late 17thC turned fruitwood goblet.

4.5in (11.5cm) high

$2,500-3,500 WW

An early 18thC turned boxwood salt.

3.75in (9.5cm) high

$600-800 WW

An 18thC turned yew spice castor, with a threaded pierced finial, with restoration.

5in (12.5cm) high

$700-900 WW

A pair of 18thC mahogany wassail cups and covers.

Wassail comes from the Old Norse 'ves heill', meaning 'be well and in good heath'. Wassail bowls were used to serve the hot mulled cider typically drunk at toasts and as part of the ancient English ritual (wassailing) intended to ensure a good apple harvest. Although it was also a riotous drunken festival, the ritual was taken very seriously, particularly in areas such as Devon where the apple was an important part of the local economy.

9in (22cm) high

$1,200-1,800 SWO

An 18thC turned laburnum goblet, with four hairline cracks.

3.5in (9cm) high

$300-500 WW

A late 18th/early 19thC Baltic birch kovsh, in the form of a bird, carved with leaf scrolls.

7in (17.5cm) high

$5,000-6,000 WW

A late 18thC *lignum vitae* wassail bowl and cover, with brass acorn finial.

11in (28cm) high

$650-850 DA&H

An 18thC turned sycamore salt.

4.5in (11.5cm) diam

$500-700 WW

A pair of early 19thC turned rosewood eggcups.

3in (7.5cm) high

$300-500 WW

A pair of 19thC treen urns and covers, the bases stamped 'GG'.

16.75in (43cm) high

$1,000-1,500 CHEF

An 18thC *lignum vitae* pestle and mortar.

9in (24cm) high

$3,000-4,000 SWO

A mid-18thC turned *lignum vitae* pestle and mortar.

6in (15cm) high

$300-500 WW

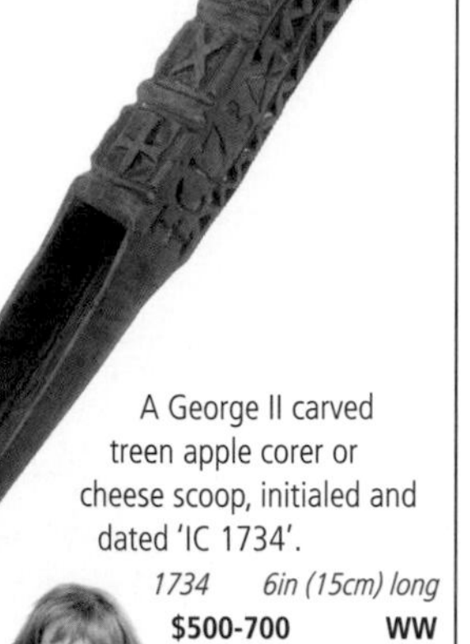

A George II carved treen apple corer or cheese scoop, initialed and dated 'IC 1734'.
1734 *6in (15cm) long*
$500-700 **WW**

A George III treen stay busk, with a heart-shaped finial, with floral, geometric and heart decoration, initialed and dated 'MB 1794'.
1794 *12.5in (31.5cm) long*
$1,200-1,800 **WW**

A large 18thC French walnut tobacco rasp, carved with the Royal Arms of France and in reverse with 'Amselme'.

'Amselme' refers to Father Anselm (1625-94), the French genealogist.
19.5in (49.5cm) long
$2,000-3,000 **GORL**

A Regency carved treen and bone-inlaid knitting sheath, inscribed 'Eleanor Stokoe June 14 1813,' inlaid with a bone heart and two diamonds, carved with a diamond, a heart, a spade, a club, two circular cross motifs and an open hand.
1813 *6in (15cm) long*
$400-600 **WW**

Judith Picks: James I/Charles I Nutcracker

Nuts have been a significant part of the food supply since the beginning of time and, over the years, man has created ingenious ways to open the shells. The oldest known metal nutcracker dates to the 3rdC or 4thC BC. By the 15thC wood carvers in France and England were creating beautiful wooden nutcrackers. Nutcrackers are alluded to in 'The Canterbury Tales' and even Leonardo DaVinci spent some time working out how best to crack nuts. I have been a collector of treen for many years. Finding good 18thC treen is becoming more difficult but to find a dated walnut nutcracker from the early 17thC is extraordinary. It operates, as many contemporary nutcrackers do today, by inserting a nut into the circular aperture and winding a thumbpiece with a screw thread. But the exciting thing about this particular example is that it is carved with floral motifs and inscribed and dated 'JOHN BAKER 1625'. The inscription, with a date on the cusp of the reigns of James I and Charles I, was the reason it rose high above a $550-750 estimate. Rarity and desirability added to age and condition – a full house!

A rare James I/Charles I treen nutcracker, inscribed 'JOHN BAKER 1625', carved with paterae, floral and foliate motifs and stars.
1625 *3.25in (8cm) long*
$18,000-22,000 **DN**

A Malby's terrestrial globe, in a varnished treen box, the globe with twelve printed gores.
c1877 *Globe 3in (7.5cm) diam*
$2,500-3,500 **TOV**

An 18thC Welsh turned sycamore mealey beg (covered butter bowl).
4in (10cm) diam
$800-1,200 **WW**

A mahogany coaster, with a carved horse head terminal, on turned wheels.
19in (48.5cm) long
$650-750 **WW**

A pair of late George III turned walnut coasters.
6in (15cm) diam
$800-1,200 **DN**

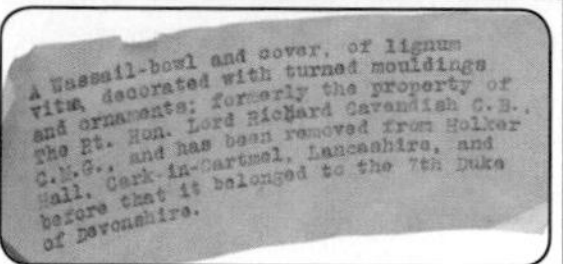
A Wassail-bowl and cover, of lignum vitae decorated with turned mouldings and ornaments; formerly the property of the Rt. Hon. Lord Richard Cavendish C.B., C.M.G., and has been removed from Holker Hall, Cark-in-Cartmel, Lancashire, and before that it belonged to the 7th Duke of Devonshire.

A Regency carved betel nut snuff box, modeled as a sixty gun man-of-war, with inscription 'SNUFF BOX CARVED BY ONE OF NAPOLEON'S STAFF, LONGWOOD, ST. HELENA, 1819', one lid with representation of Napoleon.
1819 *7in (17.5cm) long*
$2,000-3,000 **DN**

A South-German carved, painted and gilded limewood group of a Gothic Madonna and Child, Mary standing holding a pear, with some peeling to the paintwork.
c1470 *35in (90cm) high*
$50,000-70,000 **DOR**

ESSENTIAL REFERENCE - THE HOLY KINSHIP

The Holy Kin were Jesus's extended family, descending from his maternal grandmother St Anne. While some theologians believe that Anne was only married once, others believe that she was married three times and each marriage produced one daughter: Mary (the mother of Jesus), Mary of Clopas and Mary Salome.

- **According to this tradition, Anne is therefore the grandmother of five of the twelve disciples: John the Evangelist, James the Greater, James the Less, Simon and Jude.**
- **Anne's sister, Hismeria (or Esmeria), was the mother of John the Baptist's mother, Elizabeth, and of a second child, Eluid, who was in turn the grandfather of St Servatius.**
- **The Holy Kinship was a popular theme in religious art throughout Germany and the Low Countries, especially during the late 15thC and early 16thC.**

A probably Rhineland carved and painted limewood group of the Holy Kinship.
c1480 *30in (75cm) high*
$40,000-60,000 **SWO**

An Antwerp carved walnut relief of 'The Adoration of the Three Kings', with Joseph, Mary enthroned and the infant Jesus on her lap, with remains of old paintwork.
c1490 *17.75in (45cm) high*
$10,000-15,000 **DOR**

A 16thC German carved, painted and gilded oak figure of an enthroned pope, missing four fingers.
42in (106cm) high
$3,000-5,000 **DOR**

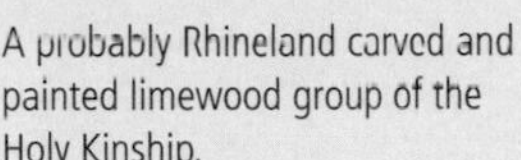

A late 17thC Continental painted wood and composition relief of the Madonna and Child, inscribed 'AVE MARIS STELA'.
24.75in (63cm) high
$10,000-15,000 **DN**

A carved pine relief of 'God the Father Over Clouds', from the workshop of Thomas Schwanthaler (1634-1707), with remains of old paintwork.

Schwanthaler came from a family of sculptors and is arguably the most important Austrian sculptor of the latter 17thC. He was regarded as a 'genius, playboy and prankster'.
c1690 *31in (80cm) wide*
$3,000-4,000 **DOR**

An Upper Austria/Salzburg full-round carved limewood figure of 'Christ at the Whipping Post', with traces of old paintwork, missing one finger.
c1700 *46in (117cm) high*
$3,000-4,000 **DOR**

An Upper Austria/Saltzurg Baroque carved and painted limewood group of St Joseph with the Infant Jesus, with some peeling to paintwork.
c1730 *53in (135cm) high*
$5,000-7,000 **DOR**

An Upper Austria/Salzburg Baroque carved and painted limewood figure of Christ as 'Man of Sorrows', with some peeling to paintwork.

c1730 *28in (70cm) high*

$4,000-6,000 **DOR**

A Baroque unstained full-round carved limewood figure of 'Maria Immaculata', in dynamic pose over clouds with two winged angels.

This masterly Baroque carving is by a sculptor from Styria (now south-eastern Austria).

c1740 *33in (84cm) high*

$5,000-7,000 **DOR**

A Salzburg Baroque carved, painted and gilded limewood angel's head, with some peeling to paintwork.

c1750 *8in (20cm) high*

$800-1,200 **DOR**

A Salzburg Baroque carved, painted and gilded wood figure of Mary 'Immaculata', with two angels.

c1760 *15in (38cm) high*

$3,000-4,000 **DOR**

An 18thC Italian carved, painted and gilded figure of a 'Dog with Torch' (a symbol of St Dominic), with glass eyes.

According to legend, St Dominic's pregnant mother dreamt that she would give birth to a dog with a torch that would 'burn the world'. St Dominic went on to found the Order of Preachers/the Dominicans.

18in (45cm) wide

$2,500-3,500 **DOR**

A South German carved limewood figure of St Mary, previously part of a crucifixion group, missing one finger.

c1790 *34in (87cm) high*

$5,000-7,000 **DOR**

A 19thC Neapolitan carved crèche figure, with glass eyes, original clothing and bagpipes.

16in (40.5cm) high

$2,500-3,500 **SWO**

Jailhouse Carvers

A rare American Jailhouse Carvers model of a horse and carriage, signed 'Ed Walters E.P. C2341'.

This is a unique example from this group of artisans and possibly the only example signed by its maker.

c1921 *24in (61cm) wide*

$5,000-7,000 **POOK**

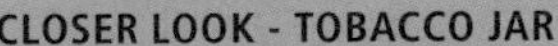

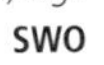

A late 19thC 'Black Forest' carved bear epergne, with a green glass trumpet vase.

18.75in (48cm) high

$3,500-4,500 **SWO**

CLOSER LOOK - TOBACCO JAR

The Black Forest carving industry originated in the town of Brienz, Switzerland.

The quality of Black Forest carving varies as much as the number of households that are involved in this cottage industry. This is significant when you consider that, by 1910, there were some thirteen hundred carvers plying their trade in the locality of Brienz.

This fox is particularly well carved and has much extra detail, which adds to his overall charm.

Bears are common subjects of Black Forest carvings, as they are the symbol for the nearby city of Bern. A fox fisherman, on the other hand, is a very unusual subject. It is also charming and appealing.

This tobacco jar has immense cross-market appeal, as it is likely to appeal to collectors of smoking, fishing and fox memorabilia, as well as collectors of Black Forest carvings!

A 19thC Black Forest carved tobacco jar, in the form of a fox fisherman.

15.5in (39.5cm) high

$12,000-18,000 **GORL**

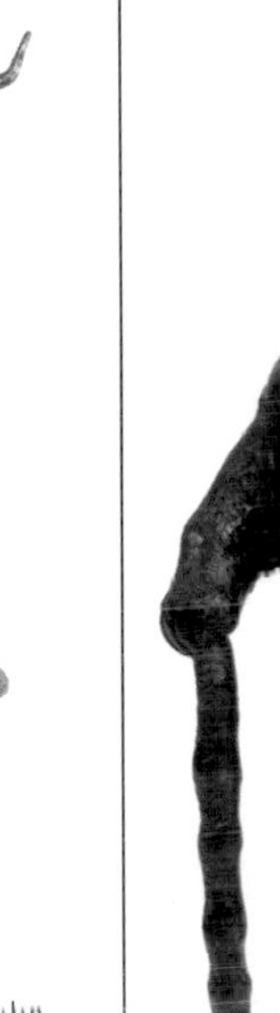

A Black Forest hall stand in the form of a carved bear with cub, the base with metal liner, missing one branch.

c1900 *77in (196cm) high*

$3,500-4,500 **DN**

A Black Forest carved figure of a bear with a walking stick.

c1900 *19in (48cm) high*

$3,000-4,000 **SWO**

A 19thC Black Forest carved tobacco jar in the form of a bear on a toboggan.

12.5in (32cm) high

$5,000-7,000 **GORL**

A large 19thC Black Forest carved tobacco jar in the form of four bears around a tree stump.

17in (43.2cm) high

$5,000-7,000 **GORL**

A 19th century Black Forest carved and painted inkwell in the form of a cockerel.

8.5in (21.5cm) high

$1,500-2,500 **GORL**

THE CLOCKS, WATCHES & SCIENTIFIC INSTRUMENTS MARKET

The clock market has been relatively stable over the past few years. Good-quality clocks in original condition and by important makers are still doing very well. London makers have always tended to be the most sought-after, but collectors are also focusing on the numerous skilled provincial clockmakers and these clocks are also beginning to fetch quite strong prices.

Thirty years ago, the clock and barometer market was dominated by specialists, with most good clocks selling to a handful of dealers and collectors. The market was for good clocks in unrestored condition. They were mainly interested in the movement.

However, there is a new group of buyers entering the market who are interested in the aesthetics of a clock, and will accept sensitive restoration, especially when it comes to early clocks. These buyers are also looking at quality decorative clocks, such as good quality boulle examples. Decorative mantel clocks if very stylish will also find a market.

Smaller clocks, for example carriage clocks and small bracket clocks, which fit in well with modern houses, have been popular. Recently Dreweatts have sold some very good table clocks including a Charles II walnut table clock, by John Wise, London, for over \$100,000 (see p.293) and a George II mahogany-veneered table clock, by Delander, London, c1730 for over \$40,000 (see p.294).

The tallcase clock market has continued to display two distinct trends. The most desirable 17thC and early 18thC examples by well-known makers, again particularly London makers, have done well. However, mid-to late 18thC and 19thC large mahogany clocks have proved difficult to sell.

Lantern clocks from the First Period of lantern clockmaking, particularly if they are new to the market and in unrestored condition, are still getting strong prices. Unfortunately there are many fake lantern clocks, so if in doubt buy from a specialist dealer or auction house.

Skeleton clocks have remained popular, particularly if the clock has unusual features. Automaton clocks can also be highly desirable.

Wristwatches by the prestigious brands continue to do very well. In 2012 Antiquorum sold a rare Patek Philippe 18ct gold astronomic, minute-repeating wristwatch for \$542,500. The same auction house also sold a gilt-brass, enamel and pearl-set pocket watch, by Bovet, Fleurier, decorated with an enamel scene attributed to Amédée Champod, for more than \$70,000.

Barometers have been slow sellers unless by a top name such as Daniel Quare or John Patrick. Unusual features help, and in general good-quality 18thC examples are selling better than 19thC. Dealers report that they are finding some younger buyers, so the market may well improve.

Left: A George II mahogany-veneered table clock, by Delander, London. See p.294.
Far Left An 18ct gold chronometer pocket watch, John Roger Arnold, London. See p.301.

A Charles II walnut and oyster laburnum-marquetry tallcase clock case.

c1680 *76in (193cm) high*

$25,000-35,000 **DN**

An oak eight-day tallcase clock, by Thomas Wise, London, the five-finned pillar outside countwheel bell striking movement with anchor escapement, the 10in (25cm) dial with subsidiary seconds dial and calendar aperture and signed, formerly ebonized, case with replacements.

Thomas Wise (d.1698) was apprenticed to his father, the eminent clockmaker John Wise, in 1678 and gained his freedom in 1686.

c1690 and later *89in (209cm) high*

$10,000-15,000 **DN**

A William and Mary walnut and marquetry eight-day tallcase clock, by John Clowes, London, the five-finned pillar outside countwheel bell striking movement, case with restoration.

John Clowes is recorded as working in London 1673-1713.

c1690 *78in (198cm) high*

$15,000-20,000 **DN**

A small William III ebonized 30-hour tallcase clock, by Samuel Aldworth, Oxford, the five-finned pillar outside countwheel bell striking movement with Knibb-type pendulum suspension incorporating butterfly nut pendulum regulation, the dial plate signed, case with repairs.

Samuel Aldworth was apprenticed to John Knibb of Oxford 1673-80 and continued to work with him until 1689. Many features of this clock are directly influenced by Knibb and its case was almost certainly made by Knibb's casemaker. In 1697 Aldworth moved to London and by 1720 he had moved to Childrey, Oxfordshire.

c1690 *78in (198cm) high*

$15,000-20,000 **DN**

A William III walnut and floral marquetry eight-day tallcase clock, by John Finch, London, the five-finned pillar inside countwheel bell striking movement with anchor escapement, the 11in (23cm) brass dial with ringed winding holes, calendar aperture and subsidiary seconds dial, on later molded skirt.

Thomas Finch is recording as working from St Martins, London, until c1689. This clock can be stylistically dated to the end of the 17thC. The three crowns engraved on the dial may commemorate the unification of the three kingdoms of England, Scotland and Ireland under William III.

c1695 *82in (208cm) high*

$25,000-35,000 **DN**

A William III walnut and floral-marquetry eight-day tallcase clock, by Thomas Power, Wellingborough, the five-finned and latched pillar outside countwheel bell striking movement.

Thomas Power was born in c1630. He was working in Wellingborough by the 1660s and continued until his death in 1709.

c1695 *85in (205cm) high*

$15,000-20,000 **DN**

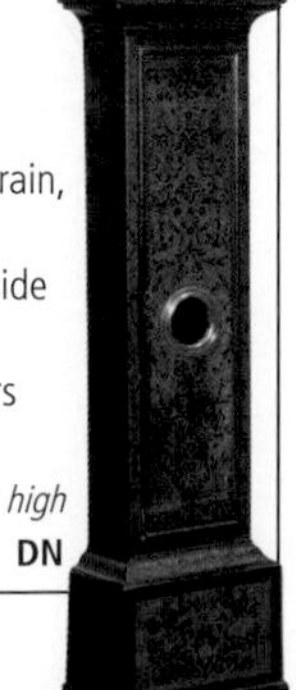

A Queen Anne walnut and arabesque-marquetry quarter-striking eight-day tallcase clock, by Jeremiah Hartley, Norwich, the two-train, five-finned pillar movement with inside countwheel cut for striking the quarters on two bells.

85in (215cm) high

$7,000-10,000 **DN**

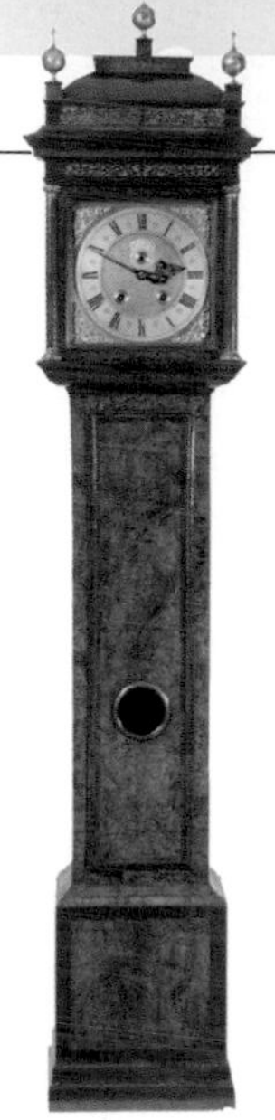

A rare burr elm and walnut three-month tallcase clock, by Morgan Lowry, Leeds, the six-pillar movement with an anchor escapement and outside countwheel striking on a bell, the dial with subsidiary seconds.

c1715 *102.5in (260cm) high*

$35,000-45,000 **TEN**

A Queen Anne ebonized 30-hour tallcase clock, by Robert Rouch, Bristol, the posted countwheel bell-striking movement with anchor escapement.

Robert Rouch is recorded as working in Bristol c1725-55.

87in (220cm) high

$5,000-7,000 **DN**

A Queen Anne red japanned tallcase clock, by William Moore, London, with a brass and steel dial, with subsidiary seconds dial and date aperture.

c1715 *100in (254cm) high*

$30,000-40,000 **L&T**

A burr walnut three-month tallcase clock, by Simon DeCharmes, London, the movement and dial supplied for the clock by Claude DuChesne, the eight-finned pillar rack and bell striking movement with five-wheel trains, with pull quarter-repeat on six bells, dated.

Claude DuChesne and Simon DeCharmes were both of French Huguenot immigrant extraction. DuChesne originated from Paris and was made a free brother of the Clockmakers Company in 1693; De Charmes was made a free brother in 1691. Both specialized in producing very distinctive high-quality clocks usually of complex specification, with many examples playing music or bearing astronomical features. Most were exported to Northern Europe. Clocks of three-month duration are extremely rare.

[illegible] *107in (271cm) high*

$45,000-55,000 **DN**

A George I walnut eight-day musical tallcase clock, by James Green, Althorpe, the five-finned pillar triple train movement with inside countwheel hour striking on a bell and playing a choice of four tunes on eight bells three times a day.

c1720 *86.5in (219cm) high*

$6,000-7,500 **DN**

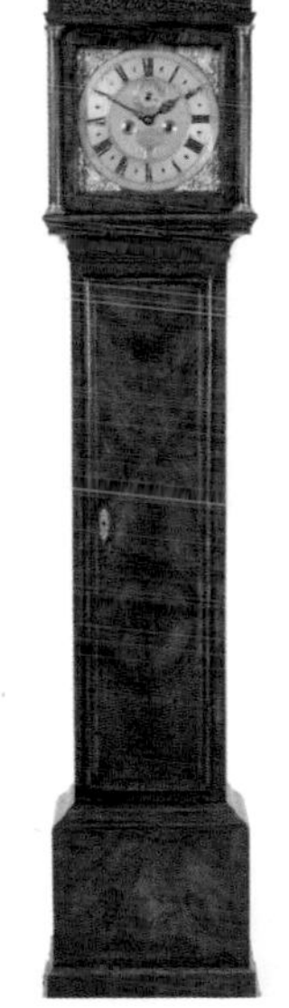

A walnut eight-day tallcase clock, by John Marsden, London, the five-pillar movement with anchor escapement and inside countwheel striking on a bell, the dial with winding holes, date aperture and subsidiary seconds, with restorations.

c1730 *87.5in (220cm) high*

$8,000-12,000 **TEN**

A George II walnut eight-day tallcase clock, by Samuel Berry, London, with five-pillar rack and bell striking movement.

Samuel Berry is recorded as being admitted as an apprentice in 1698, gaining his freedom of the Clockmakers' Company in 1705 and working until 1743.

c1735 *96.5in (245cm) high*

$5,000-7,000 **DN**

Miller's Compares

Both these clocks are by London makers but the clock by the excellent maker Benjamin Taylor is superior. It has a quarter-striking musical eight-day movement striking the quarters on two bells and playing a choice of six airs on eight bells every hour. This fine clock has the rare feature of two-in-one quarter striking where both the quarters and the hours are sounded from the same train. The clock on the left is a good clock, but has a much simpler movement.

The pagoda-pedimented case has a blind-fret-fronted swan-neck frieze.

The subsidiary selection dials have chime/not chime and song/jig/minuet/gavot/song/jig tune.

The brass break-arch dial has subsidiary seconds and calendar dials.

The five-pillar rack and bell-striking movement has one pillar removed.

A George III mahogany eight-day tallcase clock, by Williams, London, with five-pillar rack and bell striking movement, with 12in (30cm) brass break-arch dial.

c1780 *94.5in (240cm) high*

$4,000-6,000 **DN**

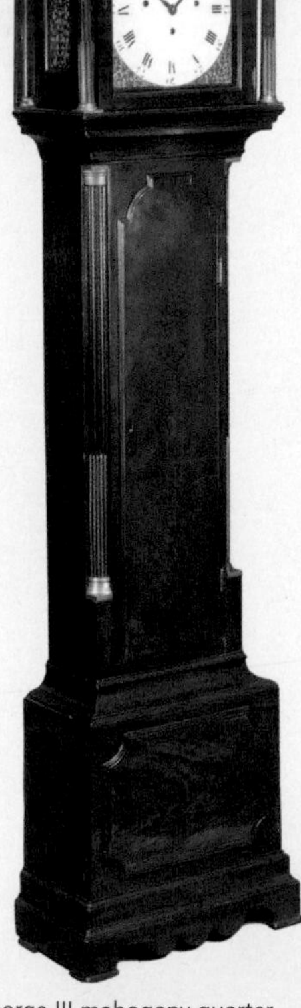

A George III mahogany quarter-striking musical eight-day tallcase clock, by Benjamin Taylor, London, the five-pillar triple train movement striking the quarters on two bells and playing a choice of six airs on eight bells every hour.

Benjamin Taylor is recorded as working from Lombard Street, London, 1773-1800.

c1780 *99in (252cm) high*

$12,000-18,000 **DN**

A japanned eight-day tallcase clock, by John Simpson, London, the four-pillar movement with anchor escapement and rack striking on a bell, the 12in (30.5cm) brass dial with subsidiary seconds and date aperture.

c1750 *97in (247cm) high*

$4,000-6,000 **TEN**

A rare mid-18thC inlaid oak musical 30-hour tallcase clock, by Thomas Bilbie, Chew Stoke, with three-train posted movement, the going and strike trains laid out one in front of the other and both driven via Huygen's endless chain with a shared weight, with anchor escapement.

87in (220cm) high

$8,000-12,000 **DN**

A mid-18thC Dutch walnut and marquetry eight-day tallcase clock, by Jan. Gobels, Amsterdam, the five-finned pillar rack and bell striking movement with rolling moonphase calibrated for the lunar month, lacking motionwork.

93in (237cm) high

$5,000-7,000 **DN**

An oak eight-day tallcase clock, by Simcock, Prescot, the four-pillar movement with deadbeat escapement and rack striking on a bell, the 13in (33cm) brass dial with subsidiary seconds and engraved 'On TIME'S date depends uncertain ETERNITY', with rolling moonphase.

c1780 *87.5in (220cm) high*

$7,000-10,000 **TEN**

A mahogany eight-day tallcase clock, by Blair Flight, Kenross, the four-pillar movement with attached falseplate stamped 'Osborne', anchor escapement and rack striking, bell missing, the 14in (35.5cm) painted dial with date aperture and subsidiary seconds, with rolling moon in the arch.

89in (226cm) high

$3,000-4,000 TEN

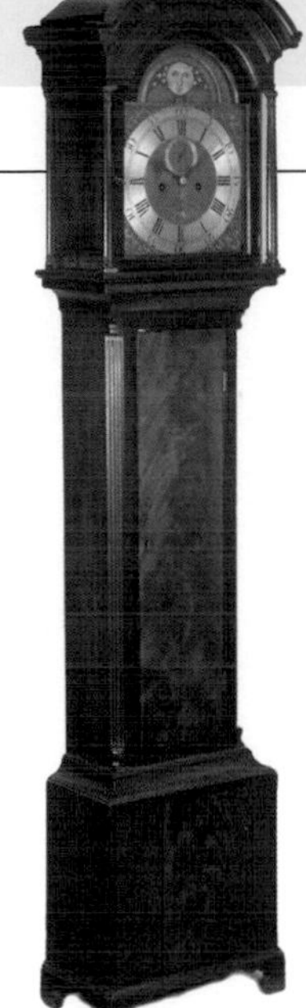

A mahogany eight-day tallcase clock, by Josiah Bartholemew, Sherborne, with five pillar rack and bell striking movement, the arch with rolling moonphase incorporating landscape, now in a break-arch case.

c1800 *83in (210cm) high*

$3,500-4,500 DN

ESSENTIAL REFERENCE - REGULATORS

Made from the 18thC, a regulator is a precise timekeeper designed to regulate other clocks.

- **Most regulators have plain cases, although French regulators may have ormolu mounts.**
- **To maximize precision, regulators were fitted with a gridiron, wood-rod or mercurial compensated pendulum and a deadbeat escapement with jeweled bearings to reduce friction.**
- **The chapter ring on a regulator usually displays minutes, with subsidiary dials for hours and seconds.**

A mahogany tallcase regulator, by George Stephenson, Warminster, the single weight driven six-pillar movement with deadbeat escapement driven by Harrison's maintaining power, the 13in (33cm) regulator dial with subsidiary seconds, with hour dial and signed.

c1830 *85in (213cm) high*

$8,000-12,000 TEN

A Scottish mahogany eight-day tallcase clock, by K Murdoch, Ayr, the four-pillar movement with anchor escapement and rack striking on a bell, the 14in (35.5cm) painted dial with subsidiary seconds, date and signed, the arch depicting a figural lake scene.

c1820 *86in (218cm) high*

$2,000-3,000 TEN

A Sheraton Revival chiming tallcase clock, by S Smith & Son, London, the triple weight driven movement with deadbeat escapement, eight hammers quarter striking onto eight tubular bells and a further hammer striking a further tubular bell for the hours, the 14in (35.5cm) dial with subsidiary seconds.

c1900 *107.5in (270cm) high*

$18,000-22,000 TEN

An Edwardian carved walnut quarter-chiming tallcase clock, retailed by Kemp Brothers, Bristol, the four-pillar triple train movement with deadbeat escapement, Harrison's maintaining power and chiming a choice of two airs on a graduated set of eight tubular gongs with hour strike on a further gong.

104in (264cm) high

$15,000-20,000 DN

An 18thC Delaware walnut tallcase, by Samuel Bispham, Wilmington, the brass dial with moonphase dial, calendar and demi-chapter ring.

94in (239cm) high

$30,000-40,000 FRE

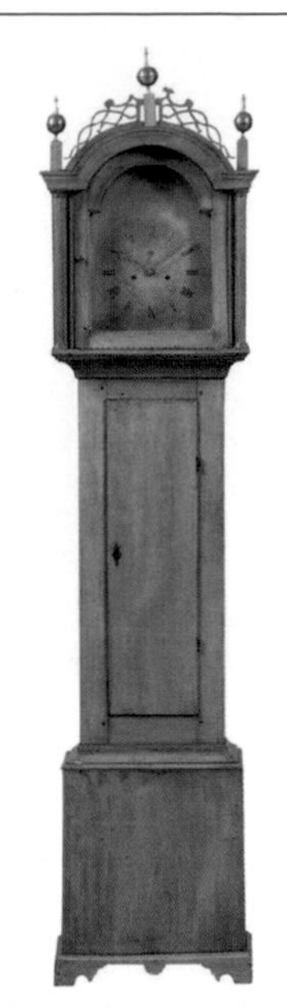

A late 18thC Massachusetts Chippendale maple eight-day tallcase clock, by John Bailey II, Hanover, the weight-powered movement with skeletonized plates, refinished, restored.

94in (239cm) high

$3,000-4,000 SK

A Pennsylvania Chippendale walnut eight-day tallcase clock, by Jacob Sallade (Solliday), Bucks County, signed.

c1780 93in (236cm) high

$12,000-18,000 POOK

A Massachusetts Federal carved mahogany eight-day tallcase clock, by Aaron Willard, Roxbury, the painted iron dial with moonphase dial, inscribed 'J. Minott 131', with paper maker's label engraved by Paul Revere and printed in red ink.

c1790 94in (239cm) high

$15,000-25,000 SK

An 18thC Delaware walnut tallcase, by Samuel Bispham, Wilmington, the brass dial with moonphase dial, calendar and demi-chapter ring.

94in (239cm) high

$30,000-40,000 FRE

A Pennsylvania cherrywood tallcase clock, by Bernard Hendel, Carlisle, with painted moonphase dial, Arabic hour chapter ring and outer seconds ring.

c1800 88in (224cm) high

$10,000-15,000 FRE

A Pennsylvania Chippendale cherrywood eight-day tallcase clock, by Isaac Chandlee, Nottingham, Chester County, with painted face, signed.

c1800 94.75in (241cm) high

$25,000-35,000 POOK

A Massachusetts painted pine 30-hour tallcase clock, by S. Hoadley, Plymouth, signed.

This clock retains its original boldly grained surface.

c1820 83.75in (213cm) high

$10,000-15,000 POOK

CLOSER LOOK - LOUIS XIV BRACKET CLOCK

Two fine 'Religieuse' spring clocks by Gaudron are illustrated in Reinier Plomp's 'Early French Pendulum Clocks 1658-1700'. The movement of this clock, although slightly later, is remarkably similar to those pictured in Plomp's book.

A pewter veneer has been applied to the iron dial plate, which has then been polished and finished to simulate mother-of-pearl.

The chapter ring is very finely engraved and pierced.

The backplate is signed 'Gaudron A Paris'.

Antoine Gaudron is recorded in G H Baillie's 'Watchmakers & Clockmakers of the World' as working from c1675. In 1689 he was established at Place Dauphine at 'La Perle' and then at 'La Renommee' in 1709. He died a wealthy man in 1714.

A French Louis XIV ormolu-mounted tortoiseshell bracket clock, by Antoine Gaudron, Paris, the six back-pinned baluster pillar movement of two week duration with large spring barrels, verge escapement with silk suspension and cycloidal cheeks, and high position numbered countwheel to the upper right hand corner of the backplate for striking the hours and once at the half hour with a vertically pivoted hammer on a bell mounted within the top of the case.

c1700 *21in (53cm) high*

$10,000-15,000 **DN**

A late 17thC ebony-veneered striking bracket clock, by Henry Godfrey, London, the six-pillar movement converted to anchor escapement, quarter repeating work removed in a basket top case.

c1695 *14in (37cm) high*

$15,000-20,000 **WW**

A Queen Anne ebonized bracket clock, by Christopher Gould, London, the five-finned pillar single fusee movement with verge escapement, with pull quarter repeat and alarm.

Christopher Gould, who gained his freedom in 1682, is generally regarded as one of the leading makers from the 'Golden Period' of English clockmaking. His work was of such high quality that only the very wealthy could afford his clocks.

c1710 *14in (36cm) high*

$20,000-30,000 **DN**

A German ebonized eight-day bracket clock, by Laurentius Müller, Freiburg, with quarter hour striking on three bells, verge escapement with chain and fusee, dated.

1739 *27.5in (68.5cm) high*

$15,000-20,000 **KAU**

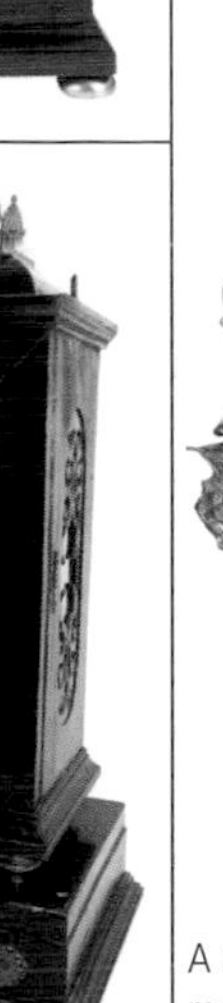

An early 18thC Dutch verge ebonized two-train bracket clock, the turned pillars striking on a bell, the base inset with a small drawer.

Clock 15in (38cm) high

$2,000-3,000 **GHOU**

A mid-18thC French ormolu-mounted boulle bracket clock and wall bracket, by Le Fubure, LeHavre, the two train outside countwheel bell striking movement with four baluster turned pillars, converted from verge escapement to anchor.

58in (147cm) high

$8,000-12,000 **DN**

A late 18thC brass-mounted mahogany pad-top bracket clock, by Robert Flight, Bath, the five-pillar twin fusee bell-striking movement now with anchor escapement.

14in (36cm) high

$10,000-15,000 DN

A late 18thC ebonized eight-day bracket clock, by John Crucifix, London, striking on a bell, carillon striking on six bells, verge escapement with chain and fusee, restored.

15in (39.5cm) high

$12,000-18,000 KAU

A George III ebonized bracket clock, by Thomas Grignion, London, the six-pillar twin fusee rack and bell striking movement with verge escapement.

From c1730 to 1750, Thomas Grignion (1713-84) worked in partnership with his father, who had previously been employed in the workshop of Daniel Quare. Grignion continued the business alone until 1775 when he went into partnership with his son, also named Thomas.

c1775 *14in (36cm) high*

$12,000-18,000 DN

A Louis XV 'corne verte' eight-day pendulum clock, signed 'Bellot a Toul', inscribed 'Par Belloz Horloger à Toul aux Evéchez', with oblong spring-motion, verge escapement, half-hour striking mechanism on bells.

Bellot is associated with high-value 18thC clocks. He founded the 'Manufacture de Versailles' in 1795.

44in (112cm) high

$6,500-7,500 DOR

A George III mahogany bracket clock, by William Robinson, London, the five-pillar twin fusee bell-striking movement with verge escapement, with a later Gothic fretwork wall bracket (not shown).

c1780 *19in (49cm) high*

$12,000-18,000 DN

An ebonized bracket clock, by Robert Bertrand, London, the single fusee movement with anchor escapement, on later seatboard.

c1790 *20in (52cm) high*

$5,000-7,000 TEN

A late 18thC brass-mounted mahogany pad-top bracket clock, by Robert Flight, Bath, the five-pillar twin fusee bell-striking movement now with anchor escapement.

14in (36cm) high

$10,000-15,000 DN

A Regency brass-inlaid mahogany lancet-shaped bracket clock, by Brockbank & Atkins, London, the five pillar twin fusee bell striking movement with anchor escapement.

The firm Brockbanks was established when John and Myles Brockbank went into partnership in the early 1790s. The business became Brockbanks & Grove when George Grove was taken into partnership in 1812, later becoming Brockbank and Atkins when George Atkins was taken into partnership after Grove's death in 1814. The firm was well known for producing fine marine chronometers.

20in (50cm) high

$5,500-6,500 DN

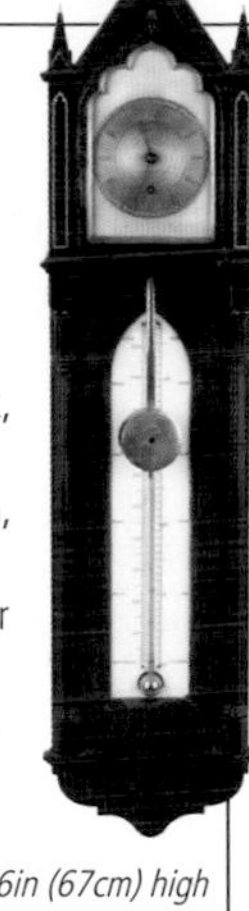

An unusual Regency Gothic Revival brass-inlaid rosewood wall-mounted bracket clock, with thermometer, by William Payne, London, the single fusee movement with anchor escapement, the lower backboard inset with an ivory-scaled mercury thermometer.

26in (67cm) high

$3,500-4,500 DN

A William IV brass-inlaid goncalo alves bracket clock, by John Cross, Trowbridge, the five-pillar twin fusee bell striking movement with deadbeat escapement.

c1830 35in (88cm) high

$10,000-15,000 DN

A William IV brass-mounted ebonized bracket clock, by Arnold & Dent, London, the five-pillar twin fusee bell striking movement with anchor escapement.

Celebrated clock and chronometer makers John Roger Arnold and Edward Dent formed a partnership in 1830 and soon built a reputation for producing clocks, watches and marine chronometers of the highest quality. In 1837 they were granted the Royal Warrant. The partnership was dissolved in 1840.

c1835 19.5in (49cm) high

$3,000-4,000 DN

A rosewood bracket clock, by Thomas Cox Savory, London, the four-pillar single-fusee movement with anchor escapement.

Thomas Cox Savory is recorded as working in London 1839-57.

c1850 14.25in (36.5cm) high

$5,000-7,000 DN

A Victorian brass-inlaid miniature bracket clock, by T. Hammond, Manchester, the four-pillar single fusee movement with anchor escapement.

c1850 11in (28cm) high

$2,000-3,000 DN

A late Victorian satinwood and gilt-brass mounted director's bracket clock, the repeating three train movement striking a peel of eight bells and five gongs, with bracket (not shown).

Clock 25in (63.5cm) high

$5,000-7,000 WW

A late 19thC gilt-brass mounted quarter chiming bracket clock, the four-pillar triple fusee movement with rise/fall regulation, chiming the quarters on eight-bells and striking the hour on a gong, the base with presentation plaque reading 'EDWARD HARDCASTLE, FROM THOMAS USBORNE. A MEMENTO OF THE FEW DAYS DURING 1892 THEY SERVED TOGETHER IN THE HOUSE OF COMMONS'.

25in (64cm) high

$4,000-6,000 DN

A Louis XV ormolu and white marble mantel clock, modeled with Jason presenting the golden fleece to King Aeëtes, the dial signed 'Viger à Paris', movement no.1175.

c1750 *14in (36cm) high*

$10,000-15,000 **GORL**

A mid-18thC Italian Baroque fruitwood mantel clock, attributed to Abraham Chavane, the single-train movement chiming on two bells and with pull repeater.

17.5in (44cm) high

$4,000-6,000 **SK**

A Louis XVI marble eight-day mantel clock, signed 'Feron à Paris', with half-hour striking mechanism on bells and thread suspension.

c1780 *14in (36cm) high*

$5,500-6,500 **DOR**

A French Empire bronze and ormolu mantel clock, mounted with a cherub seated on a dog.

18in (46cm) high

$12,000-18,000 **GORB**

A Biedermeier one-day commode clock, by Mathias Müllner, Vienna, with Viennese hour striking mechanism, some restoration.

c1820 *20in (52cm) high*

$2,500-3,500 **DOR**

An early 19thC French gilt and silvered-bronze mantle clock, depicting a trumpeting figure atop a winged horse.

23.25in (59cm) high

$3,500-4,500 **LHA**

An early 19thC Continental satinwood, mahogany and parquetry mantel clock, with a platform lever escapement, with key.

18.25in (46cm) high

$6,500-7,500 **WW**

An early 19thC French marble and ormolu eight-day obelisk mantel clock, with outside count wheel, striking on a bell.

22in (56cm) high

$6,500-7,500 **WW**

A French ormolu eight-day mantel clock, with half hour striking on a bell, missing pendulum and key.

c1830 *15in (36cm) high*

$800-1,200 **KAU**

A French ormolu and bronze mantel clock, the twin barrel movement with silk suspension, outside countwheel striking on a bell, the movement backplate stamped 'Arera' and numbered '292'.

c1830 *17.5in (43cm) high*

$7,000-10,000 **TEN**

A Louis Philippe ormolu and patinated-bronze eight-day mantel clock, the enamel dial signed 'Giteau, Palais Royal No. 140, Paris', the striking movement with silk suspension.

c1835 *20in (52cm) high*

$5,500-6,500 **DN**

A French 19thC ormolu and porcelain mantel clock, with 'Vincenti 1855' drum movement.

19in (48cm) high

$6,500-7,500 **CHEF**

A Second Empire ormolu and bronze figural two train mantel clock, the movement with outside countwheel.

18.5in (47cm) high

$3,000-4,000 **GHOU**

A 19thC French ormolu and white marble mantel clock, by Rollin, Paris.

c1860 *19in (48cm) high*

$5,000-7,000 **GORL**

A 19thC French ormolu 'pendule d'officier' mantel clock, with chain-driven two-train movement, quarter chiming on a bell.

With handle 9in (22.5cm) high

$5,000-7,000 **BELL**

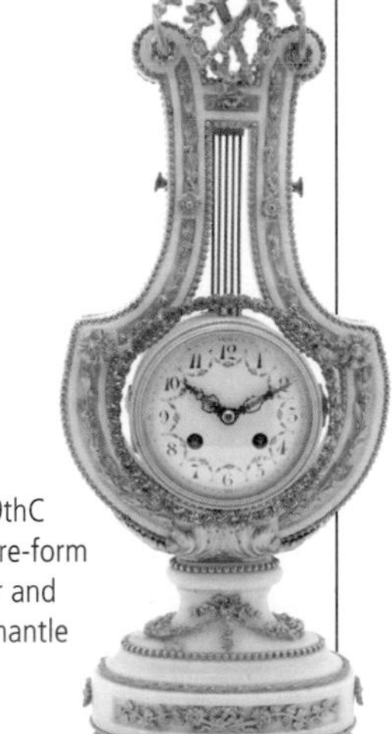

A late 19thC French lyre-form alabaster and ormolu mantle clock.

21.5in (55cm) high

$5,000-7,000 **LHA**

A 19thC French ormolu and Sevres-style porcelain mantel clock, retailed by Ellis Bros. of Exeter, the movement stamped 'J.B.D.'.

c1870 *20in (51cm) high*

$5,000-7,000 **GORL**

A 19thC French Louis XV-style red boulle mantel clock, the movement stamped 'P. Japy et Cie', dated.

1878 *13.75in (35cm) high*

$3,500-4,500 **GORL**

A late 19thC Viennese Gothic Revival silver-gilt and enamel mantel clock.

7in (17.5cm) high

$5,000-7,000 **L&T**

A Louis XVI-style ormolu and red marble mantel clock, with figures of a fairy and Apollo, with half-striking movement.

c1880 *28in (71cm) high*

$6,500-7,500 **SK**

A late 19thC French ormolu eight-day mantel clock, depicting Napoleon Bonaparte, the movement faintly inscribed 'T.C. Cugghe(?)...et Cie, Paris', with count wheel strike and pendulum, the lower section with applied patriotic scenes and military iconography and inscribed 'Toulon', 'Mantour' and 'Lodi' (Napoleonic battles).

17.5in (44cm) high

$6,500-7,500 **SK**

A late 19thC French ormolu four-glass mantel clock, retailed by 'Howell James & Co, Paris', with visible escapement.

c1900 *13in (33cm) high*

$3,500-4,500 **GORL**

A large French champlevé and ormolu temple-form mantle clock, by Japy Freres, with twin-train movement, signed.

c1900 *21in (53.3cm) high*

$35,000-45,000 **WAD**

An American Empire-style mahogany eight-day mantel clock, the time and 'house' strike movement with lever escapement, the dial inscribed 'CHELSEA CLOCK CO. BOSTON, U.S.A.', serial no.35022, dated.

According to a certificate issued by the Chelsea Clock Company on 8th May 2008, this clock was shipped from the factory on 29th July 1909 and sold to G S Kern.

1909 *24.5in (62cm) high*

$6,500-7,500 **SK**

An Edwardian mahogany double fusee mantel clock, by John Carter, 28 St Swithins Lane, London, signed.

11.75in (30cm) high

$3,000-4,000 **GHOU**

CLOSER LOOK - CHARLES II TABLE CLOCK

The casting of the carry handle is very distinctive.

The wheel-work has a finned-collet design and the stopwork has a pronounced disc cam to the fusee.

The movement is of substantial construction, which, while not particularly unusual for the period, is a desirable feature in an antique clock.

The detail design and layout of the movement does not conform with the prevalent Fromanteel/Tompion/Knibb and East/Jones schools of clockmaking.

A Charles II walnut table clock, by John Wise, London, the seven double-baluster turned latched pillar twin fusee movement with bolt-and-shutter maintaining power, the gilt-brass latched dial with calendar aperture and shutters engraved with male and female profile portraits.

Although several early tallcase and lantern clocks by John Wise senior are known, table clocks by Wise are extremely rare. This clock has excellent family provenance.

c1675 *14.in (37cm) high.*

$100,000-150,000 **DN**

A late 17thC William III quarter-repeating ebony table clock, by Richard Colston, London, the fully-latched seven-finned pillar rack and bell striking movement with verge escapement, with alarm.

Richard Colston was made freeman of the Clockmakers Company in 1682. He ceased to pay quarterage in 1702.

14in (36cm) high

$40,000-60,000 **DN**

Automaton Clock

A German ormolu and ebonized-oak automaton table clock, Augsburg, modeled as a dog, with verge fusee going train, with star wheel activating eye movement, the standing barrel strike activating tail.

c1670 *8in (19cm) high*

$30,000-40,000 **WAD**

A late 17thC pull quarter repeating verge table clock, by John Bushman, London, the seven baluster pillar movement with verge escapement, rack striking on a bell.

Clocks by John Bushman (b.1691) are held at the Victoria & Albert Museum in London, UK, and the Metropolitan Museum of Art in New York, USA. Bushman was made a brother of the Clockmakers Company in September 1692 and is thought to have worked as a clock- and watchmaker in London until 1725.

c1695 *18in (45cm) high*

$25,000-35,000 **TEN**

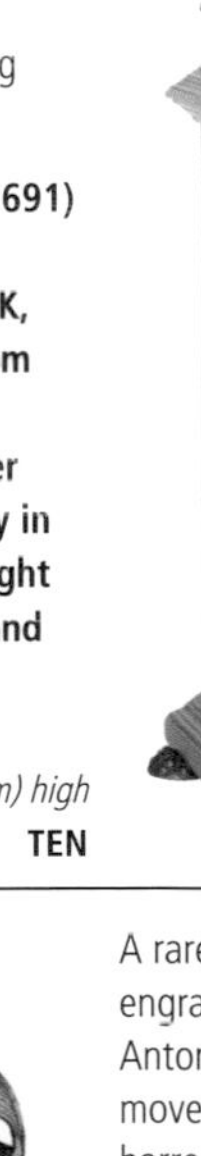

A rare small Italo-Germanic engraved-brass table clock, by Antonio Ferci, Asti, the four-pillar movement with engraved standing barrel and verge escapement, with pull quarter repeat and alarm.

The fact that this clock has a 'silent pull' repeat mechanism (which strikes the hours and quarters on demand only) and an alarm suggests that it was designed for use in the bedroom.

c1700 *8in (20.5cm) high*

$25,000-35,000 **DN**

CLOSER LOOK - TABLE CLOCK

Richard Haughtin was apprenticed to Peter Wise and became free of the Clockmakers Company in 1689. The last known record of him dates to 1714.

This is a very early use of the break-arch dial.

The damascened steel signature boss is extremely rare on any clock. Most of Haughtin's clocks are signed with his Fetter Lane address.

This clock is intricately decorated, featuring burnished gilding to both dial and movement and engraving to the backcock and rise/fall arm.

The attention to detail displayed in this clock and its sophisticated design is reminiscent of the work of Daniel Quare, particularly whilst he was in partnership with Stephen Horseman.

A Queen Anne brass-mounted quarter-repeating ebony table clock, by Richard Haughtin, London, the five-finned and knopped pillar twin fusee movement with verge escapement.

19in (47cm) high

$15,000-20,000 **DN**

A George II walnut table clock, by Robert Smith, London, the twin train fusee movement with anchor escapement and striking on a bell.

16in (40cm) high

$6,500-7,500 **L&T**

ESSENTIAL REFERENCE - DANIEL DELANDER

Daniel Delander was apprenticed to Charles Halstead in 1692. He was known to be working in Thomas Tompion's workshop in 1693 and continued working with Tompion after gaining his freedom in 1699. The attractive proportions and detail in the finish of Delander's clocks show Tompion's influence.

- **Later he set up on his own, working from Devereux Court before moving to 'within Temple Bar', Fleet Street from where he is thought to have worked until his death in 1733.**
- **He is best known for his small walnut precision tallcase clocks with duplex escapements made during the 1720s.**
- **Daniel Delander was succeeded by his son, Nathaniel, who gained his freedom of the Clockmakers' Company in 1721. He is recorded working from Fleet Street and later the Royal Exchange. He was appointed Master of the Clockmakers' Company in 1747 and died in 1762.**

A George II mahogany-veneered table clock, by Delander, London, the six-pillar bell striking movement with verge escapement and pull quarter repeat, with carved moldings, with some losses to veneers, lacking pendulum.

c1730 *16.5in (42cm) high.*

$40,000-60,000 **DN**

A George II brass-mounted ebonized table clock, by Charles Clay, London, the seven-finned pillar twin fusee movement with verge escapement, with pull quarter repeat and alarm, some restoration.

Charles Clay, who originated from near Huddersfield, gained his freedom of the Clockmakers Company before 1716. In 1723 he was appointed Clockmaker in His Majesty's Board of Works and in 1731 supplied the turret clock for the gateway at St James's Palace. He specialized in and experimented with musical mechanisms and is now best known for his organ clocks, one of which is in Windsor Castle.

c1730 *19in (49cm) high*

$10,000-15,000 **DN**

A George III lacquer table clock, by John Parker, London, the six-pillar twin fusee movement with verge escapement, some restoration.

17.5in (44cm) high

$15,000-20,000 **DN**

A George III brass-mounted mahogany musical table clock, by Henry Favre, London, the seven-pillar triple fusee movement striking the hours on a large bell and at the half hour on a smaller bell, with four tunes on nine bells with thirteen hammers, with verge escapement.

c1800 *24in (61cm) high*

$15,000-20,000 **DN**

Judith Picks

If you want an elaborate clock by an excellent maker that will be noticed, here it is! This is not about the clock movement: this is about this clock as a 'looker'. Everything about the case is designed to impress, with the pierced enamel panels and lapis lazuli veneers, surmounted by enameled figures of knights and gladiators. The corners are marked with enamel columns surmounted by additional figures of warriors. This is a top quality piece of late 19thC decorative art.

An Austrian enamel, silver and lapis lazuli table clock, attributed to Hermann Boehm, Vienna, with enameled figures of knights and gladiators.

c1880 *15in (38cm) high*

$30,000-40,000 **FRE**

A mahogany table clock, by Thomas Southall, Stafford, the twin fusee movement with verge escapement and striking on a bell.

c1820 *19in (48cm) high*

$6,500-7,500 **TEN**

A 19thC French eight-day bedside table clock, the single mainspring movement with crown wheel and verge escapement, the skeletonized rotating chapter ring illuminating the time by the lighted candle at the back.

13.5in (34cm) high

$6,500-7,500 **SK**

An oak chiming table clock, by Oldfield, Liverpool, with triple fusee movement, quarter chiming eight hammers onto eight bells or four hammers striking four gongs and a further hammer striking a gong for the hours.

c1890 *18in (46cm) high*

$2,000-3,000 **TEN**

A walnut chiming table clock, the triple fusee movement with anchor escapement, the backplate stamped 'Peerless', the dial with slow/fast, chime/silent and chime on eight bells/Westminster.

c1890 *28in (71cm) high*

$4,000-6,000 **TEN**

A late 19thC French Renaissance-style engraved gilt-brass eight-day table clock, by Matieu Planchon, Paris, the two train gong striking movement with 'VINCENTI & Cie, MEDAILLE D'AGANT 1855' medallion and stamped 'PLANCHON, PALAIS-ROYAL'.

Matieu Planchon was apprenticed to his father and worked for several of the leading French makers, including Robert Houdin, before setting up business at Palais Royal, Paris in 1890. He specialized in high-end novelty clocks, such as floating turtle timepieces and recreations of Renaissance models. The scale of this clock suggests it was made for an exhibition.

26in (65cm) high

$15,000-20,000 **DN**

A rare 'First Period' brass lantern clock, unsigned, the short-duration posted countwheel bell-striking movement formerly with verge and balance-wheel escapement now with verge and external short bob pendulum, with an oak wall bracket.

This London-style clock can be stylistically dated to the 1630s and loosely compared to examples by makers such as Peter Closon, William Sellwood and Francis Foreman. The thistle decoration is unusual and suggests the clock could have Scottish origins.

c1635 *17in (42cm) high*

$12,000-18,000 DN

An early 'Third Period' brass lantern clock, the movement and frame attributed to the Fromanteel Workshop, the two train posted movement with double-cut hoop wheel, iron countwheel and conversion to anchor escapement, the current dial signed 'Gibbon, London'.

This lantern clock retains many early features such as separately wound trains, heavily tapered arbours and iron countwheel. Its value is lowered by heavy modifications. Evidence indicates that it originally had a verge escapement and short pendulum.

c1660 *17in (44cm) high*

$3,000-4,000 DN

Tallcase

A late 17thC ebonized oak and pine 'tallcase' lantern clock case, with external iron strap-hinges, brass drop handle and molded aperture, on later skirt,

Original 'tallcase' cases for lantern clocks are very rare, mainly because lantern clocks were predominantly designed to hang from the wall. The construction of this type of case (often termed 'pencil case') with its slender trunk continuing to the floor helps date this example to the late 17thC. Early 18thC lantern cases tended to resemble contemporary tallcase clock cases. The mixed use of woods suggests the clock was designed with the intention of taking a painted finish, in this case ebonisation.

76in (193cm) high

$7,000-9,000 DN

A Charles II brass lantern clock, by John London, Bristol, the posted countwheel bell-striking movement with early conversion to anchor escapement, lacking pendulum and weight.

John London is first recorded gaining his freedom of the City of Bristol as a gunsmith on 2nd June 1675. He is perhaps best known for being the first Bristol-based maker of tallcase clocks. A handful of eight-day movements and one complete 30-hour example survive.

c1675 *16.5in (42cm) high*

$20,000-30,000 DN

A Charles II brass two-handed lantern clock, unsigned but possibly by Marcos Peres, the posted countwheel bell-striking movement formerly with verge escapement, now with anchor escapement.

c1680 *15in (39cm) high*

$3,500-4,500 DN

A Charles II brass lantern clock, by George Thomlinson, London, the posted countwheel bell-striking movement formerly with verge balance wheel escapement now with anchor escapement, with contemporary oak 'tallcase' case.

George Thomlinson is recorded as working 1674-81.

c1680 *84in (214cm) high*

$3,000-4,000 DN

A late 17thC brass lantern clock, the movement with later anchor escapement.

15in (38cm) high

$2,500-3,500 GHOU

ESSENTIAL REFERENCE - CARRIAGE CLOCKS

Carriage clocks are small, spring-driven clocks that are housed in plain or gilt-brass cases. They have a carrying handle at the top and often have a fitted case allowing them to be taken on travels.

- **The carriage clock was developed in c1796 by Abraham-Louis Breguet.**
- **Carriage clocks were popular in France and England from the mid- to late 19thC.**
- **They are typically set with glass or, more rarely, enamel or porcelain panels.**
- **They are typically fitted with a platform escapement. This is sometimes visible through a glazed aperture on the top of the case.**

An engraved gorge-cased eight-day grande sonnerie carriage clock, the movement strikes and repeats on two bells, with alarm.
c1870 *5.75in (15cm) high*
$12,000-18,000 **DR**

A French gilt-brass and enamel striking and repeating carriage clock, with twin barrel movement and lever escapement, the backplate numbered '1703'.
c1880 *7.5in (19cm) high*
$5,000-7,000 **TEN**

A gilt-brass quarter-striking carriage clock, by G F Frodsham, London, the twin barrel movement with lever escapement, signed.
c1880 *10in (25cm) high*
$12,000-18,000 **TEN**

A large 19thC Swiss gilt-brass eight-day grande sonnerie carriage clock, unsigned, the two-train movement with horizontal lever escapement with split bimetallic balance engraved 'Cesare Schepers, Firenze, 1883' to the platform, with alarm and push-button repeat.
8in (20.5cm) high
$8,000-12,000 **DN**

A gilt-brass striking and repeating carriage clock, retailed by E White, Paris, the twin-barrel movement with silvered platform lever escapement and striking on a gong.
c1890 *6.25in (16cm) high*
$1,200-1,800 **TEN**

A gilt-brass grand sonnerie carriage clock, the twin barrel movement with lever escapement, quarter and hour striking, with alarm.
c1890 *8in (20cm) high*
$4,000-6,000 **TEN**

A late 19thC French Tiffany & Co. ormolu and champlevé carriage clock, the movement striking on a gong, signed.
9.5in (24cm) high
$2,000-3,000 **GHOU**

An early 20thC gilt-brass carriage clock, retailed by Stewart Dawson & Co. Ltd., Regent Street, the French movement striking on a gong, in a leather carrying case.
5in (14.5cm) high
$300-400 **WHP**

A mid-19thC brass skeleton clock, unsigned, the single fusee movement with anchor escapement and passing strike, the marble base with glass dome (not shown).

18in (46cm) high

$650-750 **DN**

A Victorian brass skeleton clock, by Viner, London, the twin-train fusee movement with anchor escapement and striking on a bell, on a rosewood base with glass dome (not shown).

Clock 15in (39cm) high

$8,000-12,000 **L&T**

A 1970s lacquered-brass 'Concorde' skeleton clock, by Fred Whitlock for Dent, London, the five-pillar A-shaped pierced plates with compound 'dumb bell' pendulum, with Harrison's grasshopper escapement, on mahogany base with glass cover (not shown).

This skeleton clock was conceived and constructed by Fred Whitlock for retail by Dent and is based on a design by Martin Burgess. Approximately 25 examples were constructed during the 1970s with a further batch of around ten produced from unused parts discovered in c2000.

30in (75cm) high overall

$6,500-7,500 **DN**

A late 19thC Swiss painted tinplate figural 'clock pedlar' clock, unsigned, the miniature spring-driven movement with long pendulum.

Although this clock is unsigned other identical examples signed 'Leser, Bern' are known.

15in (38cm) high

$3,000-4,000 **DN**

A brass and nickled automation industrial boiler clock, with barometer and thermometer, the automation wheel driving a central piston pump.

c1900 *18.5in (47cm) high*

$30,000-40,000 **TEN**

A 19thC French automaton 'bontemps' clock, each bird moving in the foliage and drinking from the imitation stream.

28in (71cm) high

$15,000-20,000 **JN**

A Congreve-style single fusee rolling ball triple dial brass clock, under a glass dome (not shown).

18in (46cm) high

$4,000-6,000 **GHOU**

An Egyptian Revival gilt-brass striking clock garniture, retailed by West & Son, Paris, the clock with twin barrel movement and striking on a gong.

c1870 *Clock 22.5in (57cm) high*

$1,200-1,800 **TEN**

A 19thC French ormolu and champlevé clock garniture, the clock with Japy Freres movement.

Clock 20.5in (52cm) high

$5,000-7,000 **GORB**

A French Egyptian Revival bronze, marble and onyx clock garniture, the clock signed 'Vincenti & Cie.', with countwheel movement striking bell.

c1880 *Clock 23in (58.5cm) high*

$3,000-4,000 **WAD**

A 19thC Japanese-style silver-plate and enameled clock garniture, the clock by Japy Freres, with twin train movement striking on bell.

Clock 15in (38cm) high

$3,000-4,000 **ECGW**

A late 19thC French 'Noir Belge' marble and bronze clock garniture, the clock with eight-day bell striking movement with visible Brocot escapement, the figures signed 'O.Semaire'.

Clock 22in (55cm) high

$1,000-1,500 **DN**

A Tiffany & Co. ormolu and marble clock garniture, with French movement.

c1900 *Clock 17.5in (44cm) high*

$3,000-4,000 **DRA**

A late 19thC cloisonné clock garniture, the clock with eight-day movement striking on a bell, stamped 'G A F, Miller & Sons 17543' and 'P.L. F R E'.

Clock 19.75in (50cm) high

$10,000-15,000 **WW**

A French Louis XVI-style ormolu and marble figural clock garniture, the clock with eight-day bell striking movement.

c1900 *Clock 13in (33cm) high*

$4,500-5,500 **DN**

Hague Clock

A late 17thC and later Dutch marquetry Hague clock, unsigned, with four baluster-turned pillars, with later anchor escapement.

In 1656 Christiaan Huygens (1629-95) built the world's first pendulum clock, which was far more reliable than any previous mechanical timepiece. Other clockmakers in the Hague copied his design and the resulting instruments became known as Hague clocks.

21in (54cm) high

$10,000-15,000 **DN**

A Charles II walnut 30-hour striking hooded wall clock, by John Knibb, Oxford, the four-finned pillar outside countwheel striking movement with verge escapement and crown wheel alarm, with alarm, lacking bell and weights.

John Knibb (1650-1722) was apprenticed to his older brother, Joseph, in c1664, and took over his Oxford workshop in 1670. Clocks by Knibb are highly sought after.

c1685 *13.75in (35cm) high*

$65,000-75,000 **DN**

A Queen Anne wall clock, by Thomas Wightman, London, the four-finned pillar single train two-handed movement with verge escapement and separately wound alarm mechanism, with alarm.

Thomas Wightman is recorded as working in Lombard Street 1701-45, becoming master of the Clockmakers Company in 1737.

23in (58cm) high

$8,000-12,000 **DN**

A George III ebony-strung mahogany eight-day hooded wall clock, by Andrew Rich, Bridgwater, the four-pillar single train two-handed movement with anchor escapement, with alarm.

Andrew Rich is recorded as working in Bridgwater 1819-31. Stylistically this clock dates from the late 18thC, which suggests Rich's career as a clockmaker predates known records. This clock is very rare as its complicated mechanism and ebony-strung case would have made it expensive at the time.

c1795 *31in (79cm) high*

$3,000-4,000 **DN**

An early 19thC oak wall clock, by Whitmore & Son, Northampton, the four-pillar single train two-handed movement with anchor escapement, half-seconds pendulum and separately wound alarm mechanism sounding on a bell.

William Whitmore & Son are recorded as working in Northampton from c1830.

29.25in (54cm) high

$3,000-4,000 **DN**

A Victorian mother-of-pearl inlaid rosewood drop-dial wall clock, by Alexander Barrett, Whitchurch, with five-pillar twin fusee bell striking movement.

29in (73cm) high

$1,200-1,800 **DN**

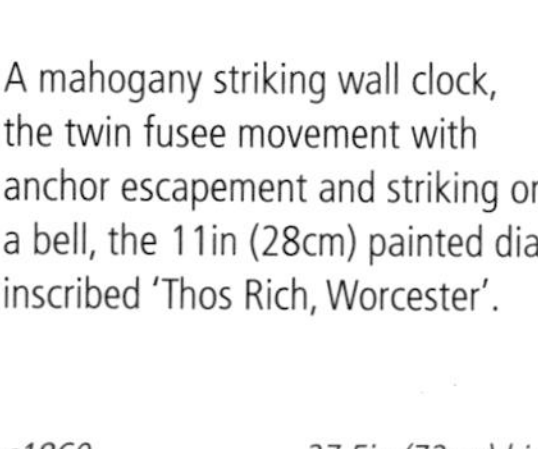

A mahogany striking wall clock, the twin fusee movement with anchor escapement and striking on a bell, the 11in (28cm) painted dial inscribed 'Thos Rich, Worcester'.

c1860 *27.5in (72cm) high*

$800-1,200 **TEN**

FIND OUT MORE...

G H Baillie, 'Watchmakers & Clockmakers of the World', NAG Press, new edition 2006

J K Bellchambers, 'Somerset Clockmakers', Courtyard Press, new edition 1986

F J Britten, 'Old Clocks & Watches and their Makers', Lightning Source UK, new edition 2012

Brian Loomes, 'The Early Clockmakers of Great Britain', NAG Press, new edition 1982

A J Moore, 'The Clockmakers of Somerset 1650-1900', author published, 1998

An early 18thC five-minute repeating verge pocket watch, signed 'Gr. Heinrich Haehnel', the verge movement with pierced cock, the repoussé silver case decorated with lovers, the pierced inner case engraved with scrolls, animals and a view of a town.

2in (5cm) diam

$3,500-4,500 **GORB**

A gold pair-cased quarter-repeater pocket watch, signed 'Paul Dupin, London' (1710-67), the verge fusee movement with fusee winding, pierced and engraved balance cock, flat three armed steel balance, and Tompion-type regulator disc, the repoussé case depicting Mercury and Proserpine.

2in (5cm) diam

$7,000-10,000 **DN**

A 22ct gold pair-cased rack-lever pocket watch, by P Litherland & Co, Liverpool, no.840, with bell-shaped balance cock, the three-wheel train with flat steel balance, fusee and one way slide, the case stamped 'RP'.

1797 *2in (5.5cm) diam*

$2,500-3,500 **SK**

An 18ct gold savage two-pin lever-escapement pocket watch, by Litherland, Davies & Co, Liverpool, no.8480, the four-wheel train with round steel balance and Berrolas' Patent quarter-repeating crown activated action, fusee, the case with maker's mark 'TH' for Thomas Helsby.

1815 *2in (5cm) diam*

$3,000-4,000 **SK**

An 18ct gold chronometer pocket watch, by John Roger Arnold, London, no.1748, with full-plate lever fusee movement, with diamond endstone to the balance cock, with two-arm monometallic 'Z' balance, the case with maker's mark 'TH' for Thomas Hardy.

John Roger Arnold (1769-1843) was the son of John Arnold, the famous British watch and clock maker. He began working with his father in 1783 before moving to Paris as an apprentice to Abraham-Louis Breguet in 1792. He became Master of the Clockmakers' Company in 1817. After the death of Arnold Snr, John Roger continued on his own, upholding his father's reputation as one of the leading watch and clock makers of his age.

1808

$10,000-15,000 **DN**

An enameled and diamond-set gold pocket watch, by John Marie, London, no.402, with pillar verge movement, the reverse with enameled panel of lovers.

c1820 *2.25in (5.5cm) diam*

$3,500-4,500 **GORB**

A Swiss gold minute-repeating calendar and chronograph pocket watch, no.13244, with month, day, seconds and moon phase dials.

2.5in (6cm) diam

$5,500-6,500 **SK**

Amédée Champod Watch

A gilt-brass, enamel and pearl-set pocket watch, by Bovet, Fleurier, the enamel scene attributed to Amédée Champod, made for the Chinese market, with free-standing barrel, Jacot duplex escapement and three-arm steel balance, signed Bovet in Chinese characters.

Amédée Champod (1834-1913) dropped out of school at eleven and began working at the age of sixteen, becoming one of the most celebrated enamel painters of the 19thC. He studied with Huguenin and Sauerländer and with Charles Glardon who had a strong impact on his style. Champond specialized in hunting scenes, such as the one shown here, although this scene is distinguished by having a large snake attack the group as opposed to a tiger, which is more common.

c1870 *2.25in (6cm) diam*

$80,000-120,000 **ATQ**

A rare 18ct pink-gold pocket watch, by A Lange & Söhne, Glashütte B/Dresden, retailed by H Hulsmann, Frankfurt, no.27424, with 16 jewels, straight line Glashütte lever escapement, gold escape wheel and pallet fork, cut bimetallic compensation balance, blued Breguet balance spring and index regulator, the case with initials 'SOC', with yellow-gold filled chain and fob.

c1910 *2in (5cm) diam*

$5,000-7,000 **ATQ**

An Audemars Piguet 'End of Days' PVD-coated stainless steel automatic chronograph wristwatch, case no.E25979, from a limited edition of 500 in collaboration with Arnold Schwarzenegger, with 54 jewels, straight-line lever escapement, monometallic balance adjusted to heat, cold, isochronism and 5 positions, 21ct gold rotor, with registers, tachometer, date, with PVD-coated stainless steel buckle.

c2000 *1.75in (4.5cm) diam*

$35,000-45,000 **ATQ**

An Audemars Piguet 'Quantieme Automatique' skeletonized platinum wristwatch, no.144, movement no.367409, the 38-jeweled movement cal. 2120/2 adjusted to five positions and temperature, with glucydur balance and engraved 21ct gold-edged rotor, with subsidiary dials for day, date, month and moon phase, on black crocodile strap.

1.5in (3.5cm) wide

$25,000-35,000 **DN**

A Blancpain 'Léman Flyback' stainless steel chronograph grande date wristwatch, no.175, with 42 jewels, straight-line lever escapement, monometallic balance adjusted to five positions, with 18ct white-gold rotor, with stainless steel deployant clasp.

c2008 *1.5in (4cm) diam*

$6,500-7,500 **ATQ**

A Breitling 18ct rose-gold chronomat wristwatch, movement no.1250, case no.606284, with slide/rule bezel, with second and 45-minute recording subsidiary dials, with black leather strap.

c1950 *1.25in (3.5cm) diam*

$5,000-6,000 **DRA**

A Cartier 'Tank Francaise' stainless steel wristwatch, ref. 2302, no.189392BB, with 20-jeweled automatic movement cal. 120 ETA 2000-1, the case inscribed 'Mazal Tov/Graduating with a 1st/Love Mum and Dad', with stainless steel bracelet.

c1980 *1.5in (3.5cm) wide*

$1,200-1,800 **DN**

A 1990s Corum Romulus 18ct gold wristwatch, with quartz movement.

1in (3cm) diam

$2,000-3,000 **KAU**

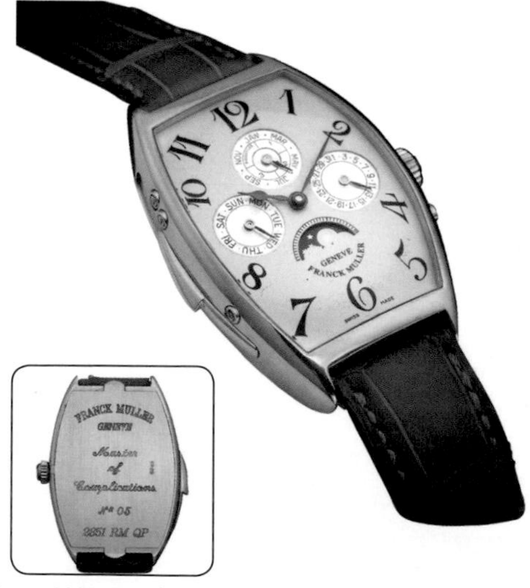

A rare 2000s Franck Muller 18ct gold astronomic, minute-repeating wristwatch, ref. 2851 RM QP, no.05, with 32 jewels, straight-line lever escapement, monometallic balance, swan-neck micrometer regulator, with perpetual calendar and moon phases, with an 18ct gold buckle.

1.25in (3cm) wide

$70,000-90,000 **ATQ**

A Garrard 18ct gold automatic wristwatch, no.'033/130', from a limited edition, with subsidiary seconds, the case back with the Royal coat-of-arms, the strap with a gold fold-over clasp.

$4,000-6,000 **TOV**

An International Watch Company 'Novecento' 18ct gold wristwatch, ref. 2552, no.2572370, movement no.2624754, the 21-jeweled IWC movement cal. 1822, the dial with subsidiary seconds, with black lizardskin strap, with original box.

1987 1.75in (4.5cm) wide

$5,000-7,000 DN

An International Watch Co. 18ct pink-gold wristwatch, ref. 5021, case no.2920080, with 66 jewels, straight-line lever escapement, monometallic balance adjusted to five positions, with secular perpetual calendar, moon phases and seven-day power reserve indicator, with an 18ct pink-gold deployant clasp.

c2004 1.75in (4.5cm) diam

$25,000-30,000 ATQ

A 1990s Jaeger LeCoultre 'Odysseus' 18ct gold astronomic, chronograph wristwatch, ref. 165.7.3., no.0764, with subsidiary date, pulsometer and moon phases, with an 18ct pink- and yellow-gold link bracelet.

1.5in (3.5cm) diam

$7,000-9,000 ATQ

A Jaeger-LeCoultre 18ct pink-gold reversible wristwatch, ref. 250.2.86, no.1989068, with 18 jewels, straight-line lever escapement, monometallic balance adjusted to four positions, with an 18ct pink-gold deployant clasp.

c1996 1in (2.5cm) wide

$7,000-9,000 ATQ

Judith Picks

This Omega watch would be collectable with no provenance, but the added value to an Elvis collector is that it was definitely owned and worn by 'The King'. Charlie Hodge was a member of the Foggy Bottom Boys gospel group and a long-time friend of Elvis Presley. They became close friends when they were drafted into the army. They traveled to Europe together as bunkmates and spent significant time together while stationed in Germany. Hodge worked for Elvis throughout the 1970s, providing back-up vocals and guitar. As detailed in the accompanying letter, Elvis gifted the Omega to Hodge after he repeatedly told Elvis that he admired the piece. Hodge additionally states that he 'lived at Graceland... for 16 years until Elvis' passing'.

An Omega 'Constellation' stainless steel and pink-gold capped chronometer wristwatch, previously owned by Elvis Presley, ref. KO 2943, no.16881537, with 24 jewels, straight-line lever escapement, monometallic balance, the dial with date aperture, with gold-plated buckle, with letter of attestation from Charlie Hodge.

c1960 1.5in (3.5cm) diam

$60,000-80,000 ATQ

A rare Jaeger-LeCoultre 'Master Grand Tradition' 18ct gold wristwatch, ref. 186.0.35.S., case no.2649302, from a limited edition of 300, with 47 jewels, one-minute tourbillon carriage, lateral lever escapement with one-minute tourbillon regulator with polished steel cage and three equidistant arms, with 18ct gold double deployant clasp.

1.5in (4cm) diam

$70,000-90,000 ATQ

A Longines 'Dolce Vita' 18ct gold lady's wristwatch, ref. 1155026, case no.33411432, with subsidiary seconds.

c2009

$1,500-2,500 DOR

An Omega 'Speedmaster' stainless steel chronograph wristwatch, from a limited series of 1357/5957, made for the 50th anniversary of the Omega 'Speedmaster' moon watch, the reverse with Speedmaster monogram and inscribed 'Flight-qualified by NASA for all manned space missions; the first and only watch worn on the moon', with stainless steel bracelet with deployant clasp.

2007 1.75in (4.5cm) wide

$3,000-4,000 TEN

ESSENTIAL REFERENCE - PATEK PHILIPPE

Patek Philippe was founded in 1839 in Geneva, Switzerland and has become famous for its high quality watches.

- **Patek Philippe pioneered the perpetual calendar, split-seconds hand, chronograph, and minute repeater in watches.**
- **Stainless steel Patek Philippe watches are highly sought after, as they are surprisingly rarer than gold examples.**
- **Some of the most expensive and complicated watches were made by Patek Philippe for multimillionaire watch collectors Charles Packard of Warren, Ohio and Henry Graves Jr of New York.**
- **To celebrate its 150th anniversary in 1989, Patek Philippe created one of the most complicated mechanical watches ever made, the 'Calibre 89', which had 39 complications.**
- **The Patek Philippe symbol of an ornate cross was first used on the 'Calatrava' range of 1932.**

A Patek Philippe 'Gondolo Calendario' 18ct pink-gold wristwatch, ref. 5135 R, case no.4378944, no. 3424798, with 34 jewels, straight-line lever escapement, Gyromax balance adjusted to heat, cold, isochronism and 5 positions, with annual calendar, moon phases, 24-hour indication, with 18ct pink-gold buckle.

2006 *1.5in (4cm) wide*

$35,000-45,000 **ATQ**

A rare Patek Philippe 18ct gold astronomic, minute-repeating wristwatch, ref. 5016, case no.2972553, no. 1905060, with 28 jewels, one-minute tourbillon regulator, Gyromax balance adjusted to heat, cold, isochronism and five positions, with retrograde perpetual calendar, moon phases, with custom gray dial, with gold buckle.

Reference 5016 is one of the most complicated wristwatches ever produced by Patek Philippe. Custom-ordered dials were available to only the most important clients, resulting in very few unique examples.

2001 *1.25in (3.5cm) diam*

$550,000-650,000 **ATQ**

A Piaget gold wristwatch, with manual movement, with square-form engine-turned decoration, the associated integrated gold band with French control marks.

$2,000-3,000 **WW**

A Patek Philippe 18ct wristwatch, case no.686640-2526, movement no.61554, with 30 jewels, 18ct gold rotor, adjusted to heat, cold, isochroism and five positions, with subsidiary seconds, with detachable, adjustable 18ct bracelet.

1.5in (4cm) diam

$30,000-40,000 **DRA**

A Patek Philippe 'Gondolo' 18ct gold wristwatch, ref. 5014, no.4170967, movement no.1880970, with subsidiary seconds, the 18-jeweled movement cal. 215 adjusted to heat and cold isochronism and five positions, with a black crocodile strap.

c1990 *1.5in (3.5cm) wide*

$15,000-20,000 **DN**

A rare Patek Philippe 18ct gold astronomic, minute-repeating wristwatch, ref. 3974, case no.1906057, with 39 jewels, straight-line lever escapement, Gyromax balance adjusted to heat, cold isochronism and five positions, with perpetual calendar, leap year indication and moon phases, with an 18ct gold buckle.

To celebrate its 150th anniversary in 1989, Patek Philippe launched its first production minute-repeating perpetual calendar wristwatch, ref no.3974. According to early 1990s Patek Philippe publications, each watch required four years of development and assembly and includes 467 parts.

1992 *1.5in (3.5cm) diam*

$400,000-500,000 **ATQ**

A Piaget 18ct gold and diamond lady's watch, with 17 jewels and unadjusted movement, with replaced tiger's eye dial.

Strap 6.5in (16.5cm) long

$3,500-4,500 **DRA**

A rare Piaget diamond-set 18ct white-gold bracelet watch, ref. 4154, case no.91322, no.9503895, with 18 jewels, straight-line lever escapement, monometallic balance adjusted to five positions and temperatures, the dial, case and bracelet channel-set with 498 baguette-cut diamonds.

c2002 *1in (2.5cm) wide*

$15,000-20,000 **ATQ**

A rare Rolex 'Padellone' Perpetual stainless steel chronometer wristwatch, ref. 8171, with 22 jewels, straight-line lever escapement, with triple date and moon phases, with stainless steel buckle.

Rolex has only ever produced two models of moon phase watches. These are reference 8171, which features a snap on back and which was only produced in very small numbers in the late 1940s and early 1950s, and reference 6062, which features an Oyster screw-down back.

c1950 *1.5in (4cm) diam*

$65,000-75,000 ATQ

A rare Rolex 'Submariner' Oyster Perpetual stainless steel automatic wristwatch, ref. 5508, case no.??1298, with 26-jeweled lever-movement cal. 1520, with luminous hands, with associated stainless steel bracelet and another bracelet.

Sean Connery wore a Rolex 'Submariner' in the first Bond films. Roger Moore also wore a 'Submariner' and the early models, including ref. 5008 (shown here), are now so closely associated with the films that they are known as 'James Bond watches'.

1958 *1.5in (4cm) wide*

$8,000-12,000 TEN

A rare Rolex 'Submariner' Oyster Perpetual stainless steel automatic wristwatch, ref. 5513, with 26-jeweled self-winding lever-movement cal. 1520, with luminous hands, with associated stainless steel bracelet.

Reference 5513 was introduced in 1962 and is one of the most collectable 'Submariners' on the market today.

1968 *1.75in (4.5cm) wide*

$5,500-6,500 TEN

A Rolex Oyster Perpetual 18ct gold and stainless steel automatic lady's wristwatch.

1in (3cm) diam

$2,000-3,000 KAU

A Rolex 'Cosmograph Daytona' 18ct gold chronograph wristwatch, ref. 16528, no.5158753, movement no.75943, the 31-jeweled movement cal. 4030 adjusted to five positions and temperature, with a gold block-link bracelet with fold-over clasp.

c1993 *2.5in (4cm) diam*

$12,000-18,000 DN

A rare Tornek-Rayville 'TR-900 'stainless steel dive watch, made for the US Navy, the bi-directional revolving black bezel with luminous unit indication, the screw-back engraved with military markings

This watch was used on patrol in Vietnam 1967-68.

c1965

$40,000-60,000 SK

A Universal 'Aero-Compax' stainless steel chronograph wristwatch, no.'882.424', with mechanical lever movement, with subsidiary seconds, 30-minute and 12-hour registers, with leather strap and steel deployant clasp.

c2000 *1.5in (4cm) diam*

$1,200-1,800 TEN

A Vacheron Constantin 'Malte' 18ct white-gold dual time regulator automatic wristwatch, ref. 42005, case no.729245, movement no.909799, with 31-jeweled nickel-finished lever-movement cal. 1206, with 18ct yellow-gold finished rotor, with brown custom-made alligator strap with Vacheron Constantin 18ct white-gold buckle.

$12,000-18,000 LHA

CLOSER LOOK

The decorative 'hood' superstructure, which incorporates ebonized spiral-twist columns and brass finials, emulates the design of late 17thC tallcase clocks.

The hood is similar to those shown in John Patrick's advertisement of c1710 (reproduced in Nicholas Goodison's 'English Barometers 1680-1860').

The silvered break-arch scale and cistern cover are both later. The bulb-cistern tube has been replaced.

John Patrick (1654-1730) was the first English instrument maker to specialize in barometers and is credited with the invention of portable barometers. He sometimes mounted mirrors in the same frame as his angle barometers to balance the design and help people decide what clothes to wear depending on the weather.

Edwin Banfield suggests in 'Barometers Stick or Cistern Tube' that the use of fretwork in a barometer case indicates a date prior to 1700.

A William & Mary and later olivewood cistern-tube stick barometer, in the manner of John Patrick, London, with arched pediment, fretwork, cross-grain veneers and ebonized edges, with restoration and replacements.

c1695 and later *47in (120cm) high*

$2,500-3,500 **DN**

A rare Queen Anne walnut cistern-tube stick barometer, in the manner of John Patrick, London, with Royal Society scale thermometer, with some restoration, with replaced thermometer scale.

The Royal Society scale thermometer was devised by Robert Hooke in 1664. Unlike previous liquid thermometers, Hooke's invention used a fixed point (in this case, the freezing point of water) to zero the scale. His other innovation was to represent every degree by an equal increment of volume: about 1/500th of the volume of the thermometer liquid per degree. By scaling it in this way, Hooke showed that a standard scale could be established for all sizes of thermometer. Hooke's original thermometer became known as the standard of Gresham College and was used by the Royal Society until 1709.

c1710 *41in (105cm) high*

$5,000-7,000 **DN**

A George III mahogany stick barometer, signed 'Shuttleworth, London', the brass register with vernier scale, with visible mercury tube and turned circular cistern.

35in (90cm) high

$2,000-3,000 **TOV**

ESSENTIAL REFERENCE - JESSE RAMSDEN

Jesse Ramsden (1731-1800) is arguably the greatest scientific instrument maker of all time. He was also an inventor and wrote various booklets on scientific instruments.

- **After serving an apprenticeship with a cloth-worker, he apprenticed himself to a mathematical instrument maker in 1758.**
- **He set up his own business in Haymarket, St James's, London in 1768, and moved to 199 Piccadilly in 1772.**
- **Ramsden specialized in dividing engines (devices used to mark graduations on measuring instruments). He also made highly accurate sextants, theodolites and vertical circles for astronomical observatories, as well as other instruments, including barometers.**
- **He was elected to the Royal Society in 1786.**

A George III mahogany bowfront stick barometer, signed 'Ramsden, London', with concealed tube and single vernier silvered register.

39in (98cm) high

$12,000-18,000 **TEN**

A George III mahogany bowfront stick barometer, by Dollond, London, with a silvered register over a hygrometer, thermometer and an ebonized urn-shaped cistern cover.

37.5in (98cm) high

$5,500-6,500 **SWO**

A George III mahogany stick barometer, by Miller, Edinburgh, with hygrometer above thermometer and barometer.

39in (99cm) high

$5,000-6,000 **L&T**

A Regency mahogany bowfront cistern-tube stick barometer, by Barrauds, London, with ebony line-inset edges, with glazed rectangular silvered vernier register and mercury Fahrenheit thermometer, with ivory vernier adjustment disc and ebonized urn-shaped cistern cover.

Paul Philip Barraud is recorded as working 1796-1820. In partnership with W Howells and G Jamison, he was charged with making Thomas Mudge's marine timekeepers. Barraud's firm was continued by his sons and became Barraud and Lund in 1839.

39in (99cm) high

$5,500-6,500 DN

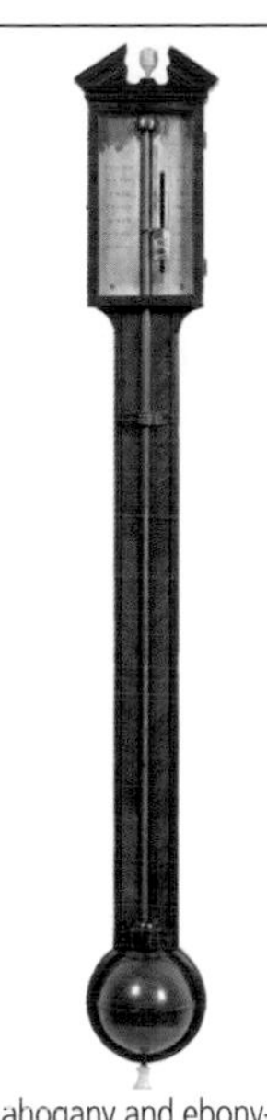

A mahogany and ebony-strung stick barometer, signed 'H Davis, London', with break-arch pediment, hinged door, exposed mercury tube, silvered single vernier, with turned cistern cover.

c1810 39in (99cm) high

$2,000-3,000 TEN

ESSENTIAL REFERENCE - SYMPIESOMETER

- **The sympiesometer was invented by Alexander Adie of Edinburgh in 1818 as an alternative to the standard marine barometer.**
- **It works by measuring the movement of colored almond oil and hydrogen in a syphon tube. An increase in air pressure causes the oil to be pushed out of the lower reservoir and into the tube, compressing the hydrogen gas into the upper reservoir. The air pressure is therefore indicated by the position of the top of the oil.**
- **Hydrogen expands and contracts with variations in temperature. This means that, before atmospheric pressure can be ascertained, the sliding pressure scale of the sympiesometer needs to be adjusted based on readings from the thermometer.**
- **Sympiesometers are less susceptible to the motion of a ship than mercury barometers and can be easily calibrated for variances in temperature.**

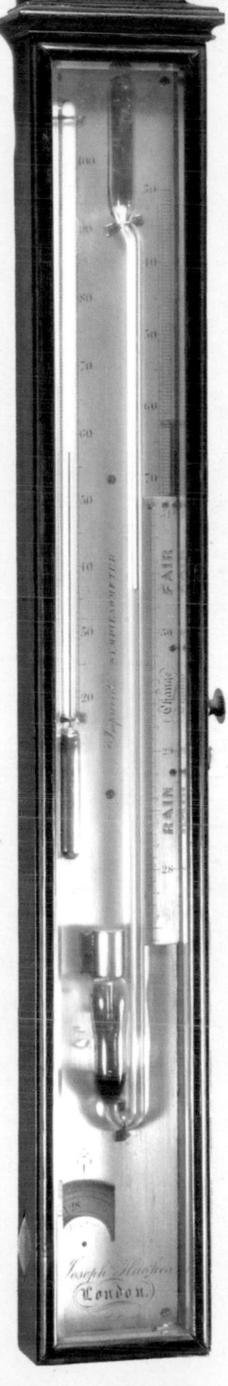

An early Victorian rosewood sympiesometer, by Joseph Hughes, London, with oil and hydrogen gas-filled syphon tube against a Fahrenheit thermometer, with Fahrenheit scale mercury thermometer.

Joseph Hughes is recorded as working from various addresses in London 1822-78.

23in (59cm) high

$5,000-7,000 DN

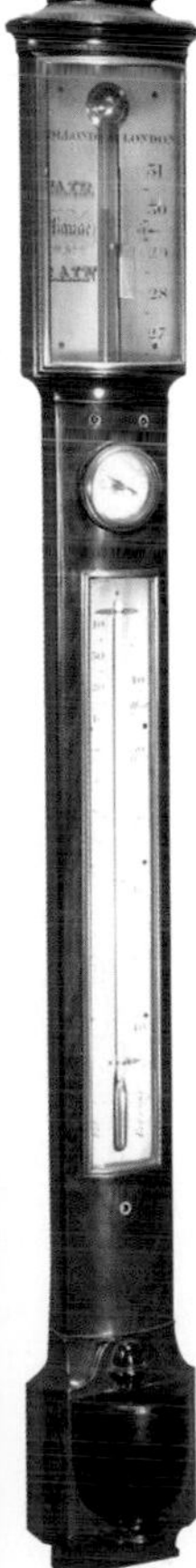

An early 19thC George III mahogany bowfront cistern-tube stick barometer, by Dollond, London.

Peter Dollond (1730-1820) began working as an optician in 1750 and became renowned for producing high-quality instruments. For more information see 'Miller's Antiques Handbook & Price Guide 2012-2013' p.303.

40in (101cm) high

$12,000-18,000 DN

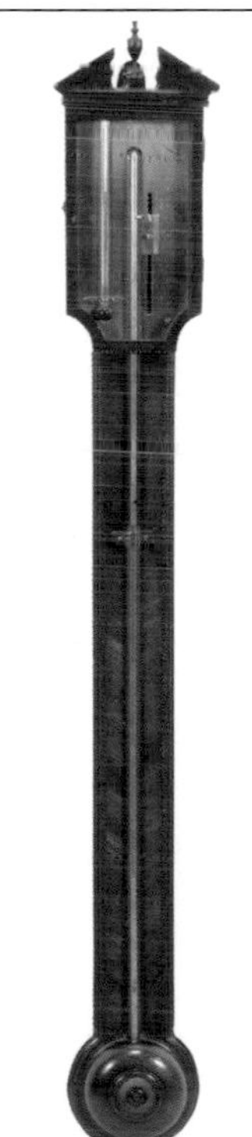

A George III parquetry-strung mahogany bulb cistern-tube stick barometer, signed 'Keate'.

c1810 38in (97cm) high

$1,500-2,500 DN

A Regency rosewood stick barometer, by D McGregor & Co, with ivory dial above a thermometer and brass reservoir.

36in (91cm) high

$2,500-3,500 GORL

An early Victorian rosewood and mother-of-pearl-inlaid bowfront ship's stick barometer, by Stebbing and Co., Southampton, with two-piece ivory vernier register and glazed Fahrenheit thermometer, with brass cylindrical cistern, missing bracket.

37.5in (94cm) high

$3,000-4,000 **DN**

A Victorian oak Admiral Fitzroy Storm barometer, signed 'Negretti & Zambra instrument makers to her Majesty, 1 Hatton Gardens E.C, 122 Regent St.W, & 59 Cornhill, EC, Patent No.444', with vernier scale and thermometer.

The firm of Negretti and Zambra traded from 11 Hatton Gardens, London, 1850-59.

41.25in (105cm) high

$1,200-1,800 **WW**

A Regency mahogany cistern-tube ship's stick barometer, by Joseph Cetti & Co., London, with door enclosing silvered vernier register, the inside door with applied Centigrade thermometer, with part-ebonized cistern cover, missing bracket.

Joseph Cetti & Co. are recorded as working from 25 Redlion Street, Holborn, London 1816-39.

c1820 *39in (99cm) high*

$4,500-5,500 **DN**

A gilt-metal ship's barometer, signed 'Dolland, London, by Appointment to the Queen', with concealed mercury tube, double vernier scale, thermometer tube and turned cistern, missing brackets.

c1870 *38in (96cm) high*

$700-1,000 **TEN**

A rare William IV mahogany cistern-tube angle barometer, in the manner of John Whitehurst of Derby, with angled silvered glazed scale signed 'Birchall' and dated, the trunk with figured veneers, kingwood-crossbanding and cockbeading.

An 'M Birchall' is recorded as working in Derby c1770-90. This barometer may have been made by him, or by a member of the Whitehurst family before being signed and retailed by Birchall.

1835 *37in (93cm) high*

$15,000-20,000 **DN**

A rare early 19thC George III mahogany dial barometer, signed 'Spear 23 Capel St. DUBLIN', with ivory vase-finial to the swan neck pediment above a 7in (17.5cm) silvered register, with Fahrenheit thermometer.

Richard Spear is recorded as working from 23 Capel Street, Dublin 1793-1809.

40in (101cm) high

$15,000-20,000 **DN**

Double-tube

A rare George III inlaid mahogany double tube/contra-barometer, by Balthazar Knie, Edinburgh, with parquetry-inlaid chevron frieze above silvered scale inscribed 'MADE BY MR. KNIE, 1800'.

The development of the double-tube barometer is generally attributed to Robert Hooke (1635-1703), who demonstrated a related instrument to the Royal Society in 1668. In a contra-barometer, a narrow tube of oil is attached to the syphon end of a double-bulbed tube of mercury. The oil-filled tube 'magnifies' the movements of the barometer and thus allows for the taking of more precise readings. Double-tube barometers are also called 'contra'-barometers as the mercury level decreases in height with an increase in air pressure.

1800 *45in (114cm) high*

$12,000-18,000 **DN**

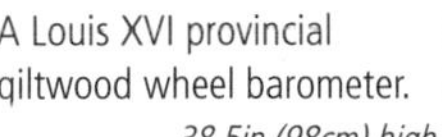

A Louis XVI provincial giltwood wheel barometer.

38.5in (98cm) high

$300-400 LC

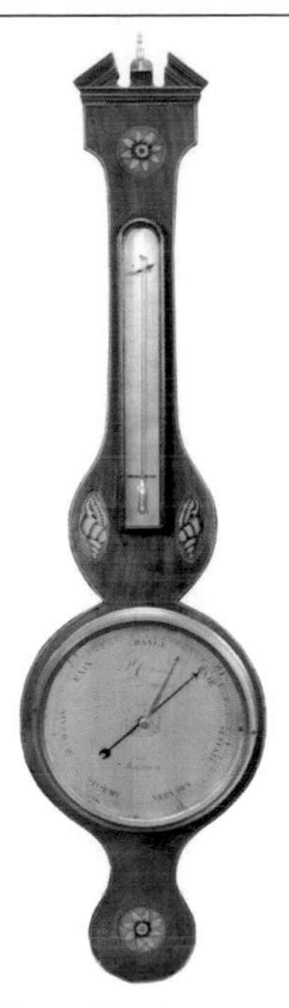

A George III mahogany and marquetry aneroid wheel barometer, the paper register signed 'P Caminada'.

c1800 39in (100cm) high

$600-800 DN

An early 19thC mahogany wheel barometer, by Zanfrini & Gugeri, Blandford, with a hygrometer, thermometer, dial and engraved level.

42.5in (108cm) high

$1,500-2,500 SWO

An early 19thC mahogany wheel barometer, by Zebroni & Co., Halton Street, Edinburgh

39in (99cm) high

$1,000-1,500 A&G

A rare rosewood wheel barometer, by Dan Robinson, Bradford, with 6in (15cm) register, hygrometer, thermometer and spirit level silvered dial.

28.5in (98cm) high

$1,500-2,500 TEN

A rare late George III satinwood wheel barometer, by Vecchio, Nottingham, with 10in (25.5cm) silvered register, Fahrenheit thermometer, hygrometer and spirit level, with line-inlaid borders.

42in (107cm) high

$1,000-1,500 DN

A Regency mahogany wheel barometer, by John Somalvico, London, with 10in (25.5cm) silvered register, Fahrenheit thermometer, hygrometer and spirit level, with ebony- and box-stringing.

Several makers named J Somalvico are recorded as working in Hatton Gardens, London in the early 19thC.

44in (112cm) high

$1,000-1,500 DN

A late 19thC carved walnut wheel barometer, by Negretti & Zambra, London, with 10 in (25cm) silvered register and Fahrenheit and Centigrade thermometer, with pediment centered balustrade and with panel fronted drop-section.

44in (113cm) high

$2,500-3,500 DN

A late 19thC mahogany and ormolu-mounted barometer, with a painted pottery dial and ivory thermometer.

37.5in (97cm) high

$1,500-2,500 SWO

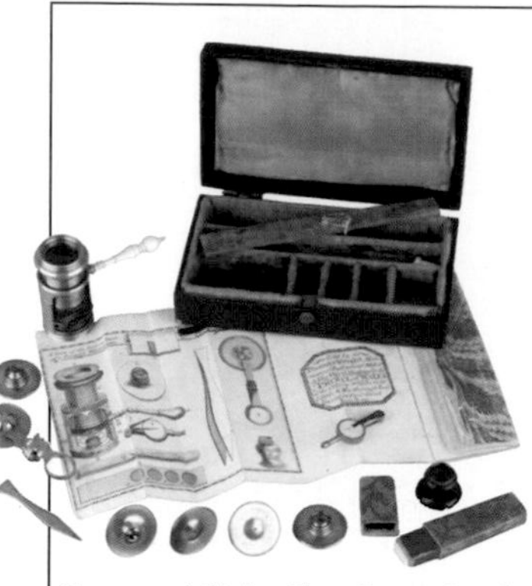

A rare George II brass screw-barrel portable microscope, attributed to Thomas Wright, London, with objective lens opposing threaded insert fitted with a condensing lens, with ivory handle, with accessories and spare objectives, in fishskin-covered box, with original printed instruction booklet.

Thomas Wright senior is recorded as working from The Orrery and Globe, Fleet Street, London 1718-47. He received a Royal appointment to George II in 1727. The screw-barrel microscope was invented at the end of the 17thC by Dutchman Nicolaas Hartsoeker (1654-1725) and was introduced to England by James Wilson.

Box 6in (15.5cm) wide

$8,000-12,000 **DN**

An early George III Culpeper-type microscope, with lignum vitae top section above green vellum and rayskin, with a central oculus and slots for mounting accessories, the mahogany base with pivoted mirror and drawer containing four objectives, with original oak box, missing some accessories.

$20,000-30,000 **DN**

An early 19thC lacquered-brass and mahogany chest microscope, by John Snart, London, with rack and pinion focus, plano-concave mirror and accessories including five objectives, tweezers, eighteen mineral and biological specimen slides and ivory-cased mica apertures.

14.5in (37cm) high

$7,000-10,000 **WAD**

An early 19thC ivory and brass pocket botanical microscope, with threaded aperture for two eye-pieces, steel and ivory pincer, in red morocco-covered case.

This type of microscope was introduced in 1798 by W & S Cary and remained popular for much of the 19thC.

6in (15cm) long

$1,500-2,500 **CM**

A lacquered-brass portable aquatic microscope, by Robert Banks, London, rack and pinion focus with ivory slip insert and tool post holes to rim, with pivoted mirror beneath, attached to original mahogany box containing some accessories.

Robert Ban(c)ks Junior is recorded as succeeding his brother Anthony Oldiss Bancks in c1796. He received an appointment to George IV in 1820 and then another to William IV in 1830. The design of this microscope is probably derived from a model developed by John Ellis in c1752. The main difference being that this design focuses by up/down movement of the stage rather than the lens.

c1820 *4in (10.5cm) high*

$2,500-3,500 **DN**

A lacquered-brass 'achromatic engioscope' (botanical microscope), signed 'Andrew Pritchard, 162 Fleet St. London', with hinged candle socket with bull's-eye lens, yew arm rest, and rack and pinion focus, in walnut case with five drawers of accessories including two sides of original manuscript instructions and a magnification rate card, both in Pritchard's handwriting, with a copy of Pritchard's 'History of Infusoria'.

c1840 *Box 12in (30.5cm) high*

$22,000-28,000 **CM**

A large brass binocular compound microscope, signed 'Baker, 244 High Holborn, London', in a mahogany box, with accessories including large and small stage forceps, objectives and eyepieces, light condensers and prism polariser.

c1870. *Box 15in (39cm) high*

$1,500-2,500 **WW**

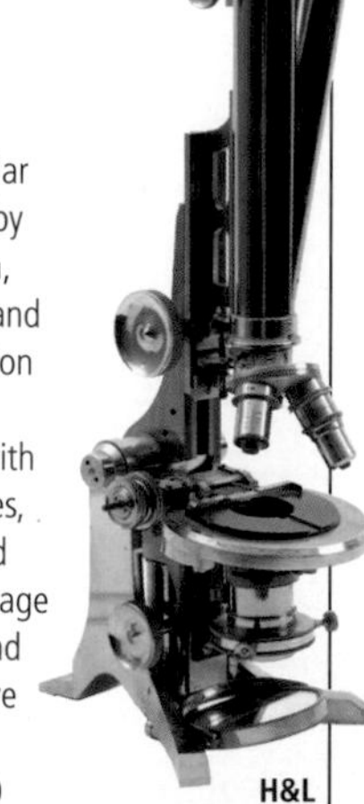

A lacquered brass binocular microscope, by Ross, London, with course and rack and pinion focus, triple nose piece with two objectives, with rack and pinion sub-stage condenser and plano concave mirror.

$3,000-4,000 **H&L**

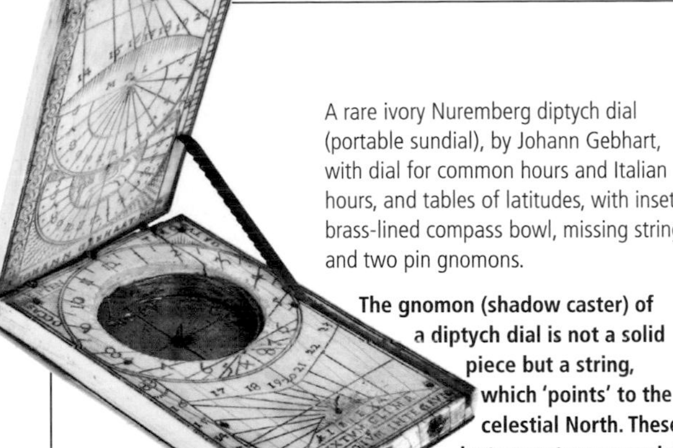

A rare ivory Nuremberg diptych dial (portable sundial), by Johann Gebhart, with dial for common hours and Italian hours, and tables of latitudes, with inset brass-lined compass bowl, missing string and two pin gnomons.

The gnomon (shadow caster) of a diptych dial is not a solid piece but a string, which 'points' to the celestial North. These instruments were mainly produced in Nuremberg from the late 15thC, usually in ivory.

1500 *3in (9.5cm) long*

$12,000-18,000 CM

A horizontal brass sundial, by Johann Engelbrecht, with hinged gnomon and plummet for latitudes from 30 65 degrees, signed 'Fecit Ioan Engelbrecht Beraunae in Bohem', with wood base.

c1780 *4.5in (11cm) high*

$2,500-3,500 DOR

A probably late 18thC silver Butterfield-type compass/sundial, signed 'Macquart Paris', the horizontal plate engraved with hour scales, the folding gnomon with a bird support, the reverse engraved with latitudes of cities, with leather case.

2.5in (6.5cm) long

$2,500-3,500 ROS

ESSENTIAL REFERENCE - DOUBLE HORIZONAL DIALS

Double horizontal dials (also named Oughtred-types after their inventor William Oughtred) have two scales. The hour can read using the angled side of the gnomon while the vertical supporting edge shows the lines of solar declination, the ecliptic and the right ascension of the sun.

- **As well as the time, double horizontal dials could therefore demonstrate the motion of the sun throughout the day and year, the altitude of the sun and its azimuth and the position of the sun on the ecliptic.**
- **They were most popular in the mid-late 17thC. Very few were made after 1700.**
- **Double horizontal dials are mentioned twice in Samuel Pepys's diary. On 3rd June, 1663: 'Up betimes, and studying my double diall... Dean Honiwood comes to me, who dotes mightily upon it and I think I must give it him.' And on the following day, 4th June: 'Home by water, where by and by comes Dean Honiwood, and I showed him my double horizontal diall, and promise to give him one, and that shall be it.'**

A 17thC 'double horizontal' brass sundial, by Elias Allen, later signed 'Jon. Seller excut Londini', the plate engraved with solar declination and hours.

Elias Allen (c1588-1653) was renowned in his day. He was Master of the Clockmakers Guild 1637-38 and had a close relationship with contemporary mathematicians, including William Oughtred. John Seller (1632-97) was a leading mathematical practitioner and mapmaker who enjoyed the Royal patronage one year and was jailed in Newgate the next. It seems likely that Seller acquired the remaining stock of Allen's workshop on Allen's death and passed a few instruments off as his own work.

c1640 *8in (20cm) diam*

$15,000-20,000 CM

A 19thC French noon-day cannon dial, signed 'Lusardi, Opticien à Valenciennes', with nickel-plated brass fittings including calibrated arcs supporting burning lens assembly and cannon on location slide, on marble base.

10in (25.5cm) diam

$5,000-7,000 CM

An Edwardian silver hunting-cased pocket compass/sundial, by Negretti & Zambra, London, the maker's mark erased, with a hinged hour ring for 'North Lats' and 'South Lats', the silver case engraved with 'Equation' and a table below, with leather Garrard & Co. case.

1908 *2in (5cm) diam*

$4,500-5,500 DN

Judith Picks

These good early globes are by a controversial maker. Louis Charles Desnos (1725-1805) was an important 18thC instrument maker, cartographer and globe maker based in Paris, France. Desnos was the Royal Globemaker to the King of Denmark, Christian VII. As a publisher, Desnos is often associated with Zannoni and Louis Brion de la Tour (1756-1823). Despite, or perhaps because of, the sheer quantity of maps Desnos published, he acquired a poor reputation among serious cartographic experts, who considered him undiscerning and unscrupulous regarding what he published. Desnos consequently had a long history of legal battles with other Parisian cartographers and publishers of the period. It is said that he published everything set before him without regard to accuracy,

A pair of terrestrial and a celestial globes, by Louis Charles Desnos, Paris, each with twelve hand-colored copper-plate gores, both with the coat-of-arms of Abel François Poisson de Vandières and inscriptions, the horizontal rings with copperplate overlays showing the signs of the zodiac, etc, on turned and ebonized wood supports, the terrestrial globe with damage.

1768 , 1770

$70,000-90,000 **DOR**

A Louis XVI celestial globe, by Jean Fortin, Paris, with twelve gores, with meridian and horizon rings and four quadrant supports, missing stand.

1780 *Globe 8in (20cm) diam*

$3,000-4,000 **FRE**

A pair of Regency terrestrial and a celestial table globes, by J & W Cary, the terrestrial with twelve hand-colored gores with an analemma, numerous explorers' tracks, notes and dates, and trade winds in the Indian Ocean, the celestial with twelve split half-gores, on original stands, with colored meridian rings.

1816 *18in (45.5cm) high*

$15,000-20,000 **CM**

A pair of American terrestrial and celestial table globes, by Wilson's & Co., Albany, NY, on a stands with turned supports and ball feet, with crack to celestial and wear to terrestrial surface.

c1845 *5.15in (13cm) high*

$6,500-7,500 **SK**

A terrestrial library globe, by D Reimer & H Kiepert, with twice 24 gores on a metal sphere, the ebonized wood stand with tripod and octagonal horizon, with damage.

Heinrich Kiepert (1818-99) is arguably one of the most important scholarly cartographers of the mid-late 19thC. Among many achievements, he created some of the first detailed ethnic maps of Germany, Austria-Hungary and the Balkan Peninsula. Kiepert maintained a long association with the publisher Dietrich Reimer.

c1900 *31in (80cm) diam*

$25,000-30,000 **DOR**

A terrestrial globe, by Ludwig Jul. Heymann, with twelve lithographed gores on a cardboard sphere, with inscription 'ERD-Globus / 10 Cent. / N. d. neuesten Quellen entw. / Berlin. / Ludw. Jul. Heymann.', supported by a cast-metal figure of Hercules, on turned wood stand.

c1900 *4in (10cm) diam*

$1,500-2,500 **DOR**

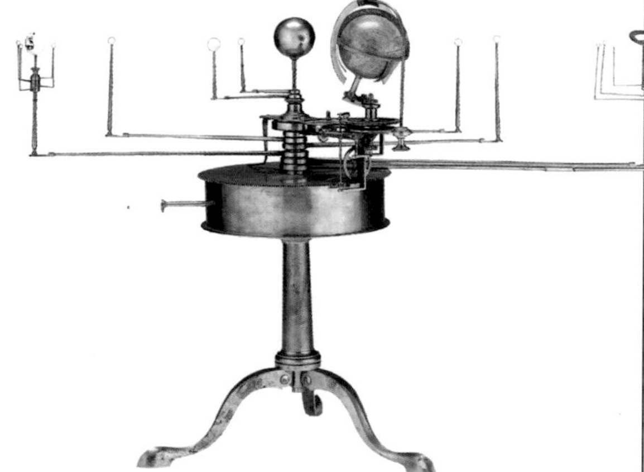

A rare Regency grand orrery, signed 'Harris & Co.', with a fixed brass sun and articulated mechanical brass armatures, the Earth represented by a 3in (7.5cm) globe labeled 'Lane's Improved Globe, 1818', the other planets represented by ivory spheres, the case engraved with month, date and Zodiac rings and inscribed 'Harris & Co. 50 Holborn London'.

c1820 *33in (84cm) long*

$50,000-60,000 **FRE**

An embossed leather, cardboard and paper revolving celestial map, by A Klippel, published by Lehrmittel-Anstalt A Klodt, on turned wood stand.

c1910 *18in (46cm) high*

$1,200-1,800 DOR

An early 19thC compass, inscribed 'Abraham, Bath', in mahogany case.

Abraham was instrument maker to the Duke of Gloucester and the Duke of Wellington.

Case 3.75in (9.5cm) wide

$700-1,000 GHOU

A probably early 20thC Islamic brass astrolabe, engraved with decoration and approximate calibre, with four double-sided plates.

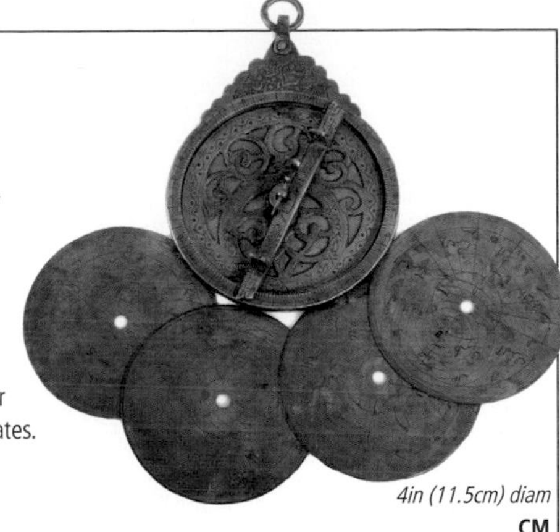

4in (11.5cm) diam

$1,200-1,800 CM

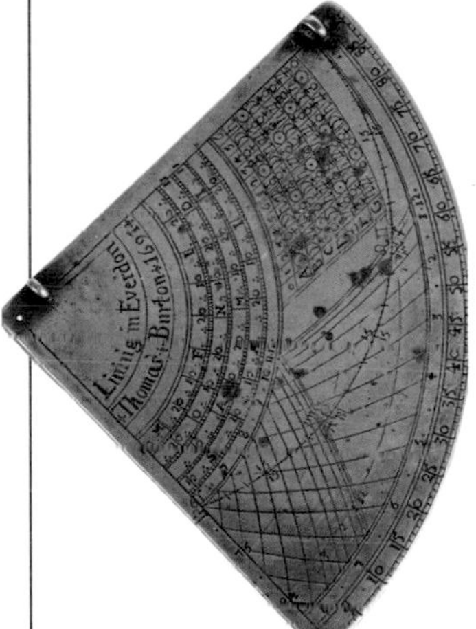

A late 17thC Gunter-type quadrant, by John Checkley, the obverse inscribed 'Living in Everdon / *Thomas * Burton * 1691 *', with degree and declination scales, table of trigonometrical scales and solid sights, the reverse with a calendar scale and perpetual calendar.

1691 *4in (12cm) diam*

$8,000-12,000 CM

A Victorian table top achromatic stereoscope, by Smith, Beck & Beck, no.231, the walnut cabinet base with pigeon holes for slides, with original instruction manual and approximately 260 card mounted slides and ten glass slides by various makers, with lift-off boxed cover.

1862 *18.25in (33cm) high*

$12,000-18,000 DA&H

A late Victorian floor-standing stereoscopic viewer, signed 'J Lizars, 101 & 107 Buchanan Street, Glasgow', with revolving mechanism for stereoscope cards, the walnut case with drawer, with slides of the Boer War by Underwood & Underwood.

49in (125cm) high

$2,500-3,500 L&T

A black-lacquered brass 'Dr. Brewsters Patent Kaleidoscope', by P Carpenter, Birmingham, the eyepiece signed 'P. CARPENTER, SOLE MAKER', the opposing end inscribed 'DR. BREWSTER'S PATENT KALEIDOSCOPE', in original mahogany and ebony-strung box with ten loose object-filled filters and other accessories.

Philip Carpenter is recorded as working from various addresses in Birmingham 1808-33. He was the sole maker of 'Dr. Brewster's Patent Kaleidoscope', which was invented by Scottish scientist Sir David Brewster in 1817.

c1825 *Kaleidoscope closed 6.25in (16cm) long*

$8,000-12,000 DN

A lacquered brass-kaleidoscope, on rectangular mahogany base.

c1860 *9in (22cm) high*

$1,200-1,800 DOR

A 19thC field-surgeon's set, by Downs Bros., comprising twelve steel tools with ebony handles, in a mahogany case.

Case 13.5in (34cm) wide

$1,000-1,500 GORL

A rare probably Dutch phaenophthalmotrope, with a pair of carved fruitwood model eyes in lacquered-brass gimbal-mounts on tapered columns.

The phaenophthalmotrope was invented by the Dutch ophthalmologist Franciscus Donders (1818-89), who was a specialist in eye diseases. It was designed to show the movements of the eye to students and is a 'junior' version of the more sophisticated ophthalmotrope.

c1870-1900 *8in (20cm) high*

$4,000-6,000 **CM**

A lead-filled brass heliostat, signed 'R. Fuess, Berlin', the clockwork-driven equatorial mount with semi-circular scale and adjustable stage for the planar beveled mirror.

A heliostat is a mirrored device that turns (compensating for the sun's movement in the sky), thus keeping sunlight reflected toward a predetermined target.

11in (28cm) high

$5,500-6,500 **SK**

A 1920s brass sunshine recorder, by Casella, London, no.1670, with spherical burning-lens support and curved brass holder for recording papers, on a wood base, with around 40 blank papers.

11in (28cm) high

$1,200-1,800 **CM**

A mahogany-cased barograph, by Short & Mason, no.3115, with an eight-tier vacuum and a cylinder-platform escapement, with a chart drawer.

15in (38cm) high

$1,500-2,500 **WW**

A rare Austrian brass and iron tachymetric measuring instrument for river-bed surveying, signed 'Ganser & Co Wien No. 51297', with adjustable wood plane table, with original case (not shown).

Case 24in (62cm) wide

$3,500-4,500 **DOR**

A rare 17thC German gilt-brass measuring instrument, signed 'Thomas Pregell Fecit in Zwickau A 1629', probably for use with artillery, the half-circle with scales from 18-0 and 0-18, the ruler with scales from 0-100, with losses.

Thomas Pregell or Prögel (b.1592) is known to have worked in Nuremberg in 1617 and in Zwickau in 1629.

28in (72cm) long

$30,000-40,000 **DOR**

A possibly unique complete drawing-instrument magazine, by George Adams II, London, the inner lid with hinged recess containing three lacquered-brass scale rules, two signed, the upper tray with brass and steel instruments, the lower tray with a signed Haywood-type 'L' square, a set of 24 unused watercolor cakes by Reeves and a porcelain mixing tray, in a mahogany case with satinwood banding, in unused condition.

George Adams II was the scientific instrument maker to George III.

c1783 *12in (32cm) wide*

$30,000-40,000 **CM**

An early 20thC 'Diera' mechanical calculator, by Adix, with original case.

After 1906 *10in (26cm) wide*

$3,000-4,000 **DOR**

A set of helmholtz-pattern resonators, comprising fourteen spun and lacquered-brass spheres with raised nipples, inscribed with numbers from 150 to 800, on display base.

Largest 9in (23cm) diam

$3,000-4,000 **CM**

Mounted chronometer

An adapted 30-hour pocket chronometer mounted as a mantel clock, signed 'JOHN ARNOLD / LONDON', no.92, the 2in (5cm) dial with subsidiary seconds, with engraved balance cock with O Z balance, with damage.

Originally conceived as a pocket chronometer, this watch was adapted early in its life, possibly by John Roger Arnold, and placed in a marine case with gimbal mounts. This, in turn, has been cut down and turned into a mantel clock.

c1785 *5in (12.5cm) wide*

$8,000-12,000 CM

A Victorian two-day marine chronometer, by Richard Hornby, Liverpool, the four-pillar full-plate movement with Harrison's maintaining power and Earnshaw-type spring detent escapement, with subsidiary seconds and power reserve dials, in a brass-bound mahogany case.

Richard Hornby is recorded as working in Liverpool 1814-51.

c1840 *6in (14.5cm) wide*

$5,000-7,000 DN

A Victorian two-day marine chronometer, signed 'Thomas Porthouse, maker to the Admiralty, 10 Northampton Square, London', the movement with Harrison's maintaining power and Earnshaw's spring detent escapement, with subsidiary seconds and power reserve dials, in a brass-bound mahogany case.

c1850 *6in (15.5cm) high*

$5,000-6,000 TEN

A two-day marine chronometer, signed 'Bliss & Creighton, New York', no. 1897, the chain fusee split plate movement with spring detent escapement, with 56-hour up-down indicator, with subsidiary seconds, in brass-bound mahogany case, with an outer padded mahogany box.

Inner case c1850 *7.75in (20cm) high*

$3,500-4,500 SK

A rare Victorian two-day marine chronometer, signed 'W.Shepherd Liverpool', the movement with a Hartnup balance and Earshaw's spring detent escapement, with subsidiary seconds and power reserve dials, in brass-bound mahogany case with vacant ivory and brass cartouche, with key.

Case 7.5in (19.5cm) high

$20,000-30,000 A&G

A two-day marine chronometer, retailed by 'S Bright & Co, Buxton', no.453, the movement with Harrison's maintaining power and Earnshaw's spring detent escapement, with subsidiary seconds and power reserve dials and later minute hand, in a brass-bound rosewood case.

This chronometer was sold with a photocopy of a chronometer ratings certificate dated 2008 and the service sales invoice.

c1880 *7in (19cm) high*

$1,500-2,000 TEN

A rare 4-orbit two-day marine chronometer, signed 'Hamilton, Lancaster, P.A., U.S.A.', no.221, the 14-jewel movement Earnshaw-type escapement with uncut stainless steel balance, Invar cross-arm and Elinvar helical balance spring, with subsidiary seconds, weeks, days and power dials, in brass-bound mahogany case, with key.

1944 *7in (19cm) wide*

$12,000-18,000 CM

A 17in (43cm) mahogany octant, signed 'Benjamin Cole 136 Fleet St. London / Iann Crick 1759', with vernier scale, with pinhole sights, interchangeable shades and inset note plate behind.

Benjamin Cole II (1737-1813) was apprenticed to his father, also Benjamin. A Cole quadrant typically cost between 18s and 25s.

19in (50cm) high

$5,000-6,000 CM

An 18in (45.5cm) mahogany and boxwood octant, by Benjamin Martin, London, the mahogany index arm with ivory-edged fiducial scale with clamp, with two pin hole sights, three interchangeable shades, mirrors and wooden rests behind, with original fitted case, inscribed 'William : Guy : Heath : 1765'.

As Martin had long since stopped making this pattern by 1765 (the vernier scale was commonly fitted by then), it is plausible that this octant was bought second hand for Heath while he was a young midshipman. This would explain the childish, over-sized inscription on the lid. Benjamin Martin (1714-82) spent most of his life working in Crane Court off Fleet Street, London. He specialized in Hadley's quadrants (or octants, as they are known). He apprenticed and employed some notable future makers, including Gabriel Wright and William Jones.

c1760 *22in (56cm) high*

$8,000-12,000 CM

ESSENTIAL REFERENCE - SINGER'S PATENT

Samuel Singer (1796-c1887) was a serious sportsman who grew frustrated with conventional compasses because they could not be read at night. As a consequence he invented and patented a compass that became a design classic and was in use for about fifty years.

- **His design featured a mother-of-pearl card set on a jeweled pivot, with the northern half of the card painted black with white symbols, and the southern with black symbols. This could be easily read in low light.**
- **The patent ran 1861-68, although later cards are often marked 'Singer's Patent'. Singer himself was swindled out of his patent rights early on and he died in penury.**
- **Trinity House (the General Lighthouse Authority for England and Wales) gave the Singer's Patent compass glowing reviews.**
- **The British and Swiss armies used pocket versions.**
- **Marine versions are the rarest form.**
- **Singer's Patent compasses remained in production until around 1906 when luminous dials (painted with radium paint) began to be common.**

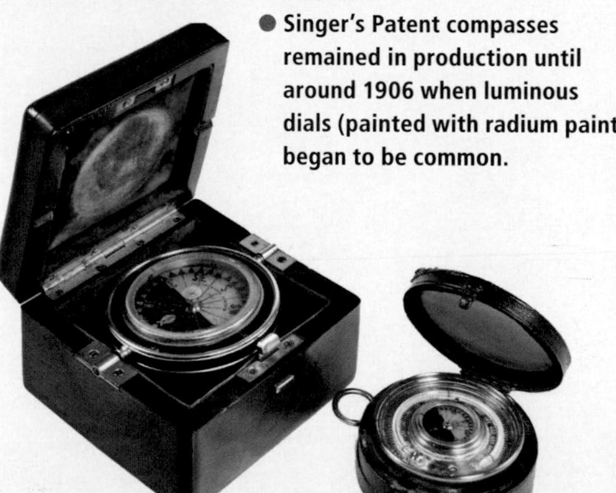

A rare Singer's patent marine night compass, by Elliott Bros., London, the 2in (5cm) mother-of-pearl card signed and numbered 'Elliott Bros London 23661 / SINGER'S PATENT', set in a gilt-brass gimbal-mounted bowl with needle lock, in mahogany box, with defective needle lock.

c1865 *4in (10cm) wide*

$4,000-6,000 CM

A late 19thC pocket weather-compendium set, signed 'J.B. Dancer, Optician, MANCHESTER', the obverse with aneroid barometer with 2in (5cm) silvered register, the reverse with thermometer surrounding a miniature Singer's Patent night compass, in double-sided cloth case.

2.5in (6.5cm) diam

$650-750 CM

An ebonized octant, by Spencer Browning & Rust, London, retailed by W. Heaton, Newcastle upon Tyne, with brass mounts, inlaid ivory scale and marked cartouche, in a fitted case.

Brass arm 14in (36cm) long

$1,000-1,500 A&G

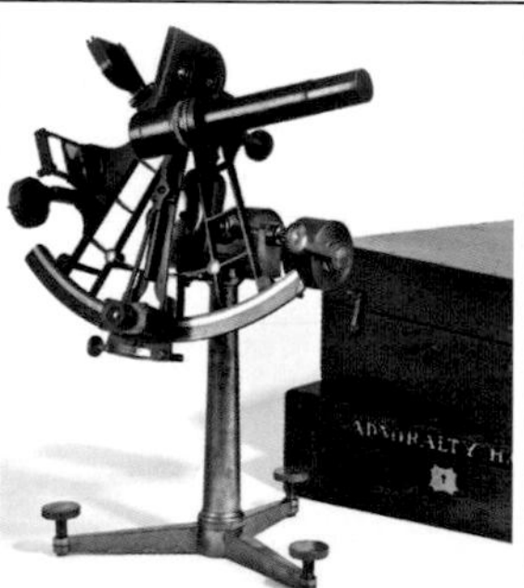

An 8in (20.5cm) oxidized-brass sextant, by Henry Hughes & Son Ltd, London, numbered '5970', with silvered vernier scale, hinged vernier magnifier platform, sighting telescopes with cross-hairs, mirrors and shades, with fitted box with accessories and test certificate for 1907, with a 19thC counter-weighted stand, stamped 'H.O. 4' for the Hydrographic Office, with box of issue.

Sextant 13in (33cm) wide

$3,000-4,000 CM

An unusual probably 19thC small liquid-type binnacle compass, with 5in (12.5cm) high-visibility Chetwynd-type acetate card on rocking pivot, in static bowl with threaded drain cock, with lamp and mahogany body.

12in (32cm) high

$1,000-1,500 CM

Judith Picks: Scrimshaw

Due to the number of fakes we are presented with, experts are always suspicious when we see a piece of scrimshaw, particularly when we see one of such quality and with so many really desirable features, such as the patriotic symbols and historical portrait on this example. The quality of the carving and attention to detail is exceptional, as is the use of color. The authenticity, quality, historical importance and rarity of this piece account for the high price.

An early/mid-19thC New England patriotic scrimshaw whale's tooth, the obverse with a ship and an eagle holding an American flag under a row of thirteen stars, the reverse with a portrait of Grace Darling.

Grace Darling was an English lighthouse-keeper's daughter, who was famed during her lifetime for participating in the rescue of survivors from the shipwrecked 'Forfarshire' in 1838.

6.25in (16cm) high

$100,000-150,000 **POOK**

A 19thC scrimshaw whale's tooth, the obverse with a whaling scene, the reverse with a portrait of the Marquasa Princess, with minor cracks.

7.5in (19cm) long

$5,000-7,000 **SK**

A rare 19thC scrimshaw whalebone 'pick wick', the turned handle with steel pick, the base incised with foliate motifs and inscribed 'CAPtn. DEXTER BELLOWS', lined with shark skin.

A pick wick was used to raise the short wick of an oil lamp.

3in (9cm) high

$3,000-4,000 **CM**

A 19thC American sailor's-sweetheart scrimshaw whalebone stay busk, one side decorated with a whaling scene, the other with lover's motifs and American patriotic symbols, highlighted in red ink, inscribed 'BARON'.

12in (32cm) long

$2,000-3,000 **CM**

A 19thC narwhal tusk walking stick, with corkscrew twist, with silver cap.

30in (76cm) long

$4,000-6,000 **CM**

A rare 19thC scrimshaw whale's tooth pipe, decorated with geometric patterns, a whaling scene and a profile entitled 'META'.

This pipe is desirable not only because of its rarity, but also due to its complicated construction. The carver used the tooth root as a natural 'pipe' and the contrast between the root and tooth is still clearly visible. The fact that it has so clearly been frequently used - see, the heavily carbonized bowl, tooth-marked and nicotine-stained mouth piece - further adds to its appeal.

3in (9.5cm) long

$6,500-7,500 **CM**

A scrimshaw whale's tooth, by William A. Gilpin, Wilmington, Delaware, the obverse with a sailor, an eagle and a banner reading 'Free Trade and Sailors Rights,' the reverse with 'The Corsair's Farewell'.

The artist William A Gilpin was formerly known as the 'Ceres A Artisan.' There are only two other teeth with this image.

c1838-45 *7in (18cm) long*

$10,000-15,000 **SK**

A 19thC scrimshaw, carved and inlaid whale bone walking cane, with marine ivory pommel, inlaid with mother-of-pearl, abalone and tortoiseshell.

37.5in (95cm) long

$8,000-12,000 **L&T**

Judith Picks: Titanic Medals

In November 2012 I went to a Titanic exhibit in Fort Worth, Texas and was given the name of a passenger. At the end of the exhibit we found out if we lived or died – I lived. Even as RMS 'Carpathia' steamed back to New York after picking up those who had survived the sinking, several First Class passengers - led by Mrs. J J 'Molly' Brown - formed themselves into the 'Titanic' Survivors' Committee. Apart from its desire to aid those made destitute by the disaster, the Committee wished to reward Captain Rostron and his crew for saving so many lives. Captain Rostron was presented with a silver cup while every member of the crew aboard 'Carpathia' received a specially commissioned medal. Gold medals were presented to 'Carpathia's captain and senior officers. The junior officers were given silver, while members of the crew had bronze. Medals in gold are excessively rare, those in silver are very rare and those in bronze are more common, with probably well in excess of 250 being struck.

An R.M.S. 'Carpathia' silver medal awarded for the rescue of the survivors from the Titanic, Dieges & Clust, New York, the obverse with RMS 'Carpathia' among icebergs and lifeboats, the reverse with inscription 'PRESENTED TO THE CAPTAIN, OFFICERS & CREW OF R.M.S. CARPATHIA, IN RECOGNITION OF GALLANT & HEROIC SERVICES FROM THE SURVIVORS OF THE S.S. TITANIC, APRIL 15TH', with original ribbon.

$12,000-18,000 CM

A 19thC sailor's woolwork picture, depicting a Royal Navy frigate within laurel wreath, patriotic flags and symbols.

22in (57cm) wide

$1,500-2,500 CM

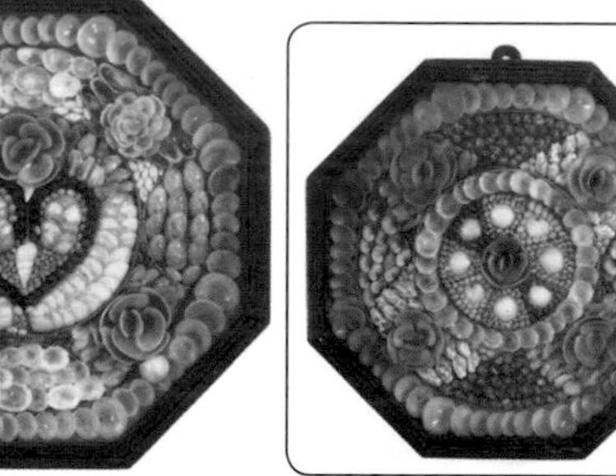

A 19thC sailor's 'Sweetheart', with two octagonal shell arrangements, one centered by a segmental circular device, the other by a heart.

8in (21.5cm) wide

$1,500-2,500 WHP

A 19thC carved and painted ship's figurehead in the form of a gentleman, mounted with red scroll, green foliage and blue sash, with restoration.

34in (86.5cm) high

$5,000-6,000 A&G

A 19thC carved pine ship's figurehead in the form of a lady dancing a jig, with some original paintwork.

56in (142cm) high

$20,000-25,000 SWO

A ship builder's model of the motor ship 'Adrian', built by Messers Rolland werft, Bremen, for Medcalf Coasters Ltd, dead weight 1,158 tons, net 966, dated, in glazed mahogany case.

1957 *32in (82cm) high*

$2,500-3,500 A&G

A large ship's wheel, with turned handles, brass plates and iron center boss.

c1880 *72in (182cm) diam*

$3,000-4,000 L&T

A 6-bolt copper and brass diver's helmet, Siebe, Gorman & Co. Ltd., numbered '12380', the air inlet with sprung non-return valve, telephone inlet with blanking nut.

9in (48.5cm) high

$5,500-6,500 CM

A mid-19thC Swiss music box, by Nicole Frères, no. 34593, the 19.75in (50cm) cylinder playing sixteen airs, in a rosewood and foliate marquetry case.

29.25in (74cm) wide

$3,000-4,000 **TEN**

A large 19thC Swiss music box, no.4573, with four 13in (33cm) cylinders playing 32 airs, in a walnut case.

37in (94cm) wide

$4,000-6,000 **GORL**

A sublime harmony music box, by G Baker & Co., no.15085, playing ten airs, in a walnut case with birds-eye maple cover, on a mahogany stand.

43in (109cm) high

$3,000-4,000 **ROS**

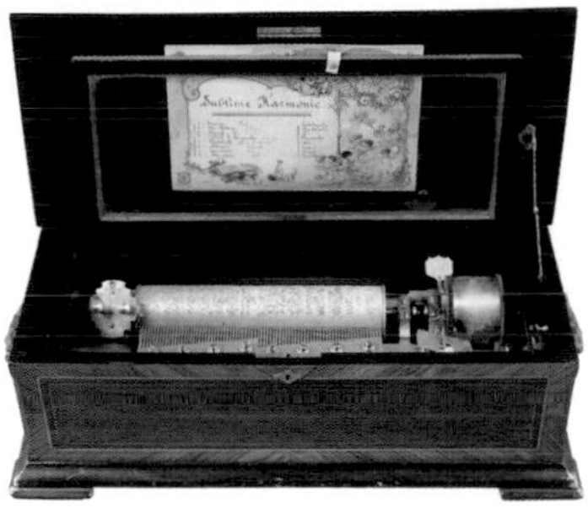

A Swiss sublime harmony music box, by Mermod Frères, no.40032, the 11in (30cm) cylinder playing eight airs, with two part comb, Jacot's Patented Safety Check and Change-Repeat selection dial, in a mahogany-veneer and marquetry case.

25.25in (64cm) wide

$2,000-3,000 **SK**

A German coin-operated disc music box, by Polyphon, in a mahogany-veneered case, with 21 discs.

c1880–90 *37.5in (97cm) high*

$6,500-7,500 **KAU**

A German upright Symphonia disc music box, with 40 discs, in a walnut-veneered case, with turned and fluted columns and two comb and star wheel assemblies, the disc bin with five pull-out shelves and two drawers.

82in (208cm) high

$5,000-7,000 **SK**

A Swiss interchangeable Ideal Piccolo music box, by Mermod Frères, no.52358, last patent date 1887, with seven 11in (30cm) cylinders, in a mahogany-veneered and ebonized case with drawer, the movement with Jacot's Patented Safety Check, with low table and drawer.

The airs include 'The Star Spangled Banner', 'Oh! Christmas Tree', 'I wish I Were in Dixie' and 'Columbia, the Gem of the Ocean'.

Box 31.5in (80cm) wide

$4,000-6,000 **SK**

One of a pair of George II silver candlesticks, by Lewis Pantin, London, with spool-shaped capitals, with shouldered and knopped stems, on molded bases.
1736 *6.5in (17cm) high 28oz*
$4,000-6,000 pair **DN**

A set of four George II silver candlesticks, by William Gould, London, with spool-shaped capitals and detachable drip-pans engraved with a crest, with knopped stems and shell shoulders, on square bases with shell motifs.
1746 *9in (23cm) high 102.4oz*
$12,000-18,000 **WW**

Snips & Snuffer Stand

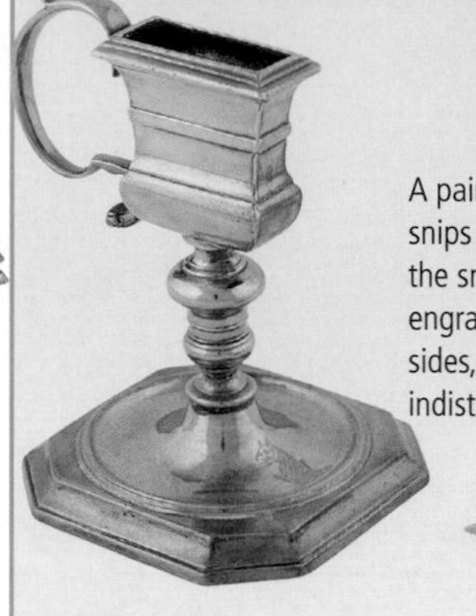

A pair of George I Britannia silver candle snips and an associated snuffer stand, the snips by Simon Panton I, London, engraved with an armorial to both sides, the stand of the same date with indistinct maker's mark, crested.
1719 *Stand 7.75in (17.5cm) high*
$10,000-15,000 **L&T**

ESSENTIAL REFERENCE - JOHN & WILLIAM CAFE

Little is known of John Cafe (or possibly Case) other than that he registered his mark with Goldsmiths in 1742 and was active 1740–57.

- **He specialized in the manufacture of candlesticks, chambersticks, snuffers and trays.**
- **His business went bankrupt in 1757 and was taken over by Cafe's brother William.**
- **William Cafe was apprenticed to his brother in 1742 and to Simon Jouet in 1746.**
- **He registered his mark in 1757 and became a prolific maker of cast candlesticks.**

A pair of George II silver candlesticks, by John Cafe, London, with urn-shaped capitals and detachable drip-pans, the stems and bases with foliate-scroll decoration, engraved with armorials.
1755 *10in (27cm) high 42oz*
$5,500-6,500 **WW**

A pair of rare George II silver candlesticks, by Robert Gordon, Edinburgh, with detachable sconces, the knopped stems on square bases.
1750 *8.5in (21cm) high 35oz*
$9,000-11,000 **L&T**

A pair of Scottish George II silver candlesticks, by Ebenezer Oliphant, Edinburgh, the spreading knops with scrolls and Turks' heads, the bases with Rococo cartouches and Turks' heads.
1751 *8.75in (22cm) high*
$4,000-6,000 **L&T**

One of a pair of Georgian silver candlesticks, maker's mark 'IP' possibly for John Priest.
c1757 *9.5in (24cm) high 28.8oz*
$3,500-4,500 pair **POOK**

A pair of George III silver candlesticks, maker's mark 'TD', London, with beaded borders, crested, with detachable drip-pans.
1785 *5in (15.5cm) high*
$400-600 **WW**

A matched set of four George III silver candlesticks, two by William Cafe, two unmarked, all London, the pierced Classical terminals with detachable sconces, the bases with gadroon borders and shell and scroll details.

1759 *12.25in (31cm) high*

$8,000-12,000 **L&T**

A set of four George III silver Corinthian-column candlesticks, by William Adby I, London, with detachable drip-pans, the bases with foliate decoration, loaded.

1764 *13in (33.5cm) high*

$10,000-15,000 **WW**

A set of four early George III silver candlesticks, by Ebenezer Coker, London, the reel capitals with rope-twist borders and detachable sconces, the bases with shells and scroll outline.

1764 *10.5in (26.5cm) high 86.55oz*

$15,000-20,000 **DN**

A pair of George III silver candlesticks, probably by John Carter, London, the spool shaped capitals with gadroon borders and detachable drip-pans, the knopped stems with scroll shoulders.

1768 *10.5in (26.5cm) high 40oz*

$5,000-7,000 **WW**

A pair of George III silver candlesticks, by John Winter, John Parsons and Charles Hall, Sheffield, with fluted urn-shaped capitals, with foliate and beaded borders, crested and with motto.

1779 *10in (28cm) high*

$3,000-4,000 **WW**

A pair of George III silver candlesticks, by John Scofield, London, the part-fluted urn capitals with detachable drip-pans, engraved with armorials.

1784 *11.75in (30cm) high 38oz*

$7,000-10,000 **WW**

A pair of George III silver candlesticks, maker's mark 'TD', London, with beaded borders, crested, with detachable drip-pans.

1785 *5in (15.5cm) high*

$400-600 **WW**

A pair of George III silver candlesticks, by John Parsons & Co., Sheffield, with fluted decoration.

1792 *12.5in (29.5cm) high*

$1,500-2,000 **WW**

A Georgian silver chamberstick and snuffer, by Henry Chawner, engraved with a bear.

c1794-95 *4in (10cm) high 7.3oz*

$1,000-1,500 **POOK**

A pair of George III silver candlesticks, by John Green, Roberts, Mosley & Co., Sheffield, with reeded borders, fluting and lappet decoration, with detachable nozzles, loaded.

11.5in (29.5cm) high

$10,000-15,000 **DN**

A pair of German Empire silver-gilt candle sticks, by Johann Samuel Schoenberg, Nuremberg.

c1810 *9.25in (23.5cm) high 27.5oz*

$5,500-6,500 **KAU**

A pair of George IV silver foliate baluster candlesticks, by S C Younge & Co., Sheffield, with detachable drip-pans.

1820 *7.5in (20.5cm) high*

$1,000-1,500 **WW**

A set of four George IV silver candlesticks, by John Watson, Sheffield, decorated with foliate scrolls, engraved with armorials, with detachable sconces, loaded.

1822 *13.25in (34cm) high*

$4,000-6,000 **DN**

A pair of George IV silver candlesticks, by John and Thomas Settle, Sheffield, with fluted columns and foliate-scroll borders.

1823 *12.5in (30cm) high*

$1,500-2,500 **WW**

A pair of Victorian silver candlesticks, by William Hutton & Sons, London, decorated with shell and scrolls, with detachable nozzles, loaded.

1896 *12in (30cm) high*

$550-750 **TEN**

A set of four Tiffany & Co. silver reeded baluster candlesticks, loaded.

1912, 1913 *9.75in (25cm) high*

$8,000-12,000 **LHA**

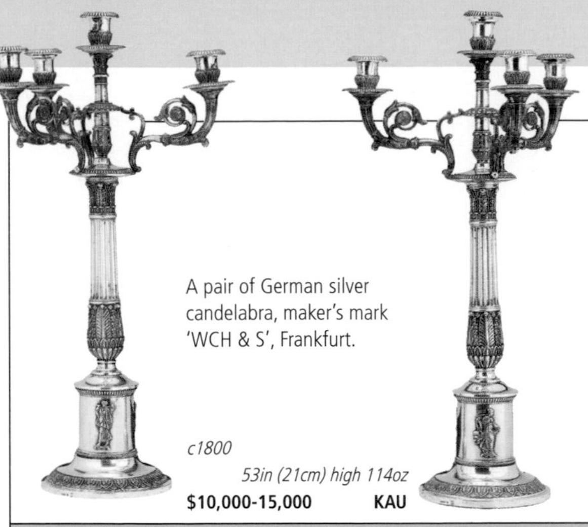

A pair of German silver candelabra, maker's mark 'WCH & S', Frankfurt.

c1800 *53in (21cm) high 114oz*

$10,000-15,000 KAU

A George III silver candelabrum, by John Edward Terrey, London, the stem with acanthus leaf mounts and shell and foliate scroll borders, with a central light and three detachable part-fluted scroll arms with urn-shaped capitals, on foliate-scroll shell bracket feet, engraved with an armorial and a crest, loaded.

1819 *25in (60.5cm) high*

$4,000-6,000 WW

ESSENTIAL REFERENCE - BARNARD & CO.

Barnard & Sons is one of Britain's oldest silversmiths. Its origins can be traced back to Anthony Nelme's company, which was founded in c1680.

- **In 1829 Edward Barnard I took over the firm, with his sons Edward II, John and William. The firm became known as Edward Barnard & Sons. Edward Barnard I retired in 1846 and the company continued under the direction of his sons.**
- **Barnard & Sons specialized in formal dining ware and commemorative pieces.**
- **In 1977 Edward Barnard & Sons Ltd. became a subsidiary of Padgett & Braham Ltd.**

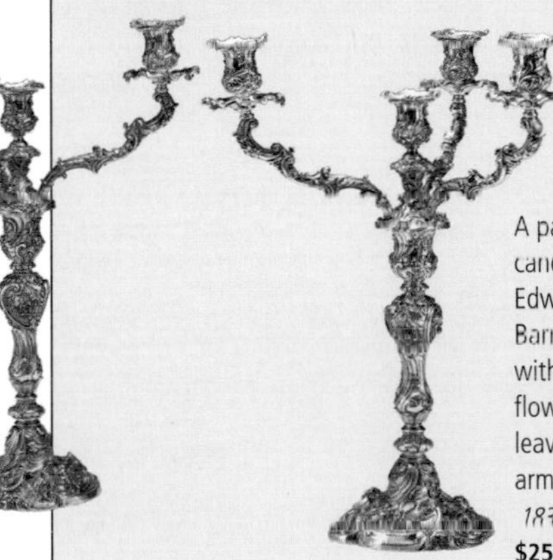

A pair of William IV silver candelabra, by Edward, Edward Jr., John and William Barnard, London, decorated with C- and S-scrolls, flowerheads and acanthus leaves, with three detachable arms.

1831 *22.5in (57cm) high 320oz*

$25,000-35,000 FRE

A Victorian silver testimonial candelabrum, by Elkington & Co., Birmingham, with a ram and ewe beneath an oak tree with three branches, with presentation inscription from the Royal Agricultural Society.

1850 *22.5in (57cm) high 128oz*

$6,000-8,000 MAB

A pair of late Victorian silver candelabra, by Hunt & Roskell (Alfred Benson & Henry Hugh Webb), London, with detachable sconces, with double C-scroll branches, the reeded tapered stems with swags, crested, loaded.

1891 *15in (38cm) high Branches 42oz*

$7,000-10,000 DN

A pair of Victorian silver candlelabra, maker's mark 'JKB', London, the stem with floral swags around Classical roundels, with three scrolling candle branches.

1891 *17.75in (45cm) high*

$6,500-7,500 L&T

A large 20thC silver menorah, with eight floral-scrolled candle branches, with detachable shammash and oil jug, marked 'Hadad'.

The Shammash is the ninth 'servant' light on the eight-branched menorah of Hanukkah. It is a utilitarian light used to light the eight 'holy' lights.

39in (99cm) high

$6,500-7,500 DRA

An Elizabeth I silver chalice and paten, maker's mark of an arrow piercing 'H', London, engraved with foliate-strapwork girdle.

1576 *8.25in (21cm) high 10oz*

$12,000-18,000 **MAB**

A late 17thC German silver-gilt tankard, probably Augsburg, embossed with seascape scenes within foliate-scroll borders, with caryatid scroll handle, with lion finial.

c1590 *7.5in (16.5cm) high 12oz*

$9,000-11,000 **WW**

Judith Picks

While this form of communion cup is well recorded for the Edinburgh and East Lothian area, these examples are of a particularly high quality. The overall shape and form, while restrained in design, shows a great skill and quality in manufacture. But the important fact that adds most to their value is that they were gifted by Alexander Seton, 1st Earl of Dunfermline, Lord Fyvie and Lord Urquhart, Baron of Fyvie and Pinkie, Pluscarden, etc (1555-1622), who was a hugely influential figure in late 16thC/early 17thC law and society. He represented King James VI (I of England) at the highest level in Scotland and in 1604 he was elevated to Lord Chancellor of Scotland until 1622. He was also heavily involved in the uniting of the two crowns of Scotland and England.

A pair of Scottish James VI (I of England) communion cups, by George Crauiford, Edinburgh, Deacon's mark for James Denniestoun, the feet with borders of foliage, flowerheads an S-scroll panels.

1619-21 *8.5in (21.5cm) high 19.5oz*

$120,000-140,000 **L&T**

A Charles I silver wine cup, maker's mark 'FW', London, the bowl pricked with initials 'NT' surrounded by scrolls, on triple-knopped stem with spreading foot.

1630 *6.25in (16cm) high 7oz*

$14,000-16,000 **MAB**

A Scottish Charles I silver communion cup, by Robert Gardyne II, Dundee, engraved 'EX DONO IACOBI SMITH MERCATORIS', on knopped baluster stem with foliate decoration to lower knop, the base with flat chased foliate border.

This cup is one of three gifted to the Steeple Kirk of Dundee. All bear the same inscription and decoration. These three cups are among the earliest communion plate in Dundee.

c1640 *9in (23cm) high 19.3oz*

$40,000-60,000 **L&T**

A Charles II silver cup and cover, maker's mark 'IS', London, with bands of laurel and acanthus leaves, with presentation inscription, with two S-scroll handles.

1679 *8in (20.5cm) high 29.3oz*

$5,500-6,500 **AH**

A Charles II silver mug, by George Garthorne, London, with reeded neck, the body with chinoiserie prick dot decoration.

1683 *4.5in (11.5cm) high 10oz*

$6,500-7,500 **GORL**

A James II silver tapered cylindrical tankard, maker's mark 'RP', London, chased with a foliate lower band, later engraved with crest.

1685 *8.25in (21cm) high 41.5oz*

$6,500-7,500 DN

A German parcel-gilt silver tankard, by Daniel Schwestermüller, Augsburg.

c1688-89 *7.5in (19.5cm) high 32oz*

$15,000-20,000 KAU

A Swedish parcel-gilt silver tankard, by Sven Jönsson Wallman, Gothenburg, the lid inset with a medallion surrounded by foliate engraving, the chased scroll handle with shield terminal, on pomegranate and foliate feet.

c1690 *7.5in (19.5cm) high 42oz*

$15,000-20,000 MAB

A silver-gilt tumbler, by Johann Philipp Schuch I, Augsburg, the base with monogram 'AJT'.

c1700 *5in (11cm) high 7oz*

$12,000-18,000 KAU

A rare Queen Anne silver tankard, by John Seatoune, Edinburgh, the S-scroll handle with tapered beaded rib flanked by stylized acanthus cut-card work and engraved initials 'ST', the knopped finial with cut card stylized foliate decoration.

1702 *7.75in (19.5cm) high 35.5oz*

$14,000-16,000 L&T

ESSENTIAL REFERENCE - GEORGE WICKES

George Wickes (1698-1761) was a leading Rococo silversmith. The quality of his work is sometimes compared to that of Paul de Lamerie.

- **He was apprenticed to Simon Wastell from 1712. He entered his first mark in 1722.**
- **He established his firm in 1735 in London. This company later became Garrad & Co. (see p.336).**
- **In 1735 Wickes was appointed Goldsmith to Frederick Prince of Wales.**
- **His most famous commissions include the Pelham Gold Cup, made to designs by William Kent, and a table service consisting of 170 pieces made for the Earl of Leinster.**

A large silver caudle cup, maker's mark 'ST' possibly for Robert Stokes.

c1705-06 *4.75in (12cm) high 9.2oz*

$5,000-7,000 POOK

A Queen Anne silver flagon, by Nathaniel Lock, London, the scroll handle terminating in a heart-shaped cartouche.

1712 *12in (30.5cm) high 40oz*

$15,000-25,000 WW

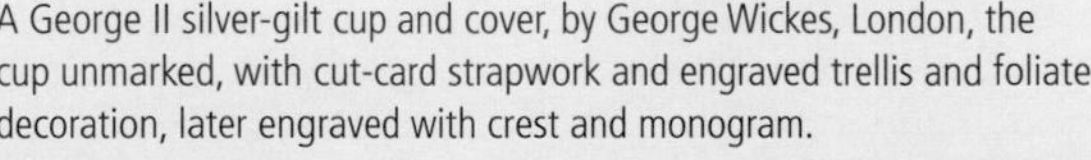

A George II silver-gilt cup and cover, by George Wickes, London, the cup unmarked, with cut-card strapwork and engraved trellis and foliate decoration, later engraved with crest and monogram.

c1735 *15in (37.5cm) high 160oz*

$12,000-18,000 WW

An 18thC German parcel-gilt tankard, possibly by Johannes Beckhardt Aurifaber, Augsburg, with chased foliate scroll borders, with a foliate cone finial.

1749-51 *7.5in (17cm) high 14oz*

$5,000-7,000 **WW**

A Georgian silver caudle cup, by William Cripps.

c1763-64 *3.5in (9cm) high 4.4oz*

$700-1,000 **POOK**

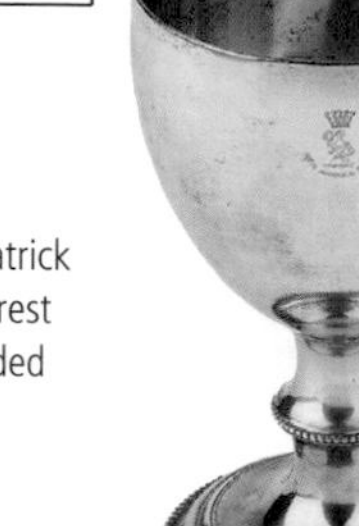

A pair of George III silver goblets, by Patrick Robertson, Edinburgh, engraved with crest and motto, on waisted stems with beaded knops.

1779 *6in (15cm) high 17oz*

$5,500-6,500 **L&T**

A George III silver tankard, by James Sutton, London, later embossed with foliate decoration and a coursing scene of two greyhounds chasing a hare.

1780 *7.5in (20.5cm) high 27oz*

$3,000-4,000 **WW**

A Georgian silver mug, by Hester Bateman, the base engraved with an elaborate armorial.

1782-83 *6in (15cm) high 18.9oz*

$3,000-4,000 **POOK**

A George III silver-gilt two-handled cup and cover, by Solomon Hougham, London, engraved with the arms of the Vintners Company and a presentation inscription, with leaf-capped scroll handles.

1801 *10in (28.5cm) high 40oz*

$2,500-3,500 **WW**

A Victorian silver flagon, by Robert Hennell, London, chased with fruiting vines and two C-scroll cartouches, one containing horses and birds, the other with presentation inscription, the finial modeled as a mare and foal.

1858 *15.5in (39.5cm) high 95oz*

$10,000-15,000 **TEN**

A late Victorian silver two-handled tazza, by Gilbert Marks, London, embossed and chased with poppies and foliate decoration, the foot with rose hip decoration.

1896 *12.5in (32.5cm) high 60oz*

$30,000-40,000 **WW**

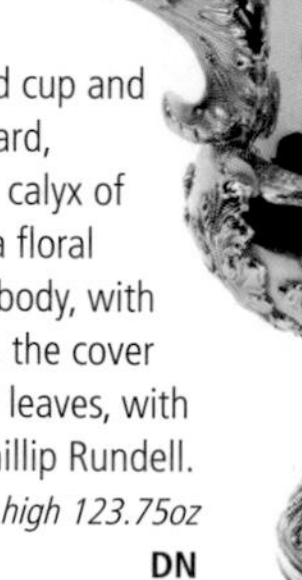

A silver campana-shaped cup and cover, by Sebastian Garrard, London, with an applied calyx of leaves and flowers and a floral frieze around the upper body, with bellflower scroll handles, the cover chased with flowers and leaves, with earlier thistle finial by Phillip Rundell.

Cup 1911 *15.5in (39cm) high 123.75oz*

$6,500-7,500 **DN**

A George I Irish silver bullet-shaped teapot, by Thomas Lilly, Dublin, with possibly later handle.

1723 *5.25in (13.5cm) high 12oz*

$12,000-18,000 **GORL**

A George I silver tea kettle, engraved with an armorial and motto 'TENE FIDEMTHE', with turned wooden grip, on associated stand.

1718 *15in (39cm) high*

$3,500-4,500 **MEA**

A George I Britannia silver teapot, by Jonah Clifton, London.

1724 *6in (15cm) high 14oz*

$5,000-7,000 **MAB**

A George II silver tapered bullet-shaped teapot, by James Mitchelson, Edinburgh, the hinged cover with flat chased border and decoration to hinge, with acorn finial.

1732 *6.5in (16.5cm) high 21oz*

$8,000-12,000 **L&T**

A George II silver bullet-shaped teapot, by James Ker, Edinburgh, with chased floral and scroll border and cartouches, with S-scroll spout and handle, the interior pierced grill with star and scroll motifs.

The intricate grill is a feature noted on a small handful of high quality mid-18thC Scottish teapots.

1735 *6in (15cm) high 23oz*

$3,000-4,000 **L&T**

A George III silver teapot, by Robert Hennell, London, engraved with foliage and later presentation inscription.

1794 *10in (28cm) wide 14oz*

$550-750 **WW**

An Irish George III silver tea kettle and stand, Dublin, the kettle chased with flowers and scrolls, engraved with an armorial and crest, with double caryatid handle and bird head spout, the stand on caryatid legs with shell feet.

c1760 *81.1oz*

$5,500-6,500 **MEA**

A Philadelphia silver teapot, by Harvey Lewis, with engraved monogram, with flame finial, the base inscribed 'J. Tatnall to S. Lea 5 Mo. 28th 1813'.

c1813 *7.5in (19cm) high 18.3oz*

$1,000-1,500 **POOK**

An early Victorian silver baluster teapot, by Charles Reily and George Storer, London, chased with a chinoiserie landscape, with a floral finial and chased bamboo and foliate handle, with presentation inscription.

1839 *10in (25.5cm) high 31.5oz*

$2,500-3,500 **DN**

An Irish George I silver coffee pot, by David King, Dublin.

David King was active 1690-1737, serving a period as Master Warden of the Company of Goldsmiths, as well as being on the Common Council of the City of Dublin. King Street was named after him.

1727 *9.25in (23.5cm) high 26oz*

$5,000-7,000 **MAB**

A George II silver coffee pot, by Edward Feline, London, engraved with a scrollwork cartouche, with molded borders, with an acorn finial, with wooden scroll handle.

1727 *9in (23cm) high 24.8oz*

$1,500-2,500 **TEN**

A George II silver coffee pot, by Gabriel Sleath, London, engraved with an armorial with foliate scroll mantling, with a wooden side handle.

1729 *7.5in (21.5cm) high 22oz*

$2,500-3,500 **WW**

Judith Picks

The ovoid coffee urn is perhaps the most unique design seen in Scottish silver. Where the inspiration for this design emanates from still remains a mystery. Even the use of these urns has caused debate, although the general consensus now seems to be that they are a form of coffee urn, rather than water urn as previously believed. During the main period these urns were manufactured (c1719-67) very few standard pouring coffee pots were produced. This may be because within contemporary accounts it's clear that coffee is considered medicinal and should 'be drunk as hot as one can bear'. This shape in combination with the use of a burner (now lacking) would have meant the contents could have been kept hot!

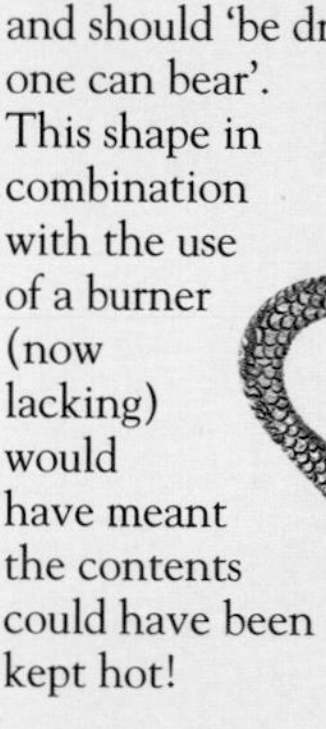

A rare Scottish George II silver coffee urn, Edinburgh, with chased borders of flowerheads and foliate scrolls, with serpent handles, with ebony finial and spigot-handle, on leaf-capped cabriole legs with paw feet.

c1744-59 *11in (29cm) high 55oz*

$18,000-22,000 **L&T**

A George II silver coffee pot, maker's mark 'TR', London, engraved with a widow's armorial, with an acorn finial, with a wooden scroll handle.

1729 *9in (23cm) high*

$2,500-3,500 **TEN**

A rare Scottish George II silver coffee pot, by James Ker, Edinburgh, the rim of fruits and flowerheads within Rococo scrolls and shells, with engraved armorial and crest, with S-scroll fruitwood handle.

1740 *10.5in (26.5cm) high 32oz*

$9,000-11,000 **L&T**

A George III silver coffee pot, London, later engraved with an armorial, with flame finial.

1774 *10in (27.5cm) high 30oz*

$2,500-3,500 **WW**

A George IV Rococo silver coffee pot, by Paul Storr for Storr & Mortimer, London, profusely chased with flowers around a crest, with ivory spacers.

1825 *10.5in (26.5cm) high 31oz*

$3,500-4,500 **MAB**

A George III silver tea set, by Solomon Hougham, London, with gadroon borders and scroll handles, with engraved foliate decoration, on ball feet.

1816 *30oz*

$1,500-2,500 **WW**

A Victorian silver tea and coffee service, by Walter and John Barnard, London, decorated with exotic birds and bamboo, with engraved monograms.

1833 *Coffee pot 8.25in (21cm) high 59.5oz total*

$2,500-3,500 **A&G**

A Victorian silver tea and coffee service, by Edward and John Barnard, London, decorated with scrollwork, fruit and floral designs, with urn finials.

1857 *Coffee pot 11in (28cm) high 76oz*

$2,500-3,500 **A&G**

A Victorian silver tea and coffee service, by Frederick Elkington, London, the engraved shoulders applied with bosses, the collars and bodies with applied foliage, the tea and coffee with ivory spacers.

1875 *Coffee pot 11in (28cm) high 87.95 oz*

$3,500-4,500 **DN**

A Victorian silver teaset, by A Rhodes for Manoah Rhodes & Son, London, chased with scrolling foliage, with pierced everted rims, with leaf-capped scroll handles.

1897 *10in (25.5cm) high 87.5oz*

$1,500-2,500 **TEN**

A Victorian silver tea and coffee service, by Martin Hall & Co., Sheffield, embossed with floral foliate and scroll-work cartouches, the four lidded pieces with floral finials and ivory spacers, the kettle stand on grotesque beast legs with foliate feet, with tray (not shown). Kettle on stand

1899-1900 *15in (38cm) high 176oz total*

$9,000-11,000 **SK**

An Edwardian silver tea set, by Elkington & Co., Glasgow, chased with strapwork cartouches containing Robert Burns scenes and surrounded by thistles and flowerheads, with further cartouches containing monograms.

1909 *Water pot 9in (23cm) high 72.8oz*

$6,500-7,500 **L&T**

An 18thC silver tea caddy, by John Newton, later embossed with foliate scroll decoration, engraved with an armorial, with pull-off cover and slide-off base.

5in (14cm) high 7.5oz

$1,200-1,800 WW

A pair of George III silver tea caddies, covers and mixing bowl, by Samuel Taylor, London, chased with flowers and scrolls, with flowerhead finials, in a Regency silver-mounted sarcophagus-shaped casket, probably John Wakefield, London.

Caddies 1763 27oz 5in (12.5cm) high

$8,000-12,000 GORL

A pair of George III silver-gilt tea caddies, by Samuel Taylor, London, embossed and chased with chinoserie figures and Classical settings, within foliate borders, with floral finials, engraved with armorials.

1765 5in (13.5cm) high 22oz

$6,000-8,000 WW

A pair of early George III silver tea caddies and sugar box, by William Plummer, London, chased with a woman holding a cornucopia, and with Rococo foliate panels, with lion finials, in original shagreen case and with two filigree caddy spoons.

1767, 1768 Caddies 5.75in (14.5cm) high 39oz total

$8,000-12,000 HT

A George III silver tea caddy, by Crispin Fuller, London, with part-fluted decoration, with urn finial.

1796 7in (18cm) high 15oz

$2,500-3,500 WW

A George III silver tea caddy, by Charles Aldridge & Henry Green, London, with bright-cut Neo-classical decoration, with vasiform finial.

1780 13.5oz

$2,000-3,000 WHP

A Victorian silver tea caddy, by Charles Stuart Harris, London, with chinoiserie and Rococo figures in foliate-scroll settings, with a figural finial, on scroll bracket feet.

1896 5in (12.5cm) high 16oz

$1,000-1,500 WW

Strainer

A George I silver strainer, London, maker's mark '?T', with pierced scroll decoration.

1721 7.5in (16.5cm) wide 2oz

$2,500-3,500 WW

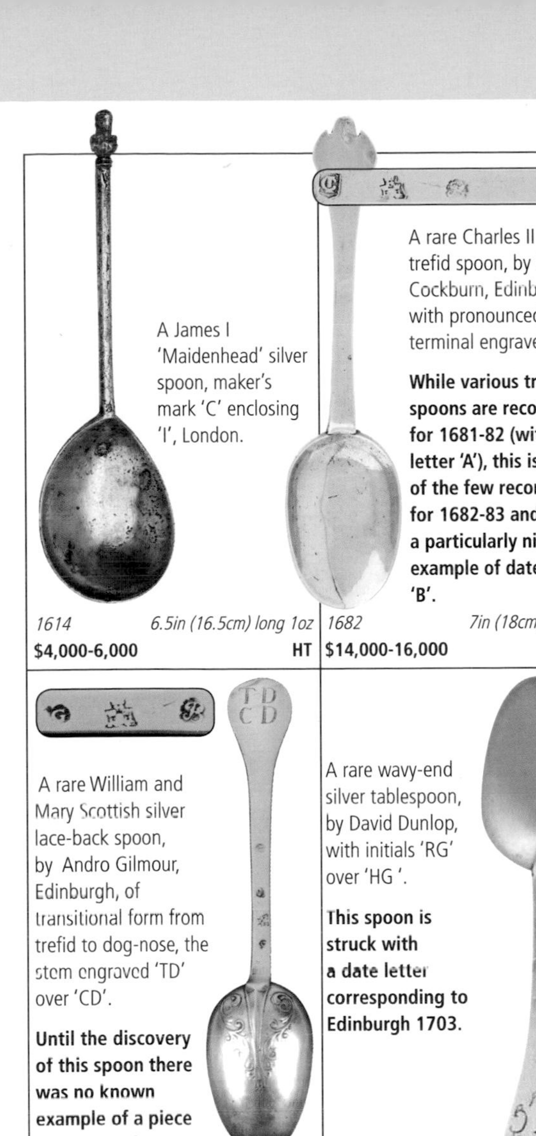

A James I 'Maidenhead' silver spoon, maker's mark 'C' enclosing 'I', London.

1614 *6.5in (16.5cm) long 1oz*
$4,000-6,000 **HT**

A rare Charles II silver trefid spoon, by James Cockburn, Edinburgh, with pronounced trefid terminal engraved 'EK'.

While various trefid spoons are recorded for 1681-82 (with date letter 'A'), this is one of the few recorded for 1682-83 and is a particularly nice example of date letter 'B'.

1682 *7in (18cm) long 2oz*
$14,000-16,000 **L&T**

A rare William and Mary Scottish silver lace-back spoon, by Andro Gilmour, Edinburgh, of transitional form from trefid to dog-nose, the stem engraved 'TD' over 'CD'.

Until the discovery of this spoon there was no known example of a piece by Andro Gilmour.

1692 *7.75in (19.5cm) long 1.8oz*
$20,000-30,000 **DN**

A rare wavy-end silver tablespoon, by David Dunlop, with initials 'RG' over 'HG '.

This spoon is struck with a date letter corresponding to Edinburgh 1703.

c1703 *1.7oz*
$9,000-11,000 **WW**

Judith Picks

As the oldest type of flatware, spoons have existed since Ancient Rome, at least. In medieval times, innkeepers expected their well-heeled customers to supply their own spoons. Indeed, the phrase 'born with a silver spoon in his mouth' actually reveals quite a bit about the time: whether or not one had a spoon, not to mention its quality and value, spoke volumes about an individual's socio-economic status. The spoon is the only item of 14thC, 15thC or 16thC silver that is readily available to the collector. They have been made in most counties of England, Scotland and Ireland – but rather oddly no early Welsh spoons survive. Or do they? In spoon collecting 'old' or 'early' relates to any spoon pre-1700 in date. These form the most valuable collections. Prices in excess of $1,500 are not unusual and particularly rare spoons, as shown by this example, can attain well over $50,000.

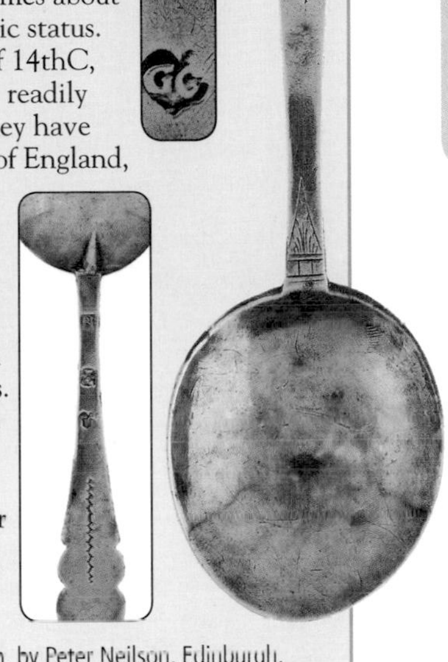

A rare Charles I silver disc-end spoon, by Peter Neilson, Edinburgh, Deacon's mark George Cleghorn, the terminal engraved 'BB' with date '1575' above foliate decoration to stem.

1648-50 or 1655-57 *7.25in (18.5cm) long 1.6oz*
$50,000-60,000 **L&T**

A Hanoverian silver tablespoon, by John Walker, with plain rattail, with scratched initials 'WL' over 'CF' over 'TL'.

c1725 *1.5oz*
$2,000-3,000 **WW**

A silver Hanoverian tablespoon, by Alexander Shirras, with initials 'GMG'.

This is a fine spoon of a heavy gauge.

c1750 *2.5oz*
$5,000-7,000 **WW**

A French silver olive spoon, with Old English thread edge and pierced foliate bowl, later initialed.

c1770 *11in (28cm) long 4.3oz*
$1,200-1,800 **TEN**

A set of six Victorian Scottish silver 'King's' pattern tablespoons, by J & W Marshall, Edinburgh, crested.

1843 *15.5oz*
$250-350 **WW**

A rare George I Britannia silver shaving jug, by John Chartier, London, with leather-covered S-scroll handle, the hinged cover with secondary hinged spout cover.
1715 *7.75in (20cm) high 18oz*
$6,500-7,500 **L&T**

A George II silver cream jug, by Louis Cuny, London, with leaf-capped scroll handle.
1731 *5in (10cm) high 5oz*
$2,000-3,000 **WW**

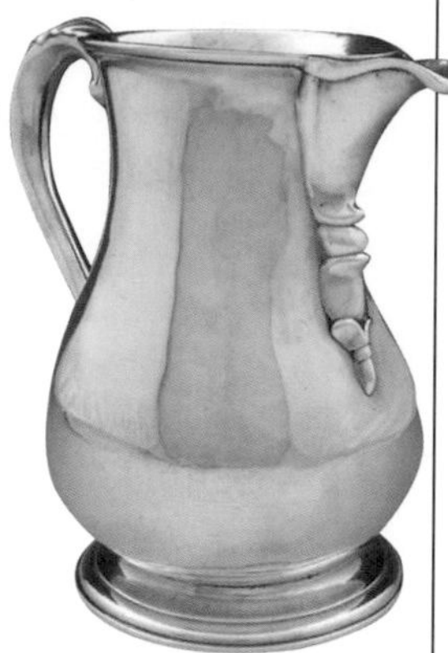

A George II silver beer jug, by William Shaw and William Priest, London, with leaf-capped scroll handle, later electroplated.
1756 *10in (23cm) high 48oz*
$6,000-8,000 **WW**

A George III silver cream jug, by Charles Chesterman, London, engraved with an armorial, with wavy girdle and scroll handle, with gilt interior.
1781 *6in (16.5cm) high 4oz*
$400-600 **SWO**

A George III Irish provincial silver cream jug, by Carden Terry and John Williams, Cork, with part-fluted decoration below drapes and foliate decoration, engraved with a monogram.
c1810 *5in (13.5cm) high 5oz*
$2,500-3,500 **WW**

A George III silver milk jug, London.
1812 *5oz*
$150-250 **WHP**

A Victorian silver claret jug, by Robert Hennell, London, retailed by C F Hancock, profusely embossed with foliate panels and pastoral scenes, with naturalistic vine-clasped handle, with water lily finial.
1854 *12.5in (32cm) high 38oz*
$5,000-7,000 **L&T**

ESSENTIAL REFERENCE - HUNT & ROSKELL

The company that would become Hunt & Roskell was founded by Paul Storr in 1819. It traded as Storr & Co. 1819-22, Storr & Mortimer 1822-38, Mortimer & Hunt 1838-43 and Hunt & Roskell 1843-97.

- **John Samuel Hunt was Storr's nephew and become a partner in the firm in 1826.**
- **Former watchmaker and merchant of Liverpool, Robert Roskell joined the firm in 1844 and remained a partner until his death in 1888.**
- **Hunt & Roskell were Silversmiths and Jewellers to Queen Victoria.**
- **John Samuel Hunt died in 1865 and was succeeded by his son, John Hunt (d.1879).**
- **In 1889 the firm was taken over by J W Benson and continued in business as Hunt & Roskell Ltd. until c1965.**

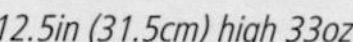

A Victorian Renaissance Revival silver 'Cellini' pattern ewer, by Hunt & Roskell, London, with strapwork, lobes, masks and animals, with monogram 'ER', with gilt interior.
1869 *12.5in (31.5cm) high 33oz*
$3,500-4,500 **MAB**

A pair of George III silver sauce tureens, covers and stands, by Sebastian and James Crespell, London, with beaded borders and pineapple finials, engraved with armorials.

1774 *9.25in (23.5cm) wide 57oz*

$10,000-15,000 **GORL**

A set of five George III silver serving dishes, by Naphthali Hart, London, comprising a soup tureen, pair of sauce tureens and pair of entree dishes, with rearing lion finials and shell and gadroon borders, on claw feet.

1807, 1812 *Soup tureen 15in (38cm) wide 309oz total*

$22,000-28,000 **GORL**

A George III silver two-handled soup tureen and cover, by Thomas Robins, London, engraved with an armorial and crest, with leaf-capped fluted scroll handles, on foliate capped paw feet, the cover with fluted decoration.

1810 *15.5in (39.5cm) wide 106oz*

$12,000-18,000 **WW**

One of a pair of George III silver vegetable tureens and covers, by William Burwash, London, engraved with armorials, with pomegranate finials, on Sheffield plate stands with paw feet and reeded leaf-capped handles.

1815 *10.5in (27cm) high*

$3,500-4,500 pair **TEN**

One of a pair of George III silver entree dishes and covers, by Kirkby, Waterhouse & Co., Sheffield, engraved with an armorial and crest, with gadroon and scroll borders, with detachable handles, the warming bases with large paw feet.

1817, 1818 *14in (35.5cm) long 206 oz*

$8,000-12,000 pair **LC**

A William IV soup tureen, by Paul Storr for Storr & Mortimer, London, with acanthus-capped handles, in a later fitted case, with silver 'Fiddle' pattern soup ladle, London.

1836 *Tureen 13.75in (35cm) wide 95oz*

$12,000-18,000 **L&T**

One of pair of early Victorian silver sauce tureens and covers, by John Waterhouse for Edward Hatfield & Co., Sheffield, on foliate feet, the covers with shell and scroll rims.

1837 *8.75in (22.5cm) long 75.85oz*

$5,000-7,000 pair **DN**

A pair of Edwardian silver entree dishes and covers, by Walker & Hall, Sheffield, with gadroon edges, with detachable handles.

1902 *29cm (11.5in) long 132.35oz*

$5,000-6,000 **DN**

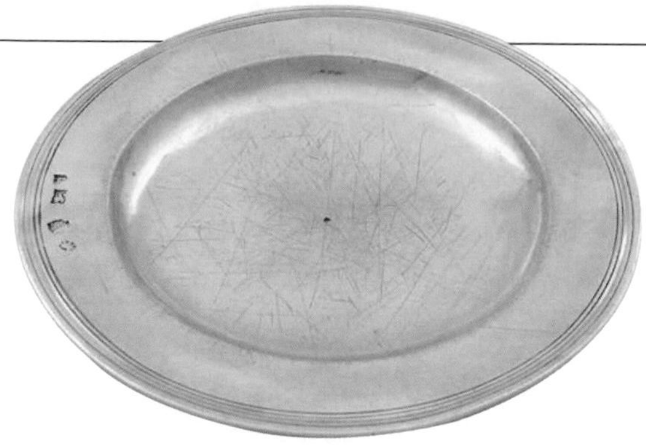

An Elizabeth I silver-gilt dish, maker's mark of a sun, London, with thread border.

1577 *5in (15cm) diam 4oz*

$10,000-15,000 **WW**

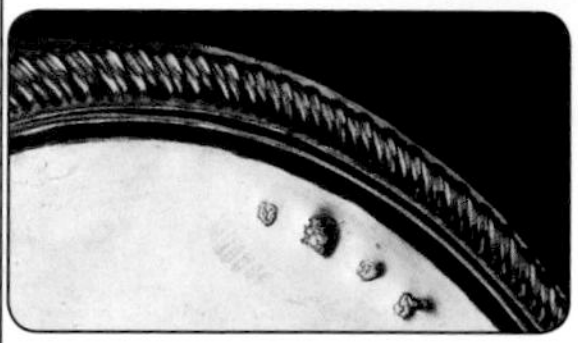

A rare William II (III of England) silver tazza, by John Yourston, Edinburgh, with domed gadroon semi-spiraled edge, with engraved initial 'B' to underside.

This appears to be one of the earliest recorded tazzas. John Yorstoun first appears within the records of the Incorporation of Goldsmiths of the City of Edinburgh as apprentice to his father George Yorstoun on 25th January 1688. He was admitted a Freeman of the Incorporation on 16th October 1697.

1698 *8.75in (22.5cm) diam 11.5oz*

$15,000-20,000 **L&T**

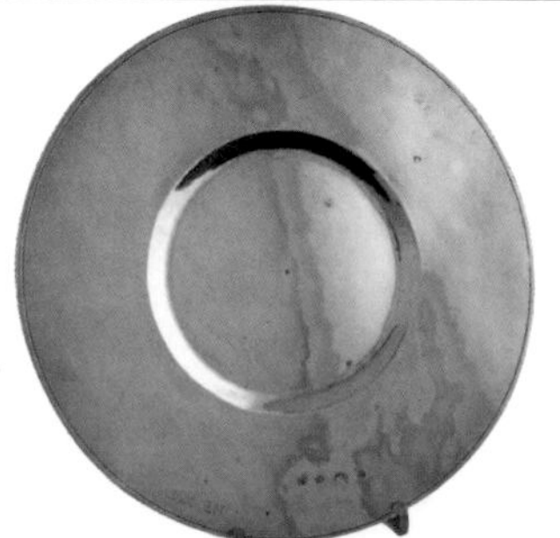

A Charles II silver paten, maker's mark 'TH' with crescent above, London.

1664 *9.5in (24cm) diam 10.5oz*

$5,500-6,500 **GORL**

A George I silver salver, by John Tuite, London, later engraved with an armorial, with a raised mold rim, on scroll feet.

1726 *12.25in (31cm) diam 38.25oz*

$2,500-3,500 **DN**

A Georgian silver waiter, by Paul De Lamerie, engraved with an armorial, with piecrust rim, on scrolled cabriole legs.

1731-32 *5.5in (14cm) wide 5.9oz*

$8,000-12,000 **POOK**

A George II silver salver, by George Hindmarsh, London, engraved with an armorial, on pad feet.

1732 *11.5in (29cm) diam*

$1,500-2,500 **TEN**

A Georgian silver waiter, by George Hindmarsh, London, engraved with an armorial, with piecrust rim, on hoof feet.

1737-38 *6.25in (16cm) wide 6.5oz*

$2,500-3,500 **POOK**

A George II silver serving plate, by George Hindmarsh, London, engraved with an armorial, with grapevine and reeded border.

1742 *15in (37cm) diam 54oz*

$6,500-7,500 **WW**

A George III silver salver, by Richard Rugg, London, with shell and scroll border, initialed within rocaille cartouche, on knurl feet.
1763 *14in (35.5cm) diam 39.1oz*
$1,500-2,500 **TEN**

A set of three George III silver course dishes, by Thomas Heming, London, with gadroon edges, crested.
1780 *12.25in (31cm) diam 73oz*
$3,500-4,500 **DN**

A George III silver circular salver, by John Scofield, London, engraved with an armorial and crest, with a beaded rim, on beaded feet.
1783 *13.75in (35cm) diam 41.95oz*
$3,500-4,500 **DN**

A pair of George III silver meat dishes, by William Stroud, London, with gadroon borders, crested and with motto.
1807 *17.25in (44cm) diam 116oz*
$5,000-7,000 **LC**

A pair of Irish George III silver salvers, by John Lloyd, Dublin, with swag-and-bead border, engraved with armorials, on shell bracket feet.
1782 *12.5in (30.5cm) diam 61oz*
$6,500-7,500 **WW**

A set of five George III silver plates, possibly by William Simons, London, with gadroon border.
1794 *10in (24cm) diam 90oz*
$3,000-4,000 **WW**

A George III silver salver, by Peter and William Bateman, London, with gadroon border, engraved with an armorial, on gadroon bracket feet.
1805 *12.5in (33cm) diam 32oz*
$2,000-3,000 **WW**

A large Irish silver platter, by Robert Breading, Dublin, with engraved armorial, with gadroon border.
c1808 *22.25in (57cm) wide 80.1oz*
$6,000-8,000 **POOK**

A George III silver salver, by William Burwash, London, engraved with an armorial, with gadroon and shell border, on foliate-capped paw bracket feet.
1817 *10in (25.2cm) diam 26oz*
$3,000-4,000 **WW**

A George IV silver salver, by Paul Storr, London, chased and engraved with flowers, with punched decoration, the center engraved with an armorial, with a shell and foliate border, on shell and vine feet.

1820 *10.25in (26cm) diam 29.9oz*

$12,000-18,000 **DN**

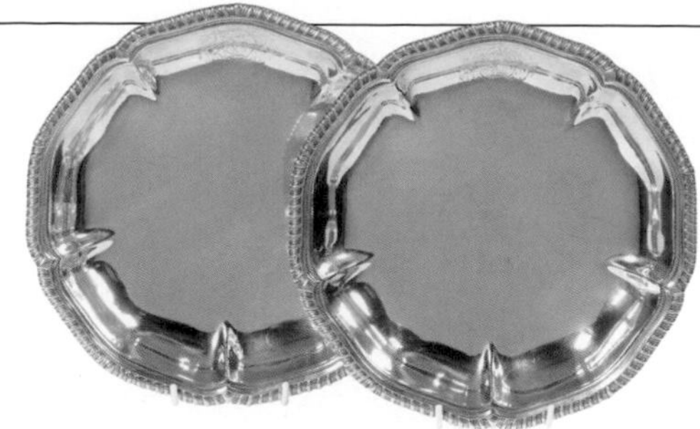

A pair of George IV silver vegetable dishes, by Robert Garrard, London, retailed by Garrards, Panton St, with gadroon rims.

1821 *10in (26cm) diam 45.4oz*

$1,500-2,500 **TEN**

A George IV silver salver, by Barak Mewburn, London, chased with flowers and foliage, with a shell, foliate and scroll rim, on shell and foliate panel supports with scroll feet, engraved with an armorial.

1829 *22.5in (57.5cm) diam 144oz*

$10,000-15,000 **DN**

ESSENTIAL REFERENCE - GARRARD & CO.

In 1802 Robert Garrard I (1760-1818) took over the firm founded by George Wickes (see p.325). He was succeeded by his son Robert II (1793-1881) in 1818. Garrard & Co. subsequently gained many important commissions, partly due to the decline of the great firm Rundell, Bridge & Rundell in the 1820s.

- **Garrard & Co. became Royal Goldsmith and Jeweller to King William IV in 1830 and Crown Jeweller to Queen Victoria in 1843. The company still retains the Royal warrant.**
- **The company's success depended on its useful wares for the dining table, which were showy but solid. It is best known, however, for elaborate presentation silver.**
- **Garrard & Co. merged with Asprey in 1999.**

A set of five Victorian silver plates, by Robert Garrard, London, with shell and gadroon border, crested and with motto.

1869 *10in (25.5cm) diam 105.6oz*

$3,000-4,000 **WW**

A Victorian silver two-handled presentation wine tray, by Martin, Hall & Co, London, with a gadroon rim, with presentation inscription, on four nub feet, with ebony handle-grips.

1881 *29in (74.5cm) wide 159oz*

$1,500-2,500 **TEN**

A late Victorian silver tray, by Charles Boyton II, London, engraved with reserves of fruit and flowers, the rim with a bellflower band inside beaded edge with foliage.

1895 *27.5in (70cm) wide 98.1oz*

$5,000-7,000 **DN**

A 20thC silver salver, by the Goldsmiths & Silversmiths Co. Ltd, London 1931, engraved 'Presented to Lady May Cambridge by the Household of the Prince of Wales on her marriage October 1931' and five facsimile signatures, with a molded raised border, on three claw-and-ball feet.

Lady May Cambridge, born Princess May of Teck (1906-94), was a descendant of the British Royal Family, a great-granddaughter of Queen Victoria.

14.5in (37cm) diam 41.95 oz

$1,500-2,500 **DN**

A William III Britannia silver bleeding bowl, by Charles Overing, London, the pierced handle with prick dot engraved initials.

1699 *5in (15.5cm) long 4oz*

$4,000-6,000 **WW**

A George II silver sugar bowl, by Archibald Ure, Edinburgh, with molded rim, crested.

1731 *4.75in (12cm) diam 5.5oz*

$2,000-3,000 **L&T**

CLOSER LOOK - GEORGE I SLOP/SUGAR BOWL

This bowl is currently the earliest recorded Scottish three-footed slop/sugar bowl. Bowls with lion-headed paw feet became common in Ireland from c1735, but this bowl pre-dates that by a decade.

Other makers who employed lion-headed paw feet this motif include Paul De Lamerie.

The large size of this bowl suggests it may have been used for slops, rather than sugar. Other sugar bowls of the period are smaller, partly due to the high cost of sugar.

A George I silver footed slop/sugar bowl, by James Ker, with engraved armorial and crest, on three lion-headed paw feet, the underside with scratch weight '11=12'.

1726 *5.5in (14cm) diam 11.5oz*

$10,000-15,000 **L&T**

A Belgian silver bowl, maker's mark 'IDP' possibly for Jean-François Dupont, Liege, the interior rim with with foliate panels.

1740 *6.75in (17.5cm) diam*

$7,000-10,000 **MAB**

A rare George II silver bleeding bowl, by Dougal Ged, Edinburgh, the pierced handle with scroll and foliate details, with later engraved monogram.

1749-50 *6in (15cm) wide 4.5oz*

$5,000-7,000 **L&T**

An Edwardian silver two-handled rose bowl, by Williams Ltd., Birmingham, with cut-card decoration and wavy-edge border, engraved with an armorial and presentation inscription, on wooden base.

1904 *With base 12in (30.5cm) high 72oz*

$3,500-4,500 **WW**

An Edwardian silver-gilt Monteith bowl and stand, by Elkington & Co., Birmingham, the castellated rim with putti masks and scrolls, with lion head ring handles, engraved with a Victoria Cross, dated '1918' and with presentation inscription, on a wooden plinth.

Alan Jerrard enjoyed the distinction of being the only aerial Victoria Cross recipient of the long and bitter campaign fought on the 'Italian Front' during the Great War. He was known as the 'Pyjama VC' because he was captured by the enemy while wearing only pyjamas under his flight uniform.

1907 *13.75in (35cm) diam 130oz*

$15,000-20,000 **WW**

A Edward VII silver Montieth bowl, by Edward Barnard & Sons, London, the rim with C-scroll notches centered by putti masks, the sides with lion-headed armorial cartouches, with lion head ring handles.

1906 *13.5in (34cm) diam 108oz*

$6,500-7,500 **FRE**

A pair of rare George III silver script wine labels, in the form of 'Calcavella' and 'Frontiniac'.
c1780
$1,000-1,500 LC

A George III silver 'RUM' label, by James Hine, London, with foliate engraving.
1791 *1.75in (4.5cm) wide*
$120-180 GORL

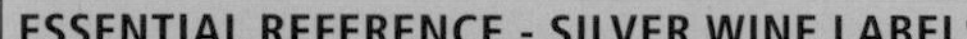

ESSENTIAL REFERENCE - SILVER WINE LABELS

Before the introduction of silver wine labels (or 'bottle tickets') in c1740, wine was typically labeled with hand-written parchment labels.

- **Silver wine labels were usually slightly curved so as to fit closely. They typically hung around the neck of the bottle on a chain or, later, a wire hoop.**
- **Most were stamped from sheet silver.**
- **Common shapes include oblongs, ovals, crescents and escutcheons, although wine labels were also produced in the shapes of anchors, scallop shells and vine leaves, etc. Heavy, cast designs featuring grapes and vines with putti holding scrolls were made in the early 19thC.**
- **Few wine labels were made after the 1850s, due to a Licensing Act of 1860, which required wine merchants to label all bottles before sale.**

A set of three Irish George IV silver wine labels, by John Teare Jarr, Dublin, with chased decoration, incised 'VIN.DE.GRAVE', 'FRONTIGNIAL' and 'MADEIRA'.
1820-25
$2,000-3,000 WW

A Victorian silver wine label, by C Rawlings & W Summers, London, cast with putti, incised with 'SHERRY'.
1838
$150-250 WW

A rare George III silver wine label, by John Robins, London, with bright-cut border, incised 'MALMZEY-MADEIRA'.
1792
$2,000-3,000 WW

An unusual Scottish George II silver wine/spirit taster, by John Clarke, Edinburgh, with twin V-neck spouts and S-scroll handles.
1748-49 *4in (10cm) wide 2oz*
$2,500-3,500 L&T

A George III silver wine funnel, by William Burwash, London, with gadroon rim and reeded spout, with detachable strainer.
1814 *6in (15cm) long 6.8oz*
$650-850 L&T

A set of four George III silver wine coasters, by John Roberts & Co., Sheffield, with fruiting vine decoration, the wooden bases with silver bosses engraved with armorials.
1809 *5.5in (14cm) high*
$7,000-9,000 GORL

A George III silver wine cooler, by William Pitts, London, with applied fruit and foliate garlands and molded foliage, crested and engraved 'Sic Fidem Teneo', with ram's head handles, with detachable silver liner and collar.
1803 *11in (28cm) high 118.9oz*
$12,000-18,000 SK

A rare William and Mary silver miniature tankard, by George Manjoy, London, with hinged cover, with embossed foliate border.
1692 *2.5in (4.5cm) high 0.6oz*
$6,500-7,500 **WW**

A set of twelve George I silver toy dinner plates, by David Clayton, London, two with scratch initials.
c1725 *2.5in (3cm) diam 1oz*
$4,000-6,000 **WW**

An 18thC Dutch silver miniature hearth brush, by Arnoldus Van Geffen, Amsterdam, with a baluster handle and ring terminal.
1731 *2.5in (6.5cm) long 0.3oz*
$500-700 **WW**

An 18thC Dutch silver miniature press, by Paulus de Soomer, Amsterdam, the screw-down cover with two detachable plates, with a pierced scroll frieze.
1756 *2.5in (9cm) high 2.8oz*
$3,000-4,000 **WW**

A late 17thC silver filigree counter box, with sixteen filigree counters.
2in (5cm) high 2oz
$1,000-1,500 **WW**

A William III silver counter box, by Francis Garthorne, London, engraved with an armorial, with 36 counters (after Simon van de Passe) depicting English monarchs.
c1700 *1in (2.5cm) high 3.75oz*
$7,000-10,000 **LC**

An Edwardian silver goat pin cushion and pin dish, by Allday & Lovekin, Birmingham, in the form of a goat pulling a cart, the cart with a shell body.
1909 *6.25in (16cm) long*
$1,500-2,500 **WW**

An Edwardian silver bear pin cushion, by Pithey & Co., Birmingham, with movable arms and legs, with ring attachment.
1909 *1.5in (4cm) high*
$1,200-1,800 **WW**

A late Victorian silver lady's walnut-form pocket necessaire, by S Mordan & Co., London, with powder box, mirror, scent bottle and pin holder.
1900 *2in (5cm) long*
$4,000-6,000 **LC**

A George II silver acorn nutmeg grater, by David Field, London, with swirl fluted screw-off cover, with steel grater.
1750-60 *1.25in (3cm) long 0.4oz*
$1,200-1,800 **WW**

A George III silver nutmeg grater, by Samuel Pemberton, Birmingham, with pull-off cover, with beaded border.
1799 *2.5in (3.5cm) long 0.3oz*
$650-850 **WW**

A silver-gilt pomander, with pierced scroll and engraved decoration, with a central screw thread and ball, with a chain and ring attachment.
2.5in (6.5cm) long
$12,000-18,000 **WW**

A George II silver sauce boat, maker's mark 'CL' possibly for Charles Leslie, Dublin, with leaf-capped scroll handle.
c1740 *6.75in (17cm) long 10.5oz*
$5,000-7,000 **WW**

A pair of George II silver sauce boats, by William Woodward.
1746-47 *4.25in (11cm) diam*
$3,000-4,000 **POOK**

A rare Scottish George II silver sauce boat, by Robert Gordon, Edinburgh, the rim chased with foliage, with dolphin S-scroll handle, on hoof feet.

Only six examples of Scottish sauceboats with this sort of flying-scroll dolphin handle survive. All known examples were made by high-quality makers.

1752-53 *6.75in (17cm) long 7oz*
$8,000-12,000 **L&T**

A George III silver cream boat, possibly by John Bayley, London, with crimped border, with leaf-capped and beaded handle, on scroll-capped scroll feet, crested.
1766 *6in (15.5cm) long 5.4oz*
$1,000-1,500 **WW**

A pair of George IV silver sauce boats, by the Lias Brothers, London, with gadroon borders, engraved with an armorial, with leaf-capped scroll handles, on shell-capped hoof feet.
1824 *8.5in (21.5cm) long 28oz*
$4,000-6,000 **WW**

ESSENTIAL REFERENCE - SILVER BASKETS

Silver baskets for holding bread, fruit, cake and sweetmeats are known from the early 17thC, although most surviving examples date from c1730 onward.

- **Silver baskets were initially hand-pierced. From the late 18thC this technique was reserved only for the finest examples, with all other pierced parts being mass-produced using a fly-punch.**
- **Late 18thC baskets tend to be thinner than earlier pieces and consequently tend to be less valuable.**
- **Regency and Victorian baskets were often unpierced. Such baskets were instead decorated with embossing or chasing. Victorian baskets tend to be comparatively affordable.**
- **Many baskets are engraved with a coat-of-arms on the body.**
- **Piercing is vulnerable to damage and should be checked carefully. You should also inspect any basket without a handle to ensure the handle has not been removed.**

A George III silver swing-handled cake basket, by John Lawford and William Vincent, London, with applied foliate decoration, ears of corn and flies, the base embossed with ears of corn.
1763 *15in (35cm) wide 32oz*
$3,000-4,000 **WW**

A George III silver fruit basket, by Elizabeth Aldridge, London, with scroll and floral border, with beaded ribbed decoration and pierced quatrefoils and stars, crested, on shell feet, with clear glass liner.

Edward Aldridge specialized in pierced work, particularly baskets, and was one of the most highly respected basket makers of his time. On his death in 1765 his widow Elizabeth continued the business using her own unregistered mark.

1766 *16in (41cm) wide 72oz*
$15,000-20,000 **CHOR**

An Edwardian silver-gilt cake basket, by Charles Stuart Harris & Sons, London, retailed by Asprey, with pierced foliate scroll decoration, the border with insects, masks and corn, engraved with an armorial, on mask-capped scroll feet.

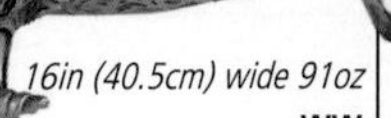

1908 *16in (40.5cm) wide 91oz*
$7,000-10,000 **WW**

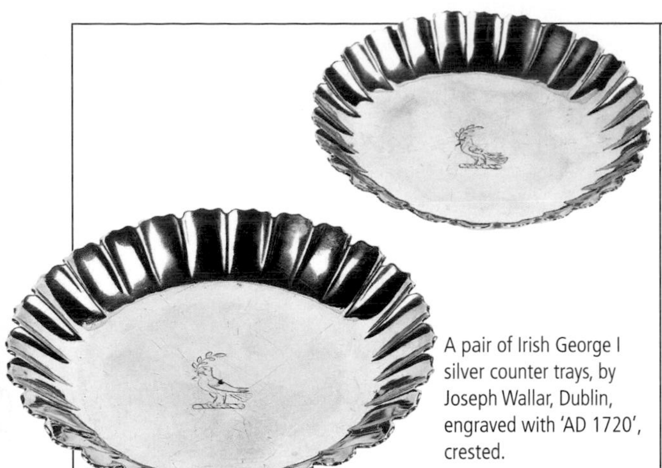

A pair of Irish George I silver counter trays, by Joseph Wallar, Dublin, engraved with 'AD 1720', crested.

1719 4.25in (11cm) diam

$2,500-3,500 L&T

A set of four William IV silver shell dishes, by Paul Storr for Storr & Mortimer, London, on periwinkle-shell feet, crested.

1830 5.5in (14cm) wide 21oz

$7,000-10,000 MAB

A William III Irish silver castor, maker's mark 'CW', Dublin, with domed foliate pierced and engraved cover, with ball finial and bayonet fittings.

1700 7.25in (18.5cm) high

$3,500-4,500 TEN

A pair of Queen Anne silver sugar casters, by William Ged, Edinburgh, the covers with engraved foliate borders and 'AMO PROBUS', and lattice pierced sections, with acorn finials, crested.

1708 Tallest 8.75in (22cm) high 19.5oz

$8,000-12,000 L&T

A George III silver Rococo castor, by Samuel Wood, London, with foliate scroll decoration, the foot with swag and scroll decoration, engraved with an armorial.

1761 7in (18cm) high 8.2oz

$800-1,200 WW

An early George III silver Warwick cruet frame, by John Delmester, London, engraved with an armorial, with shell feet, fitted with one large and two small casters with pierced and wrythen-fluted covers.

1761 Frame 10in (25.5cm) high 47.3 oz

$3,500-4,500 LC

A George III silver cruet frame, by Samuel Hennell, London, with gadroon border, the wire-work frame with leaf supports, on shell bracket feet, crested, with four cut-glass sauce bottles.

1818 7in (18cm) high 13oz

$1,000-1,500 WW

An early Victorian silver shell cruet stand, by Paul Storr, London, with three inset silver rings and dolphin-form handle, on conch-shell feet.

1838 9.25in (25cm) wide 22.8oz

$4,000-6,000 SK

A George III silver oil and vinegar stand, maker's mark 'RP' possibly for Robert Piercy, London, with gadroon border and leaf-capped scroll handle, on shell feet, with two silver-mounted cut-glass bottles with hinged crested covers and shell thumb-pieces.

1767 10in (23cm) high 15oz

$3,000-4,000 WW

A 17thC Spanish silver pyx, cover and interior bowl, engraved with a crucifix and birds, the lid with turned finial, stamped 'Sevilla, Szera?', missing applied crucifix.

A pyx or pix is a small container used by churches to carry the consecrated host to those unable to come to a church in order to receive Holy Communion.

4.5in (11.5cm) diam 13 oz

$10,000-15,000 GORL

A Georgian silver water urn, maker's mark 'IS' with stars above and below.

c1767-68 20in (51cm) high 68.1oz

$3,500-4,500 POOK

CLOSER LOOK - GEORGE III SILVER COLLARS

The presentation of silver prize dog collars is a tradition in Scotland, but surviving examples are rare. As few as seven pairs are recorded.

These collars are the second earliest recorded example of silver prize collars.

This pair are plainer in style than other surviving examples. This is due to their earlier date and the fact they were retained by the winner. Some later examples were re-engraved each year and given to subsequent winners.

That this pair still have their original chains is unusual.

Greyhound racing was considered a pastime for gentlemen and the upper classes. This is reflected in the high quality prizes, such as these collars, presented by the clubs.

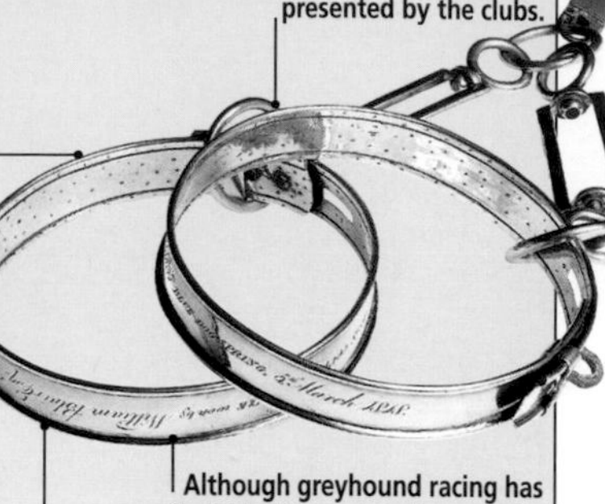

Although greyhound racing has diminished in popularity over the years, it is still a popular sport and there are many collectors of racing memorabilia. This cross-market interest is reflected in the value of these silver collars.

A rare pair of George III silver prize greyhound collars, by Robert Gray & Sons (Of Glasgow), Edinburgh, with alternating long and circular link chains.

1817 4.25in (11cm) diam 8oz total

$20,000-30,000 L&T

A Georgian silver dish cross, with maker's mark 'BD'.

c1774-75 11in (28cm) wide 16.1oz

$4,500-5,500 POOK

An early Victorian silver centerpiece, by Mathew Boulton, Birmingham, the leafy trailing column with leaf-cast scrolled branches supporting glass bowls, the base with panels of scrolling foliage, on paw feet.

1839 21.75in (55cm) high 152oz

$12,000-18,000 AH

A George IV silver-gilt centerpiece, designed by John Flaxman, by John Bridge, London, engraved with two armorials of the John Mayne family, with John Bridge 1823 mark to shell and Richard Garrard 1847 to base. 1823,

This centerpiece is believed to be a prototype for a set of four soup tureens in the Royal Collection.

1847 7.5in (44cm) high 361oz

$220,000-280,000 BARB

A large German silver centerpiece on stand, by G Hossauer, Berlin, partially gilt.

c1853 18.5in (47cm) high 145.5oz

$10,000-15,000 KAU

A matched pair of silver table ornaments, in the form of grouse, by Edward Barnard & Sons, London, with chased plumage.

1967, 1969

Tallest 6in (15.5cm) high 41.45oz

$3,500-4,500 DN

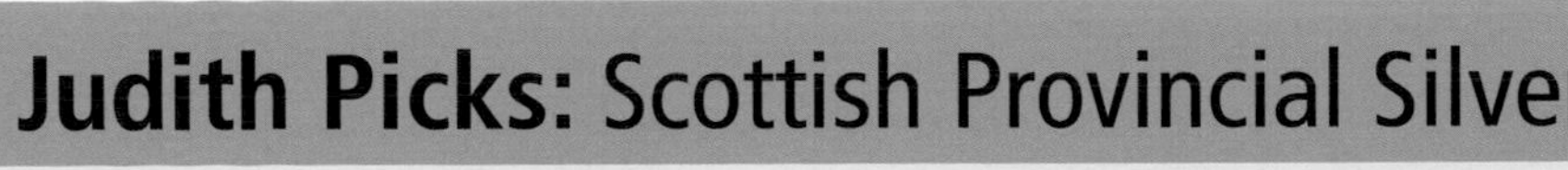

Judith Picks: Scottish Provincial Silver

Over the years Scottish provincial silver has become very collectible and highly sought after. For many reasons town silversmiths seldom sent their plate to Edinburgh or Glasgow to be assayed and then hallmarked. Instead, they marked the silver with a maker's mark or town mark or many combinations of these and other marks. Apart from the towns shown here, silver can be found with marks for Aberdeen, Arbroath, Ballater, Banff, Berwick on Tweed, Castle Douglas, Cupar, Dumfries, Fochabers, Forres, Greenock, Inverness, Iona, Leith, Montrose, Oban, Paisley, Perth, St Andrews, Shetland, Tain and Wick.

A George II Scottish provincial silver waiter, by Robert Luke, Glasgow, with arch and crescent border around chased band of shell, scroll and floral displays, crested, on double scroll and hoof feet.

This representation of the Glasgow town mark is extremely rare. Still following the tree, fish, bell and ring components of the standard mark (taken from the town arms), it is here represented in segments within the punch cartouche, rather than the truer representation from the town arms.

c1740 *8in (21cm) diam 10.5oz*

$2,500-3,500 **L&T**

A rare Scottish provincial silver quaich, by Charles Fowler, Elgin, the lugs with wriggle-work border, one with initials 'CS'.

This is currently the only fully-marked Elgin quaich recorded.

4.75in (12cm) wide 2.25oz

$10,000-15,000 **L&T**

A rare Scottish provincial silver mug, by Charles Fowler, Elgin, with reeded rim, foot and girdle, engraved with initials 'IG'.

Items of Elgin hollow ware are rare.

3in (7.5cm) high 3.7oz

$15,000-20,000 **L&T**

A pair of rare Scottish provincial silver cauldron salts, by John Steven, Dundee, with reeded rims, engraved with initials 'ED', each on three hoof feet.

3in (7.5cm) diam 7.4oz

$6,500-7,500 **L&T**

A rare Scottish provincial silver wine label, by William Ferguson, Peterhead, inscribed 'RED-PORT', with belcher-link chain.

While a small number of wine labels by William Ferguson are recorded most have Edinburgh hallmarks, suggesting they were produced in Edinburgh by another maker and overstruck by Ferguson. This piece, which has simpler decoration than other Ferguson labels and only carries local Peterhead marks, is likely to have been made by Ferguson, rather than simply retailed by him.

2.5in (6.5cm) wide 0.5oz

$5,000-7,000 **L&T**

A set of six George III Scottish provincial silver 'Oar' pattern teaspoons, by William Constable, Dundee, with the additional mark of Ziegler, Edinburgh 1809, the terminals with initials.

2oz

$250-350 **WW**

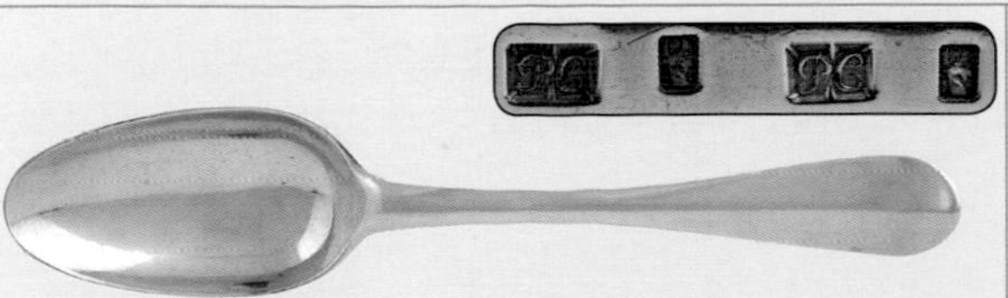

A rare Scottish provincial silver 'Hanoverian' pattern tablespoon, by Peter Cuthbertson, Canongate, with engraved initials 'AR/IR'.

Items by Peter Cuthbertson are particularly rare and, to date, only a small amount of flatware has been recorded.

7.75in (20cm) long 2.5oz

$15,000-20,000 **L&T**

An extremely rare Scottish provincial silver 'Fiddle' pattern toddy ladel, by John Mackie, Ellon, with chamfered edges.

This appears to be one of only a very small number of recorded marked Ellon pieces.

6.5in (16.5cm) long

$10,000-15,000 **L&T**

One of a pair of Old Sheffield plate wine coolers, with part-fluted decoration and gadroon borders, engraved with an armorial and crest, the handles with satyr's mask bosses, with liners.
c1815 *10in (25cm) high*
$1,200-1,800 pair **WW**

A pair of Victorian silver-plated wine coolers, by Elkington & Co., with ruffled rims, the sides applied with branches and vines, on acanthus-cast socle foot, with detachable liners.
1845 *11in (28cm) high*
$3,000-4,000 **FRE**

A pair of Victorian electroplate wine coasters, by Elkington & Co., with interwoven wirework sides and vine leaf rims, the walnut bases inset with crested roundels.
c1870 *7in (18cm) diam*
$800-1,200 **TEN**

A Victorian electroplate centerpiece, by Elkington & Co., the rockwork base with a stag beneath palm trees supporting a cut glass bowl.
c1870-80 *20in (51cm) high*
$2,000-3,000 **TEN**

A Victorian Neo-classical electroplate candelabrum and plateau, the stylized Corinthian stem with dragons supports, on a lobed spreading base, the plateau with a Gothic-style arcaded border, on scroll feet.
c1885 *Candleabrum 28in (71cm) high*
$8,000-12,000 **L&T**

Judith Picks

This impressive piece by Elkington & Co. is an electroplate copy of 'The Milton Shield', originally by Leonard Morel-Ladeuil (c1820-88). The central panel depicts the Archangel Raphael telling Adam and Eve of the 'war in heaven', in which the Archangel Lucifer rebeled against God and was expeled from heaven. The outer borders show further scenes from Milton's epic poem 'Paradise Lost'.

The elaborate and skilful workmanship on such a large piece was intended to raise the prestige and public awareness of the manufacturer, Elkington & Co. This in turn helped to sell the firm's standard mass-produced goods, such as tea wares and cutlery.

The original silver and damascened iron 'Milton Shield' was made for the 1867 Paris exhibition and took three years to produce. It was awarded the gold medal for the artist and was bought by the Victoria and Albert Museum where it remains on exhibition.

An electroplate copy of 'The Milton Shield', by Elkington & Co., decorated with scenes from Milton's Paradise Lost.
34.25in (87cm) high
$4,000-6,000 **L&T**

A Victorian electroplate centerpiece and mirror plateau, by Walker & Hall, pattern no.51351, the base with a pair of greyhounds and fruit-laden vines supporting three baskets with glass liners and a bowl support, the plateau with vines.
c1890
26.5in (67.5cm) high overall
$4,000-6,000 **MAB**

A pewter sweetmeat dish, attributed to Francis Bassett I, New York City, New York, incised with owner's initials 'IZ & CZ' and the date '1728' and foliate decoration.

1728 *8.75in (22cm) diam*

$90,000-120,000 **FRE**

An 18thC possibly West Country pewter charger, stamped 'M' beneath a crown twice, maker's marks rubbed.

15in (37.5cm) diam

$200-300 **DN**

A mid-late 18thC Massachusetts pewter plate, by Semper Eadam, Boston, with intitials 'HFO'.

8.5in (21cm) diam

$800-1,200 **FRE**

A 17thC pewter flagon, inscribed to the main body with two armorials and 'One of the three flaggons given by Mrs Hannah Gwynn to ye Company of Shoomakers in Gloc. An Dm 1688', 'Daniel Brian Master, Richard White, Thomas Ready Wardens', missing lid.

c1688 *10.5in (27cm) high*

$4,000-6,000 **DN**

A mid-late 18thC American pewter pint mug, Boston, with owner's initials 'AD'.

4.5in (11.5cm) high

$5,000-7,000 **FRE**

A 19thC pewter coffee pot, by James Dixon & Sons.

10.75in (27cm) high

$90-120 **DA&H**

A Victorian copper and brass tea urn.

22in (55cm) high

$60-80 **ROS**

A 19thC pierced copper and brass bedwarmer, the pierced lid applied with an eagle, with initials 'MHSI', with '1713' to obverse and '1773' to reverse, with turned wooden handle.

40in (102cm) long

$300-500 **POOK**

Ormolu Urn

A 20thC ormolu model of a twin handled urn, with bead-cast rim above frieze of putti, the handles cast as putti seated on serpents.

14.5in (37cm) high

$3,000-4,000 **DN**

An early 18thC heavy baluster wine glass, the bowl engraved with Queen Anne's Royal Cipher, on an inverted tear baluster stem and folded foot.
c1702 *7.25in (18.5cm) high*
$15,000-20,000 **FLD**

An early 18thC baluster wine glass, the round funnel bowl with a solid base with tear inclusion, on an inverted baluster knop with tear inclusion and small basal knop.
6in (15cm) high
$4,000-5,000 **DN**

A wine glass, the rounded funnel bowl engraved with Bacchus below the inscription 'CAPIENS CAPIOR', on a solid double-baluster stem with terraced foot.
c1730 *7.5in (17cm) high*
$3,000-4,000 **TEN**

A heavy baluster wine glass, the thistle bowl with solid base, on a hollow acorn knop over a basal knop and folded foot.
c1700 *7.5in (18cm) high*
$5,500-6,500 **TEN**

A heavy baluster wine glass, the conical bowl with solid base, on a heavy ball knop and folded foot.
c1710 *7in (17cm) high*
$5,000-6,000 **TEN**

A deceptive baluster wine glass, the funnel bowl on a flattened cushion knop and baluster stem with folded conical foot.
c1710 *5in (12.5cm) high*
$1,500-2,000 **DN**

A baluster goblet, the bell bowl with solid base and tear inclusion, on an annular knop, inverted baluster stem and basal knop.
c1720 *7in (18cm) high*
$2,500-3,500 **DN**

A balustroid wine glass, the bell bowl on an upper flattened knop and lower baluster knop.
c1740 *7in (17cm) high*
$700-1,000 **TEN**

A 'Newcastle' light baluster wine glass, the drawn trumpet bowl engraved with stylized foliage, on a cushion knop and inverted baluster stem.
c1750 *7.5in (19cm) high*
$1,500-2,000 **DN**

A wine glass, the bell bowl on multi-series air-twist stem.

c1740 *6.5in (16.5cm) high*

$400-600 **RGA**

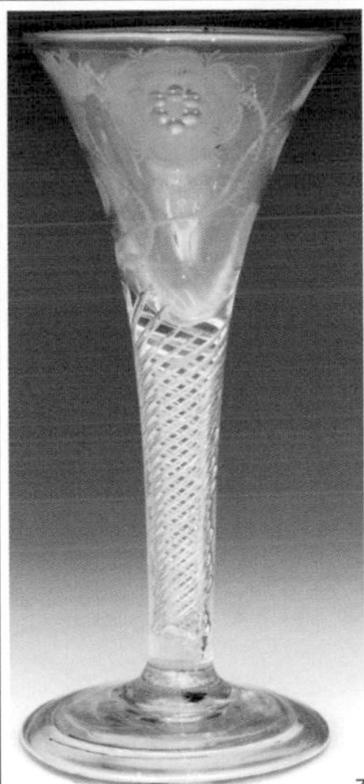

A mid-18thC Jacobite wine glass, the trumpet bowl engraved 'Redeat' and with dog roses and oak leaves, on a multi-series air-twist stem with conical foot.

7.25in (18.5cm) high

$1,500-2,000 **FLD**

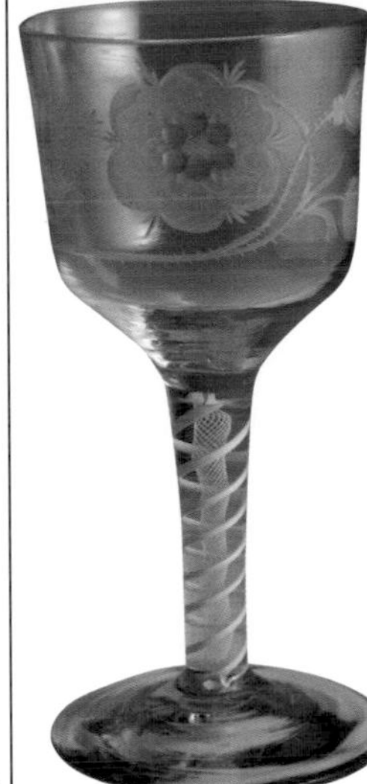

A large mid-18thC Jacobite wine glass, engraved with a rose, rosebud and butterfly, on a thick multi-series opaque-twist stem.

8in (20cm) high

$1,500-2,000 **WW**

A set of six wine glasses, the round funnel bowls on double-series opaque twist stems with conical feet.

c1760 *6.25in (16cm) high*

$2,000-3,000 **DN**

A wine glass, the ogee bowl engraved with insects, flowers and foliage, on a double-series opaque-twist stem with conical foot.

c1760 *6in (15cm) high*

$1,500-2,000 **DN**

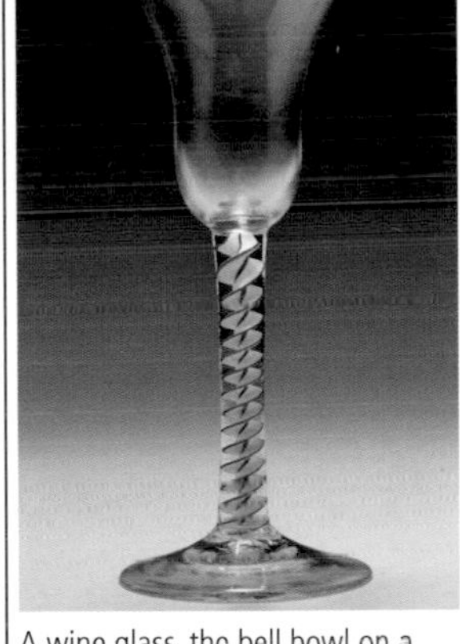

A wine glass, the bell bowl on a blue and white corked screw stem.

c1760 *6.75in (17cm) high*

$6,500-7,500 **RGA**

A wine glass, the ogee bowl engraved with lily-of-the-valley, on a red and white corked screw stem.

c1760 *5.25in (13.5cm) high*

$6,500-7,500 **RGA**

A rare set of six green wine glasses, the ogee bowls on double-series opaque-twist stems with conical feet.

c1760 *5.75in (14.5cm) high*

$30,000-40,000 **DN**

An unusual wine glass, the bell bowl on a double-knopped single-series opaque-twist stem.

c1760 *6.25in (16cm) high*

$500-700 **PC**

A rare Hanoverian wine glass, the bowl engraved with the White Horse of Hanover beneath a scroll inscribed 'LIBERTY', with a rose to reverse, on a double-knopped air-twist stem.

c1760 *6in (15.5cm) high*

$5,000-6,000 **WW**

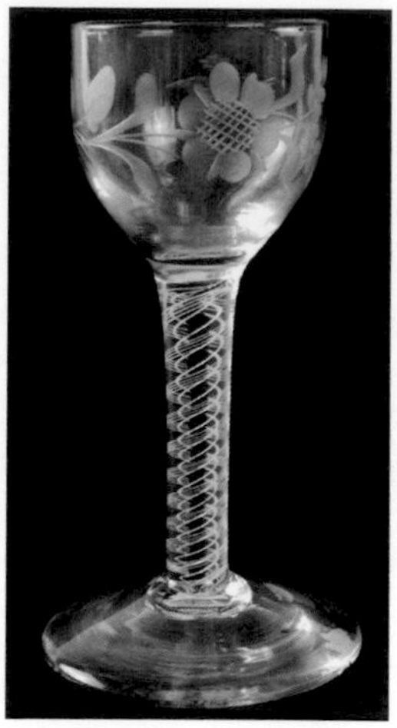

A wine glass, the ovoid bowl engraved with a bird and flower spring, on a blue cable and white opaque-twist stem with a conical foot.

c1770

$2,500-3,500 **DN**

A 'Lynn' ale glass, the funnel bowl stipple-engraved with the initials 'PM', on a double-series opaque-twist stem comprising spiral threads around a central gauze, with circular foot.

c1765 *6.75in (17cm) high*

$2,000-3,000 **TEN**

A pair of ale glasses, the funnel bowls gilded with barley and hops, on a double-series opaque-twist stem comprising a single multiple-ply band around a central corkscrew, with circular foot.

c1765 *8in (20.5cm) high*

$3,000-4,000 **TEN**

An ale glass, the funnel bowl on a triple-series opaque-twist stem comprising a multiple-ply spiral band around a triple-spiral tape and a solid vertical cable, with circular foot.

c1770 *7in (18cm) high*

$1,200-1,800 **TEN**

A large early wine glass, the conical bowl on a square-section teardrop pedestal stem with folded foot, the foot scratched 'C Gullett'.

c1720 *8in (20cm) high*

$1,000-1,500 **WW**

A pair of 18thC wine glasses.

c1770 *6in (15cm) high*

$2,000-3,000 **GORL**

An 18thC 'Amen' wine glass, the trumpet-shaped bowl diamond-point engraved with a crown, a cipher with small '8', an anthem and 'AMEN', on a plain drawn stem with folded foot.

Known as the Lennoxlove 'Amen' glass.

7in (17.5cm) high

$80,000-120,000 **HALL**

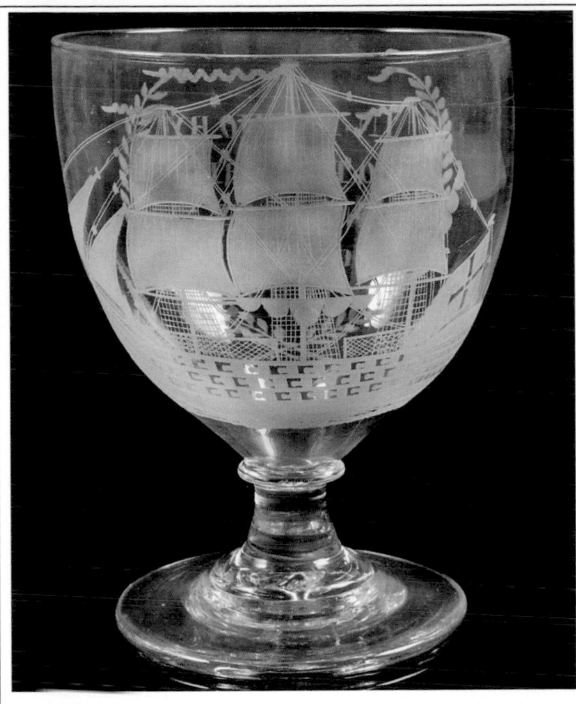

A large early 19thC engraved commemorative rummer for Admiral, Lord Nelson, engraved with HMS 'Victory', the reverse inscribed 'IN. MEMORY OF. LORD NELSON OCTR. 21 1805' within a laurel wreath.

7.5in (19cm) high

$4,000-5,000 **DN**

A large commemorative crested rummer, the funnel bowl engraved with an armorial and the motto 'GRADATIM', the reverse with initials 'JA', on 'lemon squeezer' foot, with some chips.

c1780 *9.25in (23.5cm) high*

$800-1,200 **DN**

A Sunderland Bridge rummer, the tapered bucket bowl engraved with a ship beneath the Iron Bridge and inscribed 'SUNDERLAND BRIDGE', on a capstan stem, with chip.

c1825 *6in (14.5cm) high*

$150-250 **DN**

A commemorative rummer for the Tarporley Hunt, the funnel bowl engraved 'QUAESITUM MERITIS' and 'SUCCESS TO THE TARPORLEY HUNT' within floral wreaths.

'Quaesitum Meritis' (the search for rewards) appears in the poem 'Tarporley Hunt' (1833) by Rowland Egerton-Warburton (1804-1891), member and one-time president of the Tarporley Hunt Club meeting.

c1840 *4.25in (10.5cm) high*

$1,000-1,500 **DN**

A mid-18thC Jacobite tumbler, engraved with a moth and carnation sprays.

5.25in (13.5cm) high

$1,500-2,500 **DN**

A mid-late 18thC Jacobite tumbler, engraved with a large rose and smaller single flower stem.

3.75in (9.5cm) high

$1,200-1,800 **WW**

A tumbler, engraved with the High Level Bridge, Newcastle.

c1851 *4in (10cm) high*

$350-450 **A&G**

An unusual pair of 19thC water glasses, enameled with freshwater fish among reeds.

6in (14.5cm) high

$1,000-1,500 **WW**

A Victorian silver-mounted claret jug, by James & Nathaniel Creswick, London, the glass body engraved with fruiting vines, the mounts similarly cast, with grape-stalk finial.

1853 *13in (33cm) high*

$2,000-3,000 **TEN**

A Victorian slice-cut claret jug.

c1840 *14.25in (36cm) high*

$500-700 **RGA**

A mid-18thC 'Sugarloaf' decanter, engraved with stylized flowers and insects, with a scalloped disc stopper.

c1770 *11in (28cm) high*

$700-1,000 **FLD**

A Regency slice-cut triple-ring ship's decanter.

c1820 *10in (25.5cm) high*

$1,000-1,500 **RGA**

A set of three Victorian ruby-flashed and engraved glass decanters, decorated with bands of fruiting vines, in a silver-plated stand.

Decanters 14.5in (37cm) high

$300-500 **DN**

A pair of Victorian silver-plate-mounted decanters, the stoppers cast with fruiting vines, the handles as Bacchanalian figures.

15in (38cm) high

$1,500-2,500 **DN**

A set of three Victorian decanters.

c1880 *11.25in (28.5cm) high*

$1,000-1,500 **RGA**

A pair of Edwardian ship's decanters, with mushroom stoppers.

c1910 *8.25in (21cm) high*

$1,000-1,500 **PC**

A pair of early Victorian silver-mounted green glass bottles, by Charles Reily & George Storer, London, the stopper and mount with fruiting vines.

1838 *15.75in (40cm) high*

$1,200-1,800 **DN**

A large mid-18thC Bohemian wine glass, the bowl profusely engraved with strapwork, chinoiserie figures and other motifs, on faceted knop and stem with red and gilt twist.

12.5in (30.5cm) high

$5,000-6,000 **DOR**

An early 16thC German ribbed tumbler.

c1500 *3.5in (8.5cm) high*

$10,000-15,000 **FIS**

A 17thC German tumbler.

2.5in (6.5cm) high

$5,000-6,000 **FIS**

A Bohemian footed tumbler, probably by Freidrich Egermann, enameled in pink, silver-yellow, lilac and pale blue, engraved with foliate and floral tendrils.

c1835-40 *5in (15.5cm) high*

$3,000-4,000 **DOR**

An early 20thC Austrian 'Knieriemm, Leim, Zwirn, das liederliche Kleeblatt' tumbler, engraved with three medallions enameled with characters from the play 'Lumpazivagabundus'

4.25in (11cm) high

$4,000-5,000 **DOR**

A large Bohemian lidded goblet, possibly by Franz Pohl, engraved with a deer in a forest landscape.

c1860 *20.5in (51cm) high*

$5,500-6,500 **FIS**

A rare Austrian enameled and gilt lidded goblet, from the workshop of Gottlob Samuel Mohn, Vienna, inscribed 'Mich erzeugen nur die Alpen', signed 'Mohn f. Wien' and dated.

1818 *12.5in (32cm) high*

$12,000-18,000 **KAU**

A Bohemian silver-mounted alabaster-glass jug, silver-painted with leaves and floral tendrils, the silver lid modeled as a faun on rockwork and flowers, with Viennese wheel hallmark.

1844 *12.5in (30cm) high*

$3,500-4,500 **DOR**

A rare German silver-gilt-mounted bottle.

1700

5.75in (14.5cm) high

$6,500-7,500 **FIS**

A pair of 19thC Bohemian enameled portrait vases, with portraits of maidens.

10.15in (26cm) high

$1,500-2,500 **LHA**

A mid-late 19thC Bohemian enameled vase, with four panels of flowers.

15in (37cm) high

$2,000-3,000 **DOR**

An unusual Georgian goldfish bowl.
c1800 *9in (23cm) high*
$650-850 **RGA**

A late 17thC half-size 'Shaft and Globe' bottle, patinated and partly iridescent.

This bottle was dug up in Booksellers' Row, the Strand, London, May 1894. Until the Victoria Embankment was constructed in the 1860s, the Strand was just a muddy riverside bridle path linking the City and Westminster.
c1660-75 *8in (19.5cm) high*
$8,000-12,000 **TEN**

A mallet-shaped wine bottle, with string rim.
c1725 *7.75in (20cm) high*
$550-750 **DN**

A large sealed wine bottle, applied with a circular seal for 'R Wilkins, Potterne, 1805'.
c1805 *10.5in (26.5cm) high*
$1,500-2,000 **WW**

ESSENTIAL REFERENCE - STIEGEL GLASS

Henry William Stiegel (1729–85) was a German ironmaster and glassmaker who immigrated to the USA in 1750. There he established three glassworks, of which the best known was the Manheim Glassworks (established in 1763).

- **Steigel glass forms are comparable to period Bohemian vessels. They were usually made in low-lead, greenish gray glass, often with engraved or wheel-cut decoration.**
- **All Stiegel's factories closed in 1774 due to financial problems.**
- **The term 'Stiegel glass' is generally applied to most 18thC American pattern-molded wares. It is difficult to positively attribute glass to one of Stiegel's factories. Many fakes are known.**

A rare 17th/early 18thC Mughal ruby-glass hookah base, decorated in gilt with poppies and geometric bands.
6.75in (17cm) high
$70,000-90,000 **L&T**

An American Stiegel molded amethyst-colored glass flask, in a diamonds above flute pattern.
c1770 *5in (13cm) high*
$7,000-9,000 **POOK**

A George III flat-cut blue scent bottle.
c1770 *6in (15cm) high*
$500-700 **RGA**

A rare panel-molded sweetmeat glass, with air-beaded knop and dumbbell baluster.
c1730 *6.5in (16.5cm) high*
$2,000-3,000 **RGA**

A 19thC Clichy carpet-ground millefiori paperweight, including one purple, one green, six pink-and-green and four white Clichy rose canes, in a white stave basket.

3in (7.5cm) diam

$15,000-20,000 **JDJ**

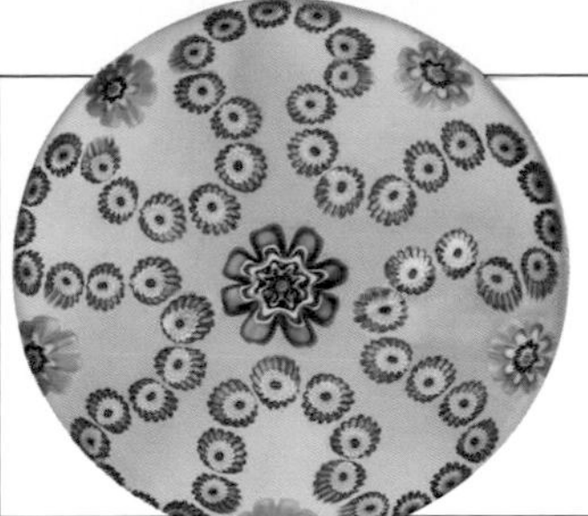

A large 19thC Clichy millefiori paperweight, with five loops of pink and white canes divided by blue 'pastry mold' canes and centered by a green 'pastry mold' star cane.

3.5in (9cm) diam

$2,000-3,000 **RGA**

A 19thC Clichy paperweight, with large 'pastry mold' canes including a pink Clichy rose, on an 'upset muslin' ground and divided by white muslin.

3in (7.5cm) diam

$2,500-3,500 **RGA**

A Clichy scrambled millefiori paperweight, including a pink-and-green Clichy rose, with scratches.

c1850 *2.5in (8cm) diam*

$1,000-1,500 **TOV**

A miniature Clichy millefiori paperweight, with nineteen spaced multicolored flowerheads

c1850 *2.25in (5.5cm) diam*

$400-600 **TEN**

A 19thC French possibly Clichy sulphide paperweight, with a profile of Queen Victoria.

3in (7.5cm) diam

$500-700 **RGA**

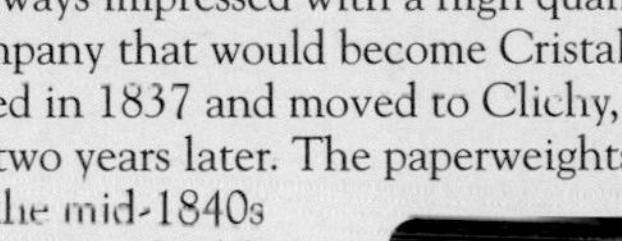

Judith Picks

I once tried my hand at making a paperweight at Selkirk Glass in the Scottish Borders with disastrous results - I am therefore always impressed with a high quality example. The company that would become Cristallerie de Clichy was founded in 1837 and moved to Clichy, then a suburb of Paris, two years later. The paperweights that it produced from the mid-1840s to the late 1850s are now highly desirable. The colors of Clichy weights tend to be richer than those of rivals Baccarat and St Louis. This is a typical, highly complex weight with the famous Clichy rose featuring prominently. It has a central green and white millefiori cane surrounded by two concentric rings of millefiori canes including 16 pink and white roses. There are eight circlets of millefiori canes and a garland of pink and green rose canes surrounding the design.

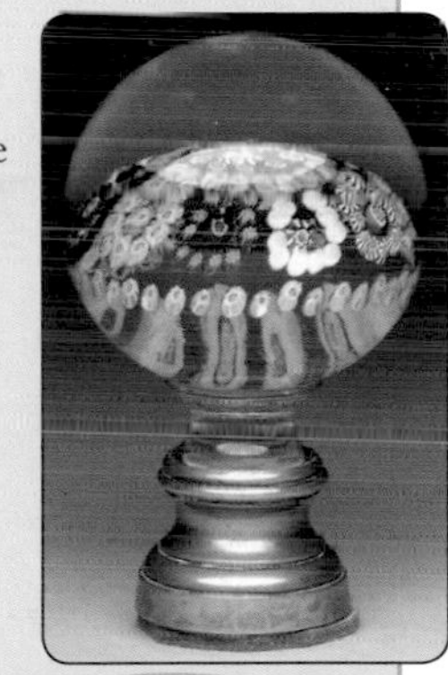

A 19thC Clichy millefiori newel post, including sixteen pink-and-white Clichy roses, with original metal hardware.

3.75in (9.5cm) diam

$12,000-18,000 **JDJ**

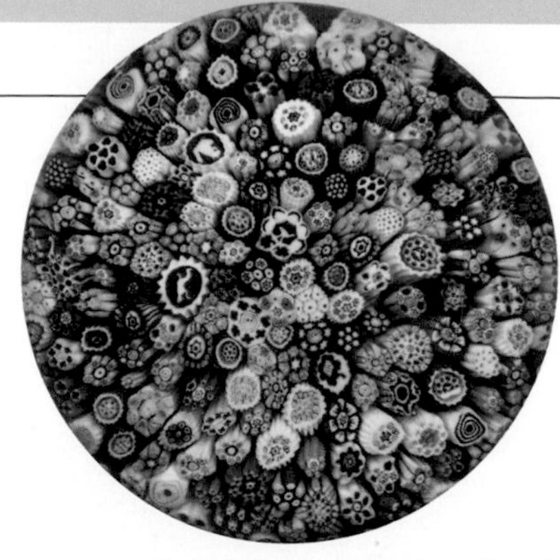

A Baccarat carpet-ground millefiori paperweight, including whirl, star, arrowhead and Gridel canes, signed and dated.

1847 *3.25in (8cm) diam*

$6,500-7,500 **RGA**

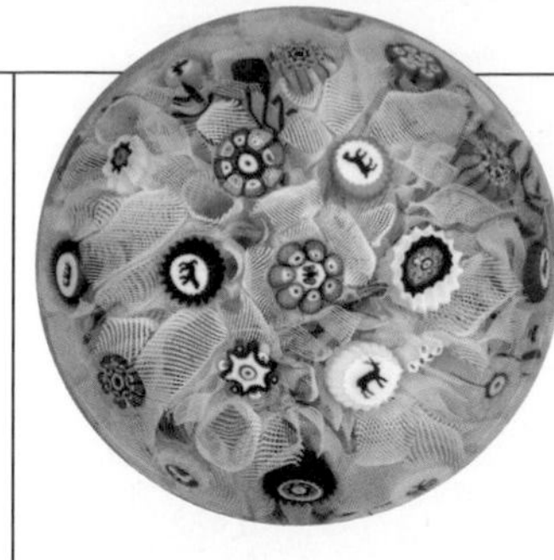

A Baccarat millefiori paperweight, including Gridel canes, on a latticino and colored bands ground, signed and dated.

1848 *2.75in (7cm) diam*

$4,500-5,500 **DOR**

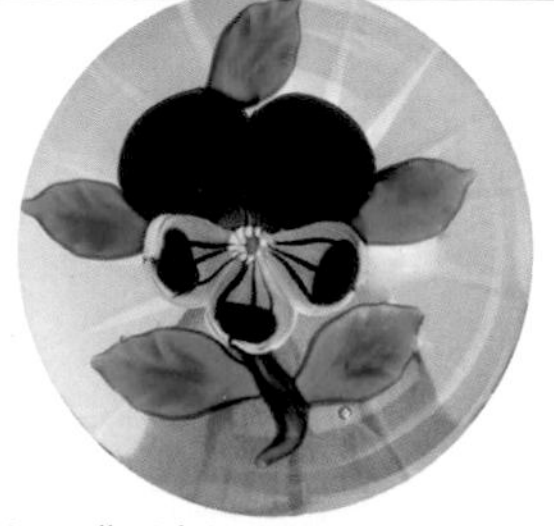

A small 19thC Baccarat pansy paperweight, with star-cut base.

2.5in (6.5cm) diam

$500-700 **RGA**

A large 19thC Baccarat blue-and-white primrose paperweight, with star-cut base.

3.25in (8cm) diam

$2,000-3,000 **RGA**

A rare 19thC St Louis 'Clematis' paperweight, on an amber flash base, with faceted sides.

3.5in (9cm) diam

$2,500-3,500 **RGA**

Paperweight Chalice

A 19thC Baccarat paperweight chalice, with four panels of loosely packed millefiori canes, with spiral lattice stem and further canes to foot, with gilding, in a presentation case.

6.75in (17cm) high

$15,000-17,000 **JDJ**

A 19thC St Louis 'Dahlia' paperweight, with five tiers of blue-striped petals and eight green leaves, with star-cut base.

3in (7.5cm) diam

$20,000-30,000 **JDJ**

A 19thC English Bacchus millefiori paperweight.

George Bacchus & Sons was a 19thC glass manufacturer in Birmingham, UK. The company produced a very small number of paperweights (around 400-500) in the late 1840s/early 1850s. These pieces were predominantly in soft, pastel colors and whites. The weight shown is typical of the company's output.

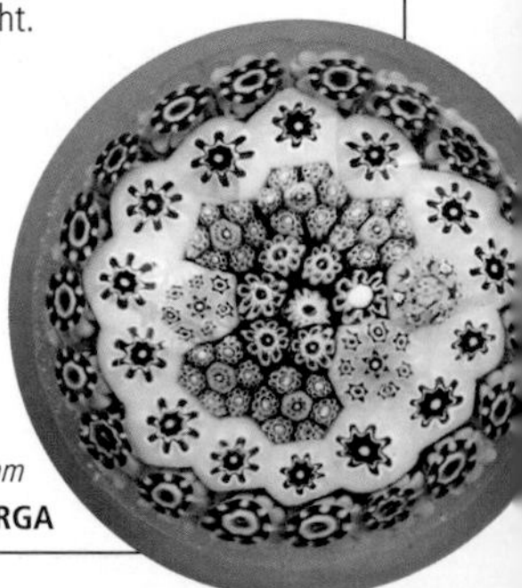

3.25in (8.5cm) diam

$3,000-4,000 **RGA**

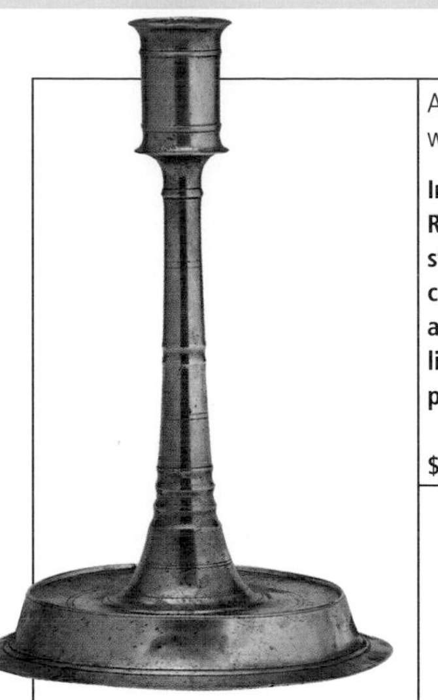

A Nuremberg patinated brass candlestick.
c1520 *7.5in (21.5cm) high*
$2,500-3,000 **KAU**

A 17thC Dutch brass Heemskerk candlestick, with ridged ball-type knopped stem.

In 'Old Domestic Base-Metal Candlesticks' Ronald Michaelis states that the 'ridged ball' stems that are typical of early Heemskerk candlesticks were superseded by 'inverted acorn' types by mid-17thC. It is therefore likely that the candlestick shown was produced before 1650.

7.5in (19cm) high
$1,000-1,500 **DN**

A pair of William III/Queen Anne brass candlesticks, with knopped stems and diamond bases.
c1700 *7in (17.5cm) high*
$500-700 **DN**

A mid-18thC William III-style brass candlestick, with knopped stem, the square base with concave drip tray.

Michaelis suggests provincial makers in the reign of George II were still making candlesticks of this form due to a reluctance to adopt the styles of the day.

9in (22.5cm) high
$200-300 **DN**

A near pair of French Rococo ormolu candelabra, in the manner of Messonier, one with crowned 'C' poincon (stamp).
1745-49 *Taller 15in (38cm) high*
$4,500-6,500 **LC**

A pair of mid-18C brass three-part candlesticks.
7in (18cm) high
$250-350 **TRI**

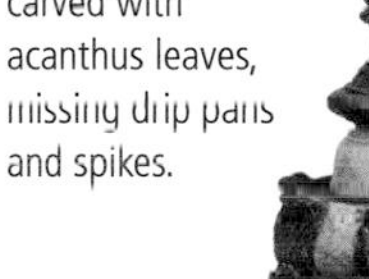

A pair of large 18thC Baroque carved and painted candle holders, carved with acanthus leaves, missing drip pans and spikes.
$4,000-6,000 **DOR**

A pair of French Empire brass and painted candlesticks, the capitals in the form of three female African heads, the bases with egg-and-dart border.
12in (30cm) high
$3,500-4,500 **GORB**

A pair of Regency gilt and patinated metal candelabra, on fluted columns and foliate bases, with paw feet, later electrified.
24in (61cm) high
$1,200-1,800 **L&T**

A pair of Louis XVIII bronze and ormolu candelabra, in the form of Classical figures holding cornucopia issuing scrolled candle-branches suspending later chains, on marble plinths mounted with vine leaves.
c1815 *30.75in (78cm) high*
$15,000-17,000 **MEA**

A pair of cut glass and ormolu-mounted luster candlesticks, in the manner of Baccarat.

c1825 *14in (35.5cm) high*

$3,500-4,500 **DN**

CLOSER LOOK - CANDELABRA

These candelabra are extremely decorative and in the style of Robert Adam.

They display particularly fine details, such as six scrolling and one stiff central candle arm in the form of flowering stems.

The white marble vasiform bodies are mounted with jasperware plaques of putti and ormolu rams' heads and floral swags – all features favored by Adam.

They have distinctive toupie feet.

A pair of ormolu, marble and jasperware-mounted candelabra, in the manner of Robert Adam, later electrified.

36in (91cm) high

$30,000-40,000 **FRE**

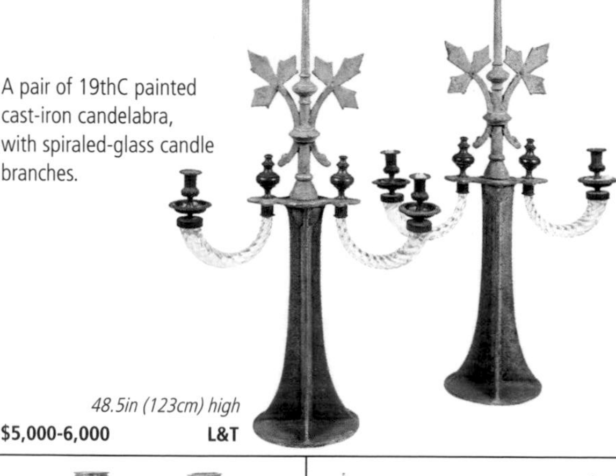

A pair of 19thC painted cast-iron candelabra, with spiraled-glass candle branches.

48.5in (123cm) high

$5,000-6,000 **L&T**

A pair of 19thC and later Continental ormolu and patinated-bronze candlesticks, with berry- and foliate-cast sockets above caryatids on plinths, the plinths incised with figures, on paw feet and triform bases.

13in (33cm) high

$5,000-6,000 **DN**

A pair of 19thC Louis XVI-style ormolu candelabra, the candle branches terminating in sphinx busts, the base cast with Classical figures and laurel garlands, on marble base, later electrified.

28in (71cm) high

$5,500-6,500 **FRE**

A pair of 19thC ormolu and patinated-bronze candelabra, in the form of putti holding vases issuing candle branches, on engine-turned plinths with goats' heads and associated Siena marble plinths, one damaged, later electrified.

Without fittings 27.5in (70cm) high

$10,000-15,000 **MEA**

An Austrian Lobmeyr glass and gilt-metal-mounted candelabrum, Vienna.

Designed 1877 *20in (50cm) high*

$4,500-5,500 **DOR**

(For silver candlesticks, see pp.320-23.)

A pair of 19thC painted spelter candlesticks, in the form of a jockey and a bookie, by Eugène Guillaume, signed.

12.5in (31.5cm) high

$2,000-3,000 **SWO**

One of pair of Irish George II Waterford cut-glass chandeliers, each with an inverted dish corona hung with linked swags and drops, the five candle branches with star drip-pans and tulip-shaped nozzles, one with replacements.

42in (107cm) high

$35,000-45,000 pair **MEA**

An Irish George II probably Waterford cut-glass chandelier, the baluster column with lozenge decoration above an inverted corona hung with drops, the scroll and overhanging branches with star-shaped drip-pans hung with drops, with restoration and replacements.

44in (112cm) high

$50,000-60,000 **MEA**

A large late George III cut-glass chandelier, the inverted dish corona above a baluster column and eight arrow-shaped candle-branches above eight scrolled candle-branches with lobed drip-pans in a bowl, all hung with drops, with ball terminal.

60in (152cm) high

$70,000-80,000 **MEA**

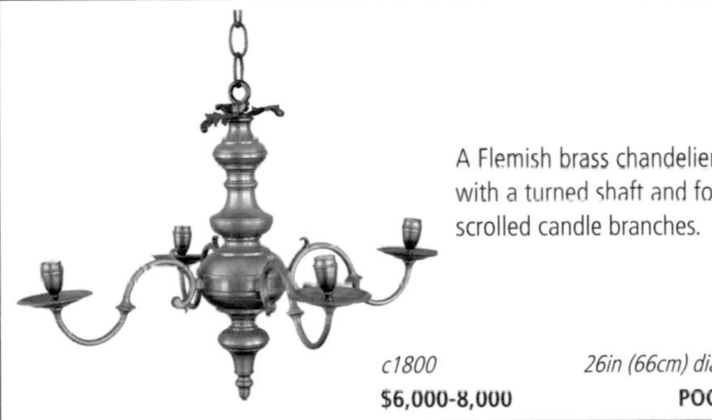

A Flemish brass chandelier, with a turned shaft and four scrolled candle branches.

c1800 *26in (66cm) diam*

$6,000-8,000 **POOK**

An early 19thC Baccarat glass and gilt-metal-mounted chandelier, with eight candle branches, the drip-pans signed 'Baccarat', later electrified.

32.5in (80cm) high

$10,000-15,000 **DOR**

A Biedermeier gold-painted wooden chandelier, with six candle branches and a ceiling crown, with restoration and replacements.

35in (90cm) high

$3,000-4,000 **DOR**

A late 19thC Spanish Baroque-style wrought iron and rock crystal chandelier, with three tiers of scrolls hung with glass and crystal drops, enclosing crystal orb, with gold-painted accents, later electrified.

36in (91cm) high

$3,500-4,500 **SK**

ESSENTIAL REFERENCE - CHANDELIERS

Glass chandeliers were first made in Britain in the early 18thC. The many facets of the glass drops were designed to reflect candle light.

- **Early 18thC British glass chandeliers followed the lines of brass prototypes, featuring curved arms attached to a central column made of spheres.**
- **Later 18thC examples were increasingly Rococo in style, often with two layers of arms fixed to a plate around the center stem.**
- **During the Regency period, chandeliers were often characterized by a cascade of hanging droplets, which created a curtain-like effect around the central stem.**

A Victorian-style cobalt-blue glass chandelier, with six scrolled branches with hurricane lamp shades, with gilt accents and hung with prisms.

37.5in (95cm) high

$7,000-8,000 **FRE**

A 19thC carved and painted chandelier, in the form of a mermaid holding a cornucopia and a fork, with cast antlers, with cracks and some losses.

47.5in (120cm) high

$5,000-6,000 **DOR**

A 20thC 18thC-style patinated-metal chandelier, the ten foliate-cast candle branches with foliate-cast drip-pans, with openwork foliate-cast stem.

18.5in (47cm) high

$550-750 **DN**

A large 20thC Austrian Lobmeyr glass and bronzed-metal chandelier, Vienna, with sixteen candle branches in two tiers, with replacements.

37in (95cm) diam

$6,000-7,000 **DOR**

A large 18thC-Continental-style carved and silvered wooden chandelier, with fourteen acanthus candle-branches in two tiers.

71in (180cm) high

$35,000-45,000 **DN**

A late 20thC Austrian Bakalowits cut-glass and ormolu 'Oriental Empire' chandelier, model no.2195, with eight satellite lights.

39in (100cm) high

$6,000-7,000 **DOR**

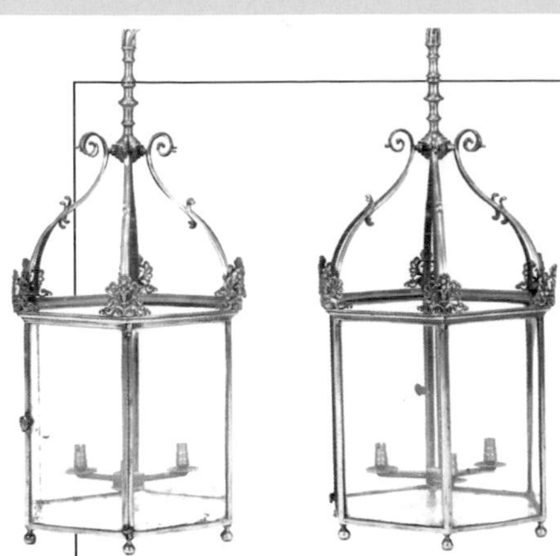

A pair of 19thC brass and glazed hall lanterns, with scrolling supports terminating in anthemion mounts, with three internal branches fitted for electricity.

31.5in (80cm) high

$9,000-11,000 **DN**

A 19thC George III-style brass and glazed hall lantern, with six foliate-cast supports and foliate-cast feet, later electrified.

27.5in (70cm) high

$4,500-5,500 **DN**

A late Victorian brass and leaded-glass hall lantern, with castellated gallery and foliate-cast uprights.

20in (51cm) high

$550-750 **DN**

A large late 19thC wrought-iron court lantern, with floral and foliate decoration, with later gold-paint and wall fitting, missing glazing.

51.25in (130cm) wide

$4,000-6,000 **DOR**

A pair of Victorian giltwood girandoles.

39in (100cm) high

$8,000-12,000 **DN**

One of a pair of Victorian brass gas wall appliqués, with crimped pink glass shades on scrolling branches, later electrified.

c1870 *12in (31cm) high*

$250-350 pair **DN**

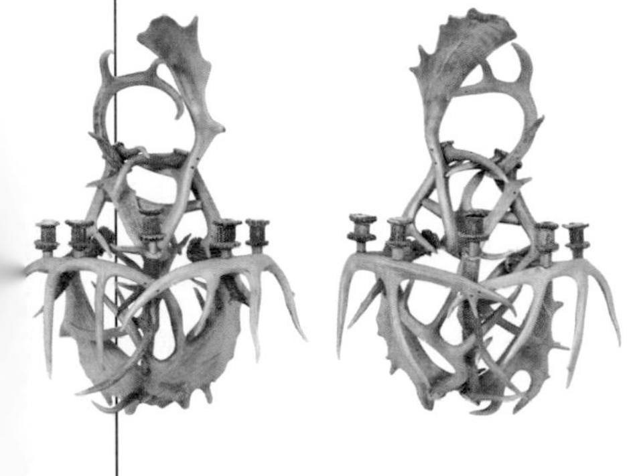

A pair of rare Austro-German fallow and white-tailed deer antler wall appliqués, each with five candle holders.

c1870 *31in (78cm) high*

$3,500-4,500 **TEN**

One of a pair of late 19thC Louis XV-style ormolu appliques, with laurel leaf- and berry-cast candle branches above a Bacchic mask.

24.5in (62cm) high

$5,000-6,000 pair **DN**

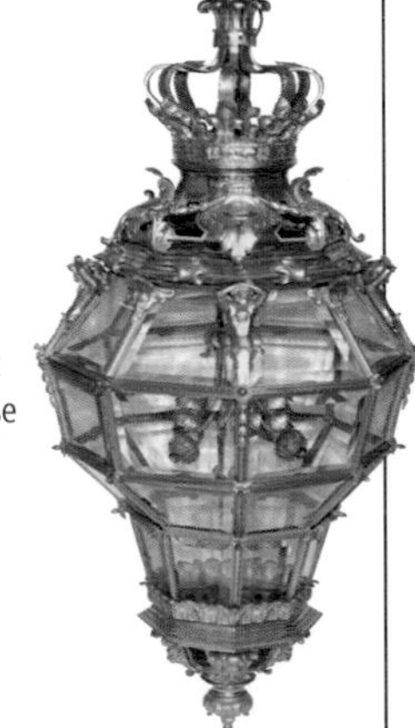

An ormolu lantern, with a crown over caryatid and pendant husk mounts, the base with cats' heads and acanthus, with nine internal flowerhead light fittings.

65in (167cm) high

$12,000-18,000 **TEN**

A pair of Regency ormolu and cut-glass colza oil lamps, hung with glass beads and pendants, the branches with panther head finials supporting light fittings, on foliate-cast bases.

c1815 *23in (59cm) high*

$3,500-4,500 **DN**

A pair of mid-19thC Argand lamps, signed 'Cox, New York', later electrified.

23in (58cm) high

$3,000-4,000 **DRA**

A pair of Venetian carved blackamoor lamps, on turned socle bases, on gilt and later ebonized plinths.

60in (152.5cm) high

$8,000-12,000 **WW**

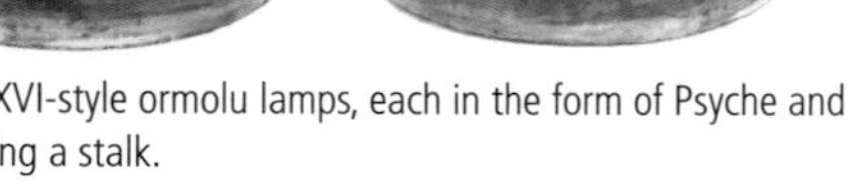

A pair of Louis XVI-style ormolu lamps, each in the form of Psyche and two putti climbing a stalk.

24in (61cm) high

$12,000-18,000 **DOY**

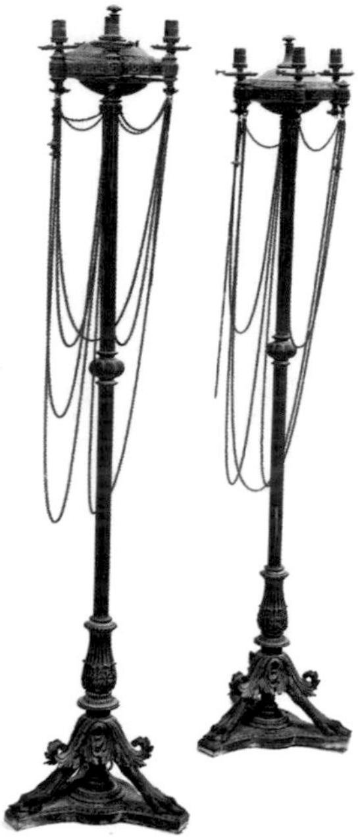

A pair of 19thC Neo-classical-style bronze standard lamps, the reeded stems on acanthus-cast triform bases with paw feet, with glass shades.

c1860 *63in (159cm) high*

$5,500-6,500 **L&T**

A pair of large Belle Époque ormolu and verde antico marble candelabra, in the form of the Three Graces supporting an urn issuing six candle branches centered by riser with flame finial, the bases decorated with Neo-classical motifs.

46in (117cm) high

$5,500-6,500 **WAD**

A pair of Louis XV-style ormolu-mounted verde antico marble urns mounted as lamps, the handles modeled as putti masks and scrolling acanthus, with foliate mounts to body and base.

c1900

Urns 15.5in (39cm) high

$5,000-6,000 **SK**

A pair of early 20thC French gilt-metal table lamps, in the form of foliate-cast urns with handles cast as berried sprigs, on marble bases.

10.5in (26.5cm) high

$350-450 **DN**

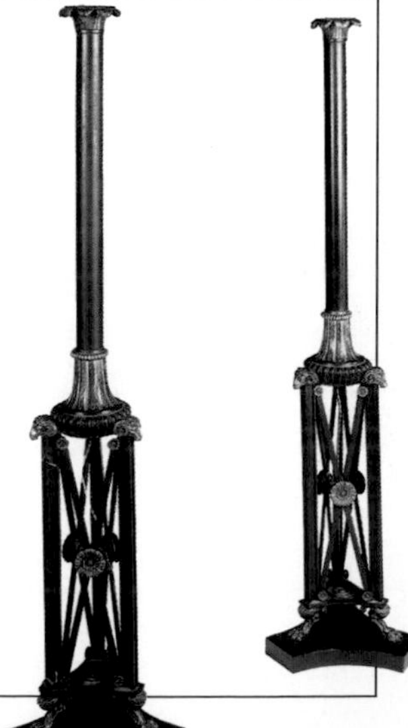

A pair of 20thC Neo-classical-style patinated bronze standard lamps, on openwork triform bases surmounted by rams' heads, on claw feet, with marble bases.

56.75in (144cm) high

$10,000-15,000 **L&T**

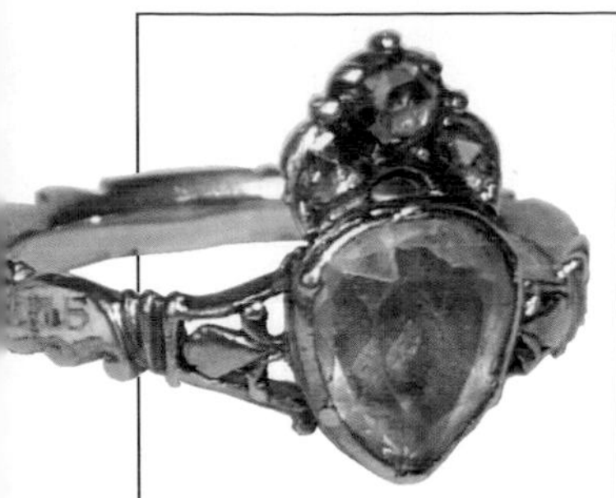

A George II diamond mourning ring, with woven hair under a rock crystal cover, mounted in gold, champlevé enameled 'J Town OB: 27 Jan: 1755 A.E:75'.

$2,500-3,500 SWO

A George III topaz and diamond ring.

$1,200-1,800 WW

A George III garnet and diamond ring, the garnet surmounted by diamond-set foliate motif, mounted in silver and gold.

$2,500-3,500 WW

A Georgian seven-stone ring, set with oval-shaped rubies in closed-back gold settings.

$3,500-4,500 LC

A Georgian citrine ring, with a locket behind the stone, mounted in gold, engraved 'J H Sherwood AR ob 10 Aug: 1770AE: 33'.

1770 *Size N*

$2,500-3,500 DN

A George III diamond ring, mounted in gold.

Size O

$650-850 GORL

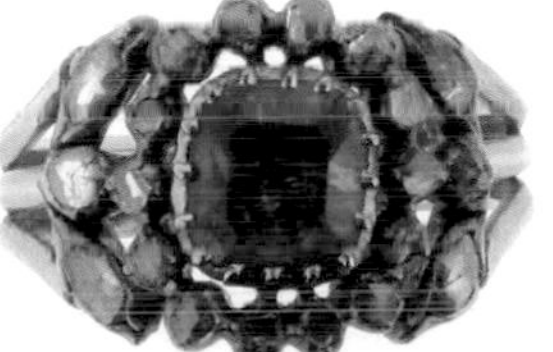

A George III emerald and diamond ring, mounted in silver and gold.

$1,200-1,800 WW

A Georgian ruby and diamond memorial ring, mounted in gold, the shank chased 'Anne Luxford OBt Mar 17?2 AE23'.

$1,500-2,500 DN

ESSENTIAL REFERENCE - GEORGIAN JEWELRY

Before the discovery of large deposits of gold in the USA in the 1840s and diamonds in South Africa in the 1870s, some jewelry that was no longer fashionable was dismantled and refashioned.

- **One of the most distinctive Georgian ring forms was the 'giardinetto' (small garden) ring, which featured a bouquet of gemstones. During the later Georgian period, Neo-classical rings with small cameos and intaglios were popular.**
- **In the late 18thC diamond pins in gold or silver were popular. Typical designs included sunbursts, crescents, stars and simple flowerheads.**
- **Late 18thC earrings were invariably made in the girandole or 'chandelier' design, which featured a large gemstone with three matching stones suspended beneath.**
- **Mourning jewelry became extremely popular in the 19thC due to Queen Victoria spending most of her reign in mourning for her husband Albert, who died in 1861. However, mourning jewelry was known from the 17thC. Georgian mourning jewelry included memento mori rings, which were often decorated with black enamel.**

A George III diamond cluster ring, the central brilliant-cut diamond claw-set within a surround of diamonds, with diamond-set shoulders, mounted in gold-backed silver.

c1770 *Central diamond 1.53ct*

$18,000-22,000 DN

A George III sapphire and diamond cluster ring, the sapphire within a double surround of old-cut diamonds, mounted in gold-backed silver, with a Harvey & Gore case.

c1800 *Diamonds 1.4ct*

$15,000-20,000 DN

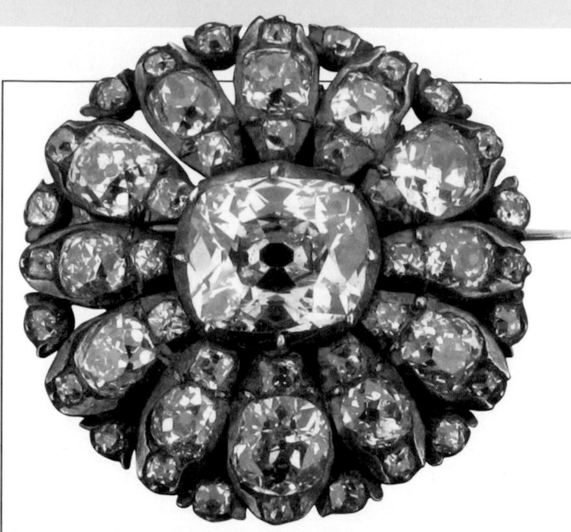

A George III diamond pin, mounted in silver and gold, with detachable pin mount.

Provenance: The vender's great-great-grandfather was the 6th Earl of Mayo and Viceroy of India from 1869 until his assassination in 1872. Family tradition holds that the pin came from India and possibly from the Viceroy.

1in (2.5cm) wide

$15,000-20,000 **WW**

An 18thC diamond feather pin, mounted in gold-backed silver, with a removable pin fitting and further later pin fitting, in a Harvey & Gore leather case.

c1770 *3.5in (8.5cm) wide*

$1,500-2,500 **DN**

A pair of George III diamond drop earrings, mounted in silver and gold.

$4,000-6,000 **WW**

A Georgian malachite-cameo and diamond rivière necklace, the cameos depicting putti, with foil-backed rose-cut diamonds in cut-collets and pearls, mounted in 14ct gold and silver-topped gold.

15.5in (39.5cm) long

$3,500-4,500 **DRA**

A Regency gold and amethyst necklace and earrings set, the necklace claw-set with mixed-cut amethysts in cannetille mounts and with a flexible woven gold collar.

Cannetille is similar to filigree, with designs created from fine wires or thinly hammered metal, jewelry with cannetille popular in the 1820s and '30s.

c1820 *Necklace 16in (40.5cm) long*

$10,000-15,000 **DN**

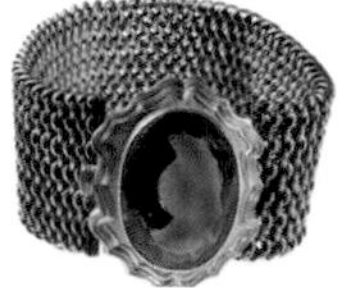

A pair of Regency gold and amethyst bracelets, the woven gold bracelets with mixed-cut amethyst clasps in scrolled mounts.

c1820 *7in (17.5cm) long*

$5,500-6,500 **DN**

A Regency gold, pink topaz and half-pearl necklace and earrings set, the necklace with a detachable pendant and five clusters set with pink topazes in cut-down closed-back settings within half pearl and gold filigree surrounds, in a Victorian case with a hand-written history of the necklace dated 1938.

c1820 *Necklace 16.25in (41cm) long*

$12,000-18,000 **DN**

An early 19thC gold belcher-link chain, interspersed with star-decorated belcher-links, the clasp in the form of a hand set with a ruby, in a fitted case.

49.5in (126cm) long

$30,000-40,000 **L&T**

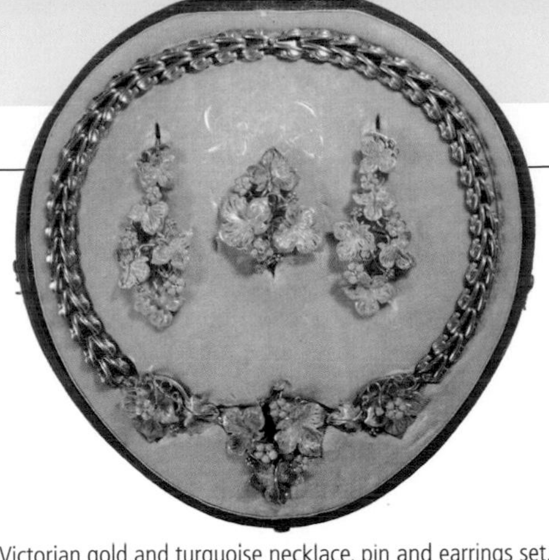

A mid-Victorian gold and turquoise necklace, pin and earrings set, with two-color gold leaves and turquoise forget-me-not clusters, the necklace with a chevron-link chain, in its original case.

c1870 *Necklace 17.25in (44cm) long*

$7,000-10,000 **DN**

A Victorian jet heart pendant, carved with a floral motif.

2.5in (5cm) high

$350-450 **TEN**

A late 19thC peridot and diamond suite, with 23 bright-cut peridots with diamond surrounds and diamond arabesque links, mounted in silver-topped gold.

This suite is fully transformable for wear as collar, fringe, girandole and earrings. Fittings for a tiara have been lost.

c1890 *Peridot 324ct*

$150,000-200,000 **DRA**

CLOSER LOOK - CAMEO

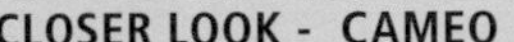

The gold and enamel chain sensitively complement the cameo.

The hardstone has been intricately carved to give the hair and hair ornament a naturalistic appeal.

Mythological subjects were popular during the early 19thC.

The contrast between dark and light is particularly successfully utilized on this piece.

A Victorian hardstone cameo, depicting a Greek youth, mounted in 18ct gold, with 14ct gold and enamel chain.

Pendant 2.5in (6.5cm) high

$8,000-12,000 **DRA**

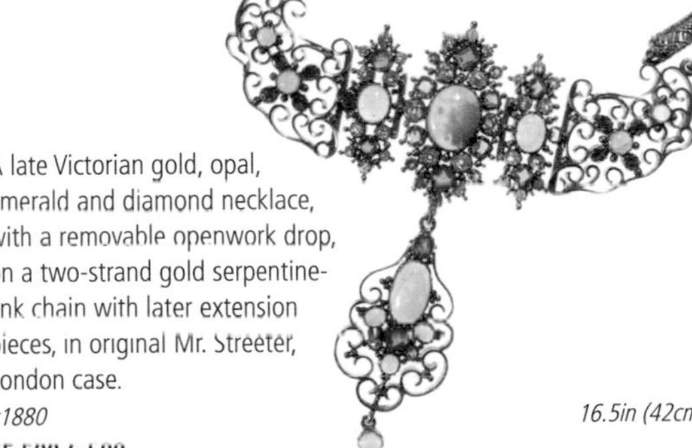

A late Victorian gold, opal, emerald and diamond necklace, with a removable openwork drop, on a two-strand gold serpentine-link chain with later extension pieces, in original Mr. Streeter, London case.

c1880 *16.5in (42cm) long*

$5,500-6,500 **DN**

A late Victorian natural pearl, diamond and ruby pendant, the garland set with rose-cut diamonds and a ruby, mounted in gold-backed silver.

1.25in (3cm) high

$3,000-4,000 **DN**

A late Victorian diamond pendant, the central old-brilliant-cut diamond surrounded by old-cut diamonds, mounted in gold-backed silver, with removal pin fitting, the chain with diamond-cluster clasp.

c1890 *Pendant 1.25in (3cm) diam*

Central diamond 2.3ct

$12,000-18,000 **DN**

A Victorian gold and diamond portrait pin/pendant, with four old-European-cut diamonds.
c1897 *Portrait 1in (2.5cm) diam*
$300-400 **LHA**

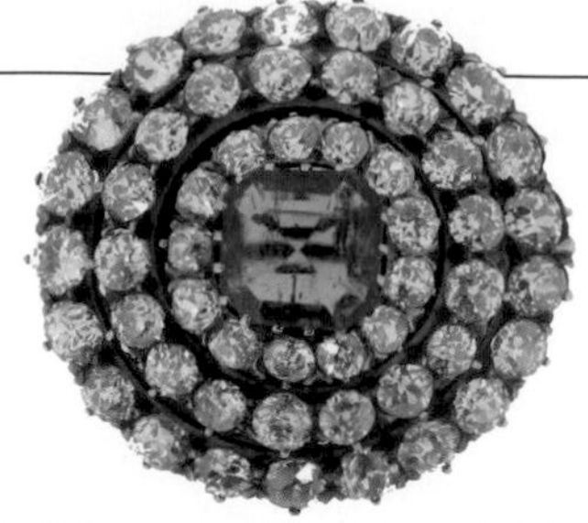

A late Victorian emerald and diamond pin/pendant, the emerald-cut emerald within three surrounds of cushion-shaped diamonds, mounted in silver and gold.
1in (2.5cm) diam
$7,000-10,000 **WW**

A Victorian diamond foliate pin, with cushion-shaped diamonds, mounted in silver and gold, the central diamond possibly later.
1.25in (3.5cm) wide
$6,500-7,500 **WW**

An Italian 18ct gold and micromosaic pin and earrings set, by the Vatican mosaic workshop, Rome, depicting doves and a rose branch within a geometric border, with old restoration.
c1885 *Pin 1.5in (4cm) diam*
$4,500-5,500 **DRA**

A demantoid-garnet and diamond salamander pin, with old-brilliant-cut diamonds and ruby eyes, mounted in 14ct gold.
c1900 *2.5in (6.5cm) long*
$4,000-6,000 **DRA**

A 19thC possibly Russian enamel, gold and diamond serpent pin, with mine-cut diamond to head and rose-cut diamond eyes.
1.5in (4cm) diam
$1,500-2,500 **DRA**

A late Victorian diamond swallow pin, set with rose-cut diamonds and a ruby eye, mounted in silver, with a gold removable pin frame.
c1890 *1.75in (4.5cm) long*
$2,500-3,500 **DN**

A late Victorian pearl and diamond double-heart pin/pendant, the gray half-pearls surrounded by old-brilliant-cut diamonds, with a gray pearl and diamond drop, the top with further diamonds and a bouton pearl, mounted in gold-backed silver, in an S J Phillips case, with a modern chain.
c1890
$10,000-15,000 **DN**

A Victorian Royal presentation gold pin, the reverse with glazed panel enclosing a lock of hair, inscribed 'Presented by Her Majesty Queen Victoria to Mrs MacGovan of Callander, Invertrossachs Sept 10th 1869', in original fitted case with trade label to interior for 'Abud Collingwood & Sons, Jeweller to the Queen and HRH the Prince of Wales, 46 Conduit Street W'.
1.5in (4cm) diam
$5,000-7,000 **L&T**

A late 19thC gold and Swiss-enamel bangle, pin and earring set, with plaques depicting a ladies in 18thC costume en habille with rose-cut diamonds.

c1880 *Bangle 2in (5cm) diam*

$3,500-4,500 **DN**

A mid-19thC Anglo-Indian gold swami-style bangle (kadakam), the articulated hinged panels depicting Hindu gods, in a Victorian case.

Following the 1875-76 official visit of the Prince of Wales to India, the Indian Museum in South Kensington held an exhibition of the gifts he'd received during that tour. These included silverware and jewelry in the swami style made by P Orr & Sons of Madras. A 19thC trade catalog noted that bangles like this were among the company's most popular designs.

c1890 *2.25in (5.5cm) diam*

$9,000-11,000 **DN**

A Victorian 14ct gold, seed pearl and enamel cuff bracelet.

c1880 *2.25in (5.5cm) diam 1.42oz*

$1,200-1,800 **LHA**

A Victorian gold and pearl bracelet, the applied plaque with initials 'M & P'.

7in (18cm) long 2.43oz

$12,000-18,000 **WW**

A 19thC Renaissance Revival sapphire and diamond hinged-bangle, mounted in pierced silver-topped gold.

1.48oz 7.5in (19cm) diam

$12,000-18,000 **DRA**

A Victorian gold, turquoise and diamond bracelet, the central hinged disc opening to reveal a glazed compartment, on a flexible serpentine-link bracelet with a concealed snap-clasp.

c1870 *7in (18cm) long*

$2,000-3,000 **DN**

A Victorian pierced and chased gold bracelet, the hinged central panel decorated with an exotic bird and opening to a photograph, the other panels with exotic plants, in fitted case.

6.5in (16.5cm) long

$30,000-40,000 **L&T**

A Victorian turquoise serpent bracelet, with rose-cut diamond eye, mounted in silver-topped gold.

2oz

$8,000-12,000 **DRA**

JEWELRY

A Victorian gold and amethyst bracelet, the central amethyst surrounded by cabochon amethysts and rose-cut diamonds, with a glazed compartment to reverse, the palmette-link bracelet with a concealed clasp.
c1870 *6.75in (17.5cm) long*
$4,000-6,000 **DN**

A late Victorian gold and pietra dura bracelet, depicting flower sprays, with foliate cluster connecting links.
c1880 *7.25in (18.5cm) long*
$1,500-2,000 **DN**

A gold 'SOUVENIR' folding bracelet, the bracelet folding away into a stylized book, with three bands of turquoise cabochons, in a Hacock case.
$5,000-7,000 **WW**

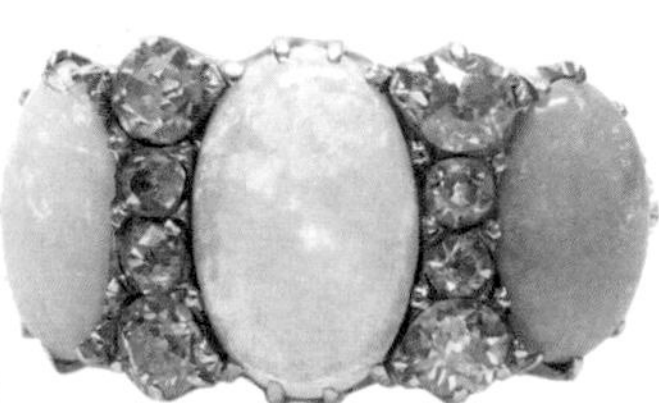

A Victorian opal and diamond ring, the cabochon opals spaced by rows of old-cut-diamonds, mounted in yellow-metal.
Size K Diamonds 0.50ct
$700-1,000 **TEN**

A Victorian sapphire and diamond ring, the emerald-cut sapphire surrounded by cushion-shaped diamonds,mounted in silver and gold, in a case.
Size P Sapphire 7.25ct
$30,000-40,000 **WW**

A pair of early Victorian diamond drop earrings, with large old-brilliant-cut diamonds surrounded by old-cut diamonds, with later post fittings, in a leather-bound case.
c1850 *1.5in (4cm) long Diamonds 4.6ct*
$15,000-20,000 **DN**

A pair of late 19thC gold earrings, with wirework decoration.
3in (7.5cm) long
$2,000-3,000 **DN**

An early 19thC Egyptian Revival gold serpent ring.
0.67oz
$3,000-4,000 **WW**

A late Victorian diamond memorial ring, the central hairwork panel with a diamond-set 'G' beneath rock crystal and surrounded by rose-cut diamonds, the reverse with inscription.
1882
$2,500-3,500 **DN**

A late Victorian turquoise half-hoop ring, Birmingham, the turquoise cabochons spaced with rose-cut diamonds, mounted in 18ct gold, with case.
1900 *Size L*
$700-1,000 **WW**

A Liberty & Co. gold and opal ring, designed by Archibald Knox, with stamped marks.
1902
$5,000-7,000 **WW**

An Arts & Crafts sapphire and pearl pin, in the manner of John Paul Cooper for the Artificers' Guild, with wirework decoration.
$500-700 **DN**

A French Art Nouveau 18ct gold, silver, diamond and pearl pin.
c1900 *2.5in (4.5cm) high Diamonds 2.2ct*
$2,500-3,500 **KAU**

An Arts & Crafts silver and gold 'Phyllida' pendant, by Arthur & Georgie Gaskin, Birmingham, set with chalcedony and tourmaline cabochons, on chain.
c1930 *Pendant 2.75in (7cm)*
$12,000-18,000 **TEN**

A French Art Nouveau diamond pin, mounted in platinum.
2.5in (4.5cm) wide Diamonds 1.12ct
$1,500-2,500 **KAU**

An Art Nouveau diamond pin, with old-brilliant-cut diamonds and a rose-cut diamond, mounted in platinum-topped gold.
c1910 *2in (5cm) long Diamonds 2ct*
$5,000-7,000 **DN**

An Art Nouveau opal and demantoid-garnet peacock-feather pin, attributed to Karl Rothmuller, Munich, mounted in platinum-topped gold.
c1900 *Main opal 8ct*
$12,000-18,000 **DRA**

An Art Nouveau opal, garnet and enamel 'Winged Love' ring, with rose-cut diamond accents, mounted in 18ct gold, inscribed '1895 Herbert Dorothy'.
1895
$3,500-4,500 **DRA**

A Belle Époque aquamarine and diamond pendant, with a scroll border of diamond-set fleur-de-lys, mounted in platinum, with a platinum chain.
$6,500-7,500 **WW**

A Belle Époque diamond and pearl bracelet/necklace, the bracelet set with pearls and circular- and rose-cut diamonds on a lattice ground, with silver necklace-extender.
c1900 *Necklace 9in (22.5cm) long*
$15,000-20,000 **WW**

A Belle Époque platinum, oriental pearl and rose-cut diamond 'Marie Antoinette' necklace, after the 18thC rivière necklace by Boehmer et Bassenge, restrung.

Known as the 'Queen's necklace', the original was an excessive diamond ornament. The public's reaction to its expense contributed to the French Revolution.
$7,000-10,000 **DRA**

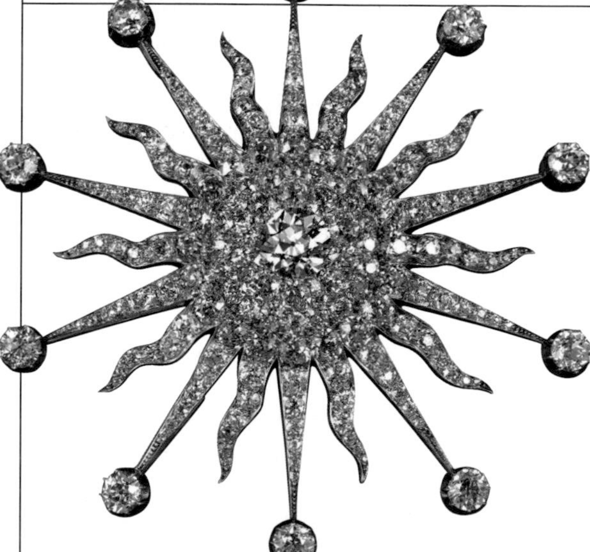

A Fin de Siècle sun pin, the transitional brilliant-cut diamonds mounted in silver and gold, with detachable pin mount and hair ornament fitting, in fitted case.

Provenance: Mary Caroline, Countess of Lovelace (widow of Ralph, 2nd Earl of Lovelace and grandson of Lord Byron) and then by descent.
c1900 *3.25in (8cm) diam*
$50,000-70,000 **WW**

ESSENTIAL REFERENCE - BELLE ÉPOQUE

The Belle Époque (c1871-c1914) was a period in French history that was characterized by optimism, peace and new technology.

- **New artistic movements, such as Art Nouveau, the Symbolist movement, Fauvism, Expressionism and early Modernism, were developed during the Belle Époque.**
- **Literature was characterized by increased realism and naturalism by authors such as Guy de Maupassant and Émile Zola.**
- **Popular musical styles included salon music and operetta by notable composers such as Johann Strauss III, Franz Lehár and Claude Debussy.**
- **Modern dance began to emerge as a serious force in the theatre. The Ballets Russes and performers such as Loie Fuller had a strong influence on the work of Belle Époque artists and designers.**

A Belle Époque amethyst and diamond pendant, with rose-cut diamonds, on a link chain, in fitted case.
$4,000-6,000 **WW**

A Belle Époque diamond pin, millegrain-set with a transitional-cut diamond surrounded by circular-cut diamonds and lattice sections.
2in (5cm) diam
$15,000-20,000 **WW**

A Belle Époque diamond articulated pin, with old-brilliant-cut and old-cut diamonds, mounted in platinum topped gold.
c1910 *2.25in (6cm) long*
Central diamond 2.08ct
$25,000-35,000 **DN**

A Belle Époque sapphire and diamond pendant necklace, mounted in yellow- and white-metal.
c1900
$1,500-2,500 **WHP**

A pair of Belle Époque diamond drop earrings, mounted in gold.
2in (5cm) long
$3,000-4,000 **GORL**

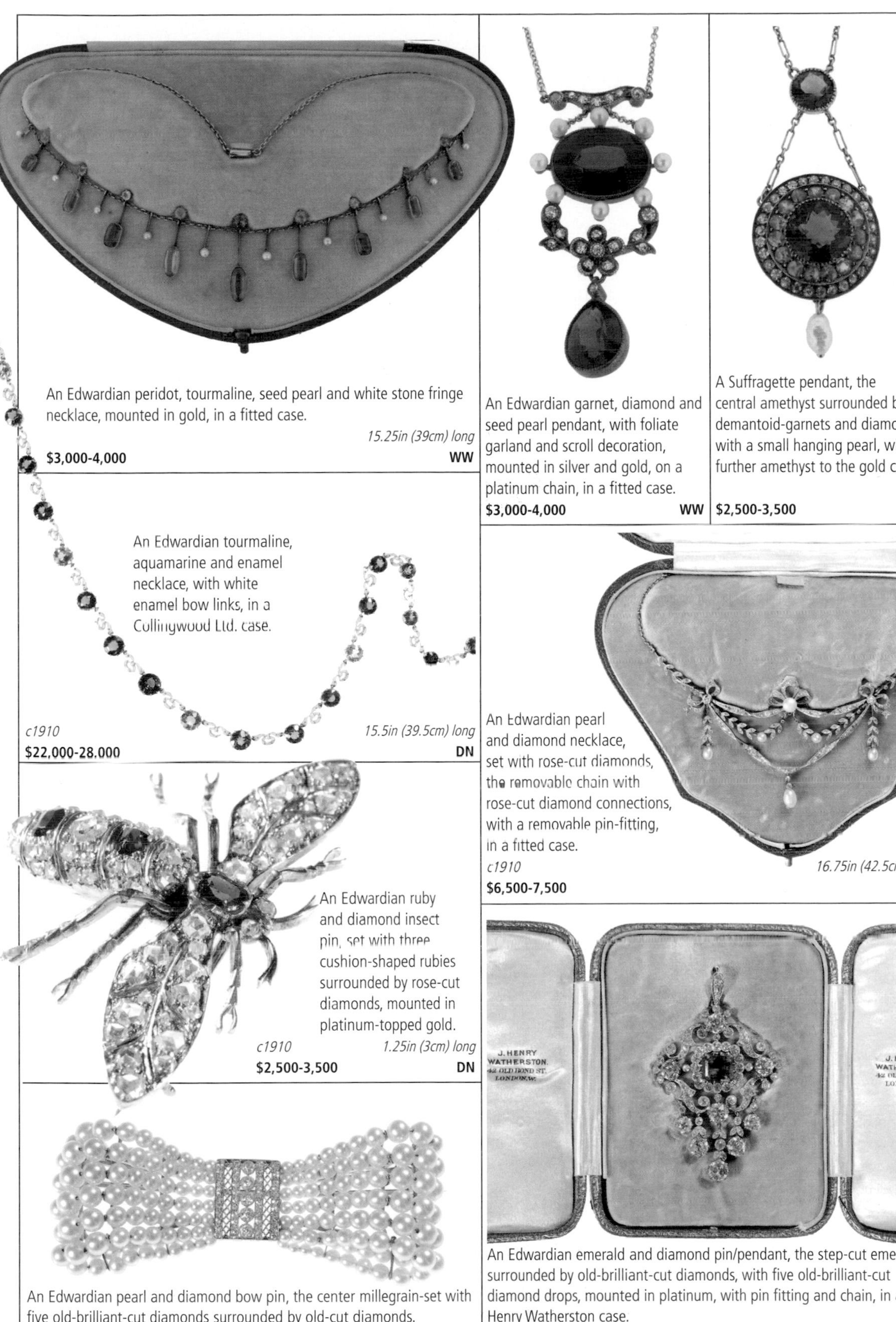

An Edwardian peridot, tourmaline, seed pearl and white stone fringe necklace, mounted in gold, in a fitted case.

15.25in (39cm) long

$3,000-4,000 **WW**

An Edwardian garnet, diamond and seed pearl pendant, with foliate garland and scroll decoration, mounted in silver and gold, on a platinum chain, in a fitted case.

$3,000-4,000 **WW**

A Suffragette pendant, the central amethyst surrounded by demantoid-garnets and diamonds, with a small hanging pearl, with a further amethyst to the gold chain.

$2,500-3,500 **WW**

An Edwardian tourmaline, aquamarine and enamel necklace, with white enamel bow links, in a Collingwood Ltd. case.

c1910 *15.5in (39.5cm) long*

$22,000-28,000 **DN**

An Edwardian pearl and diamond necklace, set with rose-cut diamonds, the removable chain with rose-cut diamond connections, with a removable pin-fitting, in a fitted case.

c1910 *16.75in (42.5cm) long*

$6,500-7,500 **DN**

An Edwardian ruby and diamond insect pin, set with three cushion-shaped rubies surrounded by rose-cut diamonds, mounted in platinum-topped gold.

c1910 *1.25in (3cm) long*

$2,500-3,500 **DN**

An Edwardian pearl and diamond bow pin, the center millegrain-set with five old-brilliant-cut diamonds surrounded by old-cut diamonds.

c1910

$4,000-6,000 **DN**

An Edwardian emerald and diamond pin/pendant, the step-cut emerald surrounded by old-brilliant-cut diamonds, with five old-brilliant-cut diamond drops, mounted in platinum, with pin fitting and chain, in a J Henry Watherston case.

c1910 *Diamonds 5.15ct*

$15,000-20,000 **DN**

An Art Deco diamond bracelet, set with old-brilliant-cut and old-cut diamonds.
c1935 *7in (18cm) long Diamonds 7.8ct*
$9,000-11,000 **DN**

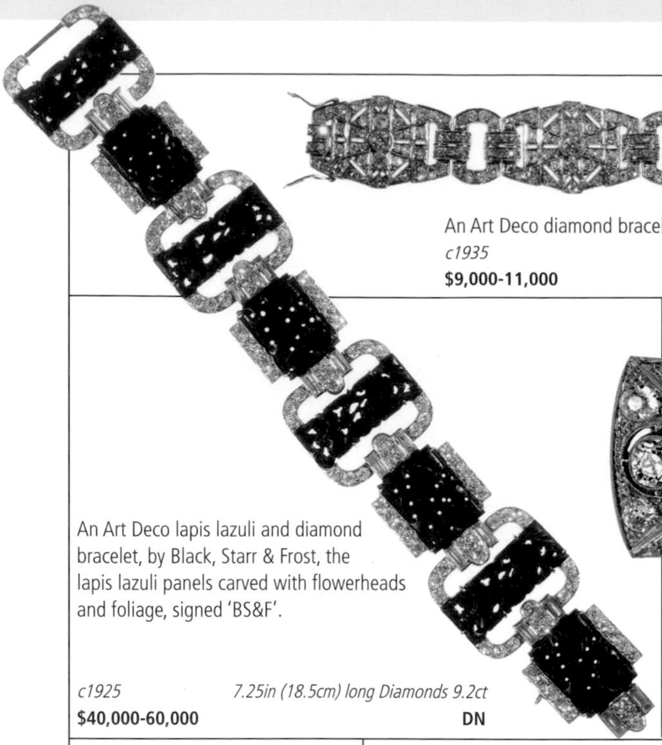

An Art Deco lapis lazuli and diamond bracelet, by Black, Starr & Frost, the lapis lazuli panels carved with flowerheads and foliage, signed 'BS&F'.
c1925 *7.25in (18.5cm) long Diamonds 9.2ct*
$40,000-60,000 **DN**

A French Art Deco diamond pin, mounted in platinum.
c1925 *2.5in (6.5cm) wide Diamonds 4.6ct*
$7,000-10,000 **KAU**

A Georg Jensen silver pin, depicting a doe and a squirrel.
2.5in (4.5cm) wide
$700-1,000 **TEN**

An Art Deco diamond pin, set with one transitional brilliant-cut diamond surrounded by baguette-cut, triangle-cut, old-cut, and transition-cut diamonds, mounted in platinum and white gold.
Diamonds 8.1ct
$12,000-18,000 **DOR**

A pair of French Art Deco diamond, aquamarine, garnet and hardstone clips, with carved lapis lazuli and black onyx scroll sections, signed 'RR', possibly for Robert and Robert.
4.75in (12cm) wide
$5,000-7,000 **WW**

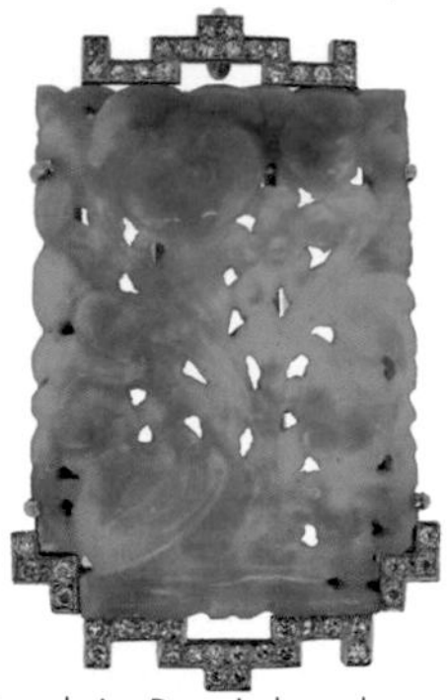

A French Art Deco jade and diamond pin/pendant, the geometric terminals set with diamonds, mounted in white gold.
2.25in (5.5cm) wide
$4,000-6,000 **WW**

An Art Deco diamond pin, set with circular-cut and baguette-cut diamonds, mounted in platinum.
$5,000-7,000 **WW**

An Art Deco platinum and colored-diamond bar pin, with five diamond and pearl drops.
2in (5.5cm) wide
$6,500-7,500 **LSK**

An Art Deco Cartier-style giardinetto pin, set with diamonds and gems carved as flowers and foliage.
2in (5cm) wide
$9,000-11,000 **L&T**

A pair of Art Deco diamond, turquoise and onyx earrings, mounted in platinum.

1.75in (4.5cm) long Diamonds 2.3ct

$8,000-12,000 **DRA**

A pair of French Cartier emerald, diamond and onyx revised earrings, mounted in platinum, with black enamel borders, marked 'Cartier', repurposed from a Jabot pin.

c1920 *1in (2.5cm) long*

$12,000-18,000 **DRA**

A pair of French Art Deco diamond and conch-pearl earrings, set with brilliant-cut and marquise-cut diamonds, mounted in platinum, with French control marks.

1.5in (4cm) long

$9,000-11,000 **L&T**

An Art Deco diamond plaque ring, mounted in platinum and white gold.

Size P 1/2

$3,000-4,000 **WW**

Judith Picks

I am well known for my love of costume jewelry, but I could certainly be tempted by these classic Art Deco diamond earrings! René Boivin's jewelry was initially rich, elegant and elaborate in the taste of the late 19thC, but soon the jewels that he and his very talented wife Jeanne produced began drawing inspiration from Cubist and Art Deco designs. The house of Boivin was among the most innovative in their designs and their workmanship was impeccable. When Jeanne Boivin died in 1959, the house was taken over by Louis Girard, who continued to produce many of the earlier designs, adapting them as necessary to changes in fashion. In April of 1991, the house of Boivin was purchased by the Asprey Group.

A pair of French diamond earrings, pavé-set with old-brilliant-cut and old-cut diamonds, the posts with indistinct French poincons, in a suede René Boivin Joaillier case.

2.25in (6cm) long Diamonds 5.8ct

$50,000-70,000 **DN**

A Dutch Art Deco diamond and onyx ring, mounted in 14ct white gold.

Principal diamond 1.1ct

$5,000-7,000 **KAU**

An Art Deco emerald and diamond ring, box-set with a trap-cut emerald within brilliant cut and single-cut diamonds, the shoulder set with step-cut emeralds.

$5,000-7,000 **L&T**

An Art Deco sapphire ring, the mixed-cut sapphire between shoulders collet-set with eight-cut diamonds, signed 'Chaumet', numbered '19461', with rubbed French poincons.

c1935 *Size L Sapphire 13.9ct*

$80,000-120,000 **DN**

A Cartier diamond ring, claw-set with a brilliant-cut diamond between two baguette-cut diamond, signed 'Cartier London'.

Principal diamond 4.5ct

$30,000-40,000 **L&T**

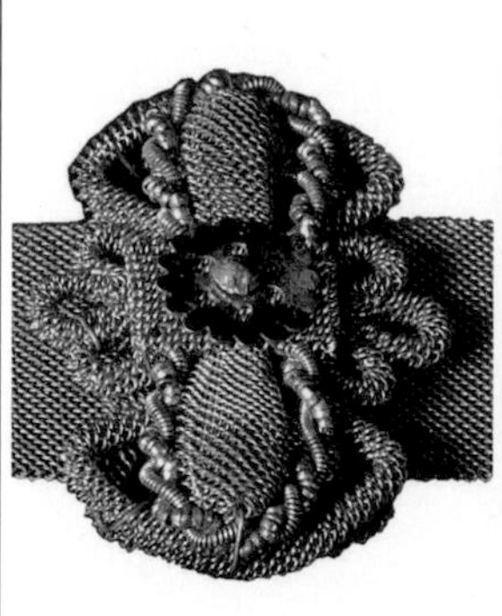

A Georgian cut-steel choker, with steel wirework buckle-motif, with woven-steel eyelet fittings.

c1780 *15in (36cm) long*

$350-450 **DN**

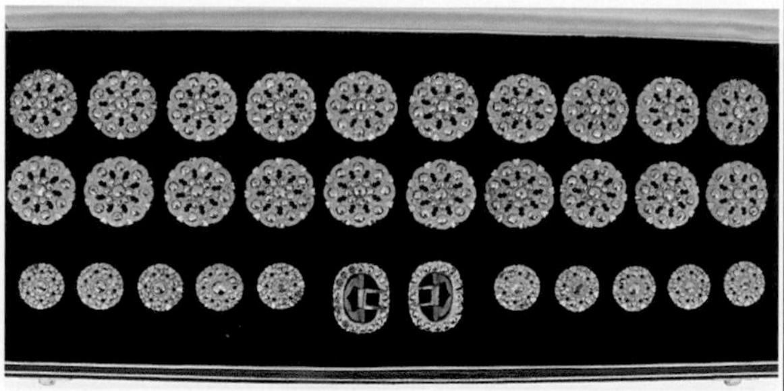

A set of thirty late George III cut-steel buttons and two buckles, in a fitted case.

Larger buttons 1in (2.5cm) diam

$2,000-3,000 **WW**

A pair of Georgian gold, paste and half-pearl earrings, the pastes claw-set in closed-back cut-down collets, with later screw fittings.

c1780 *2.5in (4cm) long*

$1,000-1,500 **DN**

A pair of Georgian silver and paste earrings, the colorless pastes in closed-back settings.

c1800 *2.5in (6cm) long*

$1,000-1,500 **DN**

A Georgian gold and paste pin, the pale-blue pastes claw-set in closed-backed cut-down collets.

c1800 *3.25in (8.5cm) wide*

$2,500-3,500 **DN**

An Arts & Crafts copper and cloisonné pendant, depicting a maiden with a Glasgow-style rose in her hair, on a handmade copper chain.

Pendant 3.25in (8cm) long

$1,200-1,800 **DN**

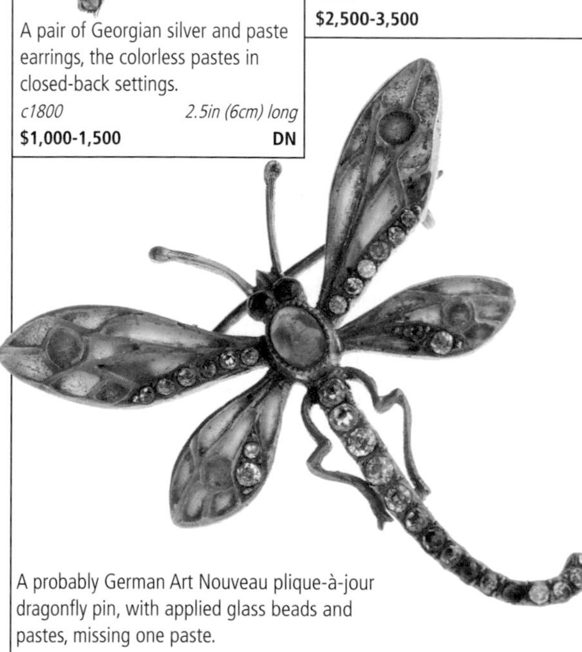

A probably German Art Nouveau plique-à-jour dragonfly pin, with applied glass beads and pastes, missing one paste.

1.5in (4cm) long

$200-300 **DN**

A 19thC white metal, paste and diamond fleur-de-lys pin, set with graduated old-mine-cut pastes and small rose-cut diamonds, in a leather case.

2.25in (6cm) high

$2,500-3,500 **L&T**

A late 19thC French silver and paste fringe necklace, in an Au Vieux Paris box.

13in (33cm) long

$2,000-3,000 **GORL**

ESSENTIAL REFERENCE - ALEXIS KIRK

- **Alexis Kirk was born in California. He studied jewelry design at the Rhode Island School of Design, RI and at the Boston Museum School of Fine Arts, MA, USA.**
- **In the 1960s he founded a workshop in Newport, RI. He established his firm in 1969.**
- **His clients included the Duchess of Windsor and Jackie Onassis.**
- **He won the American Fashion Critics 'Coty' Award in 1970 and the Great American Design Award in 1974.**
- **His jewelry is inspired by Hollywood movies, such as 'Jaws', and exotic travel. Middle Eastern, Aztec and other cultural motifs are common.**

Three Alexis Kirk cork, wood and gilt-metal beaded necklaces, designed for the Duchess of Windsor, signed 'Alexis Kirk', in later leather case embossed 'WE'.
$3,500-4,500 DN

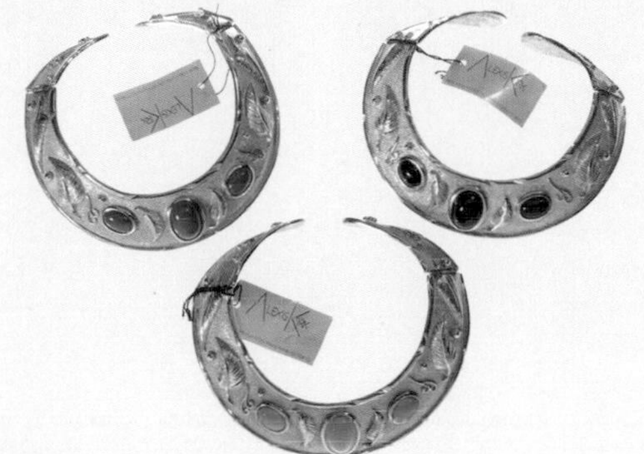

A set of three Alexis Kirk gilt-metal collars, set with faux onyx, faux coral and faux turquoise cabochons, all signed 'Alexis Kirk'.
$500-700 DN

Two 1970s Alexis Kirk gilt-metal necklaces and a ring, from the 'Art To Wear Collection' inspired by his designs for the Duke and Duchess of Windsor, signed 'Alexis Kirk', in card boxes.
$400 600 DN

Two Alexis Kirk gilt-metal collars, one in the form of an undulating sunburst, the other decorated with basket-weave patterns, signed 'Alexis Kirk'.
$250-350 DN

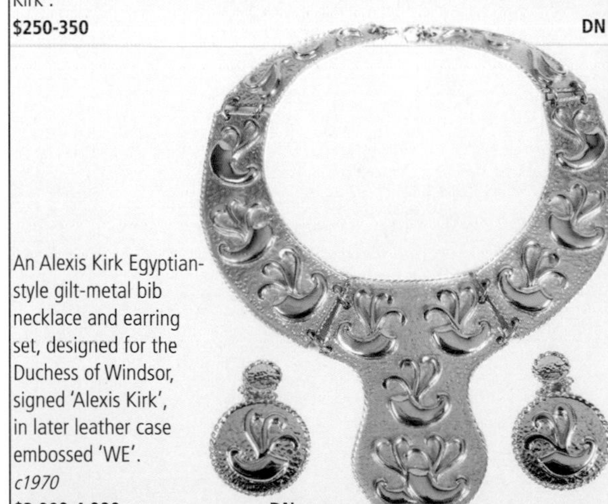

An Alexis Kirk Egyptian-style gilt-metal bib necklace and earring set, designed for the Duchess of Windsor, signed 'Alexis Kirk', in later leather case embossed 'WE'.
c1970
$3,000-4,000 DN

An Alexis Kirk gilt-metal and simulated lapis lazuli necklace and ring set, designed for the Duchess of Windsor, signed 'Alexis Kirk', in later leather case embossed 'WE'.
c1970
$3,500-4,500 DN

An Alexis Kirk Middle-Eastern-style gilt-metal body sculpture necklace, made for the Duchess of Windsor, signed 'Alexis Kirk', in later leather case embossed 'WE'.
c1970
$4,000-6,000 DN

A Hanna Bernhard turquoise and bronze face pendant, on chain.

Pendant 6.25in (16cm) high

$700-1,000 **SCA**

A 1950s Hattie Carnegie gilt-metal 'Aztec' pin, set with faux jade, faux coral and diamanté, marked 'HATTIE CARNEGIE' with copyright symbol.

2.5in (6cm) high

$300-500 **CRIS**

A Chanel Novelty Co. enameled iris pin, set with diamanté, marked 'Chanel'.

The Chanel Novelty Co. was a division of Reinad, a costume jewelry company based in New York City.

c1940 *3.5in (8.5cm) high*

$1,500-2,500 **CRIS**

A Chanel amethyst-crystal sautoir, stamped 'Chanel/1981'.

1981 *60in (152.5cm) long*

$1,200-1,800 **LHA**

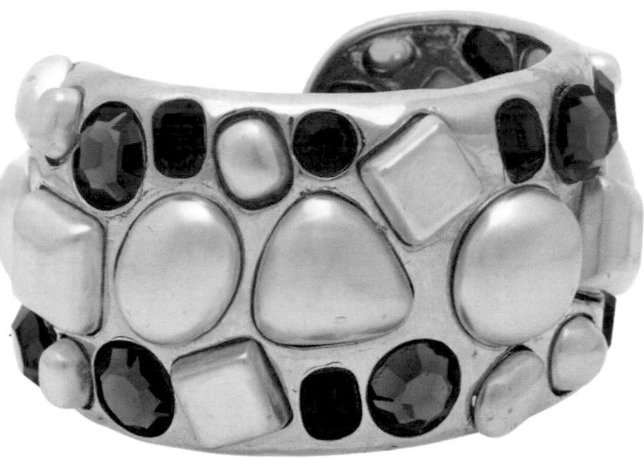

A 1980s Chanel faux sapphire and faux pearl cuff bracelet, stamped 'Chanel'.

6.5in (16.5cm) diam

$3,000-4,000 **LHA**

A Coppola e Toppo green beaded Jabot-style necklace, labeled 'Coppola e Toppo'.

$2,000-3,000 **LHA**

An Oscar de la Renta necklace, designed by Iradj Moini, with multicolor charms suspended from three large link chains, stamped 'Oscar de la Renta'.

$1,200-1,800 **LHA**

A 1920s Deposé articulated diamanté fur clip and earrings.

Clip 5in (12.5cm) high

$1,500-2,500 **CRIS**

A Christian Dior faux emerald and faux ruby necklace and earrings set, marked 'CHRISTIAN DIOR' with copyright symbol, dated.

1961 *Necklace 13in (33cm) long*

$2,500-3,500 **CRIS**

A pair of 1950s Florenza gilt-metal earrings, set with faux topaz, peridot and pearls, marked 'FLORENZA' with copyright symbol.

1.25in (3cm) diam

$60-80 **CRIS**

A 1950s Joseff of Hollywood 'Russian gold' lily of the valley pin and earrings set, marked 'JOSEFF HOLLYWOOD'.

Pin 5in (13cm) high

$500-700 **CRIS**

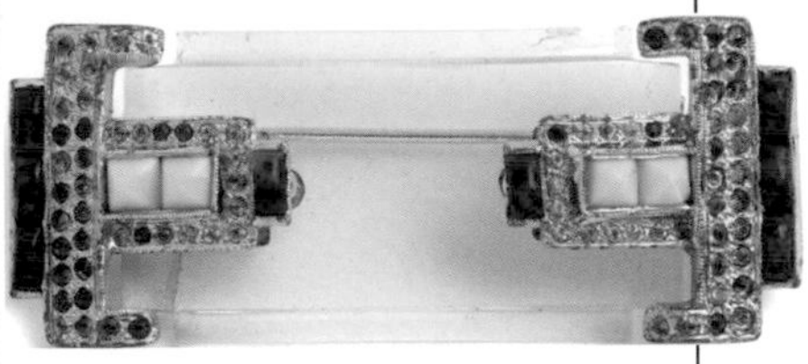

A 1930s KTF Lucite and rhodium-plated pin, set with colorless and blue rhinestones, marked 'KTF'.

2.25in (5.5cm) wide

$150-250 **CRIS**

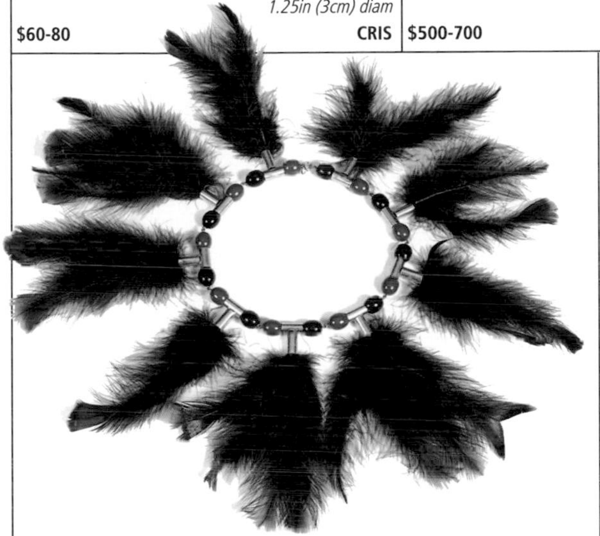

A bead and feather necklace, possibly designed by Cliff Nicholson, the beads of faux coral, onyx and gilt-metal, in later leather case embossed 'WE'.

This necklace was formerly owned by the Duchess of Windsor.

c1970

$5,000-7,000 **DN**

A 1940s Reja Sterling gilt-metal 'Asian' head pin, set with diamantés, faux rubies and faux amethysts, marked 'Reja'.

2.75in (7cm) high

$1,000-1,500 **CRIS**

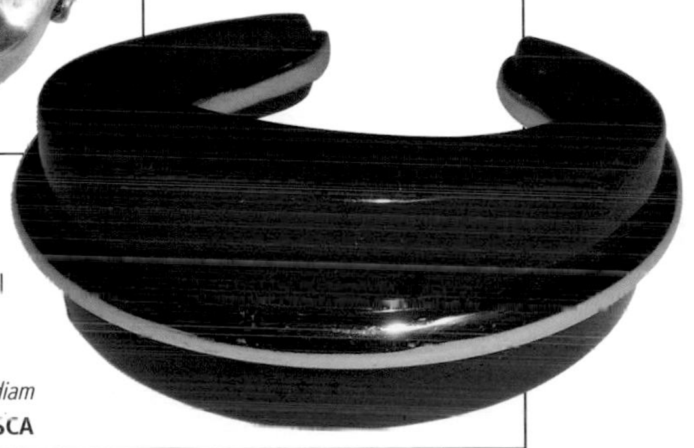

A 1970s-80s Yves Saint Laurent acrylic bangle, with gilt-metal frame, stamped 'YSL'.

3.5in (9cm) diam

$500-700 **SCA**

An Yves Saint Laurent bib necklace and earrings set, made by Atelier Gripoix, the necklace set with colored paste cabochons, signed 'Yves Saint Laurent', the earrings signed 'YSL', in card box.

Necklace 17.75in (45cm) long

$2,500-3,500 **DN**

A 1950s Elsa Schiaparelli gilt-metal flower-spray pin, set with fantasy moonstone pastes and aurora borealis rhinestones, unmarked.

2.75in (7cm) high

$300-500 **CRIS**

A 2000s Larry Vrba flower pin, signed 'Larry Vrba'.

$500-700 **SCA**

A late 18thC gold-mounted bloodstone egg vinaigrette, the body with engraved strap decoration, the cover with enameled border and inscription.

1.75in (4.5cm) high

$2,000-3,000 WW

A George III silver Nelson commemorative vinaigrette, by Matthew Linwood, Birmingham, the cover engraved with a portrait of Lord Nelson within a cartouche inscribed 'ENGLAND EXPECTS EVERYMAN WILL DO HIS DUTY', the grill stamped with an image of HMS 'Victory' and 'VICTORY TRAFALGAR OCR 21 1805'.

1805

$5,000-7,000 L&T

A rare Scottish provincial silver clam-shaped vinaigrette, by David Pirie, Aberdeen, the gilt interior with hinged pierced and engraved foliate grill.

1.75in (4.5cm) wide

$6,500-7,500 L&T

A George IV silver vinaigrette, by Mary Ann and Charles Reily, London, the cover inset with an enameled lake scene, with engine-turned sides and base and foliate-scroll border, the grille with pierced flower decoration.

1828 *2.5in (4cm) wide*

$6,500-7,500 WW

A William IV silver novelty vinaigrette, in the form of an urn with raised floral borders, by C Rawlings and W Summers, London, the pull-off cover secured by a chain.

1834 *2.75in (7 cm) high 2oz*

$6,500-7,500 LC

A William IV silver-gilt vinaigrette, by Nathaniel Mills, Birmingham, in the form of a George I snuffbox, the cover with a field of quatrefoils and chased foliate border, the grille pierced with scrolls and flowers.

1835 *1.5in (4cm) wide*

$2,000-3,000 TEN

A Victorian silver castle top vinaigrette, by Nathaniel Mills, Birmingham, the lid engraved with a view of Gloucester Cathedral.

1843 *1.5in (4cm) wide*

$2,000-3,000 TEN

A Victorian silver-gilt vinaigrette, by James Collins, Birmingham, engraved with foliate scrolls, the cover set with a hardstone engraved with an inscription, the grill with foliate-scroll decoration.

1845 *2.5in (4.5cm) wide*

$1,500-2,500 WW

A Victorian silver castle top vinaigrette, by Nathaniel Mills, Birmingham, the lid engraved with a view of Worcester, initialed 'ML'.

1847 *2.5in (4.5cm) wide 1oz*

$1,200-1,800 TEN

A 19thC gold vinaigrette, in the form of a book, the spine set with four rose-cut diamonds, the hinged cover monogrammed.

1.25in (3cm) wide 0.6oz

$1,200-1,800 WW

ESSENTIAL REFERENCE - VINAIGRETTES

A vinaigrette is a small box containing a sponge soaked in aromatic vinegar, which is held in place with a perforated grille under a hinged lid. The purpose of a vinaigrette was similar to the pomander, in that it could be inhaled to mask bad smells or counteract faintness.

- **Most vinaigrettes were produced from c1770 to c1900.**
- **Early examples tend to be quite small. From the early 1800s, vinaigrettes were typically larger (often up to 1.5in/4cm wide) and were more elaborately decorated. Designs from this later period include floral and foliate designs, as well as designs with figures and animals within raised floral and shell borders.**
- **Vinaigrettes were typically made from silver or gold. The interior of the box was always gilt-lined to prevent the liquid from eating into the metal.**
- **Most vinaigrettes had a small ring to one side, which allowed the owner to wear it on a necklace or chatelaine.**

A Swiss gold and enamel vinaigrette, enameled with green and gold foliate decoration, the interior lid with painted enamel plaque of vessels on a Swiss lake.
c1850 *1in (2.5cm) wide*
$3,000-4,000 **TEN**

A Victorian silver castle top vinaigrette, in the form of a purse, by John Tongue, Birmingham, the cover with a view of Windsor Castle, chased with scrolls, with chain and finger ring.
1851 *1in (2.5cm) high 0.5oz*
$1,500-2,500 **LC**

A Victorian silver novelty vinaigrette, in the form of a railwayman's lantern, by H W Dee, London, with a revolving, three-color lens.
1870 *1.25in (3.5cm) high 1.5oz*
$2,000-3,000 **LC**

A Victorian silver vinaigrette, by James Fenton, Birmingham.
1866 *1.25in (3cm) wide 0.3 oz*
$300-500 **LC**

A Victorian silver combined vinaigrette, compass, photo frame and coin holder, in the form of a globe, by H W Dee, London, retailed by Jenner & Co.
1875 *1.25in (3cm) diam 2oz*
$3,500-4,500 **LC**

A Victorian silver vinaigrette, by H W Dee, London, in the form of a shield, with floral scroll chasing, monogrammed.
1873 *1.75in (4.5cm) wide 1.2oz*
$3,000-4,000 **LC**

A Victorian silver vinaigrette, in the form of a carnation, by E H Stockwell, London, initialed 'F.B.', in original case.
4.5in (11.5 cm) long 2.8oz
$7,000-10,000 **LC**

A Victorian silver vinaigrette, in the form of a walnut, by Sampson Mordan, London.
c1880 *1.35in (3.5 cm) wide 0.6oz*
$3,500-4,500 **LC**

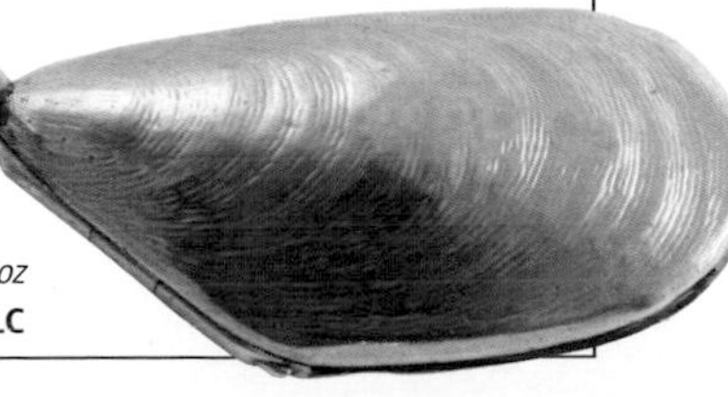

A Victorian silver vinaigrette, in the form of a mussel shell, by Sampson Mordan, London, the grille pierced with scrolls.
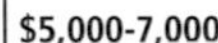
1881 *1.75 (4.5cm) wide 0.4oz*

$5,000-7,000 **LC**

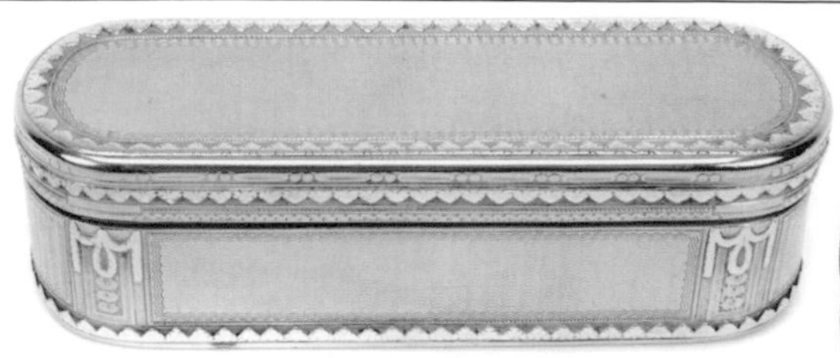

A French Louis XV two-color gold snuff box, maker's mark 'PD', Paris.

A handwritten note inside reads, 'Gold snuffbox The property of Walter Spencer Stanhope MP said to have been a well known & popular snuffbox in the time of Wm Pitt'. This seems to refer to Walter Spencer-Stanhope (1749-1822) of Horsforth and Leeds, Yorkshire. He was a politician and industrialist whose family fortune had been made through the iron trade. He was a supporter of William Pitt the younger and of William Wilberforce.

1768-74 *9cm (3.5in) wide 4oz*
$6,000-8,000 **DN**

A late 18thC French two-color gold, tortoiseshell and lacquer snuff box, maker's mark 'LV'?, Paris, the hinge mounts replaced.

2.5in (6.5cm) wide
$2,000-3,000 **DN**

A William IV 18 ct gold snuff box, London, makers mark possibly 'Thomas Ingelton', with engraved boars head crest to the cover, dated.

1834 *3in (7.5cm) wide 4oz*
$3,000-4,000 **ROS**

An early 19thC gold musical snuff box, the cover with chased panel depicting musical trophies, with original case.

2.5in (6.5cm) wide
$12,000-18,000 **HT**

A 19thC French gold and enamel snuff box, the cover with enamel plaque depicting a maiden weighing Cupid against a butterfly, cast with fruit and floral and foliate designs.

3.25in (8.5cm) wide 3.9oz
$15,000-20,000 **SK**

A rare Scottish gold-mounted horn snuff mull, with applied emblem and motto of St Andrew, the cover set with Montrose agate, with chained implements, including pricker, spoon, rake, rabbit's paw and ivory hammer, with display stand.

12.5in (32cm) long
$8,000-12,000 **L&T**

A Jacobite gold-mounted tortoiseshell snuff mull, the cover and base inset with panels engraved with monograms, the cover with Jacobite rose.

1.75in (4.5cm) high
$2,000-3,000 **L&T**

An early 19thC Italian gold-mounted granite and micromosaic snuff box, the micromosaic in the style of Giacomo Raffaelli, depicting a duck and duckling.

3.5in (8.5cm) diam
$10,000-15,000 **L&T**

A rare early 19thC French gold-mounted tortoiseshell and ivory snuff box, the cover with carved ivory diorama probably depicting the Battle of the Chesapeake, in leather case.

The Battle of the the Chesapeake (5th September 1781) was the crucial naval battle in the American War of Independence.

3.5in (9cm) wide
$10,000-15,000 **MAI**

A William and Mary silver 'squeeze-action' spice/snuff box, maker's mark 'WF' crowned, the cover engraved with a squirrel within foliate-scroll decoration.
c1690 *2.5in (4cm) wide 0.5oz*
$2,500-3,500 **WW**

A George III silver snuff box, in the form of a fox head, maker's mark 'WP', London.
1792 *3.5in (8.5cm) long 5.3oz*
$8,000-12,000 **CHEF**

A George III Irish provincial silver snuff box, by Joseph Gibson, Cork.
c1795
3in (7.5cm) wide 2oz
$6,500-7,500 **LC**

A George III silver-gilt snuff box, by Joseph Ash I, London, the cover embossed with a Classical scene and foliate-scroll decoration, the sides chased with shells.
1809 *2.5in (8cm) wide 5oz*
$1,500-2,500 **WW**

ESSENTIAL REFERENCE - NATHANIEL MILLS

Nathaniel Mills & Sons was a 19thC company of Birmingham silversmiths, well known for producing high quality silver boxes, vinaigrettes, snuff boxes and card cases.

- **Nathaniel I (1746-1840) was never listed as an apprentice. He registered his first mark in 1803 as a partner in the jewellers Mills & Langston.**
- **In 1825 Mills registered an individual mark 'N.M' from a new address in Caroline Street, Birmingham. Production now began on silver, rather than jewelry.**
- **Between 1825 and 1855, the firm registered six further marks, although these showed little variation in style other than clipped corners and the inclusion of a pellet between the 'N' and the 'M'.**
- **Nathaniel Mills I was succeeded in his business by his sons, Nathaniel II, William and Thomas. All three had previously been partners in the company.**
- **Nathanial II introduced many new techniques, such as engine-turning, stamping and casting.**
- **Many of the most collectible Nathaniel Mills boxes were made during c1840 and 1853. Most of these boxes were made by William or Thomas Mills, rather than Nathaniel II.**

A large William IV silver castle top snuff box, by Joseph Wilmore, Birmingham, the cover with a view of the Houses of Parliament surrounded by raised floral borders, the sides chased with flowers and scrolls.
1834 *3.75in (10cm) wide 8.5oz*
$5,000-7,000 **LC**

A William IV silver table snuff box, by John Jones, London, the cover with high-relief scene from the Battle of Waterloo, with engine-turned sides and base.
1836 *3.75in (9.5cm) wide 11.5oz*
$4,000-6,000 **LC**

An early Victorian silver castle top snuff box, by Nathaniel Mills, Birmingham, the cover with a view of Abbotsford.
1836 *2.75in (7cm) wide*
$1,500-2,500 **H&L**

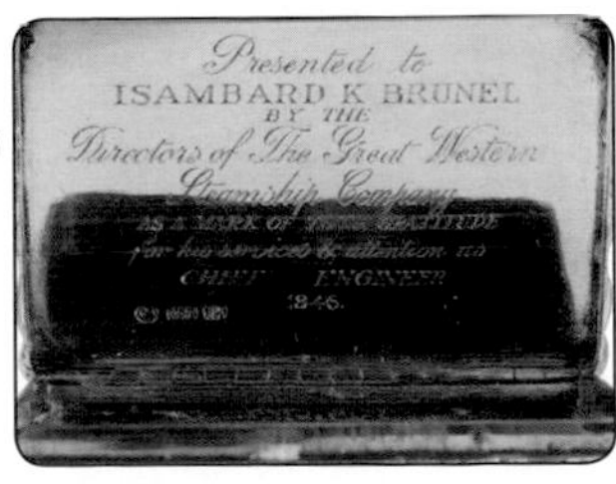

A silver presentation snuff box, by Nathaniel Mills, Birmingham, the cover engraved with SS 'Great Britain', the inside inscribed 'presented to ISAMBARD K BRUNEL...'.
1846 *4.91oz*
$30,000-40,000 **J&J**

A rare Victorian silver 'patent' snuff box, by W C Williams & Sons, Birmingham, engraved with scrolls, the cover enclosing a small 'bridge' surmounted by a pair of small saucers.

This box enabled the user to take snuff using only one hand and without soiling it with snuff. The box is inverted and then righted again, leaving a small heap of snuff on each saucer. The cover is then opened and the saucers are placed under each nostril prior to a snort. The design was registered 12/1/1850 no. 2145.

1849 *3in (7.5cm) wide 2oz*

$2,500-3,500 **LC**

A 19thC silver double snuff box, engraved with two armorials.

2.5in (7.5cm) wide

$3,000-4,000 **WW**

A Victorian silver snuff box, by Edward H Stockwell, London, decorated in relief with a pair of birds.

1877 *4in (10cm) wide 4oz*

$1,800-2,200 **SWO**

An early 18thC silver-mounted terrapin shell snuff box, the mount chased with foliate-scroll decoration.

c1725-30 2.5in (7.5cm) wide

$1,500-2,500 **WW**

An Irish George III silver and hardstone snuff box, by James Keating, Dublin.

1795 *3in (8cm) wide*

$2,000-3,000 **WW**

A Victorian Scottish silver-mounted ram's head snuff mull, maker's mark 'PW', Edinburgh, with compartments for snuff and cigars, the covers and thistle terminals all set with cut paste stones, with chained implements, including spoon, rake, pick, mallet and rabbit's paw.

1860 *12.25in (31cm) high*

$7,000-10,000 **WAD**

A 19thC silver-mounted nautilus shell snuff mull, maker's mark 'RC'.

Possibly the work of Lyon & Twinam or an Indian Colonial maker.

9.75in (25cm) high

$5,000-7,000 **WAD**

A late 19thC Portuguese silver and micromosaic snuff box, Lisbon, depicting the Colosseum.

1886-1938 *2.75in (7cm) wide*

$12,000-18,000 **GORB**

A Scottish provincial silver snuff box, by William Robb, Ballater, the cover set with mother-of-pearl and citrine, with applied fret-cut foliate decoration.

1917 *3in (7.5cm) wide*

$2,500-3,500 **L&T**

An 18thC probably Italian tortoiseshell snuff box, with piqué and inlaid decoration of buildings, with damage.

This form of decoration is very rare.

3in (7.5cm) wide

$4,000-6,000 **LC**

A mid-18thC Jacobite gilt-copper and tortoiseshell snuff box, the interior of the false upper lid painted in reverse on glass with a portrait of Bonnie Prince Charlie, the sides chased with flowers and foliage.

3.25in (8cm) diam

$4,000-6,000 **MAB**

A mid-18thC German possibly Meissen porcelain snuff box, the cover enameled with a Classical bust to one side and a portrait of a lady to the reverse (shown), the body decorated in the Kakiemon palette.

3.75in (9.5cm) wide

$4,000-6,000 **GORL**

A George II copper-gilt snuff box, the cover depicting Hercules and Minerva, the interior with a portrait of a young man.

c1750 *3in (8cm) wide*

$1,500-2,500 **TEN**

A late 18thC German enamel table snuff box, the cover depicting a coastal landscape with castle, the sides with flower sprays

5.5in (14cm) wide

$500-700 **DN**

An early 19thC papier-mâché snuff box, painted with figures and horses outside an inn.

3.7in (9.5cm) diam

$800-1,200 **DN**

A 19thC horn snuff box, in the form of a bicorn hat, carved in low-relief with Napoleon Bonaparte on horseback.

3in (8cm) wide

$400-600 **TOV**

A 19thC tortoiseshell snuff box, the cover inset with a miniature of the 'Punishment of Cupid', with pique borders.

3in (7.5cm) diam

$1,200-1,800 **DN**

A 19thC lacquer snuff box, by Stobwasser, Brunswick, the cover painted with the 'Birth of Venus', the interior inscribed 'Gerburt der Venus, Stobwasser Fabrik in Braunschweig, 6274'.

4in (10cm) diam

$2,500-3,500 **WW**

A Victorian silver and enamel vesta case, London, depicting the King of Diamonds, and engraved 'F.P. from A.E.A., 3rd Oct. 1903'.

1884 *1.75in (4.5cm) high*

$1,500-2,500 **ROS**

A Victorian silver novelty vesta case, in the form of a footballer's leg kicking a ball, maker's mark 'SB&S', Birmingham, embossed 'C&M PATENT', with later inscription 'JIM to JOE'.

1884 *2.5in (6cm) high 0.5oz*

$1,200-1,800 **L&T**

A Victorian silver novelty vesta case, in the form of a boar, by Thomas Johnson, London, with button thumb press and spring-loaded cover.

1885 *2.75 (7cm) wide 1.25oz*

$2,500-3,500 **LC**

A Victorian silver vesta box, by Alfred Fuller, London, retailed by 'J & G Beaskey, St. James's St.', the closure in the form of an arm thumping a grotesque mask, the cover applied with an oyster shell and a rodent, on four vesta-form feet, with three vestas.

1886 *3in (8cm) wide 5.5oz*

$3,000-4,000 **LC**

ESSENTIAL REFERENCE - SAMPSON MORDAN

Sampson Mordan (1790-1843) founded his company in 1815. He subsequently became known for producing high quality, small, silver items, such as vesta cases, desk seals and particularly propeling pencils.

- **In 1822 Mordan registered a patent for the propeling pencils he had developed with John Isaac Hawkins. Mordan, who had bought out Hawkins, then entered into a business partnership with Gabriel Riddle, an established stationer. From 1823 to 1837, they manufactured and sold silver mechanical pencils marked 'SMGR'. After 1837, Mordan continued to sell silver pencils as S Mordan & Co.**
- **During the late 19thC, the firm supplied many articles, often in novelty shapes, to notable retailers, such as Asprey & Sons and Walter Thornhill & Co.**
- **The company closed in 1941 and the name and rights were sold to Edward Baker.**
- **Some of the best Sampson Mordan propeling pencils are featured in Kenneth Bull's book, 'The KB Collection of Pencils'.**

A Victorian novelty silver-gilt and enameled vesta case, in the form of a sentry box, by Sampson Mordan & Co., London, with enameled sentry panel.

1886 *2.25in (5.5cm) high*

$5,000-7,000 **GORB**

A late Victorian silver novelty vesta box, in the form of a carriage lantern with a red glass lens, by Samuel Jacobs, London, the cover with a compartment for stamps.

1894 *2in (5.5cm) high 3oz*

$3,000-4,000 **LC**

A rare late Victorian silver vesta case/vinaigrette, by William Hutton & Sons, Birmingham, monogrammed 'A.E.B.'.

1899 *2.5in (6.5cm) wide 1.6oz*

$4,000-6,000 **WW**

A late Victorian silver and enamel vesta case, by Sampson Mordan & Co., London, one side painted with a hunting scene.

1899 *2.25in (5.5cm) wide*

$2,000-3,000 **TOV**

A Victorian silver castle top card case, by Nathaniel Mills, Birmingham, engraved with view of St Paul's Cathedral.

1850 *3.75in (9.5cm) high*

$1,500-2,500 **GORL**

A Victorian silver castle top card case, maker's mark 'DP', Birmingham, chased with a view of York Minster.

1856 *4in (10cm) high*

$1,000-1,500 **TEN**

CLOSER LOOK - SCOTTISH CARD CASE

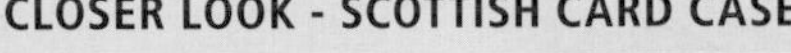

Although Birmingham-made card cases of Scottish views (mainly the Scott Monument) are not rare, Edinburgh-made card cases of this type are.

Edinburgh-made card cases with multiple views are particularly rare.

The four cartouches show Edinburgh Castle, the Scott Monument, Holyrood Palace, and the Assembly Hall and Tolbooth Church.

George Carstairs is a well-known and collectible maker.

A rare Scottish silver multi-view castle top card case, by George Carstairs, Edinburgh, engraved with a view of Calton Hill and the Royal High School, the reverse engraved with 'HJR' and cartouches of views.

1857 *3.7in (9.5cm) high 2.5oz*

$5,500-7,500 **L&T**

A Victorian mother-of-pearl card case.

4in (10.5cm) high

$200-300 **LSK**

A Queen Anne Britannia silver tobacco box, by Edward Courthope, London, the cover engraved with a monogram.

1712 *3.75in (9.5cm) wide 3.5oz*

$3,000-4,000 **WW**

An early 18thC Dutch parcel-gilt and brass tobacco box, decorated in relief with chinoiserie landscapes.

4.5in (11.5cm) wide

$3,000-4,000 **GORL**

An Austrian partial-gilt silver tobacco box, maker's mark 'FS'.

c1813 *2.5in (8.5cm) wide 4.1oz*

$550-750 **KAU**

A 19thC European Renaissance Revival silver, enamel and stone-set jewel casket, maker's mark 'AGB', the lid with enameled silver figures of St George and the dragon, the sides mounted with masks, dragons and flowerheads, the lid set to the interior with an enameled landscape under glass, with damage.

6in (15cm) high

$10,000-15,000 **SK**

A 19thC Dieppe carved and paste-set ivory triptych figure of Edward VI, opening to reveal scenes from his life including King Henry VIII surrounded by figures from the church, and Elizabeth I.

8.25in (21cm) high

$5,000-7,000 **RTC**

A pair of 19thC probably Dieppe carved ivory busts of Classical figures, on socle bases and columns.

6.25in (16cm) high

$3,000-4,000 **TOV**

A 19thC Continental carved ivory figure of a putto holding a bow and arrow, on an ebonized turned base.

Figure 12in (30cm) high

$4,000-6,000 **TOV**

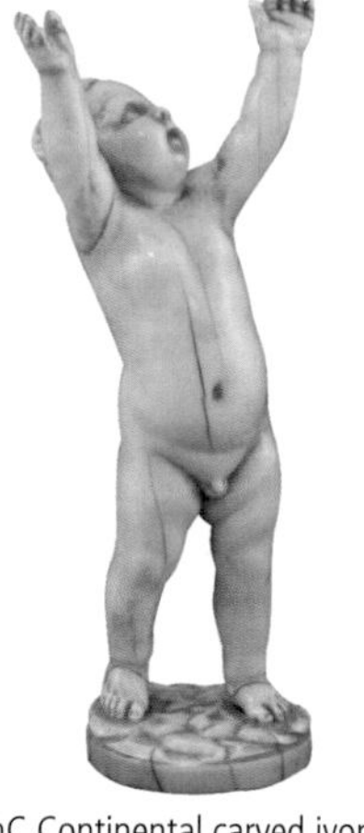

A 19thC Continental carved ivory figure of a putto reaching upward.

6.25in (16cm) high

$2,000-3,000 **GORL**

A set of six 19thC Dieppe carved ivory figures of musicians, on treen bases modeled as barrels.

Tallest 5.75in (14.5cm) high

$2,500-3,500 **GORB**

A 19thC Dieppe carved ivory triptych figure of a noblewoman in a feathered hat, with hinged skirt opening to interior scene of an artist's studio.

8.75in (22cm) high

$3,500-4,500 **WAD**

A 19thC French carved ivory figure of St Joseph, holding an open book and cruciform staff.

7in (18cm) high

$1,000-1,500 **L&T**

A late 19thC Continental carved ivory triptych figure of an archbishop, collet-set with blue and red stones, opening to reveal scenes from the life of Christ.

9.25in (23cm) high

$5,000-7,000 **SK**

A late 19thC Continental carved ivory triptych figure of an archbishop, collet-set with multicolored stones and small painted beads, opening to scenes of Christ on the cross and mourning angels, on wood block base.

Ivory 12.75in (33cm) high

$5,500-6,500 **SK**

An 18thC French carved ivory snuff rasp, with a shell terminal, carved with Diana, fruit, leaves and scrolls, the back panel decorated with a lady holding a lamp above Cupid, with damage.

7.5in (19cm) high

$2,000-3,000 WW

An 18th century Continental turned ivory goblet, with engraved reeded bands, with chips.

4.75in (12cm) high

$4,000-6,000 GORL

A 19thC Anglo-Indian carved ivory temple.

7in (18cm) high

$2,500-3,500 GORL

A 19thC gold-mounted ivory seal, with engraved carnelian matrix and armorial.

3.75in (9.5cm) long

$1,200-1,800 GORB

A mid-19thC Dieppe Ivory-framed wall mirror, the frame carved with leaves, interspersed with putti playing instruments and surmounted by two mermaids flanking an armorial.

This mirror bears French Royal insignia. The three fleur-de-lys are for the King and the dolphin is for the dauphin.

34.75in (88cm) high

$18,000-22,000 DN

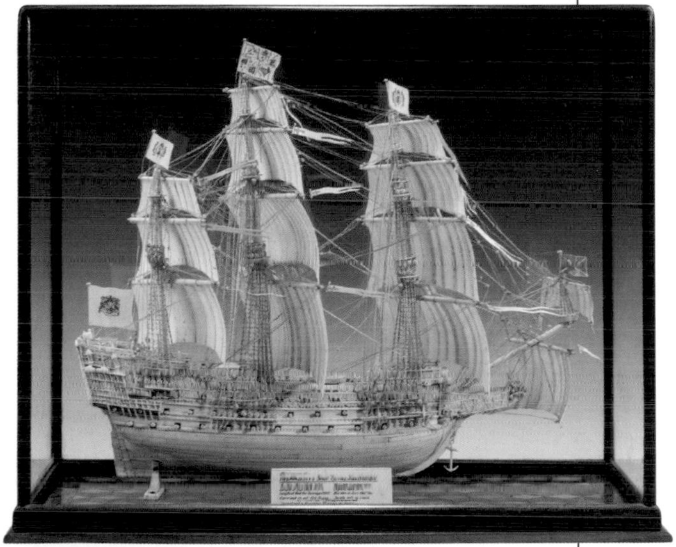

A Viennese silver-mounted ivory table tabernacle, partially enameled, set with rubies, sapphires, emeralds and pearls.

c1870 *12in (29.5cm) high*

$6,500-7,500 DOR

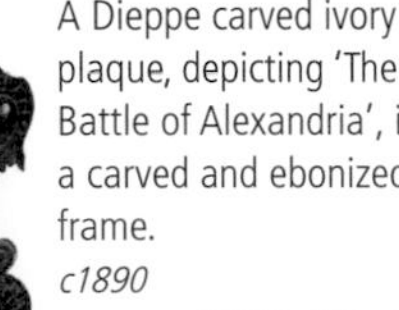

A Dieppe carved ivory plaque, depicting 'The Battle of Alexandria', in a carved and ebonized frame.

c1890

25.25in (64cm) wide

$7,000-10,000 TEN

A rare ivory model of HMS 'Royal Sovereign', by A W Kiddie, with a planked and pinned hull, the rigging tied with either human hair or cat gut, on original parquetry and mahogany base, in original case.

Provenance: This model was given by A W Kiddie to his son, George Arthur Kiddie, and then by descent through the family.

c1917 *23.5in (59.5cm) long*

$70,000-90,000 RGA

An 18thC watercolor-on-ivory portrait miniature of a gentleman in military garb, the reverse with lock of hair, inscribed with initials 'JLC'.

3in (7.5cm) high

$10,000-15,000 **POOK**

A tempera-on-ivory portrait miniature of a lady, by Pierre Louis, inscribed 'Madame A. De C...' and signed.

5in (11.5cm) high

$3,000-4,000 **KAU**

A watercolor-on-ivory portrait miniature of George, 5th Duke of Gordon, by William Singleton, signed and dated.

1783 *1.5in (4cm) high*

$4,000-6,000 **L&T**

A watercolor portrait miniature of a lady, by Samuel Shelley, signed 'Sam. Shelley, No.7 Henrietta Street, Cov. Garden', in a gold frame, in a leather case.

$2,000-3,000 **SWO**

An American watercolor-on-ivory portrait miniature of a gentleman, by Robert Field, signed with initials 'RF' and dated, the case with a lock of hair behind the monogram 'HCM'.

This miniature reportedly depicts a Philadelphia gentleman named Henry C Mercken.

1798

Miniature 3in (7.5cm) high

$12,000-18,000 **SK**

An early 19thC watercolor-on-ivory miniature portrait of Lord Nelson, in a gilt-metal frame.

1.75in (4.5cm) diam

$1,200-1,800 **FRE**

A pair of 19thC miniature portraits of a lady and gentleman.

3in (7.5cm) high

$3,000-4,000 **LC**

A watercolor-on-ivory portrait miniature of Sophia Brunel MacCarthy née Hawes, by Augusta Cole, signed and dated, in a gilt-metal frame, in a velvet-lined case.

2.5in (4.5cm) high

$2,500-3,500 **TOV**

A mid-19thC American School watercolor-on-ivory portrait miniature of a gentleman, in a gold frame with embossed floral decoration and braid of hair.

2.5in (6.5cm) high

$500-700 **POOK**

An 18thC steel corkscrew, with tamper ends.

$1,200-1,800 **WW**

A Charles Hull 'Presto' corkscrew, with cracks and heavy wear.

Hull's (incomplete) patent document covered a corkscrew with a worm that is pushed into the cork, rather than turned as is usual. Once the worm has been fully inserted, a ratchet is engaged enabling the cork to be pulled out without rotating the worm. The button on the handle releases the mechanism. Examples are hard to find.

$1,000-1,500 **WW**

A late 18thC Soho patent steel corkscrew, stamped 'Obstando Promov's', with treen handle and brush.

4in (10cm) long

$2,000-3,000 **GORL**

Judith Picks

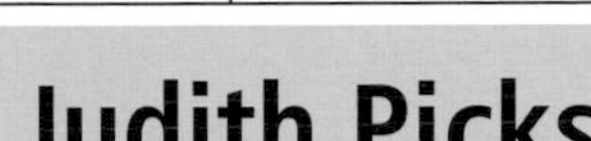

Where would we be without a good corkscrew? The first corkscrew model designed by Robert Jones & Son of Cheapside, Birmingham in 1840, distinctive for a narrow barrel and a single spike, can usually be bought for around $1,500. However, his short-lived second model corkscrew is perhaps the most desirable of the many Victorian patent corkscrews. Registered in 1842, two years after Robert Jones issued his first corkscrew patent, it is distinguished by the two spikes partially concealed within a bronze barrel, which are designed to spear the cork, while the helix pulls it from the bottle.

A Robert Jones second patent corkscrew.

This is a good example that retains its original rosewood handle and brush and a pleasing patina to the barrel.

$20,000-30,000 **GTH**

A Thomason 1802 patent corkscrew, patent no.2617, with turned fruitwood raising-handle, the barrel with Royal armorial marked 'Thomason's Patent Ne Plus Ultra'

$4,000-6,000 **WW**

A Thomason 'Autumnal' barrel corkscrew, with a turned bone handle and brush, with small repair.

$3,000-4,000 **WW**

A Thomason 'Gothic' barrel corkscrew, with a shaped bone handle.

$4,000-6,000 **WW**

An English variant Dowler's patent serpent corkscrew, with a later turned wooden handle, the serpent raising-handle with remains of bristles, the barrel with an applied plaque marked 'DOWLER' and 'PATENT'.

$6,500-7,500 **WW**

A 19thC 'King' patent brass and steel corkscrew, patent no.6064 with turned wooden handle.

11in (28cm) long

$300-400 **GORL**

A 19thC Dowler-type corkscrew, with turned bone handle, the brass barrel with applied armorial.

7in (18cm) long

$250-350 **GORL**

A Heeley's Empire double-lever corkscrew, with traces of bronze paint.

Patent 1890

$3,000-4,000 **WW**

A George III sailor-made engraved horn beaker, engraved with a British ship, a cutter, a mermaid and a martial trophy, with inscription, with silver-colored collar.

Inscription reads: 'The Flying Nautilus For The Palermo Lasses Care To Thy Coffin Adds A Nail No Doubt While Every Flowing Bumper Drives Another Out. May The Merry Arse Never Wear A Ragged Petticoat, May The Falling Woman Suck Seed In Her Undertaking * Finished At Sea Off Maritimo By IQ Septr 23 1812 Nautilus' and 'And Redwing In Company'.

1812 *4.75in (12cm) high*

$2,500-3,500 **DN**

A Pennsylvania horn beaker, inscribed 'William Faulks Anno 1775 Dom, Lancaster County Penna of Cocalico Township', the handle with cutout heart and crosshatch decoration.

1775 *4.25in (11cm) high*

$4,000-6,000 **POOK**

An early 19thC horn beaker, engraved with town scenes above British ships, with a silver-colored collar.

The scenes include the Royal Pavilion (Brighton) and Sunderland Bridge.

3.75in (9.5cm) high

$1,500-2,500 **DN**

A pair of Victorian Scottish provincial silver-mounted horn beakers, by George Jamieson & Son, Aberdeen, with glass bases.

c1860 *8in (20.5cm) high*

$1,000-1,500 **WW**

A Polish silver Torah shield (tas), maker's mark 'AR', Warsaw, with applied symbols, the border chased with flowerheads and foliate-scrolls, with an associated English silver pendent shield inscribed in Hebrew.

1876 *10.25in (26cm) high 20oz*

$5,500-6,500 **MAB**

A late 19thC German silver Torah shield (tas), with applied symbols, chased with foliage, stamped '750', with associated English silver pendent shield.

12.5in (32cm) high 31oz

$3,000-4,000 **MAB**

An Edwardian silver Torah shield (tas), by Moses Salkind, London, with applied symbols, with scroll and foliate chased border, inscribed in English and Hebrew, missing plaque box cover.

1909 *12in (30.5cm) high 26oz*

$2,000-3,000 **MAB**

A George V silver Torah shield (tas), by Jacob Rosenzweig, London, with applied symbols, with matted foliage, flowerheads and chased scroll border, missing one Tablet of the Law door and plaque box cover.

1919 *12in (30.5cm) high 30oz*

$1,500-2,500 **MAB**

A pair of Victorian silver Torah finials (rimmonim), by Hilliard & Thomason, Birmingham, die-stamped with foliage, with damage, missing upper finials.

1875 *11.5in (29cm) high 19oz*

$4,000-6,000 **MAB**

A pair of George V silver Torah finials (rimmonim), by Jacob Rosenzweig, London, embossed with foliage and with cast bracket central sections, hung with bells (some missing).

1918 *14in (35.5cm) high 32oz*

$1,200-1,800 **MAB**

A Russian silver Torah crown, maker's mark (in cyrillic) poorly struck, Minsk (or Warsaw), chased with flowers and lions, with bells pendent from stags (three missing), the bells later English replacements, with eagle finial.

1893 *14.75in (37.5cm) high 32oz*

$7,000-9,000 **MAB**

An eastern European silver Torah crown, the openwork crown centered by a single bell, missing finials, with sliding inscribed staves.

c1900 *12.5in (32cm) high 28oz*

$2,500-3,500 **MAB**

A mid-19thC German/Austro-Hungarian silver filigree spice tower (besamim), the pull-off lid surmounted by a gilt flag inscribed in Hebrew, the solid collar inscribed in Hebrew and English, with damage, in original fitted case.

8.5in (21.5cm) high 4oz

$3,000-4,000 **MAB**

A George IV silver-gilt and ivory ink stand, by John Bridge, London, the cover with flambeau taper holder, enclosing a removable cut-glass inkwell, the ivory carved with naked women and dolphins, the base engraved with a band of convolvulus.

Provenance: The use of a possibly antique ivory section looks back to German plate of the 17thC and is typical of the early 19thC historicism promoted by the Prince Regent (later George IV).

1829 *13cm (5in) high*

$30,000-40,000 DN

A Victorian silver novelty inkwell, in the form of an owl, by Charles Thomas & George Fox, London, with glass eyes, with faceted blue glass liner, the rim with inscription.

1844 *3.75in (9.5cms) high 7oz*

$5,000-7,000 LC

A Victorian silver-gilt inkstand, in the form of a stag on rocks, by John S Hunt, London, on a burr-walnut base, fitted with two later ink bottles.

1850 *11in (28cm) wide*

$4,000-6,000 LC

An Edwardian silver novelty inkwell, in the form of a sedan chair, by Sampson Mordon & Co., London, the front hinged to reveal a molded glass inkwell.

1906 *3.7in (9.5cm) high*

$3,000-5,000 L&T

A Victorian silver writing compendium, by Henry William Dee, London, inscribed with monogram 'MLG', the interior with two folding candle/sealing-wax holders, a hinged inkwell, a combined vesta box and wafer seal box, a dip pen and pencil.

1878 *4in (10.5cm) long 12.25oz*

$2,000-3,000 LC

An Edwardian silver regimental novelty inkwell, in the form of a Light Infantry glengarry bonnet, by Percy Edwards Ltd., London, the plume lifting out for use as a dip pen, the interior with a glass ink bottle.

1909 *3.75 (9cm) long 4.7oz*

$3,000-4,000 LC

A Victorian novelty silver-mounted glass scent bottle, in the form of a champagne bottle, by Sampson Mordan & Co., London.

c1870 *5in (12.5cm) long*

$8,000-12,000 LC

A Victorian silver scent flask, in the form of a tulip flower with leaves, by E H Stockwell, London, one leaf engraved with a fish, engraved with registered no.'43966'.

The scent vessel is accessed by pushing up the flower stem against spring pressure.

1886 *4.25in (11cm) long 3.5oz*

$5,000-7,000 LC

A late Victorian silver novelty scent bottle, in the form of a squirrel, by E H Stockwell, London, with sprung-hinged head, with button release.

The date letter has been partially lost in texturing.

c1890 *2in (5.5cm) high 1.9oz*

$2,500-3,500 LC

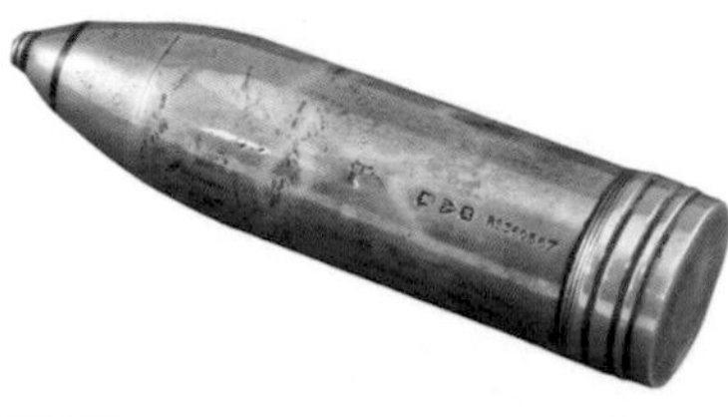

A late Victorian novelty silver and enameled double-ended scent bottle, in the form of a bomb shell, by H M Emanuel & Son, Chester.

1900 *3.5in (9cm) long*

$350-450 GORL

An early 17thC Scottish Burgh seal, probably by David Milne, Edinburgh, the matrix with armorial shield scroll and flowerheads enclosed in a motto '+S'.COMUNE. BVRGH. DE. ANSTREVTHER. EISTER.', with turned ebony baluster handle.

To date, only one other marked pre-1700 Scottish silver seal has been recorded. This previously unrecorded armorial falls well before the first record taken of Scottish Burgh and Corporate seals in 1672 and is, therefore, the earliest representation of a Burgh seal for the 'Royal Burgh of Kilrenny, Anstruther Easter, Anstruther Wester'.

1613-14 *2in (5cm) diam*

$65,000-75,000 L&T

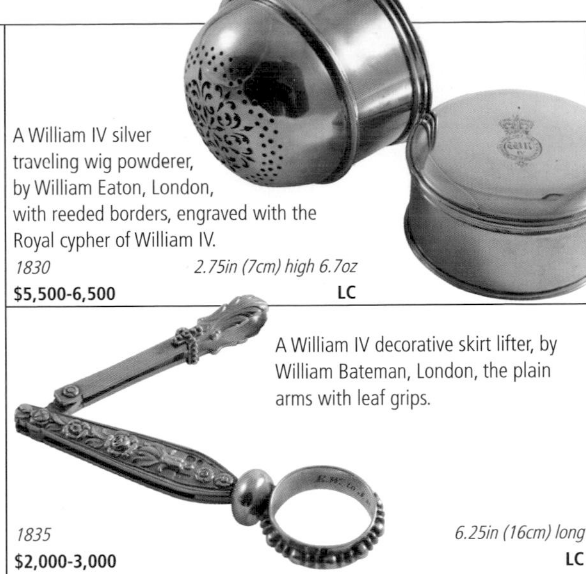

A William IV silver traveling wig powderer, by William Eaton, London, with reeded borders, engraved with the Royal cypher of William IV.

1830 *2.75in (7cm) high 6.7oz*

$5,500-6,500 LC

A William IV decorative skirt lifter, by William Bateman, London, the plain arms with leaf grips.

1835 *6.25in (16cm) long*

$2,000-3,000 LC

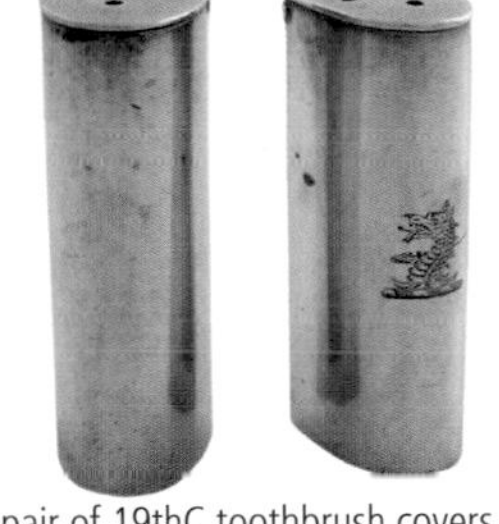

A pair of 19thC toothbrush covers, unmarked, with hinged covers, crested.

2.5in (5.5cm) high

$150-250 WW

An Edwardian silver spirit flask and two pull-off beakers, by the Goldsmiths and Silversmiths Company, London.

1909 *7.5in (19cm) high 22oz*

$1,500-2,500 WW

A 19thC French silver-gilt singing bird box, the case chased with foliate scrolls, birds and musical trophies.

3.75in (10cm) wide

$5,000-7,000 FRE

An Austrian Biedermeier silver musical box, by Georg Dobitsch, Vienna, the lid chased with a scene of the first giraffe in Vienna, the barrel mechanism with two melodies.

3.75in (9.5cm) wide

$3,500-4,500 DOR

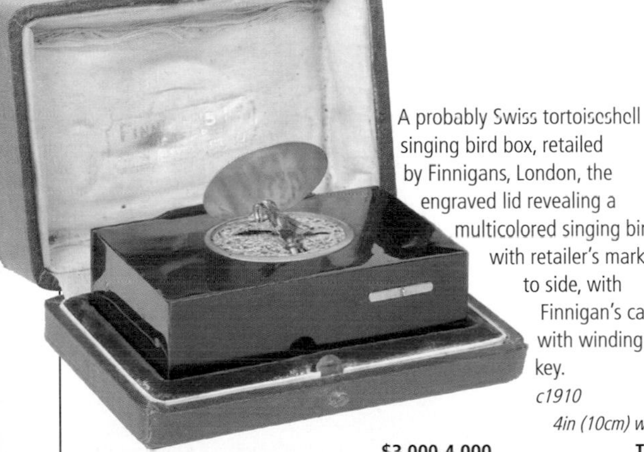

A probably Swiss tortoiseshell singing bird box, retailed by Finnigans, London, the engraved lid revealing a multicolored singing bird, with retailer's mark to side, with Finnigan's case, with winding key.

c1910

4in (10cm) wide

$3,000-4,000 TEN

A 20thC silver-gilt music box, set with gemstones, treated stones and imitation pearls, with enameled decoration, with wooden interior.

9in (22.5cm) wide

$15,000-20,000 DOR

An early 17thC Prussian silver-mounted amber tankard, probably Königsberg, the body carved with birds, fruit and scrolls, the foot with a frieze of animals, the wooden cover with finial in the form of a boy, with restoration.

10.25in (26cm) high

$20,000-30,000 **LC**

CLOSER LOOK - AMBER CHALICE

The male and female portraits are perhaps emblematic of marriage.

This chalice is not carved from a single nugget of fossilized resin. It was fashioned from thinly-cut plates of amber, decorated in low relief, and then joined together using adhesives. This technique was developed in the amber-making center of Königsberg in the 17thC.

Similar examples have been attributed to Jacob Heise, a member of the amber workers' guild. Heise worked for the court in Königsberg 1654–1663.

Artefacts made of 'Baltic gold' (amber) were fashionable among the highest classes of society in the 17thC.

This chalice is severely damaged - the bowl and stem have become detached from the foot and had to be held together with Blu-Tack for this photograph! The rarity and quality of the piece ensured a high value, regardless.

A 17thC Prussian silver-gilt-mounted amber chalice, probably Gdansk or Königsberg, carved with panels of floral-scrolls alternating with panels of male and female portraits above swags of fruit, the stem carved as a kneeling man, with major damage.

8.25in (21cm) high

$400,000-500,000 **LC**

A late 19th/early 20thC Italian marmo siena and marble-mounted model of an urn with the 'Doves of Pliny'.

9in (23cm) high

$1,000-1,500 **DN**

A 19thC Italian coral figure of Leda and the swan, on an oval malachite base, in a leather case.

3.5in (9cm) high

$3,000-4,000 **GORL**

A mid-late 19thC Viennese silver, lapis lazuli and enamel vase, makers mark 'HR', the rim and foot painted with figures in a garden, the handles surmounted with cats.

5in (12.5cm) high

$2,500-3,500 **WAD**

A Boucheron silver-mounted rock crystal table seal, with a Greek key border, engraved 'Boucheron Paris' to underside.

c1910-20 *2in (5cm) high*

$5,500-6,500 **L&T**

One of a set of three late 19thC Italian pietra dure panels, in ebonized molded frames.

Largest 6.25in (16cm) wide

$1,500-2,500 set **DN**

A small early 19thC Italian micromosaic panel, depicting a figure before a waterfall, in a black papier-mâché frame.

The waterfall is perhaps the Falls at Tivoli.

2.75in (7cm) diam

$5,500-6,500 **DN**

An agate cameo, by William Brown (1748-1825), depicting Napoleon, signed BROWN.

2.25in (5.5cm) high

$12,000-18,000 **M&K**

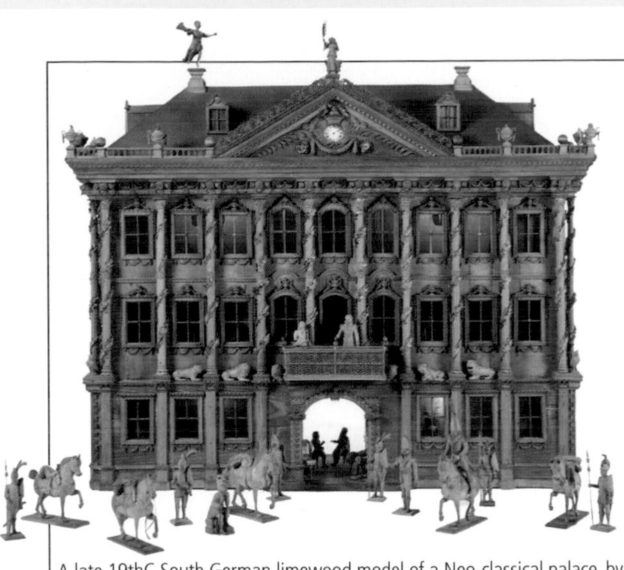

A late 19thC South German limewood model of a Neo-classical palace, by C Herman Bruckner, with around thirty carved figures of soldiers, guards, dogs and the proprietor of the house with his family and his servants.

48.75in (124cm) wide

$20,000-30,000 **L&T**

A 19thC Flemish limewood high-relief carved plaque, depicting an uprising in a townscape, in molded frame.

Frame 32.5in (83cm) high

$5,500-6,500 **L&T**

A bone Janus-head carving, with Christ's head to one side and a skull to the other.

$12,000-18,000 **DURR**

A Napoleonic prisoner-of-war bone automaton, modeled as four ladies at various pursuits and two children dancing.

4.75in (12cm) high

$2,000-3,000 **HT**

A pair of mid-19thC ebony carvings of the king and queen of Kandi, with damage.

8.75in (22.5cm) high

$1,200-1,800 **SWO**

A 19thC probably German turned rhinoceros horn vase and cover.

8.75in (19.5cm) high

$50,000-70,000 **WW**

A plaster cast of a salmon, in an oak frame inscribed 'Caught by Mrs Morison in Lower Shaw, Mountblalry on 1¼in Brown Wing Killer, 21st Oct. 1924, 61lbs, Length 52¼in, Girth 34in'.

Clementina 'Tiny' Morison wrote to her friend Lt. Col. W Keith (who had lost a very large fish in the same pool the previous year) reporting the catch: 'I rushed down, put my hands in his gills and dragged him up onto the bank. He looked enormous lying there - a huge male fish, well hooked but a beautiful shape and colored. Sim [the gamekeeper] said 'My goodness, he is over 50lb I believe'. I had no idea what a prize he was. We sent him to Aberdeen by the first train to get a plaster cast made.' It remains the biggest salmon ever caught on a fly in the UK.

$10,000-15,000 **MBA**

A black-painted plaster bust of Mercury, by Robert Shout, Holborn.

c1810

$2,000-3,000 **MEA**

One of a pair of French Empire tôle peinte tureens and covers, decorated with riverside landscapes, with pineapple finials.

c1800 *8.75in (22cm) high*

$3,500-4,500 pair **L&T**

An early 20thC Continental enamel bell push, with sage-green enamel on an engine-turned ground, with English import marks for London 1910.

c1910 *2.25in (6cm) diam*

$350-450 **WW**

A 19thC papier-mâché desk stand, by Jennens & Bettridge, inlaid with mother-of-pearl, gilt with foliage, with two glass inkwells flanking a stamp box.

12in (31cm) wide

$300-400 **MOR**

A possibly 17thC Continental feather collage picture, depicting 'S.MICHAEL ARCHANGELVS', within a titled border with geometric motifs, in glazed frame.

8.5in (21.5cm) high

$8,000-12,000 **TEN**

A Victorian shell-work architectural diorama, depicting a country house in shells, paper, mirror panels, moss and other natural materials, in a stained wooden case.

37in (94cm) wide

$3,000-4,000 **L&T**

An open steel razor, reputedly once owned by Robert Burns, the tapering green-stained cow horn handle with rocaille-embossed terminal, with a vellum case bearing an old label inscribed: 'Razor which belonged to Robt. Burns Poet', with handwritten note of providence.

Razor 6in (16cm) long

$3,000-4,000 **L&T**

A wooden charka, used by Gandhi.

18in (45.5cm) long

$50,000-70,000 **MM**

Judith Picks: Gandhi's Spectacles

These very simple steel-rimmed spectacles are synonymous with Mahatma Gandhi. Born on October 2, 1869, in Porbandar, India, he studied law and came to advocate for the rights of Indians, both at home and in South Africa. Gandhi became a leader of India's independence movement, organizing boycotts against British institutions in peaceful forms of civil disobedience. He was killed by a fanatic in 1948.

A very ironic and fitting quote from the great man is: 'An eye for an eye only ends up making the whole world blind'.

A pair of steel-rimmed spectacles, owned by Gandhi, in original metal case.

$65,000-85,000 **MM**

A Russian silver and cloisonné tea-glass holder and spoon, by Grachev, St Petersburg, decorated with stylized flowers and foliage, with twisted-rope and beaded borders, with maker's mark and purity mark '88', with souvenir inscription, the glass insert engraved with flowers.
c1900 *3.5in (9cm) high*
$8,000-12,000 FRE

A set of six Russian silver and plique-à-jour tea-glass holders, by Antip Kuzmichev, Moscow, with purity mark '88'.
1892 *7.69oz*
$6,500-7,500 DRA

A Russian silver and cloisonné kovsh, by 6th Artel, Moscow.
c1899-1908
4.5in (11cm) long
$2,000-3,000 TEN

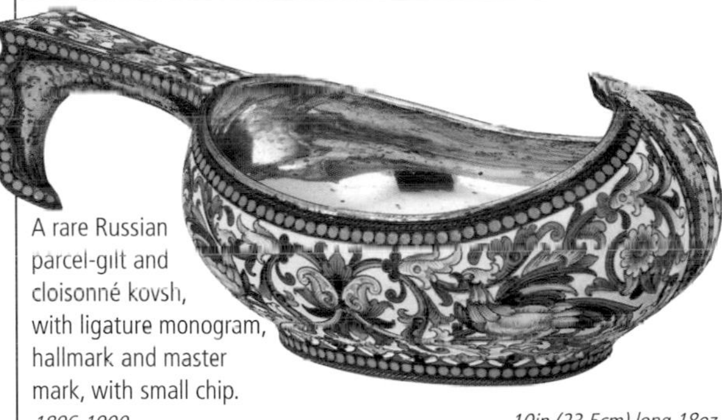

A rare Russian parcel-gilt and cloisonné kovsh, with ligature monogram, hallmark and master mark, with small chip.
1896-1900 *10in (23.5cm) long 18oz*
$25,000-30,000 KAU

An early 20thC Russian silver and shaded-cloisonné kovsh and spoon, decorated with stylized foliate panels and turquoise beads, with rope-twist borders, with purity mark '84' and maker's mark.
6.25in (16cm) long
$6,500-7,500 FRE

ESSENTIAL REFERENCE - PLIQUE-À-JOUR

- **Plique-à-jour is an enamel technique that is similar to cloisonné, except that there is no backing to the enamel. This feature means light can shine through the enamel, hence the name 'plique-à-jour', which means 'letting in the daylight' in French. There are various methods of creating this effect.**
- **Filigree plique-à-jour: A design is created from wires that are worked over a metal form and later soldered together. Ground enamels are added to each cell created by the wire frame and fired in a kiln. This technique is sometimes known as 'Russian plique-à-jour'.**
- **Pierced plique-à-jour: A sheet of metal is pierced to create the design. The resulting cells are then filled with ground enamel and fired.**
- **Cloisonné on mica or copper: The design is created on a base of mica or thin copper. This underlayer is subsequently peeled off (mica) or etched away with acid (copper) to leave enamel windows.**

A late 19thC Russian silver and plique-à-jour enamel tumbler, by P Ovchinnikov, Moscow, decorated with floral and foliate panels, with twisted-rope borders, with purity mark '88'.
3in (7.5cm) high
$5,500-6,500 FRE

A Russian silver and cloisonné kovsh, decorated with foliage, with spurious marks.
6.5in (17cm) long 6oz
$2,500-3,500 LHA

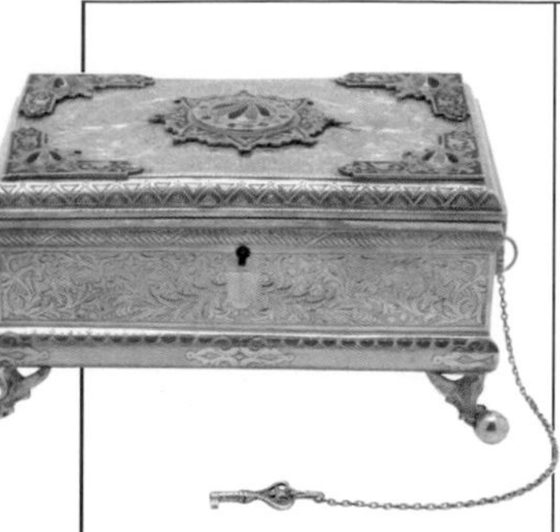

A Russian silver and champlevé table casket.
1893 *6in (15cm) wide 14oz*
$4,000-6,000 LHA

A 19thC Russian silver and cloisonné box and cover, by Viktor Savinkov, Moscow, decorated with geometric patterns, with purity mark '91'.
1876 3.5in (9cm) wide 17oz
$12,000-18,000 GORL

A Russian silver and shaded-cloisonné egg, by 11th Artel, Moscow, with purity mark '84'.
1908-17 *2.5in (6.5cm) high 2.3oz*
$8,000-12,000 SK

A Russian silver-gilt and cloisonné cigarette case, by Alexander Lubavin, St Petersburg, decorated with herons among scrolling foliage, on a stippled gilded ground, with purity mark '88'.
1893-1917 *5.5oz 4in (10cm) wide*
$2,500-3,500 DRA

A Russian silver and cloisonné cigarette case, by Ivan Khlebnikov, decorated with stylized foliage and a monogram, the interior later dated '25'.
1908-17 *4.25in (10.5cm) wide*
$5,500-6,500 WW

An early 20thC Russian silver-gilt and shaded-cloisonné basket, by 11th Artel, Moscow, decorated with flowers and geometric motifs on a stippled gilt ground, with twisted-rope borders, with maker's mark and purity mark '84'.
4.5in (11.5cm) high
$7,000-10,000 FRE

A Russian silver-gilt and cloisonné spoon, Moscow, the bowl decorated with a cathedral.
c1896-1908
6.5in (17cm) long 1.4oz
$6,000-8,000 LHA

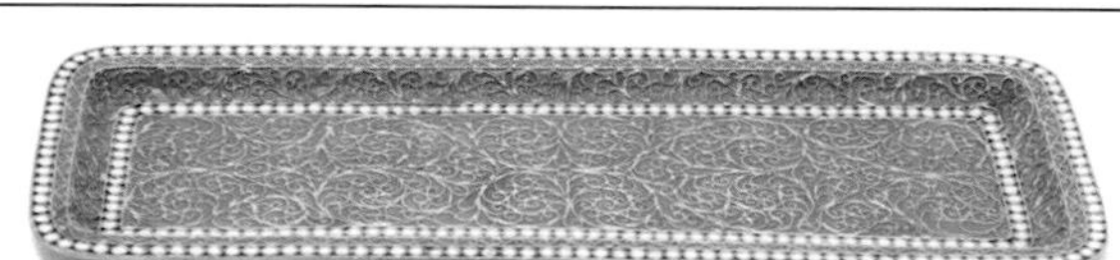

A Russian silver-gilt and cloisonné tray, by Gustav Klingert, decorated with scrolls.
1892 *5.75in (15cm) wide 2.3oz*
$3,000-4,000 LHA

A Russian silver and cloisonné three-piece tea service, possibly by Nikomor Zotov, decorated with foliate motifs and turquoise beads, with purity mark '84'.
Teapot 6in (15cm) high
$8,000-12,000 FRE

A Russian Fabergé page turner, by Carl Fabergé, Moscow, with painted silver-gilt and cloisonné handle and wood blade, in a fitted case.
1908-17 *14.5in (37cm) long*
$35,000-45,000 WAD

A Russian Fabergé silver card case, the cover with a two-color gold foliate flourish and '1899', the gilt interior with leather-pocket, with Russian double-headed eagle mark and Fabergé mark, with purity mark '84'.

c1899 *3.75in (9.5cm) long*

$3,000-4,000 TEN

A Russian Fabergé gold, ruby and diamond cufflinks and stud set, by August Frederik Hollming, the ruby set in yellow gold, the circular-cut diamonds in white gold, with purity marks '72' and '750'.

$7,000-10,000 L&T

Two settings from a Russian Fabergé silver fish service for twelve, St Petersburg.

1899-1903

Knives 8.5in (22cm) long 53.8oz

$4,000-6,000 set LHA

A Russian gold and diamond presentation cigarette case, by Yakov M Rosen, St Petersburg, the lid with applied Imperial double eagle in diamonds, with sapphire cabochon.

This cigarette case belonged to Tsar Nicholas II.

1908-17 *4in (10cm) wide 6.6oz*

$20,000-30,000 DOR

Four pieces from a rare Russian niello and parcel-gilt thirteen-piece tea set, Moscow, with purity mark '84' and ivory handles and spacers, with hallmark, city mark, assayer's mark and maker's mark.

Niello is a black mixture of copper, silver and lead sulphides. It is used as an inlay on engraved or etched metal.

c1895 *Teapot 5in (14cm) high 53oz*

$40,000-50,000 set KAU

A Russian silver serving tray, Moscow.

1891

Total 23.25in (59cm) wide 56.4oz

$2,500-3,500 LHA

An 18thC Russian silver bullet-shaped teapot, possibly by Yakov Semyonov Maslennikov, Moscow, with a composition loop handle, the date worn.

c1787 *7.25in (18.5cm) long 7.5oz*

$700-1,000 DN

A Russian silver and marble inkwell, St Petersburg, on a Rococo scrolling base with purity mark '88'.

9.5in (24cm) wide

$2,500-3,500 LHA

A Russian silver and leather portfolio, by 2nd Artel, Moscow, depicting a bearded Boyar reading a document, with inset cityscape panel, opening to various compartments.

1912-16 *Silver 17in (43cm) high*

$25,000-30,000 LHA

A 9ct gold bracelet with fourteen Russian miniature Easter eggs, the eggs unmarked or by various makers including Gabriel Nykänen, set variously with diamonds, rubies and sapphires.

c1900

$18,000-22,000 DN

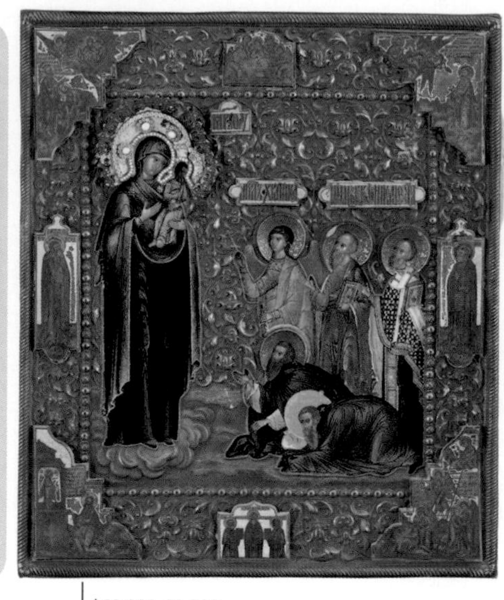

An 18thC Russian silver-gilt and tempera on wood icon, depicting 'The Mother of God appears to St Zosima and St Sawwatij', the oklad set with gemstones.

12.25in (31cm) high

$40,000-60,000 **KAU**

An 18thC Russian icon, depicting the ascension of Christ surrounded by Saints.

12in (31.5cm) high

$1,200-1,800 **BELL**

A late 18thC Russian gilt and polychrome icon, depicting Our Lady of Kazan, in a gilt shadowbox frame.

6.5in (17cm) high

$800-1,200 **FRE**

A Russian silver-gilt and enamel icon, depicting the Fedorovskaya Mother of God.

1896 *12in (30cm) high*

$1,200-1,800 **FRE**

A Russian embossed brass and painted icon, depicting the Madonna, with Cyrillic text, the edge stamped '84,1871, IR, Fabergé', the reverse with various inscriptions.

12.25in (31cm) high

$1,500-2,500 **WW**

Judith Picks: Icon

At the moment, prices for Chinese ceramics are making headlines, but I think prices for Russian artworks will soon be joining them. Rich Russian collectors have been buying back their heritage over the past few decades and prices have been rising as a consequence. Historically, the highest prices for Russian antiques have gone to enamels, particularly those by famous makers, such as Fabergé. Icons have been less sought after, perhaps due to collectors not necessarily being religious and the lower intrinsic value of the materials, but this trend is changing. Icons are increasingly being appreciated for their artistic and historical value and the best pieces can fetch thousands of dollars. This icon shows what can happen with the right combination of maker (in this case the Imperial court artist), good provenance linking the icon to the Imperial family and the 'wow' factor in its design. The fact that the repoussé halos may have been by Fabergé can't have hurt!

An early 20thC Russian icon, by Nikolai Sergeevich Emelianov, depicting the Mother of God of the Sign flanked by St Nicholas and St Seraphim, the silver repoussé haloes with possibly later Fabergé marks, in carved wood frame probably from the workshop of Olovyanishnikov.

Emelianov was the court artist. Provenence: Owned by Colonel Dmitrii Nikolaivich Loman, aninner-circle aide to Nicholas II and Alexandra.

Frame 23in (58.5cm) high

$650,000-750,000 **JACK**

A Russian silver and enamel icon, depicting the Madonna and Child, with spurious marks.

12.75in (32cm) high

$3,000-4,000 LHA

A Russian tempera on wood and silver icon, depicting Our Lady of Kazan, the oklad scroll engraved and embossed.

An oklad (also known as a riza or revement) is a metal cover protecting an icon.

7in (18cm) high

$550-750 DN

A 20thC Russian silver and cloisonné icon, by Pavel Ovchinnikov, Moscow, depicting Our Lady of Kazan, the oklad applied with enameled haloes and drapes.

10.5in (26.5cm) high

$15,000-20,000 MAB

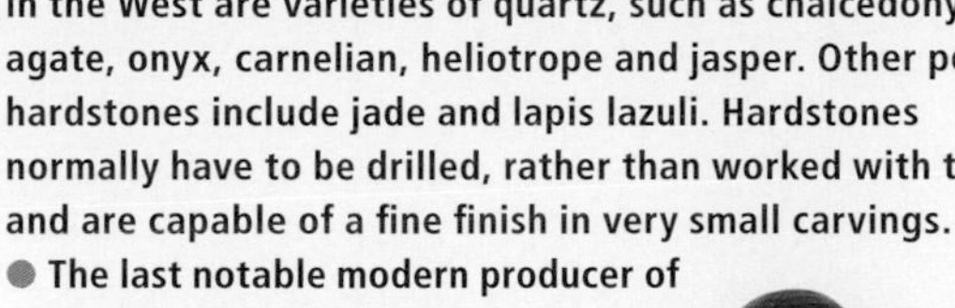

ESSENTIAL REFERENCE - HARDSTONE CARVING

Most of the hardstones that have been traditionally carved in the West are varieties of quartz, such as chalcedony, agate, onyx, carnelian, heliotrope and jasper. Other popular hardstones include jade and lapis lazuli. Hardstones normally have to be drilled, rather than worked with tools, and are capable of a fine finish in very small carvings.

- **The last notable modern producer of hardstone carvings was Peter Carl Fabergé (1846-1920).**
- **Fabergé's figures were typically less than 4in (10cm) long or wide.**
- **Subjects included animals, human figures and plants. Elephants and pigs are among the most common animals depicted, with some of the rarest being custom-made models of the pets of the British Royal family.**

A 20thC Russian-style hardstone figure of a gypsy, with brilliant-cut diamond eyes, gold earrings and silver necklace.

7.5in (19cm) high

$5,000-7,000 MAB

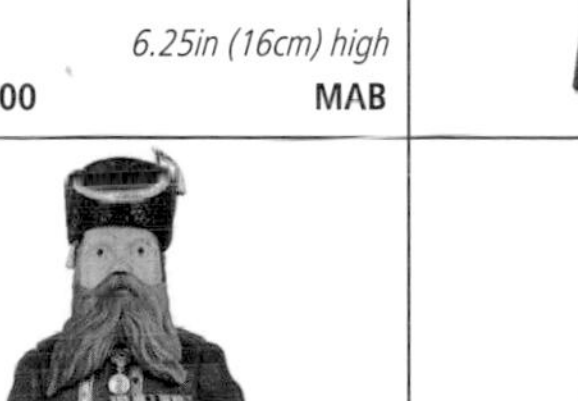

A 20thC Russian-style hardstone figure of a boyar, with gold fastenings to coat and oxidized silver cane.

6.25in (16cm) high

$3,000-4,000 MAB

A 20thC Russian-style hardstone figure of 'The Balalaika Player', after Carl Fabergé, with agate bench and coat, lapis lazuli breeches, gold belt and enameled balalaika.

4.75in (12cm) high

$4,000-6,000 MAB

A 20thC Russian-style hardstone figure of a wine seller, with crystal jug and mugs.

7.75in (20cm) high

$3,500-4,500 MAB

A 20thC Russian-style hardstone figure of a Imperial army officer, with gold and enamel trimmings and silver medals.

7.5in (19cm) high

$4,000-6,000 MAB

A 20thC Russian-style hardstone figure of a Cossack officer, with gold and silver details and sapphire eyes.

6.75in (17cm) high

$3,500-4,500 MAB

A 20thC Russian-style hardstone figure of a coachman, the lapis lazuli coat set with gold and enamel, with sapphire eyes.

3.5in (9cm) high

$1,500-2,500 MAB

A mid-late 18thC Russian St Petersburg porcelain dish and cover, painted with flowers, with gilt edging, with underglaze blue mark.

1762-96 *15in (39cm) diam*

$5,000-7,000 DOR

A Russian 'jeweled' porcelain cup and saucer, the cup with a portrait of Alexander II and gilt Imperial eagles, the saucer with a gilt laurel wreath band, crown and Imperial eagle, marked 'MFZ'. Cup

4in (10cm) high

$700-1,000 FRE

A 19thC Russian porcelain plate, painted with Hope suckling the infant Cupid, within a gilt border, broken and riveted.

10in (24.5cm) diam

$2,000-3,000 WW

A late 19thC Russian St Petersburg porcelain plate, from the 'Livadia' yacht service, the green border painted with chain links interspersed with anchors, set with a reserve depicting an Imperial crown, with underglaze green mark.

The Imperial steam yacht 'Livadia' was built for Alexander II at the Glasgow yard of John Elder & Co. in 1880 to an unorthodox design by Rear-Admiral Popov. She proved so unstable that she was seriously damaged on her commissioning voyage to Sebastopol. Alexander II was assassinated the following year and the vessel was stripped of its opulent contents.

10in (25cm) diam

$1,500-2,500 L&T

A Russian St Petersburg porcelain side plate, from the 'Raphael' dessert service, made for the Tsarskoye Selo Palace, decorated with Cupid riding a dolphin within borders painted with rustic vignettes, with crowned Imperial insignia and dated.

1894 *6.75in (17cm) diam*

$4,000-6,000 GORL

An early 20thC Russian St Petersburg porcelain vase, decorated with putti holding a mirror among clouds, with crowned mark, dated.

1901 *12in (30.5cm) high*

$20,000-30,000 GORL

A mid-late 19thC Russian glass and gilt-metal-mounted vase, St Petersburg, the colorless glass body overlaid with cobalt blue glass.

13in (34cm) high

$6,500-7,500 DOR

A Russian amethyst-glass and ormolu-mounted tazza.

c1870 *7.5in (19cm) high*

$4,000-6,000 WAD

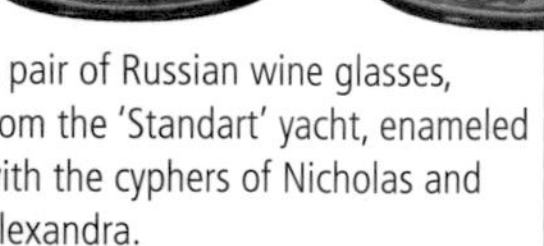

A pair of Russian wine glasses, from the 'Standart' yacht, enameled with the cyphers of Nicholas and Alexandra.

Provenance: Acquired in Paris pre-1939 as having been part of the furnishings of the Imperial Russian yacht 'Standart'.

4.75in (12cm) high

$14,000-16,000 LC

A 19thC Russian bone- and ivory-veneered casket, probably Arkangel, the lid decorated with a cherub and dated, on bun feet.

1828 *10.25in (26cm) wide*

$4,000-6,000 **L&T**

A 19thC Russian bone-veneered pocket-watch stand, probably Arkangel.

9in (23cm) high

$2,500-3,500 **L&T**

A mid-19thC Russian watercolor-on-ivory miniature of a Russian nobleman.

4in (10cm) high

$12,000-18,000 **KAU**

A Russian lacquered encrier, with paper dispenser and two hinged inkwells with glass inserts, decorated with figures.

11in (28cm) wide

$300-400 **LHA**

A 19thC Russian ormolu group of a carthorse pulling a wagon.

11in (28cm) long

$3,500-4,500 **FRE**

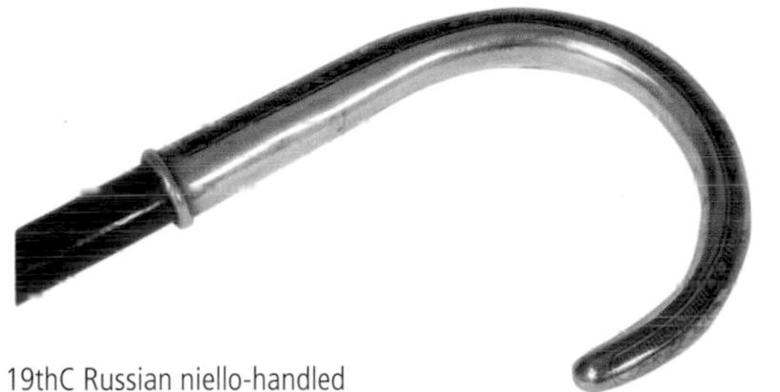

A 19thC Russian niello-handled walking stick, decorated with panels of a peasant, a peacock and foliate motifs, with ebonized cane.

37in (94cm) long

$800-1,200 **L&T**

A late 19thC Russian Imperial rosewood, silver and enamel tea caddy, by Pavel Sazikov, the silver strapwork initialed 'KC', with birch-lined interior, with various marks, including those of Kostroma.

8in (21cm) high

$8,000-12,000 **TEN**

A late 19thC Russian birch walking cane, the handle engraved with crown and 'CIIAJA 1890r'.

36in (91.5cm) long

$200-300 **WW**

A late 19thC/early 20thC Russian brass twin-handled samovar.

21in (54cm) high

$80-120 **DN**

A Russian Fabergé copper pot, with brass handles.

5in (12.5cm) diam

$5,000-7,000 **DOY**

A 19thC carved marble pilaster/fireplace edge in the form of a winged faun, with rich floral decoration, with small chips.

55in (140cm) high

$12,000-18,000 **DOR**

A late 18thC French sandstone fireplace, with some wear and small losses.

59in (150cm) wide

$5,500-6,500 **DOR**

A 19thC George III-style carved pine fireplace, with inverted breakfront top, the frieze carved with egg-and-dart and shells, the pilasters with urn and bellflowers, with carrara marble slips.

61.75in (157cm) wide

$2,000-3,000 **DN**

An early 19thC-style carrara and porphyry fireplace, with inverted breakfront shelf and canted inner edge, the porphyry pilasters with molded capitals and blocks.

75in (191cm) wide

$8,000-12,000 **DN**

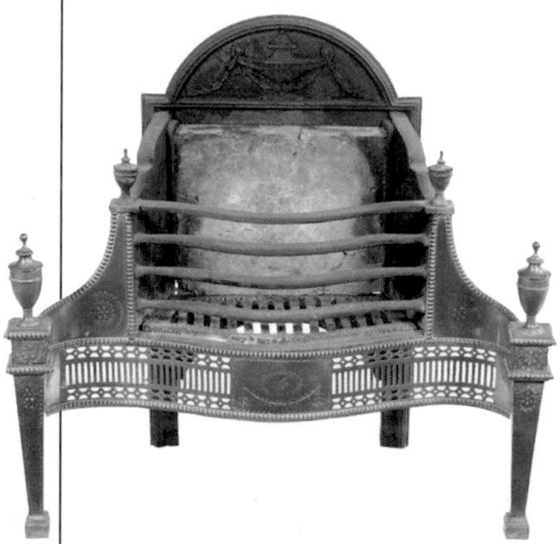

A George III-style brass and cast-iron firegrate, by Thomas Elsley, the arched back cast with an urn, the serpentine front with engraved and pierced decoration, the back stamped 'ELSLEY LIMITED LONDON'.

31.75in (80.5cm) wide

$3,000-4,000 **WW**

A late Victorian cast- and wrought-iron firegrate, with three rails to the front and sides, on bracket feet.

66in (106cm) wide

$2,500-3,500 **DN**

A 19thC cast-iron fireback, decorated with two lions, with some wear.

32.5in (80cm) high

$1,200-1,800 **DOR**

One of a pair of Rococo ormolu andirons, each with a seated chinoiserie figure.

14in (36cm) high

$6,500-7,500 pair LC

A pair of 18thC-French-style bronze sphinx andirons, modeled with feather plumes, ribbon-tied fur collars and paneled capes, the ebonized bases inlaid with brass marquetry bands.

15in (35cm) high

$5,000-7,000 DN

One of a pair of late 19thC Continental Neo-classical gilt-metal andirons, modeled with flambeau urns on pedestals with swagged balustrading between.

17.5in (44cm) wide

$550-750 pair DN

ESSENTIAL REFERENCE - FEDERAL STYLE

The American version of Neo-Classicism, Federal style appeared in the 1780s and continued until the 1830s. It reflected the confidence and prosperity of the newly formed United States of America.

- **Important government buildings of the time, such as the White House, were designed in the Federal style.**
- **Federal furniture was constructed on a slightly grander scale than British Neo-classical furniture, and used less uniform techniques and materials.**
- **One of the most characteristic shapes of Federal furniture is the circular wall mirror with a characteristic wide, ogee-molded frame around a 'bulls-eye' glass.**
- **Notable Federal cabinet-makers include Benjamin Randolph of Philadelphia, John and Thomas Seymour of Boston and Duncan Phyfe of New York City.**

A pair of Federal brass and cast-iron andirons, in the manner of R. Whittington, topped by urns, with claw-and-ball feet, monogrammed and dated.

1797 *30.75in (78cm) high*

$10,000-15,000 DRA

A pair of American bronze figural andirons in the form of Native Americans, by Louis McClellan Potter (1873-1912), stamped 'Roman Bronze Works' and signed.

22in (56cm) high

$6,500-7,500 SK

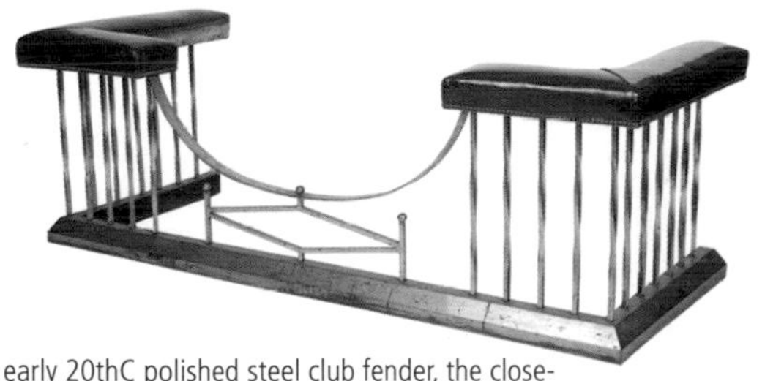

An early 20thC polished steel club fender, the close-nailed red leather seat raised on spiral twist supports and plinth base.

73in (185.5cm) wide

$3,000-4,000 L&T

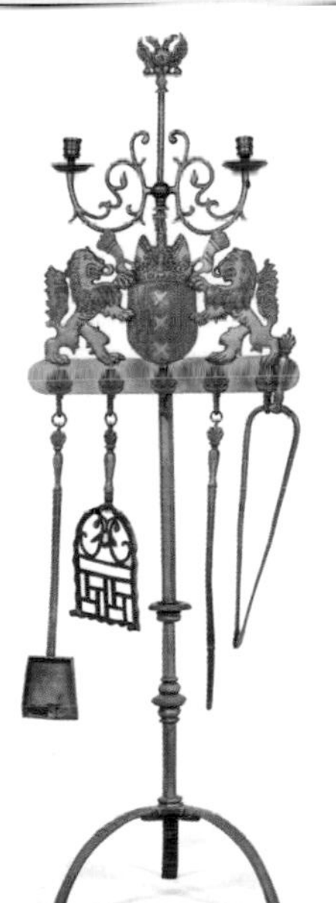

A set of four late 19thC fire tools and frame, the trefoil brass frame with candle holders and a shield emblem flanked by lions.

Frame 51in (130cm) high

$2,500-3,500 DOR

A set of wrought-iron firetools on stand, by Thornton & Downer, comprising tongs, shovel and poker, each with twist and punched decoration.

27.5in (71cm) high

$1,000-1,500 WW

A pair of 19thC Italian modified Baroque-style marble columns, with shaped bases, with chips.

52in (131cm) high

$14,000-16,000 **DOR**

A pair of Continental marble pedestals, with fluted columnar shafts.

35.5in (90cm) high

$3,000-4,000 **LHA**

A pair of marble urns and pedestals, the urns of squat campana form, the round columns with hexagonal bases.

55in (140cm) high

$5,500-6,500 **L&T**

An Italian carved serpentine-marble pedestal, the revolving, square top on a tapered spiral-carved shaft, with waisted socle and octagonal base.

c1880 *43in (109cm) high*

$1,000-1,500 **DN**

A pair of late 19thC Neo-Classical ebonized hardwood columns, the tapered square-section forms with bronze applications, with some wear.

39in (100cm) high

$3,000-4,000 **DOR**

A pair of Victorian marble-mounted satinwood pedestal columns, with turned fluted shafts, with stepped plinth bases.

c1890 *43.25in (110cm) high*

$2,500-3,500 **DN**

A pair of late 19thC French Doric-style vert d'estours marble and bronze-mounted columns, with tapered entasis-shaped shafts, on circular bases.

89in (226cm) high

$10,000-15,000 **DN**

A pair of 20thC red and white marble-mounted columns, with integral square plinths and acanthus-carved capitals.

41.75in (106cm) high

$2,000-3,000 **DN**

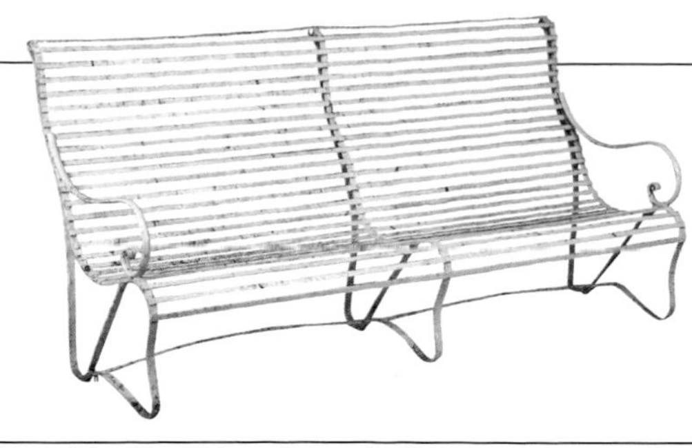

A Regency painted ironwork garden bench.

c1800 *71.5in (183cm) wide*

$2,500-3,500 **CHEF**

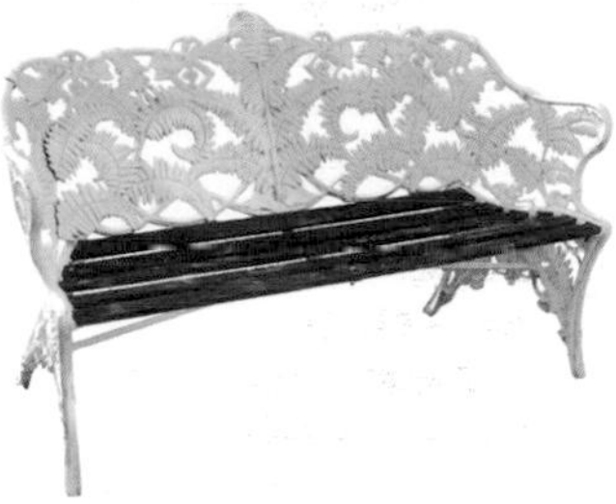

One of a pair of Coalbrookdale 'fern and blackberry' pattern cast-iron garden benches, stamped' C B DALE CO' and with registration numbers, with replaced wood seat slats, repainted.

This design appears as seat no.29 in the 1875 Coalbrookdale castings catalog.

c1900 *56in (143cm) wide*

$5,000-7,000 pair **DN**

A mid-late 19thC provincial garden bench, of side panel construction, with two frieze drawers, with some weathering.

95in (240cm) wide

$6,500-7,500 **DOR**

A pair of iron garden benches, with slatted backs and seats, on scrolling supports.

45.5in (116cm) wide

$2,500-3,500 **LHA**

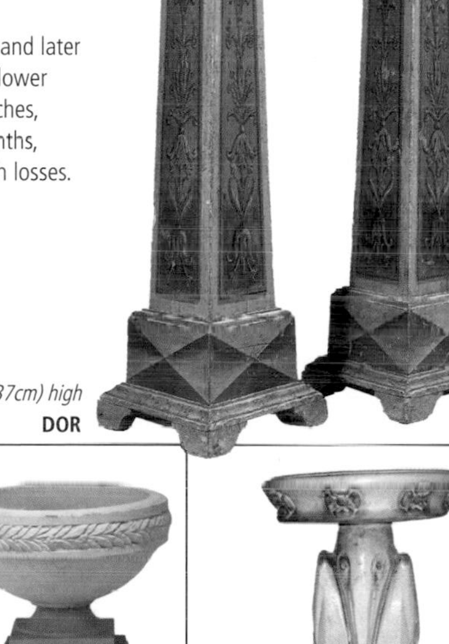

A pair of 17thC and later Italian painted flower stands, the Marches, with molded plinths, cracked and with losses.

54in (137cm) high

$8,000-12,000 **DOR**

A Coalbrookdale pottery trough, the sides cast with a central figure and poultry within foliate scrolls, with impressed factory marks and registration mark, with some damage.

33in (85cm) long

$500-700 **H&L**

A large 19thC stone vase on plinth, after the antique, decorated with a marble female mask and terracotta garlands, with some chips.

33in (85cm) high

$6,500-7,500 **DOR**

A pair of 20thC Galloway urns, on separate square pedestal bases, signed.

19in (48cm) diam

$3,000-4,000 **DRA**

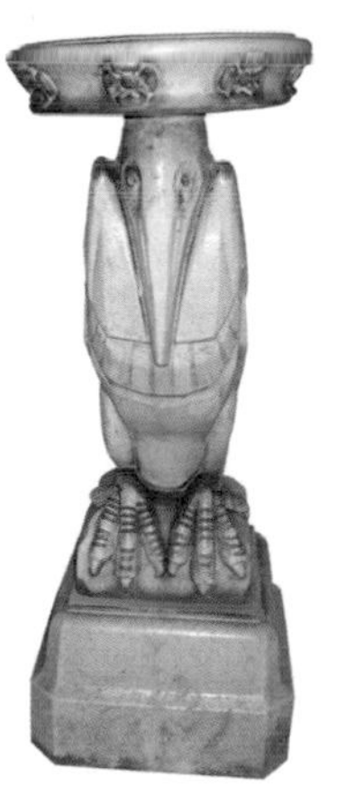

A late 19thC stoneware birdbath, the column in the form of a grotesque bird.

31in (79cm) high

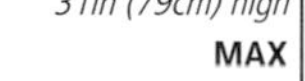

$1,500-2,500 **MAX**

ESSENTIAL REFERENCE - HEINRICH VON FERSTEL

Heinrich von Ferstel (1828-83) is often credited as one of the architects of 'modern' Vienna. He trained at the Polytechnic Institute under Eduard van der Nüll, August Sicard von Sicardsburg and Rösner.

- **His professional work began at the atelier (workshop) of his uncle, Stache. While there he worked on the Chapel of Saint Barbara in the Cathedral of Saint Stephen, as well as on various Bohemian castles**
- **He was strongly inspired by Renaissance architecture, particularly after his travels to Italy in 1854.**
- **He returned to Vienna in 1856. His important works of this period include the votive church (Votivkirche), which was later proposed as a model for Westminster Cathedral in London, the Austro-Hungarian Bank and the Stock Exchange. Later designs include the palace of Archduke Ludwig Victor, the Austrian Museum of Applied Art and the University of Vienna.**
- **In 1879 he was raised to the rank of Freiherr (baron).**

A pair of mid-late 19thC Baroque-style terracotta figures of tritons, after designs by Heinrich von Ferstel, one with a horn, the other with a trident, both on rectangular section bases.

Provenance: These statues were reputedly once mounted on the Stock Exchange building in Vienna.

Taller 65in (165cm) high

$20,000-30,000 DN

A late 19thC Italian marble figure of a woman, with a marble pedestal.

Figure 25.25in (64cm) high

$2,000-3,000 POOK

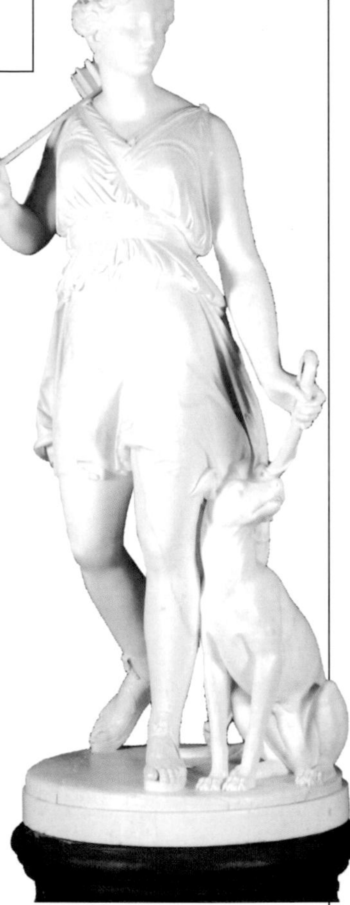

A late 19thC life-size white and gray-veined carrara marble figure of Diana, after Giovanni Maria Benzoni (1809-1873), modeled with arrows and with a seated lurcher, with separate base and associated tapering terracotta stand embossed with flowers and reeded bands, with minor restoration.

This statue was originally carved for use as a headstone before being abandoned under a privet hedge in the 1960s.

93.25in (237cm) high

$50,000-60,000 FLD

A Continental painted terracotta figure of David, after Michelangelo, on a square base.

66.25in (168cm) high

$4,000-6,000 L&T

An early 20thC lead model of a peacock.

23.5in (60cm) high

$800-1,200 DN

A late 19th/early 20thC copper wall-mounted architectural eagle figure, with weathered verdigris surface.

66in (168cm) wide

$9,000-11,000 SK

An 18thC Continental carved marble plaque, carved in relief with a portrait profile of an angel.

12.25in (31cm) diam

$15,000-20,000 L&T

Judith Picks

Having visited Chatsworth House before filming an episode of the BBC 'Antiques Roadshow', we were privileged to get a private tour of the house. I was amazed to see The Chatsworth tazza, the largest known Blue John one-piece ornament, and the Shore urn, which is the largest of its type. They were quite simply glorious. Derbyshire Blue John (also known as Derbyshire Spar, or simply Blue John) is a semi-precious mineral, a form of fluorite with bands of a purple-blue or yellowish color. In the UK it is found only at Blue John Cavern and Treak Cliff Cavern at Castleton in Derbyshire. During the 19thC, it was mined for its ornamental value and mining continues today on a small scale. These are superb examples of the unique Derbyshire fluorspar.

Additionally, the ormolu mounts, in the manner of the great French bronzier Pierre-Philippe Thomire, are particularly fine.

A pair of 19thC ormolu-mounted Blue John campana-shaped pedestal urns, with cherub-form handles, the mounts in the manner of Pierre-Philippe Thomire, on black marble plinths.

15.25in (38.5cm) high

$250,000-300,000 TEN

A pair of late 18th/early 19thC Blue John vases, with knopped spreading columns with circular bases, with marble and Blue John paneled plinths, with minor damage.

13.5in (34cm) high

$22,000-28,000 TRI

A Regency and later ormolu-mounted Blue John urn and cover, with flambeau cast finial and foliate cast and lobed socle, the plinth with alabaster top, Blue John sides, on a marmo nero Belgio base.

16in (41cm) high

$15,000-20,000 DN

An early 19thC Blue John vase, on a single knop column with a spreading base, on a black slate plinth, with minor stress fractures.

11in (28cm) high overall

$2,500-3,500 TRI

A pair of 19thC Blue John urns and covers, with white marble and 'Blue John' pedestals, with repairs.

10in (25.2cm) high

$5,000-7,000 BELL

A pair of late 18thC ormolu-mounted Blue John cassolettes, with twin scroll handles and ram's head mounts, on stepped square bases.

Cassolettes are small braziers in which aromatic materials can be burned.

9in (23cm) high

$55,000-65,000 GORL

A pair of 19thC ormolu-mounted Blue John obelisk candelabra, the mounts in the manner of Pierre-Philippe Thomire, the eagle-headed, foliate-sheathed branches with rosette terminals and campana nozzles, the ormolu bases applied with lilies within tied laurel wreaths, with black marble bases.

20in (51cm) high

$20,000-30,000 TEN

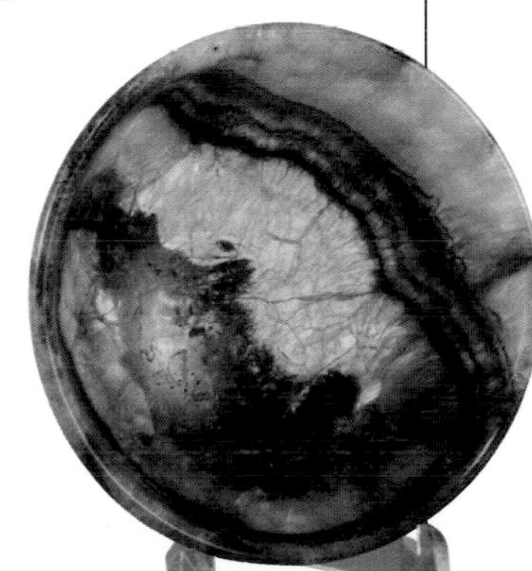

A 19thC Blue John bowl.

5in (12.5cm) diam

$2,000-3,000 GORL

A 19thC swell-body copper running horse weather vane, with verdigris surface.

31.25in (79cm) wide

$2,000-3,000 **POOK**

A mid-19thC gilt-copper prancing 'Arabian' horse weather vane, attributed to A L Jewell & Co., Waltham, Massachusetts, with boss eyes, on a shaped-iron base, with stand.

33in (84cm) long

$10,000-15,000 **SK**

A late 19th/early 20thC copper and cast-iron horse and jockey weather vane, the horse with cast-iron head, with stand.

30in (76cm) long

$7,000-9,000 **SK**

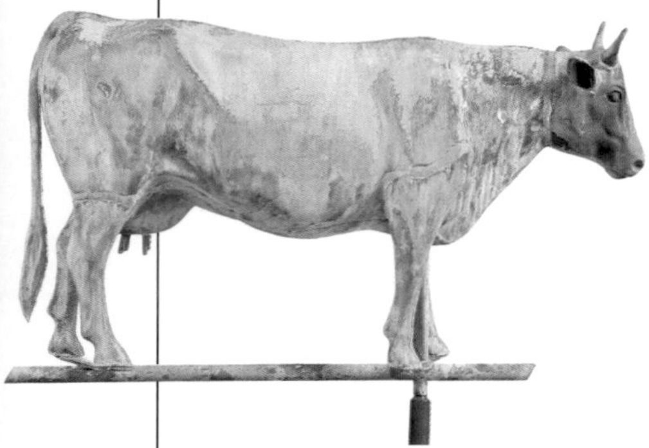

A late 19thC copper cow weather vane, with verdigris surface, on a copper rod, with stand.

27in (69cm) long

$6,500-7,500 **SK**

A copper and zinc steer weather vane, Waltham, Massachusetts, with a zinc head by Cushing & White, with verdigris surface.

30in (76cm) long

$35,000-45,000 **POOK**

A late 19thC gilt-copper ram weather vane, by L W Cushing, Waltham, Massachusetts, with original horns, on a copper rod, with stand.

29.5in (75cm) long

$15,000-20,000 **SK**

A late 19th/early 20thC gilt-copper codfish weather vane, with corrugated sheet-copper fins, with minor surface wear.

31.5in (80cm) long

$12,000-18,000 **SK**

An early 20thC silver-painted gilt-copper fish weather vane, possibly by E G Washburne & Co., with traces of gilt, with stand.

30in (76cm) long

$5,000-7,000 **SK**

A late 19thC copper butterfly weather vane, attributed to J W Fiske, New York, with copper-wire antennae and legs, with yellow and verdigris surface, on copper rods with orb terminals, with stand.

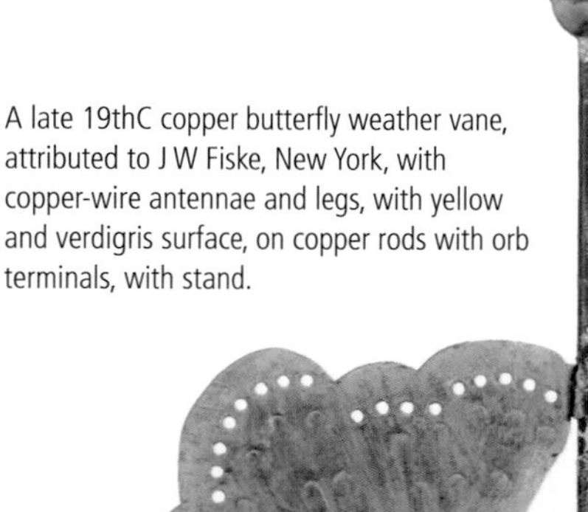

22.25in (56.5cm) long

$50,000-70,000 **SK**

Whirligig

A Pennsylvania carved and painted pine whirligig in the form of a policeman, with original painted surface in mint condition.

Whirligigs are typically powered by the wind and were probably invented by either farmers or sailors. Today they are a well-established sub-category of folk art and are increasingly valued by collectors.

c1860-70 *22in (56cm) high*
$20,000-30,000 POOK

An Austrian black marble vessel, from the Stadtpalais Liechtenstein in Vienna, with some chips.

Originally commissioned by Count Kaunitz in 1691, the still unfinished palace was sold to Prince Johann Adam I of Liechtenstein in 1694. It was completed under the direction of architects Gabriele di Gabrieli and Domenico Martinelli in 1711. The finished building is considered the first important high Baroque building in Vienna.

c1710 *22in (55.5cm) diam*
$8,000-12,000 DOR

A pair of ormolu-mounted serpentine marble urns.

16in (41cm) high
$4,000-6,000 LC

A late Victorian brass and cast-iron door porter in the form of a fox's head, the stem cast as a whip.

18in (46cm) high
$700-1,000 DN

A mid-late 17thC funerary wrought-iron cross, with three cross bars ending in scrolls, with minor restoration.

40in (100cm) high
$3,000-4,000 DOR

A late Victorian oak country-house postbox, the drawer to base with embossed brass handle, stamped 'Regency Post Box No. 437 WT'.

24in (61cm) high
$6,000-8,000 GORL

A pair of wrought-iron gates, the open scrolling decoration further adorned with leaves.

c1900 *71.25in (181cm) high*
$1,000-1,500 LHA

A 19thC giltwood and red lacquer door surround, the openwork frame carved with ho ho birds, clouds and scrolling foliage.

143in (364cm) wide
$4,000-6,000 L&T

An Afshar rug, with plants and an urn issuing flowers, within with a fawn stepped-leaf and rosette border and blue guard stripes.

63in (161cm) long

$2,000-3,000 **TEN**

A Bidjar rug, with stylized vines around a medallion framed by indigo spandrels within samovar borders and guard stripes.

155in (391cm) long

$3,500-4,500 **TEN**

A Feraghan rug, with a central medallion and floral patterns within ivory borders.

240in (609.5cm) long

$12,000-18,000 **POOK**

A Feraghan Sarouk rug, with a central medallion, floral pattern and blue field with corners.

c1910 *144in (366cm) long*

$5,000-6,000 **POOK**

A late 19thC Hamadan runner.

136in (345cm) long

$3,000-4,000 **FRE**

ESSENTIAL REFERENCE - HERIZ

The town of Heriz in Persia produced rugs during the 19thC and 20thC. These rugs were typically of wool on cotton, but in the late 19thC some were of silk.

- **Heriz designs often have an overall repeated pattern or a central medallion, which is often star-shaped. Such designs are based on formal town carpet designs.**
- **Heriz rugs are distinguished by a more angular rendering of the design elements than other Persian rugs.**
- **During the 19thC typical colors included ivory, terracotta and pale blues. Stronger colors were popular in the 20thC. Rugs with white grounds are extremely rare and can be valuable.**
- **Heriz rugs are very tough and hardwearing. This is reputedly due to the major deposit of copper underneath the mountain Heriz stands on. Traces of copper are found in the drinking water of sheep, who subsequently grow high quality wool.**

A late 19thC/20thC Heriz rug, with indigo star medallion and small spandrels, within red rosette and stylized vine border and cream bands.

230in (584cm) long

$8,000-12,000 **L&T**

An early 20thC Heriz rug, with central medallion and wide banded border.

214in (544cm) long

$10,000-15,000 **DRA**

A Heriz rug, with repeating floral pattern.

c1900 *169in (429cm) long*

$15,000-20,000 **POOK**

An early 20thC Isfahan rug, with red medallion suspending pendants and indigo spandrels.

149in (378cm) long

$7,000-10,000 **L&T**

An Isfahan rug.

87.5in (220cm) long

$1,000-1,500 **TEN**

A Karajah runner.

163in (414cm) long

$800-1,200 **TEN**

A 1920s Kashan silk rug.

77.5in (198cm) long

$8,000-12,000 **KAU**

A possibly Kashan Mottisham silk rug, with some wear.

115in (292cm) long

$7,000-10,000 **LC**

A late 19th/early 20thC Khamseh rug.

80in (204cm) long

$2,000-3,000 **L&T**

A Khorosan rug.

186in (472cm) long

$3,000-4,000 **IMC**

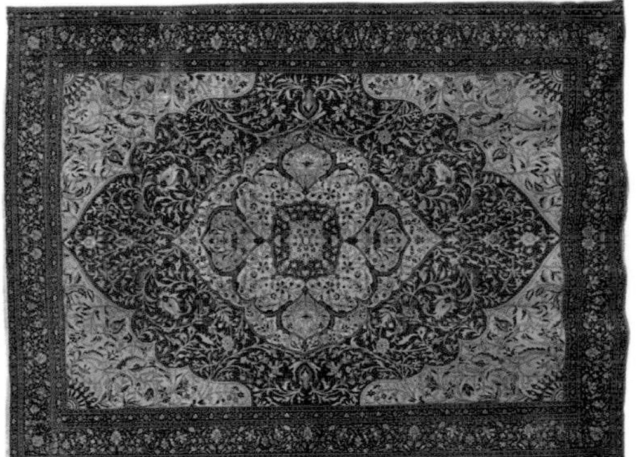

A Kirman rug.

c1900

144in (366cm) long

$6,500-7,500 **POOK**

A large Kirman rug.

330in (840cm) long

$12,000-18,000 **CHEF**

A Malayer rug.
103in (330cm) long
$2,000-3,000 **MEA**

A Mashad rug.
c1930 *213in (541cm) long*
$7,000-9,000 **POOK**

A Mashad rug.
c1930 *73in (186cm) long*
$800-1,200 **WW**

A Qashqai rug.
85in (216cm) long
$1,000-1,500 **GORL**

A Sarouk rug.
122in (310cm) long
$1,200-1,800 **LHA**

A Saroukh rug, with trees, plants, figures and animals.
177in (450cm) long
$8,000-12,000 **TEN**

A late 19thC Senneh rug.
77in (196cm) long
$3,500-4,500 **FRE**

A Senneh rug, Kurdistan.
c1900 *81in (206cm) long*
$3,000-4,000 **TOV**

A Serapi rug.
c1900 *146in (371cm) long*
$10,000-15,000 **POOK**

A late 19th/early 20thC Sultanabad rug.

267.75in (680cm) long

$6,500-7,500 L&T

A Tabriz rug.

196in (498cm) long

$2,500-3,500 LHA

A 20thC Tabriz rug, with central medallion surrounded by birds.

138in (350.5cm) long

$5,500-6,500 DRA

A late 19thC Ziegler rug, Sultanabad, with palmette and foliate design, within indigo rosette-and-vine border, within bands.

208in (528cm) long

$60,000-80,000 L&T

A late 20thC Ziegler-style rug.

141in (358cm) long

$4,000-6,000 MEA

An early 20thC northwest Persian rug.

248in (630cm) long

$8,000-12,000 L&T

Judith Picks: Ziegler Rug

This carpet came from Elveden Hall in Suffolk, which was lavishly refurbished by the Guiness family in 1894. Purchases included 23 Ziegler carpets, then considered to be the finest Oriental carpets on the market. The contents of Elveden Hall were sold in 1984. Many of the larger Ziegler carpets sold for prices in excess of $50,000 each. Zieglers, a Manchester-based firm dealing in the export of cotton, established offices in Turkey and Iran during the third quarter of the 19thC. The firm opened an office in Sultanabad, West Iran in the 1870s and quickly moved into carpet production. Zieglers organized weaving on a cottage industry basis. They supplied local weavers with loans, looms, cotton, wool and dyes. New designs were commissioned and old ones adapted specifically to suit European and American homes. Today Ziegler carpets are still considered the most desirable weavings on the market.

A Ziegler 'Mahal' rug, with lattice design of palmettes and flowerheads, within madder borders of scrolling vines, within guard stripes.

140in (356cm) long

$40,000-60,000 TEN

ESSENTIAL REFERENCE - KARABAGH

Karabagh is a rug-producing area of the Caucasus that borders north Persia. Many high quality rugs were produced in the area during the 17thC, 18thC and 19thC.

- **Karabagh rugs have long, thick piles.**
- **Designs are based on earlier classic forms, both Persian and Anatolian. One of the most characteristic Karabagh rug designs is the 'eagle' or 'sunburst' design, which originated in the village of Chelaberd. Karabagh rugs also sometimes feature European floral or Rococo-inspired designs, although these are crudely interpreted.**
- **The best quality rugs from this area are found in bright, vibrant colors that are not brash or conflicting.**

A late 19thC Karabagh Chelaberd rug, the ends reduced, the sides re-bound, with repairs and re-knotting.
107in (271cm) long
$7,000-10,000 DOR

A Karabagh runner, with boteh design.
c1910 *310in (787cm) long*
$4,000-6,000 POOK

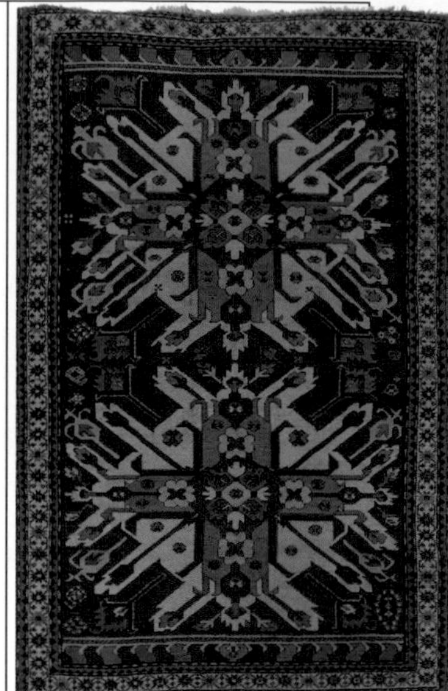

An Eagle Kazak throw rug.
80in (203cm) long
$5,500-6,500 POOK

An early 20thC Kazak 'Tree' rug, with Karabagh-style medallion.
91in (232cm) long
$2,500-3,500 L&T

A late 19thC Kuba prayer rug.
56.5in (144cm) long
$2,000-3,000 WW

An early 20thC Shirvan runner, with repeating boteh pattern.
129in (328cm) long
$2,000-3,000 LHA

A Shirvan rug.
c1910 *73in (185cm) long*
$3,000-4,000 POOK

A Shirvan rug.
100in (251cm) long
$8,000-12,000 DN

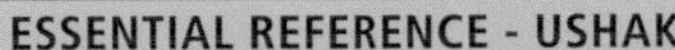

A mid-late 20thC Hereke silk rug, with inscription.

171.75in (275cm) long

$12,000-18,000 L&T

A Ladik prayer rug, the stepped Mihrab flanked by lemon yellow spandrels with ewers.

75in (191cm) long

$700-1,000 TEN

ESSENTIAL REFERENCE - USHAK

Ushak in western Turkey has been a center of rug-making since at least the 15thC.

- **The town is credited with the creation of many iconic Turkish designs, such as 'Lottos' and 'Holbeins' (named due to their appearance in paintings by those artists in the early 16thC).**
- **It is known for large 'medallion' and 'star' rugs, influenced by Ottoman court designs.**
- **After the 17thC, the market waned and rug production went into decline.**
- **Demand returned with the 19thC European fashion for 'Orientalist' design. As the town did not have enough skilled weavers left to meet demand, it turned to neighbouring villages and towns for help. These weavers had a more tribal style, using larger knots and longer pile on an all wool foundation.**
- **19thC Ushak rugs are consequently a fusion of tribal styles and older Ushak designs, as well as an incorporation of simplified Persian-style floral patterns.**
- **Rugs from this period were woven to fit European and American rooms.**

A late 19thC Ushak rug.

255in (648cm) long

$15,000-20,000 L&T

A late 19thC Ushak rug.

260in (660cm) long

$30,000-40,000 L&T

A Turkish silk rug, the field with gardens, animals, and trees, within a border of wild animals.

c1880 126in (320cm) long

$6,000-8,000 POOK

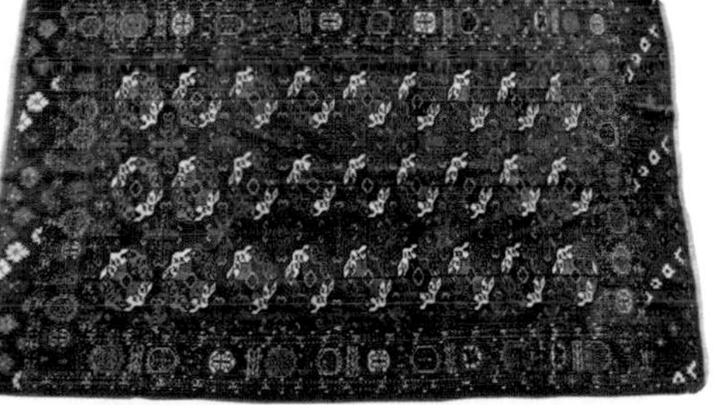

An unusual Turkoman rug, Emirate of Bukhara, the field with three rows of nine large guls, within borders of octagons containing hooked motifs, within mirror borders and barber pole guard stripes, the elams with stepped medallions.

The main gul is clearly of the Tekke tribe, but the elams suggest a Yomut origin. This may be the result of a Yomut bride marrying into the Tekke tribe.

122in (309cm) long

$6,500-7,500 TEN

A Turkoman Ersari rug, Amu-Darja.

c1850 119.25in (303cm) long

$12,000-18,000 DOR

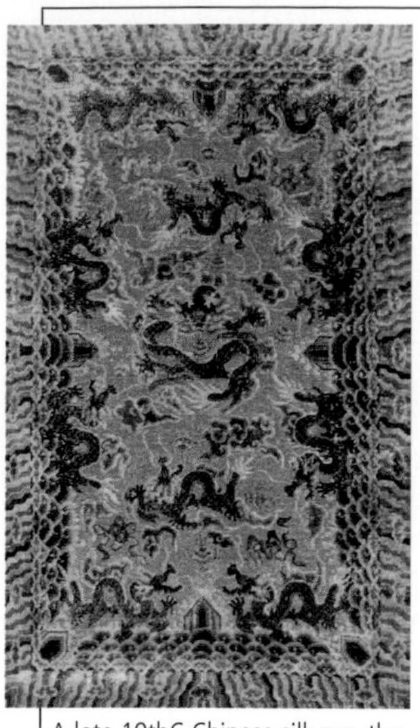

A late 19thC Chinese silk rug, the field with dragons and pearls.

85in (216cm) long

$5,500-6,500 **GORL**

A Chinese Peking rug.

c1900 *810in (2,057cm) long*

$2,000-3,000 **POOK**

A late 19thC Indian Agra rug, with scrolling blue strapwork-lattice and palmette pattern.

178.5in (454cm) long

$50,000-70,000 **L&T**

An Indian Agra rug.

c1930 *159in (404cm) long*

$5,500-6,500 **POOK**

One of five sections of probably British late 19th/early 20thC 'Turkey' runner.

Largest 228.5in (580cm) long

$7,000-9,000 set **L&T**

An Indian Mahal rug.

c1920 *1,111in (2,822cm) long*

$6,000-8,000 **POOK**

A late 19thC British Axminster Savonnerie-style rug, rewoven, cut and repaired.

282in (716cm) long

$20,000-25,000 **MEA**

An American Pennsylvania hooked 'Domestic Zoo' rug, by Magdalina Briner.

This may be the largest Briner rug extant.

c1870 *115in (292cm) long*

$12,000-18,000 **POOK**

A late 19th/early 20thC American hooked rug.

40.5in (103cm) long

$8,000-12,000 **POOK**

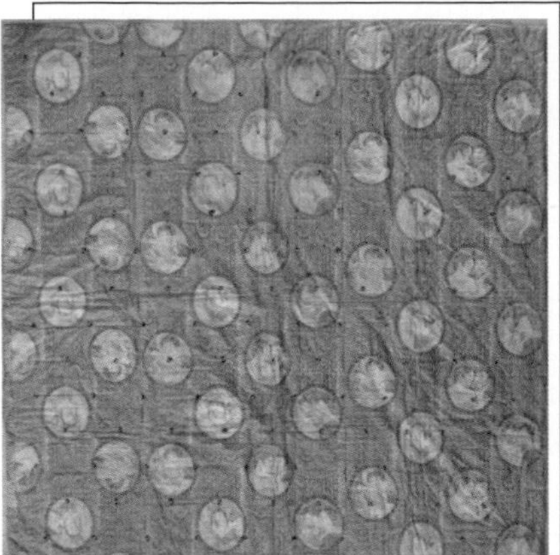

An early 19thC chintz quilt.

71in (180cm) long

$350-450 **POOK**

CLOSER LOOK - QUILT

The intricate pattern on this quilt is characteristic of quilts made in Balitmore in the 1840s and '50s by a group of women belonging to the Methodist church.

The heart-shaped floral wreath is flanked by American flags inscribed 'Gen'l Jackson/The Hero of New Orleans'. This patriotic detail is likely to appeal to American buyers.

Album quilts (quilts composed of squares of different motifs, generally a group effort) are among the most sought after and elaborate appliqué quilts.

The individual squares on an album quilt are often signed by their makers. This example has seven squares signed with ink or a stamped signature and four signed with stitched initials.

One of the center squares is signed and dated, 'By Miss Mary Ann Grooms/Democracy is my Motto/ Baltimore/1847'.

A Baltimore, Maryland pieced and appliquéd cotton album quilt.

99in (251cm) long

$15,000-20,000 **SK**

A Lebanon County, Pennsylvania 'tumbling block' friendship quilt.

1845-46 *85in (216cm) long*

$1,200-1,800 **POOK**

A mid-19thC New Jersey or Maryland 'Bethlehem star' album quilt, signed 'ELW'.

111.5in (283cm) long

$12,000-18,000 **POOK**

A Connecticut or New York album quilt, with mofits including the American flag, flowers, harp, starbursts, etc., several signed 'Litchfield' and 'Woodstock', dated.

1852 *88in (224cm) long*

$3,000-4,000 **POOK**

An American chintz appliqué crib quilt, inscribed verso 'Made for Mary Steele McCulloch by her Grandma Foulke in her 93rd year May 6 1854'.

1854 *41in (104cm) long*

$3,000-4,000 **POOK**

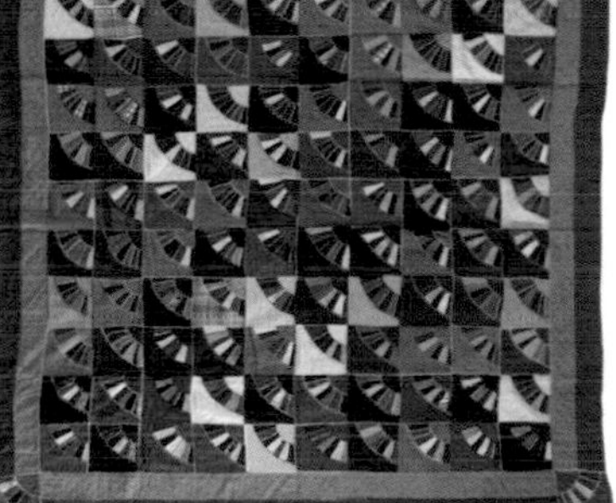

A late 19thC Pennsylvania fan quilt.

75.5in (192cm) long

$300-500 **POOK**

Judith Picks: Suffragette Quilt

The tradition of quilting for worthy causes has its roots in the female benevolent associations. Evangelical Protestantism, social reform, sewing, and fundraising were closely related in these societies. The WCTU addressed the issue of the eight-hour work day, child care for working women, vocational training, prison reform, and suffrage. These signature quilts generated funds in two ways. Individuals donated money to have their signatures on the quilt, and later the finished quilt itself was sold or raffled. Red on white is the most common color combination for signature quilts, because of the fastness of Turkey red dye, but orange, blue, old rose and gold were also used in combination with white. Although the signature quilt has fallen out of fashion, fund-raising quilts are still popular.

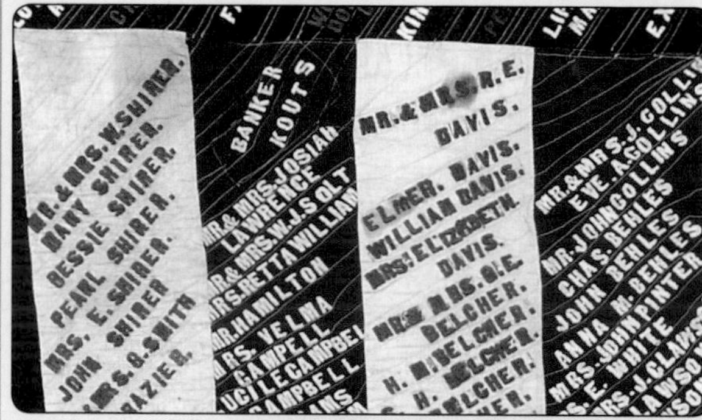

A late 19thC probably New York embroidered, pieced cotton Suffragette fund-raising quilt, decorated with the Stars and Stripes, embroidered with names.

74in (188cm) long

$15,000-20,000 **SK**

An early 20thC Lancaster County, Pennsylvania Amish pieced crib quilt.

43in (109cm) long

$4,000-6,000 **POOK**

A 20thC patriotic pieced and appliqué quilt, with four American flags surrounding an eagle holding an American flag and a shield.

88in (223.5cm) wide

$5,000-7,000 **POOK**

An unusual appliqué quilt, the field with red polka dots, within a red border.

c1920

$700-1,000 **POOK**

A Pennsylvania schoolhouse quilt.

c1930 *76in (193cm) wide*

$350-450 **POOK**

A Lancaster County, Pennsylvania Amish quilt, with a sawtooth-diamond in a square.

c1940 *81in (206cm) wide*

$1,000-1,500 **POOK**

A mid-late 16thC Flemish biblical tapestry fragment, with later plain border, reduced.

99in (252cm) high

$7,000-10,000 L&T

A mid-late 16thC Flemish biblical tapestry fragment, reduced.

This fragment is a part of the 'Abraham' series at Hampton Court. The subject it belongs to is no.8, Eliazar's oath to Abraham and departure in quest of Rebecca. The kneeling figure is Eliazar.

78in (198cm) high

$1,500-2,500 L&T

A late 16thC Flemish biblical tapestry, Oudenaarde, depicting a scene from the story of David and Bathsheba, missing border, with wear and restoration.

94in (240cm) wide

$4,000-6,000 L&T

An early 17thC Flemish tapestry border fragment, later mounted.

72.75in (185cm) high

$2,000-3,000 WW

A 17thC Flemish hunting tapestry, with brown scrolling vine border.

65in (164cm) high

$1,500-2,500 L&T

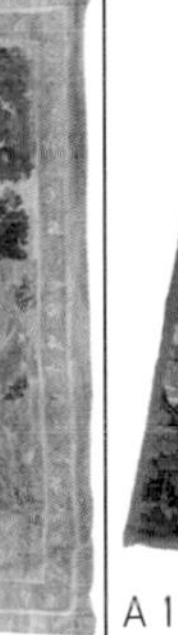

A 17thC Flemish verdure tapestry, depicting a woodland landscape.

85in (215cm) high

$7,000-10,000 DN

A 17thC Flanders tapestry, depicting a king grappling with a Roman soldier before a court.

119in (302cm) wide

$7,000-10,000 SK

A 17thC Flemish tapestry.

82.25in (209cm) high

$7,000-10,000 DN

A 17thC French tapestry, depicting a waterfall and ho ho birds.

89in (226cm) high

$2,500-3,500 GORL

An 18thC North European verdure tapestry.

81in (205cm) high

$2,000-3,000 **TOV**

An 18thC Brussels verdure tapestry fragment, with added borders of flowers, parrots and dogs, with some restoration and re-weavings.

96.5in (246cm) high

$12,000-18,000 **WW**

An 18th/19thC Flanders tapestry.

110in (278cm) high

$5,000-7,000 **KAU**

An Aubusson tapestry panel, with later backing.

c1860 *77.5in (194cm) high*

$6,500-7,500 **DN**

A late 19thC Aubusson portière, centered by a coat-of-arms above motto.

Provenance: This portière was made for Anne-Louis-Hercule Felix, Duc de la Salede Rochemaure (1856-1915) and was hung at the Chateau de Clavieres. The duke was described in his time as a megalomaniac but was also noted for his biography of Pope Gilbert and a work on the Catalan Troubadours.

173.25in (440cm) wide

$2,000-3,000 **DN**

ESSENTIAL REFERENCE - AUBUSSON TAPESTRIES

Tapestries have been woven in the French town Aubusson and the nearby village of Felletin from the early 16thC. Aubusson is distinguished from the other major French tapestry makers, Gobelins and Beauvais, in that Aubusson weavers worked in their own homes, rather than in a central factory.

- **In 1665 Aubusson was granted the title of Royal manufactory.**
- **Production largely ceased following the Revocation of the Edict of Nantes in 1685 as many of the Aubusson weavers were Huguenots. They consequently escaped to the Low Countries and the UK.**
- **The tapestry weaving industry in Aubusson was revived in 1732. Designs included copies of Gobelins and Beauvais tapestries, images derived from contemporary prints and scenes from the 'Fables of La Fontaine'.**
- **Reproductions of earlier tapestries were made in the 19thC.**
- **Tapestries are still produced in Aubusson.**

Four panels of late 17thC Aubusson tapestry, mounted as a four-leaf screen.

81.5in (207cm) high

$10,000-15,000 **MEA**

A French Renaissance needlework wall hanging, depicting the children of Israel.
c1600-20 *78in (198cm) high*
$35,000-45,000 **DUK**

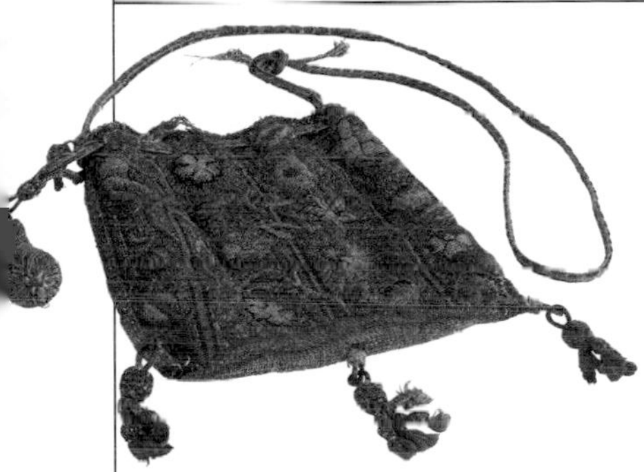

A rare Charles I silk and silver-thread needlework purse.

At this time purses were seldom used to hold money, they were more often used for holding sewing supplies or 'sweet bags'.
c1630 *4.75in (12cm) wide*
$15,000-20,000 **L&T**

A mid-17thC Continental woolwork picture, with a dated cartouche and two armorials.
1632 *35.5in (90cm) wide*
$4,000-6,000 **DN**

A Charles II embroidered and stumpwork picture, in a chionoiserie frame.
c1680 *With frame 22in (56cm) wide*
$7,000-10,000 **DN**

A late 17thC stumpwork and sequin-worked picture, in a walnut frame.
With frame 22in (56cm) wide
$1,000-1,500 **DN**

A late 17thC silkwork panel, in a velvet frame, with losses to stitching.
Overall 11in (28cm) high
$1,500-2,000 **GORL**

A Charles II beadwork basket, initialed 'EG'.
24in (61cm) wide
$25,000-35,000 **POOK**

A late 17thC polychrome and silver needlework panel, with appliqué needlepoint detailing, in a later frame.

14in (35cm) wide

$5,500-6,500 **TOV**

A William III petit point needlework panel, signed 'Elizabeth Clarke February 12th 1692', in later frame.

9.75in (25cm) wide

$3,000-4,000 **GORL**

An early 18thC needlework picture, in a frame.

60in (152cm) high

$6,500-7,500 **L&T**

A woven and embroidered picture, depicting the Austrian Imperial double-eagle with a large coat-of-arms, with glass stones and imitation pearls, with later fabric backing, framed.

c1860 *26in (67cm) high*

$7,000-10,000 **DOR**

A George III silkwork picture, depicting the Judgement of Solomon, in later frame.

30.5in (77cm) high

$700-1,000 **DN**

A Victorian woolwork picture, depicting a British man-of-war, surrounded by four ships and four flags, in a maple frame.

22.5in (59cm) wide

$1,500-2,500 **SWO**

A late 19thC Victorian silkwork bed cover, fringed and lined.

122in (310cm) long

$3,000-4,000 **L&T**

A 19thC gros point woolwork panel, depicting a Cavalier spaniel, in a Hogarth-style frame.

18in (46cm) wide

$700-1,000 **TOV**

A Queen Anne petit and gros point sampler, by Nellie Yetts, worked with a verse, birds and Adam and Eve by the Tree of Life, dated, with some moth holes, framed.

1708 *14.5in (37cm) high*

$2,000-3,000 **GORL**

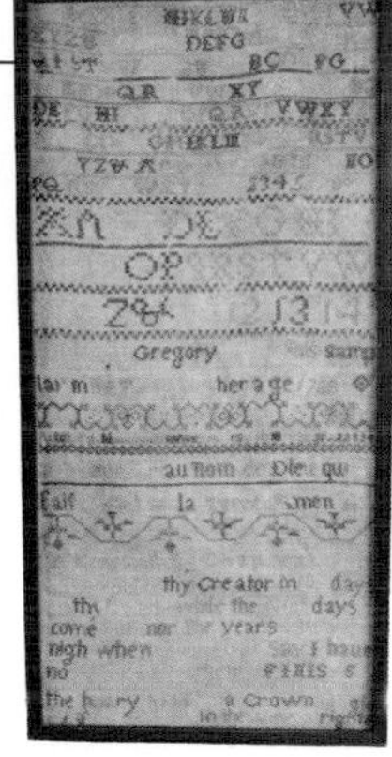

A George II sampler, worked with alphabetic, numerical and Biblical text within foliate borders, framed.

1738 *17.5in (46cm) high*

$300-500 **DN**

A George III needlework sampler, initialed 'MN', worked with a verse, animals, house and flowers, dated, framed.

The positioning of the date (with one digit in each corner of the main panel) is very unusual.

1773 *16.25in (41cm) high*

$4,000-6,000 **GORL**

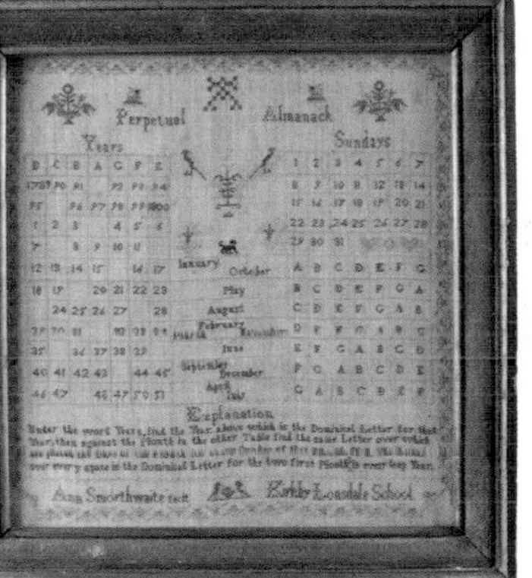

A George III perpetual almanack sampler, by Ann Smorthwaite, Kirkby Lonsdale School, framed.

1789 *13.5in (34cm) high*

$5,500-6,500 **WW**

A Dracut, Massachusetts silk-on-linen sampler, worked with 'MARTHA BRADLEY BORN JANUARY THE 31 IN Ye YEAR 1774 AGD TWELVE YEARS'.

13in (33cm) high

$7,000-10,000 **SK**

A probably English silk-on-linen sampler, by 'Mary Caddick Nov. 12 180, worked with a verse and farmyard scene, in a giltwood frame.

21.5in (55cm) high

$3,000-4,000 **SK**

CLOSER LOOK - SAMPLER

This is a really good example of a family sampler.

The text records the vital statistics of Elizabeth Whitley 'born the 17th November 1763 in Paxton 4 miles from Harrisburgh in Dauphin County...', and John Ward (no birth date given) who were married in 1783, and their nine children.

This sampler is of a similar to design to ones executed by students attending the school of Mrs Leah (Bratten) Galligher (later Maguire) in 1797–1826 at Lancaster and Harrisburg, Pennsylvania.

Similar examples of Susquehanna Valley samplers are illustrated and discussed in Betty Ring's book 'Girlhood Embroidery: American Samplers, Pictorial Needlework 1650-1850'.

A late 18th/early 19thC Susquehanna Valley silk-on-gauze-over-linen sampler, Harrisburg, Pennsylvania, worked with compartmented designs bordering a family record.

14in (36cm) wide

$7,000-10,000 **SK**

A Chester County, Pennsylvania silk-on-linen sampler, by Sarah E Garrett, taught by E Passmore, dated.

1820 *22in (56cm) wide*

$10,000-15,000 **POOK**

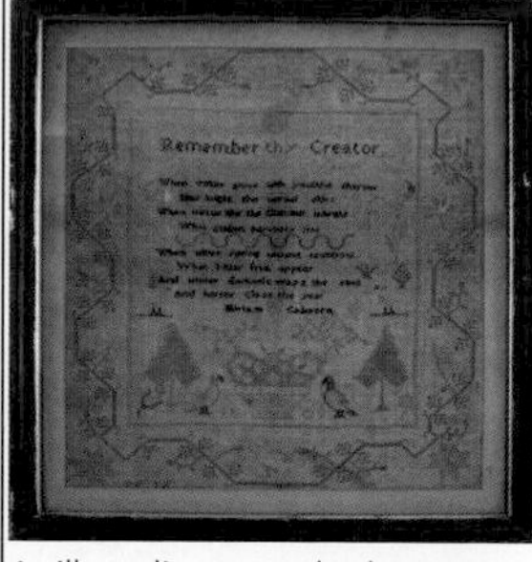

A silk-on-linen sampler, by Miriam Cobourn, dated.

1809 *15.75in (40cm) high*

$1,000-1,500 **POOK**

A Chester County, Pennsylvania Westtown school sampler, by Elizabeth Adams, dated.

1813 *16in (40.5cm) wide*

$4,000-6,000 **POOK**

A Midwest wool-on-linen needlework sampler, by Mary Blades.

c1830 *12in (30.5cm) wide*

$4,000-6,000 **POOK**

An American silk-on-linen sampler, by Cevilla Funk, dated.

1832 *16.25in (41cm) high*

$1,000-1,500 **POOK**

An early 19thC needlework sampler, by Helen McEwen Allan, worked with a verse tablet above floral urns, trees and a house flanked by thistles and trees, dated, framed.

20in (51cm) high

$2,000-3,000 **L&T**

An 18thC Ottoman machine-woven silk panel, framed.

43in (109cm) wide

$10,000-15,000 **CHEF**

A 19thC Turkish Kaaba-door bullionwork panel, with Koranic scripts and the Turkish Royal cypher within foliate bands.

103in (40.5cm) high

$12,000-18,000 **GORL**

A rare New York woven coverlet, signed 'Sarah S. Pomeroy 1838 B. French Weaver in Clinton'.

1838 *86in (218cm) long*

$2,000-3,000 **POOK**

A Continental velvet appliqué-on-linen, with central crest.

111in (282cm) wide

$4,000-6,000 **LHA**

A mid-18thC court waistcoat, heavily brocaded in silver-gilt with a floral pattern.
$800-1,200 TOV

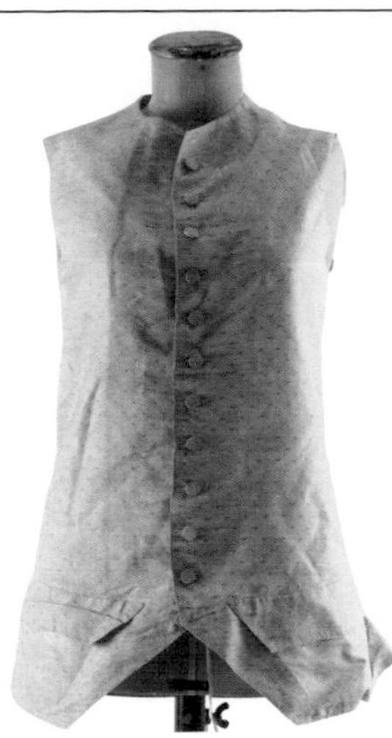
A Regency silk brocade waistcoat.
27.5in (70cm) long
$250-350 GORL

An 18thC embroidered silk waistcoat, with flowers around the pockets, buttons and collar and scattered sprigs to the front.
c1775
$1,500-2,500 A&G

A mid-19thC silk bodice and skirt, with applied jet beading.

This outfit was sold with a Victorian photograph of a lady wearing it.
$500-700 TOV

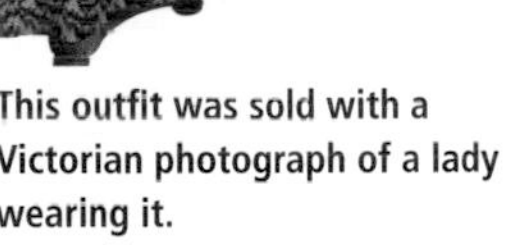

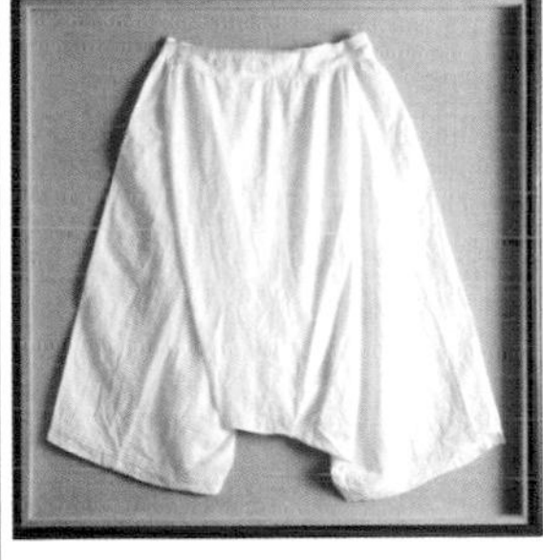
A pair of Queen Victoria's silk bloomers, embroidered 'VR2', framed.
35in (89cm) wide
$15,000-20,000 L&T

A pair of Queen Victoria's kid gloves, embroidered 'VR', framed.
15.5in (39cm) long
$4,000-6,000 L&T

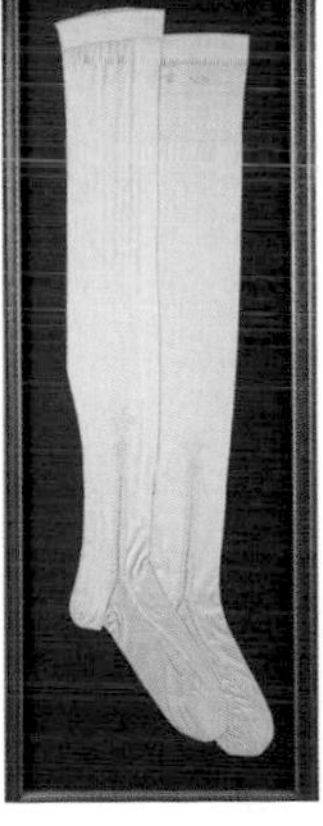
A pair of Queen Victoria's silk stockings, embroidered 'VR', framed.

These stockings were sold with framed photographs of John Meakin and Ann Birkin, 'Hosiery Weaver and Hosiery Embroideress for Her Majestys (sic) the Queen'.
36.5in (93cm) long
$10,000-15,000 L&T

Judith Picks

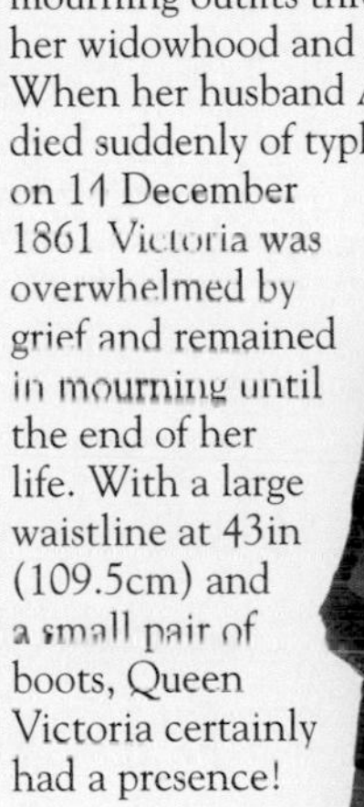

This outfit worn by Queen Victoria comprises a silk taffeta and bomberdine bodice and matching grograin skirt. A black straw hat complete with mourning veil richly decorated with silk ribbons and lace is mounted with an ostrich feather. The hat was made by the royal milliner Robert Heath of Hyde Park Corner. The garments date to the 1880s and include her silk undergarments, comprising a pair of silk bloomers and a chemise. Both objects are monogrammed VR (Victoria Regina). Also included are a pair of Queen Victoria's leather booties. The garments were high fashion of the day as Queen Victoria was conscious of wearing mourning outfits throughout her widowhood and her reign. When her husband Albert died suddenly of typhoid on 14 December 1861 Victoria was overwhelmed by grief and remained in mourning until the end of her life. With a large waistline at 43in (109.5cm) and a small pair of boots, Queen Victoria certainly had a presence!

A collection of Queen Victoria's clothes.
$12,000-18,000 HAN

A Balenciaga black silk evening gown, labeled 'Balenciaga/99121'.
54in (137cm) long
$3,000-4,000 **LHA**

An early 20thC Callot Soeurs green brocade evening coat, with metallic lace trim and floral closure, labeled 'Callot Souers 6 Rue de la Paix'.
$1,000-1,500 **LHA**

A Chanel blue tweed jacket, labeled 'Chanel/66576'.
$2,000-3,000 **LHA**

A Chanel gold and pink skirt suit, with raised gold-colored metallic detail, labeled 'Chanel/05799', with matching wool jersey camisole.
$2,000-3,000 **LHA**

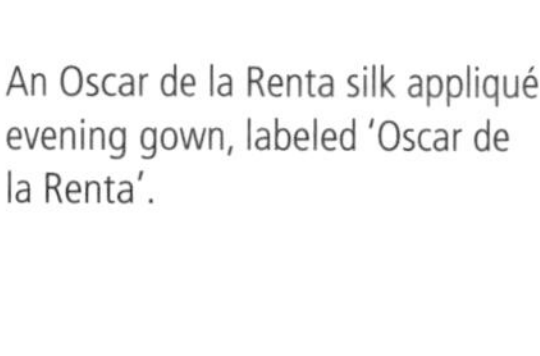

An Oscar de la Renta silk appliqué evening gown, labeled 'Oscar de la Renta'.

$2,000-3,000 **LHA**

A Jean Dessès aqua-blue lace evening dress, fully lined, labeled 'Jean Dessès Rd. Pt. Champs-Elysees Paris'.
c1958
$1,500-2,500 **LHA**

A Christian Dior black lace and silk evening gown.
51in (129.5cm) long
$2,000-3,000 **LHA**

A Galanos yellow evening gown, with sequin and bead detail, labeled 'Galanos'.
56in (143cm) long
$1,000-1,500 **LHA**

A 1980s Givenchy navy-blue satin evening gown, with seam detail at waist, labeled 'Givenchy'.
Size 42
$550-750 **LHA**

A Gucci red suede jacket, with alligator trim, labeled 'Gucci'.
48in (122cm) long
$1,000-1,500 **LHA**

A 1980s Norma Kamali orange three-piece parachute ensemble, labeled 'Omo Norma Kamali'.

$2,000-3,000 LHA

A probably 1930s Kiviette pink silk faille gown, the pleated fitted bodice with boning, labeled 'Kiviette'.

$800-1,200 LHA

A 1930s Germaine Monteil silk gown, labeled 'Germaine Monteil', with a matching embroidered cropped vest and red silk sash.

$1,500-2,500 LHA

A Thea Porter silk-chiffon patchwork kaftan, labeled 'Thea Porter Couture'.

$3,000-4,000 LHA

An Yves Saint Laurent 'leopard' silk evening gown, with a gold-painted design, labeled 'Yves Saint Laurent'.

This dress was photographed by Helmut Newton for a 1993 advertising campaign.

Size 36

$2,000-3,000 LHA

An Yves Saint Laurent brocade evening gown, with green and colorless rhinestone trim, labeled 'Yves Saint Laurent/016439/I.Magnin'.

$1,200-1,800 LHA

A Philippe Venet silk-chiffon evening gown and duster, labeled 'Phillipe Venet'.

$800-1,200 LHA

A Gianni Versace black moire-taffeta and jewel-encrusted jacket, decorated with Classical motifs, labeled 'Gianni Versace Couture'.

$1,500-2,500 LHA

A unique Clifford Yong reverse-painted mink coat, reverses to phoenix painting, signed 'Clifford Yong'.

51in (129.5cm) long

$5,000-7,000 DRA

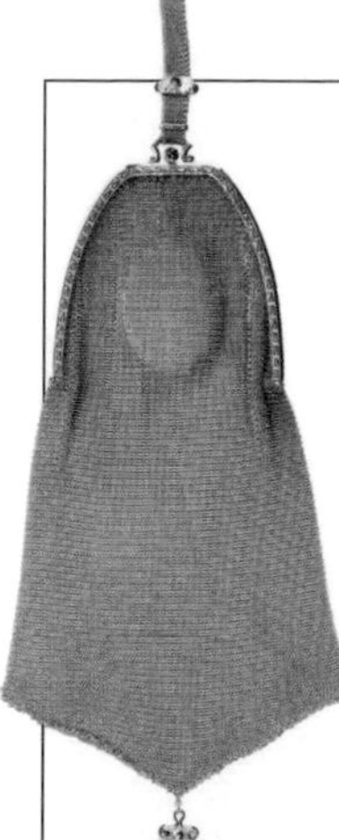

A Durand & Co. gold-mesh evening bag, with seed pearl tassel and sapphire slide and thumbpiece, with gold-cased mirror.

c1910

16in (40.5cm) long 5.6oz

$5,000-7,000 DRA

A 9ct-gold-framed mesh evening bag, with cabochon sapphire clasp.

6.25in (16cm) wide

$3,000-4,000 TEN

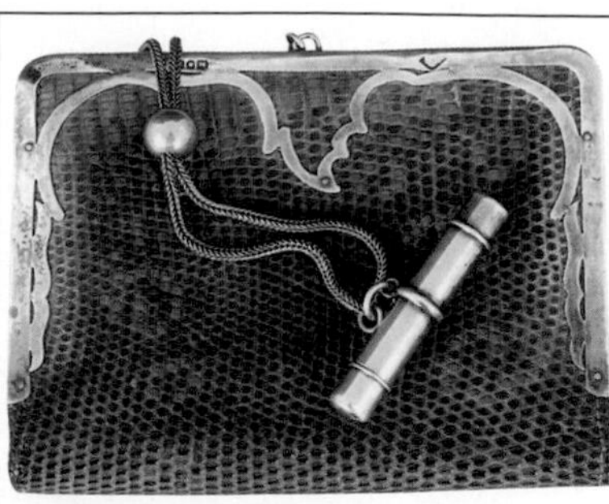

An Edwardian crocodile-skin and silver-mounted evening bag, maker's mark 'KW', London, with foxtail chain clasp terminating in pencil.

1904

$250-350 FLD

A 1920s possibly French glass evening bag, with pressed glass flowerheads below beeded-mesh and expandable brass collar.

$150-250 FLD

A Chanel black leather tote, with chainlink and leather straps, stamped 'Chanel'.

14in (35.5cm) wide

$3,000-5,000 LHA

ESSENTIAL REFERENCE - CHANEL

Gabrielle 'Coco' Chanel (1883-1971) was a French fashion designer, who, among other achievements, is renowned for re-defining the 'little black dress' and the most famous perfume of all time: Chanel No.5.

- **Chanel opened a millinery shop in Paris in 1910, a boutique in Deauville in 1912 and a Couture House in Biarritz in 1915. In 1918 she opened a Couture House at 31 rue Cambon in Paris.**
- **Her style was encapsulated in her designs for formal yet simple suits, well-cut dresses, quilted purses and costume jewelry, especially pearls.**
- **Chanel launched the 2.55 quilted purse in February 1955, naming the bag after the date of its introduction.**
- **Her fashion house survives today.**

A Chanel pressed-silk hardsided 'Coco' purse, printed with Coco Chanel's face, stamped 'Chanel'.

11.5in (29cm) wide

$2,500-3,500 LHA

A Chanel black quilted-linen purse, with chainlink straps, stamped 'Chanel'.

13in (33cm) wide

$1,200-1,800 LHA

A Chanel olive-green quilted caviar-leather bag, with logo closure, stamped 'Chanel'.

12.5in (31.50cm) wide

$2,000-3,000 LHA

A rare Chanel red alligatorskin 'Classic' purse, Y03587, with white-metal hardware and a leather strap.

This bag, with authenticity card no. 12153633, requires a CITES licence to be exported outside the European Union.

c2008 *10.5in (26cm) wide*

$18,000-22,000 DN

A Longchamp 'Le Pliage 1621' printed canvas purse, designed by Tracey Emin, with leather trimmings, with dustbag.

c2004 *13in (33cm) wide*

$1,500-2,500 **DN**

A 1960s Hermès black crocodileskin 'Sac Mallette' purse, with gilt-metal hardware, with stamped marks, with dustbag.

12.25in (31cm) wide

$5,500-6,500 **DN**

An Hermès black calfskin 'Passe-Guide' purse, with a long shoulder strap, gold frame, stamped 'Hermès'.

This purse was more expensive than other Hermès calfskin purses because it was the only one with a rounded and curved base, made on a wooden form.

9in (23.5cm) wide

$5,500-6,500 **LHA**

An Hermès red calfskin 'Kelly' bag, with lock and key sheath, with matching shoulder strap, stamped 'Hermès'.

12in (32cm) wide

$3,500-4,500 **LHA**

An Hermès forest green crocodileskin 'Birkin' bag, with gold hardware, with matching lock and key sheath, stamped 'Hermès Paris'.

This bag sold with CITES papers required for export.

2006 *12in (30cm) wide*

$25,000-30,000 **LHA**

A Judith Leiber tiger minaudière bag, with a hidden chain shoulder strap, stamped 'Judith Leiber'.

7in (18cm) long

$2,000-3,000 **LHA**

A Louis Vuitton bucket bag and pouchette, the suede multicolor fringe with charms, with suede interior, with dustbag.

10.5in (26.5cm) wide

$3,000-4,000 **DRA**

A Louis Vuitton leather trunk, with a central strap and three trays, with label reading 'Paris London 782021'.

24in (62cm) wide

$2,500-3,500 **SWO**

Judith Picks

The American film star, Fred Astaire, was doubtless just the sort of money-no-object client Louis Vuitton had in mind when they launched their 'Sac Tennis' range in the 1970s. Most of the cases in the range were made to accommodate the smaller scale vintage racquets so, the covers at least, are of limited use today (a more current model, with natural cowhide leather trims, retails for several thousand dollars), but that was of little concern to the All England Law Tennis Club, who eyed this stardust-sprinkled lot for the Wimbledon Lawn Tennis Museum.

A Louis Vuitton tennis racquet cover, ball bag and racquet holdall, owned by Fred Astaire.

$1,200-1,800 **JN**

A Goyard canvas dresser trunk, stamped 'E. Goyard'.

41in (104cm) wide

$10,000-15,000 **LHA**

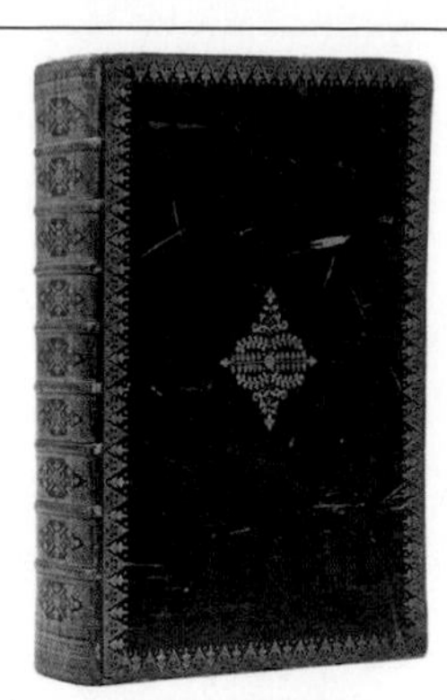

'The Holy Bible', published by John Baskerville, printer to the University of Cambridge, bound in contemporary calf, without list of subscribers.

1763

$5,500-6,500 BLO

'The New Testament Of Our Lord and Saviour Jesus Christ: Newly Translated out of the Original Greek; And with the former Translations Diligently Compared and Revised', published by Robert Aitken, bound in contemporary calf, in early 20thC Hyman Zucker box.

Robert Aitken (1734-1802) was a printer, publisher and engraver. He was born in Dalkeith, Scotland and emigrated to America in 1769. In 1777 Aitken published the New Testament breaking the Crown's monopoly on the production of the King James Bible. The first complete Bible followed in 1781-82. The venture was a financial failure despite official approval from the newly instituted Congress.

1777

$200,000-300,000 BLO

'The Holy Bible. Containing the Old and New Testaments: With the Apocrypha', published by Isaiah Thomas, Worcester, MA, with engraved frontispiece and 49 plates, bound in contemporary calf.

The edition was the first folio bible printed in the USA.

1791

$6,500-7,500 LHA

ESSENTIAL REFERENCE - THE KELMSCOTT PRESS

The Kelmscott Press was established by William Morris (1834-96) in 1891 in London.

- **During its period of operation, the press produced 53 books (totaling around 18,000 copies).**
- **Morris designed two typefaces based on 15thC models for the press. The Roman 'Golden' type, which was inspired by the type of Venetian printer Nicolaus Jenson, and the black letter 'Troy' type.**
- **Kelmscott books are notable for their harmony of type and illustration. Care was taken with all aspects of production, including the paper, the type and the letter spacing. Designs were strongly influenced by medieval artwork.**
- **The press closed in 1898.**

Chaucer, Geoffrey, 'The Works', edited by F S Ellis, one of 425 copies on Perch paper, printed by the Kelmscott Press, with 87 wood-engraved illustrations designed by Edward Burne-Jones, with wood-engraved title, borders and initials designed by William Morris, bound in later white pigskin.

The most important work from the Kelmscott Press. Morris began discussing the project in 1891 and finally issued the book to subscribers in June 1896, a few weeks before his death.

1896

$55,000-65,000 BLO

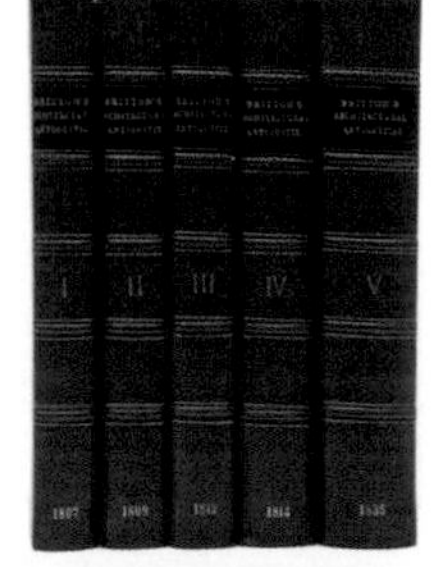

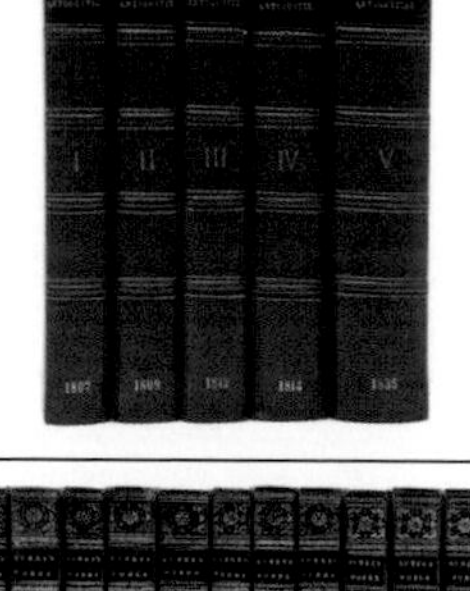

Britton, John, 'The Architectural Antiquities of Great Britain', with engraved titles and plates, bound in modern half morocco over marbled boards.

1807-35

$550-750 BLO

Burke, Edmund, [The Works], bound in contemporary calf, gilt with morocco labels.

1801-27

$3,000-4,000 DN

Cook, Captain James, '[Third Voyage] A Voyage to the Pacific Ocean', second edition, published by H Hughs for G Nicol and T Cadell, with 23 engraved charts, bound in contemporary calf, with a volume of 41 loose plates and maps from Anson's 'Voyage round the World'.

1785

$3,000-4,000 BLO

Darwin, Charles, 'Narrative of the Surveying Voyages of His Majesty's Ships Adventure and Beagle...', first edition, first issue, published by Henry Colburn, London, with eight maps and 48 plates, rebound.

1839

$25,000-30,000 LHA

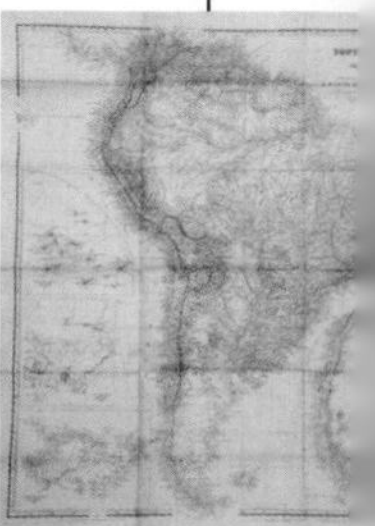

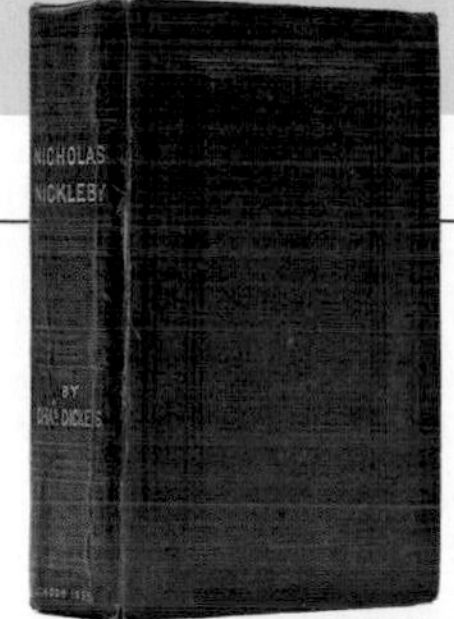

Dickens, Charles, 'The Life and Adventures of Nicholas Nickleby', first edition in book form, with 39 engraved plates, with original green cloth.
1839
$6,500-7,500 BLO

Doyle, Arthur Conan, 'The Hound of the Baskervilles', an early edition, published by McClure, Phillips & Co., New York City, signed by the author, with original red cloth.

Provenance: The Conan Doyle collection of Mary Jakeman, lady's maid to Sir Arthur and Lady Conan Doyle.
1902
$8,000-12,000 SWO

ESSENTIAL REFERENCE - CHARLES DICKENS

Charles Dickens (1812-70) rose to fame with the publication of 'The Pickwick Papers' in 1836 and subsequently wrote 14 further novels, fives novellas and hundreds of short stories and non-fiction articles.

- **Most of Dickens's novels were originally published in monthly or weekly instalments. Once the series was complete, many readers then had the instalments bound together as a book. You can check if a copy is bound from instalments by looking for stab holes in the margins where the instalments were originally bound in wrappers.**
- **Perhaps his most famous work, 'A Christmas Carol', was never serialized, but was instead published as a stand–alone novella by Chapman & Hall in 1843.**

Dickens, Charles, 'Bleak House', first edition in the original installments, published by Bradbury & Evans, London, with 40 etched plates, in original blue wraps, in custom cloth slipcase.
1852-53
$2,000-3,000 LHA

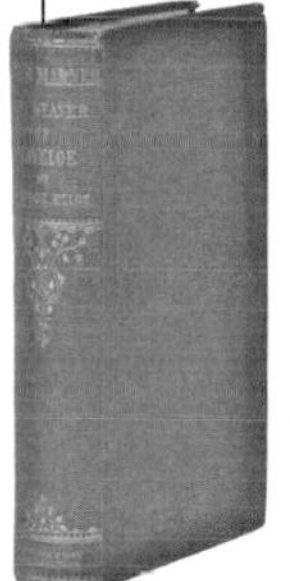

Elliot, George, 'Silas Marner: The Weaver of Raveloe', first edition, published by Blackwood, with 20pp. advertisements, with original orange cloth.
1861
$2,000-3,000 DW

Gaskell, Elizabeth Cleghorn, 'Cranford', first edition, in original green cloth, rebacked.
1853
$1,000-1,500 DW

Morris, F O, 'A History of British Birds, fourth edition, published by John C Nimmo, London, with 394 hand-colored plates.
1895-97
$1,000-1,500 LHA

Newton, Sir Isaac, 'The Mathematical Principles of Natural Philosophy', first edition in English, translated by Andrew Motte, printed for Benjamin Motte at the Middle-Temple-Gate, London, with 47 engraved plates, bound in contemporary calf, rebacked.

Provenance: Stamped 'J Herschel', probably for Colonel John Herschel (1837-1921), son of the mathematician and astronomer Sir John Frederick William Herschel. With a note reading, 'This book to become the property of W.F.H. Waterfield in due course of time, should he settle down in England..., F.H., 1923'. The 'F.H.' is probably Francisca Herschel, daughter of Sir John. 'Waterfield' is most likely the renowned American astronomer.
1729
$45,000-55,000 BLO

Weatherly, Frederic E, 'A Happy Pair', illustrated by Beatrix Potter, first edition, published by Hildesheimer & Faulkner, London, and Geo. C Whitney, New York City, with 6 chromolithograph illustrations signed 'H.B.P.', in modern green morocco box.
1890
$25,000-35,000 BLO

Potter, Beatrix, 'The Tale of Peter Rabbit', first trade edition, published by F Warne & Co., London, with color illustrations, with owner's inscription, with original green boards.
1902
$3,000-4,000 DW

Radcliffe, Ann, 'The Italian', first edition, printed for T Cadell Jun. and W Davies, bound in contemporary half calf over marbled boards.

1797

$1,500-2,500 DN

Raleigh, Sir Walter, 'The Historie of the World', printed for Robert White, with eight maps, with additional engraved title, missing engraved portrait.

1666

$2,500-3,500 BLO

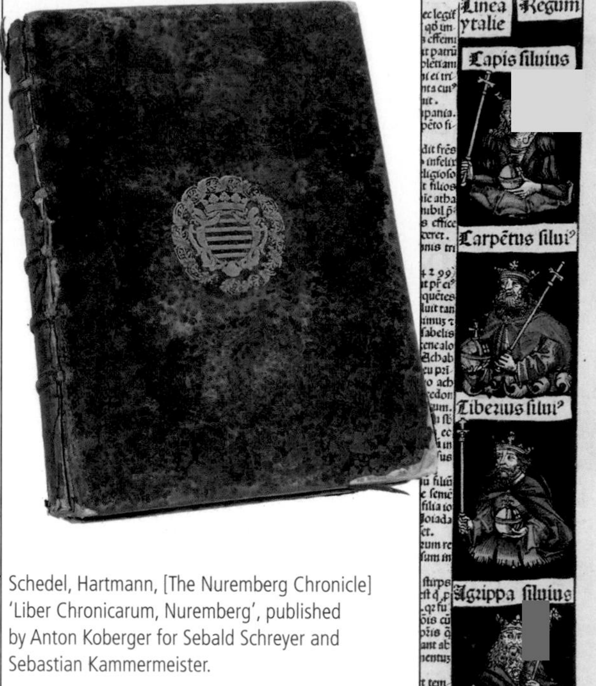

Schedel, Hartmann, [The Nuremberg Chronicle] 'Liber Chronicarum, Nuremberg', published by Anton Koberger for Sebald Schreyer and Sebastian Kammermeister.

1493

$150,000-200,000 HT

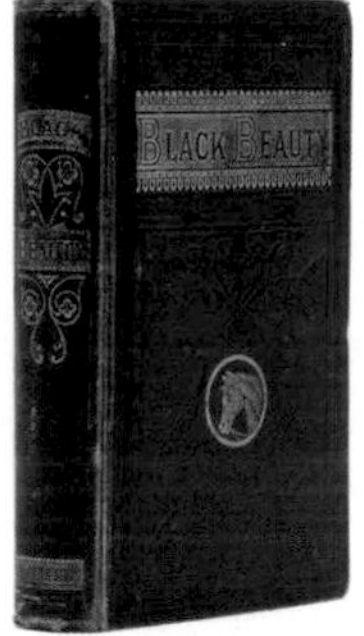

Sewell, Anna, 'Black Beauty', first edition, published by Jarrold & Sons, Norwich, with 8pp. advertisements, with owner's inscription, with original blue cloth.

A rare copy of this internationally acclaimed and successful children's classic, purported to be the sixth bestseller in the English language.

1877

$3,000-4,000 BLO

Shelley, Percy Bysshe, 'The Poetical Works', published by the Kelmscott Press, one of 250 copies on Flower paper, with wood-engraved title, borders and initials designed by William Morris, bound in original limp vellum with silk thongs.

1894-95

$5,000-7,000 BLO

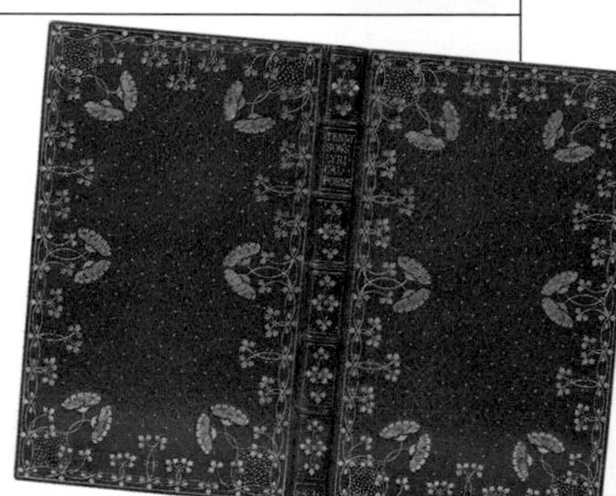

Tennyson, Lord Alfred, 'Lyrical Poems', first edition, published by Effingham Wilson, London, with advertisements at the end, bound in green morocco.

1830

$3,000-4,000 L&T

Tolstoy, Leo, 'War and Peace', first edition in English, translated from the French by Clara Bell, published by William S Fottsberger, New York City, with original morocco and later cloth slip-case.

1886

$5,500-6,500 BLO

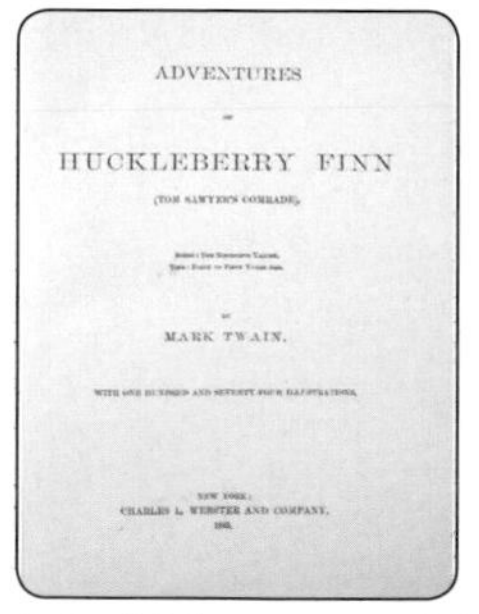
ADVENTURES

OF

HUCKLEBERRY FINN

(TOM SAWYER'S COMRADE.)

BY

MARK TWAIN.

NEW YORK:
CHARLES L. WEBSTER AND COMPANY.

Twain, Mark [Clemens, Samuel L], 'The Adventures of Huckleberry Finn (Tom Sawyer's Comrade.)', first American edition, published by Charles L Webster, New York City, with original green cloth.

1885

$2,500-3,500 LHA

Verne, Jules, 'Twenty Thousand Leagues Under the Sea', first American edition, published by James R Osgood, Boston, with original green cloth.

This edition is exceedingly rare, as most of the copies printed reportedly perished in the Great Boston Fire of 1872.

1873

$3,500-4,500 LHA

Asbjørnsen, Peter Christen and Moe, Jørgen E, 'East of the Sun and West of the Moon', one of 500 copies, signed by the artist, with 25 color plates by Kay Nielsen, signed by the artist, bound in pictorial vellum, in original slip case.

1914

$15,000-20,000 **BLO**

[Bradley, Katharine Harris and Cooper, Edith Emma], Field, Michael, 'Whym Chow Flame of Love', first edition, one of 27 copies, privately printed by the Eragney Press.

Bradley and Cooper wrote collectively under the pseudonym of Michael Field. 'Whym Chow' was a celebration of their much-loved dog, who died in 1906. Apart from each other, Whym Chow was their closest companion and such was the depth of their feeling for him that after his death they underwent a religious crisis that led to their conversion to Roman Catholicism.

1914

$10,000-15,000 **DW**

Chopin, Kate, 'The Awakening', first edition, published by Herbert S Stone & Co., Chicago and New York City, with original pictorial green cloth, with owner's signature.

The controversy over the strong sexual and liberal themes in 'The Awakening' dissuaded the publisher from printing a second run. Few copies of this edition appear on the market.

1899

$4,500-5,500 **SWA**

ESSENTIAL REFERENCE - AGATHA CHRISTIE

Agatha Christie (1890-1976) is the best-selling novelist of all time, having sold nearly four billion copies of her books. Although she wrote some romances, she is best known for her crime novels featuring famous characters Hercule Poirot and Miss Marple.

- **Christie's play, 'The Mousetrap', holds the record for the longest initial run. It opened in 1952 and is still running.**
- **In 1955 she was the first recipient of the Mystery Writers of America's highest honour, the Grand Master Award.**
- **Christie's global popularity makes first editions of her novels very desirable.**
- **As Christie's popularity grew, print runs increased. This means that while early books, such as 'Poirot Investigates', are rare and valuable, many first editions of her later books survive. These later books can now be very affordable.**

Christie, Agatha, 'Poirot Investigates', first edition, with 14pp. advertisements, with loose publisher's editor review copy slip, with dust jacket and original yellow cloth.

The dust jacket is very rare.

1924

$65,000-75,000 **DW**

Christie, Agatha, 'Death on the Nile', first edition, published by Collins Crime Club, with small owner's inscription, with 4pp. advertisements, with restored dust jacket and orange cloth.

1937

$4,000-6,000 **DW**

Christie, Agatha, 'The Hound of Death', first edition, with original cloth and dust jacket.

1933

$250-350 **BLO**

Christie, Agatha, 'Ten Little Niggers', first edition, with one page of advertisements, with owner's inscription, with original dust jacket and orange cloth.

1939

$4,000-6,000 **DW**

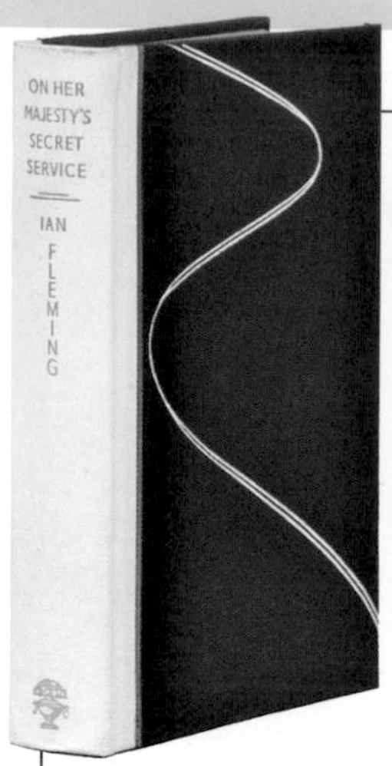

Fleming, Ian, 'On Her Majesty's Secret Service', limited edition of 250 signed by the author, with color portrait frontispiece, with original vellum-backed boards, with glassine wrapper.

1963

$8,000-12,000 DW

Fleming, Ian, 'You Only Live Twice', first edition, published by Jonathan Cape, London, inscribed by the author, 'To Celestial Hiscock-san from Grateful Fleming-san', with unclipped dust jacket.

1964

$8,000-12,000 LHA

Forester, E M, 'A Passage to India', first edition, published by E Arnold, with 3pp. advertisements, with loose 4pp leaflet, with dust jacket and original red cloth, with modern slipcase.

1924

$5,000-7,000 DW

Gernsback, Hugo, 'Ralph 124C 41+. A Romance of the Year 2660', first edition, published by The Stratford Company, Boston, with bookplate signed by the author to Roy V Hunt, with 11 plates by Frank R Paul, with clipped dust jacket and original blue cloth, dust jacket with tape repairs.

Gernsback originally serialized this work in his 'Modern Electrics' magazine. The annual Hugo Awards, named in his honour, continue to highlight his contributions to the formation of science-fiction as a viable literary genre.

1925

$6,500-7,500 SWA

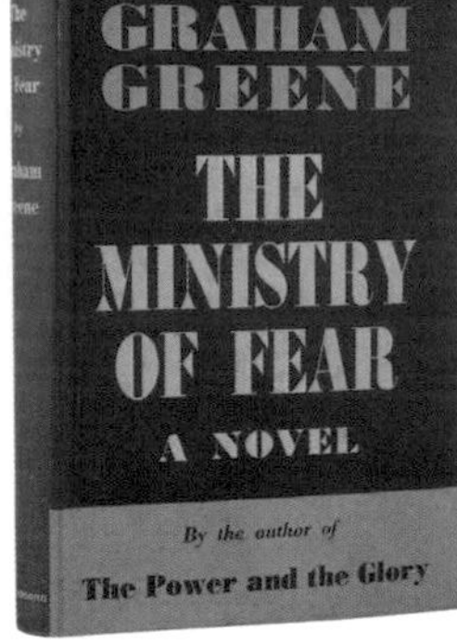

Greene, Graham, 'The Ministry of Fear', first edition, published by Heinemann, London, with unclipped dust jacket and yellow cloth.

1943

$18,000-22,000 GORL

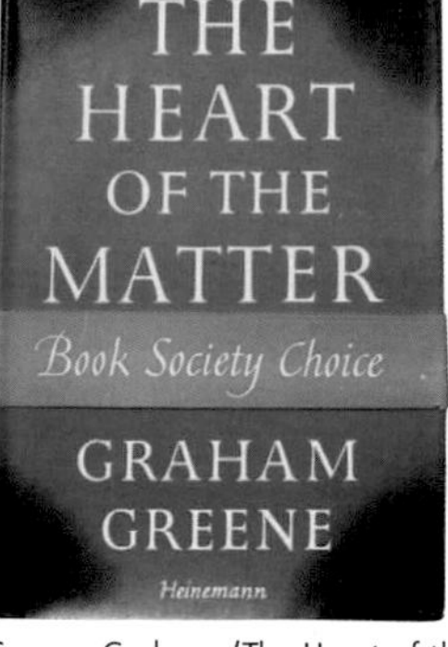

Greene, Graham, 'The Heart of the Matter', first edition, published by Heinemann, London, with unclipped dust jacket, book society wrap around and blue cloth.

1948

$2,000-3,000 GORL

Herbert, Frank, 'Dune', first edition, published by Chilton, Philadelphia, signed by the author, with dust jacket and blue cloth.

'Dune' was the first novel to win both the Hugo and Nebula awards. It was made into a feature film in 1984 and a SciFi Channel mini-series in 2000.

1965

$5,000-7,000 SWA

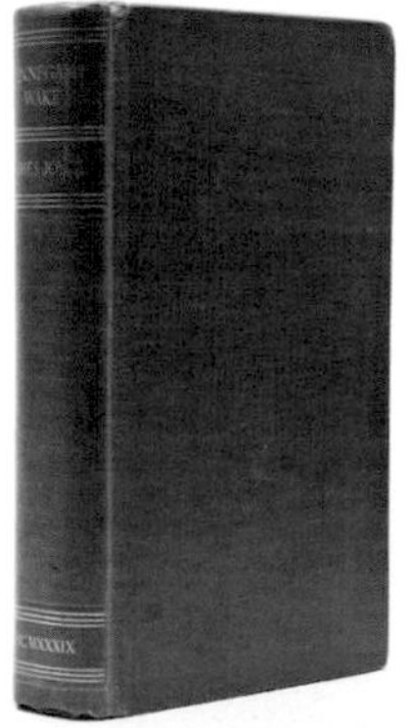

Joyce, James, 'Finnegans Wake', first edition, published by Faber & Faber, London, one of 425 copies signed by the author, with original red cloth.

1939

$6,500-7,500 BLO

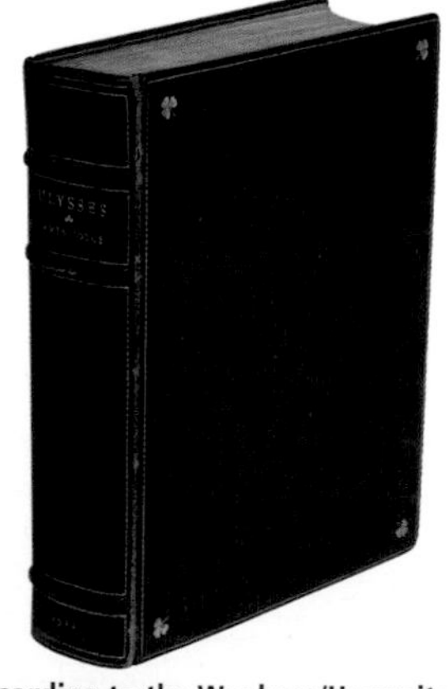

Joyce, James, 'Ulysses', first edition of 150 copies on vergé d'arches and one of the 'Giant Joyce' copies, published by Shakespeare & Company, Paris, rebound in brown morocco, with original Greek blue wrappers.

According to the Woolmer/Horowitz Census, p.120, this was the copy given to Sybil Amhurst on May 11, 1922. This issue became known as the 'Giant Joyce' because its dimensions were larger than those of the other editions.

1922

$15,000-20,000 SWA

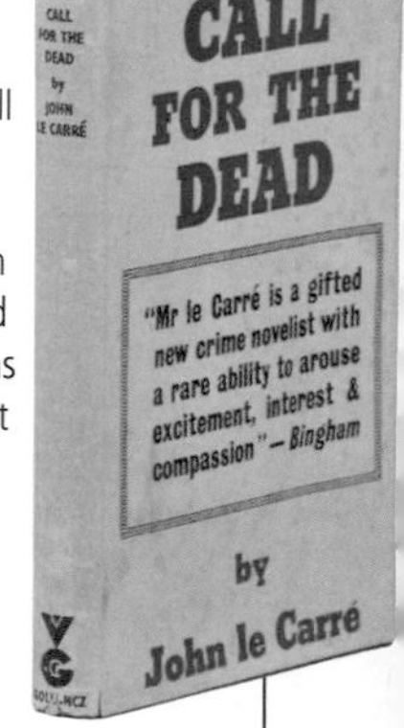

Le Carre, John, 'Call For the Dead', first edition, inscribed by the author 'John Le Carre, aka David Cornwell, Christmas 2004. With my best wishes! D.C.', with dust jacket and original cloth, with custom-made half morocco foldover box.

This is the author's first book and the first appearance of George Smiley.

1961

$3,000-4,000 DW

Lessing, Doris, 'The Golden Notebook', first edition, with dust jacket, with some damage.
1962
$250-350 **BLO**

Lewis, C S, [The Chronicles of Narnia], first editions, with some pen marks and light restoration, with dust jackets and original cloth.
1950–55
$15,000-20,000 **BLO**

[Lewis, C S], Hamilton, Clive, 'Dymer', first edition, published by J M Dent & Sons, London, with dust jacket and original blue cloth.

'Dymer' is a narrative poem in the epic tradition. Lewis began writing it in 1916 and completed it in 1925. The first edition had a limited print run and very few examples have survived.
1926
$2,500-3,500 **GORL**

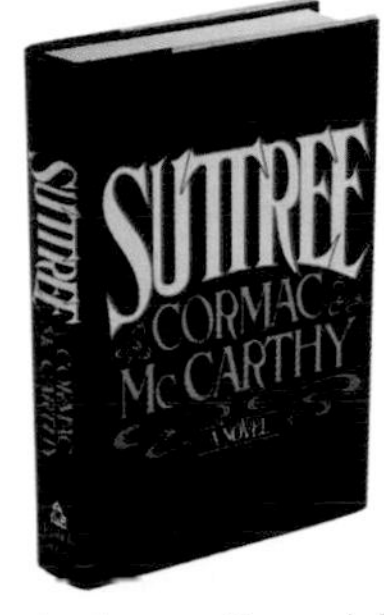

McCarthy, Cormac, 'Suttree', first edition, published by Random House, New York City, with dust jacket and original cloth, without the remainder stamp, sold with an advance uncorrected proof copy of the same book.
1979
$4,000-6,000 **SWA**

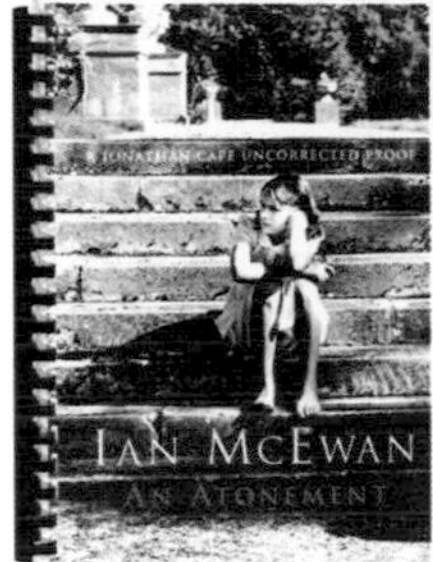

McEwan, Ian, 'Atonement', uncorrected proof copy, signed by the author on title, ring-bound with original cover design.

Seemingly very rare as probably only small number of advance copies were produced.
2001
$700-1,000 **BLO**

Meyer, Stephenie, 'Twilight', first English edition, with dust jacket and original boards.
2006
$400-600 **BLO**

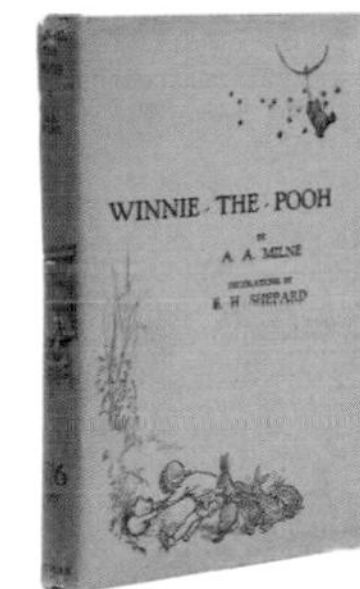

Milne, A A, 'Winnie-the-Pooh', first edition, published by Methuen, London, with dust jacket and original green cloth.
1926
$1,000-1,500 **LHA**

Milne, A A, [The Christopher Robin books], comprising 'When We Were Very Young', 'Winnie-the-Pooh', 'Now We Are Six', 'House at Pooh Corner', first editions, published by Methuen, London, in custom buckram chemises, in cloth slipcase.
1924–28
$4,000-6,000 **SWA**

Nabokov, Vladimir, 'Lolita', first edition, published by Olympia Press, Paris, with owner's inscription, with old repair, with publisher's wrappers.

'Lolita' was not published in the USA or the UK until 1959.
1955
$5,000-7,000 **SWA**

Orwell, George, 'The Road to Wigan Pier', first edition, published by Gollancz, London, with dust jacket and original blue cloth, with letter from Gollancz stating,'I enclose herewith a copy of Road to Wigan Pier, By George Orwell which we are publishing on Monday March 8th, Sheila Lynd'.
1937
$12,000-18,000 **GORL**

Raymond, Jean Paul, 'Beyond the Threshold', translated from the French and illustrated by Charles Ricketts, printed at the Curwen Press, with original morocco with gilt design by Charles Ricketts.

1929

$2,000-3,000 DW

Rushdie, Salman, 'Midnight's Children', first edition, first issue, with signed inscription from the author, with original cloth-backed boards.

This example was presented by the author to a colleague of his during his time in advertising.

1981

$3,000-4,000 BLO

Thompson, Flora, 'Lark Rise', first edition, with illustrations by Lynton Lamb, with clipped dust jacket and original cloth.

This is first book in the Candleford trilogy, now a popular BBC series.

1939

$1,200-1,800 BLO

Judith Picks

J K Rowling's first Harry Potter book, 'Harry Potter and the Philosopher's Stone', is one of the most sought after modern first editions on the market. Harry may be famous now, but when the 'Philosopher's Stone' was published Bloomsbury had no idea whether it would sell. Reputedly, they printed a mere 500 copies as part of the first print run of the first edition. These true first editions have a full line of numbers leading down to a '1' on the imprint page and do not have a dust jacket.

Most of the 500 copies were sold to British libraries or schools and are consequently in very bad condition today, but such is the boy wizard's popularity that even a very battered first edition of 'Harry Potter and the Philosopher's Stone' can fetch over $1,500! This example, on the other hand, is the closest to mint condition that book-specialist auctioneer Bloomsbury have ever seen. Consequently, the price is nothing short of magical.

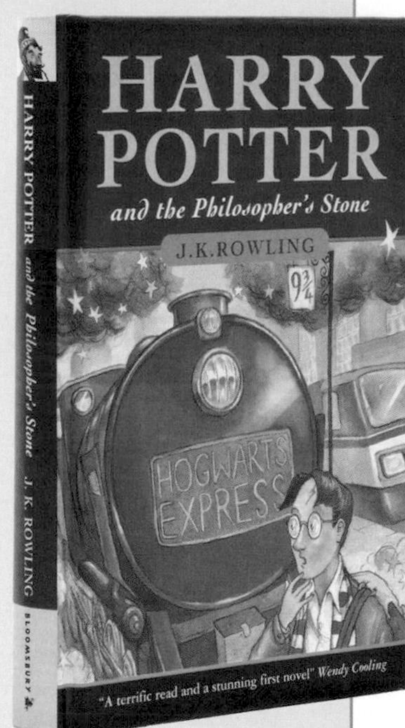

Rowling, J K, 'Harry Potter and the Philosopher's Stone', first edition, first impression, with original pictorial boards.

1997

$35,000-45,000 BLO

Tolkien, J R R, [The Lord of the Rings], first editions, 'The Fellowship of the Ring' and 'The Two Towers' second impressions, 'The Return of the King' first impression, with folding maps, with original dust jackets and red cloth.

1954–55

$800-1,200 DW

Waugh, Evelyn, 'Brideshead Revisited', first edition, published by Chapman & Hall, London, with unclipped dust jacket and original red cloth.

1945

$4,000-6,000 GORL

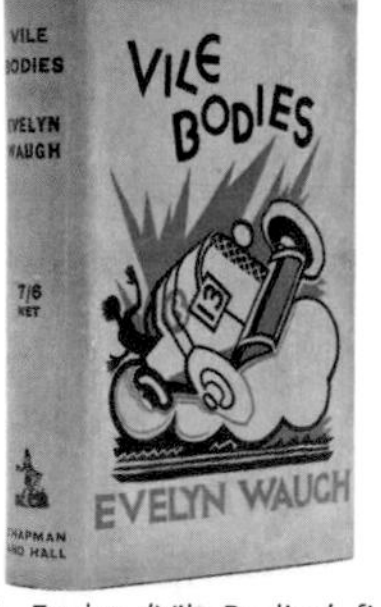

Waugh, Evelyn, 'Vile Bodies', first edition, published by Chapman & Hall, London, with dust jacket and original patterned boards, with 2pp. reviews of 'Decline & Fall' at end, with professional restoration.

The dust jacket is very rare.

1930

$4,000-6,000 BLO

Woolf, Virginia, 'The Voyage Out', first edition, published by Duckworth, London, signed 'E.H.R.Altounyan/ 1915', with 22pp. advertisements, with original green cloth.

Earnest Haig Riddell Altounyan was friends with the Woolfs and visited them on several occassions. This was Virginia Woolf's first book.

1915

$1,000-1,500 BLO

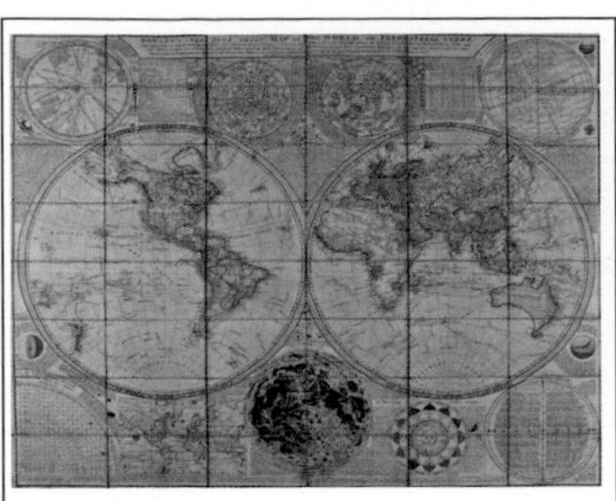

Bowles, Carrington, 'Bowles's New Four-Sheet Map of the World, or Terrestrial Globe', with original hand-coloring.

c1780 *50in (126cm) wide*

$4,000-6,000 **BLO**

Cary, John, 'Cary's New Pocket Plan of London, Westminster and Southwark', with partial hand-coloring, linen-backed.

1798 *24in (60.5cm) wide*

$600-800 **TOV**

Cruchley, G F, 'Cruchley's New Plan of London', with original hand-coloring, with minor repairs.

c1828 *37.5in (93cm) wide*

$2,000-3,000 **BLO**

Faden, William, 'Plan of The Operations of General Washington, against The Kings Troops in New Jersey from The 26th of December 1776 to The 3d January 1777', with partial hand-coloring, trimmed and framed.

1777 *15.5in (39cm) wide*

$8,000-12,000 **FRE**

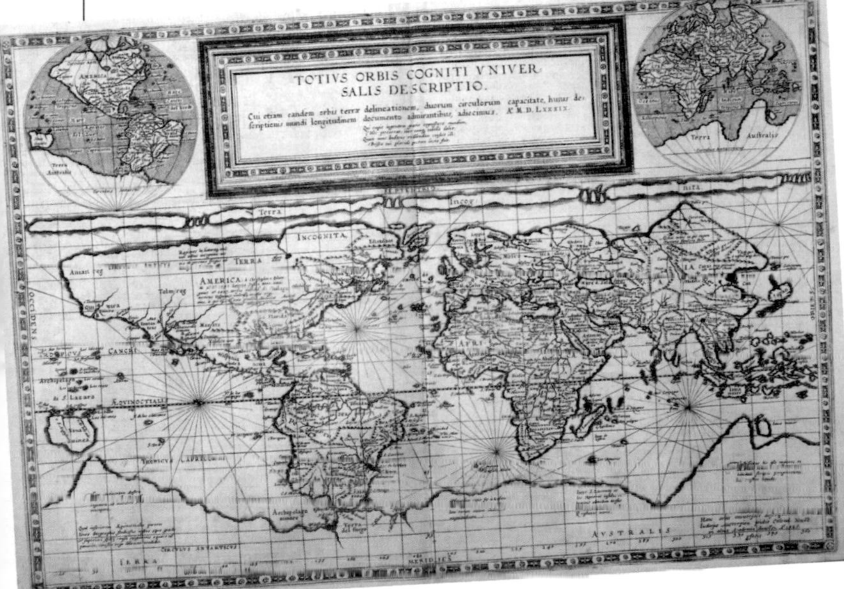

De Jode, G, 'Totius Orbis Cogniti Universalis Descriptio ...', copperplate.

Gerard De Jode and his son, Cornelis, produced a series of maps published in the 'Speculum Orbis Terrae ...', an atlas intended to rival the already successful 'Theatrum ...' of Abraham Ortelius. The 'Speculum' failed after only two editions, meaning this map is rare.

1589-93 *20in (51cm) wide*

$30,000-40,000 **JPOT**

Greenwood, C, 'Map of the County Palatine of Chester', published by Wakefield, W Fowler & C Greenwood, with original hand-coloring, linen-backed.

1819 *60in (154.5cm) wide*

$2,000-3,000 **BLO**

Greenwood, C & J, 'Map of London from An Actual Survey made in the Years 1824, 1825 and 1826', published by Greenwood, Pringle & Co., engraved with original hand-coloring, linen-backed.

1827 *75in (188cm) wide*

$13,000-15,000 **BLO**

Hondius, Jodocus, 'Terra Sancta quæ in Sacris Terra Promissionis ol. Palestina, the Holy Land', with North oriented to the left, with hand-coloring.

c1610 *19in (49.5cm) wide*

$300-500 **BLO**

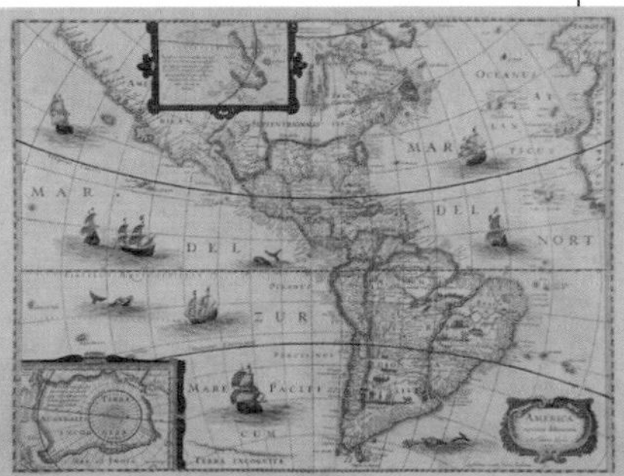

Hondius, Jodocus II, 'America Noviter Delineata', with insets of the North and South Poles, with hand-coloring, with minor repairs.

c1636 *20in (50cm) wide*

$1,500-2,500 **BLO**

CLOSER LOOK - COLORED MAP

This map is the first to depict the New World as an entity and the first to use the term 'Mare Pacificum' to denote the Pacific Ocean.

It depicts a relatively accurate South America and West Indies.

Japan is shown as 'Zipangri', but is located very close to the American west coast.

North America is shown with a clearly defined Florida but with a narrow isthmus linking the north-east 'Francisca' to 'Terra Florida'.

A legend on the South American mainland indicates the presence of 'Canibali'.

This map is rarely found with original hand-coloring.

Munster, S, 'Die Neuwen Inseln / So Hinder Hispanien ...', with original hand-coloring.
1540-61 *13.5in (34cm) wide*
$10,000-15,000 **JPOT**

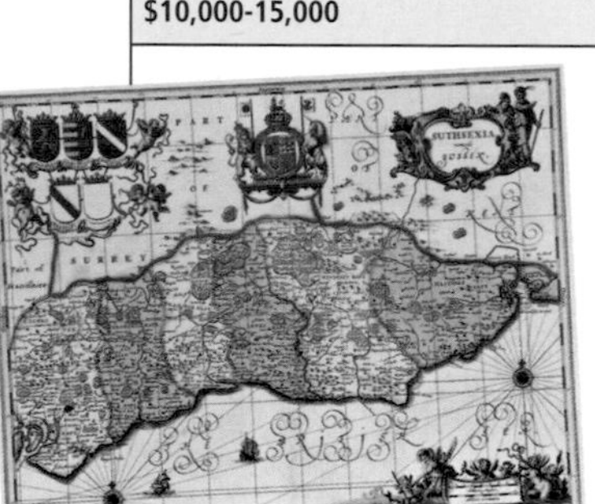

Jansson, Jan, 'Suthsexia' [Sussex], with hand-coloring.
c1650 *20in (50cm) wide*
$550-750 **BLO**

Middleton, Captain Christopher T, 'To the King, This Chart of Hudson's Bay & Straits, Baffin's Bay, Strait Davis & Labrador Coast &c. is most humbly Dedicated…'.
1743 *25in (66.5cm) wide*
$6,500-7,500 **BLO**

Montanus, B A, 'Benedict Arias Montanus Sacrae Geographiae Tabulam', copperplate, printed in Hebrew, Greek, Latin and Syraic.

The map primarily serves a theological purpose in identifying the distirbution of the Tribes of Israel. It is also renowned for the depiction of a landmass emerging from the Indian Ocean where Australia would soon be plotted.
1571 *20.75in (53cm) wide*
$7,000-9,000 **JPOT**

Schedel, Heinrich, [Map Of The Ptolemaic World from the Nuremberg Chronicle].
1493 *20in (51cm) wide*
$20,000-30,000 **JPOT**

Ortelius, A, 'Maris Pacifici', with original outline color.

This map is from the first 'modern' atlas - 'Abraham Ortelius's 'Theatrum Orbis Terranum'. It is one of the most famous and important atlas maps ever produced. It was the first printed map to focus on the Pacific Ocean.
1589-1603 *9.25in (49cm) wide*
$10,000-15,000 **JPOT**

Schenk, Peter, 'Planisphaerium Coeleste', with original color.

This map is based on the constellations of Hevelius and the format of Eimmart.
c1705 *22in (56cm) wide*
$3,500-4,500 **JPOT**

CLOSER LOOK - MAP OF PTOLEMAIC WORLD

At this stage in mapping, the Indian Ocean is shown with a distinctive Indian peninsula and is no longer bound by a southern section of land linking Africa and Asia.

The map was woodblock printed in black with some black letterpress text. In a further pass through the press, letterpress place names were added in red ink.

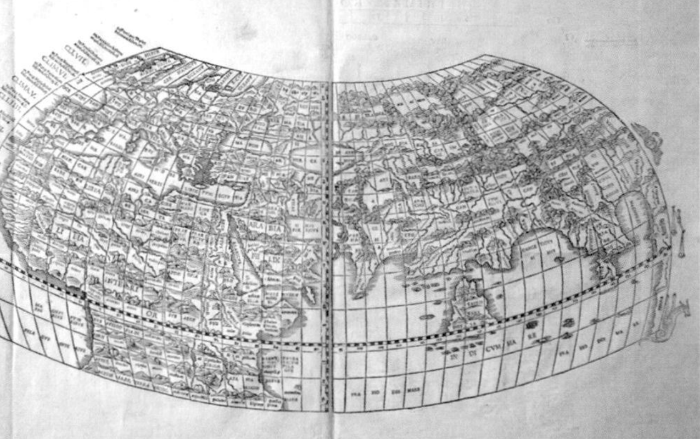

The British Isles are here shown in non-Ptolemaic style.

This is one of the first examples of two-color map printing.

The unusual shape of the map clearly implies that the world is a sphere.

Sylvanus, Bernard, Untitled [Map Of The Ptolemaic World],

22in (56cm) wide

$20,000-30,000 **JPOT**

'A New Map of the North Part of America Claimed By France ...', with hand-coloring.

This map is an English cartographic counter-blast. French mapmakers had depicted France as owning all the land watered by the Mississippi and its tributaries, thus limiting the English to a narrow belt of land along the eastern seaboard. This map shows the English laying claim to larger areas of land including the Carolinas.

1720-c1730 *40.25in (102cm) wide*

$6,500-7,500 **JPOT**

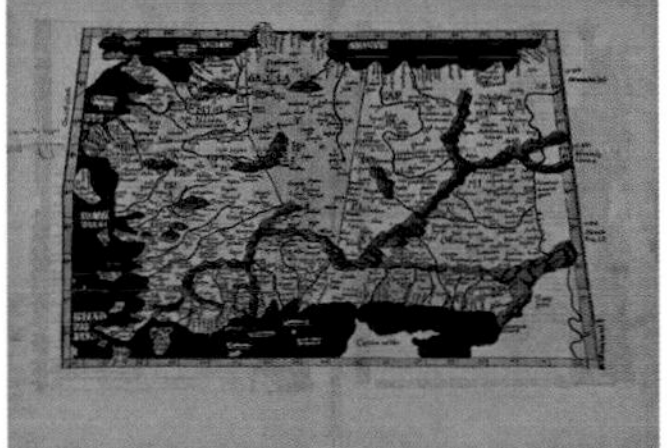

Waldseemüller, Martin and Fries, Lorenz, 'Tabula I Asiae Ptolemaic map of Asia Minor', with original hand-coloring.

c1535 *22.5in (54cm) wide*

$1,200-1,800 **BLO**

Speed, John, 'Sussex Described and Divided into Rapes', published by Sudbury & Humble, with hand-coloring, heightened with gold, trimmed.

c1614 *20in (50cm) wide*

$500-700 **BLO**

Tallis, John, 'Tallis's Illustrated Plan of London and its Environs in commemoration of the Great Exhibition of Industry of all Nations 1851', with paneled border of 49 views of buildings and monuments, with original hand coloring, linen-backed.

1851 *30in (74cm) wide*

$2,000-3,000 **BLO**

Traveling Fan

Balster, T, 'The Ladies Travelling Fan of England and Wales', copperplate with original color.

This elegant Georgian artefact details the roads and the towns distances from London.

1788 *16.25in (43cm) wide*

$10,000-15,000 **JPOT**

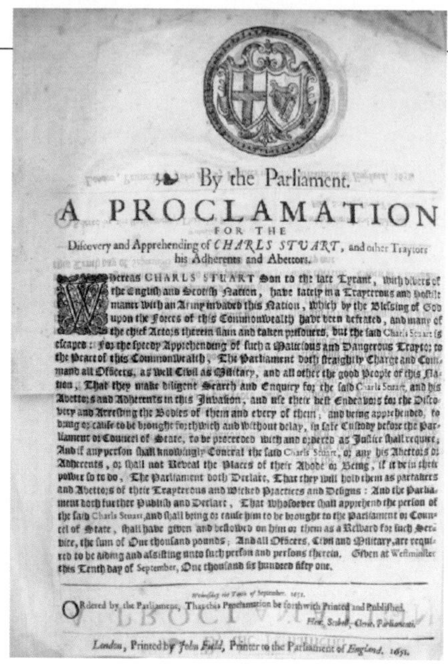

By the Parliament.

A PROCLAMATION

FOR THE

Discovery and Apprehending of CHARLS STUART, and other Traytors his Adherents and Abettors.

Whereas CHARLS STUART Son to the late Tyrant, with divers of the English and Scottish Nation, have lately in a Traytorous and hostile manner with an Army invaded this Nation, which by the Blessing of God upon the Forces of this Commonwealth have been defeated, and many of the chief Actors therein slain and taken prisoners, but the said Charls Stuart is escaped: For the speedy Apprehending of such a Malicious and Dangerous Traytor to the Peace of this Commonwealth, The Parliament doth straightly Charge and Command all Officers, as well Civil as Military, and all other the good People of this Nation, That they make diligent Search and Enquiry for the said Charls Stuart, and his Abettors and Adherents in this Invasion, and use their best Endeavors for the Discovery and Arresting the Bodies of them and every of them; and being apprehended, to bring or cause to be brought forthwith and without delay, in safe Custody before the Parliament or Councel of State, to be proceeded with and ordered as Justice shall require; And if any person shall knowingly Conceal the said Charls Stuart, or any his Abettors or Adherents, or shall not Reveal the Places of their Abode or Being, if it be in their power so to do, The Parliament doth Declare, That they will hold them as partakers and Abettors of their Traytorous and Wicked Practices and Designs: And the Parliament doth further Publish and Declare, That whosoever shall apprehend the person of the said Charls Stuart, and shall bring or cause him to be brought to the Parliament or Councel of State, shall have given and bestowed on him or them as a Reward for such Service, the sum of One thousand pounds; And all Officers, Civil and Military, are required to be aiding and assisting unto such person and persons therein. Given at Westminster this Tenth day of September, One thousand six hundred fifty one.

Wednesday the Tenth of September, 1651.

Ordered by the Parliament, That this Proclamation be forthwith Printed and Published.

Hen: Scobell, Cleric. Parliament.

London, Printed by John Field, Printer to the Parliament of England. 1651.

An English Civil War proclamation 'for the discovery and Apprehending of Charles Stuart and other Traytors his Adherents and Abettors'.

This proclamation was issued following the defeat of the King's army at the Second Battle of Worcester. Charles I fled (what is now known as) 'King Charles House' and began his historic ride to Boscabel in Staffordshire where he hid in the oak tree before finally making his slow progress throughout the country to the coast where he made his escape to the continent.

14in (35.5cm) high

$70,000-90,000 **MM**

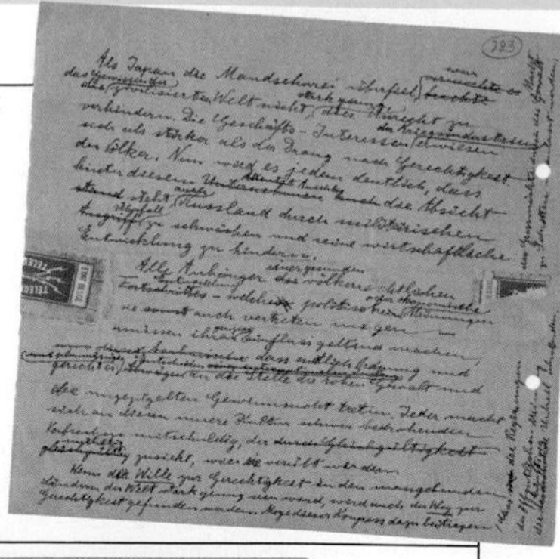

A draft of a speech on the Japanese invasion of Manchuria by Albert Einstein, on verso of a telegram to Einstein requesting that he attend an anti-war convention in Amsterdam, with certificate of authenticity.

1932 *7.75in (20cm) wide*

$30,000-40,000 **BLO**

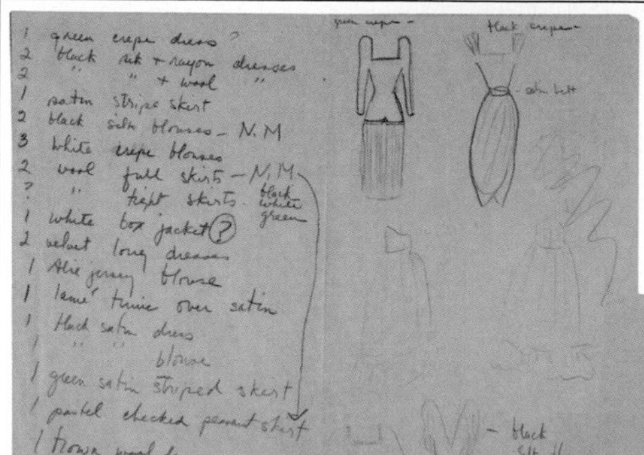

A duplicated typescript for 'Comedy of Murders' with manuscript corrections and additions by Charlie Chaplin, comprising forty pages, with four pencil sketches, bound in modern morocco box.

1946

$30,000-40,000 **BLO**

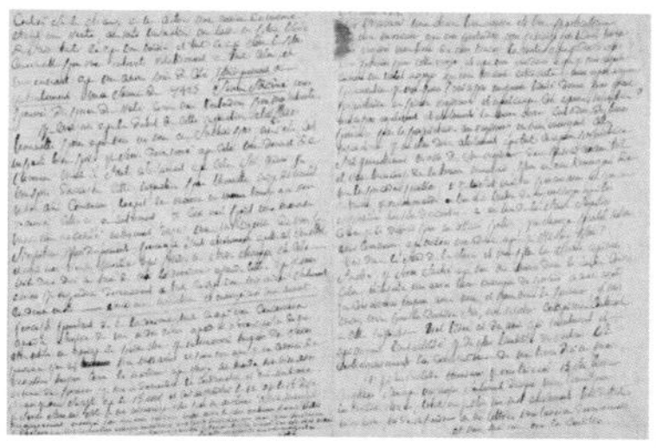

A long autograph letter from the Marquis de Sade, comprising four pages addressed to Gaspard-François-Xavier Gaufridy.

In this letter, Sade complains that he is sick and needs money.

1796

$7,000-9,000 **BLO**

An autograph letter from Mary Shelley, comprising three pages to Cyrus Redding.

In this letter Shelley refuses permission to make an engraving from an unfinished portrait of Percy Shelley. Provenance: Betty T Bennett (1935-2006), Professor of Literature and Dean of the College of Arts and Sciences (1985-97) at American University. authority on the life of Mary Shelley and editor of 'The Letters of Mary Shelley, 1980-88'.

$10,000-15,000 **BLO**

An autographed photograph of Oscar Wilde, signed and inscribed 'rien n'est vrai, que le beau', photograph by Napoleon Sarony, framed and glazed.

A very rare large format photograph, taken during Wilde's American tour in 1882. The quote 'rien n'est vrai, que le beau' (only the beautiful is true) is taken from Alfred de Musset.

12.75in (32.5cm) high

$20,000-25,000 **BLO**

An autographed photograph of Charles Lindbergh with the 'Spirit of St Louis', signed and inscribed 'To Waterman Fountain Pen'.

The aviator Charles Lindbergh piloted the first solo non-stop flight across the Atlantic in 1927.

8in (21cm) high

$1,000-1,500 **L&T**

An autographed photograph of Queen Elizabeth II and Prince Philip, dated, framed, with two related letters from the Private Secretary to the Queen.

1981 *13.25in (33.5cm) high*

$1,200-1,800 **DN**

A George I doll, with carved wooden head and torso, the gesso-covered and painted head with glass eyes and a sparse human hair wig, with mortise-and-tenon jointed wooden arms and legs, with original silk brocade dress, multiple petticoats, silk hat and brocade shoes, in a mahogany and walnut-veneered display case.

c1720 *Doll 25in (64cm) high*

$55,000-65,000 **SK**

A George II wooden doll, with brown glass eyes and original hair, with embroidered silk dress.

19in (48cm) high

$8,000-12,000 **POOK**

A carved and painted wooden mother with baby doll, with original hand sewn clothing.

c1800 *11in (28cm) high*

$4,000-6,000 **POOK**

Judith Picks

Infrequently on the 'Antiques Roadshow' we come across an early wooden doll. These so-called 'Queen Anne' dolls were made throughout the late 17thC and 18thC, not just in the reign of Queen Anne. English doll makers of this period were renowned for their fine and delicate work, although most remain anonymous. The doll's detailed clothing reveals the work of either a very accomplished amateur (possibly a lady from a wealthy family indulging her passion for needlework) or that of a professional dressmaker. These dolls were expensive purchases and rarely played with. This doll has a gesso-covered and painted head, lower arms and legs with one-piece head and torso, with black glass eyes, long swan-like neck. The doll is jointed at the shoulders, elbows, hips and knees with detail articulation at the elbows to allow greater movement than is normally found with this type of doll. She has elongated separately carved fingers. The wig is upswept brown human hair. One point that is of particular importance to collectors is that all paint surfaces appear to be original.

A mid-18thC wooden doll.

24in (61cm) high

$40,000-60,000 **JDJ**

A George III wooden doll, with painted face and carved ears, with original clothes, missing wig.

This is an extremely fine doll, which has a beautiful, delicate expression. As well as retaining nearly all her original finish, she appears to be dressed in her original clothes, which are in excellent, unfaded and untorn condition.

25in (64cm) high

$30,000-40,000 **H&L**

A Grodnertal wooden doll, the gesso-covered and painted shoulder head with painted hair, with a patterned gauze dress with lace trim and straw bonnet.

c1820 *7in (18cm) high*

$2,000-3,000 **SK**

A papier-mâché 'Milliner's Model' doll, with hair kid body and wooden limbs, with 'Apollo Knot' hairstyle, with pink printed dress.

The doll displays the first place ribbon from 'The National Doll and Toy Collectors Club Regional' in 1972. The 'Apollo Knot' hairstyle was popular among women in the 1830s and '40s.

c1840 *18in (45.5cm) high*

$3,000-4,000 **SK**

A papier-mâché 'Milliner's Model' doll, with original blue and white printed cotton dress, in a walnut shadow box featuring fabric flowers.

Dolls like this were created in the mountain hamlets of Germany's Thuringian Forest in the early 1800s.

c1850 *Doll 12in (30cm) high*

$1,500-2,500 **SK**

A cabinet-size Bru bisque-head bébé, with paperweight eyes and open/closed mouth, the head and shoulder incised 'Bru Jne 2', with original mohair wig, on white leather 'Chevrot'-style body with hinged joints, with wooden lower legs and bisque forearms, the original Bru black leather shoes impressed '2' and 'Bru Jne Paris'.

12.5in (32cm) high

$30,000-40,000 **JDJ**

A Bru bisque-head bébé, with paperweight eyes, closed mouth and molded bosom, the head incised 'Bru Jne 5', with kid body and bisque lower arms, with original cotton dress and Bru shoes marked 'Bru Jne 5', with original necklace and earrings, missing wig and two fingers.

c1885 *15in (38cm) high*

$20,000-30,000 **SK**

ESSENTIAL REFERENCE - BRU

The famous Parisian company, Bru Jeune et Cie was founded in 1866 by Leon Casimir Bru.

- **Bru was known for making very fine bisque-headed fashion dolls and bébé, which exhibited delicate molding and painting in a realistic style.**
- **Dolls were marked either with 'Bru (Jeune)' or a circle and dot.**
- **Bru was one of the founding members of the Société Francaise de Fabrication de Bébé et Jouets, which formed in 1899.**

A Bru bisque-head 'circle dot' bébé, with paperweight eyes and an open/closed mouth, the shoulder plate incised 'Bru Jne 7', with original mohair wig and cork pate, with gusseted leather torso, kid-over-wood upper arms and bisque forearms, the bisque arms replaced.

20.5in (52cm) high

$12,000-18,000 **JDJ**

An 1890s Bru bisque-head bébé, with paperweight eyes and closed mouth, the head incised 'Bru Jne R10', the articulated wood and composition body stamped 'Bébé Bru No.10'.

23in (58cm) high

$5,000-7,000 **JDJ**

A Gauthier bisque-head 'block letter' bébé, with paperweight eyes and closed mouth, the head incised 'F.7.G.', on bisque shoulder plate, with gusseted leather body, with bisque forearms.

18.5in (47cm) high

$10,000-15,000 **JDJ**

An early Jumeau bisque-head portrait doll, with paperweight eyes, the head with artist's check mark in red, marked 'L' and 'Z' or '7', with an '8 ball body'.

This doll corresponds in size to the smallest first series portrait dolls, which are normally mark '4/0'.

12.5in (31.5cm) high

$7,000-9,000 **JDJ**

A Kammer & Reinhardt bisque doll, model no.109, with painted features and jointed composition body, missing one shoe.

10.5in (27cm) high

$2,500-3,500 **GORL**

A Kammer & Reinhardt art-reform doll, model no.104, the bisque head marked 'K*R 104', with original wig, body and embroidered trachten-ware costume.

This model is extremely rare - only two or three others are known to exist. This example is in exceptional condition.

1910 *20in (51cm) high*

$220,000-350,000 **THE**

ESSENTIAL REFERENCE - LENCI

- **Elena and Enrico Scavini began to create dolls and toys using felt made near their home town of Turin, Italy, in 1920. They later registered the name Lenci, which was also Elena's nickname.**
- **In the early 20thC, Lenci dolls became well known for their naturalistic molding and painted felt faces.**
- **Lenci dolls' bodies were modeled, rather than stuffed. Their hair was made of mohair and was sewn into their heads.**
- **The Lenci factory was destroyed during World War II.**

A 1920s Lenci felt boy doll, in Turkish costume.

This boy's eyes are sideways glancing, giving him a slightly sullen appearance. Dolls with sideways-glancing eyes were popular in the 1920s.

17in (43cm) high

$800-1,200 **SAS**

A Kestner bisque boy doll, with painted face, google eyes, brown mohair wig and jointed limbs.

5in (13cm) high

$250-350 **AH**

A Kestner bisque-head doll, with glass sleeping eyes and closed mouth, with blonde wig, with joined composition limbs and body, marked 'K Made in Germany'.

23.5in (60cm) high

$1,800-2,200 **AH**

An Armand Marseille bisque-head baby doll, the bisque head with glass sleeping eyes, open mouth and pierced ears, with composition bent-limbed body, marked '362/0.K'.

17.5in (44cm) high

$400-600 **AH**

An Armand Marseille bisque-head doll, with glass sleeping eyes and open mouth, with mohair wig, with composition body and jointed composition limbs, marked '390 A 7 1/2 M'.

26in (66cm) high

$150-250 **AH**

A Schoenau & Hoffmeister bisque-head 'Princess Elizabeth' doll, with sleeping eyes and open mouth, with jointed composition body.

24in (61cm) high

$800-1,200 **GORL**

An SFBJ bisque-head 'Joyce' doll, with sleeping eyes and open mouth, the head marked '60/6', with brown wig.

23in (58cm) high

$300-400 **RW**

A Simon & Halbig bisque-head 'Jutta' doll, with glass sleeping eyes, open mouth and pierced ears, with mohair wig, with jointed composition limbs and body, marked '1348 Jutta S & H 16'.

35in (89cm) high

$700-1,000 **AH**

A German bisque-head dollhouse soldier, with cloth body, bisque lower arms and molded black boots.

c1900 *7.5in (19cm) high*

$1,500-2,500 **SK**

An Izannah Walker oil-painted-cloth doll, with some paint wear.

Izannah Frankford Walker was born in 1817 and worked in Rhode Island, USA. From as early as 1840, she operated a cottage industry making pressed cloth dolls. These dolls resemble primitive folk portraits from the mid-1800s. In 1873 she applied for a patent for her particular process of making an unbreakable doll.

c1860 *19.5in (50cm) high*
$10,000-15,000 **SK**

A 19thC Chinese porcelain-head doll, with a silk robe embroidered with a phoenix.

11in (27cm) high
$400-600 **WW**

A late 19thC Jumeau bisque-head automaton doll, with brown eyes and closed mouth, the swivel head marked 'Déposé Téte Jumeau 4', with mechanism and music box, with restoration to head and renewal to clothes.

17.5in (47cm) high
$4,000-6,000 **KAU**

A Jumeau clown automaton doll, the head marked 'Tete Jumeau 4', with original clothing, the movement causing the figure to beat the drum, clap cymbals and turn his head, with original box.

10.5in (26.5cm) high
$15,000-20,000 **JDJ**

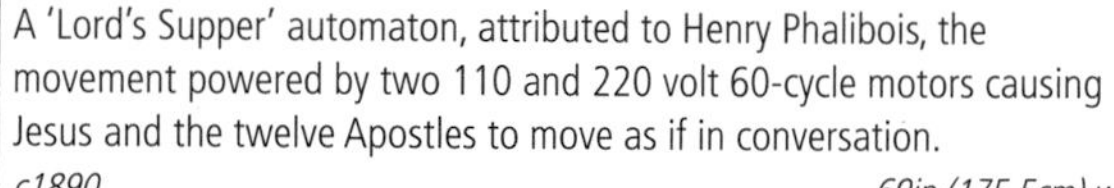

A 'Lord's Supper' automaton, attributed to Henry Phalibois, the movement powered by two 110 and 220 volt 60-cycle motors causing Jesus and the twelve Apostles to move as if in conversation.

c1890 *69in (175.5cm) wide*
$15,000-20,000 **SK**

ESSENTIAL REFERENCE - GUSTAVE VICHY

Gustave Vichy was born in 1839 in Paris, France. His father Antoine Michel Vichy, a watch and clock maker, and his mother Geneviève set up the Vichy company in 1862.

- **In 1866, Gustave Vichy took over the company. He mainly developed automata while his wife dressed the figures.**
- **The Vichy company became part of a group of businesses that thrived in Paris 1860-1910. This period is known as the 'Golden Age of Automata'.**
- **One of Vichy's models won the Grand Prix at the Great Exhibition of 1900.**

A Gustave Vichy black smoker automaton, the composition head with glass eyes and traces of hair, with mechanical movement to the eyes, mouth and neck, the papier-mâché body with mechanical arms and composition hands, with original clothes and monocle.

c1880 *27.5in (70cm) high*
$15,000-20,000 **L&T**

An early 20thC painted doll's house, with a double-opening front, opening to four rooms with wallpaper and paint finish, with some faults and playwear.

26in (67cm) wide
$1,200-1,800 **TOV**

A 1950s Tri-ang wooden 'Coronation' doll's house, opening to five rooms and a garage, unfurnished.

26.75in (68cm) high
$120-180 **DN**

Judith Picks

Who can resist an early Steiff bear, particularly one with a face like this honey-colored bruin? The German company Steiff (founded 1886) are considered the best maker. Before World War II, bears tended to have long limbs with large upturned paw pads, pronounced snouts and humped backs. They were usually made from mohair and feel solid, as they were stuffed with wood shavings or kapok. This is a desirable large bear with good color, in excellent condition and has 'eye appeal'.

An early Steiff honey-colored teddy bear, missing button

c1904 24in (61cm) high

$10,000-15,000 JDJ

A Bing golden mohair teddy bear, with a vertically-stitched nose.

All of the larger Bing bears, from 16in (41cm) upward, have vertically-stitched noses, while the smaller bears have horizontally-stitched noses.

c1925 16in (41cm) high

$2,000-3,000 TBW

A 1930s Chad Valley white mohair-plush teddy bear, with Rexine paw pads, brown glass eyes and remains of chest label.

17in (43cm) high

$800-1,200 BEJ

A Chiltern pale-gold mohair-plush 'Hugmee' teddy bear, with velvet paw pads and amber and black glass eyes.

15in (38cm) high

$550-750 BEJ

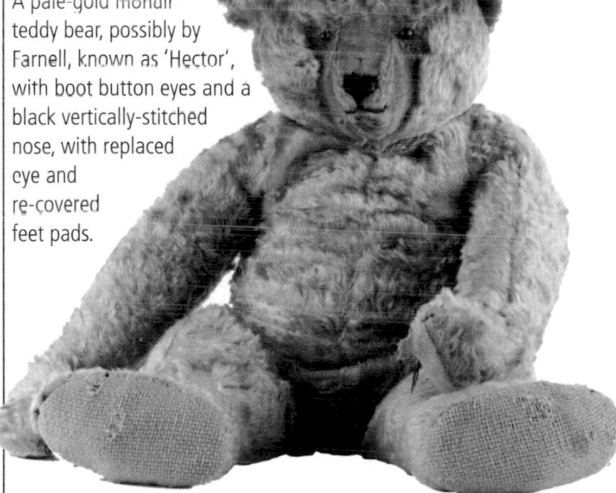

A pale-gold mohair teddy bear, possibly by Farnell, known as 'Hector', with boot button eyes and a black vertically-stitched nose, with replaced eye and re-covered feet pads.

c1920 30.25in (77cm) high

$1,200-1,800 DN

A 1920s Ideal cinnamon mohair-plush teddy bear, with felt paw pads, small amber colored glass eyes and a long snout.

15in (38cm) high

$1,200-1,800 BEJ

A 1960s golden mohair 'Cheeky' teddy bear, with label to foot.

10in (25.5cm) high

$250-350 PC

An early 20thC Steiff mohair teddy bear, with shoe button eyes and a swivel head.

16in (40.5cm) high

$3,500-4,500 POOK

Fox

A gold mohair fox soft toy, with glass eyes, a black vertically-stitched nose and a jointed neck.

11.75in (30cm) long

$150-250 DN

An Arcade cast-iron 'Acf' bus, with opening passenger door.

11in (28cm) long

$5,500-6,500 **BER**

A Hubley cast-iron 'Popeye On Motorcycle', the motorcycle tank embossed 'Patrol', Popeye with moving arms, with intact clicker and original pull string with ball end, copyright King Features.

This example carries a factory tag as it was a showroom display piece, making it possibly the finest known example.

1928 *6.75in (17cm) long*

$20,000-25,000 **BER**

A Schoenhut clown with roller chimes and cast-iron horses, with re-painting to clown's face.

16.5in (42cm) long

$5,000-7,000 **BER**

A small Vindex cast-iron 'P&H' steam-powered shovel.

Vindex was a line of cast-iron toys manufactured by the National Sewing Machine Company.

11.5in (29cm) long

$8,000-12,000 **BER**

A Wilkins pressed-steel horse-drawn wagon, with some wear to spokes.

16in (40.5cm) long

$3,000-4,000 **BER**

A rare 1930s French enameled cast-iron 'Mickey Mouse' money bank, with original paint, with raised marks to feet and embossed lettering to ears.

This bank was often found in French school rooms where it was used as an instructional tool, teaching children how to save money.

8.5in (21.5cm) high

$5,000-7,000 **JDJ**

A Bing steam-operated brass fire engine, the vertical boiler with operating water pump, on later cast-metal horse-drawn-pattern vehicle, with later fabrication and painting.

c1902 *11.75in (30cm) long*

$4,000-6,000 **SAS**

A rare German hand-painted lead Santa Claus money bank, with repair to trap.

6.25in (16.5cm) high

$10,000-15,000 **BER**

A 1930s American-style tinplate cord-driven 'Tin Lizzy' open-topped car, by Arnold, made in US Zone Germany, missing windscreen 'glass'.
c1945
$600-800 **W&W**

A Bing tinplate clockwork 'Brake' car, with original paint.

The Bing 'Brake' is one of a celebrated range of more than a dozen automotive toys that appear in the firm's 1902 catalog.
c1902 *9.5in (24cm) long*
$25,000-30,000 **WHP**

A Bing tinplate clockwork open tourer, cat ref. 10480/3, with replaced white metal lamps, with chips and scratches.
c1912 *12.25in (31cm) long*
$2,500-3,500 **SAS**

A Brimtoy tinplate clockwork 'route 657' trolleybus, with moveable trolley arm, motor inoperative, trolley arm becoming detached.
9in (23cm) long
$300-500 **W&W**

A Bub tinplate clockwork open tourer, with simulated leather seats, with glazed windscreen, with chauffeur.
c1927 *13in (33cm) long*
$2,500-3,500 **SAS**

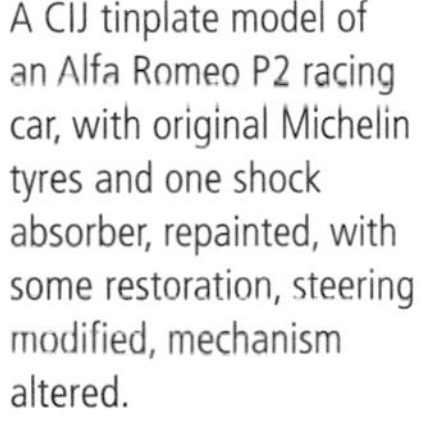

A CIJ tinplate model of an Alfa Romeo P2 racing car, with original Michelin tyres and one shock absorber, repainted, with some restoration, steering modified, mechanism altered.
20in (52cm) long
$1,200-1,800 **TOV**

A late 19thC Carette clockwork tinplate 'vis-a-vis', with original driver, with working motor.
6.5in (16.5cm) long
$650-750 **W&W**

An early 1900s Gunthermann tinplate clockwork limousine, with original chauffeur, with opening rear doors, with replacement wheel hubs, with working motor.
7.5in (19cm) long
$1,200-1,800 **W&W**

A Fischer tinplate clockwork limousine, with rear opening doors, with chauffeur, with twin lamps.
c1912 *11in (28cm) long*
$4,000-6,000 **SAS**

A Lehmann tinplate clockwork four-wheeled 'horseless carriage', with chauffeur.
5in (10cm) high
$400-600 **WHP**

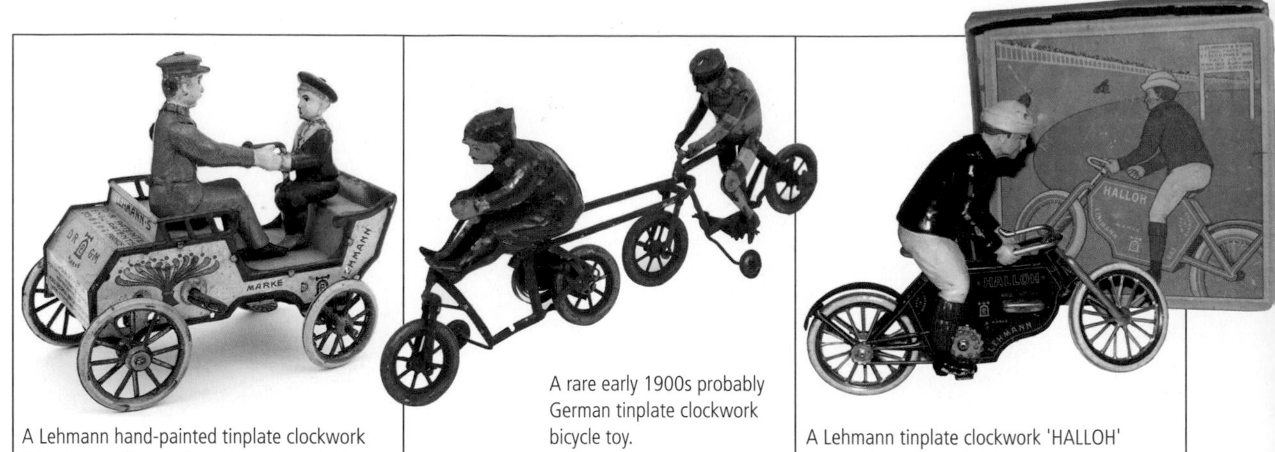

A Lehmann hand-painted tinplate clockwork 'Naughty Boy' vis-a-vis, with tired mechanism.
$700-1,000 **W&W**

A rare early 1900s probably German tinplate clockwork bicycle toy.
11in (28cm) long
$6,500-7,500 **W&W**

A Lehmann tinplate clockwork 'HALLOH' motocycle, with original box.
$6,500-7,500 **WHIT**

A German tinplate clockwork station porter and trolley, the trunk lithographed with destination labels.
4.5in (11.5cm) long
$300-500 **DN**

A rare Lehmann flywheel-drive 'The Lehmann Family Walking Down Broadway', EPL no.260, missing dog, stick and rack strip to operate flywheel.
c1900
$3,000-4,000 **SAS**

Märklin Bi-plane

A rare Märklin and Zeppelin-Luftschiffe tinplate clockwork 'Farman' bi-plane, with original instructions and parts.
$20,000-30,000 **WHIT**

A Fernand Martin tinplate clockwork 'English solider in France' figure, with felt suit, with early re-solder and re-paint, gun in need of re-soldering.
8.25in (21cm) high
$6,500-7,500 **BER**

A rare German lithographed-tinplate clockwork deep sea diver, the diver with propeller blades.
7in (18cm) high
$6,500-7,500 **BER**

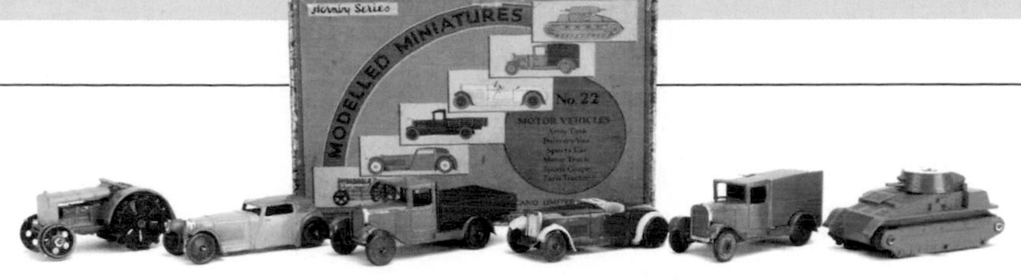

A rare pre-war Hornby Series 'MODELLED MINIATURES' set, no.22, all with pre-Dinky Toys Hornby Series cast on underside, with box.

1933-34

$25,000-30,000 SAS

A Dinky pre-war 1st type lead-cast 'ENSIGN CAMERAS' van, with faint corrosion.

$3,000-4,000 SAS

A Dinky 'FODEN 14-TON TANKER', no.504, with first-type cab, with box.

1952-57

$350-450 DN

A rare Dinky special issue 'TRIUMPH Herald', no.189, with original box.

These special issues were ordered by Standard-Triumph of Coventry and apparently dispatched directly to the dealerships from Binns Road.

1959

$2,500-3,500 SAS

DINKY TOYS Gift Sets

A rare Dinky commercial vehicles 'Gift Set No.2', comprising 'Bedford End Tipper', 'Farm Produce Wagon', 'Land-Rover', 'Tanker' and 'Austin Covered Wagon', with original box and insert, with some paint chips.

$1,500-2,500 SAS

A Dinky 'CAR CARRIER WITH TRAILER', no.983, with slightly damaged box, with card packing pieces.

1958-63

$550-750 DN

A French Dinky 'Renault 4L Van' 'P&T', no.518 (561).

This model is a possible prototype for no.561. It utilizes the no.518 'Renault 4L' model with a steel baseplate.

$2,000-3,000 VEC

A French Dinky limited edition 'Peugeot 404' fire car, no.525H (525HC), with detached rear seat, missing roof and aerial.

1964

$2,500-3,500 VEC

A French Dinky Junior 'OPEL KADETT', no.106, with some tarnishing and rubbing to paintwork, with mint box.

$1,000-1,500 VEC

A French Dinky 'CITROËN PRESIDENTIELLE', no.1435, with some plating-loss to front bumper, with box and leaflet, missing plastic 'bubble'.

$550-750 VEC

A Dinky 'ARMY STAFF CAR', no.675, with plain card box.

$700-1,000 VEC

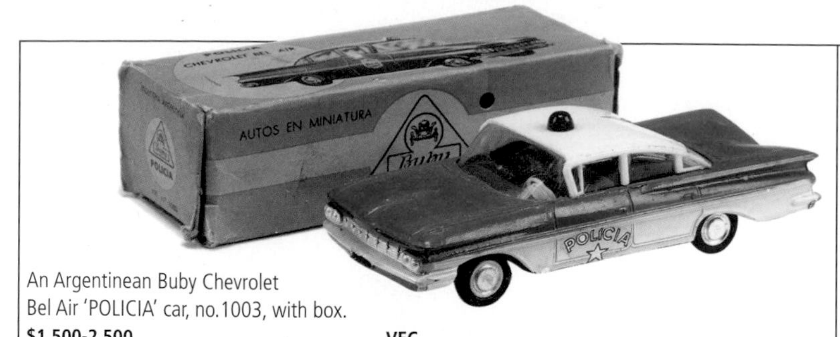

An Argentinean Buby Chevrolet Bel Air 'POLICIA' car, no.1003, with box.

$1,500-2,500 **VEC**

A Lion Toys 'Renault DAUPHINE', no.145, with fatigue crack to bonnet, with box.

$2,000-3,000 **VEC**

A Diapet Datsun 'FAIRLADY' Convertible, no.D113, made by Yonezawa Toys, with box.

$1,800-2,200 **VEC**

A Lion Toys 'DKW', no.147, with box.

$1,800-2,200 **VEC**

A rare Matchbox 1-75 series 'No.5' London bus, with 'FREMLINS' adverts, in mint condition, with box.

This model has unrecorded but professionally-produced printed advertisements and is believed to be a Code 2 release. These models were distributed by Fremlins brewery in their original unaltered Matchbox boxes to selected corporate customers.

c1960 *2.25in (5.5cm) long*

$650-750 **DN**

A Japanese Micro Pet 'SUBARU 360', no.1, with friction motor, with box.

$10,000-15,000 **VEC**

A Japanese Micro Pet 'DATSUN LIGHT VAN', no.17, with friction motor, in carded picture box.

$2,500-3,500 **VEC**

A Japanese Micro Pet 'HILLMAN MINX', no.15, with friction motor, with box.

$3,000-4,000 **VEC**

A Taiseiya 'CHERRYCA PHENIX SERIES' 'TAXI', no.PHE35, with corrosion to one side, with box.

$1,000-1,500 **VEC**

A 19thC Continental papier-mâché clockwork cat, the movement causing the cat to move its head from side to side.

22.5in (57cm) high

$1,000-1,500 **WW**

A German papier-mâché jester pull-toy, with mechanical wooden body, with cotton outfit and hat with Dresden paper trim, on a wheeled marbleized-paper-covered platform, the tip of nose re-glued.

16in (41cm) high

$1,000-1,500 **SK**

A Schoenhut 'KO-KO The Inkwell Clown' figure, with hat and original clothes, missing two felt buttons, with some wear.

Koko the Clown was created by Max Fleisher in 1919 and this toy was produced by Schoenhut in the 1920s. 'KO-KO' is the largest and rarest of the Schoenhut clowns and the most sought after. Fewer than ten 'KO-KO's are known. This example is particularly desirable as it includes his Schoenhut pin back button.

$4,000-6,000 **BER**

A rare Schoenhut 'Teddy Roosevelt Safari' Arab figure, with original clothing, head wrapping and beard, with replaced sword, pistol and rifle with some damage to clothing.

Theodore Roosevelt's post-Presidency trip to Africa in 1909 was big news by the time Schoenhut came out with a toy playset based on the adventure in 1909-12. This 'Arab' is perhaps the hardest of the Safari figures to obtain.

1909-12 *7.5in (19cm) high*

$4,000-6,000 **JDJ**

Two rare Britains 'British Camel Corps' figures, from set no.131.

1909

$2,500-3,500 **SAS**

A Haffner 'British General on a horse' figure, missing one fetlock.

3in (7.5cm) high

$1,200-1,800 **SAS**

An early 1900s Georg Heyde & Co. artillery set, made for French market, with some paint wear, with box.

The Heyde company was founded in Dresden, Germany, by Georg Heyde in 1872. Heyde models are not marked, but they can be distinguished by their fragile, elegant appearance and by the variety of poses available within sets. The Heyde factory was destroy in 1945 in the allied bombing of Dresden.

Box 10in (25.5cm) wide

$8,000-12,000 **BER**

A rare Georg Heyde & Co. 'Engl. [English] Balloon Detachment N. 737' set, comprising a painted tinplate airship, observation balloon, winch wagon with four-horse team, and members of the 'Prussian' British infantry, in original slightly damaged display box marked 'Charles Morrell, 868 Oxford Street, London W'.

c1910 *Airship 9in (23cm) long*

$20,000-30,000 **SAS**

A rare Georg Heyde & Co. 'The Viceroy's Elephant' figure, from the 'Delhi Durbar Procession' set, with mahout and gold howdah, Viceroy and Vicerene, assistant and punkawallah.

$5,500-6,500 **SAS**

A Bing tinplate clockwork torpedo boat, cat. ref. 13079, with pairs of forward and aft guns and torpedo tubes, with repair to one wheel, with replaced anchors and chains.

c1902 *23.5in (60cm) long*

$7,000-10,000 **SAS**

A Bing tinplate clockwork torpedo boat, no.13957/2, with nickel and cat ventilators, with original box.

c1906-09 *39in (99cm) long*

$25,000-35,000 **BER**

A Bing tinplate clockwork super dreadnought battleship, cat. ref. 155/116, with rotating forward, aft and side gun turrets, with some corrosion.

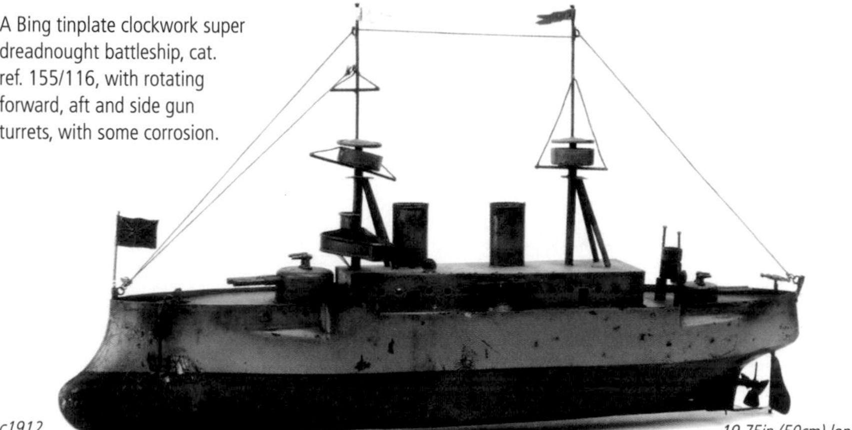

c1912 *19.75in (50cm) long*

$3,000-4,000 **SAS**

A mid-19thC Buchner clockwork paddle-wheel steamer, with flat lead people, with canopy cover at stern, with some paint flaking and re-painting.

7in (18cm) long

$15,000-20,000 **BER**

A Fischer lithographed tinplate gunboat penny toy, with two lifeboats, with some corrosion to hull.

9.5in (24cm) long

$500-700 **BER**

A Fleischmann tinplate clockwork liner, with single-screw, with two Red Ensigns.

c1950 *13in (33cm) long*

$700-1,000 **SAS**

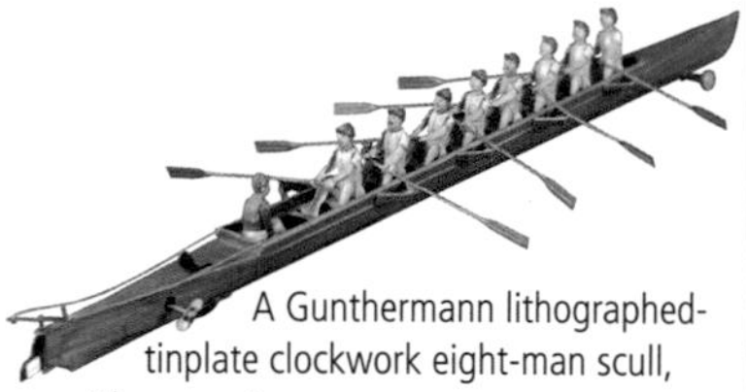

A Gunthermann lithographed-tinplate clockwork eight-man scull, with coxswain.

This is an exceptionally detailed toy with the same synchronized rowing action as the real thing.

29in (73.5cm) long

$30,000-40,000 **BER**

A Rock & Graner steam-powered 'KAISER WILHELM' paddle-wheel steamer, no.2111, with bell at bow.

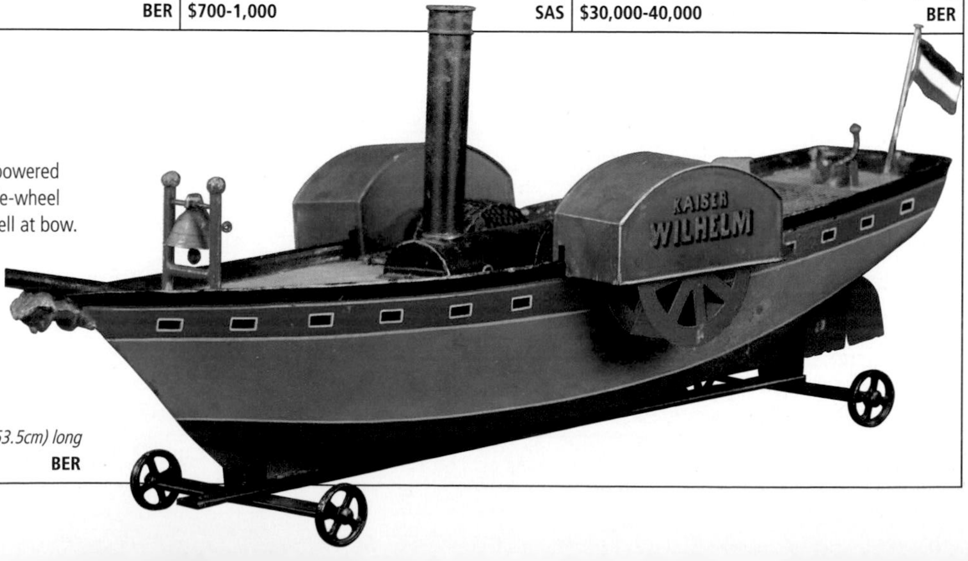

c1875 *21in (53.5cm) long*

$50,000-70,000 **BER**

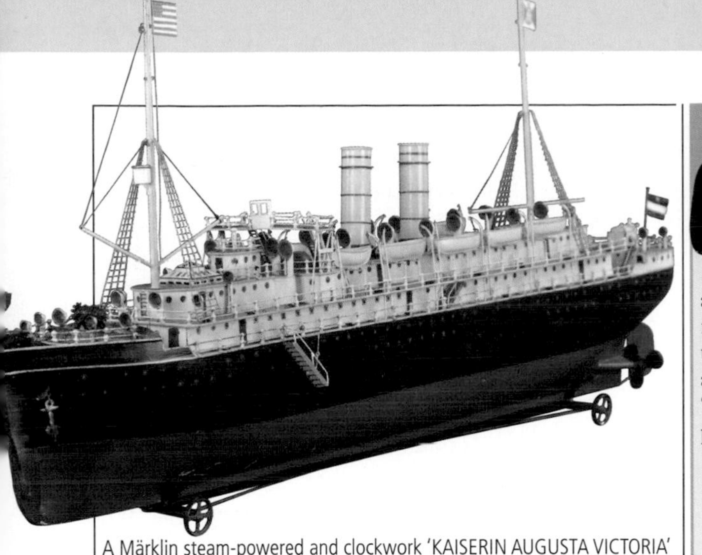

A Märklin steam-powered and clockwork 'KAISERIN AUGUSTA VICTORIA' liner, model no.5050/11D, with some paint chips.

The real liner, on which this model is based, was billed as the largest in the world. This Märklin toy is the largest in their toy fleet and exceptionally detailed.

c1913 *20in (51cm) long*

$140,000-180,000 BER

A Märklin tinplate clockwork 'PROVIDENCE' paddle-wheel steamer, model no.1071, with passenger benches and bridge, with minor restoration, with one replaced lifeboat.

Märklin left no detail on this model unemembellished, with particular highlights including the painted curtains and the windows and the ornately stamped seating area. With the sea captain at the foredeck, this majestic ship conjures the image of sheer luxury at sea.

c1900-02 *26in (66cm) long*

$250,000-300,000 BER

Judith Picks

With the build-up of naval power in the early 20thC, young boys were keen to acquire model battleships. Today these are some of the rarest Märklin toys as many were submerged in water and rusted. This steamer was made at the height of the factory's creative genius in c1900-02 and also graces the dust cover of the book 'Allure of Toy Ships'. It's a spectacular piece. Märklin envisioned a toy that recreated the luxury of an early paddle-wheeler. With details such as hand-painted lower deck curtains and six figures of the captain and crew, this toy does indeed exude the luxury of the steamer with the utmost artistic perfection.

A Märklin tinplate clockwork 'CHICAGO' paddle-wheel steamer, model no.1080/2, with minor restoration.

c1900-02 *31in (78.5cm) long*

$270,000-350,000 BER

A rare Märklin 'first series' tinplate spirit-fired 'HMS TERRIBLE' battleship, with some minor replacements, missing lifeboats.

HMS 'Terrible' was a British battleship, which was involved in the relief of Ladysmith in 1899 and served in the Boxer Rebellion in 1900.

c1904 *25in (62cm) long*

$160,000-200,000 SAS

A Märklin 'first series' tinplate clockwork 'NEW YORK' battleship, model no.1092/115, with fully appointed upper deck, with one replaced mast, with original box.

c1905 *27.5in (70cm) long*

$110,000-180,000 BER

A Märklin tinplate clockwork 'NEW YORK' cruiser battleship, model no.5103, with gun turrets, stairs to observation towers and bridge, four lifeboats and two masts with crow's nest.

c1909 *16in (40.5cm) long*

$80,000-120,000 **BER**

A Märklin tinplate clockwork 'BLENHEIM' riverboat, model no.50/40/34.

c1909 *13in (33cm) long*

$30,000-40,000 **BER**

A Märklin tinplate steam-powered 'MARYLAND' battleship, model no.5128D/9, with gun turrets, lifeboats on cranes, four-tiered mast, twin funnels, multi-deck observation decks, with stairs and guns on all sides.

c1915 *36in (91.5cm) long*

$150,000-200,000 **BER**

A Märklin 'second series' 'BROOKLYN' battleship, model no.5130 D/9, with gun turrets at multiple levels and angles, armored crow's nest and cranes suspending lifeboats.

c1915 *38in (96.5cm) long*

$120,000-180,000 **BER**

ESSENTIAL REFERENCE - MÄRKLIN

Gebrüder Märklin (Märklin Brothers) was founded in 1859 by Theodor Friedrich Wilhelm Märklin (1817-66) in Göppingen in Baden-Württemberg, Germany.

- **In 1891 the company acquired the Ludwig Lutz tinplate toy factory and combined their handmade techniques with processes of mass-production.**
- **By 1900 Marklin had become the market leader in clockwork and steam-powered model trains.**
- **A wide range of other toys, including model cars, boats and stationary steam engines, were also produced.**
- **Production ceased temporarily during World War II, with tinplate manufacture being abandoned completely in 1950.**
- **Märklin is still one of the largest toy manufacturers in Europe.**

A Märklin tinplate clockwork 'CARMANIA' British-market liner, cat. ref. 5050/9, with 32 ventilators, two masts, ten lifeboats, detailed bridge and wheel-house, with some re-painting.

c1912 *38.5in (98cm) long*

$50,000-70,000 **SAS**

A Märklin tinplate clockwork liner, cat. ref. 5050/9, renamed 'Star of India', with major re-painting, with replaced anchors and chains.

c1919 *38.5in (98cm) long*

$3,000-4,000 **SAS**

A 1930s Märklin tinplate clockwork submarine, model no.5031/57, with enhanced paint to railings.

22in (56cm) long

$8,000-12,000 **BER**

An ACE Trains 0-gauge electric A4 4-6-2 'OSPREY' locomotive and tender, RN no.4494, with box and packing.

$1,500-2,000 W&W

A Bassett-Lowke war-time issue 0-gauge clockwork 0-6-0T locomotive, RN no.78.

This is rare example of an outside cylinder LMS class 3P Suburban Tank locomotive.

$1,200-1,800 W&W

A Beeson 3-rail 0-gauge electric 4-4-0 locomotive and tender, no.937, with power pick-up in tender and full inside motion to locomotive.

$20,000-30,000 TEN

A Beyer Garratt 3in (7.5cm) gauge 2-8-0-0-8-2 'SAMUEL JACKSON' locomotive, RN no.4, built by A William G Tucker.

William Tucker was a well-known locomotive builder in the 1950s and '60s. The nameplate on this locomotive commemorates Samuel Jackson who became the Works Director at Beyer Peacock Locomotive builders. Jackson was also the draughtsman who prepared the first works drawings for these famous locomotives.

66in (167.5cm) long

$30,000-40,000 DN

A 1920s Bing for Bassett-Lowke clockwork LSWR 0-4-4 tank locomotive, RN no.109, with slight re-painting, with two dents and chipping.

$5,000-7,000 SAS

A Bing 3-gauge clockwork MR 0 4 0 locomotive and tender, RN no.2631, similar to cat. ref. 17592/3, with replacement tender coal rail, with some re-painting, missing lamp.

c1912

$6,500-7,500 SAS

A Carette 3-gauge steam-powered NER 4-4-0 locomotive and tender, RN no.1619, similar to cat. ref. 513/67, with cast-iron frames, with re painting, with old corrosion and pitting to cast-iron areas.

c1911

$8,000-12,000 SAS

A Carette 3-gauge NER bogie luggage van, RN no.1325, with replaced wheels, with re-painted roofs, with glazing added.

$5,000-7,000 SAS

A 2-rail electric class-4 CR 4-4-0 'Dunalastair' locomotive and bogie tender, RN no.767, built by Geoff Holt and painted by Keith King.

15in (41cm) long

$4,500-5,500 SAS

A Hornby 0-gauge electric 'Schools Class' 4-4-0 'ETON' locomotive and tender, no.4, RN no.900.

$1,500-2,500 W&W

A Hornby Dublo 3-rail 4-6-2 BR Princess Coronation Class 'CITY OF LIVERPOOL' locomotive, no. 3226, RN no.46247, with box and instruction booklet dated '2/59'.

1959

$650-850 VEC

A Hornby 0-gauge electric LMS E220 4-4-2 'Special Tank' locomotive, RN no.6954.

$550-750 VEC

An early Märklin 1-gauge clockwork 0-2-2 locomotive and tender, cat. ref. 1021, with minor repairs and re-painting.

1899

$2,500-3,500 SAS

A Märklin tinplate electric GNR 4-4-0 locomotive and tender.

Locomotive 9in (23cm) long

$400-600 ECGW

A Märklin 0-gauge clockwork L&NWR 4-6-0 locomotive and tender, RN no.66, in need of restoration.

$1,500-2,500 A&G

A 7in (18cm) gauge model of the LMS 'Pacific' 4-6-2 'DUCHESS OF BUCCLEUCH' locomotive and tender, RN no.6230, built by Harry Powell, the paintwork and lettering by Louis Raper.

113in (287cm) long

$280,000-300,000 DN

A Hornby 0-gauge E2E engine shed.

$800-1,200 VEC

A rare Märklin French-market 1-gauge tinplate 'Gare Centrale', cat. ref. 2013, the interior with ticket hall, kiosk, barrier and waiting room with two chairs, two benches and a table, with original etched glass windows, with paint loss and creasing, with replacement bell.

1902-19

13.75in (34cm) long

$10,000-15,000 SAS

An 1896 Athens Olympic Games bronze second prize medal, designed by Jules Chaplain.

There were no gold prize medals awarded at the inaugural modern Olympic Games of 1896. The winner received a silver medal, the runner-up a bronze.

$30,000-40,000

An 1896 Athens Olympic Games bronze participation medal, designed by N Lytras, struck by Honto-Poulus.

$1,000-1,500 **GBA**

A 1904 St Louis Olympic Games athlete's participation medal, Dieges & Clust, New York.

The version of this medal presented to officials has a loop at the top and was worn as a badge.

$20,000-30,000 **GBA**

A 1908 London Olympic Games 15ct gold first prize winner's medal, awarded to an unknown Australian player for rugby, designed by Bertram Mackennal, struck by Vaughton & Son, Birmingham.

The recipient of this medal was one of the touring Wallabies team, who provided the only opposition to Great Britain in the entry for the Olympic rugby competition. The Great Britain team was effectively the Cornwall county rugby team.

$20,000-25,000 **GBA**

A 1908 London Olympic Games silver second prize medal, awarded to Great Britain's Walter Tysall for gymnastics, designed by Bertram Mackennal, in original case.

Walter Tysall (1880-1955), the three times British gymnastics champion, was the first Great British competitor to win a gymnastics medal and was also the last to medal in the gymnasium before Louis Smith won an individual medal - the bronze - at Beijing precisely one hundred years later in 2008.

$6,500-7,500 **GBA**

A 1908 London Olympic Games silver second prize medal, awarded to Great Britain's Arthur Warren J Cumming for the Special Figures for Men, designed by Bertram Mackennal.

This was the first Olympic silver medal awarded for a winter sport. Arthur Cumming finished runner-up in the Special Figures to the Russian skater Nikolai Panin. The Special Figures never appeared as part of an Olympic program thereafter.

$10,000-15,000 **GBA**

The 1912 Stockholm Olympic Games silver-gilt first prize medal, awarded to Great Britain's Jennie Fletcher for the 100 metres Freestyle Relay, designed by Erik Lindberg & Bertram Mackennal.

$20,000-30,000 **GBA**

A rare 1908 London Olympic Games silver-gilt marathon judge's badge, Vaughton & Son, Birmingham.

$15,000-20,000 **GBA**

A 1908 London Olympic Games silvered-bronze judge's badge, Vaughton & Son, Birmingham.

$2,000-3,000 **GBA**

A 1908 London Olympic Games second prize diploma, awarded to Great Britain's Dora Boothby in the ladies' tennis singles, lithograph after John Bernard Partridge.

21in (53.5cm) wide

$7,000-9,000 GBA

A 1912 Stockholm Olympic Games first prize diploma, awarded to a Great Britain soccerer, designed by Professor Olle Hjortzberg, mounted.

For the second successive Olympic Games, Great Britain won the gold medal in the soccer competition, beating Hungary 7-0, Finland 4-0 and, in the final, Denmark 4-2.

25.5in (65cm) wide

$15,000-20,000 GBA

BULLETIN DU COMITÉ INTERNATIONAL
JEUX OLYMPIQUES

A set of the first three issues of 'Bulletin du Comite International des Jeux Olympiques' (the Olympic Review), each comprising four pages.

1894-95

$12,000-18,000 GBA

A pair of 1906 Athens Intercalated Olympic Games tickets, issued for the first day, with circular and star shaped clippings.

$1,500-2,500 GBA

A silver inkpot, by Vaughton & Son, Birmingham, mounted with two enameled roundels of artistic interpretations of the 1908 London Olympic Games participation medal design.

1908 *3.5in (9cm) high*

$8,000-12,000 GBA

A Sèvres 1924 Paris Olympic Games first prize porcelain vase, designed by Octave Denis Victor Guillonnet, decorated by Bracquemond with gilt laurel branches and pâte-sur-pâte medallions depicting Olympic sports.

1924 *13in (33cm) high*

$12,000-18,000 GBA

A 1948 London Olympic Games aluminium torch, designed by Ralph Lavers, the bowl pierced with Olympic Rings and 'XIVth OLYMPIAD 1948, OLYMPIA TO LONDON, WITH THANKS TO THE BEARER', with torch bearer's letter of invitation, runner's instructions and photographs.

This torch was carried by Mr J Brinton between Chudleigh Police Station and Toll Cottage, Rixey Park, at Chudleigh Knighton turning in Devon.

16in (40.5cm) high

$10,000-15,000 GBA

A 1911 FA Cup 15ct gold winner's medal, awarded to Robert Torrance of Bradford City, inscribed '1911, CHALLENGE CUP, WINNERS, BRADFORD CITY, R.TORRANCE'.

Robert 'Bob' Torrance joined Bradford City in 1908 and was predominantly a reserve for his first three years, including in the 1911 FA Cup final. William 'Willie' Gildea was injured during the game and was replaced by Torrance in the re-play at Old Trafford. Torrance played superbly and was many commentators' choice as Man of the Match. Afterward Torrance became a regular first teamer.

$20,000-30,000 GBA

A 1961-62 Soccer League Championship 9ct gold medal, inscribed 'THE Soccer LEAGUE, CHAMPIONS, DIVISION 1, SEASON 1961-62, IPSWICH TOWN F.C., J. COMPTON', in original box.

This medal was awarded to Ipswich Town left-back John Compton for his part in the Suffolk club's historic Championship winning season of 1961-62 under the stewardship of Alf Ramsey.

$10,000-15,000 GBA

A 1966 European Cup gold and enamel winner's medal, inscribed 'COUPE DES CLUBS CHAMPIONS EUROPEENS', the reverse inscribed 'VAINQUEUR, 1966'.

Real Madrid beat Partizan Belgrade 2-1 in the final played at the Heysel Stadium, Brussels.

$6,500-7,500 GBA

A 1973 FA Cup 9ct gold runners-up medal, inscribed 'THE Soccer ASSOCIATION, CHALLENGE CUP, RUNNERS-UP', with original case.

Provenance: Sold together with a signed letter of provenance from Allan Clarke of Leeds United. In one of the most famous FA Cup finals, underdogs Sunderland from the Second Division beat the mighty Leeds United through a goal by Ian Porterfield.

$5,000-7,000 GBA

A 1892 West Bromwich Albion v Aston Villa English Cup final match ball on stand, the ball gilded, painted and with inscription, surmounted by a stuffed and mounted song thrush.

$30,000-40,000 MM

A red long-sleeved England no.20 jersey, issued to Ian Callaghan for the 1966 World Cup final.

For the 1966 World Cup final Umbro produced a red jersey plus a spare for all 22 members of the England squad in order to cover the final team selection. Callaghan was issued with the no.20 jersey in the England squad but played in just one of the games. The jersey shown was therefore not required.

$5,500-6,500 GBA

A 1973-74 Soccer League Division One Champion's presentation in the form of a 9ct gold medal plaque, awarded to Allan Clarke, inscribed 'THE Soccer LEAGUE, CHAMPIONS DIVISION 1'.

Provenance: Sold with a signed letter of provenance from Allan Clarke.

1973-74 *4in (10cm) wide*

$8,000-12,000 GBA

A white long-sleeved Tottenham Hotspur no.9 jersey, worn by Alan Gilzean in the 1967 FA Cup final, with a Cup final rosette.

Provenance: Sold with a letter of provenance from a previous vendor confirming that, as a child, he was given the jersey directly by Alan Gilzean in c1980.

$10,000-15,000 GBA

An autographed white long-sleeved England no.7 jersey, issued to David Beckham for the 1998 World Cup, signed 'Best Wishes, David Beckham.'

This jersey was never worn.

1998

$2,000-3,000 GBA

A 1950 World Cup England cap, worn by Henry Cockburn, inscribed 'WORLD CUP 1950 TOURNAMENT'.

Manchester United's Henry Cockburn was selected for the England squad at their first World Cup appearance in 1950 but did not start in any of England's three games.

$2,000-3,000 GBA

A red 1966-67 Wales international cap, worn by Gary Sprake, inscribed '1966-67 S', with label marked 'G. Sprake'.

Provenence: Sold with a letter of authenticity signed by Gary Sprake. Gary Sprake's only Welsh appearance in the season of 1966-67 was in the home international v Scotland, which doubled-up as a European Championship qualifying match. The game ended 1-1.

$1,500-2,500 GBA

A rare 1899 Derby County v Sheffield United official FA Cup final program, for the match played at the Crystal Palace 15th April, with old sellotape repairs and minor losses.

1899

$10,000-15,000 **GBA**

A 1901 Tottenham Hotspur v Sheffield United FA Cup final program, for the match played at the Crystal Palace 20th April, with old sellotape repairs and some losses.

1901

$20,000-30,000 **GBA**

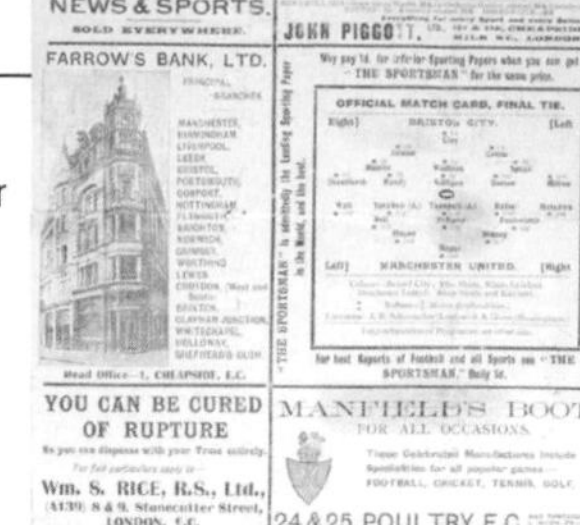

A rare 1909 Manchester United v Bristol City FA Cup final official program, for the match played at the Crystal Palace 24th April, with old sellotape repairs.

1909 saw Manchester United's first ever appearance in a FA Cup final and was the first of their record 11 FA Cup wins to date. This example is the first 1909 FA Cup final program ever offered at auction.

1909

$40,000-60,000 **GBA**

A 1912 Barnsley v West Bromwich Albion FA Cup final program, for the match played at the Crystal Palace 20th April, with old sellotape repairs.

1912

$10,000-15,000 **GBA**

A 1929 Bolton Wanderers v Portsmouth FA Cup final program, for the match played 27th April.

1929

$1,200-1,800 **GBA**

A rare 1939 England v Scotland wartime international match program, for the match played at Newcastle United 2nd December.

This was the first wartime England home game. The gate for the match was just 15,000, which may explain the program's rarity.

1939

$10,000-15,000 **GBA**

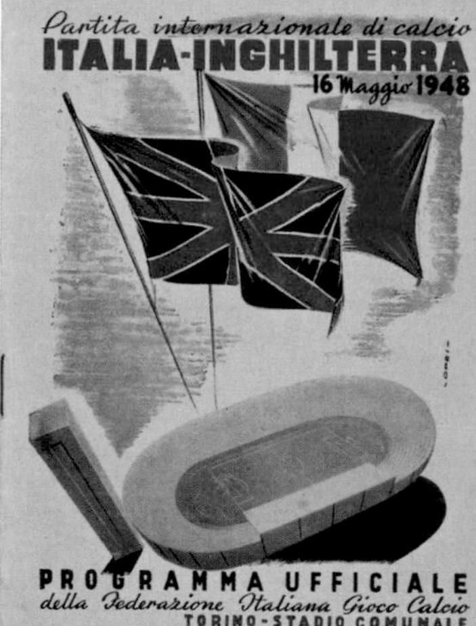

A rare 1948 Italy v England international match program, for the match played at the Stadio Comunale, Torino, 16th May.

1948

$4,000-6,000 **GBA**

A rare 1934 World Cup poster, designed by Luigi Martinati, printed by Grafiche, Roma/Milano, strung at upper margin as issued.

9.5in (24cm) high

$10,000-15,000 **GBA**

An official international match pennant, received by England captain Billy Wright from Hungary captain Ferenc Puskás before the match played at Wembley Stadium 25th November 1953, with a match ticket, souvenir brochure and photograph of the teams.

The 25th November 1953 was a watershed for English and international soccer. Hungary inflicted a devastating 6-3 defeat over England at Wembley Stadium. Until this day the mother country of soccer had never lost an international match at home to overseas opposition. English managers were forced, for the first time, to look to Europe to understand the training and tactical advances that were being made there. At the forefront of this movement was Manchester United's Matt Busby.

1953

Pennant 22.75in (58cm) long

$15,000-20,000 **GBA**

A rare Zutsei Bros., Sialkot late long-nose beech short spoon, with full wrap-over brass sole plate and hide grip with underlisting.

The Garrison golf club in Sialkot was founded during the height of the British Empire rule in Pakistan for members of the armed forces and is still in existence today.

c1890

$1,000-1,500 **MM**

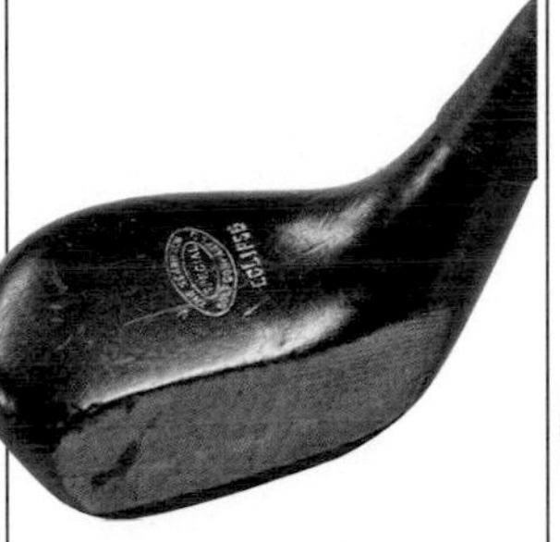

An unusual St Andrews Golf Club persimmon 'Eclipse' driver, with rounded toe and curved sole, with original full-length hide grip, unused.

$250-350 **MM**

A rare Fred Whiting, West Cornwall 'Legh's Patent' integral-face putter, without grip.

c1906

$1,200-1,800 **MM**

A box of Ocobo 27 1/2 guttie golf balls, comprising eight unused golf balls, six in their original wrappers, and two used golf balls, with original Ocobo sleeve box.

'Ocobo' is a trade name of the J B Halley Company.

c1894

$4,000-6,000 **MM**

A rare papier-mâché advertising figure of 'Silver King Man', the base stamped 'Patent no 208 063 Made in England'.

There are reputedly only 15 examples of this figure in existence.

c1910 *14in (35.5cm) high*

$10,000-15,000 **MM**

A rare papier-mâché advertising figure of 'Penfold Man', smoking a cigarette instead of the usual pipe, the base inscribed 'He played a PENFOLD'.

c1930 *20.5in (52cm) high*

$2,000-3,000 **MM**

A rare Doulton Lambeth stoneware jug, decorated with golfing figures, with Doulton mark and production numbers, the silver rim hallmarked Sheffield.

1900 *8in (20cm) high*

$1,200-1,800 **MM**

A rare 1965 Open Golf Championship competitor's badge and autographed photograph of the winner Peter Thomson.

$700-1,000 **MM**

A Rye Golf Club 9ct gold and enamel 'Colt Medal', the reverse engraved 'E G Maltby 1929'.

1929

$500-700 **MM**

A silver presentation golf-themed desk set, by George Edwards & Sons, Birmingham, with presentation inscription, crested.

1924 *11in (28.5cm) wide 51oz*

$4,000-6,000 **GBA**

A rare 1938 US Open Championship brass 'season ticket' badge, inscribed '42nd Open Championship Season Ticket June 4-11 1938 No. 388'.

2.5in (6.5cm) wide

$300-500 **MM**

The 'Arkle' bridle, the bit inscribed 'ARKLE 19.4.1957, RETIRED 8.10.68'.

Provenance: Sold with letters of authentication.

$20,000-30,000 **GBA**

The 'Manna' 1925 Derby silks, worn by Steve Donoghue when winning the 1925 Derby, by Merry & Co., St James Street, London, framed.

Provenance: Sold with a signed letter of provenance confirming that the silks were acquired from the trainer Fred Darling of Beckhampton.

Frame 34in (86.5cm) high

$6,500-7,500 **GBA**

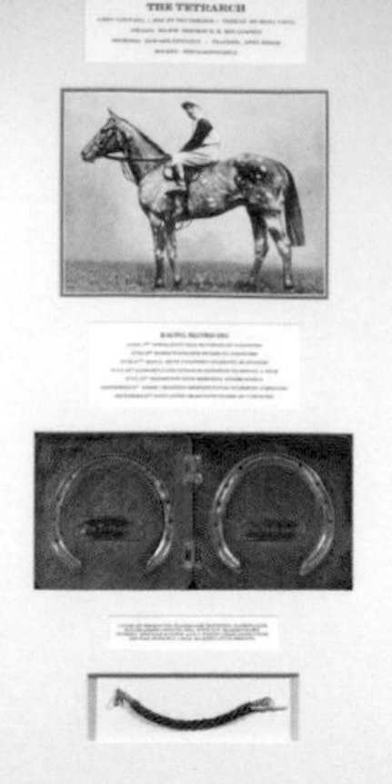

A framed display containing a pair of the Tetrach's racing plates and a plait of his tail hair, the shoes set into oak panels with silver plaques by Robert Pringle & Sons, London, the horse hair with 9ct gold fittings.

The Tetrarch was an unbeaten racehorse known as 'The Spotted Wonder' due to his highly unusual coat markings. He was bred in Ireland in 1911 and sold to Major Demot McCalmont.

Frame 37in (94cm) high

$8,000-12,000 **GBA**

A complete set of racecards for Lester Piggott's Derby wins.

$1,500-2,000 **GBA**

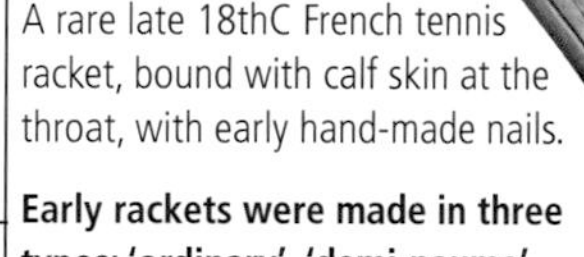

A Cartier racing 'finishing post' stickpin, set with old-mine-cut diamonds and French-cut rubies, signed 'CARTIER PARIS', numbered, stamped with French control marks, with a leather case.

3in (7.5cm) high

$4,000-6,000 **L&T**

A rare late 18thC French tennis racket, bound with calf skin at the throat, with early hand-made nails.

Early rackets were made in three types: 'ordinary', 'demi-paume' and 'en battoir'. This may be a rare example of either of the two latter descriptions.

$30,000-40,000 **GBA**

An early 19thC real tennis racket, with unusual stringing pattern, with uncovered real tennis balls.

$3,000-4,000 **GBA**

A mid-late 19thC Henry Malings of Woolwich tilt-head lawn tennis, stamped with maker's mark and Royal coat-of-arms, with original stringing, with some broken strings.

$3,000-4,000 **GBA**

An early 20thC H J Gray & Sons cast-iron tennis ball cleaner, rusted.

15in (36cm) high

$120-180 **FLD**

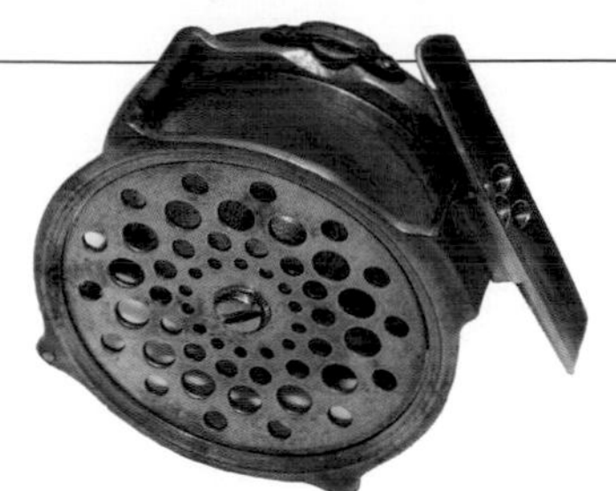

An early Hardy 'Bougle' 3in (7.5cm) alloy dry-fly reel, the face plate stamped with logos, 'Rod in Hand Border' and 'Bougle Reel'.

1906

$3,000-4,000 MM

An early 'Coxon Aerial' four-spoke 3.5in (9cm) reel, with tension regulator ivorine handles, mahogany backplate and brass star back and ratchet button.

$1,500-2,500 MM

A Hardy 'Perfect' brass 4.5in (11.5cm) salmon fly reel, the winding plate impressed 'Rod in Hand Oval' and 'Hardy Pat', with ivory handle.

$4,000-6,000 MM

A Seifert & Söhne mahogany-veneered billiards table, with five billiards balls, with damage and losses.

$6,500-7,500 DOR

A silk scorecard commemorating A C MacLaren's innings for Lancashire v Somerset at Taunton in 1895, in need of restoration.

This innings still remains a record high score for an Englishman in First Class Cricket.

$1,000-1,500 GBA

An early American gold, silver, enamel and jeweled 'Holske International Challenge' boxing belt, R T Hewitson & Co., Boston, MA, the central panel set with a locket containing a photograph of Jem Carney.

This belt was awarded to Jem Carney as Light Weight Champion of the World.

1887

$15,000-20,000 GBA

A rare commemorative gold medal, presented by the Melbourne Cricket Club to the English cricketer E F S Tylecote in commemoration of the first Ashes Test Series in 1882-83, the reverse inscribed 'E.F.S. TYLECOTE, 1882-3', marks indistinct.

Identical medals were presented to all gentlemen members of The Hon. Ivo Bligh's England team to Australia in 1882-83.

$6,500-7,500 GBA

An Arai racing helmet, worn by Joey Dunlop, with Snell number 'A 0873470' and Arai serial number labels, with replaced screws, with some deterioration of the inner foam.

In 2005 Joey Dunlop was voted the fifth greatest motorcycling icon ever by 'Motor Cycle News' readers. It is thought that this helmet was the first to carry the distinctive black symmetrical outlines that soon became recognized as Joey Dunlop's trademark.

1983-84

$6,500-7,500 GBA

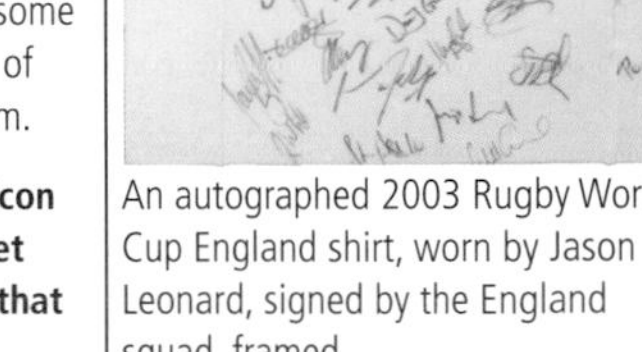

An autographed 2003 Rugby World Cup England shirt, worn by Jason Leonard, signed by the England squad, framed.

2003 *Frame 36in (91.5cm) high*

$800-1,200 GBA

ESSENTIAL REFERENCE - BEMBE

The Bembe live in eastern Democratic Republic of the Congo, where there are around 250,000 members, and western Tanzania, where there are around 360,000 members. Their social organisation was based on the matrimonial clan. The chief in charge of the village, the nga-bula, mediated with the ancestors.

- **The Bembe carve numerous kinds of wooden figures, many of which represent spirits. Female mukuya fetish figures, such as the one shown, were traditionally thought of as a household protective statues.**
- **The Bembe also carve several different kinds of masks, the most notable being antelope horn masks (elande).**

An early 20thC Bembe female mukuya fetish figure, Democratic Republic of the Congo, with classic body scarification and features, her eyes inlaid with ivory, both arms re-attached, with losses.

6in (15cm) high

$2,500-3,500 DRA

A carved ivory horn, probably Congo, decorated with a procession of figures in native and western dress.

16in (40.5cm) long

$5,000-7,000 GORL

An early/mid-20thC Dan carved wood zakpai mask, Ivory Coast, set with animal teeth and remains of red textile.

These masks were traditionally used in annual races.

9in (23cm) high

$2,500-3,500 DRA

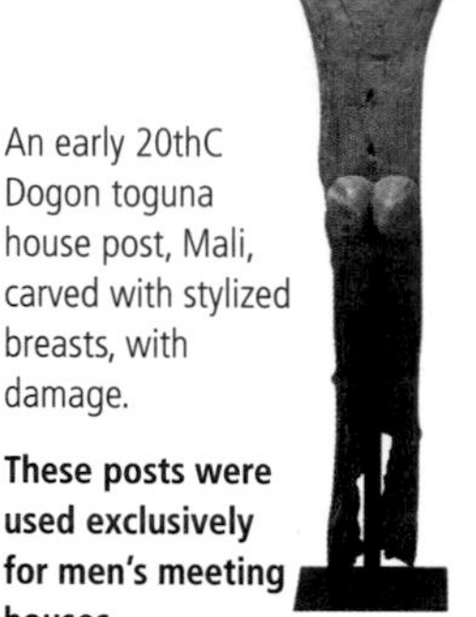

An early 20thC Dogon toguna house post, Mali, carved with stylized breasts, with damage.

These posts were used exclusively for men's meeting houses.

55in (140cm) high

$1,500-2,500 DRA

ESSENTIAL REFERENCE - DAN

The Dan tribe (also known as the Gio) live in the West African countries of Liberia and the Ivory Coast. There are approximately 350,000 members of the group, united by the Dan language. The Dan are primarily farmers of cattle and staple crops, such as rice, cassava and maize.

- **The Dan are known for their wooden masks, which are worn with full-body costumes and have different functions in Dan society. For example, the 'Deangle' mask becomes the guardian and intermediary of the uncircumcised boys' initiation camp, while 'Gaegon' masks are primarily used for singing and entertainment.**
- **'Lu me' (wooden people) figures are rare, with male figures being especially rare. Most examples are female and represent the preferred wife of the chief. They confer prestige to their owners.**

A Fang carved wood head, with metal eyes, with stylized coiffure and long tapered neck, with wood loss.

15.5in (39cm) high

$2,000-3,000 SK

A mid-20thC Ibo parade bust, Nigeria, with stylized tattoos and ritual scars.

34in (86cm) high

$1,200-1,800 DRA

A Dan carved wood mask, with red cloth over eyes, pierced at the edge for attachment, with losses.

8.25in (21cm) high

$1,500-2,500 SK

A Kuba carved wood king's figure, wearing ornaments including a sash with cowrie shell decoration, with some rodent damage to eyes and nose.

18.5in (47cm) high

$5,500-6,500 **SK**

A carved wood female figure, possibly Lwena, Angola, with headdress containing ritual material.

9.25in (23cm) high

$2,500-3,500 **SK**

A late 19thC Mboum headdress, Cameroon, with stylized cowrie shell images, accented with kaolin and adorned with kola nuts.

34.5in (88cm) high

$2,500-3,500 **DRA**

An early to mid-20thC Mbundu mask, Angola, with classic coffee-bean eyes, with some restoration to stress fractures.

Such masks are worn during the initiation of young men into adulthood.

15.5in (39cm) high

$1,500-2,500 **DRA**

A Teke carved wood power figure, the torso encased in a remnant-encrusted magic bundle.

13.25in (34cm) high

$1,800-2,200 **SK**

ESSENTIAL REFERENCE - CITES

CITES (the Convention on International Trade in Endangered Species of Wild Fauna and Flora) is an international agreement between governments, which aims to ensure that international trade in wild animals and plants does not threaten their survival. It covers over 30,000 live specimens and products derived from live animals.

- **All import and export of species covered by the Convention has to be authorized through a licencing system.**
- **CITES was drafted as a result of a resolution adopted in 1963 at a meeting of members of The World Conservation Union. The final text of the convention was agreed by 80 countries in 1973 and CITES entered in force in 1975.**
- **As of 2013, CITES is now upheld by 178 countries.**
- **Antiques (defined as specimens significantly altered from their natural state for jewelry, adornment, art, utility or musical instruments, before 1st June 1947) are exempt from CITES. Uncarved horns could not be considered antique.**

A 19thC East African rhino horn knobkerrie.

20in (51cm) long

$15,000-20,000 **GORL**

A 19thC East African rhino horn knobkerrie.

17.5in (44.5cm) long

$15,000-20,000 **GORL**

A 19thC Sudanese turned rhino horn cup.

3.25in (8.5cm) high

$10,000-15,000 **GORL**

A 19thC Sudanese turned rhino horn cup,

This piece has CITES permission. However, it is unlikely that a re-export license, outside of the EU, would be granted.

2.75in (7cm) high

$5,500-6,500 **GORL**

Judith Picks

I was very lucky to be introduced to Inuit Art by Duncan McLean of Waddingtons in Toronto many years ago and I've filmed some exceptional pieces on the 'Antiques Roadshow' here in the UK. The sculptor Ennutsiak was born in the Nunavik region of Quebec in 1896. This 'Migration Scene' recounts the harrowing journey many of the Inuit make on a skin boat or 'umiak', paddling through breaking ice floes to reach safety. Ennutsiak was the father of Nuveeya Ipellie and grandfather of Seepee and Alooktook Ipellie. He died in Iqualit, Nunavut.

'Migration Scene' in stone and ivory, by Ennutsiak (1896-1967), E7-603, Iqaluit.
1960 *15in (38cm) long*
$100,000-150,000 **WAD**

'Dancing Polar Bear', in stone, by Davie Atchealak (1947-2006), E7-1182, Iqaluit, signed in Roman.
18in (45.5cm) high
$8,000-12,000 **WAD**

'Windswept Musk Ox', in stone and antler, by Lucassie Ikkidluak (b.1949), E7-765, Lake Harbour, signed in syllabics, dated.
2008 *11in (28cm) long*
$4,000-6,000 **WAD**

ESSENTIAL REFERENCE - OSUITOK IPEELEE

Osuitok Ipeelee (1923-2005) learned to carve by watching his father, Ohotok.

- **He sold his first ivory carving in the 1940s and was already highly regarded for his artistry by the time that James Houston (who played an important role in the recognition of Inuit art) arrived in 1951.**
- **In the late 1950s, Ipeelee participated in Houston's printmaking program.**
- **His work was part of the 'Sculpture/Inuit. Sculpture of the Inuit: Masterworks of the Canadian Arctic' show that toured the world 1971-73.**
- **His sculptures gradually became more stylized and minimal.**
- **Ipeelee is one of the most important and influential Inuit sculptors. His work is in international collections, including the National Gallery of Canada, the Metropolitan Museum of Art in New York City, USA, and the Vatican Collection, Italy.**
- **In 2004, Osuitok received the Lifetime Aboriginal Art Achievement Award.**

'Owl', in stone, by Osuitok Ipeelee (1923-2005), E7-1154, Cape Dorset, signed in syllabics.
13.5in (34.5cm) high
$20,000-30,000 **WAD**

'Kneeling Mother with Child in her Amaut', in stone, by Osuitok Ipeelee (1923-2005), E7-1154, Cape Dorset.

An amaut is the hood on an Inuit woman's parka. It is used to carry a child.

c1975 *25.5in (65cm) high*
$30,000-40,000 **WAD**

'Owl with Arctic Hare', in stone, by Osuitok Ipeelee (1923-2005), E7-1154, Cape Dorset, signed in syllabics.
17in (43cm) high
$20,000-30,000 **WAD**

'Shaman Transformation', in stone, by Sharky Nuna (1918-1979), E7-883, Cape Dorset.
c1965 *10.25in (26cm) high*
$800-1,200 **WAD**

'Shaman with Inset Face and Antlers', in stone and antler, by Josiah Nuilaalik (1928-2005), E2-385, Baker Lake, signed in syllabics.
13.25in (33.5cm) high
$10,000-15,000 **WAD**

'Bird With Outstretched Wings', in stone, by Lukta Qiatsuk (1928-2004), E7-1060, Cape Dorset, signed in syllabics.

8.75in (22cm) high

$5,500-6,500 **WAD**

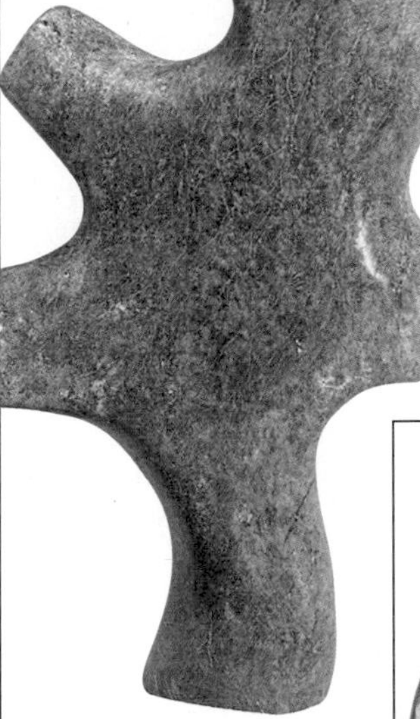

'Dancing Polar Bear', in stone and ivory, by Pauta Saila (1916-2009), E7-990, Cape Dorset.

1998 10.5in (26.5cm) high

$7,000-10,000 **WAD**

'Caribou', in stone and ivory, by Joe Talirunili (1893-1976), E9-818, Povungnituk, signed in Roman.

7in (18cm) wide

$2,500-3,500 **WAD**

'Drummer', in stone and antler, by George Tataniq (1910-91), E2-179, Baker Lake, signed in syllabics.

8.25in (21cm) high

$7,000-10,000 **WAD**

'Faces', in stone, by John Tiktak (1916-81), E1-266, Rankin Inlet, signed in syllabics.

5.5in (14cm) high

$5,000-7,000 **WAD**

'Falcon', in stone, by Ovilu Tunnillie (b.1949), E7-779, Cape Dorset, signed in syllabics.

12in (30.5cm) high

$3,000-4,000 **WAD**

'Seated Musk Ox', in stone and antler, by Judas Ullulaq (1937-1998), E4-342, Gjoa Haven, signed in syllabics.

10in (25.5cm) high

$3,500-4,500 **WAD**

'Inukshuk Man', in stone and antler, by Judas Ullulaq (1937-1998), E4-342, Gjoa Haven, signed in syllabics.

An inukshuk is a sculptural form of unworked stones. It is used by the Inuit to mean 'someone was here' and 'you are on the right path'. The word 'inukshuk' means 'in the likeness of a human'.

10in (25.5cm) high

$2,000-3,000 **WAD**

'The Return Of The Sun', by Kenojuak Ashevak (1927-2013), E7-1035, Cape Dorset, stonecut, edition 23/50.

1961 *26in (66cm) wide*

$7,000-10,000 **WAD**

'Complex Of Birds', by Kenojuak Ashevak (1927-2013), E7-1035, Cape Dorset, stonecut, edition 35/50.

1960 *25.25in (64cm) wide*

$10,000-15,000 **WAD**

'Four Musk Oxen', by Osuitok Ipeelee (1923-2005), E7-1154, Cape Dorset, skin stencil, edition 25/30.

Ipeelee was already well known as a sculptor when he made this sealskin stencil print, 'Four Musk Oxen', in 1959. The oxen are seen with hunter's eyes: in flight, but potent and dangerous to approach.

1959 *19.5in (49.5cm) wide*

$12,000-18,000 **WAD**

'An Inland Spirit', by Ohotaq Mikkigak (b.1936), E7-1009, Cape Dorset, sealskin stencil.

1961 *25in (63.5cm) wide*

$8,000-12,000 **WAD**

'Inside the Igloo to Talk', by Jessie Oonark (1906-1985), E2-384, Baker Lake, stonecut and stencil, edition 31/40.

1987 *23in (58.5cm) wide*

$1,500-2,500 **WAD**

'Hunting Owls', by Joe Talirunili (1893-1976), E9-818, Povungnituk, stonecut, edition 15/30.

1963 *26.25 (66.5cm) wide*

$1,500-2,500 **WAD**

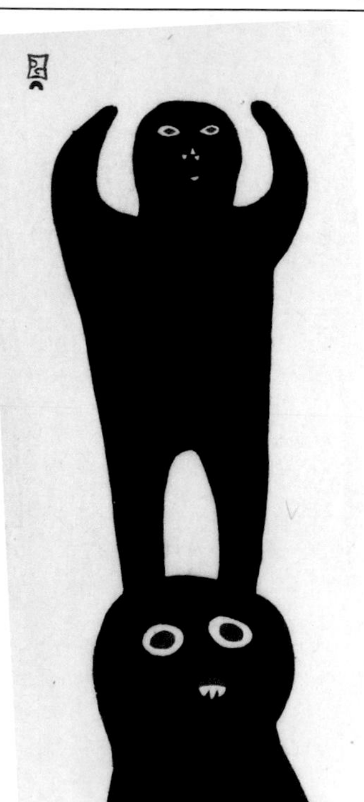

'Seal Thoughts Of Man', by Tudlik (1890-1966), E7-1050, Cape Dorset, stonecut, edition 46/50.

1959 *24in (61cm) high*

$20,000-30,000 **WAD**

'Bird Dream Forewarning Blizzard', by Tudlik (1890-1966), E7-1050, Cape Dorset, stone block, edition 7/30.

1959 *19.75in (50cm) high*

$20,000-30,000 **WAD**

A Californian coiled basketry bowl, decorated with hourglass and diagonal stacked diamond motifs.

c1900 *17.5in (44cm) diam*

$4,000-6,000 **SK**

CLOSER LOOK - HAIDA GREASE BOWL

The bowl would have been used for serving rich foods such as oolichan (candlefish) grease, a butter-like condiment eaten with dried fish or meats.

This is a high-status and rare object.

It would have been brought out during feasts or potlatches celebrating the rank and lineage of chiefs.

It is carved and painted in the form of a stylized seal.

A mid-19thC Northwest Coast Haida grease bowl.

12in (30.5cm) wide

$120,000-180,000 **J&H**

A Californian coiled basketry bowl, decorated with six standing human figures.

c1900 *17in (43cm) diam*

$3,000-4,000 **SK**

A Californian Yokuts coiled basketry bowl, decorated with four bands of rattlesnake motifs, with three sections of zigzag designs.

c1900 *10in (25cm) diam*

$7,000-10,000 **SK**

A late 19thC Northwest Coast Tlingit carved wood shaman figure, carved holding a serpent with an animal head to its chest.

8.5in (22cm) high

$7,000-10,000 **SK**

ESSENTIAL REFERENCE - TLINGIT

The Tlingit are an indigenous people living in the Pacific Northwest Coast of North America. Art and spirituality are important parts of the Tlingit culture and even everyday objects, such as boxes and spoons, are profusely decorated and imbued with spiritual power and historical beliefs.

- **The tribe is known for their 'Chilkat' blankets (dancing blankets), which are made from Cedar bark and mountain goat wool. A common pattern is an abstract whale.**
- **Baskets are typically geometric, though some also feature whales.**

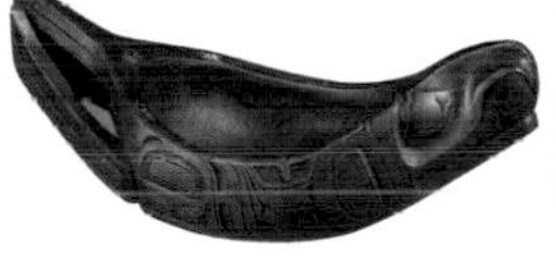

A late 19thC Northwest Coast carved wood bowl, in the form of a stylized seal, with abalone inlay at rim.

10.5in (27cm) long

$3,500-4,500 **SK**

A mid-late 19thC Northwest Coast Tlingit carved and painted wood finial, decorated with avian and animal forms, with sea-lion whisker attachments.

20in (51cm) long

$65,000-75,000 **SK**

An early 19thC Alaskan Athabaskan shot pouch, the beaded leather bag and strap on trade cloth with incised powder horn.

Bag 6.5in (17cm) long

$8,000-12,000 **DRA**

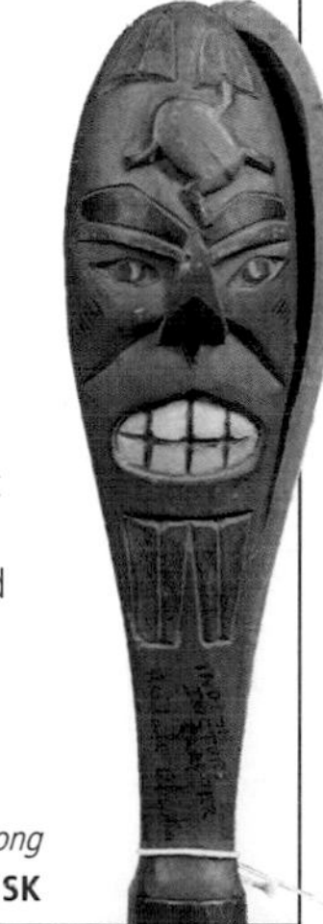

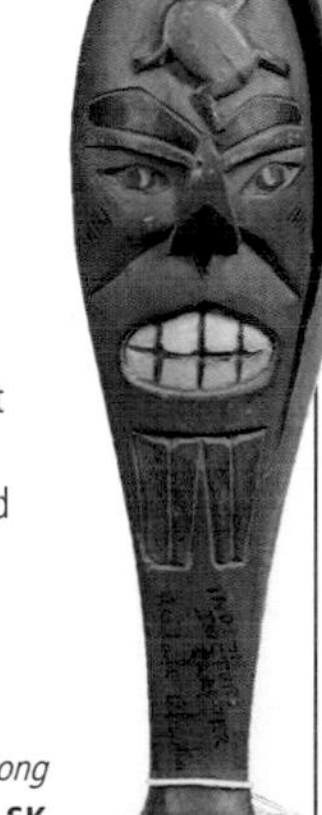

A late 19thC Northwest Coast carved wood clapper, inscribed on the handle 'Indian Doctor's Clapper, Haidah Alaska'.

9.5in (24cm) long

$1,000-1,500 **SK**

A pair of mid-19thC Northeast beaded and quilled hide and cloth moccasins, with some quill and bead loss.

9.5in (24cm) long

$5,000-7,000 **SK**

A pair of late 19thC Ute beaded hide man's leggings, decorated with American flags and brass hawk bells.

31in (79cm) long

$5,000-7,000 **SK**

A late 19thC Great Lakes Ojibwa pipe, the black steatite bowl with lead and catlinite inlays, decorated with brass tacks and file branding.

27in (69cm) long

$6,500-7,500 **SK**

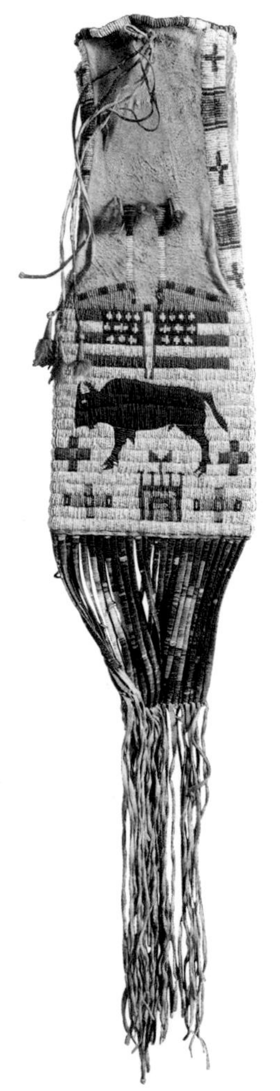

A late 19thC Central Plains Lakota beaded and quilled hide pipe bag, decorated with two American flags over a single bison, the reverse with geometric and cross motifs and a horse.

35in (89cm) long

$25,000-30,000 **SK**

A rare Plains carved wood triple-blade gunstock club, set with three butcher knife blades marked 'Lamson and Goodnow Mfg. Co. Patent March 6, 1860', decorated with brass tacks, some missing.

c1860 *38.75in (98cm) long*

$40,000-60,000 **SK**

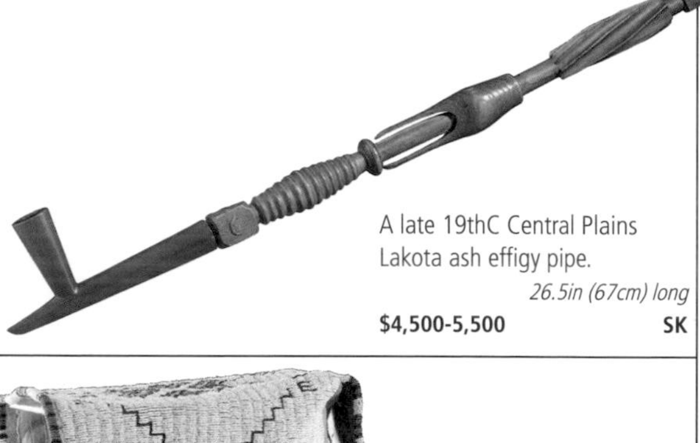

A late 19thC Central Plains Lakota ash effigy pipe.

26.5in (67cm) long

$4,500-5,500 **SK**

A late 19thC Central Plains Lakota beaded hide and cloth cradle.

24.5in (62cm) high

$10,000-15,000 **SK**

A late 19thC Central Plains Lakota beaded hide vest, the back decorated with four American flags and the name 'T.S. Cord', with restoration and bead loss.

18in (46cm) long

$2,500-3,500 **SK**

A pair of late 19thC Central Plains beaded hide woman's high-top moccasins.

16in (41cm) high

$4,000-6,000 **SK**

A late 19thC Central Plains beaded hide leggings, decorated with beaded strips with geometric designs.

31in (79cm) long

$3,000-4,000 **SK**

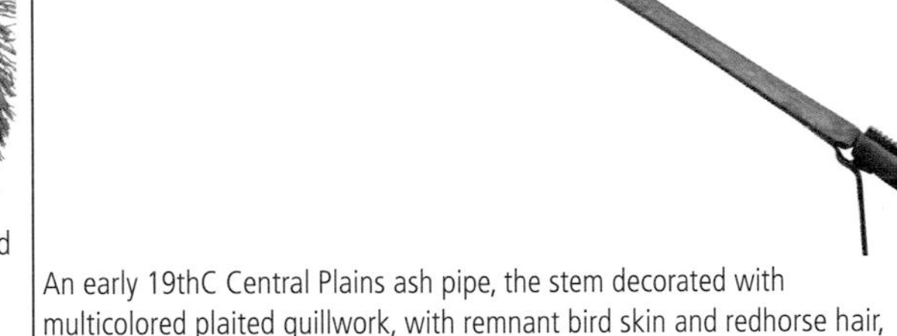

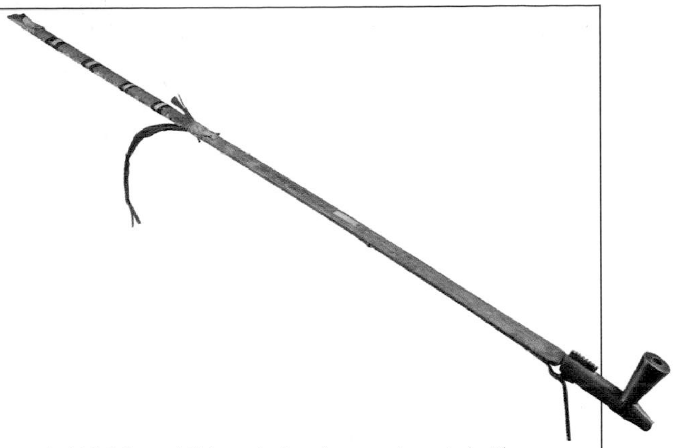

An early 19thC Central Plains ash pipe, the stem decorated with multicolored plaited quillwork, with remnant bird skin and redhorse hair, with old tag reading 'Pipe Stem, Sioux Indian'.

41in (104cm) long

$20,000-30,000 **SK**

A late 19thC Central Plains Lakota beaded and quilled hide pipebag, decorated with American flags, the reverse with two mounted warriors chasing a buffalo.

With fringe 40.5in (103cm) long

$25,000-30,000 **SK**

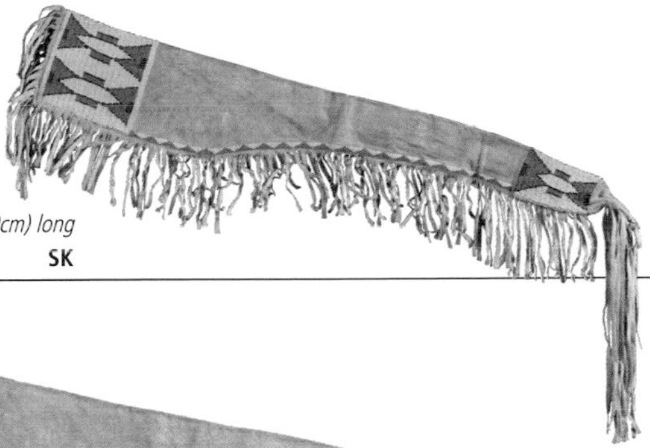

A Central Plains Lakota beaded hide rifle scabbard.

c1900 *39in (99cm) long*

$4,000-6,000 **SK**

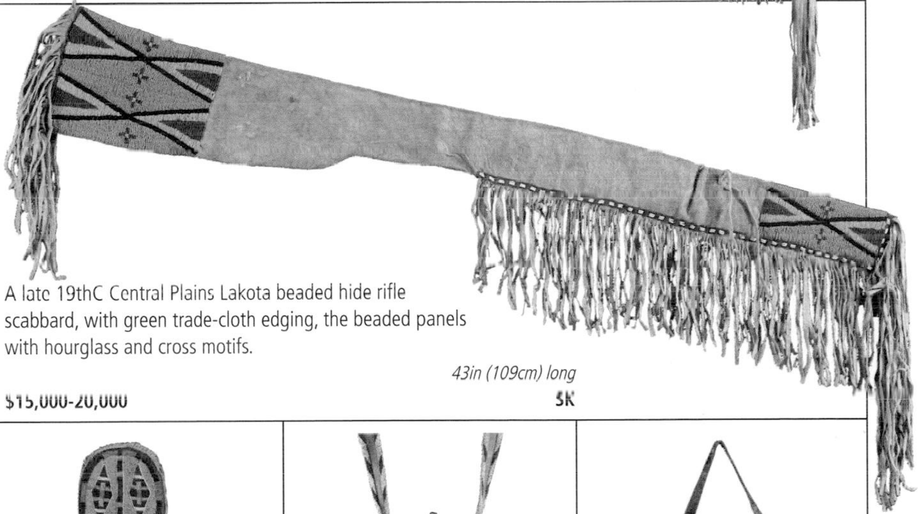

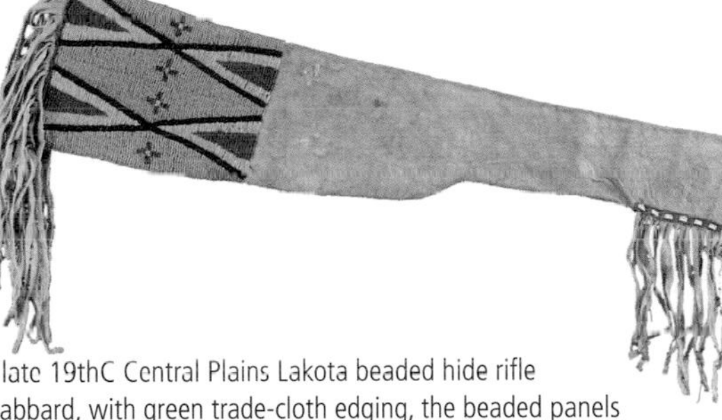

A late 19thC Central Plains Lakota beaded hide rifle scabbard, with green trade-cloth edging, the beaded panels with hourglass and cross motifs.

43in (109cm) long

$15,000-20,000 **SK**

A large early 20thC Northern Plains Crow beaded wood, hide and cloth cradle, with a commercial doll.

33in (84cm) long

$5,000-7,000 **SK**

A late 19thC Northern Plains Crow partial bridle.

With cheek straps 17in (43cm) long

$2,500-3,500 **SK**

A late 19thC Southern Plains Kiowa beaded commercial-leather and hide dispatch bag.

11in (28cm) long

$12,000-18,000 **SK**

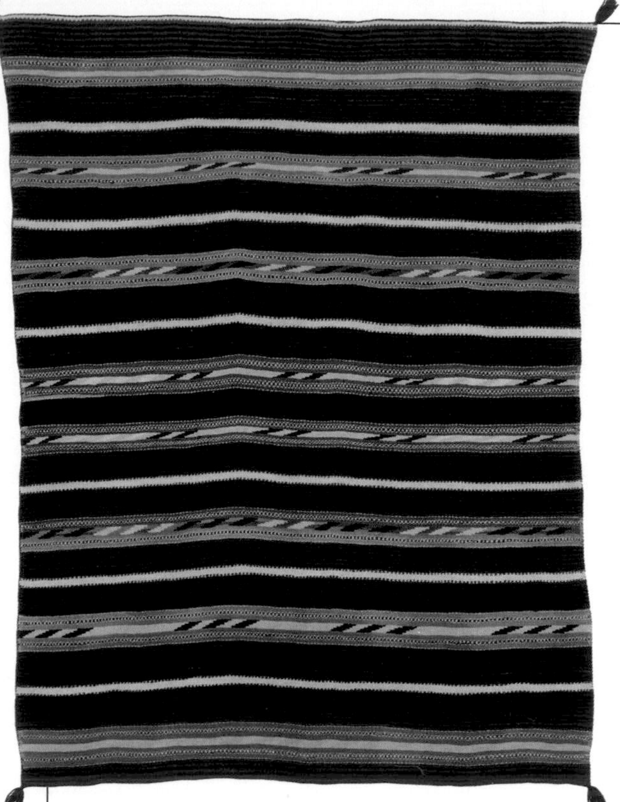

A Southwest Navajo Late-Classic-Period 'Moqui' blanket, woven with commercial and hand-spun yarns, with some restoration.

During the Late Classic Period (c1800-68), the Navajo made three types of serape-style blankets, all of which were longer than they were wide. The 'Moqui' (or Moki) pattern consisted of alternating stripes of indigo and natural brown, often separated by narrow white stripes. Early traders thought these blankets were made by the Hopi, hence they the name 'Moqui': the Spanish word for the Hopi people.

64in (163cm) long

$25,000-30,000 SK

A Southwest Navajo Late-Classic-Period child's blanket.

Provenance: Collected by William Wallace Borst in Colorado while working for the Denver and Rio Grand Railroad.

c1860 47in (119cm) long

$12,000-18,000 SK

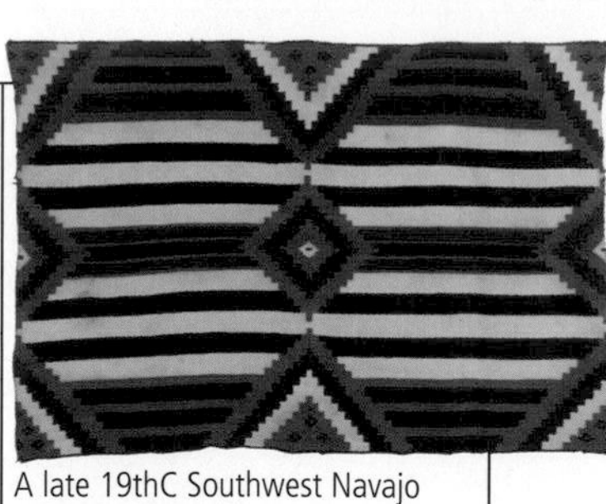

A late 19thC Southwest Navajo weaving, in natural and synthetic dyed homespun wool, in a third phase chief's pattern.

76in (193cm) long

$8,000-12,000 SK

An early 20thC Southwest Navajo weaving, in natural and synthetic dyed homespun wool.

64in (163cm) long

$2,000-3,000 SK

An early 20thC Southwest Navajo regional weaving, Two Grey Hills, in natural homespun wool.

The community of Two Grey Hills is known for bordered rugs with geometric patterning in natural sheep's colors of tan, brown, gray, black and white.

82.5in (210cm) long

$6,500-7,500 SK

A mid-20thC Southwest Navajo regional weaving, in natural and synthetic dyed wool.

84.5in (215cm) long

$4,000-6,000 SK

A Southwest Hopi carved wood kachina doll, depicted wearing a green tablita.

13.75in (35cm) high

$650-850 SK

A Southwest carved blackware bowl, Santa Clara, signed 'Margaret Tafoya, Santa Clara Pue. N. Mex', with small chip.

9.5in (24cm) diam

$2,500-3,500 SK

A pair of late 19thC Apaché beaded hide high-top moccasins.

17.5in (44cm) high

$5,500-6,500 SK

A Pre-Columbian Mexican Olmec carved jade figure.

c1150-550 BC *1.75in (4.5cm) high*

$1,500-2,500 **SK**

A Pre-Columbian Peruvian Chavin carved stone mortar, in the form of a fanged feline with curled tail.

c500-100 BC *7in (18cm) long*

$4,000-6,000 **SK**

A Pre-Columbian Argentinian Condorhuasi carved stone mortar, in the form of a fanged feline, with damage to tail and one fang.

c200 BC-300 AD *8.5in (22cm) long*

$2,000-3,000 **SK**

A Pre-Columbian Costa Rican carved jade pendant, with avian and caiman heads.

c300-700 AD *4.75in (12cm) high*

$3,000-5,000 **SK**

A Pre-Columbian Mexican Teotihuacan pottery incensario, the lid representing Quetzalcoatl, with a feather headdress with abstract bird designs, repaired from parts.

c600-800 AD *18in (46cm) high*

$3,000-5,000 **SK**

A Pre-Columbian Taino carved bone vomit stick, the handle carved as a Zemi figure.

8in (20cm) long

$3,500-4,500 **SK**

A Pre-Columbian Costa Rican Pataky-style pottery jaguar tripod bowl, Nicoya Peninsula.

c1000-1500 AD *15.5in (39cm) long*

$6,500-7,500 **SK**

A Pre-Columbian Costa Rican Guanacaste-style pottery incensario, with repairs and clay loss.

c1000-1200 AD *19in (48cm) high*

$500-700 **SK**

An Inca Pre-Columbian Peruvian carved wood kero, carved with a lizard/jaguar peering over the rim.

c1400-1500 AD *8in (20cm) high*

$2,000-3,000 **SK**

A 19thC Aboriginal brass breastplate/king plate, engraved 'Billy King of Walloon' between an emu and a kangaroo.

7in (18cm) wide

$15,000-20,000 **SWO**

A 19thC New Zealand Maori Tiki carved wood figure, with later gold pigment at eyes.

Provenance: Collected by Rev. Alfred Fairbrother, Baptist minister to the Maoris, 1882-85.

10in (25cm) high

$12,000-18,000 **SK**

A 19thC New Zealand Maori carved wood billhook hand club, the handle with grotesque mask finial.

Provenance: Collected by Rev. Alfred Fairbrother, Baptist minister to the Maoris, 1882-85.

14.75in (37cm) long

$5,000-7,000 **SK**

A 19thC New Zealand Maori Tiki hei (greenstone pendant).

6in (15cm) high

$5,500-6,500 **SK**

A 19thC New Zealand Maori carved taiaha (long club), the finial with fourteen serrated-edged haliotis-shell inlaid 'eyes'.

62.5in (159cm) long

$4,000-6,000 **SK**

A 19thC New Zealand Maori whale bone kotiate (club), the handle with a carved mythological head with inset abalone shell eyes.

Provenance: Collected in the early 20thC.

15in (39cm) long

$30,000-40,000 **L&T**

A New Zealand Maori Waka huia (feather box and cover), with rauponga decoration, with tiki mask handles, the lid with stylized interlocking figure lifts.

Rauponga decoration consists of a row of dog-tooth notches (pakati), surrounded on each side with parallel grooves (haehae) and ridges (raumoa). Rauponga is one of the patterns very often used to fill in spaces on minor carvings and on boxes and weapons.

15.75in (39.5cm) wide

$6,500-7,500 **WW**

Judith Picks

These ceremonial forks, or 'Ai cula ni bokola', are often referred to as 'cannibal forks', suggesting that they were primarily used for cannibalistic rituals. In fact, they were implements reserved for priests and chiefs who, 'as living representatives of the gods', were prohibited from touching food with their hands. They therefore ate everything with the forks, including the flesh of their tribal enemies at ritual feasts. Forks became a way of displaying power and influence, with decorated or elaborate examples denoting higher status.

From left to right:
A 19thC Fiji Islands ceremonial or cannibal fork.

13.5in (34.25cm) long

$9,000-11,000

A 19thC carved wooden Fiji Islands ceremonial or cannibal fork.

10.5in (26.5cm) long

$12,000-18,000

A 19thC Fiji Islands carved wood ceremonial or cannibal fork.

17in (46cm) long

$5,500-6,500

A 19thC Fiji Islands wooden ceremonial or cannibal fork.

9.6in (24.5cm) long

$5,550-6,500

Two Fiji Islands ceremonial or cannibal forks (one upright).

Larger 7.5in (19.5cm) long

$9,000-11,000

A 19thC Fiji Islands wooden ceremonial or cannibal fork.

7.5in (19cm) long

$6,500-7,500 **MART**

A 19thC Polynesian carved wood war club, Marquesas Islands, with projecting tiki heads, with incised stylized devices on the lower section.

60.5in (154cm) long

$55,000-65,000 **SK**

An early 20thC Bornean Dayak bidayuh clan mask, depicting a shaman.

These masks were used in ritual dances.

11in (28cm) high

$1,200-1,800 **DRA**

An early to mid-20thC Bornean Kayan/Kenyah Dayak hudoq mask, with bone fangs and rattan basketry helmet, the eyes with small mirrors, the horn appendages reglued.

These masks were typically used in agricultural dances. The painted red, black and white designs mimick rainforest vines.

20in (51cm) high

$1,200-1,800 **DRA**

An early 20thC Indonesian Sumba Island limestone memorial sculpture, with erosion consistent with tribal use.

These were used locally as markers for sacred sites.

21.5in (55cm) high

$1,500-2,500 **DRA**

A 19thC Polynesian carved wood stilt step, Marquesas Islands.

14.5in (37cm) high

$4,500-5,500 **SK**

A mid-20thC Papua New Guinea carved wood gable mask, Sepik River, depicting an ancestral spirit face.

91in (231cm) long

$1,000-1,500 **DRA**

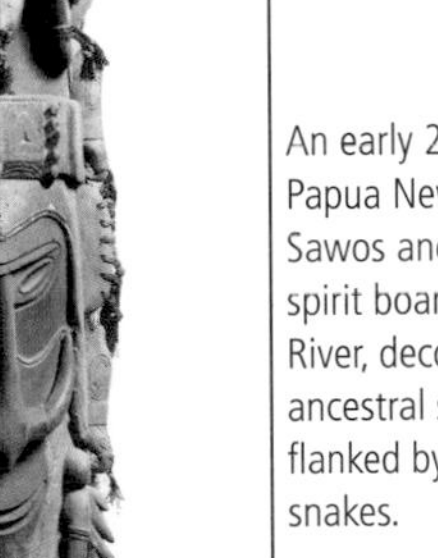

A mid-20thC Papua New Guinea carved wood totem, Ramu River, decorated with avian and canine figures and an ancestral face, with cassowary bird feathers.

The cassowaries are very large flightless birds, native to the tropical forests of New Guinea and north-eastern Australia.

91in (231cm) long

$2,500-3,500 **DRA**

An early 20thC Papua New Guinea Sawos ancestral spirit board, Sepik River, decorated with ancestral spirit masks flanked by birds and snakes.

79.5in (202cm) long

$4,000-6,000 **L&T**

A Scottish 2-bore steel flintlock belt pistol, with engraved silver and brass decoration, with traces of a signature at the base.

c1700 *15.5in (39cm) long*

$20,000-30,000 **TDM**

A pair of flintlock sidelock cannon-barreled pistols, by David Wynn, London, signed 'Wynn, London', with walnut butts, with silver side plates and grotesque masks.

David Wynn (d.1729) started business in St James, Westminster, London in 1720. He was free of the Gunmakers' Company by redemption as of 7th April 1715.

c1730 *Barrel 4.25in (10.5cm) long*

$4,000-6,000 **L&T**

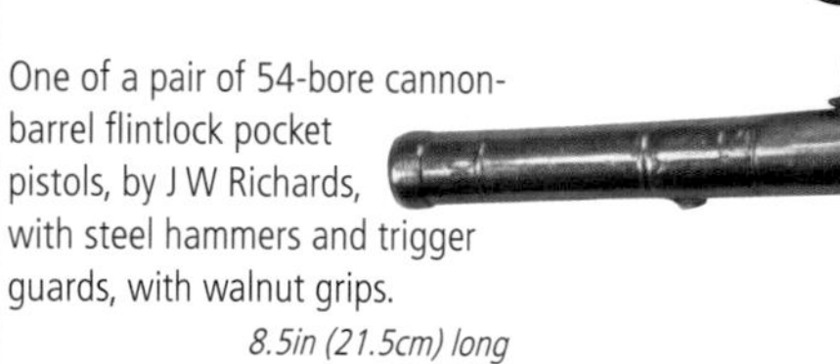

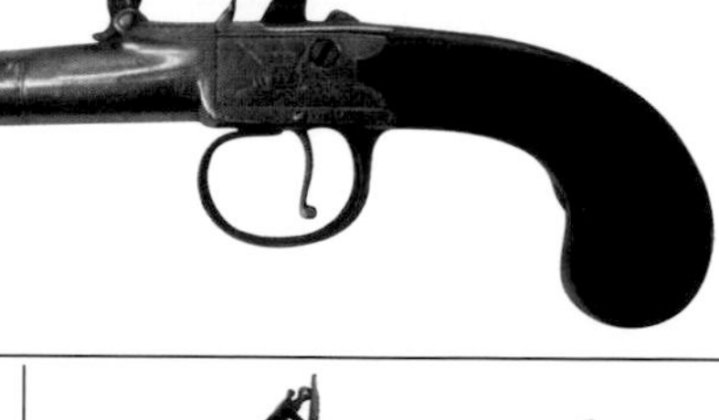

One of a pair of 54-bore cannon-barrel flintlock pocket pistols, by J W Richards, with steel hammers and trigger guards, with walnut grips.

8.5in (21.5cm) long

$2,500-3,500 pair **A&G**

A pair of 25-bore flintlock dueling pistols, by John Twigg, London, the barrels and locks signed, the barrel stamped with barrelsmith's mark, crowned 'IT' and London proof marks, engraved with beadwork at the breech, the breech tang and trigger-guard engraved with flowerheads, the walnut stock carved with a shell, with horn-tipped ramrods.

c1766-70 *15.25in (38.8cm) long*

$15,000-20,000 **TDM**

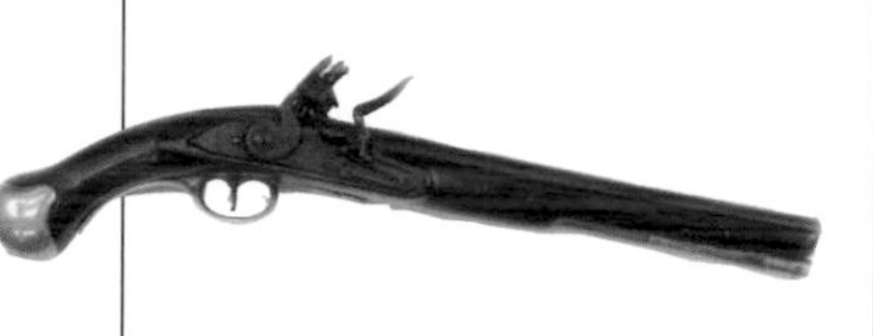

A naval service flintlock pistol, the lock with an unbridled frizzen.

19.5in (49.5cm) long

$2,500-3,500 **WW**

A pair of 18thC Turkish silver-inlaid flintlock pistols.

14in (35.5cm) long

$7,000-10,000 **JN**

An Indian flintlock dagger pistol, with steel lock and spring-loaded bayonet operated when the trigger is pulled, the gilt-metal butt with cast foliate decoration and inset with semi precious stones.

c1770 *15in (96cm) long*

$10,000-15,000 **L&T**

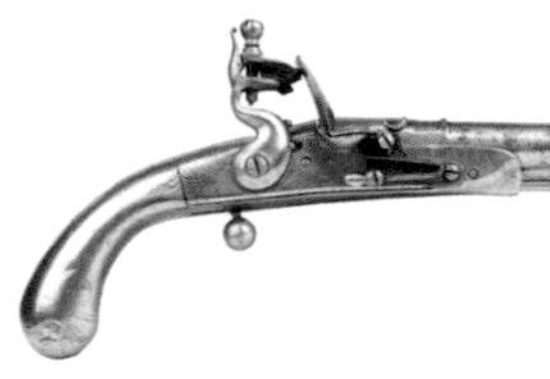

A Scottish 17-bore flintlock steel and silver lobe-butt pistol, with four-stage barrel, with original belt-hook steel ramrod.

c1770 *10in (25cm) long*

$3,000-5,000 **L&T**

A cased pair of 18thC officer's pistols, by Innes, Edinburgh, the engraved locks with safety slides signed 'Innes', the barrels engraved 'Edinburgh', with walnut full-stocks, with associated case and accessories, with restoration, with replacement ramrods.

c1780 *35.56in (14cm) long*

$6,500-7,500 **L&T**

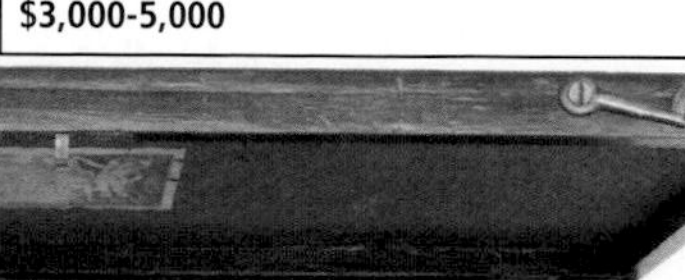

A cased pair of 25-bore flintlock dueling pistols, signed 'H. W. Mortimer Gunmaker to His Majesty', with figured walnut full-stocks, the barrels and locks signed, with engraved steel mounts, with original case and some accessories.

Harvey Walklate Mortimer was made Gunmaker in Ordinary to George III in 1783.

c1785-90 *15.5in (39.5cm) long*

$25,000-30,000 **TDM**

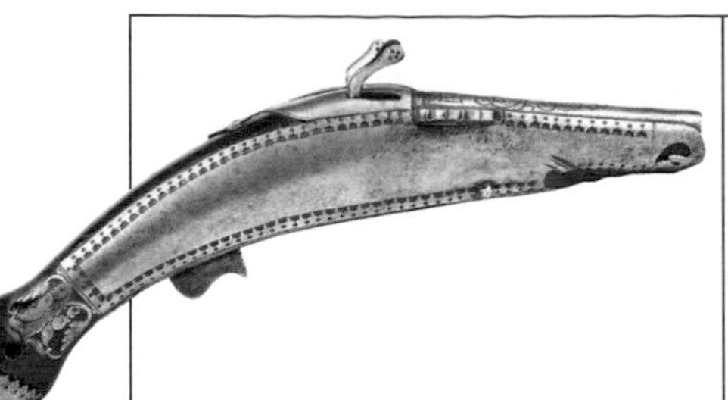

An Indian 28-bore matchlock double-barrel pistol, missing ramrod.

c1790 *9in (22cm) long*

$5,500-6,500 **L&T**

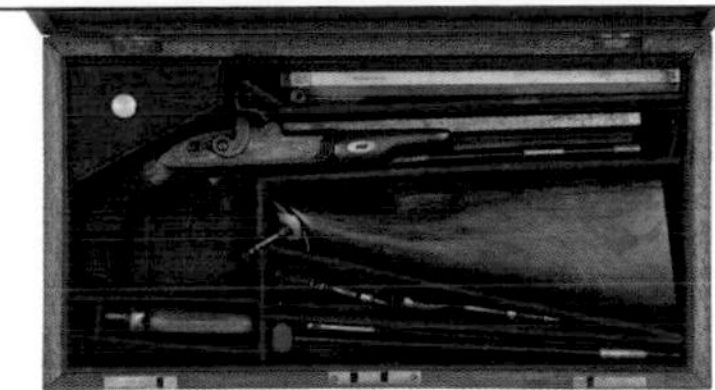

A cased 30-bore percussion pistol/carbine, by Robertson, Haddington, the barrel engraved 'Haddington', the lock engraved with scrolls and signed 'Robertson', with walnut half-stock, with steel mounts, with original case containing interchangeable rifled barrel, walnut shoulder stock and accessories.

16.5in (42cm) long

$20,000-30,000 **W&W**

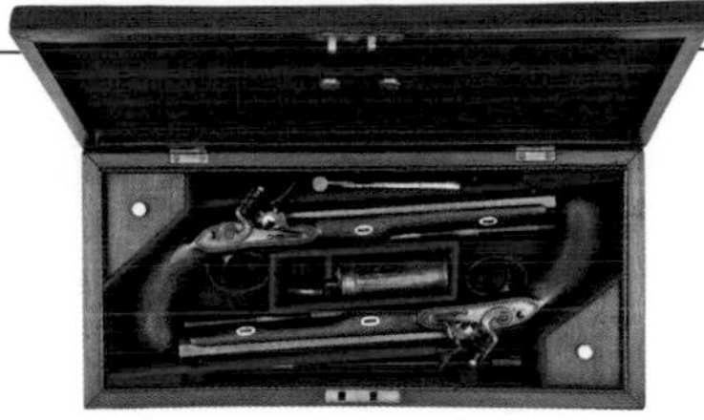

A cased pair of 26-bore flintlock dueling pistols, by Joseph Manton, London, no.1563 the octagonal twist barrels inlaid with gold, with rainproof pans, the plates engraved with fern tip borders and signed 'Joseph Manton London', the walnut full-stocks inlaid with silver, with steel mounts, with original case and accessories.

1801 *15in (38cm) long*

$20,000-30,000 **W&W**

A cased pair of 38-bore flintlock dueling pistols, by John Manton & Son, Dover Street, London, no. 10129, the octagonal barrels signed and stamped with Galway census numbers '3575' and '3576', with barrelsmith's mark, the breeches and tangs engraved with scrolls of foliage and inlaid with platinum, the walnut half-stocks with silver escutcheons, with original brass-tipped ramrods, with original case and some accessories.

1827 *15in (38cm) long*

$50,000-70,000 **TDM**

A rare boxed pair of Moore 'No.1' silver- and gold-plated derringers. nos.4092 and 4138, cal. 41 RF., engraved with foliate arabesque patterns, the barrels marked 'MOORE'S PAT. F.A. CO. BROOKLYN, N.Y.' and patent date '1863', with original box.

According to 'Flayderman's Guide to Antique American Firearms', around 3,000 Moore 'No.1' derringers were produced 1860-65.

$30,000-40,000 **JDJ**

A Victorian percussion service holster pistol, cal. 0.577, the lock plate stamped 'Tower 1857' and crowned 'V.R.', with walnut stock and grip.

16in (40.5cm) long

$2,500-3,500 **A&G**

A rare Reid silver-plated 'knuckle duster' pistol, no.6040, cal. 41, the top strap marked 'J. REID'S DERRINGER' with patent date, the frame engraved with foliate arabesque patterns.

According to 'Flayderman's Guide to Antique American Firearms', only c150 of these pistols were produced 1870-72, making this an extremely rare American pistol.

$40,000-60,000 **JDJ**

CLOSER LOOK - LE PETIT PROTECTOR

The cartridges are glued into place and are not removable.

The ring is in good condition with the steel parts retaining nearly all their original bright blue.

The six-shot revolving cylinder has a spring detent bolt and is manually rotated with knurled bead at the top of cylinder.

The pinfire cartridge was invented by Casimir Lefaucheux in 1828 and was one of the earliest practical designs of a metallic cartridge. The priming compound in such cartridges is ignited by striking a small pin that protrudes from just above the base of the cartridge.

Reputedly, 'Le Petit Protector' was sold mainly to gamblers.

A cased 'Le Petit Protector' ring/pistol, no.NSN, cal. 4mm, with German-silver finger loop, engraved 'Le Petit Protector' and with acanthus motifs, with original leather and silver case, with five pinfire cartridges.

$30,000-40,000 **JDJ**

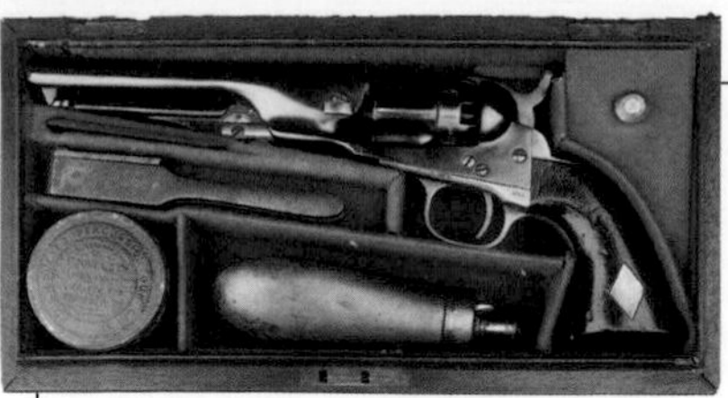

A cased Colt .36 calibre revolver, with brass frame and trigger guard, the walnut grip inlaid with silver, with case and accessories.

11in (27cm) long

$6,500-7,500 L&T

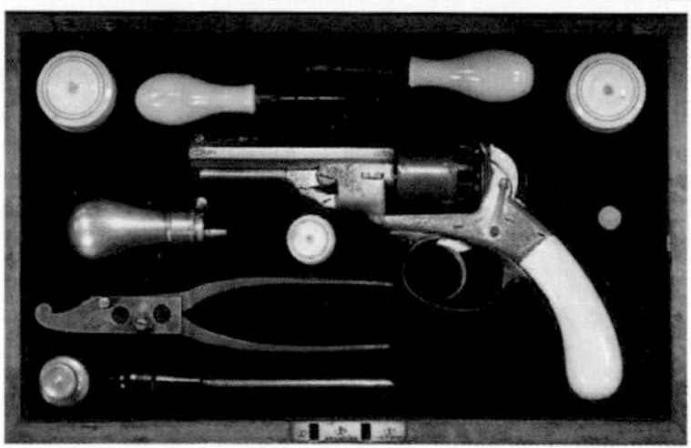

A cased Victorian 110-bore gilt-metal and ivory presentation percussion cap revolver, signed 'James Beattie, 205, Regent Street, London', no.2731, the hexagonal barrel with Victoria and London proof marks, with original case and accessories.

$6,500-7,500 GORL

CLOSER LOOK - COLT ARMY REVOLVER

This revolver has a crisp, brilliant shiny bore and no evidence of ever having been fired.

'OWA' stands for Orville Wood Ainsworth, who was the ordnance sub-inspector at the Colt factory for the first 13 months of the single-action army revolver's production (October 1873-November 1874). Colt single-action army revolvers produced during this period are rare and valuable.

The ejector rod housing is of the first type, with bull's eye ejector rod head.

The base pin is of the original type, with dimpled front end.

This revolver was produced in 1874 during the height of the Indian wars where the majority of martially marked single-actions were shipped to various cavalry units serving from Texas, New Mexico, Arizona and all the way to Montana.

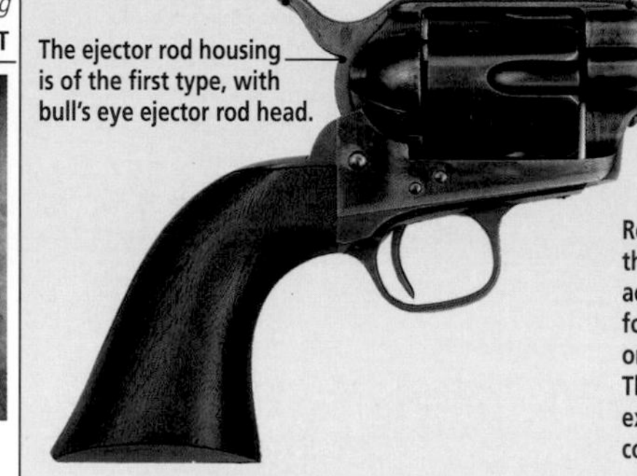

Revolvers from this series of single actions are seldom found with any original finish. This revolver is in exceptionally good condition.

A Colt cavalry single-action army revolver, no.12473. cal. 45 Colt, the walnut grip with 'OWA' cartouche, the backstrap and grip with 'A' inspector initials.

1874

$200,000-300,000 JDJ

A Colt 'Banker's Special' revolver, no.320264, cal. 38 Colt, engraved by Arnold Griebel with foliate patterns, one sideplate inlaid 'HMG', the other with a boar's head, the buttstrap inscribed 'ENGR. BY A. GRIEBEL', with ivory grips, with a Safariland brown leather holster.

Given the deluxe treatment (even the screw heads are engraved) and the inlaid initials, it seems likely that this revolver was engraved for one of Griebel's family members.

$8,000-12,000 JDJ

A rare Smith & Wesson engraved 'No.3' third-model Russian single-action revolver, no.49727, cal. 44 Russian, engraved by L D Nimschke with foliate arabesque patterns, the muzzle signed 'L.D.N. / N.Y.', the keyhole-shape barrel engraved with patent date 'AUG 24 69' and 'W.C. DODGE'S PATENT EXTRACTOR', with pearl grip.

The third model Russian was made in fairly large quantities. However, extremely few are so profusely engraved.

$120,000-180,000 JDJ

A rare Colt sheriff's model single-action army revolver, no.145300, cal. 45 Colt, marked with two-line address, calibre marking, '45M', two-line patent dates and rampant Colt in a circle, with rampant Colt hard rubber grips.

Barrel 3in (7.5cm) long

$350,000-400,000 JDJ

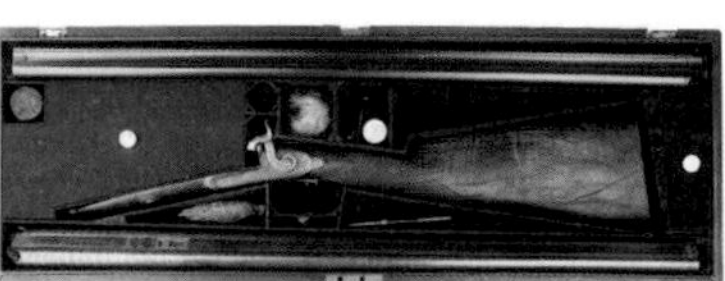

A cased Scottish 16-bore percussion sporting gun-rifle, signed 'Charles Ingram, Glasgow', complete with a set of rifled barrels, with folding leaf sights 100, 150 and 200 yards all signed, with case and some accessories.

c1850 *28in (71cm) long*

$10,000-15,000 L&T

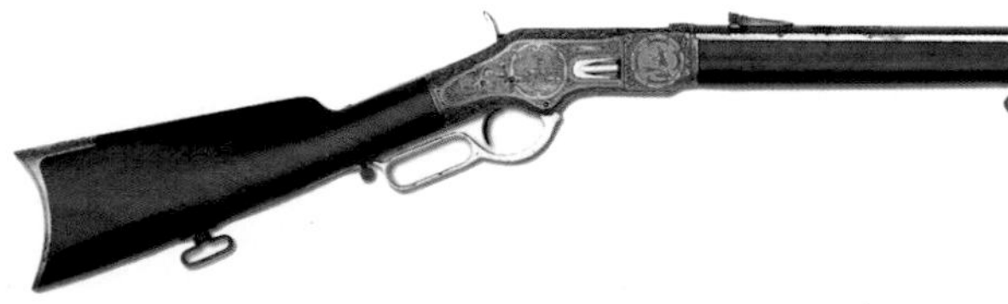

A Winchester relief-engraved 'Model 1866' lever-action rifle, no.96741, cal. 44 RF Henry, probably engraved by John Ulrich with hunting scenes and foliate arabesque patterns, with a gold-washed Beech's combination front sight and a reproduction Henry 900 yard ladder rear sight, with crotch-walnut stock.

This rifle was purchased recently by well-known dealer and collector LeRoy Merz from the great-great grandson of the former King of Spain. By repute, the rifle was presented personally to the king by Oliver Winchester.

$350,000-400,000 JDJ

A 17thC probably European dagger, with double-edged wavy blade and oak handle.

12in (30cm) long

$500-700 **CAPE**

A Caucasian silver-mounted Kindjal, the hilt decorated with gilt and niello scrolls, wire work and bosses, the hilt and scabbard stamped '84X KHK'.

Blade 15in (38cm) long

$5,000-7,000 **A&G**

A 19thC Indian jade-hilted dagger, the blade with reinforced back-edge, the silver ferrule engraved with stylized foliage, the pommel set with a red paste, with silver-mounted leather-covered wooden scabbard.

14in (35.5cm) long

$3,000-4,000 **TDM**

A 19thC Indian dagger, the recurved double-edged blade with reinforced tip and long fullers, decorated with gilt koftgari, the steel hilt in the form of a bird's head and decorated with flowerheads, with wooden scabbard.

14in (35.5cm) long

$1,500-2,500 **TDM**

A 19thC Balkan silver-mounted dagger, the watered-steel blade double-edged toward the point, the silver ferrule repoussé-decorated with scrolls, beadwork and foliage, the ivory grip set with turquoises in silver settings, with silver repoussé-decorated scabbard set with turquoises.

10.5in (27cm) long

$2,000-3,000 **TDM**

A Scagel hunting knife, the brass hilt with leather, red fiber and silver spacers and a silver plate to base, the blade with maker's mark and Kris mark, with original leather sheath.

Scagel's bird's head pommel knives are relatively rare.

10.25in (26cm) long

$20,000-30,000 **JDJ**

A Scagel camp knife, with brass guard, Scagel-style stacked handle and long whitetailed-deer antler pommel, the blade with maker's mark and Kris mark, with Joseph Dieken leather sheath, the knife and sheath in mint condition.

13.5in (34.5cm) long

$50,000-70,000 **JDJ**

ESSENTIAL REFERENCE - WILLIAM SCAGEL

William 'Bill' Scagel (1873-1963) was born in Michigan, USA. Before he began making the knives he is now best known for in c1910, he was a sheet-metal worker in the shipping industry. He also worked as a gunsmith, a machinist and a builder of bridges.

- **He designed and built his own machining and forging equipment and powered his home and workshop with a windmill, old submarine batteries and a Cadillac engine.**
- **The distinctive layered handles of Scagel knives were made from objects that were easy to acquire from the area around Scagel's Michigan workshop.**
- **Although contemporary reports suggest he was viewed as a potentially murderous eccentric, Scagel is known to have performed acts of kindness, such as making free leg braces for children with polio.**

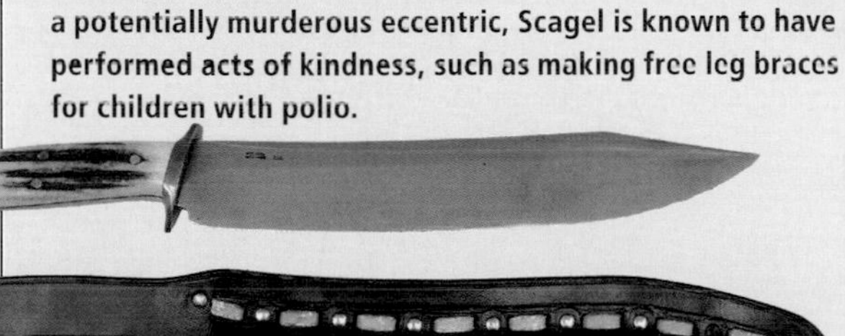

A rare large Scagel 'VL&A' Bowie knife, the brass hilt mounted with elk-stag antler, the blade with maker's stamp and 'USA' and 'VL&A', with original leather Scagel sheath, the blade and sheath in mint condition.

All of Scagel's grind lines are clear.

1929 or earlier *15in (38cm) long*

$55,000-65,000 **JDJ**

Tiger-claw Dagger

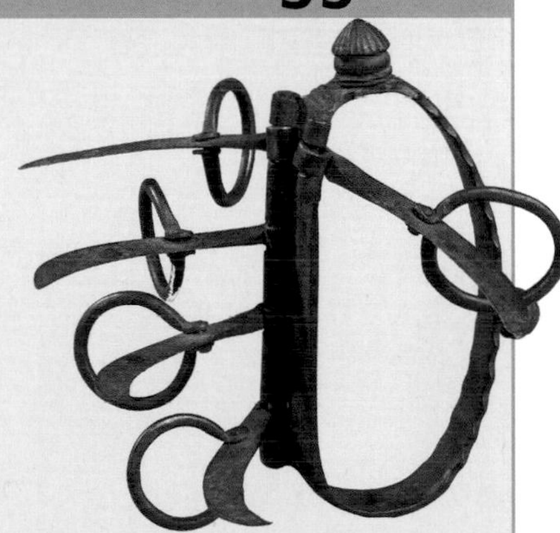

A 19thC Indian 'tiger-claw' dagger (bagh nakh), with five hooked blades mounted with rings.

4.5in (11.5cm) high

$2,000-3,000 **TDM**

CLOSER LOOK - RENAISSANCE SWORD

The decoration is in the manner of Heinrich Aldegrever of Paderborn (1502-c1555).

The distinguished quality of the present sword places it among a small group of highly decorated pieces of the same date. The closest example to the present sword is that of King Gustav Vasa of Sweden, attributed to an unknown Brunswick maker, dating to c1535-40.

The top panel is decorated with the winged figure of Justice. The panel below is decorated with the figure of Death above the date.

A German Renaissance silver-mounted hand-and-a-half sword, the earlier double-edged blade engraved 'I.N.R.I.' and with cross-and-orb mark on each face, with silver-gilt steel hilt, with original silver-gilt scabbard, part replaced, engraved with figures and dated.

'I.N.R.I. stands for 'I sus Nazar nus, R x I dae rum', which translates as 'Jesus the Nazarene, King of the Jews'.

1540 *Blade 37.5in (95cm) long*
$70,000-100,000 **TDM**

A 17thC Scottish basket-hilted broadsword, the German double-edged blade with three narrow fullers and struck on both sides with a circle and a cross, the iron hilt with 'Beaket Neb' forward guard.

37in (93cm) long
$10,000-15,000 **L&T**

A mid-17thC cup-hilted rapier, the diamond-section blade with armorial mark on the ricasso, with old repairs, with light rust.

54in (137cm) long
$2,000-3,000 **HT**

A 17thC cup-hilt rapier, the diamond-section blade inscribed 'D. Francisco-Toledo', with associated grip.

41.75in (106cm) long
$1,500-2,500 **DN**

A Scottish basket-hilted broad sword, the double-edged German blade with three fullers, the iron basket pierced with hearts and circles.

c1680 *Blade 31.5in (80cm) long*
$12,000-18,000 **L&T**

A 17th/18thC hanger, the single-edged blade with three-quarter length fuller, with brass half-basket hilt and later wooden grip.

A hanger is similar to a cutlass.

36in (91.5cm) long
$700-1,000 **A&G**

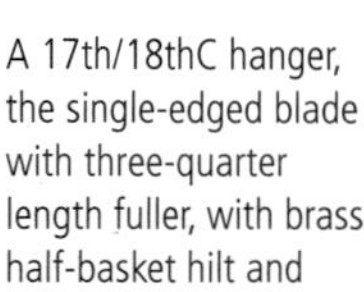

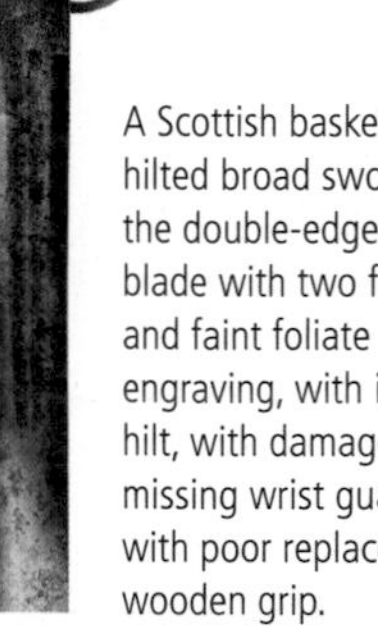

A Scottish basket-hilted broad sword, the double-edged blade with two fullers and faint foliate engraving, with iron hilt, with damage, missing wrist guard, with poor replacement wooden grip.

c1700 *94in (38cm) long*
$5,000-7,000 **L&T**

An early 18thC hunting sword, the curved fullered blade with running fox and orb armorer's marks, the brass hilt enameled with foliage and an animal head.

25.75in (65.5cm) long
$4,000-6,000 **WW**

A Scottish basket-hilted sword, the double-edged fullered blade engraved with crowned 'GR', maker's name 'Harvey' and date, the steel hilt pierced with hearts and circles, the wooden grip with original fishskin covering and brass binding.

1762 *Blade 35.75in (91cm) long*
$5,500-6,500 **TDM**

A silver-mounted hunting sword, the curved blade double-edged for the last third, the silver hilt chiseled with designs, with lion's head pommel and green-stained ivory grip, maker's mark 'HI', London, with original silver-mounted leather scabbard.

1777 *Blade 24.15in (61.5cm) long*

$3,000-4,000 **TDM**

A late 18thC/19thC Indian pattissa, the earlier steel blade decorated with silver koftgari flowers and foliage, fitted with long shaped panels, with iron talwar-form hilt, with original silver-mounted leather-covered wooden scabbard.

Blade 31.75in (80.5cm) long

$2,500-3,500 **TDM**

A French small sword, the double-edged blade with gilt and blue decoration, the steel hilt and pommel chiseled and blued with Neo-classical motifs, bound with silver wire, missing scabbard.

c1790 *34.5in (87cm) long*

$5,500-6,500 **L&T**

A French Senior Republican officer's sabre, with single-edged 'Petite Montmorency'-type blade, the brass hilt with lion's head pommel, the guard and knuckle guard pierced with scrollwork and lozenges, bound with copper wire.

c1790-95 *Blade 26.5in (67.5cm) long*

$1,200-1,800 **DN**

A '1796 pattern' heavy cavalry officer's sword, the German blade inscribed 'J. J. Runkel, Solingen', with etched and gilt decoration, the gilt-brass hilt bound with silver wire, with original scabbard impressed with two fleur-de-lys, probably for the Third Dragoon Guards, and the initials 'J. C.'.

During the early part of the French Revolutionary War, the British Army launched an expeditionary force into France. John Gaspard Le Marchant, serving as a brigade major during the conflict, noted the clumsy design of the heavy, over-long swords and decided to revolutionize the design. Working in collaboration with the Birmingham sword cutler Henry Osbor, he designed a new sabre, which was adopted by the British Army as the '1796 pattern' light cavalry sabre.

Blade 32.25in (82cm) long

$2,500-3,500 **TDM**

A '1796 pattern' light cavalry officer's sword, the curved shallow-fullered blade with etched and gilt decoration, the steel stirrup-hilt with langets, with original steel scabbard.

Blade 32.75in (83cm) long

$2,500-3,500 **DN**

An '1805 pattern' naval officer's sword, the fullered and blued blade engraved with British motifs, the gilt hilt with ivory grip and lion pommel, the knuckle guard engraved 'Used by Lord Nelson and presented by him to Lieutenant Edward Gascoine Palmer.', the gilt-mounted leather scabbard with similar inscription and monogram 'HN'.

38in (96.5cm) long

$5,000-7,000 **WAD**

A rare late 19thC infantry officer's presentation sword, the blade with presentation inscription, the ivory hilt ith chased and embossed guard with 'VR' cartouche, the silver-plated scabbard engraved with coats-of-arms and floral motifs.

1887 *40in (101.5cm) high*

$2,000-3,000 **HT**

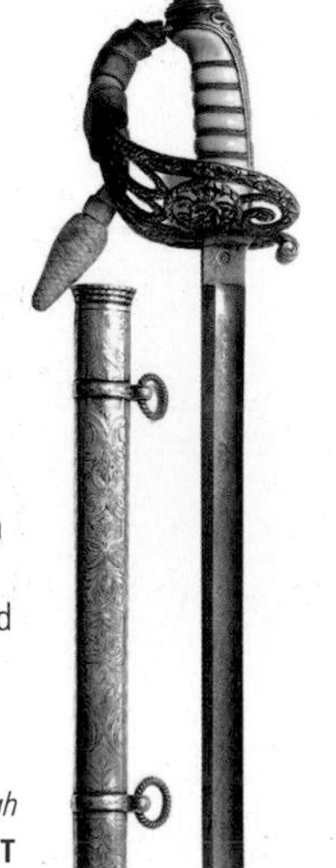

An Iraq War presentation sword, with a chrome-plate blade and gilt hilt, the original red velvet case with inscribed brass plaque.

This sword is believed to have been presented to a Major General of the Syrian Arabic Delegation and brought to the UK by a British serviceman.

$700-1,000 **DN**

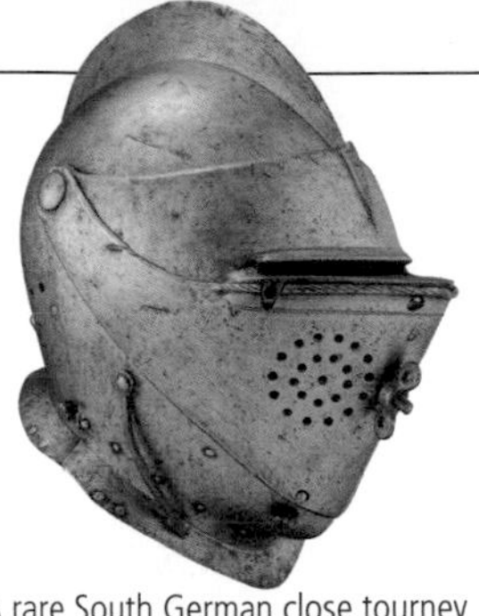

A rare South German close tourney helmet, Augsburg or Dresden, with spring-catch with button release, missing plume-holder and gorget-plates.

The strongly stepped visor, the provision for a reinforcement, the overall form and the weight of this helmet is reminiscent of the well-known group of armors made for the Elector Christian I of Saxony (1560-91).

c1590 *10.75in (27cm) high*

$35,000-45,000 TDM

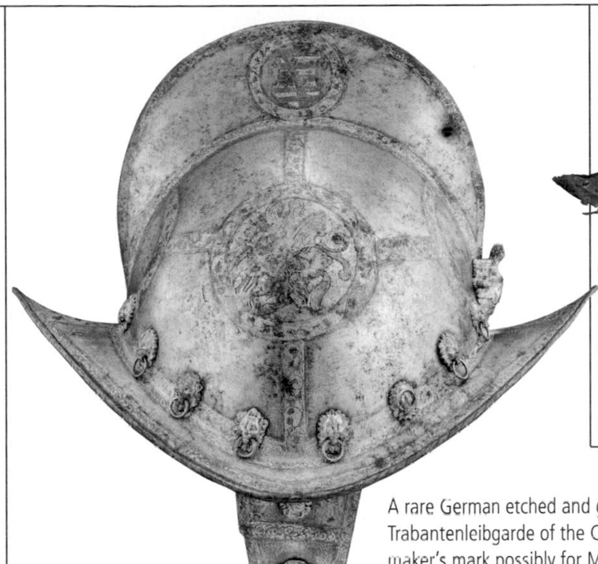

A rare German etched and gilt comb morion, for the Saxon Trabantenleibgarde of the Christian II, Elector of Saxony, maker's mark possibly for Martin Schneider, Nuremberg, with sixteen gilt-brass lions' heads and plume holder in the form of a herm, etched and gilt with scrolls and coats-of-arms.

11.75in (30cm) high

$50,000-70,000 TDM

An English pikeman's pot helmet, probably Greenwich, formed of two pieces joined by a low comb, with a fragment of a plume-holder, with losses.

c1630 *9in (23cm) high*

$1,500-2,500 TDM

A mid-17thC Dutch lobster-tail helmet, with lobster tail, ear flaps and sliding nasal bar adjusted by a butterfly bolt.

11in (28cm) high

$3,000-4,000 HT

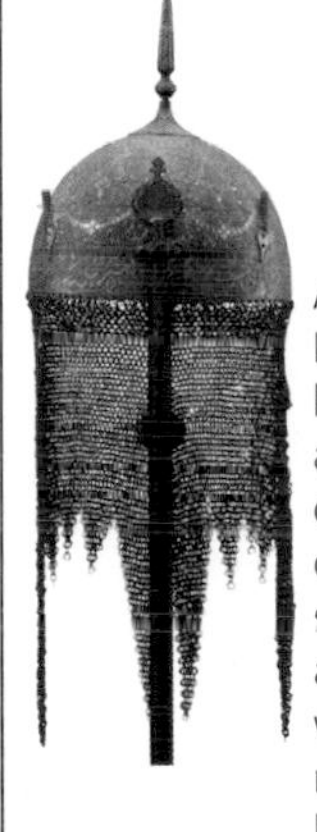

A 19thC Indo-Persian kulah khud, etched and gilt with calligraphy and cartouches of scrolling flowers and foliage, with mail neck-defense of butted links.

11in (28cm) high

$5,000-7,000 TDM

A 19thC Persian helmet, decorated with figures, birds and foliage, with script panel.

12in (30cm) high

$800-1,200 GORL

A rare South German infantry breastplate, probably by Wolfgang Großschedel, Landshut, with etched bands and borders of scrolling foliage, flowerheads, reclining nudes and trophies of arms, with minor damage.

Wolfgang Großschedel (d.c1562) was first recorded working for the British King Henry VIII in the royal workshops at Greenwich in 1517/18, but he returned to Landshut soon afterward and became a citizen there in 1521. From around 1550, he started to receive patronage from both the Spanish and Imperial courts. The decoration on this breastplate resembles that on a series of armors thought to have been delivered by him in 1560 for the use of the Emperor and his companions in a Vienna tournament of that year.

c1560 *17in (35.5cm) high*

$25,000-30,000 TDM

A late 16thC and later European composite half-set of armor, comprising close helmet, one-piece breastplate of peascod form and backplate, large symmetrical pauldrons and fully articulated 16thC vambraces.

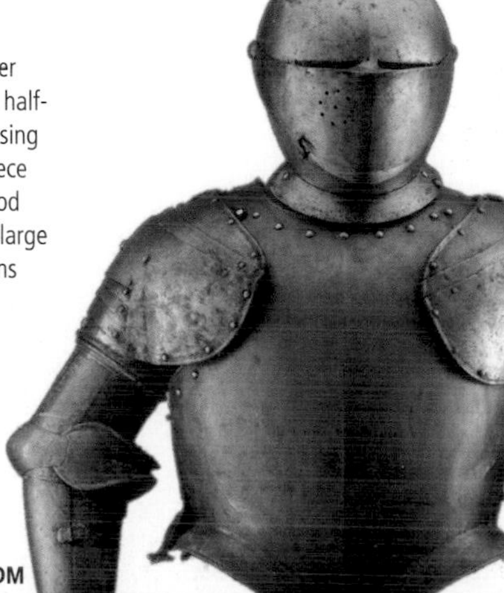

$8,000-12,000 TDM

A rare late 18thC staff officer's undress frock coat, with epaulettes to both shoulders, the straps with embroidered badge of crowns within a blue strap-and-buckle titled 'GARRISON STAFF', with silver-plated buttons.

$4,000-6,000 TDM

A lieutenant-general's undress coatee, with twist loops arranged in threes, with gilt-metal general officer's buttons.

1811-25

$4,000-6,000 TDM

A company officer's short-tailed coatee for the 52nd (The Oxfordshire) Regiment of Foot, the buttons embossed '52' within a laurel wreath, missing two buttons and light infantry pattern 'wing' epaulettes.

This jacket was worn by John Hart while serving with his regiment at the battle of Waterloo, as well as in the subsequent pursuit of the defeated French army and in the occupation of France.

1814-16

$25,000-30,000 TDM

A Hungarian k und k Major General of the Cavalry's complete gala uniform, complete with officer's sword cupola and cavalry officer's sword, model no.1869, with mannequin.

The boots are of brown leather, rather than the regulation black.

1910-11

$25,000-30,000 DOR

A rare World War I RAF lieutenant's tunic, with pilot's wings, with gilt crown/eagle badges, with a pair of overalls, marked 'S F J Fells'.

$1,200-1,800 W&W

An Imperial Russian officer's full dress tunic, the cuffs embroidered 'I', the shoulder straps with crowned 'WM' and 'NII' cypher, the buttons with Imperial eagle, with associated breast badge.

$1,200-1,800 W&W

A naval officer's bicorn hat, epaulettes and sword belt, by Gieves Ltd, with tin case painted 'J.F. Harvey, R.N.'.

$700-1,000 A&G

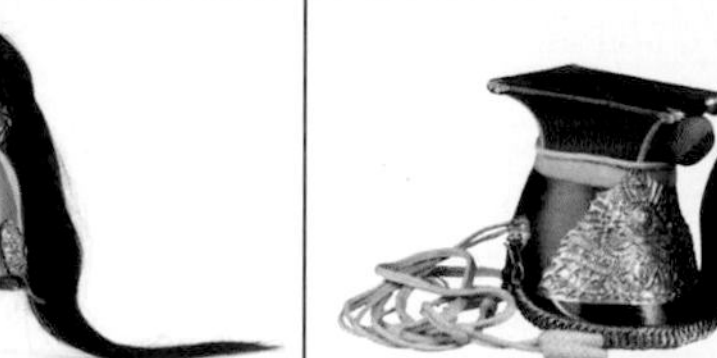

An enlisted ranks gilt-metal helmet for the 6th Inniskilling Dragoons, the front rayed plate with Royal coat-of-arms and honour scroll inscribed 'WATERLOO', the title band inscribed 'INNISKILLING DRAGOONS', with black horsehair plume.

1843 - 47

$5,000-7,000 DN

An officer's lance cap of the 'FIFTH ROYAL IRISH LANCERS', with embossed brass plate and lion's head ear bosses, the red and yellow wool rosette with 'VR' brass button, with stained hair plume, with stamped numbers and small paper label to visor.

8.5in (22.5cm) high

$1,000-1,500 A&G

An infantry officer's helmet for 'THE KINGS OWN YORKSHIRE LIGHT INFANTRY', signed 'J.R. Gaunt & Son Ltd, 53, Conduit Street, London', the brass spike embossed with Yorkshire roses, the brass and steel plate on black felt body, with Yorkshire rose ear bosses and felt backed brass linked chin-chain, with maker's label, in tin case.

11in (28cm) high

$1,200-1,800 A&G

A Military General Service medal, awarded to James Ashcroft, 48th Regiment of Foot, with clasps for 'ALBUHERA', 'BUSACO' and 'TALAVERA'.

$2,500-3,500 DN

An 1815 Waterloo medal, awarded to Sergeant Joseph Jackson, 2nd Battalion, 30th (Cambridgeshire) Regiment of Foot, the original ring suspension replaced with clasp engraved 'PENISULA 30th REGT'.

1815

$5,000-7,000 DN

An 1841-42 China War medal, awarded to Lieutenant William Bailey, HMS Vixen, the medal mounted as a pin.

1841-42

$800-1,200 WW

A Crimea medal, awarded to G Weller, 2nd Battalion Rifle Brigade, with clasps for 'SEBASTOPOL', 'INKERMANN' and 'ALMA'.

$650-850 A&G

An 1881 Afghanistan medal, awarded posthumously to Private H Martin, 66th Regiment of Foot.

On the 27th of July 1880, at the battle of Maiwand, 2,700 British and Indian troops, including the 66th Foot (later the Royal Berkshires), engaged an Afghan force of over 25,000. Although hugely outnumbered and with many young recruits who had not completed weapons training, the 66th fought with extraordinary bravery. After finally being over-run, the 66th fell back but a group of around 200 rallied on the bank of a ravine at Khig. The group were surrounded and their commanding office was dead, but they fought on, effecting a second stand in a small mud-walled garden, until the remaining officer's and men of the 66th gave their lives protecting the regimental colors.

$3,000-4,000 DN

An Army of India medal, awarded to William Fordyce Blair, Mate RN, with clasp for 'AVA'.

$6,500-7,500 L&T

An 1878-80 Afghanistan Medal, awarded to Corporal C Thompson, 2/15th Regiment of Foot.

1878-80

$250-350 A&G

An 1882 Egypt medal, awarded to Private G Tester, 1st Royal Sussex Regiment, with clasps for 'ABU KLEA', 'THE NILE 1884-85', 'EL-TEB_TAMAAI' and 'SUAKIN 1884'.

1882

$1,500-2,500 GORL

An 1879 South Africa medal, awarded to Private W Greenaway, 1-24th Regiment of Foot, with clasp.

1879

$1,200-1,800 TEN

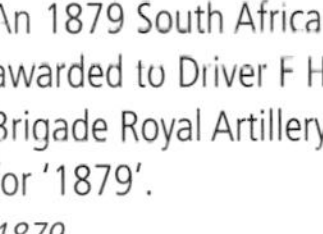

An 1879 South Africa medal, awarded to Driver F H Galpin, 5th Brigade Royal Artillery, with clasp for '1879'.

1879

$1,200-1,800 DN

A 1909 India General Service medal, awarded to Private J C Morgan, RAF, with clasp for 'Waziristan 1925'.

$1,200-1,800 TEN

A 1918 Royal Naval Meritorious Service medal, awarded to Deckhand H Burman, Royal Naval Reserve.

$650-850 DN

A Royal Artillery enameled and diamond badge, set with rose-cut diamonds, the banner inscribed 'UBIQUE QUO FAS ET GLORIA DUCUNT', with case.

1.5in (3.5cm) wide

$650-850 **L&T**

A Victorian helmet plate for the 'HANTS RIFLE VOLUNTEERS'.

$250-350 **W&W**

A 1869 pattern shako plate for the 22nd (Cheshire) Regiment.

$300-500 **W&W**

A Victorian glengarry badge for the '2ND VOLR BATTN' 'ROYAL SUSSEX'.

$200-300 **W&W**

A mid-19thC Royal Horseguards officer's buckle.

4in (10cm) high

$1,000-1,500 **A&G**

An American Revolutionary War powder horn, decorated with a ship, anchor, crown, gun and tomahawk, inscribed 'Adam Fischer Merland1775', 'Liberty/J. Braberdy/or Death' and 'Kil or be Kild', missing plug.

1775 *13.5in (34cm) long*

$2,000-3,000 **SK**

A late 19thC scrimshaw powder horn, decorated with masonic and other symbols.

12.5in (32cm) long

$1,500-2,500 **TRI**

A gunner's powder horn, the wooden base with screw-in plug and brass nozzle.

13in (33cm) long

$200-300 **W&W**

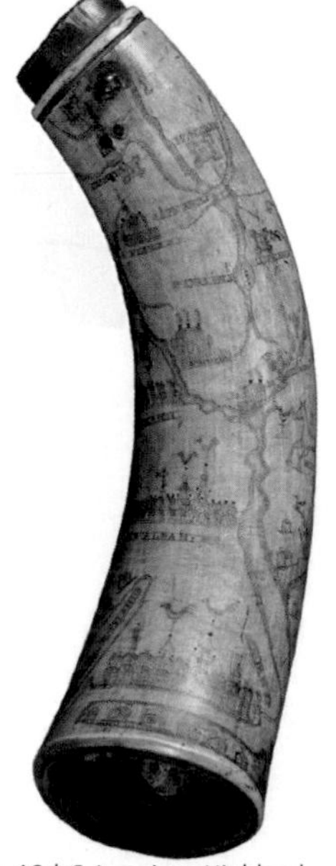

An 18thC American Highland militia power horn, engraved with a map of New York depicting forts, settlements and rivers of strategic importance during the early stages of the French Indian War.

c1756 *10.25in (26cm) long*

$15,000-20,000 **LA**

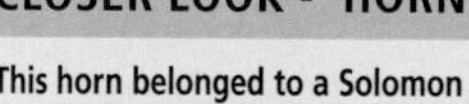

CLOSER LOOK - HORN

This horn belonged to a Solomon Lumbard, a Revolutionary War soldier born in Lebanon, Connecticut, who fought in the Battle of Bunker Hill (Massachusetts) and the Battle of White Plains (New York).

The inscription 'ELIR ELIPH BEN' appears to be contemporary with the rest of the scrimshaw and may refer to the names of the maker's family.

This horn was discovered more than 30 years ago in an old house in West Virginia. It was purchased from a carpenter preparing to demolish the house who stated that it was discovered inside a cupboard.

This horn is in remarkable condition and has aged to an attractive medium yellow color.

The decoration represents a primitive style associated with some of the best 18thC American folk art.

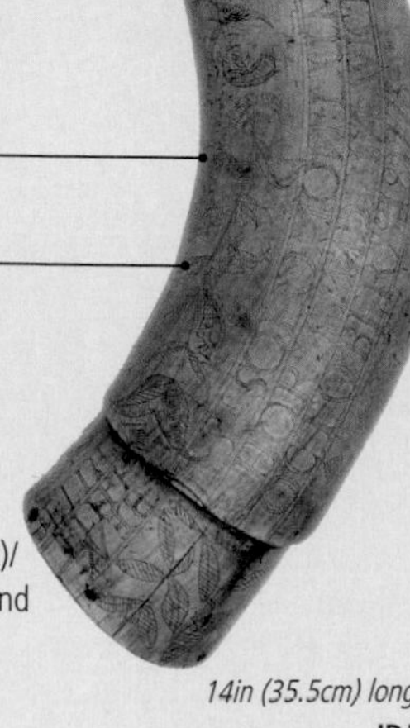

An American Revolutionary War scrimshawed powder horn, inscribed 'SOLOMON LUMBARD HIS HORN MADE IN WICKED CAMBRIDG (sic)/ OCTOBER ye 18 1775', 'LIBERTY 1775' and 'ELIR ELIPH BEN', with wooden plug.

1775 *14in (35.5cm) long*

$20,000-30,000 **JDJ**

A Polish war axe, with a spike and a disgorger on the head, the disgorger decorated with scrolls.

c1580 63in (25cm) high

$3,000-4,000 **L&T**

A mid-19thC boarding axe, the painted head decorated with gilt foliage and stamped 'N', 'WD' and with an arrow mark.

Head 8in (20cm) long

$2,000-3,000 **W&W**

A spitfire pilot's axe, the blade stamped 'CHILLINGTON METALAX', the patented rubber handle marked 'TESTED 20,000 VOLTS'.

15.5in (39.5cm) long

$200-300 **WW**

A late 18thC/early 19thC mahogany and brass truncheon, inscribed 'St. Mary Redcliffe Ward 1800'.

18.25in (46cm) long

$650-850 **DN**

A Victorian ebonized, painted and gilt wooden truncheon, with a crowned 'VR' above a naive crest of a boar's head.

15in (38cm) long

$250-350 **A&G**

A rare late 16thC Venetian leather-covered wooden parade shield, made for the bodyguard of Wolf Dietrich von Raitenau, Prince Archbishop of Salzburg, tooled and lacquered with foliate-scrolls, with professional restoration.

This shield is one of a series made in the time of Wolf Dietrich von Raitenau, who ruled as Prince Archbishop of Salzburg, 1587-1612. An inventory of 1669, now in the archives of the Städtisches Museum, Salzburg, mentions 398 gilded and painted shields. The fashion for Turkish-style arms is recorded in Europe as early as the mid-16thC.

22.5in (57cm) diam

$30,000-40,000 **TDM**

A 19thC Indo-Persian painted hide dhal shield, decorated with scrolling foliage, with four decorated brass bosses.

19in (48cm) diam

$350-450 **DN**

Judith Picks: Dettingen Standard

This is the earliest standard known to exist of a regiment of cavalry of the line in the British regular army. The Battle of Dettingen was fought on 16th June 1743 during the War of the Austrian Succession (1740-48). The cornet that carried this standard at Dettingen was Henry Richardson. Dettingen was the last time that a British monarch - in this case King George II - personally commanded his troops in battle. In the battle, the French launched a huge cavalry attack against the British left wing, which would have been overrun had not three regiments of British cavalry, with Ligonier's Horse in the center, intervened. During the cavalry battle, Ligonier's three standards became the object of concerted and repeated French attempts to capture them. The British troops successfully prevented their attempts and the standard was not made a trophy by the French. After the battle, Cornet Richardson was presented with the standard that his gallantry had preserved from capture.

The 'Dettingen Standard', for the 8th (Ligonier's) Regiment of Horse, decorated in gold and silver lace and wire, decorated with lions rampant, military motifs and the crest and motto of John (or Jean-Louis) Ligonier, the obverse and reverse sides mounted separately.

c1743 *22in (56cm) high*

$50,000-70,000 **TDM**

A large Egyptian Naqada I-II period red clay bowl, the interior painted in a red slip with horizontal patterns.

The Naqada period covers the pre-Pharaonic age of ancient Egypt. This pre-dynastic period lasted from around 4400 BC to 3000 BC, which is broken down into three distinct periods of developement (denoted by Roman numerals). The Naqada I period involved advancements centered on the town of Naqada in Upper Egypt. The later periods saw the spread of the advancements and the emergence of leading famillies who would later develop into the nobility and priesthood of the Pharaonic periods.

3900-3300 BC *9.5in (24cm) diam*

$1,200-1,800 **BC2AD**

A rare 7th/6thC BC Greek 'plastic' aryballos in the form of a warrior's head, modeled wearing a decorated Corinthian helmet.

The term 'plastic' refers to the manufacturing process of any piece made from pressing wet clay into a pre-formed mold. These warrior heads seem to have been of eastern Greek origin, manufactured mainly at Ephesus and Rhodes. It is unknown whether they were commemorative pieces or grave goods indicating the deceased's military past.

3.5in (9cm) high

$3,500-4,500 **BC2AD**

An Egyptian faience ushabti of Horudja, holding a hoe and a flail, with a seed bag on his back, with damage to ankles.

c600 BC 8in (21.5cm) high

$8,000-12,000 **WW**

A mid-6thC BC Attic black-figure column-krater, decorated with an owl, ibex and birds.

10in (25cm) diam

$5,500-6,500 **G&M**

A large Attic black-figure lekythos, decorated by the Acheloos Painter with a fight between two heroes (maybe the fight for the arms of Achilles), with extensive restoration.

520-510 BC *12in (31.5cm) high*

$4,000-6,000 **G&M**

A 5th/4thC BC Greek transport amphora, with sea-encrustations.

26in (65cm) high

$2,500-3,500 **G&M**

A 5thC BC Attic black-figure amphora, one side decorated with warriors, the other with a man, a woman and a lion, perhaps depicting Peleus chasing Thetis, with restoration.

6.75in (17cm) high

$4,500-5,500 **WW**

A rare 5thC-3rdC BC earthenware amphoriskos, with a modern stand.

This particular style and size of vessel has had its origins attributed to the Phoenician unguents industry, with examples being found across the Mediterranean. The main center of manufacture appears to have been the coastal areas of northern Syria.

9.5in (24cm) high

$650-850 **BC2AD**

A pair of Egyptian Late Period blue-glazed bichrome ushabtis, both with chips to faces, on a modern stand.

Early ushabtis were often inscribed with passages from the 'Book of the Dead', but this custom declined during the Late Period. This decline was a result of fewer people knowing how to read hieroglyphs and also due to new foreign deities becoming widely worshiped, a development that hastened the abandonment of traditional funerary practices.

664-332 BC

With stand 4.75in (12cm) high

$1,000-1,500 **BC2AD**

A 4thC BC Roman Gnathia lekythos, with cross-hatched decoration to body, with wave and banded decoration to shoulder, with chips to base.

Gnathia vases are named after the ancient Roman city of Gnathia (now Egnazia) where the first examples of the style were discovered in the mid-19thC.

7in (17cm) high

$650-850 **BC2AD**

An Apulian kantharos, decorated by the 'Stoke-on-Trent' Painter with female heads, with minor losses.

320-310 BC *8in (19cm) high*

$1,800-2,200 **G&M**

An Apulian red-figure oinochoe, decorated with a seated lady and a standing winged bearer, perhaps Eros, on an anthemion ground.

c300 BC *3in (8cm) high*

$2,000-3,000 **WW**

A 3rdC BC Greek Hellenistic period hollow terracotta figure of a lady, holding a fruit.

9in (23cm) high

$1,500-2,500 **BC2AD**

A 1stC BC-1stC AD Roman ceramic cup, with applied decoration of vines, with green and brown glaze, with restoration.

6in (15.5cm) diam

$5,000-7,000 **G&M**

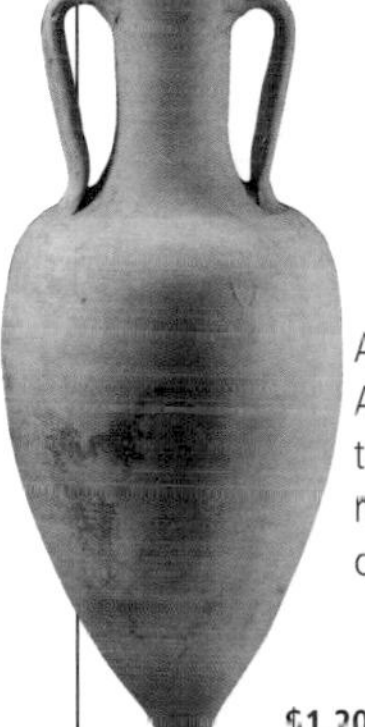

A 1stC BC-1stC AD Roman ceramic transport amphora, missing foot, with crack.

33in (83cm) high

$1,200-1,800 **G&M**

A 3rdC AD Roman twin-handled amphoriskos, with applied decoration of vines and a hare.

6.25in (16cm) high

$700-1,000 **BC2AD**

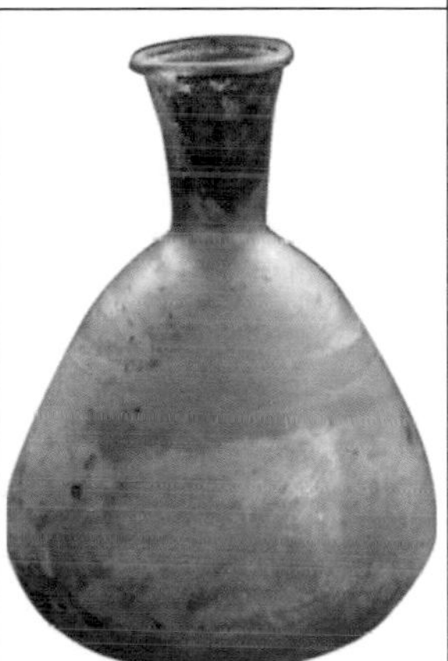

A large 1st/2ndC AD Roman glass flask, with turned lip and bulbous body, with some areas of iridescence.

6.5in (17cm) high

$300-500 **BC2AD**

A 3rd/4thC AD Roman manganese glass amphora jug, with green handle.

6.25in (16cm) high

$1,000-1,500 **GORL**

Cinerarium

A 1st/2ndC AD Roman blue-green glass cinerarium, with traces of purple and gold iridescence, with damage.

A cinerarium is a place for keeping the ashes of a cremated body.

15.75in (40cm) high

$30,000-40,000 **AS&S**

A 4th/5thC AD Roman green glass trailed bottle.

3in (7.5cm) high

$300-500 **GORL**

A 10thC AD Islamic green glass flared jug.

4in (10cm) high

$120-180 **GORL**

An Egyptian Late Period bronze figure of Osiris, holding a flail and crook.

712-332 BC *10in (25cm) high*

$15,000-20,000 **SWO**

A early Bronze Age Anatolian copper model of a coach drawn by a bull, with green patina, with damage to one wheel.

c2500 BC *9in (22cm) long*

$5,000-7,000 **G&M**

A 7thC-4thC BC Egyptian Late Period bronze figure of Isis with the Horus-child, with green patina, with damage to one horn.

4in (11cm) high

$3,000-4,000 **G&M**

A 5thC-3rdC BC Celtiberian bronze figure of a man, with green patina.

2.5in (6cm) high

$1,500-2,000 **G&M**

An Egyptian Ptolemaic gypsum head of a Pharaoh, with surface chips.

c300 BC

11in (28cm) high

$12,000-18,000 **WW**

A 5th/4thC BC Greek bronze oinochoe, with old professional restoration.

6in (16cm) high

$2,500-3,500 **G&M**

A 2nd/3rdC BC Roman marble statue of a girl, with Greek inscription to base, missing head, right hand and left arm.

27in (70cm) high

$12,000-18,000 **G&M**

A Greek bronze kotyle, with reddish patina, the foot re-attached, with minor loss.

c350-300 BC *8in (19.5cm) diam*

$5,500-6,500 **G&M**

A 2nd/3rdC AD Roman iron folding chair.

21in (52.5cm) wide

$15,000-20,000 **G&M**

An etched part slice from the 'Arispe' meteorite.

Several masses of this coarse octahedrite meteorite were found 1896-98, 15 and 25 miles from Arispe, Sonara, Mexico.

28in (17cm) long 26oz

$4,500-5,500 L&T

A fragment of the 'Gibeon' iron meteorite.

The 'Gibeon' meteorite (found in the Namibian Desert, Africa) was first reported by a Captain J E Alexander in 1836. When cut, polished and etched with acid, 'Gibeon' reveals a pattern called Widmanstätten figures - a crystal structure formed by nickel-rich and nickel-poor metallic bands as a result of an extremely low rate of cooling over thousands or millions of years. Widmanstätten structure is often used as absolute proof of the meteoric origin of iron meteorites, as it is not something that can be copied or forged in a lifetime.

8.75in (22cm) long 335oz

$2,500-3,500 L&T

A 'Campo del Cielo' iron meteorite.

'Campo del Cielo' translates as 'Valley of the Sky'. The name is applied to a group of iron meteorites and the area they were found in Gran Chaco, Argentina. This example fell more than 4,000 years ago.

11in (28cm) high 811.5oz

$4,000-6,000 GORL

A fusion-crusted stone fragment from the 'El Hammami' meteorite.

After a bright fireball and loud detonations, this meteorite fell into the desert in Western Algeria in 1995. Local tribesmen collected many of the stones and broke them open in search of 'hidden treasures' sent from heaven.

4.25in (11cm) long 46oz

$650-750 L&T

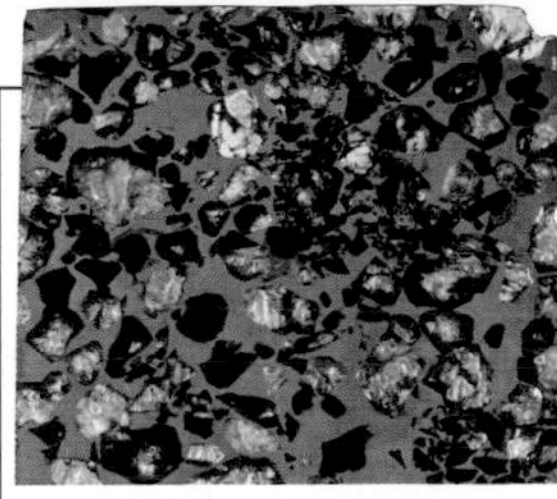

A polished slice of the 'Esquel' pallasite meteorite, containing translucent pale yellow-green crystals held in the silvery iron matrix.

The 50.75lb mass of the 'Esquel' meteorite was discovered by an Argentine farmer in 1951. It has become one of the most renowned pallasites for the quality of the gem peridot olivine crystals that fill its interior.

1.75in (4.5cm) long 5oz

$2,000-3,000 IMC

Left: A rhodium-plated ring made from the 'Gibeon' meteorite.

This example was shown to and briefly worn by Buzz Aldrin at a special dinner held at the Natural History Museum, London, UK in 2000.

0.75in (2cm) diam

$1,000-1,500 L&T

Right: A rhodium-plated ring made from the 'Gibeon' meteorite.

0.5in (1.5cm) diam

$900-1,100 L&T

A large mass from the 'Hambleton' pallasite (stony-iron) meteorite, with polished end piece.

The 'Hambleton' meteorite was discovered in the North Yorkshire, UK, in 2005. Pallasites are extremely rare. They are formed deep within the core/mantle boundary layer of a large asteroid, and account for just 1 per cent of all known meteorites. This makes 'Hambleton' the most scientifically interesting meteorite recovered within the UK to date. This example is the largest piece of the 'Hambleton' meteorite in existence.

204.5oz

$20,000-30,000 L&T

Several tumble-polished fragments of the 'Henbury' iron meteorite.

This meteorite was found in Henbury, Australia in 1931. The shape and condition of the crater walls indicate an explosive origin.

16.5oz total

$400-600 L&T

A tiny fragment of the 'Nakhla' 'Mars rock' meteorite.

This meteorite of Martian stone fell in the Abu Hommus district of Egypt in 1911. The 'Nakhla' meteorite has been extensively researched and studied amid renewed claims of fossilized Martian bacterial lifeforms found within the stony matrix.

$2,500-3,500 L&T

An etched end piece of the 'Wabar' iron meteorite.

This meteorite is reported to have fallen during a thunderstorm in 1863 in Rub'al Khali, Saudi Arabia. Several craters associated with the meteorite are filled with drifted sand and surrounded by abundant silica glass. This indicates that they are relatively recent.

4in (10cm) long 30oz

$4,000-6,000 L&T

An etched part end piece from the 'Zerhamra' iron meteorite.

This meteorite was found in Zerhamra, Algeria, in 1967. It underwent re-heating and re-crystallisation while still in space, creating an unusual appearance to the cut and etched faces.

2.75in (7cm) long 8oz

$5,000-7,000 L&T

A French violin, labeled 'Ch. J.B. Colin-Mezin, Luthier a Paris...1913', signed.

14.15in (36cm) long

$1,500-2,000 GHOU

A violin, labeled 'Giuseppe Ornati, fece in Milano Anno 1923, G. O. M.', with the maker's inked oval brand above the label.

14.25in (36cm) long

$1,500-2,000 GHOU

Stroviol Violin

A Stroviol practise violin, possibly by Evans, with original large horn and replacement smaller horn, with original tooled leather case.

The Stroviol violin (or horn-violin) is a violin that amplifies sound through a metal horn, rather than a wooden sound box. It was patented by electrical engineer John Matthias Augustus Stroh in 1899. The stroviol violin was very useful in the early days of phonographic recording, as the sound was much louder and could be directed toward a recording device. Although the sound produced is louder than that of a standard violin, it is also harsher and more grating. On early records the Stroviol violin can be recognized by its characteristically thin whining tone.

$700-1,000 GHOU

A French viola, labeled 'Ch J B Collin-Mézin...Paris', the bow stamped 'Charles Buthod A Paris', cased, with an additional silver-mounted bow.

Body 15.5in (39.5cm) long

$5,000-7,000 SWO

A 19thC German violoncello, Mittenwald, with bow, with soft case.

29.25in (74.5cm) long

$1,500-2,500 GHOU

A late 19thC German double bass, with 'Edward Withers of London' repairer's label, the scroll signed 'H.D. Curtis'.

Body 45in (115cm) long

$45,000-55,000 GORL

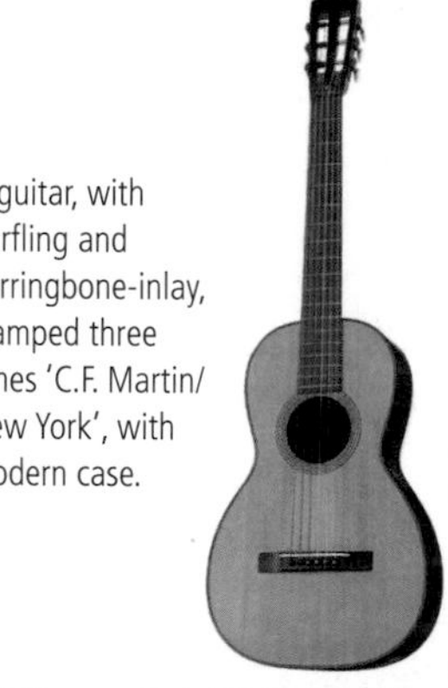

A guitar, with purfling and herringbone-inlay, stamped three times 'C.F. Martin/ New York', with modern case.

c1860 Body 17.75in (45cm) long

$1,200-1,800 FRE

A Rickenbacker 'Roger McGuinn' 12-string electric guitar, serial no.A39958, no.'826/1000', with certificate of authenticity, with case.

1990

$4,000-6,000 DN

A Tunbridgeware seven-stringed fretless banjo.

10in (25.5cm) diam

$550-750 GHOU

A 19thC satinwood and parcel-gilt 45-string concert harp, the brass plate stamped 'Frederick Grosjean, 11 Soho Square, London, improved patent, no.1030', with leaf-carved scrolling toes and six pedals.

69in (174cm) high

$2,000-3,000 TEN

A boxwood and ivory-mounted flute, by 'Rudall & Rose no. 15 Piazza, Covent Garden, London no. 984', with seven silver keys.
c1827
$3,500-4,500 **GHOU**

A French silver flute, by 'L.L Louis-Lot Paris 136 Brevete, no. 136', with gold lip-plate, with case and separate case for head joint.
$10,000-15,000 **GHOU**

A cocuswood flute, by 'Rudall & Rose no. 15 Piazza, Covent Garden, London, no.937', with eight silver keys.
c1830
$2,500-3,500 **GHOU**

A stained-pearwood bassoon, by 'W Milhouse, London, 337 Oxford Street', with six brass keys.
c1820
$1,200-1,800 **GHOU**

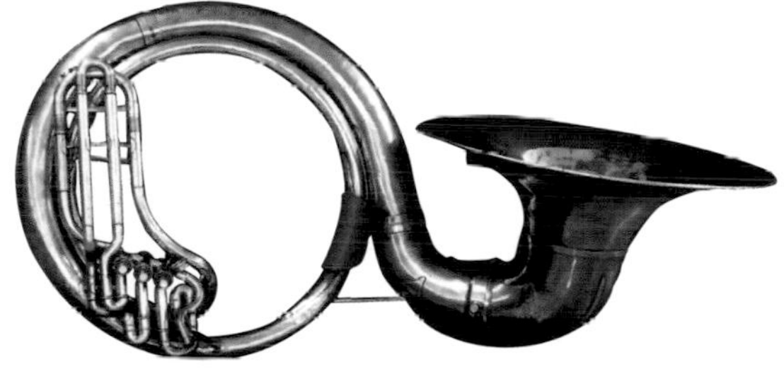

A Besson & Co. silver-plated B flat sousaphone, with soft case.
$1,000-1,500 **GHOU**

ESSENTIAL REFERENCE - SQUARE PIANOS

- **Square pianos were introduced in the mid-1770s and were an immediate success as they had a sweeter tone than harpsichords and were half the price.**
- **They were produced into the early 20thC by German, British, French and American makers before being superseded by grand and upright pianos.**
- **Most square pianos appearing at auction have been converted into other items, such as sideboards or cocktail cabinets. They usually make around a few hundred dollars.**
- **According to restorer Michael Cole of Cheltenham: 'In recent years there has been a renaissance when these long-neglected instruments have been appreciated for their fine craftsmanship and the beautiful effects that they impart to classical period music.'.**

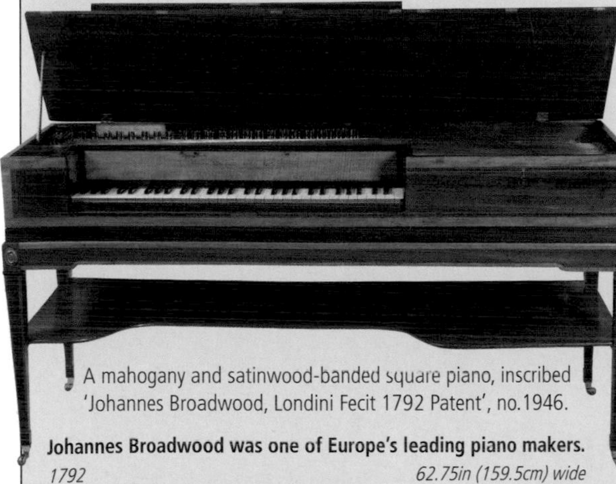

A mahogany and satinwood-banded square piano, inscribed 'Johannes Broadwood, Londini Fecit 1792 Patent', no.1946.

Johannes Broadwood was one of Europe's leading piano makers.
1792 *62.75in (159.5cm) wide*
$3,000-4,000 **HT**

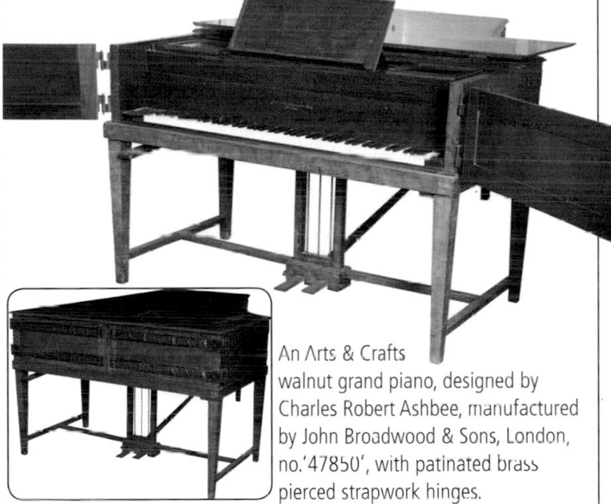

An Arts & Crafts walnut grand piano, designed by Charles Robert Ashbee, manufactured by John Broadwood & Sons, London, no.'47850', with patinated brass pierced strapwork hinges.

Ashbee's designed his first piano for his wife Janet in 1900. It was square and reflected the piano forms of the late 18thC but with hinged doors to the front. This example, produced four years later, retains many of the features of Ashbee's first design although the case encloses the more usual grand piano frame.
c1904 *61in (155cm) wide*
$15,000-20,000 **L&T**

A mahogany 'Model A' grand piano, by C Bechstein, Berlin, on three turned and tapered simulated-rosewood legs with brass toes and castors.
c1900
$5,500-6,500 **TEN**

THE DECORATIVE ARTS MARKET

Following the pattern of other collecting areas, the Decorative Arts market has seen high prices for high-end items while mid-to-low-end goods have struggled. Many Doulton wares are quite simply unfashionable. Demand for the Royal Doulton figures has fallen dramatically and only the prototypes, limited production and rare colorways are fetching good money. There is little demand for 'dull'-colored Doulton stoneware and faience. That said, I recently attended an antiques fair where the dealers reported some stirring of interest, so perhaps an up-turn is on the way.

Moorcroft and Martin Brothers have continued to perform well. A unique James Macintyre flambé 'Carp' vase sold at Woolley & Wallis in 2012 for a world record price of $55,000 (see p.515). In 2013 Rago Arts sold a rare early Martin Brothers bird tobacco jar for over $30,000 (see p.512). Rare Clarice Cliff patterns and shapes continue to command high prices and the same is true of Wedgwood 'Fairyland Luster' ceramics.

In contrast, the Ohio school, including Rookwood and Roseville, has had several quiet years, with few exciting pieces coming onto the market. However, Van Briggle, from Colorado, has been much in demand. For example, in 2013 a flame and foliate motifs vase with bronzed handles by Yosakichi Asano sold at Rago Arts for over $40,000 (see p.523).

20thC silver has continued to sell well, particularly pieces by Charles Robert Ashbee and Omar Ramsden. Rare and unusual Liberty pieces are in great demand – in 2013 Reeman Dansie sold a particularly fine silver and enamel biscuit box for over $50,000 (see p.573).

In glass, it is the big names that continue to sell, particularly Daum, Gallé, Lalique, Loetz and Tiffany. In 2013 Anderson & Garland achieved a world record when a Lalique cire-perdue glass 'Deux Figures Femmes Aillees' sold for over $500,000 (see p.550).

Bronze and ivory figures by Demêtre Chiparus and Ferdinand Preiss have also performed extremely well. In 2011 Bonhams sold a bronze figure of 'The Riding Crop', by Bruno Zach for $150,000 (see p.589). Unfortunately there are spelter and ivorene fakes around, so buyers must be cautious and buy from a reputable source.

In 2012 there was an incredible Tiffany sale at Michaan's, which included a Tiffany 'Dragonfly' table lamp that sold for over $150,000 (see p.567).

The sale of early 20thC furniture has been unspectacular, but when something fresh and with very good provenance appears so do the collectors. This was the case with the Charles Rennie Mackintosh music cabinet sold at Robertson's in Scotland in 2013 (see p.542). It sold for over $70,000.

Right: A chryselephantine figure of a dancer representing the Assyrian Queen, Semiramis. $280,000-320,000 MACK

Left: A Tiffany silver-gilt-mounted 'Favrile' glass cabinet vase. See p.556.

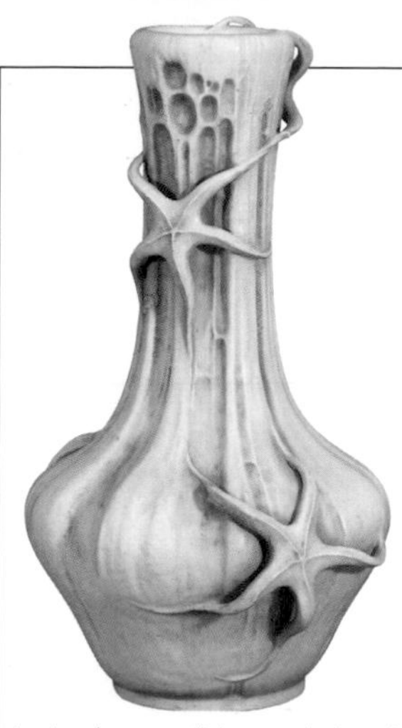

An Amphora starfish vase, designed by Paul Dachsel, impressed 'AMPHORA 3648/3', incised 'PD'.

c1905-10 *15.5in (39cm) high*

$5,000-7,000 **WAD**

Am Amphora vase, designed by Eduard Stellmacher, with an applied dragon.

This is a rare and highly desirable design from the highpoint of the company's production, which ran from c1894 until c1904: the year Stellmacher left the company, following designer Paul Dachsel the year before. Plants, animals, mythical creatures and designs inspired by Gustav Klimt and Alphonse Mucha, were typical of Amphora designs from this period.

26.25in (67cm) high

$15,000-20,000 **GORL**

A pair of Riessner & Kessel Amphora vases, with applied mermaids holding nets of fish and weed, with impressed marks, with minor damage.

19in (48cm) high

$2,000-3,000 **WW**

An Ernst Wahliss Amphora vase, with an applied heron and frog, with blue depose stamp and 'Made in Austria 4709'.

22in (56cm) high

$1,000-1,500 **DRA**

A rare Amphora Louis Wain planter, signed 'Louis Wain, Futurist Cat', stamped 'Imperial Amphora Austria' and numbered 'RGNo.637132'.

1914 *11in (28cm) high*

$6,500-7,500 **DRA**

An early 20thC Riessner, Stellmacher & Kessel Amphora bust of a lady, with red 'R St. K' mark.

15.75in (40cm) high

$2,000-3,000 **DRA**

An early 20thC Ernst Wahliss Amphora bust of a lady, with red 'Turn Wien Depose' crown and 'Made in Austria' marks.

17in (43cm) high

$1,500-2,000 **DRA**

An Amphora figure of a young Dutch girl, with impressed marks.

31in (78.5cm) high

$1,000-1,500 **AH**

A Berlin Art Nouveau vase, painted with a semi-clad nymph.

16.5in (42cm) high

$2,500-3,500 GORL

A Berlin Art Nouveau vase, painted with a portrait of a maiden by E Volk.

8in (20cm) high

$650-850 GORL

A Berlin Art Nouveau vase, painted with a semi-clad maiden by E Koch.

6.75in (17cm) high

$650-850 GORL

Two Berlin Art Nouveau cabinet plates, painted by E Volk.

Largest 9.75in (25cm) diam

$1,500-2,000 GORL

A C H Brannam vase, decorated with incised and applied fish, the neck with flowers and beads, signed 'C.H. Brannum', dated.

1886 13.5in (34cm) high

$500-700 TRI

An early 20thC C H Brannam model of a cat, signed 'C H Brannum, Baron', dated.

1911 12.25in (31cm) high

$500-700 TRI

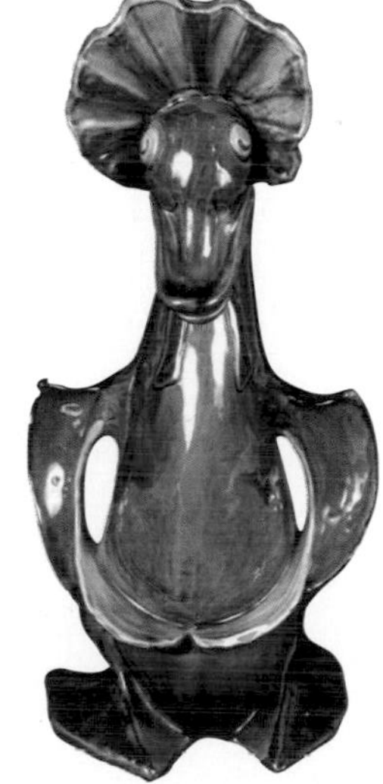

A C H Brannam model of a duck, with impressed marks.

11.75in (30cm) high

$400-600 DN

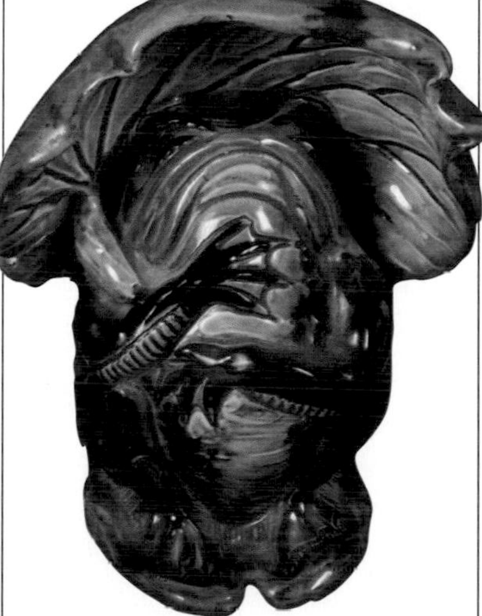

A C H Brannam model of a frog, with incised marks, dated.

1901 8in (20.5cm) high

$1,500-2,500 DN

A Clarice Cliff Fantasque Bizarre 'Green Autumn' bowl, with black printed 'Wilkinson' mark, with some paint losses.
1930-34 *8.75in (22cm) diam*
$650-850 **DN**

A Clarice Cliff Bizarre 'Blue Autumn' pattern dish, with 'Bizarre' and 'Honeyglaze' mark.
c1931 *17.5in (42cm) diam*
$4,000-6,000 **FLD**

A 1930s Clarice Cliff 'Brangwyn' panel, no.27, hand-painted with a tropical forest containing figures, flowers and animals.

First exhibited in Olympia in 1933, 'The British Empire Panels' were designed by Frank Brangwyn and commissioned by Lord Iveagh for the House of Lords to commemorate deceased peers. The original panels are now on display at Swansea Civic Center. Clarice Cliff adapted designs from three of the Brangwyn panels for limited edition wall plaques, which were produced by Royal Staffordshire pottery.
17in (43.5cm) diam
$2,000-3,000 **ROS**

A Clarice Cliff 'Crocus' 33-piece breakfast set.
$2,500-3,500 **SWO**

A miniature Clarice Cliff Bizarre 'Green Erin' bottle-vase, with printed factory mark.
2.5in (6.5cm) high
$1,500-2,500 **WW**

A Clarice Cliff Bizarre 'Gayday' yo-yo vase, with 'Bizarre' mark.
9in (23cm) high
$4,000-6,000 **GORL**

A Clarice Cliff 'House & Bridge' sugar sifter, with printed factory marks to base.
c1931 *5.25in (13.5cm) high*
$2,000-3,000 **L&T**

A Clarice Cliff Fantasque Bizarre 'House & Bridge' plate.
10in (23cm) diam
$1,000-1,500 **SWO**

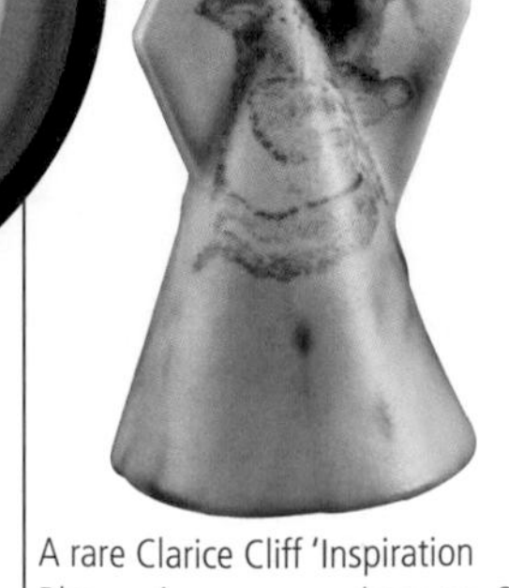

A rare Clarice Cliff 'Inspiration Blossom' yo-yo vase, shape no. 37
10in (23cm) high
$4,500-5,500 **GORL**

A Clarice Cliff Bizarre 'Inspiration Lily' coffee set, with printed and painted marks.

c1930

$12,000-18,000 **SWO**

A Clarice Cliff Bizarre 'Applique Blue Lugano' tankard coffee can and saucer, with printed and painted marks.

2.5in (6cm) high

$1,000-1,500 **WW**

A Clarice Cliff 'May Avenue' Conical sugar sifter, with printed factory marks.

c1933 *5.75in (14.5cm) high*

$10,000-15,000 **L&T**

A Clarice Cliff Bizarre 'Mountain' Conical sugar sifter, with printed factory mark, with cracks.

6in (14cm) high

$2,000-3,000 **WW**

A Clarice Cliff 'Red Roofs' Conical coffee service, with 'CAFE AU LAIT' and 'Bizarre' marks, with some minor paint scuffs.

Cliff's 'Red Roofs' pattern was only produced 1931-32. The pattern features a cottage with an orange-colored climber plant up its side, a fence alongside and a green tree. An orange flower is painted on the reverse. During the same two-year period, the cafe-au-lait sponging process was used on several Bizarre and Fantasque patterns, including 'Bobbins', 'Summerhouse' and 'Autumn'.

c1931

$3,000-4,000 **FLD**

A Clarice Cliff Bizarre 'Solomon's Seal' Stamford teapot and cover, with black printed 'Wilkinson' mark.

5in (13cm) high

$500-700 **DN**

A Clarice Cliff Bizarre 'Shark's Teeth' bowl, with printed mark.

9in (23.5cm) diam

$2,000-3,000 **WW**

A rare Clarice Cliff Fantasque Bizarre 'Summerhouse' Conical coffee set for six.

Coffee pot 7in (18cm) high

$4,500-5,500 **WW**

A Clarice Cliff Bizarre 'Sunray' water jug.

7.5in (18cm) high

$1,200-1,800 **WHP**

A Clarice Cliff Bizarre 'Orange Trees & House' Conical coffee set for four.

$3,000-4,000 **SWO**

A Clarice Cliff 'Orange Trees & House' Conical sugar sifter, with printed factory marks.

c1930 *5.5in (14cm) high*

$1,500-2,500 **L&T**

A Clarice Cliff Bizarre 'Brookfields' Trieste Tea for Two nine-piece set, with printed marks and impressed '10/35'.

1935 *Teapot 5in (13cm) high*

$1,500-2,500 **TEN**

A unique Clarice Cliff hand-modeled figure of an Arabian man, with incised mark, with printed date and 'Wilkinsons'.

Provenance: This figure remained the personal property of Clarice Cliff and formed part of her estate, which was auctioned on the 1st and 2nd of March 1973 following her death.

1924 *8.25in (21 cm) high*

$2,500-3,500 **FLD**

A Clarice Cliff novelty figure of a laughing cat, with 'Bizarre' mark.

5in (15cm) high

$3,000-4,000 **FLD**

Judith Picks

Clarice Cliff's fame and success in the 1930s are hard to fully appreciate now, but at that time there was no such thing as a 'career woman'. She was a true innovator - it was her ability to design both the patterns and also the shapes those patterns were to decorate that distinguished Cliff above any other designers in the Staffordshire Potteries at this time.

Along with the 'Age of Jazz' figures, the 'Lido Lady' ashtray (shape no.561) is quintessentially the most Deco shape Clarice Cliff ever created. The lady is so 'of her time', with her hands provocatively on her hips, the swimsuit, wide bottomed trousers and fashionably bobbed hair.

This ashtray was produced in two sizes. This is the larger one and has a square ashtray base; the smaller one is circular. As a functional item, many of these ashtrays would have been damaged and thrown away over the years so undamaged examples are extremely rare. The original price was three shillings in 1930/31 - which was not inexpensive.

A Clarice Cliff novelty figure of a 'Lido Lady', with 'FANTASQUE' and 'Bizarre' marks.

c1932 *6.5in (16.5cm) high*

$10,000-15,000 **FLD**

A Della Robbia sgraffito-decorated faience vase, designed and decorated by Charles Collis and Lizzie Wilkins, with incised factory marks, incised 'C' and 'JF', painted 'L.W.'.

c1900 *11.5in (29cm) high*

$5,000-7,000 L&T

ESSENTIAL REFERENCE - DELLA ROBBIA

The Della Robbia Pottery was established in Birkenhead, Merseyside, UK, in 1894 by Harold Rathbone (1881-1911), who had been a student of Ford Madox Brown, and the sculptor Conrad Dressler (1856-1940). Dressler left in 1897 to establish the Medmemham Pottery in Buckinghamshire.

- **The pottery was named after the Italian Renaissance sculptor Luca della Robbia.**
- **Giovanni Carlo Valentino Manzoni joined Della Robbia in early 1894, leaving to establish his own pottery, the Minerva Art Ware Manufacturers, in Hanley in 1895. He returned to Della Robbia in 1898.**
- **Della Robbia pottery featured lustrous lead glazes and often used patterns of interweaving plants with heraldic and Islamic motifs.**
- **Pieces are typically marked with a hand-drawn ship as well as the initials of the designer and decorator, and sometimes the date.**
- **The pottery closed in 1906 due to high running costs.**

A pair of Della Robbia earthenware ewers, unmarked.

14in (35cm) high

$1,000-1,500 FLD

A Della Robbia vase, incised and painted with vines, incised 'JS' and '59'.

8in (21.5cm) high

$800-1,200 WW

A Della Robbia wall mirror, modeled with fairies and harebells, inscribed 'D. R. 316 M. de C.'.

c1900 *23in (58.5cm) high*

$5,500-6,500 SWO

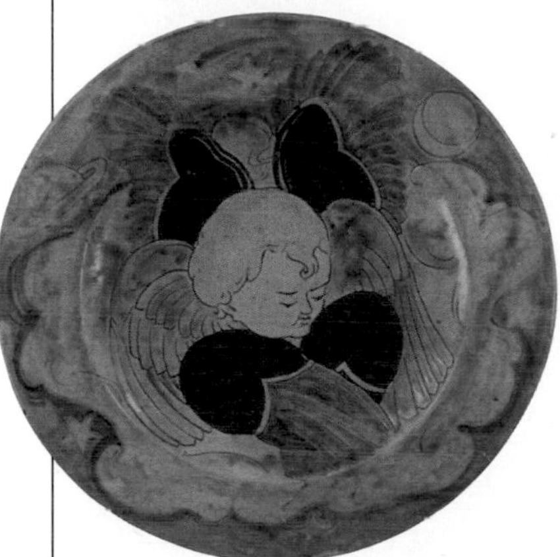

A Della Robbia plate, by Cassandia Annie Walker, incised and painted with a cherub, with incised marks including 'CAW', dated.

1900 *10in (26.5cm) diam*

$550-650 WW

A Della Robbia charger, by Charles Collis, with incised ship device mark and 'C', numbered '304'.

c1900 *15in (38cm) diam*

$1,500-2,500 SWO

A Della Robbia stoneware plaque, by Conrad Dressler, with painted marks to reverse, with damage, dated.

1904 *21in (54cm) high*

$1,500-2,500 WW

A Doulton Lambeth salt-glaze stoneware vase, by Hannah Barlow and an unidentified assistant, numbered '513'.
c1892 *14.25in (36cm) high*
$3,000-4,000 **SK**

A Doulton Lambeth stoneware vase, by Hannah Barlow, incised with dogs and cats, with 'BHB' monogram and impressed mark, broken and repaired at neck.
c1891-1902 *12.5in (31.5cm) high*
$1,000-1,500 **DN**

A Doulton Lambeth salt-glazed stoneware figure of a Boer War Soldier, modeled by John Broad, incised 'J. Broad Sc.', with impressed mark.
c1901 *12in (31cm) high*
$1,500-2,500 **DN**

A Doulton Lambeth salt-glazed stoneware figure of Nelson, modeled by John Broad, the plinth molded 'NELSON 1805-1905', incised 'J. Broad Sc.', with impressed marks.
c1905 *7.75in (19.5cm) high*
$650-850 **DN**

A Doulton Lambeth stoneware model of a recumbent Ibex.
5in (12.5cm) wide
$1,200-1,800 **GORL**

A Doulton Lambeth 'The Finding of Moses' tile panel, with title and 'The gift of the DEAN and CHAPTER', the forty 6in (15cm) tiles painted with the pharaoh's daughter finding Moses, with painted mark 'Doulton Lambeth'.
60in (153cm) high
$15,000-20,000 **TEN**

ESSENTIAL REFERENCE - GEORGE TINWORTH

George Tinworth (1843-1913) was a wood carver and pottery modeller, best known for the stoneware figures he designed for Doulton Lambeth from 1866. He also produced vases and plaques for Doulton.

- **At the age of 19, he pawned his overcoat to pay for evening classes at the Lambeth School of Art in Kennington Park Road, London.**
- **He was friends with Wallace Martin (one of the Martin Brothers, see pp.512-13) and some of his models are similarly grotesque. Religious subjects are also common in Tinworth's work, as are groups of animals, particularly mice.**
- **John Ruskin described Tinworth's religious plaques as being 'full of fire and zealous faculty'.**

A rare Doulton Lambeth terracotta figure of 'The Jester', modeled by George Tinworth, signed and inscribed.
c1900 *11.25in (29cm) high*
$8,000-12,000 **SK**

A Doulton Lambeth 'Waning of the Honeymoon' vase, modeled by George Tinworth, with impressed marks.
4.75in (12cm) high
$4,000-6,000 **FLD**

A Doulton Lambeth mouse chess piece, modeled by George Tinworth, modeled as a pawn holding a shield, incised 'TG' and impressed 'Doulton Lambeth E...D'.

2.5in (6.5cm) high

$1,000-1,500 DN

Two Royal Doulton mouse chess pieces, modeled by George Tinworth, modeled as a castle and a bishop, both incised 'TG' and impressed 'Doulton Lambeth'.

Largest 3.25in (7.5cm) high

$3,000-4,000 DN

A Doulton Lambeth stoneware vase, by George Tinworth, with parrot handles, the shoulders with salamanders, with impressed mark inside rim, 'TG' monogram, with filled firing cracks.

This vase is of exhibition quality. Despite its magnificence, there is no record of it ever being exhibited. This was probably as a result of the extensive firing cracks.

25in (64cm) high

$6,500 7,500 DN

A Royal Doulton 'Sung' vase, designed by Charles Noke, with printed and painted marks.

10in (25cm) high

$2,000-3,000 WW

A Royal Doulton model of a matador and bull, modeled by Peggy Davies, under the direction of Doulton Fine China.

This is one of 500 made for worldwide distribution in 1964. This example was the only one imported into New Zealand for retail sale. It has its original dated receipt and was priced at NZD725 (equivalent to $620).

1966 26in (66cm) long

$3,000-4,000 DS

A matched pair of Royal Doulton Titanian Ware vases, painted by Robert Allen, with printed factory mark, stamped '1361/A', painted 'RA 9390'.

10in (26cm) high

$2,500-3,500 TEN

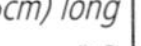

A Royal Doulton Lambeth Titanian Ware porcelain vase, decorated by Harry Allen, titled to the base, numbered '1,692', signed and dated.

1917 8.5in (22cm) high

$3,000-4,000 SK

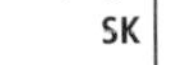

A Royal Doulton Lambeth vase, by Mark V Marshall, with an applied dragon.

14.75in (37.5cm) high

$3,500-4,500 GORL

A Royal Doulton 'Sung' flambé rhinoceros, designed by Charles Noke, signed 'Noke' with 'Sung' mark, with some damage.

15.5in (39cm) long

$3,000-4,000 **FLD**

A Royal Doulton 'Sung' flambé elephant, designed by Charles Noke, painted 'Doulton England' and 'Noke Sung'.

17.75in (45cm) long

$6,500-7,500 **DN**

A Royal Doulton flambé model of a lion.

8.75in (22.2cm) high

$5,500-6,500 **GORL**

A Royal Doulton figure of 'A Spook', HN51, designed by Harry Tittensor, with titanian-type glaze to robe and orange glazed face, on onyx dish base,.

1916-36 *7in (17.5cm) high*

$10,000-15,000 **GORL**

A Royal Doulton figure of 'An Elizabethan Lady', HN309, designed by Ernest W Light.

1918-38 *9.5in (24cm) high*

$1,800-2,200 **GORL**

A rare Royal Doulton figure of 'Dolly', HN355, designed by Charles Noke.

1919-38 *7.25in (18.5cm) high*

$5,500-6,500 **CENC**

A rare Royal Doulton figure of 'Harlequinade', HN711, designed by Leslie Harradine.

1925-40 *7in (18cm) high*

$2,000-3,000 **CENC**

A Royal Doulton figure of 'The Proposal (man)', HN725, designer unknown.

1925-38

5.5in (14cm) high

$1,000-1,500 **CENC**

A rare Royal Doulton figure of 'The Proposal (lady)', HN788, designer unknown.

1926-40

5.75in (22cm) high

$3,000-4,000 **CENC**

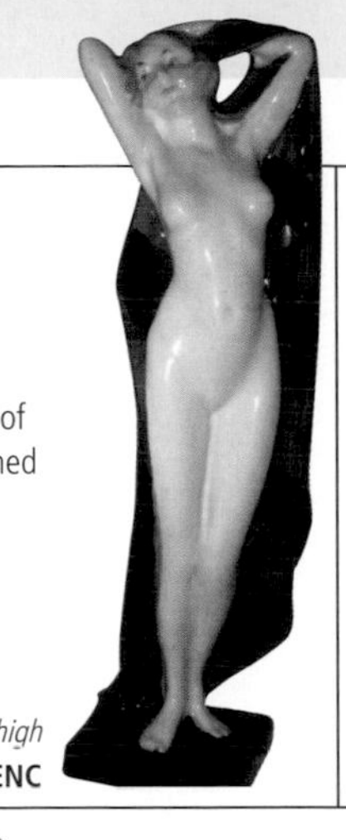

A Royal Doulton figure of 'Circe', HN1250, designed by Leslie Harradine.

1927-36

7.5in (19cm) high

$1,800-2,200 **CENC**

A Royal Doulton figure of 'Scotties', HN1281, designed by Leslie Harradine.

1928-36 *5.5in (14cm) high*

$1,200-1,800 **CENC**

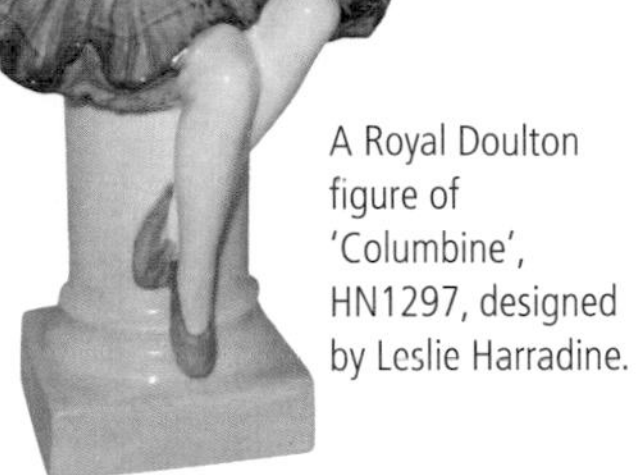

A Royal Doulton figure of 'Columbine', HN1297, designed by Leslie Harradine.

1928-40 *6in (15cm) high*

$800-1,200 **CENC**

A Royal Doulton figure of 'Siesta', HN1305, designed by Leslie Harradine.

1928-40 *4.75in (12cm) high*

$2,000-3,000 **CENC**

A rare Royal Doulton figure of 'Sunshine Girl', HN1344, designed by Leslie Harradine.

1929-38 *5in (12.5cm) high*

$5,000-6,000 **CENC**

A Royal Doulton figure of 'Dreamland', HN1481, designed by Leslie Harradine.

1931-37 *4.75in (12cm) high*

$5,000-7,000 **CENC**

A Royal Doulton figure of 'Gwendolen', HN1503, designed by Leslie Harradine.

1932-49 *6in (15cm) high*

$650-850 **CENC**

A Royal Doulton figure of 'Modena', HN1845, designed by Leslie Harradine.

1938-49 *7.25in (18.5cm) high*

$1,000 1,500 **CENC**

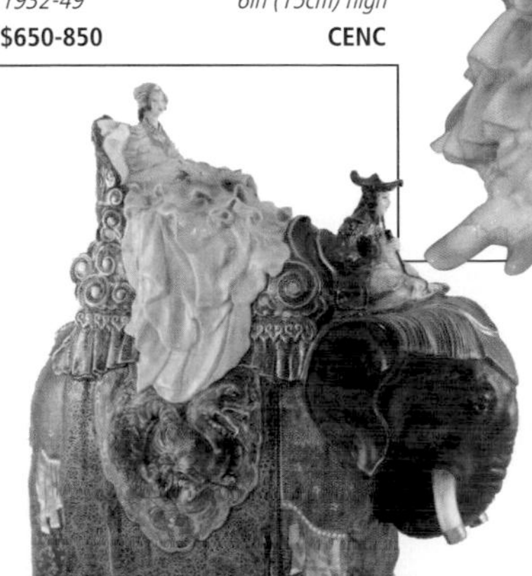

A Royal Doulton figure of 'Princess Badoura', HN2081, designed by Harry Tittensor and Harry E Stanton.

1952- *22in (56cm) wide*

$3,000-4,000 **GORL**

An early 20thC cold-painted terracotta figure of a young fisherboy, attributed to Regina Goldscheider, Vienna, with a trademark plaque.

47.25in (120cm) high

$12,000-18,000 **AH**

A late 19thC Goldscheider cold-painted terracotta figure, impressed with facsimile signature 'Goldscheider' and model no.'1620/1/17'.

54in (138cm) high

$3,500-4,500 **ROS**

A Goldscheider terracotta bust of a Nubian slave girl, modeled holding a scallop-shell dish, label partially lost.

22in (55cm) high

$6,500-7,500 **SWO**

A Goldscheider figure of 'Helen', designed by Ernst Seger (1868-1939), model no.'3697/46/65', with black factory mark.

c1909 22in (55.5cm) high

$2,500-3,500 **DOR**

A Goldscheider alabaster figure of a seated nude, model no.4625.K.54, designed by E Tell, with incised marks and inlaid coin mark, on a stone base.

c1908 13.75in (38cm) high

$2,500-3,500 **DOR**

A Goldscheider figure of a dancing girl, signed and stamped '7776 1'.

16.5in (42cm) high

$1,200-1,800 **IMC**

A Goldscheider figure of 'Festive Rhythm', after the dancer Mary Wigman, model no.8706/211/7, with a factory label to base, with black factory mark and impressed marks, with repaired crack.

c1939 14.75in (37.5cm) high

$1,200-1,800 **DOR**

A rare Goldscheider figure of a female dancer, model no.5543, designed by Josef Lorenzl, inscribed 'AS' and 'D.5.X11', with impressed marks, signed.

19.75in (50cm) high

$5,500-6,500 **HT**

A Goldscheider figure of a girl, model no.8711, with impressed and printed marks, with restoration to hands.

15in (38cm) high

$1,800-2,200 **WW**

A Goldscheider figure of 'Tricorne' (a girl in a carnival costume), model no.'5658/179/16', designed by Stefan Dakon, with black factory mark and impressed marks, with restoration.

c1927 *13in (32.5cm) high*

$2,500-3,500 **DOR**

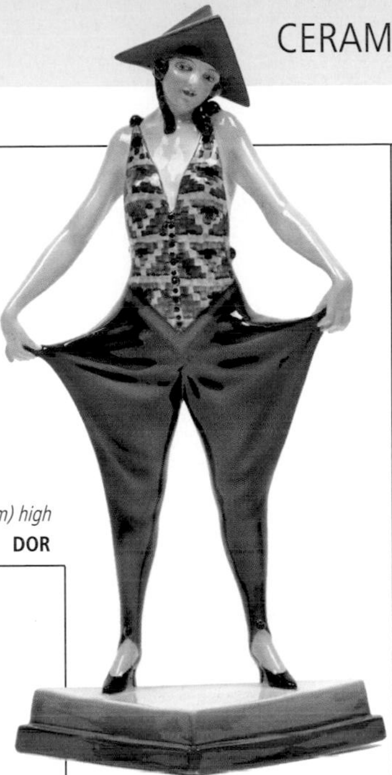

A Goldscheider figure of a woman in a bathing costume walking her Borzoi, model no.8117, designed by Stefan Dakon.

c1939 *12.5in (33cm) high*

$3,000-4,000 **SWO**

A Goldscheider figural lamp base, model no.6912, designed by Stefan Dakon, with impressed factory marks and facsimile signature, with chip.

12in (30.5cm) high

$1,000-1,500 **WW**

A Goldscheider figure of a ski girl, model no.7149.

12in (30.5cm) high

$2,000-3,000 **GORL**

A Goldscheider figure of a female dancer, with black printed mark and impressed model no.'5822.639.6'.

18in (46cm) high

$2,000-3,000 **AH**

A Goldscheider figure of a woman with a guitar, model no.6901, designed by Stefan Dakon, with printed and impressed marks.

17in (42cm) high

$2,000-3,000 **WW**

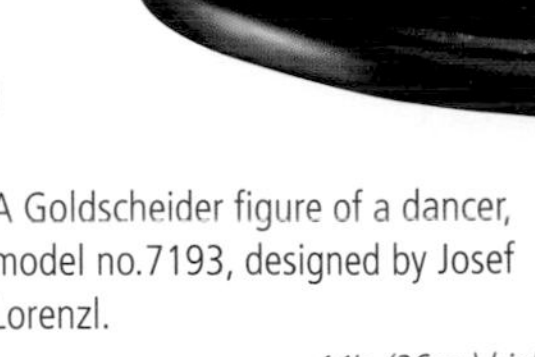

A Goldscheider figure of a dancer, model no.7193, designed by Josef Lorenzl.

14in (36cm) high

$2,000-3,000 **GORL**

A rare Grueby vase, glazed in matt green, with circular pottery stamp.

9.5in (24cm) high

$6,500-7,500 **DRA**

A Grueby two-color vase, modeled by Ruth Erickson, with Grueby Pottery stamp and 'RE BL 13-08'.

Ruth Erickson worked at Grueby c1899–1910.

8.5in (21.6cm) high

$5,000-7,000 **DRA**

ESSENTIAL REFERENCE - GRUEBY

William H Grueby (1867-1925) began his career in ceramics at the J & J G Low Art Title Works, Chelsea, MA, USA. He was briefly in partnership with Eugene R Atwood in 1892 before he established his own pottery, the Grueby Faience Company, in 1894.

- **The Grueby Faience Company specialized in handmade tiles and slip-cast vessels, which were typically glazed in organic tones of green, yellow and ocher.**
- **In 1908 the pottery went bankrupt.**
- **In 1910 William H Grueby opened a new firm, the Grueby Faience & Tile Company, which made architectural wares.**
- **In 1920, this company was bought by the C Pardee Works, NJ, which continued to make Grueby-style tiles until the late 1920s.**

A Grueby melon-shaped vase, modeled by Ruth Erickson with leaves, with blue-gray glaze, with circular pottery stamp and paper label 'RE'.

11in (28cm) high

$6,500-7,500 **DRA**

A Grueby vase, modeled with with two rows of leaves, glazed in matt green, with circular faience stamp no.'180'

20in (51cm) high

$20,000-30,000 **DRA**

A Grueby tile, decorated with a yellow tulip, signed 'ES', with remnant of paper label.

6in (15cm) wide

$1,500-2,500 **DRA**

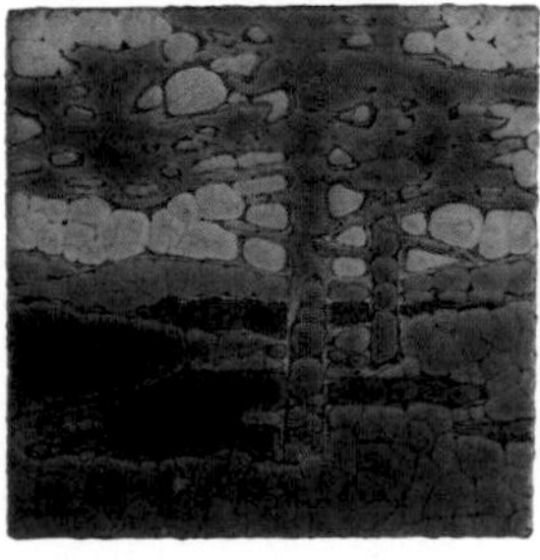

A Grueby 'The Pines' trivet tile, unmarked.

6in (15cm) wide

$3,000-4,000 **DRA**

An early 20thC Grueby tile, decorated with turtle under leaves, unsigned, with heavy restoration.

$1,000-1,500 **DRA**

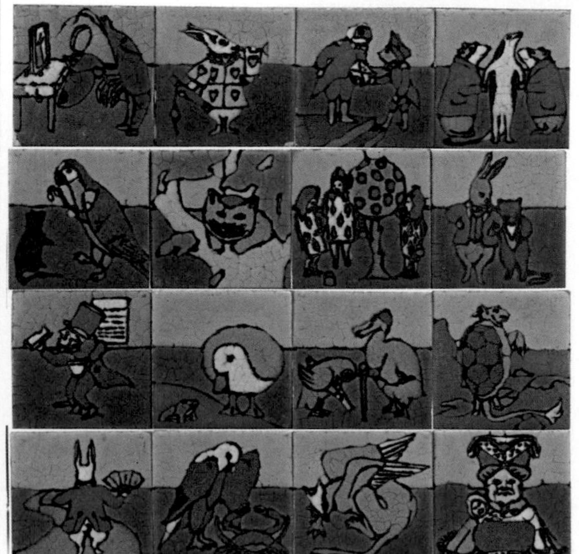

A rare collection of sixteen Grueby 'Alice in Wonderland' tiles, designed by C Pardee, numbered, some with artist initials.

c1915

Each 4in (10cm) wide

$15,000-20,000 **DRA**

A pair of Brown-Westhead, Moore & Co. majolica vases and covers, the finials in the form of fruit.

15in (39cm) high

$2,500-3,500 **WHP**

Two 19thC Portuguese majolica fish bowls, Caldas da Rainha, one impressed 'M Mafra Caldas, Portugal', one damaged.

Longest 15in (37cm) long

$2,000-3,000 **MAR**

A Portuguese Palissy-style majolica charger, Caldas da Rainha, with a toad and serpent in mortal combat, with impressed marks, with restored chips.

c1880 *16in (40.5cm) diam*

$1,200-1,800 **DN**

A late 19thC Portuguese Palissy-style majolica dish, with small chips.

14in (36cm) diam

$2,500-3,500 **DN**

A George Jones majolica game-pie dish and cover, with extensive damage.

13in (33cm) wide

$3,500-4,500 **A&G**

A Portuguese Palissy-style majolica ewer and cover, Caldas da Rainha, with frog knop and lizard handle.

c1900 *15in (40.5cm) high*

$500-700 **TEN**

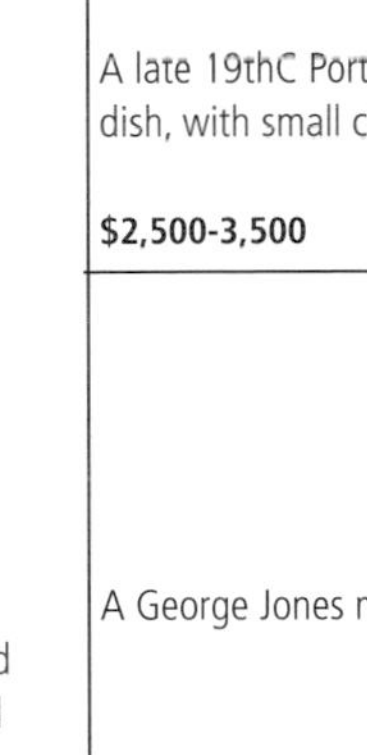

A George Jones majolica centerpiece.

10in (25cm) high

$7,000-10,000 **WHP**

One of a set of six George Jones majolica dishes, marked 'G J & Sons' and with Victorian registration mark.

10in (26cm) diam

$6,500-7,500 set **LC**

A George Jones majolica cheese stand and cover, modeled as a thatched straw hive, with registration mark, with restoration.

1872 *13.5in (34cm) high*

$7,000-10,000 **WW**

ESSENTIAL REFERENCE - MINTON

Thomas Minton (1765–1836) trained as an engraver at Caughley and is credited with developing the 'Willow' pattern. In 1796 he founded the Minton ceramics factory in Stoke-on-Trent.

- **In c1798 Minton began to produce cream-colored bone china. A slump in the economy caused production of bone china to cease in 1816. It resumed in 1822.**
- **In 1849 Joseph-François Léon Arnoux, a ceramicist from Sèvres, became art director. Among his innovations was the development of majolica.**
- **Minton's merged with Royal Doulton in 1968.**

A Minton majolica quatre-lobed jardinière and stand, with impressed mark and date code, with restoration.

1867 *23in (58cm) high*

$1,500-2,500 **WW**

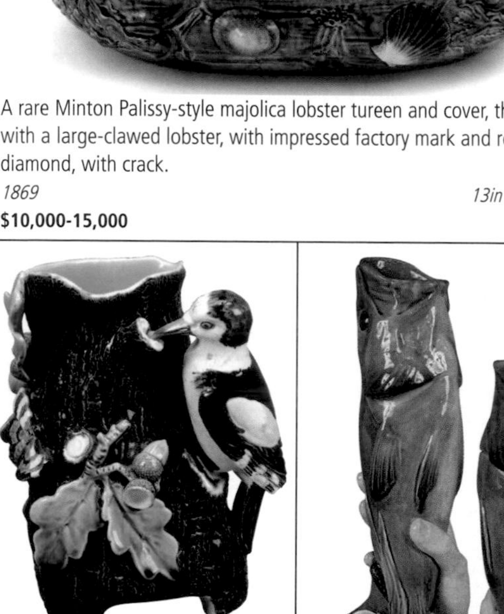

A rare Minton Palissy-style majolica lobster tureen and cover, the cover with a large-clawed lobster, with impressed factory mark and registration diamond, with crack.

1869 *13in (34cm) wide*

$10,000-15,000 **WW**

A Minton majolica vase, modeled as a tree-trunk with woodpecker, model no.1558, with printed and impressed marks, with date code, with damage and loss.

1870 *7in (18cm) high*

$5,500-6,500 **DN**

A pair of Minton majolica vases, model no.1321, with impressed marks, with minor restoration.

1868 *10in (23cm) high*

$2,000-3,000 **TOV**

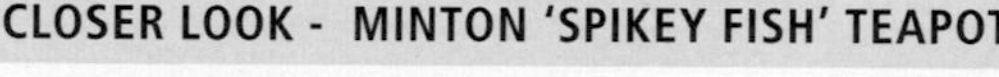

A Minton majolica oyster dish, modeled with tiers of shells with a fish and eel finial, with impressed numbers and date code, with a small chip.

1872 *10in (25cm) high*

$2,500-3,500 **WW**

CLOSER LOOK - MINTON 'SPIKEY FISH' TEAPOT

This teapot embodies the humor and quirkiness of majolica designs of the late 19thC.

All the elements are here – it is modeled as a strange blue fish riding on green waves.

The spout protrudes from the mouth and the cover has a spiky dorsal fin as the knop.

The handle is formed from seaweed with a snail shell as the thumb-rest.

Victoriana at its exuberant best!

A 19thC Minton majolica 'Spikey Fish' teapot, stamped 'Minton', with chips and restoration.

7.25in (18.5cm) high

$10,000-15,000 **DRA**

A 19thC Palissy-style majolica dish.

15.25in (39cm) diam

$2,000-3,000 **FRE**

A pair of late 19thC majolica wall brackets, modeled by Hughes Protat, with impressed mark.

15.75in (40cm) high

$1,500-2,500 **CAPE**

A late 19thC Wedgwood majolica basket, cover and stand.

8.5in (22cm) high

$3,000-4,000 **GORL**

A Royal Worcester majolica fish pitcher, with chip.

1886 *12in (31cm) high*

$350-450 **WW**

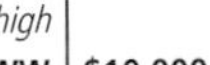

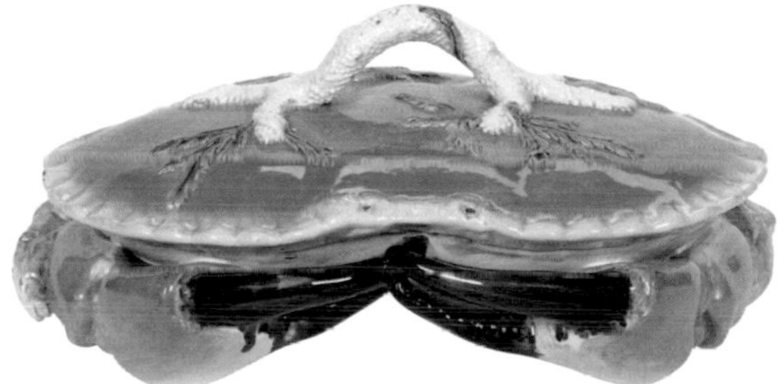

A late 19thC majolica crab-form sauce tureen.

14in (35cm) wide

$10,000-15,000 **TEN**

A Continental majolica game bird cache pot and stand, the stand model no. 1203, with impressed marks and initialed 'BF'.

c1875 *15in (39cm) high*

$6,500-7,500 **TEN**

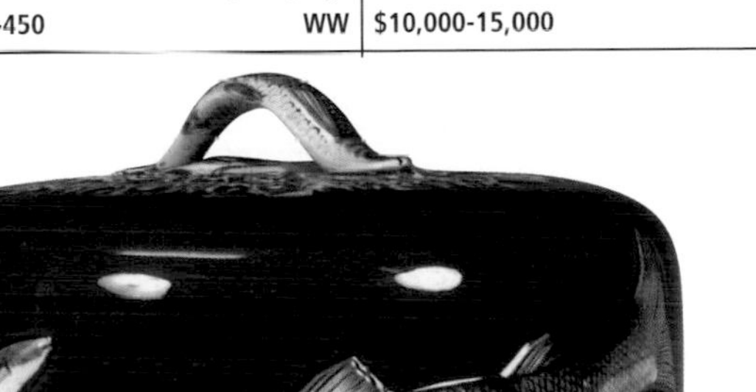

A 19thC majolica cheese dish and cover.

9in (24cm) high

$1,200-1,800 **L&T**

A late 19thC creamware teapot and cover, modeled as a monkey painted in majolica colours,with slight damage to the cover.

9in (23cm) high

$700-1,000 **WW**

A late 19thC Continental majolica jardinière and stand.

54.25in (138cm) high

$3,000-4,000 **L&T**

A Martin Brothers stoneware bird tobacco jar, inscribed 'R.W. Martin & Bros. London and Southall' and marked '10-1887'.

1887 *8.5in (22cm) high*

$25,000-30,000 **SK**

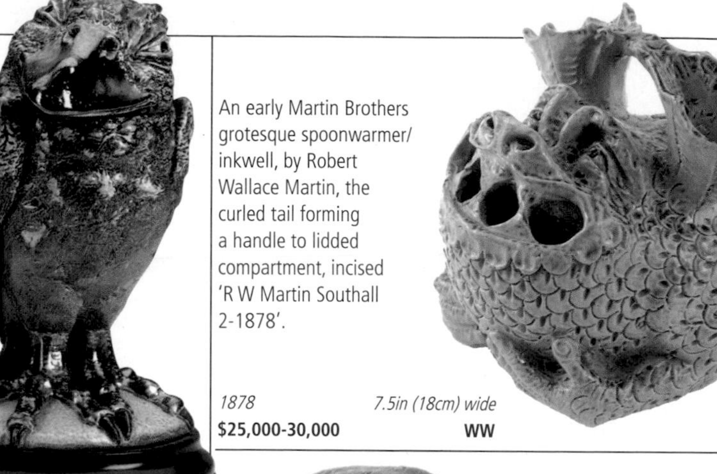

A Martin Brothers stoneware bird tobacco jar, signed 'Martin Bros, London, Southall, 5-1897'.

1897 *8.5in (22cm) high*

$30,000-40,000 **DRA**

An early Martin Brothers grotesque spoonwarmer/inkwell, by Robert Wallace Martin, the curled tail forming a handle to lidded compartment, incised 'R W Martin Southall 2-1878'.

1878 *7.5in (18cm) wide*

$25,000-30,000 **WW**

Judith Picks

The one rule of valuing antiques is that something does not have to be a thing of beauty to be very valuable – it just has to be rare and desirable. I was reminded of this when I came across this grotesque model. The Martin Brothers fame derives from their models of grotesque birds, jars and face-pots. These were made by hand in stoneware, each piece was unique and individual.

The Martin Brothers can be thought of as eccentric, but at the time there was a Gothic Revival spreading through out the country, and the Martin Brothers wares were reminiscent of the Middle Ages. This tonsured figure grasping his chest with long bony figures with pointed nails and casting a slight sideways glance with a seriously maniacal smile could be out of 'Lord of the Rings' or your worst nightmare. But nightmare turned to dream when you see the value.

A rare Martin Brothers stoneware grotesque jar and cover, incised 'R W Martin & Bros, London & Southall 10-1900'.

1900 *6.5in (16.5cm) high*

$100,000-150,000 **WW**

A rare Martin Brothers stoneware monkey jar and cover, incised '11-1903 Martin Bros, London & Southall', with exhibition paper label, with hairline crack.

1903 *10in (23cm) high*

$30,000-40,000 **WW**

A Martin Brothers stoneware face jug, incised 'R W Martin & Bros., London and Southall 31.1.1911'.

1911 *5in (15cm) high*

$8,000-12,000 **SWO**

A Martin Brothers stoneware vase, inscribed 'R W Martin & Bros, London and Southall, 11-1886'.

1886 *8in (20cm) high*

$3,000-4,000 **SWO**

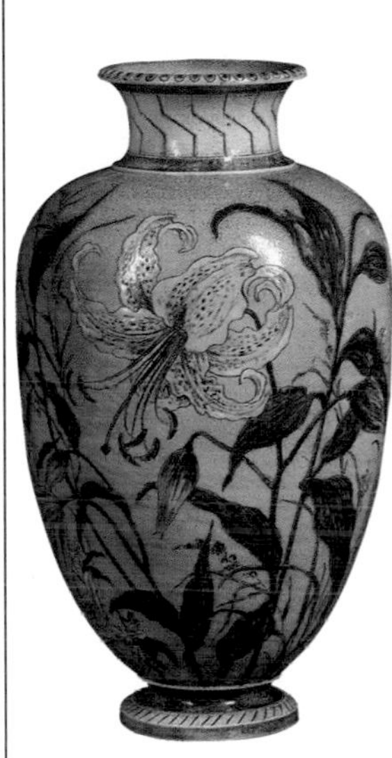

A large Martin Brothers stoneware vase, inscribed '9-1889, RW Martin & Bros, London & Southall'.

1889 *16.5in (42cm) high*

$10,000-15,000 **SK**

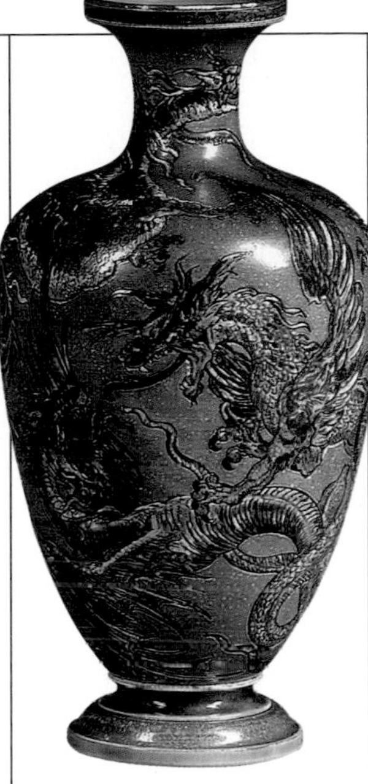

A Martin Brothers stoneware 'Dragon' vase, incised 'R.W. Martin & Bros. London & Southall', dated.

1892 *9.5in (24cm) high*

$5,000-7,000 **SK**

A Martin Brothers stoneware gourd-shaped vase, incised '6-1907 Martin Bros London & Southall'.

1907 *4.5in (11.5cm) high*

$2,000-3,000 **TEN**

A Martin Brothers stoneware 'Eskimo' jug, with ear handle.

1903 *14.25in (36cm) high*

$12,000-18,000 **SK**

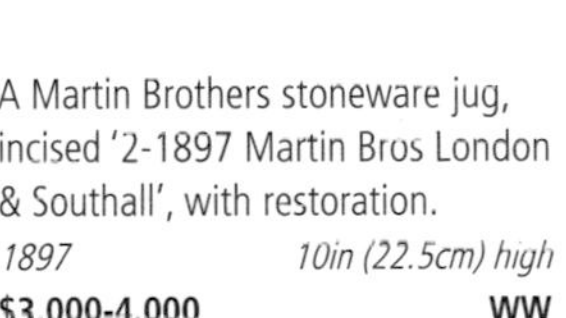

A Martin Brothers stoneware jug, incised '2-1897 Martin Bros London & Southall', with restoration.

1897 *10in (22.5cm) high*

$3,000-4,000 **WW**

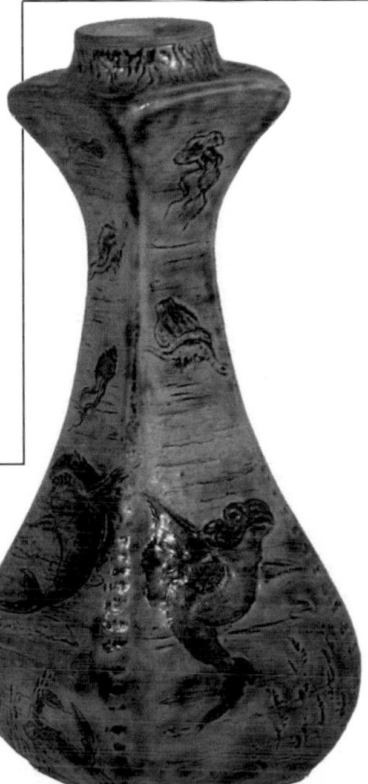

A Martin Brothers stoneware aquatic candlestick, incised '3-1907 Martin Bros, London & Southall', drilled to base probably at the factory.

1907 *7in (18.5cm) high*

$5,000-7,000 **WW**

A Martin Brothers stoneware mug, inscribed 'Alice', incised '12-1893, Martin Bros, London & Southall'.

This mug might relate to the Martin Brothers' sister Alice Martin.

1893 *3.75in (9.5cm) high*

$1,200-1,800 **WW**

A Martin Brothers stoneware jardinière, incised '10-1892, Martin Bros London & Southall', with restuck glaze chip and hairline.

1892 *7.5in (21cm) high*

$8,000-12,000 **WW**

ESSENTIAL REFERENCE - MINTON ART POTTERY

- **The Minton Art Pottery studio was opened under the directorship of W J Coleman in 1871.**
- **It was opened with the stated aim that 'eminent artists, ladies especially, may be induced to paint upon porcelain and majolica'.**
- **The Kensington Gore building was destroyed by fire in 1875.**
- **As the first art pottery studio to be opened, the Minton studio was very influential.**

A probably Minton earthenware dish, designed by A W N Pugin, decorated with Gothic motifs.
c1860 *12.5in (34cm) diam*
$1,000-1,500 **SWO**

A Minton Art Pottery, Kensington Gore charger, painted by Rebecca Coleman, stamped, impressed and signed, with crack and stapled.
1871-75 *19in (48.5cm) diam*
$1,000-1,500 **TRI**

A Minton Art Pottery Studio charger, painted by William S Coleman, with a female nude holding a fan, with printed factory mark, signed, with chip and minor repair.
15.25in (39cm) diam
$12,000-18,000 **WW**

A pair of Minton Secessionist vases, with printed marks and date code.
1910 *12.5in (32cm) high*
$500-700 **GORB**

A pair of late 19thC Minton Aesthetic vases, with gilt factory marks to bases, with minor faults.
7.5in (19cm) high
$550-750 **TOV**

A pair of Minton 'cloisonné' vases, designed by Christopher Dresser, with impressed marks.
6.5in (17cm) high
$1,500-2,500 **GORL**

A Minton Art Pottery, Kensington Gore jardinière, stamped 'Mintons Art Pottery Studio, Kensington Gore', with impressed marks.
c1871-75 *8in (20cm) diam*
$2,000-3,000 **TRI**

A Minton, Hollins & Co. tile, with impressed marks.
11in (28cm) wide
$1,200-1,800 **WW**

A Minton two-tile panel, painted by Linnie Watt, with children picnicing in a wooded landscape, signed, framed.
Tiles 15.75in (40cm) long
$5,000-7,000 **WW**

A unique James Macintyre & Co. flambé 'Carp' vase, by William Moorcroft, with impressed Burslem mark, with painted green signature.

This was a world record price for a Moorcroft vase.

12in (30.5cm) high

$55,000-65,000 WW

A James Macintyre & Co. Florian 'Harebell' vase, designed by William Moorcroft, with printed brown mark, with painted green signature.

1902-04 *7.75in (20cm) high*

$5,000-7,000 AH

A pair of James Macintyre & Co. Florian 'Poppy' vases, designed by William Moorcroft, with brown painted Florian ware mark and green signature.

c1903 *12in (30.5cm) high*

$5,500-6,500 HT

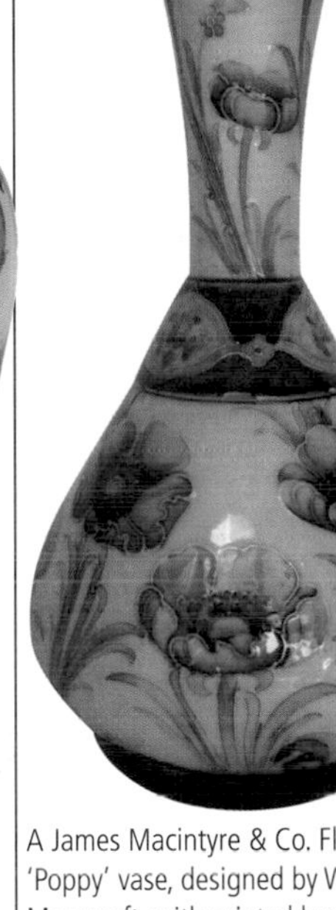

A James Macintyre & Co. Florian 'Poppy' vase, designed by William Moorcroft, with printed brown factory mark and 'Rd No. 401753', impressed '163', with painted green signature.

c1904 *9in (24cm) high*

$3,000-4,000 TEN

A James Macintyre & Co. 'Revived Cornflower' tea set, designed by William Moorcroft, with printed marks, initialed 'WM' in green.

Teapot 4.7in (12cm) high

$5,500-6,500 FLD

A James Macintyre & Co. jardinière, designed by William Moorcroft, decorated with sprays of roses, tulips and forget-me-nots, with printed marks, with painted signature.

c1907 *11in (28cm) high*

$2,500-3,500 CHEF

A Moorcroft Pottery 'Hazledene' centerpiece bowl.

15.25in (39cm) diam

$5,500-6,500 POOK

A Moorcroft Pottery 'Hazeldene' wafer box and cover, designed by William Moorcroft, printed 'Made for Liberty & Co.' and 'RdNo. 397964', with painted green signature 'William Moorcroft des', the lid with some damage.

6in (15cm) wide

$7,000-9,000 FLD

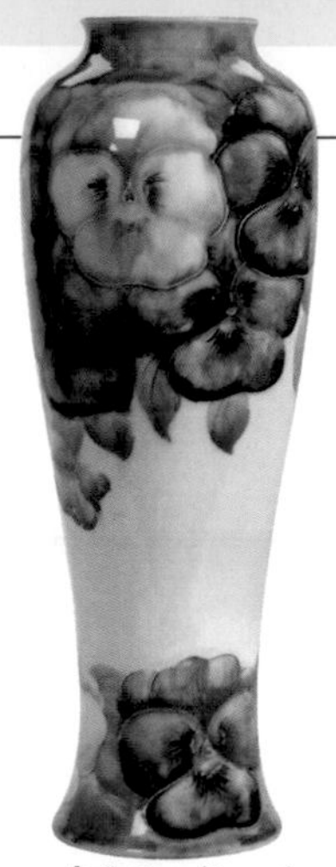

A Moorcroft Pottery 'Pansy' vase, with printed brown factory mark, with painted green signature, with impressed numbers.

c1914 *12in (29.5cm) high*

$4,000-6,000 **TEN**

A pair of miniature James Macintyre & Co. 'Pansy' vases, designed by William Moorcroft, initialed in green.

3in (7.6cm) high

$7,000-9,000 **GORL**

A pair of Moorcroft Pottery 'Spanish' vases, designed by William Moorcroft, impressed 'Moorcroft, Burslem, England' and '24', with green signatures, the newer vase with glue-repair to neck.

The 'Spanish' design was introduced in 1910 and was made until the 1930s. It combines the flowing linear style of the early Florian wares with the richer colors of 'Pomegranate' and later patterns. Darker greens and blues are scarcer than greeny-beige.

1915 and 1918 *10in (26.5cm) high*

$6,500-7,500 **H&L**

Judith Picks

The prices paid for Moorcroft, particularly early Moorcroft, have constantly risen over a period when the work of other potteries has suffered. Moorcroft collectors have consistently kept the prices strong. William Moorcroft was an innovator and although the vase here is not the most visually exciting, it shows Moorcroft continuing to push the boundaries. The flambé kiln was introduced at Cobridge in 1919 and in production by 1921. It was difficult to control so William Moorcroft allowed pieces to develop in the kiln, reveling in the varied effects it could produce. He continued to develop the technique and actually delighted in the unpredictability of each piece and the eccentricity of the colors produced. The almost metallic finish on this vase could well be an example of his experimentation. Moorcroft was very secretive about the flambé firings and insisted that he should control the ovens himself.

A Moorcroft Pottery flambé 'Eventide' vase.

c1925 *9.25in (23cm) high*

$1,500-2,500 **A&G**

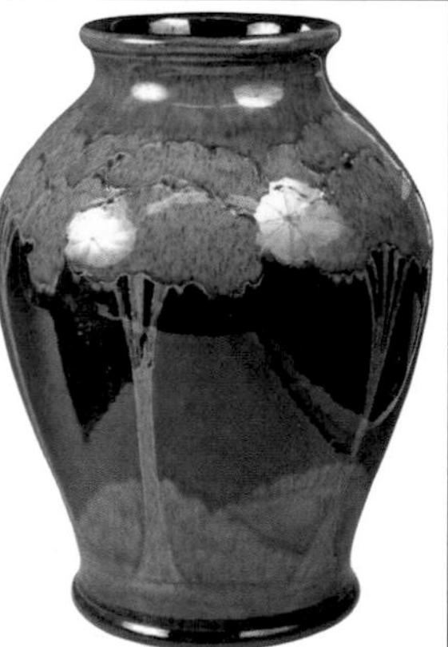

A large Moorcroft Pottery 'Moonlit Blue' vase, with green facsimile signature, with impressed marks, with crazing and star-crack to base.

c1924 *14.75in (37.5cm) high*

$8,000-12,000 **SWO**

A Moorcroft 'Leaf and Fruit' salt-glazed vase, with painted and impressed signatures, a small part of rim re-glued.

1928-34 *6in (15cm) high*

$2,500-3,500 **A&G**

A Moorcroft Pottery flambé lidded bowl, with tube-lined decoration of fish among reeds, with impressed marks and painted initials.

1930-38 *5.5in (14cm) diam*

$5,000-7,000 **AH**

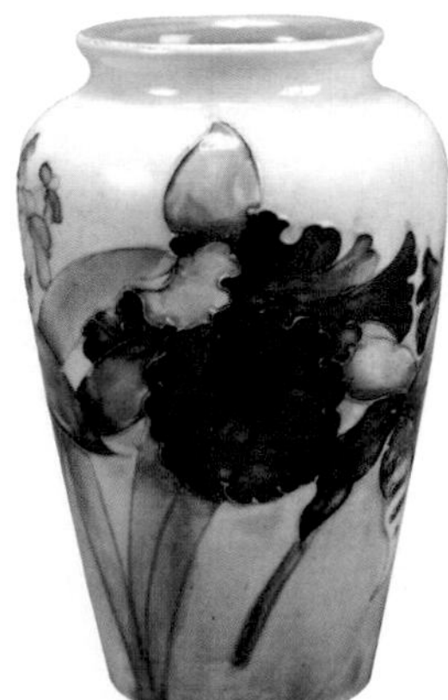

A Moorcroft 'Orchid' vase, with impressed and painted marks, with remains of label 'Potters to the late Queen Mary'.

1953-78 *8in (20cm) high*

$400-600 **DN**

An early Newcomb College jar, slip-decorated by Harriet Joor with palm fronds, marked 'NC/HJ/JM/U'.
c1905 *16in (40.5cm) high*
$7,000-9,000 **DRA**

A Newcomb College vase, decorated by Katherine Walker, carved with dogwood, marked 'NC/JM/KW/BT78/Q'.
1907 *5in (12.5cm) high*
$12,000-18,000 **DRA**

A Newcomb College vase, decorated by Marie De Hoa LeBlanc.
1908 *9in (23cm) high*
$2,500-3,500 **SK**

A Newcomb College Transitional vase, decorated by Henrietta Bailey with pine trees, marked 'NC/HB/JM/165/HT73'.
1915 *12in (30.5cm) high*
$10,000-15,000 **DRA**

A Newcomb College vase, decorated by A F Simpson marked 'NC/SK43/500/JH AFS'.
1930 *6in (15cm) high*
$5,500-6,500 **DRA**

A Newcomb College match holder, decorated by an unknown artist, with marks.
2.5in (6.5cm) high
$700-1,000 **DRA**

A North Dakota School of Mines vase, decorated by Flora Huckfield, with circular indigo stamp and 'FLH'.
9.5in (24cm) high
$15,000-20,000 **DRA**

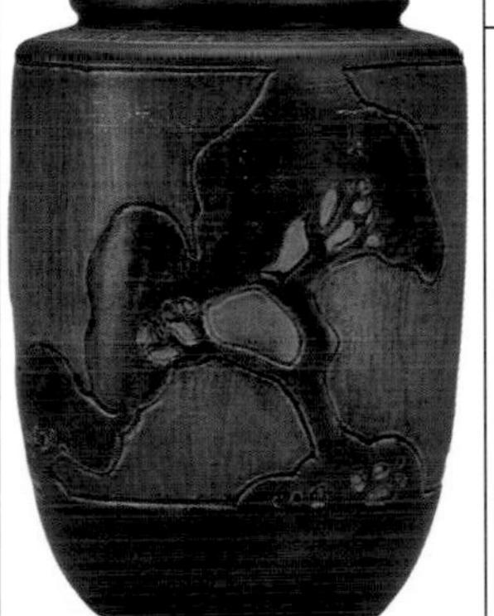

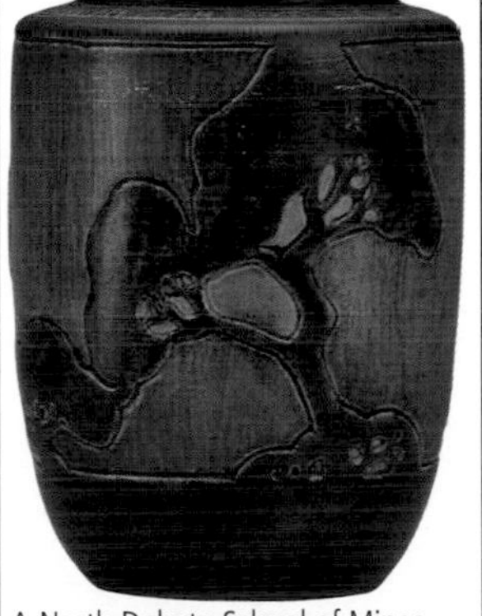

A North Dakota School of Mines commemorative vase, decorated by Margaret Cable, carved with 'Awarded by the 1934 All-American Turkey Show Grand Forks N.D. for Excellence'.
1934 *8in (20.5cm) high*
$4,000-6,000 **DRA**

A North Dakota School of Mines covered vessel, decorated by Ruth Schnell, inscribed 'For my son Richard from mother, 4/10 1945', signed, with circular indigo stamp.
1945 *6.5in (16.5cm) high*
$3,000-4,000 **DRA**

A North Dakota School of Mines vase, decorated by L Whiting, stamped mark.
1942 *4.5in (11.5cm) diam*
$700-1,000 **DRA**

A George Ohr dimpled and ruffled vessel, stamped 'G.E.OHR Biloxi, Miss.'.

3.5in (9cm) high

$7,000-9,000 **DRA**

A George Ohr vase, in mottled gun-metal, raspberry and green glaze, stamped 'G.E. OHR, Biloxi, Miss.'.

6in (15cm) high

$4,000-6,000 **DRA**

A George Ohr dimpled and ruffled vase, stamped 'G.E.OHR Biloxi, Miss.'.

3.75in (9.5cm) high

$5,000-7,000 **DRA**

A George Ohr sculptural pitcher, of marbleized clays, with script signature.

4.5in (11.5cm) high

$8,000-12,000 **DRA**

A George Ohr corseted vase, with in-body twist, in green and brown sponged-on glaze, on burnt-siena ground, stamped 'G.E.Ohr, BILOXI'.

4in (10cm) high

$5,000-7,000 **DRA**

A George Ohr white-clay squat vessel, with ruffled rim, with script signature.

3.5in (9cm) high

$3,500-4,500 **DRA**

A George Ohr squat vessel, stamped 'G.E. OHR, Biloxi, Miss.'.

3in (7.5cm) high

$3,500-4,500 **DRA**

A large George Ohr dimpled vessel, with folded rim, stamped 'G.E.OHR Biloxi, Miss.', with original price tag of '$85'.

6in (15cm) high

$15,000-20,000 **DRA**

A Poole Pottery 'Holly' vase, shape no.949, decorated in pattern 'LG' designed by Truda Carter, decorated by Anne Hatchard, with impressed mark and decorator's mark.

13.75in (35cm) high

$5,500-6,500 FLD

A Poole Pottery vase, decorated in pattern 'TZ', decorated by Marjorie Batt, with impressed and painted marks.

9.5in (24cm) high

$1,800-2,200 WW

A Poole Pottery 'Leaping Gazelle' vase, decorated pattern 'TZ' designed by Truda Carter, with impressed marks.

7.5in (16cm) high

$250-350 FLD

A Poole Pottery vase, decorated in pattern 'JR' designed by Ruth Pavely, with hairline crack.

8in (20cm) high

$400-600 WW

A 1920s Poole Pottery vase, decorated in pattern 'PN', with impressed and painted marks, with minor damage.

6.75in (17cm) high

$2,000-3,000 FLD

Judith Picks

The Poole Pottery artist Guy Sydenham produced this figure of a rhino calf as part of a very small series of African Animals he created with his associate, Beatrice Bolton, in the late 1970s. This naturalistic model and its mother were both for sale at the Poole factory. The calf was then priced at £180 ($300). Just one other rhino calf is known to exist. The 16in (40cm) long Sydenham-Bolton rhino cow (the mother) is even more valuable than the baby! It sold in December 2012 for $13,500, despite having a re-glued horn. Both models were on display in a photograph showing the Queen and Prince Philip at the Poole factory

A Poole Pottery stoneware model of a baby rhinoceros, designed by Guy Sydenham and Beatrice Bolton, with a small 'fleabite' chip to the ear.

Late 1970s *10in (25cm) long*

$10,000-15,000 COT

A Poole Pottery figure of a child, designed by Phoebe Stabler, stamped 'Carter Stabler Adams, Poole, England'.

6.75in (17cm) high

$800-1,200 SWO

A Poole Pottery figure of a 'Picardy Peasant', designed by Phoebe Stabler, with stamped mark.

10.5in (27cm) high

$800-1,200 DUK

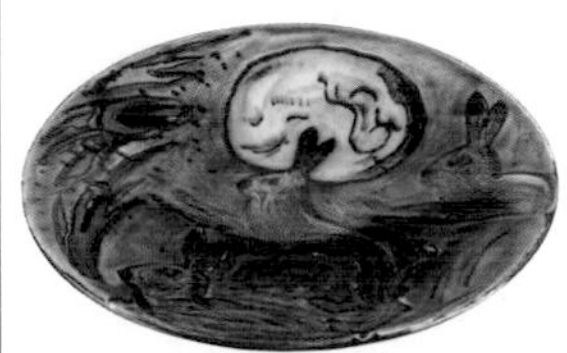

A unique Poole Studio 'Dancing Hares' charger, decorated by Anita Harris, signed and dated '00', marked '1/1'.

2000 *16in (41cm) diam*

$650-850 A&G

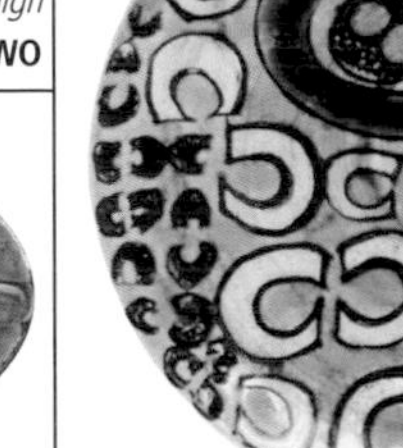

A Poole Studio plaque, probably decorated by Tony Morris with printed 'TV' mark.

8in (20.5cm) diam

$1,000-1,500 FLD

An early Rookwood covered jar, decorated by Fannie Auckland, marked 'Rookwood Pottery Cin O 1881 F.A.'.

1881 *8in (20cm) high*

$800-1,200 **DRA**

A Rookwood 'dull finish' porcelain urn, decorated by Artus Van Briggle.

1891 *12.5in (32cm) high*

$3,000-4,000 **DRA**

ESSENTIAL REFERENCE - KATARO SHIRAYAMADANI

Kataro Shirayamadani (1865–1948) was born in Kanazawa, Japan.

- **Before working at Rookwood, he worked at Fujiyama, an important retail and decorating shop in Boston.**
- **He was hired by Rookwood in 1887, with the specific goal of bringing a Japanese influence to the pottery. He continued to work at the company until his death.**
- **He also designed many of the company's molds.**
- **He typically decorated the entire surface of a vase, rather than just the 'front'.**
- **He is considered by many to be Rookwood's greatest artist.**

A Rookwood relief 'Iris' glaze vase, decorated by Matt Daly with hyacinths, with flame mark and '604 C M. A. Daly'.

1900 *12in (30.5cm) high*

$3,000-4,000 **DRA**

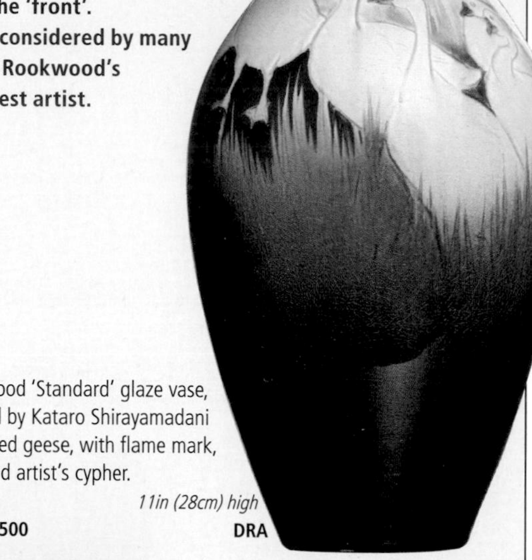

A Rookwood 'Standard' glaze vase, decorated by Kataro Shirayamadani with incised geese, with flame mark, '745A' and artist's cypher.

1898 *11in (28cm) high*

$6,500-7,500 **DRA**

A Rookwood carved 'Sea Green' vase, decorated by Anna Marie Valentien, modeled with a nude woman wrapped around its rim, with flame mark, '162Z' and 'A.M.V.' marks.

1900 *3.25in (8.5cm) high*

$20,000-30,000 **DRA**

A Rookwood carved and painted 'Black Iris' vase, decorated by Kataro Shirayamadani, with flame mark, '07B/W' and artist's cypher, with short glazed-over firing line to footrim.

1901 *17.5in (44.5cm) high*

$30,000-40,000 **DRA**

A Rookwood 'Matt' glaze lamp base, decorated by William P McDonald, with flame mark, '323AZ' and 'WMD' marks, with factory oil font, chimney and hand-painted milk-glass globe.

1902 *Total 29.5in (75cm) high*

$3,000-4,000 **DRA**

A Rookwood 'Iris' glaze vase, decorated by Lenore Asbury, with hollyhocks, with flame mark, '939B', 'L.A.' and 'W' marks.

1907 *9.75in (25cm) high*

$2,500-3,500 DRA

A Rookwood marine 'Scenic Vellum' vase, decorated by Frederick Rothenbusch with sailboats, with flame mark, '399C' and 'FR'.

1908 *9in (23cm) high*

$4,000-6,000 DRA

A Rookwood 'Iris' glaze vase, decorated by Kataro Shirayamadani, with flame mark, '907C' amd artist's cypher.

1908 *13.5in (34.5cm) high*

$18,000-22,000 DRA

A Rookwood matt glaze faience umbrella stand, decorated with geese, with flame mark, 'XI' and '1235AY'.

1911 *26in (66cm) high*

$4,000-6,000 DRA

A Rookwood 'Standard' glaze ewer, decorated by Rose Fechheimer with lilies, with marks.

1914 *10in (25cm) high*

$400-600 DRA

A large Rookwood 'Scenic Vellum' plaque, decorated by Sallie Coyne, in a contemporary Arts & Crafts frame.

Sallie Coyne (1876-1939) was a decorator at Rookwood 1891-c1931.

Plaque 12in (30.5cm) wide

$10,000-15,000 DRA

A Rookwood 'Scenic Vellum' plaque, decorated by Charles McLaughlin, with flame mark and signature, in original frame.

1915 *Plaque 8in (20.5cm) wide*

$5,000-7,000 DRA

A Rookwood 'Scenic Vellum' vase, decorated with a landscape.

10.5in (27cm) high

$2,500-3,500 POOK

A Rookwood 'Wax Mat' glaze vase, decorated by Elizabeth Barrett, with a portrait of a lady and blossoms, with flame mark and '6197F' mark, with artist's cypher.

1943 *4.75in (12cm) high*

$2,000-3,000 DRA

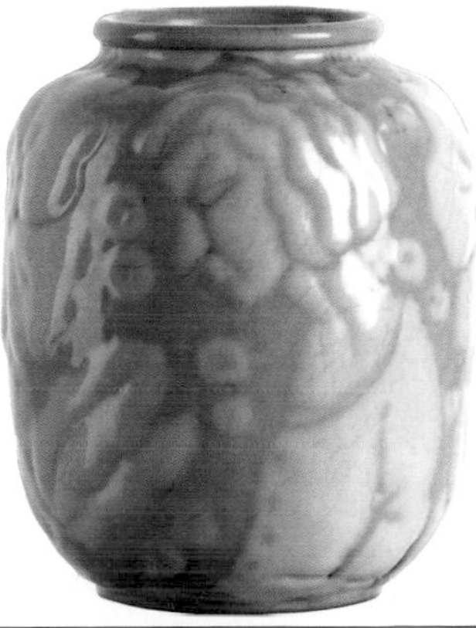

A Roseville 'Blackberry' vase, unmarked.

12in (30cm) high

$800-1,200 **DRA**

A Roseville 'Della Robbia' vase, carved with cherry branches, marked 'GB', with restored drill hole to base and restoration to neck.

11.25in (28.5cm) high

$3,000-4,000 **DRA**

A Roseville 'Dogwood I' umbrella stand, with 'RV' ink mark, with small chip.

20in (51cm) high

$1,000-1,500 **DRA**

A Roseville brown 'Ferrella' vase, with short tight line to rim.

10in (25cm) high

$700-1,000 **DRA**

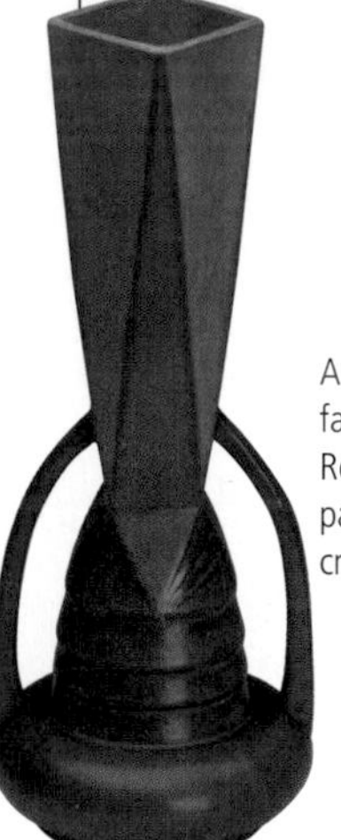

A Roseville 'Futura' faceted vase, with Roseville silver paper label, with cracks.

14in (36cm) high

$2,500-3,500 **DRA**

A Roseville green 'Pinecone' ice-lip pitcher, shape no.1321, with stamped marks.

$500-700 **DRA**

A Roseville 'Rozane', vase, decorated by Hester Pillsbury with nasturtium, with 'Rozane' medallion, minor stilt pull.

8.5in (22cm) high

$300-500 **DRA**

A rare Roseville 'Rozane' 'Olympic' vase, depicting 'Persia and Ionia Yoked to the Chariot of Xerxes', signed and titled.

14.5in (37cm) high

$5,500-6,500 **DRA**

A Roseville 'Sunflower' vase, unsigned.

10.5in (27cm) high

$1,500-2,500 **DRA**

A Roseville 'Sunflower' jardinière, unmarked.

9in (23cm) high

$1,200-1,800 **DRA**

A Roseville 'Vista' floor vase, unmarked.

18in (46cm) high

$800-1,200 **DRA**

ESSENTIAL REFERENCE - VAN BRIGGLE

Artus Van Briggle (1869-1904) trained at the Beaux Arts Academy and the Julian Art School in France. During the 1890s he worked as a decorator for Rookwood, before leaving in 1899 for Colorado Springs, CO, due to his tuberculosis.

- **In Colorado he established a pottery where he produced matt-glazed pottery in the Art Nouveau style.**
- **After his death, the pottery was carried on by his widow, Anna. She moved to a larger factory in 1907 before selling it in 1912.**
- **The pottery is still active today, making copies of Van Briggle's original wares.**

A Van Briggle vase, with bronzed handles by Yosakichi Asano, incised 'AA VAN BRIGGLE 228 1903 III'.

Yosakichi Asano had designed metalware for Rookwood during Van Briggle's time at that pottery.

1903 *11in (28cm) high*

$40,000-60,000 DRA

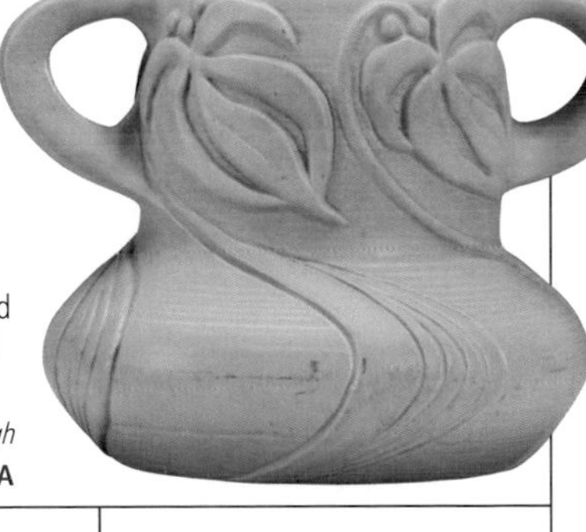

A Van Briggle vase, decorated with Virginia creeper, incised 'AA VAN BRIGGLE 1902 III'.

1902 *7.5in (19cm) high*

$8,000-12,000 DRA

A Van Briggle spherical bottle, decorated with a spider and Native American symbols, in bright green glaze, incised 'AA VAN BRIGGLE 1902 III'.

1902 *5in (12.5cm) high*

$4,000-6,000 DRA

A Van Briggle vase, decorated with Native American symbols, in blue glaze, incised 'AA VAN BRIGGLE/1902/III', stamped '15', with 'XXIII' in marker.

1902 *4.75in (12cm) high*

$1,200-1,800 DRA

A Van Briggle vase, decorated with trumpet flowers, in green and burgundy glaze, incised 'AA VAN BRIGGLE 1903 III 197'.

1903 *6in (15cm) high*

$3,000-4,000 DRA

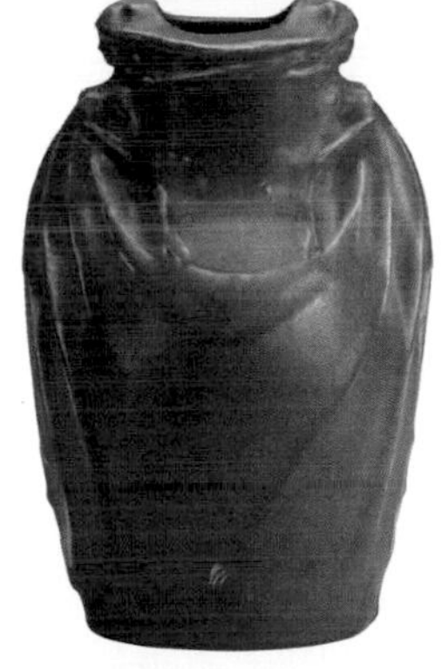

A Van Briggle 'Dos Cabezas' vase, in lavender glaze, incised 'AA VAN BRIGGLE 1905'.

1905 *8.25in (21cm) high*

$10,000-15,000 DRA

A Van Briggle vase, decorated with poppy pods, in mauve glaze, incised 'AA VAN BRIGGLE 1905 V 21'.

1905 *3.75in (9.5cm) high*

$700-1,000 DRA

A 1920s Wedgwood Fairyland Luster 'Sycamore Tree with Feng Hwang'/'Bridge, Ship and Tree' vase, decorated in pattern no.'Z5360', with printed mark.

8in (20.5cm) high

$15,000-20,000 **SK**

A 1920s Wedgwood Fairyland Luster 'Jeweled Tree with Cat and Mouse and Copper Trees' vase and cover, decorated in pattern no.'Z4966', printed mark.

11.25in (28.5cm) high

$25,000-30,000 **SK**

A 1920s Wedgwood Fairyland Luster 'Imps on a Bridge'/'Tree House' vase, shape no.2465, decorated in pattern no.Z4968 designed by Daisy Makeig-Jones, with gilt factory mark and other marks, with restored chip.

16.7in (42.5cm) diam

$20,000-30,000 **TEN**

A 1920s Wedgwood fairyland luster 'Woodland Bridge/Garden of Paradise' K'ang Hsi bowl, decorated in pattern no.Z4968, designed by Daisy Makeig-Jones, with gilt factory mark and other marks.

7in (18cm) diam

$5,000-7,000 **TOV**

A Wedgwood Fairyland Luster 'Garden of Paradise'/'Jumping Faun' Melba bowl, decorated in pattern no.'Z4968', with printed mark.

c1920 *8in (20.5cm) diam*

$15,000-20,000 **SK**

A 1920s Wedgwood Fairyland Luster 'Fairy Gondola' lily tray, the exterior decorated with flying geese, with printed mark.

13in (33cm) diam

$20,000-30,000 **SK**

A Wedgwood Fairyland Luster 'Ghostly Wood' malfrey pot and Cover, designed by Daisy Makeig-Jones, Portland vase mark and painted Z4968, incised 2312.

13in (33cm) high

$55,000-65,000 **SWO**

Judith Picks

Eric William Ravilious was an English painter, designer, book illustrator and wood engraver. He was born in London in 1903 and grew up in Eastbourne. He studied at the Eastbourne School of Art and the Royal College of Art and later taught in both. He was introduced to Tom Wedgwood in 1935 and designed for the pottery from 1936-40. One of his most memorable designs was his commemorative mug to mark the planned coronation of Edward VIII in 1937. Ravilious was appointed official war artist in 1940. He died in 1942 while on a Royal Air Force air sea rescue mission off Iceland. This was Ravilious's last design for Wedgwood.

A Wedgwood Queensware mug, commemorating the Wedgwood factory's move to Barlaston in 1940, printed with 'Designed by Eric Ravilious'.

4in (10.5cm) high

$3,000-5,000 **DN**

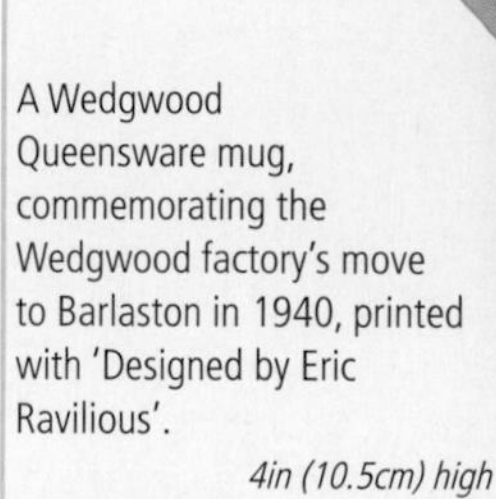

A Wedgwood earthenware moon flask, designed by Norman Wilson, with impressed and printed marks.

9in (22.5cm) high

$300-500 **WW**

ESSENTIAL REFERENCE - WEMYSS

Wemyss Ware was first made at the Scottish Fife Pottery (est. c.1790) in 1882. During the main period of production, the pottery was run by Robert Methven Heron. Bohemian artist Karel Nekola was in charge of the painting shop from 1883.

- **Typical Wemyss shapes include pig and cat figures, jug and basin sets, tablewares and candlesticks. Typical patterns include fruit, thistles and cabbage roses.**
- **In 1930 the rights and molds were sold to the Bovey Tracey Pottery, Devon.**
- **Griselda Hill pottery began to make modern Wemyss ware in 1985.**

A Wemyss model of a pig, impressed 'Wemyss Ware/R. H. & S./ T. Goode & Co.', with restoration.
c1900 *17in (43cm) long*
$2,500-3,500 **L&T**

A Wemyss model of a pig, decorated with thistles, impressed 'R.H & S' and stamp for 'Thomas Goode, London', with damage.
17in (43cm) long
$3,500-4,500 **DN**

A Wemyss model of a pig, decorated by Joe Nekola, painted 'Nekola/ Pinxt', printed 'Plichta/ London/England'.
post 1930 *18in (46cm) long*
$2,000-3,000 **L&T**

A Wemyss model of a sleeping piglet, decorated with cabbage roses, impressed and painted 'Wemyss', with small repair.
6.5in (16.5cm) long
$7,000-10,000 **T&F**

A Wemyss model of a cat, in pink glaze, with inset glass eyes, impressed 'Wemyss Ware'.
c1900 *12.75in (32.5cm) high*
$10,000-15,000 **L&T**

One of a rare pair of Wemyss models of 'marmalade' cats, with green glass eyes, painted 'Wemyss'.
12.75in (32.5cm) high
$10,000-15,000 pair **SWO**

A Wemyss model of a cat, in the manner of Gallé, with impressed and painted marks, with damage.
12.75in (32.5cm) high
$6,500-7,500 **SWO**

A Wemyss model of a cat, decorated with thistles, with inset glass eyes, with green painted 'Wemyss Ware Made in England'.
post 1930 *12.5in (32cm) high*
$2,500-3,500 **TOV**

A rare Wemyss model of a rabbit, printed 'T. Goode & Co.', with hairline cracks.

This very rare rabbit is one of only two known examples.
c1900 *6.25in (16cm) long*
$5,500-6,500 **L&T**

An early 20thC Wemyss 'Cabbage Roses' ewer and basin, decorated by James Sharp, with impressed and painted 'Wemyss'.

Basin 15in (38.5cm) diam

$1,000-1,500 L&T

A Wemyss 'Cabbage Roses' button, impressed 'Wemyss'.

c1900 *1.5in (4cm) diam*

$3,500-4,500 L&T

A Wemyss 'Cabbage Roses' hat pin, impressed 'Wemyss'.

c1900 *1.5in (4cm) diam*

$1,500-2,500 L&T

An early 20thC Wemyss 'Thistles' hat pin, impressed 'Wemyss'.

1.5in (3.5cm) diam

$2,000-3,000 L&T

An early 20thC Wemyss 'Thistles' Kenmore vase, marked 'T. Goode & Co.'.

15in (38cm) high

$1,500-2,500 L&T

An early 20thC Wemyss 'Gentian Violets' slop-pail and cover, impressed 'Wemyss'.

11in (29cm) high

$3,000-4,000 L&T

A Wemyss 'Harebells' pin tray, impressed 'Wemyss Ware/ R.H.& S.'.

c1900 *5.25in (13.5cm) diam*

$4,000-6,000 L&T

A Wemyss 'Daffodils' stationery rack, decorated by James Sharp, incised 'WEMYSS', with minor hairline cracks.

c1900 *8.75in (22cm) wide*

$5,500-6,500 L&T

An early 20thC Wemyss honeycomb box, cover and tray, painted 'Wemyss Ware' and impressed 'Wemyss'.

Tray 7in (18.5cm) diam

$1,500-2,000 L&T

A Wemyss 'Earlshall' cream jug, impressed and painted 'Wemyss'.

4.75in (12cm) high

$1,500-2,500 TEN

A Wemyss 'Earlshall' mug, with inscription; 'A LITTLE HEALTH A LITTLE WEALTH A LITTLE HOUSE WITH FREEDOM AND AT THE END A LITTLE FRIEND WITH LITTLE CAUSE TO NEED HIM.', impressed 'WEMYSS'.

c1915 *5.5in (14cm) high*

$1,500-2,500 L&T

ESSENTIAL REFERENCE - FREDERICK RHEAD

Frederick Hurten Rhead (1880-1942) was born in England and immigrated to the USA in 1902. He is known for pottery with incised decoration and for designing the extremely successful tableware range 'Fiesta' in 1936.

- **Rhead's first American position was managing Vance Faience (late Avon Faience) from 1902.**
- **Rhead worked briefly at the Weller Pottery in 1904 and was artistic director of the Roseville Pottery 1904-08.**
- **He and his wife ran a pottery in Santa Barbara 1913–17.**
- **Rhead was hugely influential in the development of studio pottery in the USA. This was as a result of his teaching at the University City Pottery, MO, in 1910 and at the Arequipa Pottery, CA, 1911-13, as well as his writing. He also designed for Arequipa.**

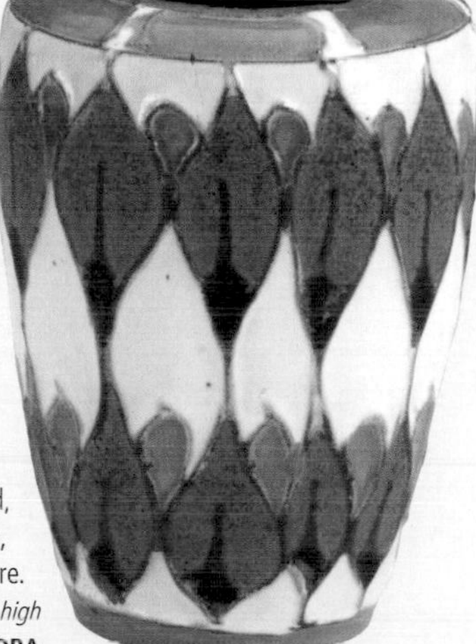

An Arequipa cabinet vase, designed by Frederick Rhead, with squeezebag decoration, with blue and white signature.

3.5in (9cm) high

$12,000-18,000 **DRA**

An Arequipa bowl, designed by Frederick Rhead, with squeezebag decoration of trees, with circular Arequipa stamp.

10in (25.5cm) diam

$6,500-7,500 **DRA**

A Bretby vase, no.2022, with a dragon in relief, with impressed marks, missing one of the dragon's whiskers.

15.75in (40cm) high

$300-500 **DN**

A Burmantoft glazed faience plaque, designed by Pierre Mallet and sculpted by Edward Hammond, signed, in wooden frame.

Total 45.75in (116cm) high

$2,000-3,000 **DN**

A Carlton Ware 'Red Devil' (Mephistopheles) dressing table set, with printed marks.

$8,000-12,000 **FLD**

A Cantagalli luster charger, decorated with elephants, with painted mark, with small chip.

13in (33.5cm) diam

$3,500-4,500 **WW**

A Carlton Ware 'River Fish' vase, shape no.777, decorated with a stylized fish over a water scene, with printed and painted marks.

7.5in (21cm) high

$1,500-2,000 **FLD**

A Carlton Ware coffee set, no.1582, decorated with stylized flowers and stars.

$1,000-1,500 **DA&H**

A Clewell copper-clad vase, on Vance-Avon blank, stamped 'Vance & Co. 139', with some interior losses to copper.

9.5in (24cm) high

$800-1,200 **DRA**

An Essevi Art Deco wall mask of a masked girl and a monkey.

11in (28cm) high

$1,500-2,500 **GORL**

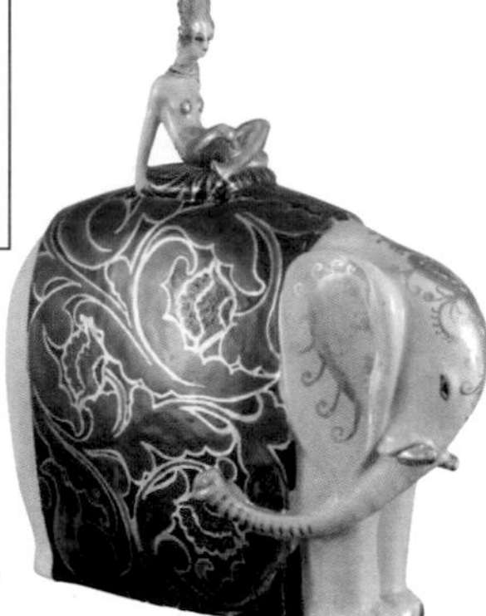

A Faenza faience group of a lady riding an elephant, probably by the Minardi Brothers, with damage.

11.5in (29cm) wide

$5,500-6,500 **GORL**

A Richard-Ginori 'Circo' twenty-piece tea set, designed by Gio Ponti, comprising seven cups and saucers, three plates, teapot, sugar bowl and creamer, with maker's marks.

$4,000-6,000 set **DRA**

A Richard-Ginori bowl, designed by Gio Ponti, decorated with gilt animal tamers, marked 'RICHARD-GINORI PITTORIA DI DOCCIA, 1688 E'.

Ponti was art director of Richard-Ginori of Milan from 1923 to 1930.

Designed 1928 *5.75in (14.5cm) diam*

$2,000-3,000 **QU**

Judith Picks

This, to me, is an Art Deco masterpiece. It embodies the optimism and modernity of the early 1930s. It was created in earthenware with black and vibrant blue glazes and a jazzy New York theme - tilting skyscrapers, flags, stars and other symbols. The 'Jazz' bowl was designed by ceramicist Viktor Schreckengost, who was a prolific American industrial designer. He was asked to design a punch bowl with a New York theme while he was working at the Cowan Pottery Co. in Rocky River, Ohio. The client turned out to be Mrs Franklin D Roosevelt, and the bowl turned out to be the first of a series (and first of three that she ordered) that he designed. It is estimated there are between 20 and 50 of these bowls, though the exact number is unknown. The fabulous expression of the Art Deco spirit, the presidential connection and the limited number produced add to its desirability.

A large Cowan 'Jazz' bowl, designed by Viktor Schreckengost (1906-2008), signed, stamped 'COWAN' with floral mark.

c1931 *16in (40.5cm) diam*

$100,000-150,000 **DRA**

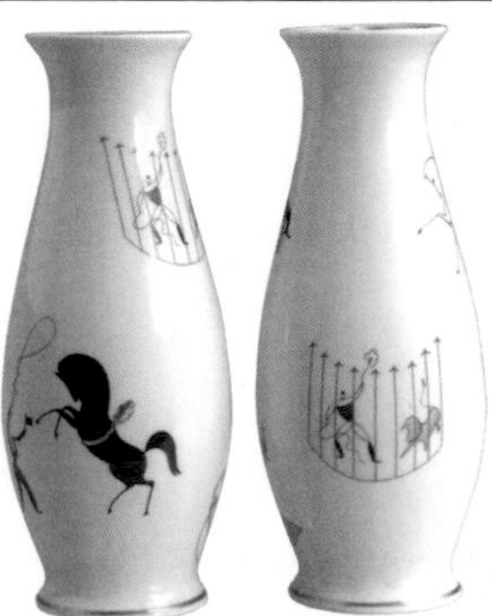

A pair of Richard-Ginori vases, designed by Gio Ponti, with maker's marks and 'MADE IN ITALY, 36-11'.

Designed c1925 *7.5in (19cm) high*

$2,500-3,500 **QU**

A mid-20thC Gustavsberg 'Argenta' vase, designed by Wilhelm Kåge, with maker's mark to base.

10.2in (26cm) high

$2,000-3,000 **KAU**

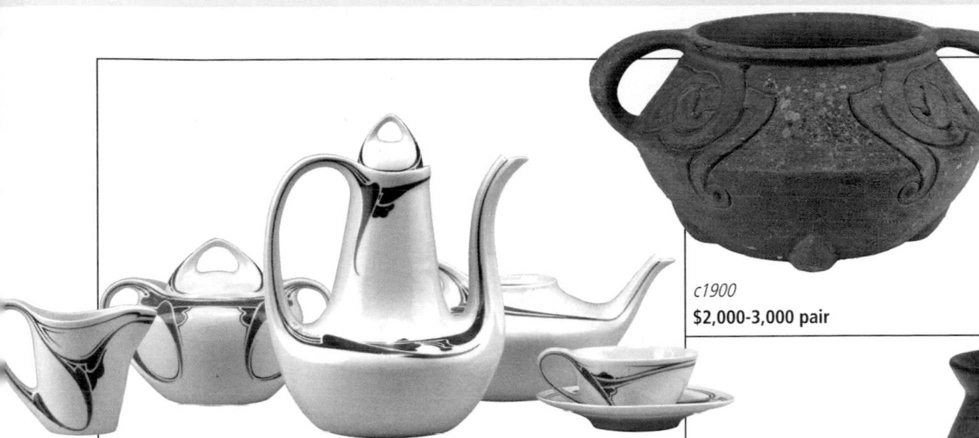

One of a pair of 'Compton' terracotta jardinières, designed by Archibald Knox, with Celtic inspired decoration, with molded 'Designed and Manufactured by Liberty & Co.' mark.

c1900 *25.2in (64cm) wide*

$2,000-3,000 pair **L&T**

A Louis Lourioux nine-piece coffee and tea set, designed by Maurice Dufrène, made for La Maison Moderne.

Louis Lourioux (1874–1930) began producing ceramics in Foëcy, France, in 1902. After his death, the pottery was run by his wife until 1949.

Coffee pot 9in (22.5cm) high

$6,500-7,500 **QU**

A Marblehead vessel, with incised decoration by Arthur Baggs, with incised 'AB T' and shipmark.

4in (10cm) high

$7,000-10,000 **DRA**

A Marblehead vase, incised and painted by Arthur Hennessey, with irises, with stamped shipmark and 'HT'.

4.25in (11cm) high

$3,000-4,000 **DRA**

An early 20thC Marblehead vase, marked.

9.5in (24cm) high

$650-850 **DRA**

A Maw & Co. red luster vase, decorated with seated figures, with swan handles.

1890-91 *9in (23cm) high*

$10,000-15,000 **DURR**

A Pewabic vase, with an iridescent silver glaze dripping over lapis blue matte, stamped 'PEWABIC DETROIT'.

10in (25.5cm) high

$10,000-15,000 **DRA**

A Pierrefonds high-fired stoneware vase, shape no.602, with blue impressed marks.

10in (25cm) high

$400-600 **WW**

A Pierrefonds high-fired stoneware vase, model no.603, with impressed mark.

8in (21cm) high

$500-700 **WW**

A Pilkington's earthenware vase, designed by Richard Joyce, molded with running gazelles, decorated in 'sang de boeuf' glaze, with printed mark and monogram.

9in (22.9cm) high

$2,000-3,000 **HT**

A Pilkington's vase, decorated by C E Cundall, with impressed and inscribed marks, dated.

1907 *3.25in (8cm) high*

$2,000-3,000 **HT**

A Royal Dux figure of a maiden, no.1257, modeled by Alois Hampel, signed, with pink pad mark.

16in (41cm) high

$650-850 **DN**

A Rozenburg Art Nouveau 'Den Haag' vase, with painted marks, with artist cypher, with restoration.

10in (25cm) high

$300-500 **WW**

A Ruskin Pottery high-fired vase, impressed 'Ruskin England', dated.

1926 *14in (36cm) high*

$1,500-2,500 **DN**

A 1920s Ruskin Pottery vase, the cream base glaze graduating to 'sang de boeuf' and rich magenta, impressed 'Ruskin/ England'.

15.5in (39cm) high

$2,500-3,500 **L&T**

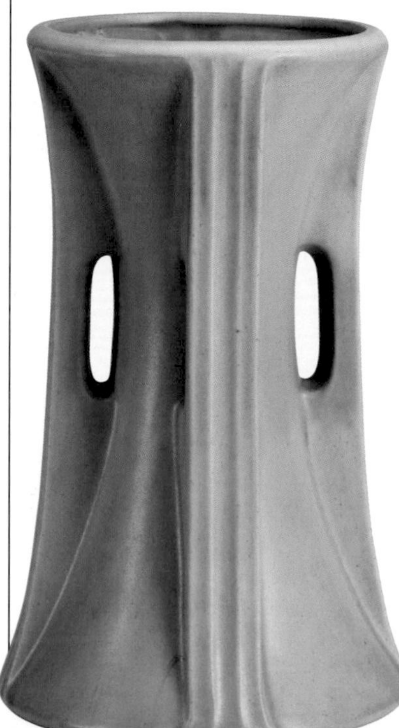

A Teco buttressed vase, stamped 'Teco'.

This is an exceptionally tall, finely sculpted example.

18in (45.5cm) high

$50,000-70,000 **DRA**

A Teco vase, with pierced quatre-lobed shoulder, incised 'Teco 113'.

6in (15.5cm) high

$1,500-2,500 **WW**

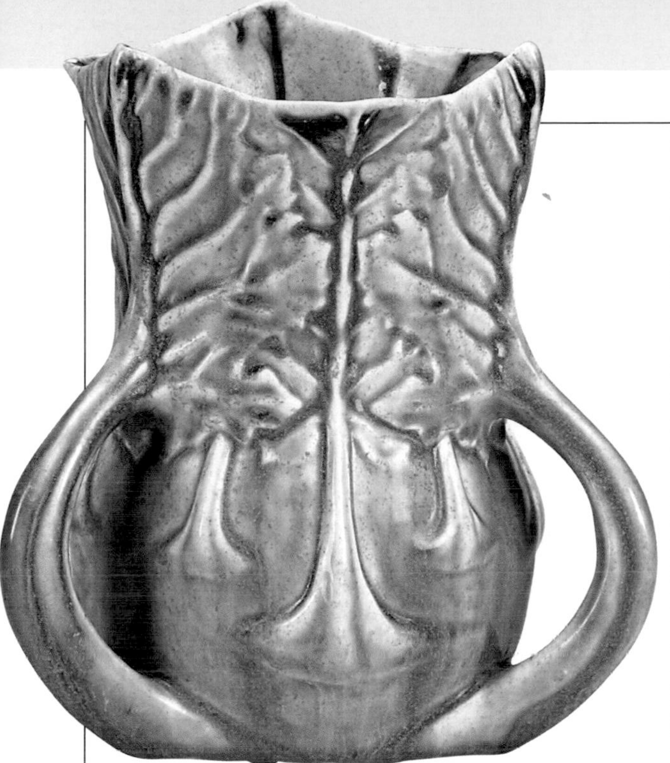

A rare Louis Comfort Tiffany glazed ceramic vessel, inscribed 'L. C. T. Pottery P 490'.

6.5in (16.5cm) high

$15,000-20,000 **DRA**

An early 20thC Volkmar bowl, in 'Persian Blue' glaze, signed.

11.75in (30cm) diam

$650-850 **DRA**

A W J Walley vase, in mottled red and ivory glaze, stamped 'WJW'.

4.5in (11.5cm) high

$2,500-3,500 **DRA**

A Weller 'Muskota' model of an elephant, stamped 'Weller', with restoration.

13in (33cm) long

$800-1,200 **DRA**

A Weller 'Hudson Scenic' bud vase, decorated with rabbits, etched 'Weller Pottery' and artist's monogram 'J.G.'.

6in (15cm) high

$1,200-1,800 **DRA**

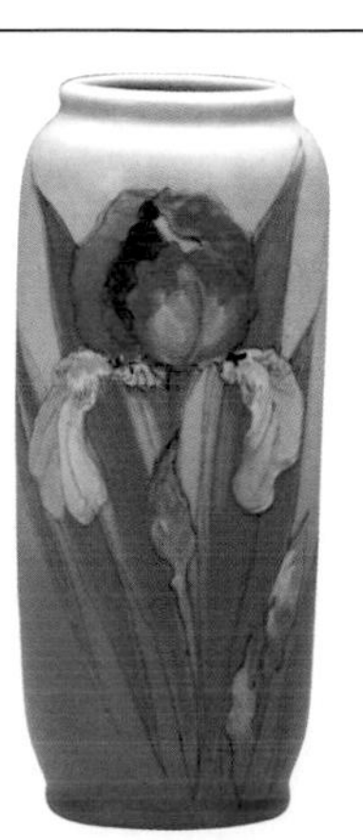

A Weller 'Hudson' vase, decorated by Sarah Timberlake, with kiln stamp.

9in (23cm) high

$800-1,200 **DRA**

A Weller 'Sicard' bud vase, signed 'Weller Sicard'.

6in (15cm) high

$1,000-1,500 **DRA**

A Weller 'Louwelsa' vase, decorated by Hester Pillsbury with roses, stamped 'Louwelsa Weller', 'HP' and numbered.

19in (48cm) high

$350-450 **DRA**

A late 19thC vase, painted in the manner of William de Morgan with Persian flowers, unmarked.

13in (33.5cm) high

$1,500-2,500 **DN**

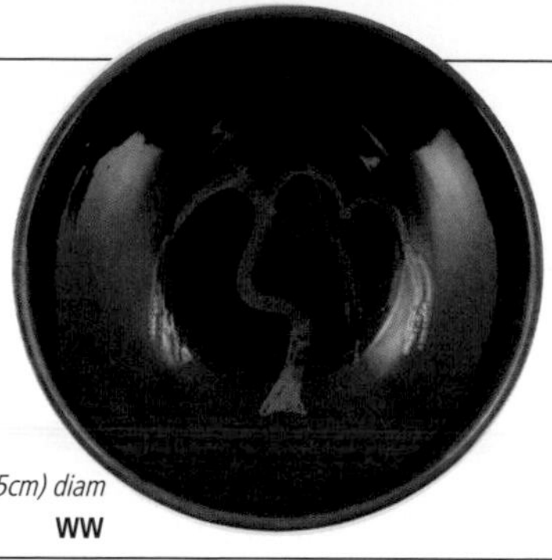

A Lowerdown Pottery stoneware bowl, by David Leach (1911-2005), resist-decorated in tenmoku with a willow tree, with impressed seal mark.

15in (38.5cm) diam

$1,500-2,500 **WW**

A 1960s earthenware bowl, by Otto and Gertrud Natzler, in white, cobalt and brown volcanic glaze, with paper label, marked 'H958'.

10in (25.5cm) diam

$20,000-30,000 **DRA**

A stoneware vase, by Katharine Pleydell-Bouverie (1895-1985), with impressed seal mark.

4in (10cm) high

$500-700 **WW**

A stoneware bottle-vase, by Dame Lucie Rie (1902-1995), in spiraling purple and pale blue glaze, with impressed seal mark, with restoration.

10in (24.5cm) high

$2,500-3,500 **WW**

A porcelain 'Byzantine' bowl, by Dame Lucie Rie (1902-1995), decorated with a bronze-clour flower motif, with impressed seal mark.

8in (20.5cm) diam

$12,000-18,000 **WW**

ESSENTIAL REFERENCE - CHARLES VYSE

Charles Vyse (1882-1971) and his wife Nell (1892-1967) founded a pottery studio in Chelsea in 1919. There they produced studio pottery and slip-cast figures based on London characters.

- **Charles was apprenticed to Doulton as a modeller and designer at the age of 14 in 1896 and created many of their most popular models.**
- **The Vyses' studio pottery included revivals of Oriental forms and glazes, as well as hand-decorated Art Deco stoneware.**
- **In 1940 the studio was damaged in an air raid. After World War II Charles started making character figures again with Barbara Waller.**
- **He retired in 1963.**

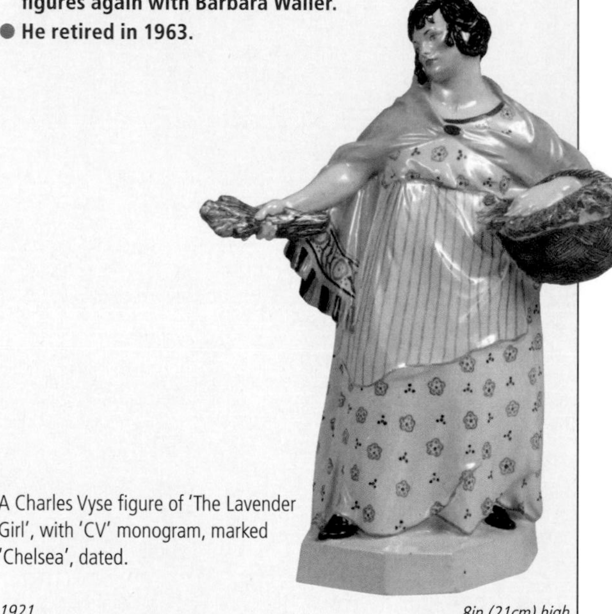

A Charles Vyse figure of 'The Lavender Girl', with 'CV' monogram, marked 'Chelsea', dated.

1921 *8in (21cm) high*

$1,500-2,500 **SWO**

A Charles Vyse figure of 'The Midday Rest', incised 'C. Vyse, Chelsea', on an ebonized base, dated.

1931 *7.5in (20cm) high*

$6,500-7,500 **SWO**

A Charles Vyse figure of 'Market Day, Boulogne - Vegetables', incised 'C. Vyse, Chelsea', on an ebonized base, dated, with chips.

1931 *7.5in (21.5cm) high*

$10,000-15,000 **SWO**

A late 19thC Gothic Revival oak bookcase, in the manner of A W N Pugin.

88in (224cm) high

$5,000-7,000 **DN**

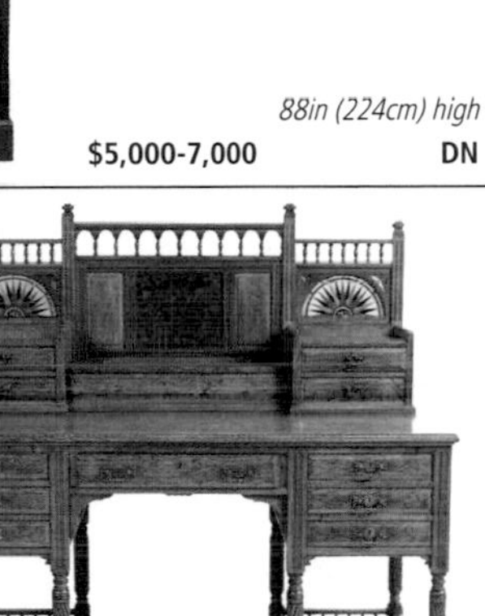

A Gothic Revival oak desk, in the manner of J P Seddon, the back with marquetry radial sun design.

55in (137cm) high

$1,500-2,500 **WW**

A Victorian Gothic Revival mahogany writing cupboard/ bookcase.

By repute this piece was commissioned for a Fellow of King's College Cambridge and echoes the architectural features of King's College Chapel.

c1850 *69in (175cm) high*

$3,000-5,000 **DN**

A Victorian Gothic Revival oak cabinet, carved with St Barbara and bishop saints.

53in (135cm) high

$700-1,000 **GORL**

A late 19thC Gothic Revival carved oak twin-pedestal desk.

50.5in (128cm) wide

$2,500-3,500 **DN**

Four of a set of seventeen Gothic Revival oak dining chairs, in the manner of A W N Pugin, twelve chairs lacking upholstery.

c1880

$10,000-15,000 set **DN**

A late Victorian Gothic Revival pollard-oak-framed chaise longue, with Pugin-style carving.

80in (203cm) long

$1,500-2,500 **SWO**

A set of four Gothic Revival oak dining chairs, by Holland & Sons, with stamped marks.

37in (94.5cm) high

$2,500-3,500 **DN**

A Gothic Revival hardwood dressing-table mirror, designed by A W N Pugin for the House of Lords, unmarked.

See Paul Atterbury & Clive Wainwright's 'Pugin' (V&A Catalog) p.131 plate 230 for a chair from the House of Lords with a comparable Tudor rose motif.

31in (78cm) high

$1,200-1,800 **WW**

An American Aesthetic Movement mahogany two-part sideboard, the upper section carved with dragons, large foliate panels, scrollwork and leaftips.

c1875 *88in (224cm) high*

$5,500-6,500 **SK**

An Aesthetic Movement golden-oak museum cabinet, the doors with Aesthetic brass cabinet fittings and ebony inlay, with locks by Cope & Collinson.

75in (190.5cm) high

$1,500-2,500 **A&G**

An Aesthetic Movement ebonized and burr-walnut desk, with gilt-incised decoration.

c1880 *54in (137cm) wide*

$1,500-2,500 **L&T**

An Aesthetic Movement bamboo jardinière, with Wedgwood 'Midsummer Night's Dream' tiles designed by Helen J A Miles, with molded marks.

c1878 *32in (82cm) high*

$1,800-2,200 **DN**

Judith Picks

Louisine and Henry O Havemeyer were influential and enthusiastic art collectors and patrons during America's 'Gilded Age'. The imposing Havemeyer mansion on Fifth Avenue at 66th Street, completed in 1892, featured interiors designed by New York designers Louis Comfort Tiffany and Samuel Colman. It is rare to find complete interiors designed by these two luminaries. They were charged with creating interiors that would showcase the Havemeyer's extensive and diverse collection. The resulting design would herald a uniquely American Aesthetic style, incorporating exotic elements from Japan, India, Persia and natural motifs in unusual and fresh applications.

This settee was inspired by Near Eastern design and decorated with elaborately carved floral patterns recalling Indian motifs. The double-arched crest is densely decorated with peacocks nestled and feeding amongst meandering stylized tendrils, leaves and various species of blossoms. The tapering reeded legs end in unusual claw and glass-ball feet.

A Louis Comfort Tiffany and Samuel Colman carved and parcel-gilt ash settee, in the Near-Eastern style.

c1890-91 *67.75in (172cm) wide*

$400,000-500,000 **DOY**

A British Aesthetic Movement ebonized-framed armchair.

34in (87cm) high

$80-120 **WW**

A pair of Aesthetic Movement ebonized-beechwood elbow chairs, designed by E W Godwin, with 'Japanesque' fretwork backs, unmarked, one chair with a reglued spindle.

$7,000-10,000 **SWO**

A late 19thC Aesthetic Movement painted and giltwood overmantel mirror.

55in (138cm) high

$2,000-3,000 **DN**

A Gustav Stickley bookcase, with mitred mullions, with early signature.

c1901 *56in (142cm) wide*

$15,000-20,000 **DRA**

A Gustav Stickley china cabinet, model no.815, with burned-in mark.

64.25in (163cm) high

$5,500-6,500 **DRA**

A Gustav Stickley chest-of-drawers, model no.913, designed by Harvey Ellis, with hammered strap hardware, with paper label and red decal.

50.75in (129cm) high

$15,000-20,000 **DRA**

A Gustav Stickley sideboard, model no.814 variant, with unusual exposed through-tenons, with paper label and red decal.

66in (167.5cm) wide

$5,000-7,000 **DRA**

A Gustav Stickley 'Bride's' chest, with iron hardware, with cedar lining, with large red decal.

40.5in (103cm) wide

$25,000-30,000 **DRA**

A Gustav Stickley drop-arm 'Morris' chair, with burned-in mark.

37in (94cm) high

$5,500-6,500 **DRA**

A set of eight Gustav Stickley ladderback dining chairs, model nos.349 1/2 and 349 1/2A, with original leather seats, with branded marks.

c1912 *37.5in (95.5cm) high*

$7,000-10,000 **DRA**

A Gustav Stickley fixed-top dining table, model no.634 variant, with unusual pedestal base, on casters, with paper label and burned-in mark.

c1912 *60in (152.5) diam*

$5,500-6,500 **DRA**

An L & J G Stickley slatted bow-arm rocking chair, with drop-in spring seat, with handcraft label.

37in (94cm) high

$3,000-4,000 **DRA**

An L & J G Stickley bookcase, with 'The Work of...' decal.

55.25in (140.5cm) high

$3,500-4,500 **DRA**

An L & J G Stickley cabinet, with strap hardware, with handcraft label.

70.5in (179cm) high

$15,000-20,000 **DRA**

An L & J G Stickley bookcase, model no.642, with chamfered back, with handcraft decal.

c1907-12 *55in (139.5cm) high*

$4,000-6,000 **DRA**

An L & J G Stickley trestle table, with lower shelf, with L & J G decal.

48in (122cm) wide

$1,200-1,800 **DRA**

A Charles Rohlfs dresser, with saw mark.

52in (132cm) wide

$12,000-18,000 **DRA**

A rare Charles Rohlfs oak coal-hod, with carved 'R'.

c1898-99 *30in (76cm) diam*

$40,000-50,000 **DRA**

ESSENTIAL REFERENCE - CHARLES ROHLFS

Charles Rohlfs (1853-1936) was an American furniture designer whose unique style combined Arts & Crafts forms with Art Nouveau decoration, such as sinuous carved motifs. He also made use of fretwork.

- **He opened the Charles Rohlfs Workshop in Buffalo, NY, in 1898. It remained open until 1928.**
- **Rohlfs' furniture was mostly made from oak.**

A rare Charles Rohlfs carved barrel chair, with carved 'R' and date.

1902 *35in (89cm) high*

$15,000-20,000 **DRA**

A rare Charles Rohlfs carved rocking chair, with carved 'R' and date.

1902 *36in (91.5cm) wide*

$12,000-18,000 **DRA**

A Robert 'Mouseman' Thompson oak paneled hall wardrobe, adzed all over, with wrought-iron hinges and handle, with carved recessed mouse signature.

1931 *48in (122cm) wide*

$10,000-15,000 **TEN**

A 1930s Robert 'Mouseman' Thompson oak paneled cupboard, with wrought-iron butterfly-shaped hinges and latch handles, with recessed mouse signature.

48in (122cm) wide

$7,000-10,000 **TEN**

A Robert 'Mouseman' Thompson paneled oak chest-of-drawers, with carved mouse signature.

c1930 *41in (103cm) wide*

$10,000-15,000 **TEN**

A Derek 'Lizardman' Slater oak sideboard, adzed and paneled, signed with a lizard.

The wood carvers and furniture makers of Yorkshire (who work with oak and sign almost all of their pieces with a 'critter' or creature) are known, not surprisingly, as 'critters'.

72in (183cm) wide

$10,000-15,000 **DN**

A set of eight Derek 'Lizardman' Slater oak and leather dining chairs, each signed with a lizard.

35.75in (91cm) high

$2,000-3,000 **DN**

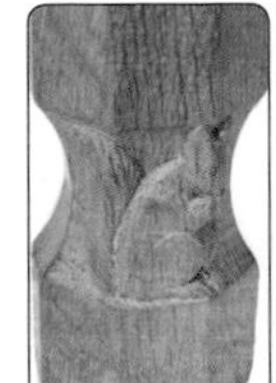

A Wilf 'Squirrelman' Hutchinson oak display cabinet, signed with a squirrel.

Wilfred Hutchinson trained at the 'Mouseman' workshops 1951-57. He started on his own in 1957 at Husthwaite, Yorkshire. The business still operates today overseen by his son, Trevor.

42in (107cm) wide

$2,500-3,500 **DN**

A Peter 'Rabbitman' Heap oak sideboard, with iron hinges and latch.

Peter Heap trained at the Mouseman workshops in the 1950s and '60s. He set up his own workshop in Wetwang, Yorkshire, in 1970.

72in (183cm) wide

$3,000-4,000 **MOR**

Judith Picks

This table forms part of a collection of Arts & Crafts furniture made in the early 1920s for Liberty & Co.'s magnificent Tudor building in Great Marlborough Street, London. The building was designed by Edwin Thomas Hall and his son Edwin Stanley Hall at the height of the 1920s fashion for the Tudor revival and constructed from the timbers of two 19thC men-of-war battleships: HMS 'Impregnable' and HMS 'Hindustan'. After World War II, a more reactionary attitude toward architecture and design was understandable. The new building demonstrated craft of the highest quality and attention to detail and reflected the Arts & Crafts values of 'truth to material', which had played such an important part in the foundation of the company and the goods that it sold.

A Liberty & Co. oak center table, designed by Edwin T Hall and Edwin S Hall, the planked top later inset with brass metre rule.
c1924 *60in (152.5cm) long*
$3,000-5,000 **L&T**

One of a pair of Liberty & Co. oak occasional tables, designed by Edwin T Hall and Edwin S Hall.
c1924 *24.75in (63cm) high*
$4,000-6,000 pair **L&T**

A Liberty & Co. fumed-oak center table, designed by Sir Robert Lorimer, the top with pegged construction, with chamfered frieze.
c1924 *34in (86.5cm) diam*
$6,500-8,500 **L&T**

A Liberty & Co. limed oak center table, designed by Sir Robert Lorimer (1864-1929), the molded top with later inset brass metre rule.
c1924 *59.75in (152cm) long*
$8,000-12,000 **L&T**

A Liberty & Co. oak hall cupboard, with 'Liberty and Co, London, W' ivorine label.
72in (182cm) high
$2,500-3,500 **L&T**

A Liberty & Co. oak 'Thebes' stool, with applied Liberty label.
12in (31cm) wide
$3,000-5,000 **WW**

A mahogany table, attributed to Edward William Godwin, possibly for Liberty & Co.
31in (80cm) wide
$1,000-1,500 **DN**

A 'Turkish' side table, possibly retailed by Liberty & Co., inset with bone, mother-of-pearl and pewter, unsigned.
22.5in (56cm) high
$1,000-1,500 **WW**

Two of a set of eight oak dining chairs, in the manner of Liberty & Co., reupholstered.
c1900
$3,000-5,000 set **SWO**

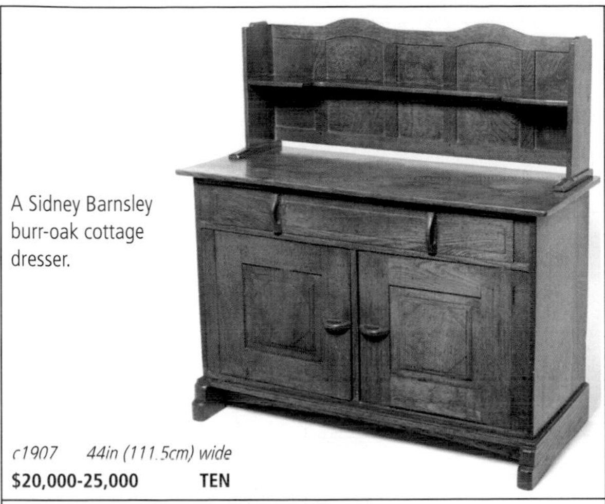

A Sidney Barnsley burr-oak cottage dresser.

c1907 44in (111.5cm) wide

$20,000-25,000 TEN

A Byrdcliffe mahogany cabinet, carved with Latin motto 'Magna Est Veritas Et Praevalet' and in Greek, unsigned.

37.5in (95.5cm) wide

$5,000-7,000 DRA

A set of six Ernest Gimson ash ladderback rush-seated chairs, unmarked.

38in (97cm) high

$2,500-3,500 TEN

ESSENTIAL REFERENCE - ERNEST GIMSON

In 1890 Earnest Gimson (1864-1919) was a founder member of the short-lived furniture company Kenton & Co. Following the company's collapse in 1893, Gimson and two other former members, Sidney and Earnest Barnsley, moved to Gloucestershire in the Cotswolds.

- **In 1900 Gimson established a furniture workshop in Cirencester. He later moved to larger workshops at Daneway House in Gloucestershire.**
- **He was a leading figure in the Arts & Crafts movement and in what became known as the Cotswold School.**
- **Gimson believed that design was not something to be added once the work was finished, rather it should come from the careful use of proportion and construction, choice and knowledge of materials, tools and techniques.**
- **He was inspired by nature, Byzantine and Islamic arts, 17thC and 18thC British furniture and the Arts & Crafts tradition.**
- **Gimson also designed metalware.**

An Ernest Gimson oak chest-of-drawers, the drawers with hammered handles and chip-carved dividers, the carcass with exposed dovetail joints.

38.5in (98cm) high

$15,000-20,000 DUK

A Harden drop-arm settee, with paddle arms.

60in (152cm) wide

$400-600 DRA

A Lifetime 'Puritan' settle, unmarked.

74in (188cm) wide

$1,500-2,000 DRA

A Lifetime 'Puritan' server, with Paine Furniture tag.

60in (152.5cm) long

$1,500-2,000 DRA

A rare Limbert oak dresser, with bell, with the Mission Inn logo, with branded mark.

Provenance: Designed for the Mission Inn, Riverside, California, USA.

54in (137cm) wide

$8,000-12,000 DRA

A Limbert server, model no.125, with branded mark.

c1906-10 *52in (132cm) wide*

$5,000-7,000 DRA

A Limbert double-oval library table, model no.158, unsigned.

c1906 *48in (122cm) diam*

$10,000-15,000 DRA

A Plail Brothers barrel rocker, with drop-in spring seat, unmarked.

29.5in (75cm) high

$1,500-2,500 DRA

A Roycroft 'Ali Baba' bench, with orb and cross mark.

42in (106.5cm) wide

$10,000-15,000 DRA

A Roycroft mahogany child's chair, with carved orb and cross mark.

29in (74cm) high

$800-1,200 DRA

A Roycroft library table, with orb and cross mark.

48in wide

$3,000-4,000 DRA

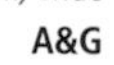

A Gordon Russell oak 'Enstone' sideboard, designed by W H Russell, Broadway, Worcestershire.

c1935 *66in (168cm) wide*

$2,000-3,000 A&G

A Gordon Russell oak 'Wishbone' table, with pegged joints, unsigned.

60in (153cm) wide

$1,800-2,200 WW

Shapland & Petter

A Shapland & Petter oak and marquetry 'compactum' wardrobe and dressing chest.

The Shapland & Petter factory was established in 1854 in Barnstaple by cabinetmaker Henry Shapland (1823–1909), who later took accountant Henry Petter into partnership. Shapland & Petter furniture was made using a combination of up-to-date machinery and skilled craftsmanship.

Wardrobe 45.75in (116cm) wide

$1,500-2,500 **DN**

An Arthur Simpson of Kendal 'Cuban' mahogany side cabinet, with original label for 'Arthur W. Simpson, The Handicrafts, Kendal'.

77in (195cm) wide

$3,000-5,000 **LC**

A George Walton oak wardrobe.

c1900 *74in (188cm) high*

$6,500-7,500 **L&T**

A George Walton 'Abingwood' chair.

First used for John Rowntree's café in Scarborough in 1896/7, the 'Abingwood' chair was a blend of a perceived 'Old English' style and Arts & Crafts revivalism. The chair was also used in the Billiard Room in Miss Cranston's Buchanan Street Tea Rooms in Glasgow.

$3,500-4,500 **DUK**

An Arts & Crafts burr-oak table, probably designed by Philip Webb.

22in (57cm) high

$5,500-6,500 **TEN**

A Glasgow School Arts & Crafts oak and inlaid dresser, attributed to Wylie & Lochhead, with 'Glasgow rose' decoration, stamped '5682' over '3322' over '2'.

82in (208.5cm) high

$3,000-5,000 **DN**

An Arts & Crafts oak settle, with rush back-panels.

177in (450cm) wide

$2,000-3,000 **SWO**

A late Victorian Arts & Crafts Middle Eastern-style walnut twin-pedestal desk, inlaid with bone and mother-of-pearl star motifs.

55in (139cm) wide

$5,000-7,000 **TOV**

A Charles Rennie Mackintosh overpainted-wood and painted-steel coat and stick stand, with four square insets for drip trays, missing trays.

c1904 *80in (202.5cm) high*

$30,000-40,000 L&T

A Windsor armchair, designed by Charles Rennie Mackintosh, overpainted in dark blue over pale green.

This chair was designed by Mackintosh for the Dutch Kitchen, Argyle Street Tearooms, Glasgow, in 1906.

c1906 *30in (76cm) high*

$5,000-7,000 L&T

A beech high stool, designed by Charles Rennie Mackintosh.

The stool was made for Queen Margaret Medical College, Glasgow. The treatment of the stretchers appears to echo those of the domino table designed by Mackintosh in 1898 for the Argyle Street Tea Rooms.

c1894 *26.75in (68cm) high*

$2,000-3,000 L&T

An oak domino table, attributed to Charles Rennie Mackintosh.

The design of this table appears to be an amalgam of scale drawings produced by Mackintosh for a domino table in c1897 and a table photographed by the 'Studio' magazine in the same year. The example illustrated in the 'Studio' demonstrates differences from the drawing. The example shown here may have been a prototype or special commission. However, it remains untraced.

c1897 *26.5in (67cm) high*

$4,000-6,000 L&T

A Cassina stained-black sideboard, after a design by Charles Rennie Mackintosh, the back section inset with enameled glass mosaic rose, bound with lead, enclosed with inlaid mother-of-pearl squares, unmarked.

64in (162.5cm) wide

$1,500-2,000 TEN

A stained-birch day bed, designed by Charles Rennie Mackintosh, the cushion upholstered in dark-gray corduroy, with replacements and restoration.

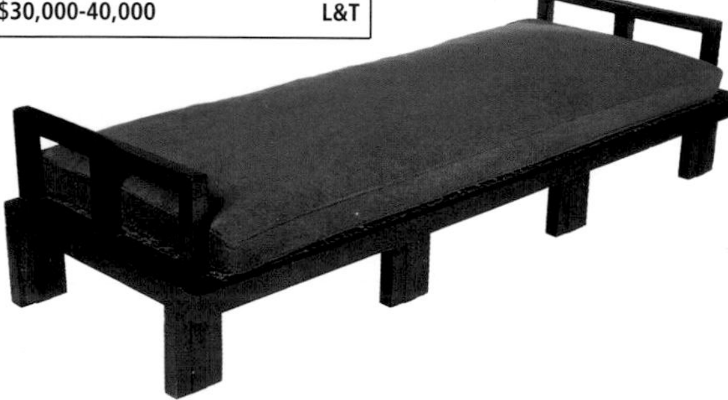

The original design for this day bed survives in the Glasgow University Collection under the title 'Couch in Ladies Common Room'. The wood is to be 'birch stained dark and waxed' and the upholstery of 'mouse gray corduroy'. Once it had served its time in the Ladies' Common Room the couch was transferred to the Sculpture Room where it was used as the model's couch.

c1910 *84.25in (214cm) long*

$5,000-7,000 L&T

A Guthrie & Wells oak press cupboard, designed by Charles Rennie Mackintosh, the doors with applied decorative strap hinges, the door handles replaced.

c1894 *57.75in (146.5cm) wide*

$5,500-6,500 L&T

Judith Picks

This Arts & Crafts music cabinet is a hitherto lost design by Charles Rennie Mackintosh. Research shows that a watercolor for the design is in the collection of the Hunterian Museum and Art Gallery in Glasgow. Signed and dated 1898, it is inscribed Music Cabinet for Mrs Pickering, Braxfield, Lanark. A stenciled or embroidered panel would have covered the shelves below the stained glass. Mackintosh produced cabinets with the same distinctive cornice for other clients during the same year, including those made for the Edinburgh printer Alex Seggie. This proven attribution to a Mackintosh design accounts for the high value.

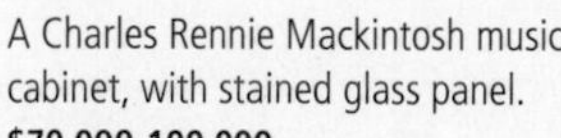

A Charles Rennie Mackintosh music cabinet, with stained glass panel.

$70,000-100,000 ROK

A Carlo Bugatti walnut corner chair, inlaid with stained walnut, parchment, cord, bone, pewter and brass, with later leather-upholstered seat.

c1902 *28in (72cm) high*

$12,000-18,000 **L&T**

A Peter Wylie Davidson brass wall mirror, the frame repoussé-decorated and pierced with opposing peacock, inset with abalone shell, stamped signature 'P. Wylie Davidson'.

c1900

$3,000-4,000 **L&T**

A George Montague Ellwood mahogany, inlaid and leaded-stained-glass bureau, designed for J S Henry.

50in (126cm) high

$6,500-7,500 **DN**

A nest of three Émile Gallé marquetry tables, inlaid in specimen woods with sea holly in a mountain landscape, cottages in a landscape and boats at sea, each with marquetry signature 'GALLÉ'.

c1900 *Largest 22.75in (58cm) wide*

$3,000-5,000 **L&T**

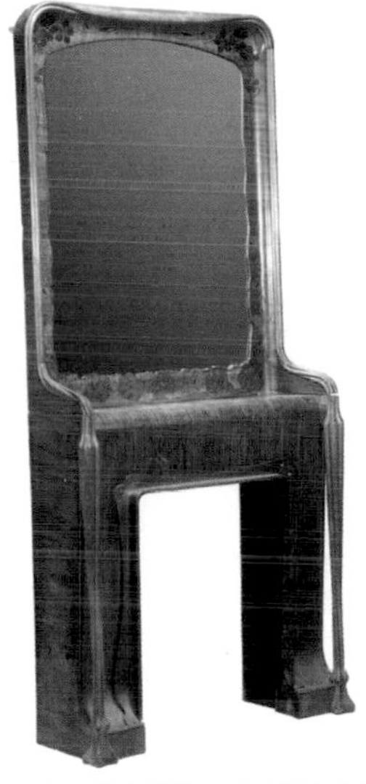

A Louis Majorelle walnut and marquetry mantelpiece and mirror, in two sections.

Provenance: This mantelpiece was owned by Peter Grant (1935-1995), who was, most famously, the manager of the band Led Zeppelin. Grant formed his collection of Art Nouveau furniture and pictures while touring America and Europe with the band in the 1970s.

96.5in (245cm) high

$5,000-7,000 **DN**

An Art Nouveau inlaid mahogany display cabinet, attributed to Morris & Co.

74in (189cm) high

$5,000-7,000 **TEN**

An Art Nouveau mahogany and marquetry display cabinet, inlaid with swirling foliage and plant motifs, with label for Christopher Pratt, Bradford.

77.75in (197.5cm) high

$3,000-5,000 **HT**

A Raleigh mahogany inlaid music cabinet, decorated with stylized panels with bulrush inlay.

61.5in (156cm) high

$2,000-3,000 **SWO**

A Shapland & Petter mahogany writing desk, inlaid with specimen woods, mother-of -pearl, brass and copper in stylized honesty motifs, stamped to drawer lock.

c1900 *43in (109cm) wide*

$5,000-7,000 **L&T**

ESSENTIAL REFERENCE - ERNEST TAYLOR

Ernest Archibald Taylor (1874-1951) was born in Greenock, Scotland, one of seventeen children.

- **He was initially apprenticed as an engineer and designer in the shipbuilding firm Scott & Co., where he worked until 1898.**
- **In 1898 he began studying at the Glasgow School of Art, where his fiancée, Jessie Marion King, was also a student.**
- **Taylor then gained employment with the Glasgow cabinet-makers Wylie & Lochhead. He won great acclaim for his furniture at the 1901 Glasgow International Exhibition.**
- **Taylor and King married in 1908 and moved to Paris where they established an art school known as the Shieling atelier.**
- **Prior to her marriage, Jessie had purchased a house at Kirkcudbright and, at the outbreak of World War I, she and Taylor returned there. They subsequently became involved in the Kirkcudbright art community, which was seen as the 'Scottish St Ives'.**

One piece from Ernest Archibald Taylor mahogany bedroom suite, designed for Wylie & Lochhead, Glasgow, comprising a wardrobe, a washstand, a bedside cabinet and a wall mirror formerly from a dressing table.

c1900 *Wardrobe 87.5in (222cm) wide*

$4,500-5,500 suite **L&T**

An Ernest Archibald Taylor mahogany hanging wall cabinet, designed for Wylie & Lochhead, the doors inset with stained glass panels of Glasgow roses.

c1900 *57.5in (146cm) wide*

$3,500-4,500 **L&T**

An Art Nouveau mahogany and satinwood marquetry settee.

c1900 *52.5in (134cm) wide*

$1,200-1,800 **DN**

An Art Nouveau mahogany breakfront display cabinet.

47.5in (123cm) wide

$1,200-1,800 **TOV**

An Art Nouveau inlaid mahogany sideboard.

c1890 *71.75in (182cm) wide*

$2,000-3,000 **SWO**

An Art Nouveau mahogany and marquetry display cabinet, with retailer's label 'James Simpson & Sons, Glasgow'.

c1900 *46.5in (118cm) wide*

$2,000-3,000 **L&T**

An early 20thC Art Nouveau mahogany hall stand.

80in (202cm) high

$2,000-3,000 **DN**

An Art Nouveau wrought-iron plant stand.

47in (119.5cm) high

$3,000-4,000 **SK**

An Edgar Brandt wrought-iron dressing-table mirror.

This design is illustrated on p.164 of 'Edgar Brandt' by Joan Khar, New York, 1999.

17in (43cm) high

$2,000-3,000 DUK

A pair of French Art Deco wrought-iron and macassar-ebony occasional tables, in the manner of Edgar Brandt.

27.5in (70cm) high

$5,000-7,000 GORL

A Gordon Russell Workshops drinks cabinet, designed by Eden Minns, the walnut upper section with two sliding mirror doors above a sycamore interior, the doors with intarsia work in various woods, on a macassar-ebony stand, fully labeled.

Eden Minns was the firm's chief designer.

1935 *60in (152.5cm) high*

$2,500-3,500 TEN

A pair of Koloman Moser elm-veneered chairs, designed for court carpenter K.U.K. Müller, Vienna, inlaid with friezes of maple, the backrests with a dove holding an olive twig in maple, rosewood and mother-of-pearl.

1904 *37.25in (94.5cm) high*

$300,000-400,000 QU

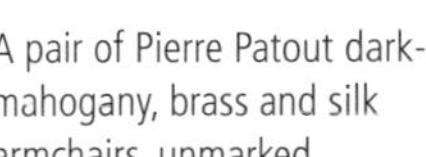

A pair of Pierre Patout dark-mahogany, brass and silk armchairs, unmarked.

These armchairs were from the first-class dining room of the SS 'Normandie'.

c1935 *34.5in (88cm) high*

$5,500-6,500 DRA

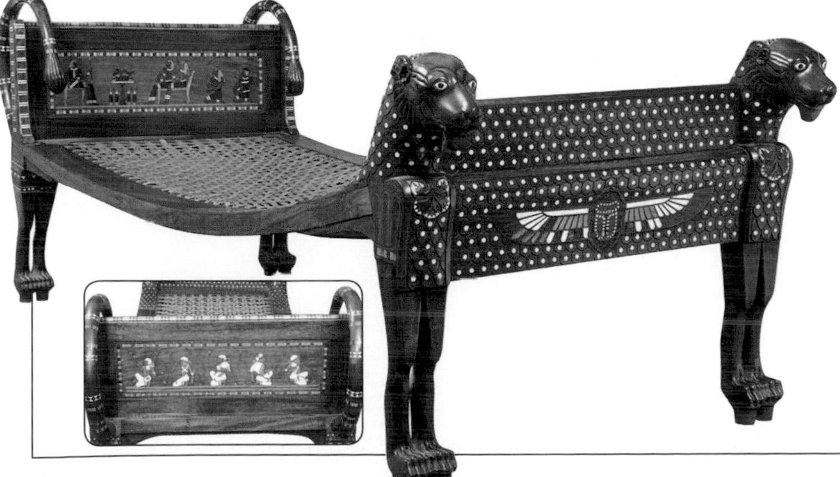

An Egyptian Revival mahogany and bone-inlaid chaise longue, decorated with pharaonic figures, attendants and Horus surrounded by scales, on lion monopode forelegs and monopode back legs with lion tails.

An almost identical chaise longue is featured in the film 'The Ten Commandments' starring Charlton Heston, Yul Brynner and Anne Baxter. The film was released in 1956 but this example is almost certainly much earlier.

c1922-36 *84.75in (215.5cm) long*

$40,000-60,000 DOY

One of a pair of Art Deco macassar-ebony and brass armchairs, inlaid with satinwood, unmarked.

34in (86cm) high

$3,000-4,000 pair **DRA**

Two early 20thC Egyptian Revival carved-walnut and bone-inlaid chairs, on animalistic legs, one with paw feet, the other with hoof feet.

35.5in (90cm) high

$10,000-15,000 **DN**

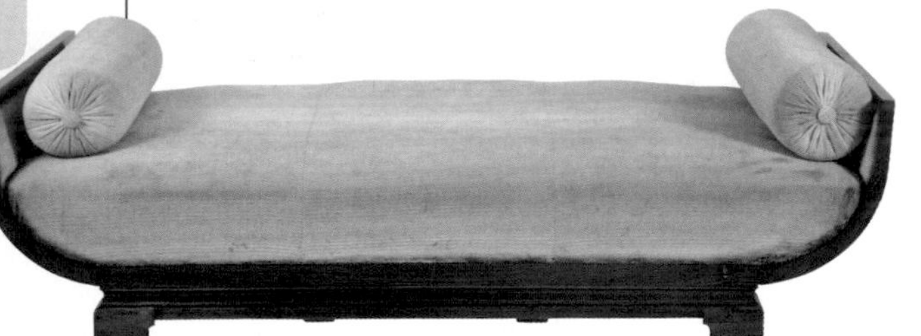

An Art Deco walnut day bed, with scrolled ends, the fabric dirty, missing some piping.

83.5in (212cm) long

$2,500-3,500 **SWO**

An Art Deco walnut-veneered console table, with restoration.

c1930-35 *38.5in (98cm) long*

$5,500-6,500 **DOR**

An Art Deco mahogany and thuja-burl-veneer sideboard, with marble top, with original mounts, with wear.

c1930-35

75in(191cm) wide

$2,500-3,500 **DOR**

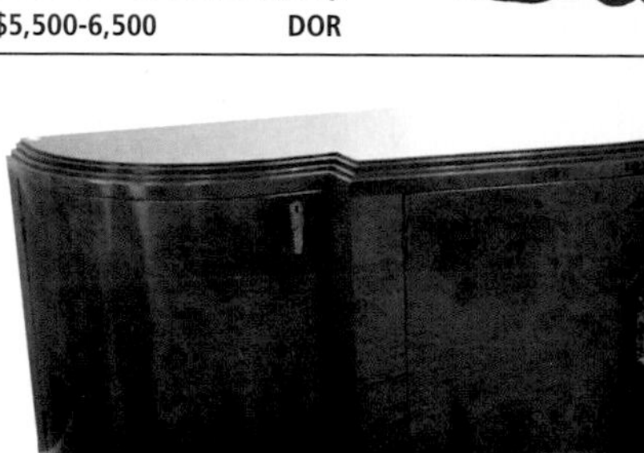

A large Art Deco burr-walnut sideboard, with a central relief metal panel, opening to a burr-maple interior, on silvered reeded-supports.

97.5in (250cm) wide

$6,500-7,500 **SWO**

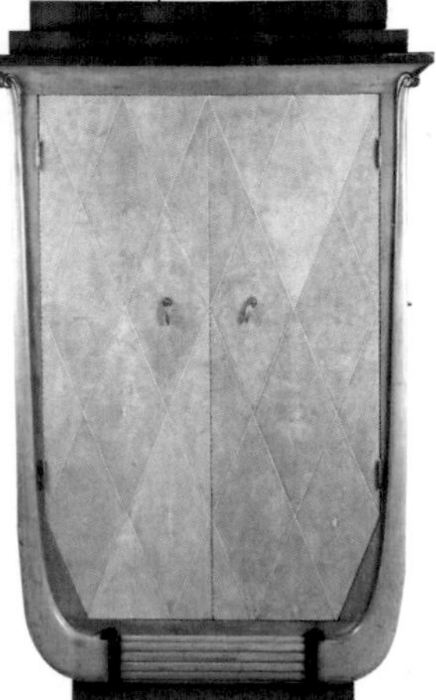

An Art Deco sycamore and rosewood dressing cabinet, with shagreen doors, opening to reveal a triple mirror with a retractable light above, the side doors opening to shelves and drawers.

75in (190cm) high

$10,000-15,000 **SWO**

An Art Deco two-part walnut- and Caucasian walnut-veneered desk, designed in Vienna, the fall front opening to marquetry-decorated interior, with restoration.

c1935 *61in (155cm) high*

$10,000-15,000 **DOR**

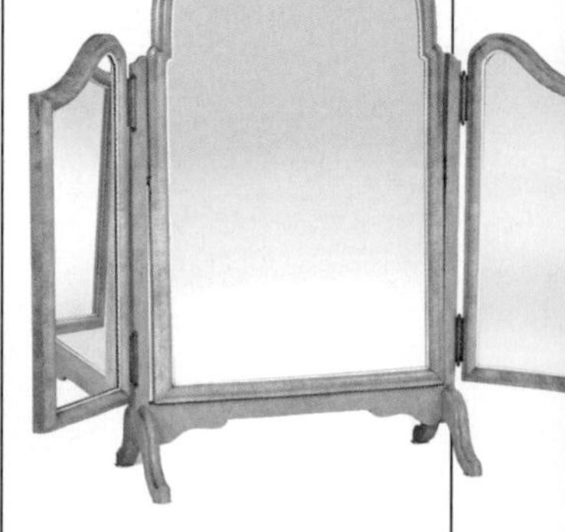

An Art Deco shagreen and ivory triptych dressing-mirror, one of the hinges inscribed '9287 YW/-/-'.

35in (88.5cm) wide

$4,000-6,000 **TEN**

A Daum cameo and enameled glass 'Prairie' vase, signed in gold 'Daum Nancy', with Cross of Lorraine.

5.5in (14cm) high

$18,000-22,000 **JDJ**

A Daum cameo glass vase, wheel-engraved and with a martelé ground, signed 'Daum Nancy', with Cross of Lorraine, with applied paper label '43'.

This vase comes with original retailer's label, which reads, 'Vase/ 4/11/01/ £7/II/'.

c1900 *5in (12.5cm) high*

$15,000-20,000 **L&T**

A Daum cameo glass vase, etched with bats, the transparent glass overlaid with yellow-green and brown glass, signed 'Daum Nancy', with Cross of Lorraine.

c1900 *13in (33cm) high*

$7,000-10,000 **KAU**

A Daum cameo glass vase, acid-etched with poppies against a martelé ground, signed 'Daum Nancy', with Cross of Lorraine.

c1902 *11.5in (29cm) high*

$4,000-6,000 **TRI**

CLOSER LOOK - DAUM 'SNAIL' VASE

This is a complicated multi-layer design.

This was a top-end, high quality vase made by one of Daum's most skilled craftsmen.

The cameo decoration of grapevines, leaves and grape clusters is done in green, gray and purple vitrified glass against a brown shading to yellow background.

The vase is adorned with an applied snail and several applied cabochon grapes giving the vase a somewhat three-dimensional feel.

A Daum cameo glass 'Snail' vase, etched with grapevines, leaves and grape clusters, signed 'Daum Nancy', with Cross of Lorraine.

c1905 *10in (25.4cm) high*

$15,000-20,000 **JDJ**

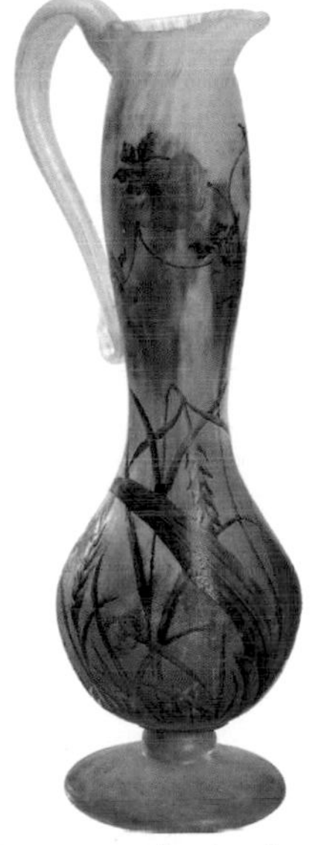

A Daum cameo glass jug, decorated with orchid flowers, signed 'Daum Nancy'.

c1905 *12.5in (33cm) high*

$4,000-6,000 **KAU**

A Daum cameo glass 'Crocus' vase, designed by Henri Bergé, wheel-engraved with buds on a martelé ground, signed 'DAUM NANCY', with Cross of Lorraine.

1906 *12in (30.5cm) high*

$10,000-15,000 **QU**

A Daum cameo and enameled glass 'Mushroom' bowl, designed by Henri Bergé, model no.'3054', enameled with three types of mushrooms, acid-etched in low and deep relief, engraved with the model no.

1907 *5.5in (13.5cm) high*

$15,000-20,000 **FIS**

A Daum enameled glass vase, enameling with a winter landscape, signed 'Daum Nancy' in enamel.

c1910 *4in (11cm) high*

$5,000-7,000 WW

A Daum enameled glass vase, enameled with a summer landscape, signed 'Daum Nancy BS' in enamel.

9in (22cm) high

$4,000-6,000 WW

A Daum cameo glass vase, wheel-carved with iris, with gilded accents on frosted ground, signed 'Daum Nancy', with Cross of Lorraine.

7.25in (18cm) high

$1,200-1,800 DRA

A Daum enameled glass vase, enameled with sweetpea stems, signed, with painted 'HW' monogram.

2.5in (7cm) high

$1,800-2,200 WW

A Daum ribbed, cameo and enameled glass vase, signed 'Daum Nancy', with Cross of Lorraine.

c1910 *23.75in (60.5cm) high*

$8,000-12,000 DN

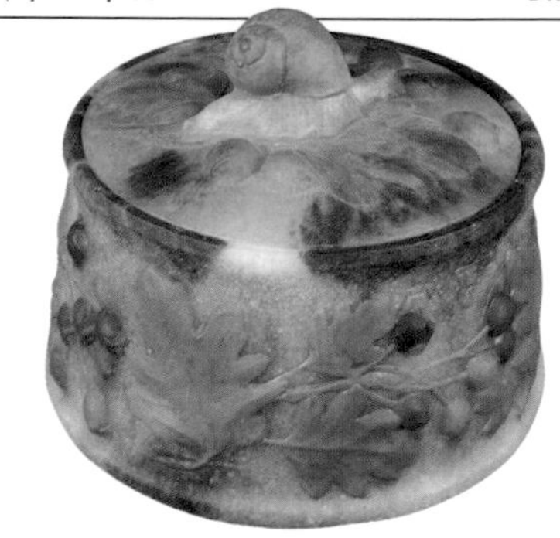

A Daum pâte-de-verre and enameled glass box, the cover with a snail finial.

3.5in (8.5cm) high

$10,000-15,000 DOY

An early 20thC Daum cameo and enameled glass vase, signed.

3in (8cm) high

$1,200-1,800 FLD

A Daum acid-etched lemon-yellow glass vase, signed 'Daum Nancy'.

c1930 *10in (25.5cm) high*

$2,000-3,000 L&T

A 1930s Art Deco Daum glass vase, cased with pale celadon fired enamel over a deep cinnamon ground, signed, with Cross of Lorraine.

12.5in (32cm) high

$6,500-7,500 FLD

An Émile Gallé cameo glass 'Chêne lorrain' vase, martelé-cut with twigs of durmast oak, signed 'Gallé'.
1889-95 *8in (20.5cm) high*
$30,000-40,000 **QU**

An Émile Gallé enameled glass vase, enameled and gilded with a male figure, signed 'Gallé'.
1895-1900 *9.5in (24cm) high*
$10,000-15,000 **FIS**

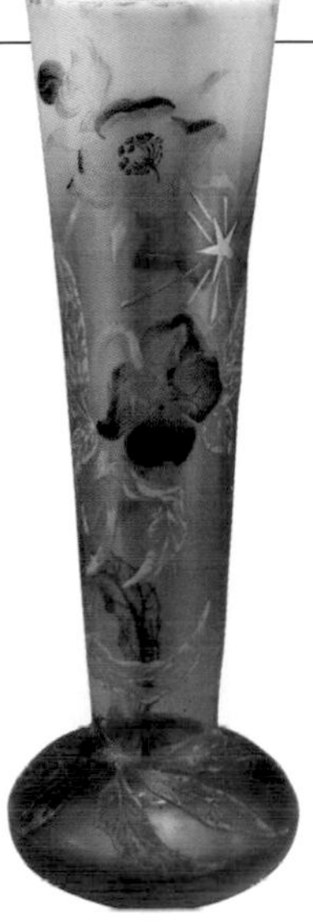

An Émile Gallé enameled glass 'Hellebore' vase, enameled and gilded with Christmas flowers, signed 'Gallé déposé'.
1897-1900 *17.5in (44.5cm) high*
$7,000-10,000 **QU**

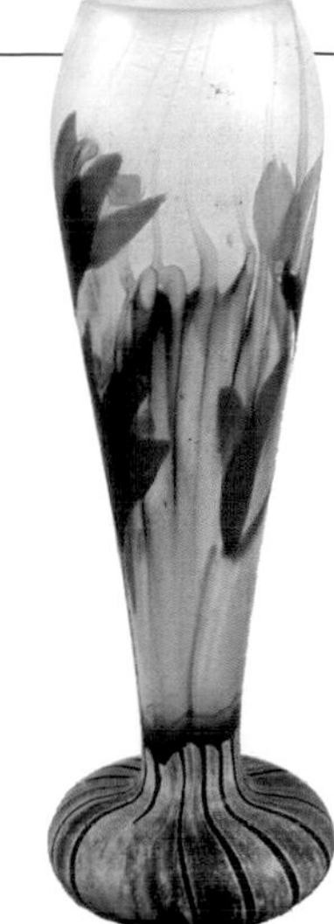

An Émile Gallé marquetry glass 'Crocus' vase, with fancy intaglio signature, inscribed on reverse 'Le Safran des Alpes Dis aux petits que les etes sont courts M. Valmare'.
c1900 *8.25in (21cm) high*
$20,000-30,000 **POOK**

A pair of Émile Gallé cameo glass vases, with applied raspberry cabochons, signed with intaglio marks 'Gallé'.
c1900 *8.5in (22cm) high*
$10,000-15,000 **WAD**

An Émile Gallé cameo glass 'windowpane' vase, decorated with plums in a multitude of blues, signed 'Gallé'.

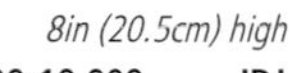

8in (20.5cm) high
$7,000-10,000 **JDJ**

An Émile Gallé cameo glass vase, acid-etched with blossoms, signed 'Gallé'.
c1900 *11in (28cm) high*
$5,500-6,500 **DOY**

An Émile Gallé cameo glass vase, etched with blue and purple flowers against a yellow ground, signed.
11.75in (30cm) high
$6,500-7,500 **BELL**

An Émile Gallé cameo glass vase, the yellow glass overlaid with brown slipper orchids, signed.
7in (17.5cm) high
$2,500-3,500 **WW**

A René Lalique blue glass 'Albert' vase, model no.958, the handles modeled as falcons' heads, engraved 'R.Lalique, France'.

c1925 *6.75in (17cm) high*

$3,000-4,000 **GORL**

Miller's Compares

This vase is arguably the most famous vase associated with René Lalique. The 'Bacchantes' vase displays the young priestesses of Bacchus. The finish of the background is very sculptural and the surface could almost be mistaken for 'cire-perdue' glass. The vases were produced in clear, gray, colored and also in the rare opalescent glass. The difference in value is purely that the vase on the left is a pre-1937 opalescent and the one on the right is a post 1945 sepia.

The opalescence of this example is a really deep and rich striking blue/white color. It is further enhanced with the original blue staining.

A René Lalique clear, frosted and opalescent glass 'Bacchantes' vase, model no.997, wheel-etched 'R. LALIQUE/FRANCE', with small chip to foot.

Designed 1927 *9.5in (24cm) high*

$30,000-40,000 **L&T**

A Lalique frosted glass 'Bacchantes' vase, model no.997, with sepia patina, unmarked.

c1945-50 *9.5in (24cm) high*

$5,500-6,500 **DRA**

Judith Picks

Technically challenging and rare, cire perdue (lost wax) casts are the most sought of Lalique glass. The method results in completely unique, one-off pieces of art. This vase was particularly desirable for its subject matter - two winged female nudes with outstretched arms. The design was previously known only from a line drawing. It bears a full and partial thumbprint to the base, which is as close as a collector will ever get to one of the luminaries of 20thC glass.

A René Lalique cire-perdue glass 'Deux Figures Femmes Aillees' vase, model no.415, decorated with two winged female nudes, inscribed 'No 1/4' '415-22, wheel-engraved 'R Lalique'.

1922 *6.25in (16cm) high*

$500,000-600,000 **A&G**

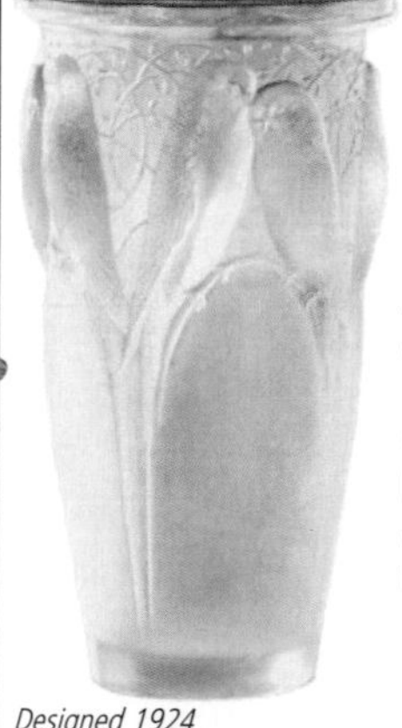

A Lalique opalescent glass 'Ceylan' vase, model no.905, with blue patina, wheel-engraved 'R Lalique France'.

Designed 1924 *9.5in (24cm) high*

$6,500-7,500 **SWO**

A René Lalique red glass 'Formose' vase, model no.934, molded 'R Lalique', cracked.

Designed 1924 *7in (18cm) high*

$700-1,000 **WW**

A René Lalique clear and frosted yellow glass 'Moissac' vase, model no.992, wheel-cut 'R.LALIQUE FRANCE'.

Designed 1927 *5in (12.5cm) high*

$2,500-3,500 **DRA**

A René Lalique frosted black-amethyst-glass 'Montargis' vase, model no.1022, molded 'R.LALIQUE FRANCE', engraved 'R. Lalique France no.1022'.

c1930 *8.25in (21cm) high*

$4,000-6,000 **WAD**

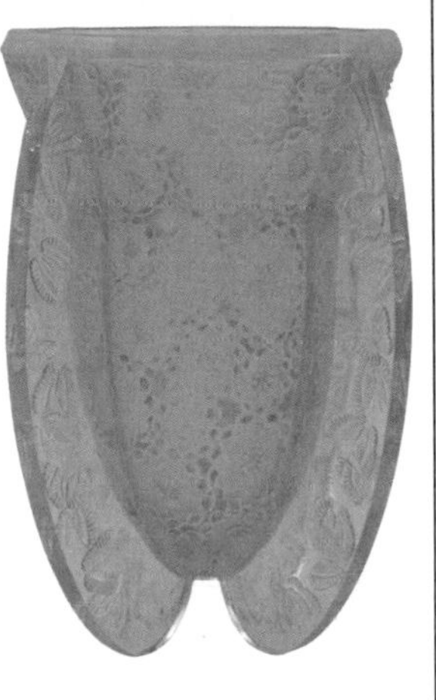

A René Lalique clear and frosted glass 'Papillons' vase, model no.10-899, with sepia staining to body, acid-etched 'R Lalique France', with small chip to foot.

Designed 1936 *9in (22.5cm) high*

$5,000-7,000 **WW**

A René Lalique enameled and frosted glass 'Pensée' vase, model no.928, enameled in black and aubergine, intaglio 'R Lalique'.

c1920 *6in (14cm) high*

$5,000-7,000 **WW**

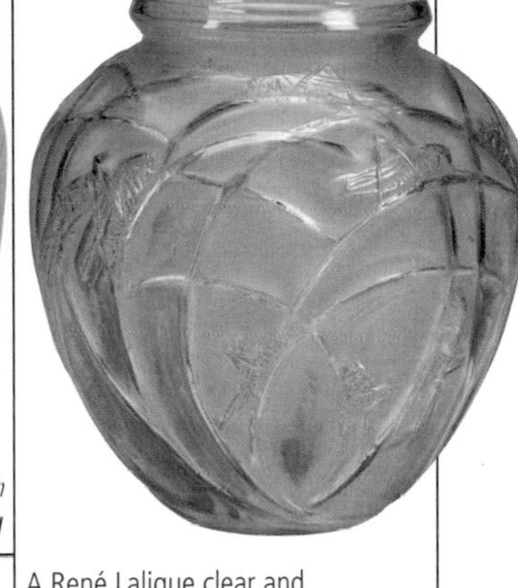

A René Lalique clear and frosted glass 'Sauterelles' vase, model no.888, decorated with grasshoppers and partial turquoise and blue patina, engraved 'Lalique France'.

c1912 *10.75in (27.5cm) high*

$5,000-7,000 **DRA**

A René Lalique opalescent glass 'Saint Francois' vase, model no.1055, stenciled 'R Lalique'.

Designed 1930

7.25in (18.5cm) high

$3,000-4,000 **WW**

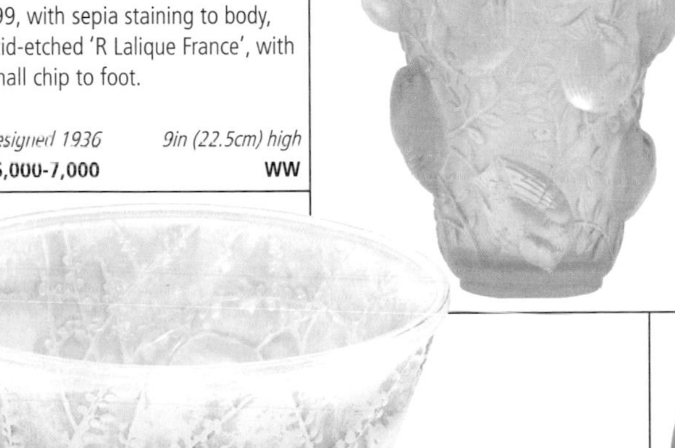

A René Lalique opalescent glass 'Senart' vase, model no.1098, molded with squirrels, with blue staining, stenciled 'R. Lalique/ France'.

Designed 1934 *8.25in (21cm) high*

$6,500-7,500 **L&T**

A René Lalique yellow glass 'Tourbillons' vase, model no.973, wheel-cut 'R Lalique France', with bruise to top rim.

Designed 1926 *8in (20.5cm) high*

$5,500-6,500 **WW**

A René Lalique frosted and opalescent glass 'Deux Colombes' clock, model no.727, molded 'R. LALIQUE/ FRANCE', with replaced movement.

Designed 1926 *8.75in (22cm) high*

$5,500-6,500 **L&T**

A René Lalique opalescent glass 'Inseparables' clock, model no.765, with blue patina, intaglio 'R Lalique'.

c1926 *4in (11cm) high*

$4,000-6,000 **WW**

A modern Lalique frosted colorless glass 'Masque de Femme' plaque, with faint signature 'Lalique France'.

12.5in (32cm) wide

$3,500-4,500 **DOY**

ESSENTIAL REFERENCE - LOETZ

- **The Loetz (or Lötz) factory was founded by Johann Baptist Eisner in 1836 in the Bohemian village of Klostermühle.**
- **In 1840 the company was taken over by Johann Loetz.**
- **After his death in 1851, it was taken over his widow Susanne Gerstner-Loetz. Pieces produced during this period are often referred to as 'Loetz Witwe'.**
- **By the end of the 19thC Loetz's grandson, Max Ritter von Spaun, had made the company into one of the greatest glassworks in central Europe.**
- **Loetz was known for innovative techniques, organic forms and bold use of color. The company patented iridescent glass in 1895.**
- **Notable designers include Maria Kirschner, Josef Hoffmann and Koloman Moser.**
- **The company closed in 1947.**

A Loetz glass 'Phänomen' vase, designed by Franz Hofstötter for the Paris World Fair 1900, marked 'Phänomen Gre 353'.
1900 *7.5in (19.5cm) high*
$20,000-30,000 QU

A Loetz glass vase, designed by Franz Hofstötter, decorated with several pulled patterns, signed 'Loetz Austria'.
10.5in (26.5cm) high
$25,000-30,000 DRA

A Loetz glass 'Phänomen' 'Gre 829' pattern vase, in lemon-yellow cased glass trailed with silver-yellow and blue striped bands.
c1900 *5in (13.5cm) high*
$3,000-4,000 DOR

A Loetz glass 'Phänomen' 'Gre 1/4' pattern vase, with yellow opalescence, carved 'Loetz Austria'.
c1900 *5in (12.5cm) high*
$5,000-7,000 DOR

A Loetz glass 'Phänomen' 'Gre 358' pattern vase, designed by Franz Hofstötter for the 1900 Paris World Fair, cased in opalescent yellow trailed with silver-yellow bands and orange and brown veined bands, carved 'Loetz Austria'.
1900 *13in (32.5cm) high*
$18,000-22,000 DOR

A Loetz glass 'Phänomen' vase, carved 'Loetz Austria'.
c1900 *5.5in (14cm) high*
$10,000-15,000 DOR

A large Loetz glass 'Titania' vase, unsigned.
11in (28cm) high
$15,000-20,000 DRA

A Loetz glass and gilt-metal-mounted 'Creta Pampas' vase, the mount with three handles.
c1900 *7.5in (17cm) high*
$2,500-3,500 DOR

A Loetz glass 'Phänomen' 'Gre 2/450' pattern vase, carved 'Loetz Austria'.
1902 *7.3in (18.5cm) high*
$8,000-12,000 DOR

A Venini & C. slightly iridescent glass 'a Bollicine' vase, designed by Carlo Scarpa, acid-stamped 'venini murano'.

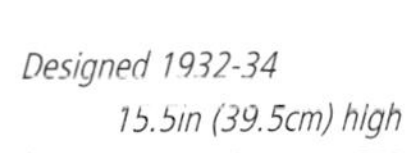

Designed 1932-34 *15.5in (39.5cm) high*
$8,000-12,000 **QU**

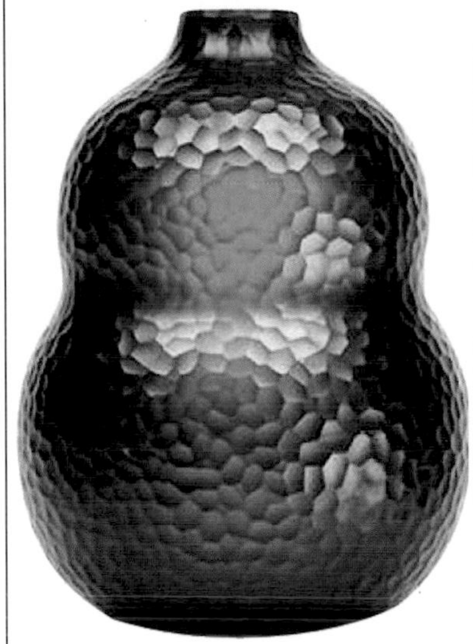

A Venini & C. glass 'Battuto' vase, designed by Carlo Scarpa, with acid-etched factory mark.
Designed 1940 *7.5in (17.5cm) high*
$6,500-7,500 **DOR**

A Venini & C. glass 'Inciso' vase, designed by Carlo Scarpa, cased in colorless glass over rust-red, with cut surface, acid-stamp 'venini murano'.
Designed 1940 *9.25in (23.5cm) high*
$12,000-18,000 **QU**

A Venini & C. glass 'Fazzoletto' vase, designed by Paolo Venini and Fulvio Bianconi, etched 'Venini, Murano, Italia'.
Designed 1949 *10.25in (26cm) high*
$500-700 **SWO**

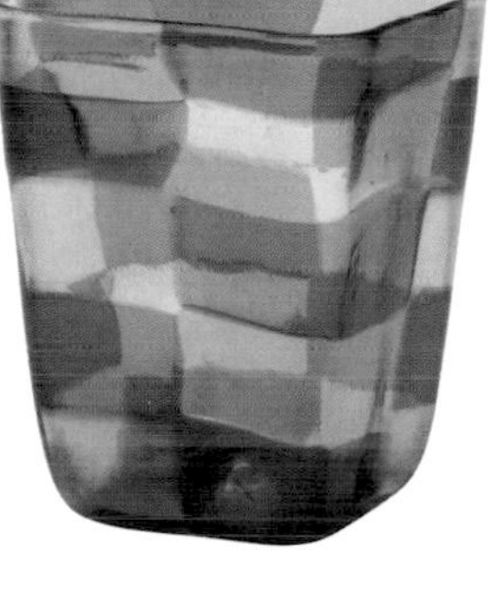

A Venini & C. glass 'Pezzato' vase, designed by Fulvio Bianconi, with platelets of yellow, moss-green, clear and purple glass, acid-stamped 'venini murano ITALIA'.
Designed 1950-51 *5.25in (13cm) high*
$4,000-6,000 **QU**

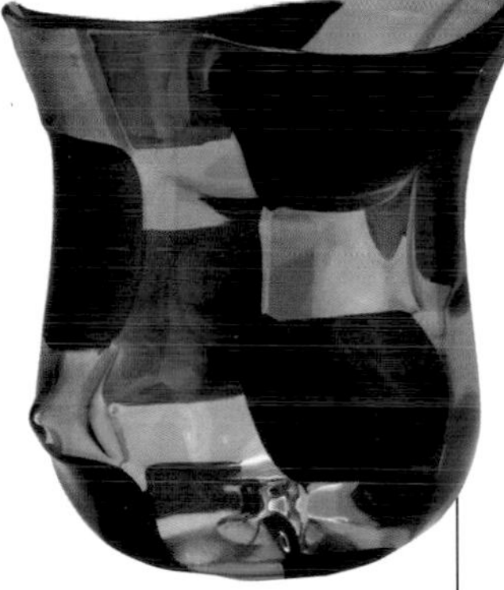

A Venini & C. glass 'Pezzato' vase, designed by Fulvio Bianconi, unsigned.
Designed c1950-51 *6.75in (17cm) high*
$8,000-12,000 **QU**

A Venini & C. glass 'Scozzese' vase, designed by Fulvio Bianconi, acid-stamped 'venini murano ITALIA'.
Designed c1954
11.75in (29.5cm) high
$30,000-35,000 **QU**

A Venini & C. glass prototype 'Zanfirico Mosaico' vase, designed by Paolo Venini, unsigned.
c1954 *14.5in (36.5cm) high*
$10,000-15,000 **QU**

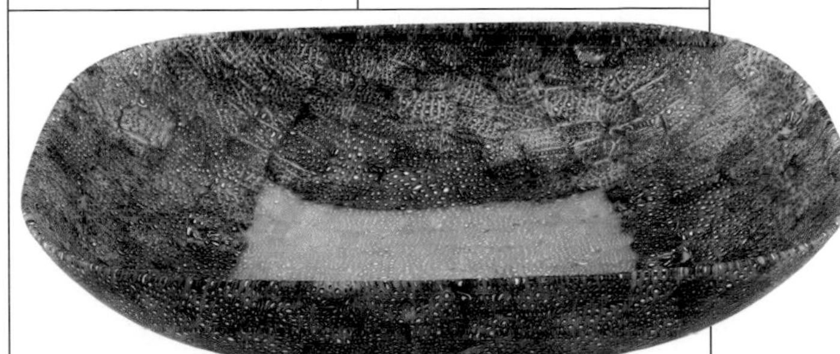

A Venini & C. glass 'Murrine' bowl, designed by Ludovico Diaz de Santillana, unsigned.
Designed c1959 *9.25in (23.5cm) long*
$20,000-25,000 **QU**

An Aureliano Toso slightly iridescent glass 'Oriente Firenzio' vase, designed by Dino Martens, model no.5270, includes webs, 'zanfirico' bands and a large murrine in white and dark purple, with two apertures.

Designed c1954 *13.5in (34cm) high*
$10,000-15,000 **QU**

An Aureliano Toso glass double-gourd vase, designed by Dino Martens, model no.5497, with combed blue and red threads, with label.

1954 *12.5in (32cm) high*
$2,500-3,500 **FIS**

ESSENTIAL REFERENCE - AVEM

In 1932 a group of glassblowers set up Arte Vetraria Muranese (AVeM) on the island of Murano in Venice, Italy. They produced pieces to their own designs and commissioned further designs from Italian painters. This approach was immediately successful as the wine glasses designed by painter Vittorio Zecchin for AVeM received acclaim at the Venice Biennale in the same year AVeM was founded.

- **Giulio Radi was artistic director 1939-52.**
- **Giorgio Ferro (b.1931) became artistic director in 1952. His acclaimed designs include vases and jugs in asymmetric shapes, with multiple necks and handles and a distinctive iridescent finish.**
- **Ferro and his father Galliano left AVeM in 1955 to found Vetreria Galliano Ferro.**
- **Other notable designers to work for AVeM included Dino Martens and Anzolo Fuga.**

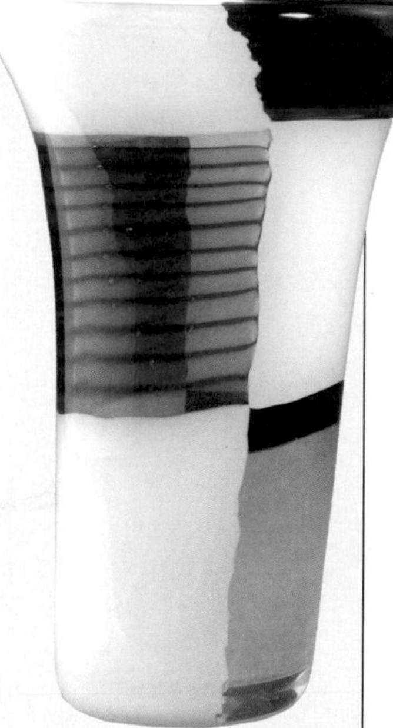

An AVeM glass 'Bandiere' vase, designed by Anzolo Fuga.

Designed 1955 *13.25in (33.5cm) high*
$5,500-6,500 **QU**

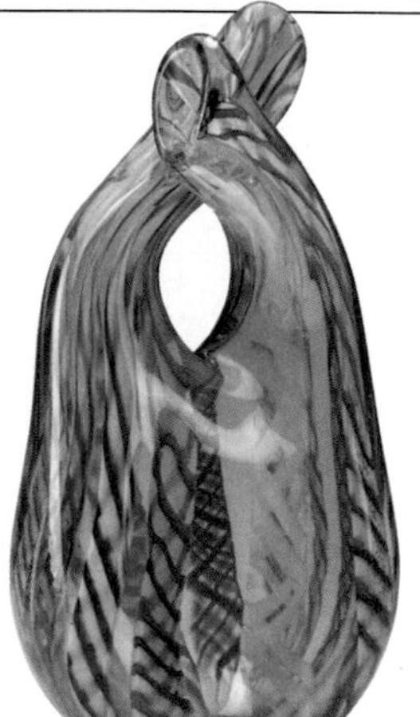

A 1960s AVeM cased 'ribbon' glass bottle, with acid- etched circular mark.

12.75in (32.5cm) high
$3,000-4,000 **DRA**

A Vetreria Artistica Barovier & C. glass vase, designed by Ercole Barovier.

Designed 1920 *11in (28.5cm) high*
$30,000-35,000 **QU**

A Vetreria Artistica Barovier & C. glass 'Primavera' vase, designed by Ercole Barovier.

Pieces from the rare 'Primavera' glass range have a clear, slightly milky, bubbly and craqueled appearance. The handles and rim of this example are of a black gather.

Designed 1929-30 *13.25in (33.5cm) high*
$150,000-200,000 **QU**

A Barovier & Toso glass 'Saturneo' vase, designed by Ercole Barovier, with gold foil and fused murrines, with maker's decal.

Designed 1951 *7in (18cm) high*
$7,000-9,000 **QU**

A Barovier & Toso glass 'Egeo' vase, designed by Ercole Barovier, with fused murrines in green, milky white and purple.

Designed 1960 *10.5in (27 cm) high*
$30,000-40,000 **QU**

An MVM Cappellin & C. glass 'Lattimo' vase, designed by Carlo Scarpa, acid-stamped 'MVM Cappellin Murano'.

Designed 1929/30 *13.5in (34cm) high*

$20,000 30,000 **QU**

An MVM Cappellin & C. iridescent glass 'pasta vitrea' ewer, designed by Carlo Scarpa, decorated with fused burst silver foil.

'Pasta vitrea' glass is made to look like ceramic.

Designed 1929/30 *9.25in (23.5cm) high*

$10,000-15,000 **QU**

An unusual Cenedese 'Aquarium' lamp, on chrome metal frame.

7.75in (20cm) wide

$800-1,200 **WW**

A Fratelli Toso glass 'Millepiedi' vase, designed by Ermanno Toso, with 'Kiku' murrines, with label.

c1950-55 *13.75in (35cm) high*

$25,000-30,000 **FIS**

A Fratelli Toso glass 'Cattedrale' vase, designed by Pollio Perelda, with large murrines, with original label.

1957 *11.5in (29.5cm) high*

$15,000-20,000 **FIS**

A Vetreria Artistica Archimede Seguso glass 'Merletto Irregulare' vase, designed by Archimede Seguso, with partially white 'merletto' web and green layers.

Designed 1953 *14in (36cm) high*

$15,000-20,000 **QU**

A Vetreria Artistica Archimede Seguso glass 'Merletto' vase, designed by Archimede Seguso, with bands of white 'merletto' web and purple drips, inscribed '6835', with remains of paper labels.

Designed 1954 *11.75in (30cm) high*

$20,000-25,000 **QU**

A Vetreria Vistosi glass and copper 'Pulcini' bird sculpture, designed by Alessandro Pianon, unmarked.

Designed 1961-62 *8.5in (21.5cm) high*

$8,000-12,000 **DRA**

A complete set of five Vetreria Vistosi glass and copper 'Pulcini' birds, designed by Alessandro Pianon, all applied with round murrines as eyes, inscribed 'Made in Italy Murano', one bird with paper label.

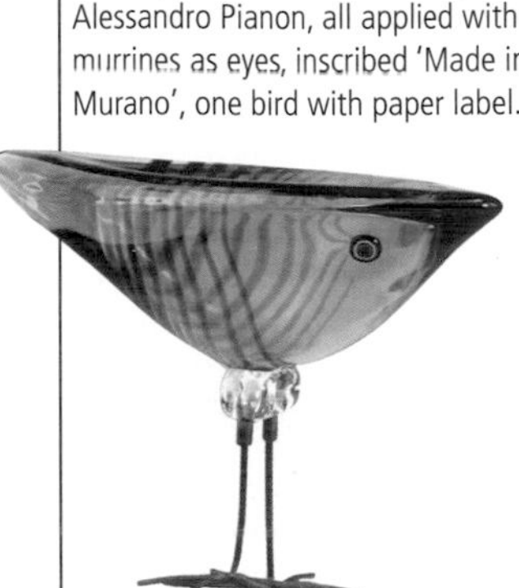

Designed 1961-62 *Tallest 12.5in (32cm) high*

$30,000-40,000 **QU**

A Tiffany gold 'Favrile' glass floriform vase, etched 'L.C.T. M7566'.

Louis Comfort Tiffany trademarked 'Favrile' (from the old French word for handmade) on November 13, 1894.

14.5in (37cm) high

$7,000-10,000 DRA

A Tiffany glass vase, with steel-blue and metallic luster, signed 'Louis C. Tiffany, 0 16500', with original paper label 'TIFFANY FAVRILE GLASS REGISTERED TRADEMARK GDTCO'.

1901 *12in (30.5cm) high*

$45,000-55,000 QU

A Tiffany 'Favrile' glass vase, signed 'L.C. Tiffany Favrile 1526-8620 G'.

1900-10 *13.25in (33.5cm) high*

$2,500-3,500 QU

A Tiffany 'Favrile' glass vase, decorated with trailed green leaves and vines, with gold luster with pink and blue highlights, signed '5135C L.C. Tiffany-Favrile'.

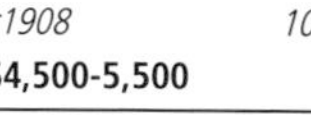

c1908 *10.5in (27cm) high*

$4,500-5,500 DOY

A Tiffany 'Favrile' glass 'Calla Lily' paperweight vase, inlaid with green and brown leaves and three white blossoms, signed '3002 G L.C. Tiffany-Favrile'.

c1912 *16.5in (42cm) high*

$40,000-50,000 DOY

ESSENTIAL REFERENCE

Louis Comfort Tiffany (1848-1933) established Tiffany Glass & Decorating Co. (later Tiffany Studios) in 1885 and the Stourbridge Glass Company (later Tiffany Furnaces) in 1893.

- **With the assistance of English glassmaker Arthur J Nash (1849-1934), Tiffany refined and developed the technique of iridizing glass. The resulting 'Favrile' range was launched in 1894 and was an immediate success. Other iridescent ranges, such as 'Lava', followed.**
- **Tiffany created innovative plant-inspired Art Nouveau forms, such as the 'Jack-in-the-Pulpit' vase.**
- **Tiffany Furnaces was dissolved in 1924.**

A Tiffany glass 'Jack-in-the-Pulpit' vase, inscribed 'L.C.T. 3059'.

The domed circular foot is uncharacteristic of the 'Jack-in-the-Pulpit' model, suggesting that this may have been an early form that was modified later.

12.5in (32cm) high

$120,000-180,000 MIC

A Tiffany silver-gilt-mounted 'Favrile' glass cabinet vase, the glass inscribed 'L.C.T. B1285', the mount by La Maison Vever, Paris, impressed 'VEVER PARIS' with a boar's head hallmark.

The Maison Vever was one of France's foremost jewellers. Around the turn of the century, the company designed a number of mounts in precious materials for Tiffany glassware. Siegfried Bing undoubtedly served as liaison between La Maison Vever and Tiffany.

c1900 *3in (8cm) high*

$42,000-55,000 MIC

An early 20thC Tiffany 'Favrile' glass vase, with polished pontil, signed 'L.C.T. D821 Louis C. Tiffany', with 'Tiffany Favrile Glass Trademark' paper label.

6.25in (16cm) high

$5,000-7,000 SK

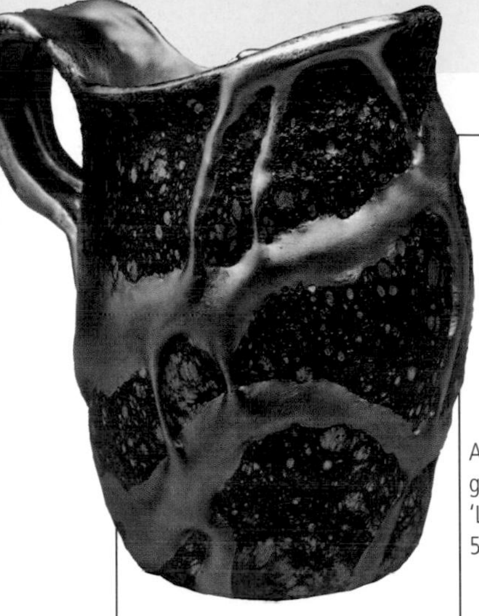

A Tiffany 'Lava' glass ewer, inscribed 'L.C.Tiffany-Favrile 606K', with enameled accession no.'L88.2 GAT'.

The 'Lava glass' technique pioneered by Tiffany was possibly inspired by his visit to Mount Etna in Sicily during one of its eruptions. Different metallic oxides were mixed within the glass. This created an iridescent 'lava-flow' and black voids.

4.5in (11.5cm) high

$300,000-350,000 **MIC**

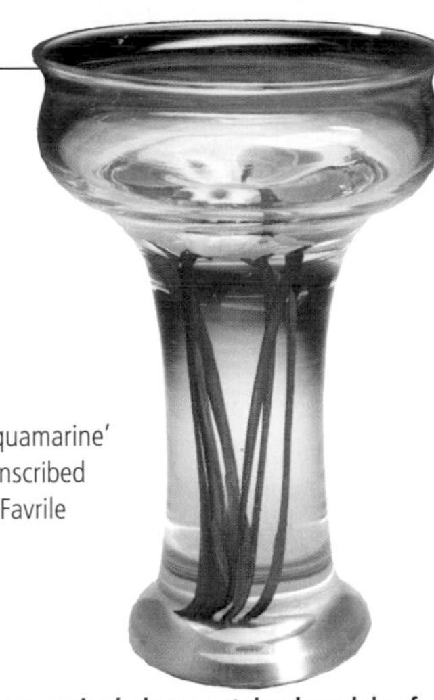

A Tiffany 'Aquamarine' glass vase, inscribed 'L.C.Tiffany-Favrile 5202G'.

Tiffany's 'Aquamarine' glass contained models of aquatic plants and other marine life fashioned from small colored glass canes that the glassblower pulled into their required forms with a metal hook not unlike a crochet needle. At various stages in the process, the composition was encased in layers of clear or tinted glass gathered on a blow-pipe from a crystal pot. The result provided the viewer with the impression of looking into a fishbowl or pond, with the best examples providing a sense of motion within the water.

1911/12 *10in (25cm) high*

$65,000-75,000 **MIC**

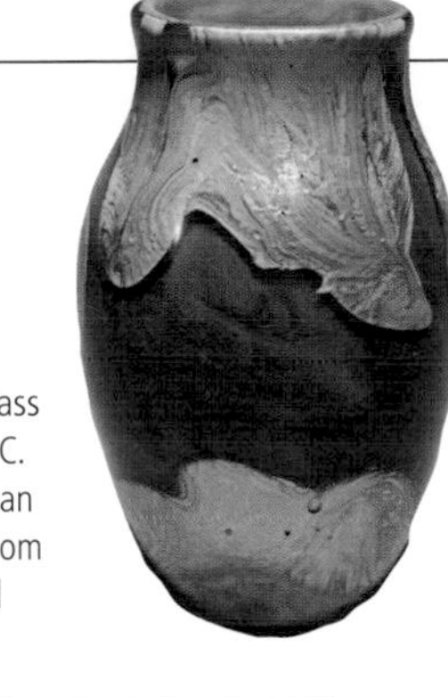

A Tiffany 'Cypriote' glass vase, inscribed 'Louis C. Tiffany M2698', with an original paper label from 'The Tiffany Glass and Decorating Co.'.

With his 'Cypriote' glass, Louis Comfort Tiffany sought to simulate the qualities of glass excavated from archaeological sites on Cyprus. To replicate the devitrified surfaces of buried artefacts, particles of metallic oxides were applied to a mass of molten glass. This created a chemical reaction that, in turn, pitted the surface of the glass when it was held to a flame. Another technique used involved a gather of molten glass rolled over a marver (steel plate) covered in pulverized silica rock - this process also pitted the surface of the glass. Often additional decorative elements, such as silvery-blue leaves on trailing stems, were applied to the encrusted ground before it was iridized.

7in (18cm) high

$40,000-50,000 **MIC**

A Tiffany 'Morning Glory' glass paperweight vase, inscribed 'L.C. Tiffany-Favrile 3309J'.

The glassmakers at Tiffany Studios faced an on-going challenge in their creation of 'Morning Glory' glass. Leslie H Nash later noted that in countless hours of unsuccessful experimentation, five different types of glass were employed in multiple reactive firings and coolings in the attempt to create the 'most beautiful prismatic colors' of the flower. International recognition of the firm's ultimate achievement in this endeavour was provided by the award of First Honourable Mention by the jury at the 1914 'Salon of La Société des Artistes Français' in Paris.

6.5in (16.5cm) high

$45,000-55,000 **MIC**

A Tiffany glass 'Millefiori' paperweight vase, with an intercalaire pattern comprising white millefiori buds and twigs, inscribed 'L.C. Tiffany Favrile 8510n'.

1919 *6.5in (16.5cm) high*

$15,000-20,000 **QU**

A Tiffany glass 'Parakeets and Goldfish Bowl' tea screen, manufactured by the Jewelry Department at Tiffany & Co., with opaque and plique-à-jour enamel, in 18kt gold frame inscribed 'TIFFANY & CO.PP', in carved boxwood stand.

This tea screen required a variety of enameling techniques and required several trips to the firing kiln to achieve the different degrees of translucency in the enamel. According to John Loring in 'Louis Comfort Tiffany at Tiffany & Co.', tea screens were used to shield spirit lamps under the hot-water kettles in tea services.

With stand 8in (20.5cm) high

$320,000-370,000 **MIC**

A Tiffany 'Apple Blossom' window, depicting an apple tree in full bloom before a cloud-streaked sky and water, with a metal tag impressed 'Tiffany Studios New York'.

c1915 *50in (127cm) high*

$120,000-180,000 **MIC**

ESSENTIAL REFERENCE - GABRIEL ARGY-ROUSSEAU

Joseph-Gabriel Argy-Rousseau (1885–1953) was a French ceramicist turned glassmaker. He is best known for his Art Deco pâte-de-verre and pâte-de-cristal glass vases.

- **In 1921 Argy-Rousseau met gallery and glassworks owner Gustave Moser-Millot with whom he established the Société Anonyme des Pâtes de Verre d'Argy-Rousseau. The firm developed their pâte-de-verre technique for six months and built new workshops before beginning to regularly commission work from 1923 onward.**
- **Common motifs include flowers, insects, animals and the female form. Scenes from ancient mythology, such as 'Le Jardin des Hespérides', were also used.**
- **Argy-Rousseau's pâte-de-verre and pâte-de-cristal designs are usually signed 'G. Argy-Rousseau'.**
- **He also produced vessels in clear glass that were decorated with colored enamels. These are typically signed 'G.A.R'.**

A Gabriel Argy-Rousseau pâte-de-verre glass 'Vase à la Chevelure' vase, molded 'G Argy-Rousseau, France'.
c1928 *7in (19cm) high*
$12,000-18,000 **TEN**

A 1920s Gabriel Argy-Rousseau pâte-de-verre glass vase, decorated with spiders, webs and brambles, marked 'G. ARGY-ROUSSEAU' and '7848'.
4.5in (11.5cm) high
$10,000-15,000 **FIS**

An early 20thC Baccarat Art Nouveau glass and ormolu ink-stand, the glass molded as a cresting wave, mounted with an ormolu mermaid, marked 'Baccarat'.
9.5in (24cm) long
$12,000-18,000 **SK**

A Burgun, Schverer & Co. silver-mounted glass 'Cyclamens' vase, by Malvézieux aîné, signed 'VERRERIE D'ART DE LORRAINE, BS & Co', with Cross of Lorraine with thistle.

Burgun, Schverer & Co. was founded in 1711 in Alsace-Lorraine, France. The company produced glass for Gallé to his designs from 1885. After World War II it became Verrerie de Meisenthal.
1896-1903 *5.5in (14cm) high*
$8,000-12,000 **QU**

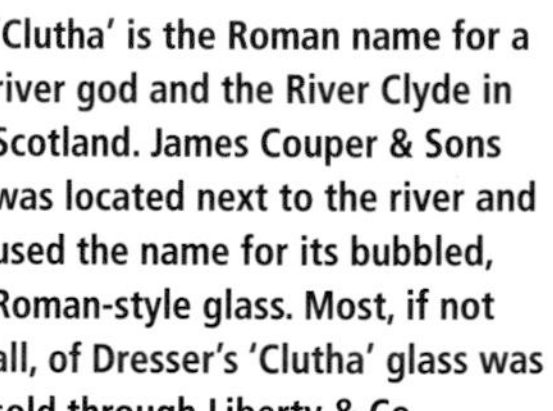

A James Couper & Sons 'Clutha' glass bottle vase, designed by Dr Christopher Dresser, the neck decorated with a blue trailed line, with two-tone green ground, with acid-etched signature.

'Clutha' is the Roman name for a river god and the River Clyde in Scotland. James Couper & Sons was located next to the river and used the name for its bubbled, Roman-style glass. Most, if not all, of Dresser's 'Clutha' glass was sold through Liberty & Co.
11.75in (30cm) high
$7,000-10,000 **FLD**

A Durand glass 'King Tut' vase, in lustered blue and cobalt, unsigned.
7in (18cm) high
$1,200-1,800 **DRA**

A Thomas Webb & Sons cut-crystal vase, engraved by William Fritsche, with palm trees carved against applied bulbous knobs, signed 'Webb', '1674' and 'W. Fritsche'.

William Fritsche was born in Meistersdorf, Bohemia, in 1853. In 1868 he immigrated to the UK and joined Thomas Webb & Sons in Stourbridge. Fritsche was a skilled matt-engraver and also developed the technique of carving and polishing glass so it appeared like natural rock crystal.
8.25in (21cm) high
$12,000-18,000 **JDJ**

A Holmegaard glass vase, designed by Per Lütken, dated.
1961
$300-400 **SWO**

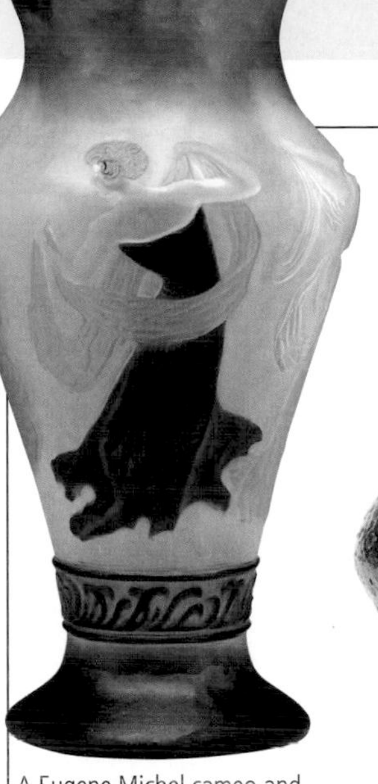

A Eugene Michel cameo and intaglio-carved glass vase, decorated with four maidens depicting the four seasons, signed in cameo 'E. Michel'.

12in (30.5cm) high

$55,000-65,000 **JDJ**

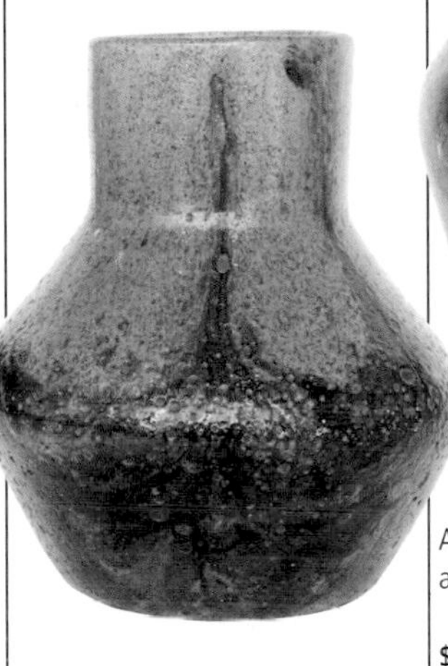

A Monart glass vase, shape GA, size V, 'stoneware'-decorated with pulled black over a mottled tonal green ground.

9in (23cm) high

$1,500-2,500 **FLD**

A Monart glass vase, with aventurine flecks.

9in (23cm) high

$300-400 **SWO**

A Moser glass vase, cut and acid-etched with fish and a seahorse, with acid-etched mark.

c1930 *7.5in (19cm) high*

$1,800-2,200 **SWO**

A Moser glass vase, the amber-colored body with applied blue glass rim and rigaree at the foot, decorated with an applied glass lizard or komodo dragon, unsigned.

Rigaree is a form of appliquéd glass decoration that appears as crimped, ribbon-like highlights. It was sometimes used on Victorian art glass.

11.5in (29cm) high

$5,500-6,500 **JDJ**

A large Moser glass vase, in two parts, with three-dimensional applied birds, cherries, flowers, stems and leaves, the ruffled rim and the foot trimmed in gold, with old, professional, minor repair.

29.5in (75cm) high

$30,000-35,000 **JDJ**

A pair of Moser glass decanters, decorated with applied birds, insects, grape leaves, stems and clusters on a shaded amberina background, both marked '2467', one with remnants of original paper label.

14.5in (37cm) high

$20,000-25,000 **JDJ**

A Moser cranberry-glass bowl, enameled and gilt with a landscape.

11in (28cm) diam

$400-600 **LHA**

A Moser glass vase, with wheel-carved decoration, signed 'Moser Karlsbad'.

10in (25cm) wide

$1,200-1,800 **POOK**

A Muller Frères cameo glass vase, decorated with peonies, molded 'Muller Fres Lunéville'.

c1925 *18in (45cm) high*

$5,000-7,000 **DOR**

An Orrefors glass 'Ariel' vase, by Edvin Öhrström, with etched signature and factory marks.

8in (21cm) high

$1,200-1,800 **WW**

A molded glass figure of 'Donna', by Pablo Picasso and Egidio Costantini, from the 'Nymphs and Fauns' series, with authentification certificate from Egidio Costantini.

1956 *11.5in (29cm) high*

$10,000-15,000 **FIS**

A Societé Anonyme des Verrerie Schneider glass 'Campanules' floor vase, acid-etched with stylized bellflowers, on a frosted ground, needle-etched 'Le Verre Français'.

1920-25 *21.75in (55.5cm) high*

$3,000-4,000 **DOR**

A Societé Anonyme des Verrerie Schneider glass 'Myrtilles' vase, acid-etched with stylized berries, on a frosted ground, signed 'Charder' and 'Le Verre Français'.

1927/28 *16.5in (42cm) high*

$3,000-4,000 **DOR**

A 1920s Steuben double-etched glass 'Chinese' pattern bowl, attributed to Frederick Carder, model no.5002, cased in rosaline-glass over alabaster.

10.25in (26cm) diam

$1,200-1,800 **SK**

ESSENTIAL REFERENCE - QUEZAL

- **Quezal was founded in Brooklyn, New York City, NY, USA, in 1901 by two former employees of Tiffany.**
- **The company was named after a South American bird noted for its colorful plumage.**
- **Quezal made no innovations, instead preferring to simply reproduce Tiffany's production methods and style. Although they were by no means original, Quezal's pieces were of a very high quality.**
- **Decoration tends to be more regular than on Tiffany examples. Pulled-feather designs are typical. Undecorated pieces are rare.**
- **The company closed in 1925 as iridescent glass fell out of fashion.**

A Quezal iridescent glass vase, with pulled and twisted feathering, marked 'Quezel, N. Y.'.

11in (28cm) high

$8,000-12,000 **FRE**

A post-war Skruf glass 'Thalatta' vase, designed by Bengt Edenfalk, with internal 'Ariel' design of repeat abstract forms, with engraved signature.

7in (18cm) high

$1,000-1,500 **FLD**

A Steuben blue iridescent glass 'Aurene' bowl, etched 'Steuben Aurene 2697'.

9.75in (25cm) diam

$700-1,000 **DRA**

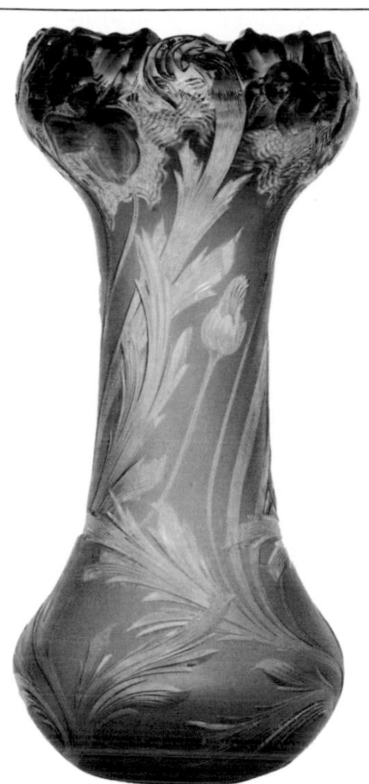

A Stevens & Williams Art Nouveau glass vase, designed by Frederick Carder, probably cut by Orchard.

The original artwork for this vase is published in '20th Century British Glass' by Charles R Hajdamach and shows the illustration monogrammed 'FC 1901'. This illustration matches Stevens & Williams pattern number 27810, registered on the 12th November 1901.

c1901 *12.6in (32 cm) high*

$15,000-20,000 FLD

A pair of late 19thC Stevens & Williams glass vases, after designs by John Northwood.

9.25in (23.5cm) high

$1,500-2,500 FLD

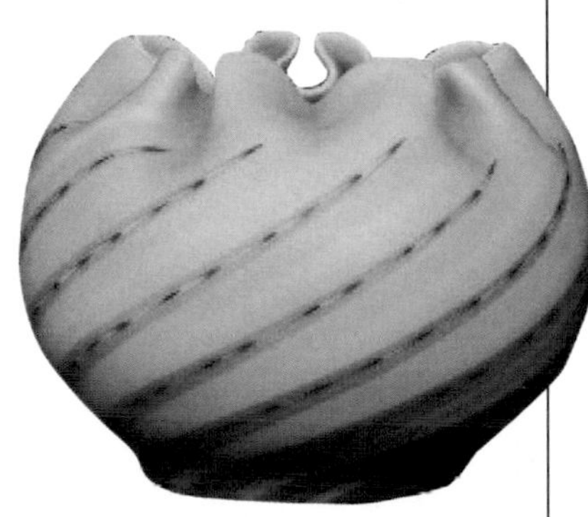

One of a pair of late 19thC Stevens & Williams glass 'Osiris' posy bowls, both marked 'PATENT'.

3.5in (9cm) high

$2,000-3,000 pair FLD

An early 20thC Stevens & Williams hock glass, the double-cased bowl engraved with three exotic birds.

8in (20.5cm) high

$3,000-4,000 FLD

An early 20thC Stevens & Williams glass posy vase, cased in ruby over citron and polished intaglio-cut.

4.25in (11cm) high

$1,000-1,500 FLD

An Edwardian Stevens & Williams clear crystal decanter, cut with a clematis over a trellis, possibly by Joshua Hodgetts.

15.75in (40cm) high

$2,000-3,000 FLD

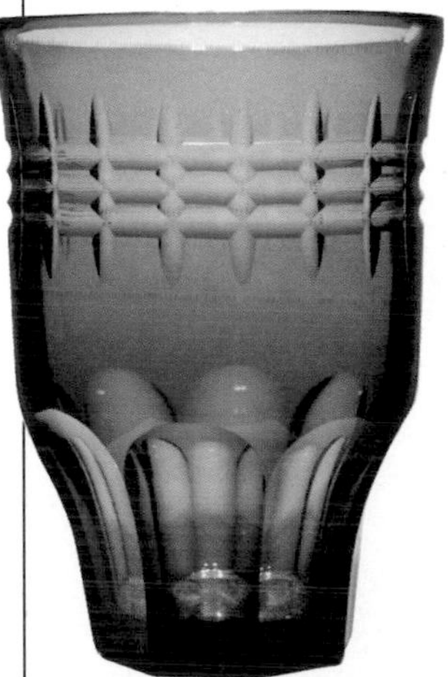

A large 1930s Stevens & Williams glass vase, designed by Keith Murray.

11.75in (30cm) high

$2,000-3,000 FLD

A Stourbridge citron-yellow and white cameo glass vase.

c1880 *6in (15cm) high*

$2,000-3,000 DN

A 19thC Edward Varnish & Co. glass goblet, flash-cut with Gothic-style arches, with inset tablet mark to base.

7in (18cm) high

$1,000-1,500 FLD

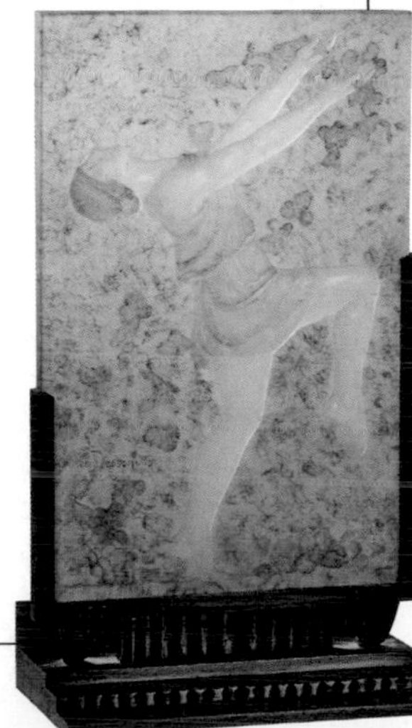

An Amalric Walter pâte-de-verre glass plaque, designed by Jean Descomps, signed 'Jean Descomps' and 'A Walter/Nancy', with a steel base and stepped plinth, wired for electricity.

c1925 *19.25in (49cm) high*

$10,000-15,000 L&T

A late 19thC Thomas Webb & Sons novelty glass spirit flask, attributed to Dr Christopher Dresser, in the form of a mythical beast, with restoration.

10in (26cm) long

$3,000-4,000 **FLD**

A late 19thC Thomas Webb & Sons cameo glass vase.

9.25in (23.5cm) high

$2,500-3,500 **FLD**

A 19thC Thomas Webb & Sons cameo glass 'Andromeda' plaque, designed by George Woodall, with engraved signature, with original leather presentation case.

One of only three cameos of 'Andromeda'. The other two remain within the Woodall family. The figure was modeled on George Woodall's daughter, Connie.

6.5in (16.5cm) high

$40,000-50,000 **FLD**

A James Powell & Sons, Whitefriars glass decanter, with silver mount and cover, stamped 'JATS London', with Japanese ivory netsuke finial.

1885 *8in (20cm) high*

$1,200-1,800 **WW**

A James Powell & Sons, Whitefriars flint-glass decanter, designed by Harry Powell, from the 'Minerbi' service, unmarked.

9in (23cm) high

$1,500-2,500 **WW**

A Whitefriars cinnamon glass 'Drunken Bricklayer' vase, designed by Geoffrey Baxter, pattern no.9673.

This shape was produced 1967-77.

Designed 1966 *8.25in (21cm) high*

$200-300 **DN**

ESSENTIAL REFERENCE - WHITEFRIARS

The glassworks that would become known as Whitefriars was founded in the 17thC in London. In 1834 it was acquired by James Powell (1774–1840) and became known as James Powell & Sons. The company was officially named Whitefriars from 1962, but collectors often refer to earlier pieces by this name.

- **19thC production included hand-blown glass in historical styles, as well as designs for William Morris.**
- **Pieces from the mid-20thC are most sought after today. Most were produced by Geoffrey Baxter (1922-95), who joined the company in 1954. Baxter's designs include Scandinavian-inspired pieces in the 1950s and strongly colored, textured ranges in the late 1960s and 1970s.**
- **Whitefriars closed in 1980.**

A James Powell & Sons, Whitefriars glass vase, probably designed by Harry Powell, unsigned.

10in (24cm) high

$2,500-3,500 **WW**

A James Powell & Sons, Whitefriars glass vase, designed by Edward Spencer, applied with prunts and a rigoree band, unsigned.

5in (12.5cm) high

$800-1,200 **WW**

A large Whitefriars 'Textured' range willow glass 'Banjo' vase, designed by Geoffrey Baxter.

Designed 1966 *12.25in (31cm) high*

$1,200-1,800 **FLD**

A pair of Bohemian electroplated and silver-mounted glass vases.

c1900–20 *14.5in (37cm) high*

$2,500-3,500 **DOR**

A Dubarry glass perfume bottle, designed by Julien Viard, made by Depinoix, the stopper modeled as an Egyptian Princess.

c1920 *4in (10cm) high*

$2,000-3,000 **SWO**

An early Émile Gallé enameled glass perfume bottle, signed 'Crystallerie d'Émile Gallé, Nancy'.

4.25in (11cm) high

$4,000-6,000 **DRA**

A René Lalique glass Le Lilas De Gabilla perfume bottle, inscribed 'Le Lilas De Gabilla', with original box.

3.5in (9cm) high

$2,000-3,000 **POOK**

A René Lalique glass 'Bouquet de Faunes' perfume bottle, for Guerlain, molded 'Guerlain Paris', with original black leather case.

c1925 *4in (10cm) high*

$1,000-1,500 **DRA**

A René Lalique metal-mounted perfume bottle, decorated with maidens, signed 'R. Lalique France', the atomizer stamped 'Made in France'.

3.5in (9cm) high

$400-600 **LHA**

A René Lalique glass 'Dans La Nuit' perfume display bottle, for Worth, signed 'Lalique France', missing stopper.

7.5in (19cm) high

$250-350 **DRA**

A René Lalique glass 'Pavots d'Argent' perfume bottle, for Roger et Gallet, with raised mark 'France'.

c1927 *3.25in (8.5cm) high*

$650-850 **DRA**

Thomas Webb

A Thomas Webb & Sons cameo glass scent bottle, carved with putto, butterflies, flowers and tassels, with a silver stopper, marks rubbed, maker 'HA'.

Thomas Webb (1802–69) established his glassworks in 1837 near Stourbridge, West Midlands. It produced a varied range of decorative glass, including cameo glass, 'Alexandrite', iridescent glass and 'Queen's Burmese'. In 1920 the company joined with the Edinburgh & Leith Flint Glass Co. to become Webb's Crystal Glass Co. Cut-glass pieces were produced during the Art Deco and post-war period. The company closed in 1990.

c1885 *5.5in (14cm) high*

$15,000-20,000 **M&K**

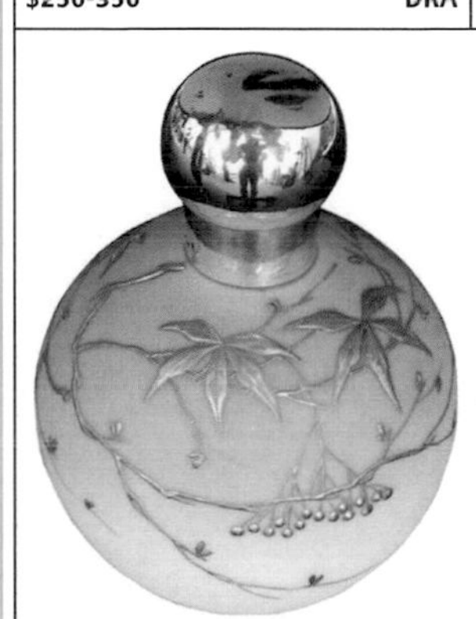

A late 19thC Thomas Webb & Sons 'Queen's Burmese' glass scent bottle, gilded by Jules Barbe, with a silver hallmarked stopper.

5in (13cm) high

$1,500-2,500 **FLD**

A Liberty & Co. 'Tudric' pewter mantel clock, designed by Archibald Knox, with copper dial above blue enamel panel, the single barrel movement stamped 'Lenzkirch' and 'No.493737', with later platform escapement, stamped 'Tudric 0367'.

6.5in (17cm) high

$5,000-6,000 **AH**

A Liberty & Co. pewter carriage clock, with a blue and green enameled dial, copper chapter ring and French movement.

4.75in (12cm) high

$4,000-6,000 **GORL**

A Liberty & Co. 'Tudric' pewter mantel clock, designed by Archibald Knox, the dial with blue and green mottled enamel, with a Lenzkirch movement, stamped '0370'.

c1900 *8in (20.5cm) high*

$10,000-15,000 **L&T**

A Liberty & Co. 'Tudric' pewter mantel clock, designed by Archibald Knox, serial no. '0367', with copper dial above blue and green enameled plaque, stamped 'TUDRIC'.

c1900 *6.25in (16cm) high*

$2,500-3,500 **L&T**

A Tiffany Studios 'Turtle Back' tile clock, with iridescent blue, green and purple tiles set in bronze, the dial signed 'Tiffany & Co.'.

13in (33cm) high

$80,000-100,000 **MIC**

An Arts & Crafts silver mantel clock, attributed to Edith Dawson, decorated in the Moorish style, with ivory columns and feet, the dome enameled with peacocks, unmarked.

c1900 *8in (20cm) high*

$5,500-6,500 **L&T**

Davidson

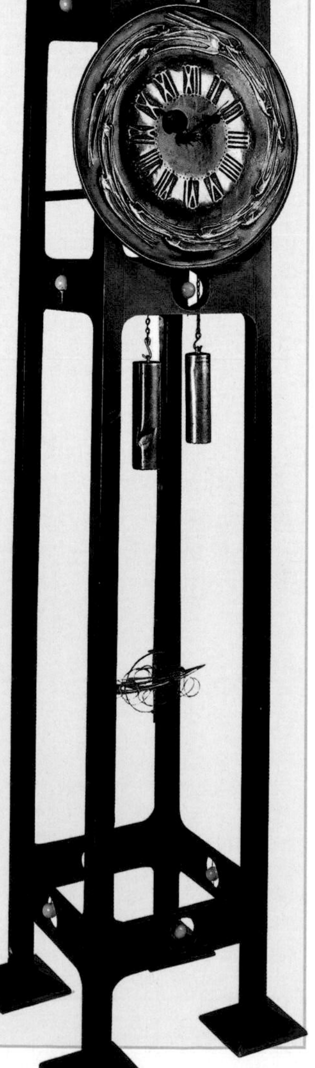
A 'Swallows' longcase clock, designed by Peter Wylie Davidson, the repoussé decoration enclosed by a frieze of stylized swallows.

Davidson was a significant figure at the Glasgow School of Art, where he was the Technical Instructor for metalwork for 38 years, from the late 1890s until his retirement in 1935.
His creative and technical virtuosity, drive and clarity of instruction led the GSA s metalwork department to become internationally venerated by 1900.
This clock is possibly a collaboration with Charles Rennie Mackintosh. The swallows' flight motif around the clock face is a distinctive Davidson element, which can be seen on his best pieces. It is also a classic 'Glasgow School' motif.

c1902 *47in (119.5cm) high*

$30,000-40,000 **L&T**

A Douglas Clock Company silver mantle clock, stamped 'DCC Birmingham'.

1901 *7.5in (18cm) high*

$5,500-6,500 **WW**

A Scottish School copper mantel clock, with embossed silvered dial, with inscription 'Tempus Fugit'.

c1910 *9.5in (24cm) high*

$700-1,000 **L&T**

A William Moorcroft 'Big Poppy' mantel clock, the white-metal base stamped 'SILVER'.

5in (14.5cm)

$12,000-18,000 **TEN**

A Richard Ginori majolica clock, the two-train movement striking on a bell, with underglaze blue factory mark and '186-279', the movement with impressed 'Japy Frères Medaille d'Honneur' medallion, with loss to one shell.

1842-60

$2,500-3,500 **WES**

A Jules Vieillard, Bordeaux faience clock, for Maple & Co., Paris, with impressed factory marks.

c1880 10.5in (27cm) high

$1,000-1,500 **L&T**

An Elkington & Co. ebonized mantle clock, designed by Lewis F Day, for Howell & James, with French twin-train movement.

c1880 15.5in (39cm) high

$550-750 **L&T**

An Amalric Walter pâte-de-verre clock, designed by Henri Bergé, decorated with bees and orchid, signed 'Bergé SC AWALTER NANCY'.

4.5in (11.5cm) high

$3,000-4,000 **DRA**

A 1920s Cartier onyx-cased 'Milestone' desk clock, set with rose diamonds and coral panels, with eight-day movement, engraved 'Cartier, Paris' and 'No.1627', with some damage.

4in (10cm) high

$80,000-120,000 **CAN**

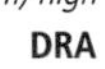

A rare Cartier Art Deco rock crystal, enamel and diamond-set strut desk timepiece, with lever movement, signed 'Cartier 119', numbered '6981', with original pink leather fitted case.

c1925 5in (12.5cm) high

$100,000-150,000 **TEN**

A Cartier lacquer and gilt-metal alarm clock, no.15958, ref. 7509, in box.

3.5in (9cm) high

$500-700 **DN**

An Elizabeth Burton copper and abalone-shell lamp shade, unmarked.

15in (38cm) wide

$3,000-4,000 **DRA**

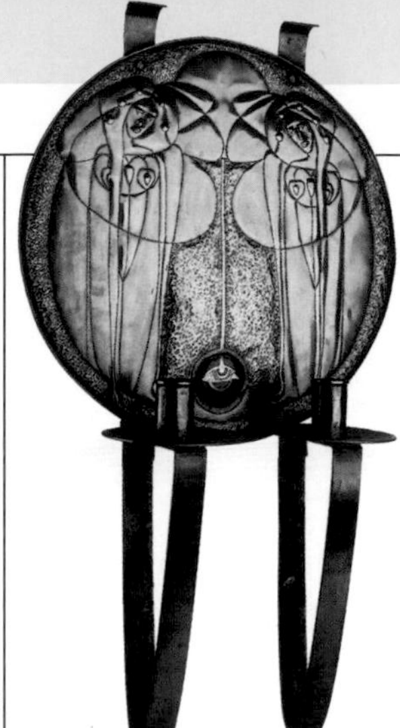

A copper and enamel wall sconce, in the manner of Margaret and Frances MacDonald.

27.75in (70.5cm) high

$7,000-10,000 **L&T**

A Roycroft hammered-copper three-socket table lamp, with Steuben glass shade, with orb and cross mark.

16.5in (42cm) high

$8,000-12,000 **DRA**

A Gustav Stickley copper, iron and vaseline-glass lantern, designed by Harvey Ellis, model no.204, unmarked.

13.5in (34.5cm) high

$15,000-20,000 **DRA**

A Gustav Stickley hammered copper wall sconce, with Quezal gold 'hammered' glass shade, etched 'Quezal', with original faceted screws.

19.5in (50cm) high

$3,500-4,500 **DRA**

A Samuel Yellin wrought-iron floor lamp, stamped 'Samuel Yellin'.

67in (170cm) high

$8,000-12,000 **FRE**

A Samuel Yellin wrought-iron and brass adjustable floor lamp, marked 'Samuel Yellin'.

55in (139.5cm) high

$10,000-15,000 **DRA**

One of three Arts & Crafts wrought-iron and copper ceiling lamps.

c1900 *58.75in (149cm) high*

$1,200-1,800 set **L&T**

An Arts & Crafts hammered-copper three-light lamp, in need of rewiring.

12.5in (31.5cm) high

$2,500-3,500 **DN**

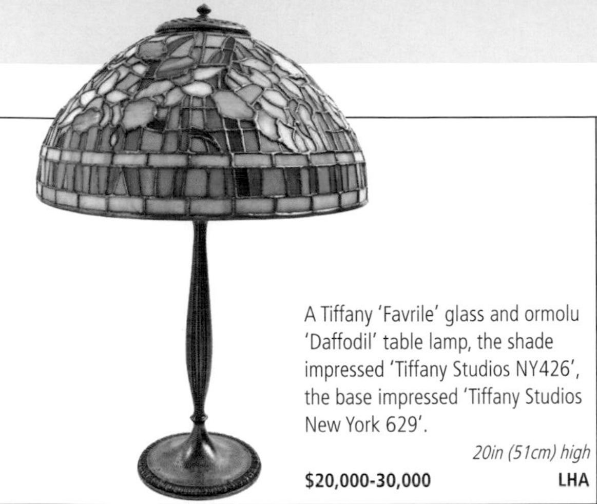

A Tiffany 'Favrile' glass and ormolu 'Daffodil' table lamp, the shade impressed 'Tiffany Studios NY426', the base impressed 'Tiffany Studios New York 629'.

20in (51cm) high

$20,000-30,000 **LHA**

A Tiffany 'Daffodil' table lamp, the shade impressed 'TIFFANY STUDIOS NEW YORK 1449', the base impressed 'TIFFANY STUDIOS NEW YORK and 28621', with Tiffany Glass & Decorating Co. logo.

This base is a wonderful example of 'Favrile' glass blown through bronze.

21in (53.5cm) high

$130,000-180,000 **MIC**

Miller's Compares: 'Dragonfly' Lamps

The first 'Dragonfly' lamp is a reasonably simple example in a less pleasing colorway. The second lamp is more complex. It has seven dragonflies with olive green bodies and beautiful multi-colored wings with yellow, pink and amber all set against a green background of heavily mottled glass. The third 'Dragonfly' shade is mounted on one of the most sought after and rare bases. The base is decorated with three dragonflies in heavy relief bronze and an inlay of iridescent mosaic 'Favrile' glass tiles, which continue up the shaft of the base.

A Tiffany 'Dragonfly' table lamp, impressed 'Tiffany Studios New York', one light fitting needs professional restoration.

c1900-20 *17.5in (46.5cm) high*

$35,000-50,000 **DOR**

A Tiffany 'Dragonfly' table lamp, signed 'Tiffany Studios New York 1495', on bronze mock-'Turtle Back' base, signed 'Tiffany Studios New York 587'.

26in (66cm) high

$70,000-120,000 **JDJ**

This lamp features confetti 'Favrile' glass forming the wings of the blue-bodied dragonflies.

A Tiffany 'Dragonfly' table lamp, the shade impressed 'TIFFANY STUDIOS NEW YORK NY 1585', the base impressed 'TIFFANY STUDIOS NEW YORK 356'.

Shade 1913, Base 1906 *20in (51cm) high*

$150,000-200,000 **MIC**

A Tiffany 'Nasturtium' table lamp, the shade signed 'Tiffany Studios New York', the bronze trumpet base signed 'Tiffany Studios New York 573'.

26in (66cm) high

$60,000-75,000 **JDJ**

A Tiffany 'Venetian/Ninth Century' table lamp, the shade impressed 'TIFFANY STUDIOS NEW YORK 515-6', the base impressed 'TIFFANY STUDIOS NEW YORK 515'.

This lamp is part of both the 'Venetian' and 'Ninth Century' desk set patterns. The base has glass cabochons that simulate rubies and garnets, which were worn as personal adornment by 9thC nobility and wealthy merchant class.

20in (51cm) high

$115,000-140,000 **MIC**

A miniature or 'pony' Tiffany 'Wisteria' table lamp, model no.3349, the shade impressed 'TIFFANY STUDIOS NEW YORK', the base impressed 'TIFFANY STUDIOS NEW YORK 249'.

In the firm's literature 'pony' refers to certain miniature models. Today's collectors refer to such models as miniatures.

1906 *15.5in (39.5cm) high*

$100,000-140,000 **MIC**

A Tiffany table lamp, with 'Lemon Leaf' shade and 'Papyrus' base, the base stamped 'TIFFANY STUDIOS NEW YORK 627', the shade numbered '1470'.

24in (61cm) high

$20,000-30,000 DRA

An early 20thC Tiffany 'Brickwork' shade on an bronze oil font base, the shade signed 'Tiffany Studios New York 142', later electrified.

18.5in (47cm) high

$6,500-7,500 SK

An early 20thC Tiffany patinated-bronze desk lamp, model no.320, with drop blossom shades, base marked 'Tiffany Studios New York'.

8in (20cm) high

$2,500-3,500 FRE

A Tiffany 'Favrile' glass and ormolu ten-light 'Lily' table lamp, the base stamped 'Tiffany Studios New York, 381', the shades inscribed 'L.C.T'.

22in (56cm) high

$30,000-40,000 LHA

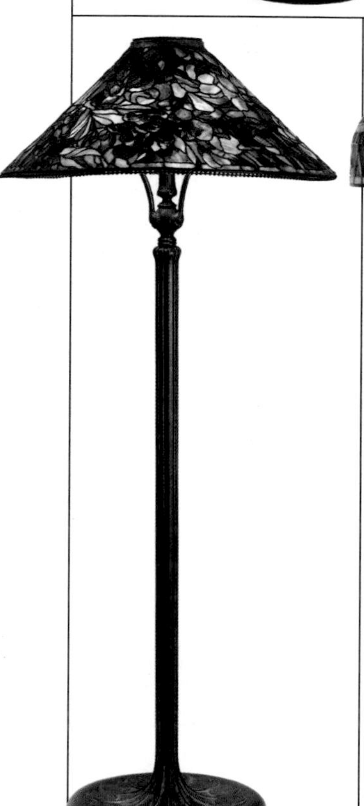

A Tiffany 'Favrile' glass and patinated-bronze floor lamp, the shade stamped, the base marked 'Tiffany Studios, New York' and stamped '28623' and '10/10'.

c1900-10 *70in (177.5cm) high*

$200,000-250,000 KAU

A Tiffany 'Favrile' glass and patinated bronze 'Tulip' floor lamp, stamped 'Tiffany Studios', on a bronze 'Junior' base, stamped 'Tiffany Studios, New York, 387'.

60.75in (154.5cm) high

$80,000-120,000 LHA

A Tiffany bronze 'Moorish' chandelier, with seven 'Favrile' glass shades, the shades etched 'LCT Favrile', the frame unmarked.

36.5in (92.5cm) high

$50,000-70,000 DRA

A Tiffany 'Alamander' chandelier, decorated with blossoms against a background of mottled confetti glass, impressed 'Tiffany Studios, New York'.

28.25in (72cm) diam

$220,000-280,000 MIC

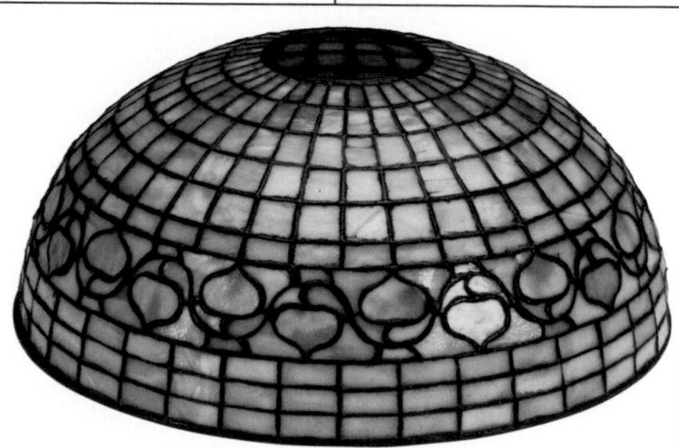

A Tiffany 'Acorn' lamp shade, stamped 'TIFFANY STUDIOS NEW YORK 1435-143'.

15.5in (39.5cm) diam

$8,000-12,000 DRA

A Duffner & Kimberly 'Oak Leaf' table lamp, the three-socket base decorated with an Art Nouveau leaf pattern.

24in (61cm) high

$10,000-15,000 **JDJ**

ESSENTIAL REFERENCE - DUFFNER & KIMBERLY

The Duffner & Kimberly Co. was established in New York City, NY, in 1905 by stained-glass designer Oliver Speers Kimberly (1871–1956) and Francis Joseph Duffner (1860–1929), who had extensive experience of the lighting industry. The company introduced its first lamps in 1906.

- **Notable designers included chief designer Gazo Foudji (1853–1916) and John Gordon Guthrie (1874–1961), both of whom had previously worked for Tiffany. Hamilton Tappan Howell (1872–1952) was responsible for many of the striking early lamp designs.**
- **Duffner & Kimberly filed for bankruptcy in 1911. Duffner dissolved the partnership and left the firm, which was reorganized in 1911 into the Kimberly Company, which closed in 1913.**

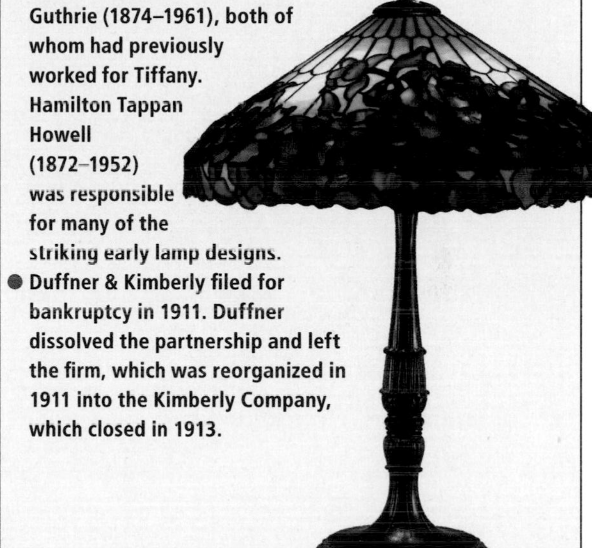

A Duffner & Kimberly 'Peony' table lamp, the bronze base decorated with stylized acanthus leaves, with 'Duffner & Kimberly Co. New York' tag.

32in (81.5cm) high

$50,000-70,000 **JDJ**

A Handel slag-glass boudoir lamp, the shade pierced with a tropical scene, the base decorated with a woodland scene and stamped 'Handel'.

14in (36cm) high

$1,200-1,800 **DRA**

An early 20thC Handel slag-glass lamp shade, decorated with a landscape scene of trees and a river.

22.25in (57cm) diam

$6,500-7,500 **SK**

A Pairpoint puffy 'Azalea 'lamp, the shade decorated with pink, red and white azaleas against a green leafy background, the base signed 'Pairpoint Mfg. Co. 3095' and Pairpoint logo, the shade signed 'Patent Appl'd For'.

19in (48.5cm) high

$20,000-30,000 **JDJ**

A Handel slag-glass and patinated-bronze floor lamp, the shade and base stamped 'Handel'.

65in (165cm) high

$7,000-10,000 **DRA**

A Riviere table lamp, unmarked.

24in (61cm) high

$7,000-10,000 **DRA**

A Wilkinson table lamp, the shade with a tuck-under design, accentuated by Oriental poppies, the base with stylized Art Nouveau decoration, with minor restoration to leadwork on shade.

The shade and base have the locking pins, which are the trademark of Wilkinson Co., Brooklyn, NY, USA.

30in (76cm) high

$8,000-12,000 **JDJ**

ESSENTIAL REFERENCE - MAURICE BOUVAL

Maurice Bouval (1863–1916) was a French sculptor, who worked in the Art Nouveau style from c1880.

- **He was a pupil of Alexandre Falguière.**
- **Bouval's work usually incorporated the female form combined with floral imagery, such as water lilies, lotuses and poppies. Smaller pieces were often gilded.**
- **His most famous works are 'Ophelia', 'Femme assise', 'Jeune femme', 'Le Sommeil', 'Femme aux pavots' and 'Le Secret et la Pensive'.**
- **His bronzes were cast by at least three different foundries: Colin, Jollet and Thiebaut Frères.**
- **He participated in the 1890 Exposition Universelle in Paris and was a member of the Société des Artistes Français.**
- **As well as sculptures, Bouval also designed a wide range of light fixtures, including wall brackets, candelabra, candlesticks and table lamps.**
- **His works are usually signed 'M. Bouval'.**

One of a pair of Art Nouveau ormolu figural wall sconces, by Maurice Bouval, with Schneider glass shades, the bronze signed 'M. Bouval', the glass signed 'Schneider'.

13in (33cm) high

$12,000-18,000 pair **SK**

A W A S Benson copper and brass electrolier, the 'lotiform' ceiling rose stamped 'Benson' and with registration mark '386811', the Whitefriars vaseline glass shades with registration number '290976', with slight chip to one shade.

Both registration numbers correspond to ones registered to W A S Benson.

30in (76cm) high

$8,000-12,000 **A&G**

A Daum cameo glass table lamp, decorated with landscape, trees and river, marked 'DAUM NANCY'.

1910-15 *20.5in (52cm) high*

$12,000-18,000 **FIS**

A Doulton 'Silicon Ware' oil lamp, in the form of an owl, with brass mounts and foot, with Hinks's duplex burner, with impressed mark.

1883 *17.25in (44cm) high*

$6,500-7,500 **M&K**

A Fulham Pottery table lamp, by Quentin Bell, with incised signature, the hand-painted lampshade initialed 'QB' and 'CM'.

10in (25.5cm) high

$1,200-1,800 **DN**

An early 20thC Émile Gallé acid-etched cameo glass ceiling lamp.

15.75in (40cm) diam

$8,000-12,000 **DOY**

An early 20thC Émile Gallé cameo glass lamp, acid-etched with clematis and leaves, the illuminated base with conforming decoration.

15.5in (39.5cm) high

$40,000-50,000 **DOY**

A Goldscheider patinated-terracotta floor lamp in the form of a maiden, by Stanislaus Capèque, signed and with factory mark, impressed 'Production Réservée' and '3139/39/3'.

c1900 *46in (116.5cm) high*

$5,000-7,000 **L&T**

An Art Nouveau pewter and nautilus-shell table lamp, by Gustav Gurschner, with mark to base.

14in (36cm) high

$3,500-4,500 GORL

An Art Nouveau bronze table lamp, by Charles-Émile Jonchery, marked 'C E Jonchery'.

Charles-Émile Jonchery (1873-1937) was the son of the sculptor Émile Jonchery. He worked in Auguste Rodin's workshop and participated in the Paris Salons during the early 20thC.

c1900 *14.4in (36.5cm)*

$6,500-7,500 QU

A Loetz table lamp, the brass foot by Argentor, Vienna, marked.

1899 *17.5in (43.5cm) high*

$6,500-7,500 QU

ESSENTIAL REFERENCE - MONART

Monart glass was made at the Moncrieff Glassworks (est.1865) in Scotland from 1924. The range was designed by glassblower Salvador Ysart (1878-1955) and his sons.

- **The mottled effect was achieved by rolling glass gathers in enamel and then coating in a layer of clear glass before blowing in shape.**
- **Production of Monart ceased in 1939. It resumed on a smaller scale after World War II under Paul Ysart, Salvador's eldest son.**

A Monart glass table lamp, the mushroom shade with adjustable brass support, the clear glass with swirling lemon and white inclusions and with further green and pink inclusions, with original paper label 'VII.P/23.390'.

c1930 *14.5in (37cm) high*

$3,000-4,000 L&T

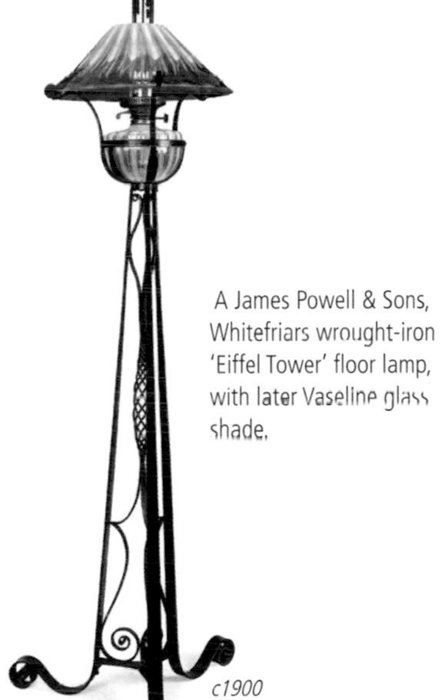

A James Powell & Sons, Whitefriars wrought-iron 'Eiffel Tower' floor lamp, with later Vaseline glass shade.

c1900

66.5in (169cm) high

$2,000-3,000 L&T

One of a pair of Austrian cold-painted bronze and brass candelabra, one with foxes and mallard ducks, the other with foxes and cats.

c1920 *12.5in (32cm) high*

$3,000-4,000 pair SK

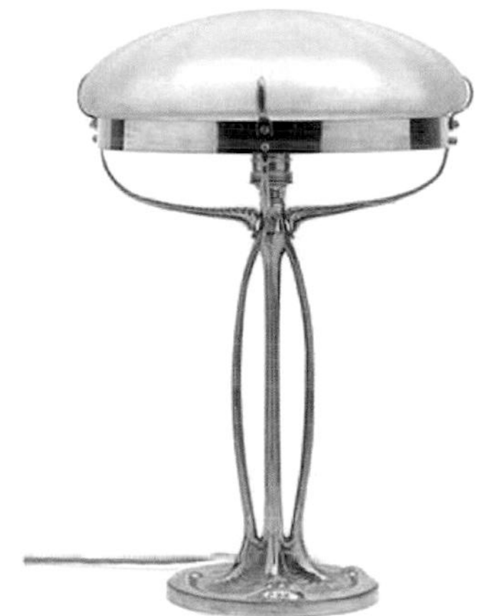

A Bohemian one-light brass table lamp, with matted and acid-textured glass shade.

c1900 *20in (51cm) high*

$5,000-7,000 DOR

A pair of Art Deco gilt-metal table lamps, with globular glass shades.

These lamps are copies of the ground lighting from the 1924 British Empire Exhibition, Wembley, UK.

1924 *24in (60cm) high*

$5,000-7,000 L&T

Judith Picks

The items on this page belonged to Augustus Welby Northmore Pugin (1812-52). When Pugin's former home, The Grange in Ramsgate, passed to Benedictine monks in 1928, Charles Pugin Purcell inherited the contents. These items were exhibited in 1994 at the Victoria & Albert Museum's exhibition 'Pugin: A Gothic Passion'. These metalwares were all designed by Pugin for his own use at the Grange and accordingly most pieces bear his coat-of-arms and all were in his possession and handled by him.

A pair of John Hardman & Co. silver salts, designed by A W N Pugin, Birmingham, the borders engraved 'without me is no savour'.
1838 *4in (10.5cm) diam*
$25,000-30,000 **SWO**

A pair of John Hardman & Co. gilt-brass candlesticks, designed by A W N Pugin, Birmingham, engraved with Pugin's coat-of-arms.
c1844 *13.75in (35cm) high*
$120,000-180,000 **SWO**

A silver-plated bowl, designed by A W N Pugin engraved with Pugin's coat-of-arms.
c1845 *6.5in (16.5cm) diam*
$2,000-3,000 **SWO**

A pair of silver-plated storage canisters, designed by A W N Pugin, the covers engraved 'B' and 'C', the bases with the Pugin crest.
c1845 *4.75in (12cm) high*
$5,500-6,500 **SWO**

A pair of John Hardman & Co. silver-plated tazzas, designed by A W N Pugin, Birmingham, the bowls with central roundels engraved with a knight's helmet and foliage.

This pair of tazzas (a rare example of Pugin's domestic metalwork) are two of only four known to survive today.
c1846 *6.75in (17.5cm) high*
$35,000-45,000 **SWO**

A pair of John Hardman & Co. gilt-brass candlesticks, designed by A W N Pugin, Birmingham, each with a knop set with four moonstones, missing one sconce.
c1846 *12.5in (32cm) high*
$6,500-7,500 **SWO**

A John Hardman & Co. gilt-brass altar vase, designed by A W N Pugin, Birmingham, with an enameled plaque to both sides.

This was probably used by Pugin in his private chapel at 'The Grange', Ramsgate.
c1850 *10.5in (26.5cm) high*
$2,500-3,500 **SWO**

E W Pugin

A Gothic Revival enameled brass candlestick, the design attributed to Edward Welby Pugin, inscribed 'ALLELUIA', unsigned.

Edward Welby Pugin was the eldest son of Augustus Welby Northmore Pugin.
7.5in (17.5cm) high
$1,200-1,800 **WW**

A Liberty & Co. silver and enamel 'Cymric' spoon, designed by Archibald Knox, stamped 'L & CO CYMRIC'.

7.75in (19cm) long

$4,000-6,000 **DRA**

A Liberty & Co. silver and enamel biscuit box, designed by Archibald Knox, Birmingham, with embossed tendril and knot decoration, the base engraved '1903'.

1900 *7.75in (19.5cm) high 28oz*

$50,000-70,000 **REEM**

A Liberty & Co. silver 'Cymric' tea canister and cover, designed by Archibald Knox, Birmingham, enameled with bands of Celtic knotwork, marked 'L&CO/ CYMRIC/691'.

1905 *4in (10cm) high*

$5,500-6,500 **L&T**

A Liberty & Co. silver and enamel 'Cymric' photo frame, designed by Archibald Knox, Birmingham, marked 'L&C/ CYMRIC'.

1904 *8in (20.5cm) high*

$4,500-5,500 **L&T**

A Liberty & Co. Aesthetic Movement silver bowl, London, with stamped marks and simulated Japanese mark.

1895 *4in (10cm) diam*

$550-750 **WW**

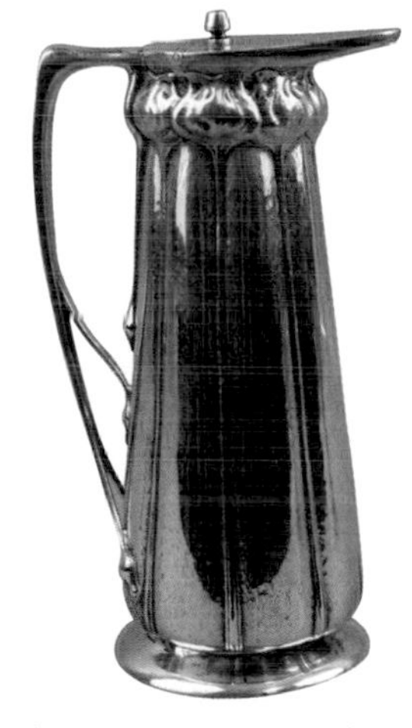

A Liberty & Co. Art Nouveau silver claret jug, Birmingham.

1901 *24.5oz*

$5,000-7,000 **DA&H**

A Liberty & Co. 'English Pewter' vase, designed by Archibald Knox, model no.0927, cast with a band of stylized honesty, with stamped marks.

11in (29cm) high

$800-1,200 **WW**

A pair of Liberty & Co. pewter 'Tudric' candlesticks, designed by Archibald Knox, model no.0219, cast with stylized ivy leaf friezes, with stamped marks.

5in (10cm) high

$1,500-2,000 **WW**

A Liberty & Co. pewter and enamel 'Tudric' tea service and tray, designed by Archibald Knox, serial nos.0231, cast with foliage and set with enamel roundels, with stamped marks.

c1910 *Tray 19.5in (49cm) wide*

$4,000-6,000 **L&T**

A Liberty & Co. pewter 'Tudric' wall mirror, designed by Archibald Knox, cast with Celtic knots, with applied ivorine label.

35in (90cm) wide

$4,000-6,000 **WW**

A Liberty & Co. pewter and Moorcroft-pottery 'Tudric' tray, designed by Archibald Knox, model no.044, cast with whiplash foliage, with a Moorcroft 'Pomegranate' shield, with stamped marks.

10in (25.5cm) diam

$1,500-2,500 **TEN**

A Liberty & Co. pewter 'Tudric' tobacco jar and cover, designed by Archibald Knox, model no.0193, with stamped marks.

5in (13cm) high

$2,500-3,500 **WW**

A Liberty & Co. 'English Pewter' biscuit box, stamped 'English Pewter 0237 Made in England'.

5in (12.5cm) high

$2,500-3,500 **DN**

A Ramsden & Carr silver christening bowl and spoon, inscribed 'Omar Ramsden et Alwyn Carr Me Fecerunt MCMX'.

1908/09 *Bowl 6.25in (15.5cm) diam 10.2oz*

$1,500-2,500 **DN**

A Ramsden & Carr silver chalice, London, set with eight garnet cabochons.

1909 *5.5in (14cm) high 9oz*

$12,000-18,000 **WW**

A Ramsden & Carr silver tea caddy, London, chased with a stylized octopus, incised 'OMAR RAMSDEN ET ALWYN CARR ME FECERUNT MCMXIII'.

1913 *4.5in (11cm) high 11.25oz*

$10,000-15,000 **LC**

An Omar Ramsden silver and Limoges-enamel salver, London, signed 'LC', stamped 'OR'.

1918 *5in (13cm) diam*

$2,000-3,000 **WW**

An Omar Ramsden silver hot water jug, London, the base incised 'OMAR RAMSDEN ME FECIT'.

1921 *7.75in (19.5cm) high 17.3oz*

$6,500-7,500 **LC**

An Omar Ramsden silver and 9ct gold cigarette case, London, the cover applied with a silver plaque depicting Crispin and Crispinian, the patron saints of cordwainers, cutting leather and making a shoe, engraved 'OMAR RAMSDEN ME FECIT MCMXXII', with stamped marks.

Provenance: This cigarette case, recorded as number 888 in Ramsden's workbooks, was commissioned by George William Poulton, a Kettering shoe manufacturer.

1922 *4.5in (11.5cm) long 7oz*

$8,000-12,000 **DN**

A pair of Arts & Crafts electroplated candlesticks, in the manner of Omar Ramsden, the knopped stems set with four garnet cabouchons, unmarked.

7.5in (20cm) high

$4,000-6,000 **WW**

A pair of Omar Ramsden silver grape scissors, London, with a Tudor rose boss.

1924 *5in (15.5cm) long 4oz*

$2,000-3,000 **WW**

An Omar Ramsden silver and enamel matchbox cover, London, stamped 'OR' and 'Omar Ramsden Me Fecit'.

1936 *2.5in (6cm) wide*

$2,000-3,000 **WW**

An Omar Ramsden silver and walnut mazer bowl, London, stamped OR' and 'Omar Ramsden Me Fecit'.

A mazer is a type of Germanic drinking vessel, traditionally made of maple wood.

1925 *8in (21.5cm) diam*

$4,000-6,000 **WW**

An Omar Ramsden silver-mounted shagreen casket, London, with walnut interior, the silver base with inscription.

The inscription reads, 'This casket of hand wrought silver mounted shagreen i.e. English walnut covered with the abraded skin of the China ray-fish, was made by Omar Ramsden'.

1927 *6.5in (16.5cm) wide*

$5,500-6,500 **MAB**

A Ramsden & Carr pepperette, inscribed 'YOUNG LAUGHTER MAKES THE OLD WORLD GAY', stamped 'Ramsden & Carr'.

3.75in (9.5cm) high

$1,500-2,500 **WW**

An Omar Ramsden silver cup and cover, London, stamped 'OR' and 'Omar Ramsden Me Fecit'.

1931 *10in (26cm) high*

$7,000-10,000 **WW**

An Omar Ramsden silver desk inkwell, London, made for the Queen's 22nd London Regiment, stamped 'OR' and 'Omar Ramsden Me Fecit', with glass liner.

1926 *6in (16cm) diam*

$3,000-4,000 **WW**

Leslie Durbin

A silver hot water/chocolate pot, Leslie Durbin, London, on three cast scroll cherub feet

Leslie Durbin was a pupil of Omar Ramsden and he purchased Ramsden's pattern books and stock. The design for the feet on this pot is from a Ramsden design.

1954 *12in (31cm) high 36oz*

$1,800-2,200 **WW**

Judith Picks

Johan Rohde (1856-1935) began designing products for Jensen in 1906. Rohde's designs are highly stylized in comparison to Jensen's more natural Art Nouveau style. In 1913 Rohde committed to designing solely for Jensen. Many of his pieces were quintessentially modern and well ahead of their time: pitcher 432 was one such piece. Designed in 1920, Jensen believed the 432's design so advanced that it was held back from production until 1925. Since then, this jug has been admired for over 90 years, demonstrating the enduring appeal of its design and its ability to transcend a century's worth of design.

A George Jensen silver jug, designed by Johan Rohde, model no.432A, with artist's monogram and maker's mark.
1945-77 *10in (23cm) high 19oz*
$4,000-6,000 **DOR**

A Georg Jensen silver butter dish and cover, with import marks for George Stockwell, London, with clear glass liner.
c1924 *5in (15.5cm) diam 6oz*
$1,500-2,000 **WW**

A Georg Jensen silver bowl.
1933-44 *7.75in (19.5cm) diam 22.16oz*
$3,000-4,000 **LHA**

A Georg Jensen silver footed-bowl, probably designed by Ove Brobeck, marked 'DESSIN OB, DENMARK GEORG JENSEN', 'STERLING, 641, B.', designed c1920.
Post 1945 *7in (17.5cm) diam*
$4,000-6,000 **QU**

A Georg Jensen silver 'Continental' 125-piece cutlery set, all pieces hallmarked.

This set was designed in 1906. The example shown has never been used.
Post 1945 *153.6oz*
$6,500-7,500 **DOR**

A Georg Jensen silver 'Blossom' tray, model no.2H.
c1945-51 *14.25in (36cm) wide 20oz*
$4,000-6,000 **DOY**

A pair of Georg Jensen silver 'Grape' candlesticks.
Post 1945 *6in (15cm) high 22oz*
$5,000-7,000 **DOY**

A Georg Jensen silver sauceboat, model no.296, with a scrolling handle ending in a grape cluster.
Post 1945 *9in (23cm) wide 19oz*
$3,000-4,000 **DOY**

A Georg Jensen silver cocktail shaker, designed by Harald Nielson, model no.462C, stamped 'Georg Jensen & Wendel'.
1945-51 *12in (30.5cm) high 28oz*
$5,000-7,000 **GORL**

A Georg Jensen silver 'Cosmos' tea service, designed by Johan Rohde, model nos.'45A' and '45C', the tray model no.241C, with Jensen hallmarks.
Post 1945 *Coffee pot 9.5in (24cm) high 155oz*
$15,000-20,000 **DOY**

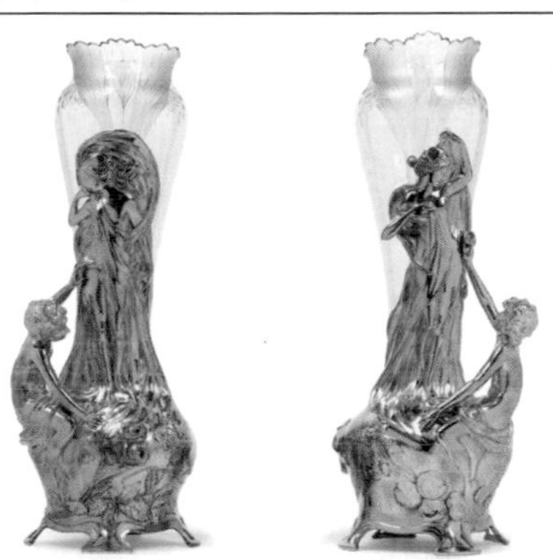

A pair of WMF silver-plated vases, model no.185, the bodies decorated with figures and floral tendrils, with impressed factory marks, with glass liners.
c1900 *20in (50cm) high*
$8,000-12,000 **DOR**

A WMF electroplated comport, in the form of a lily pad with maiden, marked '246'.
c1900 *11.5in (29cm) wide*
$2,000-3,000 **L&T**

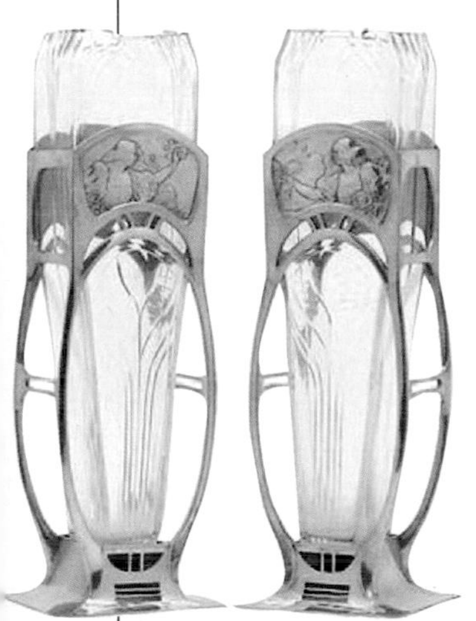

A pair of WMF silver-plated vases, model no.241, decorated with girls picking flowers, with impressed factory marks, with glass liners.
c1900-05
$4,000-6,000 **DOR**

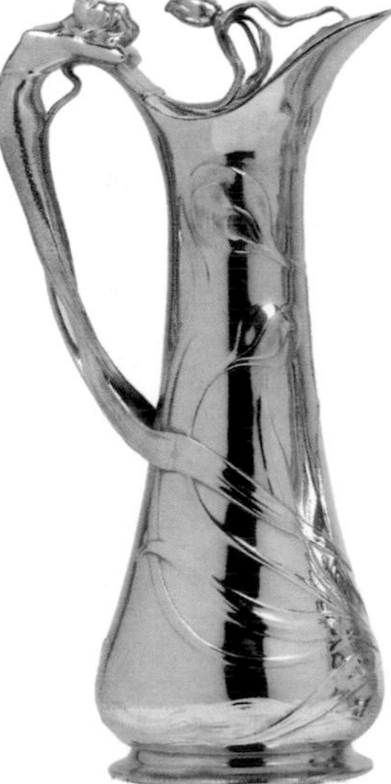

A WMF polished metal wine jug, model no.138D, with mermaid handle and floral finial, marked.
c1905 *14.75in (37.5cm) high*
$2,500-3,500 **DOR**

A WMF polished metal service dish, model no.169, manufactured by A Köhler & Cie, Vienna, with impressed factory mark.

c1905 *9.5in (24cm) high*
$2,000-3,000 **DOR**

A WMF copper and enamel vase, with a cloisonné enamel frieze of stylized birds and chequer banding, with stamped factory marks.
c1930 *12.5in (32cm) high*
$1,000-1,500 **L&T**

Judith Picks

Both of these vases were signed Elkington & Co in 'wires' within the design and were shown at the Philadelphia Centenary Exhibition of 1876. Elkington's was the only leading British silversmiths to show at Philadelphia, and a lithograph for 'The Art Journal' showing their display includes a very similar vase. While their manufacture appears to copy Japanese cloisonné wire techniques, the Birmingham firm made their interpretations using electro-deposition (rather than wires) to create cavities for the enamels. They produced the line for only a few years. These are extremely rare and in superb condition.

A pair of Elkington & Co. cloisonné and ormolu vases, one decorated with flamingos, dragonflies and an exotic bird among irises and water lilies, the other with a hawk and garden birds in a lakeland landscape beyond.

1876 *27in (71cm) high*

$150,000-200,000 **APAR**

A Gorham & Co. Aesthetic Movement mixed-metal vase, decorated in the Japanesque style with a beetle, cranes, swallows and butterflies.

c1881 *7.75in (19.5cm) high*

$6,500-7,500 **DOY**

A pair of Art Nouveau silver and enamel vases, by the Goldsmiths & Silversmiths Company, London.

1902 *7.75in (19.5cm) high*

$2,000-3,000 **WW**

A rare Victorian jewel-decorated flask, designed by William Burges, decorated with wire work, the detachable cloisonné top with cut and cabochon semi-precious stones, the flask engraved 'W Burges in remembrance of Tommy Deane his pupil MDCCCLXXIV'.

Tommy Deane, who went on to become architect Sir Thomas Manly Deane, was making a name for himself internationally when Burges designed this flask. The original design is in the Victoria & Albert Museum, London. Interest in Burges' designs was revived in 2011 when Geoffrey Munn, an expert on the BBC's Antiques Roadshow, said he would be delighted to see a piece of jewelry designed by the 19thC architect. In response, a woman took a piece along to a subsequent show that was valued at $58,000.

7.5in (19cm) high

$80,000-120,000 **HARR**

A silver and enamel dressing table mirror, by the Adie Brothers, Birmingham.

1928 *12.25in (31.5cm) high*

$2,500-3,500 **WW**

A mid 20thC Limoges enameled copper vase, designed by Camille Fauré, 'impasto'-enameled with flowering branches, signed in gilt 'FAURÉ, LIMOGES, FRANCE', with signed label.

11.5in (29cm) high

$12,000-18,000 **WAD**

A Marie Zimmermann silver and enamel covered-box, with a Victorian sardonyx hardstone cameo, stamped 'MZ' and 'STERLING'.

2.75in (7cm) wide

$10,000-15,000 **DRA**

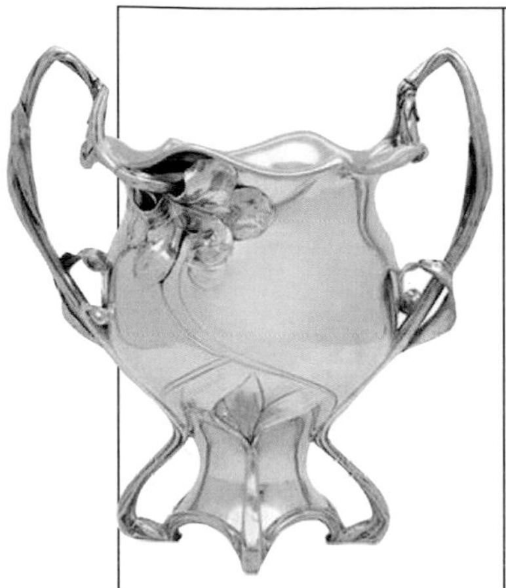

A silver wine cooler, decorated with irises, marked 'MR', 'KB', '875' and with a six-pronged star.

c1900 *12.5in (34cm) high 94oz*

$15,000-20,000 **DOR**

A pair of silver-plated candlesticks, designed by Edward Spencer, marked to base 'Edward Spencer/ DEL/380'.

c1900 *9in (23cm) high*

$2,000-3,000 **L&T**

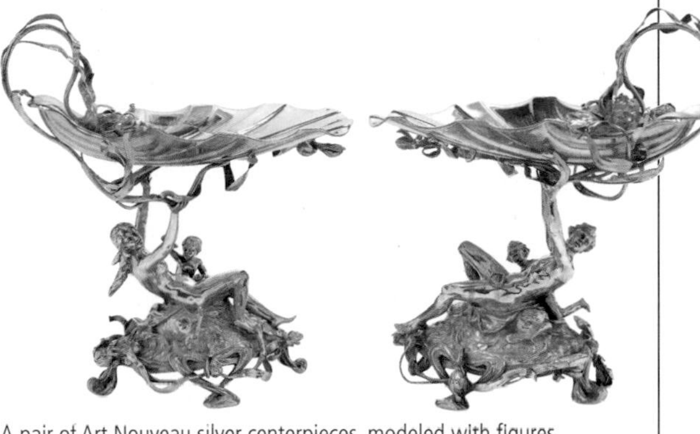

A pair of Art Nouveau silver centerpieces, modeled with figures supporting shellwork bowls, marked 'Lazarus Posen Veuve', with German government mark.

1888 *14in (36.5cm) high 156.8oz*

$22,000-28,000 **DOR**

A Tiffany parcel-gilt 'Ninth Century' desk set, comprising a photo frame, blotter ends and magnifying glass, stamped 'Tiffany Studios New York'.

Frame 8in (20.5cm) high

$4,500-5,500 **DRA**

A pair of Adolf Amberg silver candelabra, by Bruckmann & Söhne, Heilbronn, with German hallmarks and eagle, one marked '800', the other '925'.

22in (56cm) high

$55,000-65,000 **QU**

Guild of Handicraft

A Guild of Handicraft's silver and chrysoprase butter dish and knife, designed by Charles Robert Ashbee, London.

Ashbee founded the Guild of Handicraft in 1888. In 1902 he moved his craftsmen to Chipping Camden, UK. It was voluntarily wound up in 1908.

1900 *Dish 4.5in (11.5cm) diam 6.2oz*

$15,000-20,000 **DN**

A Black, Starr & Frost silver-gilt and jade vase, with dragon-form handles, stamped 'BLACK, STARR & FROST STERLING', with an eagle and star symbol and '552 PATENT APPLIED FOR'.

10.5in (26.5cm) high

$6,000-8,000 **DOY**

A Henrik Moller Arts & Crafts silver 'Dragestil' covered cup, Trondhiem, Norway, decorated with Viking imagery, with abstract owl finial, marked '830'.

c1900 *17.5in (44.5cm) high 59.6oz*

$10,000-15,000 **SK**

A Birmingham Guild of Handicraft Arts & Crafts silver beaker, Birmingham.

1901 *5in (13cm) high 8oz*

$2,000-3,000 **WW**

A silver vase, by Georg Adam Scheid, Vienna, with glass inset, marked with Diana's head and 'GAS'.

1905 *41.5in (105.5cm) high*

$15,000-20,000 **QU**

Two Wiener Werkstätte silver sardine slices, designed by Josef Hoffmann, from the 'Round Model' cutlery set, model no.S894, marked 'JH' and 'WW', with maker's mark 'JF', Diana's head and rose marks.

Designed 1907 *5in (12.5cm) long*

$8,000-12,000 **DOR**

A Bruckmann & Söhn silver tazza, Heilbronn, missing glass liner.

c1910 *14in (35cm) high 31oz*

$2,500-3,500 **DOR**

A Gorham silver seven-piece tea and coffee service.

c1911-13 *Kettle 13.25in (33.5cm) high 229oz*

$7,000-10,000 **DOY**

An Irish Arts & Crafts goblet, by Wakely & Wheeler, Dublin.

1912 *11.5in (29cm) high 26oz*

$4,000-6,000 **TEN**

A Tiffany & Co. silver seven-piece tea and coffee service, pattern no.18389.

Kettle 12.5in (32cm) high 272oz

$10,000-15,000 **DOY**

A 20thC Peter Bruckmann & Söhne silver five-piece tea and coffee set, Heilbronn, with maker's mark and '800'.

Coffee pot 10in (23cm) high 80oz

$3,500-4,500 KAU

A J C Klinkosch silver goblet, Vienna, marked 'JCK'.

1922 11in (29cm) high 25oz

$1,200-1,800 DOR

A J C Klinkosch silver goblet, Vienna, model no.11427, marked 'JCK' and '800'.

J C Klinkosch was one of the best silversmiths in Vienna who worked for the Emperor Franz Josef.

c1922 10in (27cm) high 12oz

$4,000-6,000 DOR

An H G Murphy Falcon Works silver cigarette box and cover, London, with stamped marks.

Revered during his lifetime, Harry Murphy was Britain's leading Jewelry designer of the early 20thC. One of the first to be nominated Royal Designer for Industry, he encapsulated that early 20thC dream, the successful marriage of art and industry.

1934 5in (12cm) high

$10,000-15,000 WW

A 1930s Art Deco silver and ivory-mounted vase, by Charles Boyton, London, with engraved inscription, signed.

1937 10in (25.5cm) high 19oz

$1,500-2,000 GORL

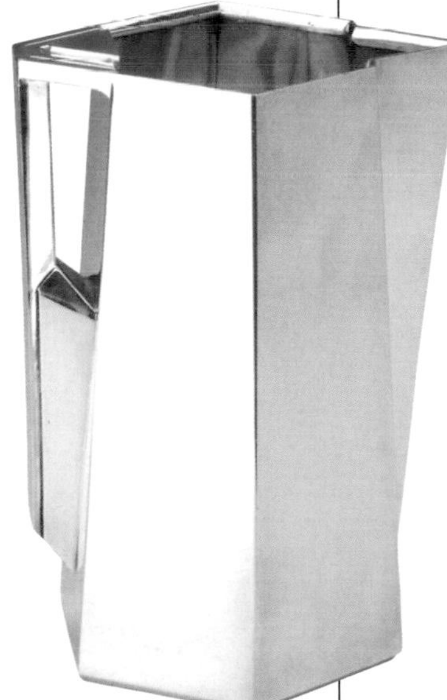

A Tiffany & Co. silver jug, designed by Frank Lloyd Wright, marked '57.3 OT'.

This jug was designed by Frank Lloyd Wright for the Imperial Hotel in Tokyo in 1918.

1985 10.25in (26cm) high

$4,500-5,500 DRA

An Adie Bros. Art Deco silver three-piece tea service, designed by Harold Stabler, Birmingham.

1936 Teapot 7.75in (20cm) long 28.35oz

$4,000-6,000 DN

An H G Murphy Falcon Works silver beaker, London, with stamped marks.

1938 4in (10cm) high

$5,500-6,500 WW

DECORATIVE ARTS

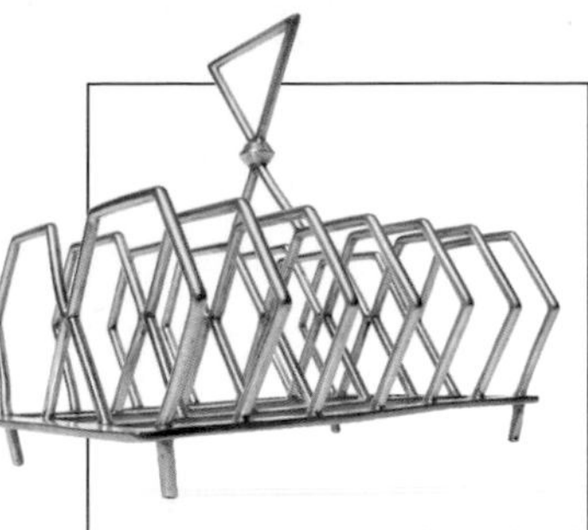

A James Dixon & Sons electroplated toast rack, designed by Dr Christopher Dresser, stamped 'EP JD&S 68 Chr Dresser'.

c1879 *7.5in (16cm) long*

$5,000-7,000 **TEN**

A Gorham Manufacturing Co. Art Nouveau silver-colored-metal and glass 'Athenic' vase, 'no.D847', with stamped marks and date code.

In 1891 William Codman, a London silversmith, went to the USA at the request of the director of Gorham, Edward Holbrook. Codman established a workshop devoted to handmade Art Nouveau silver that would then be sold under the name 'Athenic'. The forms were inspired by Greek models.

1901 *25.5cm (10in) high*

$2,500-3,500 **DN**

An F W Quist silver-plated coffee set, designed by Paul Follot, marked 'P. Follot, F.W.Q.E'.

1902 *Coffee pot 7.5 (19cm) high*

$4,500-5,500 **QU**

A Wiener Werkstätte silver-plated vase, designed by Josef Hoffmann, manufactured by Josef Berger, with rose mark and monograms of Josef Hoffmann and Josef Berger.

1904 *9.5in (24cm) high*

$65,000-75,000 **QU**

An F W Quist Art Deco silver-plated six-piece tea and coffee service, Esslingen, with rosewood handles and finials, with marks.

c1925 *Coffee pot 7.25in (18.5cm) high*

$1,500-2,500 **DOR**

A Walther & Wagner Metallwarenfabrik chrome-plated hot-water pot, designed by Wilhelm Wagenfeld, Schleiz.

c1930 *6in (15cm) high*

$25,000-35,000 **QU**

A Russel Wright spun-aluminum and walnut-lidded bowl, stamped 'Russel Wright'.

c1930 *8.5in (21.5cm) diam*

$4,000-6,000 **DRA**

A pair of nickel-plated vases, designed by Edgar Brandt and George Bastard, for the French ocean liner SS 'Normandie', marked 'C.G.T.' for the Compagnie Generale Transatlantique.

c1935

$6,500-7,500 **DRA**

A James Dixon & Sons electroplated sugar basin and milk-jug, designed by Dr Christopher Dresser, model no.2294, with stamped marks and facsimile signature.

3.75in (9.5cm) high

$2,500-3,500 **WW**

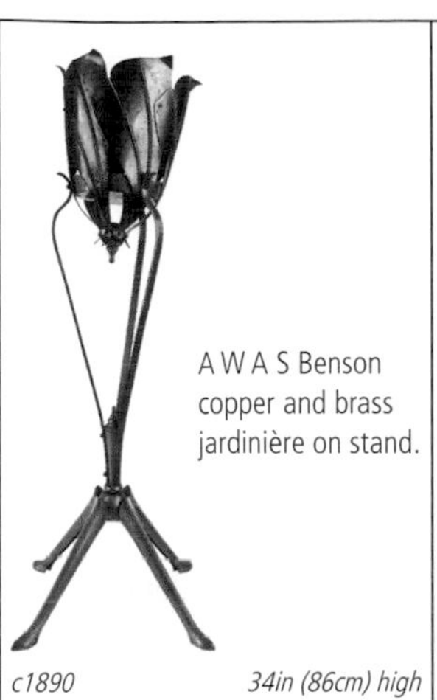

A W A S Benson copper and brass jardinière on stand.

c1890 *34in (86cm) high*

$2,500-3,500 **L&T**

A Dirk Van Erp hammered copper pitcher, with open box windmill mark.

7.75in (19.5cm) high

$3,000-4,000 **DRA**

A pair of Art Nouveau bronze vases, by Jean Garnier, cast with nymphs, with brass liners, signed.

13in (33cm) high

$2,000-3,000 **GORL**

A K M Seifert & Co. brass candlestick, designed by Richard Mueller, Dresden.

1900-01 *12.5in (31.5cm) high*

$3,000-4,000 **QU**

A John Pearson Arts & Crafts copper charger, no.2252, decorated with a galleon and sea monster, signed and dated.

1895 *24in (61cm) diam*

$4,000-6,000 **GORL**

A Shreve & Co. copper lidded bowl, designed by Joseph Heinrichs, with silver, horn and stone arrowheads, with bison finial, stamped 'SHREVE & CO COPPER AND SILVER'.

7.5in (18.5cm) high

$25,000-30,000 **DRA**

A Tiffany ciborium, inscribed '15594 TIFFANY & Co. MAKERS 18KT SOLID GOLD C 1634', in original velvet-lined box.

A ciborium is a covered chalice containing the consecrated wafers or pieces of bread served during the sacrament of Holy Communion.

1903 *11.75in (30cm) high 44.17oz*

$100,000-150,000 **MIC**

A Gustav Stickley hammered copper oversized coal bin, with circular 'Als Ik Kan' stamp.

19.5in (49.5cm) high

$8,000-12,000 **DRA**

A pair of late 19thC French bronze ewers.

38in (97cm) high

$3,500-4,500 **FRE**

An Italian bronze figure of 'Augustus Prima Porta', after the antique, by Benedetto Boschetti, stamped 'Fonderia Neulli', on a marble column.

Bronze 45.5in (116cm) high

$20,000-25,000 **LHA**

A pair of late 17thC French patinated-bronze figures of 'Bacchus' and 'Amphitrite', after Louis Garnier and Michel Anguier, with later bronze bases.

$10,000-15,000 **DN**

A bronze group of two wrestlers, after the antique.

c1870 *23in (59cm) high*

$2,500-3,500 **TEN**

A bronze group of Venus teased by two putti, after Luca Madrassi, signed 'L. Madrassi Paris'.

Luca Madrassi (1848-1919) was born in Tricesimo, Italy, and studied in Italy and Paris, where he was a pupil of Pierre-Jules Cavalier. He exhibited at the Salon des Artistes Français 1881-96 and at the Nationale from 1896. He specialized in busts, statuettes and allegorical groups.

c1885 *29in (73cm) high*

$4,000-6,000 **TEN**

A 19thC French bronze figure of a river god, after the antique.

12in (30cm) long

$1,000-1,500 **FRE**

A bronze figure of a Roman soldier, by Émile Louis Picault (1833-1915), inscribed 'E. Picault Scup./Salon des Beaux Arts'.

31.5in (80cm) high

$6,500-7,500 **FRE**

A bronze figure of a 'Running Athlete', after the antique.

19in (48cm) high

$1,000-1,500 **FRE**

An Italian School patinated bronze figure group of 'Laocoön and his Sons', after the antique, on a marble stand.

This depicts a scene from Virgil's 'Aeneid' in which the Trojan priest Laocoön is bitten and strangled by sea snakes.

c1900 *23in (59.5cm) high*

$5,000-7,000 **SWO**

A bronze statue of a kneeling woman, by Joseph Mario Korbel (1882-1954), signed 'Mario Korbel/1929 No.1', stamped 'Roman Bronze Works, N.Y.'.

11.5in (29cm) high

$5,000-7,000 **FRE**

F. H. Rhead/University City $637,500 10/26/12

ESSENTIAL REFERENCE - A E CARRIER-BELLEUSE

- **Albert-Ernest Carrier-Belleuse (1824-1887) was born in Anizy-le-Château in northern France.**
- **He made his reputation with his sculpture 'Salve Regina' (1861). Notable later works include 'Baccante' (1863) and 'The Messiah' (1867).**
- **He was highly regarded by Napoleon III who would introduce him as 'Notre Clodion': 'our Clodion', refering to the French Rococo sculptor Claude Michel (1738-1814).**
- **Carrier-Belleuse worked for Minton, UK, 1850-55 and in Brussels in c1871.**
- **He was one of the founder members of Société Nationale des Beaux-Arts.**
- **He was made an officer of the Légion d'Honneur in 1862.**
- **Auguste Rodin worked as his assistant 1864–70.**

A French bronze figure of 'L'Enlevement d'Hippodamie', by Albert-Ernest Carrier-Belleuse, signed, with 'Bronze Garanti au Titre' mark and 'L'Enlevement" title plaque.

25.5in (65cm) high

$25,000-30,000 **FRE**

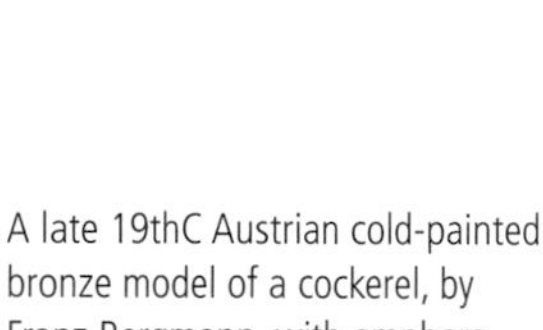

A late 19thC Austrian cold-painted bronze model of a cockerel, by Franz Bergmann, with amphora mark.

12.25in (31cm) high

$10,000-15,000 **L&T**

An early 20thC Austrian cold-painted bronze figural boudoir lamp, probably by Franz Bergmann, depicting an Egyptian merchant seated on a rug.

11.75in (30cm) high

$7,000-10,000 **SK**

An Austrian cold-painted bronze table-lamp base, by Franz Bergmann, in the form of woman playing a lute on a camel's back, the camel lead by a man carrying a rifle and sword, marked 'B' in a shield.

14.5in (37cm) high

$12,000-18,000 **HT**

An early 20thC Austrian cold-painted bronze bust of a Moor, by Franz Bergmann, with amphora mark, signed 'GESCH', on an onyx base.

12.5in (32cm) high

$4,000-6,000 **L&T**

A late 19thC Tiffany & Co. ormolu figure of a lute player, by Albert-Ernest Carrier-Belleuse, marked.

27in (69cm) high

$6,000-8,000 **DRA**

A French bronze figure of 'Octopus Dancer', by Louis Chalon (1866-1916), stamped 'Louchet' and 'L. Chalon'.

21in (53cm) high

$55,000-65,000 **FRE**

A pair of bronze busts of 'The Venus Africaine' and 'Saïd Abdallah, De La Tribu De Mayac, Royaume De Darfour', after Charles-Henri-Joseph Cordier (1827-1905).

19.5in (49cm) high

$35,000-45,000 **L&T**

An American bronze figure of 'The Crest of the Wave', by Harriet Whitney Frishmuth (1880-1980), inscribed and dated, stamped 'Gorham Co. Founders/QFHL', on a marble base.

1925 *21in (53cm) high*

$5,500-6,500 **LHA**

A pair of French ormolu figures of a samurai and bijin, attributed to Émile-Coriolan-Hippolyte Guillemin (1841-1907).

c1875 *25in (63cm) high*

$15,000-20,000 **TEN**

A cold-painted bronze figure of 'Serena', by Josef Lorenzl (1892-1950), signed, on an onyx base.

14.5in (36.5cm) high

$2,000-3,000 DN

A French bronze figure of 'David Après le Combat', by Marius-Jean-Antonin Mercié (1845-1916), with 'Collas Reduction' seal, on a marble column.

28.75in (73cm) high

$12,000-18,000 SK

An Art Deco silvered-bronze group of 'Illumination', by C Mirval, signed.

c1930 *30in (76.5cm) high*

$6,000-8,000 DN

An Art Deco ormolu figure of a Russian dancer, by Paul Philippe (1870-1930), signed, on an onyx base, one finger detached but present.

15.5in (39.5cm) high

$4,000-6,000 GORB

A French parcel-gilt bronze group of 'Salammbô Chez Matho', by Theodore Rivière (1857-1912), marked 'Carthage', 'Susse Fes Edt.', 'Susse Freres Editeurs Paris' stamp, stamped 'H' for the foundry Ciseleur Hubert.

This group is based on Flaubert's novel 'Salammbô (1862). It shows Matho kneeling before the high priestess and was exhibited at the Salon des Artistes Français 1895 and the Exposition Universelle 1900.

16in (41cm) high

$8,000-12,000 SWO

A bronze figure of a nude, by Victor Heinrich Seifert (1870-1953), on a marbled stone base, inscribed in the plinth.

c1900 *27.5in (71cm) high*

$7,000-10,000 DOR

A French bronze figure of 'Fortune', by Augustin Edme Moreau-Vauthier (1831-93), inscribed 'Moreau Vauthier/1878', with foundry mark 'RÉDUCTION MÉCANIQUE A.COLLAS BREVETÉ'.

1878 *51.25in (130cm) high*

$10,000-15,000 FRE

A bronze figure of 'Bohemienne', by Emmanuel Villanis (1858-1914), signed, with foundry stamp for B L Paris.

13.25in (33.5cm) high

$2,000-3,000 DN

A bronze and ivory figure of 'Connoisseur', by Bruno Zach, on a stone base.

c1930 *10in (25cm) high*

$6,500-7,500 DOR

An American bronze model of 'The Four Horsemen of the Apocalypse', by Lee Lawrie (1877-1963), inscribed 'LEE LAWRIE', with foundry mark for the Roman Bronze Works, NY.

This sculpture was commissioned by Rex Ingram for the premiere of his 1921 film 'The Four Horsemen of the Apocalypse'. The film was ground-breaking, critically acclaimed and the highest grossing film of the year. Lee Lawrie is widely known for his public works, such as the Atlas bronze in Rockefeller Center. He did not typically accept private commissions, as he believed art should be enjoyed by the masses. However, Ingram had been one of Lawrie's favorite students at Yale and the film's subject matter appealed to the sculptor's sensibilities.

24in (61cm) high

$20,000-30,000 **FRE**

ESSENTIAL REFERENCE - PIERRE-JULES MÊNE

French animalière Pierre-Jules Mêne (1810–79) is considered a pioneer of animal sculpture. He specialized in small bronzes of domestic animals, such as horses, cows, bulls, sheep and dogs.

- **Mêne established the first of his foundries in 1837.**
- **In 1861 he received the Légion d'Honneur.**
- **Due to Mêne's popularity in his own time, most of his bronzes were made in large editions.**
- **After his death, his final foundry was run by his son-in-law, Auguste Cain, who continued to produce high quality bronzes until 1879. The foundry was closed in 1894 and many of the models were sold to Susse Frères.**

A bronze group of 'L'Accolade', by Pierre-Jules Mêne (1810-79), signed 'P J MÊNE'.

20in (53cm) long

$12,000-18,000 **TEN**

A bronze model of Queen Alexandra's barouche horse 'Splendour', by Herbert Haseltine (1877-1962), signed and dated, with foundry mark.

1910 *17in (43cm) high*

$15,000-20,000 **FRE**

A bronze model of 'Cheval de Course', by Pierre-Jules Mêne, signed.

This model is considered one of Mêne's best. It was modeled in the 1860s and is no.35 in the sculptor's catalog.

17in (44cm) wide

$6,500-7,500 **SWO**

A bronze group of 'Chasse à la Perdrix', by Pierre-Jules Mêne, signed P J MÊNE' and dated.

1847 *15in (41cm) long*

$5,000-7,000 **TEN**

A bronze model of 'Chief Baron Par The Baron Caladenia', by Jules Moigniez (1835-94), signed 'J MOIGNIEZ', inscribed 'GOELZER PARIS'.

15in (35.5cm) high

$5,000-7,000 **TEN**

An early 20thC German bronze model of an ostrich, after Joseph Franz Pallenberg, signed and dated, inscribed 'Dusseldf. BRONCIBILD GIESSEREI Gmbh', on marble plinth.

1906 *19.25in (49cm) high*

$5,500-6,500 **M&K**

A bronze and ivory group of a satyr with maiden, by Antoine Bouraine, signed, on stone base, with cracks to ivory.

c1925 *18.5in (47cm) high*

$6,500-7,500 **FRE**

An early 20thC Art Nouveau bronze and ivory figure, by A Cassmann, signed.

15.5in (39cm) high

$3,000-4,000 **LHA**

A Romanian ormolu and ivory figure of a young girl, by Démetre H Chiparus (1886-1947), inscribed 'Chiparus' and '5402', on a marble base.

7.75in (20cm) high

$3,500-4,500 **FRE**

A bronze and ivory figure of a peasant girl, by Giuseppe Joseph D'Aste (1881-1945), on a marble base.

c1900 *15in (30cm) high*

$2,500-3,500 **DOR**

An Art Deco ormolu and ivory figure of the 'Dance of Carthage', by Claire-Jeanne Roberte Colinet, no.19, with a bronze medallion marked 'L.M. PARIS J.L', on a marble base.

12.25in (31cm) high

$25,000-30,000 **DOY**

A bronze and ivory figure of 'Harlequinade', by A Gilbert, signed, marked 'Made in France', with impressed foundry mark, on an onyx base.

c1930 *20.5in (52cm) high*

$7,000-10,000 **FRE**

A cold-painted bronze and ivory figure of 'Sonny Boy', by Ferdinand Preiss (1882-1943), signed, on onyx base.

c1930 *8.25in (21cm) high*

$5,500-6,500 **L&T**

Judith Picks

While I was a student in Edinburgh in the early 1970s I spotted an Art Deco bronze and ivory sculpture in an antique shop. Priced at £165 ($250) it was out of my reach. How I wish I had taken out a loan! This is Bruno Zach's iconic masterpiece and is one of the most famous of all the Art Deco bronzes. The sculptor specialized in depictions of dominating women and the statue shows a girl dressed in an off-the-shoulder negligee, stockings and high heels and holding a riding crop behind her back. Little is known about Bruno Zach (1891-1935). Born in Austria, he is most associated with Berlin between the wars and his work conjures up the world of Christopher Isherwood's novels and the Oscar winning film 'Cabaret'. He depicted the dream mistresses of the demi monde of Berlin,

A green- and gilt-patinated bronze figure of 'The Riding Crop', by Bruno Zach, signed and with monogram on base.

c1930 *32.75in (83cm) high*

$150,000-200,000 **BON**

A French Art Nouveau bronze pedestal bust of 'Cendrillon', by Emmanuel Villanis (1858-1914), signed, with foundry stamp 'Vrai Bronze Garanti Paris'.

'Cendrillon' is a chamber comic opera by Pauline Viardot, based on the story of Cinderella. The work was first premiered in Viardot's Parisian salon on 23 April 1904.

c1905 *24in (62cm) high*

$5,500-6,500 **TEN**

A French Art Nouveau bronze bust of 'Mignon', by Emmanuel Villanis (1858-1914), signed, titled and stamped 'E.V. 85 LU Salon'.

1896 *15in (37cm) high*

$2,500-3,500 **TEN**

A 19thC Art Nouveau carved alabaster bust.

26in (66cm) high

$1,200-1,800 **FRE**

A British alabaster sculpture of 'Daphne', by Stephen M Wiens (1871-1956), signed 'S. Wiens/ Sculpst/1919'.

1919 *70in (178cm) high*

$20,000-30,000 **L&T**

A late 19thC/early 20thC alabaster bust, by Umberto Stiaccini, signed 'U Stiaccini Firenze'.

11in (28cm) high

$500-700 **DN**

An American marble sculpture of 'Fragelina', by Attilio Piccirilli (1866-1945).

Italian-born sculptor Piccirilli studied in Rome, before immigrating to New York City, NY, USA, in 1888. His father Guiseppe and five brothers were all marble cutters and sculptors. They worked from the Piccirilli studio in the Bronx.

50in (127cm) high

$30,000-40,000 **FRE**

ESSENTIAL REFERENCE - WHARTON ESHERICK

Wharton Esherick (1887-1970) was an American craftsman and sculptor, who worked in Paoli, PA.

- **He learned wood and metal working at Manual Training High School, drawing and printmaking at the Pennsylvania Museum School of Industrial Art and painting at the Pennsylvania Academy of Fine Arts.**
- **In the early 1920s he began sculpting in wood. By 1926 his sculpture was being exhibited at the Whitney in New York.**
- **Esherick's sculptures are often large and abstract. Many of his subjects were directly related to his long-term involvement with the community of actors and artists connected to Rose Valley's Hedgerow Theatre.**
- **Esherick is perhaps best known for his furniture, which is typified by sinuous, organic lines and demonstrates a sculptor's eye for space and form (see p.597).**

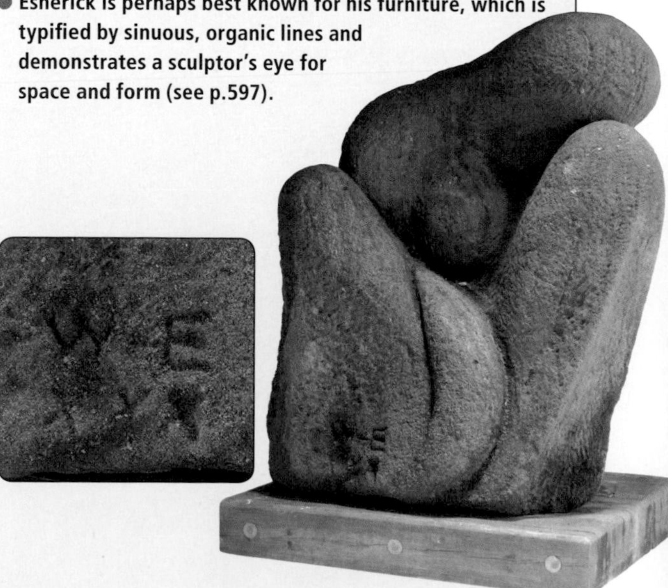

An Alabama-sandstone sculpture of 'Andante', by Wharton Esherick, signed and dated.

This sculpture was displayed in front of the Fairhope Hotel, Fairhope, AL, USA.

1930 *33in (84cm) high*

$70,000-90,000 **DRA**

A late 19thC/early 20thC Italian marble sculpture of 'The Three Graces', after Antonio Canova.

33in (84cm) high

$20,000-30,000 **LHA**

A bronze sculpture of 'Adam', by Wharton Esherick, signed, titled and dated.

1926 *15.75in (40cm) high*

$35,000-45,000 **DRA**

An Arts & Crafts Donegal-style carpet, in the manner of Alexander Morton and G K Robertson.

In 1898 Alexander Morton & Co. established carpet-weaving workshops in Donegal on the north coast of Ireland. This was a desirable location as the cost of labor was low and the venture created jobs in an economically-depressed area.

142.5in (365cm) long

$10,000-15,000 DN

One of a set of five cushion covers made from Morris & Co. 'Bird' pattern jacquard wool fabric, the fabric designed by William Morris (1834-96).

24.75in (63cm) wide

$2,000-3,000 set L&T

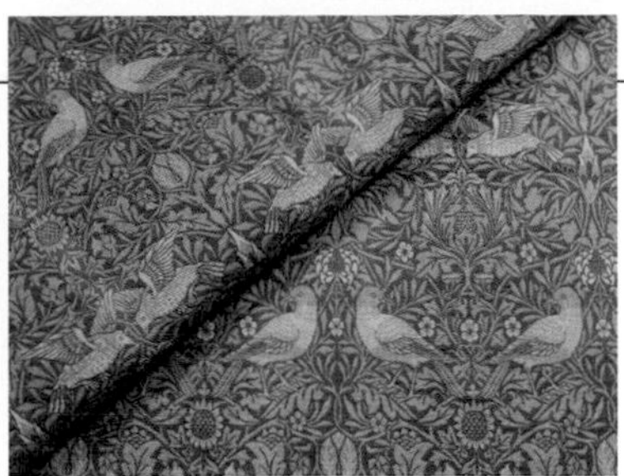

A panel of Morris & Co. 'Bird' pattern jacquard-wool fabric, designed by William Morris.

100in (255cm) high

$3,000-4,000 TEN

A Quayle & Tranter Ltd., Kidderminster 'Hunting' rug, designed by George Bain (1881-1968), the Celtic knotwork medallion surrounded by huntsmen and animals.

Scottish art teacher George Bain almost single-handedly revived interest in Celtic and Insular art in the 20thC. His book 'Celtic Art: The Methods of Construction' was published in 1951 and became highly influential on its re-issue in 1971. The book described and illustrated more than 200 historical examples of Celtic designs. It also gave detailed instructions for creating similar interlace, spiral and trumpet designs.

c1948 144in (366cm) long

$3,500-4,500 L&T

A late 19thC Morris & Co. embroidered panel, with cord and wool appliqué embroidery.

24.75in (63cm) high

$1,800-2,200 L&T

A silk embroidery, attributed to Morris & Co., framed.

17in (43.5cm) wide

$500-700 WW

A late 19thC woolwork embroidery, after Selwyn, framed and glazed.

22.5in (57cm) wide

$4,000-6,000 L&T

A James Templeton & Co. wool rug, designed by Frank Brangwyn, with artist's monogram.

113in (288cm) wide

$3,000-4,000 WW

A Pre-Raphaelite School silkwork embroidered roundel, mounted in a velvet slip, framed.

c1870 Roundel 12.5in (32cm) diam

$1,500-2,500 L&T

THE MODERN DESIGN MARKET

Where other areas have faltered financially, interest in and prices for out-standing post World War II design has in many cases quadrupled. The market is fed by the quantity of items available. Design in this period was totally international and, with the added impetus of the internet, so is the collecting market. Moreover, many pieces are found in large numbers and are consequently relatively affordable, making this area accessible to younger buyers. The styles are also in tune with a younger taste.

While the seeds of Mid-century Modern lay in the Scandinavian 'Soft Modernism' of the 1930s, the designers who started working during and after World War II were excited by the possibilities of new materials and the demands of an enthusiastic consumer class. Designers such as Charles and Ray Eames in the US said their mission was 'getting the most of the best to the greatest number of people for the least amount of money'. Of course many of the Eames' original designs can no longer be purchased for 'the least amount of money' as they are now highly prized as icons of design. An untitled Eames plywood sculpture, designed in 1943, sold for over $380,000 in 2008. If it came back on the market today I would estimate it at over $1,200, 000.

Many other designers are also fetching record sums. In mid-2012 Christie's New York sold a unique Isamu Noguchi fossil marble table, commissioned in 1948 by Mr and Mrs Dretzin, for nearly $3,000,000.

The Modern Movement is by its very nature diverse. It covers the great studio craftsmen, such as furniture makers George Nakashima and Wharton Esherick, and potters such as the Natzlers and Peter Voulkos. It also covers 1960s plastic and Postmodern pieces by designers such as Joe Colombo and Ettore Sottsass. There is something in this area to suit all tastes and pockets. For example, Stuart Devlin, noted Australian/British silver- and goldsmith, designed some highly individual furniture in the 1970s, like the love seat on p.596.

Glass from the 20thC greats – the designers and factories of Scandinavia and Murano – continues to sell really well. Buyers like the vibrant colors and modern forms. Big names are another plus factor and prices for the work of luminaries, such as Murano-trained American designer Dale Chihuly, have quadrupled in recent years. Other glass artists who have pioneered new techniques in the US include Mary Ann 'Toots' Zynsky whose 'Ramingo' vessel on p.616 sold for $25,000 at Rago Arts.

A newcomer to the growing 20thC glass stable is Post-War Czech glass, triumphed by my friend and colleague Mark Hill in his book 'High Sklo, Low Sklo'. Currently, the low end of the market ($50-500) is the most populated. As people get more comfortable with the unusual names of the designers, this market seems set to rise.

Above: A Dale Chihuly glass 'Macchia' group. See p.613.
Left: A Jack Earl glazed ceramic 'The What Kind of Dog is That Dog' sculpture. See p.612.

One of a pair of Alvar Aalto laminated-birch and velvet 'Tank' lounge chairs, for Artek, unmarked.

c1950 *31in (79cm) wide*

$8,000-12,000 pair **DRA**

A pair of Jacques Adnet bronze and leather campaign benches, unmarked.

25.5in (65cm) wide

$3,000-4,000 **DRA**

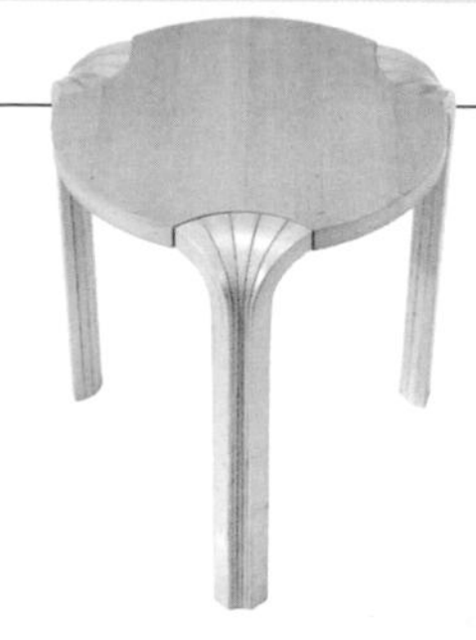

An Alvar Aalto bent-plywood fan-legged stool, for Artek.

Designed 1954 *17.5in (44cm) high*

$250-350 **FRE**

A Jacques Adnet black leather and brass daybed, unmarked.

77.5in (197cm) long

$8,000-12,000 **DRA**

An early Ron Arad steel 'Well Tempered Chair', for the Vitra Edition.

The 'Well Tempered Chair' was designed in 1986. This example is from the first production series comprising approximately 50 pieces, all of which were composed of four steel bands each. In the subsequent production series (until 1993), an additional steel plate was mounted underneath the seat.

1986 *37in (95cm) high*

$12,000-18,000 **DOR**

A Jacques Adnet chrome-plated-steel and smokey-glass bar trolley, unmarked.

29in (74cm) high

$3,000-4,000 **DRA**

A Ron Arad patinated-steel and leather 'Spring' daybed, manufactured by Moroso, Italy.

This daybed (designed 1990) is based on Arad's 'After Spring' daybed, which was produced by Ron Arad Associates in 1990.

c1994 *91in (230cm) long*

$25,000-30,000 **DOR**

Franco Albini

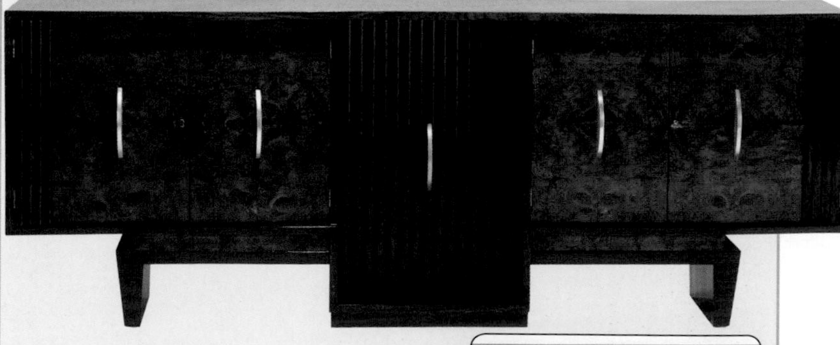

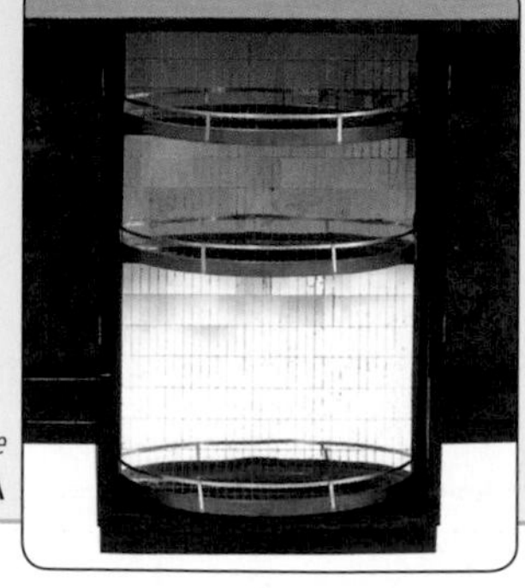

A 1940s Franco Albini rosewood, burlwood and mahogany cabinet, with nickel-plated hardware and mirrored interior, unmarked.

Franco Albini (1905-77) worked in the studio of Gio Ponti until 1930 when he established his own design and architecture practice. His designs epitomize Italian Rationalism.

92in (234cm) wide

$8,000-12,000 **DRA**

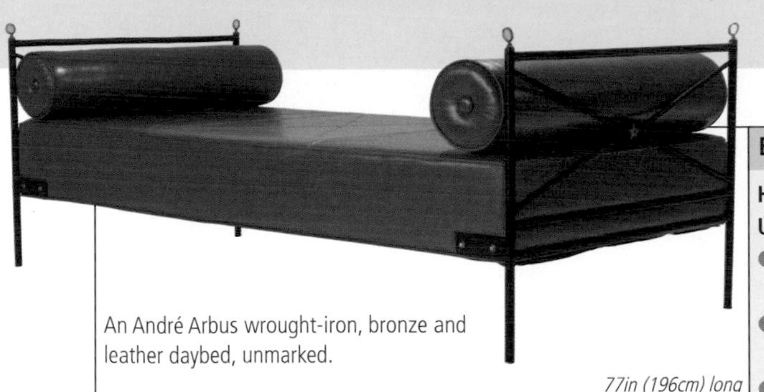

An André Arbus wrought-iron, bronze and leather daybed, unmarked.

77in (196cm) long

$10,000-15,000 **DRA**

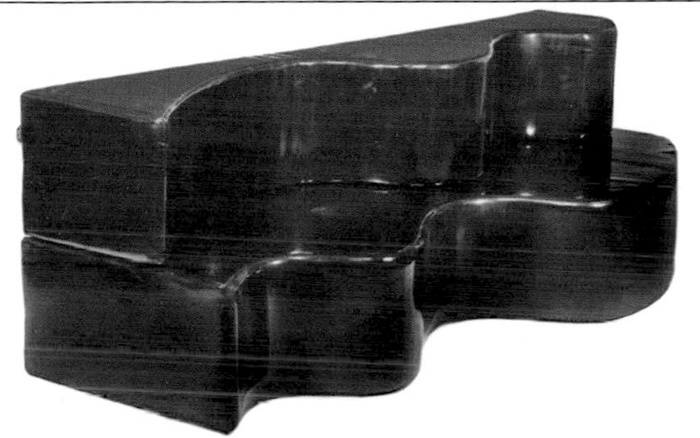

An Archizoom Associati 'Superonda' unit, for Poltronova, comprised of interlocking vinyl-covered sculptural forms, with fabric label 'Poltronova Made in Italy'.

Designed 1966 *93in (236cm) long*

$1,200-1,800 **DN**

ESSENTIAL REFERENCE - HARRY BERTOIA

Harry Bertoia (1915-78) was born in Italy and settled in the USA in 1930.

- **He studied at the Cranbrook Academy 1937-39 and later taught metalwork there 1939-43.**
- **He is best known for his wire mesh and tubular steel 'Diamond' chair, designed 1950 for Knoll.**
- **As well as furniture, Bertoia is known for his 'Sonambient' sculptures (see p.622).**

A Harry Bertoia 'Bird' chair and ottoman, with welded-steel frame.

This was part of Bertoia's 1952 collection of bent-steel furniture for Knoll.

Chair 40.25in (102cm) high

$2,500-3,500 **FRE**

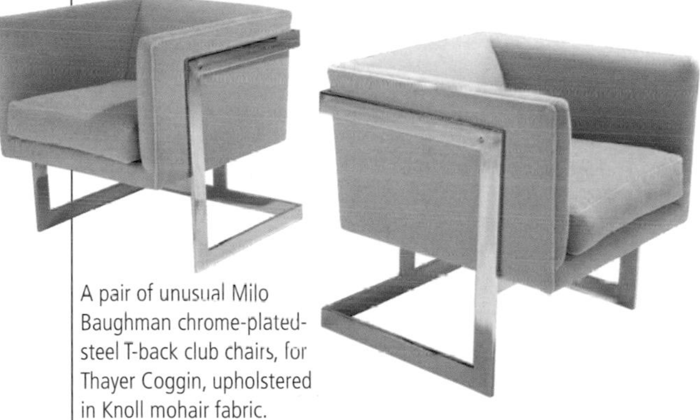

A pair of unusual Milo Baughman chrome-plated-steel T-back club chairs, for Thayer Coggin, upholstered in Knoll mohair fabric.

26in (66cm) high

$5,000-7,000 **DRA**

A 1940s Osvaldo Borsani onyx, mahogany and brass dining table, for Atelier Varedo, unmarked.

After completing his studies at the Politecnico di Milano, Borsani joined the family business Atelier Varedo (later Arredamento Borsani) as a furniture designer.

39.5in (100.5cm) diam

$6,500-7,500 **DRA**

A black-lacquered cocktail cabinet, attributed to Osvaldo Borsani, with white-alloy revealed hinges, handles and sabots.

50in (127cm) high

$2,500-3,500 **DN**

A Hans Brattrud laminated-rosewood lounge chair, for Hove Møbler, with a tilt mechanism, with suede and vinyl upholstery.

41in (104cm) high

$3,000-4,000 **DN**

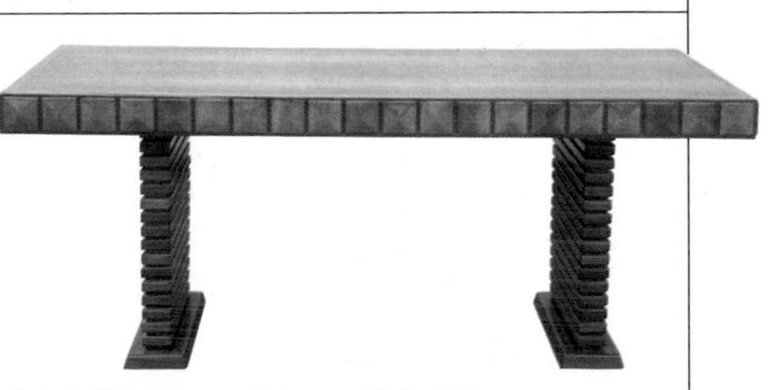

A Paolo Buffa Japanese-maple-veneered dining table.

c1940 *77.5in (197cm) long*

$2,500-3,500 **QU**

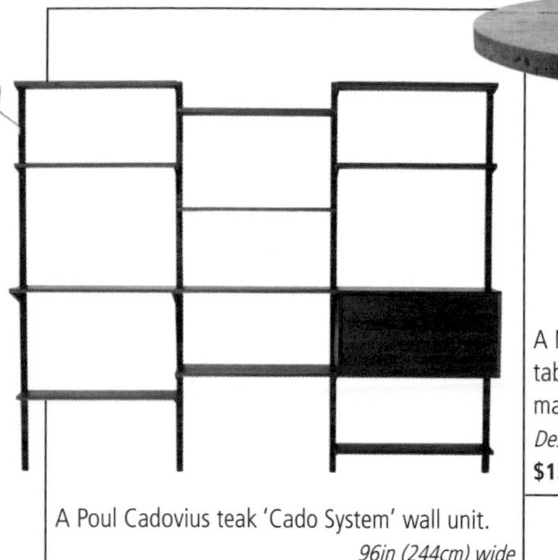

A Poul Cadovius teak 'Cado System' wall unit.
96in (244cm) wide
$1,200-1,800 **DRA**

A Mario Ceroli firwood 'Rosa dei Venti' dining table, the top decorated with a compass pattern, marked 'Ceroli Poltronova'.
Designed 1974 *64.5in (164cm) diam*
$12,000-18,000 **QU**

A pair of floral side tables, attributed to Arthur Court, with gilt-metal bases and glass tops.
19in (48cm) diam
$1,200-1,800 **DRA**

A Joe D'Urso prototype 'Supper' table, with mahogany planks above a black brushed-steel base with casters.

This example was part of a house designed by D'Urso in Easthampton, MA, USA. It is a prototype of a design later put into production by Donghia and was designed in the mid-1960s.
124in (315cm) wide
$5,500-6,500 **FRE**

A burl-walnut and satinwood desk, possibly designed by Donald Deskey, for the Company of Master Craftsmen.
c1935 *46in (117cm) wide*
$1,500-2,500 **FRE**

Judith Picks

In 1974 Stuart Devlin engaged craftsman Brian Martin to produce his furniture designs. This piece is believed to be a one-off. It harks back to the traditional Victorian loveseat but with a totally modern twist. His four maxims say a lot about this designer: That the future is much more important than the past. That creativity is paramount. That skill is fundamental. That the justification for being a designer is to enrich the way people live and work.

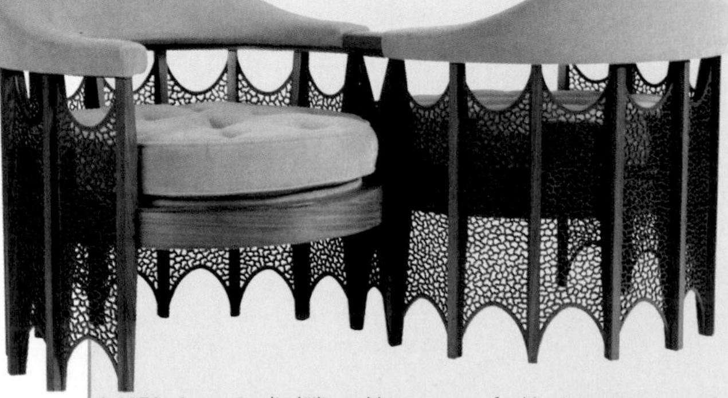

A 1970s Stuart Devlin 'Filigree' love seat, crafted by Brian Martin, each seat with 19 rosewood-laminated panels.
31in (79cm) wide
$6,500-7,500 **TEN**

A Nanna Ditzel teak desk, model no.93/4, for Søren Willadsen, the drawers with recessed handles, on Y-profile legs.
Designed 1958 *69in (175cm) wide*
$3,500-4,500 **DN**

A pair of Dorothy Draper fruitwood and fur stools, unmarked.
26in (66cm) wide
$5,500-6,500 **DRA**

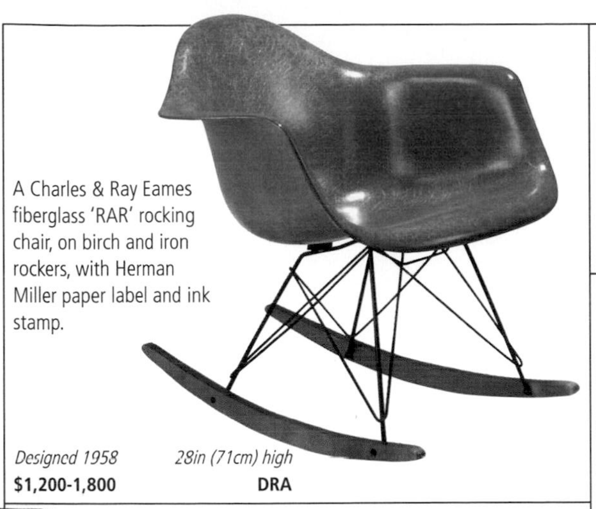

A Charles & Ray Eames fiberglass 'RAR' rocking chair, on birch and iron rockers, with Herman Miller paper label and ink stamp.

Designed 1958 *28in (71cm) high*

$1,200-1,800 **DRA**

A Charles & Ray Eames walnut, birch, laminate, lacquered-masonite and chrome-plated-steel 'ESU 200' unit, for Herman Miller, unmarked.

47in (119.5cm) wide

$8,000-12,000 **DRA**

A Charles Eames & Eero Saarinen Honduran-mahogany storage unit, for Red Lion, unmarked.

Provenance: Organic Design competltion.

1941 *79.5in (202cm) high*

$8,000-12,000 **DRA**

A late 1950s Charles & Ray Eames rosewood and black leather lounge chair and ottoman, model nos.670 and 671, with Herman Miller paper labels.

Chair 32.5in (82.5cm) high

$7,000-10,000 **DRA**

A Wharton Esherick oak and cherrywood tiered stand, carved 'WE 1965'.

1965 *34.75in (88.5cm) high*

$50,000-60,000 **DRA**

A Wharton Esherick coffee table, inscribed 'To Buckety Bill from Maggie Grant, 1952.'.

1952 *38in (97cm) wide*

$35,000-45,000 **FRE**

A Paul Evans sculpted-bronze and glass dining table, on a serpentine base, signed 'PE 73'.

1973 *96in (244cm) long*

$7,000-10,000 **DRA**

A pair of Paul Evans brass-veneered sofas, with upholstered seats and cushions, with 'Paul Evans Inc.' labels.

1975 *54in (137cm) wide*

$5,500-6,500 **FRE**

A Paul Evans chrome-plated-steel and burl-maple cabinet, for Directional, unmarked.

72in (183cm) long

$6,500-7,500 **DRA**

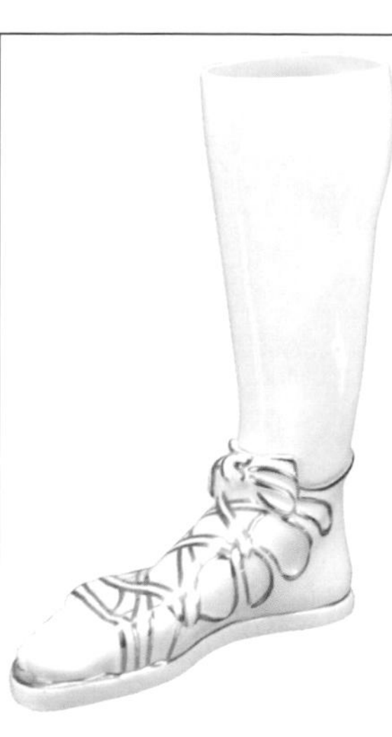

A Piero Fornasetti pottery 'Roman Foot' umbrella/stick stand, with black printed mark.

22.5in (57cm) high

$650-850 **DN**

A 1950s Piero Fornasetti lithographed-steel 'Alsatian Dog' umbrella stand, unmarked.

34in (86.5cm) high

$6,500-7,500 **DN**

ESSENTIAL REFERENCE - PIERO FORNASETTI

Piero Fornasetti (1913-88) was an Italian painter, sculptor, designer and engraver.

- **He studied at Milan's Brera Academy of Fine Art 1930-32.**
- **In the 1930s he designed glass for Venini.**
- **He began collaborating on furniture and interiors with Gio Ponti in 1940.**
- **Fornasetti was heavily influenced by Greek and Roman architecture and often mixed images from antique engravings with Trompe L'Oeil and surreal effects. His work often features a strong use of black and white, and motifs such as the sun.**

A Piero Fornasetti 'Corinthian Capital' chair, marked '22 di 40/92', maker's label 'FORNASETTI MILANO MADE IN ITALY'.

This example was produced in 1992.

Designed c1955 *36.5in (92.5cm) high*

$1,500-2,500 **QU**

A 1950s Piero Fornasetti magazine stand, lithographed with Classical building-facades, with metal divisions and feet, labeled 'Fornasetti Milano Made in Italy'.

16.5in (42cm) wide

$1,500-2,000 **SWO**

A Jean-Michel Frank iron, oak and stitched-leather console table, with 'Comte Buenos Aires' metal tag.

47in (119cm) wide

$15,000-20,000 **DRA**

A 1940s Paul Frankl lacquered-cork and lacquered-mahogany coffee table, for Johnson Furniture Co., with stenciled numbers.

48in (122cm) wide

$7,000-10,000 **DRA**

An Elisabeth Garouste 'Entrelacs' buffet, with patinated-bronze handles and feet, with lilac-lacquered interior, signed and numbered.

This buffet is no.1 from the limited edition of 25.

2005 *54in (136cm) wide*

$25,000-30,000 **DOR**

An Alexander Girard stool, for Herman Miller, on polished aluminum base.

15.75in (40cm) diam

$2,000-3,000 **DRA**

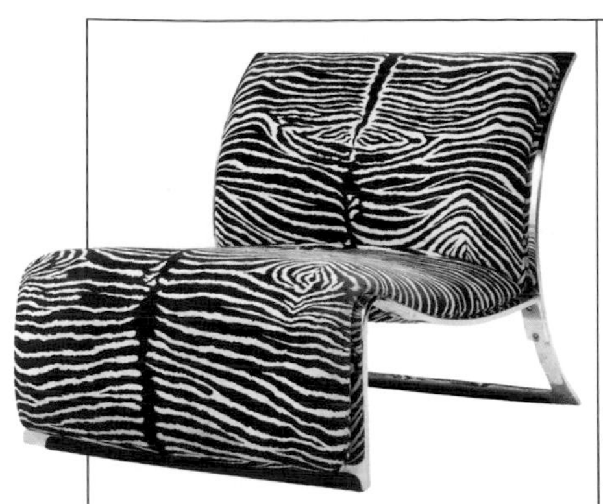

One of a pair of Vittorio Introini lounge chairs, upholstered in zebra-pattern brushed fabric, on flat steel frames.

32in (81cm) high

$1,200-1,800 pair **DRA**

An Arne Jacobsen 'Egg' chair, for Fritz Hansen, with original foil label.

This example is from the original issue (c1961) of this chair. Provenance: It was purchased by an architect who worked for Arne Jacobsen.

Designed 1958

$4,000-6,000 **FLD**

A Louis XVI-style ebonized-mahogany and brass-mounted bureau plat, attributed to Maison Jansen.

Maison Jansen was a Paris-based interior decoration firm, founded in 1880 by Dutch-born Jean-Henri Jansen. The firm closed in 1989.

c1960 *71in (179.5cm) wide*

$12,000-18,000 **L&T**

A Pierre Jeanneret teak desk, designed for the Base Building in Chandigarh, India, the top covered with replaced green leather, inscribed 'DIT/CT-7'.

1952–56 *48in (122cm) wide*

$15,000-20,000 **DOR**

A 1970s Charles Hollis Jones lacquered console table, unmarked.

86.5in (220cm) wide

$5,500-6,500 **DRA**

ESSENTIAL REFERENCE - FINN JUHL

Finn Juhl (1912-89) studied architecture at the Royal Danish Academy of Fine Art, Copenhagen, graduating in 1934.

- **He was influenced by the abstract sculptor Jean Arp.**
- **From 1937 to 1959 he collaborated with cabinetmaker Niels Vodder.**
- **He opened an office in 1945 in Copenhagen.**
- **Juhl helped popularize the use of teak in Danish design.**
- **His most famous design is the 'Chieftain' chair (1949).**
- **He taught at the School of Interior Design, Copenhagen, 1945-55.**
- **His furniture is typically organically shaped. Many of his chairs feature a 'floating' back and seat.**

A Finn Juhl teak dining table, for France & Søn, with two leaves.

c1961 *Closed 72.75in (185cm) long*

$3,000-4,000 **FRE**

A Finn Juhl teak and teak-veneered sideboard, manufactured by Niels Vodder, Copenhagen.

This sideboard was designed to also be used as a room divider.

Designed 1954 *94.5in (240cm) wide*

$20,000-30,000 **QU**

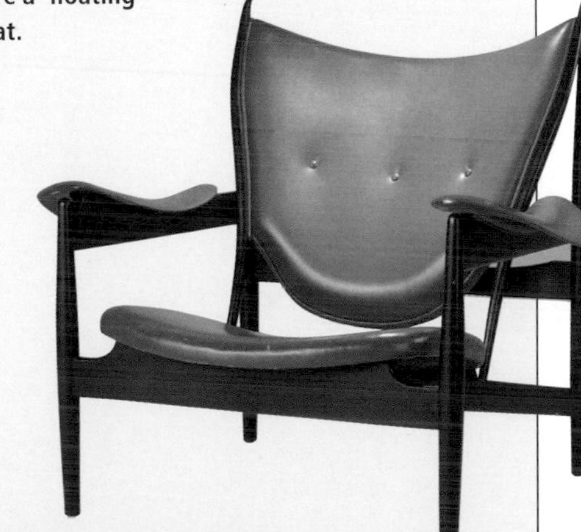

A Finn Juhl teak and leather 'Chieftain' chair, for Niels Roth Andersen, unmarked, designed in 1949.

c1980 *41in (104cm) high*

$5,500-6,500 **DRA**

ESSENTIAL REFERENCE - VLADIMIR KAGAN

German born designer Vladimir Kagan (b.1927) immigrated to the USA in 1938. By the early 1950s he had become known for innovative, sculptural furniture. Typical designs have splayed legs and sinuous frames.

- **He studied architecture at Columbia University, New York City, NY, graduating in 1946.**
- **Kagan started designing in 1946.**
- **In 1947 he went to learn cabinetmaking from the ground up at the woodworking shop of his father Illi Kagan, a master cabinetmaker.**
- **He opened his first shop in East 65th Street, New York City, NY, in 1948. The shop moved to 57th Street in 1950.**
- **Kagan's furniture is held in numerous museum collections, including the V&A, London, and the Vitra Design Museum, Weil am Rhein, Germany.**

A rare Vladimir Kagan oak 'Floating Curve' sofa, with wool upholstery, unmarked.

87in (221cm) wide

$12,000-18,000 **DRA**

One of a pair of 1990s Vladimir Kagan 'Nautilus' lounge chairs, upholstered in ultrasuede, on swivel bases.

36in (91cm) high

$2,500-3,500 pair **DRA**

A Vladimir Kagan oak queen-size headboard, flanked by integrated marble-topped nightstands.

Headboard 156in (396cm) wide

$1,500-2,500 **DRA**

A 1950s Vladimir Kagan mosaic glass, brass and walnut occasional table, for Dreyfuss, unmarked.

24.25in (64cm) diam

$10,000-15,000 **DRA**

A late 1960s Vladimir Kagan walnut-framed upholstered sofa, model no.150BC, unmarked.

118in (300cm) long

$20,000-30,000 **DRA**

A 1950s Vladimir Kagan walnut and wool wing lounge chair and ottoman, model no.503, for Dreyfuss, unmarked.

Chair 41in (104cm) high

$15,000-20,000 **DRA**

A 1950s Vladimir Kagan walnut and wool adjustable lounge chair, model no.VK100, for Dreyfuss, branded.

$5,500-6,500 **DRA**

Judith Picks

I fell in love with the furniture of Poul Kjærholm when I visited and wrote about his home in Denmark and met his widow, the architect Hanne Kjaerholm. Poul Kjærholm (1929-80) learned the craft traditions of woodwork as an apprentice to a cabinetmaker at the age of 15, after which he graduated from the Danish School of Arts and Crafts, where he had studied with the designer Hans Wegner, in 1952. Kjærholm designed modern functionalist furniture that was praised for its understated elegance and clean lines. He softened International style rationalism with naturalistic Nordic design.

This early design combines tubular steel and moulded aluminum. Fewer than 25 examples of the 'Moulded Aluminum Chair' were produced, all of which date from 1953.

A rare and early Poul Kjaerholm 'Moulded Aluminum Chair', manufactured by Chris Sorensen, Denmark, on tubular-steel legs.
1953 *25in (63cm) high*
$35,000-45,000 **DOR**

A John Kapel walnut dresser, for Glenn of California, with stenciled marks.
c1960 *83.25in (211cm) wide*
$1,200-1,800 **DRA**

A 1950s Poul Kjaerholm chrome-plated-steel, leather and plywood 'PK 80' daybed, for E Kold Christensen, stamped with logo.
75in (190.5cm) long
$15,000-20,000 **DRA**

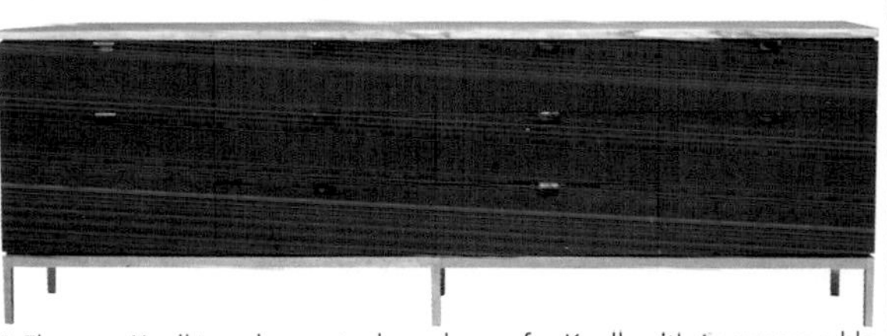

A Florence Knoll ten-drawer teak credenza, for Knoll, with Carrera marble top, unmarked.
74.5in (189cm) wide
$3,000-4,000 **DRA**

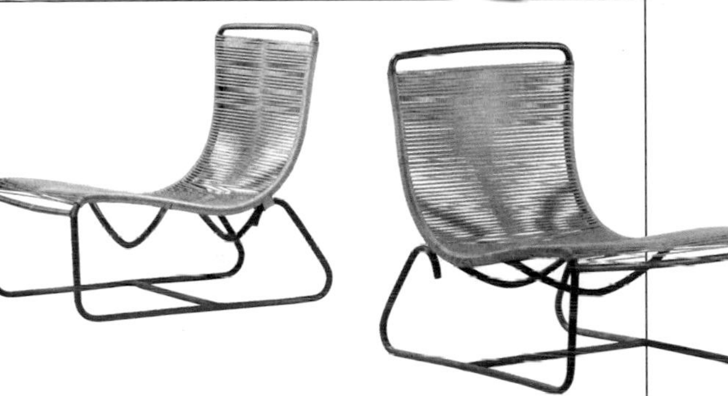

A pair of 1950s Walter Lamb verdigris-patinated-bronze and flagline lounge chairs, unmarked.
29in (73.5cm) high
$5,500-6,500 **DRA**

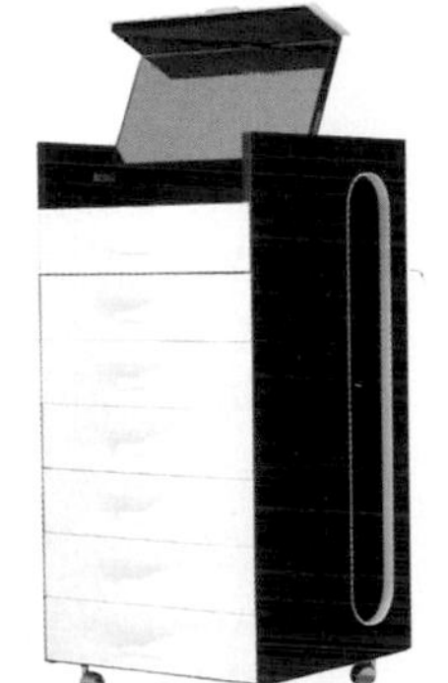

A Raymond Loewy eight-drawer macassar and acrylic valet chest, marked 'DF2000 Made in France'.
42in (107cm) high
$3,000-4,000 **DRA**

A Sam Maloof walnut and ebony rocking chair, with black leather upholstery, with carved signature.
c1970 *44.5in (113cm) high*
$30,000-40,000 **DRA**

An Enzo Mari beech table, manufactured by Simon International, Milan.
Designed 1973 *54.75in (139cm) wide*
$8,000-12,000 **QU**

A pair of 1960s Ludwig Mies van der Rohe stainless-steel and leather 'Barcelona' chairs and ottomans, for Knoll, unmarked.

Chair 30.5in (77.5cm) high

$5,000-7,000 **DRA**

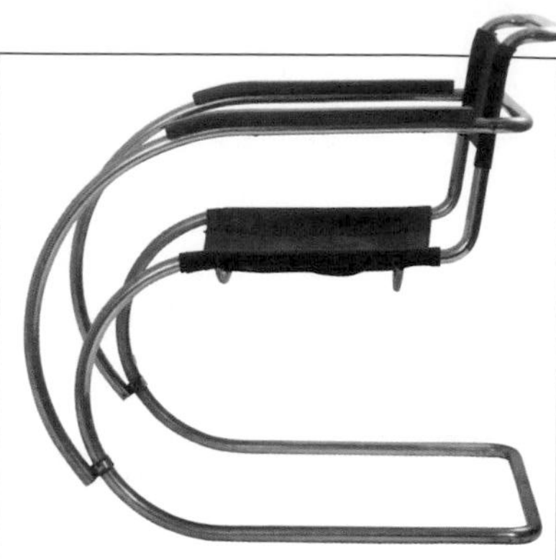

An early 1930s Ludwig Mies van der Rohe chrome-plated 'Weissenhof MR 20' armchair, for Thonet.

This is an early execution of the 'MR 20' chair. The early date is confirmed by the plug connection (without screws) in the back, the two expansion bails below the seat, the wood on the armrests and the joining of the armrests to the frame.

Designed 1927 *32in (81.5cm) high*

$10,000-15,000 **QU**

A Børge Mogensen '2213' sofa, manufactured by Fredericia Furniture, with original black leather, on teak feet.

Designed 1962 *87in (221cm) long*

$3,000-4,000 **FRE**

Two Børge Mogensen teak and brass cabinets, one with five drawers, the other with two doors over shelves, unmarked.

1958 *35.5in (90cm) high*

$10,000-15,000 **DRA**

A pair of Carlo Mollino mahogany-framed armchairs, upholstered in replaced red bouclé, with adjustable backrests.

c1950 *33in (85cm) high*

$8,000-12,000 **DOR**

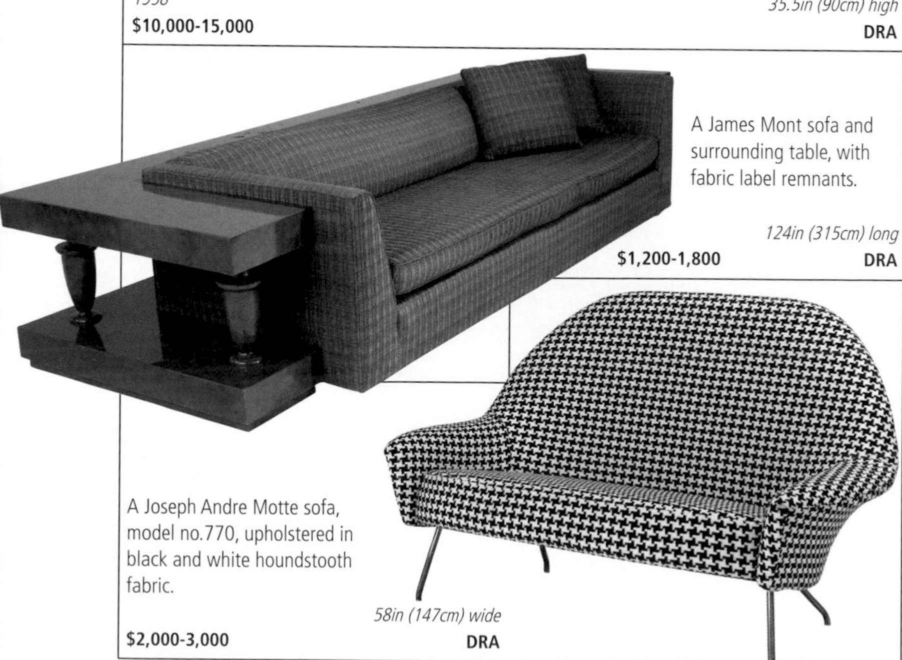

A James Mont sofa and surrounding table, with fabric label remnants.

124in (315cm) long

$1,200-1,800 **DRA**

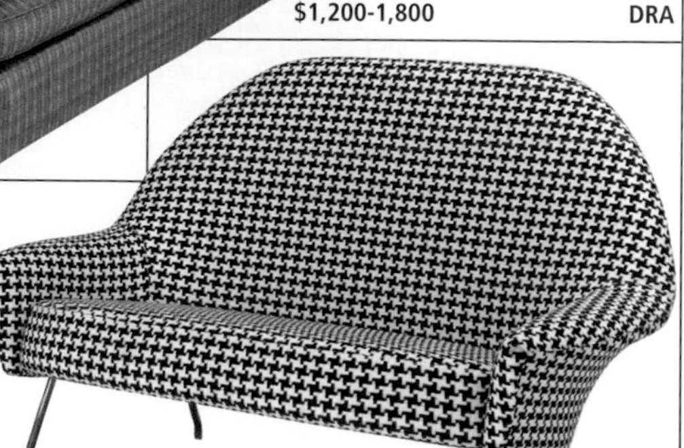

A Joseph Andre Motte sofa, model no.770, upholstered in black and white houndstooth fabric.

58in (147cm) wide

$2,000-3,000 **DRA**

A rare Pascale Mourgue burnt-iron and imitation-leather 'Face à Face' fallfront desk and chair, with magnet lock, chair not shown.

In 1985 Mourgue was awarded the Prix de la Création for this piece.

1985 *Desk 27in (67.5cm) wide*

$2,500-3,500 **DOR**

ESSENTIAL REFERENCE - GEORGE NAKASHIMA

George Nakashima (1905-90) is known as the father of the American Craft Movement.

- **He studied architecture in Seattle and at the Massachusetts Institute of Technology, graduating in 1931.**
- **He learned traditional Japanese carpentry while interned in a US camp 1942-43.**
- **In 1946 he set up a 'craft furniture' studio in New Hope, Pennsylvania.**
- **As well as privately commissioned furniture produced in his own studio, Nakashima also designed furniture for Knoll, including the 'Straight Back Chair'.**
- **Nakashima is best known for his tables topped with large wood slabs with smooth tops but unfinished natural edges.**

A George Nakashima French-olive, burl-ash and walnut 'Minguren II' coffee table, signed, with name of original owner and dated.

1982-83 *42.5in (106.5cm) long*

$55,000-65,000 **DRA**

A George Nakashima English-claro-walnut coffee table, with 'Odakyu' base, signed and dated.

1988 *32in (81cm) wide*

$12,000-18,000 **FRE**

A George Nakashima 'Kornblut' walnut cabinet, signed and dated.

1989 *22in (56cm) high*

$15,000-20,000 **FRE**

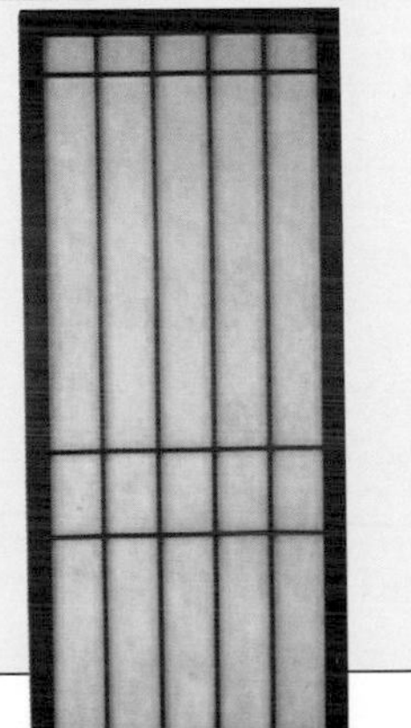

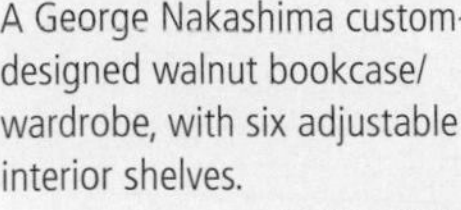

A George Nakashima custom-designed walnut bookcase/ wardrobe, with six adjustable interior shelves.

79.25in (201cm) high

$4,000-6,000 **DRA**

A pair of George Nakashima 'Wohl' walnut tables.

1956 *26.5in (67cm) wide*

$6,500-7,500 **FRE**

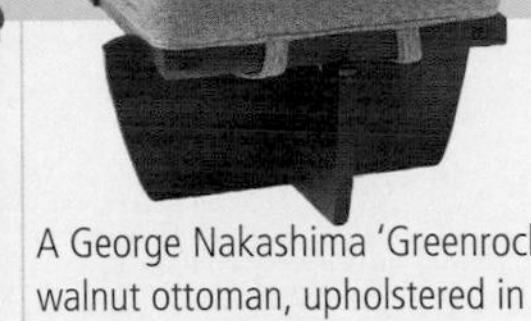

A George Nakashima 'Greenrock' walnut ottoman, upholstered in chenille.

This fabric was hand-selected by Nakashima and is unique to this 'Greenrock' ottoman.

1982 *21.25in (54cm) wide*

$7,000-10,000 **FRE**

A George Nakashima 'Odakyu' cabinet, with Asa-no-ha sliding doors, signed and dated.

'Asa-no-ha' (hemp leaf) is a traditional Japanese pattern. This cabinet was sold with a copy of Nakashima Special Commissions invoice, Full Circle, Inc.

1986 *57.75in (147cm) wide*

$30,000-40,000 **FRE**

A George Nakashima cherrywood credenza, with canvas-backed doors, unmarked.

78.25in (199cm) wide

$8,000-12,000 **DRA**

A pair of George Nakashima walnut 'Cushion' chairs, unmarked.

33in (84cm) wide

$6,500-7,500 **DRA**

A George Nakashima walnut bench, unmarked.

60in (152cm) wide

$8,000-12,000 **DRA**

One of a pair of George Nelson vinyl and enameled-steel 'Coconut' chairs, on chrome-plated-steel legs, with Herman Miller metal tags.

c1950 *41.5in (105cm) high*

$5,000-7,000 pair **DRA**

A George Nelson rosewood, porcelain and aluminum 'Thin Edge' dresser, for Herman Miller, unmarked.

46.75in (118.5cm) wide

$7,000-10,000 **DRA**

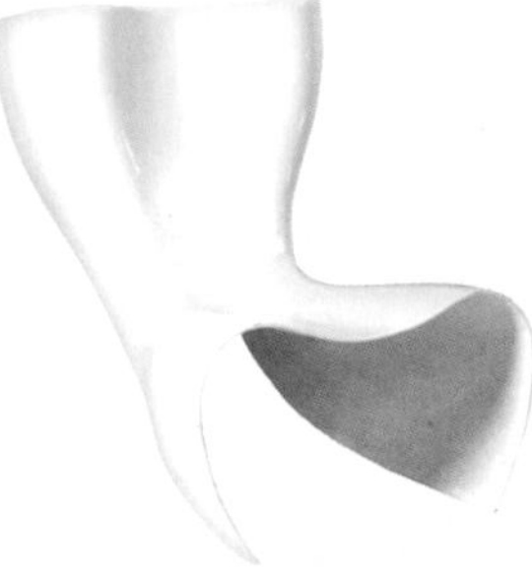

A Marc Newson fiberglass 'Felt' chair, probably manufactured by Cappellini, with polished aluminum leg, unmarked.

33in (84cm) high

$1,500-2,500 **WW**

An Isamu Noguchi walnut and chrome-plated-steel rocking stool, model no.85T, for Knoll, unmarked.

c1955 *14in (36cm) diam*

$5,500-6,500 **DRA**

A set of six Pace Collection chrome-plated-steel and leather barstools, unmarked.

28in (71cm) high

$5,000-7,000 **DRA**

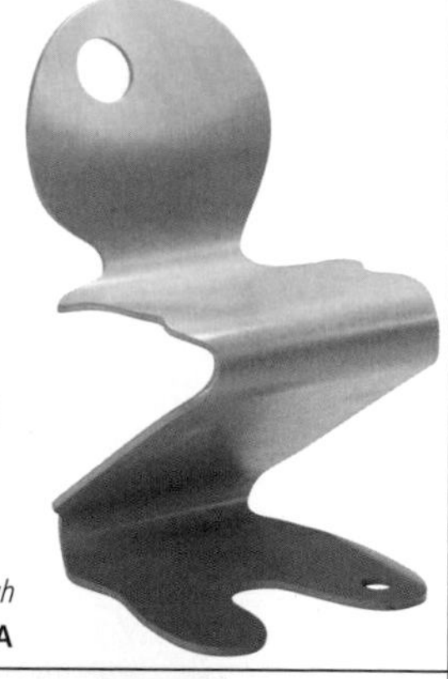

Two Verner Panton 'Pantonic' laminated side chairs, for Studio Hag, unmarked.

Taller 36.5in (93cm) high

$1,500-2,500 **DRA**

A Verner Panton red-lacquered laminated-wood 'Party Set', comprising five stools and a table, for A Sommer, Germany, with black imitation-leather seat cushions.

The 'Party Set' was only produced 1965-67.

Designed 1965 *Table 20in (50cm) diam*

$4,000-6,000 **DOR**

An Ico Parisi veneered sideboard, the glass top with red lacquer, with patinated-brass fittings.

Designed c1958 *52.75in (134cm) wide*

$12,000-18,000 **QU**

A rare Tommi Parzinger mahogany-framed upholstered wing chair, unmarked.

46in (117cm) high

$3,000-4,000 **DRA**

A 1950s Tommi Parzinger undulating mahogany and brass cabinet, for Parzinger Originals, unmarked.

84in (213.5cm) wide

$30,000-40,000 **DRA**

A set of ten Michel Péclard ivory-lacquered laminated-wood stacking stools, for Horgen Glarus, Switzerland, with paper labels 'AIFD', designed in 1960.

These stools are the first model of Péclard's stacking stool. This is confirmed by their reinforced bottoms. 'AIFD' is the manufacturer's code for 1964.

1964 *18in (46cm) high*

$5,000-7,000 **DOR**

A Charlotte Perriand black-stained hardwood stool, for Steph Simon, Paris, designed in 1947.

c1956 *13in (32cm) diam*

$5,000-7,000 **DOR**

One of a pair of Gio Ponti walnut 'Ninfea' folding chairs, for Fratelli Reguitti, Italy, with cane seats.

Designed 1958 *27in (69cm) high*

$10,000-15,000 pair **DOR**

A Phillip Lloyd Powell walnut bench.

96in (244cm) wide

$15,000-20,000 **FRE**

A Gio Ponti walnut three-door cabinet, for Singer & Sons, Italy, unmarked.

71in (180.5cm) wide

$12,000-18,000 **DRA**

A 1960s Phillip Lloyd Powell sculpted and chip-carved American-black-walnut sofa, unmarked.

78.5in (200cm) wide

$20,000-25,000 **DRA**

A Jean Prouvé & Jules Leleu armchair and side table, manufactured by Les Ateliers Jean Prouvé, Nancy, designed for the Martel de Janville Sanatorium, Passy, with replaced seat cushion.

c1934 *Table 20in (50cm) long*

$6,500-7,500 **DOR**

A set of four Jean Prouvé black-lacquered steel and laminated wood 'Standard' chairs, model no.4, manufactured by Les Ateliers Jean Prouvé, Nancy, designed in 1934.

c1950 *32in (81cm) high*

$25,000-30,000 **DOR**

A Jean Prouvé red-lacquered tubular-iron and laminated-oak 'Visiteur' armchair, manufactured by Les Ateliers Jean Prouvé, Nancy, with oak armrests and ball feet, designed in 1942.

c1950 *29in (74cm) high*

$35,000-45,000 **DOR**

One of a pair of steel-framed armchairs, attributed to Gustavo Finali Pulitzer, manufactured by Artlex, Milan.

Designed 1960s *36.5in (93cm) high*

$8,000-12,000 pair **QU**

A 1940s Gerrit Rietveld painted wood 'Military' stool, branded 'H.G.M. G.A.v.d. GROENEKAN DE BILT NEDERLAND'.

17.5in (44.5cm) high

$5,500-6,500 **DRA**

A Willy Rizzo lounge chair and ottoman, embroidered 'Willy Rizzo', 'Hand crafted in Italy' label.

Chair 41in (104cm) high

$500-700 **DRA**

A late 1950s T H Robsjohn-Gibbings mahogany cabinet, with decal Widdicomb label.

63in (160cm) high

$10,000-15,000 **DRA**

A T H Robsjohn-Gibbings walnut dresser, with gilded-porcelain pulls, with fabric Widdicomb label.

69.75in (177cm) wide

$2,000-3,000 **DRA**

A pair of Gilbert Rohde mahogany and leather dressers, for Herman Miller.

44.5in (113cm) wide

$3,000-4,000 **DRA**

A Richard Schultz aluminum '42' contour chaise longue, for Knoll, with woven Dacron mesh seat.

Designed 1967 *58in (147cm) long*

$1,200-1,800 **FRE**

A Walter Schulz tubular-steel chair, manufactured by Schapermöbel, Frankfurt.

Designed 1929 *29.5in (74.5cm) high*

$3,000-4,000 **QU**

One of a pair of Don Shoemaker jacaranda and leather lounge chairs, manufactured by Señal SA, with rocking seats, unmarked.

In the 1950s and '60s these chairs were advertised as the 'Sling Casual' chairs. Don Shoemaker is the most important representative of Mexican Modernism furniture design.

c1960 *33.25in (84cm) high*

$5,000-7,000 pair **DRA**

An André Sornay sycamore armoire, with copper-inlaid decoration, unmarked.

66in (168cm) wide

$3,000-4,000 **DRA**

A Hugo Cesar Tonti iron, wood and bone console table, unmarked.

Tonti is a famous Argentinian artist and furniture maker.

78.25in (199cm) long

$5,000-7,000 **DRA**

Aldo Tura

An Aldo Tura bar cabinet, manufactured by Tura, Milan, the wooden frame covered with kid leather, decorated with an architectural pattern, with glass interior, one glass marked 'Vetro CB Seveso'.

c1960 *54in (136cm) high*

$10,000-15,000 **QU**

One of a pair of Guglielmo Ulrich walnut and mohair lounge chairs, unmarked.

31in (79cm) high

$5,000-7,000 pair **DRA**

A Ueli Berger, Eleanora Peduzzi-Riva & Heinz Ulrich leather twenty-two-channel 'Non-Stop' sofa, for De Sede/Stendig, unmarked.

Arm section 41in (104cm) long

$10,000-15,000 **DRA**

One of a pair of Hans Wegner oak armchairs, model no.CH-22, branded 'Designer/Hans J. Wegner/made in Denmark/by Carl Hansen & Son/ Odense Denmark', embossed '80'.

Designed 1950 *29in (73cm) high*

$5,000-7,000 pair **DOR**

A 1960s Hans Wegner teak-framed 'Papa Bear' chair, stamped, with metal control label for A P Stolen, Denmark.

Designed 1951 *39in (99cm) high*

$4,000-6,000 **DRA**

A Hans Wegner mahogany 'PP505 Cowhorn' chair, for Johannes Hansen, with leather seat, with applied label.

Provenance: Reputedly from the estate of the managing director (UK) of Finmar.

28.75in (73cm) high

$3,500-4,500 **WW**

A Lawrence Weiner bamboo 'Axis' chair, for Meta-Memphis, Milan, the oak backrest with copper inlays.

This example is no.11 from the limited edition of 25.

1991 *61in (154cm) high*

$6,500-7,500 **DOR**

A Franz West 'Uncle' armchair, model no.P278.

A unique piece (designed in 2001) from the limited edition featuring different variations of this model (all produced from 2005). The 'Uncle' chair rarely occurs as an armchair.

2006 *33in (85cm) high*

$7,000-10,000 DOR

A Robert Whitley walnut Windsor rocking chair, inscribed 'An original furniture design by Robert C. Whitley Solebury, Bucks County, PA.'

c1960 *40.5in (103cm) high*

$4,000-6,000 DRA

A pair of Edward Wormley leather and mahogany 'Spinneybeck' wing armchairs, for Dunbar, unmarked.

37in (94cm) high

$12,000-18,000 DRA

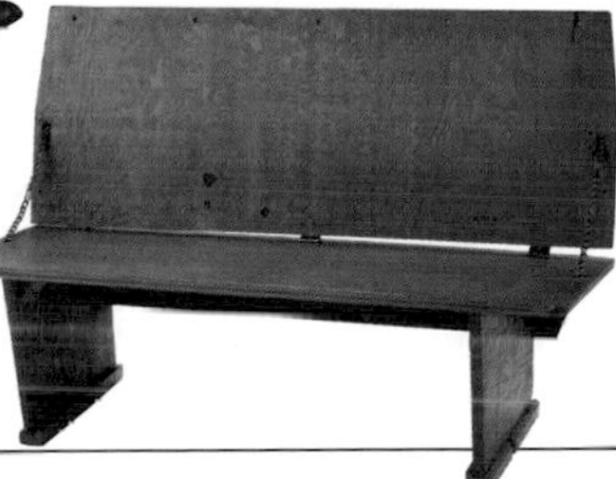

A Frank Lloyd Wright plywood bench, branded 'FLW51'.

Provenance: Meeting House, First Unitarian Society, Madison, WI, USA.

1951 *42in (107cm) high*

$2,000-3,000 DRA

ESSENTIAL REFERENCE - SORI YANAGI

Sori Yanagi (1915-2011) was a Japanese designer, known for combining traditional Japanese craftsmanship and new techniques in his furniture.

- **He studied painting and architecture at the Tokyo School of Fine Arts from 1934.**
- **He was influenced by Le Corbusier.**
- **He worked in Charlotte Perriand's Toyko office 1900-42.**
- **In 1952, he founded the Yanagi Industrial Design Institute,**
- **The 'Butterfly' stool (1954) is perhaps his most famous design. The shape is representative of a butterfly's wings or the gateway to a Shinto shrine.**
- **As well as furniture, he also designed lighting, glass objects, cutlery, toys, metro stations and cars.**

A Sori Yanagi rosewood 'Butterfly' stool, manufactured by Tendo, with brass hardware, unmarked.

17.5in (44cm) high

$3,000-4,000 DRA

One of a pair of birch lounge chairs, attributed to Russel Wright, with original vinyl upholstery.

31in (79cm) high

$1,200-1,800 pair DRA

A pair of lacquered-walnut dressers, for Grosfeld House, with tooled-leather fronts and nickel-plated brass handles, unmarked.

36.5in (93cm) wide

$3,000-4,000 DRA

One of a pair of walnut and leather lounge chairs, in the style of Ib Kofod-Larsen, unmarked.

32in (81cm) high

$5,500-6,500 pair DRA

A Design Institute of America console table, with brass, chrome and enameled-metal base and plate glass top.

47.75in (121cm) wide

$1,200-1,800 DRA

A Laura Andreson earthenware bowl, covered in semi-matt glaze, signed 'Laura Andreson 1955'.

1955 *5.25in (13cm) diam*

$1,200-1,800 **DRA**

An Arzberg 'Fantasia' tea-for-one set, designed by Matteo Thun, with printed marks, with original box.

Teapot 4.25in (11cm) high

$120-180 **WW**

A Piero Fornasetti ceramic jar and cover, printed with a frieze of book spines, with printed factory mark.

9.75in (25cm) high

$400-600 **WW**

A Rosenthal 15-piece 'TAC2' coffee set, designed by Walter Gropius and Louis McMillen.

Designed 1969

Coffeepot 9in (23cm) high

$8,000-12,000 **QU**

A James Melchert 'reassembled' glazed stoneware tile, signed and dated.

1998 *14in (36cm) high*

$1,500-2,500 **DRA**

Judith Picks

Pablo Picasso (1881-1973) was one of the great, or perhaps the greatest, 20thC painter, but his ceramics were also remarkable. All of Picasso's ceramics were produced at the Madoura pottery run by Suzanne and Georges Ramié in Vallauris in the south of France. Picasso first visited the pottery in 1946 and returned every year. In 24 years over 633 pieces were created in limited editions. Familiar themes included portraits, bull-fighting scenes and nature – birds, goats and fish. Edition Picasso ceramics were made in multiples of 25 to 500.

At Christie's in June 2012 a new world record price was paid for a Picasso ceramic edition. The 'Grand vase aux femmes voilées' realized $1,177,000.

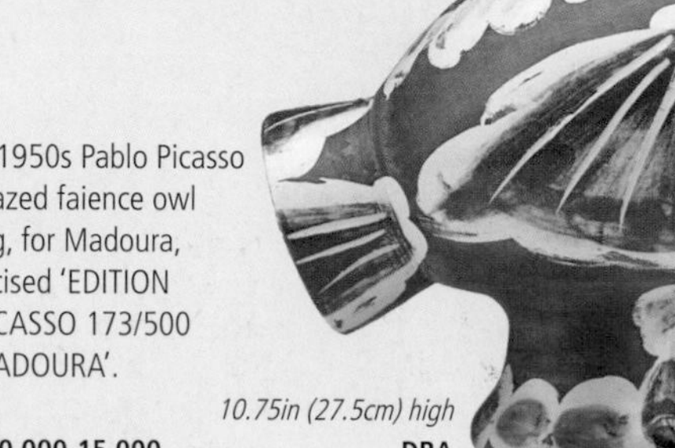

A 1950s Pablo Picasso glazed faience owl jug, for Madoura, incised 'EDITION PICASSO 173/500 MADOURA'.

10.75in (27.5cm) high

$10,000-15,000 **DRA**

A Wiener Werkstätte glazed ceramic vessel, designed by Hilda Jesser, stamped 'WW MADE IN AUSTRIA 974'.

c1920 *9in (23cm) high*

$3,000-4,000 **DRA**

A Pablo Picasso glazed faience plate, for Madoura, signed 'N.202 EDITION PICASSO 14/500 MADOURA'.

10in (25.5cm) diam

$5,500-6,500 **DRA**

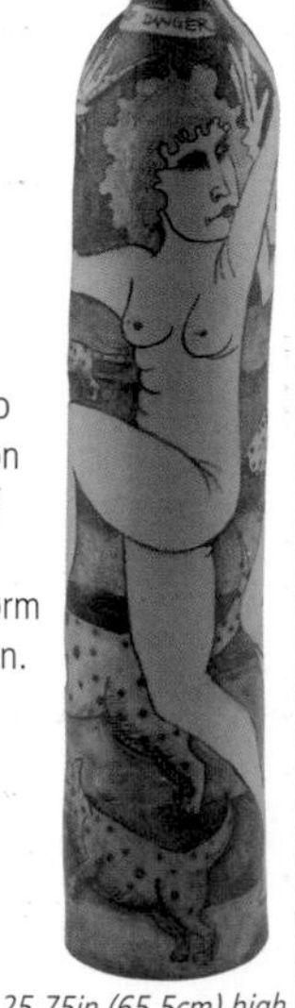

A tall Amanda Popham 'Grant This Day' bottle vase and cover, painted with two dancing nudes on a background of spotty dogs, the stopper in the form of a nude woman.

2007 *25.75in (65.5cm) high*

$400-600 **WW**

ESSENTIAL REFERENCE - AXEL SALTO

Danish designer Axel Salto (1889-1961) is renowned for his nature-inspired sculptural forms and his rich glazes.

- **Salto's work can be divided into three main categories. 'Fluted' pieces were based on simple repetitive patterns. The 'budding' style was reputedly inspired by chestnuts and eucalyptus fruits, while the 'sprouting' style was inspired by growing plants.**
- **After meeting Picasso and Matisse in Paris in 1916, Salto decided to found an arts journal, 'Klingen'.**
- **He won numerous awards, including the Grand Prix at the Milan Triennale 1951.**
- **He worked at Royal Copenhagen from the 1930s until his death.**

A Royal Copenhagen glazed stoneware vase, designed by Axel Salto, stamped 'Royal Copenhagen Denmark', etched 'SALTO 20561'

8.5in (21.5cm) high

$5,500-6,500 **DRA**

A Royal Copenhagen glazed stoneware 'Budding' vase, designed by Axel Salto, stamped 'Royal Copenhagen Denmark', etched 'SALTO 21454'.

4.5in (11.5cm) high

$4,000-6,000 **DRA**

An Adrian Saxe glazed ceramic 'Ampersand' teapot, with cactus lid, inset with crystals, signed and dated.

1998 *11.25in (28.5cm) high*

$12,000-18,000 **DRA**

A Toshiko Takaezu glazed stoneware garden stool, with rattle, unmarked.

1965-70 *21in (53.5cm) high*

$10,000-15,000 **DRA**

A Toshiko Takaezu glazed porcelain 'Moonpot' vessel, with rattle, incised 'TT'.

7.75in (19.5cm) high

$4,000-6,000 **DRA**

A Dennis Chinaworks limited edition 'Dogwood' vase, designed by Sally Tuffin, no.10/25, applied with bees, with printed and painted marks, dated.

2006 *12in (30.5cm) high*

$550-750 **WW**

A Dennis Chinaworks limited edition 'Peacock' vase and cover, designed by Sally Tuffin, no.'16/40', with printed and painted marks, dated.

2007 *12.25in (31cm) high*

$800-1,200 **WW**

A Peter Voulkos glazed figural stoneware platter, signed.

14.5in (37cm) wide

$10,000-15,000 **DRA**

A Peter Voulkos slab-built stoneware charger, decorated with a figure, signed.

14in (35.5cm) diam

$8,000-12,000 **DRA**

A Beatrice Wood luster-glazed ceramic bowl, with metallic teal glaze, signed 'BEATO.'

4.75in (12cm) diam

$1,500-2,500 **FRE**

A Beatrice Wood ceramic chalice, decorated with mother and child medallions, signed 'BEATO B181, BWTF#283'.

10.5in (26.5cm) high

$4,000-6,000 **DRA**

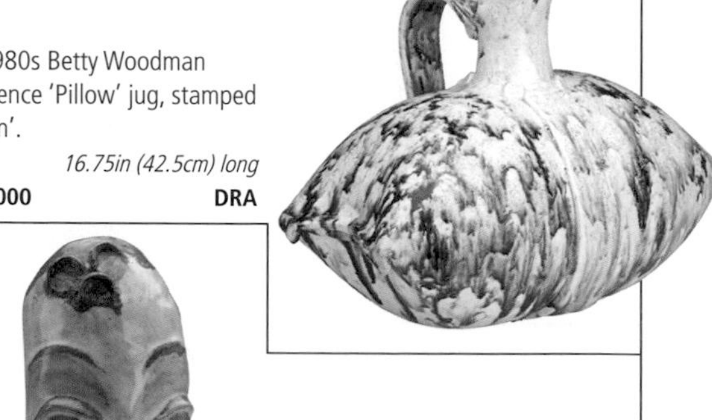

A large 1980s Betty Woodman glazed faience 'Pillow' jug, stamped 'Woodman'.

16.75in (42.5cm) long

$5,000-7,000 **DRA**

A Wiener Werkstätte glazed ceramic bust, designed by Gudrun Baudisch-Wittke, stamped 'G B WW no.345 MADE IN AUSTRIA no. 7'.

9.5in (24.5cm) high

$8,000-12,000 **DRA**

A Jack Earl glazed ceramic 'The What Kind of Dog is That Dog' sculpture, signed 'Jack Earl Ohio 1976'.

This sculpture was made for the Kohler Foundation in WI, USA.

1976 *25in (64cm) long*

$5,000-7,000 **DRA**

A John Maltby stoneware 'Royal Barge' sculpture, with applied metal decoration, on painted wood base with painted title, date and signature, with impressed seal mark.

2007 *15.25in (39cm) high*

$1,200-1,800 **WW**

A John Maltby stoneware group of '3 Figures (St Ives)', with impressed seal mark, with painted signature and title.

16.25in (41cm) wide

$1,500-2,500 **WW**

A Tom Rippon porcelain sculpture of 'Chicago'.

1975 *21in (53cm) wide*

$250-350 **DRA**

A large Sunkoo Yuh glazed stoneware 'Congregation' sculpture, unsigned.

1999 *80in (203cm) high*

$15,000-20,000 **DRA**

A Vic Bamforth & Allister Malcolm clear crystal 'Heroes of Glass' vase, with engraved signatures, no.'13/33'.

The glass is internally decorated with a hand-painted frieze depicting landmarks, individuals and dates relating to the Stourbridge Glass Industry and the International Festival of Glass.

7.5in (19cm) high

$2,000-3,000 **FLD**

CLOSER LOOK - 'MACCHIA' GROUP

Derived from the Latin 'macula', the Italian word 'macchia' means a stain.

Chihuly found modern equivalencies for filigree designs (latticinio) and woven glass (varo tessuto).

The undulating forms of Chihuly's 'Macchia' objects can be seen as a critique of the handkerchief shapes that Fulvio Bianconi designed in the 1940s.

A Dale Chihuly amber and red glass eight-piece 'Macchia' group, the largest piece signed and dated.

2005 *Largest 12.75in (33.5cm) long*

$30,000-40,000 **DRA**

An early Howard Ben Tré glass vase, signed 'Ben Tré Pilchuck 77'.

Howard Ben Tré is a pioneer in the use of cast glass as a sculptural medium.

1977 *4.5in (11.5cm) high*

$650-850 **DRA**

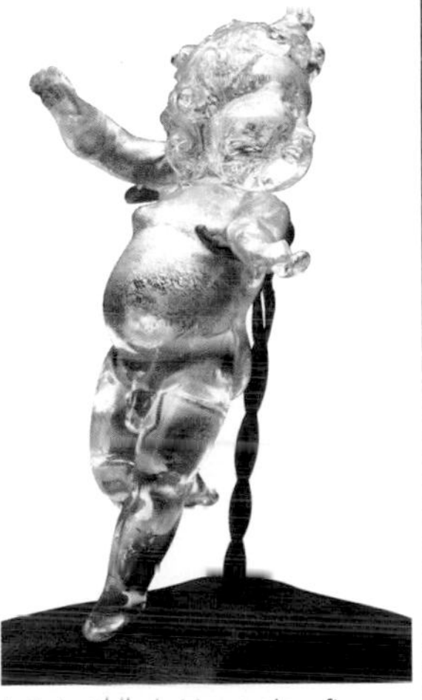

A Dale Chihuly blown glass figure of a putto, with gold foil inclusions.

6.5in (17cm) high

$1,200-1,800 **DRA**

A Dale Chihuly cobalt, red and gold glass 'Piccolo' vase, unsigned.

16.5in (42cm) high

$5,000-7,000 **DRA**

A large late 20thC Ieslyn Davies glass 'Tutti Frutti' bowl, for Blowzone, cased in six colors and decorated with elliptical cuts, unsigned.

9.5in (24cm) diam

$1,500-2,500 **FLD**

A Laura De Santillana blown and compressed glass 'Dawn II' sculpture, signed and dated.

2002 *15.5in (39.5cm) high*

$15,000-20,000 **DRA**

A unique John Ford glass 'Graal' vase, cased in clear crystal over 'Reflex Blue', 'Gorgeous Grape' and 'Burnt Sienna' glass, decorated with stylized fish, signed and dated, no.'1/1', with box and certificate.

2000 *12in (31cm) high*

$2,000-3,000 **FLD**

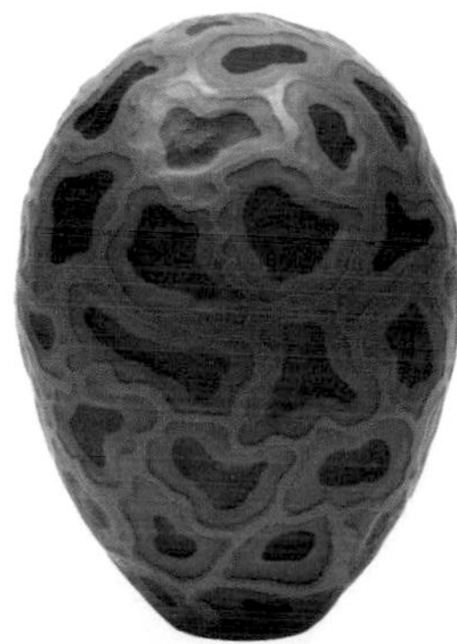

A Monica Guggisberg & Philip Baldwin glass 'Tricolor African' vase, Paris, carved with a 'giraffe' pattern, with carved signature 'B/G 02 # B 1252'.

2002 *12in (30cm) high*

$5,000-7,000 **DOR**

A Jonathan Harris & Allister Malcolm hand-blown glass vase, with a swirled tonal-blue, celadon-green and silver-aventurine ground, internally decorated with silver-leaf carp, with engraved signature, no.'8/33'.

7in (18cm) high

$5,000-7,000 **FLD**

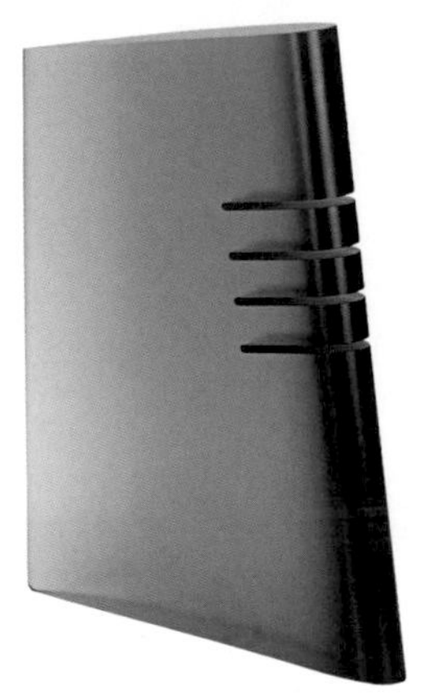

A Petr Hora cast, cut and polished glass sculpture, signed and dated.

2000 *16.5in (42cm) high*

$3,000-4,000 **DRA**

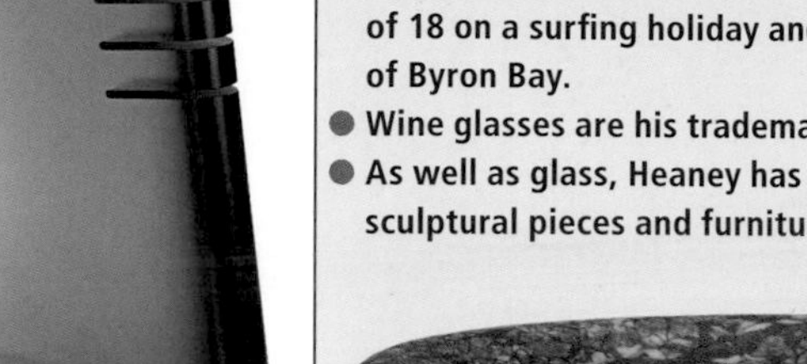

ESSENTIAL REFERENCE - COLIN HEANY

After working as a sculptor, Colin Heaney began to make art glass in 1982, having largely taught himself to blow and manipulate hot glass.

- **He was born in Canada, but traveled to Australia at the age of 18 on a surfing holiday and stayed, settling in the town of Byron Bay.**
- **Wine glasses are his trademark.**
- **As well as glass, Heaney has produced fabricated sculptural pieces and furniture using mixed media.**

A Colin Heaney blown glass and metallic powder 'Red Mortar' bowl, signed and dated, marked 'M208'.

1998 *7.25in (18.5cm) high*

$5,500-6,500 **DRA**

A rare Jon Kuhn glass 'Golden Expanse' sculpture, with internal flakes of colored glass and gold foil, on a metal stand.

2005 *15.75in (40cm) high*

$8,000-12,000 **FIS**

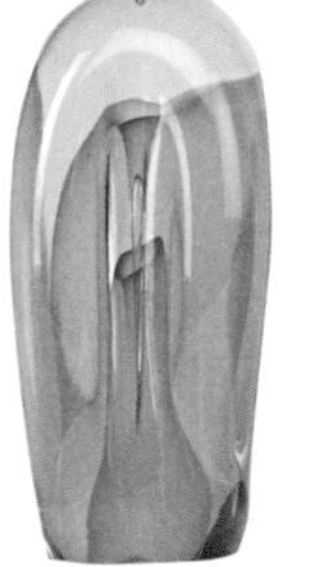

A Dominick Labino glass sculpture, from the 'Emergence' series, signed and dated.

1976 *8.25in (21cm) high*

$2,500-3,500 **DRA**

A Stanislav Libenský & Jaroslava Brychtová molded and polished glass sculpture, for Železnobrodské Sklo, decorated with fish.

1969 *7in (18cm) high*

$3,000-4,000 **FIS**

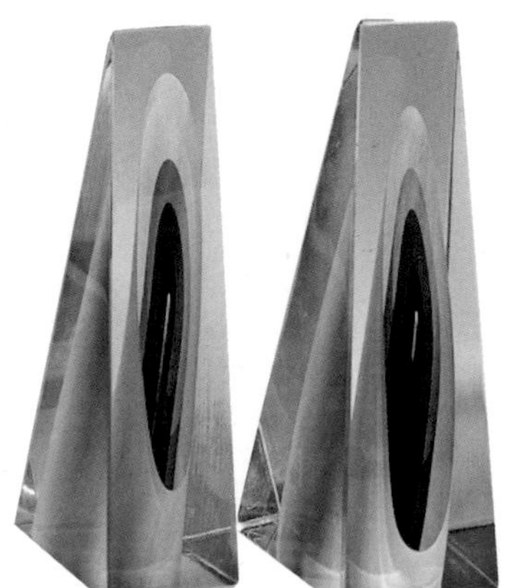

A pair of Harvey K Littleton glass 'Triangular Section' sculptures.

1981 *10in (25.5cm) high*

$6,500-7,500 **FIS**

A John Littleton & Kate Vogel blown glass 'Acrobag' vessel, signed and dated.

1993 *16.25in (41.5cm) high*

$2,000-3,000 **DRA**

A Charles Lotton iridescent glass 'Jack in the Pulpit' vase, with pulled internal decoration, signed and dated.

1991 *16in (41cm) high*

$1,000-1,500 **LHA**

A Richard Marquis blown and sculpted glass 'Whole Elk Tower #2', vessel, decorated with zanfirico rods, unsigned.
2001 *12.25in (31cm) high*
$7,000-9,000 **DRA**

A William Morris blown glass 'Untitled Vessel', signed and dated.
1984 *14in (35.5cm) high*
$10,000-15,000 **DRA**

ESSENTIAL REFERENCE - WILLIAM MORRIS

William Morris (b.1957) was born in Carmel, CA and now lives in the Pacific Northwest, USA. He was educated at California State University and Central Washington University.

- **He worked as Dale Chihuly's gaffer (lead glassblower) in the early 1980s.**
- **He is influenced by archaeology, ancient pagan cultures and Murano glass.**
- **Morris is known for his treatment of surface texture. He achieves these effects using various techniques, such as sprinkling powdered glass and minerals onto a blown surface, etching and acid washing.**

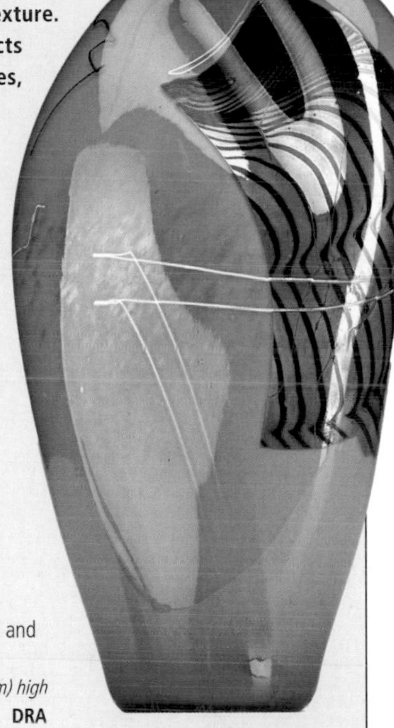

A William Morris blown glass vase, with red lip wrap, signed and dated, marked '305'.
1980 *11.5in (29.5cm) high*
$2,000-3,000 **DRA**

A William Morris glass 'Stonehenge' vase, signed and dated.
1984 *12.25in (31cm) high*
$7,000-10,000 **DRA**

A 1980s Philip Moulthrop glass 'Turned Mimosa' spherical bowl, signed 'Philip Moulthrop Mimosa'.
8in (20.5cm) high
$3,000-4,000 **DRA**

A 1980s Orient & Flume iridescent glass vase, with pulled silver glass over a cobalt ground, signed and dated 'Orient & Flume D 50'.
1983 *10.5in (27cm) high*
$200-300 **LHA**

A Michael Pavlik cut, polished and laminated glass 'Virtual Equinox Series #1721' sculpture, marked '1771', signed and dated.
1982 *9.5in (24cm) high*
$10,000-15,000 **DRA**

A miniature Barry Sautner & Doug Merritt glass vase, carved in bas-relief with interlocking circles, signed and dated 'Barry Sautner Doug Merritt Vandermark GPCL #1'.
1984 *3in (7.5cm) high*
$650-850 **DRA**

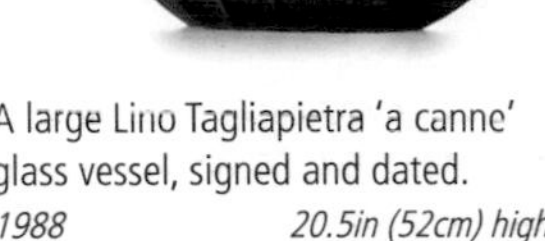

A large Lino Tagliapietra 'a canne' glass vessel, signed and dated.
1988 *20.5in (52cm) high*
$12,000-18,000 **DRA**

An early Steve Tobin blown and sandblasted glass 'Cityscape' bowl, signed and dated.

1984 *21.75in (55cm) diam*

$1,000-1,500 DRA

A Bertil Vallien sand-cast glass 'Head Resting I' sculpture, with etched signature and 'Kosta Boda unique BVAUN 97041'.

1997 *7.75in (19.5cm) long*

$5,500-6,500 DRA

An Elliot Walker & Richard P Golding hand-blown vase, internally decorated with applied flowers and foliage, with engraved marks.

7.75in (20cm) high

$1,200-1,800 FLD

A Tsuchida Yasuhiko glass 'One's Will' vessel, overlaid in marbled opalescent beige, with red rimline, carved 'Tsuchida Yasuhiko', titled and dated.

2007 *10in (25cm) high*

$5,500-6,500 DOR

A Giorgio Vigna limited edition iridescent glass 'Fior d'acqua' vase, from the 'Millenium III' collection for Venini, signed and marked '37/99'.

In 1999 Venini commissioned ten works by the designers who featured in the most recent Venini collection: Gae Aulenti, Emmanuel Babled, Mario Bellini, Rodolfo Dordoni, Monica Guggisberg, Philip Baldwin, Alessandro Mendini, Alejandro Ruiz, Ettore Sottsass, Giorgio Vigna, and Marco Zanini. All the pieces commissioned were made in limited editions of 99.

1999 *21.3in (54cm) high*

$2,000-3,000 FIS

A Tsuchida Yasuhiko glass 'Cubism Vessel' vase, internally decorated with red meshwork, partially cased in violet, with silver foil inclusions and colored bands, the exterior martelé-cut, with violet rimline, with carved signature and date.

2000 *10in (23.5cm) high*

$6,000-8,000 DOR

ESSENTIAL REFERENCE - MARY ANN 'TOOTS' ZYNSKY

Mary Ann 'Toots' Zynsky (b.1951) graduated from the Rhode Island School of Design, RI, in 1973. She also studied at the Haystack Mountain School of Crafts in Deer Isle and the Pilchuck Glass School, where she was a contemporary of Dale Chihuly.

- **She worked as assistant director and head of the hot shop for New York's Experimental Glass Workshop (Urban Glass).**
- **She is best known for glass vessels created using the 'filet de verre' technique, which she developed in 1982. 'Filet de verre' is the process of pulling glass threads from hot glass canes.**
- **Her glass vessels are represented in over 70 international museum collections, including the Metropolitan Museum of Art in New York and the Smithsonian in Washington.**

A Mary Ann 'Toots' Zynsky fused and thermo-formed glass bowl, from the 'Tierra del Fuego' series, signed 'Z'.

1988 *13in (33cm) diam*

$10,000-15,000 DRA

A Mary Ann 'Toots' Zynsky glass 'Folto' vase, for Venini, Murano, with incised signature, with old factory label.

This vase was designed in 1984 in Boston, USA.

1989 *10in (25.5cm) high*

$2,500-3,500 DOR

A large Mary Ann 'Toots' Zynsky 'filet-de-verre' glass 'Ramingo' vessel, signed 'Z'.

8.5in (21.5cm) diam

$25,000-30,000 DRA

A silver rose bowl centerpiece, by Graham K Arthur, London the detachable grille with sixteen candle/flower holders and two domed and pierced flower holders, inscribed 'designed and made by Graham K Arthur, 1970'.

1970 *11in (27.5cm) diam 65oz*

$6,000-8,000 **WW**

A parcel-gilt silver 'Aurum' goblet, by Desmond Clen-Murphy, London, no.'198/600'.

These goblets were made to commemorate Chichester Cathedral's ninth centenary.

1976 *6.5in (17cm) high 10.2oz*

$400-600 **DN**

A pair of 1930s Donald Deskey aluminium and enameled-steel andirons, unmarked.

17.75in (45cm) high

$5,500-6,500 **DRA**

A Stuart Devlin silver-gilt limited edition 'surprise' egg, London, with bark texturing, the interior with three enameled trembling flowers, no.'10'.

1968 *3in (7cm) high 5oz*

$500-700 **DN**

A Stuart Devlin parcel-gilt silver jug, London, with a gilt band of irregular wirework on a matted ground, with falcon crest.

This jug was presented as a President Falcon Award by the Hambro Life Assurance's Falcon Club in 1979.

1979 *7.5in (19cm) high 15oz*

$2,000-3,000 **MAB**

ESSENTIAL REFERENCE - STUART DEVLIN

Stuart Devlin (b.1931) was born in Australia and studied gold- and silversmithing at the Royal Melbourne Institute of Technology, Melbourne and the Royal College of Art, London.

- **In 1964 he designed Australia's first decimal coinage.**
- **He opened a workshop in London in 1965.**
- **In 1982 he was made Goldsmith to the Queen.**
- **He was Prime Warden of the Goldsmith's Company in 1996-97.**
- **Devlin has designed furniture (see p.596), interiors, jewelry and stainless steel, but is best known for his silver, which often features contrasts between shiny silver surfaces and textured gold.**

A Stuart Devlin parcel-gilt silver salver, London, with a textured gilt rim, stamped with a falcon crest.

This salver was presented as a President Falcon Award by the Hambro Life Assurance's Falcon Club in 1978.

1978 *14in (35.5cm) diam 40oz*

$2,000-3,000 **MAB**

A set of eight Stuart Devlin parcel-gilt silver wine goblets, the gilt-washed bowls with beaten effect exterior, on silver-gilt stems.

1973 *6.25in (16cm) high 56oz*

$5,000-7,000 **TEN**

A silver footed-bowl, Leslie Gordon Durbin, London, with hand-beaten interior and exterior, with maker's mark 'LGD'.

1971

$2,000-3,000 **TEN**

A David Mellor silver four-piece 'Pride' tea service, Walker & Hall, Sheffield, the pots with leather-covered handles and ebonized wood finials, the teapot with re-covered handle.

The 'Pride' tea service was designed by David Mellor in 1958. In 1959 it won a Council of Industrial Design award for both aesthetic and practical reasons.

1962/63 *69oz*

$3,000-4,000 **TEN**

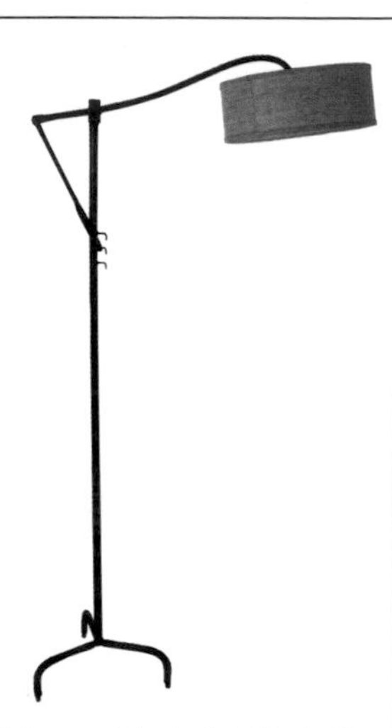

A Jacques Adnet adjustable leather floor lamp, with drum shade, stamped 'Made in France'.

67in (170cm) high

$3,000-4,000 DRA

A Jacques Adnet leather and brass table lamp, unmarked.

26.75in (68cm) high

$3,000-4,000 DRA

An Arredoluce chrome-plated-brass three-arm floor lamp, with enameled steel shades, stamped 'Arredoluce Monza Italy'.

c1950 81in (206cm) high

$8,000-12,000 DRA

An Arredoluce brass floor lamp, with blue-painted aluminum shade, marked 'Made in Italy. Arredoluce Monza'.

Designed c1955

69.25in (176cm) high

$4,500-5,500 QU

ESSENTIAL REFERENCE - CASTIGLIONI BROTHERS

Livio (1911-79), Pier Giacomo (1913-68) and Achille Castiglioni (1918-2002) graduated from the Polytechnic Institute of Milan, Italy, in 1936, 1937 and 1944 respectively.

- **Livio and Pier Giacomo set up a studio in 1938. Achille joined in 1944, while Livio left in 1952.**
- **Pier Giacomo and Achille are known for such famous designs as the 'Arco' lamp (1962) and the 'Allunaggio' (moonlanding) seat (1966).**
- **They helped establish the ADI (Associazione per il Disegno Industriale) in 1956.**
- **Achille Castiglioni continued to work at his Milan studio until his death. It is now open to the public as Studio Museum Castiglioni.**

An Achille Castiglioni & Pier Giacomo Castiglioni 'Arco' floor lamp, for Flos, unmarked.

98.5in (250cm) high

$1,500-2,500 DRA

An Arteluce '1098' floor lamp, designed by Cini Boeri.

Designed 1968

47.5in (121cm) high

$1,500-2,500 QU

An Achille Castiglioni plastic pendant lampshade, for Flos.

c1960 19in (48cm) high

$250-350 FRE

An Achille Castiglioni chrome-plated and plastic 'Frisbi' ceiling lamp, for Flos, with maker's label and mark.

Designed 1978 23.5in (60cm) diam

$400-600 QU

A Colombini & Guzzetti perspex and aluminum 'Psycho' table lamp, manufactured by Lamperti, Italy.

Designed 1971 18in (46cm) high

$12,000-18,000 QU

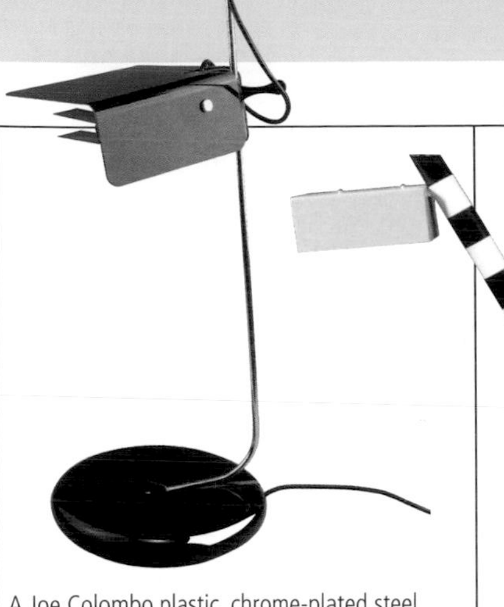

A Joe Colombo plastic, chrome-plated steel and metal 'Anubis' table lamp, manufactured by Forma e Funzione, Varese, marked 'made in italy', 'FORMA e FUNZIONE VARESE' and 'Designer Joe Colombo'.

1969 *25.5in (65cm) high*

$1,000-1,500 **QU**

A Memphis painted tubular-metal 'Oceanic' table lamp, designed by Michele de Lucchi.

Designed 1980 *29.25in (74cm) high*

$1,000-1,500 **QU**

A Stuart Devlin parcel-gilt silver three-light candelabrum and four matching parcel-gilt candle holders and shades, London.

1969

$12,000-18,000 **WW**

A Bruno Gecchelin chrome-plated-steel and marble 'Mezzaluna' floor lamp, manufactured by Skipper, Milan.

Designed 1975 *91.75in (233cm) high*

$800-1,200 **QU**

A Franca Helg aluminum and perspex '601' table lamp, manufactured by Arteluce, labeled 'AL ARTELUCE MILANO'.

Designed 1963 *16.5in (42cm) high*

$8,000-12,000 **QU**

A Poul Henningsen copper, enameled-copper and chrome-plated-steel 'Artichoke' ceiling lamp, for Louis Poulsen, Denmark, with Louis Poulsen paper label.

1965 *Body 30in (76cm) diam*

$4,000-6,000 **DRA**

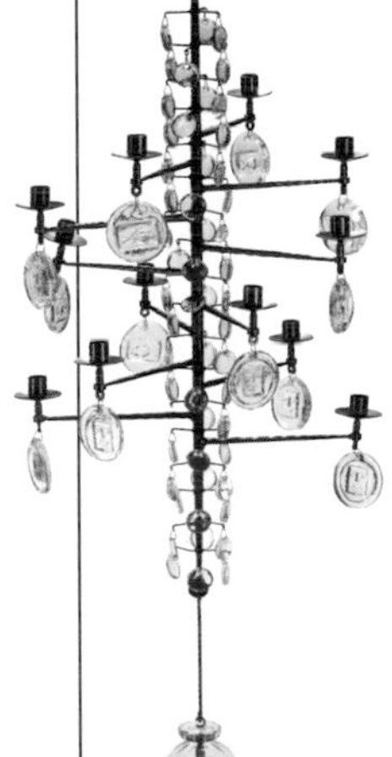

A 1950s Erik Höglund enameled wrought-iron and glass hanging candelabrum, manufactured by Boda Nova Glassworks and Axel Strömberg Ironworks, unmarked.

34in (86.5cm) high

$5,500-6,500 **DRA**

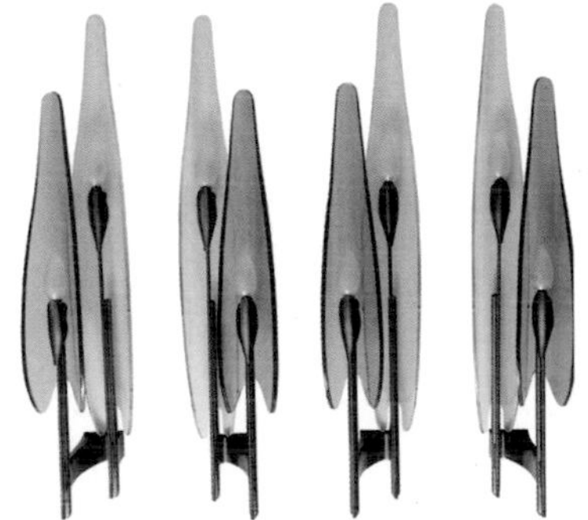

A set of four Fontana Arte brass and glass 'Dalia' wall sconces, attributed to Max Ingrand.

Designed c1955 *29.5in (75cm) high*

$6,500-7,500 **QU**

A Curtis Jere brass ceiling lamp, signed and dated.

1975 *22.5in (57cm) high*

$1,000-1,500 **DRA**

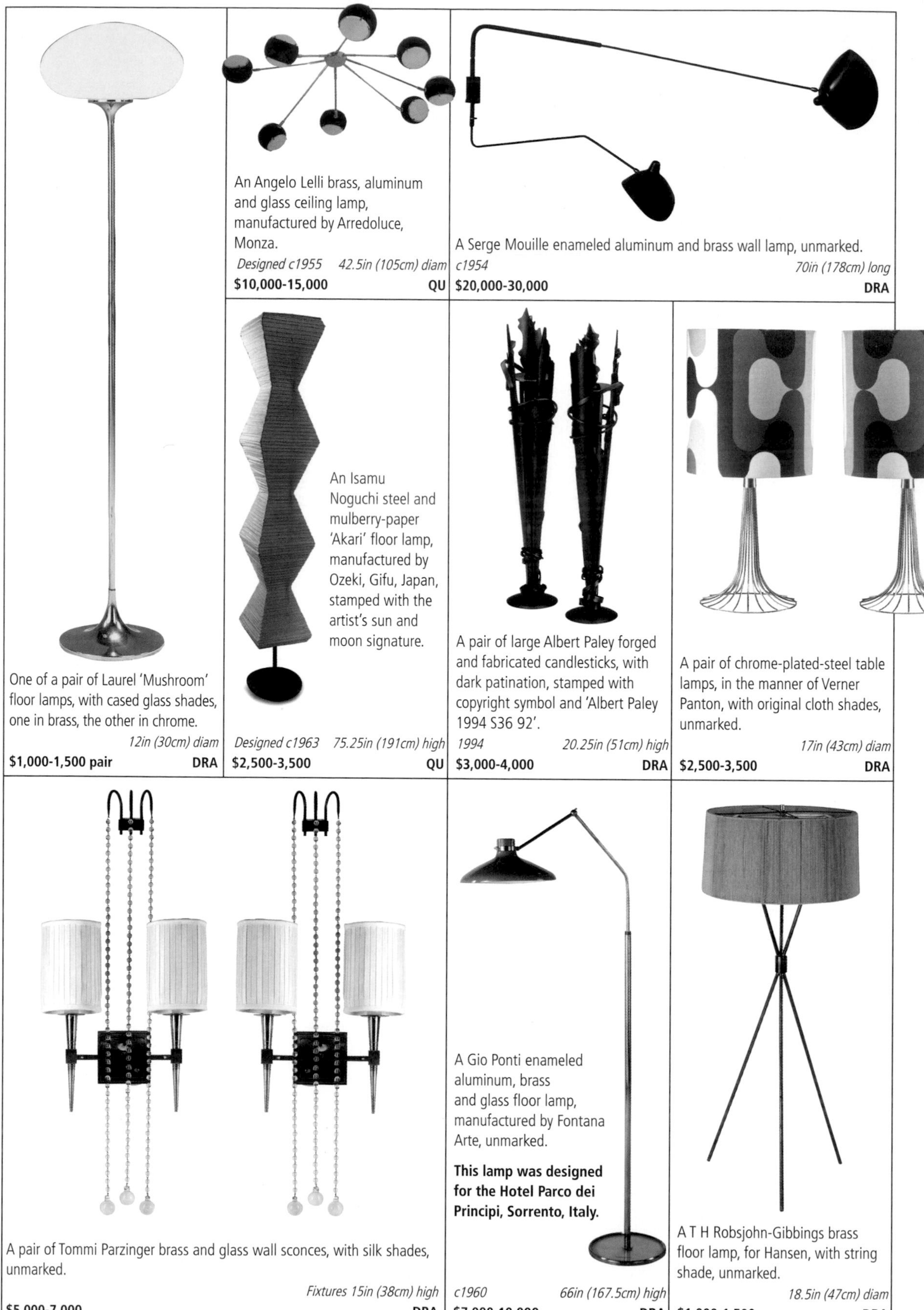

An Angelo Lelli brass, aluminum and glass ceiling lamp, manufactured by Arredoluce, Monza.

Designed c1955 *42.5in (105cm) diam*

$10,000-15,000 **QU**

A Serge Mouille enameled aluminum and brass wall lamp, unmarked.

c1954 *70in (178cm) long*

$20,000-30,000 **DRA**

One of a pair of Laurel 'Mushroom' floor lamps, with cased glass shades, one in brass, the other in chrome.

12in (30cm) diam

$1,000-1,500 pair **DRA**

An Isamu Noguchi steel and mulberry-paper 'Akari' floor lamp, manufactured by Ozeki, Gifu, Japan, stamped with the artist's sun and moon signature.

Designed c1963 *75.25in (191cm) high*

$2,500-3,500 **QU**

A pair of large Albert Paley forged and fabricated candlesticks, with dark patination, stamped with copyright symbol and 'Albert Paley 1994 S36 92'.

1994 *20.25in (51cm) high*

$3,000-4,000 **DRA**

A pair of chrome-plated-steel table lamps, in the manner of Verner Panton, with original cloth shades, unmarked.

17in (43cm) diam

$2,500-3,500 **DRA**

A pair of Tommi Parzinger brass and glass wall sconces, with silk shades, unmarked.

Fixtures 15in (38cm) high

$5,000-7,000 **DRA**

A Gio Ponti enameled aluminum, brass and glass floor lamp, manufactured by Fontana Arte, unmarked.

This lamp was designed for the Hotel Parco dei Principi, Sorrento, Italy.

c1960 *66in (167.5cm) high*

$7,000-10,000 **DRA**

A T H Robsjohn-Gibbings brass floor lamp, for Hansen, with string shade, unmarked.

18.5in (47cm) diam

$1,000-1,500 **DRA**

A large Venini backlit glass-tile wall sculpture, no.952, on brass grid, unmarked.

c1960 *56in (142cm) long*

$5,000-7,000 **DRA**

A pair of Hugo Cesar Tonti iron and parchment table lamps, inscribed 'Tonti, Argentinian'.

28.5in (72cm) high

$3,000-4,000 **DRA**

A Robert Sonneman enameled and chrome-plated steel floor lamp, with adjustable arm.

73in (185cm) high

$650-850 **DRA**

A pair of 1970s Italian chrome lamps, each with six bulbs radiating from waist and a single bulb from top, with long shag fringes.

18in (46cm) high

$5,000-7,000 **FRE**

A Gino Sarfatti '1063' floor lamp, for Arteluce, Milan, labeled 'ARTELUCE MILANO'.

Designed 1953/54

84.75in (215cm) high

$25,000-35,000 **QU**

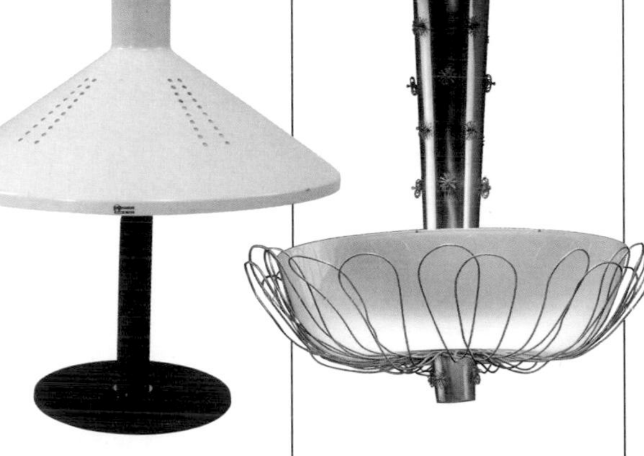

A Gino Sarfatti chrome-plated and painted steel '609' table lamp, for Arteluce, Milan, marked 'ARTELUCE MILANO MADE IN ITALY'.

Designed 1972 *20.75in (53cm) high*

$5,500-6,500 **QU**

A large Paavo Tynell brass ceiling lamp, manufactured by Taito Oy, Helsinki, with yellowish opal-glass shade.

Designed c1950 *27.5in (70cm) diam*

$12,000-18,000 **QU**

A Stilnovo brass and glass table/wall lamp, with maker's label.

Designed c1955 *15.75in (40cm) high*

$2,000-3,000 **QU**

An Ettore Sottsass methacrylate and chrome-plated 'Asteroide - Mod. L 012' lamp, manufactured by Francesconi & C., Roncadelle, for Design Center, marked 'DESIGN CENTRE', labeled 'made in Italy'.

Designed 1968

29in (73.5cm) high

$4,000-6,000 **QU**

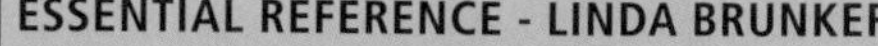

A Harry Bertoia patinated-bronze sculpture.

30in (76cm) wide

$25,000-35,000 **DRA**

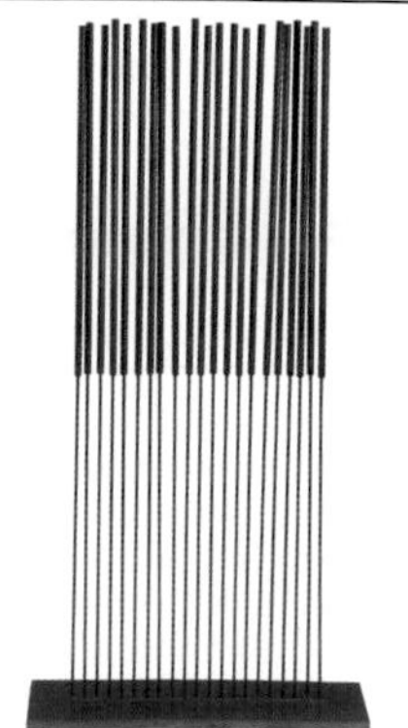

A Harry Bertoia brass 'Sonambient' sculpture, with four 33-rpm records of Sonambient music.

24in (61cm) high

$15,000-20,000 **DRA**

A Harry Bertoia patinated-bronze two-rod 'Sonambient' sculpture, unmarked.

Provenance: Acquired directly from the artist.

c1970 *83in (211cm) high*

$15,000-20,000 **DRA**

ESSENTIAL REFERENCE - LINDA BRUNKER

Linda Brunker was born in Dublin in 1966.

- **She studied at the National College of Art & Design 1983-88.**
- **She immigrated to the USA in 2005.**
- **In the late 1980s, she began to develop her 'open filigree' technique of casting in bronze.**
- **Her sculptures are typically based on the human form and have a strong spiritual and ecological quality.**
- **Natural elements such as leaves, feathers or starfish are used to give shape to figures that are later cast in bronze.**
- **Her works are in various collections worldwide and she has had many solo and group exhibitions.**

A Linda Brunker bronze 'Oak' sculpture of a figure with foliage.

This was the first piece Linda Brunker made in her signature 'open filigree' style.

c1988 *40in (102cm) wide*

$12,000-18,000 **ECGW**

A John Coen bronze 'Gathering Light' sculpture.

16in (41cm) high

$4,000-6,000 **SWO**

A Gianni Colombo glass and metal 'Strutturazione Fluida' kinetic object, manufactured by Gruppo T, Milan, powered by an electric motor, marked 'Strutturazione Fluida di Gianni Colombo Disegno 1960 Copia N. Cinque Voltaggio 220 Made in Italy'.

Designed 1960 *19in (48.5cm) high*

$20,000-30,000 **QU**

A Mario Dal Fabbro carved and ebonized wood sculpture, signed twice and dated, with stand.

1978 *16.75in (42.5cm) high*

$5,500-6,500 **DRA**

A Claire Falkenstein welded copper and Venetian glass fusion sculpture.

23in (58cm) high

$6,500-7,500 **DRA**

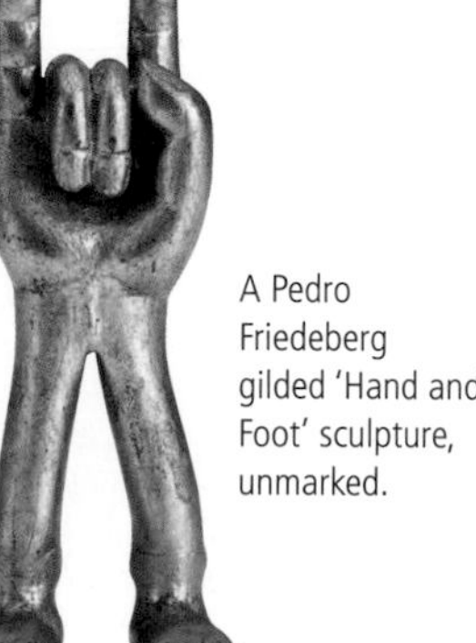

A Pedro Friedeberg gilded 'Hand and Foot' sculpture, unmarked.

5.25in (13cm) high

$1,200-1,800 **DRA**

An Oswaldo Guayasamín stylized brass bust, marked 'TALLER Guayasamín'.

14in (36cm) high

$2,000-3,000 **DRA**

A Barbara Hepworth 18ct gold 'Mincalo' sculpture, signed with initials, numbered and dated 'BH 5/12 1971', with London hallmark, on marble base, designed 1971.

Commissioned by the Morris Singer Foundry, London as part of the 'Artists in Gold' series. The sculptors Barbara Hepworth, Michael Ayrton, Lynn Chadwick, Elisabeth Frink, Enzo Plazzotta, Kenneth Armitage, Cesar and William Chattaway were commissioned to create sculptures specially suited to being cast in gold. Each design had a maximum edition of no more than 12.

Cast 1975 *Total 10.5in (27cm) high*

$70,000-90,000 **GORL**

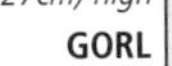

A Klaus Ihlenfeld phosphorus-bronze 'Bamboo Growth' sculpture, stamped 'KI'.

8.5in (22cm) high

$3,000-4,000 **DRA**

A Philip Jackson bronze figure of 'Mistress of the Ca' D'Oro', with mid-brown patination and polished detail, signed and marked with an O bisected by a sloping line.

c2001 *15.5in (38.5cm) high*

$15,000-20,000 **DN**

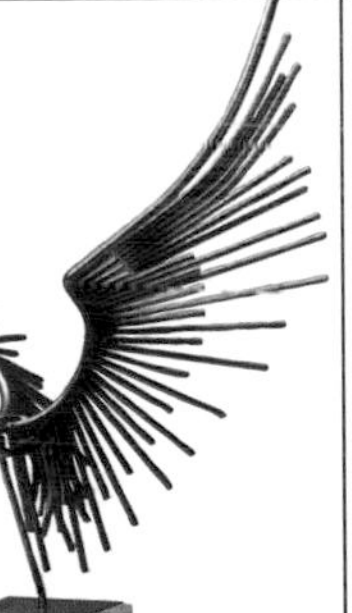

A Curtis Jere gilt-wire sculpture of a hawk, signed 'C. Jere 1978', on a marble base.

1978 *27in (69cm) high*

$300-500 **DRA**

An Eduardo Paolozzi bronze 'Portrait of Matta' bust, with medium-brown patination, signed 'E. Paolozzi'.

Designed c1980 *4.5in (11.5cm) high*

$2,000-3,000 **DN**

A Fernando la Pinto steel sculpture, unmarked.

c1961 *63in (160cm) long*

$2,500-3,500 **DRA**

ESSENTIAL REFERENCE - BARBARA HEPWORTH

Barbara Hepworth (1903-75) is one of the most important figures in modern sculpture.

- **She won a scholarship to study at the Leeds School of Art 1920-21. There she was a contemporary of Henry Moore. She won a further scholarship to study at the Royal College of Art 1921-24.**
- **She was married to sculptor John Skeaping and then to painter Ben Nicholson.**
- **Her first major solo exhibition was held in Temple Newsam, Leeds in 1943.**
- **She bought Trewyn Studio, St Ives, in 1949.**
- **Hepworth won the Grand Prix of the 1959 São Paolo Bienal.**
- **One of her best-known works is 'Single Form' (1961-64), which is housed at the United Nations Building, NY.**
- **Following her death, her studio was opened as the Barbara Hepworth Museum and Sculpture Garden. From 1980 it has been run by the Tate.**

A Barbara Hepworth polished bronze 'Squares' sculpture, no.2/9, signed, with Morris Singer foundry initials, dated, on plinth.

1969 *9in (23cm) high*

$90,000-110,000 **GORL**

A Grupo Strum green polyurethane foam 'Pratone' object, manufactured by Gufram, Balangero, marked 'PRATONE", GUFRAM MULTIPLE 24, PRATONE 4/200'.

Designed 1970 *54.75in (139cm) wide*

$15,000-20,000 **QU**

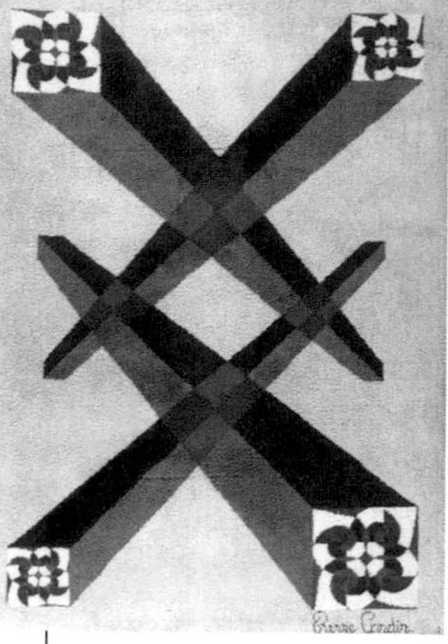

A Pierre Cardin wool 'Concorde 1' rug, signed, with fabric label.

108in (274cm) long

$3,000-4,000 **DRA**

CLOSER LOOK - ALEXANDER CALDER TAPESTRY

In the early 1970s Alexander Calder designed 14 wall tapestries (of which this is one) as part of a charitable project to help those affected by the devastating 1972 earthquake in Managua, Nicaragua.

All Calder's tapestries were woven from native grasses dyed with vegetable colors.

Circles and ellipses are extremely difficult to weave using traditional methods.

All Calder's tapestries were limited to 100 examples of each design.

This design, 'Turquoise', is one of the most popular Calder tapestries, as it strongly evokes his famous mobiles.

An Alexander Calder maguey fibre 'Turquoise' tapestry, for Bon-Art, woven 'Calder 75', '21/100' and copyright symbol, with fabric label.

1975 *84.5in (215cm) long*

$12,000-18,000 **DRA**

A large Kay Bojesen teak articulated monkey, stamped 'Kay Bojesen Denmark'.

18in (46cm) high

$2,000-3,000 **DRA**

A Tapio Wirkkala veneered 'Leaf dish', manufactured by Soinne & Kni, Helsinki.

22.25in (56.5cm) long

$50,000-60,000 **QU**

A Michelle Holzapfel turned and carved walnut vase, signed and dated.

1989 *11.5in (29cm) high*

$1,500-2,500 **SK**

A Gilbert Rohde burlwood-veneered and chrome 'World's Fair Clock', for Herman Miller, with brass tag.

13.25in (34cm) wide

$3,000-4,000 **DRA**

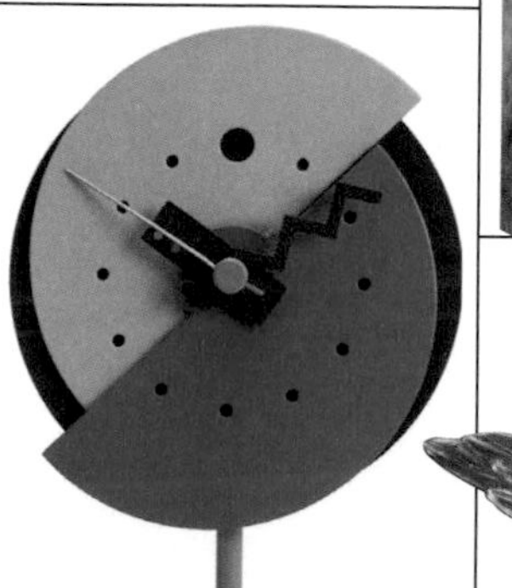

A Syohe Imihara 'Neos' table clock, marked.

4in (10cm) diam

$200-300 **DRA**

A Pedro Friedeberg mahogany and gilt figural 'Angel' clock, signed.

19in (48cm) high

$5,000-7,000 **DRA**

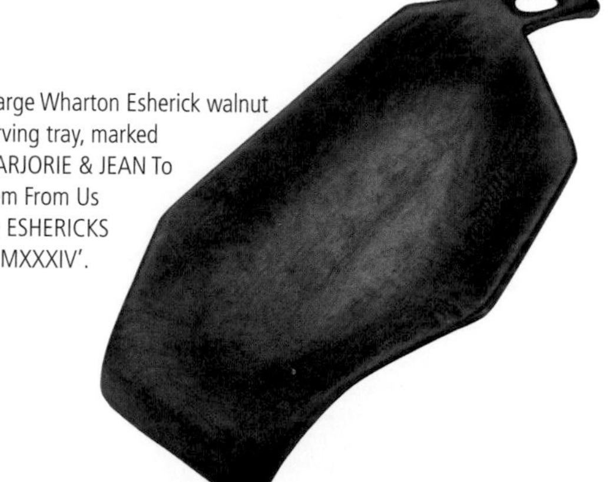

A large Wharton Esherick walnut serving tray, marked 'MARJORIE & JEAN To Them From Us The ESHERICKS MCMXXXIV'.

Provenance: Given by the artist to Marjorie Content and Jean Toomer, thence by descent.

1934 *28in (71cm) long*

$20,000-30,000 **DRA**

'JOB', designed by Alphonse Mucha, printed by F Champenois, Paris, with creases and marks.

22.25in (59cm) high

$9,000-11,000 **DN**

'LE RUBIS', designd by Alphonse Mucha, no. 1461, printed by F Champenois, Paris.

1908 *45in (114.5cm) high*

$8,500-9,500 **DN**

CLOSER LOOK - 'REVERIE'

This was one of Mucha's most popular designs.

This design exists in several variations, as Champenois capitalized on its popularity and sold it to many different clients.

This variant (without text) was sold by literary and artistic review 'La Plume' to collectors and connoisseurs.

The orange and yellow colours are unusual for Mucha.

The composition is classically Mucha's, with the maiden depicted in front of a halo (albeit larger and more intricate than normal) filled with floral stylization.

['Reverie'], designed by Alphonse Mucha, printed by F Champenois, Paris, in excellent condition, framed.

1897 *26in (66cm) high*

$18,000-22,000 **SWA**

'RISCHARDSQUELLE', designed by Koloman Moser, printed by Friedrich Sperl, Vienna, with restoration and repaired tears.

Kolomon Moser was a key figure in the Austrian Secession and much of his graphic work was done on behalf of that group. His commercial posters are quite rare. One of several variations, this poster was first printed in 1899 in a smaller size, without the bottom line of text or the image of the bottle itself.

c1908 *73.5in (187cm) wide Sold for*

$12,000-14,000 **SWA**

'HARDEN GRENADE - EXTINCTEUR', designed by Paul Berthon, with repaired tears, framed.

The combination of Art Nouveau patterns with the practical applications of a life-saving device is handled in a deft and sure manner.

1900 *49in (124.5cm) high*

$2,000-3,000 **SWA**

'MUSÉE GRÉVIN les Fantoches de JOHN HEWELT', designed by Jules Chéret, printed by Les Ateliers d'Art Liturgique Chéret, Paris, in excellent condition.

1900 *49in (124.5cm) high*

$6,000-7,000 **SWA**

['Fruit and Flower'], designed by Alphonse Mucha, one of two decorative panels, in excellent condition.

1897 *26.5in (67.5cm) high*

$16,000-18,000 pair **SWA**

'Palais de Glace', designed by Jules Chéret, printed by Chaix, Paris, from a supplement in 'Courrier Français' supplement on March 1, 1896, in excellent condition.

1896 *22.75in (58cm) high*

$5,000-6,000 **SWA**

'ABSINTHE ROBETTE', designed by Henri Privat-Livemont, printed by J L Goffart, Brussels, with creases, framed.

1896 *43in (109.5cm) high*

$12,000-14,000 **SWA**

'LA RÉFORME le 21 Novembre Le Masque Anarchiste', designed by Henri Privat-Livemont, printed by Trommer & Staeves, Brussels, with restoration and repaired tears.

Unusually for an other Art Nouveau work, this image uses the style to depict a gory, eye-catching scene. Even the decorative border, exhibiting traditional floral motifs, contains images of death, blood and mutilation.

1897 *62in (157.5cm) wide*

$5,000-7,000 **SWA**

'Lait Pur Stérilisé', designed by Théophile-Alexandre Steinlen, printed by Charles Verneau, Paris, with restoration.

The first poster Charles Verneau printed for Steinlen, 'Lait Pur Stérilisé' became an instant success and remains an iconic image of the period. Steinlen used green for the outline, as opposed to black, which adds to the soft feel of the image.

1894 *55.25in (140cm) high*

$16,000-18,000 **SWA**

'COCORICO', designed by Théophile-Alexandre Steinlen, printed by Charles Verneau, Paris, with folds and creases, framed.

'Cocorico' was a magazine published between 1898 and 1902. As a literary and artistic publication, its main role was to promote the Art Nouveau movement. Its primary artists included Steinlen, Alphonse Mucha and Georges de Feure.

1899 *54in (137cm) high*

$15,000-20,000 **SWA**

'Jane Avril', designed by Henri de Toulouse-Lautrec, printed by Imprimerie Chaix, Paris, with restoration, framed.

Toulouse-Lautrec designed three posters promoting Jane Avril's theatrical performances, of which this is the first.

1893 *50in (93cm) high*

$45,000-65,000 **SWA**

'La revue blanche', designed by Henri de Toulouse-Lautrec, printed by Edward Ancourt, Paris, in excellent condition.

1895 *50.25in (127.5cm) high*

$25,000-30,000 **SWA**

Judith Picks

Bruant was one of Lautrec's earliest supporters. One year after Lautrec designed his first poster for the Moulin Rouge, Bruant recognized the potential that such potent artwork could have for his own career. This is Lautrec's third poster for the performer. It is his sparest design for Bruant, with the performer turning his back to the viewer and glancing over his left shoulder, to reveal his face in profile. Now reduced to a few elemental shapes, this forceful hieroglyph served as Bruant's logo in a variety of formats. The broad strokes, flat colours, detailed representation of the singer's face, and the implied arrogance of the performer who would turn his back on his public all served to make this an iconic image.

['Aristide Bruant Dans Son Cabaret'], designed by Henri de Toulouse-Lautrec, printed by Charles Verneau, Paris, with repaired tears, framed.

1893 *54in (137cm) high*

$75,000-95,000 **SWA**

['Cycles Michael'], designed by Henri de Toulouse-Lautrec, lithograph in colors, printed by Imprimerie Chaix, Paris, linen-backed, in excellent condition.

1896 *50in (127cm) wide*

$10,000-15,000 **DN**

'CHARLES FROHMAN PRESENTS WILLIAM GILLETTE IN SHERLOCK HOLMES', designed by John Stewart Browne, printed by David Allen & Sons Ltd., framed but not glazed.

28.75in (73cm) high

$9,000-11,000

'ANTIBES', desgined by Roger Broders, printed by Lucien Serre, Paris, in excellent condition.

F Scott Fitzgerald and his wife Zelda stayed in this Riviera town in 1926 and it was during his time there that he began writing his novel 'Tender is the Night'.

c1928 *42in (106.5cm) high*

$12,000-14,000 **SWA**

'KNSM', designed by Willem Frederick Ten Broek, linen-backed, in excellent condition, framed.

37in (94cm) high

$6,000-8,000 **SWA**

'BITTER CAMPARI', designed by Leonetto Cappiello, printed by Devambez, Paris, in excellent condition.

1921 *38.75in (98.5cm) high*

$6,000-8,000 **SWA**

'CHOCOLATE TALMONE AU LAIT', designed by Jean Carlu, printed by Réunis, Paris, with restoration and minor losses, framed.

This is an early, rare and previously unreferenced work by Carlu.

c1924 *61.25in (155.5cm) high*

$4,000-5,000 **SWA**

'GRAND-SPORT', desgined by A M Cassandre, printed by Hachard & Cie., Paris, in excellent condition.

This is one of the first fashion advertising posters to show the direct influence of Cubism. The manner in which the legibility and message are achieved, through a strict geometrical approach tempered with shimmering airbrush treatment around the solid colors, became the artist's signature.

1925 *31.5in (80cm) high*

$15,000-17,000 **SWA**

'RAYON DES SOIERIES', designed by Maurice Dufrène, printed by Imprimerie Chaix, Paris, linen-backed.

1930 *47in (119cm) high*

$1,500-2,500 **DRA**

'BAL DE LA GRANDE OURSE', designed by Auguste Herbin, printed by Kaplan, Paris, with restoration and repaired tears.

1925 *46in (118cm) high*

$3,500-4,500 **SWA**

'BITTER BONOMELLI MILANO', designed by Maga (Giuseppe Magagnoli), printed by Creazione Marzo, with repaired tears.

1922 *78.25in (199cm) high*

$3,500-4,500 **SWA**

'CONTINENT VIA HARWICH', designed by Tom Purvis, printed by The Dangerfield Printing Co., Ltd., London, linen-backed.

c1930 *40in (102cm) high*

$800-1,200 **DN**

'INTERNATIONALE HYGIENE-AUSSTELLUNG DRESDEN', designed by Franz Von Stuck, printed by Leutert & Schneidewind, Dresden, with creases.

This image was extremely popular and resonated throughout the German graphic landscape. It was stolen by a cigarette company, cartooned in Lustige Blätter and later, in 1930, was revamped by Billy Petzold.

1911 *23.5in (58.5cm) high*

$3,500-4,500 **SWA**

'LUX', designed by an unknown designer, printed by Fretz Frères, Zurich, with restoration and losses, framed.

50in (127cm) high

$1,500-2,500 **SWA**

'I WANT YOU FOR U.S. ARMY', designed by James Montgomery Flagg, printed by Leslie-Judge Co., New York, in excellent condition, framed.

This is arguably the best-known American poster of all time.

1917 *40in (101.5cm) high*

$14,000-16,000 **SWA**

'TEAMWORK BUILDS SHIPS', designed by William Dodge Stevens, printed by Forbes, Boston, with repaired tears.

This poster was issued by the US Shipping Board, an entity formed in 1916 to restore greatness to America's merchant marine fleet.

c1918 *50in (127cm) wide*

$4,000-6,000 **SWA**

'LET US GO FORWARD TOGETHER', designed by an unknown designer, printed by J Weiner, London, in excellent condition.

The caption for this poster is taken from Winston Churchill's first speech as Prime Minister to the House of Commons on 13 May 1940.

1940 *29.75in (75.5cm) high*

$4,500-5,500 **SWA**

['To Revenge and Redemption'], designed by Gabriel & Maxim Shamir, with repaired tears.

1945 *26.5in (67cm) high*

$5,000-6,000 **SWA**

'THE JEWISH WELFARE BOARD', designed by Josef Foshko, printed by The Hegemen Print, New York, in excellent condition.

The text in Yiddish reads, 'Not sure he is all right.'

1918 *28in (71cm) high*

$5,000-6,000 **SWA**

'SHARE', designed by Alfred F Burke, printed by Sackett & Wilhelms Co., Brooklyn, with restoration.

Depicting America offering her bounty to Jewish refugees, this is one of the finest and rarest of the World War I Judaic posters.

c1917 *40.25in (102cm) high*

$6,000-8,000 **SWA**

'1938 CHRYSLER', designed by an unknown designer, in excellent condition.

It is unusual that such a bright image, infused with pre-war optimism and designed for such a prominent American company should be unrecorded.

1938 *49.5in (126cm) high*
$5,500-6,500 **SWA**

'UNION PACIFIC SUN VALLEY IDAHO', designed by Augustus Moser, with restoration and repaired tears.

c1940 *34.5in (88cm) high*
$12,000-14,000 **SWA**

'CANADA welcomes U.S. CITIZENS NO PASSPORTS', designed by Peter Ewart, in excellent condition.

1940 *35.75in (90cm) high*
$4,000-6,000 **SWA**

'The New EMPIRE STATE EXPRESS', designed by Leslie Ragan, printed by Brett Lithographing Co., in excellent condition.

1941 *40.75in (103.5cm) high*
$6,000-8,000 **SWA**

'SUN VALLEY KETCHUM, IDAHO', designed by Dwight Clark Shepler, with minor restoration.

c1940 *35in (89cm) high*
$9,000-11,000 **SWA**

'CAUTERETS', designed by Léon Constant-Duval, printed by Via-Deco, Paris, linen-backed, in excellent condition.

41in (104cm) high
$750-950 **DN**

'ST PIERRE DE CHARTREUSE', designed by Roger Broders, printed by Vaugirard, Paris, linen-backed, in excellent condition.

39.5in (101cm) high
$1,300-1,600 **DN**

'WASHINGTON AMERICAN AIRLINES', designed by Edward McKnight Kauffer, in good condition.

1948 *40in (102cm) high*
$300-400 **DN**

'Griffon', designed by J Hugo d'Alesi, framed.

77.5in (196cm) high
£1,800-2,200 **TEN**

'ZOE MELEKE AND HER TROUPE OF TRAINED CANARIES', designed by an unknown designer, printed by H A Thomas, New York, with minor soiling.

c1885 *37.25in (94.5cm) high*

$3,500-4,500 **SWA**

'HON. W. F. CODY BUFFALO BILL', designed by J B, printed by Forbes Co., Boston & New York, with remnant of text banner, with losses.

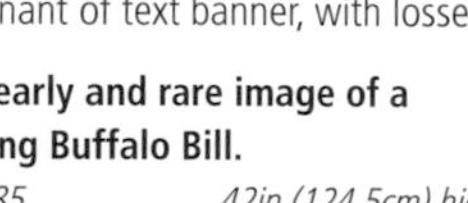

An early and rare image of a young Buffalo Bill.

c1885 *42in (124.5cm) high*

$20,000-25,000 **SWA**

CLOSER LOOK - 'W.F. CODY BUFFALO BILL'

This exceptionally rare poster is comprised of scenes from Cody's life.

This poster features the bust of President William McKinley, elected in 1897.

This French poster is more colourful than the American variation, printed by the Enquirer Litho. Company in Cincinnati in 1899.

Most of the images on this poster previously appeared on two earlier Buffalo Bill posters, 'Scenes in the Life of Col. W. F. Cody' (1895) and 'Chief of Scouts and Guide for U.S. Army' (c1888). The two vignettes that do not appear on either previous poster are: Cody Day at the Omaha Exposition and an image of Bill's first cabin.

'W.F. Cody BUFFALO BILL', printed by Weiners CH. Wall, Paris, with restoration and repaired tears.

c1905 *39in (99cm) high*

$16,000-18,000 **SWA**

'A JUST DECISION' 'FAIRNESS KEEPS FRIENDS', designed by Willard Frederic Elmes, printed by Mather & Co., Chicago, with restoration and losses.

1926 *48in (122cm) high*

$2,500-3,500 **SWA**

'A Loyal Man Speaks Well of His Friends', designed by an unknown designer, printed by Mather & Co., Chicago, in excellent condition.

1924 *48in (122cm) high*

$5,000-6,000 **SWA**

'SECESSION 49. AUSSTELLUNG', designed by Egon Schiele, printed by Albert Berger, Vienna, mounted on Japan, with minor restoration, framed.

The people around the table have been identified as various artist friends of Schiele's (who is seated at the top of the poster). The empty seat opposite him is said to be intended for Gustav Klimt, who died about a month prior to the exhibition's opening.

1918 *26in (66cm) high*

$30,000-35,000 **SWA**

['Opium'], designed by the Stenberg brothers (Vladimir and Georgii), printed by Sovkino, Moscow, with minor losses.

This 'documentary' about opium was written by Osip Brik and directed by Vitaly Zhemchuzny, both members of LEF (Left Front of Art). Its title refers to the phrase, 'Religion is opium for the masses'. To promote this daunting subject, the Stenberg Brothers designed this poster depicting a member of the clergy and a member of the proletariat together on a playing card.

1930 *36.5in (93cm) high*

$12,000-14,000 **SWA**

'VERWENDE STETS NUR GAS', designed by Walter Dexel.

Dexel was closely associated with the Bauhaus and became one of the most prominent practitioners of Constructivism.

1924 *25in (63.5cm) wide*

$27,000-30,000 **SWA**

UK PERIOD	USA PERIOD	FRENCH PERIOD	GERMAN PERIOD
Elizabethan *Elizabeth I* (1558-1603)			
Jacobean *James I* (1603-1625)		**Renaissance**	**Renaissance** (to c1650)
Carolean *Charles I* (1625-1649)	**Early Colonial**	**Louis XIII** (1610-1643)	
Cromwellian *Commonwealth* (1649-1660)			
Restoration			
Charles II (1660-1685) *James II* (1685-1688)			**Renaissance/ Baroque** (c1650-1700)
		Louis XIV (1643-1715)	
William and Mary (1689-1694)	**William and Mary** (1689-1694)		
William III (1694-1702)	**Dutch Colonial**		
Queen Anne (1702-1714)	**Queen Anne**		
			Baroque (c1700-1730)
Early Georgian		**Régence** (1715-1723)	
George I (1714-1727) *George II* (1727-1760)	**Chippendale** *From 1750*	**Louis XV** (1723-1774)	**Rococo** (c1730-1760)
		Louis XVI (1774-1792)	**Neoclassicism** (c1760-1800)
Late Georgian *George III* (1760-1811)	**EARLY FEDERAL** (1790-1810) *American Directoire* (1798-1804) *American Empire* (1804-1815)	**Directoire** (1792-1799)	**Empire** (c1800-1815)
		Empire (1799-1815)	
Regency *George III* (1812-1820)		**Restauration** (1815-1830)	
George IV (1820-1830)	**Later Federal** (1810-1830)	*Louis XVIII* (1814-1824) *Charles X* (1824-1830)	**Biedermeier** (c1815-1848)
William IV (1830-1837)		**Louis Phillipe** (1830-1848)	**Revivale** (c1830-1880)
Victorian *Victoria* (1837-1901)	**Victorian**	**2nd Empire** (1848-1870)	
Edwardian *Edward VII* (1901-1910)		**3rd Republic** (1871-1940)	**Jugendstil** (c1880-1920)

Every antique illustrated in Miller's Antiques has a letter code which identifies the dealer or auction house that sold it. The list below is a key to these codes. In the list, auction houses are shown by the letter A and dealers by the letter D. Some items may have come from a private collection, in which case the code in the list is accompanied by the letters PC. Inclusion in this book in no way constitutes or implies a contract or a binding offer on the part of any of our contributors to supply or sell the goods illustrated, or similar items, at the prices stated.

A&G Ⓐ
ANDERSON & GARLAND
Anderson House, Crispin Court, Newbiggin Lane, Westerhope, Newcastle upon Tyne, Tyne and Wear, NE5 1BF, UK
Tel: 0044 191 430 3000
www.andersonandgarland.com

AH & HT Ⓐ
HARTLEY'S
Victoria Hall, Little Lane, Ilkley, West Yorkshire, LS29 8EA, UK
Tel: 0044 1943 816363
www.andrewhartleyfinearts.co.uk

APAR Ⓐ
ADAM PARTRIDGE AUCTIONEERS & VALUERS
Withyfold Drive, Macclesfield, Cheshire, SK10 2BD, UK
Tel: 0044 1625 431 788
www.adampartridge.co.uk

AS&S Ⓐ
ANDREW SMITH & SON
The Auction Rooms, Manor Farm, Itchen Stoke, Nr. Winchester, Hampshire, SO24 0QT, UK
Tel: 0044 1962 735988
www.andrewsmithandson.com

ATQ Ⓐ
ANTIQUORUM
595 Madison Avenue, Fifth Floor, New York, NY 10022
Tel: 212 750-1103
www.antiquorum.com

BARB Ⓐ
BARBERS FINE ART
The Mayford Centre, Smarts Heath Road, Woking, Surrey, GU22 0PP, UK
Tel: 0044 1483 728939

BC2AD Ⓓ
BCIIAD
www.bc2ad.co.uk

BE & H&L Ⓐ
BEARNES, HAMPTON & LITTLEWOOD
St Edmund's Court, Okehampton Street, Exeter, Devon, EX4 1DU, UK
Tel: 0044 1392 413100
www.bearnes.co.uk

BEJ Ⓓ
BÉBÉS ET JOUETS
Tel: 0044 131 3325650
bebesetjouets@tiscali.co.uk

BELL Ⓐ
BELLMANS
New Pound Wisborough Green, Billingshurst, West Sussex, RH14 0AZ, UK
Tel: 0044 1403 700858
www.bellmans.co.uk

BER Ⓐ
BERTOIA AUCTIONS
2141 Demarco Drive, Vineland, NJ 08360
Tel: 856 692 1881
www.bertoiaauctions.com

BLO Ⓐ
DREWEATTS & BLOOMSBURY
Bloomsbury House, 24 Maddox Street, London, W1 S1PP, UK
Tel: 0044 20 7495 9494
www.bloomsburyauctions.com

BON Ⓐ
BONHAMS
101 New Bond Street, London, W1S 1SR, UK
Tel: 0044 20 7447 7447
www.bonhams.com

BRI Ⓐ
BRIGHTWELLS
Easters Court, Leominster, Herefordshire, HR6 0DE, UK
Tel: 0044 1568 611166
www.brightwells.com

CAN Ⓐ
THE CANTERBURY AUCTION GALLERIES
40 Station Road West, Canterbury, Kent, CT2 8AN, UK
Tel: 0044 1227 763337
www.thecanterbury auctiongalleries.com

CAPE Ⓐ
CAPES DUNN & CO.
The Auction Galleries, 38 Charles Street, Manchester, M1 7DB, UK
Tel: 0044 161 2731911
www.capesdunn.com

CENC Ⓓ
CENTRAL COLLECTABLES
www.centralcollectables.com

CHEF Ⓐ
CHEFFINS
Clifton House, 1 & 2 Clifton Road, Cambridge, Cambridgeshire, CB1 7EA, UK
Tel: 0044 1223 213343
www.cheffins.co.uk

CHOR Ⓐ
CHORLEY'S
Prinknash Abbey Park, Near Cheltenham, Gloucestershire, GL4 8EU, UK
Tel: 0044 1452 344499
www.simonchorley.com

CHT Ⓐ
CHARTERHOUSE
The Long Street Salerooms, Sherborne, Dorset, DT9 3BS, UK
Tel: 0044 1935 812277
www.charterhouse-auctions.co.uk

CLV Ⓐ
CLEVEDON SALEROOMS
Kenn Road, Kenn, Clevedon, Bristol, Somerset, BS21 6TT, UK
Tel: 0044 1934 830111
www.clevedon-salerooms.com

CM Ⓐ
CHARLES MILLER
11 Imperial Road, London, SW6 2AG, UK
Tel: 0044 20 7806 5530
www.charlesmillerltd.com

COT Ⓐ
COTTEES AUCTIONS
The Market, East Street, Wareham, Dorset, BH20 4NR, UK
Tel: 0044 1929 552826
www.cottees.co.uk

CRIS Ⓓ
CRISTOBAL
26 Church Street, Marylebone, London, NW8 8EP, UK
Tel: 0044 20 7724 7230
www.cristobal.co.uk

DA&H Ⓐ
DEE, ATKINSON & HARRISON
The Exchange Saleroom, Driffield, East Yorkshire, YO25 6LD, UK
Tel: 0044 1377 253151
www.dahauctions.com

DMC Ⓐ
DUMOUCHELLES ART GALLERY
409 East Jefferson Avenue, Detroit, MI 48226
Tel: 313 963 6255
www.dumouchelle.com

DN Ⓐ
DREWEATTS & BLOOMSBURY
Donnington Priory Salerooms, Donnington, Newbury, Berkshire, RG14 2JE, UK
Tel: 0044 1635 553553
www.dnfa.com/donnington

DOR Ⓐ
DOROTHEUM
Palais Dorotheum, Dorotheergasse 17, 1010 Vienna, Austria
Tel: 0043 1515600
www.dorotheum.com

DOY Ⓐ
DOYLE NEW YORK
175 East 87th Street, New York, NY 10128
Tel: 212 427 2730
www.doylenewyork.com

DR Ⓐ
DEREK ROBERTS ANTIQUES
25 Shipbourne Road, Tonbridge, Kent, TN10 3DN, UK
Tel: 0044 1732 358986
www.qualityantiqueclocks.com

DRA Ⓐ
RAGO ARTS
333 North Main Street, Lambertville, NJ 08530
Tel: 609 397 9374
www.ragoarts.com

DS Ⓐ
DUNBAR SLOANE
12 Akepiro Street, Mt Eden, Auckland, New Zealand
Tel: 0064 4721367
www.dunbarsloane.co.nz

DURR Ⓐ
DURRANTS
The Old School House, Peddars Lane, Beccles, Suffolk, NR34 9UE, UK
Tel: 0044 1502 713490
www.durrants.com

DUK Ⓐ
DUKE'S
The Dorchester Fine Art Salerooms, Weymouth Avenue, Dorchester, Dorset, DT1 1QS, UK
Tel: 0044 1305 265080
www.dukes-auctions.com

DW Ⓐ
DOMINIC WINTER
Mallard House, Broadway Lane, South Cerney, Cirencester, Gloucestershire, GL7 5UQ, UK
Tel: 0044 1285 860006
www.dominic-winter.co.uk

ECGW Ⓐ
EWBANK CLARKE GAMMON WELLERS
The Burnt Common Auction Rooms, London Road, Send, Woking, Surrey, GU23 7LN, UK
Tel: 0044 1483 223101
www.ewbankauctions.co.uk

FIS Ⓐ
AUKTIONHAUS DR FISCHER
Trappensee-Schößchen, D-74074 Heilbronn, Germany
Tel: 0049 7131155570
www.auctions-fischer.de

FLD Ⓐ
FIELDINGS AUCTIONEERS
Mill Race Lane, Stourbridge, West Midlands, DY8 1JN, UK
Tel: 0044 1384 444140
www.fieldingsauctioneers.co.uk

FRE Ⓐ
FREEMAN'S
1808 Chestnut Street, Philadelphia, PA 19103
Tel: 215 563 9275
www.freemansauction.com

G&M Ⓐ
GORNY & MOSCH
Maximiliansplatz 20, 80333 Munich, Germany
Tel: 0049 89/24 22 643-0
www.gmcoinart.de

GBA Ⓐ
GRAHAM BUDD AUCTIONS
PO Box 47519, London, N14 6XD, UK
Tel: 0044 20 83662525
www.grahambuddauctions.co.uk

GHOU Ⓐ
GARDINER HOULGATE
Bath Auction Rooms, 9 Leafield Way, Corsham, Wiltshire, SN13 9SW, UK
Tel: 0044 1225 812912
www.gardinerhoulgate.co.uk

GORB Ⓐ
GORRINGES
Terminus Road, Bexhill-on-Sea, East Sussex, TN39 3LR, UK
Tel: 0044 1424 212994
www.gorringes.co.uk

GORL Ⓐ
GORRINGES
15 North Street, Lewes, East Sussex, BN7 2PD, UK
Tel: 0044 1273 472503
www.gorringes.co.uk

GTH Ⓐ
GREENSLADE TAYLOR HUNT
Priory Sale Room, Winchester Street, Taunton, Somerset, TA1 1QE, UK
Tel: 0044 1823 332525
www.gth.net

H&C Ⓐ
HISTORICAL & COLLECTABLE
Kennetholme, Midgham, Reading, Berkshire, RG7 5UX, UK
Tel: 0044 1189 712420
www.historicalandcollectable.com

HALL Ⓐ
HALLS
Battlefield, Shrewsbury, Shropshire, SY4 3DR, UK
Tel: 0044 1743 450700
www.hallsestateagents.co.uk/fine-art

HAN Ⓐ
HANSONS AUCTIONEERS
Heage Lane, Etwall, Derbyshire, DE65 6LS, UK
Tel: 0044 1283 733 988
www.hansonsauctioneers.co.uk

HARR Ⓐ
HARRISON AUCTIONS
Jubilee Auction Rooms, Phillips Yard, Marlborough Road Pewsey, Wiltshire, SN9 5NU, UK
Tel: 0044 1672 562012
www.jubileeauctions.com

HICK Ⓓ
HICKMET FINE ART
85 Portobello Road, London, W11 2QB, UK
Tel: 0044 1342 841 508
www.hickmet.com

HW Ⓐ
HOLLOWAY'S
49 Parson's Street, Banbury, Oxfordshire, OX16 5NB, UK
Tel: 0044 1295 817777
www.hollowaysauctioneers.co.uk

IMC Ⓐ
I M CHAIT
9330 Civic Center Drive Beverly Hills, CA 90210
Tel: 310 2850182
www.chait.com

J&H Ⓐ
JACOBS & HUNT
26 Lavant Street, Petersfield, Hampshire, GU32 3EF, UK
Tel: 0044 1730 233933
www.jacobsandhunt.com

J&J Ⓐ
JONES & JACOB
Watcombe Manor Saleroom Ingham Lane, Watlington, Oxfordshire, OX49 5EJ, UK
Tel: 0044 1491 612810
www.jonesandjacob.com

JACK Ⓐ
JACKSON'S
2229 Lincoln Street, Cedar Falls, IA 50613
Tel: 319 277 2256
www.jacksonsauction.com

JDJ Ⓐ
JAMES D JULIA INC
PO Box 830, Fairfield, ME 04937
Tel: 207 453 7125
www.juliaauctions.com

JN Ⓐ
JOHN NICHOLSONS
Longfield, Midhurst Road, Fernhurst, Haslemere, Surrey, GU27 3HA, UK
Tel: 0044 1428 653727
www.johnnicholsons.com

JPOT Ⓓ
JONATHAN POTTER LTD.
125 New Bond Street, London, W1S 1DY, UK
Tel: 0044 20 7491 3520
www.jpmaps.co.uk

KAU Ⓐ
AUKTIONSHAUS KAUPP
Hauptstrasse 62, 79295 Sulzburg, Germany
Tel: 0049 763450
www.kaupp.de

L&T Ⓐ
LYON & TURNBULL
33 Broughton Place, Edinburgh, Midlothian, EH1 3RR, UK
Tel: 0044 131 5578844
www.lyonandturnbull.comk

LA Ⓐ
DAVID LAY FRICS
Penzance Auction House, Alverton, Penzance, Cornwall, TR18 4RE, UK
Tel: 0044 1736 361414
www.davidlay.co.uk

LC Ⓐ
LAWRENCE'S FINE ART AUCTIONEERS
The Linen Yard, South Street, Crewkerne, Somerset, TA18 8AB, UK
Tel: 0044 1460 73041
www.lawrences.co.uk

LHA Ⓐ
LESLIE HINDMAN AUCTIONEERS
1338 West Lake Street, Chicago, IL 60607
Tel: 312 280 1212
www.lesliehindman.com

LOW Ⓐ
LOWESTOFT PORCELAIN AUCTIONS
Surrey Street, Lowestoft, Suffolk, NR32 1LJ, UK
Tel: 0044 1296 892736
www.lowestoftchina.co.uk

LSK Ⓐ
LACY SCOTT & KNIGHT
10 Risbygate Street, Bury St. Edmunds, Suffolk, IP33 3AA, UK
Tel: 0044 1284 748600
www.lsk.co.uk

M&K Ⓐ
MELLORS & KIRK
The Auction House, Gregory Street, Nottingham, NG7 2NL, UK
Tel: 0044 115 979 0000
www.mellorsandkirk.co.uk

MAB Ⓐ
MATTHEW BARTON LTD.
25 Blythe Road, London, W14 0PD, UK
Tel: 0044 20 7806 5545
www.matthewbartonltd.com

MAI Ⓐ
MOORE ALLEN & INNOCENT
The Cirencester Salerooms, Burford Road, Cirencester, Gloucestershire, GL7 5RH, UK
Tel: 0044 1285 646050
www.mooreallen.co.uk

MAR Ⓐ
FRANK MARSHALL & CO.
Marshall House, Church Hill, Knutsford, Cheshire, WA16 6DH, UK
Tel: 0044 1565 653284
www.frankmarshall.co.uk

MART Ⓐ
MARTEL MAIDES LTD.
Cornet Street, St Peter Port, Guernsey, GY1 2JX, UK
Tel: 0044 1481 722700
www.martelmaidesauctions.com

MAX Ⓐ
MAXWELLS
133A Woodford Road, Woodford, Stockport, Cheshire, SK7 1QD, UK
Tel: 0044 161 4395182
www.maxwells-auctioneers.co.uk

MBA Ⓐ
MULBERRY BANK AUCTIONS
26A St Vincent Crescent,
Glasgow, G3 8LH, UK
Tel: 0044 141 2258181
www.mulberrybankauctions.com

MEA Ⓐ
MEALY'S
'The Old Cinema', Chatsworth Street, Castlecomer, County Kilkenny, Ireland
Tel: 00353 56 4441229
www.mealys.com

MIC Ⓐ
MICHAAN'S
2751 Todd Street, Alameda, CA 94501
Tel: 510 740 0220
www.michaans.com

MM Ⓐ
MULLOCK'S
The Old Shippon, Wall under Heywood, Church Stretton, Shropshire, SY6 7DS, UK
Tel: 0044 1694 771771
www.mullocksauctions.co.uk

MOR Ⓐ
MORPHETS
6 Albert Street, Harrogate, North Yorkshire, HG1 1JL, UK
Tel: 0044 1423 530030
www.morphets.co.uk

PBE Ⓐ
PAUL BEIGHTON AUCTIONEERS
16 Woodhouse Green, Thurcroft, Rotherham, South Yorkshire, S66 9AQ, UK
Tel: 0044 1709 700005
www.pbauctioneers.co.uk

PC ⓅⒸ
PRIVATE COLLECTION

POOK Ⓐ
POOK & POOK
463 East Lancaster Avenue, Downington, PA 19335
Tel: 610 269 4040
www.pookandpook.com

QU Ⓐ
QUITTENBAUM
Theresienstrasse 60, D-80333 Munich, Germany
Tel. 0049 89 273702125
www.quittenbaum.dem

REEM Ⓐ
REEMAN DANSIE
No. 8 Wyncolls Road, Severalls Business Park, Colchester, Essex, CO4 9HU, UK
Tel: 0044 1206 754754
www.reemandansie.com

RGA Ⓓ
RICHARD GARDNER ANTIQUES
Eastrop House, 3 East Pallant, Chichester, West Sussex, PO19 1TR, UK
Tel: 0044 1243 533772
www.richardgardnerantiques.co.uk

ROK Ⓐ
ROBERTSONS OF KINBUCK
Main Street, Kinbuck, Dunblane, Perthshire, FK15 0NQ, UK
Tel: 0044 1786 822603
www.robauctions-dunblane.co.uk

ROS Ⓐ
ROSEBERY'S
74-76 Knight's Hill, West Norwood, London, SE27 0JD, UK
Tel: 0044 20 8761 2522
www.roseberys.co.uk

RTC Ⓐ
RITCHIES
777 Richmond Street West, Toronto, Ontario, M6J 2L8, Canada
Tel: 416 364 1864
www.ritchies.com

RW Ⓐ
RICHARD WINTERTON AUCTIONEERS
The Lichfield Salerooms, Cross Keys, Lichfield, Staffordshire, WS13 6DN, UK
Tel: 0044 1543 251081
www.richardwinterton.co.uk

SAS Ⓐ
SPECIAL AUCTION SERVICES
81 New Greenham Park, Newbury, Berkshire, RG19 6HW, UK
Tel: 0044 8456 044 669
www.specialauctionservices.com

SCA Ⓓ
SCARAB ANTIQUES
Tel: 0044 2081 335895
www.scarabantiques.com

SHAP Ⓐ
SHAPES
Bankhead Medway, Sighthill, Edinburgh, EH11 4BY, UK
Tel: 0044 131 4533222
www.shapesauctioneers.co.uk

SK Ⓐ
SKINNER INC.
The Heritage on the Garden, 63 Park Plaza Boston, MA 02116
Tel: 617 350 5400
www.skinnerinc.com

SWA Ⓐ
SWANN GALLERIES
104 East 25th Street, New York, NY 10010
Tel: 212 254 4710
www.swanngalleries.com

SWO Ⓐ
SWORDERS
14 Cambridge Road, Stansted Mountfitchet, Essex, CM24 8GE, UK
Tel: 0044 1279 817778
www.sworder.co.uk

T&F Ⓐ
TAYLER & FLETCHER
London House, High Street, Bourton-on-the-Water, Gloucestershire, GL54 2AP, UK
Tel: 0044 1451 821666
www.taylerandfletcher.co.uk

TBW Ⓓ
TEDDY BEARS OF WITNEY
99 High Street, Witney, Oxfordshire, OX28 6HY, UK
Tel: 0044 1993 706616
www.teddybears.co.uk

TDM Ⓐ
THOMAS DEL MAR LTD.
25 Blythe Road, London, W14 0PD, UK
Tel: 0044 207 602 4805
www.thomasdelmar.com

TEN Ⓐ
TENNANTS
The Auction Centre, Leyburn, North Yorkshire, DL8 5SG, UK
Tel: 0044 1969 623780
www.tennants.co.uk

THE Ⓐ
THERIAULT'S
PO Box 151, Annapolis, MD 21404
Tel: 800 638 0422
www.theriaults.com

TOV Ⓐ
TOOVEY'S
Spring Gardens, Washington, West Sussex, RH20 3BS, UK
Tel: 0044 1903 891955
www.tooveys.com

TRI Ⓐ
TRING MARKET AUCTIONS
Brook Street, Tring, Hertfordshire, HP23 5EF, UK
Tel: 004 1442 826446
www.tringmarketauctions.co.uk

VEC Ⓐ
VECTIS AUCTIONS
Fleck Way, Thornaby, Stockton on Tees, North Yorkshire, TS17 9JZ, UK
Tel: 0044 1642 750616
www.vectis.co.uk

W&W Ⓐ
WALLIS & WALLIS
West Street Auction Galleries, Lewes, East Sussex, BN7 2NJ, UK
Tel: 0044 1273 480208
www.wallisandwallis.co.uk

WAD Ⓐ
WADDINGTON'S
111 Bathurst St., Toronto, Ontario M5V 2R1, Canada
Tel: 416 504 9100
www.waddingtons.ca

WES Ⓐ
WESCHLER'S
909 E Street NW, Washington, DC 20004
Tel: 202 628 1281
www.weschlers.com

WHP Ⓐ
W & H PEACOCK
26 Newnham Street, Bedford, Bedforshire, MK40 3JR, UK
Tel: 0044 1234 266 366
www.peacockauction.co.uk

WHT Ⓐ
WHITE'S AUCTIONS
Middleboro, MA 02346
Tel: 508 947 9281
www.whitesauctions.com

WW Ⓐ
WOOLLEY & WALLIS
51-61 Castle Street, Salisbury, Wiltshire, SP1 3SU, UK
Tel: 0044 1722 424500
www.woolleyandwallis.co.uk

INDEX TO ADVERTISERS

This is a list of auctioneers that conduct regular sales. Auction houses that would like to be included in the next edition should contact us at info@millers.uk.com.

ALABAMA

Flomaton Antique Auction
PO Box 1017, 320 Palafox Street, Flomaton 36441
Tel: 251 296 1850
www.flomatonantiqueauction.com

Vintage Auctions
Star Rte Box 650, Blountsville, 35031
Tel: 205 429 2457

ARIZONA

Dan May & Associates
4110 North Scottsdale Road, Scottsdale, 85251
Tel: 480 941 4200

Old World Mail Auctions
2155 W. Hwy, 89A, Ste 256, Sedona, 86336
Tel: 928 282 3944
www.oldworldauctions.com

ARKANSAS

Hanna-Whysel Auctioneers
3403 Bella Vista Way, Bella Vista, 72714
Tel: 501 855 9600

Ponders Auctions
1504 South Leslie, Stuttgart, 72160
Tel: 870 673 6551
www.pondersauctions.com

CALIFORNIA

Bonhams & Butterfields
7601 Sunset Blvd, Los Angeles, 90046
Tel: 323 850 7500
220 San Bruno Ave, San Francisco, 94103
Tel: 415 861 7500
580 Madison Avenue
New York, New York 10022
Tel: 212 644 9001
www.bonhams.com

I M Chait Gallery
9330 Civic Center Drive, Beverly Hills, 90210
Tel: 310 285 0182
www.chait.com

Cuschieri's Auctioneers & Appraisers
863 Main Street, Redwood City, 94063-1901
Tel: 650 556 1793

eBay, Inc.
2005 Hamilton Ave, Ste 350, San Jose, 95125
www.ebay.com

H R. Harmer
2680 Walnut Ave, Suite AB
Tustin, 92780
Tel: 714.389.9178

Michaan's
2751 Todd Street, Alameda, 94501
Tel: 510 740 0220
www.michaans.com

San Rafael Auction Gallery
634 Fifth Avenue, San Rafael, 94901
Tel: 415 457 4488
www.sanrafaelauction.com

L H Selman Ltd.
123 Locust St, Santa Cruz, 95060
Tel: 800 538 0766
www.paperweight.com

Slawinski Auction Co.
251 King Village Rd, Scotts Valley, 95066
www.slawinski.com

Sotheby's
9665 Wilshire Boulevard, Beverly Hills, 90212 2320
Tel: 310 274 0340
www.sothebys.com

NORTH CAROLINA

Robert S Brunk Auction Services Inc.
PO Box 2135, Asheville, 28802
Tel: 828 254 6846
www.brunkauctions.com

Raynors' Historical Collectible Auctions
1687 West Buck Hill Rd, Burlington, 27215
Tel: 336 584 3330
www.hcaauctions.com

SOUTH CAROLINA

Charlton Hall Galleries Inc.
7 Lexington Drive, West Columbia, 29170
Tel: 803 799 5678
www.charltonhallauctions.com

COLORADO

Pacific Auction
1270 Boston Ave, Longmont, 80501
Tel: 303 772 7676
www.pacificauction.com

Pettigrew Auction Company
1645 South Tejon Street, Colorado Springs, 80906
Tel: 719 633 7963

Priddy's Auction Galleries
5411 Leetsdale Drive, Denver, 80246
Tel: 800 380 4411

Stanley & Co.
Auction Room, 395 Corona Street, Denver, 80218
Tel: 303 355 0506

CONNECTICUT

Braswell Galleries
1 Muller Avenue, Norwalk, 06851
Tel: 203 847 1234
www.braswellgalleries.com

Framefinders
Edward Balfour, 401 Hamburg Rd, Lyme, 06371
www.framefinders.com

The Great Atlantic Auction Company
2 Harris & Main Street, Putnam, 06260
Tel: 860 963 2234

Norman C Heckler & Company
79 Bradford Corner Road, Woodstock Valley, 06282
Tel: 860 974 1634
www.hecklerauction.com

Lloyd Ralston Toys
549 Howe Ave, Shelton, 06484
Tel: 020 3924 5804
www.lloydralstontoys.com

Winter Associates Inc.
21 Cooke Street, PO Box 823, Plainville, 06062
Tel: 860 793 0288
www.auctionsappraisers.com

NORTH DAKOTA

Curt D Johnson Auction Co.
4216 Gateway Drive, Grand Forks, 58203
Tel: 701 746 1378
www.curtdjohnson.com

SOUTH DAKOTA

Fischer Auction Company
239 Haywire Ave, Long Lake, 57457
Tel: 800 888 1766/605 577 6600
www.fischerauction.com

FLORIDA

Auctions Neapolitan
1100 1st Ave South, Naples 34102
Tel: 239 262 7333
www.auctionsneapolitan.com

Burchard Galleries/ Auctioneers
2528 30th Ave North, St Petersburg, 33713
Tel: 727 821 1167
www.burchardgalleries.com

Arthur James Galleries
615 East Atlantic Avenue, Delray Beach, 33483
Tel. 561 278 2373

Kincaid Auction Company
3809 East Hwy 42, Lakeland 33801
Tel: 800 970 1977
www.kincaid.com

Albert Post Galleries
809 Lucerne Ave, Lake Worth, 33460
Tel: 561 582 4477

TreasureQuest Auction Galleries Inc.
8447 S.E. Retreat Drive, Hobe Sound, 33455
Tel: 772 546 4853
www.tqag.com

GEORGIA

Arwood Auctions
26 Ayers Ave, Marietta, 30060
Tel: 770 423 0110

Great Gatsby's
5180 Peachtree Industrial Blvd, Suite 107, Atlanta, 30341
Tel: 770 457 1903
www.greatgatsbys.com

My Hart Auctions Inc.
PO Box 2511, Cumming, 30028
Tel: 770 888 9006
www.myhart.net

Red Baron's Auction Gallery
6450 Roswell Rd, Atlanta, 30328
Tel: 404 252 3770
www.redbaronsantiques.com

Southland Auction Inc.
3350 Riverwood Parkway, Atlanta, 30339
Tel: 770 818 2418

IDAHO

The Coeur d'Alene Art Auction
8836 North Hess St, Suite B, Hayden, 83835
Tel: 208 772 9009
www.cdaartauction.com

INDIANA

AAA Historical Auction Service
2110 McConnell Drive, New Haven, 46774
Tel: 260 493 6585

Heritage Auction Galleries
5335 North Tacoma Ave, Suite 24, Indianapolis, 46220
Tel: 317 257 0863
www.historical.ha.com

Lawson Auction Service
1731 Central Ave, Columbus, 47201
Tel: 812 372 2571
www.lawsonauction.com

Schrader Auction
950 North Liberty Drive, Columbia City, 46725
Tel: 800 451 2709
www.schraderauction.com

Stout Auctions
529 State Road East, Williamsport, 47993
Tel: 765 764 6901
www.stoutauctions.com

Strawser Auctions
200 North Main, PO Box 332, Wolcotville, 46795
Tel: 260 854 2859
www.strawserauctions.com

ILLINOIS

Bloomington Auction Gallery
300 East Grove Street, Bloomington, 61701
Tel: 309 828 5533
www.bloomingtonauctiongallery.com

The Chicago Wine Company
835 N. Central, Wood Dale, 60191
Tel: 630 594 2972
www.tcwc.com

Hack's Auction Center
400 W. Third St, Pecatonica, 61063
Tel: 815 239 1436
www.hacksauction.com

Leslie Hindman Inc.
1338 West Lake St, Chicago, 60607
Tel: 312 280 1212
www.lesliehindman.com

Mastro Auctions
17542 Chicago Ave, Lansing, 60438
Tel: 708 889 9380
www.legendaryauctions.com

Sotheby's
188 East Walton Place, Chicago
60611
Tel: 312 475 7900

Susanin's Auction
900 S. Clinton, Chicago, 60654
Tel: 312 832 9800
www.susanins.com

John Toomey Gallery
818 North Boulevard, Oak Park,
60301
Tel: 708 383 5234
www.johntoomeygallery.com

IOWA

Jackson's Auctioneers & Appraisers
2229 Lincoln Street,
Cedar Falls, 50613
Tel: 319 277 2256
www.jacksonsauction.com

Tubaugh Auctions
1702 8th Ave, Belle Plaine, 52208
Tel: 319 444 2413
www.tubaughauctions.com

KANSAS

CC Auction Gallery
416 Court Street, Clay Center,
67432
Tel: 785 632 6062

Spielman Auction
2259 Homestead Road, Lebo, 66856
Tel: 316 256 6558

KENTUCKY

Hays & Associates Inc.
120 South Spring Street, Louisville,
40206
Tel: 502 584 4297

Steffen's Historical Militaria
PO Box 280, Newport, 41072
Tel: 859 431 4499

LOUISIANA

Estate Auction Gallery
3374 Government Street,
Baton Rouge, 70806
Tel: 504 383 7706

New Orleans Auction Galleries
801 Magazine Street, New Orleans,
70130
Tel: 504 566 1849
www.neworleansauction.com

MAINE

Cyr Auctions
100 Lewiston Road, Route 100
North, Gray, 04039
Tel: 207 657 5253
www.cyrauction.com

James D Julia Auctioneers Inc.
PO Box 830, Fairfield, 04937
Tel: 207 453 7125
www.jamesdjulia.com

Randy Inman Auctions Inc.
PO Box 726, Waterville, 04903-0726
Tel: 207 872 6900
www.inmanauctions.com

Thomaston Place Auction Galleries
PO Box 300, Thomaston, 04861
Tel: 207 354 8141
www.thomastonauction.com

MARYLAND

Hantman's Auctioneers & Appraisers
PO Box 59366, Potomac, 20859
Tel: 301 770 3720
www.hantmans.com

Ilsennock Auctions & Appraisals Inc.
4106B Norrisville Road, White Hall,
21161,
Tel: 410 557 8052
www.isennockauction.com

Richard Opfer Auctioneering Inc.
1919 Greenspring Drive, Lutherville,
Timonium, 21093-4113
Tel: 410 252 5035
www.opferauction.com

Sloans & Kenyon
7034 Wisconsin Ave, Chevychase,
20815
Tel: 301 634-2330
www.sloansandkenyon.com

Theriault's
PO Box 151, Annapolis, 21404
Tel: 410 224 3655
www.theriaults.com

MASSACHUSETTS

Douglas Auctioneers
241 Greenfield Road, Route 5,
South Deerfield, 01373
Tel: 413 665 2877
www.douglasauctioneers.com

Eldred's
1483 Route 6A, East Dennis, 02641
Tel: 508 385 3116
www.eldreds.com

Grogan & Company Auctioneers
22 Harris Street, Dedham, 02026
Tel: 781 461 9500
www.groganco.com

Shute Auction Gallery
850 West Chestnut St, Brockton,
02401
Tel: 508 588 0022

Skinner Inc.
63 Park Plaza, Boston, 02116
Tel: 617 350 5400
274 Cedar Hill St, Marlborough,
01752
Tel: 508 970 3000
www.skinnerinc.com

White's Auctions
2 Middleboro, 02346
Tel: 508 947 9281
www.whitesauctions.com

Willis Henry Auctions Inc.
22 Main Street, Marshfield, 02050
Tel: 781 834 7774
www.willishenry.com

MICHIGAN

Frank H. Boos Gallery
2830 W. Maple Road, Suite 104,
Troy, 48084
Tel: 248 643 1900

DuMouchelle Art Galleries Co.409 East Jefferson Ave, Detroit,
48226
Tel: 313 963 6255
www.dumouchelles.com

MINNESOTA

Tracy Luther Auctions
2548 East 7th Ave, St. Paul, 55109
Tel: 651 770 6175

Rose Auction Galleries
P.O. Box 270435, St. Paul, 5512
70435
Tel: 612 484 1415
www.rosegalleries.com

MISSOURI

Ivey Selkirk Auctioneers
7447 Forsyth Blvd, Saint Louis,
63105
Tel: 314 726 5515
www.iveyselkirk.com

Simmons & Company Auctioneers
40706 East 144th Street,
Richmond, 64085-8033
Tel: 816 776 2936
www.simmonsauction.com

MONTANA

Allard Auctions
PO Box 1030, St. Ignatius, 59865
Tel: 460 745 0500
www.allardauctions.com

Stan Howe & Associates
4433 Red Fox Drive,
Helena, 59601
Tel: 406 443 5658 / 800 443 5658

NEW HAMPSHIRE

Paul McInnis Inc. Auction Gallery
One Juniper Road, North Hampton,
03862
Tel: 603 964 1301
www.paulmcinnis.com

Northeast Auctions
93 Pleasant St, Portsmouth, NH
03801
Tel: 603 433 8400
www.northeastauctions.com

R O Schmitt Fine Art
PO Box 162, Windham, 03087
Tel: 603 432 2237
www.roschmittfinearts.com

NEW JERSEY

Bertoia Auctions
2141 De Marco Dr, Vineland, 08360
Tel: 856 692 1881
www.bertoiaauctions.com

Dawson & Nye
128 American Road, Morris Plains,
07950
Tel: 973 984 8900
www.dawsonandnye.com

Rago Arts & Auction Center
333 North Main Street,
Lambertville, 08530
Tel: 609 397 9374
www.ragoarts.com

NEW MEXICO

Altermann Galleries
Santa Fe Galleries, 225 Canyon
Road, Santa Fe, 87501
www.altermann.com

NEW YORK

Antiquorum
595 Madison Avenue, Fifth Floor,
New York, 10022
Tel: 212 750-1103
www.antiquorum.com

Christie's
20 Rockefeller Plaza, New York, 10022
Tel: 212 636 2000
www.christies.com

Copake Auction Inc.
266 RT. 7A, Copake, 12516
Tel: 518 329 1142
www.copakeauction.com

Samuel Cottone Auctions
15 Genesee Street, Mount Morris,
14510
Tel: 716 658 3180

Doyle New York
175 East 87th Street, New York, 10128
Tel: 212 427 2730
www.doylegalleries.com

Guernsey's Auction
108 East 73rd St, New York, 10021
Tel: 212 794 2280
www.guernseys.com

William J Jenack Auctioneers
62 Kings Highway Bypass, Chester,
10918
Tel: 845 469 9095
www.jenack.com

Keno Auctions
1127 East 69th Street, New York, 10021
Tel: 212 734 2381
www.kenoauctions.com

Mapes Auction Gallery
1729 Vestal Parkway, West Vestal,
13850
Tel: 607 754 9193
www.mapesauction.com

Phillips de Pury & Company
450 West 15 Street, New York, 10011
Tel: 212 940 1200
www.phillipsdepury.com

Sotheby's
1334 York Ave, New York, 10021
Tel: 212 606 7000
www.sothebys.com

Stair Galleries
549 Warren Street, Hudson, 12534
Tel: 518 751 1000
www.stairgalleries.com

Sterling Auction House
4757 Route 55, Swan Lake, 12783
Tel: 845 913 6816
www.sterlingauctionhouse.com

Swann Galleries Inc.
104 East 25th Street,
New York, 10010-2977
Tel: 212 254 4710
www.swanngalleries.com

OHIO

Belhorn Auction Services
PO Box 20211, Columbus, 43220
Tel: 614 921 9441
www.belhorn.com

Cincinnati Art Galleries LLC
225 East 6th Street, Cincinnati,
45202
Tel: 513 381 2128
www.cincinnatiartgalleries.com

The Cobbs Auctioneers LLC
Noone Falls Mill, 50 Jaffrey Road,
Petersborough, 03458
Tel: 603 924 6361
www.thecobbs.com

Cowan's Historic Americana Auctions
6270 Este Ave, Cincinnati, 45232
Tel: 513 871 1670
www.cowanauctions.com

Garth's Auction Inc.
2690 Stratford Rd,PO Box 369,
Delaware, 43015
Tel: 740 362 4771
www.garths.com

Treadway Gallery Inc.
2029 Maidson Road,Cincinnati,
45208
Tel: 513 321 6742
www.treadwaygallery.com

Wolf's Auction Gallery
1239 West 6th Street, Cleveland,
44113
Tel: 216 575 9653

OKLAHOMA

Buffalo Bay Auction Co.
825 Fox Run Trail, Edmond, 73034
Tel: 405 285 8990
www.buffalobayauction.com

OREGON

O'Gallery
228 Northeast Seventh Ave, Portland,
97232
Tel: 503 238 0202
www.ogallerie.com

PENNSYLVANIA

Noel Barrett
PO Box 300, Carversville, 18913
Tel: 215 297 5109
www.noelbarrett.com

William Bunch Auctions
1Hillman Drive, Chadds Ford,
Philadelphia 19317
Tel: 610 558 1800
www.williambunchauctions.com

Concept Art Gallery
1031 South Braddock Avenue,
Pittsburgh, 15218
Tel: 412 242 9200
www.conceptgallery.com

Freeman's
1808 Chestnut St, Philadelphia,
19103
Tel: 610 563 9275
www.freemansauction.com

Hunt Auctions
256 Welsh Pool Road, Exton, 19341
Tel: 610 524 0822
www.huntauctions.com

Pook & Pook Inc.
463 E. Lancaster Ave, Downington,
19335
Tel: 610 269 4040
www.pookandpook.com

Sanford Alderfer Auction Co.
501 Fairgrounds Road, PO Box 640,
Hatfield, 19440
Tel: 215 393 3023
info@alderauction.com

Charles A. Whitaker Auction Co.,
1002 West Clivedon St,
Philadelphia, 19119
Tel: 215 817 4600
www.whitakerauction.com

RHODE ISLAND

Gustave White Auctioneers
37 Bellevue, Newport, 02840
Tel: 401 841 5780

TENNESSEE

Kimball M Sterling Inc.
125 West Market Street,
Johnson City, 37604,
Tel. 423 920 1471
www.sterlingsold.com

TEXAS

Austin Auctions
8414 Anderson Mill Road, Austin,
78729
Tel: 512 258 5479
www.austinauction.com

Dallas Auction Gallery
2235 Monitor St, Dallas, 75207
Tel: 214 653 3900
www.dallasauctiongallery.com

Heritage Auction Galleries,
3500 Maple Ave, 17th Floor, Dallas,
75219
Tel: 800 872 6467
www.ha.com

UTAH

America West Archives
PO Box 100, Cedar City, 84721
Tel: 435 586 9497
www.americawestarchives.com

VERMONT

Eaton Auction Service
3428 Middle Brook Rd, Fairlee,
05045
Tel: 802 333 9717
www.eatonauctionservice.com

VIRGINIA

Green Valley Auctions Inc.
2259 Green Valley Lane,
Mount Crawford, 22841
Tel: 540 343 4260
www.greenvalleyauctions.com

Ken Farmer Auctions & Estates
105 Harrison Street, Radford, 24141
Tel: 540 639 0939
www.kenfarmer.com

Phoebus Auction Gallery
Tel: 757 722 9210
www.phoebusauction.com

WASHINGTON DC

Seattle Auction House,
5931 4th Avenue South, Seattle, 98108
Tel: 206 764 4444
www.seattleauctionhouse.com

Weschler's
909 East Street NW,
Washington, 20004-2006
Tel: 202 628 1281 / 800 331 1430
www.weschlers.com

WISCONSIN

Milwaukee Auction Galleries
1919 North Summit Ave, Milwaukee,
53202
Tel: 414 271 1105

Schrager Auction Galleries Ltd.
PO Box 10390, 2915 North Sherman
Blvd, Milwaukee, 53210
Tel: 414 873 3738
www.schragerauctions.com

CANADA

ALBERTA

Arthur Clausen & Sons, Auctioneers
11802 - 145 Street, Edmonton T5L 2H3
Tel: 780 451 4549
www.clausenauction.com

Hall's Auction Services Ltd.
5240 1A Street S.E., Calgary, T2H 1J1
Tel: 403 640 1244
www.hodginshalls.com

Hodgins Art Auctions Ltd.
5240 1A Street S.E., Calgary, T2H 1J1
Tel: 403 640 1244
www.hodginshalls.com

Lando Art Auctions
11130-105 Avenue N.W., Edmonton,
T5H 0L5
Tel: 780 990 1161
www.landoartauctions.com

BRITISH COLUMBIA

Maynards Fine Art Auction House
415 West 2nd Avenue,
Vancouver V5Y 1E3
Tel: 604 876 6787
www.maynards.com

Robert Derot Associates
P.O. Box 52205, Vancouver, V7J 3V5
Tel: 604 649 6302
www.robertderot.com

Waddington's West
3286 Bellevue Road, Victoria, V8X 1C1
Tel: 250 384 3737
www.waddingtonsauctions.com

Heffel Fine Art Auction House
2247 Granville Street, Vancouver
V6H 3G1
Tel: 604 732 6505
www.heffel.com

ONTARIO

Empire Auctions
165 Tycos Drive, Toronto M6B 1W6
Tel: 416 784 4261
www.empireauctions.com

Ritchies
777 Richmond Street West, Toronto,
M6J 2L8
Tel: 416 364 1864
www.ritchies.com

A Touch of Class
92 College Crescent, Barrie L4M 5C8
Tel: 888 891 6591
www.atouchofclassauctions.com

Waddington's
111 Bathurst Street, Toronto M5V 2R1
Tel: 416 504 9100
www.waddingtonsauctions.com

Walkers
81 Auriga Drive, Suite 18, Ottawa
K2E 7Y5
Tel: 613 224 5814
www.walkersauctions.com

Deveau Galleries, Robert Fine Art Auctioneers,
299 Queen Street, Toronto, M5A 1S7
Tel: 416 364 6271 www.
deveaugalleries.com

Heffel Fine Art Auction House,
13 Hazelton Avenue, Toronto M5R 2E1
Tel: 416 961 6505
www.heffel.com

Sotheby's
9 Hazelton Avenue, Toronto M5R 2E1
Tel: 416 926 1774
www.sothebys.com

QUEBEC

Empire Auctions
5500, rue Paré, Montréal H4P 2M1
Tel: 514 737 6586
www.montreal.empireauctions.com

Iegor - Hôtel des Encans
872, rue Du Couvent, Angle Saint-Antoine Ouest, Montréal H4C 2R6
Tel: 514 842 7447
www.iegor.net

Montréal Auction House
5778 St. Lawrent Blvd., Montréal,
H2T 1S8
Tel: 514 278 0827
http://pages.videotron.com/encans

Pinneys Auctions
2435 Duncan Road (T.M.R.),
Montréal, H4P 2A2
Tel: 514 345 0571
www.pinneys.ca

Specialists who would like to be listed in the next edition, or have a new address or telephone number, should contact us at info@millers.uk.com. Readers should contact dealers before visiting to avoid a wasted journey.

AMERICAN PAINTINGS

James R Bakker Antiques Inc.
248 Bradford Street,
Provincetown, MA 02657
Tel: 508 487 9081
www.bakkerart.com

Jeffrey W Cooley
The Cooley Gallery Inc, 25 Lyme Street, Old Lyme, CT 06371
Tel: 860 434 8807
www.cooleygallery. com

AMERICANA & FOLK ART

American West Indies Trading Co. Antiques & Art
27315 Barbuda Lane, Summerland Key, FL 33042
Tel: 305 872 3948
www.goantiques.com/members/awindiestrading

Augustus Decorative Arts Ltd.
Tel: 215 587 0000
www.portrait-miniatures.com

Axtell Antiques
1 River Street, Deposit, NY 13754
Tel: 607 467-2353
www.axtellantiques.com

Thomas & Julia Barringer
26 South Main Street, Stockton, NJ, 08559
Tel: 609 397 4474
tandjb@voicenet.com

Bucks County Antique Center
Route 202, Lahaska, PA 18931
Tel: 215 794 9180

Sidney Gecker
226 West 21st Street, New York, NY 10011
Tel: 212 929 8769
www.sidneygecker.com

Garthoeffner Gallery Antiques
Tel: 717 471 4694
garthgallery@comcast.net
www.garthoeffnergallery.com

Allan Katz Americana
25 Old Still Road,
Woodbridge, CT 06525
Tel: 203 393 9356
www.allankatzamericana.moonfruit.com

Olde Hope Antiques Inc.
P.O. Box 718, New Hope, PA 18938
Tel: 215 297 0200
www.oldehope.com

Pantry & Hearth,
994 Main Street South,
Woodbury, CT 06798
Tel: 203 263 8555
www.pantryandhearth.com

Raccoon Creek Antiques
Box 276, 208 Spangsville Road,
Oley, PA 19547
www.raccooncreekantiques.com

J B Richardson
6 Partrick Lane,Westport, CT 06880
Tel: 203 226 0358

Cheryl & Paul Scott
P.O. Box 835, 232 Bear Hill Road,
Hillsborough, NH 03244
Tel: 603 464 3617
riverbendfarm@tds.net

The Splendid Peasant
992 Foley Road, Sheffield, MA 01257
Tel: 413 229 8800
www.splendidpeasant.com

The Stradlings
1225 Park Avenue, New York, NY 10028
Tel: 212 534 8135

Patricia Stauble Antiques
180 Main Street, PO Box 265,
Wiscasset, ME 04578
Tel: 207 882 6341
www.staublechambersantiques.com

Throckmorton Fine Art
145 East 57th Street, 3rd Floor,
New York, NY 10022
Tel: 001 212 223 1059
www.throckmorton-nyc.com

Jeffrey Tillou Antiques
39 West Street, PO Box 1609,
Litchfield, CT 06759
Tel: 860 567 9693
www.tillouantiques.com

ANTIQUITIES

Frank & Barbara Pollack
1214 Green Bay Road,
Highland Park, IL 60035
Tel: 847 433 2213
barbarapollack@comcast.net

ARCHITECTURAL ANTIQUES

Garden Antiques
Katonah, NY 10536
Tel: 212 744 6281
www.bi-gardenantiques.com

Hurst Gallery
53 Mt. Auburn Street,
Cambridge, MA 02138
Tel: 617 491 6888
www.hurstgallery.com

Cecilia B Williams
12 West Main Street, New Market, MD 21774
Tel: 301 865 0777

ARMS & MILITARIA

Faganarms
33915 Harper Avenue, Clinton Township. MI 48035
Tel: 586 465 4637
www.faganarms.com

BAROMETERS

Barometer Fair
PO Box 25502, Sarasota, FL 34277
Tel: 941 400 7044
www.barometerfair.com

BOOKS

Bauman Rare Books
535 Madison Avenue,
New York, NY 10022
Tel: 212 751 0011
www.baumanrarebooks.com

CARPETS & RUGS

John J Collins Jr. Gallery,
40R Merrimac Street, Brown's Wharf,
Newburyport, MA 01950
Tel: 978 462 7276
www.bijar.com

Karen & Ralph Disaia
Oriental Rugs Ltd, 23 Lyme Street,
Old Lyme, CT 06371
Tel: 860 434 1167
www.orientalrugsltd.com

D B Stock Antique Carpets
464 Washington Street, Wellesley, MA 02482
Tel: 781 237 5859
www.dbstock.com

CERAMICS

Charles & Barbara Adams
289 Old Main Street,
South Yarmouth, MA 02664
Tel: 508 760 3290
adams_2430@msn.com

Mark & Marjorie Allen
300 Bedford St, Suite 421,
Manchester, NH 03101
Tel: 603 644 8989
www.antiquedelft.com

Jill Fenichell
By appointment Tel: 212 980 9346
jfenichell@yahoo.com

Mellin's Antiques
PO Box 1115, Redding, CT 06875
Tel: 203 938 9538
www.mellinsantiques.com

Philip Suval, Inc
1501 Caroline Street, Fredericksburg, VA 22401
Tel: 540 373 9851
jphilipsuval@aol.com

COSTUME JEWELRY

Aurora Bijoux
Tel: 215 872 7808
www.aurorabijoux.com

Deco Jewels Inc.
131 Thompson Street, New York, NY 10012
Tel: 212 253 1222

Terry Rodgers & Melody
1050 2nd Ave, New York, NY 10022
Tel: 212 758 3164
www.melodyrodgers.com

Roxanne Stuart
Tel: 215 750 8868
gemfairy@aol.com

Bonny Yankauer
bonnyy@aol.com

CLOCKS

Kirtland H. Crump
387 Boston Post Road, Madison, CT 06443
Tel: 203 245 7573
www.crumpclocks.com

RO Schmitt Fine Art
PO Box 162, Windham, NH 03087
Tel: 603 432 2237
www.roschmittfinearts.com

DECORATIVE ARTS

Susie Burmann
23 Burpee Lane, New London, NH 03257
Tel: 603 526 5934
rsburmann@tds.net

H L Chalfant Antiques
1352 Paoli Pike, West Chester, PA 19380
Tel: 610 696 1862
www.hlchalfant.com

Brian Cullity
18 Pleasant Street, PO Box 595,
Sagamore, MA 02561
Tel: 508 888 8409
www.briancullity.com

Gordon & Marjorie Davenport
4250 Manitou Way, Madison, WI 53711
Tel: 608 271 2348
GMDaven@aol.com

Ron & Penny Dionne
55 Fisher Hill Road, Willington, CT 06279
Tel: 860 487 0741

Peter H Eaton Antiques
24 Parker St, Newbury, MA 01951
Tel: 978 465 2754
www.petereaton.com

Gallery 532
142 Duane St, New York, NY 10013
Tel: 212 219 1327
www.gallery532tribeca.visualnet.com

Leah Gordon Antiques
Gallery 18, Manhattan Art & Antiques Center, 1050 Second Avenue, New York, NY 10022
Tel: 212 872 1422
www.leahgordon.com

Samuel Herrup Antiques
116 Main St, PO Box 248, Sheffield, MA 01257
Tel: 413 229 0424
www.samuelherrup.com

High Style Deco
224 West 18th Street, New York, NY 10011
Tel: 212 647 0035
www.highstyledeco.com

R Jorgensen Antiques
502 Post Road (US Route 1), Wells, ME 04090
Tel: 207 646 9444
www.rjorgensen.com

Bettina Krainin
289 Main St, Woodbury, CT 06798
Tel: 203 263 7669
www.bettinakraininantiques.com

William E Lohrman
248 Rte 208, New Paltz, NY 12561
Tel: 845 255 6762

Lorraine's
23 Battery Park Avenue, Asheville, NC 28801
Tel: 828 251 1771
www.lorrainesantiques.com

Gary & Martha Ludlow Inc.
616 Rotunda Ave, Akron, OH 44333
Tel: 330 576 6189
www.ludlowantiques.com

Macklowe Gallery
667 Madison Ave, New York, NY 10021
Tel: 212 644 6400
www.macklowegallery.com

Milly McGehee
P.O. Box 666, Riderwood, MD 21139
Tel: 410 653 3977
millymcgehee@comcast.com

Jackson Mitchell Inc.
5718 Kennett Pike, Wilmington, DE 19807
Tel: 302 656 0110
JacMitch@aol.com

Lillian Nassau
220 East 57th Street, New York, NY 10022
Tel: 212 759 6062
www.lilliannassau.com

Perrault-Rago Gallery
333 North Main Street, Lambertville, NJ 00530
Tel: 609 397 9374
www.ragoarts.com

Sumpter Priddy Inc.
323 South Washington Street, Alexandria, VA 22314
Tel: 703 299 0800
www.sumpterpriddy.com

James L Price Antiques
831 Alexander Spring Road, Carlisle, PA 17013
Tel: 717 243 0501
jlpantiques@earthlink.net

R J G Antiques
P.O. Box 60, Rye, NH 03870
Tel: 603 433 1770
www.rjgantiques.com

John Keith Russell Antiques Inc.
110 Spring Street, PO Box 414, South Salem, NY 10590
Tel: 914 763 8144
www.jkrantiques.com

Israel Sack
730 Fifth Avenue, Suite 605, New York, NY 10029
Tel: 212 399 6562

Lincoln & Jean Sander
235 Redding Road, Redding, CT 06896
Tel: 203 938 2981
sanderlr@aol.com

Kathy Schoemer American Antiques
PO Box 173, 38 Lynn Hill Road, Acworth, NH 03601
Tel: 603 835 2105
www.kathyschoemerantiques.com

Thomas Schwenke Inc.
50 Main Street North, Woodbury, CT 06798
Tel: 203 266 0303
www.schwenke.com

Jack & Ray Van Gelder
Conway House, 468 Ashfield Road, Conway, MA 01341
Tel: 413 369 4660

Van Tassel/Baumann American Antiques
690 Sugartown Road, Malvern, PA 19355
Tel: 610 647 3339

Anne Weston & Associates LLC
43 Pray St, Portsmouth, NH 03801
Tel: 603 431 0385
www.anne-weston.com

DOLLS

Sara Bernstein Antique Dolls & Bears
Englishtown, NJ 07726
Tel: 732 536 4101
www.sarabernsteindolls.com

Theriault's
PO Box 151, Annapolis, MD 21404
Tel: 410 224 3655
www.theriaults.com

FURNITURE

American Antiques
161 Main Street, PO Box 368, Thomaston, ME 04861
Tel: 207 354 6033
acm@midcoast.com

Antique Associates
PO Box 129W, 473 Main Street, West Townsend, MA 01474
Tel: 978 597 8084
www.aaawt.com

Antiquebug
Frank & Cathy Sykes, 85 Center St, Wolfeboro, NH 03894
Tel: 603 569 0000
www.antiquebug.com

Barbara Ardizone Antiques
P.O. Box 433, 62 Main Street, Salisbury, CT 06068
Tel: 860 435 3057
www.barbaraardizone.com

Artemis Gallery
Wallace Rd, North Salem, NY 10560
Tel: 914 669 5971
www.artemisantiques.com

Joanne & Jack Boardman
2719 Greenwood Acres, Dekalb, IL 60115
Tel: 815 756 359
boardmanantiques@comcast.net

Boym Partners Inc.
131 Varick Street, Ste. 915, New York, NY 10013
Tel: 212 807 8210
www.boym.com

Joan R Brownstein
24 Parker St, Newbury, MA 01951
Tel: 978 465-1089
www.joanrbrownstein.com

Carswell Rush Berlin Inc.
PO Box 0210, Planetarium Station, New York, NY 0024-0210
Tel: 212 721 0330
www.american-antiques.net

Evergreen Antiques
1249 Third Ave, New York, NY 10021
Tel: 212 744 5664
www.evergreenantiques.com

Douglas Hamel Antiques
56 Staniels Road, Chichester, NH 03234
Tel: 603 798 5912
www.shakerantiques.com

Eileen Lane Antiques
150 Thompson Street, New York, NY 10012
Tel: 212 475 2988
www.eileenlaneantiques.com

Lost City Arts
18 Cooper Square, New York, NY 10003
Tel: 212 375 0500
www.lostcityarts.com

Alan Moss
436 Lafayette Street, New York, NY 10003
Tel: 212 473 1310
www.alanmossny.com

GENERAL

Alley Cat Lane Antiques
Tallahassee, FL 32303
Tel: 850 294 5073
www.rubylane.com/shops/alleycat-lane

Bucks County Antiques Center
Route 202, 8 Skyline Drive, Lahaska, PA 18914
Tel: 215 794 9180

Camelot Antiques
7871 Ocean Gateway, Easton, MD 21601
Tel: 410 820 4396
www.about-antiques.com

Manhatten Arts & Antiques Center
1050 Second Avenue, 55th-56th Street, New York, NY 10022
Tel: 212 355 4400
www.the-maac.com

Showcase Antiques Center
Route 20, Sturbridge, MA 01566
Tel: 508 347-7190
www.showcaseantiques.com

South Street Antique Markets
615 South 6th Street, Philadelphia, PA 19147
Tel: 215 592 0256

GLASS

Brookside Art Glass
16 Sconticut Neck Rd, 312 Fairhaven, MA 02719
Tel: 508 993 9434
www.wpitt.com

Holsten Galleries
Elm Street, Stockbridge, MA 01262
Tel: 413 298 3044
www.holstengalleries.com

Antiques by Joyce Knutsen
Tel: 315 637 8238 (Summer)
Tel: 352 567 1699 (Winter)

Paul Reichwein
2321 Hershey Ave, East Petersburg, PA 17520
Tel: 717 569 7637

JEWELRY

Ark Antiques
PO Box 3133, New Haven, CT 06515
Tel: 203 498 8572

Arthur Guy Kaplan
PO Box 1942, Baltimore, MD 21203
Tel: 410 752 2090
rkaplan8350@comcast.net

LIGHTING

Chameleon Fine Lighting
223 East 59th Street, New York NY 10022
Tel: 212 355 6300
www.chameleon59.com

MARINE ANTIQUES

Hyland Granby Antiques
P.O. Box 457, Hyannis Port, MA 02647
Tel: 508 771 3070
www.hylandgranby.com

METALWARE

Wayne & Phyllis Hilt
176 Injun Hollow Road, Haddam Neck, CT 06424-3022
Tel: 860 267 2146
www.hiltpewter.com

ORIENTAL

Marc Matz Antiques
75 Main Street, Wiscasset, Maine 04578
Tel: 802 592 3383
www.marcmatz.com

Mimi's Antiques
1984 San Marco Blvd. Jacksonville, FL 32207
Tel: 904 399 1218
www.mimisonline.com

PAPERWEIGHTS

The Dunlop Collection
PO Box 6269, Statesville, NC 28687
Tel: 704 871 2626 or (800) 227 1996

SCIENTIFIC INSTRUMENTS

Edison Gallery
Susanin's, 900 South Clinton Street, Chicago, IL 60607
Tel: 312 832 9800
www.edisongallery.com

SILVER

Alter Silver Gallery Corp.
Gallery 49A & 50, 1050 Second Ave, New York, NY 10022
Tel: 212 750 1928 or917 848 1713
aftersilvergallery@mac.com

Argentum
The Leopard's Head, 472 Jackson St, San Francisco, CA 94111
Tel: 415 296 7757
www.arguentum-theleopard.com

Chicago Silver
www.chicagosilver.com

Jonathan Trace
PO Box 418, Rifton, NY 12471
Tel: 914 658 7336

Imperial Half Bushel
831 North Howard Street, Baltimore, MD 21201
Tel: 410 462 1192
www.imperialhalfbushel.com

TEXTILES

Pandora de Balthazar
201 E. Austin St, Round Top, TX 78954
Tel: 979 249 2070
www.pandoradebalthazar.com

Colette Donovan
98 River Road, Merrimacport, MA 01860
Tel: 978 346 0614
colettedonovan@adelphia.net

M Finkel & Daughter
936 Pine Street, Philadelphia, PA 19107
Tel: 215 627 7797
www.samplings.com

Cora Ginsburg
19 East 74th Street, New York, NY 10021
Tel: 212 744 1352
www.coraginsburg.com

Nancy Goldsmith
New York, NY
Tel: 212 696 0831

Andrea Hall Levy
PO Box 1243, Riverdale, NY 10471
Tel: 646 441 1726
barangrill@aol.com

Stephen & Carol Huber
40 Ferry Road, Old Saybrook, CT 06475
Tel: 860 388 6809
www.antiquesamplers.com

Fayne Landes Antiques
593 Hansell Road, Wynnewood, PA 19096
Tel: 610 658 0566

Charlotte Marler
Booth 14, 1528 West 25th Street, New York, NY 10010
Tel: 212 367 8808
char_marler@hotmail.com

Stephanie's Antiques
28 West 25th Street, New York, NY 10010
Tel: 212 633 6563

TRIBAL ART

Arte Primitivo
Howard S. Rose Gallery, 3 East 65th Street, Suite 2, New York, NY 10065
Tel: 212.570.6999
www.arteprimitivo.com

Marcy Burns American Indian Arts
520 East 72nd Sreet, New York, NY 10021
Tel: 212 439 9257
www.marcyburns.com

Domas & Gray Gallery
Tel: 518 392 3913
www.domasandgraygallery.com

Hurst Gallery
53 Mount Auburn Street, Cambridge, MA 02138
Tel: 617 491 6888
www.hurstgallery.com

Morning Star Gallery
513 Canyon Road, Santa Fe, NM 87501
Tel: 505 982 8187
www.morningstargallery.com

Myers & Duncan
12 East 86th Street, Suite 239, New York, NY 10028
Tel: 212 472 0115
jmyersprimitives@aol.com

Elliot & Grace Snyder
PO Box 598, South Egremont, MA 01258
Tel: 413 528 3581
www.elliotandgracesnyder.com

Trotta-Bono American Indian Art
PO Box 34, Shrub Oak, NY 10588
Tel: 914 528 6604
www.trottabono.com

20THC DESIGN

Mix Gallery
10 North Union Street, Lambertville, NJ 08530
Tel: 609 773 0777
www.mixgallery.com

Moderne Gallery
111 North 3rd Street, Philadelphia, PA 19106
Tel: 215 923 8536
www.modernegallery.com

Modernism Gallery
1500 Ponce de Leon Blvd., 2nd Floor, Coral Gables, FL 33134
Tel: 305 442 8743
www.modernism.com

R Gallery
82 Franklin Street, New York, NY 10013
Tel: 212 343 7979
www.r20thcentury.com

CANADIAN SPECIALISTS

CANADIANA

Antiquites Gerard Funkenberg & Jean Drapeau
900 Massawippi, North Hatley, Quebec, J0B 2C0
Tel: 819 842 2725

The Blue Pump
178 Davenport Road, Toronto, Ontario, M5R 172
Tel: 416 944 1673
john@thebluepump.com

Ingram Antiques & Collectibles
669 Mt. Pleasant Road, Toronto, Ontario M4S 2N2
Tel: 416 484 4601

CERAMICS

Cynthia Findlay
284 King Street West, 1st Floor, Toronto, Ontario M5V 1J2
Tel: 416 260 9057
www.cynthiafindlay.com

Pam Ferrazzutti Antiques
1235 Fairview St, Suite 222, Burlington, Ontario L75 2K9
Tel: 416 260 0325
www.pamferrazzuttiantiques.com

FINE ART

Barbara M Mitchell
Tel: 416 699 5582
fineartsbarbara@hotmail.com

FURNITURE

Croix-Crest Antiques
49 Mary Street, St. Andrews, New Brunswick E5B 1S5
Tel: 506 529 4693

Faith Grant
The Connoisseur's Shop Ltd.
1156 Fort Street, Victoria, British Columbia V8V 3K8
Tel: 250 383 0121
www.faithgrantantiques.com

Lorenz Antiques Ltd.
701 Mount Pleasant Rd, Toronto, Ontario M4S 2N4
Tel: 416 487 2066
info@lorenzantiques.com

Maus Park Antiques
289 Pinehurst Road, Paris, Ontario N3L 3E2
Tel: 416 454 7778
www.mausparkantiques.ca

Milord Antiques
1870 Notre-Dame St W., Montréal, Quebec H3L 1M6
Tel: 514 933 2433
showroom@milordantiques.com

Richard Rumi & Co. Antiques
55 Woodlawn Ave, Mississauga, Ontario, L5G 3K7
Tel: 905 274 3616
www.rumiantiques.com

Shand Galleries
Toronto Antiques Centre, 276 King Street West, Toronto, Ontario, M5V 1J2
Tel: 416 260 9056

GENERAL

Can/Am Antiques
www.canamauctionzone.com

Floyd & Rita's Antiques
Toronto Antiques Centre, 276 King Street West, Toronto, Ontario, M5V 1J2
Tel: 416 260 9066
www.floydrita.com

Toronto Antiques Centre
284 King Street West, 1st Floor, Toronto, Ontario, M5V 1J2
Tel: 416 260 9057
www.torontoantiquesonking.com

JEWELRY

Fraleigh Jewellers
1977 Yonge Street, Toronto, Ontario, M4S 1Z6
Tel: 416 483 1481
www.fraleigh.ca

Fiona Kenny Antiques
PO Box 11, 18 Front St. N., Thorold, Ontario, L2V 3Y7
Tel: 905 682 0090
www.fionakennyantiques.com

ORIENTAL

Pao & Molkte Ltd.
Four Seasons Hotel, 21 Avenue Road, Toronto, Ontario, M5R 2G1
Tel: 416 925 6197
www.paoandmoltke.com

Topper Gallery
1111 Finch Avenue West, Toronto, Ontario, M3J 2E5
Tel: 416 663 7554
www.topperart.com

SILVER

Richard Flensted-Holder
By appointment only
Tel: 416 961 3414

Louis Wine Ltd.
150 Cumberland St, Yorkville, Toronto, Ontario, M5R 1A8
Tel: 416 929 9333
www.louiswine.com

TRIBAL

Jamieson Tribal Art
Golden Chariot Productions, 468 Wellington West Street, Suite 201, Toronto, Ontario, M5V 1E3
Tel: 416 569 1396
www.jamiesontribalart.com

Page numbers in **bold** refer to pages with special features

PA
1957

Horses in Action

Horses in Action

Angela Sayer

Exeter Books
NEW YORK

First published in the USA in 1982
by Exeter Books
Exeter is a trademark of Simon & Schuster
Distributed by Bookthrift
New York, New York

ISBN 0-89673-126-X

Printed in Italy

Contents

The Taming of the Horse

Today's horse in all its variety of types, shapes and colours is said to have descended from three basic ancestral root stocks, namely, the Steppe, the Forest and the Plateau horses of prehistory. Even before the diversification of horses into these three types, their common ancestors, according to the fossil record, appear to have originated in North America and crossed to Europe and Asia over the great Bering land bridge which then joined the continents. From the diminutive *Eohippus*, or dawn horse, *Equus* gradually evolved and apparently found conditions particularly ideal in Europe, Asia and Africa. It prospered in those parts of the world but eventually became extinct in the Americas about 8000 years ago and the Western Hemisphere was to be without horses until the arrival of Christopher Columbus in Haiti during 1490. This intrepid explorer carried 30 horses aboard his ships and by the time of his death in 1506, had created breeding establishments on various islands in the West Indies. When Herman Cortez landed in Mexico 13 years later, he took ashore five mares and 11 stallions and the horse once again trod the land of its birth.

The Steppe horse had a short stocky body with long slender limbs and narrow hooves. Its head was large with a concave profile and long ears. It is thought to have been sandy dun in colour, blending in with its environment, and its dark mane stood erect along its

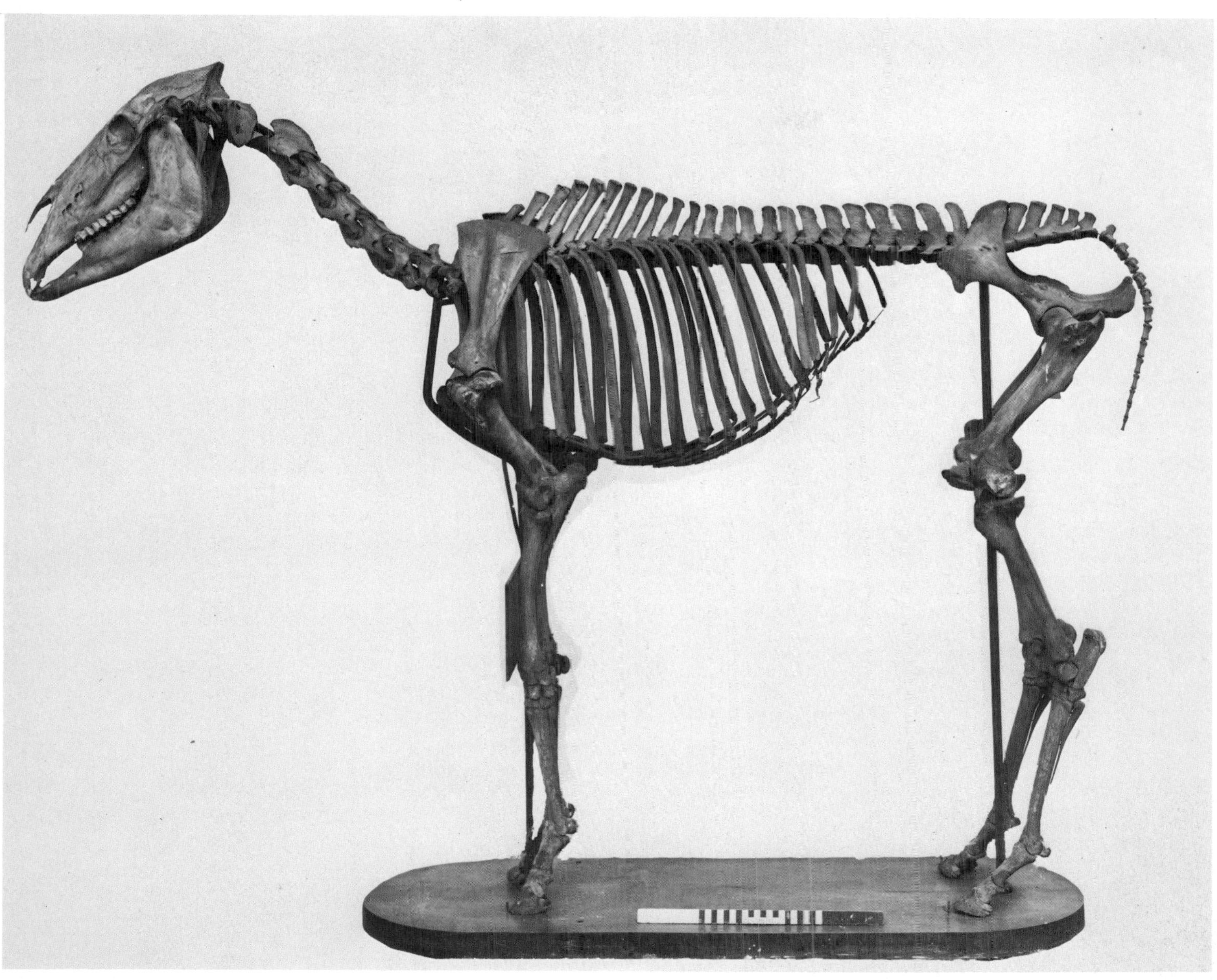

A skeleton of the Mongolian Wild Horse, *Equus caballus przewalskii*, among the first of horse types to be domesticated. Natural History Museum, London.

Left: Pre-historic man was well acquainted with the horse, as may be seen by the striking wall paintings deep within the caves of Lascaux, in France's Dordogne region. Musée du Louvre, Paris.

thick neck. It probably had dark legs and feet and vestigial zebra stripes on its legs, with an eel-mark along the spine. It was a gregarious creature, always alert to any sign of danger and ready to run from attackers when necessary, clearing any natural obstacles in its path. Virtually unaltered relatives of this type still exist today and are known as the Mongolian Wild Horse or Poljakof. Isolated for centuries in the Great Gobi Desert, well away from human interference, herds of these horses existed in their natural state until discovered in 1881 by a Russian explorer, Colonel N. M. Przwalski. He was travelling in the Kobdo district of Western Mongolia when he first observed herds of such horses and christened the species *Equus caballus przwalskii*. Once the existence of the herds became common knowledge in the region, massive hunts were organized to run down and kill the animals for their hides and meat, and until the governments of Mongolia and China intervened, the wild horses were in danger of extinction. Today, successful breeding herds of Mongolian Wild Horses are preserved in zoos and parks throughout the world and retain all the characteristics of those discovered by Przwalski a century ago.

The modern Mongolian Pony is descended from the Wild Horse and is kept in large herds by the Mongolian peoples of today. The mares are milked for three months after foaling and their milk is made into yoghurt and cheese or fermented to produce *kumiss*, a potent drink. The ponies are also used in herding, haulage and as pack animals and provide good quality leather and meat.

More sturdily built than the Steppe variety, the Forest Horse had a thicker, longer body and shorter legs with large rounded hooves adapted for traversing soft marshy ground. Its broad head was concave between the eyes and convex at the muzzle, rather similar to the head of the modern moose or elk. This characteristic enabled it to eat efficiently tender young shoots and to browse on the bark and branches of young forest trees. It is

Right: This handsome pair of Przewalski horses are seen in a modern zoo enclosure where the breed is being carefully preserved.

Below: The extinct Tarpan has been reconstructed by scientific breeding programmes. Lighter in build than the Przewalski horse, the Tarpan is thought to be the ancestor of our modern riding horses and ponies.

thought to have had a long mane and thick, low-set tail and was probably a dark dun in colour with mottled markings helping to conceal its bulk in the dappled light of the leafy glades. It is from this Forest Horse that we believe that most of today's heavy horse breeds descended.

The Plateau Horse or Tarpan officially became extinct in 1887, having been hunted to its demise in the quest for easy meat and hides. Small and shy it was very fast over short distances and was pursued by teams of mounted men working in relays who considered such hunting an exciting and profitable sport. Eventually, the horse's close descendants were gathered together and several zoological parks started programmes of selective genetically planned breeding, in order to reconstruct the Plateau Horse in its original form. The Tarpan is thought to be the ancestor of our present-day riding horses and lightweight ponies. It stands about 13 hands high and has a lightly constructed body with long slender limbs and neat, rounded hooves. Its small, narrow head has a straight or sometimes concave profile, it has neat ears and large eyes. In varying shades of dun, the Tarpan's coat often displays zebra markings on the legs and an eel-mark down its spine.

It is clear from dated evidence that early man knew the horse well, for drawings made on cave walls around

Even today, the Egyptians find the ass is invaluable for carrying heavy loads over rough ground and in high temperatures.

Left: Wild asses were tamed and used for pack work before the horse was harnessed. This onager is carved on an Egyptian temple wall at Thebes, dated around 2000 B.C.

30000 B.C. clearly depict a predominance of equine subjects. By the advent of the New Stone Age, the drawings were more carefully executed and suggested the use of the horse in magic, religious or hunting rituals. Oxen and wild asses were tamed and used for draught and pack work, long before man tried to harness horses. Saharan rock drawings of the fifth millenium clearly show oxen, while Egyptian drawings of the same date discovered in the Eastern Desert show asses with packs and oxen drawing heavy loads. Meanwhile in Eurasia the first pack and saddle animals were reindeer and it was not until 2000 B.C. that the horse was eventually harnessed to the service of man.

The first written record of the use of the horse is attributed to the reign of Hammurabi, a king and lawgiver of Babylon who lived from 1728 B.C.–1686 B.C. By 1500 B.C. Kikkulis, Master of the Horse to the King of Hittites, had a treatise chipped out of stone advocating the care necessary in the training and feeding of horses; it emphasized the fact that a good diet was required to enable the horse to gallop swiftly over long distances and explained how kindness in training made the animal more co-operative.

Controversy rages as to whether the horse was first ridden or harnessed to chariots. It is quite obvious that chariots and draught harness would be more likely to survive over the ages than the flimsy thongs and primitive bits used by a rider. It must be agreed, however, that the very earliest drawings depict small horses drawing chariots of various designs.

Early herdsmen were quick to exploit the horse and learned the best methods of husbandry, training and control. They soon began to ride, identifying themselves as much as possible with their herds' natural leaders. Some wild herds are led by senior mares, so the most successful herders rode similar mares to lead or drive their horse stock to new pastures. Before long, selective breeding practises were established as mares and stallions were chosen for desirable characteristics, and specimens with particular features such as size, speed or stamina were selected for certain purposes.

The agricultural aspects of riding and driving evolved naturally from two different aspects of herdsmanship. Riding was a natural and decisive aid to herd management, movement and control, while carting and haulage became necessary when stock was kept on permanent pasture. In warfare, although the horse was first used to draw chariots into battle, it was soon discovered that mounted warriors had more flexibility and speed. The size of available horses within a region probably had a bearing

Above left: The horse was first used to draw light chariots. This Egyptian relief shows King Rameses II taking part in a buffalo hunt.

Left: The Hittites, too, were quick to realize the speed and power of the horse. This relief showing a lion hunt is dated 1000 B.C. Archaeological Museum, Ankara.

Above: Eventually the horse was ridden into battle and one of the most successful of all mounted leaders was Alexander, shown here in a detail from a mosaic at Pompeii. Museo Nazionale, Naples.

on the way in which they were used. A fairly small pony could be used quite satisfactorily to draw a chariot but would not be strong enough to carry an armed man.

Around the year 450 B.C. Herodotus wrote 'The limitless plains beyond the lower Danube are peopled by the Sigynnes who dress like Medes. The winter coat of their horses is five fingers thick but they are small, blunt nosed and driven only in harness being too small to carry a man.'

Skill as well as courage was needed when warriors exchanged their chariots for warhorses. Great modifications had to be made in weaponry, and the skills of equitation had to be acquired. Various types of bits and bridles were used and later, saddles gave comfort on long rides, but it was to be many years before the stirrup was invented, providing riders with more secure seats.

In 1929 a Soviet archaeologist Dr. Rudenko excavated a series of *kurgans* or burial mounds dating to the 5th century B.C. They were situated near Pazyryk in a high valley of the Althai Mountains of Western Mongolia. The tombs were rectangular shafts lined with felt hangings, and due to a freak series of climatic conditions, all the contents had been perfectly preserved in ice. This proved to be a momentous find, for among the relics were the bodies of 69 horses, complete with all their accoutrements. Not only were the external features virtually free from decomposition, but all the internal organs and even the stomach contents were well preserved. The horses discovered were of four types ranging in height from 13 to 15 hands. The tallest were similar to today's Arabians in conformation with small concave heads, arched necks and short backs. They had fine clean legs with good bone and were mostly golden dun in colour with black points. Their use as riding animals was confirmed by the saddles and bridles buried with them. The shortest groups were of much more common type, stocky in build and were buried with the harness used to draw the wagon which had been employed as a hearse for the burial. The other two groups were of intermediate types, and were probably utility animals. All the stomach contents showed evidence of

Right: Today's desert Arabian, ridden by sightseeing tourists, often wears a collection of ill-fitting leather tackle.

The first equestrians controlled their mounts by means of simple bridles and bits, riding naturally without saddles. Museo Barracco, Rome.

grain feeding, and the fact that systematic breeding was practised was obvious as the geldings had all been castrated before maturity. No foals were found, but some of the clothing in the tomb was trimmed with foal-fur.

When Alexander the Great journeyed on towards his conquest of India he came upon some wondrous horses in the kingdom of Bactria on the northern slopes of the Afghan mountain ranges. He traded with locals and remounted his troops on the impressive animals. Horses had been bred in the area for many years, in fact two local ancient tribal names, 'Zariaspai' and 'Arimaspai', mean literally 'golden horses' and 'well-schooled horses'. The King of Bactria refused to sell horses to the Emperor of China in the 2nd century B.C., despite the offer of much gold, and eventually a mighty battle ensued during which the Chinese captured 30 of the coveted 'heavenly blood-sweating horses' and some 3000 halfbred mares and stallions. From these beginnings the Chinese built a strong horse-breeding industry and considerably increased the efficiency of their cavalry units, making them all but invincible.

Bactrian horses spread through to neighbouring Turkestan but eventually Bactria and Turkestan were conquered by the Arabs during the 8th century. Horse breeding continued in this vast region over the centuries and the animals were constantly upgraded. By the 13th century, Marco Polo travelled through the area and reported that its horses were of excellent quality and very swift, with superb legs and hard hooves which never needed shoes, despite the stony ground. He also mentioned the fact that in northern Afghanistan there was said to be a race of horses descended from Bucephalus, the famous warhorse of Alexander the Great, each of which was possessed of strange distinctive markings upon its forehead in the form of a star and crescent moon.

Military Horses

In its wild state the horse is a true pacifist, a herbivore whose natural form of defence is to gallop swiftly away from danger. It does not, therefore, require much imagination to appreciate the length of time needed from the animal's first domestication to develop its decisive role on the battlefields of the civilized world. The earliest use of the horse in war came with the invention of the wheel which allowed the construction of primitive chariots. The Mesopotamians constructed simple vehicles with four solid wheels, and these were drawn by pairs of onagers. At that time the soldiers fought with axes and javelins, for apparently the bow was unknown. The Standard of Ur is a double-sided panel inlaid with mother-of-pearl figures set in a background of lapis lazuli. Discovered in the tomb of a great ruler at Ur, it dates back to about 2100 B.C. and graphically shows Sumerian battle scenes on one side, with the king himself inspecting his captives. The detail is remarkable and the construction of the chariots made quite clear.

Below: The Standard of Ur, dated about 2100 B.C., showing Sumerian war chariots along the bottom row, with a supply wagon above. British Museum, London.

Bottom: A charioteer from the temple of Queen Hatshepsut of Egypt, 1490–1475 B.C.

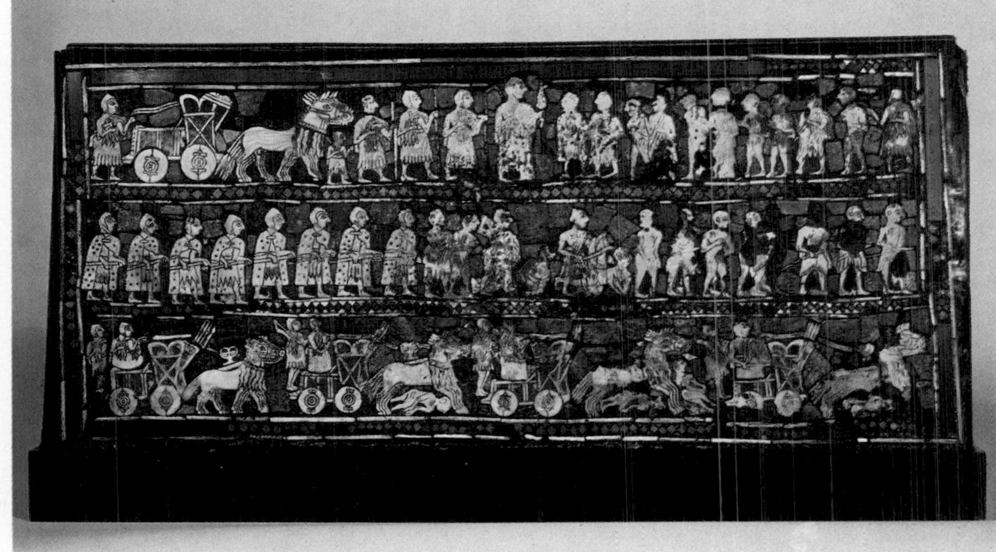

When the fertile Nile Valley was invaded by the Hyksos, or Shepherd Kings, around 1650 B.C., the army of the Pharaoh consisted entirely of infantry. The Hyksos with their war chariots swept victoriously through the Delta lands, quickly achieving an almost bloodless victory. The Egyptians quickly realized the advantages of such war machines, especially on hard level ground. By the time of the withdrawal of the Hyksos and the rise of the Egyptian New Empire in 1550 B.C., Egypt had established its own military superiority and its chariot corps had become the elite of its regular army. With typical skill and ingenuity the ruling classes devised spoked wheels for their carefully designed chariots, and through judicious crossbreeding with horses from the Phoenician coast, had developed strong fast animals.

The Egyptian charioteers formed units in battle and, now armed with efficient bows as well as javelins, proved a formidable force. The war chariot became heavier but more sophisticated in design, and any damage sustained in battle was quickly repaired by teams of specialized carpenters and wheelwrights. The influence of the Arabian in the breeding of chariot horses at this time is apparent from frescoes on temple walls decorated by the ancient Egyptians. In Thebes Museum is a low relief of great beauty and immense detail. It shows Rameses II in his ornate war chariot at the Battle of Kadesh in 1296 B.C. The chariot is drawn by two magnificent, spirited and prancing stallions with long fine limbs and proudly arched necks. Their polls, crests and backs are protected with heavy and finely decorated clothing and the harness seems simple but obviously effective. Reins

pass from the fine bridle through rings in the collar and are tied together behind the Pharaoh's waist, allowing him to control the pair, but leaving his hands and arms free to draw his powerful bow. During this battle, Rameses began by being totally out-manoeuvred by the opposing Hittite commanders, but due to the efforts of his superior charioteers and the might and accuracy of the compact, long-range bows, the Egyptian king finally won the day.

When the Israelites were banished from Egypt in 1230 B.C. they were without horses and, in fact, disdained such creatures, associating them with memories of the Pharaohs' armies. The early books of the Old Testament are full of derogatory references to the horse and it was ordered that any warhorse captured in battle should be hocked or houghed. This was one of the cruellest tortures that could be meted out to a horse for it consists of hamstringing the animal by slashing through and severing the powerful Achilles tendon just above the hock. A horse so mutilated was effectively immobilized, able only to squat painfully on its haunches awaiting a long and lingering death.

David is recorded as the first Israelite king to retain some of the horses of defeated armies. He chose the finest of the animals for the use of his court and from these presumably were bred many of the horses later owned by his son, King Solomon, who took over the throne in 974 B.C. The Old Testament's First Book of Kings confirms the wisdom of Solomon's rule. His armies were well disciplined, expertly trained and properly organized. The horses were carefully treated and well fed and the King could boast a formidable force. Chapter four, verses 26-28 tell us 'And Solomon had forty thousand stalls of horses for his chariots and twelve thousand horsemen, and those officers provided victual . . . they lacked nothing. Barley also and straw for the horses, and dromedaries brought they unto the place where the officers were, every man according to his charge.'

The armies of Assyria fought with all their neighbours in the Near and Middle East; they were strong, disciplined warriors and the first people to develop a separate cavalry. Some of the wars they waged were defensive, and planned to protect the kingdom against invasion

Above: Detail from the bronze gates of Shalmaneser III, 835–824 B.C., showing his army of charioteers in the wars against Syria. British Museum, London.

Above right: This black basalt relief dated around 800 B.C. clearly shows the harnessing and control of the chariot of that time. Archaeological Museum, Ankara.

Right: The Ancient Greeks soon became skilled in horsemanship and bred horses for racing as well as warfare and draught purposes. British Museum, London.

from the north and northwest from the Armenians and the Kashshu. To the south and west, however, the Assyrians fought aggressively with the object of increasing and strengthening their territorial boundaries. Assyrian chariots were heavy and designed to carry four or five soldiers and were, therefore, only effective on level ground. In hilly areas the cavalry came into its own and, armed with spears and bows, the riders worked in pairs, one to steer the horses and hold aloft a large protective shield while his partner, a skilled bowman, loosed his arrows at the enemy. It was during this period that larger horses were bred, capable of carrying armed warriors into battle. This, in turn, became a turning point for the chariot which gradually lost its importance in battle and was slowly relegated to use as a racing vehicle.

The Ancient Greeks exercised the utmost care and skill in breeding both light and heavy horses for specific purposes. Fine-spirited horses were used for chariot racing, a favourite sport of princes and the very rich, and studs were established for breeding swift and handsome stock. In warfare, the Greeks placed greater dependence on their infantry than on cavalry units, and the warhorse was undervalued while the racehorse was prized. Records of Ancient Greek horses abound in all forms including beautiful bronzes. The

Above: Bronze statuette of a Greek cavalryman of about 550 B.C. showing his protective helmet and some body armour. British Museum, London.

Left: Today's military horse often takes on a different role. This is *Hercules*, drum horse of the Mounted Troop of the Household Cavalry.

light horses were depicted as small compact animals with rather concave heads and strong clean legs. The horses were often controlled with light bridles and were ridden bareback.

By the year 530 B.C. Cyrus the Great of Persia had extended his empire across the Middle East from the lands of Bactria through Mesopotamia and into Babylon, east as far as the Oxus and west to the Bosphorus – his victories were made possible by a combination of courageous charioteers and heavily armoured warhorses. Herodutus recorded the exploits of the Persian armies and noted '. . . no man dared face them . . .' When Cambyses, the successor of Cyrus, also conquered Egypt, the whole of the Ancient Orient was secured under Persian rule. Cambyses left no successor to the throne and it was decided that the seven princely candidates should ride out of the city gates at dawn, and the rider of the first horse to neigh should be crowned the King of Kings. Oibares, who was Master of the Horse to Prince Darius, was determined that his master should be the successor and devised a cunning scheme. He went to his breeding stud and rubbed his hand over a mare in breeding condition, then covered the scented hand within the folds of his robe. As the prince passed through the gates, Oibares held up his hand as though in greeting to his master whereupon the fine stallion on which Darius was mounted, neighed loudly. Historian Herodotus records that Darius, after his coronation, erected a fine statue to the glory of Oibares and the stallion. He restored peace to his great empire and ruled wisely and well.

Horsemanship and Training

Xenophon was an Athenian writer of note. As well as compiling several historical and philosophical books, he produced *Hippike* and *Hippicarchakos*, important treatises on horsemanship and cavalry training, around the year 360 B.C. The books explain the desirable features of horses for all purposes, and describe the perfect troop horse saying that it should be 'sound-footed, gentle, sufficiently fleet, ready and able to undergo fatigue, and first and foremost, obedient. . .'. Going on to discuss the disobedient horse he says 'but he often plays the part of a very traitor . . .'. It is interesting to read that muzzles were used on the stallions whenever they were handled without bridles, and that all training and schooling were carried out over natural ground. Xenophon emphasized the importance of producing a balanced and collected mount so that it moves in a 'graceful and striking manner . . .'. He deplores the practise of jerking the animal's mouth or heeling its sides '. . . most people think that this is the way to make him look fine; but they only produce an exactly contrary effect – they positively blind their horses by jerking the mouth up instead of allowing them to see where they are going, and by spurring, and whipping, frighten them into confusion so that they run headlong into danger. This is the way horses behave that are fretted into ugly and ungraceful action. But if you teach your horse to go with a light hand on the bit, yet to carry his neck high and bend his head you will make him do exactly what he himself delights in. . . .'

A Persian relief of the 5th century B.C. shows a different style of protective helmet worn by a skilled horseman while schooling his powerful stallion from the ground.

Xenophon rose through the cavalry ranks from troop leader to general and took a leading role during the mercenary attack organized by Cyrus the Younger for the dethronement of Artaxerxes. After a fierce confrontation during which Cyrus was killed, it was Xenophon who proved himself to be the hero of the day by safely leading the army of 10 000 Greeks through Persian territory to the Black Sea.

As well as advocating effective methods of horsemanship and training Xenophon actively encouraged the upgrading of riding horse stock, suggesting careful selection of animals for breeding. He stressed the importance of good conformation '. . . his feet should be hollow and ring like cymbals, the pastern sloping but not too much so. The horse should have good bones, supple knees, powerful shoulders and a broad chest; the neck should not sag, but be arched like the neck of a fighting cock.' Nowhere in his writings does Xenophon give the height of the horse, but the horses of his time are represented by those prancing across the Parthenon frieze executing their parade paces. This great work was completed ten years before the birth of Xenophon, and his description of the ideal horse compares well with these stone examples 'being compact, well coupled with fine legs and heads . . .'. The comparative scale of the riders to the horses would indicate an average size of about 14 hands.

In the 4th century B.C. King Philip of Macedon developed the use of cavalry from his exalted position as leader of the Greek confederation. He is even credited with having conceived and initiated the first full charge of a mounted troop. Previously, the cavalry had fought as individuals, each selecting an adversary and fighting hand to hand.

Following the teachings of Xenophon, the king instituted periods of drill and exercises for the training of both horses and their riders to fight in a coordinated way; eventually the massed charge was attempted. Philip's son Alexander was born in 356 B.C. and learned the art of horsemanship from a very tender age. When he reached the age of 13 years he was placed in the care

The Romans trained their horses carefully, encouraging them to arch their necks and to respond to light signals from the reins. Villa Albani, Rome.

of Aristotle to be instructed in the arts of politics and war. He was thoroughly trained to be expert in all aspects of weaponry and cavalry-style riding and at 18 years of age fought valiantly at his father's side at the Battle of Chaeronea. Here, his skill and tactics in the deployment of his cavalry and his great personal courage resulted in an overwhelming victory. Two years later, in 336 B.C., Philip of Macedon was assassinated and the throne passed to the 20-year-old Alexander. His many famous battles and victories, including those against Darius III of Persia, earned him the title of Alexander the Great.

Alexander himself accredited most of his success to his superb cavalry units and he personally had one of the most celebrated warhorses in history. The story of Alexander's acquisition of his horse was related by both Pliny and Plutarch who recorded King Philip's purchase of the great stallion for a large sum, and his subsequent anger when he found the animal ill-tempered and unmanageable. No one was able to mount the horse and the king ordered the groom to return him to his stable. Alexander, then aged 12, begged his father to allow him to try his luck and wagered the value of the horse against his success or failure. Amid much teasing laughter from the assembled noblemen, Alexander coaxed the horse and quietly turned him to face into the sun. He had noticed the animal's tendency to shy away from his own shadow, and gambled that his tactics would work. The horse settled down and within moments Alexander was astride his back. He trotted around the courtyard, then turned out to gallop across the open parkland. Philip was as amazed at the feat as were the rest of the onlookers and when his son returned on the calm stallion he pronounced 'You must seek out a kingdom worthy of you, Macedonia is not broad enough for you.' The horse, Bucephalus, became Alexander's favourite mount from that day and accompanied him throughout his military career. He was first charger and as such was never ridden on march or in reviewing the troops, but whenever Alexander was preparing to enter battle, he called for the horse, mounted up and led the attack.

Bucephalus was 30 years old when he carried Alexander into the battle of Hydaspes in which Porus, King of India, was defeated in 327 B.C. The stallion fought as valiantly as his master in the thick of the skirmishing, surrounded by attackers on all sides, and took spear and javelin wounds in the neck and flanks. Mortally wounded, the horse turned and carried Alexander, quite unscathed, to safety before collapsing. The king was consumed with grief at the loss of his horse and had the stallion buried with full military honours at the spot where his armies had crossed the Hydaspes river. He ordered a city to be built there and named it after the great horse. The name, Bucephalus, came from the Greek

Right: Despite their skill on horseback and the quality of their small horses, the Roman generals preferred to employ their infantry whenever possible. Musei Vaticani.

Below: This mosaic from Pompeii shows Darius routed by the army of Alexander the Great at Issus in 333 B.C., when in Syria Alexander met the Persian's main force for the first time. Museo Nazionale, Naples.

Right: A bronze horseman taken from the lid of a 6th century B.C. Greek bowl. Such mounted warriors would feign retreat, then turn to fire at their bewildered pursuers.

Opposite page: An armoured and well-mounted Roman cavalryman. The breastplate and breechings are decorated with brass ornaments, a tradition still continued to this day by heavy horse enthusiasts.

boukephalos, meaning bull-headed, and according to some writers he was so named because of a star and blaze on his forehead in the shape of a bull's head with horns. It is more likely, however, that the name refers to the horse's exceptionally broad forehead and wide poll, distinctive features of a breed of Thessalian horses, described by Aristophanes and seen in samples of the sculpture of that time.

The Role of the Cavalry

At first the Romans despised the horse and relied upon the strength of their legions of infantry, but as time went by, they came to realize the value of the swift-moving, flexible force offered by the well-trained cavalry unit. Tacitus observed that the European horse-soldiers were mounted on 'slow and ugly' Gallic horses, animals obviously descended from the original wild horses of Eurasia. The Romans preferred quality in their chargers and celebrated individual horses were treated with reverence. Virgil wrote *Georgics circa* 30 B.C. and in it he described the Roman horse of war thus: 'His neck is carried erect; his head is small; his belly short; his back broad. Brawny muscles swell upon his noble chest. A bright bay or a good gray is the best colour; the worst is white or dun. If from afar the clash of arms be heard, he knows not how to stand still; his ears prick up, his limbs quiver, and snorting, he rolls the collected fire under his nostrils. And his mane is thick, and reposes tossed right back on his right shoulder. A double spine runs along to his loins.'

Little money was spent on the early Roman cavalry and its military role consisted mainly of clearing up straggling groups of retreating forces. When the Romans were confronted by Hannibal, the Carthaginian general, they reckoned without his superiority as a cavalry officer. As a child, Hannibal had been sworn to eternal enmity with Rome, an oath he never forgot, and he is best known for his crossing of the Alps with elephants. Having traversed the mountains in 15 days Hannibal formed his platoons, with the elephants in the centre and his cavalry on the flanks.

Between the elephants and the horses were units of infantry, the division being necessary to prevent the horses panicking at the scent of the mighty pachyderms. The Numidians who formed the cavalry were very impressive, each mounted upon a well-equipped, strong, fit horse of Arabian stock. In contrast the Romans rode small ponies and attacked without formation. As they galloped towards the formed columns their mounts scented the elephants and panicked and in the resulting pandemonium the Romans suffered a crushing defeat.

In 55 B.C. led by Caesar, two legions invaded the shores of Britain. Of a total of 10000 men, 600 were cavalry and many of their horses were lost overboard in the violent storms encountered as the Roman ships approached the English coast. As the infantry tried to land, it was attacked by hordes of barbarous Britons, riding tough and tireless ponies. Eventually the Britons retired and the exhausted Romans rallied around their standard on the shore. When the invaders tried to forage for grain, they were again attacked by the Britons, painted with blue woad, and, this time, driving

The statue on London's Westminster Bridge commemorating Boadicea, Queen of the Iceni, who died in A.D. 61.

A detail from the Bayeux tapestry, showing the simple saddlery of the time and the use of stirrups, providing the extra stability necessary for wielding such formidable weapons. Musée de la Reine Mathilde, Bayeux.

chariots drawn by pairs of ponies. Roman intelligence had not prepared its army for such force and tactics, and it was only the presence of Caesar that endowed the legions with sufficient encouragement to press their invasion. Eventually after much bloodshed the Romans gained a foothold in Britain which was to last five hundred years.

In Britain's East Anglian region lived the Iceni, a tribe led by Queen Boadicea, who was flogged by a Roman commander and had two of her daughters violated. In the year A.D. 61 with their neighbours, the Trinobantes, the Iceni rose in vengeance against the Romans and attacked Colchester, London and St. Albans. Boadicea wore a scarlet cloak and drove at the head of her army in her war chariot, the long knives embedded in its wheels literally mowing down the Roman lines. In one raid alone, a township of 500 civilians was slaughtered and it was estimated by Tactitus, the Roman historian, that this Celtic queen and her charioteers managed to kill a total of 70 000 of their enemies, almost destroying the Roman power. When the revolt was eventually quelled, Boadicea committed suicide by swallowing poison. Incredible though it might seem, the Romans learned little from their defeats; they failed to develop their cavalry and continued to rely on infantry which they considered to be invincible.

The fall of Rome was gradual, the Empire crumbling slowly away. One significant blow which helped to erode its foundations occurred in the battle of Adrianpole in A.D. 378 when Gothic horsemen rode down and virtually annihilated the Roman divisions. As Rome fell, a grand master of military horse warfare was born who was to earn the nickname of the Scourge of God. He was Attila, King of the Huns, and he and his barbaric soldiers were feared for their cruelty and vandalism. Attila almost lived in the saddle of his splendid Tartary-bred charger. He even had his dining table set with the finest silver and his favourite delicacies, then lifted aloft so that he could eat from his exalted mounted position. Attila was a master of mounted tactics and it is said that he commanded 300 000 horsemen in one of his final battles.

At Châlons sur Marne, he split his cavalry into three wings to descend on his enemy in a huge arc. When Attila died in A.D. 453, his horsemen in their thousands rode around the bier in which their idol's remains were enclosed within

As armour and weapons became heavier, the warhorse had to be capable of carrying such burdens into battle and the Great Horse or Destrier evolved. British Library, London.

three magnificent coffins. Respects were paid for a period of several days, funeral songs were sung and rousing martial music played. Then their King was buried with all his most valuable spoils of war.

The horse had achieved a vital role as a military machine and the possession of an efficient cavalry wing was considered essential by any warring faction. As the centuries passed, various refinements were developed to aid in riding efficiently and over long distances. Perhaps the most important of all was the evolution in the 8th century of the stirrup giving stability and therefore greater fighting power to horsemen.

Although the Saxons, like the early Romans, disregarded the horse in war and preferred to rely on infantry, they venerated the horse as a cult symbol and used it for transport and hunting. The first Saxon chieftains to land in Britain were the brothers, Hengist (named from the German *Hengst* or stallion) and Horsa (from the English 'horse'). Their lack of cavalry proved the Saxon's downfall in 1066, for when William of Normandy faced Harold at the Battle of Hastings, his archers and infantry were led by a thousand horsemen, partially armoured and heavily armed. Despite efficient wielding of their mighty 5 ft Danish battle axes, the Saxons were defeated. The Bayeaux tapestry was completed within a few years of the decisive battle and provides more than two hundred accurate pictures of horses and their accoutrements. The horses were all stallions and all appear to have been of one type, fairly light in build and about 14 hands in height for the riders' legs hang far below the girths. The cavalrymen wore only light armour of chainmail, thin links of metal sewn to leather tunics, and, therefore, had no need of heavyweight warhorses.

The Age of Chivalry

In the 12th century, as the Order of Chivalry spread throughout Europe, many noblemen joined the ranks of mounted knights, with their strict code of conduct and high moral ideals. The fully armoured knight needed a great horse to carry him, and animals were specially bred up to size. King John imported more than one hundred fine Flanders stallions into Britain and these were crossed with mares from France, Lombardy and the Low Countries. Up to 17 hands in height, the warhorse was of typical cold-blood type with a Roman nose, thick, heavily feathered legs and a massive body. Known as the Destrier, the great horse was able to carry 420 lb (224 kg) upon its back, and so ponderous did it become that it proved eventually to cause its own downfall. Lacking manoeuvrability, the great horse could not be ridden on the march and it was liable to become bogged down in wet or marshy ground. Its major drawback, however, was its enormous food requirement, necessitating a wagon train of forage to accompany the unit.

Horses similar to this fine Percheron colt were imported into Britain from France and the Low Countries and crossed with King John's stock from Flanders, to produce warhorses.

A battle scene, taken from a mid 13th-century French manuscript. The combatants wear chainmail and protective helmets with visors, but the horses are vulnerable. Pierpont Morgan Library, New York.

The glory of the Destrier was recorded around 1183 by William Fitzstephen, secretary to Thomas a Becket, who wrote, 'In the suburbs immediately outside one of the gates there is a smooth field both in fact and name [this refers to Smithfield which was situated just outside one of the gates of the City of London]. On every sixth day of the week unless it be a major feast day on which solemn rites are prescribed, there is a much frequented show of fine horses for sale. Thither come all the Earls, Barons and Knights who are in the city and with them many of the citizens whether to look on or to buy. It is a joy to see . . . the costly Destriers of graceful form and goodly stature with quivering ears, high necks and plump buttocks . . . their limbs tremble impatient of delay, they cannot stand still. When the signal is given they stretch forth their limbs, they gallop away, they rush on with obstinate speed.'

Fitzstephen also wrote about the young men of those times, eager to train and prepare for future battles: 'Every Sunday in Lent, after dinner, a fresh swarm of young gentles goes forth on war horses . . . from the households of Earls and Barons come young men not yet invested with the belt of Knighthood, that they may there contend together. Each one of them is on fire with the hope of victory.

In contrast to the heavyweight Destrier, the mountain pony breeds of Scotland and Wales provided economic and agile mounts for the cavalry of Robert the Bruce who employed effective hit-and-flee techniques against the English at the Battle of Bannockburn in 1314. In the battle almost everyone was mounted, and although the English outnumbered the Scots by three to one, it was their size and weight that proved to be their downfall. Edward II and his men charged the pikes of the Scots and their Destriers were mortally wounded. Their heavy armour totally immobilized the unseated knights and the agile Scots were able to gallop in to the kill on their fleet ponies.

The Celtic armies of Scotland and Wales used light arms. Their native ponies were able to live on sparse natural forage and were hardy and strong. The men themselves had spartan qualities and carried little in the way of equipment or provisions, eating only once a day and training regularly in order to remain fit during battles. Their leaders rode larger horses, bred from native stock crossed with imported Oriental stallions. In the Middle East and Asia Minor, lighter and more agile Oriental horses were bred and when West met East in the Crusades, these lightly armed and finely mounted horsemen gained superiority over the ironclad and ponderous knights.

The Asian Warriors

While the knights and their chargers ruled the battlefields of Europe in the late Middle Ages, two of the greatest horse soldiers of history came to power in the vastness of Asia Minor. Genghis Khan was known as the Perfect Warrior and even his name inspired terror in lesser mortals. Born in 1164, the son of a Mongol chief, he was first called Temujin but changed this later to Genghis Khan, meaning the Khan of all Khans. He became supreme ruler of the Mongols and Tartars, taking over an army when only 14 years of age, following the death of his father. Later he invaded China and eventually his empire stretched from Siberia to the Persian Gulf and from the Volga to the Pacific Ocean.

Genghis Khan is reputed to have been responsible for the deaths of five million people. He employed sophisticated battle techniques and gloried in the defeat of his enemies. He was a strict disciplinarian and a superb leader, sure of the respect of all his men. His cavalry was superb, well-trained, well-mounted and superbly equipped. They understood that their lives depended upon their horses and cared for them accordingly. On rough terrain, strips of yak skin were tied for protection over the hooves of their unshod mounts, and the animals' rations and nosebags were carried on the march. When food was desperately short, each of the men would sustain himself with a little blood taken from a vein in his horse's neck. Genghis Khan reviewed his troops before battle; mounted on a milk-white stallion. His saddle and bridle were ornately decorated with silver escutcheons and he sat as one with his horse. Throughout his life he loved horses more than people, and ever since his death in 1227 and his secret burial at the edge of the Gobi desert, a ghostly white horse is said to make an annual trek, galloping across the sands to stand all night over the buried bones of the Great Khan.

One hundred years after the death of Genghis Khan, Timur-i-lane was born, destined to become Tamurlaine the Great, a chieftain of central Asia who set out to establish a world empire. Tamur-

The conquest of Constantinople, from the Chronicles of the 4th Crusade attributed to Geoffrey de Villehardouin. Bodleian Library, Oxford.

Left: Genghis Khan conquered a vast empire during his military career. This illustration from Book 2, Part 1 of the *History of the Mongols* shows his battle with the Khitai and Jurje tribes at Hunegen Dabaan during his march on China. Gulistan Library, Teheran.

Right: Charles I, an accomplished horseman and advocate of the curb bit, designed to bend the horse's neck at the crest, showing the desired effect in a portrait by Van Dyck. National Gallery, London.

Below: The Great Khan, unable to make a frontal attack on North China which was protected by the Great Wall, struck first at Tangut, where his Mongol strategy, ideal for fighting on the Steppes, proved inconsistent with the storming of fortresses. Miniature from the *History of the Mongols*. Gulistan Library, Teheran.

laine believed that military success could only be achieved by the possession of the finest and best-trained horses in all the world. He spent enormous sums of money in order to procure superb Arabian horses, tested for their powers of speed, stamina and courage. His first major campaign was against Toktamish, descendant of Genghis Khan. Each of Tamurlaine's 100000 cavalrymen was given two horses and a set of weapons including bow, lance and scimitar. This army of horsemen moved across country on a 30-mile wide front, covering 1800 miles in three months. When they decided to stop, the central columns halted and the wings swept round in a huge circle, encompassing much game which was swiftly killed. This well-mounted and disciplined army moved invincibly on, taking all in its path. Tamurlaine swept south as far as Persia, then west to fight against the Syrians who had been joined by the Egyptians. As he camped in preparation for an attack on the Turkish Empire, Turkish King Bayozid hastened back from his own wars, bringing 200000 fighting men. The cunning Tamurlaine anticipated Bayozid's tactics and skirted round behind his enemy, taking Ankara and seizing all the Turkish supply wagons. Although Tamurlaine's cavalry totally destroyed Bayozid's troops, the King was captured but treated as an honoured guest by the chieftain.

Decline of the Heavy Horse

Henry VII was a very practical King who passed laws prohibiting the export of Britain's precious horses. He was anxious to upgrade the standard of his warhorses and it was decreed that all 'entires' should be kept stabled, so that breeding could be controlled. From this we have our term 'stallion' or the 'stalled one', and it was at this time that horsekeepers found it more practical to begin gelding their horses.

Henry VII's son, Henry VIII, had a great love for the horse and went to extreme lengths to obtain the finest horses and to become an accomplished horseman. When he eventually met Francis I of France at The Field of the

Cloth of Gold, he was surprised and very upset to find that the French cavalry was better mounted than was his own, a bitter blow for a man who liked to shine in any company.

Succeeding monarchs did their utmost to improve the horses of Britain but with little success and by the reign of Charles I, the breeding and keeping of quality warhorses had dramatically declined. The heavy horse as a war machine had, in any case, been superceded. The invention of the long pike made a major impact on all the battlefields of Europe at that time. Powder and shot also came into use and the ordinary infantryman armed with his musket became more than a match for any charging horseman.

Oliver Cromwell proved himself to be one of the finest cavalry officers of all time and showed an intelligent understanding of the characteristics required of the military horse of his time. He confiscated much of the fine Arab stock in the country and set up stud farms, sending some of the best stallions to Ireland to be crossed with the hardy Irish pony strain. Having dispensed with the last of the Destriers, Cromwell sent his agents abroad to buy the best Oriental horses that they could find. The Protector's cavalry became very efficient, each soldier being expected to care for, feed and protect his personal mount. This attitude and care for detail produced a disciplined and effective fighting force.

The First Horse Schools

It was during the reign of Charles II that the first Horse Schools were established. The Merry Monarch seized Cromwell's Arab stud, and imported fine breeding stock which became known as the Royal Mares. His personal regiments were instructed in the skills of equitation, and finely mounted, were known as the Household Cavalry. The Household Cavalry was, in turn, divided into the Life Guards, the Royal Horse Guards and the King's Dragoon Guards.

Though the 18th century was called the Age of Reason, battles raged

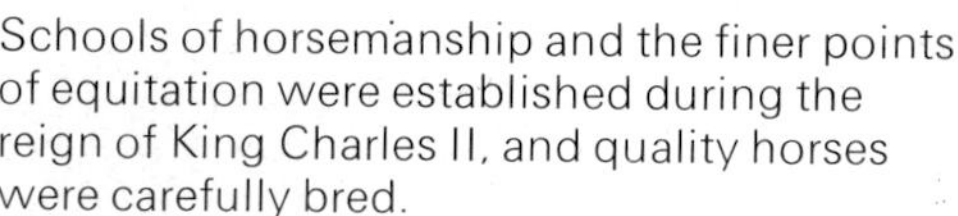

Schools of horsemanship and the finer points of equitation were established during the reign of King Charles II, and quality horses were carefully bred.

By the end of the 18th century, warfare had changed dramatically and cavalry suffered in the face of gunfire.

throughout the great states of Europe, and despite increased use of artillery, armies still maintained cavalry units. In 1717 a book was published entitled *The Complete Horseman*. Written by the equerry to the French king it gave precise details of the care and training of military and other horses. It describes the Italian method of training horses by kindness instead of by brutality, and the popularity of those desiring to become accomplished equestrians to take themselves off to Naples for two or three years' intensive training.

Much fighting continued through the century, and despite the increasing use of carbine and bayonet, brave cavalry charges were made and great battles won and lost. France continued to produce the finest horses and large tracts of suitable land in Normandy, Anjou and Navarre were given over to the raising of stock. In January 1790 the Revolution foolishly decreed that horse breeding should be suppressed, and it was not until 1806, when most of the best horses had disappeared, that Napoleon attempted to reorganize affairs. He brought Arab horses from far and wide and established a productive stud. He was a great admirer of the Oriental horse and wrote 'A good Arab stallion is the world's best horse, far better than the Thoroughbred for improving all breeds.'

The horse schools ensured that the cavalry units of Britain as well as the rest of Europe, were fit, efficient and very well trained. Changes of technique in cavalry units' employment were devised and studied, too, and Napoleon, surely the greatest of all cavalry commanders, exploited every effective battle plan it was possible to devise.

War in America

Meanwhile across the Atlantic, 1775 saw the outbreak of the American War of Independence and the emergence of George Washington as its first great general. Although he had received a military education he found great problems in handling the large bodies of untrained men at his disposal. It was to be this untrained quality of his men, however, that eventually caused the overthrow of the British Army after an eight-year struggle. Just like the ancient Britons who bravely faced the invading Roman legions, the young Americans rode out of the woods and hills, struck down their enemy, then retreated swiftly to safety. They were natural horsemen and their horses had been born and raised to cope with the local terrain. The war was long, hard and bitter and many men and animals on both sides died in the struggle for supremacy.

The North American Indians had acquired their first horses by the end of the 18th century – until that time they had fought most of their battles on foot. Their skill in handling horses grew rapidly and changed their fighting methods dramatically. Resistance to having their land settled by immigrant farmers and their buffalo herds annihilated became something more than token. The Indian Wars were fierce and bloody and it was to be many years before the last bands of proud indiginous Americans were forced into reservations.

Less than a century after the War of Independence, the American Civil War broke out. In this war the role of the horse was considerably changed; it was used mainly for communications, reconnaissance and transport. At the outset the Southern States with their traditions of horse breeding and riding were strongly placed at the outbreak of the war. Most of their recruits were from the rural areas, and each boy brought his own horse. The Southern gentlemen, too, were proud to go off to war and took along their finest-bred saddlehorses. In contrast, the Northern armies had to purchase their horse stock and often had to content themselves with very inferior animals.

Battles raged for four years during which 250000 young men and countless horses died lingering, painful deaths from severe wounds. As the numbers of horses declined, mustangs and tough cow ponies were shipped in to take their places, and even Indian ponies were bought to join the cavalry ranks. Names of men like J. E. B. Stuart joined those of Jackson, Sherman, Grant, Lee and others in the files of the famous. At last, with a large proportion of his men unhorsed, General Robert E. Lee wrote despondently to Jefferson Davis, 'Unless

Above: In the American West, the native Indians had also discovered the advantages of using horses in warfare and had become skilled riders and fearless warriors. This painting by Charles M. Russell, 'Sioux meets Blackfoot', hangs in the Thomas Gilcrease Institute of American History and Art in Tulsa, Oklahoma.

Left and right: In the American Civil War the role of the horse was mainly one of communications, reconnaissance and transport. Today, groups of enthusiasts re-enact famous battle scenes and events, such as these riders at Pioneer Arizona, near Phoenix.

Horses were used extensively in the Boer War, 1899–1902. Here soldiers are collecting forage for all the animals back at their camp.

Above: The victorious charge of the British Heavy Brigade at the Battle of Balaclava in 1854. National Army Museum, London.

Above left: The gun teams awaiting orders during the Crimean War, 1853–1856.

the men and animals can be subsisted the army cannot be kept together and our present lines must be abandoned . . .'. This was not to be, and within a month of penning those lines, Lee surrendered to the North at Appomattox.

After the Civil War American cavalry forces turned their attentions towards attacks on the Indians. Sherman and Sheridan, both former Union generals, were the worst offenders. They set out to kill all the Indian leaders and Sheridan chose George Custer as his assistant. In June 1876 General Sherman ordered Sheridan to begin a campaign against tribes in the Black Hills, an area given to the Indians in a treaty of 1868. Custer and his 7th cavalry attacked an encampment of some 3000 Sioux and Cheyenne near the Little Big Horn River in the plains of Dakota, but reckoned without the skills of their enemy.

Mustered under Chiefs Sitting Bull and Crazy Horse, the Indians shot the horses and forced the soldiers into a tight group on Battle Ridge. Using dead and dying horses as barricades, Custer and his soldiers fought bravely but in vain, trying to pick off the mounted braves relentlessly circling their last stand. The incensed Indians, attacked on their ancient holy lands, perpetrated the most shattering defeat ever suffered by American soldiers at the hands of the Indian race. The great Indian Chief, Sitting Bull, explained the ferocity of the Indians in this battle: 'We did not go out of our own country to kill them; they came to kill us and got killed themselves. The Great Spirit so ordered it.'

The End of an Era

Although cavalry units were still used in the world's warfare, Colonel Henderson, the military historian, considered that only seven successful battles were won by horse soldiers from the time of Napoleon until the end of the 19th century. One of these was the victory of the British Heavy Brigade at Balaclava in 1854. (On the whole the Crimean war was fought incompetently, and the cavalry was commanded by the ageing Lord Raglan. In contrast to the success of the Charge of the Heavy Brigade, a fault in communications combined with a clash of personalities led to the disastrous Charge of the Light Brigade in which 600 men were mistakenly ordered

Today's army horses are mainly used for ceremonial occasions, and are kept in the peak of condition and carefully trained. Here a skilled officer takes part in the Sword, Lance and Revolver competition at a leading horseshow.

to gallop into the very mouths of the Russian cannon. It was at this time that the futility of the traditional role of the military horse was realized.)

In subsequent wars, horses have proved their worth in hauling heavy artillery and carrying supplies. They suffered appalling deprivation and conditions, and many thousands died of malnutrition, exhaustion, disease and dreadful wounds. At the Battle of Amiens in 1918 cavalry divisions accompanied tanks into battle, an experiment which failed dismally. The days of the warhorse were numbered, its days of glory over.

Today's military horse enjoys all its ancestor's glory, but none of the hardship, for only a few horses are used in warfare. These few are used to bring supplies and equipment to fighting men, when terrain prohibits the use of motorized transport. In Britain, and in some other countries of the world, military horses are kept to remind the people of the part they played in their history. They provide pomp, ceremony and colour at all State occasions and stir the emotions of all onlookers. Though they are no longer called upon to enter the field of battle, they will always be assured of a place in our hearts.

Police Horses

All around the civilized world, horses are used by police forces to help enforce the law and to control crowds and traffic. It has been said that one mounted policeman can do the work of 20 men on foot in riot situations.

The history of the police horse in Britain began in 1758 when two 'Persuit' horses were attached to the Bow Street offices of the Fielding brothers. Henry Fielding was the famous author of *Tom Jones*. A magistrate of Westminster, he formed the force which was to become the Thief Takers or Bow Street Runners. In the 1760s his blind step-brother and co-magistrate, Sir John Fielding, devised a scheme entitled 'A Plan for Preventing Robberies within Twenty Miles of London'. In this plan Sir John asked that a temporary regiment of light horses be stationed in the metropolitan area, and eventually the Treasury agreed to the formation of a horse patrol of eight horses including the two original Persuers. Although the experiment proved successful, the Government decided to discontinue the employment of Persuers after a period of only two years, and the Bow Street Horse Patrol was not re-formed until another 40 years had passed.

In 1767 Sir John Fielding issued a paper entitled 'A Warning to Travellers, Stage Coachmen and Others'. In it he described '. . . that gang of unhappy wretches . . .', men that lived in idleness and existed by stealing trunks and other goods from stagecoaches, wagons and carts left outside stage stops and inns. Highwaymen were common, too, and travellers were advised to sound a horn when attacked. There was no mounted patrol to aid the Norwich coach in 1775, when it was waylaid by seven highwaymen in Epping Forest. The guard fought valiantly and shot dead three of his assailants before he was finally killed.

The coming of the railways and the advent of steam changed the landscape of the countryside and rang the death knell for the stage- and mail coaches, and the very first steam-driven horseless carriages startled horses as early as 1801.

The regular Bow Street Horse Patrol formed in 1805 provided surveillance of all main roads within a radius of 20 miles (32 km) from Bow Street. Its provisional strength of 52 men and their mounts fluctuated with the price of fodder. That this was a limiting factor is underlined also by the fact that the patrolmen were not allowed to keep pigs or poultry for which they might be tempted to pilfer grain. The men employed were all ex-cavalry, they had to be over 35 years of age and happily married. They were provided with cottages adjacent to their individual patrol areas and were paid 28

Highwayman Dick Turpin, mounted on his famous mare Black Bess, clears the toll-gate at Hornsey to escape from pursuing constables.

shillings per week. The distinctive uniform consisted of blue trousers and greatcoats, a black leather hat, white gloves and steel spurred boots. With this they wore scarlet waistcoats which soon earned them the nickname of Redbreasts. The men were armed with sabres, pistols and truncheons, and carried handcuffs. Though few in numbers, the Redbreasts proved very successful, effectively protecting travellers in their area. By 1813 control of the Bow Street Horse Patrol had passed from the Chief Magistrate to the Home Secretary. In 1836 it was incorporated into Sir Robert Peel's new and unarmed police force but retained individual status and separate fields of duty.

The Bow Street Horse Patrol was not responsible for controlling riots or disturbances, both of which were common in those troubled times. It was the job of the cavalry to quell any dangerous uprisings, and in August of 1819, when a crowd of about 60 000 people congregated on St. Peter's Field in Manchester hoping to have the Corn Laws repealed, the 15th Hussars were summoned. Drawing their sabres, the cavalrymen did their work. The crowd was indeed controlled and though only a few demonstrators died, many were seriously injured. Distressing as this might seem, some force was required to control the angry crowds – the Gordon riots of 1780 had resulted in a London mob burning down 70 houses and four gaols. It was to be some years before mounted police were to take over this duty.

Left: The musical ride enacted at the 150th anniversary celebrations of London's Metropolitan Police. Though the horses wore modern tack their riders were dressed in the uniform of the old Bow Street Horse Patrol.

Left centre: The Manchester and Cheshire Yeomanry Cavalry charging the huge crowd gathered on St. Peter's Field in Manchester, an action which was later known as the Peterloo Massacre.

Left bottom: By 1890, the date of this print showing the use of horses in quelling rioters at Bow Street, protective helmets were in regular use by the Mounted Branch of the Metropolitan Police.

Right: When the first Soccer Cup Final match was played at London's Wembley Stadium in 1923 excited crowds invaded the pitch, but were successfully cleared by mounted police.

Below: Forty years later, a similar scene occurred when angry, jobless men attempted to storm the Houses of Parliament at Westminster, London.

In 1839 the Mounted Branch became a section of the Metropolitan Police, an effective force in maintaining law and order. The former 'Persuit' horses were to be used in crime prevention rather than for chasing and catching offenders, and this change of policy, giving prevention priority over detection, became the first principle of the police force. The use of mounted police in crowd control was a very gradual process. At first a dozen men on horseback were sent to Hyde Park to assist 800 ordinary policemen in controlling a meeting of some 5000 Chartists, and following the West End riots of 1886 it was decided to increase mounted forces for London. It was at this stage that mounted police finally took over from the cavalry, who were then confined to military duties.

London's mounted 'Peelers' were less flamboyant in dress than the original Redbreasts, and wore the same blue uniforms as the foot police, consisting of straight trousers and long buttoned tunics. At first they were issued with tall black hats, which were later replaced by pillbox caps, until protective helmets were devised in 1865. The practise of carrying firearms was discontinued, and the Peeler's only weapon was a heavy truncheon. Until 1885 a rattle was carried to summon help; eventually this was replaced by a shrill whistle.

In Britain the Victorian era was one of great change and the two factors which most affected the police force were the rapid rise in population generally and the unprecedented rate of urbanization. Mounted police were invaluable during the national celebrations to celebrate Queen Victoria's Diamond Jubilee and, later, among the mourning crowds, gathered to watch the passing of her funeral procession. During the reign of Edward VII and George V the suffragettes caused problems in London, and the mounted police were often called to deal with the skirmishes.

At this time the Metropolitan Mounted Branch had its strength reduced to 126 horses with 12 reserves stabled in Paddington. Main duties consisted of controlling the riders in Hyde Park's Rotten Row, a social meeting place, patrolling the commons and being on call to break up rioting mobs. At the

Police horses compete in testing competitions. Here a young horse trots neatly over poles (below) then calmly passes a noisy crowd of youths waving flags and banners, and making as much noise as they can (bottom). Another horse, a previous Championship winner, shows how it helps its rider cope with passage through a barrier (opposite right). Finally, one of London's mounted policewomen steadies her horse while a pistol is fired at close quarters (opposite bottom).

Derby race meeting of 1913 mounted police were out in force, but they were powerless to prevent Emily Davidson throwing herself to her death under the hooves of the galloping horses. This act of martyrdom was designed to call attention to the suffragette movement, and the militant women of those days seemed to be at constant war with the men of the mounted division.

When the First World War broke out, mounted police were in great demand to control the throngs of eager young men outside the recruiting offices in London's Whitehall, answering Kitchener's compelling call to arms, determined to join his New Army of the First Hundred Thousand. In Britain there was a scheme for the compulsory purchase of horses for army use, and some trained police horses joined the shipments across the Channel to France. After the war an ex-officer of the Royal Scots Greys named Colonel Laurie was appointed Assistant Commissioner. In 1919 he took over and reorganized the Mounted Branch of the Metropolitan Police, instituting methods which are still used today.

During the 1920s it was felt that the police horse had served its purpose and senior officers of the mounted division were issued with cars instead of horses. Luckily the mounted policeman was retained and plays an important role today. Most humans have an inborn respect for the strength and power of a large horse; many, in fact, are rather afraid of the animal which they consider fairly dangerous and unmanageable. Over the years famous horses and riders have emerged, having performed feats of heroism, saving lives and diverting catastrophes. No incident seems too immense or too trivial for the mounted policeman.

War broke out once more in 1939. In Britain London's police horses were evacuated to stables outside the area of prime bombing targets. Their training carried on and stood them in good stead upon their return to the devastated city of 1941 where they were threatened by bombing and great fires. Three police horses named Regal, Upstart and Olga were presented with medals given 'For Outstanding Courage during the Battle of London while serving with the Metropolitan Police Force'. The police horses of London took their rightful place protecting Winston Churchill from the cheering multitudes on VE Day when he made his triumphant 'V for Victory' sign outside the Houses of Parliament.

Training Police Horses in England

London's mounted policemen and their horses, as well as many from overseas countries, receive their training at Imber Court in Surrey, England. It was founded by Colonel Laurie in 1920 and specializes in taking suitable young horses, often unbroken and unschooled, and turning them into the steady, reliable police horses seen on our busy streets. As horses are all individuals, the time taken to achieve this goal varies, but seems to average six or seven months. The whole system at Imber Court is based on quiet and gentle handling, with suitable rewards for lessons well executed. Each horse is, at first, schooled with the trainer working from the ground. The animal learns to go in straight lines and in circles, being driven on long reins, and, during such exercises, learns to obey spoken commands. Once his confidence is gained, the first taste of 'nuisance' training is introduced and he may be shown a furled flag or a silent rattle. Long-rein driving develops the muscles and the suppleness of any horse, and such early schooling lays good foundations for later work.

Once broken to the saddle and trained in the school, the horses are ridden on the roads outside the centre in order to accustom them to all forms of road traffic. Back in the school they are encouraged to jump various obstacles and given preliminary schooling in dressage. The 'nuisance' training is continued and eventually horses are conditioned to accept just about anything to which a rowdy crowd could

subject them. They are taught to have flags and scarves waved in their faces, to accept any loud noise including gunfire and to tolerate the weight of pushing people. Police horses must stay calm near fire, stand quietly in water, step carefully over people lying on the ground and be totally immune to every form of road, rail or air traffic.

The horses come from several sources although many are bought from breeders in Yorkshire, continuing a tradition of long-standing. Less than 5 per cent of those originally selected fail to make the grade as full-fledged police horses.

At Imber Court the horses are trained by very experienced instructors and, at the end of their course, are taken over by their future riders. Only experienced officers are given novice horses, and care is taken that the pair are temperamentally suited to one another. They spend some time working together at the centre before going on duty, and in Britain most policemen keep the same horse for the duration of its working life, which averages 15 years.

In addition to the training of the horses, selected constables who apply for transfer to the Mounted Branch of the Metropolitan Police are also trained at Imber Court. A team of special horses is kept for the purpose of training these recruits.

Most of these horses are unsuited to normal duty for one reason or another. Often it is just old age which prevents the animal coping with long hours of street patrol, or involvement in a serious accident may have caused a horse to just fall short of being traffic-proof. Such horses are ideal in every way for teaching the keen young riders, many of whom have never been astride a horse before reporting to the centre. Recruits undergo a six-month intensive training programme at Imber Court, then join one of the police stables as mounted reserves, riding horses of officers absent from duty. Eventually, having completed the probationary period satisfactorily, they are given experienced horses of their own.

London's police horses are spread

Above: Police horses being worked in the indoor riding school.

Above right: *Richard*, a dappled grey gelding, ready for duty in the busy streets of London.

Right: Police horses are very effective in the gentle control of large crowds. Here happy tourists are kept safely off the road during the Changing of the Guard at London's Buckingham Palace.

Overleaf: A pair of grey police horses escort the relief guard through the London streets.

through several units. The ones used in Central London are housed in what was once Lord Lonsdale's coaching stables, now called Great Scotland Yard, just off Whitehall. The horses' stalls are on the first floor, and they go upstairs to bed, climbing a long ramp carpeted with coarse matting. Each officer is responsible for the care of his own horse and equipment, and rides patrol for about three hours each day. In special circumstances, or during emergencies, however, he and his horse may be expected to stay on duty for up to ten exhausting hours.

Each police horse has its own personal saddle tree and girth and wears a bridle with a universal, reversible portmouth bit. This has two reins and, for safety, there is a fine chain passed round the animal's neck which may be quickly clipped onto the bit during demonstrations. This is to ensure that, even if the leather reins were cut through, the officer could maintain control of his mount. The British police are unarmed and the two leather wallets which look rather like holsters on either side of the pommel are saddle bags which carry emergency items such as a lamp, a waterproof saddle cover, a small truncheon and a first-aid kit.

The horses which live in Great Scotland Yard spend a great deal of time in the region of Buckingham Palace, escorting the Guardsmen to and fro and taking part in parades and ceremonies. One of their main jobs consists of controlling the vast throngs of visitors and tourists who congregate each day to watch the Changing of the Guard ceremony, and it is an inspiring sight to watch the large patient creatures using their bulk to ease the crowds gently back to the safety of the pavement.

Police horses in other countries are trained using methods very similar to those used at Imber Court. Traffic, crowds and noise are universal hazards to which the horses must be accustomed. Different countries, naturally, have individual requirements which their horses must meet. The police horses stationed in The Hague, Holland, for example, spend a great deal of time during the summer months patrolling

The Officer-in-Charge and the Riding Master inspect men of the Royal Canadian Mounted Police, checking the turnout of each black horse and its rider's general appearance.

beaches. Their riders carry long ropes to enable them to rescue swimmers having difficulties or beachcombers trapped in quicksand.

New York's Mounted Police

In New York a mounted police division was started in 1871 with 15 horses. The Mounted Squad No. 1, as it was called, was responsible for controlling fast and reckless driving in the areas of Fifth, Sixth and Seventh Avenues from Fourteenth to Fifty-Ninth Street, and from Fourteenth to Thirty-Fourth Street on Lexington Avenue. The squad proved so successful in its work that more men were trained for mounted duty and a training stable was established in 1889, at which there were 230 police patrol horses. In the same year the Chief of Police first deployed his men in a wedge formation, designed to split any crowd into two manageable factions. The 'flying wedge' tactics have proved invaluable over the years and have been employed whenever vast crowds of marchers or rioters have threatened to get out of hand.

In 1910 the New York Police Department had over 700 horses, but their numbers gradually declined as police began to be issued with motor vehicles. Mounted policemen were still used for crowd control and could be rushed to trouble spots in large, specially designed horseboxes. After the Second World War, stabling became difficult to find and the numbers of horses were dramatically cut. The remaining horses were of mixed types but all were expected to reach the same high level of achievement in training. Today the horses are kept in brightly painted, comfortable stalls and the horses are selected by a buying committee. The buyers look for handsome bay geldings from 15.3 to 16.2 hands high, with very sound conformation and good feet. When the horses have passed through a ten-day probationary period they are expected to pass a rigorous fitness test before embarking on the intense six-month training programme.

After its full working life, the New York police horse is retired and sent to live on a pleasant farm at Otisville. Here it lives a life of luxury, being carefully tended, and in return makes a valuable contribution to human welfare by providing small amounts of blood serum to be used in the manufacture of antitoxins for diseases such as tetanus.

The Famous 'Mounties'

Perhaps the most famous mounted police force in the world is the Royal Canadian Mounted Police, affectionately known as the 'Mounties' and originally formed to patrol vast tracts of virtually uninhabited land in the Northwest Territories of Canada. The Canadian Government passed a bill in 1873 providing for a uniformed police force, made up of healthy men of good character, aged between 18 and 40 years of age, able to ride well. The Mounties took to their arduous duties willingly and well and soon gained the reputation of always getting their man. They often had to contend with more than desperate criminals, traversing miles of difficult terrain and coping with extreme weather conditions. Mounted on tough jet black horses and wearing their distinctive scarlet tunics, the Mounties commanded respect wherever they rode. During the Great War, many of the Forces' best men and horses were posted for overseas service in 1918 and suffered heavy casualties, and although horses were still used for duty between the two world wars, the Force gradually became more and more mechanized. Today, although still known by their original title, the Royal Canadian Mounted Police retain only enough horses to enable them to perform certain ceremonials and to give their celebrated Musical Ride. Presented frequently throughout Canada and occasionally in other countries, the Ride is a superb display of schooling and precision riding. The impressive horses used by the Force are bred from thoroughbred stallions and halfbred mares at their own ranch in a beautiful valley, 5000 feet above sea level, and like police horses the world over, spend long months of intensive training for their work.

The 'Mounties' perform their polished and intricate 'Musical Ride' at all types of horse shows and events. They wear traditional uniform of scarlet tunic, blue breeches with yellow stripe and a broad-brimmed hat.

Heavy Horses

Below: Dated 1899, this picture shows three heavy horses harnessed 'in line' to haul a heavy Trimmers wagon, loaded with hops.

Bottom: In France, the Breton proves its pulling power.

Opposite page: *Gilbert* and *Sullivan*, two magnificent grey Shire horses, pull their heavy brewers' dray through London's busy streets.

Until the end of the 17th century in Britain heavy horses were used only for military needs; oxen pulled ploughs and carried out all the other heavy draught work in agriculture. Over the years military horses had been bred larger in accordance with various laws passed by Parliament. An act of 1535, for example, stated that owners of farms or parks and grounds of one mile in compass, should keep 'two mares able to bear foals of a height of 13 handfuls'. A law passed in the reign of Edward VI prohibited the importation of any stallion under 14 hands, or of mares under 15 hands. Having finally bred the English Great Horse to carry immensely heavy, armoured knights, weapons improved and were made lighter, so faster horses were needed for the cavalry. Eventually, towards the end of the 18th century, roads improved and horses replaced the plodding oxen in drawing wagons. Many farmers considered oxen to be far superior to horses for agricultural work. They were said to be cheaper to feed and harness, needing only a simple yoke and traces. Oxen were placid and simple to train, undemanding, and a capital asset when their draught days were over – they were saleable as meat. It was also argued that the ox could pull better than a horse of equal size. The admirers of the draught horse maintained that it was a faster and more versatile animal and, unlike the ox, did not have to stop work in order to ruminate. The horse, as we know, eventually won the day, although in the Sussex countryside the last team of oxen worked until 1929.

The coming of mechanization to the farms sounded the death knell for many heavy horses. Today, however, they have again found favour, for it has been realized that there are many jobs they are able to perform better than machines. Horses cope well on heavy clays where constant use of heavy tractors compacts the land and, by literally destroying the soil structure, renders it unproductive.

They come into their own, too, in very wet weather and on sloping ground, when the use of machines could prove hazardous. On small farms, and on those with limited capital, a careful farmer can economically produce his crops using horsepower, especially if he is also able to grow his horses' feed. With energy costs increasing each year it is quite likely that the draught horse will be in even greater demand. Some of London's brewery companies did some careful costings, and discovered that using teams of horses to deliver barrels of beer to local publicans was more economical than using motor vehicles. This cost effectiveness was important, and the magnificent sight of the massive horses pulling smart drays also acted as mobile advertising, a bonus indeed. As well as performing a very real duty, the brewery horses are often entered at shows and many give displays for charity.

Easter Monday is a social day for London's horse owners and horse admir-

GILBERT
SULLIVAN

ers for it is the occasion of the annual Harness Horse Parade which takes place in Regents Park. Brewery horses take part and are joined by those of other companies who own treasured antique vehicles and harness. The costers show off their cobs and ponies and the Pearly Kings and Queens make their appearances dressed in their traditional costumes covered with thousands of pearl buttons. The parade lasts for hours and attracts hordes of tourists and sightseers. The turnouts do not compete but certificates are awarded by judges, looking for immaculate presentation and general fitness of the horses and ponies.

When the horse was first harnessed some 4000 years ago, a wooden yoke was used, similar to that which had proved satisfactory in harnessing oxen. It was soon found that the horse pulls in a different way from the ox, and its strongest pulling power comes from a point just in front of its shoulders. By attaching chariots to yokes fitted up on the horses' withers, a great deal of power was lost. It was also difficult to find a satisfactory method of fixing the yoke in place. With oxen, such contraptions sit across their necks between the horns and withers, and are sometimes lashed to the horns for added security. In some areas of the world, these same methods have continued unchanged to this day. Eventually a simple collar was evolved for use on the horse to keep the yoke in position. Homer, in his *Iliad*, described the modified harness used in the siege of Troy. He explains that from the yoke a simple strap of several thicknesses of leather passed round the horse's neck and from the same point of the yoke, a second strap was passed round the body, rather like a girth, and was attached to the neck strap at the withers. Another strap was fixed to the bottom of the neck strap and passed between the front legs to join the girth. A pair of horses in such harness was yoked to the chariot. Later the yoke was improved by shaping, and gradually the ends became curved. Then it was but a small step to the development of the breast harness.

The Romans loved chariot racing and were continually exploring ways in which to improve the performance of their horses. Their teams of four included two central horses being har-

Above: Chains attached to padded collars enable these horses to drag felled tree trunks up the banks of Scotland's Loch Awe.

Above right: *Jim* and *Tinker*, two working Shires, wearing their best harness, complete with brasses.

Right: In the celebrated chariot race from the MGM epic film *Ben-Hur*, careful attention was paid to the accuracy of the harness.

nessed as described above, while the two either side had been coupled to the chariot with single traces attached to neck straps. To gain more power from the *quadriga*, the two outside horses were fitted with double traces which met in front of their shoulders. Instead of the inefficient, diagonal neckstrap, the traces were now horizontal, and kept in place with a girth strap and wither pad. The pulling point was lowered and the charioteers suddenly found the extra horsepower they craved.

Many years were to pass before the padded neck collar was invented, and it was first seen in Europe in the 10th century in a form very similar to the collar of today. Shafts had been devised instead of a single pole on vehicles, and this made it possible to use a single heavy horse. The collar was shaped to sit on the horse's shoulders in such a way that it did not restrict its breathing by pressing on the windpipe and it supported rigid frames, known as hames, to take the weight of the load.

Because the pulling power came from the collar, the shafts were fixed at the correct height on either side of the horse by means of leather straps, and to prevent the weight of the shafts from bruising the horse's back, a thickly padded and modified sort of saddle was devised. Some more straps were added around the horse's rear, helping to brake the load when going downhill or stopping.

Above: In the show ring an immaculate turn-out is essential. These black Shire horses have been groomed to perfection to await judging.

Left: The profuse 'feathering' on the legs of Shire horses must be cleaned. Here fine sawdust is being used in show preparation.

Above right: Cross-bred heavy horses often work as efficiently as the larger pure-bred Shires, and may be favoured for ploughing matches.

The slow and plodding oxen had not required reins. They were directed by a few simple words of command and the tapping of a goad to move them from side to side. However, even the earliest harness horses were used at fast speeds, and, therefore, control was essential. Light bridles and bits complete with reins, probably of rope, were developed early, and only slightly modified for the agricultural and draught horses of later years. Bearing reins were also developed early, possibly as a safety measure, acting as they do as a check to excessive speed.

Although the harness has become stronger and lighter over the years, it remains remarkably similar to preserved early examples. The harness is often decorated with brass ornaments which, in the superstitious days of old were used as magical symbols to ward off evil and to ensure fertility in the fields. It is thought that the first brass ornaments worn by horses were on the accoutrements of the Saracens and some were carried back to England as souvenirs after the Crusades. Local craftsmen copied these ornaments in brass and each added his own ideas and designs. The brasses soon became popular with horsekeepers for adorning their harnesses.

At first the brasses were cut by hand from hammered sheets of brass and the first designs were necessarily simple. The cut edges were smoothed and the centres raised by hammering on the back of the design. Later, brasses were cast and over a thousand different designs became available. The original crescent design remained popular and variations on a star theme were in great demand. The brewers and other companies had their own designs cast and on special occasions, the manufacturers produced suitable commemorative brasses, a practice continued in Britain to this day.

Those who own and work heavy horses take enormous pride in their condition and turnout. A fairly plain, unadorned harness is used for general purposes, but on high days and holidays, competitions, displays or matches, most owners bring out their treasured show tackle. The leather is generally black and is kept supple by the application of oil. Buckles and decorations are generally of brass, though some old harnesses have beautiful porcelain ornaments,

Left: A modern demonstration of the haymaking techniques used in bygone days.

Right: A contented group of the Sampson Stud's Shire mares relaxing in their sunny paddock.

Below: A patient Clydesdale mare demonstrating the use of an antique wooden roller.

horses may be harnessed as a unicorn, with two abreast in front of the implement, and the third well forward and central to them. Young horses are trained by being yoked between two more experienced and docile horses and quickly learn just what is expected of them. Most heavy horses are handled a great deal as youngsters and are quiet and docile. They are accustomed to being led about and having their feet lifted, and are taught to accept the human touch all over their bodies. At two years of age a simple harness is placed on the heavy horse and it is taught to go forward in long reins, with someone at the bridle to coax and praise. Eventually the young horse learns to respond to voice commands as well as rein aids, and will go willingly and steadily on straight lines and circles. He is taught to back up evenly and to stand quietly without being tied. When the young horse is considered sufficiently muscled up, its first lessons in pulling loads commence. Initially an assistant pulls back hard on trace lines attached to the collar; later a large log or pole is used. At first the young horse may plunge in fright, but soon learns that the weight is not going to hurt him. Finally he is taught to pull various implements and learns road sense.

The Heavy Horse Breeds

The Shire. Purebred heavy horses have had a welcome revival in Britain and many other parts of the world, and it is a stirring sight to see a parade of heavy horses on show. The Shire was developed in the Midlands of England and was known as the Great Black Horse of Derbyshire. The first stallion recorded was a black called the Pankington Blind Horse, foaled in 1755, but studs of blacks are known to have existed before this date.

In 1878 the English Cart Horse Society was formed and this did a great deal to improve the standard and quality of the Shire horse. A stud book was initiated and a breed standard was drawn up. Six years later the organization's title was changed to the Shire Horse Society, and is still in existence today. The modern Shire horse must possess strength, stamina, power, docility and adaptability, combined with a good, sound constitution. It must be built as a powerful pulling machine and should be from 16.2 to 18.2 hands in height. Shire stallions and geldings weigh one ton or more, and the mares only a little less.

The breed standard calls for deep shoulders, a short strong and very muscular back, round deep ribs, a wide chest and sweeping quarters. The neck should be fairly long and arched and the head, with its slightly Roman nose, has a broad forehead, large expressive eyes and narrow nostrils. The legs are well under the body, and are massive, with good feet. Unlike the original breed standard, today's requirement is for only a moderate amount of silky feather on the legs. In action the Shire must go straight in a brisk gay manner and give every appearance of being suitable for

One of the fine Percheron mares of the Hales Stud feeding her dark grey colt foal.

Opposite page: The Belgian Ardennes, with their superb calm temperament, make ideal workers, like this pair pictured at Pioneer Arizona.

east of Paris. Here in A.D. 732 some Arabian stallions were found to have been abandoned by their Moorish riders after their defeat in the battle of Tours. These were crossed with the massive local Flemish mares, and the typical Percheron type evolved. Later infusions of Arab blood were made by the introduction of carefully selected stallions to the finest mares and all modern Percherons descend from these lines. In 1883 the Percheron Society of France was founded to safeguard the interests of the breed, and eventually exports of breeding stock were sent to the United States of America and to Britain. The British Percheron Society was formed in 1918 and during the next few years 36 stallions and 316 mares were imported from France. During the First World War many farmers serving with the British Forces in France had been highly impressed with the docility and power of the Percherons and were keen to have such horses of their own. Several achieved this aim and the breed spread rapidly throughout Britain. Although the increased use of mechanization caused a decline in the breed from the 1940s, a strong nucleus of breeding stock survived and the Percheron is again in demand, not only in Britain, but in several other countries of the world.

Only grey or black stallions are eligible for entry in the Stud Book and they should be a minimum of 16.3 hands in height. Essentially a heavy draught animal, the Percheron has a very strong body with a short back, deep shoulders and very powerful hindquarters. The strong neck is exceptionally arched in the stallions, and the head is broad between full and intelligent-looking eyes. The strong legs have big knees and hocks. The feet are of medium size and formed of a distinctive hard blue horn. This last factor combined with the absence of feathering on the legs ensures that the Percheron rarely suffers any trouble in this region. Honest and hardworking, the Percheron is docile and good-natured, but never sluggish or dull.

The Ardennes. Another French breed is the massive Ardennes, an ancient horse developed in that mountainous region which intersects the borders of France and Belgium. First recorded in dispatches sent by Julius Caesar in 57 B.C., mares of this ancient breed were crossed with Arab stallions, producing efficiently strong and active warhorses. The French Ardennes may be either bay, chestnut, roan or sorrel, with a dark mane and tail and dark feathering on the legs. The horse averages 16 hands in height and is strong and powerful but with a very gentle temperament. The Belgian Ardennes is a very similar breed from the same stock. It is generally shorter and less stocky than its French cousin and very popular for utility work especially on farms in the mountainous regions of its birth.

Horses of the Ardennes breed are very popular in the United States and may be seen in many entertainment parks doing what they do best – hauling heavy loads made up from special vehicles designed to give rides to holidaymakers and tourists. In California's Disneyland, superbly harnessed and immaculately groomed Ardennes horses draw shining, brass-bedecked trams through the streets of the park, and similar horses are used to pull stage coaches around the permanent film set of Old Tucson, Arizona.

The vast tracts of agricultural land in the United States preclude the general use of heavy horses, but utility horses, suitable for both riding and hauling, are still used on some small farms and holdings.

Harness Horses

Driving can be a delightful pastime, but reliable well-schooled ponies and horses are often very expensive to buy, and so are their vehicles and harness. Having made the initial purchase, the animal must be properly fed and housed, and regular roadwork means very regular visits from the farrier.

Horses have been used to draw carts for thousands of years, from the time, in fact, when they were used to replace the onager, an ass with a most uncertain temperament and will of its own. Even before the wheel was invented, ponies pulled sled-like vehicles and contraptions made of long poles lashed together to which goods and chattels could be tied. The coming of the wheel, however, meant that horses could pull loads much heavier than themselves. A record of horses being driven for sport dates back to 680 B.C. and describes races between teams of charioteers in an early version of the Olympic Games. Throughout the centuries specialized horses and ponies have been bred for driving purposes. Heavy breeds were selected for pulling laden farm carts, delivery vans and wagons, while teams of lighter, faster animals were required for the stage- and mail coaches. In more recent times, fine, high-stepping and elegant horses were bred for light carriage work.

By the 18th century, driving as a sport was well established and large wagers were placed on the results of matches between teams from rival owners. In Russia, about 1777, Count Alexis Grigorievich Orlov developed a breed of trotting horses and established a stud. His horses, originally bred from Arab, Thoroughbred, Dutch and Danish stock, were smart and trotted at a spanking pace, showing great powers of

The London–Manchester Mail Coach, changing horses at a London inn stop in 1825.

Harnessing the night team and lighting the lamps. A coaching print of 1840.

endurance. At the same time, the Marquess of Queensberry became the instigator of many matches between chaises, drawn by single horses.

In the early 19th century, driving became a very fashionable pastime, helped by the patronage of King George IV, then still the Prince of Wales. It was thus at this time that the Norfolk Trotter or Roadster, originally bred for farm and utility work, proved its worth, winning many of the trotting races that had become popular in East Anglia.

Although the Norfolk Trotter has died out as a breed in its own right, it lives on in the other breeds that evolved from it, including the Hackney, the American Standardbred Trotter, the Gelderlander from Holland, the Demi-Sang Trotter of France, and the Furioso of Hungary. Some experts also maintain that the useful Morgan horse can claim the Roadster in its list of forebears.

In the north of Britain before the days of coaches, goods and merchandise were carried in packs by teams of horses, led by travelling salesmen called chapmen. Their strong, good-natured and hardy horses became known as Chapman horses. Later the type became very standardized and were bred in the Cleveland district of Yorkshire. Bright bay in colour, well-made and with very good legs and feet, the Cleveland Bays were the obvious choice when, in the reign of Elizabeth I, coaches came into use.

As time went by, the formerly rutted highways were improved and the Old Cleveland Bay type was upgraded into a slightly lighter, faster horse. This was done by crossing the best mares with two Thoroughbred stallions, Manica, a son of the Darley Arabian, and Jalap, a grandson of the Godolphin Arabian. From this far-sighted breeding policy may be traced the popular horses of today's Cleveland Bay breed, often to be seen pulling the Royal carriages on state occasions. Also developed from matings between Thoroughbred and Cleveland Bay stock, the Yorkshire Coach Horse was a magnificent animal and breeding stock was exported from Britain to many parts of the world.

Today any breed of horse or pony may be used for driving so long as it has the conformation and temperament to be trained to harness work.

The Hackney

Bred solely for driving purposes, the Hackney's very exaggerated action makes it an extremely uncomfortable

Opposite page: Norwegian Fjord ponies are ideal for harness work and are very distinctive with their dun coats, dark points and mealy muzzles.

A state landau belonging to the British Royal Family, drawn here by a well-matched pair of Cleveland Bay horses.

animal to ride. This unique action, in which the knees and hocks are lifted very high, was inbred by very careful selection over a period of years. Today's Hackneys command very high prices for show driving. Although the breed may be traced back to the 14th century, its most influential ancestor was the Norfolk Trotter or Roadster, bred from Arabian and Yorkshire stock. The Hackney Horse Society was formed in 1883 and brought about a revival of smart trotting horses. A Stud Book was opened and most of today's high-stepping horses can be traced back to a stallion named Shales, the son of the Thoroughbred, Blaze. It is thought that the breed took its name from the Norman-French word for an ambling horse, *haquenée*. In the old days, a Hackney was expected to complete a distance of 17 miles within one hour, and road conditions were often less than perfect. Even today the breed is capable of trotting evenly and strongly at a very smart pace over a considerable distance.

Standing a little over 15 hands high, the Hackney Horse is generally dark brown, black, bay or chestnut. Apart from its distinctive action it is identifiable by its small convex head, neat ears and large expressive eyes. Its back is very short and it has powerful but rather straight shoulders. The quarters are muscular and the shortish legs have very strong knees and hocks. When it stands still, the Hackney holds it head very high with ears pricked and alert, giving the impression that it is about to take off at any moment. The hind legs are stretched back and the tail held high.

The introduction of Welsh and Fell Pony blood to the Hackney breed produced Hackney Ponies, virtually scaled-down versions of their larger cousins. Although these animals share the Hackney's beautiful action, they are of true pony type and, though originally bred for light delivery work in towns, are now used almost exclusively in the show ring.

All Hackney horses and ponies whose pedigrees are registered with their Society may compete at the many shows offering classes for singles, pairs and tandems. Singles are driven by one driver or 'whip' sitting in small, lightweight wagons with four pneumatic-tyred wheels. Pairs are driven to four-wheeled phaetons and tandems draw two-wheeled gigs. The driver of a

92

pair or tandem is accompanied by a groom, often dressed in full livery with white breeches and a black silk hat. Many Hackneys are driven by professional drivers or their trainers, although there are special classes for amateur drivers too, and while presentation and turnout is important, it is on their action and conformation that the animals are judged in the ring. The show performance of the Hackney does not include any road work, but many horses and ponies of the breed excel on the roads, taking part in marathon drives and private driving contests.

Classes and Events

Private driving classes are divided into those for Hackney or Hackney-type horses and ponies, and those for non-Hackney types. If entries are large, the classes are further divided by height. In such classes singles may be driven in any type of two-wheeled vehicle except trade turnouts or Hackney wagons with pneumatic tyres. At some shows pairs and tandems may be judged separately from the singles, the pairs being driven to four-wheeled vehicles and the tandems, for safety's sake, to those with two wheels. In these driving classes the turnout is important, and the judges look at several factors. The vehicle must be suitable for the horse or pony; the harness must be spotlessly clean and fitting well; and the action, conformation and behaviour of the animal are all taken into account. The horses and ponies competing in private driving classes must be well schooled, with impeccable manners in the ring and on the road, and be impervious to traffic.

Road and private coaches. Great crowd pullers at the larger shows are the divided classes for four-in-hands driven to road and private coaches. Road coaches are sometimes called stage-coaches, and are brightly painted vehicles still sporting their names and destinations as they did when carrying fare-paying passengers in years gone by. Private coaches or drags are generally more sombre, but often have a family crest or monogram on the door panels or back. Regimental coaches are similar to drags, but are painted in regimental colours with emblazoned crests. Road coaches are heavier than drags and carry 14 people as opposed to the drag's complement of 12.

Above: In the light harness class the overall presentation of the entrants is judged in addition to their performance.

Left and right: High-stepping Hackney horses are driven to light four-wheeled wagons in the show ring, in single-harness classes.

Above: A beautifully matched four-in-hand enters the show ring after completing its marathon drive on the roads.

Right: H.R.H. Prince Philip, Duke of Edinburgh, competing at Windsor in one of the Combined Driving contests that he introduced to Britain in recent years.

The road coach carries a guard traditionally clad in a scarlet frock-coat and top hat. His long horn used for blowing such signals as 'Clear the Way' and 'Pulling Up', is stowed in a leather holder. The very experienced driver of a road coach does not necessarily control a perfectly matched team, and often continues the old tradition of adding grey or odd-coloured horses so that they are more easily visible in dim light.

Private drags are generally drawn by well-matched teams, although, for the same reasons of visibility, an odd-coloured leader is often added and colour matched to the team. An all-black team might have a piebald leader for example and a bay skewbald would be put as leader to a team of bays. Drags are driven with their lamps inside the coach during daytime, and two grooms, wearing silk top hats and livery to match the coach, ride on the seat at the back.

The presentation of the coaches is noted by the judges and after the teams have taken a marathon drive over a distance of six or 12 miles on the road, their appearance, action and condition is checked. It is a splendid sight to watch the teams trotting briskly back into the arena after their marathon, with passengers smiling and horns sounding.

Combined Driving is a fairly recent innovation introduced to Britain by H.R.H. The Duke of Edinburgh who had been impressed by the sport when he saw it in Europe. It is a three-day event and tests the fitness and stamina of the driver as well as that of the horses taking part. On the first day, the entrants are judged on presentation and are expected to give a dressage test. In this they must show normal and extended trotting, turning within a limited area, halt and level rein-back. On the second day, miles of country must be covered within time limits and at varying speeds, making tight turns, going up and down steep slopes and fording streams. On the third day, control is tested as the drivers guide their animals through a series of obstacles in the ring. This event was devised to be driven with four-in-hands, when it is a particularly impressive affair to watch, but now Combined Driving contests are also arranged for singles and pairs, and horses and ponies of all types and sizes have the chance to compete.

Scurry driving is another recent innovation on the British show scene. The object is to complete a run through a series of obstacles within the ring and against the clock. Faults are incurred when any obstacle is touched or knocked over, and the winner is the one with the least faults and the fastest time. As these classes are judged solely on performance, every sort of horse and pony, in singles and pairs, is eligible to compete, and any type of vehicle may be used. Scurry competitions are fast, furious and very exciting to watch, and some of the smaller pony pairs obviously enjoy the sport immensely.

Trade classes are very popular with horse-show audiences. They are divided into two main sections, heavy and light trade, with a third section for the costers. The heavy trade classes are further divided into singles, pairs and teams of four, and at very large shows with a large number of entries, may again be divided by breeds.

The heavy horses are generally shown with appropriate trade or farm vehicles with the correct harness, or occasionally, there are classes for heavy horses to be shown harnessed and led in hand. The light trade classes are for heavy horses and ponies of any height, and although all breeds are eligible, the show stealers are the Hackneys and Welsh Cobs. The horses and ponies are also shown with appropriate trade vehicles – such as bakers' vans and milk-floats. Each must have its normal fixtures and fittings but must not be loaded. The harness must be serviceable and clean, and the driver suitably attired. The judges take into consideration the entire presentation of the turnout and the suitability of the animal to the vehicle. The manners of the horses and ponies are important and they may be expected to stand still and unattended as if on a delivery round.

The coster classes are only for costermongers' animals, and the horses and ponies may be of any size, colour or type, and shown in typical trolleys and spinners. These turnouts are very flamboyant and colourful, and often include displays of the costers' wares of vegetables, fruit, etc.

Competition in the U.S.A.

In the United States of America driving competitions have been steadily increasing in popularity with both the Carriage Association of America and the American Driving Society, each showing a steady rise in membership every year. Driving enthusiasts have a variety of competitions to enter and a calendar of such events is published regularly in a publication called *The Whip*. The American Horse Show Association has

A totally different form of harness racing takes part at big rodeo events like the famous annual Calgary Stampede. Here chuck wagons speed for the best position at the first bend in the arena.

Harness racing, in which light sulkies are used to carry the jockeys, is a popular sport throughout the world. This scene shows pacers well into their stride at a large fair in Wisconsin, U.S.A.

approved driving classes restricted to specified breeds such as the Morgan, American Saddlebred, Pony of the Americas, Hackney and Harness Pony, Arab, Welsh and so on. The harness classes are usually divided into formal classes in which a four-wheel buggy is used and informal or pleasure classes where the choice of vehicle is optional.

In formal driving classes, the greatest emphasis is placed on the quality and general performance of the competitors whereas in the pleasure classes, the manners of the horses and ponies are of prime importance.

The Morgan. A favourite American driving horse is the celebrated Morgan, which has a whole range of classes reserved expressly for its breed. Formal Morgan events are known as Park classes, in which the horses are shown harnessed to a special four-wheeled, fine-harness buggy, and are expected to go forward in an animated but very balanced fashion. In their pleasure classes, Morgan horses must show their ability at the regular trot and also at the road trot which is a fast, ground-covering pace. They must have impeccable manners at all times. The Morgan horse derives its name from the breed's foundation stallion, a tough and tenacious pony, foaled in 1789, and given as payment of a debt to a schoolmaster called Thomas Justin Morgan. The horse came from a crossbred mare, thought to have descended from a Norfolk Trotter, and although there are no accurate records, the horse's sire is said to have been True Briton, a Thoroughbred horse directly descended from the Byerley Turk. At first, Figure, as the young horse was then called, was put to work on the farm to earn his keep, and was often ridiculed for his short stature. He soon proved his worth, however, cleverly hauling timber and performing feats of strength which belied his size. His weight-pulling capacity was phenomenal and he won many contests, becoming the talk of the neighbourhood, and was referred to as 'Justin Morgan's horse'. Although he was due to be gelded, local people were keen to have him serve their mares of various types. To everyone's surprise, he proved to be a very prepotent stallion passing on his own conformation, character and size to all the foals he sired. Now known as 'Justin Morgan', the versatile little horse changed hands several times. He was found to have a great turn of speed and

Right: A fine pair of Shires ready to take their place in the Easter Harness Horse Parade in London.

Below: Scurry racing is a popular event at the larger horse shows and always attracts large crowds to cheer on competitors.

plenty of stamina and eventually began a racing career; he remained unbeaten either in harness or under saddle.

Finally, Justin Morgan was bought by the United States Army, who established a breeding stud in Vermont. The horse's offspring were all so similar that a new breed, known as the Morgan Horse was quickly standardized and rapidly gained popularity. The Morgan Horse of today may be either bay, chestnut, black or brown and is larger than Justin Morgan, standing about 15.2 hands high. It is a compact and muscular horse with powerful shoulders and a thick crested neck. It has good quarters, well-made legs and feet and a very full mane and tail. Morgans are popular family horses as they excel in riding and jumping classes as well as in harness.

Harness Racing

This is an exciting sport for both the participants and the spectators. There are harness races for trotters and pacers; in both cases the horses pull lightweight carts or sulkies behind them at great speeds around the track. The difference between the trotter and the pacer is in the gait. The former races at a fast trot or 'tormentor' with long, extended, diagonal movements of the legs, whereas the pacer or 'ambulator' action requires that the left legs go forward together, then both right legs.

In the United States of America trotting and pacing races were started by early settlers as spare-time recreation, the men backing their own horses against those of friendly rivals. Today the American Standardbred is a famous breed. The name applies to both trotters and pacers and comes from the one-mile speed-trial standard each horse must attain before being eligible to race. Trotters are expected to achieve the mile in 2 minutes 30 seconds, while pacers must cover the distance in 2 minutes 25 seconds. Predominantly Thoroughbred in background, the Standardbred also

Top: The costermongers are the traditional cockney traders of London and special classes are provided for them and their cherished cobs and ponies. Here a sturdy cob mare pulls the typical vehicle called a coster trolley.

Centre: The pacer moves at an artificial pace, and trots on the laterals rather than the diagonals as in the natural trot. Special contraptions hanging around the legs help to ensure that the gait remains unbroken.

Left: Great speeds are achieved during pacing races and the sport draws large crowds.

claims Hackney, Arab and Morgan stock in its ancestry. It may be any solid colour, and stands about 15.2 hands high. Courageous and bold in character, the Standardbred's conformation is variable, but the best horses are very muscular with powerful shoulders, chests and quarters and iron-hard legs and feet.

A number of European countries have their own particular breed of trotting horse and for years the sport has been popular in many countries. In Russia a fairly recent breed has been developed from the famous Orlov Trotter crossed with the Standardbred. Only the best of trotting stock was used in the initial crosses, and the result has been a high-performance horse known as the Métis Trotter. Harness racing was a national sport in the Netherlands long before it became popular in other European countries and the Dutch trotting breed is called the Harddraver. The special breed of France is the Anglo-Norman Trotter or Demi-Sang. These horses are raced under saddle as well as in harness, when they are expected to carry weights up to 160 lb (85 kg). Like most other trotting breeds, the Demi-Sang can trace its ancestry back to the Norfolk Trotter of old. Selective breeding began in earnest in the early 20th century and to Young Rattler, an English halfbred stallion foaled in 1811, fell the honour of founding the Anglo-Norman horse. A Stud Book was opened in 1922 and any Anglo-Norman which publicly proved its ability to trot one kilometre in 1 minute 42 seconds became eligible for entry. In 1941 entry to this Stud Book was restricted to horses from previously registered parents and since then the Demi-Sang has remained purebred. Another trotter called the Noram was developed from the Demi-Sang crossed with the American Standardbred, and horses from this breed have proved exceptionally fast and successful in several countries of the world. One Italian-bred Noram trotter, called Tornese, only 14 hands high, won prizes totalling £220 000 in eight years. Out of 210 starts, he won 129 races, was second 53 times and third 13 times. Italian race-goers are more ardent fans of the Trotter than of the Thoroughbred and have many meetings from which to choose. There is also a great interest in harness racing on the island of Sicily and the stadium at Palermo regularly rings with the cries of the cheering crowds.

Veterok is a famous Métis Trotter, bred from the Orlov and the Standardbred. Although the action of the trot is a natural one with legs moving on the diagonals, racing trotters are trained to go at an unnaturally fast speed and must not break into a canter.

Horses in Sport

Horses provide many hours of entertainment not only for their riders, owners and trainers but also for thousands of devotees who like to watch their participation in spectator sports such as polo, the rodeo and the circus. The medium of television has played an enormous role, too, in the popularization of racing, show jumping and eventing, which now have a huge following from people without any previous interest in or knowledge of equestrian sports.

Show Jumping

Originally show-jumping contests were known as 'leaping matches' and were designed to test the horses' potential in the hunting field. The Royal Dublin show in 1868 included two such events: a high-jumping competition with one fence made of three bars which could be gradually raised; and a long-jumping contest with a wide jump made from wattle hurdles. Although many such matches must have taken place in earlier years, the earliest international jumping competition is recorded as having taken place in Turin, Italy in 1901, and show jumping had been included in the Olympic Games the previous year. In the United States of America, leaping contests were popular in horse shows held in Virginia, Connecticut and Massachusetts from the middle of the 19th century, and by the time the inaugural National Horse Show was held in New York's Madison Square Garden in 1883, the sport had achieved popular support and was well established. In Britain the first International Horse Show was held in 1907 and included 12 jumping classes. In those early days the courses were unimaginative with very few, generally upright jumps spread far apart in the arena. They had easily dislodged slats, and a horse had only to flick these to pick up penalties. There were no time limits, and as a spectator sport the early jumping competition could be very boring. Furthermore, rules varied between countries which led to disagreements in international events. The formation of the Féderation Equestre Internationale in 1921 did much to improve the situation, but it was not until the years following the Second World War that show jumping as we know it today really came into its own.

Show-jumping standards are extremely high, and unless competitors have corn-fed and expertly schooled horses and ponies, they stand little chance of success, even at small local shows. The style of the rider and the conformation of his horse have no bearing whatsoever on the results; it is the horse's ability or failure to clear the obstacles, often within a set time limit, that decides the winners or losers. Jumping takes place in indoor and outdoor arenas. The rules are fairly simple and internationally instituted by the Fédération Equestre Internationale. Rather than awarding points for cleared jumps, horses receive four penalty faults for knocking down fences. A fence is considered down whether a small section is dislodged or the whole structure demolished. Faults are also incurred if a horse or rider falls. If a jump is refused or the horse circles in front of it, the penalty is three faults, while refusing a second time gains six faults. On a third refusal the horse is automatically eliminated from

Competitors at a horse show waiting to be called into the collecting ring.

In show jumping, clearing the high wall is no mean achievement.

the competition. When time limits are imposed it is usual to add one-quarter fault for each second taken over the allowed time, or if the total time is exceeded, the competitor is disqualified. There are several types of jumps, many of which are painted in bright colours and are made to look like obstacles such as 'Road Closed' signs. Five-barred and wicket gates are favourite fences, and walls are constructed to look very solid and formidable. Combination jumps are often made of double or triple sets of post-and-rail fences, and the show jumper's ability is often tested in outdoor arenas by the provision of a wide water jump and possibly a high, solid Irish bank.

Eventing

Eventing has developed naturally from the skills acquired and used in the training of cavalry horses. Every great military riding academy devised some form of combined schooling for both horses and men, with the object of first training, then testing them in a variety of situations. Like show jumping, eventing was dominated by competitors from the military forces when it first became an open spectator sport. Several European countries as well as the United States of America held events comprising combined training early in the present century, and the first such competition at international level was part of the Olympic Games of 1912. British riders involved in cross-country riding, and show jumping were not keen on the dressage component of combined-training competitions and so eventing was slow to evolve, only becoming established in Britain after the Second World War. Britain hosted the Olympic Games of 1948 and a three-day event formed part of the proceedings, held mainly at the Aldershot Army Centre in Hampshire. One of the excited spectators at this event was the Duke of Beaufort. He was impressed by the concept of the testing of combined skills of horses and riders and subsequently set aside part of the grounds of his ancestral home in Badminton, for the sole purpose of holding an annual event. The Badminton Horse Trials are perhaps the best-

known of all three-day events. Held annually in the late spring, competitors are drawn from all over the world, eager to test themselves and their horses over the formidable course.

Three-day eventing requires a high standard in three diverse fields of equestrianism. The dressage competition is held on the first day and demands skill and precision to execute the specified test to the standard required. The test is performed in an arena sectioned by markers. A series of set school movements must be executed in a period of about ten minutes, and these are designed to show off the degree of obedience and suppleness the horse has attained. Known as field dressage, the test is far less demanding than that required in top-class competitive dressage, and consists of basic school movements with a fairly complex pattern of changes in direction and pace.

On the second day of the trials comes the gruelling and spectacular endurance section. Designed to test stamina as well as ability of horse and rider, it begins with a course over a distance of about four miles over roads and tracks, to be completed in a specific time. The experienced competitor sets a pace planned to cover the distance just within the limit, but without unduly tiring his horse. The steeplechase phase follows in which riders may gain bonus points for fast times. A sensible approach is even more vital in this section as the decision must be made whether it is better to gallop on and perhaps risk a fall, or to go steadily and accurately and risk losing bonuses. At the finish of the 12 or so steeplechase fences, which cover some two and a half miles, competitors must cover more roads and tracks, allowing the horses to calm down and regain their equilibrium. Next comes a rigorous veterinary examination during which riders dismount and rest their horses. Those animals which pass as fit, then carry on to the cross-country section. This is laid out over a distance of about five miles and includes about 30 cleverly contrived fences. Described as being natural, and indeed constructed of natural materials such as logs, rustic poles, ditches and banks, the obstacles

Clearing an obstacle in fine style in an outside arena.

The cross-country section of an event often has testing obstacles like this narrow stile.

are large and formidable. This phase tests courage as well as fitness for some of the fences are very difficult to negotiate with drop landings, concealed rails and awkward angles for take-off. Many have evocative names like the Sunken Road, Cat's Cradle, Vicarage Ditch and the Ski-jump. All must be taken at a fair speed as fast times gain bonus points. Falls are heavily penalized and four refusals at any fence means disqualification.

After completing the second day, event horses are given extra care, glucose and vitamins and much attention is paid to the legs and feet. A veterinary examination is carried out, too, to ensure that each animal is fit to proceed with the third day's trial which is the show-jumping section. The jumping course is demanding and difficult requiring totally different skills to those used by the horse during the previous day when it was required to gallop fast over fixed obstacles. Compared with those at international shows, the jumps are small, but they are high enough to test the suppleness, fitness and obedience of each horse. The jumps must be taken in a prescribed sequence and faults are collected for knock-downs, refusals and falls. At the end of the three days, the points gained and lost in all three phases are tallied, determining the placings for the final awards. As in show jumping, women as well as men are constantly found among the winners of the top awards, although the sport is physically very demanding indeed. It can take several years to bring a horse up to the level of competence required for eventing and, as might be expected, such horses are of very high value.

One-day events are run by riding clubs. They are for novices, as well as intermediate and more advanced riders and their horses, and are scaled-down versions of the three-day affairs. The courses are much shorter as the competitors have to complete all three sections during one day. Being less strenuous, such events are invaluable for training young horses and building confidence, and many of today's successful trials

Left: In dressage it is important to have the horse going forward with lots of controlled impulsion.

Below: In eventing, some jumps may entail crossing water, either by clearing it, or as in this case landing in the stream before jumping out again.

3

riders began their competitive careers as children in Pony Club One-Day events.

Polo

Thought to be the oldest of all mounted sports, the game of polo is thought to have originated in Persia about 2500 years ago, where it was played by women as well as men. From there the game's popularity spread eastwards to China and westwards to Turkey, and was eventually enjoyed as an off-duty sport by British officers serving in Manipur, India, during the 19th century. The first Polo Club was formed in Calcutta towards the end of the 1850s, and on their return home after a long term of service, officers of the 10th Hussars introduced the game to Britain.

The first British polo game took place in 1871 and was played by two teams of eight players, one of whom acted as goalkeeper. This number was found to be dangerous and unwieldy in practise, and the number was soon reduced to five-a-side. By 1882 each team consisted of four players, as it does to this day. Introduced to the United States of America in the 1880s, polo became a popular sport for the well-to-do who found that their cow ponies and cutting horses made superb mounts for the game. The Argentinians were quick to realize the potential of their tough and hardy little Criollo horses in this sphere, and set about the breeding of the perfect polo pony.

Polo is played in four to six periods of play known as chukkas, each of which lasts for $7\frac{1}{2}$ minutes; there are rest intervals of three minutes between each chukka. The playing area is a field measuring 300 yards by 200 yards (274 metres by 183 metres). The goals are set at either end of the field, and the ball is hit between the posts to score. Polo players must be superb riders and very fit. They must practice for hours to develop a good eye for the ball and to be able to hit it accurately with the special long-handled mallets used in the game.

With the exception of ice hockey, polo is the fastest game in the world and can be very dangerous, especially when played on hard ground. The four players who make up each team are numbered 1, 2, 3 and Back. Each is handicapped according to his ability, and the higher the handicap, the better the player is known to be. Beginners generally start with handicaps of minus two goals and gradually progress to nought, when they are neither assets nor liabilities to their sides. Beginners often get their chance to play when a club manager attempts to even out the handicaps of two teams and

Left: Polo, the oldest of all mounted sports, has remained popular through the centuries.

Below: Jumping in style. A rider shows how to go forward with the horse, taking all his weight on his knees, leaving his mount's hindquarters free to lift clear of the obstacle.

Overleaf: The cowboy's horse plays an important role in the rodeo. It must be fit and highly trained to respond immediately to its rider's needs.

The rodeo provides great entertainment value for crowds and competitors alike. There are lots of varied events like Saddle-Bronc riding (below), Bull-Dogging (right), Calf-Roping (opposite bottom) and for the ladies, Barrel-Racing (opposite).

finds that he has one team with a total handicap of 16 while the three players of the other team have 18. By adding a player with a minus-two handicap the teams are exactly matched. Though the basic rules of polo have remained virtually unchanged through the ages, one rule that has been altered is that limiting the height of the ponies. In the first games played in the West the ponies used were about 13 hands high. In 1914 a height limit of 14.2 hands was set and at that time the agile and wiry Australian ponies became a leading force in international matches. Eventually the height limit was abolished altogether, and today's top polo ponies are generally horses of about 15 hands, bred from Thoroughbred and Argentine stock, and costing several thousands of pounds each to purchase when fully trained. Fast, obedient and capable of extremely sharp starts and stops, the top-class polo pony anticipates its rider's moves, naturally rides off opponents and appears to enjoy the game as much as everyone else.

Australia has evolved an interesting variation of polo and lacrosse, known as polocrosse. The ball is scooped up in a long stick with a net attached and is either passed between players or carried to goal. The game is fast, informal and very entertaining.

Rodeo

During the early days of the cattle industry in the American West off-duty cowboys enjoyed testing their various skills, especially at round-up time or after long trail drives, when they had money to spend on drinking and gambling. Rodeo literally means 'round-up' and during the celebrations of a completed cycle of work, informal events began on the larger ranches around 1840. In 1847 a one-ranch rodeo was planned in Santa Fe, New Mexico, and, for the first time, spectators were invited. In Deer Trail, Colorado, in 1869, the first rodeo was held involving contestants from more than one ranch, and in Pecos, Texas, in 1883, prize money was offered for the very first time.

Today's professional cowboy has one aim in life and that is to achieve the title of World Champion. This aim means that he will have to enter a total of about one hundred rodeos during an 11-month season, and to perform consistently well in arena events such as steer wrestling, calf roping, team roping, bull riding, and bronco riding with a saddle and bareback. There are hundreds of official rodeos held each year in the United States, with prize money totalling millions of dollars, and it is possible for the top competitors to become very rich indeed unless they are unfortunate enough to be hospitalized first.

Horses play important roles in rodeos; in fact the classic event is held by many to be bronco-riding. Originally unbroken or imperfectly broken range horses, the 'broncs' of today are horses trained to buck from the moment they are released from the special holding chutes in the arena. Most of these horses are owned by contract companies and are prized for their skill in unseating top riders. They are kept very well-fed and fit, and seem very calm and friendly creatures except when they feel the bucking strap tightening under their bellies, when they know they must go to work for a few seconds in the ring.

In bareback bronco riding, the horse has only a webbing surcingle around its girth. The cowboy slides onto the back of the bronco while it is enclosed within the chute and must only have one hand on the rigging. When the chute opens, the horse leaps out bucking furiously and the cowboy must observe certain rules. One arm must always be held above his shoulder line, he must roll his spurs up the horse's neck at least once and prove by throwing his feet wide that he is staying aboard by balance only. The required eight seconds before the bell rings must seem an interminable period for the cowboy, and most competitors seem to hit the dust within the first two or three seconds after leaving the chutes. In saddle bronco riding, the horse is equipped with a saddle, but the rider is not allowed to 'pull leather' by grasping the horn. He must have his feet over the bronco's shoulder as the animal hits the ground in its first buck from the chute and his free hand must not touch any part of the horse.

The cowboys have their own horses for the wrestling and roping events. These must be highly trained and very fit for they play an important part in the proceedings. In steer wrestling, two riders work as a team. The first, called the hazer, rides a line to keep the steer running straight while his partner draws alongside and leaps from his galloping horse to wrestle the steer to the ground by its horns in a movement called bulldogging. In calf roping, the horse's role is crucial. The cowboy races after a freshly released calf and throws a loop of his rope around it. In one seemingly fluid motion the horse stops dead and pulls back on the end of the rope fixed to the saddle horn, while the cowboy leaps to the ground, upturns the calf and ties

its four feet together with a special pigging string. The calf must remain immobilized for six seconds, then is released unharmed. Steer wrestling and calf roping are run against the clock; the cowboy who achieves the shortest time with the fewest penalty points is the eventual winner.

Also run against the clock is the team-roping event, which can be very spectacular. Two cowboys work as a team and the object is to rope a running steer. The first cowboy, known as the header, must get his rope neatly round and under the steer's horns, while his partner, the heeler, must rope the animal's hind legs. Team-ropers' horses are expertly trained in their job and know exactly when to run, stop, turn or pull back, and seemingly without any aids, work in perfect unison with their riders.

Members of the Girls' Rodeo Association are allowed to compete in certain events. Some girls make skilled ropers and take part in the team contests. They really have the rodeo crowd roaring in the barrel-racing competitions which combine skilled riding and co-ordination in a race against the relentless clock. Three large drums or barrels are placed in the arena at specified points and competitors must race around them forming a cloverleaf pattern, circling the first barrel in one direction and the second and third in the opposite direction. Neither horse nor rider must touch any of the barrels and knocking one over results in a five-second penalty. The girls work for long hours schooling their barrel-racing ponies which must be very fit and fast, able to go into a gallop from a standing start and have the ability to turn at speed without losing impetus. As may be expected, such ponies are highly valued and well cared-for.

In the larger rodeos, horses play other roles, taking part in great parades commemorating eipsodes in the history of the Wild West. Some are dressed in warpaint and carry impressive Indian chieftains; others are resplendent in Mexican attire with tooled black leather saddlery, heavily embossed with silver. Horses draw wagons and various old

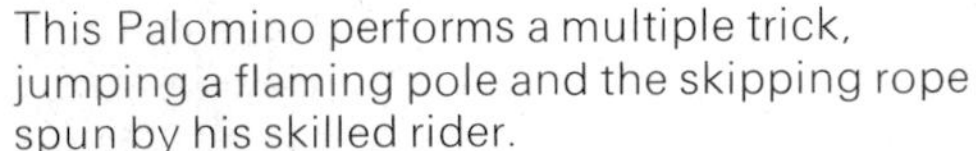

This Palomino performs a multiple trick, jumping a flaming pole and the skipping rope spun by his skilled rider.

agricultural machines. They come in all sizes, shapes and colours and the parade emphasizes the part played by the horse in the exploration, development and taming of the West during the last century or so.

Circus Horses

Horses have been a popular part of the circus since 1768 when the first trick-riders presented their daring displays to admiring and appreciative audiences. Since that time the leading circus families throughout the world have developed their own individual equestrian acts. Most of these displays consist of subtly modified or extended high-school exercises, which, when performed in time to carefully selected music by beautiful horses give the illusion of an evocative equine ballet. In some acts horses are ridden and they wear carefully designed and ornamented saddles and bridles often sporting colourful tassels or plumes. Their riders generally wear dramatic costumes designed to a theme complementing the chosen music, and adding to the illusive quality of their performances. Groups of handsome horses are also trained to perform liberty acts, in which they enter the ring in a disciplined group and, riderless, go through an intricate set of movements in response to commands given by their trainer, who works them standing in the centre of the ring. Tiny ponies and those of unusual colouring are often used to add variety to the liberty act and appeal particularly to young children in the audience. Young horses, with exceptionally good looks and that elusive quality known as presence, are chosen for the circus ring when four or five years of age. Great care is taken to ensure that they have been well reared and kindly treated, and show no traces of aggression or of having acquired bad habits. The selected horses are given a year's intensive schooling and notes are taken of any natural habits or traits which might be developed into an animal's personal display. Any animals showing potential as high-school horses are given their first lessons in classic dressage at five years of age and their schooling continues for a further two years. Other horses with very wide backs and large rumps are trained to canter steadily around the ring while acrobats, clowns and jugglers leap on, off and over them. These are the Rosinbacks, and their act is almost as old as the circus itself.

Circus horses are well fed and immaculately groomed, for they must look their best whenever they enter the ring which forms their stage. That they enjoy their work is clear to any horse-lover in the audience for they work with ears pricked, calmly waiting for every signal from the trainer. Protests have been heard and efforts made to prohibit the use of animals in the circus, and it is true to say that some animals, such as elephants and the big cats may be made to look foolish by the tricks they are expected to perform. The horse, however, performs only extensions of its natural behaviour patterns, enjoys its work and presents a spectacle which is traditional and exemplifies the very spirit of the sawdust ring.

A precarious perch for the Guttenbergs' famous bareback riding act.

Riding Horses

Opposite page: The ultimate in training and response to the rider's aids may be seen in dressage tests as performed by this splendid Hanoverian.

The riding horse should be calm and well behaved at all paces and in all situations, whether it is ridden in English or Western tackle.

The prime asset in any riding horse is that it should be quiet, well-mannered, comfortable and a pleasure to ride. A quiet horse will be well behaved while it is being groomed and saddled, and it will calmly accept the regular visits of the farrier. It will stand while being mounted and dismounted, will walk boldly into its stable or a trailer, and does not bite, kick, rear or buck. Such equine paragons result from kind careful handling from an early age, followed by correct schooling. All riding horses and ponies should be mentally and physically suited to the work expected of them.

Heavy riders need strong horses, while small riders find it easier to control lighter horses. Those animals used for trail riding and trekking must be sturdy and surefooted, and those for use in towns must be completely fearless in heavy traffic.

Once a horse has been broken in to carry a saddle and bridle, and has learned to accept a rider on its back, the riding horse or pony begins a period of schooling. This entails teaching the animal to move correctly in straight lines and circles, to start and stop smoothly and to move backwards and sideways. Most of these lessons are taught by a trainer from the ground, then later reinforced with aids given by a rider. These schooling movements form the basis of elementary dressage training, and the schooling exercises may be continued in slow stages over a period of many months to produce a dressage horse for the show ring.

Dressage is defined as the art and training of the horse in obedience, deportment and responses. Today's intricate movements and figures are refinements of exercises once used in cavalry training. It was considered vital that the warhorse should be capable of moving in all directions and be very responsive to each of its rider's requests.

Antoine de Pluvinel, a 17th century Frenchman, wrote a book on equitation which advocated the use of kindness and reward in training the horse. His somewhat revolutionary ideas were adopted and extended by François de la Guerinère, a great riding-school master based in Naples, who has been called the prophet of the art of high-school riding. Fast riding across country appealed more to the British, but European riders were prepared to exercise the patience and discipline necessary to school and ride dressage horses. Eventually, all riders came to realize that even elementary dressage training produces balance, suppleness and control in all types of riding horses, and whether they are to be used for hunting, eventing or show jumping or merely for pleasure riding, such preliminary schooling makes for better performance.

49

Right: Early handling and kind training helps to instil responsive behaviour in the young riding horse long before it is mature enough to be mounted and ridden.

Below: Eight Lipizzaner stallions in the riding hall at the Spanish Riding School of Vienna at the end of the performance of their traditional quadrille.

At international show level, competition dressage provides the most graceful of all displays of equitation, involving as it does a sequence of expertly performed, timed and controlled movements. The normal walk, trot and canter are executed in both their collected and extended forms. In the collected paces the horse is gathered in with its hocks well under the body, while in extended paces an active, free effect is seen. In addition to the basic paces, dressage horses perform such sideways movements as the half-pass, and turn right around in the pirouette. The Fédération Equestre Internationale has devised a number of set dressage tests which are recognized in most international circles. In these, each movement is specified and judges look for certain qualities in each competitor. The horse must show freedom and regularity in its paces, and give the impression of harmony, lightness and ease of movements. When working on a line, the horse must move absolutely straight and when working on a curved line, its body should bend accordingly.

The Great Lipizzaners

Perhaps the finest exhibition in the world of high-school riding can be seen at the Spanish Riding School of Vienna, the oldest and the last riding academy in which classical riding is cultivated in its purest form. The School owes its name to the fact that since its foundation in the late 16th century, only Spanish stallions, selected for their strength, nobility and intelligence, have been chosen to train in *Haute Ecole*. This training develops the mental and physical qualities of the horse until it is able to execute harmonious and balanced exercises of great complexity. The famous classical jumps, or 'schools above the ground', are produced when a perfectly supple horse is allowed to release the energy gathered during a period of intensive collection. These movements, called the Levade, the Capriole and the Courbette, are extensions of the natural behaviour of young stallions at play, indulging in mock fighting.

The famous Spanish horses used in the School were first bred in the tiny township of Lipizza in present-day Yugoslavia, the site of the former Royal Court Stud, founded in 1580. The Lipizzaners seen in today's performances are stallions bred at the Government stud at Piber. The magnificent riding hall in which the stallions perform was built between 1729 and 1735 by Josef Emanuel Fischer von Erlach. It is 180 ft long, 59 ft wide and 56 ft high (55 by 18 by 17 metres respectively) with plain white columns supporting the viewing galleries. The performance of the white horses starts with the entrance of eight young stallions, several of which still sport their dark grey juvenile coats. These are followed by four experienced stallions showing the steps and movements expected in the classical school. Then a pair of stallions perform a stately *pas de deux*. After some advanced airs displayed by seven stallions, some working between fixed pillars in the centre of the arena, a single horse gives a breathtaking performance, controlled from the ground on long reins. Next comes what the audience has been waiting for, the 'schools above the ground'. Four massive and very fit stallions work individually and execute the very vigorous and difficult leaps and kicks, and it is easy to understand why such training proved an invaluable asset in battle. Finally, eight white stallions enter the hall and carry out the intricate, dreamlike movements of the quadrille.

Showing Horses

Unlike the high-school airs performed by the great Lipizzaner stallions, the requirements of dressage tests are for basic, natural movements only, precisely executed as part of a polished and controlled performance. All riding horses benefit from a little dressage work, whether they are show jumpers, hunters or hacks, and horses parading in the show ring display their conformation and movements best after such schooling. Horse shows of various kinds are held all over the world. They may take the form of small local gymkhanas with a few jumping classes, or be part of huge agricultural shows lasting for several days, catering for all sorts of livestock, as well as offering a wide selection of equine classes. Between these two extremes there are many other types of horse show. Specialist clubs hold their own breed shows for young stock, stallions and mares with foals, all of which may be shown in-hand, and generally add some ridden classes too. There are special jumping meetings held at famous courses, and other shows incorporating dressage, eventing and driving.

Showing classes are judged on the horse's conformation, movement and style, and a very few also take into consideration the appearance and ability of the rider. In Hack and Hunter classes the horses circle within the ring while the judges appraise them closely, then they are called in one by one,

Colonel Alois Podhajsky riding one of the great white stallions at the Spanish Riding School of Vienna.

forming a line, for closer inspection. In some classes riders of the better horses will be asked to remove the saddles from their mounts so that the judge can assess conformation. In Hunter classes the judge likes to ride the most promising animals to find out which is the most comfortable. Such classes are divided into lightweight, middleweight and heavyweight hunters and the horses that compete rarely if ever have a day with hounds for fear that they might sustain an injury which could ruin their show careers!

Working Hunter classes are enjoyable to watch for the competitors not only have to walk, trot and canter around the ring, but are also expected to jump some natural-looking fences, and may have to pass between stacked hay-bales or some other such hazards. The show hack is generally crossbred but with a considerable amount of Thoroughbred blood, giving it a refined appearance. It is a horse that has its origins in the days when fashionable ladies and gentlemen rode out in the town streets and city parks. The hack must have beautiful conformation and impeccable manners, and there are ladies' classes in which it may be ridden sidesaddle when it looks particularly elegant.

Pony Classes

Ponies have show classes divided by height and those under 12 hands may be shown on the leading-rein if ridden by very small children. As well as looking for attributes of soundness and conformation, the judges of these classes expect to see a safe, quiet performance. Larger ponies are expected to have impeccable manners and to respond to all the aids given by their young riders. They must be correctly turned out and are asked to give short individual performances for the judge. In Working Pony classes more emphasis is placed on utility, and although the conformation

Left: A Lipizzaner stallion taking part in a show parade of rare horse breeds.

Right: One of the competitors gives a short 'show' of her pony's paces in a Children's Ridden Class.

Below: Perhaps the most elegant and well-mannered of all riding horses are the Show Hacks, which in the Ladies' class may be ridden sidesaddle.

of the pony is important, soundness, action and efficiency are judged more important than beauty and elegance.

The Fun of the Gymkhana

Not everyone is fortunate or wealthy enough to afford a beautiful show horse or pony, but that does not mean that they are deprived of entering some equine competitions. The gymkhana provides fun and enjoyment for riders of all ages and offers such a variety of classes that literally anyone, with any type of horse or pony, can enter. Size, shape, colour or looks are quite unimportant for gymkhana events, for it is the agility of the animal and the skill of the rider that determine who wins or loses. There are many mounted games, some of which are divided by age groups, some by heights of the ponies and some which are open to all.

One of the most popular of all gymkhana games is the Bending Race in which rows of evenly placed poles are set down the arena. The object of the race is to gallop in and out of the poles, turn at the bottom and race in and out again back to the start, which then becomes the finish. Bending is fast and furious and the horses and ponies taking part thoroughly enjoy it. Run in heats, all the heat winners then race each other for the final prizes. There are lots of musical games in which competitors ride to music in a circle around the arena. When the music abruptly stops, the riders must race to the centre of the ring, and depending on the event; place their hats on a post, or dismount and sit on chairs, and so on. There are fewer targets than competitors, and those failing to gain their goal are eliminated. Targets are removed after each round and eventually there is a single one left with two or three keen riders eyeing it intently. The music stops and only the lucky winner gains his objective. The horses and ponies which perform best in mounted games are those which respond readily to leg aids and have the happy-go-lucky sort of temperament that allows them to enter into the competitive spirit of the proceedings.

Gymkhana games are fun for ponies and their riders, and help to increase their confidence in one another.

Ponies become adept at aiding their young riders in the intricacies of the mounted games and races.

Riding Clubs

Families are loath to part with their gymkhana ponies, and even quite small animals enjoy carrying light adults and large teenagers through the intricacies of such events as sack-racing and the egg-and-spoon event. Such ponies may be loaned to other families with children, on condition that the animals are never sold, and are returned to their own old homes when their useful days are over. Tried and trusted family ponies are often loaned to centres which provide riding lessons for disabled children and young adults. It has been found that such exercise is both mentally and physically stimulating even for those who have quite serious disabilities. Expert instructors run riding centres or classes for disabled students, each of whom needs someone to handle his pony as well as someone to make sure that he stays safely in the saddle, and such helpers are generally volunteers. Even the horses and ponies taking part in the lessons seem to appreciate the problems of their riders and behave with quiet dignity as they are mounted and ridden gently in the school. Suitable ponies may be loaned for these valuable riding activities by members of various riding clubs and these clubs are a boon for those interested in, but not wealthy enough to own, valuable horses and ponies.

Membership in a riding club entitles riders to use various facilities and may also allow reduced entry to shows. Such clubs arrange lectures and shows of their own with classes designed to encourage novices and those with inexperienced mounts. The Pony Club, affiliated to the British Horse Society, has branches all over the world and is instrumental in helping to educate its members in all aspects of riding and the care of their ponies. Rallies and meetings are held throughout the year and youngsters are encouraged to join the annual camping holiday, taking along their ponies, to enjoy a concentrated level of

In the hunting field, weight-carrying horses with great stamina are used to carry large riders throughout the often tiring day.

instruction and games. Young people with a background of attending club activities grow up with a firm knowledge of horse care, and enjoy good working relationships with their horses.

Hunting

For the sport of hunting, a very special type of horse is required. It is not of any particular breed but must be bold, intelligent and capable of negotiating all manner of obstacles. It must be strong and sound enough to carry its rider for four or five hours at varying speeds including a fast gallop, and must be responsive to the aids. Hunter type varies according to the kind of country over which they are used. Over heavy clay, stocky animals fare better than Thoroughbred types, while these come into their own when the country is predominantly fast, well-drained grassland. Large, heavy riders obviously need weight-carrying hunters, while lightweight riders are best mounted on finer animals which they find easier to control. Horses are trained for the hunting field in gradual stages. First they are taught normal obedience, then they may be ridden to the meet to be introduced to hounds. Many young horses find the unaccustomed crowds of horses and hounds to be very exciting, but calm down after two or three meets. It is vital that the young horse is prevented from kicking at hounds or other horses, and such introductory lessons should be conducted in as quiet and collected a manner as possible. After getting used to the sounds, sights and smells of the hunting scene, the young horse is generally taken out with the field for an hour

or so until it learns to behave in an acceptable and calm way. Any horse that learns good manners and goes strongly and well becomes very valuable indeed for such horses are always in demand as hunters.

Holidays on Horseback

Trekking and trail-riding provide pleasurable holidays for the many people who love horses but are not fortunate enough to own them. Even novice and inexperienced riders are able to enjoy such pursuits, for the horses and ponies chosen to carry them are quiet and docile, safe and surefooted. Trekking and trail-riding centres exist in many countries of the world, often situated in very remote and beautiful places impossible to explore by car or on foot. You may ride trails in many parts of the United States of America, traverse areas of Spain, the foothills of the Himalayas and the mountains of Scotland and Wales. Locally bred horses or ponies are generally chosen by the proprietors of such centres, as these are more likely to perform well over their natural terrain. The animals are well trained and very safe to ride and it is usual for each rider to be allocated his own mount for which he is totally responsible. Novices are soon taught to groom and saddle up their charges by an expert instructor. Treks and trail-rides are led by experienced guides and usually cover miles of tracks and paths across glorious countryside. Exhilarating but at the same time restful, the quiet passage of the ponies enables their riders to catch evocative glimpses of wildlife at every turn of the trail.

Pony trekking is a fine pastime, enabling horselovers, perhaps with little riding experience, to enjoy the countryside from the saddle.

Hacking in the countryside provides perfect relaxation after a busy working week.

Hacking

Many people own quite ordinary but well-mannered horses and ponies and get all the enjoyment they require from riding out quietly in the countryside, on bridlepaths and tracks, through wooded glades and down quiet lanes. They try to avoid busy roads whenever possible, for today's heavy traffic and thoughtless drivers can prove unnerving for even the quietest of mounts. Hacking, as this gentle pursuit is called, provides good healthy outdoor exercise for both horse and rider, and can be as relaxing or invigorating as they wish. Relaxing rides through quiet copses soon rest a weary mind and allow a close look at the natural world of the woodland, with only the sound of birdsong and the quiet footfalls of the horse's hooves through the soft leaf layer. When the mind and body needs a tonic, nothing can beat a short sharp gallop along a clear ride or over the brow of a hill, riding up the headlands of a friendly farmer's field. Nothing can equal the feel of the horse's muscular shoulders moving under the saddle and the sting of the wind whipping salt tears from the eyes.

In caring for his own horse, a rider learns to read its every mood and soon builds up a rapport unequalled in relationships with any other species of animal. The horse, kept apart from others of its kind, soon begins to look upon its master as the leader of its herd. It is happy to be dominated and tries its best to behave in an acceptable way, quite content to work hard in return for the comfort of a safe home, good food and kind treatment.

Horses of the Turf

Flat Racing

The beginnings of the sport of horse racing go so far back in history that they have been virtually unrecorded, although some Hittite cuneiform tablets dated at about 3200 B.C. give specific instructions for the training of racehorses. It is known that the Ancient Chinese and Greeks staged races for mounted men, and that they prized their fastest horses, but it was not until the Roman occupation that racing was finally introduced to the British Isles. Greatly enjoyed by off-duty Roman soldiers, flat racing has been popular ever since. The first races were held on public holidays as part of festivities in market towns for the enjoyment of the populace, or as private meetings arranged by gentlemen on their own estates.

The first accurately recorded flat race in Britain was run in 1377 when the young King Richard II, while still the Prince of Wales, raced his horses against those of the Earl of Arundel. The chosen site for the match was the open heathland at the small Suffolk village of Newmarket, already a favourite society locale for feats of horsemanship, hunting and hawking. This area of East Anglia proved very popular for horse breeding and rearing of fine healthy stock at several stud farms. Royal patronage through the ensuing years did much to improve the quality and size of the racehorse, and Royal studs were also instituted in London's Hampton Court, at Eltham in Kent and in various other parts of England. In Scotland native horses were bred with Spanish and Barbary stallions, which were said to

The *Darley Arabian*, foaled in 1700 in the Syrian Desert and transshipped to England four years later, is the forebear of today's thoroughbred racehorses.

A somewhat stylized portrait of the great Godolphin Arabian, found drawing a watercart in the streets of Paris before being brought to England in 1730. Most of today's top thoroughbred horses may be traced directly back to this great stallion.

have swum ashore to Galloway from the wrecked Spanish Armada. Their offspring proved to be so swift and full of stamina that racing soon became a popular pastime throughout Scotland.

When James I came to the English throne, he and his Scottish nobles soon established regular race meetings at Newmarket. The first such sporting visit occurred on 27 February 1605. King James recognized the military importance of improving the general quality of British horses, and although hunting, hawking and coursing appealed more to his tastes than racing, he went to enormous lengths to encourage the general upgrading of horses. He imported fine Oriental horses, many chosen specially for him by the Duke of Buckingham, appointed Master of the Horse in 1616.

One of the earliest and most famous of the Eastern imports was the Markham Arabian, purchased for the sum of £154, but he did not impress anyone with much speed for it was said of him at the time, 'When he came to run, every horse beat him.' King James received many important presents of bloodstock from abroad including a large consignment of coursers from Naples and 12 mares from Denmark. All the mares at the stud in Hampton Court Palace were said to be Spanish genets and Barbs. During James' reign, races generally took the form of matches between two horses with prizes of golden bells, snaffles or cups for which the winner had to give a bond, guaranteeing to produce the trophy for competition at the next meeting. Later, these trophies were superceded by cups of silver-gilt which could be retained by the winners, and the race structure was altered so that six or more horses could compete and more circuits of the course were run to add excitement to each race. Races were started by an important official such as a sheriff or mayor; the riders had to pay an entrance fee and be distinguished from each other by the colours of their jackets and caps; and, as one account states, 'everyone that rydeth shall waye or be made in weight just tenne stone'. There was often great ceremony at the presentation of the prizes with lengthy speeches and the placing of laurel wreaths upon the heads of the winning riders.

Charles I was not particularly keen on racing, but neither did he actively discourage it or the breeding of quality horses. He was an accomplished horseman and enjoyed many equestrian pursuits including tilting at the lists. He was painted on horseback by such artists as Rubens and Van Dyck. The King's arch adversary, Oliver Cromwell, was very fond of hunting and enjoyed horse racing too. His studmaster, Mr. Place, owned a fine Arabian known as the White Turk which had considerable success on the racetrack and was a successful sire. Cromwell, who had been a notable cavalry officer, was a fine judge of horses. His stud of breeding stock was superb and his well-matched coach teams were unsurpassed even by those of royalty. Later, after the execution of the King, Cromwell added racing to cock-fighting and bull-baiting on his list of 'Forbidden Sports', mainly, it is thought, to discourage the gathering of large crowds of possible Royalists. It was not long before Charles II came to the throne, however, and racing bloomed again under this 'Merry Monarch'.

The 17th century racehorse was still a creature of varied type and rather lacking in height, and although it had the stamina necessary to run the often arduous races of the day, it lacked the exceptional turn of speed seen in the modern Thoroughbred. The King sent his Master of the Horse on expeditions to the East to seek and procure desirable foreign horses for the Royal stud. Several purchases were made and the mares, along with their immediate progeny, came to be known as the Royal Mares. Gradually, towards the end of the century, the influence of imported Arabian and Barb stallions began to show and bloodstock began to become upgraded.

The first of these horses to be mentioned in the Stud Book came through Turkish and Hungarian intermediaries. The Lister Turk was captured in the battle of Buda in 1686 and the Belgrade Turk was a fine mare, taken in 1707. Of all the Eastern imports, though, just three famous stallions form the cornerstone of the General Stud Book. They are the Byerley Turk, the Darley Arabian and the Godolphin Arabian. Today, every registered Thoroughbred has one or more of these horses at the root of its pedigree, in some cases recurring many times.

John Evelyn writing in his diary in 1683 describes having seen three fine

When the sport of horse-racing first became popular, most spectators attended on horseback and would gallop from the start to the finish to watch their fancies run home, as seen in this early print of racing at Epsom.

Many horses were trained in close proximity to the track, much as they are today.

Arabian stallions being exhibited by King Charles II in London's St. James Park. The horses had been brought from Hamburg having been captured from the Turks in the siege of Vienna. One of these was undoubtedly the Byerley Turk although he had not, at that time, acquired his name.

Robert Byerley was a rich man who acquired the stallion. He took the horse on several campaigns during King William's wars in Ireland, where the animal proved himself to be a fearless, faithful charger. When Colonel Byerley retired, he took his stallion home to Yorkshire and put him at stud where the horse founded a dynasty of racehorses, and is the ancestor of such marvels as the Tetrarch and Tourbillon. The great horse was never named, but is referred to in all records as the Byerley Turk. A purebred Arabian despite his title, the horse stood 15 hands high and was bay in colour with no white markings. The General Stud Book says of him, 'He did not cover many bred mares but was the sire of the Duke of Kingston's Sprite who was thought nearly as good as Leedes; the Duke of Rutland's Black-Hearty and Archer; the Duke of Devonshire's Basto, Lord Bristol's Grasshopper and Lord Godolphin's Byerley Gelding, all in good forms; Halloway Jigg a middling horse, and Knightley's Mare in a very good form.'

The second horse of the great trio was the Darley Arabian who was foaled in 1700 in the Syrian Desert among the Fedan Bedouin and bought by Thomas Darley, the British Consul in Aleppo, to be transshipped to England in 1704. An entry in the General Stud Book of 1803 describes him as follows: 'DARLEY'S ARABIAN was brought over by a brother of Mr. Darley of Yorkshire, who, being an agent in merchandising abroad, became member of a hunting club by which means he acquired interest to procure this horse. He was sire of Childers and also got Almanzor a very good horse; a white-legged horse of the Duke of Somerset's, full brother to Almanzor and thought to be as good but meeting with an accident he never ran in public; Cupid and Brisk, good horses; Daedalus a very fleet horse; Dart, Skipjack, Manica and Aleppo, good Plate horses though out of bad mares; Lord Lonsdale's mare in a very good form; and Lord Tracy's mare in a good one for Plates. He covered very few mares except Mr. Darley's who had very few well bred besides Almanzor's dam.' Childers, referred to in this record, was foaled in 1715. He was also known as Flying Childers and was renowned in his day as the 'fleetest horse that was ever trained in this or any other country'.

Many stories have been written about the Godolphin Arabian but it has now

The finish of the St Leger Stakes of 1836.

been established that the horse was presented by an eastern potentate to King Louis XV, who in turn gave the horse to his cook, who sold him to a tradesman. The subdued stallion was seen pulling a watercart through the streets of Paris and bought for the sum of 75 francs by a Mr. Coke, and transported to England in 1730. The General Stud Book states, 'The GODOLPHIN ARABIAN was imported by Mr. Coke at whose death he became the property of Lord Godolphin. His first employment was that of Teazer to Hobgoblin who refusing to cover Roxana she was put to the Arabian, and from that cover produced Lath the first of his get. He was also sire of Cade, Regulus, Blank . . . and what is considered very remarkable, as well as a strong proof of his excellence as a Stallion there is not a superior horse now on the turf without a cross of the Godolphin Arabian, nor has there been for several years past. He was a brown bay with no white except the off heel behind, and about 15 hands high. It is not known of what particular race of the Arab breed, indeed it has been asserted that he was a Barb. He died at Gog Magog in 1753, in or about the 29th year of his age.

'The story of his playfellow, the Black Cat must not be omitted here, especially as an erroneous account has got abroad, copied from the first introduction to the present work. – Instead of his grieving for the loss of the Cat, *she* survived *him*, though but a short time; she sat upon him after he was dead in the building erected for him, and followed him to the place where he was buried under a gateway near the running stable; sat upon him there until he was buried then went away and was never seen again, till found dead in the hay-loft.'

During the reign of George II, a chronicler of the time wrote this of the three stallions '. . . they have produced stock of vast size, bone and substance and were at the same time endowed with such extraordinary and therefore unheard of powers of speed, as to render it probable that some of them have reached nature's goal, or ultimate point of perfection . . .'

Racing was, of course, the hobby of the very rich and aristocratic at that time, and another hundred years were to pass before the true Thoroughbred emerged as the cornerstone of a vast, worldwide racing industry.

Queen Anne proved to be a great patron of racing and was responsible for the development of a beautiful racecourse conveniently close to Windsor Castle in Berkshire. Now known as 'Royal' Ascot, the first race there was run in August 1711. The horses, which had to be under six years of age, raced in three heats, each carried 12 stones

(168 lb) in weight, and the eventual winner carried off the prize of one hundred guineas.

The Jockey Club

Formed in 1752, the Jockey Club began as a small social club for gentlemen involved in racing, and one of the first members was Sir Charles Bunbury. Bunbury and Lord Derby decided to arrange a very special race at Epsom, and tossed a coin to determine after whom it should be named. Lord Derby won the toss – otherwise one of our present day classics would be known as 'the Bunbury'. When the first Derby was run in 1780, however, it was Sir Charles' colt, Diomed, who was first past the winning post. The Derby has since become one of the great events of the sporting year. Run over a distance of $1\frac{1}{2}$ miles, it is considered to be today's best all-round test of speed and stamina for three-year-old colts.

The Jockey Club has also stood the test of time, evolving into the governing body of flat racing, electing its members from those closely involved in the 'Sport of Kings'. All trainers, jockeys, officials and racecourses must hold licences granted by the Jockey Club, which has the right to revoke these without any recourse to appeal.

Once the Jockey Club took control of racing matters, rules and regulations were standardized and careful breeding records were maintained. Racing calendars were formulated, and apart from the troubled war years, the industry boomed giving enjoyment to people from all walks of life. In addition to the Derby, Britain has four other great classic races. Two of these are held in Newmarket each spring; they are for

Above: An exciting start to the 1981 Derby at Epsom.

Right: Thundering past the stand at Royal Ascot.

Young American jockey Steve Cauthen in action.

three-year-olds and are run over a course of one mile. The One Thousand Guineas is for fillies and the Two Thousand Guineas is for colts. Like the Derby, the Oaks is run at Epsom over $1\frac{1}{2}$ miles, but is for fillies only, and the season's final classic race, run in September over $1\frac{3}{4}$ miles at Doncaster, is the St. Leger.

The American Jockey Club is based in New York, but unlike its English cousin is basically a secretariat, concerning itself mainly with the registration of racing colours and bloodstock. Rules of racing vary according to the State in which it takes place, and State boards are responsible for disciplinary matters. The racing season in the United States varies also, according to climatic conditions. In the New York area, racegoers may indulge in their sport for 313 days each year, for the courses close only on Tuesdays so that the staff can enjoy a rest day, and on Christmas Day. In California, racing starts in the fall and lasts until early spring, while the Arlington meetings run from May until September.

In the United States of America the most famous of the many flat races are the Kentucky Derby, held in early May, the Preakness Stakes in late May, and, the longest of the three, the Belmont Stakes, which is run in June over $1\frac{1}{2}$ miles. In France the Grand Prix du Paris and the Prix Royal Oak are run at Longchamp, while in Chantilly is staged the important Prix du Jockey Club. Thoroughbreds travel from many parts of the world in order to take part in the great classic races, and the most successful bloodstock changes hands at enormous prices for breeding purposes. In Britain the flat-racing season lasts from March until November and horses of any age from two years old upwards may take part, although it is rare for a horse to race on the flat after it is five or six years of age.

All Thoroughbreds have their official birthday on 1 January of each year no matter when they are foaled, so most breeders aim to have mares producing early in each New Year. Late foals – those born in June for example – are at a distinct disadvantage unless very forward, being officially two years old when only chronologically 18 months. The Jockey Club rules for racing are strictly enforced and make all aspects of the sport ethical and irreproachable.

In the classic races, all runners carry identical weights but in other races weight is decided by 'condition' in which the animal's past performance and age automatically decide its weight, or it may be decided by an official handicapper. In this instance, the weights are adjusted in an attempt to even the chances of each runner.

Steeplechasing

National Hunt racing is controlled by a similar body to the Jockey Club known as the National Hunt Committee which was formed in 1866. The season lasts from August until the following May or June. The horses which take part in the sport are mostly Thoroughbreds and generally geldings rather than entire stallions and mares. National Hunt horses race for several years; in fact, many famous jumpers have found their best form between eight and 12 years of age. National Hunt has its classic races,

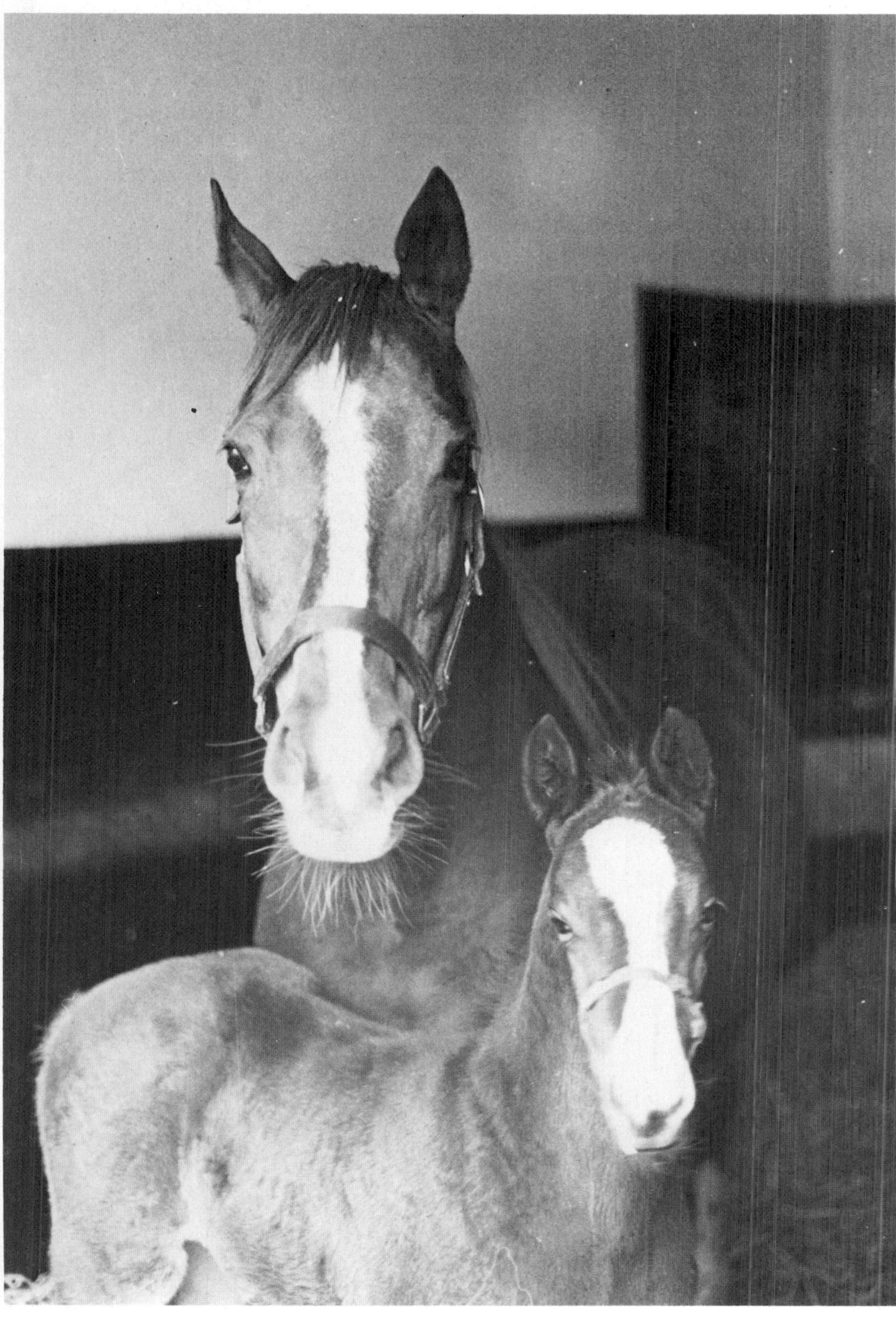

A famous thoroughbred mare passes on her striking colour and facial markings to her promising young foal.

Overleaf: Three American horses finishing well in the 1980 classic race at Newmarket, the Two Thousand Guineas: Known Fact (4), Nureyev (7) and Posse (8).

Safely over the formidable Chair fence in the Grand National Steeplechase.

too, and these test the stamina and courage of top horses and leading jockeys. The Cheltenham Gold Cup is a telling three and a half miles, over tough fences. The Champion Hurdle Challenge Cup is, as its title suggests, run over hurdles for two miles. The renowned Grand National at Aintree is over the largest and most demanding fences in the world, spread over a distance of four and a half miles.

The first steeplechase originated from the 'pounding matches' held among Irish gentlefolk during the 18th century. A leader was chosen by drawing lots and he would mount his horse and gallop off across country, choosing as difficult a course as he could, while his opponent had to follow or risk losing the race by default. The pace was often quite slow, but the daredevil attitude of the contestants attempting to clear formidable obstacles often caused frightful accidents to be suffered by both horses and riders. The winner was the rider who literally pounded his opponent to a standstill. Eventually these races became more organized and the matches were raced over agreed courses between two points or landmarks. In 1752 one of the earliest recorded steeplechases took place when a Mr. O'Calloghan raced a Mr. Blake over a distance of four and a half miles from Buttevant Church to the church of St. Leger, the steeple of which could just be seen from the starting point. The sport gained popularity as the exploits of certain horses and riders were relayed over dinner tables and in the hunting field. Great wagers were placed and

some horses were tested to the limits of their endurance. In March of 1790 a Mr. Hardy matched his horse against that of the Honourable Mr. Willoughby for a prize of 1000 guineas over a nine-mile course in Leicestershire. In November 1804 a very significant race took place over a distance of eight miles, significant because the three gentlemen who took part wore distinctive coloured jackets for the first time – Mr. Bullivant chose orange, Mr. Day was in crimson, while Mr. Frisby favoured sky blue. The first military steeplechase took place in the same year. It was held near Newcastle-upon-Tyne and involved two officers, Captains Prescott and Tucker of the 5th Light Dragoons. Over the next few years some excellent and regular steeplechase meetings were instituted. One such popular event was that held in the Vale of Aylesbury. The first Aylesbury race was instigated by a group of huntsmen who considered that the deep brooks intersecting the immense Vale would produce an unusual and exciting race for spectators and participants.

In Liverpool flat racing began in 1576 with a special race held every Ascension Day over a course of four miles, the prize being a valuable silver bell. The event continued for a few years, then interest in the sport lapsed. After a fallow period of some two hundred years a few races were organized, then discontinued once again through lack of support. Eventually, in 1827, a group of businessmen and racing enthusiasts joined forces and formed a committee to hold meetings at Aintree. They leased the land and built

Overleaf: A Grand National drama.

'So and So' parading before the 1980 Grand National at which he fell at Becher Brook.

33

30
9

a grandstand and the flat races were restarted in 1829. By 1836 a notice advertised 'a sweepstake of £10 each with £80 added for horses of all denominations 12 stones each, gentlemen riders. . . . Twenty fences in each of two circuits. Two flights of hurdles in the straight.' There were ten runners in this race and the winner was a horse called The Duke, ridden by a certain Captain Becher, a keen and fearless young horseman. In 1839 a syndicate was formed to organize the Liverpool races and a special race was arranged to cover 4 miles across country. There were 53 entries published on 6 January for the race scheduled for 26 February and the grand parade was programmed for 1 pm. The day dawned calm and bright and spectators turned out in their thousands, making their way by all manner of means and transport to the Aintree course. It was not until 3 pm that the parade finally started and the crowds saw that only 17 runners and riders intended to start in this great steeplechase. In all there were 29 demanding jumps which soon began to take their toll of horses and riders. One horse, Dictator, was killed, and at a stout wide post and rails with a brook and a drop landing, Captain Becher's mount, Conrad, was making all the running when he sustained a severe fall. The Captain, thrown clear, crept into the brook until the following horses had all jumped the obstacle then he caught his horse, remounted and finished the race. Ever since then, this particular fence, one of the most testing in the race, has been known as Becher's Brook. The eventual winner of the day was Lottery, a half-bred, foaled in 1830 and originally named Chance. The horse on this occasion was ridden by the accomplished and popular Jem Mason.

The legendary Red Rum, ridden by Brian Fletcher, being led in after winning the Grand National Steeplechase in 1974.

After two wins and two seconds in the testing race, Red Rum, ears pricked, gallops triumphantly past the post and into the history books as he wins the Grand National for the third time.

Although this race is considered to have been the first Grand National, it was originally entitled the Grand Liverpool Steeplechase, then changed to the Liverpool and National Steeplechase in 1843, before being finally called the Grand National in 1847.

Over the years public outrage has caused some of the punishing obstacles to be modified, but even so the Grand National remains the ultimate test of courage and fitness of both horse and rider. The Grand National has become a national institution, and whatever a horse's track record might be he will be sure to go down in equine history by finishing first in this renowned race.

To win the Grand National is to gain fame, but to win it more than once is phenomenal. Only six horses have achieved double success in the race, Peter Simple, Abd El Kader, The Colonel, Poethlyn, Manifesto and Reynoldstown. (The first of Poethlyn's wins occurred in 1918 when, because of the war, the race was moved to Gatwick in Sussex.) A seventh horse won the National in 1973 and in 1974, catching the public's imagination with his courage and pulling at the heartstrings of horse lovers and sportsmen alike. This was the mighty Red Rum, a living legend, for as well as joining the ranks of the dual winners he achieved second place on two other occasions and then galloped into immortality on 1 April 1977 by winning the great race for the third time. As Red Rum is a gelding and therefore useless for breeding, he retired in glory and spends his well-earned years of rest officiating at opening ceremonies of all types, raising money for various charities and making public appearances before his many fans.

The Grand National has produced outstanding performances from horses and their riders, and has become compulsive viewing even for those with little interest in any form of racing. It was estimated that last year's race was watched worldwide on seven million television screens. Overseas riders like the chance to take part in the great race, which seems to hold a particular fascination for American jockeys, two of whom rode the winners of the race, in 1965 and 1980. Nationals have been lost by sheer bad luck when bridles, reins or stirrup leathers have snapped at critical points in the race, but courageous horses have triumphed having fallen and been remounted to finish well placed after all the opposition had also taken tumbles.

In France a race considered the equivalent of the Grand National is run on the Auteuil track in Paris in June of each year. Other steeplechases are also held, but in that country the sport does not seem as popular as flat racing or harness racing. In the United States the most famous steeplechase is the Maryland Hunt Cup, but on the whole, the American racegoers seem to prefer hurdle racing to steeplechasing.

The Vintner (14) and *Dromore* (27) reach out for the dramatic dropped landing over Becher's Brook in the 1980 Grand National.

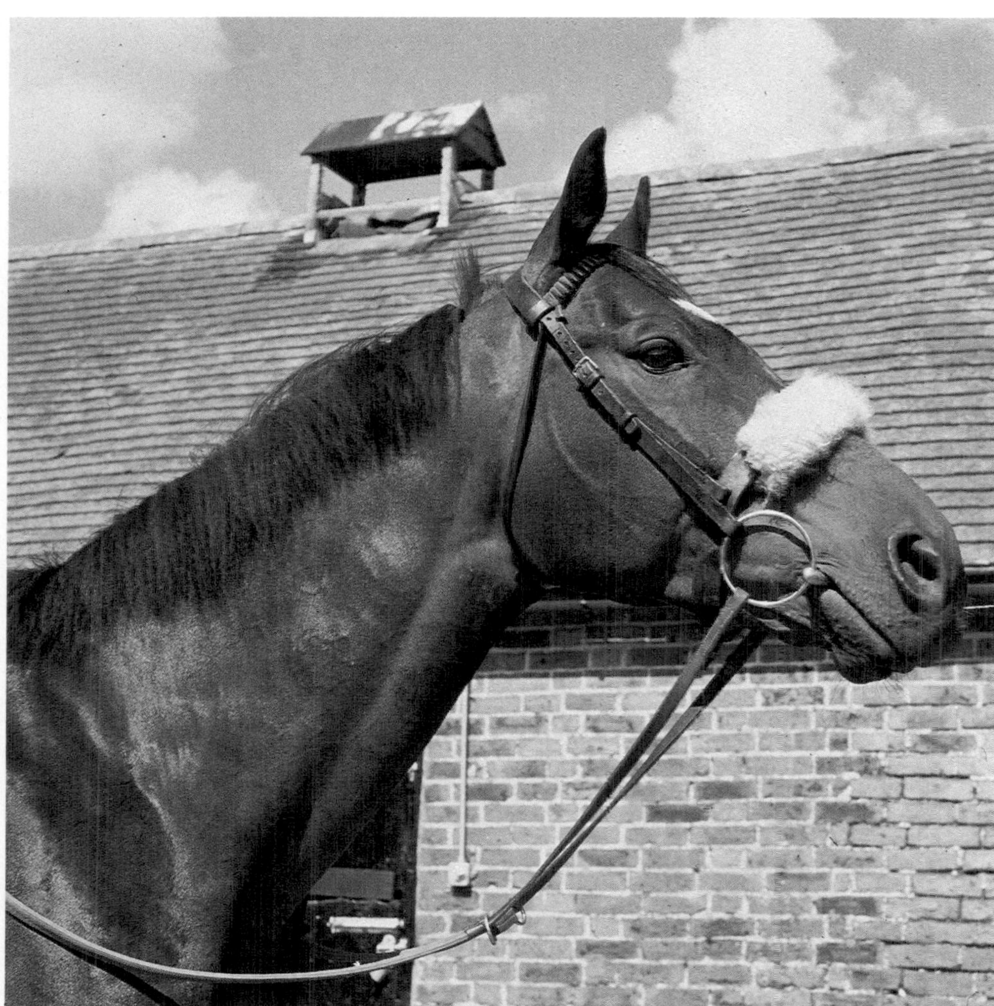

Left: A steeplechaser.

Below: On an American track, rain turns the surface to liquid mud, quickly coating Steve Cauthen and his mount *Barton Silverman*.

The Willing Workhorse

What is it that makes a large, powerful quadruped like the horse, serve and obey the comparatively small and puny biped that is man? For serve he does, and has done ever since his domestication over five thousand years ago. Man took away the horse's freedom and put the animal to work; in return he provided the horse with adequate food and water and protected it from danger. So it would seem, both sides of the partnership stood to gain from the association and had very little to lose. The horse is essentially a gregarious animal and when removed from its herd is forced to think and act as an individual. In the natural herd situation, each horse has its own place in the hierarchy. It will be subordinate to some members of its group and dominant to others. The wild-horse herd has a leader, generally a stallion, which is accepted as dominant by all other members of the community. This dominant horse earns its role by virtue of his courage and expertise in detecting and warning his companions of danger, finding the best grazing and water. His reward for his vigilance, bravery and skill comes from mating with the mares and thus perpetuating his own bloodlines.

On parade, an unusual albino gelding, hooves painted to match his immaculate coat, carries his proud owner through the streets, publicizing the rodeo.

When a human intervenes and breaks up the equine community structure by selecting a horse for use in a domesticated role, he finds that the animal transfers the loyalty naturally reserved for the herd leader to his human master. Over the years man has learned to exploit this characteristic, and this has enabled him to train the horse to perform the variety of tasks expected of it today.

Very few animals are capable of making this adjustment to their natural patterns of behaviour. The dog does it best of all and is often doubly rewarded by being allowed into the home to be treated very much as part of the family. The closer the bond between animal and master, the more responses may be elicited. The Arabs knew this and hand-fed their precious horses, stabling them inside their own tents and spending long hours petting and talking to them.

A horse has a very simple mind and it is necessary to understand its primitive principles to get the best performance and responses from it. It is very important that any horse respects its master or rider. By treating him as his leader, the horse becomes responsive and sensitive to his every command. To replace the equine stimuli of sound, smell and touch, the human conveys messages through the reins to the bit, by the pressure of legs against the animal's sides and by voice. The horse likes to have a very ordered

existence with regular routines and established times for feeding, exercising and sleeping. When it has been broken in and schooled it proves to be an obedient animal, willing to work hard and often to show pleasure at the approach of its master or other friends.

In its wild state the horse is a herbivore and exists as part of its herd, wandering freely in search of suitable grazing. It is built for defensive flight if attacked and is capable of vigorous bucking movements with its head down, designed to dislodge any large carnivore that attacks by leaping onto its back. It is equipped to bite savagely when necessary and is able to kick back hard at anything attacking from the rear. When the horse rises from a resting position on the ground it first raises the front of its body then lifts the hind end. This enables it, if startled, to kick out at the precise moment that it is up on its feet.

The horse's eyes are so placed that when it is grazing it is able to see all around. It picks at grass in a pattern and if carefully observed, it will be seen to be looking around itself constantly, forwards, backwards and to both sides. If it notices anything untoward, it will immediately stop chewing, raise its head and turn towards the object that first caused alarm, its muscles slightly tensed, and ready to run if necessary.

Horses have unusual vision allowing both close and distant objects to be focussed at the same time. An adaption to the grazing habit, this enables the most succulent of grasses to be selected, while simultaneously a watch is maintained for any possible dangers on the horizon. The horse adjusts the depth of

The horse's eyes are so placed as to give all-round vision even while the head is down for grazing.

Overleaf: Today the Mustang, descended from the horses of the Spanish Conquistadors, still roams some isolated ranges in the United States of America.

part of the animal's body. It is this muscle that also enables the horse to shiver, helping it to keep warm in very cold weather, and to dislodge biting insects when they alight on the skin, out of reach of the flicking tail.

As opposed to shivering, the horse is able to sweat, virtually at will. When it becomes overheated from exertion or excitement, sweat glands on the body and neck exude copious quantities of sweat and the horse's temperature soon stabilizes at its normal 100·3°F (37·9°C).

The horse, like the dog, quickly learns behaviour patterns considered acceptable by its human master. These are taught in careful stages and merely take the animal's natural movements and habits and mould them so that they are performed to order. The animal soon appreciates the fact that when it performs satisfactorily, it is praised and patted, but when it is disobedient, it is made to repeat the exercise until it improves. Horses are gradually conditioned into acceptance of a whole range of responses to certain stimuli, and are then said to be well-schooled. Different horses are, naturally, schooled to perform in different ways. The Thor-

Above: The fitting of blinkers has been found to improve the racing performance of many horses. This racehorse is on a training run at Keenelands, Kentucky.

Right: A horse and gharry at Luxor, Egypt, waiting patiently for a fare.

Right: Willing warhorses of the First World War, standing patiently in their lines, often overheated and overworked. Many such horses which survived shellfire and blast had to be abandoned at the end of the war, ending their days as peasants' workhorses, often half-starved and ill-used.

Below: A touch of the past: Canadian cowboys muster young semi-wild horses for their annual innoculations and veterinary check.

In contrast is the pampered show jumper, fed on the very best of good food, rugged up against all extremes of weather and shown off with pride.

oughbred has no need of the collected trot; it merely needs the ability to run well, and to produce extra power when asked. It must be taught to enter the stalls at the start of the race and to remain controlled in the paddock and on the way to the starting post.

The dressage horse must learn to gear every movement to the slightest, almost imperceptible aid given by its rider – all thoughts of a good gallop far from its mind. Yet both these horses are of almost identical type and bloodlines, they have the same physique and the same thought processes. There is no such thing as a natural racehorse or a natural dressage horse. Horses are chosen for their allotted tasks in life by careful selection of stock from the right breeding. They must also have the right conformation for their purpose, and when these factors are right, they are then trained. The trained horse becomes capable of performing all the skills necessary for its job, and is able to produce the correct responses to the instructions given by its rider, driver or handler, willingly and without question. Only in moments of great stress or excitement does the normally well-behaved and well-trained horse disobey; then it may temporarily forget every lesson it has learned from its human leader, and revert to its natural, innate behaviour patterns. Its first reaction to fear is to gallop as fast as possible away from danger, and if it is prevented from doing so, it may lash out with its heels.

The unquestioning obedience and servitude of the horse has proved its worth through the centuries. It certainly helped man change the whole course of civilization by changing him into a centaur and allowing him to terrorize his neighbours who knew nothing of the horse. It was the horse that gave armies supremacy, that raised Genghis Khan and other such leaders and allowed the founding of great empires.

Still a necessity in some parts of the world, the horse often leads a miserable life of drudgery, half-starved and abused. In the more affluent countries, the horse has become one of life's little luxuries. Pampered and kept with pride, it is a sporting companion, a cherished pet, and always, a willing worker.

More and more people are becoming interested in matters concerned with horses, and those who feel it is too late to start riding, often fulfil their need by learning to drive a horse or pony. Farmers, with every modern machine at their disposal, often have a heavy horse or two, and many children have a great desire to own a pony. It has been said that the ownership of horses is some kind of status symbol but it is more probable that it fulfils a deep-seated need in the human. It does seem that in this technological era people have a nostalgic need for things of the past, and who knows, with the depletion of many of the world's resources, the horse may well return to its full glory as a vitally important servant of man.

Acknowledgments

Alinari, Florence 12 left, 19, 20 top, 21 top; All Sport, Morden 86, 106; All Sport: Dave Bunce 104–5, 108–9; All Sport: Tony Duffy 80; All Sport: John Gichigi 111, 112–13; All Sport: Peter Greenland 105 bottom; All Sport: Robert Martin 123; All Sport: Ralph Merlino 82–83; All Sport: Steve Powell 73 centre, 73 bottom; All Sport: John Starr 110; Animal Photography: Sally Anne Thompson 69, 72 bottom, 120–121; Animal Photography: R. Willbie 124; Bodleian Library, Oxford 27; British Library, London 24; British Museum, London 13 top, 20 bottom; British Museum (Natural History), London 7; Central Press, London 39 top; Colorsport, London 79 bottom; Commissioner of Police, London 38 top, 42; Rosemary & Penelope Ellis, Devizes 59; Equestrian Photographic Services 79 top, 98; Forestry Commission 50; Werner Forman Archive, London 28 left, 28 right; Gaggiotti, Rome 21 bottom; Thomas Gilcrease, Institute of American History & Art, Tulsa, Oklahoma 33 top; Photographie Giraudon, Paris 10 bottom; Hamlyn Group Picture Library 15 bottom, 17, 22, 23, 30, 31, 35, 54 top, 55, 90 bottom, 91, 101, 102, 103; Hampshire County Museum Service, Winchester 48 top; Hirmer Fotoarchiv, Munich 14, 15 top; John Howard, Lightwater 68, 75, 76, 77, 78; Imperial War Museum, London 34 top, 34 bottom, 126 bottom; Cornelius Linfert, Hamburg 74; Jack de Lorme 70; Machatschek, Paris 48 bottom; Mansell Collection, London 37, 38 centre, 38 bottom, 99; MGM 54; Musée de l'homme, Paris 6; National Gallery, London 29; Office of the High Commissioner for Canada 46, 47; Robert Owen, Dorking 81, 90 top, 95, 107, 127 top; Antonello Perissinotto, Padua 18; Pierpont Morgan Library, New York 26; Roger-Viollet, Paris 10 top, 11; Angela Sayer, Crawley 8 top, 8 centre, 8 bottom, 12 right, 13 bottom, 16, 25, 32, 33 bottom, 36, 40 top, 40 bottom, 41 top, 41 bottom, 43 top, 43 bottom, 44, 45, 49, 52 top, 52 bottom, 53, 54 bottom, 56, 57 top, 57 bottom, 58, 60, 61, 64, 65, 67 top, 67 bottom, 72 top, 73 top, 84 top, 84 bottom, 85 top, 85 bottom, 92, 93 top, 93 bottom, 94, 96, 97, 118, 119, 122 left, 122 right, 125; Sport & General Press Agency, London 39 bottom, 66; Syndication International, London 114, 115, 116; Berne Tempest 100; The Times, London 87; John Topham Picture Library, Edenbridge 51 top; US Information Service 71.

The illustrations on page 62 and page 63 are reproduced by courtesy of HM Postmaster General.

Front cover: All Sport: Ralph Merlino
Back cover: All Sport: Robert Martin
Endpapers: Animal Photography
Title spread: Angela Sayer